The Routledge Queer Studies Reader

"It is hard to imagine a volume that could represent the field more knowingly!"

Robyn Wiegman, *Duke University, USA*

"This fresh, innovative, and significant volume demonstrates convincingly the queer moment is by no means over."

Laura Doan, *University of Manchester, UK*

"Get prepared to enter a scene of provocation, a sexy sort of maelstrom, where trans meets butch meets brown meets 'quare' meets intersex, racial, post-colonial, and disabled matters in juxtaposition, in telling combinations. Even subtleties and biting formulations appear side by side, in a queer cubism, leading both students and scholars to thoughts that will startle and seduce them."

Kathryn Bond Stockton, *University of Utah, USA*

The Routledge Queer Studies Reader provides a comprehensive resource for students and scholars working in this vibrant and interdisciplinary field.

The book traces the emergence and development of queer studies as a field of scholarship, presenting key critical essays alongside more recent criticism that explores new directions. The collection is edited by leading scholars in the field and presents:

- individual introductory notes that situate each work within its historical, disciplinary and theoretical contexts
- essays grouped by key subject areas including Genealogies, Sex, Temporalities, Kinship, Affect, Bodies, and Borders
- writings by major figures including Eve Kosofsky Sedgwick, Judith Butler, David M. Halperin, José Esteban Muñoz, Elizabeth Grosz, David Eng, Judith Halberstam, and Sara Ahmed.

The Routledge Queer Studies Reader is a field-defining volume and presents an illuminating guide for established scholars and also those new to queer studies.

Donald E. Hall is Professor and Herbert and Ann Siegel Dean of the College of Arts and Sciences at Lehigh University, USA.

Annamarie Jagose is Professor and Head of the School of Letters, Arts and Media at the University of Sydney, Australia.

Andrea Bebell is a Graduate Teaching Assistant at West Virginia University, USA.

Susan Potter is a doctoral candidate in the Department of Film, Television, and Media Studies at the University of Auckland, New Zealand Aotearoa.

Routledge Literature Readers

Also available

Literature and Globalization
Edited by Liam Connell and Nicky Marsh

The History of Reading
Edited by Shafquat Towheed, Rosalind Crone and Katie Halsey

World Literature
Edited by Theo D'haen, César Domínguez and Mads Rosendahl Thomsen

For further information on this series visit: http://www.routledge.com/literature/series

The Routledge Queer Studies Reader

Edited by

Donald E. Hall and Annamarie Jagose, with
Andrea Bebell and Susan Potter

Routledge
Taylor & Francis Group

LONDON AND NEW YORK

First published 2013
by Routledge
2 Park Square, Milton Park, Abingdon, Oxon OX14 4RN

Simultaneously published in the USA and Canada
by Routledge
711 Third Avenue, New York, NY 10017

Routledge is an imprint of the Taylor & Francis Group, an informa business

British Library Cataloguing in Publication Data
A catalogue record for this book is available from the British Library

Library of Congress Cataloging in Publication Data
The Routledge queer studies reader / edited by Donald E. Hall . . . [et al.].
    p. cm.
  Cover title: Queer studies reader
  Includes bibliographical references.
  1. Gay and lesbian studies.   I. Hall, Donald E.   II. Title: Queer studies reader.
  HQ75.15.R68 2012
  306.76'6—dc23
                                                            2011042814

ISBN: 978-0-415-56410-6 (hbk)
ISBN: 978-0-415-56411-3 (pbk)

Typeset in Perpetua/Bell Gothic
by RefineCatch Limited, Bungay, Suffolk

Printed and bound in the United States of America
by Edwards Brothers Malloy on sustainably sourced paper.

Contents

Acknowledgements

The publisher and the editors would like to thank the following for permission to reprint material under copyright:

Part 1: Genealogies

"Queer and Now", from *Tendencies*, Eve Kosofsky Sedgwick. Copyright 1993, Duke University Press. All rights reserved. Reprinted by permission of the publisher.

Judith Butler, "Critically Queer", in *GLQ: A Journal of Lesbian and Gay Studies*, Volume 1, no. 1. Copyright 1993, Duke University Press. All rights reserved. Reprinted by permission of the publisher.

"Judith Butler: Queer Feminism, Transgender, and the Transubstantiation of Sex" from *Second Skins: The Body Narratives of Transsexuality* by Jay Prosser, published by Columbia University Press (1998): 21–60. Copyright © 1998 Columbia University Press.

"The Queer Intervention" from *A History of Bisexuality* by Steven Angelides, published by University of Chicago Press. © 2001 by The University of Chicago. Reprinted by permission of the publisher.

Cathy Cohen "Punks, Bulldaggers and Welfare Queens: The Radical Potential of Queer Politics", from *GLQ: A Journal of Lesbian and Gay Studies*, Volume 3, no. 4. Copyright 1997, Duke University Press. All rights reserved. Reprinted by permission of the publisher.

E. Patrick Johnson, "'Quare' Studies, or Almost Everything I Know About Queer Studies I Learned From My Grandmother", from *Black Queer Studies*, E. Patrick Johnson, Mae G. Henderson, Eds. Copyright, 2005, Duke University Press. All rights reserved. Reprinted by permission of the publisher.

Roderick A. Ferguson, "Introduction: Queer of Color Critique, Historical Materialism, and Canonical Sociology", from *Aberrations in Black: Towards a Queer of Color Critique* (University of Minnesota Press, 2005). Used courtesy of University of Minnesota Press.

Rosemary Hennessy, "The Material of Sex", From: *Profit and Pleasure: Sexual Identities in Late Capitalism*, by Rosemary Hennessy (Copyright © 2000 by Routledge), pp. 37–73. Reproduced by permission of Taylor & Francis Books.

"Lacan Meets Queer Theory", from *Beyond Sexuality* by Tim Dean, published by University of Chicago Press. © 2000 by The University of Chicago. Reprinted by permission of the publisher.

Part 2: Sex

"Sex in Public" by Lauren Berlant and Michael Warner from *Critical Inquiry*, vol. 24, no. 2, published by University of Chicago Press. © 1998 by The University of Chicago. Reprinted by permission of the publisher.

Gregory Tosmo, "Viral Sex and the Politics of Life", in *South Atlantic Quarterly*, Volume 107, no. 2. Copyright, 2008, Duke University Press. All rights reserved. Reprinted by permission of the publisher.

Elizabeth Grosz, "Experimental Desire: Rethinking Queer Subjectivity". From: *Space, Time, and Perversion: Essays on the Politics of Bodies*, by Elizabeth Grosz (Copyright © 1995 by Routledge), pp. 207–27. Reproduced by permission of Taylor & Francis Books.

"Dinge", from *Black Gay Man: Essays* by Robert F. Reid-Pharr, published by New York University Press (2001): 85–98. © 2001 by New York University. Reprinted by permission of the publisher.

Part 3: Temporalities

Tavia Nyong'o, "Do You Want Queer Theory (or Do You Want the Truth)? Intersections of Punk and Queer in the 1970s", in *Radical History Review*, Volume 100. Copyright, 2008, MARHO: The Radical Historians Organization, Inc. All rights reserved. Reprinted by permission of the publisher, Duke University Press.

Elizabeth Freeman, "Turn the Beat Around: Sadomasochism, Temporality, History", in *differences*, Volume 19, no. 1. Copyright, 2008, Brown University and *Differences: a Journal of Feminist Cultural Studies*. All rights reserved. Reprinted by permission of the publisher, Duke University Press.

"How to Do the History of Male Homosexuality", from *How to Do the History of Male Homosexuality* by David M. Halperin, published by University of Chicago Press. © 2002 by David M. Halperin. Reprinted by permission of the publisher.

"The Future Is Kid Stuff: Queer Theory, Disidentification and the Death Drive" by Lee Edelman, from the journal *Narrative*. Copyright 1998 by The Ohio State University. Reprinted with permission.

Part 4: Kinship

David L. Eng, "Transnational Adoption and Queer Diasporas", in *Social Text*, Volume 21, no. 3. Copyright, David L. Eng. All rights reserved. Reprinted by permission of the publisher.

"Afterword: Making Queer *Familia*", in *Next of Kin*, Richard Rodriguez, pp. 167–76. Copyright, 2009, Duke University Press. All rights reserved. Reprinted by permission of the publisher.

Mark Rifkin, "Romancing Kinship: A Queer Reading of Indian Education and Zitkala-Ŝa's *American Indian Stories*", in *GLQ: A Journal of Lesbian and Gay Studies*, Volume 12, no. 1. Copyright 2006, Duke University Press. All rights reserved. Reprinted by permission of the publisher.

Elizabeth Povinelli, "Notes on Gridlock: Genealogy, Intimacy, Sexuality", in *Public Culture*, Volume 14, no. 1. Copyright, 2002, Duke University Press. All rights reserved. Reprinted by permission of the publisher.

Part 5: Affect

"AIDS Activism and Public Feelings", in *An Archive of Feelings*, Ann Cvetkovich, pp. 156–82; 202–4. Copyright 2003, Duke University Press. All rights reserved. Reprinted by permission of the publisher.

"Archiving Queer Feelings in Hong Kong" by Helen Hok-Sze Leung from *Inter Asia Cultural Studies*, vol. 8, no. 4, 2007. Reprinted by permission of the publisher (Taylor & Francis Ltd, http://www.tandf.co.uk/journals).

"Feeling Brown, Feeling Down: Latina Affect, the Performativity of Race, and the Depressive Position" by José Esteban Muñoz from *Signs: Journal of Women in Culture and Society*, vol. 31, no. 3, published by University of Chicago Press. © 2006 by The University of Chicago. Reprinted by permission of the publisher.

Sara Ahmed, "Queer Feelings". From: *The Cultural Politics of Emotion*, by Sara Ahmed (© 2004 by Sara Ahmed), pp. 144–67. Reproduced by permission of Routledge Publishing Inc./Taylor & Francis Books.

Part 6: Bodies

Iain Morland, "What Can Queer Theory Do for Intersex?", in *GLQ: Journal of Lesbian and Gay Studies*, Volume 51, no. 2, pp. 285–312. Copyright 2009, Duke University Press. All rights reserved. Reprinted by permission of the publisher.

"Transgender Butch: Butch/FTM Border Wars and the Masculine Continuum", in *Female Masculinity*, Judith Halberstam, pp. 141–73. Copyright 1998, Duke University Press. All rights reserved. Reprinted by permission of the publisher.

Robert McRuer, "Compulsory Able-Bodiedness and Queer/Disabled Existence". Reprinted by permission of the Language Association of America from *Disability Studies: Enabling the Humanities*, Sharon L. Snyder (ed.) (2002).

Wilson, Elizabeth A. "Neurological Preferences: LeVay's Study of Sexual Orientation." Originally published in *SubStance* Issue 91, 29.1 (2000): 23–28. © 2000 by the Board of Regents of the University of Wisconsin System. Reproduced by the permission of the University of Wisconsin Press.

Part 7: Borders

Jasbir Puar, "Queer Times, Queer Assemblages", in *Social Text*, Volume 23, no. 3–4, pp. 121–39. Copyright 2005, Duke University Press. All rights reserved. Reprinted by permission of the publisher.

"Queer Intersections: Sexuality and Gender in Migration Studies" by Martin Manalansan, from the journal *International Migration Review* (2006). Reproduced by permission of Wiley Blackwell.

"Border/Line Sex: Queer Postcolonialities or How Race Matters Outside the U.S." by Anjali Arondekar from *Interventions*, vol. 7, no. 2, 2005. Reprinted by permission of the publisher (Taylor & Francis Ltd, http://www.tandf.co.uk/journals).

Lucas Cassidy Crawford, "Transgender without Organs?: Mobilizing a Geo-Affective Theory of Gender Modification", from *Women's Studies Quarterly*, Volume 36, no. 3–4 (Fall–Winter 2008): 127–43. Copyright © 2008 by the Feminist Press at the City University of New York. Reprinted with the permission of the author and the publisher, www.feministpress.org.

Editors' acknowledgements

Annamarie and Donald thank their research assistants—Susan Potter and Andrea Bebell respectively—for their diligence in proofreading scanned text and most particularly for their drafting of the contextualizing headers that precede each essay in this collection. Andrea took lead responsibility for headers 1–17 and Susan for headers 18–33.

Donald would also like to offer his very deep gratitude to his many colleagues at West Virginia University, where he taught, researched and administered from 2004 to 2011. His friends there have left an indelible impression on this collection and on Donald's work as a whole. His new colleagues at Lehigh University will no doubt have a similarly profound impact on his future endeavors. He has joined an extraordinary community of faculty, staff, students and researchers.

Finally, Donald wishes to thank his partner, Bill Maruyama, for his tireless support and love through a wide variety of life transitions, large and small. Donald's part of this collection is dedicated to Bill.

International advisory board

Introduction

The queer turn

With the publication of *The Routledge Queer Studies Reader*, we pay homage to the publication, nearly twenty years previous, of *The Routledge Lesbian and Gay Studies Reader*. Consistent with the notion of performativity that was a grounding concept for one influential strand of theorizing in the 1990s, the appearance on bookshelves around the English-speaking world of the *Lesbian and Gay Studies Reader* confirmed the emergence of a new scholarly field, in so far as its own chunky materiality "constitutes as an effect the very subject it appears to express."[1] It was less its authoritative heft—weighing in at 666 pages, the *Reader* drew together forty-two essays, dwarfing every other similar title in the field to date—than the fact that, in laying a claim to the genre of the reader, it also laid claim to the broader existence of a capacious and thriving field of work, sufficiently coherent to be understood as lesbian and gay studies.

Yet, lest it seem that our salute to the *Lesbian and Gay Studies Reader* facilitates a sense that now, in the twenty-first century, its moment and the field it represents might be deferentially passed over for a more salient and critically aerodynamic queer studies, it is worth considering in a little detail the specific ways in which Henry Abelove, Michèle Aina Barale, and David M. Halperin, the editors of the *Reader*, define lesbian and gay studies. In their brief introduction, Abelove, Barale and Halperin sketch out the methodological grounds of an emergent lesbian and gay studies through analogous reference to the longer-established project of women's studies: "Lesbian/gay studies does for *sex* and *sexuality* approximately what women's studies does for gender."[2] This pithy claim is important for any historical understanding of the emergence and consolidation of not only lesbian and gay but also queer studies, since it was singled out for lengthy critique by Judith Butler, who, in an influential essay published the following year, took the *Lesbian and Gay Studies Reader* to task as a prominent example of a critical indifference to gender and a proprietary relation to sexuality that she attributed first to lesbian and gay studies and then to queer studies.[3] In suggesting in what follows that the *Lesbian and Gay Studies Reader* constituted lesbian and gay studies more complexly than Butler acknowledges, we mean to draw attention to the important ways in which the emergence and continuing development of queer studies cannot conceptually be held distinct from either feminist studies or lesbian and gay studies.

Butler contends that, in making an analogy between women's studies and lesbian/gay studies, the *Lesbian and Gay Studies Reader* authorizes the project of lesbian and gay studies via a reductive account of that of women's studies. Reading the analogy as positing gender as the proper scholarly object of women's studies while claiming sexuality for lesbian/gay studies, Butler argues that the editors of the *Lesbian and Gay Studies Reader* overlook the important feminist tradition of radical sexual theorizing in which the normative reproduction of gender supports and enables the regulation of sexuality. Moreover, they do so, she suggests, in order to provide a clear and uncontested ground for their own nascent field of scholarly operation. In light of Butler's critique, it is important to note that Abelove et al. take some care to qualify their claim. They emphasize that they do not advocate that "sexuality and gender must be strictly partitioned" and they note that the question of the proper degree of their separation is currently "a matter of lively debate and ongoing negotiation."[4] It is even more important, however, to return to their analogizing of lesbian/gay and women's studies in order to understand on what basis such an analogy is claimed. It is our contention, contra Butler, that Abelove et al. offer their analogy not as a decisive adjudication between women's and lesbian/gay studies but rather to draw a comparison between them on the grounds of their shared refusal of any identity-based foundational category, a characteristic that will soon be identified as central to a newly emergent queer studies.

The analogous turn to women's studies in the Introduction to the *Lesbian and Gay Studies Reader* occurs as part of a larger argument intended to demonstrate that lesbian/gay studies is not simply about or relevant to lesbians and gay men: "Lesbian/gay studies, in short, cannot be defined exclusively by its subject, its practitioners, its methods, or its themes. An analogy with women's studies may help to clarify this point."[5] According to Abelove et al., just as women's studies seeks less to inaugurate *women* as a new object of study than to transform existing knowledge formations by establishing "the centrality of *gender* as a fundamental category of historical analysis and understanding," so too lesbian/gay studies seeks to establish sexuality as an analytic rubric of broad relevance and importance for a diverse range of disciplinary fields and interests.[6] "What women's studies does for gender," therefore, is not to lay authoritative and sole claim to it but to demonstrate the degree to which other critical traditions—including lesbian/gay studies presumably—are diminished by being inattentive to its workings. When Abelove et al. orient their ambitions for lesbian/gay studies in analogous relation to women's studies, they do not, therefore, proprietarily claim sexuality for lesbian/gay studies, still less install gender as women's studies' only scholarly license. Rather, the key operational force of their analogy is to point up the ways that lesbian/gay studies, like women's studies, might eschew an identitarian constituency in order to insist on the pertinence of what has previously been imagined as its key term—sexuality for the former, gender for the latter—for the wider scholarly map.

If the *Lesbian and Gay Studies Reader* identifies lesbian and gay studies as importantly like women's studies in some respects, it also finds affinities between its project and the not yet institutionalized formation of queer studies. Attracted to the rubric of "queer studies" but wanting "to acknowledge the force of current usage" that favors "lesbian and gay studies," Abelove et al. admit some ambivalence about the prominence of the latter in the title for their anthology and the field it attempts to represent: "our choice of 'lesbian/gay' indicates no wish on our part to make lesbian/gay studies look less assertive, less unsettling, and less queer than it already does."[7] For far from staking out a quasi-disciplinary territory defined by the sharp-edged clarity of its scholarly objects, the *Lesbian and Gay Studies Reader* insists from the start that "lesbian/gay studies is not limited to the study of lesbians, bisexuals, and gay men," being instead already "a site for inquiry into many kinds of sexual non-conformity, including, for instance, bisexuality, trans-sexualism, and sadomasochism."[8] This positioning of lesbian/gay studies needs to be understood in relation to the early 1990s institutionalization of a lesbian and gay studies in the process of being transformed by queer activism and theory. In emphasizing non-normativity as an anti-identitarian basis for the field of lesbian and gay studies and thereby claiming as its own something more commonly ceded as the signature gesture of queer theory, the editors of the *Lesbian and Gay Studies Reader* usefully remind us that those succession narratives—with their decisive breaks, distinctive fields of operation and counterweighted waxings and wanings of influence—sometimes presumed to preside over feminist, lesbian/gay and queer theory cannot adequately capture the multiple, complex and coeval relationships that productively persist between and across those fields of continuing endeavor.

The story of queer studies' origins—what it is exactly and how it came to be—has been told many times and we don't propose to retell it here in much detail. Both of us have written book-length overviews of queer theory that detail its emergence in the early 1990s and there are several other such texts, accessible in terms both of their wide availability and writing style, that might be consulted for a richer sense of the historical and critical coordinates of queer studies' emergence than we have space to convey here.[9] But we do want to comment on the ways in which how that story is told signifies importantly for our understanding of queer studies. Telling a chronologically organized account of queer studies' emergence risks obscuring its multiple origins and influences. Single, linearly organized narratives cannot easily capture the sometimes inchoate energies of the various orders of political and scholarly work that mark the rise of queer studies. For these reasons, it remains important to narrate the emergence and continued cultural and critical life of queer studies in terms of a range of different contexts, which include feminism, radical movements of color, the lesbian and gay movements, AIDS activism, various sexual subcultural practices such as sadomasochism and butch/femme stylings, poststructuralist thought—particularly the work of Michel Foucault—postcolonialism and diasporic studies, transgender and disability studies.

   In broad stroke, queer studies is the institutionalization of a new—or at least newly visible—paradigm for thinking about sexuality that emerged simultaneously across academic and activist contexts in the early 1990s, constituting a broad and unmethodical critique of normative models of sex, gender and sexuality. This critique, which David Eng suggests "we might describe as queer studies' most important epistemic as well as political promise," is evident not only in the queer eschewal of the foundational solidity of the identity categories that traditionally grounded progressive social movements but also in its persistent refusal to consolidate its object of study, to delimit the scope of its inquiry in advance.[10] More than short-hand for "lesbian/gay"—or even the more capacious but still identity-bound LGBT—queer speaks to the unintended but profound naturalization of the dominant system of sexual classification effected by the political successes of the lesbian and gay movements, staking an alternate claim to what Gayle Rubin describes as "a pluralistic sexual ethics" organized around "a concept of benign sexual variation."[11] While arguing for the validity and significance of various marginalized sexual identities and practices—such as barebacking, bisexuality, intersex and transgender subjects, public sex cultures, pornography and sadomasochism—queer studies attempts to clear a space for thinking differently about the relations presumed to pertain between sex/gender and sex/sexuality, between sexual identities and erotic behaviors, between practices of pleasure and systems of sexual knowledge.

   Queer studies' commitment to non-normativity and anti-identitarianism, coupled with its refusal to define its proper field of operation in relation to any fixed content, means that, while prominently organized around sexuality, it is potentially attentive to any socially consequential difference that contributes to regimes of sexual normalization. Rather than separating sexuality from other axes of social difference—race, ethnicity, class, gender, nationality and so on—queer studies has increasingly attended to the ways in which various categories of difference inflect and transform each other. This kind of intersectional analysis is neither new nor an innovation of queer studies. The persistent challenge to the reification of allegedly foundational identities such as "women" or "homosexuals" has long been part of the feminist and lesbian/gay contexts from which queer studies, in part, emerges. In this anti-foundationalist tradition, recent work in queer studies has, for example, investigated the formation of sexuality alongside race, ethnicity, nationality, citizenship and diasporic identities in order to demonstrate the significant ways in which sexual and racial identities are inextricable.

As might be expected, queer studies is not a stable or hard-edged field of scholarly inquiry. Nevertheless, we attempt here a snapshot of some of the leading thematics that currently shape its field of inquiry in order to give a more broadly specified sense of the key questions and critical debates that animate queer studies in the contemporary moment. Energized by Foucault's broad critique of continuous history, there has been some stunning work in queer histories of sexuality, which endeavors to encounter, across a range of different historical periods, prior systems of sexual knowledge and orders of lived erotic experience without understanding them as rudimentary expressions of modern forms of sexuality or even in terms of "sexuality" at all.[12] Thematically related to histories of sexuality, although not always attentive to history per se, is another cluster of work that might be broadly designated in terms of queer temporalities. At its best, this work loops through those deconstructive, psychoanalytic and postcolonial intellectual traditions in which time has been influentially thought outside a model of linearity, using notions of time as cyclical, interrupted, multilayered, reversible or stalled to articulate sexuality as a temporal field.[13] Another influential and much debated strand of work in queer studies has been recently reified as a school of thought under the rubric of the antisocial thesis. Drawing strongly on psychoanalytic paradigms, this work emphasizes that sexuality is a psychic rather than a social formation and therefore promotes an anti-relational, antisocial and negative ethos that detaches sex from political expressions of alliance and community to emphasize instead the shattering effects of sexual desire and the drive's violent resistance to the ego's fantasy of identity.[14] Scholars wanting to attach different affective modes to futurity and the sphere of the political often hotly contest the nihilistic negativity of the so-called antisocial thesis.[15] Part of a broader affective turn in humanities scholarship, this work analyzes the historical foundations and phenomenological experience of the radically mixed feelings of queer political engagement in order to situate sentiment not as the property of the expressive subject but as an intricately textured field across which are negotiated conflicting claims to social legibility, human subjectivity and political agency.[16] A further important cluster of work in queer studies can be characterized as using categories of race or ethnicity to unseat naturalized understandings of what counts as social or political legibility. Framed transnationally or within specific national cultures and working within postcolonial, area or diaspora studies, this work makes visible the ways in which race, ethnicity and nationality imprint dominant understandings of sexuality.[17]

Anthologization is a delicate and testing business. On numerous occasions, we have had to balance the aspirational against the pragmatic, the potential breadth of our editorial brief reined in by the commercial realities of publication. The final format and content of this reader reflect a series of negotiations, compromises and difficult decisions. Over several months as we successively drew up variant tables of content, choosing between several equally productive and problematic possibilities and wrangling with each other over the respective value of certain ideas, authors and critical perspectives, we necessarily asked ourselves some uncomfortable questions. What presumptions were we licensing in deciding to "begin" the story of queer studies in the United States and in 1993? To what extent can a volume that reflects the anti-normative impulses of queer theory challenge the institutionalization of queer studies inherent in its own design? Can a queer studies anthology acknowledge the strong Euro-American—but more particularly North American—metropolitan bias inherent in queer studies in more than a tokenistic way and without contributing to the self-reproducing logic of the center and its peripheries?

This last question was the one that most exercised us. From the first, we wanted to edit an anthology that represented queer studies in an international frame. Acknowledging the strength of North American scholarship in the area—and even the institutional realities that see many leading international queer scholars gravitate to positions in US universities—we nevertheless wanted to avoid circulating North American knowledge formations and critical values as if they were universal. Due to various constraints—our own linguistic limitations, the lack of a budget for commissioning translations, a tight publication timeframe—we were bound to an English-language anthology but that did not lessen our commitment to valuing the broad, geographically dispersed conversation that is queer studies today. One of the first challenges we encountered relates to the translatability and limited currency of the word "queer." That English-language slur, turned defiantly against a social and discursive system abetting violence toward sexual nonconformists, reflects a culturally and historically specific dynamic of abuse and response in the US and UK. It does not translate well across languages and cultures. And not only is the term itself of limited international currency, but work in the field broadly related to it is only infrequently translated. Feeling unsatisfied with what we discovered using tradit-ional scholarly search strategies, we addressed the issue of broad and responsible international coverage with the help of a group of generous colleagues from around the world. In consti-tuting this international advisory board, the members of which are listed in the volume's front pages, we sought a diverse group of individuals who would add significantly to our disciplinary and cultural knowledge base. As editors, we first proposed to them a tentative table of contents, reflecting our best attempt at disciplinary and global coverage, and then solicited their feed-back. Their familiarity with a range of different national contexts as well as their expertise in law, the social sciences, film studies, transgender studies and ethnic and regional studies, among other fields, proved invaluable in expanding the horizon of this volume.

Another decision that we had to make early in our selection process was to settle on a working date for the inauguration of queer studies as a field. One editor felt at the outset that a responsible representation of the field must start with Gayle Rubin's seminal "Thinking Sex" from 1983. The other editor had an equivalent conviction about Leo Bersani's 1987 "Is the Rectum a Grave?" Alert readers will note that neither essay appears in this volume. Quite lengthy, those two essays are already widely available in other anthologies and could be included here only if other, more recent and less widely available essays were dropped. On balance, we decided to commit to broad coverage of newer materials. Similarly, although we initially intended not to publish abridged essays, we had to delete some passages from four lengthy book chapters, explaining their broader context in the headers that precede them.

What guided our final selections was our desire to collect essays and book chapters that represent the diversity of the field and that either have been or have the potential to be generative of new ideas and directions. We have placed bets on a few names and essays that are not yet widely known, but most of the pieces here are widely recognized as central to the field of queer studies. In these pages you will find essays from leading scholars whose work has been field defining along-side those of lesser-known and emergent scholars. We have also selected essays to represent the diverse methodological approaches taken up in queer studies, from Lacanian theory, cultural materialism, qualitative sociological analysis, science studies to Deleuzian theory.

In our first section, "Genealogies," we offer a non-chronological sketch of some of the founding narratives and preoccupations that have significantly informed queer studies. Opening with a pair of essays by Eve Kosofsky Sedgwick and Judith Butler that differently define queer as marking a space where sexuality eludes the normative consolidations of identity formation, this section then moves to a sequence of essays—by Jay Prosser, Steven Angelides and Cathy J. Cohen—that not only provides distinctive and accessible surveys or summaries of the key debates or questions in queer studies but also critiques axiomatic or central queer positions from various minoritarian perspectives. E. Patrick Johnson's and Roderick A. Ferguson's essays continue Cohen's focus on questions of race and specifically African American blackness. The materialist attention to class that marks Ferguson's essay is also evident in Rosemary Hennessy's work, which, against what it perceives as the cultural approach of most queer studies, advocates understanding sexuality within a history of capitalism. Tim Dean contributes the final essay in this section, which offers yet another version of queerness, drawing on a psychoanalytic tradition that is often pitted against the "reality"-based materialist critique.

Other useful section headings suggested themselves across the iterative process of narrowing down our selection of representative essays. "Sex" emerged as a broad heading that allows us to point to both bodily and imagined acts, as well as to sexuality, that amorphous field of meaning crosshatched by notions of identity, preference, orientation and practice. It is distinguished from the later section titled "Bodies," which focuses intently on the corporeal surface and its varying perceptions and receptions among queer and non-queer publics. The section "Temporalities" centers on the long-standing queer interest in how meaning is made in time-bound contexts and how narratives of progression and personal development both constrain and empower queers and non-queers alike. The next two sections, "Kinship" and "Affect," have a clear connection to each other in pointing broadly to interpersonal needs and modes of expression but diverge in taking us to queer interrogations of family, in the first instance, and the varying ways that emotive performance and capacities propel us, in the other. Much of this complexity is then reflected and compounded in our last section—"Borders"— which demonstrates queer theory's utility in examining transnational circulations of people, power and knowledge.

Queer studies is a contestatory conversation, one that we have sampled eclectically and, we hope, without strong bias. Nevertheless, it is clear from the essays that we have chosen that this anthology comes out of a queer studies centered primarily in the humanities and qualitative social sciences. We have not represented work in critical legal studies, the quantitative social sciences or the natural or physical sciences. Beyond showcasing the individual merits of the thirty-three essays we have collected here, we were interested in curating conversations between essays and across clusters of essays. Does Lee Edelman's capitalized "Child," emblematic of a complacently heteronormative stake in futurity, afford a different string of associations when juxtaposed with the diasporic figure of the infant Korean adoptee in the US who is central to David Eng's essay, for instance? Or in what ways does Sara Ahmed's recourse to queer feeling resonate differently in proximity to Iain Morland's challenge to queer thinking to accommodate the sometimes insensate figure of the intersex body? We have worked to find dialogue and disagreement and to allow key fissures to surface across the anthology. Even we, as editors, are not in full agreement about how best to define and demarcate the field of queer studies, although we hope that readers will concur with our sense that the registration of our differences of opinion across this anthology is more a benefit than a constraint.

Donald E. Hall

Annamarie Jagose

September 2011

Notes

1   Judith Butler, "Imitation and Gender Subordination" in *The Routledge Lesbian and Gay Studies Reader* (New York: Routledge, 1993), p. 314.

2   Henry Abelove, Michèle Aina Barale and David M. Halperin, "Introduction" in *The Routledge Lesbian and Gay Studies Reader* (New York: Routledge, 1993), p. xv. This and the following three

paragraphs are drawn in revised form from Annamarie Jagose, "Feminism's Queer Theory," *Feminism and Psychology* 19.2 (2009): 157–74.

3   Judith Butler, "Against Proper Objects," *differences: A Journal of Feminist Cultural Studies* 6.2–3: 1–26.

4   Abelove et al., "Introduction," pp. xv and xvi.

5   Abelove et al., "Introduction," p. xv.

6   Abelove et al., "Introduction," p. xv.

7   Abelove et al., "Introduction," p. xvii.

8   Abelove et al., "Introduction," pp. xv and xvii. The double-billing of bisexuality in this description—as both at the heart of the category *lesbian/gay* and part of a wider field of non-normative sexual practice or identity that is not self-evidently designated by *lesbian/gay*—is interesting. For an account of the ambivalent status bisexuality has had for both lesbian/gay and queer studies and the relationship between them, see Steven Angelides, *A History of Bisexuality* (Chicago: University of Chicago Press, 2001), an excerpt from which is reprinted as the fourth chapter of this volume.

9   See Annamarie Jagose, *Queer Theory: An Introduction* (New York: New York University Press, 1996); William B. Turner, *A Genealogy of Queer Theory* (Philadelphia: Temple University Press, 2000); Donald E. Hall, *Queer Theories* (Basingstoke: Palgrave Macmillan, 2003); Nikki Sullivan, *A Critical Introduction to Queer Theory* (Edinburgh: Edinburgh University Press, 2003) and Donald E. Hall, *Reading Sexualities: Hermeneutic Theory and the Future of Queer Studies* (London: Routledge, 2009).

10   David L. Eng, "Queering the Black Atlantic; Queering the Brown Atlantic," *GLQ: A Journal of Lesbian and Gay Studies* 17.1 (2010): 193.

11   Gayle Rubin, "Thinking Sex," *The Lesbian and Gay Studies Reader*, ed. Henry Abelove et al. (New York: Routledge, 1993), p. 15.

12   See, for instance, Carolyn Dinshaw, *Getting Medieval: Sexualities and Communities, Pre- and Postmodern* (Durham: Duke University Press, 1999); David M. Halperin, *How To Do the History of Homo sexuality* (Chicago: University of Chicago Press, 2002); Matt Houlbrook, *Queer London: Perils and Pleasures in the Sexual Metropolis, 1918–1957* (Chicago: University of Chicago Press, 2005) and Valerie Traub, *The Renaissance of Lesbianism in Early Modern England* (Cambridge: Cambridge University Press, 2002).

13   See, for instance, Elizabeth Freeman, *Time Binds: Queer Temporalities, Queer Histories* (Durham: Duke University Press, 2010); Judith Halberstam, *In a Queer Time and Place: Transgender Bodies, Subcultural Lives* (New York: New York University Press, 2005); José Esteban Muñoz, *Cruising Utopia: The Then and There of Queer Futurity* (New York: New York University Press, 2009) and Kathryn Bond Stockton, *The Queer Child, or Growing Sideways in the Twentieth Century* (Durham: Duke University Press, 2009).

14   See, for instance, Leo Bersani, *Homos* (Cambridge: Harvard University Press, 1995); Teresa de Lauretis, *Freud's Drive: Psychoanalysis, Literature, and Film* (Basingstoke: Palgrave Macmillan, 2008) and Lee Edelman, *No Future: Queer Theory and the Death Drive* (Durham: Duke University Press, 2004).

15   For an interesting account of queer studies as productively structured by an "isometric tension between queer world-making and world-shattering," see Joshua J. Weiner and Damon Young, "Queer Bonds," *GLQ: A Journal of Lesbian and Gay Studies* 17.2–3 (2011): 223–34.

16   See, for instance, Sara Ahmed, *The Promise of Happiness* (Durham: Duke University Press, 2010); Lauren Berlant, *Cruel Optimism* (Durham: Duke University Press, 2011); Ann Cvetkovich, *An Archive of Feelings: Trauma, Sexuality, and Lesbian Public Cultures* (Durham: Duke University Press, 2003); Heather Love, *Feeling Backward: Loss and the Politics of Queer History* (Cambridge: Harvard University Press, 2007); Christopher Nealon, *Foundlings: Lesbian and Gay Historical Emotion before Stonewall* (Durham: Duke University Press, 2001) and Elspeth Probyn, *Blush: Faces of Shame* (Sydney: University of New South Wales Press, 2005).

17   See, for example, Tom Boellstorff, *A Coincidence of Desires: Anthropology, Queer Studies, Indonesia* (Durham: Duke University Press, 2007); Arnaldo Cruz-Malavé and Martin F. Manalansan IV, eds, *Queer Globalizations: Citizenship and the Afterlife of Colonialism* (New York: New York University Press, 2002); Gayatri Gopinath, *Impossible Desires: Queer Diasporas and South Asian Public Cultures* (Durham: Duke University Press, 2005); Eithne Luibhéid, *Entry Denied: Controlling Sexuality at the Border* (Minneapolis: University of Minnesota Press, 2002); Fran Martin, *Situating Sexualities: Queer Representation in Taiwanese Fiction, Film and Public Culture* (Hong Kong: Hong Kong University Press, 2003) and Jasbir Puar, *Terrorist Assemblages: Homonationalism in Queer Times* (Durham: Duke University Press, 2007).

PART 1

Genealogies

Chapter 1

Eve Kosofsky Sedgwick

QUEER AND NOW

Eve Kosofsky Sedgwick was a pioneering voice in the field of queer theory whose influential publications include *Between Men: English Literature and Male Homosocial Desire* (1985), *Epistemology of the Closet* (1990) and *Tendencies* (1993), from which this chapter is taken. Additionally, Sedgwick published works of creative nonfiction and poetry: *Fat Art, Thin Art* (1994) and *A Dialogue on Love* (1999). Prior to her death in 2009, she taught graduate courses in English as Distinguished Professor at the City University of New York Graduate Center.

In "Queer and Now," Sedgwick vigorously argues against monolithic understandings of sexuality that presume sexual identity as a static identity category. In doing so, she offers several definitions of "queer," the first of which works to destabilize "common sense" approaches to sexual identity. Additionally, she notes that queer can refer to work that is not subsumed solely under gender and sexuality and explores intersectional uses of the term that acknowledge ethnicity, race and postcolonial nationalisms in relation to gender and sexual identity. Further, in a turn toward the autobiographical, Sedgwick recounts her experience with breast cancer in relation to the AIDS crisis in the early 1990s. Sedgwick asserts that both breast cancer and AIDS share a similar "discursive epistemology" in regards to discourses of "*outness*," which can lead to a transformative politics that draws attention to illnesses marked by gender and/or sexuality within public health discourse.

A motive

I THINK EVERYONE WHO does gay and lesbian studies is haunted by the suicides of adolescents. To us, the hard statistics come easily: that queer teenagers are two to three times likelier to attempt suicide, and to accomplish it, than others; that up to 30 percent of teen suicides are likely to be gay or lesbian; that a third of lesbian and gay teenagers say they have attempted suicide; that minority queer adolescents are at even more extreme risk.[1]

The knowledge is indelible, but not astonishing, to anyone with a reason to be attuned to the profligate way this culture has of denying and despoiling queer energies and lives.

I look at my adult friends and colleagues doing lesbian and gay work, and I feel that the survival of each one is a miracle. Everyone who survived has stories about how it was done

> —an outgrown anguish
> Remembered, as the Mile
> Our panting Ankle barely passed—
> When Night devoured the Road—
> But we—stood whispering in the House—
> And all we said—was "Saved"!

(as Dickinson has it).[2] How to tell kids who are supposed never to learn this, that, farther along, the road widens and the air brightens; that in the big world there are worlds where it's plausible, our demand to *get used to it*.

Epistemologies

I've heard of many people who claim they'd as soon their children were dead as gay. What it took me a long time to believe is that these people are saying no more than the truth. They even speak for others too delicate to use the cruel words. For there is all the evidence. The preponderance of school systems, public and parochial, where teachers are fired, routinely, for so much as intimating the right to existence of queer people, desires, activities, children. The routine denial to sexually active adolescents, straight *and* gay, of the things they need—intelligible information, support and respect, condoms—to protect themselves from HIV transmission. (As a policy aimed at punishing young gay people with death, this one is working: in San Francisco for instance, as many as 34 percent of the gay men under twenty-five being tested—and 54 percent of the young black gay men—are now HIV infected.)[3] The systematic separation of children from queer adults; their systematic sequestration from the truth about the lives, culture, and sustaining relations of adults they know who may be queer. The complicity of parents, of teachers, of clergy, even of the mental health professions in invalidating and hounding kids who show gender-dissonant tastes, behavior, body language. In one survey 26 percent of young gay men had been forced to leave home because of conflicts with parents over their sexual identity;[4] another report concludes that young gays and lesbians, many of them throwaways, comprise as many as a quarter of all homeless youth in the United States.[5]

And adults' systematic denial of these truths to ourselves. The statistics on the triple incidence of suicide among lesbian and gay adolescents come from a report prepared for the U.S. Department of Health and Human Services in 1989; under congressional pressure, recommendations based on this section of the report were never released. Under congressional pressure, in 1991 a survey of adolescent sexual behavior is defunded. Under the threat of congressional pressure, support for all research on sexuality suddenly (in the fall of 1991) dries up. Seemingly, this society wants its children to know nothing; wants its queer children to conform or (and this is not a figure of speech) die; and wants not to know that it is getting what it wants.

Promising, smuggling, reading, overreading

This history makes its mark on what, individually, we are and do. One set of effects turns up in the irreducible multilayeredness and multiphasedness of what queer survival means—since being a survivor on this scene is a matter of surviving *into* threat, stigma, the spiraling violence of gay- and lesbian-bashing, and (in the AIDS emergency) the omnipresence of somatic fear and wrenching loss. It is also to have survived into a moment of unprecedented cultural richness, cohesion, and assertiveness for many lesbian and gay adults. Survivors' guilt, survivors' glee, even survivors' responsibility: powerfully as these are experienced, they are also more than complicated by how permeable the identity "survivor" must be to the undiminishing currents of risk, illness, mourning, and defiance.

Thus I'm uncomfortable generalizing about people who do queer writing and teaching, even within literature; but some effects do seem widespread. I think many adults (and I am among them) are trying, in our work, to keep faith with vividly remembered promises made to ourselves in childhood: promises to make invisible possibilities and desires visible; to make the tacit things explicit; to smuggle queer representation in where it must be smuggled and, with the relative freedom of adulthood, to challenge queer-eradicating impulses frontally where they are to be so challenged.

I think that for many of us in childhood the ability to attach intently to a few cultural objects, objects of high or popular culture or both, objects whose meaning seemed mysterious, excessive, or oblique in relation to the codes most readily available to us, became a prime resource for survival. We needed for there to be sites where the meanings didn't line up tidily with each other, and we learned to invest those sites with fascination and love. This can't help coloring the adult relation to cultural texts and objects; in fact, it's almost hard for me to imagine another way of coming to care enough about literature to give a lifetime to it. The demands on both the text and the reader from so intent an attachment can be multiple, even paradoxical. For me, a kind of formalism, a visceral near-identification with the writing I cared for, at the level of sentence structure, metrical pattern, rhyme, was one way of trying to appropriate what seemed the numinous and resistant power of the chosen objects. Education made it easy to accumulate tools for this particular formalist project, because the texts that magnetized me happened to be novels and poems; it's impressed me deeply the way others of my generation and since seem to have invented for themselves, in the spontaneity of great need, the tools for a formalist apprehension of other less prestigious, more ubiquitous kinds of text: genre movies, advertising, comic strips.

For me, this strong formalist investment didn't imply (as formalism is generally taken to imply) an evacuation of interest from the passional, the imagistic, the ethical dimensions of the texts, but quite the contrary: the need I brought to books and poems was hardly to be circumscribed, and I felt I knew I would have to struggle to wrest from them sustaining news of the world, ideas, myself, and (in various senses) my kind. The reading practice founded on such basic demands and intuitions had necessarily to run against the grain of the most patent available formulae for young people's reading and life—against the grain, often, of the most accessible voices even in the texts themselves. At any rate, becoming a perverse reader was never a matter of my condescension to texts, rather of the surplus charge of my trust in them to remain powerful, refractory, and exemplary. And this doesn't seem an unusual way for ardent reading to function in relation to queer experience.

White nights

The first lesbian and gay studies class I taught was in the English Department at Amherst College in 1986. I thought I knew which five or six students (mostly queer) would show up, and I designed the course, with them in mind, as a seminar that would meet one evening a week, at my house. The first evening sixty-five students showed up—a majority of them, straight-identified.

Having taught a number of these courses by now, I know enough to expect to lose plenty of sleep over each of them. The level of accumulated urgency, the immediacy of the demand that students bring to them, is jolting. In most of their courses students have, unfortunately, learned to relinquish the expectation that the course material will address them where they live and with material they can hold palpably accountable; in gay/lesbian courses, though, such expectations seem to rebound, clamorous and unchastened, in all their rawness. Especially considering the history of denegation that most queer students bring with them to college, the vitality of their demand is a precious resource. Most often during a semester everyone will spend some time angry at everybody else. It doesn't surprise me when straight and gay students, or women and men students, or religious and nonreligious students have bones to pick with each other or with me. What has surprised me more is how divisive issues of methodology and disciplinarity are: the single most controversial thing in several under-graduate classes has been *that they were literature courses*, that the path to every issue we discussed simply had to take the arduous defile through textual interpretation.

Furthermore, it was instructive to me in that class at Amherst that a great many students, students who defined themselves as nongay, were incensed when (in an interview in the student newspaper) I told the story of the course's genesis. What outraged them was the mere notation that I had designed the course envisioning an enrollment of mostly lesbian and gay students. Their sense of entitlement as straight-defined students was so strong that they considered it an inalienable right to have all kinds of different lives, histories, cultures unfolded as if anthropologically in formats specifically designed—designed from the ground up—for maximum legibility to themselves: they felt they shouldn't so much as have to slow down the Mercedes to read the historical markers on the battlefield. That it was a field where the actual survival of other people in the class might at the very moment be at stake—where, indeed, in a variety of ways so might their own be—was hard to make notable to them among the permitted assumptions of their liberal arts education. Yet the same education was being used so differently by students who brought to it sharper needs, more supple epistemological frameworks.

Christmas effects

What's "queer"? Here's one train of thought about it. The depressing thing about the Christmas season—isn't it?—is that it's the time when all the institutions are speaking with one voice. The Church says what the Church says. But the State says the same thing: maybe not (in some ways it hardly matters) in the language of theology, but in the language the State talks: legal holidays, long school hiatus, special postage stamps, and all. And the language of commerce more than chimes in, as consumer purchasing is organized ever more narrowly around the final weeks of the calendar year, the Dow Jones aquiver over Americans' "holiday mood." The media, in turn, fall in triumphally behind the Christmas phalanx: ad-swollen magazines have oozing turkeys on the cover, while for the news industry every question turns into the Christmas question—Will hostages be free *for Christmas*? What did that flash flood or mass murder (umpty-ump people killed and maimed) do to those families' *Christmas*? And meanwhile, the pairing "families/Christmas" becomes increasingly tautological, as families more and more constitute themselves according to the schedule, and in the endlessly iterated image, of the holiday itself constituted in the image of "the" family.

The thing hasn't, finally, so much to do with propaganda for Christianity as with propa-ganda for Christmas itself. They all—religion, state, capital, ideology, domesticity, the discourses of power and legitimacy—line up with each other so neatly once a year, and the monolith so created is a thing one can come to view with unhappy eyes. What if instead there were a practice of valuing the ways in which meanings and institutions can be at loose ends with each other? What if the richest junctures weren't the ones where *everything means the same thing?* Think of that entity "the family," an impacted social space in which all of the following are meant to line up perfectly with each other:

> a surname
> a sexual dyad
> a legal unit based on state-regulated marriage
> a circuit of blood relationships
> a system of companionship and succor
> a building
> a proscenium between "private" and "public"
> an economic unit of earning and taxation
> the prime site of economic consumption
> the prime site of cultural consumption
> a mechanism to produce, care for, and acculturate children
> a mechanism for accumulating material goods over several generations
> a daily routine
> a unit in a community of worship
> a site of patriotic formation

and of course the list could go on. Looking at my own life, I see that—probably like most people—I have valued and pursued these various elements of family identity to quite differing degrees (e.g., no use at all for worship, much need of companionship). But what's been consistent in this particular life is an interest in *not* letting very many of these dimensions line up directly with each other at one time. I see it's been a ruling intuition for me that the most productive strategy (intellectually, emotionally) might be, whenever possible, to *dis*articulate them one from another, to *dis*engage them—the bonds of blood, of law, of habitation, of privacy, of companionship and succor—from the lockstep of their unanimity in the system called "family."

Or think of all the elements that are condensed in the notion of sexual identity, something that the common sense of our time presents as a unitary category. Yet, exerting any pressure at all on "sexual identity," you see that its elements include

> your biological (e.g., chromosomal) sex, male or female;
> your self-perceived gender assignment, male or female (supposed to be the same as your biological sex);
> the preponderance of your traits of personality and appearance, masculine or feminine (supposed to correspond to your sex and gender);
> the biological sex of your preferred partner;
> the gender assignment of your preferred partner (supposed to be the same as her/his biological sex);
> the masculinity or femininity of your preferred partner (supposed to be the opposite[6] of your own);
> your self-perception as gay or straight (supposed to correspond to whether your preferred partner is your sex or the opposite);
> your preferred partner's self-perception as gay or straight (supposed to be the same as yours);
> your procreative choice (supposed to be yes if straight, no if gay);
> your preferred sexual act(s) (supposed to be insertive if you are male or masculine, receptive if you are female or feminine);
> your most eroticized sexual organs (supposed to correspond to the procreative capabilities of your sex, and to your insertive/receptive assignment);

your sexual fantasies (supposed to be highly congruent with your sexual practice, but stronger in intensity);

your main locus of emotional bonds (supposed to reside in your preferred sexual partner);

your enjoyment of power in sexual relations (supposed to be low if you are female or feminine, high if male or masculine);

the people from whom you learn about your own gender and sex (supposed to correspond to yourself in both respects);

your community of cultural and political identification (supposed to correspond to your own identity);

and—again—many more. Even this list is remarkable for the silent presumptions it has to make about a given person's sexuality, presumptions that are true only to varying degrees, and for many people not true at all: that everyone "has a sexuality," for instance, and that it is implicated with each person's sense of overall identity in similar ways; that each person's most characteristic erotic expression will be oriented toward another person and not autoerotic; that if it is alloerotic, it will be oriented toward a single partner or kind of partner at a time; that its orientation will not change over time.[7] Normatively, as the parenthetical prescriptions in the list above suggest, it should be possible to deduce anybody's entire set of specs from the initial datum of biological sex alone—if one adds only the normative assumption that "the biological sex of your preferred partner" will be the opposite of one's own. With or without that heterosexist assumption, though, what's striking is the number and *difference* of the dimensions that "sexual identity" is supposed to organize into a seamless and univocal whole.

And if it doesn't?

That's one of the things that "queer" can refer to: the open mesh of possibilities, gaps, overlaps, dissonances and resonances, lapses and excesses of meaning when the constituent elements of anyone's gender, of anyone's sexuality aren't made (or *can't be* made) to signify monolithically. The experimental linguistic, epistemological, representational, political adventures attaching to the very many of us who may at times be moved to describe ourselves as (among many other possibilities) pushy femmes, radical faeries, fantasists, drags, clones, leatherfolk, ladies in tuxedoes, feminist women or feminist men, masturbators, bulldaggers, divas, Snap! queens, butch bottoms, storytellers, transsexuals, aunties, wannabes, lesbian-identified men or lesbians who sleep with men, or . . . people able to relish, learn from, or identify with such.

Again, "queer" can mean something different: a lot of the way I have used it so far in this dossier is to denote, almost simply, same-sex sexual object choice, lesbian or gay, whether or not it is organized around multiple criss-crossings of definitional lines. And given the historical and contemporary force of the prohibitions against *every* same-sex sexual expression, for anyone to disavow those meanings, or to displace them from the term's definitional center, would be to dematerialize any possibility of queerness itself.

At the same time, a lot of the most exciting recent work around "queer" spins the term outward along dimensions that can't be subsumed under gender and sexuality at all: the ways that race, ethnicity, postcolonial nationality criss-cross with these *and other* identity-constituting, identity-fracturing discourses, for example. Intellectuals and artists of color whose sexual self-definition includes "queer"—I think of an Isaac Julien, a Gloria Anzaldúa, a Richard Fung—are using the leverage of "queer" to do a new kind of justice to the fractal intricacies of language, skin, migration, state. Thereby, the gravity (I mean the *gravitas*, the meaning, but also the *center* of gravity) of the term "queer" itself deepens and shifts.

Another telling representational effect. A word so fraught as "queer" is—fraught with so many social and personal histories of exclusion, violence, defiance, excitement—never can only denote; nor even can it only connote; a part of its experimental force as a speech act is the way in which it dramatizes locutionary position itself. Anyone's use of "queer" about themselves means differently from their use of it about someone else. This is true (as it might also be true of "lesbian" or "gay") because of the violently different connotative evaluations that seem to cluster around the category. But "gay" and "lesbian" still present themselves (however delusively) as objective, empirical categories governed by empirical rules of evidence (however contested). "Queer" seems to hinge much more radically and explicitly on a person's undertaking particular, performative acts of experimental self-perception and filiation. A hypothesis worth making explicit: that there are important senses in which "queer" can signify only *when attached to the first person*. One possible corollary: that what it takes—all it takes—to make the description "queer" a true one is the impulsion *to* use it in the first person.

Current: project 1

The Golden Bowl, J. L. Austin, *Dr. Susan Love's Breast Book*, and Mme de Sévigné are stacked up, open-faced, on the chair opposite me as I write. I've got three projects braiding and unbraiding in my mind; the essays in this book mark, in different ways, their convergent and divergent progress. I see them as an impetus into future work as well.

Project 1—most of the essays in this book [*Tendencies*] embody it—is about desires and identifications that move across gender lines, including the desires of men for women and of women for men. In that sense, self-evidently, heterosexuality is one of the project's subjects. But the essays are queer ones. Their angle of approach is directed, not at reconfirming the self-evidence and "naturalness" of heterosexual identity and desire, but rather at rendering those culturally central, apparently monolithic constructions newly accessible to analysis and interrogation.

The project is difficult partly because of the asymmetries between the speech relations surrounding heterosexuality and homosexuality. As Michel Foucault argues, during the eighteenth and nineteenth centuries in Europe,

> Of course, the array of practices and pleasures continued to be referred to [heterosexual monogamy] as their internal standard; but it was spoken of less and less, or in any case with a growing moderation. Efforts to find out its secrets were abandoned; nothing further was demanded of it than to define itself from day to day. The legitimate couple, with its regular sexuality, had a right to more discretion. It tended to function as a norm, one that was stricter, perhaps, but quieter . . . .
>
> Although not without delay and equivocation, the natural laws of matrimony and the immanent rules of sexuality began to be recorded on two separate registers.[8]

Thus, if we are receptive to Foucault's understanding of modern sexuality as the most intensive site of the demand for, and detection or discursive production of, the Truth of individual identity, it seems as though this silent, normative, uninterrogated "regular" heterosexuality may not function as a sexuality at all. Think of how a culturally central concept like public/private is organized so as to preserve for heterosexuality the unproblematicalness, the apparent naturalness, of its *discretionary* choice between display and concealment: "public" names the space where cross-sex couples *may*, whenever they feel like it, display affection freely, while same-sex couples *must* always conceal it; while "privacy," to the degree that it is a right codified in U.S. law, has historically been centered on the protection-from-scrutiny of the married, cross-sex couple, a scrutiny to which (since the 1986 decision in *Bowers* v. *Hardwick*) same-sex relations on the other hand are unbendingly subject. Thus, heterosexuality is consolidated as the *opposite* of the "sex" whose secret, Foucault says, "the obligation to conceal . . . was but another aspect of the duty to admit to."[9] To the degree that heterosexuality does not function as a sexuality, however, there are stubborn barriers to making it accountable, to making it so much as visible, in the framework of projects of historicizing and hence denaturalizing sexuality. The making historically visible of heterosexuality is difficult because, under its institutional pseudonyms such as Inheritance, Marriage, Dynasty, Family, Domesticity, and Population, heterosexuality has been permitted to masquerade so fully as History itself—when it has not presented itself as the totality of Romance.

Project 2

Here I'm at a much earlier stage, busy with the negotiations involved in defining a new topic in a usable, heuristically productive way; it is still a series of hunches and overlaps; its working name is Queer Performativity. You can see the preoccupations that fuel the project already at work throughout *Epistemology of the Closet* as well as *Tendencies*, but I expect it to be the work of a next book to arrive at broadly usable formulations about them. Like a lot of theorists right now (Judith Butler and her important book *Gender Trouble* can, perhaps, stand in for a lot of the rest of us), I'm interested in the implications for gender and sexuality of a tradition of philosophical thought concerning certain utterances that do not merely describe, but actually perform the actions they name: *"J'accuse"*; "Be it resolved . . ."; "I thee wed"; "I apologize"; "I dare you." Discussions of linguistic performativity have become a place to reflect on ways in which language really can be said to produce effects: effects of identity, enforcement, seduction, challenge.[10] They also deal with how powerfully language *positions*: does it change the way we understand meaning, for instance, if the semantic force of a word like "queer" is so different in a first-person from what it is in a second- or third-person sentence?

   My sense is that, in a span of thought that arches at least from Plato to Foucault, there are some distinctive linkages to be traced between linguistic performativity and histories of same-sex desire. I want to go further with an argument implicit in *Epistemology of the Closet*: that both the act of coming out, and closetedness itself, can be taken as dramatizing certain features of linguistic performativity in ways that have broadly applicable implications. Among the striking aspects of considering closetedness in this framework, for instance, is that the speech act in question is a series of silences! I'm the more eager to think about performativity, too, because it may offer some ways of describing what *critical* writing can effect (promising? smuggling?); anything that offers to make this genre more acute and experimental, less numb to itself, is a welcome prospect.

Project 3

This project involves thinking and writing about something that's actually structured a lot of my daily life over the past year. Early in 1991 I was diagnosed, quite unexpectedly, with a breast cancer that had already spread to my lymph system, and the experiences of diagnosis, surgery, chemotherapy, and so forth, while draining and scary, have also proven just sheerly *interesting* with respect to exactly the issues of gender, sexuality, and identity formation that were already on my docket. (Forget the literal-mindedness of mastectomy, chemically induced menopause, etc.: I would warmly encourage anyone interested in the social construction of gender to find some way of spending half a year or so as a totally bald woman.) As a general principle, I don't like the idea of "applying" theoretical models to particular situations or texts—it's always more interesting when the pressure of application goes in both directions—but all the same it's hard not to think of this continuing experience as, among other things, an adventure in applied deconstruction.[11] How could I have arrived at a more efficient demonstration of the instability of the supposed oppositions that structure an experience of the "self"?—the part and the whole (when cancer so dramatically corrodes that distinction); safety and danger (when fewer than half of the women diagnosed with breast cancer display any of the statistically defined "risk factors" for the disease); fear and hope (when I feel—I've got a quarterly physical coming up—so much less prepared to deal with the news that a lump or rash *isn't* a metastasis than that it is); past and future (when a person anticipating the possibility of death, and the people who care for her, occupy temporalities that more and more radically diverge); thought and act (the words in my head are aswirl with fatalism, but at the gym I'm striding treadmills and lifting weights); or the natural and the technological (what with the exoskeleton of the bone-scan machine, the uncanny appendage of the IV drip, the bionic implant of the Port-a-cath, all in the service of imaging and recovering my "natural" healthy body in the face of its spontaneous and endogenous threat against itself). Problematics of undecidability present themselves in a new, unfacile way with a disease whose very *best* outcome—since breast cancer doesn't respect the five-year statute of limitations that constitutes cure for some other cancers—will be decades and decades of free-fall interpretive panic.

Part of what I want to see, though, is what's to be learned from turning this experience of dealing with cancer, in all its (and my) marked historical specificity, and with all the uncircumscribableness of the turbulence and threat involved, back toward a confrontation with the theoretical models that have helped me make sense of the world so far. The phenomenology of life-threatening illness; the performativity of a life threatened, relatively early on, by illness; the recent crystallization of a politics explicitly oriented around grave illness: exploring these connections *has* (at least for me it has) to mean hurling my energies outward to inhabit the very farthest of the loose ends where representation, identity, gender, sexuality, and the body can't be made to line up neatly together.

It's probably not surprising that gender is so strongly, so multiply valenced in the experience of breast cancer today. Received wisdom has it that being a breast cancer patient, even while it is supposed to pose unique challenges to one's sense of "femininity," nonetheless plunges one into an experience of almost archetypal Femaleness. Judith Frank is the friend whom I like to think of as Betty Ford to my Happy Rockefeller—the friend, that is, whose decision to be public about her own breast cancer diagnosis impelled me to the doctor with my worrisome lump; she and her lover, Sasha Torres, are only two of many women who have made this experience survivable for me: compañeras, friends, advisors, visitors, students, lovers, correspondents, relatives, caregivers (these being anything but discrete categories). Some of these are indeed people I have come to love in feminist- and/or lesbian-defined contexts; beyond that, a lot of the knowledge and skills that keep making these women's support so beautifully apropos derive from distinctive feminist, lesbian, and women's histories. (I'd single out, in this connection, the contributions of the women's health movement of the 70s—its trenchant analyses, its grass-roots and antiracist politics, its publications,[12] the attitudes and institutions it built and some of the careers it seems to have inspired.)

At the same time, though, another kind of identification was plaited inextricably across this one—not just for me, but for others of the women I have been close to as well. Probably my own most formative influence from a quite early age has been a viscerally intense, highly speculative (not to say inventive) cross-identification with gay men and gay male cultures as I inferred, imagined, and later came to know them. It wouldn't have required quite so overdetermined a trajectory, though, for almost any forty-year-old facing a protracted, life-threatening illness in 1991 to realize that the people with whom she had perhaps most in common, and from whom she might well have most to learn, are people living with AIDS, AIDS activists, and others whose lives had been profoundly reorganized by AIDS in the course of the 1980s.

As, indeed, had been my own life and those of most of the people closest to me. "Why me?" is the cri de coeur that is popularly supposed to represent Everywoman's deepest response to a breast cancer diagnosis—so much so that not only does a popular book on the subject have that title, but the national breast cancer information and support hotline is called Y-ME! Yet "Why me?" was not something it could have occurred to me to ask in a world where so many companions of my own age were already dealing with fear, debilitation, and death. I wonder, too, whether it characterizes the responses of the urban women of color forced by violence, by drugs, by state indifference or hostility, by AIDS and other illnesses, into familiarity with the rhythms of early death. At the time of my diagnosis the most immediate things that were going on in my life were, first, that I was coteaching (with Michael Moon) a graduate course in queer theory, including such AIDS-related material as Cindy Patton's stunning *Inventing AIDS*. Second, that we and many of the students in the class, students who indeed provided the preponderance of the group's leadership and energy at that time, were intensely wrapped up in the work (demonstrating, organizing, lobbying) of a very new local chapter of the AIDS activist organization ACT UP. And third, that at the distance of far too many miles I was struggling to communicate some comfort or vitality to a beloved friend, Michael Lynch, a pioneer in gay studies and AIDS activism, who seemed to be within days of death from an AIDS-related infection in Toronto.

"White Glasses," the final essay in *Tendencies*, tells more about what it was like to be intimate with this particular friend at this particular time. More generally though, the framework in which I largely experienced my diagnosis—and the framework in which my friends, students, house sharers, life companion, and others made available to me almost overwhelming supplies of emotional, logistical, and cognitive sustenance[13]—was very much shaped by AIDS and the critical politics surrounding it, including the politics of homophobia and of queer assertiveness. The AIDS activist movement, in turn, owes much to the women's health movement of the 70s; and in another turn, an activist politics of breast cancer, spearheaded by lesbians, seems in the last year or two to have been emerging based on the model of AIDS activism.[14] The dialectical epistemology of the two diseases, too—the kinds of secret each has constituted; the kinds of *outness* each has required and inspired—has made an intimate motive for me. As "White Glasses" says,

> It's as though there were transformative political work to be done just by being available to be identified with in the very grain of one's illness (which is to say, the grain of one's own intellectual, emotional, bodily self as refracted through illness and as resistant to it)—being available for identification to friends, but as well to people who don't love one; even to people who may not like one at all nor even wish one well.

My war against western civilization

That there were such people—that, indeed, the public discourse of my country was increasingly dominated by them—got harder and harder to ignore during the months of my diagnosis and initial treatment. For the first time, it was becoming routine to find my actual name, and not just the labels of my kind, on those journalistic lists of who was to be considered more dangerous than Saddam Hussein. In some ways, the timing of the diagnosis couldn't have been better: if I'd needed a reminder I had one that, sure enough, life *is* too short, at least mine is, for going head-to-head with people whose highest approbation, even, would offer no intellectual or moral support in which I could find value. Physically, I was feeling out of it enough that the decision to let this journalism wash over me was hardly a real choice—however I might find myself misspelled, misquoted, mis-paraphrased, or (in one hallucinatory account) married to Stanley Fish. It was the easier to deal psychically with having all these journalists scandalize my name because it was clear most of them wouldn't have been caught dead reading my work: the essay of mine that got the most free publicity, "Jane Austen and the Masturbating Girl," did so without having been read by a single one of the people who invoked it: it reached its peak of currency in hack circles months before it was published, and Roger Kimball's *Tenured Radicals*, which first singled it out for ridicule, seems to have gone to press before the essay was so much as *written*.[15]

Not that I imagine a few cozy hours reading *Epistemology of the Closet* would have won me rafts of fans amongst the punditterati. The attacks on me personally were based on such scummy evidential procedures that the most thin-skinned of scholars—so long as her livelihood was secure—could hardly have taken them to heart; the worst of their effects on me at the time was to give an improbable cosmic ratification (yes, actually, everything *is* about me!) to the self-absorption that forms, at best, an unavoidable feature of serious illness. If the journalistic hologram bearing my name seemed a relatively easy thing to disidentify from, though, I couldn't help registering with much greater intimacy a much more lethal damage. I don't know a gentler way to say it than that at a time when I've needed to make especially deep draughts on the reservoir of a desire to live and thrive, that resource has shown the cumulative effects of my culture's wasting depletion of it. It *is* different to experience from the vantage point of one's own bodily illness and need, all the brutality of a society's big and tiny decisions, explicit and encoded ones, about which lives have or have not value. Those decisions carry not only institutional and economic but psychic and, I don't doubt, somatic consequences. A thousand things make it impossible to mistake the verdict on queer lives and on women's lives, as on the lives of those who are poor or are not white. The hecatombs of queer youth; a decade squandered in a killing inaction on AIDS; the rapacious seizure from women of our defense against forced childbirth; tens of millions of adults and children excluded from the health care economy; treatment of homeless people as unsanitary refuse to be dealt with by periodic "sweeps"; refusal of condoms in prisons, persecution of needle exchange programs; denial and trivialization of histories of racism; or merely the pivot of a disavowing pronoun in a newspaper editorial: such things as these are facts, but at the same time they are piercing or murmuring voices in the heads of those of us struggling to marshal "our" resources against illness, dread, and devaluation. They speak to us. They have an amazing clarity.

A crazy little thing called *ressentiment*

There was something especially devastating about the wave of anti-"PC" journalism in the absolutely open contempt it displayed, and propagated, for *every* tool that has been so painstakingly assembled in the resistance against these devaluations. Through raucously orchestrated, electronically amplified campaigns of mock-incredulous scorn, intellectual and artistic as well as political possibilities, skills, ambitions, and knowledges have been laid waste with a relishing wantonness. No great difficulty in recognizing those aspects of the anti-"PC" craze that are functioning as covers for a rightist ideological putsch; but it has surprised me that so few people seem to view the recent developments as, among other things, part of an overarching history of anti-intellectualism: anti-intellectualism left as well as right. No twentieth-century political movement, after all, can afford not to play the card of populism, whether or not the popular welfare is what it has mainly at heart (indeed, perhaps especially where it is least so). And anti-intellectual pogroms, like anti-Semitic or queer-bashing ones, are quick, efficient, distracting, and almost universally understood signifiers for a populist solidarity that may boil down to nothing by the time it reaches the soup pot. It takes care and intellectual scrupulosity to forge an egalitarian politics not founded on such telegraphic slanders. Rightists today like to invoke the threatening specter of a propaganda-ridden socialist realism, but both they and the anti-intellectuals of the left might meditate on why the Nazis' campaign against "degenerate art" (Jewish, gay, modernist) was couched, as their own arguments are, in terms of assuring the instant, unmediated, and universal accessibility of all the sign systems of art (Goebbels even banning all art criticism in 1936, on the grounds that art is self-explanatory). It's hard to tell which assumption is more insultingly wrong: that the People (always considered, of course, as a monolithic unit) have no need and no faculty for engaging with work that is untransparent; or that the work most genuinely expressive of the People would be so univocal and so limpidly vacant as quite to obviate the labors and pleasures of interpretation. Anti-intellectuals today, at any rate, are happy to dispense with the interpretive process and depend instead on appeals to the supposedly self-evident: legislating against "*patently* offensive" art (no second looks allowed); citing titles as if they were texts; appealing to potted summaries and garbled trots as if they were variorum editions in the original Aramaic. The most self-evident things, as always, are taken—as if unanswerably—to be the shaming risibility of any form of oblique or obscure expression; and the flat inadmissibility of openly queer articulation.

Thought as privilege

These histories of anti-intellectualism cut across the "political correctness" debate in complicated ways. The term "politically correct" originated, after all, in the mockery by which experimentally and theoretically minded feminists, queers, and leftists (of every color, class, and sexuality) fought back against the stultifications of feminist and left anti-intellectualism. The hectoring, would-be-populist derision that difficult, ambitious, or sexually charged writing today encounters from the right is not always very different from the reception it has already met with from the left. It seems as if many academic feminists and leftists must be grinding their teeth at the way the right has willy-nilly conjoined their discursive fate with that of theorists and "deconstructionists"—just as, to be fair, many theorists who have betrayed no previous interest in the politics of class, race, gender, or sexuality may be more than bemused at turning up under the headings of "Marxism" or "multiculturalism." The right's success in grouping so many, so contestative, movements under the rubric "politically correct" is a coup of cynical slovenliness unmatched since the artistic and academic purges of Germany and Russia in the thirties.

What the American intellectual right has added to this hackneyed populist semiotic of *ressentiment* is an iridescent oilslick of elitist self-regard. Trying to revoke every available cognitive and institutional affordance for reflection, speculation, experimentation, contradiction, embroidery, daring, textual aggression, textual delight, double entendre, close reading, free association, wit—the family of creative activities that might, for purposes of brevity, more simply be called *thought*—they yet stake their claim as the only inheritors, defenders, and dispensers of a luscious heritage of thought that most of them would allow to be read only in the dead light of its pieties and its exclusiveness. Through a deafeningly populist rhetoric, they advertise the mean pleasures of ranking and gatekeeping as available to all. But the gates that we are invited to invigorate ourselves by cudgeling barbarians at open onto nothing but a *Goodbye, Mr. Chips* theme park.

What is the scarcity that fuels all this *ressentiment*? The leveraged burnout of the eighties certainly took its toll, economically, on universities as well as on other professions and industries. In secretaries' offices, in hospitals and HMOs [Health Maintenance Organizations], in network news bureaus, in Silicon Valley laboratories and beyond, the bottom line has moved much closer to a lot of people's work lives—impinging not just on whether they *have* work, but on what they do when they're there. But academic faculty, in our decentralized institutions, with our relatively diffuse status economy and our somewhat archaic tangle of traditions and prerogatives, have had, it seems, more inertial resistance to offer against the wholesale reorientation of our work practices around the abstractions of profit and the market. For some faculty at some colleges and universities, it is still strikingly true that our labor is divided up by task orientation (we may work on the book till it's done, explain to the student till she understands) rather than by a draconian time discipline; that what we produce is described and judged in qualitative as much as quantitative terms; that there is a valued place for affective expressiveness, and an intellectually productive permeability in the boundaries between public and private; that there are opportunities for collaborative work; and most importantly, that we can expend some substantial part of our paid labor on projects we ourselves have conceived, relating to questions whose urgency and interest make a claim on our own minds, imaginations, and consciences.

Millions of people today struggle to carve out—barely, at great cost to themselves—the time, permission, and resources, "after work" or instead of decently-paying work, for creativity and thought that will not be in the service of corporate profit, nor structured by its rhythms. Many, many more are scarred by the prohibitive difficulty of doing so. No two people, no two groups would make the same use of these resources, furthermore, so that no one can really pretend to be utilizing them "for" another. I see that some must find enraging the spectacle of people for whom such possibilities are, to a degree, built into the structure of our regular paid labor. Another way to understand that spectacle, though, would be as one remaining form of insistence that it is not inevitable—it is not a simple fact of nature—for the facilities of creativity and thought to represent rare or exorbitant *privilege*. Their economy should not and need not be one of scarcity.

The flamboyance with which some critical writers—I'm one of them—like to laminate our most ambitious work derives something, I think, from this situation. Many people doing all kinds of work are able to take pleasure in aspects of their work; but something different happens when the pleasure is not only taken but openly displayed. I like to make that different thing happen. Some readers identify strongly with the possibility of a pleasure so displayed; others disidentify from it with violent repudiations; still others find themselves occupying less stable positions in the circuit of contagion, fun, voyeurism, envy, participation, and stimulation. When the pleasure is attached to meditative or artistic productions that deal, not always in an effortlessly accessible way, with difficult and painful realities among others, then readers' responses become even more complex and dramatic, more productive for the author and for themselves. Little wonder then that sexuality, the locus of so many showy pleasures and untidy identities and of so much bedrock confrontation, opacity, and loss, should bear so much representational weight in arguments about the structure of intellectual work and life. Sexuality in this sense, perhaps, can *only* mean queer sexuality: so many of us have the need for spaces of thought and work where everything doesn't mean the same thing!

So many people of varying sexual practices, too, enjoy incorrigibly absorbing imaginative, artistic, intellectual, and affective lives that have been richly nourished by queer energies—and that are savagely diminished when the queerness of those energies is trashed or disavowed. In the very first of the big "political correctness" scare pieces in the mainstream press, *Newsweek* pontificated that under the reign of multiculturalism in colleges, "it would not be enough for a student to refrain from insulting homosexuals. . . . He or she would be expected to . . . study their literature and culture alongside that of Plato, Shakespeare, and Locke."[16] *Alongside?* Read any Sonnets lately? You dip into the *Phaedrus* often?

To invoke the Utopian bedroom scene of Chuck Berry's immortal *aubade*: Roll over, Beethoven, and tell Tchaikovsky the news.

Notes

1　Paul Gibson, "Gay Male and Lesbian Youth Suicide," U.S. Department of Health and Human Services, *Report of the Secretary's Task Force on Youth Suicide* (Washington, D.C., 1989), vol. 3, pp. 110–42.

2　*The Complete Poems of Emily Dickinson*, ed. Thomas H. Johnson (Boston: Little, Brown, 1960), poem 325, p. 154.

3　T. A. Kellogg et al., "Prevalence of HIV-1 Among Homosexual and Bisexual Men in the San Francisco Bay Area: Evidence of Infection Among Young Gay Men," *Seventh International AIDS Conference Abstract Book*, vol. 2 (Geneva, 1991) (W.C. 3010), p. 298.

4　G. Remafedi, "Male Homosexuality: The Adolescent's Perspective," unpublished manuscript, Adolescent Health Program, University of Minnesota, 1985. Cited in Gibson, "Gay Male and Lesbian Youth Suicide."

5　Gibson, "Gay Male and Lesbian Youth Suicide," pp. 113–15.

6　The binary calculus I'm describing here depends on the notion that the male and female sexes are each other's "opposites," but I do want to register a specific demurral against that bit of easy common sense. Under no matter what cultural construction, women and men are more like each other than chalk is like cheese, than ratiocination is like raisins, than up is like down, or than 1 is like 0. The biological, psychological, and cognitive attributes of men overlap with those of women by vastly more than they differ from them.

7　A related list that amplifies some of the issues raised in this one appears in the introduction to my *Epistemology of the Closet* (Berkeley: University of California Press, 1990), pp. 25–26.

8　Michel Foucault, *The History of Sexuality*, vol. 1: *An Introduction*, trans. Robert Hurley (New York: Pantheon Books, 1978), pp. 38–40.

9　Ibid., p. 61.

10　One of the most provocative discussions of performativity in relation to literary criticism is Shoshana Felman, *The Literary Speech Act: Don Juan with J.L. Austin, or Seduction in Two Languages*, trans. Catherine Porter (Ithaca, N.Y.: Cornell University Press, 1983); most of the current work being done on performativity in relation to sexuality and gender is much indebted to Judith Butler's *Gender Trouble: Feminism and the Subversion of Identity* (New York: Routledge, 1989).

11　That deconstruction can offer crucial resources of thought for survival under duress will sound astonishing, I know, to anyone who knows it mostly from the journalism on the subject—journalism that always depicts "deconstructionism," not as a group of usable intellectual tools, but as a set of beliefs involving a patently absurd dogma ("nothing really exists"), loopy as Christian Science but as exotically aggressive as (American journalism would also have us find) Islam. I came to my encounter with breast cancer not as a member of a credal sect of "deconstructionists" but as someone who needed all the cognitive skills she could get. I found, as often before, that I had some good and relevant ones from my deconstructive training.

12　The work of this movement is most available today through books like the Boston Women's Health Book Collective's *The New Our Bodies, Ourselves: Updated and Expanded for the Nineties* (New York: Simon and Schuster, 1992). An immensely important account of dealing with breast cancer in the context of feminist, antiracist, and lesbian activism is Audre Lorde, *The Cancer Journals*, 2nd ed. (San Francisco: Spinsters Ink, 1988) and *A Burst of Light* (Ithaca, N.Y.: Firebrand Books, 1988).

13　And physical: I can't resist mentioning the infallibly appetite-provoking meals that Jonathan Goldberg, on sabbatical in Durham, planned and cooked every night during many queasy months of my chemotherapy.

14　On this, see Alisa Solomon, "The Politics of Breast Cancer," *Village Voice* 14 May 1991, pp. 22–27; Judy Brady, ed., *1 in 3: Women with Cancer Confront an Epidemic* (Pittsburgh and San Francisco: Cleis Press, 1991); Midge Stocker, ed., *Cancer as a Woman's Issue: Scratching the Surface* (Chicago: Third Side Press, 1991); and Sandra Butler and Barbara Rosenblum, *Cancer in Two Voices* (San Francisco: Spinsters Ink, 1991).

15   Roger Kimball, *Tenured Radicals: How Politics Has Corrupted Our Higher Education* (New York: Harper & Row, 1990), pp. 145–46.

16   Jerry Adler et al., "Taking Offense: Is This the New Enlightenment on Campus or the New McCarthyism?" *Newsweek*, 24 December 1990, p. 48.

"Queer and Now" was written in 1991. Ken Wissoker thought up the title, and Mark Seltzer cheered me on with it.

Chapter 2

Judith Butler

CRITICALLY QUEER

Judith Butler has published work on philosophy, pornography, feminist and psychoanalytic theory, film, the politics of race and sexuality, and, most recently, war and grief. She is most famous for *Gender Trouble: Feminism and the Subversion of Identity* (1990) and *Bodies that Matter: On the Discursive Limits of Sex* (1993).

In "Critically Queer," Butler discusses the instability of identity formations and the power of citation and repetition as forces that bind identity categories, despite their inherent instability. Butler argues for a genealogical critique of the term "queer," analyzing how queer emerges as a discursive site that raises questions about the possibilities of force, subversion, stability, and variability within performativity. For Butler, queer must remain a protean term and a "site of collective contestation" that can be deployed through performativity within myriad political contexts. Butler argues against the voluntarist accounts of gender performance that emerged following the publication of *Gender Trouble*, and reiterates that gender performance is both involuntary and imperfect. In doing so, she reworks the notion of theatricality through performativity for contemporary queer politics.

> Discourse is not life; its time is not yours.
> (Michel Foucault, "Politics and the Study of Discourse")

EVE SEDGWICK'S RECENT reflections on queer performativity ask us not only to consider how a certain theory of speech acts applies to queer practices, but how it is that "queering" persists as a defining moment of performativity.[1] The centrality of the marriage ceremony in J.L. Austin's examples of performativity suggests that the heterosexualization of the social bond is the paradigmatic form for those speech acts which bring about what they name. "I pronounce you . . ." puts into effect the relation that it names. But where and when does such a performative draw its force, and what happens to the performative when its purpose is precisely to undo the presumptive force of the heterosexual ceremonial?

Performative acts are forms of authoritative speech: most performatives, for instance, are statements which, in the uttering, also perform a certain action and exercise a binding power.[2] Implicated in a network of authorization and punishment, performatives tend to include legal sentences, baptisms, inaugurations, declarations of ownership, statements that not only perform an action, but confer a binding power on the action performed. The power of discourse to produce that which it names is thus essentially linked with the question of performativity. The performative is thus one domain in which power acts *as* discourse.

Importantly, however, there is no power, construed as a subject, that acts, but only a reiterated acting that *is* power in its persistence and instability. This is less an "act," singular and deliberate, than a nexus of power and discourse that repeats or mimes the discursive gestures of power. Hence, the judge who authorizes and installs the situation he names (we shall call him "he," figuring this model of authority as masculinist) invariably *cites* the law that he applies, and it is the power of this citation that gives the performative its binding or confer-ring power. And though it may appear that the binding power of his words is derived from the force of his will or from a prior authority, the opposite is more true: it is *through* the cita-tion of the law that the figure of the judge's "will" is produced and that the "priority" of textual authority is established.[3] Indeed, it is through the invocation of convention that the speech act of the judge derives its binding power; that binding power is to be found neither in the subject of the judge nor in his will, but in the citational legacy by which a contemporary "act" emerges in the context of a chain of binding conventions.

Where there is an "I" who utters or speaks and thereby produces an effect in discourse, there is first a discourse which precedes and enables that "I" and forms in language the constraining trajectory of its will. Thus there is no "I" who stands *behind* discourse and executes its volition or will *through* discourse. On the contrary, the "I" only comes into being through being called, named, interpellated (to use the Althusserian term), and this discursive constitution takes place prior to the "I"; it is the transitive invocation of the "I." Indeed, I can only say "I" to the extent that I have first been addressed, and that address has mobilized my place in speech; paradoxically, the discursive condition of social recognition *precedes and conditions* the formation of the subject: recognition is not conferred on a subject, but forms that subject. Further, the impossibility of a full recognition, that is, of ever fully inhabiting the name by which one's social identity is inaugurated and mobilized, implies the instability and incompleteness of subject-formation. The "I" is thus a citation of the place of the "I" in speech, where that place has a certain priority and anonymity with respect to the life it animates: it is the historically revisable possibility of a name that precedes and exceeds me, but without which I cannot speak.

Queer trouble

The term "queer" emerges as an interpellation that raises the question of the status of force and opposition, of stability and variability, *within* performativity. The term "queer" has operated as one linguistic practice whose purpose has been the shaming of the subject it names or, rather, the producing of a subject *through* that shaming interpellation. "Queer" derives its force precisely through the repeated invocation by which it has become linked to accusation, pathologization, insult. This is an invocation by which a social bond among homophobic communities is formed through time. The interpellation echoes past interpellations, and binds the speakers, as if they spoke in unison across time. In this sense, it is always an imaginary chorus that taunts "queer!" To what extent, then, has the performative "queer" operated alongside, as a deformation of, the "I pronounce you . . ." of the marriage ceremony? If the performative operates as the sanction that performs the heterosexualization of the social bond, perhaps it also comes into play precisely as the shaming taboo which "queers" those who resist or oppose that social form as well as those who occupy it without hegemonic social sanction.

On that note, let us remember that reiterations are never simply replicas of the same. And the "act" by which a name authorizes or de-authorizes a set of social or sexual relations is, of necessity, *a repetition*. Let me, for the moment, cite Derrida:

> Could a performative utterance succeed if its formulation did not repeat a "coded" or iterable utterance, or in other words, if the formula I pronounce in order to open a meeting, launch a ship or a marriage were not identifiable as *conforming* with an iterable model, if it were not then identifiable in some way as a "citation"? . . . In such a typology, the category of intention will not disappear; it will have its place, but from that place it will no longer be able to govern the entire scene and system of utterance.
>
> (18)

If a performative provisionally succeeds (and I will suggest that "success" is always and only provisional), then it is not because an intention successfully governs the action of speech, but only because that action echoes a prior action, and *accumulates the force of authority through the repetition or citation of a prior, authoritative set of practices*. What this means, then, is that a performative "works" to the extent that *it draws on and covers over* the constitutive conventions by which it is mobilized. In this sense, no term or statement can function performatively without the accumulating and dissimulating historicity of force.

This view of performativity implies that discourse has a history[4] that not only precedes but conditions its contemporary usages, and that this history effectively decenters the presentist view of the subject as the exclusive origin or owner of what is said.[5] What it also means is that the terms to which we do, nevertheless, lay claim, the terms through which we insist on politicizing identity and desire, often demand a turn *against* this constitutive historicity. Those of us who have questioned the presentist assumptions in contemporary identity categories are, therefore, sometimes charged with depoliticizing theory. And yet, if the genealogical critique of the subject is the interrogation of those constitutive and exclusionary relations of power through which contemporary discursive resources are formed, then it follows that the critique of the queer subject is crucial to the continuing *democratization* of queer politics. As much as identity terms must be used, as much as "outness" is to be affirmed, these same notions must become subject to a critique of the exclusionary operations of their own production: for whom is outness an historically available and affordable option? Is there an unmarked class character to the demand for universal "outness"? Who is represented by *which* use of the term, and who is excluded? For whom does the term present an impossible conflict between racial, ethnic, or religious affiliation and sexual politics? What kinds of policies are enabled by what kinds of usages, and which are backgrounded or erased from view? In this sense, the genealogical critique of the queer subject will be central to queer politics to the extent that it constitutes a self-critical dimension within activism, a persistent reminder to take the time to consider the exclusionary force of one of activism's most treasured contemporary premises.

As much as it is necessary to assert political demands through recourse to identity categories, and to lay claim to the power to name oneself and determine the conditions under which that name is used, it is also impossible to sustain that kind of mastery over the trajectory of those categories within discourse. This is not an argument *against* using identity categories, but it is a reminder of the risk that attends every such use. The expectation of self-determination that self-naming arouses is paradoxically contested by the historicity of the name itself: by the history of the usages that one never controlled, but that constrain the very usage that now emblematizes autonomy; by the future efforts to deploy the term against the grain of the current ones, efforts that will exceed the control of those who seek to set the course of the terms in the present.

If the term "queer" is to be a site of collective contestation, the point of departure for a set of historical reflections and futural imaginings, it will have to remain that which is, in the present, never fully owned, but always and only redeployed, twisted, queered from a prior usage and in the direction of urgent and expanding political purposes, and perhaps also yielded in favor of terms that do that political work more effectively. Such a yielding may well become necessary in order to accommodate—without domesticating—democratizing contestations that have and will redraw the contours of the movement in ways that can never be fully anticipated.

It may be that the conceit of autonomy implied by self-naming is the paradigmatically presentist conceit, that is, the belief that there is a one who arrives in the world, in discourse, without a history, that this one makes oneself in and through the magic of the name, that language expresses a "will" or a "choice" rather than a complex and constitutive history of discourse and power which composes the invariably ambivalent resources through which a queer and queering agency is forged and reworked. To recast queer agency in this chain of historicity is thus to avow a set of constraints on the past and the future that mark at once the *limits* of agency and its most *enabling conditions*.

As expansive as the term "queer" is meant to be, it is used in ways that enforce a set of overlapping divisions: in some contexts, the term appeals to a younger generation who want to resist the more institutionalized and reformist politics sometimes signified by "lesbian and gay"; in some contexts, sometimes the same, it has marked a predominantly white movement that has not fully addressed the way in which "queer" plays—or fails to play—within non-white communities; and whereas in some instances it has mobilized a lesbian activism (Smyth), in others the term represents a false unity of women and men. Indeed, it may be that the critique of the term will initiate a resurgence of both feminist and anti-racist mobilization within lesbian and gay politics or open up new possibilities for coalitional alliances that do not presume that these constituencies are radically distinct from one another. The term will be revised, dispelled, rendered obsolete to the extent that it yields to the demands which resist the term precisely because of the exclusions by which it is mobilized.

We no more create from nothing the political terms which come to represent our "freedom" than we are responsible for the terms that carry the pain of social injury. And yet, neither of those terms are as a result any less necessary to work and rework within political discourse.

In this sense, it remains politically necessary to lay claim to "women," "queer," "gay," and "lesbian," precisely because of the way these terms, as it were, lay their claim on us prior to our full knowing. Laying claim to such terms in reverse will be necessary to refute homophobic deployments of the terms in law, public policy, on the street, in "private" life. But the necessity to mobilize "the necessary error" of identity (Spivak's term) will always be in tension with the democratic contestation of the term which works against its deployments in racist and misogynist discursive regimes. If "queer" politics postures independently of these other modalities of power, it will lose its democratizing force. The political deconstruction of "queer" ought not to paralyze the use of such terms, but, ideally, to extend its range, to make us consider at what expense and for what purposes the terms are used, and through what relations of power such categories have been wrought.

Some recent race theory has underscored the use of "race" in the service of "racism," and proposed a politically informed inquiry into the process of *racialization*, the formation of race (Omi and Winant; Appiah; Guillaumin; Lloyd). Such an inquiry does not suspend or ban the term, although it does insist that an inquiry into formation is linked to the contemporary question of what is at stake in the term. The point may be taken for queer studies as well, such that "queering" might signal an inquiry into (a) the *formation* of homosexualities (an historical inquiry which cannot take the stability of the term for granted, despite the political pressure to do so) and (b) the *deformative* and *misappropriative* power that the term currently enjoys. At stake in such a history will be the differential formation of homosexuality across racial boundaries, including the question of how racial and reproductive injunctions are articulated through one another.

If identity is a necessary error, then the assertion of "queer" will be incontrovertibly necessary, but that assertion will constitute only one part of "politics." It is equally necessary, and perhaps also equally impossible, to affirm the contingency of the term: to let it be vanquished by those who are excluded by the term but who justifiably expect representation by it, to let it take on meanings that cannot now be anticipated by a younger generation whose political vocabulary may well carry a very different set of investments. Indeed, the term "queer" itself has been precisely the discursive rallying point for younger lesbians and gay men and, in yet other contexts, for lesbian interventions and, in yet other contexts, for bisexuals and straights for whom the term expresses an affiliation with anti-homophobic politics. That it can become such a discursive site whose uses are not fully constrained in advance ought to be safeguarded not only for the purposes of continuing to democratize queer politics, but also to expose, affirm, and rework the specific historicity of the term.

Gender performativity and drag

How, if at all, is the notion of discursive resignification linked to the notion of gender parody or impersonation? If gender is a mimetic effect, is it therefore a choice or a dispensable artifice? If not, how did this reading of *Gender Trouble* emerge? There are at least two reasons for the misapprehension, one which I myself produced by citing drag as an example of performativity (taken then, by some, to be *exemplary*, that is, *the* example of performativity), and another which has to do with the political needs of a growing queer movement in which the publicization of theatrical agency has become quite central.[6]

The misapprehension about gender performativity is this: that gender is a choice, or that gender is a role, or that gender is a construction that one puts on, as one puts on clothes in the morning, that there is a "one" who is prior to this gender, a one who goes to the wardrobe of gender and decides with deliberation which gender it will be today. This is a voluntarist account of gender which presumes a subject, intact, prior to its gendering. The sense of gender performativity that I meant to convey is something quite different.

Gender is performative insofar as it is the *effect* of a regulatory regime of gender differences in which genders are divided and hierarchized *under constraint*. Social constraints, taboos, prohibitions, threats of punishment operate in the ritualized repetition of norms, and this repetition constitutes the temporalized scene of gender construction and destabilization. There is no subject who precedes or enacts this repetition of norms. To the extent that this repetition creates an effect of gender uniformity, a stable effect of masculinity or femininity, it produces and destabilizes the notion of the subject as well, for the subject only comes into intelligibility through the matrix of gender. Indeed, one might construe repetition as precisely that which *undermines* the conceit of voluntarist mastery designated by the subject in language.[7]

There is no subject who is "free" to stand outside these norms or to negotiate them at a distance; on the contrary, the subject is retroactively produced by these norms in their repetition, precisely as their effect. What we might call "agency" or "freedom" or "possibility" is always a specific political prerogative that is produced by the gaps opened up in regulatory norms, in the interpellating work of such norms, in the process of their self-repetition. Freedom, possibility, agency do not have an abstract or pre-social status, but are always negotiated within a matrix of power.

Gender performativity is not a matter of choosing which gender one will be today. Performativity is a matter of reiterating or repeating the norms by which one is constituted:

it is not a radical fabrication of a gendered self. It is a compulsory repetition of prior and subjectivating norms, ones which cannot be thrown off at will, but which work, animate, and constrain the gendered subject, and which are also the resources from which resistance, subversion, displacement are to be forged. The practice by which gendering occurs, the embodying of norms, is a compulsory practice, a forcible production, but not for that reason fully determining. To the extent that gender is an assignment, it is an assignment which is never quite carried out according to expectation, whose addressee never quite inhabits the ideal s/he is compelled to approximate.

This failure to approximate the norm, however, is not the same as the subversion of the norm. There is no promise that subversion will follow from the reiteration of constitutive norms; there is no guarantee that exposing the naturalized status of heterosexuality will lead to its subversion. Heterosexuality can augment its hegemony *through* its denaturalization, as when we see denaturalizing parodies which reidealize heterosexual norms *without* calling them into question. But sometimes the very term that would annihilate us becomes the site of resistance, the possibility of an enabling social and political signification: I think we have seen that quite clearly in the astounding transvaluation undergone by "queer." This is for me the enactment of a prohibition and a degradation against itself, the spawning of a different order of values, of a political affirmation from and through the very term which in a prior usage had as its final aim the eradication of precisely such an affirmation.

It may seem, however, that there is a difference between the embodying or performing of gender norms and the performative use of language. Are these two different senses of "performativity," or do they converge as modes of citationality in which the compulsory character of certain social imperatives becomes subject to a more promising deregulation? Gender norms operate by requiring the embodiment of certain ideals of femininity and masculinity, ones which are almost always related to the idealization of the heterosexual bond. In this sense, the initiatory performative, "It's a girl!", anticipates the eventual arrival of the sanction, "I pronounce you man and wife." Hence, also, the peculiar pleasure of the cartoon strip in which the infant is first interpellated into discourse with "It's a lesbian!" Far from an essentialist joke, the queer appropriation of the performative mimes and exposes both the binding power of the heterosexualizing law *and its expropriability*.

To the extent that the naming of the "girl" is transitive, that is, initiates the process by which a certain "girling" is compelled, the term or, rather, its symbolic power, governs the formation of a corporeally enacted femininity that never fully approximates the norm. This is a "girl," however, who is compelled to "cite" the norm in order to qualify and remain a viable subject. Femininity is thus not the product of a choice, but the forcible citation of a norm, one whose complex historicity is indissociable from relations of discipline, regulation, punishment. Indeed, there is no "one" who takes on a gender norm. On the contrary, this citation of the gender norm is necessary in order to qualify as a "one," to become viable as a "one," where subject-formation is dependent on the prior operation of legitimating gender norms.

It is in terms of a norm that compels a certain "citation" in order for a viable subject to be produced that the notion of gender performativity calls to be rethought. And precisely in relation to such a compulsory citationality that the theatricality of gender is also to be explained. Theatricality need not be conflated with self-display or self-creation. Within queer politics, indeed, within the very signification that is "queer," we read a resignifying practice in which the de-sanctioning power of the name "queer" is reversed to sanction a contestation of the terms of sexual legitimacy. Paradoxically, but also with great promise, the subject who is "queered" into public discourse through homophobic interpellations of various kinds *takes up* or *cites* that very term as the discursive basis for an opposition. This kind of citation will emerge as *theatrical* to the extent that it *mimes and renders hyperbolic* the discursive convention that it also *reverses*. The hyperbolic gesture is crucial to the exposure of the homophobic "law" which can no longer control the terms of its own abjecting strategies.

To oppose the theatrical to the political within contemporary queer politics is, I would argue, an impossibility: the hyperbolic "performance" of death in the practice of "die-ins" and the theatrical "outness" by which queer activism has disrupted the closeting distinction between public and private space, have proliferated sites of politicization and AIDS awareness throughout the public realm. Indeed, an important set of histories might be told in which the increasing politicization *of* theatricality for queers is at stake (more productive, I think, than an insistence on the two as polar opposites within queerness). Such a history might include traditions of cross-dressing, drag balls, streetwalking, butch-femme spectacles, the sliding between the "march" (NYC) and the "parade" (SF); die-ins by ACT UP, kiss-ins by Queer Nation; drag performance benefits for AIDS (by which I would include both Lypsinka's and Liza Minnelli's in which she, finally, does Judy);[8] the convergence of theatrical work with theatrical activism;[9] performing excessive lesbian sexuality and iconography that effectively counters the desexualization of the lesbian; tactical interruptions of public forums by lesbian and gay activists in favor of drawing public attention and outrage to the failure of government funding of AIDS research and outreach.

The increasing theatricalization of political rage in response to the killing inattention of public policy-makers on the issue of AIDS is allegorized in the recontextualization of "queer" from its place within a homophobic strategy of abjection and annihilation to an insistent and public severing of that interpellation from the effect of shame. To the extent that shame is produced as the stigma not only of AIDS, but also of queerness, where the latter is understood through homophobic causalities as the "cause" and "manifestation" of the illness, theatrical rage is part of the public resistance to that interpellation of shame. Mobilized by the injuries of homophobia, theatrical rage reiterates those injuries precisely through an "acting out," one that does not merely repeat or recite those injuries, but that deploys a hyperbolic display of death and injury to overwhelm the epistemic resistance to AIDS and to the graphics of suffering, or a hyperbolic display of kissing to shatter the epistemic blindness to an increasingly graphic and public homosexuality.

Melancholia and the limits of performance

Although there were probably no more than five paragraphs in *Gender Trouble* devoted to drag, readers have often cited the description of drag as if it were the "example" which explains the meaning of performativity. The conclusion is drawn that gender performativity is a matter of constituting who one is on the basis of what one performs. And further, that gender itself might be proliferated beyond the binary frame of "man" and "woman" depending on what one performs, thereby valorizing drag not only as the paradigm of gender performance, but as the means by which heterosexual presumption might be undermined through the strategy of proliferation.

The point about "drag" was, however, much more centrally concerned with a critique of the truth-regime of "sex," one which I took to be pervasively heterosexist: the distinction between the "inside" truth of femininity, considered as psychic disposition or ego-core, and the "outside" truth, considered as appearance or presentation, produces a contradictory formation of gender in which no fixed "truth" can be established. Gender is neither a purely psychic truth, conceived as "internal" and "hidden," nor is it reducible to a surface appearance; on the contrary, its undecidability is to be traced as the play *between* psyche and appearance (where the latter domain includes what appears *in words*). Further, this will be a "play" regulated by heterosexist constraints though not, for that reason, fully reducible to them.

In no sense can it be concluded that the part of gender that is performed is therefore the "truth" of gender; performance as bounded "act" is distinguished from performativity insofar as the latter consists in a reiteration of norms which precede, constrain, and exceed the performer and in that sense cannot be taken as the fabrication of the performer's "will" or "choice"; further, what is "performed" works to conceal, if not to disavow, what remains opaque, unconscious, un-performable. The reduction of performativity to performance would be a mistake.

In *Gender Trouble*, I rejected the expressive model of drag which holds that some interior truth is exteriorized in performance, but what I failed to do is to refer the theatricality of drag back to the psychoanalytic discussions that preceded it, for psychoanalysis insists that the opacity of the unconscious sets limits to the exteriorization of the psyche. It also argues, rightly I think, that what is exteriorized or performed can only be understood through reference to what is barred from the signifier and from the domain of corporeal legibility.

It would have been useful as well to bring forward the discussion of gender melancholia into the discussion of drag, given the iconographic figure of the melancholic drag queen. Here one might ask also after the disavowal that occasions performance and that performance might be said to enact, where performance engages "acting out" in the psychoanalytic sense.[10] If melancholia in Freud's sense is the effect of an ungrieved loss (a sustaining of the lost object/Other as a psychic figure with the consequence of heightened identification with that Other, self-beratement, and the acting out of unresolved anger and love),[11] it may be that performance, understood as "acting out," is significantly related to the problem of unacknowledged loss.

Where there is an ungrieved loss in drag performance (and I am sure that such a generalization cannot be universalized), perhaps it is a loss that is refused and incorporated in the performed identification, one which reiterates a gendered idealization and its radical uninhabitability. This is, then, neither a territorialization of the feminine by the masculine, nor an "envy" of the masculine by the feminine, nor a sign of the essential plasticity of gender. What it does suggest is that gender performance allegorizes a loss it cannot grieve, allegorizes the incorporative fantasy of melancholia whereby an object is phantasmatically taken in or on as a way of refusing to let it go.

The analysis above is a risky one because it suggests that for a "man" performing femininity, or for a "woman" performing masculinity (the latter is always, in effect, to perform a little less, given that femininity is often cast as the spectacular gender), there is an attachment to, and a loss refusal of, the figure of femininity by the man, or the figure of masculinity by the woman. Thus it is important to underscore that drag is an effort to negotiate cross-gendered identification, but that cross-gendered identification is not the exemplary paradigm for thinking about homosexuality, although it may be one. In this sense, drag allegorizes some set of melancholic incorporative fantasies that stabilize *gender*. Not only are a vast number of drag performers straight, but it would be a mistake to think that homosexuality is best explained through the performativity that is drag. What does seem useful in this analysis, however, is that drag exposes or allegorizes the mundane psychic and performative practices by which heterosexualized genders form themselves through the renunciation of the *possibility* of homosexuality, a foreclosure which produces a field of heterosexual objects at the same time that it produces a domain of those whom it would be impossible to love. Drag thus allegorizes *heterosexual melancholy*, the melancholy by which a masculine gender is formed from the refusal to grieve the masculine as a possibility of love; a feminine gender is formed (taken on, assumed) through the incorporative fantasy by which the feminine is excluded as a possible object of love, an exclusion never grieved, but "preserved" through the heightening of feminine identification itself. In this sense, the "truest" lesbian melancholic is the strictly straight woman, and the "truest" gay male melancholic is the strictly straight man.

What drag exposes, however, is the "normal" constitution of gender presentation in which the gender performed is in many ways constituted by a set of disavowed attachments or identifications that constitute a different domain of the "unperformable." Indeed, it may well be that what constitutes the *sexually* unperformable is performed instead as *gender identification*.[12] To the extent that homosexual attachments remain unacknowledged within normative heterosexuality, they are not merely constituted as desires that emerge and subsequently become prohibited. Rather, these are desires that are proscribed from the start. And when they do emerge on the far side of the censor, they may well carry that mark of impossibility with them, performing, as it were, as the impossible within the possible. As such, they will not be attachments that can be openly grieved. This is, then, less *the refusal* to grieve (a formulation that accents the choice involved) than a preemption of grief performed by the absence of cultural conventions for avowing the loss of homosexual love. And it is this absence that produces a culture of heterosexual melancholy, one that can be read in the hyperbolic identifications by which mundane heterosexual masculinity and femininity confirm themselves. The straight man *becomes* (mimes, cites, appropriates, assumes the status of) the man he "never" loved and "never" grieved; the straight woman *becomes* the woman she "never" loved and "never" grieved. It is in this sense, then, that what is most apparently performed as gender is the sign and symptom of a pervasive disavowal.

Moreover, it is precisely to counter this pervasive cultural risk of gay melancholia (what the newspapers generalize as "depression") that there has been an insistent publicization and politicization of grief over those who have died from AIDS; the NAMES Project Quilt is exemplary, ritualizing and repeating the name itself as a way of publicly avowing the limitless loss.[13]

Insofar as the grief remains unspeakable, the rage over the loss can redouble by virtue of remaining unavowed. And if that very rage over loss is publicly proscribed, the melancholic effects of such a proscription can achieve suicidal proportions. The emergence of collective institutions for grieving is thus crucial to survival, to the reassembling of community, the reworking of kinship, the reweaving of sustaining relations. And insofar as they involve the publicization and dramatization of death, they call to be read as life-affirming rejoinders to the dire psychic consequences of a grieving process culturally thwarted and proscribed.

Performativity, gender, sexuality

How then does one link the trope by which discourse is described as "performing" and that theatrical sense of performance in which the hyperbolic status of gender norms seems central? What is "performed" in drag is, of course, *the sign* of gender, a sign which is not the same as the body it figures, but which cannot be read without it. The sign, understood as a gender imperative, i.e. "girl!", reads less as an assignment than as a command and, as such, produces its own insubordinations. The hyperbolic conformity to the command can reveal the hyperbolic status of the norm itself, indeed, can become the cultural sign by which that cultural imperative might become legible. Insofar as heterosexual gender norms produce inapproximable ideals, heterosexuality can be said to operate through the regulated production of hyperbolic versions of "man" and "woman." These are for the most part compulsory performances, ones which none of us choose, but which each of us is forced to negotiate. I write "forced to negotiate" because the compulsory character of these norms does not always make them efficacious. Such norms are continually haunted by their own inefficacy: hence, the anxiously repeated effort to install and augment their jurisdiction.

The resignification of norms is thus a function of their *inefficacy*, and so the question of subversion, of *working the weakness in the norm*, becomes a matter of inhabiting the practices of its rearticulation.[14] The critical promise of drag does not have to do with the proliferation of genders, as if a sheer increase in numbers would do the job, but rather with the exposure of the failure of heterosexual regimes ever fully to legislate or contain their own ideals. Hence, it is not that drag *opposes* heterosexuality, or that the proliferation of drag will bring down heterosexuality; on the contrary, drag tends to be the allegorization of heterosexuality and its constitutive melancholia. As an allegory that works through the hyperbolic, drag brings into relief what is, after all, determined only in relation to the hyperbolic: the understated, taken-for-granted quality of heterosexual performativity. At its best, then, drag can be read for the way in which hyperbolic norms are dissimulated as the heterosexual mundane. At the same time these same norms, taken not as commands to be obeyed, but as imperatives to be "cited," twisted, queered, brought into relief as heterosexual imperatives, are not, for that reason, necessarily subverted in the process.

It is important to emphasize that although heterosexuality operates in part through the stabilization of gender norms, gender designates a dense site of significations that contain and exceed the heterosexual matrix. Whereas it is important to emphasize that forms of sexuality do not unilaterally determine gender, a non-causal and non-reductive connection between sexuality and gender is nevertheless crucial to maintain. Precisely because homophobia often operates through the attribution of a damaged, failed, or otherwise abjected gender to homosexuals, that is, calling gay men "feminine" or calling lesbians "masculine," and because the homophobic terror over performing homosexual acts, where it exists, is often also a terror over losing proper gender ("no longer being a real or proper man" or "no longer being a real or proper woman"), it seems crucial to retain a theoretical apparatus that will account for how sexuality is regulated through the policing and the shaming of gender.

We might want to claim that certain kinds of sexual practices link people more strongly than gender affiliation (Sedgwick 1989), but such claims can only be negotiated, if they can, in relation to specific occasions for affiliation; there is nothing in either sexual practice or in gender to privilege one over the other. Sexual practices, however, will invariably be experienced differentially depending on the relations of gender in which they occur. And there may be forms of "gender" within homosexuality which call for a theorization that moves beyond the categories of "masculine" and "feminine." If we seek to privilege sexual practice as a way of transcending gender, we might ask, at what cost is the *analytic* separability of the two domains taken to be a distinction in fact? Is there perhaps a specific gender pain that provokes such fantasies of a sexual practice that would transcend gender difference altogether, in which the marks of masculinity and femininity would no longer be legible? Would this not be a sexual practice paradigmatically fetishistic, trying not to know what it knows, but knowing it all the same? This question is not meant to demean the fetish (where would we be without it?), but it does mean to ask whether it is only according to a logic of the fetish that the radical separability of sexuality and gender can be thought.

In theories such as Catharine MacKinnon's, sexual relations of subordination are understood to establish differential gender categories, such that "men" are those defined in a sexually dominating social position, and "women" are those defined in subordination. Her highly deterministic account leaves no room for relations of sexuality to be theorized apart from the rigid framework of gender difference or for kinds of sexual regulation that do not take gender as their primary objects (i.e. the prohibition of sodomy, public sex, consensual homosexuality). Hence, Gayle Rubin's influential distinction between sexuality and gender in "Thinking Sex" and Sedgwick's reformulation of that position have constituted important theoretical opposition to MacKinnon's deterministic form of structuralism.

My sense is that now this very opposition needs to be rethought in order to redraw the lines between queer theory and feminism.[15] For surely it is as unacceptable to insist that relations of sexual subordination determine gender position as it is to separate radically forms of sexuality from the workings of gender norms. The relation between sexual practice and gender is surely not a structurally determined one, but the destabilizing of the heterosexual presumption of that very structuralism still requires a way to think the two in a dynamic relation to one another.

In psychoanalytic terms, the relation between gender and sexuality is in part negotiated through the question of the relationship between identification and desire. And here it becomes clear why refusing to draw lines of causal implication between these two domains is as important as keeping open an investigation of their complex interimplication. For if to identify as a woman is not necessarily to desire a man; and if to desire a woman does not necessarily signal the constituting presence of a masculine identification, whatever that is, then the heterosexual matrix proves to be an *imaginary* logic that insistently issues forth its own unmanageability. The heterosexual logic that requires that identification and desire are mutually exclusive is one of the most reductive of heterosexism's psychological instruments: if one identifies as a given gender, one must desire a different gender. On the one hand, there is no one femininity with which to identify, which is to say that femininity might itself offer an array of identificatory sites, as the proliferation of lesbian femme possibilities attests. On the other hand, it is hardly descriptive of the complex dynamic exchanges of lesbian and gay relationships to presume that homosexual identifications "mirror" or replicate one another. The vocabulary for describing the difficult play, crossing, and destabilization of masculine and feminine identifications within homosexuality has only begun to emerge within theoretical language: the non-academic language historically embedded in gay communities is here much more instructive. The thought of sexual difference *within* homosexuality has yet to be theorized in its complexity.

Performativity, then, is to be read not as self-expression or self-presentation, but as the unanticipated resignifiability of highly invested terms. The film *Paris Is Burning* has been interesting to read less for the ways in which the drag performances deploy denaturalizing strategies to reidealize whiteness (hooks) and heterosexual gender norms than for the less stabilizing rearticulations of kinship that the film offers. The drag balls themselves at times produce high femininity as a function of whiteness and deflect homosexuality through a transgendering that *reidealizes* certain bourgeois forms of heterosexual exchange. And yet, if those performances are not immediately or obviously subversive, it may be that it is rather in the *reformulation of kinship*, in particular, the redefining of the "house" and its forms of collectivity, mothering, mopping, reading, becoming legendary, that the appropriation and redeployment of the categories of dominant culture enable the formation of kinship relations that function quite supportively as oppositional discourse within that culture. These men "mother" one another, "house" one another, "rear" one another, and the resignification of the family through these terms is not a vain or useless imitation, but the social and discursive building of community, a community that binds, cares, teaches, shelters, and enables. This is doubtless a task that any of us who are queer need to see and to know and to learn from, a task that makes none of us who are outside of heterosexual "family" into absolute outsiders to this film. Significantly, it is here in the elaboration of kinship forged through a resignification of the very terms which effect our exclusion and abjection, a resignification that creates the discursive and social space for community, that we see an appropriation of the terms of domination that turns them toward a more enabling future.

How would one ever determine whether subversion has taken place? What measure would one invoke to gauge the extent of subversion? From what standpoint would one know? It is not simply a matter of situating performances in contexts (as if the demarcation of context is not already a prefiguring of the result), of gauging audience response, or of establishing the epistemological ground from which one is entitled to "know" such effects. Rather, subversiveness is the kind of effect that *resists calculation*. If one thinks of the effects of discursive productions, they do not conclude at the terminus of a given statement or utterance, the passing of legislation, the announcement of a birth. The reach of their signifiability cannot be controlled by the one who utters or writes, since such productions are not owned by the one who utters them. They continue to signify in spite of their authors, and sometimes against their authors' most precious intentions.

It is one of the ambivalent implications of the decentering of the subject to have one's writing be the site of a necessary and inevitable expropriation. But this yielding of ownership over what one writes has an important set of political corollaries, for the taking up, reforming, deforming of one's words does open up a difficult future terrain of community, one in which the hope of ever fully recognizing oneself in the terms by which one signifies is sure to be disappointed. This not owning of one's words is there from the start, however, since speaking is always in some ways the speaking of a stranger through and as oneself, the melancholic reiteration of a language that one never chose, that one does not find as an instrument to be used, but which one is, as it were, used by, expropriated in, as a continuing condition of the "one" and the "we," the ambivalent condition of the power that binds.

Notes

1   The following is indebted to Eve Sedgwick's "Queer Performativity" [. . .]. I thank her for the excellent essay and for the provocations, lodged in her text and perhaps most poignantly in earlier drafts, which have inspired this essay in important ways. A different version of this essay is published in Judith Butler, *Bodies That Matter* (Routledge, 1993).

2   It is, of course, never quite right to say that language or discourse "performs," since it is unclear that language is primarily constituted as a set of "acts." After all, this description of an "act" cannot be sustained through the trope that established the act as a singular event, for the act will turn out to refer to prior acts and to a reiteration of "acts" that is perhaps more suitably described as a citational chain. Paul de Man points out in "Rhetoric of Persuasion" that the distinction between constative and performative utterances is confounded by the fictional status of both: ". . . the possibility for language to perform is just as fictional as the possibility for language to assert" (129). Further, he writes, "considered as persuasion, rhetoric is performative, but considered as a system of tropes, it deconstructs its own performance" (130–31).

3   In what follows, that set of performatives that Austin terms illocutionary will be at issue, those in which the binding power of the act *appears* to be derived from the intention or will of the speaker. In "Signature, Event, Context," Derrida argues that the binding power that Austin attributes to the speaker's intention in such illocutionary acts is more properly attributable to a citational force of the speaking, the iterability that establishes the authority of the speech act, but which establishes the nonsingular character of that act. In this sense, every "act" is an echo or citational chain, and it is its citationality that constitutes its performative force.

4   This historicity of discourse implies the way in which history is constitutive of discourse itself. It is not simply that discourses are located *in* histories, but that they have their own constitutive historical character. Historicity is a term which directly implies the constitutive character of history in discursive practice, that is, a condition in which a "practice" could not exist apart from the sedimentation of conventions by which it is produced and becomes legible.

5   My understanding of the charge of presentism is that an inquiry is presentist to the extent that it (a) universalizes a set of claims regardless of historical and cultural challenges to that universalization or (b) takes an historically specific set of terms and universalizes them falsely. It may be that both gestures in a given instance are the same. It would, however, be a mistake to claim that all conceptual language or philosophical language is "presentist," a claim which would be tantamount to prescribing that all philosophy become history. My understanding of Foucault's notion of genealogy is that it is a specifically philosophical exercise in exposing and tracing the installation and operation of false universals. My thanks to Mary Poovey and Joan W. Scott for explaining this concept to me.

6   Theatricality is not for that reason fully intentional, but I might have made that reading possible through my reference to gender as "intentional and non-referential" in "Performative Acts and Gender Constitution." I use the term "intentional" in a specifically phenomenological sense. "Intentionality" within phenomenology does not mean voluntary or deliberate, but is, rather, a way

of characterizing consciousness (or language) as *having an object*, more specifically, as directed toward an object which may or may not exist. In this sense, an act of consciousness may intend (posit, constitute, apprehend) an *imaginary* object. Gender, in its ideality, might be construed as an intentional object, an ideal which is constituted but which does not exist. In this sense, gender would be like "the feminine" as it is discussed as an impossibility by Cornell in *Beyond Accommodation*.

7   In this sense, one might usefully construe the performative repetition of norms as the cultural workings of repetition-compulsion in Freud's sense. This would be a repetition not in the service of mastering pleasure, but as that which undermines the project of mastery altogether. It was in this sense that Lacan argued in *Four Fundamental Principles of Psychoanalysis* that repetition marks the failure of subjectivation: what repeats in the subject is precisely that which is not yet mastered or never masterable.

8   See Román.

9   See Kramer; Crimp and Rolston; and Sadownick. My thanks to David Román for directing me to this last essay.

10 I thank Laura Mulvey for asking me to consider the relation between performativity and disavowal, and Wendy Brown for encouraging me to think about the relation between melancholia and drag and for asking whether the denaturalization of gender norms is the same as their subversion. I also thank Mandy Merck for numerous enlightening questions that led to these speculations, including the suggestion that if disavowal conditions performativity, then perhaps gender itself might be understood on the model of the fetish.

11 See "Freud and the Melancholia of Gender" in *Gender Trouble*.

12 This is not to suggest that an exclusionary matrix rigorously distinguishes between how one identifies and how one desires; it is quite possible to have overlapping identification and desire in heterosexual or homosexual exchange, or in a bisexual history of sexual practice. Further, "masculinity" and "femininity" do not exhaust the terms for either eroticized identification or desire.

13 See Crimp.

14 This may be a place in which to think about performativity in the sense outlined here in relation to the notion of performativity offered by Ernesto Laclau in *New Reflections on the Revolution of Our Time*. [. . .]

15 Toward the end of the short theoretical conclusion of "Thinking Sex," Rubin returns to feminism in a gestural way, suggesting that "in the long run, feminism's critique of gender hierarchy must be incorporated into a radical theory of sex, and the critique of sexual oppression should enrich feminism. But an autonomous theory and polities specific to sexuality must be developed" (309).

Works cited

Appiah, Anthony. "The Uncompleted Argument: Du Bois and the Illusion of Race." *"Race," Writing and Difference*. Ed. Henry Louis Gates, Jr. Chicago, IL: U of Chicago P, 1986. 21–37.

Butler, Judith. *Gender Trouble: Feminism and the Subversion of Identity*. New York: Routledge, 1990.

—. "Performative Acts and Gender Constitution." *Performing Feminisms*. Ed. Sue-Ellen Case. Baltimore, MD: Johns Hopkins UP, 1991. 270–82.

Cornell, Drucilla. *Beyond Accommodation: Ethical Feminism, Deconstruction, and the Law*. New York: Routledge, 1992.

Crimp, Douglas. "Mourning and Militancy." *October* 51 (Winter 1989): 97–107.

Crimp, Douglas, and Adam Rolston, eds. *AIDS DemoGraphics*. Seattle: Bay Press, 1990.

de Man, Paul. "Rhetoric of Persuasion." *Allegories of Reading*. New Haven, CT: Yale UP, 1987. 119–31.

Derrida, Jacques. "Signature, Event, Context." *Limited Inc*. Ed. Gerald Graff. Trans. Samuel Weber and Jeffrey Mehlman. Evanston, IL: Northwestern UP, 1988. 1–24.

Guillaumin, Colette. "Race and Nature: The System of Marks." *Feminist Studies* 8 (1988): 25–44.

hooks, bell. "Is Paris Burning?" *Z*, June 1991: 60–64.

Kramer, Larry. *Reports from the Holocaust: The Making of an AIDS Activist*. New York: St. Martin's Press, 1989.

Laclau, Ernesto. *New Reflections on the Revolution of Our Time*. London: Verso, 1990.

Lloyd, David. "Race Under Representation." *Oxford Literary Review* 13 (Spring 1991): 62–94.

Omi, Michael, and Howard Winant. *Racial Formation in the United States: From the 1960s to the 1980s*. New York: Routledge and Kegan Paul, 1986.

Román, David. " 'It's My Party and I'll Die If I Want To!': Gay Men, AIDS, and the Circulation of Camp in U.S. Theatre." *Theatre Journal* 44 (1992): 305–27.

—. "Performing All Our Lives: AIDS, Performance, Community." *Critical Theory and Performance*. Eds. Janelle Reinelt and Joseph Roach. Ann Arbor, MI: U of Michigan P, 1992. 208–21.

Rubin, Gayle. "Thinking Sex: Notes for a Radical Theory of the Politics of Sexuality." *Pleasure and Danger*. Ed. Carole S. Vance. Boston: Routledge and Kegan Paul, 1984. 267–319.

Sadownick, Doug. "ACT UP Makes a Spectacle of AIDS." *High Performance* 13.1, no. 49 (1990): 26–31.

Sedgwick, Eve Kosofsky. "Across Gender, Across Sexuality: Willa Cather and Others." *South Atlantic Quarterly* 88 (1989): 53–72.

—. *Epistemology of the Closet*. Berkeley: U of California P, 1990.

Smyth, Cherry. *Lesbians Talk Queer Notions*. London: Scarlet, 1992.

Spivak, Gayatri Chakravorty. "In a Word: Interview with Ellen Rooney." *differences* 1.2 (Summer 1989): 124–56.

Chapter 3

Jay Prosser

JUDITH BUTLER: QUEER FEMINISM, TRANSGENDER, AND THE TRANSUBSTANTIATION OF SEX

Jay Prosser is Reader in Humanities at the University of Leeds. While Prosser works across American literature, photography, and autobiography, he is best known in queer studies for his work in transgender studies. The following piece is the first chapter of Prosser's *Second Skins: The Body Narratives of Transsexuality* (1998), an analysis of the body in transsexual autobiography.

In "Judith Butler: Queer Feminism, Transgender, and the Transubstantiation of Sex," Prosser asserts that the image of the transsexual has been central to the development of queer theory. In this excerpt, Prosser offers a critique of Judith Butler's *Gender Trouble* (1990), a text often cited for its discussion of the transgender subject's embodiment of gender performativity. Working against popular readings of Butler, Prosser asserts that Butler's brand of "queer feminism" effaces the importance of corporeal interiority for transgender experience and subjectivity. While Prosser supports institutional alliances between queer theory and transgender studies, he rejects reductionist uses of transsexual subjectivity as an *always* queer or subversive performance on the grounds that this equation reinforces binary oppositions and negates aspects of experience that are unique to transsexual subjectivity. Through a critique that counters Butler's reading of *Paris is Burning* (dir. Jennie Livingston, 1990), Prosser works against the erasure of the transsexual body.

Transgender and the queer moment

> Queer is a continuing moment, movement, motive—recurrent, eddying, troublant. The word "queer" itself means across—it comes from the Indo-European root *twerkw*, which also yields the German *quer* (transverse), Latin *torquere* (to twist), English athwart.
>
> (Eve Kosofsky Sedgwick, *Tendencies*)

IN ITS EARLIEST formulations, in what are now considered its foundational texts, queer studies can be seen to have been crucially dependent on the figure of transgender. As one of its most visible means of institutionalization, queer theory represented itself as traversing and mobilizing methodologies (feminism, poststructuralism) and identities (women, heterosexuals) already, at least by comparison, in institutionalized place. Seized on as a definitively queer force that "troubled" the identity categories of gender, sex, and sexuality—or rather revealed them to be always already fictional and precarious—the trope of crossing was most often impacted with if not explicitly illustrated by the transgendered subject's crossing their several boundaries at once: both the boundaries between gender, sex, and sexuality and the boundary that structures each as a binary category.

Even in Eve Kosofsky Sedgwick's work, which has argued most trenchantly for "a certain irreducibility" of sexuality to gender, and thus one might deduce would follow a certain irreducibility of *homo*sexuality to *trans*gender, homophobic constructions are understood to be produced by and productive of culturally normative gender identities and relations.[1] The implications of this include a thorough enmeshing of homosexual desire with transgender identification. In its claim that women in the nineteenth century served to mediate desire between men, Sedgwick's *Between Men: English Literature and Male Homosocial Desire* suggests that the production of normative heterosexuality depended on a degree of male identification—and yet importantly, the disavowal of this identification—with woman as the object of desire.[2] At the beginnings of queer therefore, in what is arguably lesbian and gay studies' first book, heterosexuality is shown to be constructed through the sublimation of a cross-gendered identification; for this reason, making visible this identification— transgendered movement—will become the key queer mechanism for deconstructing heterosexuality and writing out queer.

Sedgwick's next book foregrounds this methodological function of transgender explicitly. *Epistemology of the Closet* presents transgender as one good reason for the development of a theory of (homo)sexuality distinct from feminism. The critical visibility of transgender— "the reclamation and relegitimation of a courageous history of lesbian trans-gender role-playing and identification"—poses a challenge to lesbianism's incorporation within feminism: "The irrepressible, relatively class-nonspecific popular culture in which James Dean has been as numinous an icon for lesbians as Garbo or Dietrich has for gay men seems resistant to a purely feminist theorization. It is in these contexts that calls for a theorized axis of sexuality as distinct from gender have developed."[3] Exceeding feminism's purview of gender, transgender demands and contributes to the basis for a new queer theory; paradoxically, transgender demands a new theory of sexuality. It is transgender that makes possible the lesbian and gay overlap, the identification between gay men and lesbians, which forms the grounds for this new theory of homosexuality discrete from feminism. And it is surely this overlap or cross-gendered identification between gay men and lesbians—an identification made critically necessary by the AIDS crisis—that ushers in the queer moment.

Most recently in her autobiographical narratives and performance pieces, Sedgwick has revealed her personal transgendered investment lying at and as the great heart of her queer project. Her confession of her "identification? Dare I, after this half-decade, call it with all a fat *woman's* defiance, my identity?—as a gay man" "comes out" with the transgendered desire that has been present in her work all along.[4] Similarly in its readings, *Tendencies* derives its queer frisson openly and consistently from an identification across genders: a mobility "across gender lines, including the desires of men for women and of women for men," a transgendered traversal that in its queering (skewing and unraveling) of apparently normative heterosexuality is simultaneously a movement across sexualities.[5] To summon the queer moment, the book begins with a figure for transgender—gay men wearing DYKE T-shirts and lesbians wearing FAGGOT T-shirts.

But Sedgwick is just the tip of the iceberg. The transgendered presence lies just below the surface of most of lesbian and gay studies' foundational texts. Early work on the intersections of race, gender, and sexual identities theorized otherness as produced through a racist, homophobic, and sexist transgendering, and thus again transgendering became the means to challenging this othering. Kobena Mercer's work on the fetishizing/feminizing white gaze of Robert Mapplethorpe at the black male body; Cherríe Moraga's description of the hermaphroditic convergence of the chingón and the chingada; Gloria Anzaldúa's memory of the mita' y mita' figure in the sexual, gender, and geographic borderlands: these various cross-gendered figures emerged both as constructions and, in their articulation by these critics, deconstructions of cultural ideologies that insist on absolute difference in all identity.[6] Other early lesbian and gay studies work invested in the transgendered subject's "trans" a transgressive politics. For Teresa de Lauretis, Sue-Ellen Case, Jonathan Dollimore, and Marjorie Garber whether appearing in contemporary lesbian cinematic representations of butch/femme desire, in theatrical cross-dressing in early modern England, or as popular cultural gender-blending icons, the transgendered subject made visible a queerness that, to paraphrase Garber, threatened a crisis in gender and sexual identity categories.[7] Crucial to the idealization of transgender as a queer transgressive force in this work is the consistent decoding of "trans" as incessant destabilizing movement between sexual and gender identities. In short, in retrospect, transgender *gender* appears as the most crucial sign of queer *sexuality's* aptly skewed point of entry into the academy.

Without doubt though, the single text that yoked transgender most fully to queer sexuality is Judith Butler's *Gender Trouble: Feminism and the Subversion of Identity*.[8] *Gender Trouble*'s impact was enormous: published in 1990, appearing with the decade, it transformed transgender into a queer icon, in the process becoming something of an icon of the new queer theory itself. Yet how this actually happened, how *Gender Trouble* imbricated queer with transgender, and how the book itself was imbricated with transgender forms something of an intriguing critical phenomenon. For the embodied subject of transgender barely occupies the text of *Gender Trouble*—a book very much, after all, about subjects' failure of embodiment. As Butler herself states in remarking her surprise at the tendency to read *Gender Trouble* as a book about transgendered subjects, "there were probably no more than five paragraphs in *Gender Trouble* devoted to drag [yet] readers have often cited the description of drag as if it were the 'example' which explains the meaning of [gender] performativity." From this later point, in her 1993 essay "Critically Queer," Butler clearly challenges the equation of transgender and homosexuality, or to be precise, the construction of transgender as the only sign of a deconstructive homosexuality: "cross-gendered identification is not the exemplary paradigm for thinking about homosexuality, although it may be one."[9] Yet the effect of *Gender Trouble* was precisely to secure transgender as a touchstone of lesbian and gay theory. How did *Gender Trouble* canonize, and how was it canonized for, a theory of transgender performativity that was apparently not its substance?

In the first essay appearing in the first edition of the first academic journal devoted to lesbian and gay studies, *GLQ: A Journal of Lesbian and Gay Studies*, itself a canonical moment in queer studies, Sedgwick comments on *Gender Trouble*'s canonically queer status: "Anyone who was at the 1991 Rutgers conference on Gay and Lesbian Studies [another canonizing mechanism], and heard *Gender Trouble* appealed to in paper after paper, couldn't help being awed by the productive impact this dense and even imposing work has had on the recent development of queer theory and reading." Surmising that these invocations were not indicative of an uncomplicated loyalty to *Gender Trouble*, however, Sedgwick goes on to suggest that "the citation, the *use* of Butler's formulations in the context of queer theory will prove to have been highly active and tendentious."[10] That *Gender Trouble* was subject to a set of reiterations and recitations proliferating meanings beyond the intention of the "original" might be considered especially fitting given its own attraction toward Foucauldian proliferation as the effective means for denaturalizing copies that pretend to originality. Its argument about recitation lent an amenability to its own recitation. There's something very campy, very definitively queer, about readings that refused to adhere to the letter of Butler's argument, that refused, to use its vernacular, to "repeat loyally." The original underwent a certain overreading, playful exaggeration, a mischievous adding of emphasis, yet nevertheless remained a discernible referent.

Camp may in fact be quite fundamental to our reading of *Gender Trouble* and our understanding of its transgender import. In his introduction to his anthology on camp (one of two anthologies on camp that appeared soon after *Gender Trouble*) David Bergman nominates Butler as "the person who has done the most to revise the academic standing of camp and to suggest its politically subversive potential."[11] Bergman stakes that her success in queer studies comes in part from bringing to camp a high theoretical tone—and, we might add, from bringing camp to high theory. Pushing further on the connections between camp, queer, and the argument of *Gender Trouble*, it might be said that Butler's centrality in queer theory is in part an effect of queer's recuperation of camp and queer's recuperation *through* camp. The late eighties/early nineties, simultaneous with the beginnings of queer theory, saw the cultural and political reappropriation of camp, and the history of the term "queer" is most symptomatic of this. From homophobic epithet designating and reinforcing the other's social abjection to self-declared maker of community pride, "queer" was reclaimed precisely according to the transformative mechanisms of camp in which what has been devalued in the original becomes overvalued in the repetition. In turn, in its queer reevaluation, camp has proven a key strategy for queer theory's own institutionalization, a means by which to piggyback into the academy on (appropriating and redefining) already established methodologies. *Between Men*, for instance, deployed a distinctive camp style in subjecting canonical nineteenth-century literature to deliberate yet wonderfully subtle overreadings that brought to the surface its sexual subtexts. In its academic manifestation, camp actually comes to appear a form of queer deconstruction, not simply inverting the opposition between the original and the copy, the referent and the repetition but creating, according to Scott Long, a third space, "a stance, detached, calm, and free, from which the opposition as a whole and its attendant terms can be perceived and judged."[12] This third space, this queer deconstruction, is surely queer theory.

It is certainly this camp inversion of the expected order of terms to elucidate the construction of the original that forms the very pith of *Gender Trouble*'s theory: the subject does not precede but is an effect of the law; heterosexuality does not precede but is an effect of the prohibition on homosexuality; sex does not precede but is an effect of the cultural construction of gender. Butler's argument consistently reverses the expected history between the two terms in each formulation to bring them into a third space where each opposition as a whole can be perceived and judged. The binaries of sexual difference that undergird what Butler terms "the metaphysics of sex" are fragmented and mobilized with a Derridean flourish into sexual *différance* (*GT* 16). The driving sensibility of *Gender Trouble*'s theory is in this respect an archetypally camp one. Although the embodied transgendered subject doesn't occupy *Gender Trouble* in any substantial way, it is this camp reversal of terms that conveys the sense that the transgendered subject of drag is always in the margins of the text, the implicit referent (ironically given Butler's use of camp/drag's function to displace the referent). For it is as the *personification* of camp—the third/intermediate term that reveals the constructedness of the binary of sex, of gender, and of the sex/gender system—that queer studies has anointed the transgendered subject queer. "Critically Queer"'s reading of *Gender Trouble*'s reception is thus absolutely right. Transgendered subjects, butches, and drag queens, did come to appear the empirical examples of gender performativity, their crossing illustrating both the inessentiality of sex and the nonoriginality of heterosexuality that was the book's thesis. And those five paragraphs or so where *Gender Trouble* does explicitly address the subject in drag certainly do nothing to contradict this conception of transgender as exemplarily camp/queer/performative: *"In imitating gender, drag implicitly reveals the imitative structure of gender itself—as well as its contingency"* (*GT* 137). In this sentence (particularly given that the italics appear in the original), transgender's function is unambivalently and emphatically that of the elucidating example of gender performativity.

This chapter charts the achievement of and challenges that association, transgender/camp/queer/performativity. That transgender can emerge as a "studies" in the late nineteen-nineties, that the figure at the center of many of transgender's projects is the "gender troubler," is largely due to Butler's canonization (both the canonization of Butler and her inadvertent canonization of transgender): *"s/he"*—the transgenderist, the third camp term whose crossing lays bare and disrupts the binaries that found identity—threads prominently through the self-declared first reader in the new field of transgender studies.[13] My concern is the implication of this harnessing of transgender as queer for transsexuality: what are the points at which the transsexual as transgendered subject is not queer? The splits and shifts between the deployment of transgender and that of transsexuality within Butler's work are revealing on this count. Whereas in *Gender Trouble* the transgendered subject is used to deliteralize the matter of sex, in Butler's later *Bodies That Matter: On the Discursive Limits of "Sex,"* the transsexual in particular symbolizes a carefully sustained ambivalence around sex.[14] That Butler chooses to elucidate the limits of the transgendered subject's deliteralization of sex through the figure of a transsexual is a powerful indicator of the conceptual splitting between transsexual and queer and, indeed, of queer theory's own incapacity to sustain the body as a literal category. In transsexuality sex *returns*, the queer repressed, to unsettle its theory of gender performativity [. . .]

Queer gender and performativity

> To realize the difference of the sexes is to put an end to play.
> (Jacques Lacan and Wladimir Granoff, "Fetishism:
> The Symbolic, the Imaginary, and the Real")

Even though it is articulated only in the last of four sections in the final chapter ("Bodily Inscriptions, Performative Subversions" [*GT* 128–41]), that is in less than one-twelfth of the book, it is the account of gender performativity that is most often remembered as the thrust of *Gender Trouble*. Sedgwick illustrates: "Probably the centerpiece of Butler's recent work has been a series of demonstrations that gender can best be discussed as a form of performativity." More intriguing than the disproportionate emphasis accorded the final section of *Gender Trouble* in general remembrance, however, is the way in which *gender* performativity has become so coextensive with *queer* performativity as to render them interchangeable. Sedgwick, again, exemplifies the way in which "gender" has slipped rapidly into "queer." "Queer Performativity" (the title of her essay on James) she writes, is "made necessary" by Butler's work in and since *Gender Trouble*; and in *Tendencies* Sedgwick assigns Butler "and her important book" (*Gender Trouble*) a representative function, "stand[ing] in for a lot of the rest of us" working on queer performativity.[15] How does this slippage from gender to queer in the discussion of performativity come about, and how does *Gender Trouble* come to "stand in for" it?

While it argues that *all* gender is performative—that "man" and "woman" are not expressions of prior internal essences but constituted, to paraphrase Butler, through the repetition of culturally intelligible stylized acts—*Gender Trouble* presents the transgendered subject as the concrete example that "brings into relief" this performativity of gender (*GT* 31). In retrospect we can note that, in concretizing gender performativity with transgender, *Gender Trouble* inadvertently made possible two readings that Butler later returns to refute: first, that what was meant by gender performativity was gender theatricality; and second, that all transgender is queer is syllogistically subversive. The first assumption, that gender performativity means acting out one's gender as if gender were a theatrical role that could be chosen, led to the belief that Butler's theory of gender was both radically voluntarist and antimaterialist: that its argument was that gender, like a set of clothes in a drag act, could be donned and doffed at will, that gender *is* drag. In this reading *Gender Trouble* was both embraced and critiqued. (Even before *Gender Trouble*, however, Butler had carefully argued against any conceptualization of gender as something that could be chosen at will)[16]. In fact, Butler's notion of performativity is derived not from a Goffman-esque understanding of identity as role but from Austinian speech-act theory, crucially informed by Derrida's deconstruction of speech-act theory. Not cited in *Gender Trouble* but implicit throughout in its insistence on the cruciality of repetition as destabilizing is Derrida's reading of J.L. Austin and John Searle.[17] *Bodies That Matter* wastes little time before citing Derrida's reading (Introduction 13), and in order to clarify this speech-act sense of performativity, the new work emphasizes gender's citationality throughout. To some extent in *Bodies That Matter*, the later term, "citationality," comes to displace the former of *Gender Trouble*, "performativity." Like a law that requires citing to be effective, *Bodies That Matter* argues, sex comes into effect through our citing it, and, as with a law, through our compulsion to cite it. Butler's refiguring of sex as citational law in *Bodies That Matter* is designed to derail the understanding of gender as free theatricality that constituted the misreading of *Gender Trouble*, to clarify how gender is compelled through symbolic prohibitions. The shifts in terms in the books' titles, from "Gender Trouble" to the "Discursive Limits of 'Sex' " (both the shift from "gender" to " 'sex' " and from "trouble" to "discursive limits") run as parallel attempts to account for gender's materiality, its nonsuperficiality, and at the same time to foreground the "limits" of the "trouble" subjects can effect to its constitutive prohibitions. That "sex" appears typographically inserted in citation marks suggests sex precisely as a citation.

It is the second assumption drawn from *Gender Trouble*'s illustration of gender performativity with transgender that concerns me most: the assumption that transgender is queer is subversive. For it is this syllogism that enables Sedgwick to make that slide from gender performativity to queer performativity and that effectively encodes transgendered subjectivity as archetypically queer and subversive. It should be understood that, although it never makes such an argument, *Gender Trouble* does set up the conditions for this syllogism: transgender = gender performativity = queer = subversive. We can begin to illustrate the first part of this, the equation of transgender with gender performativity, by examining *Gender Trouble*'s reading of Beauvoir's "One is not born a woman, but rather becomes one." In Butler's reformulation of Beauvoir's famed epigram on the construction of gender nearly half a century later, it is through the suggestion of a possible transgendering that gender appears not simply constructed but radically contingent on the body. To cite Butler: "Beauvoir is clear that one 'becomes' a woman, but always under a cultural compulsion to become one. And clearly, the compulsion does not come from 'sex.' *There is nothing in her account that guarantees that the 'one' who becomes a woman is necessarily female*" (*GT* 8; my emphasis). And again: "Beauvoir's theory implied seemingly radical consequences, ones that she herself did not entertain. For instance, if sex and gender are radically distinct, then it does not follow that to be a given sex is to become a given gender; in other words, *'woman' need not be the cultural construction of the female body, and 'man' need not interpret male bodies*" (*GT* 112; my emphasis). In both citations, Butler's suggestion of a possible transgendered becoming (that men may not be males and women may not be females) not only opens up a conceptual space between gender and sex and leaves sex dispensable to the process of gendering; it also conveys that gender is not a teleological narrative of ontology at all, with the sexed body (female) as recognizable beginning and gender identity (woman) as clear-cut ending. In Butler's reading transgender demotes gender from narrative to performative. That is, gender appears not as the end of narrative becoming but as performative moments all along a process: repetitious, recursive, disordered, incessant, above all, unpredictable and necessarily incomplete. "It is, for [Butler's version of] Beauvoir, never possible finally to become a woman, as if there were a *telos* that governs the process of acculturation and construction. Gender is the repeated stylization of the body, a set of repeated acts within a highly rigid regulatory frame that congeal over time to produce the appearance of substance, of a natural sort of being" (*GT* 33).[18]

If transgender now equals gender performativity, how does this formulation come to acquire the additional equivalencies of queer and subversion? In "Critically Queer," in correcting the tendency to misread *Gender Trouble* as about transgender, Butler underscores that there is no essential identity between transgender and homosexuality: "not only are a vast number of drag performers straight, but it would be a mistake to think that homosexuality is best explained through the performativity that is drag."[19] That she must return to make this qualification, however, is again precisely because *Gender Trouble* has already produced an implicit equivalence between transgender and homosexuality, so that transgender appears as the sign of homosexuality, homosexuality's definitive *gender* style. In one claim key to this imbrication of transgender with homosexuality, "parodic and subversive convergences" are said to "*characterize* gay and lesbian cultures" (*GT* 66; my emphasis). This characterization encodes transgender as homosexual gender difference, a kind of archetypal queer gender.

Where "straight" gender occults its own performativity according to a metaphysics of substance, queer transgender reveals ("brings into relief") the performativity of all gender. Transgender "dramatizes" the process of signification by which all gendered embodiment "create[s] the effect of the natural" or real; drag's imitative workings parallel the imitative workings that structure straight genders, for all "gender is a kind of persistent impersonation that passes as the real" (*GT* x). The metaphysics of substance undergirds the naturalization of sex and of heterosexuality. What Butler terms the "heterosexual matrix," building in particular on Monique Wittig's analyses of the straight mind's naturalization of a dimorphic gender system, sustains heterosexuality as natural and naturalizes gender as sex.[20] The naturalizing mechanism works both ways, shoring up the apparent naturalness of both sex/gender and heterosexual desire. The claim to "be" a man or a woman is made possible by the binary and oppositional positioning of these terms within heterosexuality. Sex, gender, and desire are unified through the representation of heterosexuality as primary and foundational. Female, femininity, and woman appear as stable and conjoined terms through their opposition to male, masculinity, and man. Gender, in other words, appears as *identity*. What stabilizes the association and keeps the two sets discrete and antithetical is the apparent naturalness of heterosexual desire.

Queer transgender's function in *Gender Trouble* can be summarized as twofold: to parallel the process by which heterosexuality reproduces (and reproduces itself through) binarized gender identities; and at the same time to contrast with heterosexuality's naturalization of this process. For whereas the constructedness of straight gender is obscured by the veil of naturalization, queer transgender reveals, indeed, explicitly performs, its own constructedness. In other words, queer transgender serves as heterosexual gender's subversive foil. Thus in the scheme of *Gender Trouble*, heterosexual gender is assigned as ground, queer transgender as figure, dramatizing or metaphorizing the workings of heterosexuality's construction. Even in "Critically Queer," in the very same paragraph that apparently seeks to disentangle homosexuality and transgender, Butler writes that drag "exposes or *allegorizes*" the process by which heterosexualized genders form themselves.[21] Queer transgender is allegory to hetero-sexual gender's (specious, for it only veils its performativity) referentiality or literality.

Biddy Martin has described her anxiety in response to Butler's and Sedgwick's work over this tendency of "antifoundationalist celebrations of queerness" to represent queer sexu-alities as "figural, performative, playful, and fun." Martin's anxiety specifically concerns the way in which feminism, gender, and, by extension, the female body, are stabilized in this dynamic, projected by queerness as "fixity, constraint, or subjection . . . a fixed ground."[22] While agreeing that the category of woman is often subject to a degree of a priori stabilization in the very writings that call for its destabilization and proliferation, my concerns, for the following reasons, are particularly with the effective appropriation of transgender by queer. In the first instance, transgendered subjectivity is not inevitably queer. That is, by no means are all transgendered subjects homosexual. While "Critically Queer" itself points this out, *Gender Trouble*'s queer transgender illustrates a certain collapsing of gender back into sexu-ality that, in the particular process of *Gender Trouble*'s canonization, has become a tendency of queer studies: a tendency that is, as Martin suggests, the queering of gender through sexuality (and I would add of sexuality through gender). And, more crucially in regard to this first distinction, in the context of a discussion of how gender and sexual subjects have been taken up in theoretical paradigms, by no means are transgendered subjects necessarily queer even in the sense that queer has come to signify in queer studies. That is, although "queer" as a camp term has to some extent lost that referent "homosexual" and now signifies not as homo-sexual *stricto sensu* but as a figure for the performative—subversive signifier displacing referent—by no means are all transgendered subjects queer even in this figurative, nonrefer-ential sense. Butler's reading of Venus Xtravaganza in *Bodies That Matter* will work as an attempt to demonstrate just this: the way in which not every gender-crossing is queerly subversive. Yet it should be pointed out again that the fact that she must later return to disen-tangle transgender, queer, and subversion in *Bodies That Matter* as she must in the essay "Critically Queer," is due precisely to their prior entanglement in *Gender Trouble*. (Although, given the importance within Butler's theory of the dynamic of citation, the extent to which her own writing is generated through such reiterative returns should be noted as richly appropriate.)

My second reason for concern with queer's arrogation of transgender is that it allocates to nontransgendered subjects (according to this binary schema, straight subjects), the ground that transgender would appear to *only* figure; this "ground" is the apparent naturalness of sex. For if transgender figures gender performativity, nontransgender or straight gender is assigned (to work within Butler's own framework of speech-act theory) the category of the constative.

While within this framework, this allocation is a sign of the devaluation of straight gender, and conversely queer's alignment of itself with transgender gender performativity represents queer's sense of its own "higher purpose," in fact there are transgendered trajec-tories, in particular *transsexual* trajectories, that aspire to that which this scheme devalues. Namely there are transsexuals who seek very pointedly to be nonperformative, to be consta-tive, quite simply, to *be*. What gets dropped from transgender in its queer deployment to signify subversive gender performativity is the value of the matter that often most concerns the transsexual: the *narrative* of becoming a biological man or a biological woman (as opposed to the performative of effecting one)—in brief and simple the materiality of the sexed body. In the context of the transsexual trajectory, in fact, Beauvoir's epigram can be read quite differently as describing not a generic notion of gender's radical performativity but the specific narrative of (in this case) the male-to-female transsexual's struggle toward sexed embodiment. One is not born a woman, but *nevertheless* may become one—given substantial medical intervention, personal tenacity, economic security, social support, and so on:

becoming woman, in spite of not being born one, may be seen as a crucial goal. In its representation of sex as a figurative effect of straight gender's constative performance, *Gender Trouble* cannot account for a transsexual desire for sexed embodiment as *telos*. In this regard *Gender Trouble* serves to prompt readings of transsexual subjects whose bodily trajectories might exceed its framework of the theory of gender performativity.

If *Gender Trouble* enables the syllogism transgender = gender performativity = queer = subversive, it stabilizes this syllogism through suggesting as constant its antithesis: nontransgender = gender constativity = straight = naturalizing. The binary opposition between these syllogisms proliferates a number of mutually sustaining binary oppositions between *Gender Trouble*'s conceptual categories: queer versus straight; subversive versus naturalizing; performativity versus constativity; gender versus sex. The first term in each opposition is ascribed a degree of generativity that puts in question the primacy of the second. The value of this intervention lies in our recognition that it is the second term that is customarily awarded primacy and autonomy over the first. But the transsexual, as Butler later realizes in Venus Xtravaganza, ruptures these binaries and their alignment.

Because it constitutes the focal point of the transsexual trajectory (to *be* a woman) among these binaries, it is the matter of sex that is of interest to me next before Venus, not simply in its conceptually associative opposition to transgendered subjects in *Gender Trouble* but as a conceptual category in itself. Transgender certainly allows Butler to displace an expressivist model of gender where gender is the cultural expression or interpretation of sex (consolidated as bedrock) with a performative model where sex can "be shown to have been gender all along" (*GT* 8). But *Gender Trouble*'s most thorough accounting for sex as discursive effect appears in the discussion of melancholia in the second chapter, "Prohibition, Psychoanalysis, and the Production of the Heterosexual Matrix" (*GT* 35–78). Here, although the transgendered subject is not explicitly marshaled to exemplify the theory, the figure of transgender haunts the analyses, and the particular conceptualization of sex as "gender all along," as we shall see, certainly has significant implications for any theory of transsexual subjectivity.

Heterosexual melancholia and the encrypting of sex

> To recast the referent as the signified . . .
>
> (Judith Butler, "Contingent Foundations")

Butler has suggested that it was the tendency to skip over this central chapter that led to the conventional (mis)reading of *Gender Trouble* as about drag and promoting a "free play" model of gender. On two occasions she has stated that this tendency is enabled by the book's structure, by too great a thematic break between the discussion of drag and the discussion of melancholia: "The problem is that I didn't bring forward the psychoanalytic material into the discussion of performativity well enough"; "[W]hat I failed to do is to refer the theatricality of drag back to the psychoanalytic discussions that preceded it, for psychoanalysis insists that the opacity of the unconscious sets limits to the exteriorization of the psyche."[23] Butler's later work has gone on to make these moves back and forth between drag and psychoanalysis, to work the connections between gender performativity and melancholia. Melancholia later becomes a way of delimiting the "play" of gender performativity (one section in "Critically Queer" is subtitled "Melancholia and the Limits of Performance"), a means for Butler to unstick the notion of performativity from the literal performance (external display) to which it had become fixed and resituate performativity within the interior workings of the psyche. If, as Butler later writes, the drag sections of *Gender Trouble* "did not address the question of how it is that certain forms of disavowal and repudiation come to organize the performance of gender," drag as it is reworked though melancholia becomes interesting not so much for what it reveals as for what it reveals as repudiated—or rather, to follow Butler's specific psycho-analytic distinction, foreclosed. For although drag is later said to expose or to allegorize heter-osexuality, now elaborated as heterosexual melancholia, melancholia is itself constituted by the "unperformable," by what it reveals as that which cannot be revealed as such.[24]

Even without Butler's later underscoring its importance and her continued reworking of melancholia and gender performativity, however, it is difficult not to conclude that, in its thorough accounting for the construction of sex via a thorough accounting of the construction of heterosexuality, this second chapter represents the primary achievement of *Gender Trouble*. While the construction of gender and sexuality is often asserted in poststructuralist theory, this chapter details how the process of construction actually takes place through the catego-ries of culture, the psyche, and body, setting up a complex and brilliant exchange between their domains and, by extension, structuralist and psychoanalytic theory. The analyses stem from these difficult questions: If sex is "gender all along," not a prior ontological substance that gender interprets but rather gender in masquerade, how is it that gender comes to pass so effectively as sex? How does sex appear as biological bedrock, and gender as its a posteriori cultural interpretation?

The deft interlocking of theoretical paradigms, namely, Lévi-Strauss, Lacan (and to a lesser extent, Joan Rivière), and Freud gives to Butler's answering of these questions a comprehensive and authoritative feel. Her beginning premise, undergirding the work of Lévi-Strauss, Lacan, and Freud—and of course Foucault—is the productivity of cultural prohibitions. However, where psychoanalysis and structuralism both posit incest as the prohibition that produces heterosexuality, Butler argues that the incest taboo is preceded by the taboo on homosexuality, for it is this that inaugurates the positive Oedipus complex, that is, the incestuous desires in the first place. The child's compliance with the taboo on homo-sexuality ensures that his/her object-cathexis is directed toward the opposite-sexed parent. In a move designed to refute the primacy of heterosexuality over homosexuality, Butler asks: What then is the productive effect on heterosexuality of the prohibition of homosexuality? What happens to the once-desired, now-outlawed homosexual love object? Where within the subject does this object-cathexis go?

Via Lacan, Butler asserts that the lost object is incorporated through a melancholic strategy of masquerade crucial to the production of sexual difference. In Lacan's "The Meaning of the Phallus," women appear to be the phallus through a masquerade effected by a melancholic incorporation. Incorporated are the "attributes of the object/Other that is lost," and significantly for Butler, Lacan exemplifies the lost object with a female homosexual cathexis (*GT* 48).[25] The lost object, in particular "the signification of the body in the mold of the Other who has been refused," is incorporated as a mask via "melancholic identification" (*GT* 50). Lacan's account enables Butler to locate "the process of gender incorporation within the wider orbit of melancholy" and to suggest that the unresolved homosexual cathexes outlawed by the taboo on homosexuality effect the production of heterosexually invested genders: symbolic sexual difference (*GT* 50). From Lacan, Rivière's famous refusal of the distinction between the masquerade of femininity and "genuine womanliness" (and Stephen Heath's elaboration of this assertion) allows Butler to consider the mask not as concealing an interior authentic gender essence but rather as that which masquerades as this essence; the mask itself constitutes gender (*GT* 53).[26]

So far in Butler's chapter the argument has stayed within the bounds of the construction of *gender*. Butler now begins to account for the construction of *sex*, that is how sex is "gender all along." She does so by turning to Freud's writings on melancholia and incorporation ("Mourning and Melancholia" and *The Ego and the Id*, particularly its chapter, "The Ego and the Super-Ego [Ego Ideal]"), and by layering over these two other sets of psychoanalytic texts: Nicolas Abraham and Maria Torok's work on mourning, melancholia, and the processes of introjection and incorporation; and Roy Schafer's descriptions of psychic internalization and the psychoanalytic language of internalization.[27] My questions here—what happens to the matter of sex in *Gender Trouble* and what are its implications for the subject of transsexuality—can be addressed by our careful retracing and elaboration of Butler's steps through these texts.

Freud's 1917 "Mourning and Melancholia" distinguishes these two eponymous psychic states. He defines mourning as a normal finite reaction of grief, which has as its goal the resolution of the death of a loved object. Melancholia differs from mourning on all counts. First, the object is lost not necessarily through death but through, for instance, love. Second, the melancholic does not know for what he grieves: the loss remains opaque to consciousness. And thus third, in not knowing what he has lost, the melancholic *preserves* his object-loss by encrypting it and incorporating it as an identification. In this incorporation of the once-desired lost object as an identification, the melancholic regresses to an oral phase where object-cathexis and identification are confused. In 1923 in *The Ego and the Id*, Freud returns to this essay in order to normalize the workings of melancholia. He discards the opposition between mourning and melancholia and suggests that the processes distinct to melancholia should now be reconceived as part of the process of mourning. Depathologizing melancholia, he argues that its dynamic of substituting an object-cathexis for an identification is central to the formation of the ego. In fact, "it may be the sole condition under which the id can give up its objects." In particular, the dynamics of substitution and incorporation should be understood to produce normative—that is nonpathological—gendering; they function to resolve the object-cathexes of the Oedipus complex and to consolidate gender positioning. Surely significantly for Butler, although she doesn't cite this passage, Freud's example of how identification through incorporation functions to consolidate gender is one of a moment of transgendered identification: "Analysis very often shows that a little girl, after she has had to relinquish her father as a love-object, will bring her masculinity into prominence and identify herself with her father (that is, with the object which has been lost), instead of with the mother."[28]

Freud's generalization of the dynamics of melancholia, his understanding of their role in gendering (through transgendering), allows Butler to select melancholia as the response to the taboo on homosexuality in generating normative (that is heterosexual) gender positions. Heterosexuality is ensured by the cultural prohibition on homosexuality, but the once-loved homosexual object must nevertheless be processed. Because of the cultural prohibition on homosexuality, because of the cultural unnameability of homosexuality, the lost homosexual love-object (always already lost in the sense that it is forbidden) cannot be mourned—that is, articulated or named. The taboo on homosexuality effects a denial of its desired status; grief over the loss is instead turned back in on itself in an unarticulated and unconscious melancholia. At this point Butler enlists Abraham and Torok's description of mourning and melancholia as characterized by two antithetical dynamics of internalization; where mourning introjects the lost object, melancholia incorporates it. Introjection, Abraham and Torok argue, clearly developing Freud's 1917 understanding of mourning as a consciousness of loss, works on a recognition or consciousness of the absence of the object. The void left by the loss of the object is not so much "filled" by articulation of the loss—that is, language—as it makes possible language—that is, the expression of loss. The original loss (the loss of the breast) is resolved through the child's cry. The loss of the real object (originally the mother's body) is thus displaced into language or metaphorized; the mouth emptied of the breast makes possible the mouth filled with words. Melancholia, on the other hand, sets in motion a fantasy of incorporation. As a means of denying the loss, the subject imagines or fantasizes taking in the object. When the loss cannot be acknowledged and articulated via mourning, the subject imagines literally "swallowing" the object, a melancholic fantasy of literalization. As a refusal to displace loss into language, incorporation, Abraham and Torok argue, is fundamentally antimetaphoric. In this sense incorporation is a magical resolution of loss; the loss is actually not resolved at all, remaining unacknowledged and unspoken. As prohibited desire that thus cannot be mourned, Butler uses Abraham and Torok to suggest, the lost homosexual cathexis is incorporated (rather than introjected) as prohibited identification.

But if this identification is incorporated, where exactly is it incorporated? Butler asks: "If the identifications sustained through melancholy are 'incorporated,' then the question remains: Where is this incorporated space? If it is not literally within the body, perhaps it is *on* the body as its surface signification such that the body must itself be understood *as* an incorporated space" (*GT* 67). Having established that melancholia is one psychic effect of the prohibition on homosexuality in the production of heterosexual identity, this, then, is Butler's most engaging proposal. Melancholia for the lost homosexual love-object literalizes sex on the (heterosexual) body. Through Freud and Abraham and Torok, the incorporation that does the work of melancholia appears as an antimetaphorical activity "precisely because it maintains the loss as radically unnameable. In other words, incorporation is not only a failure to name or avow the loss, but erodes the conditions of metaphorical signification itself" (*GT* 68). Incorporation enacts a literalization of the loss. "As an antimetaphorical activity, incorporation *literalizes* the loss *on* or *in* the body and so appears as the facticity of the body, the means by which the body comes to bear 'sex' as its literal truth" (*GT* 68).

This interchangeability between "on" and "in" ("*on* or *in*"), this slippage between, in other words, the surface of the body and its interiority, is crucial. It sets up an equivalence between surface and interiority that is absolutely pivotal both to Butler's description of sexing as a fantasy of incorporation and to her figuring of the body *as* a psychically "incorporated space." In Abraham and Torok the literalizing dynamic of incorporation is crucially a *fantasy* of literalization. Nothing is ever literally taken in during this process of incorporation. Rather, as a means of denying its absence, the subject fantasizes "swallowing" its loss. Corporeal interiority, in this case the notion that the body has a sex, is thus indexical of the literalizing fantasy of heterosexual melancholia, its incorporative response to the prohibition of homosexuality. It is only via this fantasy of literalization that the body comes "to bear a sex" as literal truth, that gender gets inscribed on the body as sex and sex appears as the literal embodiment of gender:

> The conflation of desire with the real—that is, the belief that it is the parts of the body, the "literal" penis, the "literal" vagina, which cause pleasure and desire—is precisely the kind of literalizing fantasy characteristic of the syndrome of melancholic heterosexuality. The disavowed homosexuality at the base of melancholic heterosexuality reemerges as the self-evident anatomical facticity of sex, where "sex" designates the blurred unity of anatomy, "natural identity," and "natural desire." The loss is denied and incorporated, and the genealogy of that transmutation fully forgotten and repressed. The sexed surface of the body thus emerges as the necessary sign of a natural(ized) identity and desire. The loss of homosexuality is refused and the love sustained or encrypted in the parts of the body itself, literalized in the ostensible anatomical facticity of sex. Here we see the general strategy of literalization as a form of forgetfulness, which, in the case of a literalized sexual anatomy, "forgets" the imaginary and, with it, an imaginable homosexuality.
>
> (*GT* 71)

The denied homosexual love is thus incorporated as the "surface" of the body that yet masquerades as interior literal sex. Heterosexuals who believe that their penises and vaginas are the "cause" of their pleasure or desire literalize them and "forget" an/other body: both the (once-loved) homosexual body, the body of the other, and their own imaginary or phantasmatic body (there is an implicit binding of the homosexual to the imaginary).

Because she grounds it on a misrecognition, a mistaking of the signifier of gender for the referent of sex, of the metaphorical for the literal, Butler's description of heterosexual sexing through melancholia inevitably raises mind-boggling questions about what (nonerroneous) recognition might entail. What imaginary body (parts or surfaces) does the heterosexual male who literalizes his penis forget? Is the forgotten imaginary necessarily other than what masquerades as the real? Does this body correspond to a gendered one? Are the imaginary and the phantasmatic already gendered? Later in *Gender Trouble*, in "The Body Politics of Julia Kristeva" (*GT* 79–93), Butler critiques Kristeva's premise of a pre-Symbolic body, one situated in the murky maternal space of the semiotic before the paternal law. Butler reverses Kristeva's temporality, positioning the semiotic or the imaginary as an effect of the Symbolic, the (zone of) prohibition again productive of (the zone of) the prediscursive Kristeva conceives as primary. As this section of the final chapter of *Gender Trouble* suggests that no imaginary body can signify outside of gender, it would follow that the imaginary body in the second chapter is already gendered. Indeed Butler asserts as much in the final pages of "Prohibition, Psychoanalysis, and the Production of the Heterosexual Matrix" when she figures the imaginary or fantasized body as "an altered bodily ego . . . within the gendered rules of the imaginary" (*GT* 71). In literalizing his penis, then, might the straight man be said to forget an imaginary or fantasized vagina? Does he also forget to literalize (invest sex in) body parts that he might be said to already "have" (more than he can be said to "have" a vagina)—feet for instance? And how are *these* parts gendered in the imaginary? What exactly *are* the "gendered rules" of the imaginary? The question of the precise relations between actual heterosexual subjects and the theory of heterosexual melancholia is prompted by, though not addressed in, *Gender Trouble*'s description.

For transsexual embodiment, Butler's harnessing psychoanalytic discussions of melancholia and incorporation to the processes of gendering has two interdependent significant effects: it refigures sex from material corporeality into phantasized surface; and through this it reinscribes the opposition between queer and heterosexual already at work in *Gender Trouble*, sustaining it by once again enlisting transgender as queer.

First, Butler's deliteralization of sex depends upon her conceiving the body as the psychic projection of a surface. This conceptualization derives from a rather eclectic reading of Freud's description of the bodily ego in *The Ego and the Id*. I cite the Freud passage in full:

> A person's own body, and above all its surface, is a place from which both external and internal perceptions may spring. It is *seen* like any other object, but to the *touch*, it yields two kinds of sensations, one of which may be equivalent to an internal perception. Psycho-physiology has fully discussed the manner in which a person's own body attains its special position among other objects in the world of perception. Pain, too, seems to play a part in the process, and the way in which we gain new knowledge of our organs during painful illnesses is perhaps a model of the way by which in general we arrive at the idea of our body.
>
> The ego is first and foremost a bodily ego; it is not merely a surface entity, but is itself the projection of a surface.[29]

In the apparent periphery of a footnote, *Gender Trouble* cites from the second paragraph of this passage Freud's assertion, "the ego is first and foremost a bodily ego" (*GT* 163, n. 43). But then, in a substitution crucially significant to her conceptualization of the body as the psychic projection of a surface, Butler replaces the referent "it" in the subsequent part of the cited sentence, *which in Freud clearly refers back to the ego as bodily ego* ("The ego is first and foremost a bodily ego; *it . . .*), with the word (square bracketed, demoted—in my citation of Butler's note—to parenthetical) "body." Butler's recitation of the passage reads: "Freud continues the above sentence: '(*the body*) is not merely a surface entity, but is itself the projection of a surface'" (*GT* 163 n. 43; my emphasis). Butler's reading of Freud's assertion thus figures the body as interchangeable with the ego. That is, the body appears not only as a surface entity but as itself *the psychic projection of a surface*. Yet that it is precisely Freud's concern at this point in his essay to articulate the bodily origins of the ego, the conception of the ego as product of the body, not the body as product of the ego, is underscored by the explanatory footnote added by his editor James Strachey that appeared first in the 1927 English translation of this text immediately following the above passage—a note authorized by Freud. The note reads: "I.e. the ego is ultimately derived from bodily sensations, chiefly from those springing from the surface of the body. It may thus be regarded as a mental projection of the surface of the body."[30] Butler's reading therefore inverts the note's representation of the body as productive of the psyche ("the ego is derived from bodily sensations") and, through that square-bracketed substitution, conversely images the body as a psychic effect. The body itself becomes commensurable with the psychic projection of the body. Whereas Freud's original assertion maintains a distinction between the body's real surface and the body image as a mental projection of this surface (a distinction between corporeal referent and psychic signified), Butler's recitation collapses bodily surface into the psychic projection of the body, conflates corporeal materiality with imaginary projection. In so doing, it lets slip any notion of the body as a discernible referential category.

Her later use in *Bodies That Matter* of this same passage in *The Ego and the Id* repeats and indeed heightens this reading, even though she here (again in a footnote) addresses directly that 1927 footnote—and even though she here reads it directly as Freud's: "Although Freud is offering an account of the development of the ego, and claiming that the ego is derived from the projected surface of the body, he is inadvertently establishing the conditions for the articulation of the body as morphology" (*BTM* 258, n. 4). The modifying subordination in her syntax ("although") to which her summary of the manifest meaning of the note is confined makes clear that she recognizes that what she desires the note to articulate is not deliberate but "inadvertent." Yet in spite of this recognition, Butler continues to read against the manifest sense of the note—the description of the ego as derived from the body—in order to emphasize the antithesis: the body as morphology. This notion of body as morphology derives from a Lacanian conceptualization of the body as illusory psychic projection. Indeed, her citation of Freud appears here in her chapter on imaginary morphology, "The Lesbian Phallus and the Morphological Imaginary," where Freud's concept of the ego as a bodily ego is said to "prefigure" Lacan's mirror stage in which the body is an "idealization or 'fiction'" (*BTM* 73). But Freud's configuration of the relations between psyche and body is quite different from Lacan's. If in Lacan's mirror stage the body is the ego's misconception, in Freud's *The Ego and the Id* the body is the site of the ego's conception.[31]

Butler's inversion of Freud's formulation of the relations between psyche and body in *Gender Trouble* may also be influenced by Roy Schafer's reading of Freud's bodily ego to illustrate the illusory status of the distinctions the subject makes (and the language of psychoanalysis sustains) between what is interior and what is exterior to the body. Butler enlists Schafer's critique of internalization (in addition to Abraham and Torok's analyses) to argue that incorporation is a fantasy. Schafer proposes that, in its language of internalization, psychoanalysis literalizes the always-imaginary projections on the part of the subject between what is inside and outside. For Schafer Freud's description of the bodily ego exemplifies the original way in which the subject deludes itself into believing in the facticity of corporeal interiority. The bodily ego constitutes a perception or rather a construction of the body espoused (falsely) by the subject, not a product of the body at all but rather a misreading of it; for via the bodily ego the subject assumes wrongly that the self can be conceived as occupying a body, a materiality in space.[32] My contention is that it is precisely this point that the 1927 footnote approved by Freud seeks to emphasize. Freud's bodily ego is designed not to dematerialize the body into phantasmatic effect but to materialize the psyche, to argue its corporeal dependence.

In her critique of the queering of gender Martin has remarked on the tendency in queer studies for "surfaces [to] take priority over interiors and depths and even rule conventional approaches to them [i.e. interiors and depths] as inevitably disciplinary and constraining."[33] Butler's conceptualization of sex as a heterosexual melancholic fantasy of literalization, of sex as the phantasmatic encrypting of gender in the body, implicitly designates corporeal interiority as "disciplinary and constraining" and, conversely, privileges surface as that which breaks up interiority and reveals its status as fantasy. This prioritization of surface is emphatically occularcentric, as is *Gender Trouble*'s concomitant investment in the transgendered subject of the power to reveal sex as "gender all along" (i.e., interiority as incorporated fantasy). *Gender Trouble*'s theoretical economy of gender relies heavily on a notion of the body as that which can be seen, the body as visual surface. This is possibly most marked in its deployment of the transgendered subject to illustrate gender performativity: girls who *look like* boys and boys who *look like* girls. In this sense then, in its dependence on the visible, on body-as-surface, the theory of gender performativity does in fact work out of a definitively theatrical arena. Any claim to a sense of sexed interiority, any *feeling* of being sexed or gendered (whether "differently" or not), along with other ontological claims, is designated phantasmatic, symptomatic of heterosexual melancholia. Yet, to return to that passage in *The Ego and the Id*, Freud underlines that the bodily ego derives not so much from the perception of the body (an "external perception"), that is, from what can be seen, but from the *bodily sensations* that stem from its touching—touching here in both an active and passive sense—(an "internal perception"): "[A person's body] is *seen* like any other object, but to the *touch*, it yields two kinds of sensations, one of which may be equivalent to an internal perception."[34]

The transsexual doesn't necessarily *look* differently gendered but by definition *feels* differently gendered from her or his birth-assigned sex. In both its medical and its autobiographical versions, the transsexual narrative depends upon an initial crediting of this feeling as generative ground. It demands some recognition of the category of corporeal interiority (internal bodily sensations) and of its distinctiveness from that which can be seen (external surface): the difference between gender identity and sex that serves as the logic of transsexuality. This distinction is tactically, ingeniously, and rigorously refused by *Gender Trouble*; it is this refusal that allows for a refiguration of sex into gender. In its one mention of transsexuality *Gender Trouble* uses transsexuality to exemplify not the constitutive significance of somatic feeling but the reverse, the phantasmatic status of sex: the notion that pleasure exceeds material body parts.[35] The transsexual's often declared capacity to experience his or her body as differently sexed from its materiality certainly supports Freud's notion of a bodily ego. But, because the subject often speaks of the imaginary body as more real or more sensible, I argue that this phenomenon illustrates the materiality of the bodily ego rather than the phantasmatic status of the sexed body: the material reality of the imaginary and not, as Butler would have it, the imaginariness of material reality. That the transsexual's trajectory centers on reconfiguring the body reveals that it is the ability to feel the bodily ego in conjunction and conformity with the material body parts that matters in a transsexual context; and that sex is perceived as something that must be changed underlines its very un-phantasmatic status.

Butler's deliteralization of sex, her displacement of sex from material interiority into fantasized surface, is enabled by the production of a binary between queer and heterosexual. The second important ramification for a theory of transsexual embodiment following the refiguring of the body as visual surface, is the alignment once again of transgender with queer. Heterosexuality is engendered via the literalizing strategies of melancholia, strategies that queer through its transgendered performativity brings into relief. Heterosexuality operates by attempting to literalize sex *in* the body; queer transgender reveals this depth as surface. It is not that heterosexuality is natural and queer denaturalizing; rather, heterosexuality is natu-ral*izing*, concealing the masquerade of the natural that queer makes manifest. Even so, heter-osexuality and queer are represented as, respectively, restrictive inferiority and playful surface. If gay and lesbian cultures are said to be *characterized* by camp, parodic subversive— that is, transgendered—performances that deliteralize the apparently real of sex, hetero-sexuality is said to be *characterized* by a literalizing of the apparently real: "The conflation of desire with the real . . . is precisely the kind of literalizing fantasy characteristic of the syndrome of melancholic heterosexuality" (*GT* 71). This attribution of character effects a certain hypostatization of queer and heterosexual, simultaneously impacting queer more thoroughly with transgender. In effect Butler subjects heterosexuality to a certain degree of grounding in order to read queer *through* transgender as refiguring this ground. In operation is a generic antithesis, the queer performative coinciding with the comedic staging of the impossibility of identity, heterosexual literalization with the melancholic attempt to sustain it as absolute ground. As Butler herself implicitly acknowledges when she considers how transgendered subjects also reliteralize the gender norms in her essay on *Paris is Burning*, this pivotal antithesis of *Gender Trouble* is too neat.[36] If in *Gender Trouble* the transsexual is not distinguished from the queer transgendered subject, in *Bodies That Matter* the transsexual is specifically elected as the subject who most succinctly illustrates the limitations of the queer-ness of transgender. It is to this delimiting and the transsexual that I now turn.

Venus is burning: the transubstantiation of the transsexual

> I don't feel that there's anything mannish about me except what I might have between me down there. I guess that's why I want my sex change, to make myself complete.
>
> (Venus Xtravaganza, *Paris is Burning*)

Because it was released in 1990, hot on the heels of the publication of *Gender Trouble*, Jennie Livingston's film *Paris is Burning* often got taken up in discussions of queer identities in conjunction with Butler's book, as if the subjects of the drag ball—again, the lure of the visual example in transgendered contexts—illustrated Butler's theory of gender performa-tivity.[37] Both texts in their transgendered themes captured what seemed definitive of the queer moment. For this reason they were subject to a certain yoking together in feminist/queer studies—in our readings, course syllabi, conferences, and so on. Butler's chapter in *Bodies That Matter* on the ambivalent effects of transgender in *Paris is Burning*, "Gender is Burning: Questions of Appropriation and Subversion" (*BTM* 121–42), serves by association therefore as a return to the subject of transgender in *Gender Trouble* to mark out *its* ambivalent effects. In this sense "Gender is Burning" functions to complicate those binary syllogisms of *Gender Trouble*. The essay's thesis is that crossing identifications in the film both denaturalize and renaturalize identity norms: "*Paris is Burning* documents neither an efficacious insurrec-tion nor a painful resubordination, but an unstable coexistence of both" (*BTM* 137).

While Butler uses *Paris is Burning* in general to document the ambivalent significance of performative crossings, she uses Venus Xtravaganza as the specific lever to articulate this ambivalence: "Venus, and *Paris is Burning* more generally, calls into question whether paro-dying the dominant norms is enough to displace them; indeed, whether the denaturalization of gender cannot be the very vehicle for a reconsolidation of hegemonic norms" (*BTM* 125).

For Butler it is the particular configuration of Venus's body, gender presentation, desires, and fate that best exemplifies how transgressive crossings can simultaneously reinscribe symbolic norms. The film's representation of this Latina transsexual delimits the subversive possibilities of parodic repetitions. Yet although its argument about ambivalence pivots on the specific material ambivalence of the transsexual body, Butler's essay encodes transsexuality as metaphor in a way that sublimates into theoretical allegory the specific materiality of Venus's sex and of her death as a light-skinned Latina transsexual.

The revelation of Venus's murder in the second part of *Paris is Burning* (filmed in 1989, two years after the first encounter with Venus) is indisputably the moment that most cuts through any sense of the performativity, the fictionality of identities the film provides elsewhere, particularly in the ball scenes. That Venus is killed for her transsexuality, for inhabiting a body which, as that of a preoperative male-to-female transsexual, is not coherently female, is strongly supported by the film's narrative. Angie Xtravaganza, the mother of Venus's house, to whom the film turns to provide an account of the occurrence, firmly fixes Venus's death in the context of a transsexual narrative: "That's part of life. That's part of being a transsexual in New York City." The implication is that Venus is murdered in her hotel bedroom on being "read" by her client, killed for having a body in excess of the femaleness he imagined he was paying for; killed, then, as a transsexual. Butler isolates Venus's death as the most prominent instance in the film in which the symbolic precludes its resignification: "This is a killing that is performed by the symbolic that would eradicate those phenomena that require an opening up of the possibilities for the resignification of sex" (*BTM* 131). Yet while Butler's isolation of this moment and this citation suggest that what matters (to the client, to the film, and to Butler the critic) is Venus's transsexuality and the particular configuration of her sexed body as a male-to-female, Butler's reading of Venus's killing situates Venus's body along a binary of queer man/woman of color, in the split between which Venus's Latina, passing-as-white, transsexual body falls.

Butler attributes Venus's death first to "homophobic violence," staking that it is Venus's "failure to pass completely [that renders her] clearly vulnerable" to this violence (*BTM* 129–30). By "failure to pass completely," Butler clearly intends Venus's penis; yet the presence of the penis on Venus's body renders neither her a homosexual man (a literalization of gender surely symptomatic of the heterosexual melancholia *Gender Trouble* critiqued) nor her death an effect of homophobia. Venus presents herself unambivalently as a transsexual woman, not as a gay man or drag queen. Although the only "genetic girl" is behind the camera, it does not follow that all the bodies in *Paris is Burning* are male. Rather, the film presents a spectrum of bodies and desires, heterosexual and homosexual, in-drag, transsexual, and genetic male, with the subjects frequently articulating the distinctions between these categories in a careful self-positioning. Stating that there's nothing "mannish" about her except what she has "down there," Venus describes looking forward to sex reassignment surgery to make her "complete": in other words, a complete woman. Her identification not as a gay man or a drag queen but as an incomplete (preoperative transsexual) woman highlights the impossibility of dividing up all identities along the binary homosexual/heterosexual. If it applies to Venus at all, her desire—to be a complete woman for a man—is heterosexual, and it is more this desire in combination with her transsex that kills her: not as a homosexual man, then, but as a transsexual woman whose desire is heterosexual—or, as *the failure to be* (an ontological failure) a biological woman.

It is therefore equally inadequate to read Venus's death as equivalent to that of a woman of color, as Butler does in the second instance: "If Venus wants to become a woman, and cannot overcome being a Latina, then Venus is treated by the symbolic in precisely the ways in which women of color are treated" (*BTM* 131). Without disputing that women (of color or white) can be treated identically to Venus, and while underlining that it is crucial that Venus's passing be acknowledged as double-leveled—a race and sex crossing—again, it is not for *being* a woman of color but for failing to be one that Venus is murdered; it is the crossing, the trans movement that provokes her erasure. Her death is indexical of an order that cannot contain crossings, a body in transition off the map of three binary axes—sex (male or female), sexuality (heterosexual or homosexual), and race (of color or white): a light-skinned Latina transsexual body under construction as heterosexual and female. At work in Venus's murder is not fear of the same or the other but fear of bodily crossing, of the movement in between sameness and difference: not homo- but transphobia, where "trans" here signifies the multi-leveled status of her crossing. This interstitial space is not foregrounded in Butler's reading of Venus's death.

If for Butler Venus's death represents the triumph of the symbolic, "Gender is Burning" discovers the symbolic asserting its norms through Venus even before this moment—in particular, in her expressed desires to become a "complete woman," to marry and attain financial security. The second two are of course crucially dependent on the first: a Latina transsexual's desires for sexed realness and domestic comfort. It is to set the realization of these desires in motion that Venus is turning tricks to earn enough for her lower surgery, sex work being a not uncommon, indeed often the only means by which poor/working-class male-to-females can afford to change sex. For Butler these desires reveal the extent to which Venus, even before her murder, is subject to "hegemonic constraint":

> Clearly, the denaturalization of sex, in its multiple senses, does not imply a liberation from hegemonic constraint: when Venus speaks of her desire to become a whole woman, to find a man and have a house in the suburbs with a washing machine, we may well question whether the denaturalization of gender and sexuality that she performs, and performs well, culminates in a reworking of the normative framework of heterosexuality.
>
> (*BTM* 133)

Venus's fantasy as a Latina transsexual of becoming "real" (both achieving coherent sexed embodiment and middle-class security) and her corporeal progress in realizing this fantasy mark her out from the drag ball performers who "do" realness and who "resist transsexuality" (*BTM* 136). Butler's presupposition is twofold here: first, that inherent to *doing* realness is an agency resistant to and transformative of hegemonic constraint that the desire to *be* real lacks; and following this, that the transsexual's crossing signifies a failure to be subversive and transgressive of hegemonic constraint where it *ought* to be. Hegemony constrains Venus through the "normative framework of heterosexuality." If resisting transsexuality produces a denaturalizing agency, it is because in Butler's scheme transsexuality is understood, by definition, to be constrained by heterosexuality. By extension, to fail to resist transsexuality fully (as Venus does in hoping for a sex change) is to reliteralize sex (to be rather than perform it) according to the workings of heterosexual melancholia. While Venus's murder symptomizes the triumph of the heterosexual matrix, in her desires Venus is duped by this same heterosexual ideology into believing that a vagina will make her a woman. The heterosexual matrix is therefore already asserting its hegemony in Venus's transsexuality even before her death.

From this scheme it might appear that the binary of heterosexual = literalizing/queer = performative is still in operation in *Bodies That Matter*, with transsexuality standing in for the first term. The transgendered subject, here exemplified in the transsexual, would accordingly appear simply to have been switched from one side of the binary to the other since *Gender Trouble*. Yet Butler's essay works not to reinforce but to demonstrate the ambivalence of this binary, to delimit (not negate) the queer performativity of transgender. It is the literal ambivalence of Venus's transsexual body that allows for this new theoretical ambivalence. Venus's death represents the triumph of hegemonic norms only as it simultaneously illustrates Venus denaturalizing these norms: it is a "killing performed by the symbolic that would eradicate those phenomena that require an opening up of the possibilities for the resignification of sex." Venus's body, with penis intact, is such a phenomenon that would resignify sex. Even in her death, because of her transsexual incoherence between penis and passing-as-a-woman, Venus holds out for Butler the promise of queer subversion, precisely as her transsexual trajectory is incomplete. In her desire to complete this trajectory (to acquire a vagina), however, Venus would cancel out this potential and succumb to the embrace of hegemonic naturalization. In other words, what awards Venus the status of potential resignifier of the symbolic in Butler's scheme is the fact that Venus doesn't get to complete her narrative trajectory and realize her desires, because she still has a penis at her death. What matters for Butler is the oscillation between the literality of Venus's body and the figurative marks of her gender. Conversely, Venus's desire to close down this tension (what I am calling her desire for sexed realness, for embodied sex) curtails her capacity to resignify the symbolic. That Butler figures Venus as subversive for the same reason that Butler claims she is killed, and considers indicative of hegemonic constraint the desires that, if realized, might have kept Venus at least from this instance of violence, is not only strikingly ironic, it verges on critical perversity. Butler's essay locates transgressive value in that which makes the subject's real life most unsafe.

Butler's essay itself is structured on an ambivalence toward transsexuality in its relation to the literal, caught (twice over) both between reading transsexuality literally and meta-phorically and between reading the transsexual as literalizing and deliteralizing. That Butler assigns Venus the function of ambivalence in her effect on the literal is encapsulated in the essay's reliance on the theme of transubstantiation, a term that is conjoined to transsexuality twice in the essay, that indeed stands in for transsexuality: first, in reference to Venus; and second, in reference to Jennie Livingston's camera. First, then, Butler writes that Venus's transsexual fantasy of realness is one of transubstantiation: "Now Venus, Venus Xtravaganza, she seeks a certain transubstantiation of gender in order to find an imaginary man who will designate a class and race privilege that promises a permanent shelter from racism, homo-phobia, and poverty" (*BTM* 130). Venus's desire is here said to represent a transubstantiation of gender in that her transsexuality is an attempt to depart from the literal materiality of her sexed and raced body (and as her class is intricated with these corporeal materialities, thus also a move away from her social materiality) precisely according to a strategy that reliteral-izes sex: the acquisition of a vagina to make her a "complete woman." The term "transubstan-tiation" sustains exactly such antinomy: it conveys both literalization and deliteralization, is both performative and constative. In the Eucharistic sense of transubstantiation, that the bread and wine stand for Christ's body and blood is simultaneously a metaphorization of the materials and a literalization of the Godhead. The exchange of speech during the Eucharist between the priest ("The body of Christ") and the recipient ("Amen") contracts both into agreeing that the materials *are* literally this body. Thus, to make a connection to my discus-sion of melancholia and mourning, the Eucharistic transubstantiation functions as an incorpo-ration of the lost object (Christ), which is *also* an introjection: the object is taken in and literalized, yet at the same time the articulation of its representation ("the body of Christ") ensures its resymbolization. If Venus's transsexuality "transubstantiates" in Butler's account, then, it is because transsexuality is perceived (ambivalently) as seeking out a heterosexual melancholic literalization of sex (the vagina) precisely through a queer resignification (the quest for the vagina is the penis's deliteralization). The antithesis structuring *Gender Trouble* is rendered ambivalent through transsexuality, specifically through the representation of trans-sexuality as transubstantiation.[38]

Butler's essay goes on to displace its discussion of transsexuality and transubstantiation from the literal transsexual body of Venus to the metaphorical body of Jennie Livingston.

Butler takes up bell hooks's criticism that *Paris is Burning* is the product of a white gaze that yet occults the situatedness of this gaze, that the film is a white scripting of black bodies into a play(ground) of Otherness for white pleasure. For hooks Livingston's exclusion of her own white body from the cinematic frame misrepresents the fact that the film is a white perspective on blackness and is thereby symptomatic of the dominant cultural production of whiteness as disembodied:

> Jennie Livingston approaches her subject matter as an outsider looking in. Since her presence as white woman/lesbian filmmaker is "absent" from *Paris is Burning* it is easy for viewers to imagine that they are watching an ethnographic film documenting the life of black gay "natives" and not recognize that they are watching a work shaped and formed by a perspective and standpoint specific to Livingston. By cinematically masking this reality (we hear her ask questions but never see her), Livingston does not oppose the way hegemonic whiteness "represents" blackness, but rather assumes an imperial overseeing position that is in no way progressive or counter-hegemonic.[39]

Seemingly driven by the wish to read the film as more ambivalent than hooks's reading allows (that is both reinscriptive and subversive), Butler seeks an exception to hooks's premise of the disembodiment of the white author. Butler suggests that Livingston's body—or at least its allegorical delegate—might be discovered in the scene in which the other transsexual protagonist, Octavia St. Laurent, poses for a swimsuit shoot: "The one instance where Livingston's body might be said to appear allegorically on camera is when Octavia St. Laurent is posing for the camera, as a moving model would for a photographer. We hear a voice tell her that she's terrific, and it is unclear whether it is a man shooting as a proxy for Livingston or Livingston herself" (*BTM* 134–35). My viewing of the film differs strongly from Butler's. In my experience of this scene, the body that's shooting (and the voice that's shown originating from it) is quite *clearly* that of a white male photographer, whose photographic camera appears in the cinematic frame while Livingston's cinematic camera and her directorial body continue to remain clearly outside the frame. Livingston remains omniscient and unsituated. For Butler, however, the photographer's camera metaphorically embodies Livingston's own desire through the feminization and eroticization of Octavia's transsexual body:

> What is suggested by this sudden intrusion of the camera into the film is something of the camera's desire, the desire that motivates the camera, in which a lesbian phallically organized by the use of the camera (elevated to the status of disembodied gaze, holding out the promise of erotic recognition) eroticizes a black male-to-female transsexual—presumably preoperative—who "works" perceptually as a woman.
>
> (*BTM* 135)

If the camera as subject of the gaze is the phallus, then not only is the photographic camera's appearance within the cinematic frame the allegorical instantiation of Livingston's body, in its eroticization of the male-to-female transsexual as model perfect, the photographic camera metaphorically phallicizes Livingston's body. For in representing the male-to-female transsexual as woman as object of desire, Livingston, Butler writes, "assumes the power of 'having the phallus.'" (*BTM* 135). The camera's feminization/eroticization of the male-to-female transsexual circulates the phallus from transsexual to lesbian, a circulation that amounts to a "transsexualization of lesbian desire": "What would it mean to say that Octavia is Jennie Livingston's kind of girl? Is the category or, indeed, 'the position' of white lesbian disrupted by such a claim? If this is the production of the black transsexual for the exoticizing white gaze, is it not also the transsexualization of lesbian desire?" (*BTM* 135). Livingston's desire for the transsexual is apparently also her identification with the transsexual; or rather the moment enacts an exchange of identities, with the "real girl" acquiring a phallus (becoming transsexualized) as she represents the transsexual as a "real girl." Extending her metaphorization of transsexuality, Butler designates the camera (photographic symbolizing cinematic) the tool of this (s)exchange, the "surgical instrument and operation through which the transubstantiation occurs" that produces Octavia as woman, which "transplants" the phallus from Octavia's body to Livingston's lesbian body.

Transsexuality and transubstantiation are thus brought together for a second time in Butler's essay, now in a metaphorical context. As in Butler's discussion of Venus's fantasy, transsexuality is again implicitly defined as, rendered equivalent to, transubstantiation. How is the double dynamic of literalization and deliteralization played out in this second moment of transsexualization as transubstantiation? I suggest that Butler's reading here again depends on the literal sexed ambivalence of the preoperative male-to-female transsexual body (the woman with a penis). Yet Butler's metaphor of transsexualization, its application to the lesbian body—and the refiguring of surgery into the camera's look—in effect displaces the materiality of transsexuality, and thus the materiality of sex, to the level of figurative. First, in figuring the phallus as circulated from Octavia to Livingston, the metaphor of transsexualization pivots on, and actually originates in, Octavia's penis. We know that Octavia, like Venus, is indeed preoperative for likewise in her narrative Octavia speaks of looking forward to the surgery that will make her a "complete" woman. However, as in its process of circulation in Butler's essay this penis becomes the phallus (Livingston's camera is said to accord her the phallus, not the penis), this penis is clearly subject in its translation to Lacanian sublimation itself. Butler's metaphor of transsexualization depends upon this crucial substitution of fleshly part with symbolic signifier, a confusion between phallus and penis that certainly does not take place in the film. For while Octavia (like Venus) may yet have a penis, in no way can she be said to "have the phallus": that is, in no way is she accorded or does she assume the position of delegate of the symbolic order. Conversely, while (presumably) Livingston has no penis, her capacity to represent Octavia, Venus, and the rest of the cinematic subjects as embodied others via her authority as disembodied overseer, as hooks's essay argues so convincingly, situates her precisely in this position of the symbolic's delegate—the one who appears to have the phallus. In the context of this film by a white lesbian about black and Latino/a gay men, drag queens, and transsexuals, the penis and phallus might be said to remain not only discrete but oppositional. Worlds apart from her subjects in her whiteness, her middle-classness, her educatedness, and her "real" femaleness, Livingston's position behind the camera is that of an authority with absolute powers of representation.[40]

Moreover, Livingston appears to wield this phallic power most heavily in her representation of the transsexuals, Octavia and Venus, in particular in her representation of their fantasies. The section in the film in which Octavia and Venus are cataloguing their desiderata stands as the most explicitly edited and authored moments in the film. Their sentences, most of which begin "I want," are rapidly intercut with each other's and their visual images likewise interwoven. The technique suggests an identity of their fantasies—not only that there is a generic transsexual fantasy but that the transsexual might be conceived according to what she *lacks*; "I want" reveals all that the subject lacks. At the same time, in its location of these scenes, the cinematic apparatus occults its own framing/authoring function. Both Octavia and Venus are filmed reclining on beds in bedrooms (the viewer is led to believe the subjects' own); Octavia is even dressed for bed. The setting allows the audience to assume an intimacy with the subjects, to forget the extent to which these moments are mediated through Livingston's white female gaze—exactly the dynamic of occultation that provides fodder for hooks's critique. Elsewhere in the film it becomes evident how Livingston's camera mediates what of their lives the subjects reveal. Before her death, for instance, Venus informs Livingston that she no longer works the streets, a claim that her death, of course, proves drastically untrue. (The question of whether Venus would have continued to work the streets to save for her surgery, *of whether Venus would have been killed, had Livingston contracted her* along with the film's subjects as actors is ultimately unanswerable, though the fatal ending of Venus's narrative demands its asking.) To summarize, then: in having the power to represent the other and conceal this power, Livingston not only "has the phallus," this having enables her to represent the transsexual other—Octavia and Venus—as crucially lacking: not so much in spite of, as because of their penises. Along with race and class, the crucial structuring difference between Livingston on the one hand and Venus and Octavia on the other is sexed coherence or biological realness: the difference between the nontransgendered and the embodied transgendered subject.

If phallus and penis are antithetical in *Paris is Burning*, Livingston's "phallicization" in no way reveals her embodiment—even allegorically—as Butler claims. The difference between reality and the allegorical, between the fleshy intractability of the penis and the transcendence of the phallus could not be more marked. As her position behind it renders her unrepresented, only a disembodied voice popping questions, the camera is precisely Livingston's means to disembodiment not to her embodiment. Thus hooks's critique of the filmmaker's bodily erasure still holds. Indeed, Butler's allegorization of Livingston's body in the very vehicle for her disembodiment only places further out of reach the filmmaker's literal corporeality, the notion that Livingston has a "body that matters." And although rendering the camera a lesbian phallus might well disrupt Livingston's identity as a lesbian, it does nothing to disrupt its transcendent whiteness: the reason why hooks has problems with its overseeing position in the first place. Indeed, Butler's wish to curtail hooks's critique of Livingston's disembodiment seems queerly motivated (in both senses)—that is, until she reveals an identification with Livingston: both "white Jewish lesbian[s] from Yale" (*BTM* 133). This moment—exceptionally autobiographical for Butler—suggests that perhaps something quite personal is at stake in Butler's discovering an exception to the disembodied gaze of the auteur representing transgendered subjects. For Butler as much as for Livingston the personal investment in this representation of transgendered subjects may well be there; but the point is that in neither is it ever shown and in both this elision of whatever autobiographical stakes there are exacts the cost of objectification and derealization on the represented subjects.

Most significantly, the essay's metaphorical shifting of transsexuality from Venus's body to Livingston's camera displaces transsexuality to a realm that has nothing to do with the materiality of the body. In the context of a discussion of a film during the making of which one of the protagonists is killed for her transsexuality, for the literal configuration of her sexed body, this sublimation of transsexuality appears more prominent and, in my experience anyway, proves the most disturbing moment in Butler's oeuvre. The critic's metaphorization of the transsexual body transcends the literality of transsexuality in precisely a way in which Venus cannot—Venus who is killed for her literal embodiment of sexual difference. Even in the film we might notice that the literality of Venus's transsexual body and the facticity of her death are already subject to a glossing over. As hooks points out, the film glides over the reality of Venus's death, the moment is rapidly overridden by the spectacle of the ball, and, now that she can no longer function in the service of this spectacle, Venus is abandoned. Indeed, it might be said that not only does the filmic narrative fail to mourn Venus, it markedly includes no scenes of others' bereavement over Venus. We simply have Angie Xtravaganza's terse account of what happened to Venus overlaying footage of Venus filmed on the Christopher Street piers while she was still alive, this montage itself threatening to deny the reality, the finality of Venus's death. In metaphorizing transsexuality, Butler inadvertently repeats something of this deliteralization of the subject, her body, and her death. The substance of the transsexual body is sublimated in the move from the literal to the figurative. In the critical failure to "mourn" her death, Venus's body (surely the lost object of *Paris is Burning*), the most prominent representation we have in this film of the pain and anguish of embodying the experience of being differently sexed, is encrypted in Livingston's camera. And what is not kept in view in the film or the theory on it is the intractable materiality of that body in its present state and its peculiar sex.[41]

Queer feminism and critical impropriety: transgender as transitional object?

> The institution of the "proper object" takes place, as usual, through a mundane sort of violence.
>
> (Judith Butler, "Against Proper Objects")

In her work since *Bodies that Matter* Butler demonstrates how the founding of lesbian and gay studies as a methodology distinct from feminism has involved a privileging of subjects and categories to the exclusion of others. Her essay in the "More Gender Trouble" issue of *differences* edited by her in 1994, "Against Proper Objects," critiques the way in which lesbian and gay studies has arrogated sexuality as its "proper object" of study, defining itself through and against feminism by assigning gender as feminism's object of study. What comes to appear quite critically improper in Butler's essay is this very investment in theoretical property: both the assurance with which that attribution of the object to the other is made (in effect a restriction of the other to the object) and the claims staked in the name of this attribution and restriction—namely, lesbian and gay studies' claims to "include and supersede" feminism.[42]

Butler's essay implies that it might never be possible to claim methodological distinctness without bringing into play a degree of aggression, that every theory that grounds itself by allocating "proper objects" will be prone to this kind of critical impropriety. Undoubtedly, my attempts to wrest the transsexual from the queer inscription of transgender—and here, my criticisms of Butler's writing on Venus—are not free of aggression. From the point of view of this project, what subtends the difference in such readings is quite primal (theoretical, political, and admittedly personal): concerns about territory, belonging, creating homes; indeed, the extent to which identity is formed through our investment in external "objects"— a fundamental tenet of psychoanalysis, that definition depends on defining and "owning" objects. The question is perhaps quite simple: Where (best) does the transsexual belong? In seeking to carve out a space for transgender/transsexual studies distinct from queer studies, inevitably terrain must be mapped out and borders drawn up (a fact that doesn't render them uncrossable). Representations, subjects, and bodies (such as Venus) serve as the all-important flags that mark the territory claimed. It is additionally inevitable that the establishment of methodological grounds involves the attempt early on to circumscribe neighboring methodologies and approaches, the emphasizing of what *they* do *not* as opposed to what *we do*.

Significantly, "Against Proper Objects" conjures transsexuality in order to complicate articulations of methodological difference (although Butler's language of "domestication" suggests not my frontier-scale struggles but tiffs in the kitchen). Butler presents transsexuality as a category that, because of its "important dissonance" with homosexuality (tantalizingly, but importantly for my readings which follow, she doesn't say what this is), falls outside the domain of lesbian and gay studies ("APO" 11). Insofar as lesbian and gay studies delimits its proper object to sexuality and "refuses the domain of gender, it disqualifies itself from the analysis of transgendered sexuality altogether" ("APO" 11). Transsexuality and transgender are invoked as illustrations of the exclusions that lesbian and gay studies has performed in fixing its proper object as sexuality. Transsexuality and transgender number among the categories of "sexual minorities" Butler rightly understands Gayle Rubin insisting in 1984 made necessary a "radical theory of the politics of sexuality."[43] These categories, Butler believes, get sidelined, ironically in lesbian and gay studies' appropriation of Rubin's essay as a foundational text. As I outlined at the beginning of this chapter, my sense of the role of transgender in lesbian and gay studies is quite different: that is, the figure of transgender has, rather, proven crucial to the installation of lesbian and gay studies—its installation *as* queer. Even work purporting to focus exclusively on sexuality and not gender—I suggested Sedgwick's in particular—implicitly engages this transgendered figure and, correlatively, the axis of gender. (In her other mention of transgender and transsexuality Butler writes of Sedgwick's antihomophobic critique that "[b]y separating the notion of gender from sexuality, [it] narrows the notion of sexual minorities offered by Rubin, distancing queer studies from the consideration of transgendered persons, transgendered sexualities, transvestism, cross-dressing, and cross-gendered definition" ["APO" 24, n. 8].) Although it strongly suggests that "an analysis of sexual relations apart from an analysis of gender relations is [not] possible," Butler's essay does not address how lesbian and gay studies might *already* be engaged in gender analyses, if largely unconsciously ("APO" 9). Indeed, toward the end of Butler's interview of Gayle Rubin in the same "More Gender Trouble" issue of *differences*, Rubin provocatively hints that Butler's critique of lesbian and gay studies' exclusion of gender might amount to a tilting at windmills:

> As for this great methodological divide you are talking about, between feminism and gay/lesbian studies, I do not think I would accept that distribution of interests, activities, objects and methods. . . . I cannot imagine a gay and lesbian studies that is not interested in gender as well as sexuality. . . . I am not persuaded that there is widespread acceptance of this division of intellectual labor between feminism, on the one hand, and gay and lesbian studies on the other.[44]

That s/he has received considerably less critical attention than the cross-dresser or drag artist(e), that s/he has not been subject to the same deliberate and concentrated queer recuperation, and indeed, as is demonstrated in Butler's own work on Venus, that s/he is more likely to be deployed to signal the *unqueer* possibilities of cross-gender identifications, suggests that, above all transgendered subjects, the transsexual is more of the limit case for queer studies: the object that exceeds its purview. Yet my sense is that the reasons for transsexuality's exceeding queer lie not so much in queer's refusal of the category of gender (and thus transgender), as Butler argues, as in queer's poststructuralist problems with literality and referentiality that the category of transsexuality makes manifest—particularly in relation to the sexed body. Butler's metaphorical displacement of the literality of Venus's sex can serve to exemplify just this.

Indeed, according to Butler, it must remain "an open question whether 'queer' can achieve these same goals of inclusiveness" imagined by Rubin's radical theory of sexual politics, whether queer studies can incorporate all of the "sexual minorities" among which transgender and transsexuality might be categorized ("APO" 11). For Butler the concern is queer's *capacity* to include, a question about queer's elasticity, about how far the term "queer" will stretch. What is not a concern is whether queer *should* even attempt to expand; expansion, inclusion, incorporation are automatically invested with value. One wonders to what extent this queer inclusiveness of transgender and transsexuality is an inclusiveness *for* queer rather than for the trans subject: the mechanism by which queer can sustain its very queerness—prolong the queerness of the moment—by periodically adding subjects who appear ever queerer precisely by virtue of their marginality in relation to queer. For does not this strategy of inclusiveness ensure the conferral on queer of the very open-endedness, the mobility, and—in the language of "Against Proper Objects"—the very means by which to "rift" methodological "grounds" that queer has come to symbolize? If, as Butler writes, "normalizing the queer would be, after all, its sad finish," the project of expansion enables queer to resist this normalization (what Butler fears will be "the institutional domestication of queer thinking") that would herald its end ("APO" 21). Yet if we conceive of "finish" and "end" here not as a limitation in time but a limitation in institutional space, this limited reach is inevitable and arguably necessary for the beginnings of other methodologies, for reading other narratives from other perspectives.

What Butler does not consider is to what extent—and on what occasions—transgendered and transsexual subjects and methodologies might not wish for inclusion under the queer banner. "Against Proper Objects" assesses inclusion and the resistance to inclusion solely from the perspective of queer; it does not imagine possible resistance stemming from the putatively excluded "sexual minorities." Our discussions should address not only—or perhaps not primarily—queer's elasticity but also what is gained and lost for nonlesbian and gay subjects and methodologies in joining the queer corporation. In the case of transsexuality there are substantive features that its trajectory often seeks out that queer has made its purpose to renounce: that is, not only reconciliation between sexed materiality and gendered identification but also assimilation, belonging in the body and in the world—precisely the kinds of "home" that Butler's essay holds at bay in its critical troping of "domestication." There is much about transsexuality that must remain irreconcilable to queer: the specificity of transsexual experience; the importance of the flesh to self; the difference between sex and gender identity; the desire to pass as "real-ly-gendered" in the world without trouble; perhaps above all [. . .] a particular experience of the body that can't simply transcend (or transubstantiate) the literal.

Since *Gender Trouble*, "domestication" has figured as something of a specter in Butler's work. Domestication appears to represent the assigning of subjects and methodologies to specific categorical homes, the notion that there is an institutional place to which they belong. For the Butler of 1990 what was at stake was the domestication of gender, and concomitantly the domestication of feminism through gender's domestication beyond sexuality. *Gender Trouble* sought "to facilitate a political convergence of feminism, gay and lesbian perspectives on gender, and poststructuralist theory" to produce a "complexity of gender[,] . . . an interdisciplinary and postdisciplinary set of discourses in order to resist the *domestication* of gender studies or women['s] studies within the academy and to radicalize the notion of feminist critique" (*GT* xiii; my emphasis). As a means of resisting gender/women's studies' domestication, *Gender Trouble* marshaled lesbian and gay sexuality and, as I have suggested, lesbian and gay genders, in effect troubling or queering gender. In analyzing the way in which the sex/gender system is constructed through the naturalization of heterosexuality and vice versa, *Gender Trouble* performed its work in an interstitial space between feminism and lesbian and gay studies, producing a new methodological genre—hence my term for this: queer feminism. In this sense *Gender Trouble* constituted an attempt to queer feminism. Yet although Butler's work might be said to have always conceived of domestication—what we might term object-constancy to push further on the psychoanalytic metaphor—as restrictive, it is interesting to note that in 1994 it is no longer *feminist* but *queer* studies that she perceives to be under threat of domestication: the shift indexes the change in values of the currencies of these methodologies, the ways in which queer and gender studies have "circumscribed" feminism. In "Against Proper Objects" it is (trans)gender that returns as the supplement to trouble the domestication of (homo)sexuality, gender that "troubles" queer. This shift in Butler's theoretical "object-cathexis" is a sure a sign of queer's institutionalization (Oedipalization? with feminism as [M]Other?) if ever there was one.

To resist queer's incorporation of trans identities and trans studies is not to refuse the value of institutional alliances and coalitions (in the form of shared conferences, journals, courses, and so on). But an alliance, unlike a corporation, suggests a provisional or strategic union between parties whose different interests ought not to be—indeed, cannot totally be—merged, sublimated for cohering—or queering—the whole. In closing, it needs emphasizing that it is precisely queer's investment in the figure of transgender in its own institutionalization—and above all the methodological and categorical crossings of Butler's queer feminism—that have made it possible to begin articulating the transsexual as a theoretical subject. It can be said that, in its very origins and its early attempts at self-definition, transgender studies is allied with queer.

Notes

1 Eve Kosofsky Sedgwick, *Epistemology of the Closet* (Berkeley: California University Press, 1990), p. 16.

2 Eve Kosofsky Sedgwick, *Between Men: English Literature and Male Homosocial Desire* (New York: Columbia University Press, 1985).

3 Sedgwick, *Epistemology of the Closet*, pp. 37–38.

4 Eve Kosofsky Sedgwick, *Tendencies* (Durham: Duke University Press, 1993), p. 256.

5 Sedgwick, *Tendencies*, p. 9. Judith Butler emphasizes instead the contrast between Sedgwick's theoretical formulations on sexuality versus gender and her reading practice: "Although Sedgwick appears to defend this methodological separation [of gender and sexuality], her own readings often make rich and brilliant use of the problematic of cross-gendered identification and cross-sexual identification" (Judith Butler, "Against Proper Objects," *differences* 6, nos. 2/3 [1994]: 24, n. 8).

6 Kobena Mercer, "Looking for Trouble," in *The Lesbian and Gay Studies Reader*, ed. Henry Abelove, Michèle Aina Barale, David Halperin (New York: Routledge, 1993), pp. 350–59; Kobena Mercer, "Reading Racial Fetishism: The Photographs of Robert Mapplethorpe," in *Fetishism as Cultural Discourse*, ed. Emily Apter and William Pietz (Ithaca: Cornell University Press, 1991), pp. 307–30; Kobena Mercer, "Skin Head Sex Thing: Racial Difference and the Homoerotic Imaginary," in *How Do I Look? Queer Film and Video*, ed. Bad Object-Choices (Seattle: Bay, 1991), pp. 179–210; Cherríe Moraga, *Loving in the War Years* (New York: South End, 1983); Gloria Anzaldúa, *Borderlands, La Frontera: The New Mestiza* (San Francisco: Aunt Lute, 1987).

7 Teresa de Lauretis, "Sexual Difference and Lesbian Representation," *Theatre Journal* 40, no. 2 (1988): 155–77; Sue-Ellen Case, "Toward a Butch-Femme Aesthetic," in *Making a Spectacle: Feminist Essays on Contemporary Women's Theatre*, ed. Lynda Hart (Ann Arbor: Michigan University Press, 1989), pp. 282–99; Jonathan Dollimore, *Sexual Dissidence: Augustine to Wilde, Freud to Foucault* (Oxford University Press, 1991); Marjorie Garber, *Vested Interests: Cross-Dressing and Cultural Anxiety* (New York: Routledge, 1992).

8 Judith Butler, *Gender Trouble: Feminism and the Subversion of Identity* (New York: Routledge, 1990). Page numbers of citations will appear directly in the text after *GT*.

9 Judith Butler, "Critically Queer," in this volume, pp 24, 25.

10 Eve Kosofsky Sedgwick, "Queer Performativity: Henry James's *The Art of the Novel*," *GLQ: A Journal of Lesbian and Gay Studies* 1, no. 1 (1993): 1.

11 David Bergman, ed., "Introduction," *Camp Grounds: Style and Homosexuality* (Amherst: Massachusetts University Press, 1993), p. 11. See also Moe Meyer, ed., *The Politics and Poetics of Camp* (London: Routledge, 1994).

12 Scott Long, "The Loneliness of Camp," in *Camp Grounds*, ed. Bergman, p. 79.

13 Richard Ekins and Dave King, ed., *Blending Genders: Social Aspects of Cross-Dressing and Sex-Changing* (London: Routledge, 1996); see their introduction, p. 1.

14 Judith Butler, *Bodies That Matter: On the Discursive Limits of "Sex"* (New York: Routledge, 1993). Page numbers of citations will appear directly in the text after *BTM*.

15 Sedgwick, "Queer Performativity," p. 1; Sedgwick, *Tendencies*, p. 11.

16 Judith Butler, "Variations on Sex and Gender: Beauvoir, Wittig, and Foucault," in *Feminism as Critique*, ed. Seyla Benhabib and Drucilla Cornell (Minneapolis: Minnesota University Press, 1987), pp. 128–43.

17 Jacques Derrida, *Limited Inc* (Evanston: Northwestern University Press, 1988). Biddy Martin has also noted the importance of speech-act theory—although not of the Derridean deconstruction of it—to both Butler's and Sedgwick's theory of performativity (Biddy Martin, "Sexualities Without Genders and Other Queer Utopias," *Diacritics* 24, nos. 2/3 [1994]: 104–21). Butler's most recent book *Excitable Speech: A Politics of the Performative* (London: Routledge, 1997), just out as I go to press, is a thorough exploration of the significance of speech acts (of the relation between "speech" and "act") in the contemporary cultural sphere. Since its concerns are not primarily sex or gender, I omit discussion of it here.

18 For Butler's genealogy of Beauvoir's understanding of becoming to Sartre and Hegel and a prefiguring of key arguments in *Gender Trouble*, see Judith Butler, "Sex and Gender in Simone de Beauvoir's *Second Sex*," *Yale French Studies* 72 (1986): 34–49.

19 Butler, "Critically Queer," p. 25.

20 Monique Wittig, *The Straight Mind and Other Essays* (Boston: Beacon, 1992).

21 Butler, "Critically Queer," p. 25; my emphasis.

22 Martin, "Sexualities Without Genders," p. 104.

23 Liz Kotz, "The Body You Want: Liz Kotz Interviews Judith Butler," *Artforum* 31 (November 1992): 89; Butler, "Critically Queer," p. 24.

24 Judith Butler, "Melancholy Gender/Refused Identification," *Constructing Masculinity*, ed. Maurice Berger, Brian Wallis and Simon Watson (New York, Routledge, 1995), pp. 32, 34.

25 Jacques Lacan, "The Meaning of the Phallus," in *Feminine Sexuality; Jacques Lacan and the École Freudienne*, ed. Juliet Mitchell and Jacqueline Rose (New York: Norton, 1982), pp. 74–85.

26 Joan Rivière, "Womanliness as a Masquerade," in *Formations of Fantasy*, ed. Victor Burgin, James Donald and Cora Kaplan (New York: Methuen, 1986), p. 38; Stephen Heath, "Joan Rivière and the Masquerade," in *Formations of Fantasy*, ed. Burgin, Donald and Kaplan, pp. 46–61.

27 Sigmund Freud, "Mourning and Melancholia" (1917) *The Standard Edition of the Complete Psychological Works*, vol. 14, ed. James Strachey (London: Hogarth, 1968), pp. 239–58; Sigmund Freud, *The Ego and the Id* (1923), trans. Joan Rivière, ed. James Strachey (New York: Norton, 1989); Nicolas Abraham, "Notes on the Phantom: A Complement to Freud's Metapsychology," in *The Trial(s) of Psychoanalysis*, ed. Françoise Meltzer (Chicago: Chicago University Press, 1988), pp. 75–80; Nicolas Abraham and Maria Torok, "Introjection-Incorporation: Mourning or Melancholia," in *Psychoanalysis in France*, ed. Serge Lebovici and Daniel Widlöcher (New York: International University Press, 1980), pp. 3–16; Roy Schafer, *Aspects of Internalization* (New York: International University Press, 1968); Roy Schafer, *A New Language for Psychoanalysis* (New Haven: Yale University Press, 1976).

28 Freud, *The Ego and the Id*, pp. 24, 28.

29 Freud, *The Ego and the Id*, pp. 19–20.

30 Freud, *The Ego and the Id*, p. 20, n. 16.

31 As I understand this influence, while Lacan's imago certainly derives from Freud's concept of the ego, its debt is not so much to the ego of *The Ego and the Id* as to Freud's second model of the ego in "On Narcissism: An Introduction": the ego as distinctly nonbiological and crucially split ("Lacan's Mirror Phase," talk given by Bice Benvenuto, Center for Freudian Psychoanalysis and Research, London, October 21, 1995). See Elizabeth Grosz, *Jacques Lacan: A Feminist Introduction* (London: Routledge, 1990), pp. 24–49, for an account of the differences between Freud's two egos and the genealogy of only one to Lacan.

32 "The child seems to organize its earliest subjective experience around bodily sensations with their varying pleasure–pain properties. This early subjective experience is the 'bodily ego' that, according to Freud (1923a [*The Ego and the Id*]), is the first ego. Thus, from its very beginnings, the organization of experience implies physical referents such as are later subjectively defined as being inside and outside" (Schafer, *A New Language for Psychoanalysis*, p. 171). The "physical referents"—the "bodily sensations" that Freud posits as generating the ego—are in Schafer's scheme granted only retroactively and subjectively.

33 Martin, "Sexualities Without Genders," p. 106.

34 Freud, *The Ego and the Id*, pp. 19–20.

35 "Transsexuals often claim a radical discontinuity between sexual pleasures and bodily parts. Very often what is wanted in terms of pleasure requires an imaginary participation in body parts, either appendages or orifices, that one might not actually possess, or, similarly, pleasure may require imagining an exaggerated or diminished set of parts. . . . The imaginary condition of desire always exceeds the physical body through or on which it works" (*GT* 70–71).

36 Arguing with lesbian feminism in particular, Lynne Segal makes a case for the non-normativity of heterosexual practices, their potential (for straight feminists) for putting in question gender hierarchies: "Straight sex . . . can be no less 'perverse' than its 'queer' alternatives" (Lynne Segal, *Straight*

Sex: The Politics of Pleasure [London: Virago, 1994], p. 318). That straight should thus aspire to queer is a sure sign of the success of queer theory's "grounding" (of running aground) heterosexuality.

37   *Paris is Burning*, dir. Jennie Livingston, Miramax, 1990.

38   The queer/poststructuralist investment in figures of transgression might be read as a similar (unconscious?) appropriation of Catholic rhetoric.

39   bell hooks, *Black Looks: Race and Representation* (Boston: South End, 1992), p. 151.

40   Livingston's powers of representation extend beyond the cinematic. That Livingston knowingly and intentionally entered the drag ball world of Harlem as an authority is evident from the legal cautions she took before filming, including requiring all the participants in the film to sign a release. Two years after the film's success, all but two of the participants filed legal suits against Livingston, staking a claim in her profits. Their signatures on the release ensured the dismissal of their suits. For a discussion of the significance of this case to the circumscribed agency of the ball participants beyond the realm of the ball, see Philip Brian Harper, "The Subversive Edge: *Paris is Burning*, Social Critique, and the Limits of Subjective Agency," *Diacritics* 24, nos. 2/3 (1994): 90–103.

41   Although precisely for these reasons in current transgender studies, Venus (and Butler's reading of her) is proving seminal. Ki Namaste's critique of queer theory's representation of transgender—which appeared after my writing this—similarly argues that Butler "reduce[s] Extravaganza's transsexuality to an allegorical state" ("'Tragic Misreadings': Queer Theory's Erasure of Transgender Subjectivity," *Queer Studies: A Lesbian, Gay, Bisexual, and Transgender Anthology*, ed. Brett Beemyn and Mickey Eliason [New York: New York University Press, 1996], p. 188). While I emphasize the literality of sex and the cruciality of narrative for the transsexual, Namaste's essay goes on usefully to reinstate something of the sociological context of transgender and transsexual lives in which queer's "tragic misreadings" take place.

42   Judith Butler, "Against Proper Objects," p. 2. Page numbers of further citations will appear directly in the text after "APO."

43   Gayle Rubin, "Thinking Sex: Notes for a Radical Theory of the Politics of Sexuality," *Pleasure and Danger: Exploring Female Sexuality* (1984; reprint, London: Pandora, 1989), pp. 267–319.

44   Gayle Rubin, with Judith Butler (Interview), "Sexual Traffic," *differences* 6, nos. 2–3 (1994): 88.

Chapter 4

Steven Angelides

THE QUEER INTERVENTION

Steven Angelides holds a fellowship in the Centre for Women's Studies and Gender Research and Sociology at Monash University. He is the author of *A History of Bisexuality* (2001), from which this essay is excerpted. In addition to critical analyses of bisexuality, Angelides has also published articles on child and adolescent sexualities.

In *A History of Bisexuality*, Angelides argues that bisexuality has historically functioned as the other to more traditional notions of sexual identity, thus undermining the binary categories of hetero- and homosexuality. In this excerpt from his seventh chapter, "The Queer Intervention," Angelides critiques canonical queer theory for its inattention to the category of bisexuality, closely reading the work of leading queer theorists such as Eve Kosofsky Sedgwick, Lee Edelman, and Diana Fuss, among others. Angelides diagnoses this inattention to the category of bisexuality within queer theory as a consequence of an ongoing and problematic separation of sexuality and gender in critical discourse. He contends that, in historical and epistemological terms, bisexuality functions to regulate the axes of sexuality and gender in the ongoing discursive production of sexual identities. Therefore, he argues for the necessity of including bisexuality more fully within the critical canon of queer theory.

[. . .] Queering queer theory

> Any discourse that is based on the questioning of boundary lines must never stop questioning its own.
>
> (Barbara Johnson 1987)

IN ITS ROLE as an umbrella category for the sexually marginalized, queer has been successful in initiating a new and powerful form of political organization. Notwithstanding massive debate regarding its effectiveness,[1] queer has provided a new discursive space through which to foster political alliances across class, gender, racial, and sexual borders. Here the category of bisexuality in the present tense has for the first time found a welcoming space for the articulation of its identity. At the organizational and activist level, this queer impulse is discernible not only in the way bisexuality is being appended to many "lesbian and gay" groups, but in the way it is being incorporated into "queer" groups as a part of the very category of queer.[2] In the domain of the academy, however, the situation is markedly different. In the canonical deconstructive texts of queer theory a palpable marginalization at best, and erasure at worst, surrounds the theoretical question of bisexuality.[3] This seems to me rather odd given that [. . .] the category of bisexuality has been pivotal to the epistemic *construction* of the hetero/homosexual opposition. If this is indeed the case, ought not the category of bisexuality also figure in the *deconstruction* of hetero- and homosexuality? What is the relationship between social constructionism and deconstruction, between history and theory? It is with these questions in mind that I would like now to return to some of these canonical texts in order to interrogate the erasure of bisexuality.

[. . .T]he impetus for much queer theory has been Sedgwick's claim that any analysis of "modern Western culture" requires a "critical analysis of modern homo/heterosexual defini-tion."[4] That bisexuality has been pivotal to the discursive construction of this opposition, however, has been completely overlooked by Sedgwick. This is in large part a structural effect of the central organizing principle of her work: the trope of the closet. For Sedgwick this trope is a useful metaphor for interrogating the "relations of the known and the unknown, the explicit and the inexplicit" (3) as they have served to structure modern hetero/homo-sexual definition. Sexual definition and, indeed, meaning in Western culture itself, she quite rightly argues, have been themselves structured around, among others, the oppositions secrecy/disclosure, knowledge/ignorance, masculine/feminine, natural/artificial, same/different, active/passive, in/out. However, what Sedgwick does not consider is the fact that in the history of discourses of sexuality it is the force of these very oppositions that has served to elide bisexuality from the present tense.

[. . .B]isexuality has been rendered an artifact of our evolutionary prehistory, a state outside or prior to culture or civilization, a myth, a catachresis, and a (utopian) sexual impos-sibility. This is precisely because bisexuality cannot be represented through these binary formulations, blurring as it does any easy distinction of their terms (by in fact partaking of each of the polar terms). In order to secure its binary structure, one of the primary moves of the epistemology of the closet is to repudiate bisexuality, or else render it consonant with its binary logic. In the former, bisexuality is set up as an interior exclusion; in the latter, it is subsumed either by hetero- or homosexuality. By failing to interrogate the interior exclu-sions and binary appropriations instantiated and performed by the epistemology of the closet, Sedgwick's analysis thus falls short of analyzing its terms. And as Maria Pramaggiore argues, "closets are not definitive: they continuously dissolve and reproduce themselves. Nor are they comprehensive: the logic of the closet does not define all sexualities."[5]

Sedgwick does usefully expose the way the hetero/homosexual opposition inheres in and structures—through its "ineffaceable marking" of fundamental binarisms—modern Western thought. She also brilliantly traces the conceptual contradictions responsible for the (continuing) "modern crisis of homo/heterosexual definition" since the turn of the century. By crisis Sedgwick is not celebrating the "self-corrosive efficacy of the contradictions inherent to these definitional binarisms." In other words, discourses concerned with securing sexual defi-nition are not about to disappear as a result of an "incoherence of definition." Rather, what she is attempting to highlight is the way these contradictions drive discourses of sexuality. In the history of sexuality, therefore, "contests for discursive power" can be seen as "competitions" to "set the terms of, and profit in some way from, the operations of such an incoherence of definition." An analysis of the centrality of this definitional incoherence thus comprises the primary undertaking of *Epistemology of the Closet*. Yet despite her deconstructive labors, Sedgwick does not inquire into precisely *how* discourses of sexuality vie for "rhetorical leverage"

(11), that is, *how* modern homo/heterosexual definition is (in)coherently instantiated. As I have demonstrated throughout this discussion, bisexuality is the third term in the hetero/homosexual binary that has absorbed and regulated the contradictions inherent to the reproduction of modern sexual definition. In ignoring bisexuality and, indeed, the metonymical association of bisexuality with binary contradiction, Sedgwick's deconstructive framework does not go far enough in *critically analyzing* modern hetero/homosexual definition. Doing this more effectively would require sustained attention, as I have suggested, to the interior exclusions constitutive of the epistemology of the closet. As it stands, therefore, Sedgwick, perhaps like Foucault, appears content with a description rather than explanation of the production of hetero/homosexual definition. For theorists of bisexuality, however, such a rhetorical analysis only repeats the problematic erasure of bisexuality that is the closet's point of departure.

Diana Fuss's edited collection *Inside/Out: Lesbian Theories, Gay Theories* is another of the canonical texts of queer theory that effects a similar marginalization and erasure of bisexuality. In her introduction to this collection, Fuss follows Sedgwick's lead in analyzing the discursive mechanics of modern hetero/homosexual definition. In a brief theoretical analysis she argues that it is "another related opposition"—that of inside/outside—that provides the structural foundations for the opposition of hetero- and homosexuality. Fuss raises a series of questions in order to foreground her analysis: "How do outsides and insides come about? What philosophical and critical operations or modes produce the specious distinction between a pure and natural heterosexual inside and an impure and unnatural homosexual outside? Where exactly, in this borderline sexual economy, does one identity leave off and the other begin?" [6].

Drawing more explicitly from Derridean deconstruction, Fuss appears to be asking questions from a position that cannot fail to explore the location of bisexuality in this binary economy. First, she is alluding to the fallacy of a pure inside and a pure outside through which to distinguish hetero- from homosexuality. Second, she appears to be setting herself the task of inquiring into precisely *how* these homogeneous fallacies are epistemologically ("philosophical and critical operations") created. And third, she is directly addressing the question of the very threshold between these two sexual identities, that is, the spatial, temporal, and discursive points where the boundaries between hetero- and homosexuality are blurred. Bisexuality is unmistakably implicated in every one of these questions. Yet Fuss is confusing on this point, as is evidenced by the problematic parenthetical appearance of bisexuality in the following fourth question. She asks, "And what gets left out of the inside/outside, heterosexual/homosexual opposition, an opposition which could at least plausibly be said to secure its seemingly inviolable dialectical structure only by assimilating and internalizing other sexualities (bisexuality, transvestism, transsexualism. . .) to its own rigid polar logic?" (2).

There are a number of problems with this account. Michael du Plessis argues that the identities Fuss "lists as somehow in excess of 'homosexuality' and 'heterosexuality' are cordoned off by those parentheses from the body of her own text, taken into consideration only in order to be more insidiously expelled."[7] What I argue, though, is that this rendering of bisexuality as excessive or Other to hetero- and homosexuality implies, rather problematically, the existence of a mode of bisexuality outside the economy of (hetero)sexuality and its binary logic. As I have demonstrated throughout this discussion, however, bisexuality *as a concept of sexuality* is historically and epistemologically implicated in this binarized economy, unthinkable outside its terms. Additionally, and concomitantly, Fuss seems to come close to suggesting that the appropriation of bisexuality by the inside/outside, heterosexual/homosexual binaries works *only*, therefore, to *secure* their "seemingly dialectical structure." She overlooks the fact that not only is bisexuality internal to the dialectical structure of hetero- and homosexuality, but that bisexuality, in a different yet related definitional guise, preceded and conditioned its historical invention. That is, before its appearance in the economy of (hetero)sexuality—indeed, before the construction of this economy—bisexuality was a mythological and evolutionary concept constructed to explain the origins of male and female sex difference. Fuss is not referring to this sense of bisexuality, however. Instead, she is referring to bisexuality as a mode of sexuality. Had she historicized the dialectical structure of hetero- and homosexuality, therefore, she might have recognized that bisexuality has served *both* to secure and, simultaneously, to disrupt its boundaries. For instance, within discourses of sexology, Freudian psychoanalysis, and gay liberation, bisexuality has been invoked as an explanatory causal principle in the production of hetero- and homosexuality. Yet within the very same discourses bisexuality has been obscured from the present tense and even repudiated at the very point when it threatens to blur the boundaries between the two.[8]

In fairness to Fuss, however, it is possible that I have misread the thrust of her claim that the hetero/homosexual opposition secures "its seemingly inviolable dialectical structure only by assimilating and internalizing other sexualities (bisexuality, transvestism, transsexualism . . .) to its own rigid polar logic." A more "faithful" reading might be that, with respect to bisexuality at least, it can *only* be accommodated by the hetero/homosexual opposition if it is to conform to the inherent binary logic. In this way, some of the claims of this book with regard to the logical functioning of this opposition may appear to be in agreement with Fuss. On one hand I believe this is the case, and that my first reading interpreted this sentence by ignoring the term "only." On the other hand, however, Fuss appears to diverge from my reading of bisexuality in a way that I think justifies my original critique. To say that bisexuality is *assimilated* and *internalized* by the hetero/homosexual opposition is, as I noted above, to impute a kind of distinctness to bisexuality. This suggests that bisexuality undergoes a kind of "conversion" by binary logic and that it can exist as a mode of sexuality outside this oppositional framework. My argument, on the contrary, is that bisexuality is an epistemological part of this framework, *unthinkable outside of binary logic.*

An obvious riposte might well be that Fuss is in fact implicitly referring to a notion of bisexuality that our binary logic refuses to acknowledge and that this idea is scarcely different from what I refer to as the disavowal of bisexuality in the present tense. Even if this is the case, however, the notion of bisexuality in the present tense is also, as I have repeatedly shown, produced through the workings of binary logic. Any concept of bisexuality can only ever be one of the binary logic's *effects*. By thus situating some version of bisexuality *outside* the hetero/homosexual binary, Fuss is in fact implying precisely what my original interpretation suggests: that all versions of bisexuality *inside* the hetero/homosexual binary *only* reinforce or "secure" its "dialectical structure." Yet as we have seen, in the history of sexuality this is only part of the story. Another part is that bisexuality simultaneously *disrupts*, at every turn, and within the very terms of binary logic, the dialectical structure of hetero/homosexuality.

Fuss's figuring of bisexuality highlights a deeper problem with her invocation of the inside/outside binary. Inscribed as Other to the hetero/homosexual opposition, bisexuality is situated *outside* the monogamic and monosexual figuring of the very "couple" inside and outside. It is therefore only possible for Fuss to secure the dialectical structure of this binary *as an explanatory principle* by in turn deploying its self-constituting binary logic. The law of this logic is the law of noncontradiction. Each term in a binary, therefore, is either A or not-A. Any term that is both A and not-A, or, neither A nor not-A, is excluded. Fuss relies on this law, however, by failing to consider what it excludes: the logics of both/and, neither/nor. This effectively repudiates the Möbius-like figure that is both inside and outside simultaneously, yet reducible to neither. In reading sexuality through this structure, Fuss aims to turn the categories of hetero- and homosexuality *inside/out*. However, this only demonstrates their logical interdependence. In order to go one step further in deconstructing the hetero/homosexual structure, Fuss would need to mobilize the repudiated logics and explore the undecidable within the terms of this dialectical structure. An analysis of bisexuality as undecidable, as both inside and outside, heterosexual and homosexual (yet at the same time none of these), is one crucial way of doing this. However, for Fuss, bisexuality is not identified as the third term in this epistemological configuration, but is bracketed out of the analysis. So rather than fully expose the workings of binary logic and the exclusions it attempts to hide, Fuss in fact takes this logic at its word and reinforces its modus operandi.[9]

Yet another startling example of this tendency to render bisexuality parenthetical to queer analysis is Lee Edelman's recent book *Homographesis*. It exhibits a striking similarity to the case of Fuss. One of the primary objectives of the book is to "explore the determining relation between 'homosexuality' and 'identity' as both have been constructed in modern Euro-American societies."[10] Following Sedgwick's lead, therefore, he also locates homosexuality as central to any cultural "enterprise of . . . identity-determination" (xv). In yet another self-avowedly Derridean mode, this entails and aspires to a deconstruction of the heterosexual logic of identity. Edelman performs this analysis by tracing the rhetorical and contradictory operations of sameness and difference through which (homosexual) identity is instantiated. He suggests that homosexuality is constructed as an *anxious* effect of the very crisis of representation itself. Indeed, and more specifically, "'homosexuality'," he argues, "is constructed to bear the cultural burden of the rhetoricity inherent in 'sexuality' itself" (xiv). Homosexuality thereby stands in for and serves "to contain . . . the unknowability of the sexual" (xv).

Interestingly, Edelman affirms his project as a "work of *gay* theory" (xvi). Despite this invocation, however, the nomination "gay" is not premised on the stability of a fixed referent. Instead, it is deployed as a "signifier of resistance," a deconstructive tool used to challenge the logic of identity. In other words, homosexuality becomes the privileged deconstructive site for this project because it is " 'gay sexuality' [that] functions in the modern West as the very agency of sexual meaningfulness, the construct without which sexual meaning, and therefore, in a larger sense, meaning itself, becomes virtually unthinkable" (xv). Scrutinizing a wide range of cultural productions, *Homographesis* is indicative of the queer deconstructive impulse determined to work the opposition of hetero/homosexuality to the point of epistemological frustration.

What is most startling about Edelman's work is not the almost complete absence of any discussion of bisexuality, although this is in itself rather astonishing (bisexuality does not even make it into the book's index). Rather, it is the fact that bisexuality is called forth in the preface by way of parenthetical reference only to be dismissed as antithetical to the theoretical project of deconstruction. Curiously, however, this reference occurs in the context of Edelman locating his work under the rubric of gay theory. Like Fuss's parenthesizing of bisexuality, Edelman's takes place in one rather complex, ambiguous, and perhaps even contradictory sentence:

> By retaining the signifier of a specific sexuality within the hetero/homo binarism (a binarism more effectively reinforced than disrupted by the "third term" of bisexuality) even as it challenges the ideology of that categorical dispensation, this enterprise intends to mark its avowal of the multiple sexualities, the various modes of interaction and relation, that the hierarchizing imperative of the hetero/homo binarism attempts to discredit. (xvi)

Why does bisexuality simultaneously appear and disappear in this context despite Edelman's claim to *avow* that which the "hetero/homo binarism attempts to discredit"? It seems that Edelman is attempting to reassure readers that the theoretical entity of "gay" need not be seen as simply reiterative of the logic of identity and the hetero/homosexual opposition. Is he here attempting to respond to or to reject in advance the claim that the epistemic category of bisexuality might be equally or better positioned to expose the rhetorical operations of sameness and difference in the construction of sexual identity? If this were the case, Edelman's move would scarcely be different from an *anxious* gesture of containment. Is homosexuality the only category in the hetero/homosexual binary that provides deconstructive leverage for challenging and exposing the stability and fixity of sexual identity? What kind of reductive and essentializing labor is performed on the category of bisexuality in order to render it mere reinforcement to this binary?

Edelman appears to be undertaking, perhaps in Foucauldian fashion, an *observation* of "how 'homo' and 'hetero', 'same' and 'different', switch places" (xviii–xix) in the rhetorical operations of hegemonic discourse. Yet nowhere does he consider how the category of bisexuality might be implicated in this economy. In fact, such an analysis appears to be wittingly foreclosed in advance by unknowingly performing a "metaphorizing totalization" (11) on bisexuality. Yet in the history of discourses of sexuality [. . .] bisexuality is *both* the stabilizing and destabilizing element in the epistemic construction of sexual identity. Indeed, it has been the category through and against which sexual identity has been discursively constructed. Edelman's claim that bisexuality only reinforces the hetero/homosexual binary thus ignores the historical and epistemological figuring of bisexuality. Like "homosexuality," it cannot be represented as a fixed and stable category.

In addition to this, Edelman fails to interrogate the way in which the (absent) presence of bisexuality marks the play of sameness and difference. He quite rightly suggests that "homosexuality marks the otherness, the difference internal to 'sexuality' and sexual discourse itself" (xix). What he means is that the logic of identity has installed homosexuality in order to contain the internal crisis of meaning engendered by the "rhetoricity inherent in 'sexuality' itself" (xiv). However, he does not ask what the logic of identity must exclude or disavow in order to perform this operation. That is, how does the discourse of sexual identity ensure the mutual exclusivity of sameness and difference, hetero- and homosexuality? Clearly, bisexuality must be disavowed for these operations. For in relation to hetero- and homosexuality, bisexuality is both same and different. Edelman ignores the fact that it is the repudiation of bisexuality that makes possible, indeed makes coherent, the very switching of places between hetero and homo. His project of "locat[ing] the critical force of homosexuality at the very point of discrimination between sameness and difference" (20) therefore repeats the gesture of bisexual disavowal that sustains the logic of (sexual) identity.

In *Making Things Perfectly Queer* Alexander Doty provides one of the few self-critical comments regarding his neglect in theorizing bisexuality as a position for reading mass cultural texts: "Looking through this book, I realize I have given rather cursory attention to specifically bisexual positions. Since examining bisexuality seems crucial in many ways to theorizing nongay and nonlesbian queerness—indeed, some see bisexuality *as* queerness—I consider the absence in this book of any extended discussion of bisexuality and mass culture a major omission."[11] This realization was not enough or came too late to force a conceptual rethinking of his project, however. Even more problematically, this assertion was bracketed out from his text, marginalized to an endnote. Ruth Goldman has suggested that despite Doty's marginalization of bisexuality, his willingness to "broaden his own discourse on queerness to include bisexuality can serve as an example/foundation for other queer theorists to build upon."[12] Instead of identifying "specifically bisexual positions" or "bisexual texts,"[13] however, I would suggest that bisexuality might also be deployed as a means of troubling the opposition of identification/desire that has worked to construct as distinct the spectator positions of gay, lesbian, and heterosexual. In this way, bisexuality would represent more than a mere additive to the list of discrete categories of sexual identity. Rather, bisexuality might potentially disrupt, indeed queer, theories of spectatorship that reproduce these viewing/reading positions by reifying gender in the theorization of spectator identifications. In this context, bisexuality might better function, then, to challenge the concept of sexuality or sexual identity itself.

[. . .O]ne of the foundational principles of poststructuralist-inspired queer theory is the belief in the relationality of identity. Yet it is clear from the foregoing analysis that many of the canonized works of this body of knowledge have fallen short in their examination and application of this principle. Far from being identified as a pivotal logical and relational component of hetero/homosexuality, bisexuality has instead been parenthesized or cast outside the constitutive terms of this binarism. Bisexuality has, in other words, once again been erased from the present tense.

Gender trouble in queer theory

> Queer means to fuck with gender.
>
>   (Cherry Smyth 1991)

So how are we to understand the erasure of bisexuality in some of the fundamental works of the queer canon? Earlier I suggested that for queer theory the category of sexuality has opened up a promising discursive space for interrogating and deconstructing Western discourses constituted through the hetero/homosexual binarism. As the editors of *The Lesbian and Gay Studies Reader* point out, "Lesbian/gay[/queer] studies does for *sex* and *sexuality* approximately what women's studies does for gender."[14] To say that the work of Foucault has been enormously influential in this development is to understate the case. His genealogical account of the emergence of sexuality as coextensive with modern subjectivity has been absorbed as axiomatic to the field of queer theory.[15] It appears, however, that this productive deployment of Foucault's work has also brought with it a constraining limitation: namely, a problematic relationship to gender.

Increasingly, there is a distinct concern, particularly among feminist theorists, that the category of sexuality has become reified to the point of exclusion in discourses of queer theory. Feminism and the category of gender, so the argument goes, are being cast as redundant explanatory principles as a result of queer theory's attempt to disarticulate gender and sexuality. In this section I will begin by tracing and extending these arguments in order to put forward an argument of my own in relation to bisexuality. I will argue that despite its productive potential, the disarticulation of gender and sexuality, and the Foucauldian-inflected reification of the latter, has proceeded in such a way as to occlude bisexuality from analytic view.

Judith Butler has recently problematized the above claim made by the editors of *The Lesbian and Gay Studies Reader*. She argues that it represents an unwitting, yet *aggressive and violent*, discursive appropriation of sexuality as the "proper object" of gay/lesbian/queer studies over and against a feminism whose proper object is gender.[16] This creates, Butler suggests, more than a tendentious methodological distinction between feminism and gay/lesbian/queer studies. It serves as well to make feminist inquiry into sexuality obsolete. In interrogating the terms of the analogy between feminism and gay/lesbian/queer in her essay "Against Proper Objects," Butler claims that the analogy falls down around the editors' invocation of a Foucauldian-inflected category of "sex": "The editors lead us through analogy from a feminism in which gender and sex are conflated to a notion of lesbian and gay studies in which "sex" encompasses and exceeds the purview of feminism: "sex" in this second instance would include not only questions of identity and attribute (female or male), but discourses of sensation, acts, and sexual practice as well" (2). Butler argues that the category of "sex" is common both to feminism and gay/lesbian/queer studies, yet this "commonality must be denied" (2). The "implicit argument," she suggests, "is that lesbian and gay studies does precisely what feminism is said to do, but does it in a more expansive and complex way" (4).

Butler identifies the appropriation of Gayle Rubin's essay "Thinking Sex" as the gesture serving to authorize the methodological founding of lesbian/gay/queer studies. However, she argues that a decontextualized appropriation of Rubin's call for an analytic separation of gender and sexuality effects not only a significant "restriction of the scope of feminist scholarship" (8), but breaks the long-standing coalition between feminism and lesbian/gay studies. While I remain unconvinced of the mechanics of Butler's argument as it pivots on and is extrapolated from the editors' introduction to *The Lesbian and Gay Studies Reader*—an argument made, I should add, with almost no reference to the canonical texts of queer theory[17]— she has identified an emergent tendency that is perhaps more usefully explored through a grounded analysis of specific queer texts.[18]

Biddy Martin takes a first step in this direction in her essay "Sexualities without Genders and Other Queer Utopias."[19] She provides the basis for a more productive and grounded analysis of some of the issues raised by Butler. Despite welcoming the possibilities opened up by disarticulating gender and sexuality, like Butler, Martin is concerned also that this is taking place at the expense of feminism and important feminist destabilizations of the category of gender. Sexuality, she argues, is too often being cast as that which "exceeds, transgresses, or supersedes gender."[20] Gender, and indeed feminism, on the other hand, are increasingly being framed as fixed and constraining, hampering the celebration of queerity.[21]

Martin argues that Sedgwick's work is indicative of this tendency. In "axiom 2" of *Epistemology of the Closet*, Sedgwick attempts to keep analytically distinct the two senses of the category of sex: chromosomal sex and sex as sexuality/act/fantasy/pleasure. She goes on to suggest that the latter is "virtually impossible to situate on a map delimited by the feminist-defined sex/gender distinction."[22] Instead, Sedgwick stresses that the development of an antihomophobic discourse more suited to an analysis of sexuality "as an alternative analytic axis" is not just required, but "a particularly urgent project" (32). In collapsing sex and gender "more simply under the rubric 'gender'," Sedgwick puts forward the claim that sexuality is inflected by a form of conceptual ambiguity in a way unknown to the category of gender. Rendered the more fixed, gender is considered the *proper object* of feminist discourse and is less suited to deconstructive analysis. Sexuality, on other hand, is the more apt object of deconstruction, exceeding "the bare choreographies of procreation," perhaps even situated as "the very opposite" to chromosomal sex, to gender (29).

Martin argues that it is one thing to posit the irreducibility of sexuality and gender, but quite another to react to this, as does Sedgwick, "by making them more distinct, even opposed to one another."[23] She also objects to the way Sedgwick privileges sexuality and defines antihomophobic analysis not just against but over and above monolithic and fixed notions of both feminism and gender. For example, sexuality, argues Sedgwick, "could occupy . . . even more than 'gender' the polar position of the relational, the social/symbolic, the constructed, the variable, the representational."[24] Moreover, sex (an "array of acts, expectations, narratives, pleasures," etc.) and sexuality, unlike gender, "tend to represent the full spectrum of positions between the most intimate and the most social, the most predetermined and the most aleatory, the most physically rooted and the most symbolically infused, the most innate and the most learned, the most autonomous and the most relational traits of being" (29). Sedgwick perhaps anticipates the kind of feminist objection raised by Martin with the reassurance that she is not calling for "any epistemological or ontological privileging of an axis of sexuality over an axis of gender" (34). However, in reifying sexuality as the analytically autonomous and "apter deconstructive object" (34), Sedgwick is thus able to install the hetero/homosexual opposition as *the* pivotal organizing principle of Western thought over and above that of male/female. Sexuality thereby becomes the *proper object* not of feminist but of antihomophobic inquiry (as though the two are not overlapping).[25]

The problems encountered with this reified account of sexuality and its disarticulation from gender are made even more palpable when we examine the figure of bisexuality. As I discussed earlier, Sedgwick's epistemological mapping of the logic of the closet rests on a repudiation and erasure of bisexuality. Moreover, it has been my argument that bisexuality has in fact regulated the axes of gender and sexuality. Yet despite Sedgwick's acknowledgment that these axes are "inextricable from one another,"[26] her analysis of modern hetero/homosexual definition ignores this very crucial space of overlap between gender and sexuality. Take, for example, her attempt to map the "models" of "gay/straight definition" through which homosexuality has been articulated historically. Sedgwick offers a table with two separate horizontal rows for sexuality and gender. Each row is then vertically divided by two columns, one representing "separatist" models, the other "integrative" or "transitive" ones. On the one hand, homosexuality has been defined *sexually*: as an essentialist minority (separatist) *and* as a universal and cultural potential (integrative). On the other hand, it has been defined in terms *of gender identification*: male and female homosexual desire as a natural effect of male and female gender identification respectively (separatist) *and* as a result of cross-gender identification (integrative).[27]

While this model captures some of the contradictions and cross-identifications made possible within and between the separatist and integrative axes of homosexual definition, it remains in the end only a model, as Sedgwick herself calls it, of "gay/straight definition" (88). Bisexuality is incorporated at best only as a universalizing potential; at worst it is implicitly collapsed into hetero- and homosexualities. Sedgwick's reliance on hegemonic constructions of sexual identity thereby repeats the exclusionary gesture necessary to sustain the workings of binary logic. Moreover, her unraveling of gender and sexuality as distinct axes has left her unable to accommodate, as du Plessis points out, "people for whom sexuality and gender may match up differently." This does "damage," argues du Plessis, "to the realities of transgender sexualities and bisexual genders."[28] I would argue also that this kind of exclusionary mapping of sexuality serves to sustain the analytic distance Sedgwick has installed between feminism and gay/lesbian/queer studies. That is, bisexuality (and indeed transgenderism) is the pawn that is forced out in an act of methodological and disciplinary secessionism.

A similar tendency to privilege and reify sexuality over and against gender is apparent in Fuss's work in "Inside/Out." Fuss takes the hetero/homosexual binarism as her prioritized point of deconstructive departure. Her primary task is to expose only the interdependence of the hetero on the homo; that is, the homo as always already inside the hetero. However, rather than examine the inextricable enmeshment of the hetero/homo, inside/outside oppositions with that of male/female, Fuss follows a path similar to Sedgwick's by separating too radically gender and sexuality. This move takes place in her discussion of what is "most urgently" needed in current "gay and lesbian theory": that is, a "theory of sexual borders" that can take into account and promote organizational strategies required to address "the new cultural and sexual arrangements occasioned by the movements and transmutations of pleasure in the social field."[29] This new theory, it would seem, is a queer theory of sexuality. In the next sentence Fuss does invoke the opposition of gender, but only to dethrone it as the primary paradigm through which to read sexuality: "Recent and past work on the question of sexual difference has yet to meet this pressing need, largely because, as Stephen Heath accurately targets the problem, our notion of sexual difference all too often subsumes sexual differences, upholding 'a defining difference of man/woman at the expense of gay, lesbian, bisexual, and indeed *hetero* heterosexual reality'" (5). This quote of Heath's is also part of an argument that gender and sexuality "can and should be separated from one another."[30] However, like Rubin and Sedgwick, Heath is formulating such a claim against Catharine MacKinnon's radical feminist collapsing of sexuality as a mere expression of gender.[31] So by drawing on Heath in order to fault recent and past feminist work on sexual difference, Fuss has not exactly remained faithful to the quote's original context. She is also suggesting that the vanguard position for this new *theory of sexual borders* is not feminism but gay/lesbian/queer studies. "Gay and lesbian readers of culture," she suggests, have a "responsibility . . . to reshape and to reorient the field of sexual difference to include sexual differences."[32] Curiously, this responsibility is conferred primarily, or perhaps only, on "gay and lesbian readers." Where are antihomophobic heterosexual, feminist, bisexual, or transgendered readers of culture situated in relation to this urgent political task?

I suggest that Fuss's failure to incorporate these "others" within the vanguard of this new sexual theory is the complex product of the problematic reification of sexuality over and above gender. Let us recall the opening statement of her introduction to *Inside/Out*: "The philosophical opposition between 'heterosexual' and 'homosexual'. . . has always been constructed on the foundations of . . . the couple 'inside' and 'Outside'" (1). Here Fuss has immediately elided or at the very least suspended a discussion of gender as an opposition that also fundamentally undergirds the hetero/homosexual opposition. She does invoke gender, but only in order to foreground her deconstructive analysis of the hetero/homosexual, inside/outside binaries. Homosexuality, she quite rightly points out, "is produced inside the dominant discourse of sexual difference as its necessary outside, but this is not to say that the homo exerts no pressure on the hetero nor that this outside stands in any simple relation of exteriority to the inside" (5). Fuss indeed seems to be acknowledging the inexplicable inter-lacing of gender (sexual difference) and sexuality, the latter seen as the expurgated inside of the former. However, she appears to effect a curious analytic slippage whereby gender, or sexual difference, is invoked only to be immediately subsumed or displaced by heterosexu-ality.[33] Homosexuality is then called forth as the internally erected border that works "to define and defend" the heterosexual inside. It is identified as the subversive element "occu-pying the frontier position of inside out" in the "discourse of sexual difference," "neither completely outside" it "nor wholly inside it either."[34]

In representing (homo)sexuality as transgressive or excessive of sexual difference, Fuss is attempting to gesture toward a theory of sexuality not beholden to an analysis of gender. The axis of sexuality appears to be super-imposed on the axis of gender, subsuming gender as a subsidiary component. Lee Edelman appears to perform a similar move. He suggests that "where heterosexuality . . . seeks to assure the sameness or purity internal to the categorical 'opposites' of anatomical 'sex' . . . homosexuality would multiply the differences that desire can apprehend in ways that menace the internal coherence of the sexed identities that the order of heterosexuality demands."[35] Again, it is homosexuality that is identified as the subversive agent. I would argue, however, that this maneuver performed by Fuss and Edelman reads as an allegory of the relationship being instantiated between feminism and queer theory. Feminism is metonymically associated with gender, queer theory with (homo)sexuality, the latter in a relationship of subversive excess to the former. In other words, queer theory is that through which Fuss's new theory of sexual borders and Edelman's project of *Homographesis* can be advanced over a redundant feminism. As Butler puts it so well:

> If gender is said to belong to feminism, and sexuality in the hands of lesbian and gay [and queer] studies is conceived as liberated from gender, then the sexuality that is "liberated" from feminism will be one which suspends the reference to masculine and feminine, reinforcing the refusal to mark that difference, which is the conventional way in which the masculine has achieved the status of the "sex" which is one.[36]

Fuss's new theory of sexual borders, I would add, appears to be the exclusive domain not of antihomophobic feminists, bisexuals, and transgenders, but of "gays and lesbians." For it is they who are seen to occupy the subversive "frontier position" of homosexuality. If this is in fact the case, this move of Fuss's sits uncomfortably within a deconstructive framework concerned with challenging the identity paradigm. It would also seem at odds with a deconstructive psychoanalysis that would problematize the specious conflation of identity or subject-position and subjectivity.

Despite acknowledging the fact that homosexuality is constituted inside the discourse of gender or sexual difference, Fuss and Edelman tend to construct sexuality as synonymous with the hetero/homosexual opposition, distinct from and superimposed over the top of this discourse. Partially displacing gender, sexuality (or the hetero/homosexual opposition), is then identified as the privileged upper layer of deconstructive analysis. In other words, there is a sense in both Fuss's and Edelman's work that sexuality must first be deconstructed in order to prize it away from, and thus render it autonomous of gender. However, this reification of a sexuality disarticulated from and epistemologically privileged over gender obfuscates an analysis of their mutual interrelation. As a result, an analysis of bisexuality as the figure shoring up binary sexual identity is occluded. For it is bisexuality that has not just traversed but historically and epistemologically regulated the axes of sexuality *and* gender in the continuing production of hetero- and homosexual identities. [. . .]

Notes

1   There is a growing body of work critiquing queer theory. Among these are Sally O'Driscoll, "Outlaw Readings: Beyond Queer Theory," *Signs* 22, no. 1 (1996): 30–51; Morton, "The Politics of Queer Theory"; Harriet Malinowitz, "Queer Theory: Whose Theory?" *Frontiers* 13, no. 2 (1992): 168–84; Rosemary Hennessy, "Queer Visibility in Commodity Culture," *Cultural Critique* 29 (Winter 1994–95): 31–76; Elizabeth Grosz, "Theorising Corporeality: Bodies, Sexuality and the Feminist Academy," Interview with Wei Leng Kwok and Kaz Ross, *Melbourne Journal of Politics* 22 (1994): 3–29; Michael du Plessis, "Blatantly Bisexual; or, Unthinking Queer Theory," in *RePresenting Bisexualities: Subjects and Cultures of Fluid Desire*, edited by Donald E. Hall and Maria Pramaggiore (New York: New York University Press, 1996), 19–54; Biddy Martin, "Sexualities without Genders and Other Queer Utopias," *diacritics* 24, nos. 2 and 3 (1994): 104–21; Judith Butler, "Introduction: Against Proper Objects," *differences* 6, nos. 2 and 3 (1994): 1–26.

2   To be sure, there have been heated debates surrounding the inclusion of bisexuality in group and conference titles working under the rubric of "lesbian and gay." See, e.g., Stacey Young, "Dichotomies and Displacement: Bisexuality in Queer Theory and Politics," in *Playing With Fire: Queer Politics, Queer Theories*, edited by Shane Phelan (New York: Routledge, 1997), 63–65.

3   Michael du Plessis ("Blatantly Bisexual," 23), discusses the infamous 1991 Rutgers Lesbian and Gay Conference that dropped "bisexual" from its title. One rumor to have circulated was that one of the reasons for this decision was that *"bisexuals have not produced good theory."* Many more theorists of bisexuality and bisexual theorists have identified this erasure. For some examples, see Clare Hemmings, "Resituating the Bisexual Body," in *Activating Theory*, 118–38; Jo Eadie, "Activating Bisexuality: Towards a Bi/Sexual Politics," in *Activating Theory*, 139–70; Christopher James, "Denying Complexity: Dismissal and Appropriation of Bisexuality in Queer, Lesbian, and Gay Theory," in *Queer Studies*, 217–40; Young, "Dichotomies and Displacement," in *Playing with Fire*, 51–74.

4   Sedgwick, *Epistemology*, 1. All subsequent references will be given in text.

5   Maria Pramaggiore, "BI-ntroduction I: Epistemologies of the Fence," in *RePresenting Bisexualities: Subjects and Cultures of Fluid Desires*, edited by Donald E. Hall and Maria Pramaggiore (New York: New York University Press, 1996), 3.

6   Fuss, "Inside/Out," Z.

7   Du Plessis, "Blatantly Bisexual," 37.

8   Of course, in post-Freudian psychoanalysis this threat was contained by the outright repudiation of bisexuality's existence.

9   Ironically, Fuss ("Inside/Out," 5) points out that "the problem, of course, with the inside/outside rhetoric, if it remains deconstructed, is that such polemics disguise the fact that most of us are both inside and outside at the same time."

10   Edelman, *Homographesis*, xiv.

11   Doty, *Making Things Perfectly Queer*, 105–6; see n. 35 above.

12   Ruth Goldman, "Who Is That *Queer* Queer? Exploring Norms around Sexuality, Race, and Class in Queer Theory," in *Queer Studies: A Lesbian, Gay, Bisexual, and Transgender Anthology*, edited by Brett Beemyn and Mickey Eliason (New York: New York University Press, 1996), 117. At a conference Goldman questioned Doty on bisexuality and says he responded by suggesting that "he wasn't quite sure how to theorize about it in relation to popular culture." Maria Pramaggiore ("Straddling the Screen: Bisexual Spectatorship and Contemporary Narrative Film," in *RePresenting Bisexualities: Subjects and Cultures of Fluid Desires*, edited by Donald E. Hall and Maria Pramaggiore [New York: New York University Press, 1996]) also considers Doty's suggestion "a useful starting point from which to examine contemporary films . . . and to ask whether they invite specifically bisexual readings" (273).

13   Doty, *Making Things Perfectly Queer*, 106 n. 13. Perhaps it is this kind of construction of bisexuality that Edelman thinks simply reinforces the hetero/homosexual binary.

14   Henry Abelove et al., eds., *The Lesbian and Gay Studies Reader*, xv. The reason I have put queer in parentheses is because the editors to this reader consider "queer" a structuring part of lesbian and gay studies. "Our choice of 'lesbian/gay'," they point out, "indicates no wish on our part to make lesbian/gay studies look less assertive, less unsettling, and less queer than it already does" (xvii).

15   See, e.g., Sedgwick, *Epistemology*, 3.

16   Judith Butler, "Against Proper Objects," *differences* 6, nos. 2 and 3 (1994): 5, 6. Butler suggests that it was an unintentional move, "given that all three have made strong contributions to feminist scholarship" (5).

17   Butler, "Against Proper Objects," 23–24 n. 8, refers to Sedgwick, but only in a footnote.

18   I would argue that there is nothing problematic, per se, about insisting on the partial analytic separability of gender and sexuality, feminism and lesbian/gay studies. Such a move does not translate into a clean methodological distinction. It seems to me that the editors are fully cognizant of the fact that not only is queer *both* feminism *and* lesbian/gay studies, but that it is also, simultaneously, the force that subjects both to a critique of their founding and structuring assumptions. In this way queer is more usefully seen as a continual movement within, through, and across both feminism and lesbian/gay studies. I think the editors' choice of authors and articles in the *Reader*, and their suggestion that gay/lesbian studies is already queer, reflects this productive contradiction in a way Butler downplays. I would argue, therefore, that the editors are neither intentionally nor unintentionally ascribing *proper objects* to distinct methodologies of feminism versus lesbian/gay studies. Rather, they are attempting to flag the benefits to be gained from a partial analytic separation of gender and sexuality in order to free up the relations between the two and blur the already artificial boundaries between feminism and gay/lesbian studies. It would also seem to me that their insistence on *sex* and *sexuality* as launching points for gay/lesbian/queer studies is a means of foregrounding certain kinds of analyses that may be obscured or even foreclosed by foregrounding gender not only in "feminism" but *also* in "gay and lesbian" studies. This aids the queer project of analyzing sexuality in relation (not subordination) to gender and has the potential to bring into the field of vision those sexualities of which gender is not the most, or even *a*, salient feature. Finally, Butler claims that the editors have deployed a Foucauldian notion of sex but repudiated one of the two meanings associated with the term: that is, sex in the sense of gender. I would suggest that Butler overinterprets the Foucauldianness of the editors' use of the category of "sex." While they may have conflated "sex" and "gender," I would suggest that they are using sex to mean sexual practices, pleasures, etc. Sex in the sense of gender is, I suggest, not so much repudiated as it is perhaps suspended. It is that which is the point of commonality between feminism and gay/lesbian studies but which must be suspended in order to analyze *sex* (acts, pleasures, etc.) and *sexuality* as not only or always containable by heteronormative gender. In other words, gender is momentarily suspended in order to set them into productive *relation* with sexuality.

19   Martin, "Sexualities without Genders."

20   Biddy Martin, "Extraordinary Homosexuals and the Fear of Being Ordinary," *differences* 6, nos. 2 and 3 (1994): 101.

21   Martin, "Sexualities," 106–7.

22   Sedgwick, *Epistemology*, 29.

23   Martin, "Sexualities," 107.

24   Sedgwick, *Epistemology*, 29.

25   Morton ("The Politics of Queer Theory") has also argued that queer theorists have displaced gender with sexuality: "Today, under the pressure of the experiential and pleasure-oriented ludicism of the 1980s and 1990s, the concept of gender has become too 'serious' for the bourgeois subject: in other words, because it smacks too much of *concepts* such as 'the social'/'the economic'/ . . . gender has to be displaced by sexuality" (141). He says this about "Queer Theory in *all* its variants"

(my emphasis). While this appears to be true of Sedgwick's analysis, it is certainly problematic to generalize on behalf of all queer theorists. The work of Butler and Teresa de Lauretis, e.g., has always been calibrated by a sophisticated analysis of gender.

26   Sedgwick, *Epistemology*, 30.

27   Sedgwick, *Epistemology*, 86–90, esp. 88.

28   Du Plessis, "Blatantly Bisexual," 33. Butler, in "Against Proper Objects" (24 n. 8), argues along lines similar to du Plessis's.

29   Fuss, "Inside/Out," 5.

30   Stephen Heath, "The Ethics of Sexual Difference," *Discourse* 12, no. 2 (Spring–Summer 1990): 140–41.

31   See, e.g., Catharine MacKinnon, "Marxism, Feminism, Method and the State: An Agenda for Theory," *Signs* 7, no. 3 (1982): 515–44.

32   Fuss, "Inside/Out," 6.

33   While Lacanian influenced theorists such as Fuss might distinguish sexual difference from a more sociological category of gender, I am using gender along lines similar to Judith Butler, whereby she has attempted to construct a theory of gender which retains some of the insights of Lacanian sexual difference whilst also incorporating a transformative notion of gender. See Butler, "Against Proper Objects," 18, 24–25 n. 13. In this way, following Butler, I see the notion of sexual difference as already constituted through a matrix of gender. When I discuss the separation of gender and sexuality in the work of theorists such as Fuss, therefore, I use gender interchangeably with sexual difference.

34   Fuss, "Inside/Out," 5–6.

35   Edelman, *Homographesis*, 10.

36   Butler, "Against Proper Objects," 20. Despite the fact that Butler uses the conjunction "lesbian and gay" in this quote, she does in fact use queer and lesbian and gay interchangeably throughout the essay. In addition to this, the issue of *differences* within which the essay appears is a special issue called "More Gender Trouble: Feminism Meets Queer Theory."

Bibliography

Abelove, Henry, et al., eds. *The Lesbian and Gay Studies Reader*. New York: Routledge, 1993.

Butler, Judith. *Gender Trouble: Feminism and the Subversion of Identity*. New York: Routledge, 1990.

—. "Introduction: Against Proper Objects." *differences* 6, nos. 2 and 3 (1994): 1–26.

Doty, Alexander. *Making Things Perfectly Queer: Interpreting Mass Culture*. Minneapolis: University of Minnesota Press, 1993.

Du Plessis, Michael. "Blatantly Bisexual; or, Unthinking Queer Theory." In *RePresenting Bisexualities: Subjects and Cultures of Fluid Desire*, edited by Donald E. Hall and Maria Pramaggiore. New York: New York University Press, 1996.

Eadie, Jo. "Activating Bisexuality: Towards a Bi/Sexual Politics." In *Activating Theory: Lesbian, Gay, Bisexual Politics*, edited by Joseph Bristow and Angelia R. Wilson. London: Lawrence & Wishart, 1993.

Edelman, Lee. *Homographesis: Essays in Gay Literary and Cultural Theory*. New York: Routledge, 1993.

Fuss, Diana. "Inside/Out." In *Inside/Out: Lesbian Theories, Gay Theories*, edited by Diana Fuss. New York: Routledge, 1991.

Goldman, Ruth. "Who Is That *Queer* Queer? Exploring Norms around Sexuality, Race, and Class in Queer Theory." In *Queer Studies: A Lesbian, Gay, Bisexual, and Transgender Anthology*, edited by Brett Beemyn and Mickey Eliason. New York: New York University Press, 1996.

Grosz, Elizabeth. "Theorising Corporeality: Bodies, Sexuality and the Feminist Academy." Interview with Wei Leng Kwok and Kaz Ross. *Melbourne Journal of Politics* 22 (1994): 3–29.

Heath, Stephen. "The Ethics of Sexual Difference." *Discourse* 12, no. 2 (Spring–Summer 1990): 140–41.

Hemmings, Clare. "Resituating the Bisexual Body." In *Activating Theory: Lesbian, Gay, Bisexual Politics*, edited by Joseph Bristow and Angelia R. Wilson. London: Lawrence & Wishart, 1993.

Hennessy, Rosemary. "Queer Visibility in Commodity Culture." *Cultural Critique*, no. 29 (Winter 1994–95): 31–76.

James, Christopher. "Denying Complexity: Dismissal and Appropriation of Bisexuality in Queer, Lesbian, and Gay Theory." In *Queer Studies: A Lesbian, Gay, Bisexual, and Transgender Anthology*, edited by Brett Beemyn and Mickey Eliason. New York: New York University Press, 1996.

MacKinnon, Catharine. "Marxism, Feminism, Method and the State: An Agenda for Theory." *Signs* 7, no. 3 (1983): 515–44.

Malinowitz, Harriet. "Queer Theory: Whose Theory?" *Frontiers* 13, no. 2 (1992): 168–84.

Martin, Biddy. "Extraordinary Homosexuals and the Fear of Being Ordinary." *differences* 6, nos. 2 and 3 (1994): 100–125.

—. "Sexualities without Genders and Other Queer Utopias." *diacritics* 24, nos. 2 and 3 (1994): 104–21.

Morton, Donald. "The Politics of Queer Theory in the (Post)Modern Moment." *Genders* 17 (Fall 1993): 121–50.

O'Driscoll, Sally. "Outlaw Readings: Beyond Queer Theory." *Signs* 22, no. 1 (1996): 30–51.

Pramaggiore, Maria. "BI-ntroduction I: Epistemologies of the Fence." In *RePresenting Bisexualities: Subjects and Cultures of Fluid Desire*, edited by Donald E. Hall and Maria Pramaggiore. New York: New York University Press, 1996.

Sedgwick, Eve Kosofsky. *Epistemology of the Closet*. Berkeley and Los Angeles: University of California Press, 1990.

Young, Stacey. "Dichotomies and Displacement: Bisexuality in Queer Theory and Politics." In *Playing with Fire: Queer Policies, Queer Theories*, edited by Shane Phelan. New York: Routledge, 1997.

Chapter 5

Cathy J. Cohen

PUNKS, BULLDAGGERS, AND WELFARE QUEENS: THE RADICAL POTENTIAL OF QUEER POLITICS?

Cathy J. Cohen is the David and Mary Winton Green Professor of Political Science at the University of Chicago. She is the author of two books: *The Boundaries of Blackness: AIDS and the Breakdown of Black Politics* (1999) and *Democracy Remixed: Black Youth and the Future of American Politics* (2010). Her work focuses on American politics, with emphases in African American politics, women and politics, and lesbian and gay politics. Cohen has published articles in numerous journals including *GLQ*, where this essay originally appeared.

In "Punks, Bulldaggers, and Welfare Queens," Cohen critiques contemporary queer politics and activist groups. She argues that in its current form queer politics has failed to reach the transformative .and radical potential originally promised by queer activism and theory. According to Cohen, queer political groups tend to reinforce uncomplicated binaries, most notably the dichotomy between "heterosexual" and "queer." Moreover, Cohen identifies the ways in which queer politics privilege certain identities over others, particularly in terms of class, race, and gender. To reverse this trend, Cohen advocates a leftist, intersectional approach to queer politics and activism that accounts for multiple subjectivities. This approach, Cohen argues, elucidates the multiple and intersecting systems of power that make up our social lives.

O N T H E E V E of finishing this essay my attention is focused not on how to rework the conclusion (as it should be) but instead on news stories of alleged racism at Gay Men's Health Crisis (GMHC). It seems that three black board members of this largest and oldest AIDS organization in the world have resigned over their perceived subservient position on the GMHC board. Billy E. Jones, former head of the New York City Health and Hospitals Corporation and one of the board members to quit, was quoted in the *New York*

Times as saying, "Much work needs to be done at GMHC to make it truly inclusive and welcoming of diversity. . . . It is also clear that such work will be a great struggle. I am resigning because I do not choose to engage in such struggle at GMHC, but rather prefer to fight for the needs of those ravaged by H.I.V." (Dunlap).

This incident raises mixed emotions for me, for it points to the continuing practice of racism many of us experience on a daily basis in lesbian and gay communities. But just as disturbingly it also highlights the limits of a lesbian and gay political agenda based on a civil rights strategy, where assimilation into, and replication of, dominant institutions are the goals. Many of us continue to search for a new political direction and agenda, one that does not focus on integration into dominant structures but instead seeks to transform the basic fabric and hierarchies that allow systems of oppression to persist and operate efficiently. For some of us, such a challenge to traditional gay and lesbian politics was offered by the idea of queer politics. Here we had a potential movement of young antiassimilationist activists committed to challenging the very way people understand and respond to sexuality. These activists promised to engage in struggles that would disrupt dominant norms of sexuality, radically transforming politics in lesbian, gay, bisexual, and transgendered communities.

Despite the possibility invested in the idea of queerness and the practice of queer politics, I argue that a truly radical or transformative politics has not resulted from queer activism. In many instances, instead of destabilizing the assumed categories and binaries of sexual identity, queer politics has served to reinforce simple dichotomies between heterosexual and everything "queer." An understanding of the ways in which power informs and constitutes privileged and marginalized subjects on both sides of this dichotomy has been left unexamined.

I query in this essay whether there are lessons to be learned from queer activism that can help us construct a new politics. I envision a politics where one's relation to power, and not some homogenized identity, is privileged in determining one's political comrades. I'm talking about a politics where the *nonnormative* and *marginal* position of punks, bulldaggers, and welfare queens, for example, is the basis for progressive transformative coalition work. Thus, if there is any truly radical potential to be found in the idea of queerness and the practice of queer politics, it would seem to be located in its ability to create a space in opposition to dominant norms, a space where transformational political work can begin.

Emergence of queer politics and a new politics of transformation

Theorists and activists alike generally agree that it was in the early 1990s that we began to see, with any regularity, the use of the term "queer."[1] This term would come to denote not only an emerging politics, but also a new cohort of academics working in programs primarily in the humanities centered around social and cultural criticism (Morton 121). Individuals such as Judith Butler, Eve Sedgwick, Teresa de Lauretis, Diana Fuss, and Michael Warner produced what are now thought of as the first canonical works of "queer theory." Working from a variety of postmodernist and poststructuralist theoretical perspectives, these scholars focused on identifying and contesting the discursive and cultural markers found within both dominant and marginal identities and institutions which prescribe and reify "heterogendered" understandings and behavior.[2] These theorists presented a different conceptualization of sexuality, one which sought to replace socially named and presumably stable categories of sexual expression with a new fluid movement among and between forms of sexual behavior (Stein and Plummer 182).

Through its conception of a wide continuum of sexual possibilities, queer theory stands in direct contrast to the normalizing tendencies of hegemonic sexuality rooted in ideas of static, stable sexual identities and behaviors. In queer theorizing the sexual subject is understood to be constructed and contained by multiple practices of categorization and regulation that systematically marginalize and oppress those subjects thereby defined as deviant and "other." And, at its best, queer theory focuses on and makes central not only the socially constructed nature of sexuality and sexual categories, but also the varying degrees and multiple sites of power distributed within all categories of sexuality, including the normative category of heterosexuality.

It was in the early 1990s, however, that the postmodern theory being produced in the academy (later to be recategorized as queer theory) found its most direct interaction with the real-life politics of lesbian, gay, bisexual, and transgendered activists. Frustrated with what was perceived to be the scientific "de-gaying" and assimilationist tendencies of AIDS activism, with their invisibility in the more traditional civil rights politics of lesbian and gay organizations, and with increasing legal and physical attacks against lesbian and gay community members, a new generation of activists began the process of building a more confrontational political formation—labeling it queer politics (Bérubé and Escoffier 12). Queer politics, represented most notoriously in the actions of Queer Nation, is understood as an "in your face" politics of a younger generation. Through action and analysis these individuals seek to make "queer" function as more than just an abbreviation for lesbian, gay, bisexual, and transgendered. Similar to queer theory, the queer politics articulated and pursued by these activists first and foremost recognizes and encourages the fluidity and movement of people's sexual lives. In queer politics sexual expression is something that always entails the possibility of change, movement, redefinition, and subversive performance—from year to year, from partner to partner, from day to day, even from act to act. In addition to highlighting the instability of sexual categories and sexual subjects, queer activists also directly challenge the multiple practices and vehicles of power which render them invisible and at risk. However, what seems to make queer activists unique, at this particular moment, is their willingness to confront normalizing power by emphasizing and exaggerating their own anti-normative characteristics and non-stable behavior. Joshua Gamson, in "Must Identity Movements Self-Destruct? A Queer Dilemma," writes that

> queer activism and theory pose the challenge of a form of organizing in which, far from inhibiting accomplishments, the *destabilization* of collective identity is itself a goal and accomplishment of collective action.
>
> The assumption that stable collective identities are necessary for collective action is turned on its head by queerness, and the question becomes: *When and how are stable collective identities necessary for social action and social change?* Secure boundaries and stabilized identities are necessary not in general, but in the specific, a point social movement theory seems currently to miss.
>
> (403, original emphasis)

Thus queer politics, much like queer theory, is often perceived as standing in opposition, or in contrast, to the category-based identity politics of traditional lesbian and gay activism. And for those of us who find ourselves on the margins, operating through multiple identities and thus not fully served or recognized through traditional single-identity-based politics, *theoretical conceptualizations* of queerness hold great political promise. For many of us, the label "queer" symbolizes an acknowledgment that through our existence and everyday survival we embody sustained and multisited resistance to systems (based on dominant constructions of race and gender) that seek to normalize our sexuality, exploit our labor, and constrain our visibility. At the intersection of oppression and resistance lies the radical potential of queerness to challenge and bring together all those deemed marginal and all those committed to liberatory politics.

The problem, however, with such a conceptualization and expectation of queer identity and politics is that in its present form queer politics has not emerged as an encompassing challenge to systems of domination and oppression, especially those normalizing processes embedded in heteronormativity. By "heteronormativity" I mean both those localized practices and those centralized institutions which legitimize and privilege heterosexuality and heterosexual relationships as fundamental and "natural" within society. I raise the subject of heteronormativity because it is this normalizing practice/power that has most often been the focus of queer politics (Blasius 19–20; Warner xxi–xxv).

The inability of queer politics to effectively challenge heteronormativity rests, in part, on the fact that despite a surrounding discourse which highlights the destabilization and even deconstruction of sexual categories, queer politics has often been built around a simple dichotomy between those deemed queer and those deemed heterosexual. Whether in the infamous "I Hate Straights" publication or queer kiss-ins at malls and straight dance clubs, very near the surface in queer political action is an uncomplicated understanding of power as it is encoded in sexual categories: all heterosexuals are represented as dominant and controlling and all queers are understood as marginalized and invisible. Thus, even in the name of destabilization, some queer activists have begun to prioritize sexuality as the primary frame through which they pursue their politics.[3] Undoubtedly, within different contexts various characteristics of our total being—for example, race, gender, class, sexuality—are highlighted or called upon to make sense of a particular situation. However, my concern is centered on those individuals who consistently activate only one characteristic of their identity, or a single perspective of consciousness, to organize their politics, rejecting any recognition of the multiple and intersecting systems of power that largely dictate our life chances.

It is the disjuncture, evident in queer politics, between an articulated commitment to promoting an understanding of sexuality that rejects the idea of static, monolithic, bounded categories, on the one hand, and political practices structured around binary conceptions of sexuality and power, on the other hand, that is the focus of this article. Specifically, I am concerned with those manifestations of queer politics in which the capital and advantage invested in a range of sexual categories are disregarded and, as a result, narrow and homogenized political identities are reproduced that inhibit the radical potential of queer politics. It is my contention that queer activists who evoke a single-oppression framework misrepresent the distribution of power within and outside of gay, lesbian, bisexual, and transgendered communities, and therefore limit the comprehensive and transformational character of queer politics.

Recognizing the limits of current conceptions of queer identities and queer politics, I am interested in examining the concept of "queer" in order to think about how we might construct a new political identity that is truly liberating, transformative, and inclusive of all those who stand on the outside of the dominant constructed norm of state-sanctioned white middle- and upper-class heterosexuality.[4] Such a broadened understanding of queerness must be based on an intersectional analysis that recognizes how numerous systems of oppression interact to regulate and police the lives of most people. Black lesbian, bisexual, and heterosexual feminist authors such as Kimberle Crenshaw, Barbara Ransby, Angela Davis, Cheryl Clarke, and Audre Lorde have repeatedly emphasized in their writing the intersectional workings of oppression. And it is just such an understanding of the interlocking systems of domination that is noted in the opening paragraph of the now famous black feminist statement by the Combahee River Collective:

> The most general statement of our politics at the present time would be that we are actively committed to struggling against racial, sexual, heterosexual, and class oppression and see as our particular task the development of *integrated* analysis and practice based upon the fact that the major systems of oppression

are interlocking. The synthesis of these oppressions creates the conditions of our lives. As Black women we see Black feminism as the logical political movement to combat the manifold and simultaneous oppressions that all women of color face.

(272)

This analysis of one's place in the world which focuses on the intersection of systems of oppression is informed by a consciousness that undoubtedly grows from the lived experience of existing within and resisting multiple and connected practices of domination and normalization. Just such a lived experience and analysis have determined much of the progressive and expansive nature of the politics emanating from people of color, people who are both inside and outside of lesbian and gay communities.

However, beyond a mere recognition of the intersection of oppressions, there must also be an understanding of the ways our multiple identities work to limit the entitlement and status some receive from obeying a heterosexual imperative. For instance, how would queer activists understand politically the lives of women—in particular women of color—on welfare, who may fit into the category of heterosexual, but whose sexual choices are not perceived as normal, moral, or worthy of state support? Further, how do queer activists understand and relate politically to those whose same-sex sexual identities position them within the category of queer, but who hold other identities based on class, race, and/or gender categories which provide them with membership in and the resources of dominant institutions and groups?

Thus, inherent in our new politics must be a commitment to left analysis and left politics. Black feminists as well as other marginalized and progressive scholars and activists have long argued that any political response to the multilayered oppression that most of us experience must be rooted in a left understanding of our political, economic, social, and cultural institutions. Fundamentally, a left framework makes central the interdependency among multiple systems of domination. Such a perspective also ensures that while activists should rightly be concerned with forms of discursive and cultural coercion, we also recognize and confront the more direct and concrete forms of exploitation and violence rooted in state-regulated institutions and economic systems. The Statement of Purpose from the first Dialogue on the Lesbian and Gay Left comments specifically on the role of interlocking systems of oppression in the lives of gays and lesbians. "By leftist we mean people who understand the struggle for lesbian and gay liberation to be integrally tied to struggles against class oppression, racism and sexism. While we might use different political labels, we share a commitment to a fundamental transformation of the economic, political and social structures of society."

A left framework of politics, unlike civil rights or liberal frameworks, brings into focus the systematic relationship among forms of domination, where the creation and maintenance of exploited, subservient, marginalized classes is a necessary part of, at the very least, the economic configuration. Urvashi Vaid, in *Virtual Equality*, for example, writes of the limits of civil rights strategies in confronting systemic homophobia:

> civil rights do not change the social order in dramatic ways; they change only the privileges of the group asserting those rights. Civil rights strategies do not challenge the moral and antisexual underpinnings of homophobia, because homophobia does not originate in our lack of full civil equality. Rather, homophobia arises from the nature and construction of the political, legal, economic, sexual, racial and family systems within which we live.

(183)

Proceeding from the starting point of a system-based left analysis, strategies built upon the possibility of incorporation and assimilation are exposed as simply expanding and making accessible the status quo for more privileged members of marginal groups, while the most vulnerable in our communities continue to be stigmatized and oppressed.

It is important to note, however, that while left theorists tend to provide a more structural analysis of oppression and exploitation, many of these theorists and activists have also been homophobic and heterosexist in their approach to or avoidance of the topics of sexuality and heteronormativity. For example, Robin Podolsky, in "Sacrificing Queers and Other 'Proletarian' Artifacts," writes that quite often on the left lesbian and gay sexuality and desire have been characterized as "more to do with personal happiness and sexual pleasure than with the 'material basis' of procreation—we were considered self-indulgent distractions from struggle . . . [an example of] 'bourgeois decadence'" (54).

This contradiction between a stated left analysis and an adherence to heteronormativity has probably been most dramatically identified in the writing of some feminist authors. I need only refer to Adrienne Rich's well-known article, "Compulsory Heterosexuality and Lesbian Existence," as a poignant critique of the white, middle-class heterosexual standard running through significant parts of feminist analysis and actions. The same adherence to a heterosexual norm can be found in the writing of self-identified black left intellectuals such as Cornel West and Michael Eric Dyson. Thus, while these writers have learned to make reference to lesbian, gay, bisexual, and transgendered segments of black communities—sparingly—they continue to foreground black heterosexuality and masculinity as the central unit of analysis in their writing—and most recently in their politics: witness their participation in the Million Man March.

This history of left organizing and the left's visible absence from any serious and sustained response to the AIDS epidemic have provoked many lesbian, gay, bisexual, and transgendered people to question the relevance of this political configuration to the needs of our communities. Recognizing that reservations of this type are real and should be noted, I still hold that a left-rooted analysis which emphasizes economic exploitation and class structure, culture, and the systemic nature of power provides a framework of politics that is especially effective in representing and challenging the numerous sites and systems of oppression. Further, the left-centered approach that I embrace is one that designates sexuality and struggles against sexual normalization as central to the politics of all marginal communities.

The root of queer politics: challenging heteronormativity?

In the introduction to the edited volume *Fear of a Queer Planet: Queer Politics and Social Theory*, Michael Warner asks the question: "What do queers want?" (vii). He suggests that the goals of queers and their politics extend beyond the sexual arena. Warner contends that what queers want is acknowledgment of their lives, struggles, and complete existence; queers want to be represented and included fully in left political analysis and American culture. Thus what queers want is to be a part of the social, economic, and political restructuring of this society; as Warner writes, queers want to have queer experience and politics "taken as starting points rather than as footnotes" in the social theories and political agendas of the left (vii). He contends that it has been the absence or invisibility of lived queer experience that has marked or constrained much of left social and political theories and "have posited and naturalized a heterosexual society" in such theories (vii).

The concerns and emerging politics of queer activists, as formulated by Warner and others interested in understanding the implications of the idea of queerness, are focused on highlighting queer presence and destroying heteronormativity not only in the larger dominant society but also in extant spaces, theories, and sites of resistance, presumably on the left. He suggests that those embracing the label of "queer" understand the need to challenge the assumption of heteronormativity in every aspect of their existence:

> Every person who comes to a queer self-understanding knows in one way or another that her stigmatization is connected with gender, the family, notions of individual freedom, the state, public speech, consumption and desire, nature and culture, maturation, reproductive politics, racial and national fantasy, class identity, truth and trust, censorship, intimate life and social display, terror and violence, health care, and deep cultural norms about the bearing of the body. Being queer means fighting about these issues all the time, locally and piecemeal but always with consequences.
>
> (xiii)

Now, independent of the fact that few of us could find ourselves in such a grandiose description of queer consciousness, I believe that Warner's description points to the fact that in the roots of a lived "queer" existence are experiences with domination and in particular heteronormativity that form the basis for genuine transformational politics. By transformational, again, I mean a politics that does not search for opportunities to integrate into dominant institutions and normative social relationships, but instead pursues a political agenda that seeks to change values, definitions, and laws which make these institutions and relationships oppressive.

Queer activists experiencing displacement both within and outside of lesbian and gay communities rebuff what they deem the assimilationist practices and policies of more established lesbian and gay organizations. These organizers and activists reject cultural norms of acceptable sexual behavior and identification and instead embrace political strategies which promote self-definition and full expression. Members of the Chicago-based group Queers United Against Straight-acting Homosexuals (QUASH) state just such a position in the article "Assimilation Is Killing Us: Fight For A Queer United Front" published in their newsletter, *WHY I HATED THE MARCH ON WASHINGTON*:

> Assimilation is killing us. We are falling into a trap. Some of us adopt an apologetic stance, stating "that's just the way I am" (read: "I'd be straight if I could."). Others pattern their behavior in such a way as to mimic heterosexual society so as to minimize the glaring differences between us and them. No matter how much [money] you make, fucking your lover is still illegal in nearly half of the states. Getting a corporate job, a fierce car and a condo does not protect you from dying of AIDS or getting your head bashed in by neo-Nazis. The myth of assimilation must be shattered.
>
> . . . Fuck the heterosexual, nuclear family. Let's make families which promote sexual choices and liberation rather than sexual oppression. We must learn from the legacy of resistance that is ours: a legacy which shows that empowerment comes through grassroots activism, not mainstream politics, a legacy which shows that real change occurs when we arc inclusive, not exclusive.
>
> (4)

At the very heart of queer politics, at least as it is formulated by QUASH, is a fundamental challenge to the heteronormativity—the privilege, power, and normative status invested in heterosexuality—of the dominant society.

It is in their fundamental challenge to a systemic process of domination and exclusion, with a specific focus on heteronormativity, that queer activists and queer theorists are tied to and rooted in a tradition of political struggle most often identified with people of color and other marginal groups. For example, activists of color have, through many historical periods, questioned their formal and informal inclusion and power in prevailing social categories. Through just such a process of challenging their centrality to lesbian and gay politics in particular, and lesbian and gay communities more generally, lesbian, gay, bisexual, and transgendered people of color advanced debates over who and what would be represented as "truly gay." As Steven Seidman reminds us in "Identity and Politics in a 'Postmodern' Gay Culture: Some Historical and Conceptual Notes," beyond the general framing provided by postmodern queer theory, gay and lesbian—and now queer—politics owes much of its impetus to the politics of people of color and other marginalized members of lesbian and gay communities.

> Specifically, I make the case that postmodern strains in gay thinking and politics have their immediate social origin in recent developments in the gay culture. In the reaction by people of color, third-world-identified gays, poor and working class gays, and sex rebels to the ethnic/essentialist model of identity and community that achieved dominance in the lesbian and gay cultures of the 1970s, I locate the social basis for a rethinking of identity and politics.
>
> (106)

Through the demands of lesbian, gay, bisexual, and transgendered people of color as well as others who did not see themselves or their numerous communities in the more narrowly constructed politics of white gays and lesbians, the contestation took shape over who and what type of issues would be represented in lesbian and gay politics and in larger community discourse.

While similarities and connections between the politics of lesbians, gay men, bisexuals, and transgendered people of color during the 1970s and 1980s and queer activists of today clearly exist, the present-day rendition of this politics has deviated significantly from its legacy. Specifically, while both political efforts include as a focus of their work the radicalization and/or expansion of traditional lesbian and gay politics, the politics of lesbian, gay, bisexual, and transgendered people of color has been and continues to be much broader in its understanding of transformational politics.

The politics of lesbian, gay, bisexual, and transgendered people of color has often been guided by the type of radical intersectional left analysis I detailed earlier. Thus, while the politics of lesbian, gay, bisexual, and transgendered activists of color might recognize heteronormativity as a primary system of power structuring our lives, it understands that heteronormativity interacts with institutional racism, patriarchy, and class exploitation to define us in numerous ways as marginal and oppressed subjects.[5] And it is this constructed subservient position that allows our sisters and brothers to be used either as surplus labor in an advanced capitalist structure and/or seen as expendable, denied resources, and thus locked into correctional institutions across the country. While heterosexual privilege negatively impacts and constrains the lived experience of "queers" of color, so too do racism, classism, and sexism.

In contrast to the left intersectional analysis that has structured much of the politics of "queers" of color, the basis of the politics of some white queer activists and organizations has come dangerously close to a single oppression model. Experiencing "deviant" sexuality as the prominent characteristic of their marginalization, these activists begin to envision the world in terms of a "hetero/queer" divide. Using the framework of queer theory in which heteronormativity is identified as a system of regulation and normalization, some queer activists map the power and entitlement of normative heterosexuality onto the bodies of all hetero-sexuals. Further, these activists naively characterize all those who exist under the category of "queer" as powerless. Thus, in the process of conceptualizing a decentered identity of queer-ness, meant to embrace all those who stand on the outside of heteronormativity, a monolithic understanding of heterosexuality and queerness has come to dominate the political imagina-tion and actions of many queer activists.

This reconstruction of a binary divide between heterosexuals and queers, while discern-ible in many of the actions of Queer Nation, is probably most evident in the manifesto "I Hate Straights." Distributed at gay pride parades in New York and Chicago in 1990, the declara-tion written by an anonymous group of queers begins,

> I have friends. Some of them are straight.
>
> Year after year, I see my straight friends. I want to see how they are doing, to add newness to our long and complicated histories, to experience some continuity.
>
> Year after year I continue to realize that the facts of my life are irrelevant to them and that I am only half listened to, that I am an appendage to the doings of a greater world, a world of power and privilege, of the laws of installation, a world of exclusion. "That's not true," argue my straight friends. There is the one certainty in the politics of power: those left out of it beg for inclusion, while the insiders claim that they already are. Men do it to women, whites do it to blacks, *and everyone does it to queers.*
>
> *. . . The main dividing line, both conscious and unconscious, is procreation . . .*
> *and that magic word—Family.* (emphasis added)

Screaming out from this manifesto is an analysis which places not heteronormativity, but heterosexuality, as the central "dividing line" between those who would be dominant and those who are oppressed. Nowhere in this essay is there recognition that "nonnormative" procreation patterns and family structures of people who are labeled heterosexual have also been used to regulate and exclude *them*. Instead, the authors declare, "Go tell them [straights] to go away until they have spent a month walking hand in hand in public with someone of the same sex. After they survive that, then you'll hear what they have to say about queer anger. Otherwise, tell them to shut up and listen." For these activists, the power of heterosexuality is the focus, and queer anger the means of queer politics. Missing from this equation is any attention to, or acknowledgment of, the ways in which identities of race, class, and/or gender either enhance or mute the marginalization of queers, on the one hand, and the power of heterosexuals, on the other.

The fact that this essay is written about and out of queer anger is undoubtedly part of the rationale for its defense (Berlant and Freeman 200). But I question the degree to which we should read this piece as just an aberrational diatribe against straights motivated by intense queer anger. While anger is clearly a motivating factor for such writing, we should also understand this action to represent an analysis and politics structured around the simple dichotomy of straight and queer. We know, for instance, that similar positions have been put forth in other anonymously published, publicly distributed manifestos. For example, in the document *Queers Read This*, the authors write, "Don't be fooled, straight people own the world and the only reason you have been spared is you're smart, lucky or a fighter. Straight people have a privilege that allows them to do whatever they please and fuck without fear." They continue by stating that "Straight people are your enemy."

Even within this document, which seems to exemplify the narrowness of queer concep-tions, there is a surprising glimpse at a more enlightened left intersectional understanding of what queerness might mean. For instance, the authors continue, "Being queer is not about a right to privacy; it is about the freedom to be public, to just be who we are. It means everyday fighting oppression; homophobia, racism, misogyny, the bigotry of religious hypocrites and our own self-hatred." Evident in this one document are the inherent tensions and dilemmas many queer activists currently encounter: how does one implement in real political struggle a decentered political identity that is not constituted by a process of seemingly reductive "othering"?

The process of ignoring or at least downplaying queers' varying relationships to power is evident not only in the writing of queer activists, but also in the political actions pursued by queer organizations. I question the ability of political actions such as mall invasions (pursued by groups such as the Queer Shopping Network in New York and the Suburban Homosexual Outreach Program [SHOP] in San Francisco), to address the fact that queers exist in different social locations. Lauren Berlant and Elizabeth Freeman describe mall invasion projects as

> [an attempt to take] the relatively bounded spectacle of the urban pride parade to the ambient pleasures of the shopping mall. "Mall visibility actions" thus conjoin the spectacular lure of the parade with Hare Krishna-style conversion and proselytizing techniques. Stepping into malls in hair-gelled splendor, holding hands and handing out fliers, the queer auxiliaries produce an "invasion" that conveys a different message. "We're here, we're queer, *you're* going shopping."
>
> (210)

The activity of entering or "invading" the shopping mall on the part of queer nationals is clearly one of attempted subversion. Intended by their visible presence in this clearly coded heterosexual family economic mecca is a disruption of the agreed-upon segregation between the allowable spaces for queer "deviant" culture and the rest of the "naturalized" world. Left unchallenged in such an action, however, are the myriad ways, besides the enforcement of normative sexuality, in which some queers feel alienated and excluded from the space of the mall. Where does the mall as an institution of consumer culture and relative economic privilege play into this analysis? How does this action account for the varying economic relationships queers have to consumer culture? If you are a poor or working-class queer the exclusion and alienation you experience when entering the mall may not be limited to the normative sexual codes associated with the mall, but may also be centered on the assumed economic status of those shopping in suburban malls. If you are a queer of color your exclusion from the mall may, in part, be rooted in racial norms and stereotypes which construct you as a threatening subject every time you enter this economic institution. Queer activists must confront a question that haunts most political organizing: How do we put into politics a broad and inclusive left analysis that can actually engage and mobilize individuals with intersecting identities?

Clearly, there will be those critics who will claim that I am asking too much from any political organization. Demands that every aspect of oppression and regulation be addressed in each political act seem, and are indeed, unreasonable. However, I make the critique of queer mall invasions neither to stop such events nor to suggest that every oppression be dealt with by this one political action. Instead, I raise these concerns to emphasize the ways in which varying relations to power exist not only among heterosexuals, but also among those who label themselves queer.

In its current rendition, queer politics is coded with class, gender, and race privilege, and may have lost its potential to be a politically expedient organizing tool for addressing the needs—and mobilizing the bodies—of people of color. As some queer theorists and activists call for the destruction of stable sexual categories, for example, moving instead toward a more fluid understanding of sexual behavior, left unspoken is the class privilege which allows for such fluidity. Class or material privilege is a cornerstone of much of queer politics and theory as they exist today. Queer theorizing which calls for the elimination of fixed categories of sexual identity seems to ignore the ways in which some traditional social identities and communal ties can, in fact, be important to one's survival. Further, a queer politics which demonizes all heterosexuals discounts the relationships—especially those based on shared experiences of marginalization—that exist between gays and straights, particularly in communities of color.

Queers who operate out of a political culture of individualism assume a material independence that allows them to disregard historically or culturally recognized categories and communities or at the very least to move fluidly among them without ever establishing permanent relationships or identities within them. However, I and many other lesbian and gay people of color, as well as poor and working-class lesbians and gay men, do not have such material independence. Because of my multiple identities, which locate me and other "queer" people of color at the margins in this country, my material advancement, my physical protection, and my emotional well-being are constantly threatened. In those stable categories and named communities whose histories have been structured by shared resistance to oppression, I find relative degrees of safety and security.

Let me emphasize again that the safety I feel is relative to other threats and is clearly not static or constant. For in those named communities I also find versions of domination and normalization being replicated and employed as more privileged/assimilated marginal group members use their associations with dominant institutions and resources to regulate and police the activities of other marginal group members. Any lesbian, gay, bisexual, or transgendered person of color who has experienced exclusion from indigenous institutions, such as the exclusion many out black gay men have encountered from some black churches responding to AIDS, recognizes that even within marginal groups there are normative rules determining community membership and power (Cohen). However, in spite of the unequal power relationships located in marginal communities, I am still not interested in disassociating politically from those communities, for queerness, as it is currently constructed, offers no viable political alternative, since it invites us to put forth a political agenda that makes invisible the prominence of race, class, and to varying degrees gender in determining the life chances of those on both sides of the hetero/queer divide.

So despite the roots of queer politics in the struggles of "queer" people of color, despite the calls for highlighting categories which have sought to regulate and control black bodies like my own, and despite the attempts at decentralized grass-roots activism in some queer political organizations, there still exist—for some, like myself—great misgivings about current constructions of the term "queer." Personally speaking, I do not consider myself a "queer" activist or, for that matter, a "queer" anything. This is not because I do not consider myself an activist; in fact I hold my political work to be one of my most important contributions to all of my communities. But like other lesbian, gay, bisexual, and transgendered activists of color, I find the label "queer" fraught with unspoken assumptions which inhibit the radical political potential of this category.

The alienation, or at least discomfort, many activists and theorists of color have with current conceptions of queerness is evidenced, in part, by the minimal numbers of theorists of color who engage in the process of theorizing about the concept. Further, the sparse numbers of people of color who participate in "queer" political organizations might also be read as a sign of discomfort with the term. Most important, my confidence in making such a claim of distance and uneasiness with the term "queer" on the part of many people of color come from my interactions with other lesbian, gay, bisexual, and transgendered people of color who repeatedly express their interpretation of "queer" as a term rooted in class, race, and gender privilege. For us, "queer" is a politics based on narrow sexual dichotomies which make no room either for the analysis of oppression of those we might categorize as heterosexual, or for the privilege of those who operate as "queer." As black lesbian activist and writer Barbara Smith argues in "Queer Politics: Where's the Revolution?":

> Unlike the early lesbian and gay movement, which had both ideological and practical links to the left, black activism and feminism, today's "queer" politicos seem to operate in a historical and ideological vacuum. "Queer" activists focus on "queer" issues, and racism, sexual oppression and economic exploitation do not qualify, despite the fact that the majority of "queers" are people of color, female or working class. . . . Building unified, ongoing coalitions that challenge the system and ultimately prepare a way for revolutionary change simply isn't what "queer" activists have in mind.
>
> (13–14)

It is this narrow understanding of the idea of queer that negates its use in fundamentally reorienting the politics and privilege of lesbian and gay politics as well as more generally moving or transforming the politics of the left. Despite its liberatory claim to stand in opposition to static categories of oppression, queer politics and much of queer theory seem in fact to be static in the understanding of race, class, and gender and their roles in how heteronormativity regulates sexual behavior and identities. Distinctions between the status and the acceptance of different individuals categorized under the label of "heterosexual" go unexplored.

I emphasize the marginalized position of some who embrace heterosexual identities not because I want to lead any great crusade to understand more fully the plight of "the heterosexual." Rather, I recognize the potential for shared resistance with such individuals. This potential not only for coalitional work but for a shared analysis is especially relevant, from my vantage point, to "queer" people of color. Again, in my call for coalition work across sexual categories, I do not want to suggest that same-sex political struggles have not, independently, played an essential and distinct role in the liberatory politics and social movements of marginal people. My concern, instead, is with any political analysis or theory which collapses our understanding of power into a single continuum of evaluation.

Through a brief review of some of the ways in which nonnormative heterosexuality has been controlled and regulated through the state and systems of marginalization we may be reminded that differentials in power exist within all socially named categories. And through such recognition we may begin to envision a new political formation in which one's relation to dominant power serves as the basis of unity for radical coalition work in the twenty-first century.

Heterosexuals on the (out)side of heteronormativity

In this section I want to return to the question of a monolithic understanding of heterosexuality. I believe that through this issue we can begin to think critically about the components of a radical politics built not exclusively on identities, but on identities as they are invested with varying degrees of normative power. Thus, fundamental to my concern about the current structure and future agenda of queer politics is the unchallenged assumption of a uniform heteronormativity from which all heterosexuals benefit. I want again to be clear that there are, in fact, some who identify themselves as queer activists who do acknowledge relative degrees of power, and heterosexual access to that power, even evoking the term "straight queers." "Queer means to fuck with gender. There are straight queers, bi queers, tranny queers, lez queers, fag queers, SM queers, fisting queers in every single street in this apathetic country of ours" (anonymous, qtd. McIntosh 31).

Despite such sporadic insight, much of the politics of queer activists has been structured around the dichotomy of straight versus everything else, assuming a monolithic experience of heterosexual privilege for all those identified publicly with heterosexuality. A similar reductive dichotomy between men and women has consistently reemerged in the writing and actions of some feminists. And only through the demands, the actions, and the writing of many "feminists" and/or lesbians of color have those women who stand outside the norm of white, middle-class, legalized heterosexuality begun to see their lives, needs, and bodies represented in feminist theory (Carby; Collins; hooks). In a similar manner lesbian, gay, bisexual, and transgendered people of color have increasingly taken on the responsibility for at the very least complicating and most often challenging reductive notions of heteronormativity articulated by queer activists and scholars (Alexander; Farajaje-Jones; Lorde; Moraga and Anzaldúa; B. Smith).

If we follow such examples, complicating our understanding of both heteronormativity and queerness, we move one step closer to building the progressive coalition politics many of us desire. Specifically, if we pay attention to both historical and current examples of heterosexual relationships which have been prohibited, stigmatized, and generally repressed we may begin to identify those spaces of shared or similar oppression and resistance that provide a basis for radical coalition work. Further, we may begin to answer certain questions: In narrowly positing a dichotomy of heterosexual privilege and queer oppression under which we all exist, are we negating a basis of political unity that could serve to strengthen many communities and movements seeking justice and societal transformation? How do we use the relative degrees of ostracization all sexual/cultural "deviants" experience to build a basis of unity for broader coalition and movement work?

A little history (as a political scientist a little history is all I can offer) might be helpful in trying to sort out the various ways heterosexuality, especially as it has intersected with race, has been defined and experienced by different groups of people. It should also help to underscore the fact that many of the roots of heteronormativity are in white supremacist ideologies which sought (and continue) to use the state and its regulation of sexuality, in particular through the institution of heterosexual marriage, to designate which individuals were truly "fit" for full rights and privileges of citizenship. For example, the prohibition of marriages between black women and men imprisoned in the slave system was a component of many slave codes enacted during the seventeenth and eighteenth centuries. M.G. Smith, in his article on the structure of slave economic systems, succinctly states, "As property slaves were prohibited from forming legal relationships or marriages which would interfere with and restrict their owner's property rights" (71–72). Herbert G. Gutman, in *The Black Family in Slavery and Freedom, 1750–1925*, elaborates on the ideology of slave societies which denied the legal sanctioning of marriages between slaves and further reasoned that Blacks had no conception of family.

> The *Nation* identified sexual restraint, civil marriage, and family "stability" with "civilization" itself.
> Such mid-nineteenth-century class and sexual beliefs reinforced racial beliefs about Afro-Americans. As slaves, after all, their marriages had not been sanctioned by the civil laws and therefore "the sexual passion" went unrestrained. . . . Many white abolitionists denied the slaves a family life or even, often, a family consciousness because for them [whites] the family had its origins in and had to be upheld by the civil law.
>
> (295)

Thus it was not the promotion of marriage or heterosexuality *per se* that served as the standard or motivation of most slave societies. Instead, marriage and heterosexuality, as viewed through the lenses of profit and domination, and the ideology of white supremacy, were reconfigured to justify the exploitation and regulation of black bodies, even those presumably engaged in heterosexual behavior. It was this system of state-sanctioned, white male, upper-class, heterosexual domination that forced these presumably black *heterosexual* men and women to endure a history of rape, lynching, and other forms of physical and mental terrorism. In this way, marginal group members, lacking power and privilege although engaged in heterosexual behavior, have often found themselves defined as outside the norms and values of dominant society. This position has most often resulted in the suppression or negation of their legal, social, and physical relationships and rights.

In addition to the prohibition of marriage between slaves, A. Leon Higginbotham, Jr., in *The Matter of Color-Race and the American Legal Process: The Colonial Period,* writes of the legal restrictions barring interracial marriages. He reminds us that the essential core of the American legal tradition was the preservation of the white race. The "mixing" of the races was to be strictly prohibited in early colonial laws. The regulation of interracial heterosexual relationships, however, should not be understood as exclusively relegated to the seventeenth, eighteenth, and nineteenth centuries. In fact, Higginbotham informs us that the final law prohibiting miscegenation (the "interbreeding" or marrying of individuals from different "races"—actually meant to inhibit the "tainting" of the white race) was not repealed until 1967:

> Colonial anxiety about interracial sexual activity cannot be attributed solely to seventeenth-century values, for it was not until 1967 that the United States Supreme Court finally declared unconstitutional those statutes prohibiting interracial marriages. The Supreme Court waited thirteen years after its *Brown* decision dealing with desegregation of schools before, in *Loving v. Virginia*, it agreed to consider the issue of interracial marriages.

> (41)

It is this pattern of regulating the behavior and denigrating the identities of those heterosexuals on the outside of heteronormative privilege, in particular those perceived as threatening systems of white supremacy, male domination, and capitalist advancement that I want to highlight. An understanding of the ways in which heteronormativity works to support and reinforce institutional racism, patriarchy, and class exploitation must therefore be a part of how we problematize current constructions of heterosexuality. As I stated previously, I am not suggesting that those involved in publicly identifiable heterosexual behavior do not receive political, economic, and social advantage, especially in comparison to the experiences of some lesbian, transgendered, gay, and bisexual individuals. But the equation linking identity and behavior to power is not as linear and clear as some queer theorists and activists would have us believe.

A more recent example of regulated nonnormative heterosexuality is located in current debates and rhetoric regarding the "underclass" and the destruction of the welfare system. The stigmatization and demonization of single mothers, teen mothers, and, primarily, poor women of color dependent on state assistance has had a long and suspicious presence in American "intellectual" and political history. It was in 1965 that Daniel Patrick Moynihan released his "study" entitled *The Negro Family: The Case for National Action.* In this report, which would eventually come to be known as the Moynihan Report, the author points to the "pathologies" increasingly evident in so-called Negro families. In this document were allegations of the destructive nature of Negro family formations. The document's introduction argues that the fundamental problem, in which this is most clearly the case, is that of family structure. The evidence—not final, but powerfully persuasive—is that the Negro family in urban ghettos is crumbling. A middle-class group has managed to save itself, but for vast numbers of the unskilled, poorly educated city working-class the fabric of conventional social relationships has all but disintegrated.

Moynihan, later in the document, goes on to describe the crisis and pathologies facing Negro family structure as being generated by the increasing number of single-female-headed households, the increasing number of "illegitimate" births and, of course, increasing welfare dependency:

> In essence, the Negro community has been forced into a matriarchal structure which, because it is so out of line with the rest of the American society, seriously retards the progress of the group as a whole, and imposes a crushing burden on the Negro male and, in consequence, on a great many Negro women as well. . . . In a word, most Negro youth are in danger of being caught up in the tangle of pathology that affects their world, and probably a majority are so entrapped. . . . Obviously, not every instance of social pathology afflicting the Negro community can be traced to the weakness of family structure. . . . Nonetheless, at the center of the tangle of pathology is the weakness of the family structure.
>
> (29–30)

It is not the nonheterosexist behavior of these black men and women that is under fire, but rather the perceived nonnormative sexual behavior and family structures of these individuals, whom many queer activists—without regard to the impact of race, class, or gender—would designate as part of the heterosexist establishment or those mighty "straights they hate."

Over the last thirty years the demonization of poor women, engaged in nonnormative heterosexual relationships, has continued under the auspices of scholarship on the "underclass." Adolph L. Reed, in "The 'Underclass' as Myth and Symbol: The Poverty of Discourse About Poverty," discusses the gendered and racist nature of much of this literature, in which poor, often black and Latina women are portrayed as unable to control their sexual impulses and eventual reproductive decisions, unable to raise their children with the right moral fiber, unable to find "gainful" employment to support themselves and their "illegitimate children," and of course unable to manage "effectively" the minimal assistance provided by the state. Reed writes,

> The underclass notion may receive the greatest ideological boost from its gendered imagery and relation to gender politics. As I noted in a critique of Wilson's *The Truly Disadvantaged*, "family" is an intrinsically ideological category. The rhetoric of "disorganization," "disintegration," "deterioration" reifies one type of living arrangement—the ideal type of the bourgeois nuclear family—as outside history, nearly as though it were decreed by natural law. But—as I asked earlier—why exactly is out-of-wedlock birth pathological? Why is the female-headed household an indicator of disorganization and pathology? Does that stigma attach to *all* such households—even, say, a divorced executive who is a custodial mother? If not, what are the criteria for assigning it? The short answer is race and class bias inflected through a distinctively gendered view of the world.
>
> (33–34)

In this same discourse of the "underclass," young black men engaged in "reckless" hetero-sexual behavior are represented as irresponsible baby factories, unable to control or restrain their "sexual passion" (to borrow a term from the seventeenth century). And, unfortunately, often it has been the work of professed liberals like William Julius Wilson, in his book *The Truly Disadvantaged*, that, while not using the word "pathologies," has substantiated in its own tentative way the conservative dichotomy between the deserving working poor and the lazy, Cadillac-driving, steak-eating welfare queens of Ronald Reagan's imagination. Again, I raise this point to remind us of the numerous ways that sexuality and sexual deviance from a prescribed norm have been used to demonize and to oppress various segments of the popula-tion, even some classified under the label "heterosexual."

The policies of politicians and the actions of law enforcement officials have reinforced, in much more devastating ways, the distinctions between acceptable forms of heterosexual expression and those to be regulated—increasingly through incarceration. This move toward the disallowance of some forms of heterosexual expression and reproductive choice can be seen in the practice of prosecuting pregnant women suspected of using drugs—nearly 80 percent of all women prosecuted are women of color; through the forced sterilization of Puerto Rican and Native American women; and through the state-dictated use of Norplant by women answering to the criminal justice system and by women receiving state assistance.[6] Further, it is the "nonnormative" children of many of these nonnormative women that Newt Gingrich would place in orphanages. This is the same Newt Gingrich who, despite his clear disdain for gay and lesbian "lifestyles," has invited lesbians and gay men into the Republican party. I need not remind you that he made no such offer to the women on welfare discussed above. Who, we might ask, is truly on the outside of heteronormative power—maybe *most* of us?

Conclusion: destabilization and radical coalition work

While all this may, in fact, seem interesting or troubling or both, you may be wondering: What does it have to do with the question of the future of queer politics? It is my argument, as I stated earlier, that one of the great failings of queer theory and especially queer politics has been their inability to incorporate into analysis of the world and strategies for political mobilization the roles that race, class, and gender play in defining people's differing relations to dominant and normalizing power. I present this essay as the beginning of a much longer and protracted struggle to acknowledge and delineate the distribution of power within and outside of queer communities. This is a discussion of how to build a politics organized not merely by reductive categories of straight and queer, but organized instead around a more intersectional analysis of who and what the enemy is and where our potential allies can be found. This analysis seeks to make clear the privilege and power embedded in the categoriza-tions of, on the one hand, an upstanding, "morally correct," white, state authorized, middle-class, male *heterosexual*, and on the other, a culturally deficient, materially bankrupt, state dependent, *heterosexual*, woman of color, the latter found most often in our urban centers (those that haven't been gentrified), on magazine covers, and on the evening news.

I contend, therefore, that the radical potential of queer politics, or any liberatory move-ment, rests on its ability to advance strategically oriented political identities arising from a more nuanced understanding of power. One of the most difficult tasks in such an endeavor (and there are many) is not to forsake the complexities of both how power is structured and how we might think about the coalitions we create. Far too often movements revert to a position in which membership and joint political work are based upon a necessarily similar history of oppression—but this is too much like identity politics (Phelan). Instead, I am suggesting that the process of movement-building be rooted not in our shared history or identity, but in our shared marginal relationship to dominant power which normalizes, legitimizes, and privileges.

We must, therefore, start our political work from the recognition that multiple systems of oppression are in operation and that these systems use institutionalized categories and identities to regulate and socialize. We must also understand that power and access to dominant resources are distributed across the boundaries of "het" and "queer" that we construct. A model of queer politics that simply pits the grand "heterosexuals" against all those oppressed "queers" is ineffectual as the basis for action in a political environment dominated by Newt Gingrich, the Christian Right, and the recurring ideology of white supremacy. As we stand on the verge of watching those in power dismantle the welfare system through a process of demonizing poor and young, primarily poor and young women of color—many of whom have existed for their entire lives outside the white, middle-class, heterosexual norm—we have to ask if these women do not fit into society's categories of marginal, deviant, and "queer." As we watch the explosion of prison construction and the disproportionate incarceration rates of young men and women of color, often as part of the economic development of poor white rural communities, we have to ask if these individuals do not fit society's definition of "queer" and expendable.

I am not proposing a political strategy that homogenizes and glorifies the experience of poor heterosexual people of color. In fact, in calling for a more expansive left political identity and formation I do not seek to erase the specific historical relation between the stigma of "queer" and the sexual activity of gay men, lesbians, bisexual, and transgendered individuals. And in no way do I mean to, or want to, equate the experiences of marginal heterosexual women and men to the lived experiences of queers. There is no doubt that heterosexuality, even for those heterosexuals who stand outside the norms of heteronormativity, results in some form of privilege and feelings of supremacy. I need only recount the times when other women of color, more economically vulnerable than myself, expressed superiority and some feelings of disgust when they realized that the nice young professor (me) was "that way."

However, in recognizing the distinct history of oppression lesbian, gay, bisexual, and transgendered people have confronted and challenged, I am not willing to embrace every queer as my marginalized political ally. In the same way, I do not assume that shared racial, gender, and/or class position or identity guarantees or produces similar political commitments. Thus, identities and communities, while important to this strategy, must be complicated and destabilized through a recognition of the multiple social positions and relations to dominant power found *within* any one category or identity. Kimberle Crenshaw, in "Mapping the Margins: Intersectionality, Identity Politics, and Violence Against Women of Color," suggests that such a project use the idea of intersectionality to reconceptualize or problematize the identities and communities that are "home" to us. She demands that we challenge those identities that seem like home by acknowledging the other parts of our identities that are excluded:

> With identity thus reconceptualized [through a recognition of intersectionality], it may be easier to understand the need to summon up the courage to challenge groups that are after all, in one sense, "home" to us, in the name of the parts of us that are not made at home. . . . The most one could expect is that we will dare to speak against internal exclusions and marginalizations, that we might call attention to how the identity of "the group" has been centered on the intersectional identities of a few. . . . Through an awareness of intersectionality, we can better acknowledge and ground the differences among us and negotiate the means by which these differences will find expression in constructing group politics.

(1299)

In the same ways that we account for the varying privilege to be gained by a heterosexual identity, we must also pay attention to the privilege some queers receive from being white, male, and upper class. Only through recognizing the many manifestations of power, across and within categories, can we truly begin to build a movement based on one's politics and not exclusively on one's identity.

I want to be clear that what I and others are calling for is the destabilization, and not the destruction or abandonment, of identity categories.[7] We must reject a queer politics which seems to ignore, in its analysis of the usefulness of traditionally named categories, the roles of identity and community as paths to survival, using shared experiences of oppression and resistance to build indigenous resources, shape consciousness, and act collectively. Instead, I would suggest that it is the multiplicity and interconnectedness of our identities which provide the most promising avenue for the *destabilization and radical politicalization* of these same categories.

This is not an easy path to pursue because most often this will mean building a political analysis and political strategies around the most marginal in our society, some of whom look like us, many of whom do not. Most often, this will mean rooting our struggle in, and addressing the needs of, communities of color. Most often this will mean highlighting the intersectionality of one's race, class, gender, and sexuality and the relative power and privilege that one receives from being a man and/or being white and/or being middle class and/or being heterosexual. This, in particular, is a daunting challenge because so much of our political consciousness has been built around simple dichotomies such as powerful/powerless; oppressor/victim; enemy/comrade. It is difficult to feel safe and secure in those spaces where both your relative privilege and your experiences with marginalization are understood to shape your commitment to radical politics. However, as Bernice Johnson Reagon so aptly put it in her essay, "Coalition Politics: Turning the Century," "if you feel the strain, you may be doing some good work" (362).

And while this is a daunting challenge and uncomfortable position, those who have taken it up have not only survived, but succeeded in their efforts. For example, both the needle exchange and prison projects pursued through the auspices of ACT UP New York point to the possibilities and difficulties involved in principled transformative coalition work. In each project individuals from numerous identities—heterosexual, gay, poor, wealthy, white, black, Latino—came together to challenge dominant constructions of who should be allowed and who deserved care. No particular identity exclusively determined the shared political commitments of these activists; instead their similar positions, as marginalized subjects relative to the state—made clear through the government's lack of response to AIDS—formed the basis of this political unity.

In the prison project, it was the contention of activists that the government which denied even wealthy gay men access to drugs to combat this disease must be regarded as the same source of power that denied incarcerated men and women access to basic health care, including those drugs and conditions needed to combat HIV and AIDS. The coalition work this group engaged in involved a range of people, from formerly incarcerated individuals, to heterosexual men and women of color, to those we might deem privileged white lesbians and gay men. And this same group of people who came together to protest the conditions of incarcerated people with AIDS also showed up to public events challenging the homophobia that guided the government's and biomedical industries' response to this epidemic. The political work of this group of individuals was undoubtedly informed by the public identities they embraced, but these were identities that they further acknowledged as complicated by intersectionality and placed within a political framework where their shared experience as marginal, nonnormative subjects could be foregrounded. Douglas Crimp, in his article "Right On, Girlfriend!," suggests that through political work our identities become remade and must therefore be understood as *relational*. Describing such a transformation in the identities of queer activists engaged in, and prosecuted for, needle exchange work, Crimp writes,

> But once engaged in the struggle to end the crisis, these queers' identities were no longer the same. It's not that "queer" doesn't any longer encompass their sexual practices; it does, but it also entails a *relation* between those practices and other circumstances that make very different people vulnerable both to HIV infection and to the stigma, discrimination, and neglect that have characterized the societal and governmental response to the constituencies most affected by the AIDS epidemic.
>
> (317–18)

The radical potential of those of us on the outside of heteronormativity rests in our understanding that we need not base our politics in the dissolution of all categories and communities, but we need instead to work toward the destabilization and remaking of our identities. Difference, in and of itself—even that difference designated through named categories—is not the problem. Instead it is the power invested in certain identity categories and the idea that bounded categories are not to be transgressed that serve as the basis of domination and control. The reconceptualization not only of the content of identity categories, but the intersectional nature of identities themselves, must become part of our political practice.

We must thus begin to link our intersectional analysis of power with concrete coalitional work. In real terms this means identifying political struggles such as the needle exchange and prison projects of ACT UP that transgress the boundaries of identity to highlight, in this case, both the repressive power of the state and the normalizing power evident within both dominant and marginal communities. This type of principled coalition work is also being pursued in a more modest fashion by the Policy Institute of the National Gay and Lesbian Task Force. Recently, the staff at the Task Force distributed position papers not only on the topics of gay marriages and gays in the military, but also on right-wing attacks against welfare and affirmative action. Here we have political work based in the knowledge that the rhetoric and accusations of nonnormativity that Newt Gingrich and other right-wingers launch against women on welfare closely resemble the attacks of nonnormativity mounted against gays, lesbians, bisexuals, and transgendered individuals. Again it is the marginalized relation to power, experienced by both of these groups—and I do not mean to suggest that the groups are mutually exclusive—that frames the possibility for transformative coalition work. This prospect diminishes when we do not recognize and deal with the reality that the intersecting identities that gay people embody—in terms of race, class, and gender privilege—put some of us on Gingrich's side of the welfare struggle (e.g., Log Cabin Republicans). And in a similar manner a woman's dependence on state financial assistance in no way secures her position as one supportive of gay rights and/or liberation. While a marginal identity undoubtedly increases the prospects of shared consciousness, only an articulation and commitment to mutual support can truly be the test of unity when pursuing transformational politics.

Finally, I realize that I have been short on specifics when trying to describe how we move concretely toward a transformational coalition politics among marginalized subjects. The best I can do is offer this discussion as a starting point for reassessing the shape of queer/lesbian/gay/bisexual/transgendered politics as we approach the twenty-first century. A reconceptualization of the politics of marginal groups allows us not only to privilege the specific lived experience of distinct communities, but also to search for those interconnected sites of resistance from which we can wage broader political struggles. Only by recognizing the link between the ideological, social, political, and economic marginalization of punks, bulldaggers, and welfare queens can we begin to develop political analyses and political strategies effective in confronting the linked yet varied sites of power in this country. Such a project is important because it provides a framework from which the difficult work of coalition politics can begin. And it is in these complicated and contradictory spaces that the liberatory and left politics that so many of us work for is located.

Acknowledgments

The author would like to thank Mark Blasius, Nan Boyd, Ed Cohen, Carolyn Dinshaw, Jeff Edwards, Licia Fiol-Matta, Joshua Gamson, Lynne Huffer, Tamara Jones, Carla Kaplan, Ntanya Lee, Ira Livingston, and Barbara Ransby for their comments on various versions of this paper. All shortcomings are of course the fault of the author.

Notes

1   The very general chronology of queer theory and queer politics referred to throughout this article is not meant to write the definitive historical development of each phenomenon. Instead, the dates are used to provide the reader with a general frame of reference. See Epstein for a similar genealogy of queer theory and queer politics.
2   See Ingraham for a discussion of the heterogendered imaginary.
3   I want to be clear that in this essay I am including the destruction of sexual categories as part of the agenda of queer politics. While a substantial segment of queer activists and theorists call for the *destabilization* of sexual categories, there are also those self-avowed queers who embrace a politics built around the *deconstruction* and/or elimination of sexual categories. For example, a number of my self-identified queer students engage in sexual behavior that most people would interpret as *transgressive* of sexual identities and categories. However, these students have repeatedly articulated a different interpretation of their sexual behavior. They put forth an understanding that does not highlight their transgression of categories, but one which instead represents them as individuals who operate outside of categories and sexual identities altogether. They are sexual beings, given purely to desire, truly living sexual fluidity, and not constrained by any form of sexual categorization or identification. This interpretation seems at least one step removed from that held by people who embrace the fluidity of sexuality while still recognizing the political usefulness of categories or labels for certain sexual behavior and communities. One example of such people might be those women who identify as lesbians and who also acknowledge that sometimes they choose to sleep with men. These individuals exemplify the process of destabilization that I try to articulate within this essay. Even further removed from the queers who would do away with all sexual categories are those who also transgress what many consider to be categories of sexual behaviors while they publicly embrace one stable sexual identity (for example, those self-identified heterosexual men who sleep with other men sporadically and secretly).
4   I want to thank Mark Blasius for raising the argument that standing on the outside of heteronormativity is a bit of a misnomer, since as a dominant normalizing process it is a practice of regulation in which we are all implicated. However, despite this insight I will on occasion continue to use this phrasing understanding the limits of its meaning.
5   See Hennessy for a discussion of left analysis and the limits of queer theory.
6   For an insightful discussion of the numerous methods used to regulate and control the sexual and reproductive choices of women, see Shende.
7   See Jones for an articulation of differences between the destabilization and the destruction of identity categories.

Works cited

Alexander, Jacqui. "Redrafting Morality: The Postcolonial State and the Sexual Offences Bill of Trinidad and Tobago." *Third World Women and the Politics of Feminism*. Ed. C.T. Mohanty, A. Russo, and L. Torres. Bloomington: Indiana UP, 1991. 133–52.

Berlant, Lauren, and Elizabeth Freeman. "Queer Nationality." Warner 193–229.

Bérubé, Allan, and Jeffrey Escoffier. "Queer/Nation." *Out/Look: National Lesbian and Gay Quarterly* 11 (Winter 1991): 12–14.

Blasius, Mark. *Gay and Lesbian Politics: Sexuality and The Emergence of a New Ethic*. Philadelphia: Temple UP, 1994.

Butler, Judith. *Gender Trouble: Feminism and the Subversion of Identity*. New York: Routledge, 1990.

Carby, Hazel. *Reconstructing Womanhood: The Emergence of the Afro-American Woman Novelist*. New York: Oxford UP, 1987.

Clarke, Cheryl. "The Failure to Transform: Homophobia in the Black Community." Smith, *Home Girls* 197–208.

Cohen, Cathy J. "Contested Membership: Black Gay Identities and the Politics of AIDS." *Queer Theory/Sociology*. Ed. S. Seidman. Oxford: Blackwell, 1996. 362–94.

Collins, Patricia Hill. *Black Feminist Thought: Knowledge, Consciousness, and the Politics of Empowerment*. New York: Harper, 1990.

Combahee River Collective. "The Combahee River Collective Statement." Smith, *Home Girls* 272–82.

Crenshaw, Kimberle. "Mapping the Margins: Intersectionality, Identity Politics, and Violence Against Women of Color." *Stanford Law Review* 43 (1991): 1241–99.

Crimp, Douglas. "Right On, Girlfriend!" Warner 300–320.

Davis, Angela Y. *Women, Race and Class*. New York: Vintage, 1983.

de Lauretis, Teresa. "Queer Theory: Lesbian and Gay Sexualities." *differences* 3.2 (Summer 1991): iii–xviii.

Dunlap, David W. "Three Black Members Quit AIDS Organization Board." *New York Times* 11 Jan. 1996: B2.

Dyson, Michael Eric. *Between God and Gangsta Rap*. New York: Oxford UP, 1996.

Epstein, Steven. "A Queer Encounter: Sociology and the Study of Sexuality." *Sociological Theory* 12 (1994): 188–202.

Farajaje-Jones, Elias. "Ain't I a Queer." Creating Change Conference, National Gay and Lesbian Task Force. Detroit, Michigan. 8–12 Nov. 1995.

Fuss, Diana, ed. *Inside/Outside: Lesbian Theories, Gay Theories*. New York: Routledge, 1991.

Gamson, Joshua. "Must Identity Movements Self-destruct? A Queer Dilemma." *Social Problems* 42 (1995): 390–407.

Gutman, Herbert G. *The Black Family in Slavery and Freedom, 1750–1925*. New York: Vintage, 1976.

Hennessy, Rosemary. "Queer Theory, Left Politics." *Rethinking MARXISM* 7.3 (1994): 85–111.

Higginbotham, A. Leon, Jr. *In the Matter of Color–Race and the American Legal Process: The Colonial Period*. New York: Oxford UP, 1978.

hooks, bell. *Feminist Theory: From Margin to Center*. Boston: South End, 1984.

Ingraham, Chrys. "The Heterosexual Imaginary: Feminist Sociology and Theories of Gender." *Sociological Theory* 12 (1994): 203–19.

Jones, Tamara. "Inside the Kaleidoscope: How the Construction of Black Gay and Lesbian Identities Inform Political Strategies." Unpublished dissertation, Yale University, 1995.

Lorde, Audre. *Sister Outsider: Essays and Speeches by Audre Lorde*. New York: The Crossing P, 1984.

McIntosh, Mary. "Queer Theory and the War of the Sexes." *Activating Theory: Lesbian, Gay, Bisexual Politics*. Ed. J. Bristow and A. R. Wilson. London: Lawrence and Wishart, 1993. 33–52.

Moraga, Cherríe, and Gloria Anzaldúa, eds. *This Bridge Called My Back: Writings by Radical Women of Color*. New York: Kitchen Table/Women of Color, 1981.

Morton, Donald. "The Politics of Queer Theory in the (Post) Modern Moment." *Genders* 17 (Fall 1993): 121–45.

Moynihan, Daniel Patrick. *The Negro Family: The Case for National Action*. Washington D.C.: Office of Policy Planning and Research, U.S. Department of Labor, 1965.

Phelan, Shane. *Identity Politics: Lesbian Feminism and the Limits of Community*. Philadelphia: Temple UP, 1989.

Podolsky, Robin. "Sacrificing Queer and Other 'Proletarian' Artifacts." *Radical America* 25.1 (January 1991): 53–60.

Queer Nation. "I Hate Straights" manifesto. New York, 1990.

Queers United Against Straight-acting Homosexuals. "Assimilation is Killing Us: Fight for a Queer United Front." *WHY I HATED THE MARCH ON WASHINGTON* (1993): 4.

Ransby, Barbara, and Tracye Matthews. "Black Popular Culture and the Transcendence of Patriarchical Illusions." *Race & Class* 35.1 (July–September 1993): 57–70.

Reagon, Bernice Johnson. "Coalition Politics: Turning the Century." Smith, *Home Girls* 356–68.

Reed, Adolph L., Jr. "The 'Underclass' as Myth and Symbol: The Poverty of Discourse About Poverty." *Radical America* 24.1 (January 1990): 21–40.

Rich, Adrienne. "Compulsory Heterosexuality and Lesbian Existence." *Powers of Desire: The Politics of Sexuality*. Eds. A. Snitow, C. Stansell, and S. Thompson. New York: Monthly Review, 1983. 177–206.

Sedgwick, Eve Kosofsky. *The Epistemology of the Closet*. Berkeley: U of California P, 1990.

Seidman, Steven. "Identity and Politics in a 'Postmodern' Gay Culture: Some Historical and Conceptual Notes." Warner 105–42.

Shende, Suzanne. "Fighting the Violence Against Our Sisters: Prosecution of Pregnant Women and the Coercive Use of Norplant." *Women Transforming Politics: An Alternative Reader*. Eds. C. Cohen, K. Jones, and J. Tronto. New York: New York UP, 1997.

Smith, Barbara. "Queer Politics: Where's the Revolution?" *The Nation* 257.1 (July 5, 1993): 12–16.

—, ed. *Home Girls: A Black Feminist Anthology*. New York: Kitchen Table/Women of Color, 1983.

Smith, M.G. "Social Structure in the British Caribbean About 1820." *Social and Economic Studies* 1.4 (August 1953): 55–79.

"Statement of Purpose." Dialogue on the Lesbian and Gay Left. Duncan Conference Center in Del Ray Beach, Florida. 1–4 April 1993.

Stein, Arlene, and Ken Plummer. "'I Can't Even Think Straight': 'Queer' Theory and the Missing Sexual Revolution in Sociology." *Sociological Theory* 12 (1994): 178–87.

Vaid, Urvashi. *Virtual Equality: The Mainstreaming of Gay & Lesbian Liberation*. New York: Anchor, 1995.

Warner, Michael, ed. *Fear of a Queer Planet: Queer Politics and Social Theory*. Minneapolis: U of Minnesota P, 1993.

West, Cornel. *Race Matters*. Boston: Beacon, 1993.

Wilson, William Julius. *The Truly Disadvantaged: The Inner City, the Underclass, and Public Policy*. Chicago: U of Chicago P, 1987.

Chapter 6

E. Patrick Johnson

"QUARE" STUDIES, OR "(ALMOST) EVERYTHING I KNOW ABOUT QUEER STUDIES I LEARNED FROM MY GRANDMOTHER"

E. Patrick Johnson is Professor and Chair of the Department of Performance Studies and Professor in the Department of African American Studies at Northwestern University. A scholar, activist, and performer who writes on race, sexuality, gender, and performance, Johnson is the author of *Appropriating Blackness: Performance and the Politics of Authenticity* (2003) and *Sweet Tea: Black Gay Men of the South—An Oral History* (2008). This essay first appeared in *Text and Performance Quarterly* (2001) and was reprinted in *Black Queer Studies: A Critical Anthology* (2005).

In this essay, Johnson argues that queer theory fails to acknowledge the material realities of gays and lesbians of color. In doing so, queer theory ignores culture-specific positionalities, ignores the ways bodies are marked by and read through race- and class-specific discourses, and thereby negates the subjectivity of queers of color. Johnson responds by offering a detailed outline of a "quare" theory, a term taken from the black vernacular for "queer." Quare studies works to uncover the racialized aspects of sexuality, which Johnson demonstrates through a reading of Marlon Riggs's film *Black Is . . . Black Ain't*. Utilizing theories of performance and performativity, quare studies recuperates the subject that queer theory dismisses, while actively promoting a politics of resistance.

> I love queer. Queer is a homosexual of either sex. It's more convenient than saying "gays" which has to be qualified, or "lesbians and gay men." It's an extremely useful polemic term because it is who we say we are, which is, "Fuck You."
>
> Spike Pittsberg, in Cherry Smith, "What is This Thing Called Queer?"

I use queer to describe my particular brand of lesbian feminism, which has much to do with the radical feminism I was involved with in the early 80s. I also use it externally to describe a political inclusivity—a new move toward a celebration of difference across sexualities, across genders, across sexual preference and across object choice. The two link.

Linda Semple, in Smith, "What Is This Thing Called Queer?"

I'm more inclined to use the words "black lesbian," because when I hear the word queer I think of white, gay men.

Isling Mack-Nataf, in Smith, "What Is This Thing Called Queer?"

I define myself as gay mostly. I will not use queer because it is not part of my vernacular—but I have nothing against its use. The same debates around naming occur in the "black community." Naming is powerful. Black people and gay people constantly renaming ourselves is a way to shift power from whites and hets respectively.

Inge Blackman, in Smith, "What Is This Thing Called Queer?"

Personally speaking, I do not consider myself a "queer" activist or, for that matter, a "queer" anything. This is not because I do not consider myself an activist; in fact I hold my political work to be one of my most important contributions to all of my communities. But like other lesbian, gay, bisexual, and transgendered activists of color, I find the label "queer" fraught with unspoken assumptions which inhibit the radical political potential of this category.

Cathy Cohen, "Punks, Bulldaggers, and Welfare Queens"

Quare Etymology (with apologies to Alice Walker)[1]
   Quare (Kwâr), *n.* **1.** meaning *queer*; also, opp. of *straight*; odd or slightly off kilter; from the African American vernacular for queer; sometimes homophobic in usage, but always denotes excess incapable of being contained within conventional categories of *being*; curiously equivalent to the Anglo-Irish (and sometimes "Black" Irish) variant of queer, as in Brendan Behan's famous play *The Quare Fellow*.
   —*adj.* **2.** a lesbian, gay, bisexual, or transgendered person of color who loves other men or women, sexually and/or nonsexually, and appreciates black culture and community.
   —*n.* **3.** one who *thinks* and *feels* and *acts* (and, sometimes, "acts up"); committed to struggle against all forms of oppression—racial, sexual, gender, class, religious, etc.
   —*n.* **4.** one for whom sexual and gender identities always already intersect with racial subjectivity.
   5. quare is to queer as "reading" is to "throwing shade."

I AM GOING out on a limb. This is a precarious position, but the stakes are high enough to warrant risky business. The business to which I refer is reconceptualizing the still-incubating discipline called "queer" studies. Now, what's in a name? This is an important question when, as James Baldwin proclaims, I have "no name in the street" or, worse still, "nobody *knows* my name."[2] I used to answer to "queer," but when I was hailed by that naming, interpellated in that moment, I felt as if I was being called "out of my name." I needed something with more "soul," more "bang," something closer to "home." It is my name after all!

Then I remembered how "queer" is used in my family. My grandmother, for example, used it often when I was a child and still uses it today.[3] When she says the word, she does so in a thick, black, southern dialect: "That sho'll is a 'quare' chile." Her use of "queer" is almost always nuanced. Still, one might wonder, what, if anything, could a poor, black, eighty-something, southern, homophobic woman teach her educated, middle-class, thirty-something, gay grandson about queer studies? Everything. Or *almost* everything. On the one hand, my grandmother uses "quare" to denote something or someone who is odd, irregular, or slightly off-kilter—definitions in keeping with traditional understandings and uses of "queer." On the other hand, she also deploys "quare" to connote something excessive—something that might philosophically translate into an excess of discursive and epistemological meanings grounded in African American cultural rituals and lived experience. Her knowing or not knowing vis-à-vis "quare" is predicated on her own "multiple and complex social, historical, and cultural positionality."[4] It is this culture-specific positionality that I find absent from the dominant and more conventional usage of "queer," particularly in its most recent theoretical reappropriation in the academy.

I knew there was something to the term "quare," that its implications reached far beyond my grandmother's front porch. Little did I know, however, that it would extend from her porch across the Atlantic. Then, I found "quare" in Ireland.[5] In his *Quare Joyce*, Joseph Valente writes, "I have elected to use the Anglo-Irish epithet *quare* in the title as a kind of transnational/transidiomatic pun. *Quare*, meaning odd or strange, as in Brendan Behan's famous play, *The Quare Fellow*, has lately been appropriated as a distinctively Irish variant of *queer*, as in the recent prose collection *Quare Fellas*, whose editor, Brian Finnegan, reinterprets Behan's own usage of the term as having 'covertly alluded to his own sexuality.' "[6] Valente's appropriation of the Irish epithet "quare" to "queerly" read James Joyce establishes a connection between race and ethnicity in relation to queer identity. Indeed, Valente's "quare" reading of Joyce, when conjoined with my grandmother's "quare" reading of those who are "slightly off-kilter," provides a strategy for reading racial and ethnic sexuality. Where the two uses of "quare" diverge is in their deployment. Valente deploys "quare" to devise a queer literary exegesis of Joyce. Rather than drawing on "quare" as a *literary* mode of reading/theorizing, however, I draw on the *vernacular* roots implicit in my grandmother's use of the word to devise a strategy for theorizing racialized sexuality.

Because much of queer theory critically interrogates notions of selfhood, agency, and experience, it is often unable to accommodate the issues faced by gays and lesbians of color who come from "raced" communities. Gloria Anzaldúa explicitly addresses this limitation when she warns that "queer is used as a false unifying umbrella which all 'queers' of all races, ethnicities and classes are shored under." While acknowledging that "at times we need this umbrella to solidify our ranks against outsiders," Anzaldúa nevertheless urges that "even when we seek shelter under it ["queer"], we must not forget that it homogenizes, erases our differences."[7]

"Quare," on the other hand, not only speaks across identities, it *articulates* identities as well. "Quare" offers a way to critique stable notions of identity and, at the same time, to locate racialized and class knowledges. My project is one of recapitulation and recuperation. I want to maintain the inclusivity and playful spirit of "queer" that animates much of queer theory, but I also want to jettison its homogenizing tendencies. As a disciplinary expansion, then, I wish to "quare" "queer" such that ways of knowing are viewed both as discursively mediated and as historically situated and materially conditioned. This reconceptualization foregrounds the ways in which lesbians, bisexuals, gays, and transgendered people of color come to sexual and racial knowledge. Moreover, quare studies acknowledges the different "stand-points" found among lesbian, bisexual, gay, and transgendered people of color differences—differences that are also conditioned by class and gender.[8]

Quare studies is a theory of and for gays and lesbians of color. Thus, I acknowledge that in my attempt to advance "quare" studies, I run the risk of advancing another version of identity politics. Despite this, I find it necessary to traverse this political minefield in order to illuminate the ways in which some strands of queer theory fail to incorporate racialized sexuality. The theory that I advance is a "theory in the flesh."[9] Theories in the flesh emphasize the diversity within and among gays, bisexuals, lesbians, and transgendered people of color while simultaneously accounting for how racism and classism affect how we experience and theorize the world. Theories in the flesh also conjoin theory and practice through an embodied politics of resistance. This politics of resistance is manifest in vernacular traditions such as performance, folklore, literature, and verbal art.

This essay offers an extended meditation on and an intervention in queer theory and practice. I begin by mapping out a general history of queer theory's deployment in contemporary academic discourse, focusing on the lack of discourse on race and class within the queer theoretical paradigm. Following this, I offer an analysis of one queer theorist's (mis) reading of two black gay performances. Next, I propose an intervention in queer theory by outlining the components of quare theory, a theory that incorporates race and class as categories of analysis in the study of sexuality. Quare theory is then operationalized in the following section, where I offer a quare reading of Marlon Riggs's film *Black Is . . . Black Ain't*. The final section calls for a conjoining of academic praxis with political praxis.

"Race trouble": queer studies or the study of white queers

At the moment when queer studies has gained momentum in the academy and forged a space as a legitimate disciplinary subject, much of the scholarship produced in its name elides issues of race and class. While the epigraphs that open this essay suggest that "queer" sometimes speaks across (homo)sexualities, they also suggest that "queer" is not necessarily embraced by gays, bisexuals, lesbians, and transgendered people of color. Indeed, the statements of Mack-Nataf, Blackman, and Cohen reflect a general suspicion of the term "queer," that the term often displaces and rarely addresses their concerns.[10]

Some queer theorists have argued that their use of "queer" is more than just a reappropriation of an offensive term. Cherry Smith, for example, maintains that the term entails a "radical questioning of social and cultural norms, notions of gender, reproductive sexuality and the family."[11] Others underscore the playfulness and inclusivity of the term, arguing that it opens up rather than fixes identities. According to Eve Sedgwick, "What it takes—all it takes—to make the description 'queer' a true one is the impulsion to use it in the first person."[12] Indeed, Sedgwick suggests, it may refer to "pushy femmes, radical faeries, fantasists, drags, clones, leatherfolk, ladies in tuxedos, feminist women or feminist men, masturbators, bulldaggers, divas, Snap! queens, butch bottoms, storytellers, transsexuals, aunties, wannabes, lesbian-identified men or lesbians who sleep with men, or . . . people able to relish, learn from, or identify with such."[13] For Sedgwick, then, it would appear that queer is a catch-all not bound to any particular "identity," a notion that moves us away from binaries such as "homosexual/heterosexual" and "gay/lesbian." Michael Warner offers an even more politicized and polemical view: "The preference for 'queer' represents, among other things, an aggressive impulse of generalization; it rejects a minoritizing logic of toleration or simple political interest-representation in favor of a more thorough resistance to regimes of the normal. For academics, being interested in Queer theory is a way to mess up the desexualized spaces of the academy, exude some rut, reimagine the public from and for which academic intellectuals write, dress, and perform."[14] The foregoing theorists identify "queer" as a site of indeterminate possibility, a site where sexual practice does not necessarily determine one's status as queer. Indeed, Lauren Berlant and Michael Warner argue that queer is "more a matter of aspiration than it is the expression of an identity or a history."[15] Accordingly, straight-identified critic Calvin Thomas appropriates Judith Butler's notion of "critical queerness" to suggest that "just as there is more than one way to be 'critical,' there may be more than one (or two or three) to be 'queer.'"[16]

Some critics have applied Butler's theory of gender to identity formation more generally. Butler calls into question the notion of the "self" as distinct from discursive cultural fields. That is, like gender, there is no independent or pure "self" or agent that stands outside socially and culturally mediated discursive systems. Thus, any move toward identification is, in Butler's view, to be hoodwinked into believing that identities are discourse free and capable of existing outside the systems that those identity formations seek to critique. Even when identity is contextualized and qualified, Butler still insists that theories of identity "invariably close with an embarrassed 'etc.'"[17] Butler's emphasis on gender and sex as "performative" would seem to undergird a progressive, forward-facing theory of sexuality. In fact, some theorists have made the theoretical leap from the gender performative to the racial performative, thereby demonstrating the potential of her theory for understanding the ontology of race.[18]

But, to riff off of the now-popular phrase "gender trouble," *there is some "race" trouble here with queer theory*. More particularly, in its "race for theory,"[19] queer theory has often failed to address the material realities of gays and lesbians of color. As black British activist Helen (charles) asks, "What happens to the definition of 'queer' when you're washing up or having a wank? When you're aware of misplacement or displacement in your colour, gender, identity? Do they get subsumed . . . into a homogeneous category, where class and other things that make up a cultural identity are ignored?"[20] What, for example, are the ethical and material implications of queer theory if its project is to dismantle all notions of identity and agency? The deconstructive turn in queer theory highlights the ways in which ideology functions to oppress and to proscribe ways of knowing, but what is the utility of queer theory on the front lines, in the trenches, on the street, or anyplace where the racialized and sexualized body is beaten, starved, fired, cursed—indeed, when the body is the site of trauma?[21]

Beyond queer theory's failure to focus on materiality, it also has failed to acknowledge consistently and critically the intellectual, aesthetic, and political contributions of nonwhite, non-middle-class gays, bisexuals, lesbians, and transgendered people in the struggle against homophobia and oppression. Moreover, even when white queer theorists acknowledge these contributions, rarely do they self-consciously and overtly reflect on the ways in which their own whiteness informs their own critical queer position, and this is occurring at a time when naming one's positionality has become almost standard protocol in other areas of scholarship. Although there are exceptions, most often white queer theorists fail to acknowledge and address racial privilege.[22]

Because transgendered people, lesbians, gays, and bisexuals of color often ground their theorizing in a politics of identity, they frequently fall prey to accusations of "essentialism" or "anti-intellectualism." Galvanizing around identity, however, is not always an unintentional "essentialist" move. Many times, it is an intentional strategic choice.[23] Cathy Cohen, for example, suggests that "queer theorizing which calls for the elimination of fixed categories seems to ignore the ways in which some traditional social identities and communal ties can, in fact, be important to one's survival."[24] The "communal ties" to which Cohen refers are those that exist in communities of color across boundaries of sexuality. For example, my grandmother, who is homophobic, nonetheless must be included in the struggle against oppression in spite of her bigotry. While her homophobia must be critiqued, her feminist and race struggles over the course of her life have enabled me and others in my family to enact strategies of resistance against a number of oppressions, including homophobia. Some queer activists groups, however, have argued fervently for the disavowal of any alliance with heterosexuals, a disavowal that those of us who belong to communities of color cannot necessarily afford to make.[25] Therefore, while offering a progressive and sometimes transgressive politics of sexuality, the seams of queer theory become exposed when that theory is applied to identities around which sexuality may pivot, such as race and class.

As a counter to this myopia and in an attempt to close the gap between theory and practice, self and Other, Audre Lorde proclaims:

Without community there is no liberation, only the most vulnerable and temporary armistice between an individual and her oppression. But community must not mean a shedding of our differences, nor the pathetic pretense that these differences do not exist. . . .

> I urge each one of us here to reach down into that deep place of knowledge inside herself and touch the terror and loathing of any difference that lives there. See whose face it wears. Then the personal as the political can begin to illuminate all our choices.[26]

For Lorde, a theory that dissolves the communal identity—in all of its difference—around which the marginalized can politically organize is not a progressive one. Nor is it one that gays, bisexuals, transgendered people, and lesbians of color can afford to adopt, for to do so would be to foreclose possibilities of change.

"Your blues ain't like mine": the invalidation of "experience"

As a specific example of how some queer theorists (mis)read or minimize the work, lives, and cultural production of gays, lesbians, bisexuals, and transgendered people of color, and to lay the groundwork for a return to a focus on embodied performance as a critical praxis, I offer an analysis of one queer theorist's reading of two black gay performances. In *The Ethics of Marginality*, for example, queer theorist John Champagne uses black gay theorists' objections to the photographs of Robert Mapplethorpe to call attention to the trouble with deploying "experience" as evidentiary.[27] Specifically, Champagne focuses on a speech delivered by Essex Hemphill, a black gay writer and activist, at the 1990 OUTWRITE conference of gay and lesbian writers. In his speech, Hemphill critiqued Mapplethorpe's photographs of black men.[28] Champagne takes exception to Hemphill's critique, arguing that Hemphill's reading is "monolithic" and bespeaks "a largely untheorized relation between desire, representation, and the political."[29] What I wish to interrogate, however, is Champagne's reading of Hemphill's apparent "emotionality" during the speech.

In Champagne's account, Hemphill began to cry during his speech, to which there were two responses: one of sympathy/empathy and one of protest. Commenting on an overheard conversation between two whites in the audience, Champagne writes, "Although I agreed with much of the substance of this person's comments concerning race relations in the gay and lesbian community, I was suspicious of the almost masochistic pleasure released in and through this public declaration of white culpability."[30] Here I find it surprising that Champagne would characterize what appears to be white *reflexivity* about racial and class privilege as "masochistic," given how rare such self-reflexivity is in the academy and elsewhere. After characterizing as masochistic the two whites who sympathetically align themselves with Hemphill, Champagne aligns himself with the one person who displayed vocal disapproval by booing at Hemphill's speech:

> I have to admit that I admired the bravura of the lone booer. I disagreed with Hemphill's readings of the photographs, and felt that his tears were an attempt to shame the audience into refusing to interrogate the terms of his address. If, as Gayatri Spivak has suggested, we might term the politics of an explanation the means by which it secures its particular mode of being in the world, the politics of Hemphill's reading of Mapplethorpe might be described as the politics of tears, a politics that assures the validity of its produced explanation by appealing to some kind of "authentic," universal, and (thus) uninterrogated "human" emotion of experience.[31]

Champagne's own "bravura" in *his* reading of Hemphill's tears illuminates the ways in which many queer theorists, in their quest to move beyond the body, ground their critique in the discursive rather than the corporeal. I suggest that the two terrains are not mutually exclusive, but rather stand in a dialogical/dialectical relationship to one another. What about the authenticity of pain, for example, that may supersede the cognitive and emerges from the heart—not *for* display but *despite* display? What is the significance of a black *man* crying in public? We must grant each other time and space not only to talk *of* the body, but through it as well.[32] In Champagne's formulation, however, bodily "experience" is anti-intellectual and Hemphill's "black" bodily experience is manipulative. This seems to be an un-self-reflexive, if not unfair, assumption to make when, for the most part, white bodies are discursively and corporeally naturalized as universal. Historically, white bodies have not been trafficked, violated, burned, and dragged behind trucks because they embody racialized identities. In Champagne's analysis of "blackness," bodily "whiteness" goes uninterrogated.[33]

In order to posit an alternative reading of Hemphill's tears, I turn to bell hooks's insights regarding the ways in which whites often misread emotionality elicited through black cultural aesthetics. "In the context of white institutions, particularly universities," hooks writes, "that mode of address is questionable precisely because it moves people. Style is equated in such a setting with a lack of substance." It is hooks's belief that this transformation of cultural space requires an "audience [to] shift . . . paradigms" and, in that way, "a marginal aspect of black cultural identity [is] centralized."[34] Unlike Champagne's own diminution of the "subversive powers [and politics] of style,"[35] hooks affirms the transgressive and transformative potential of style, citing it as "one example of counter-hegemonic cultural practice" as well as "an insertion of radical black subjectivity."[36] Despite Champagne's statements to the contrary, his own reading of Hemphill constitutes himself as a "sovereign subject" within his theory of antisubjectivity, a positionality that renders him "overseer" of black cultural practices and discourse. On the other hand, Hemphill's tears, as a performance of black style that draws on emotionality, may be read as more than simply a willful act of manipulation to substantiate the black gay "experience" of subjugation and objectification. More complexly, it may be read as a "confrontation with difference which takes place on new ground, in that counter-hegemonic marginal space where radical black subjectivity is *seen*, not overseen by any authoritative Other claiming to know us better than we know ourselves."[37] In his "reading" of Hemphill, Champagne positions himself as "authoritative Other," assuming, as he does, the motivation behind Hemphill's tears.[38]

Champagne also devotes an entire chapter to *Tongues Untied*, a work by black gay filmmaker Marlon Riggs. Once again critiquing what he sees as the film's problematic reliance on "experience" as evidentiary, Champagne offers a queer reading of Riggs's film to call into question the filmic representation of blackness and class:

> In *Tongues Untied*, one of the consequences of failing to dis-articulate, in one's reading, the hybrid weave of discursive practices deployed by the film might be the erasure of what I would term certain discontinuities of class, race, and imperialism as they might interweave with the necessarily inadequate nominations "Black" and "gay." For example, much of the film seems to employ a set of discursive practices historically familiar to a middle-class audience, Black and non-Black alike. The film tends to privilege the (discursive) "experience" of middle-class Black gay men, and is largely articulated from that position. The film privileges poetry, and in particular, a poetry that seems to owe as much historically to Walt Whitman and William Carlos Williams as to Langston Hughes or Countee Cullen; moreover, the film's more overtly political rhetoric seems culled from organized urban struggles in the gay as well as Black

communities, struggles often headed by largely middle-class people. Another moment in the film that suggests a certain middle-class position is arguably one of the central images of the film, a series of documentary style shots of what appears to be a Gay Pride Day march in Manhattan. A group of black gay men carry a banner that reads "Black Men Loving Black Men Is a Revolutionary Act," apparently echoing the rhetoric of early middle-class feminism. Furthermore, the men who carry this banner are arguably marked as middle-class, their bodies sculpted into the bulging, muscular style so prominent in the gay ghettos of San Francisco and New York.[39]

Champagne's critique is problematic in several ways. First, it is based on the premise that *Tongues Untied* elides the issue of class in its focus on race and homosexuality. Champagne then goes on to demonstrate the ways in which the film speaks to a middle-class sensibility. What is missing here is an explanation as to why black middle-class status precludes one from socially and politically engaging issues of race and sexuality. Because Champagne does not provide such an explanation, the reader is left to assume that the black middle-class subject position, as Valerie Smith has suggested, "is a space of pure compromise and capitulation, from which all autonomy disappears once it encounters hegemonic power."[40] Second, in his class-based analysis Champagne reads literary selections, material goods, and clothing aesthetics as "evidence" of the film's middle-class leanings. However, he fails to recognize that the *appearance* of belonging to a particular class does not always reflect one's actual class status. In the black community, for instance, middle-class status is often performed—what is referred to in the vernacular as acting "boojee" (bourgeois). The way a black person adorns herself or publicly displays his material possessions may not necessarily reflect his or her economic status. Put another way, one might *live* in the projects but not necessarily *appear* to.[41] Champagne, however, misreads signs of class in the film in order to support his thesis that middle-class status in the film is symptomatic of deeply rooted sexual conservatism and homophobia. Incredibly, he links this conservatism not only to that of antiporn feminists but also to political bigots like Jesse Helms.[42]

I am perplexed as to why the film cannot privilege black, middle-class gay experience. Is *Tongues Untied* a red herring of black gay representation because it does not do the discursive work that Champagne wishes it to do? Is it *The Cosby Show* in "gay face" because it portrays black middle-class life (and I'm not so sure that it does)? Positioning the film in such a light seems to bespeak just the land of essentialism that Champagne so adamantly argues against. That is, he links class and epistemology to serve the purpose of his critique, yet dismisses race-based ways of knowing. Why is class privileged epistemologically while "raced" ways of knowing are dismissed? Champagne states that "to point out that Riggs's film seems to privilege the (discursive) experience of largely middle-class urban Black gay men and to employ conventions of filmmaking familiar to a middle-class audience is not, in and of itself, a criticism of the video."[43] This disclaimer notwithstanding, Champagne goes on to do a close (mis) reading of various moments and aesthetics of the film—from specific scenes to what he argues is the film's "experimental documentary" style—to substantiate his class critique.

Unlike Champagne's deployment of queer theory, the model of quare studies that I propose would not only critique the concept of "race" as historically contingent and socially and culturally constructed/performed, it would also address the material effects of race in a white supremacist society. Quare studies requires an acknowledgment by the critic of her or his position within an oppressive system. To fail to do so would, as Ruth Goldman argues, "[leave] the burden of dealing with difference on the people who are themselves different, while simultaneously allowing white academics to construct a discourse of silence around race and other queer perspectives."[44] One's "experience" within that system, however discursively mediated, is also materially conditioned. A critic cannot ethically and responsibly speak from a privileged place, as Champagne does, and not own up to that privilege. To do so is to maintain the force of hegemonic whiteness, which, until very recently, has gone uninterrogated.[45]

"Quaring" the queer: troping the trope

Queer studies has rightfully problematized identity politics by elaborating on the processes by which agents and subjects come into being; however, there is a critical gap in queer studies between theory and practice, performance and performativity. Quare studies can narrow that gap to the extent that it pursues an epistemology rooted in the body. As a "theory in the flesh," quare necessarily engenders a kind of identity politics, one that acknowledges difference within and between particular groups. Thus, identity politics does not necessarily mean the reduction of multiple identities into a monolithic identity or narrow cultural nationalism. Rather, quare studies moves beyond simply theorizing subjectivity and agency as discursively mediated to theorizing how that mediation may propel material bodies into action. As Shane Phelan reminds us, the maintenance of a progressive identity politics asks "not whether we share a given position but whether we share a commitment to improve it, and whether we can commit to the pain of embarrassment and confrontation as we disagree."[46]

Quare studies would reinstate the subject and the identity around which the subject circulates that queer theory so easily dismisses. By refocusing our attention on the racialized bodies, experiences, and knowledges of transgendered people, lesbians, gays, and bisexuals of color, quare studies grounds the discursive process of mediated identification and subjectivity in a political praxis that speaks to the material existence of "colored" bodies. While strategically galvanized around identity, quare studies should be committed to interrogating identity claims that exclude rather than include. I am thinking here of black nationalist claims of "black authenticity" that exclude, categorically, homosexual identities. Blind allegiance to "isms" of any kind is one of the fears of queer theorists who critique identity politics. Cognizant of that risk, quare studies must not deploy a totalizing and/or homogeneous formulation of identity, but rather a contingent, fragile coalition in the struggle against common oppressive forms.

A number of queer theorists have proposed potential strategies (albeit limited ones) that may be deployed in the service of dismantling oppressive systems. Most significantly, Judith Butler's formulation of performativity has had an important impact not only on gender and sexuality studies, but on queer studies as well. While I am swayed by Butler's formulation of gender performativity, I am disturbed by her theory's failure to articulate a meatier politics of resistance. For example, what are the implications of dismantling subjectivity and social will to ground zero within oppressive regimes? Does an overemphasis on the free play of signifiers propel us beyond a state of quietism to address the very real injustices in the world? The body, I believe, has to be theorized in ways that not only describe the ways in which it is brought into being but also what it *does* once it *is* constituted and the relationship between it and the other bodies around it. In other words, I desire a rejoinder to performativity that allows a space for subjectivity, for agency (however momentary and discursively fraught), and, ultimately, for change.

Therefore, to complement notions of performativity, quare studies also deploys theories of performance. Performance theory not only highlights the discursive effects of acts, it also points to how these acts are historically situated. Butler herself acknowledges that the conflation of "performativity to performance would be a mistake."[47] Indeed, the focus on performativity alone may problematically reduce performativity and performance to one interpretative frame to theorize human experience. On the other hand, focusing on both may bring together two interpretative frames whose relationship is more dialogical and dialectical.

In her introduction to *Performance and Cultural Politics*, Elin Diamond proposes such a relationship between performance and performativity:

> When being is de-essentialized, when gender and even race are understood as fictional ontologies, modes of expression without true substance, the idea of performance comes to the fore. But performance both affirms and denies this evacuation of substance. In the sense that the "I" has no interior secure ego or core identity, "I" must always enunciate itself: there is only performance of a self, not an external representation of an interior truth. But in the sense that I do my performance in public, for spectators who are interpreting and/or performing with me, there are real effects, meanings solicited or imposed that produce relations in the real. Can performance make a difference? A performance, whether it inspires love or loathing, often consolidates cultural or subcultural affiliations, and these affiliations, might be as regressive as they are progressive. The point is, as soon as performativity comes to rest on *a* performance, questions of embodiment and political effects, all become discussible.
>
> Performance . . . is precisely the site in which concealed or dissimulated conventions might be investigated. When performativity materializes as performance in that risky and dangerous negotiation between doing (a reiteration of norms) and a thing done (discursive conventions that frame our interpretations), between somebody's body and the conventions of embodiment, we have access to cultural meanings and critique. Performativity . . . must be rooted in the materiality and historical density of performance.[48]

I quote Diamond at length here because of the implications that her construal of performance and performativity have for reinstating subjectivity and agency through the performance of identity. Although fleeting and ephemeral, these performances may activate a politics of subjectivity.

The performance of self is not only a performance or construction of identity for or toward an "out there," or even merely an attachment or "taking up"[49] of a predetermined, discursively contingent identity. It is also a performance of self for the self in a moment of self-reflexivity that has the potential to transform one's view of self in relation to the world. People have a need to exercise control over the production of their images so that they feel empowered. For the disenfranchised, the recognition, construction, and maintenance of self-image and cultural identity function to sustain, even when social systems and codes fail to do so. Granted, formations or performances of identity may simply reify oppressive systems, but they may also contest and subvert dominant meaning systems. When gays, lesbians, bisexuals, and transgendered people "talk back," whether using the "tools of the master"[50] or the vernacular on the street, their voices, singularly or collectively, do not exist in some vacuous wasteland of discursivity. As symbolic anthropologist Victor Turner suggests, their performances

> are not simple reflectors or expressions of culture or even of changing culture but may themselves be active *agencies* of change, representing the eye by which culture sees itself and the drawing board on which creative actors sketch out what they believe to be more apt or interesting "designs for living." . . . Performative reflexivity is a condition in which a sociocultural group, or its most perceptive members acting representatively, turn, bend, or reflect back upon

> themselves, upon the relations, actions, symbols, meanings, codes, roles,
> statuses, social structures, ethical and legal rules, and other sociocultural
> components which make up their public selves.[51]

Turner's theory of performative cultural reflexivity suggests a transgressive aspect of performative identity that neither dissolves identity into a fixed "I" nor presumes a monolithic "we." Rather, Turner's assertions suggest that social beings "look back" and "look forward" in a manner that wrestles with the ways in which that community of folk exists in the world and theorizes that existence. As Cindy Patton warns, not everyone who claims an identity does so in the ways that critics of essentialist identity claim they do.[52]

Theories of performance, as opposed to theories of performativity, also take into account the context and historical moment of performance.[53] We need to account for the temporal and spatial specificity of performance not only to frame its existence, but also to name the ways in which it signifies. Such an analysis would acknowledge the discursivity of subjects and it would also "unfix" the discursively constituted subject as always already a pawn of power. Although many queer theorists appropriate Foucault to substantiate the imperialism of power, Foucault himself acknowledges that discourse has the potential to disrupt power: "Discourses are not once and for all subservient to power or raised up against it, any more than silences are. We must make allowances for the complex and unstable process whereby discourse can be both an instrument and an effect of power, but also a hindrance, a stumbling-block, a point of resistance and a starting point for an opposing strategy. Discourse transmits and produces power; it reinforces it, *but also undermines and exposes it, renders it fragile and makes it possible to thwart it.*"[54] Although people of color, myself included, may not have theorized our lives in Foucault's terms, we have used discourse in subversive ways because it was necessary for our survival. Failure to ground discourse in materiality is to privilege the position of those whose subjectivity and agency, outside the realm of gender and sexuality, have never been subjugated. The tendency of many lesbians, bisexuals, gays, and transgendered people of color is to unite around a racial identity at a moment when their subjectivity is already under erasure.

Elaborating more extensively on the notion of performance as a site of agency for lesbian, gay, bisexual, and transgendered people of color, Latino performance theorist José Muñoz proposes a theory of "disidentification" whereby queers of color work within and against dominant ideology to effect change: "Disidentification is [a] mode of dealing with dominant ideology, one that neither opts to assimilate within such a structure nor strictly opposes it; rather, disidentification is a strategy that works on and against dominant ideology. Instead of buckling under the pressures of dominant ideology (identification, assimilation) or attempting to break free of its inescapable sphere (counteridentification, utopianism), this 'working on and against' is a strategy that tries to transform a cultural logic from within, always laboring to enact permanent structural change while at the same time valuing the importance of local and everyday struggles of resistance."[55] Muñoz's concept of "disidentification" reflects the process through which people of color have always managed to survive in a white supremacist society: by "working on and against" oppressive institutional structures.

The performance strategies of African Americans who labored and struggled under human bondage exemplify this disidentificatory practice. For instance, vernacular traditions that emerged among enslaved Africans—including folktales, spirituals, and the blues—provided the foundation for social and political empowerment. These discursively mediated forms, spoken and filtered through "black" bodies, enabled survival. The point here is that the inheritance of hegemonic discourses does not preclude one from "disidentifying," from putting those discourses in the service of resistance. Although they had no institutional power, enslaved blacks refused to become helpless victims and instead enacted their agency by cultivating discursive weapons based on an identity as oppressed people. The result was the creation of folktales about the "bottom rail becoming the top riser" (i.e., the slave rising out of slavery) or spirituals that called folks to "Gather at the River" (i.e., to plan an escape).

These resistant vernacular performances did not disappear with slavery. Gays, lesbians, bisexuals, and transgendered people of color continued to enact performative agency to work on and against oppressive systems. Quare singers like Bessie Smith and Ma Rainey, for instance, used the blues to challenge the notion of inferior black female subjectivity and covertly brought the image of the black lesbian into the American imaginary.[56] Later, through his flamboyant style and campy costumes, Little Richard not only fashioned himself as the "emancipator" and "originator" of rock-n-roll, he also offered a critique of hegemonic black and white masculinity in the music industry. Later still, the black transgendered singer Sylvester transformed disco with his high, soaring falsetto voice and gospel riffs. Indeed, Sylvester's music transcended the boundary drawn between the church and the world, between the sacred and profane, creating a space for other quare singers, like Blackberri, who would come after him. Even RuPaul's drag of many flavors demonstrates the resourcefulness of quares of color to reinvent themselves in ways that transform their material conditions. Quare vernacular tools operate outside the realm of musical and theatrical performance as well. Performance practices such as vogueing, snapping, "throwing shade," and "reading" attest to the ways in which black gays, lesbians, bisexuals, and transgendered people demonstrate the ways of devising technologies of self-assertion and summoning the agency to resist.[57]

Taken together, performance and quare theories alert us to the ways in which these disidentificatory performances serve material ends, and they do this work by accounting for the context in which these performances occur. The stage, for instance, is not confined solely to the theater, the dance club, or the concert hall. Streets, social services lines, picket lines, loan offices, and emergency rooms, among others, may also serve as useful staging grounds for disidentificatory performances. Theorizing the social context of performance sutures the gap between discourse and lived experience by examining how quares use performance as a strategy of survival in their day-to-day experiences. Such an analysis requires that we, like Robin Kelley, reconceptualize "play" (performance) as "work."[58] Moreover, quare theory focuses attention on the social consequences of those performances. It is one thing to do drag on the club stage, yet quite another to embody a drag queen identity on the street. Bodies are sites of discursive effects, but they are sites of social ones as well.

I do not wish to suggest that quare vernacular performances do not, at times, ideologically collude with sexist, misogynist, racist, and even homophobic constructions of the Other. Lesbian, bisexual, gay, and transgendered people of color must always realize that we cannot transgress for transgression's sake lest our work end up romanticizing and prolonging our state of struggle and that of others. In other words, while we may all occasionally enjoy the pleasures of "transgressive" performance, we must transgress responsibly or run the risk of creating and sustaining representations of ourselves that are anti-gay, anti-woman, anti-transgender, anti-working class, and anti-black. Despite this risk, we must not retreat to the position that changes within the system are impossible. The social movements of the past century are testament that change is possible.

Ultimately, quare studies offers a more utilitarian theory of identity politics, focusing not just on performers and effects, but also on contexts and historical situatedness. It does not, as bell hooks warns, separate the "politics of difference from the politics of racism."[59] Quare studies grants space for marginalized individuals to enact "radical black subjectivity,"[60] by adopting the both/and posture of "disidentification." Quare studies proposes a theory grounded in a critique of essentialism and an enactment of political praxis. Thus, such theorizing may *strategically* embrace identity politics while also acknowledging the contingency of identity, a double move that Angelia Wilson adroitly describes as "politically necessary and politically dangerous."[61]

Seeing through quare eyes: reading Marlon Riggs's *Black Is . . . Black Ain't*

In Marlon Riggs's documentary, *Black Is . . . Black Ain't*, we find an example of quare theory operationalized, and hence a demonstration of the possibilities of quare. Completed after Riggs's death in 1994, this documentary chronicles his battle with AIDS and also serves as a meditation on the embattled status of black identity. *Black Is . . . Black Ain't* "quares" "queer" by suggesting that identity, although highly contested, manifests itself in the flesh and, therefore, has social and political consequences for those who live in that flesh. Further "quaring" queer, the film also allows for agency and authority by visually privileging Riggs's AIDS experience narrative. Indeed, the film's documentation of Riggs's declining health suggests an identity and a body in the process of *being* and *becoming*. Quare theory elucidates the mechanics of this both/and identity formation and, in so doing, it challenges a static reading of identity as only performativity or only performance.

In examining this issue I will first focus on how the film engages performativity, focusing as it does on problematizing notions of essential blackness. One of the ways in which the film engages this critique is by pointing out how, at the very least, gender, class, sexuality, and region all impact the construction of blackness. Indeed, even the title of the film points to the ways in which race defines, as well as confines, African Americans. The recurrent trope used by Riggs to illuminate the multiplicity of blackness is that of gumbo, a dish that consists of whatever ingredients the cook wishes to use. It has, Riggs remarks, "everything you can imagine in it."[62] This trope also underscores the multiplicity of blackness insofar as gumbo is a dish associated with New Orleans, a city confounded by its mixed-raced progeny and the identity politics that mixing creates. The gumbo trope is apropos because, like "blackness," gumbo is a site of possibilities. The film argues that when African Americans attempt to define what it means to be black, they delimit the possibilities of what blackness can be. But Riggs's film does more than just stir things up. In many ways it reduces the heat of the pot, allowing everything in the gumbo to mix and mesh, yet maintain its own distinct flavor. Chicken is distinct from andouille sausage, rice from peas, bay leaves from thyme, cayenne from paprika. Thus, Riggs's film suggests that African Americans cannot begin to ask dominant culture to accept either their difference as "others" or their humanity until African Americans accept the differences that exist among themselves.

Class represents a significant axis and divisiveness within black communities. As Martin Favor persuasively argues, "authentic" blackness is most often associated with the "folk," or working-class blacks.[63] Moreover, art forms such as the blues and folklore that are associated with the black working class are also viewed as more genuinely black. This association of the folk with black authenticity necessarily renders the black middle class as inauthentic and apolitical. In *Black Is . . . Black Ain't*, Riggs intervenes in this construction of the black middle class as "less black" by featuring a potpourri of blacks from various backgrounds. Importantly, those who might be considered a part of the "folk" questionably offer some of the most anti-black sentiments, while those black figures most celebrated in the film—Angela Davis, Barbara Smith, Michele Wallace, and Cornel West—are of the baby boomer generation. Riggs undermines the idea that "authentic" blackness belongs to the black working class by prominently displaying interviews with Davis, Wallace, and Smith. While ostracized for attending integrated schools and speaking Standard English or another language altogether, these women deny that their blackness was ever compromised. The film critiques hegemonic notions of blackness based on class status by locating the founding moment of black pride and radical black activism within black middle-class communities in the 1960s, thereby reminding us that "middle class" is also an ideological construct as contingently constituted as other social and subject positionalities.

Riggs also unhinges the link between hegemonic masculinity and authentic blackness. By excerpting misogynist speeches by Louis Farrakhan, a southern black preacher, and the leader of an "African" village located in South Carolina and then juxtaposing them with the personal narratives of bell hooks and Angela Davis, Riggs undermines the historical equation of "real" blackness with black masculinity. The narrative that hooks relates regarding her mother's spousal abuse is intercut with and undercuts Farrakhan's sexist and misogynist justification of Mike Tyson's sexual advances that eventually led to his being accused of and convicted for raping Desiree Washington. The narrative set forth by hooks's story also brackets the sexism inherent in the black preacher's and African leader's justification of the subjugation of women based on biblical and African mythology. Musically framing this montage of narratives is rap artist Queen Latifah's performance of "U-N-I-T-Y," a song that urges black women to "let black men know you ain't a bitch or a 'ho.' "[64] Riggs's decision to use Latifah's song to administer this critique is interesting on a number of levels, the most notable of which is that Latifah's own public persona, as well as her television and motion picture roles, embody a highly masculinized femininity or, alternatively, what Judith Halberstam might call "female masculinity."[65] Riggs uses Latifah's song and the invocation of her persona in the service of further disrupting hegemonic constructions of black masculinity, as well as illuminating the sexism found within the black community.

While I find the film's critique of essentialized blackness persuasive, I find even more compelling its critique of homophobia in the black community and its demand for a space for homosexual identity within constructions of blackness. As a rhetorical strategy, Riggs first points to those signifiers of blackness that build community (e.g., language, music, food, and religion). Indeed, the opening of the film with the chantlike call and response of black folk preaching references a communal cultural site instantly recognizable to many African Americans. But just as the black church has been a political and social force in the struggle for the racial freedom of its constituents, it has also, to a large extent, occluded sexual freedom for many of its practitioners, namely gays and lesbians. Thus, in those opening scenes, Riggs calls attention to the double standard found within the black church by exemplifying how blackness can "build you up, or bring you down," hold you in high esteem or hold you in contempt. Riggs not only calls attention to the racism of whites; he also calls attention to homophobia in the black community, particularly in the black church. Throughout the film, however, Riggs challenges the traditional construction of the black church by featuring a black gay and lesbian church service. Given the black church's typical stance on homosexuality, some might view this avowal of Christianity as an instance of false consciousness. I argue, however, that these black gays and lesbians are employing disidentification insofar as they value the cultural rituals of the black worship service yet resist the fundamentalism of its message. In the end, the film intervenes in the construction of black homosexuality as antiblack by propagating gay Christianity as a legitimate signifier of blackness.

Riggs's film implicitly employs performativity to suggest that we dismantle hierarchies that privilege particular black positionalities at the expense of others, that we recognize that a darker hue does not give us any more cultural capital or claim to blackness than does a dashiki, braids, or a southern accent. Masculinity is no more a signifier of blackness than femininity; heterosexuality is no blacker than homosexuality; and living in the projects makes you no more authentically black than owning a house in the suburbs. Indeed, what Riggs suggests is that we move beyond these categories and these hierarchies that define and confine in order to realize that, depending on where you are from and where you are going, black is and black ain't.

While the film critically interrogates cleavages among blacks, it also exposes the social, political, economic, and psychological effects of racism, and the role racism has played in defining blackness. By adopting this dual focus rather than exclusively interrogating black discursivity, Riggs offers a perspective that is decidedly quare. He calls attention to differences among blacks and between blacks and their "others";[66] he grounds blackness in lived experience; and he calls attention to the consequences of embodied blackness. The montage of footage from the riots in Los Angeles and the interviews with young black men who characterize themselves as "gangbangers" bring into clear focus the material reality of black America and how the black body has historically been the site of violence and trauma.

Nowhere in the film is a black body historicized more pointedly and more powerfully, however, than in the scenes where Riggs is featured walking through the forest naked or narrating from his hospital bed from which his t-cell count is constantly announced. According to Riggs, these scenes are important because he wants to make the point that not until we expose ourselves to one another will we be able to communicate effectively across our differences. Riggs's intentions notwithstanding, his naked black body serves another function within the context of the film. It is simultaneously in a state of being *and* becoming. I intend here to disrupt both of these terms by refusing to privilege identity as either solely performance or solely performativity and by demonstrating the dialogic/dialectic relationship of these two tropes.

Paul Gilroy's theory of diaspora is useful in clarifying the difference between being and becoming. According to Gilroy, "Diaspora accentuates *becoming* rather than *being* and identity conceived diasporically, along these lines, resists reification."[67] Here, Gilroy associates "being" with the transhistorical and transcendental subject and "becoming" with historical situatedness and contingency. In what follows, I supplement Gilroy's use of both terms by suggesting that "being" and "becoming" are sites of performance *and* performativity. I construe "being" as a site of infinite signification as well as bodily and material presence. "Being" calls the viewer's attention not only to "blackness" as discourse, but also to embodied blackness in that moment where discourse and flesh conjoin in performance. If we look beyond Riggs's intent to "expose" himself to encourage cross-difference communication, we find that his nakedness in the woods functions ideologically in ways that he may not wish. For example, his nakedness may conjure up the racist stereotype of the lurking, bestial, and virile black male that became popular in the eighteenth- and nineteenth-century American imaginary. On the other hand, his embodied blackness in the woods and in his hospital bed also indicate a diseased body that is fragile, vulnerable, and a site of trauma, a site that grounds black discursivity materially in the flesh. At the literal level, Riggs's black male body is exposed as fragile and vulnerable, but it also synecdochically stands in for a larger body of racist discourse on the black male body in motion. This trope of black bodily kinesthetics is manifest in various forms (e.g., the vernacular expression, "keep the nigger running"; the image of the fugitive slave; and contemporary, hypermasculinized images of black athletes). Racist readings of Riggs's black male body are made possible by the context in which Riggs's body appears—that is, the woods. Within this setting, blackness becomes problematically aligned with nature, reinscribing the black body as bestial and primal. This imagery works against Riggs's intentions—namely, running naked in the woods as a way to work through the tangled and knotty web that is identity. Indeed, the images of Riggs running naked through the woods signify in multiple troubling ways that, once let loose, cannot be contained by either Riggs's authorial intentions or the viewer's gaze. The beauty of *being*, however, is that where it crumbles under the weight of deconstruction, it reemerges in all its bodily facticity. Although Riggs's body signifies in ways that constrain his agency, his embodied blackness also enlivens a discussion of a "fleshy" nature. Whatever his body signifies, the viewer cannot escape its material presence.

Riggs's body is also a site of becoming: he dies before the film is completed. Riggs's body physically "fades away," but its phantom is reconstituted in our current discourse on AIDS, race, gender, class, and sexuality. Thus, Riggs's body discursively rematerializes and intervenes in hegemonic formulations of blackness, homosexuality, and the HIV-infected person. As a filmic performance, *Black Is . . . Black Ain't* resurrects Riggs's body such that when the film is screened at universities, shown to health care providers, viewed in black communities, or rebroadcast on PBS where it debuted, the terms and the stakes for how we think about identity and its relation to HIV/AIDS are altered. Like Toni Morrison's character Sula, Riggs dreams of water carrying him over that liminal threshold where the water "would envelop [him], carry [him], and wash [his] tired flesh always."[68] After her death, Sula promises to tell her best friend Nel that death did not hurt, ironically announcing her physical death alongside her spiritual rebirthing. Her rebirthing is symbolized by her assuming a fetal position and traveling "over and down the tunnels, just missing the dark walls, down, down until she met a rain scent and would know the water was near."[69] Riggs dreams of a similar journey through water. In his dream, Harriet Tubman serves as a midwife cradling his head at the tunnel's opening and helps him make the journey. Once on the other side, Riggs, like Sula, lives on and also makes good on his promise to return through his living spirit captured in the film. The residual traces of Riggs's body become embedded in the ideological battle over identity claims and the discourse surrounding the disproportionate number of AIDS-infected people of color. His becoming, then, belies our being.

Ultimately, *Black Is . . . Black Ain't* performs what its title announces: the simultaneity of bodily presence and absence, being and becoming. Although Riggs offers his own gumbo recipe that stands in for blackness, he does so only to demonstrate that, like blackness, the recipe can be altered, expanded, reduced, watered down. At the same time, Riggs also asks that we not forget that the gumbo (blackness) is contained within a sturdy pot (the body) that has weathered abuse; that has been scorched, scoured, and scraped; a pot/body that is in the process of becoming, but nonetheless *is*.

Unlike queer theory, quare theory fixes our attention on the discursive constitution of the recipe even as it celebrates the improvisational aspects of the gumbo and the materiality of the pot. While queer theory has opened up new possibilities for theorizing gender and sexuality, like a pot of gumbo cooked too quickly, it has failed to live up to its critical potential by refusing *all* the queer ingredients contained inside its theoretical pot. Quare theory, on the other hand, promises to reduce the spillage, allowing the various and multiple flavors to coexist—those different flavors that make it spicy, hot, unique, and sumptuously brown.

Bringin' it on "home": quare studies on the back porch

Thus far, I have canvassed the trajectory for quare studies inside the academy, focusing necessarily on the intellectual work that needs to be done to advance specific disciplinary goals. While there is intellectual work to be done inside the academy—what one might call "academic praxis"—there is also political praxis outside the academy.[70] If social change is to occur, gays, bisexuals, transgendered people, and lesbians of color cannot afford to be armchair theorists. Some of us need to be in the streets, in the trenches, enacting the quare theories that we construct in the "safety" of the academy. While keeping in mind that political theory and political action are not necessarily mutually exclusive, quare theorists must make theory work for its constituency. Although we share with our white queer peers sexual oppression, gays, lesbians, bisexuals, and transgendered people of color also share racial oppression with other members of our community. We cannot afford to abandon them simply because they are heterosexual. "Although engaged in heterosexual behavior," Cathy

Cohen writes, straight African Americans "have often found themselves outside the norms and values of dominant society. This position has most often resulted in the suppression or negation of their legal, social, and physical relationships and rights."[71] Quare studies must encourage strategic coalition building around laws and policies that have the potential to affect us all across racial, sexual, and class divides. Quare studies must incorporate under its rubric a praxis related to the sites of public policy, family, church, and community. Therefore, in the tradition of radical black feminist critic Barbara Smith,[72] I offer a manifesto that aligns black quare academic theory with political praxis.

We can do more in the realm of public policy. As Cathy Cohen so cogently argues in her groundbreaking book *The Boundaries of Blackness*, we must intervene in the failure of the conservative black leadership to respond to the HIV/AIDS epidemic ravishing African American communities.[73] Due to the growing number of African Americans infected with and contracting HIV, quare theorists must aid in the education and prevention of the spread of HIV as well as care for those who are suffering. This means more than engaging in volunteer work and participating in fund-raising. It also means using our training as academics to deconstruct the way HIV/AIDS is discussed in the academy and in the medical profession. We must continue to do the important work of physically helping our brothers and sisters who are living with HIV and AIDS through outreach services and fund-raising events, but we must also use our scholarly talents to combat the racist and homophobic discourse that circulates in white as well as black communities. Ron Simmons, a black gay photographer and media critic who left academia to commit his life to those suffering with AIDS by forming the organization US Helping US, remains an important role model for how we can use both our academic credentials and our political praxis in the service of social change.

The goal of quare studies is to be specific and intentional in the dissemination and praxis of quare theory, committed to communicating and translating its political potentiality. Indeed, quare theory is "bi"-directional: it theorizes from bottom to top and top to bottom. This dialogical/dialectical relationship between theory and practice, the lettered and unlettered, ivory tower and front porch, is crucial to a joint and sustained critique of hegemonic systems of oppression.

Given the relationship between the academy and the community, quare theorists must value and speak from what bell hooks refers to as "homeplace." According to hooks, homeplace "[is] the one site where one [can] freely confront the issue of humanization, where one [can] resist."[74] It is from homeplace that we people of color live out the contradictions of our lives. Cutting across the lines of class and gender, homeplace provides a place from which to critique oppression. I do not wish to romanticize this site by dismissing the homophobia that circulates within homeplace or the contempt that some of us (of all sexual orientations) have for "home."[75] I am suggesting, rather, that in spite of these contradictions, homeplace is that site that first gave us the "equipment for living"[76] in a racist society, particularly since we, in all of our diversity, have always been a part of this homeplace: housekeepers, lawyers, seamstresses, hairdressers, activists, choir directors, professors, doctors, preachers, mill workers, mayors, nurses, truck drivers, delivery people, nosey neighbors, and (an embarrassed?) "etc." SNAP!

Homeplace is also a site that quare praxis must critique. That is, we may seek refuge in homeplace as a marginally safe place to critique oppression outside its confines, but we must also deploy quare theory to address oppression within homeplace itself. One might begin, for instance, with the black church, which remains for some gays and lesbians a sustaining site of spiritual affirmation, comfort, and an artistic outlet. Quare studies cannot afford to dismiss, cavalierly, the role of the black church in quare lives. However, it must never fail to critique the black church's continual denial of gay and lesbian subjectivity. Our role within the black church is an important one. Those in the pulpit and those in the congregation should be challenged whenever they hide behind Romans and Leviticus to justify their homophobia. We must force the black church to name us and claim us if we are to obtain any liberation within our own communities.[77]

Regarding ideological and political conflicts in gay, lesbian, and transgendered communities of color, quare praxis must interrogate and negotiate the difference among our differences, including our political strategies for dealing with oppression and our politics of life choice and maintenance. Consequently, quare studies must also focus on interracial dating and the identity politics that such couplings invoke. Writer Darieck Scott has courageously addressed this issue, but we need to continue to explore our own inner conflicts around our and our peers' choice of sexual partners across racial lines.[78] Additionally, quare studies should interrogate another contested area of identity politics: relations between "out" and "closeted" members of our community. Much of this work must be done not in the academy but in our communities, in our churches, and in our homes.

Because I am not convinced that queer studies, theory, and activism are soon to change, I summon quare studies as an interventionist disciplinary project. Quare studies addresses the concerns and needs of gay, lesbian, bisexual, and transgendered people across issues of race, gender, and class as well as other identities and subject positions. While attending to discursive fields of knowledge, quare studies is also committed to theorizing the practice of everyday life. Because we exist in discursive as well as material bodies, we need a theory that speaks to that reality. Indeed, quare studies may breathe new life into our "dead" (or deadly) stratagems of survival.

Coda

Because I credit my grandmother for passing on to me the little bit of commonsense I still have, I conclude this essay with a story about her employment of "gaydar,"[79] a story that speaks to how black folk use "motherwit" as a "reading" strategy, as well as a way to "forget all those things they don't want to remember, and remember everything they don't want to forget."[80]

My grandmother lives in western North Carolina. When I went to live with her to collect her oral history for my dissertation, she spent a considerable amount of time catching me up on all of the new residents who had moved into her senior citizens' community. Dressed in her customary polyester cutoff shorts and cotton makeshift blouse, loosely tied sheer scarf draped around her dyed, jet black hair, legs crossed and head cocked to the side, my grandmother described to me, one by one, each of the new residents. She detailed, among other things, their medical histories and conditions, the number of children they had, their marital status, and perhaps most important, whether they were "pickles" or not. She used the term euphemistically to describe people who she believes are "not quite right in the head."

There was one resident, David, in whom my grandmother had a particular interest. I soon learned that David was a seventy-four-year-old white man who had to walk with the support of a walker and who had moved to my grandmother's community from across town. But these facts were not the most important things about David, but rather another fact that my grandmother revealed to me one day: "Well, you know we got one of them 'homalsexuals' living down here," she said, dryly. Not quite sure I had heard her correctly but also afraid that I had, I responded, "A what?" She replied, again just as dryly, "you know, one of them 'homalsexuals.'" This time, however, her voice was tinged with impatience and annoyance. Curious, yet a bit anxious about the turn the conversation was taking (I was not "out" to my grandmother), I pursued the issue further: "Well, how do you know the man's a homosexual, Grandmama?" She paused, rubbed her leg, narrowed her eyes, and responded, "Well, he gardens, bakes pies, and keeps a clean house." (She might not have gone to school, but she could most definitely *read*!) Like a moth to the flame, I opened the door to my own closet for her to walk in, and said, "Well, I cook and keep my apartment clean." Then, after a brief pause, I added, "But I don't like gardening. I don't like getting my hands dirty." As soon as the words "came out" of my mouth, I realized what I had done. My grandmother said nothing. She simply folded her arms and began to rock as if in church. The question she dare not ask sat behind her averted eyes: "You ain't quare are you, Pat?" Yes, Grandmama, quare, indeed.

Notes

1   In the opening pages of *In Search of Our Mothers' Gardens*, Alice Walker coins and defines the term "womanist" in contrast to "feminist," to mark the specificity of women of color's experiences of sexism and racism. I perform a similar critique in the move from "queer" to "quare" in order to include race and class analyses in queer theory. See Alice Walker, *In Search of Our Mothers' Gardens: Womanist Prose* (San Diego: Harcourt Brace Jovanovich, 1983), xi–xii.

2   See James Baldwin, *Nobody Knows My Name: More Notes of a Native Son* (New York: Vintage, 1993) and *No Name in the Street* (New York: Dial, 1972).

3   My grandmother made her transition on July 12, 2004, before the first reprinting of this essay. I dedicate this contribution in her memory.

4   Mae G. Henderson, "Speaking in Tongues," in *Feminists Theorize the Political*, eds. Judith Butler and Joan W. Scott (New York: Routledge, 1992), 147.

5   I have long known about the connection between African Americans and the Irish. As noted in the film *The Commitments*, "The Irish are the blacks of Europe." The connection is there—that is, at least until the Irish became "white." For a sustained discussion of how Irish emigrants obtained "white" racial privilege, see Noel Ignatiev, *How the Irish Became White* (New York: Routledge, 1995).

6   Joseph Valente, "Joyce's (Sexual) Choices: A Historical Overview," in *Quare Joyce*, ed. Joseph Valente (Ann Arbor: University of Michigan Press, 1998), 4; emphasis added.

7   Gloria Anzaldúa, "To(o) Queer the Writer: *Loca, escrita y chicana*," in *Inversions: Writing by Dykes and Lesbians*, ed. Betsy Warland (Vancouver: Press Gang, 1991), 250.

8   For more on "standpoint" theory, see Patricia Hill Collins, "The Social Construction of Black Feminist Thought," in *Words of Fire: An Anthology of African-American Feminist Thought*, ed. Beverly Guy-Sheftall (New York: New Press, 1995), 338–57.

9   Cherríe Moraga and Gloria Anzaldúa, eds., *This Bridge Called My Back: Writings by Radical Women of Color* (New York: Kitchen Table; Women of Color Press, 1983), 23.

10   Judith Butler, in *Bodies That Matter: On the Discursive Limits of "Sex"* (New York: Routledge, 1993), anticipates the contestability of "queer," noting that it excludes as much as it includes but that such a contested term may energize a new kind of political activism. She proposes that "it may be that the critique of the term [queer] will initiate a resurgence of both feminist and anti-racist mobilization within lesbian and gay politics or open up new possibilities for coalitional alliances that do not presume that these constituencies are radically distinct from one another. The term will be revised, dispelled, rendered obsolete to the extent that it yields to the demands which resist the term precisely because of the exclusions by which it is mobilized" (228–29). Moreover, there are gay, bisexual, lesbian, and transgendered people of color who embrace "queer." In my experience, however, those who embrace the term represent a small minority. At the Black Queer Studies in the Millennium conference, for example, many of the attendees were disturbed by the organizers' choice of "queer" for the title of a conference on black sexuality. So ardent was their disapproval that it became a subject of debate during one of the panels.

11   Cherry Smith, "What Is This Thing Called Queer?" in *Material Queer: A LesBiGay Cultural Studies Reader*, ed. Donald Morton (Boulder: Westview, 1996), 280.

12   Eve Kosofsky Sedgwick, "Queer and Now," in *Tendencies* (Durham: Duke University Press, 1993), 9.

13   Ibid., 8.

14   Michael Warner, "Introduction," *Fear of a Queer Planet: Queer Politics and Social Theory*, ed. Michael Warner (Minneapolis: University of Minnesota Press, 1993), xxvi.

15   Lauren Berlant and Michael Warner, "What Does Queer Theory Teach Us about X?" *PMLA* 110 (May 1995): 344.

16   Calvin Thomas, "Straight with a Twist: Queer Theory and the Subject of Heterosexuality," in *The Gay '90s: Disciplinary and Interdisciplinary Formations in Queer Studies*, eds. Thomas Foster, Carol Siegel, and Ellen E. Berry (New York: New York University Press, 1997), 83.

17   Judith Butler, *Gender Trouble: Feminism and the Subversion of Identity* (New York: Routledge, 1990), 143.

18   See, for example, Stuart Hall, "Subjects in History: Making Diasporic Identities," in *The House That Race Built*, ed. Wahneema Lubiano (New York: Pantheon, 1997), 289–99; and Paul Gilroy, " 'Race,' Class, and Agency," in *There Ain't No Black in the Union Jack: The Cultural Politics of Race and Nation* (London: Hutchinson, 1987), 15–42.

19   Barbara Christian, "The Race for Theory," *Cultural Critique* 6 (1985): 51–63.

20   Helen (charles), " 'Queer Nigger': Theorizing 'White' Activism," in *Activating Theory: Lesbian, Gay, Bisexual Politics*, eds. Joseph Bristow and Angelia R. Wilson (London: Lawrence and Wishart, 1993), 101–2.

21   I thank Michèle Barale for this insight.

22   While it is true that many white queer theorists are self-reflexive about their own privilege and indeed incorporate the works and experiences of gays, bisexuals, lesbians, and transgendered people of color into their work, this is not the norm. Paula Moya calls attention to how the theorizing of women of color is appropriated by postmodernist theorists: "[Judith] Butler extracts one sentence from [Cherríe] Moraga, buries it in a footnote, and then misreads it in order to justify her own inability to account for the complex interrelations that structure various forms of human identity." David Bergman also offers a problematic reading of black gay fiction when he reads James Baldwin through the homophobic rhetoric of Eldridge Cleaver and theorizes that black communities are more homophobic than white ones. See Paula Moya, "Postmodernism, 'Realism,' and the Politics of Identity: Cherríe Moraga and Chicano Feminism," in *Feminist Genealogies, Colonial Legacies, Democratic Futures*, eds. M. Jacqui Alexander and Chandra Talpade Mohanty (New York: Routledge, 1997), 133; and David Bergman, *Gaiety Transfigured: Gay Self-Representation in American Literature* (Madison: University of Wisconsin Press, 1991), 163–87. For other critiques of simplistic or dismissive readings of the works of gays, bisexuals, lesbians, and transgendered people of color, see Helen (charles), " 'Queer Nigger'"; Ki Namaste, " 'Tragic Misreadings': Queer Theory's Erasure of Transgender Identity," in *Queer Studies: A Lesbian, Gay, Bisexual and Transgender Anthology*, eds. Brett Beemyn and Mickey Eliason (New York: New York University Press, 1996), 183–203; and Vivien Ng, "Race Matters," in *Lesbian and Gay Studies: A Critical Introduction*, eds. Andy Medhurst and Sally R. Munt (London: Cassell, 1997), 215–31. One notable exception is Ruth Goldman's "Who is That *Queer* Queer?" in which she, as a white bisexual, calls to task other white queer theorists for their failure to theorize their whiteness: "Those of us who are white tend not to dwell on our race, perhaps because this would only serve to normalize us—reduce our queerness, if you will" (Goldman, "Who Is That *Queer* Queer?" in *Queer Studies: A Lesbian, Gay, Bisexual and Transgender Anthology*, eds. Brett Beemyn and Mickey Eliason [New York: New York University Press, 1996], 169–82).

23   For more on "strategic" essentialism, see Sue-Ellen Case, *The Domain Matrix: Performing Lesbian at the End of Print Culture* (Bloomington: Indiana University Press, 1996), 1–12; Teresa de Lauretis, "The Essence of the Triangle, or Taking the Risk of Essentialism Seriously: Feminist Theory in Italy, the U.S. and Britain," *differences* 1.2 (1989): 3–37; and Diana Fuss, *Essentially Speaking: Feminism, Nature and Difference*, London: Routledge, 1989, 1–21.

24   Cathy Cohen, "Punks, Bulldaggers, and Welfare Queens: The Radical Potential of Queer Politics?" in this volume, 84.

25   For a sustained discussion of queer activists' disavowal of heterosexual political alliances, see Cohen, "Punks, Bulldaggers, and Welfare Queens," 74–95.

26   Audre Lorde, *Sister Outsider* (Freedom, Calif: Crossing, 1984), 112–13; emphasis in original.

27   Champagne draws from Joan Scott's important essay, "The Evidence of Experience" (in *Feminists Theorize the Political*, eds. Judith Butler and Joan W. Scott [New York: Routledge, 1992], 22–40), where Scott argues that "experience" is discursively constituted, mediated by and through linguistic systems and embedded in ideology. Like all discursive terrains, the ground on which "experience" moves is turbulent and supple, quickly disrupting the foothold we think we might have on history and the "evidentiary." Scott writes: "Experience is at once always already an interpretation *and* is in need of interpretation. What counts as experience is neither self-evident nor straightforward; it is always contested, always therefore political. The study of experience, therefore, must call into question its originary status in historical explanation. This will happen when historians take as their project *not* the reproduction and transmission of knowledge said to be arrived at through experience, but the analysis of the production of that knowledge itself" (37; emphasis in original). Scott is particularly concerned here with historiographies that draw on experience as evidentiary, especially in the name

of historicizing difference. "By remaining within the epistemological frame of orthodox history," Scott argues, "these studies lose the possibility of examining those assumptions and practices that excluded considerations of difference in the first place" (24–25).

28   Robert Mapplethorpe's photographs of black gay men have been and continue to be the source of great controversy in the black gay community. The reactions to the photos range from outrage to ambivalence to appreciation. I believe the most complex reading of Mapplethorpe is found in Isaac Julien and Kobena Mercer's essay "True Confessions: A Discourse on Images of Black Male Sexuality" (in *Brother to Brother: New Writings on Black Gay Men*, ed. Essex Hemphill [Boston: Alyson, 1991]). They write: "While we recognize the oppressive dimension of these images of black men as Other, we are also attracted: We want to look but don't always find the images we want to see. This ambivalent mixture of attraction and repulsion goes for images of black gay men in porn generally, but the inscribed or preferred meanings of these images are not fixed; they can, at times, be pried apart into alternative readings when different experiences are brought to bear on their interpretation" (170).

29   John Champagne, *The Ethics of Marginality: A New Approach to Gay Studies* (Minneapolis: University of Minnesota Press, 1995), 59.

30   Ibid., 58.

31   Ibid., 58–59.

32   I thank D. Soyini Madison for raising this issue.

33   I am speaking specifically about the historical devaluing of black bodies. In no way do I mean to deny that white gay, lesbian, bisexual, and transgendered people have been emotionally, psychologically, and physically harmed. The recent murder of Matthew Shepard is a sad testament to this fact. Indeed, given the ways in which his attackers killed him (i.e., tying him to a post, beating him, and leaving him for dead), there is a way in which we may read Shepard's murder through a racial lens. What I am suggesting, however, is that racial violence (or the threat of it) is enacted on "black" bodies in different ways and for different reasons than it is on "white" bodies.

34   bell hooks, *Yearning* (Boston: South End, 1990), 21, 22.

35   Champagne, *The Ethics of Marginality*, 127–28.

36   hooks, *Yearning*, 22.

37   Ibid.

38   "Emotionality" as manipulative or putatively repugnant may also be read through the lens of gender. Generally understood as a weak (read feminine) gender performance, emotional display among men of any race or sexual orientation represents a threat to heteronormativity and therefore is usually met with disapproval.

39   Champagne, *The Ethics of Marginality*, 68–69.

40   Valerie Smith, *Not Just Race, Not Just Gender: Making Feminist Readings* (New York: Routledge, 1998), 67.

41   I do not wish to suggest that the appearance of poverty or wealth never reflects that one is actually poor or wealthy. What I am suggesting, however, is that in many African American communities, style figures more substantively than some might imagine. Accordingly, there exists a politics of taste among African Americans that is performed so as to dislodge fixed perceptions about who one is or where one is from. In many instances, for example, performing a certain middle-class style has enabled African Americans to "pass" in various and strategically savvy ways. For more on the performance of style in African American communities, see Barbara Smith, "Home" in *Home Girls: A Black Feminist Anthology* (New York: Kitchen Table; Women of Color Press, 1983), 64–72; and Joseph Beam, "Introduction: Leaving the Shadows Behind," in *In the Life*, ed. Joseph Beam (Boston: Alyson, 1986), 13–18. For a theoretical perspective on the politics of taste, see Pierre Bourdieu, *Distinction: A Social Critique of the Judgment of Taste*, trans. Richard Nice (Cambridge: Harvard University Press, 1984).

42   Champagne writes: "Like the white antiporn feminists whose rhetoric they sometimes share, intellectuals like Riggs and Hemphill may in fact be expressing in *Tongues Untied* a (middle-) class-inflected sense of disgust related to sexuality—obviously, not related to all sexuality, but to a particularly culturally problematic kind. It is perhaps thus not a coincidence at all that the rhetoric deployed by Hemphill in his reading of Mapplethorpe should be so similar to that of Dworkin, Stoltenberg, and even Jesse Helms" (*The Ethics of Marginality*, 79).

43   Ibid., 69.

44   Goldman, "Who Is That *Queer* Queer?" 173.

45   For examples of white critics who interrogate "whiteness" as an obligatory and universalizing trope, see Ruth Frankenberg, ed., *Displacing Whiteness: Essays in Social and Cultural Criticism* (Durham: Duke

University Press, 1997); Mike Hill, ed., *Whiteness: A Critical Reader* (New York: New York University Press, 1997); and David Roediger, *Towards the Abolition of Whiteness* (London: Verso, 1994).

46   Shane Phelan, *Getting Specific* (Minneapolis: University of Minnesota Press, 1994), 156.

47   Judith Butler, *Bodies That Matter*, 234.

48   Elin Diamond, ed., "Introduction," in *Performance and Cultural Politics* (New York: Routledge, 1996), 5; emphasis in original.

49   Butler, *Gender Trouble*, 145.

50   Lorde, *Sister Outsider*, 110.

51   Victor Turner, *The Anthropology of Performance* (New York: Performing Arts Journal, 1986), 24; emphasis added.

52   Cindy Patton, "Performativity and Social Distinction: The End of AIDS Epidemiology." *Performativity and Performance*, eds. Andrew Parker and Eve Kosofsky Sedgwick (New York: Routledge, 1995), 181.

53   Mary Strine, "Articulating Performance/Performativity: Disciplinary Tasks and the Contingencies of Practice," paper presented at the National Speech Communication Association conference, San Diego, November 1996, 7.

54   Michel Foucault, *The History of Sexuality, Volume 1*, trans. Robert Hurley (New York: Random House, 1990), 100–101; emphasis added.

55   José Esteban Muñoz, *Disidentifications: Queers of Color and the Performance of Politics* (Minneapolis: University of Minnesota Press, 1999), 11–12.

56   For an analysis of Bessie Smith's explicitly lesbian blues songs, see Daphne Duval Harrison, *Black Pearls: Blues Queens of the 1920s* (New Brunswick: Rutgers University Press, 1998), 103–4.

57   See Marlon Riggs, "Black Macho Revisited: Reflections of a SNAP! Queen," in *Brother to Brother: New Writings by Black Gay Men*, ed. Essex Hemphill (Boston: Alyson, 1991), 253–57; E. Patrick Johnson, "SNAP! Culture: A Different Kind of 'Reading,' " *Text and Performance Quarterly* 15.3 (1995): 121–42; and E. Patrick Johnson, "Feeling the Spirit in the Dark: Expanding Notions of the Sacred in the African American Gay Community," 21 *Callaloo* (1998): 399–418.

58   Robin D.G. Kelley, "Looking to Get Paid: How Some Black Youth Put Culture to Work," in *Yo Mama's Disfunktional!: Fighting the Culture Wars in Urban America* (Boston: Beacon, 1997), 43–77.

59   hooks, *Yearning*, 26.

60   Ibid.

61   Angelia R. Wilson, "Somewhere over the Rainbow: Queer Translating," in *Playing with Fire: Queer Politics, Queer Theories*, ed. Shane Phelan (New York: Routledge, 1997), 107.

62   *Black Is . . . Black Ain't*, dir. Marlon Riggs (Independent Film Series, 1995).

63   See Martin Favor, *Authentic Blackness: The Folk in the New Negro Renaissance* (Durham: Duke University Press, 1999).

64   Queen Latifah, "U.N.I.T.Y." from *Black Reign* (Motown, 1993).

65   Judith Halberstam, *Female Masculinity* (Durham: Duke University Press, 1998), 1–42.

66   Paul Gilroy's construction of the "Diaspora" functions similarly to what I mean here in that he propagates that "Diaspora" "allows for a complex conception of sameness and an idea of solidarity that does not repress the differences within in order to maximize the differences between one 'essential' community and others." See Paul Gilroy, "'. . . to be real': The Dissident Forms of Black Expressive Culture," in *Let's Get It On: The Politics of Black Performance*, ed. Catherine Ugwu (Seattle: Bay Press, 1995), 24.

67   Ibid.

68   Toni Morrison, *Sula* (New York: Knopf, 1973), 149.

69   Ibid.

70   I do not wish to suggest that the academy is not always already a politicized site. Rather, I only mean to suggest that the ways in which it is politicized are, in many instances, different from the ways in which "nonacademic" communities are politicized.

71   Cohen, "Punks, Bulldaggers, and Welfare Queens," in this volume, 87.

72   See Barbara Smith, "Toward a Black Feminist Criticism," in *All the Women Are White, All the Blacks Are Men, But Some of Us Are Brave*, eds. Gloria T. Hull, Patricia Bell Scott, and Barbara Smith (Old Westbury, N.Y.: Feminist Press, 1982), 157–75.

73   Cathy Cohen, *The Boundaries of Blackness: AIDS and the Breakdown of Black Politics* (Chicago: University of Chicago Press, 1999).

74   hooks, *Yearning*, 42.

75   For a critique of the notion of "home" in the African American community vis-à-vis homophobia and sexism, see Joseph Beam, "Brother to Brother: Words from the Heart," in *In the Life: A Black Gay Anthology*, ed. Joseph Beam (Boston: Alyson, 1986); Cheryl Clarke, "The Failure to Transform: Homophobia in the Black Community," in *Home Girls: A Black Feminist Anthology*, ed. Barbara Smith

(New York: Kitchen Table; Women of Color Press, 1983), 197–208; Kimberlé Williams Crenshaw, "Mapping the Margins: Intersectionality, Identity Politics, and Violence against Women of Color," *Stanford Law Review* 43 (1991): 1241–99; hooks, *Yearning*; and Ron Simmons, "Some Thoughts on the Issues Facing Black Gay Intellectuals," in *Brother to Brother: New Writings by Black Gay Men*, ed. Essex Hemphill (Boston: Alyson, 1991), 211–28.

76   Kenneth Burke, *Philosophy of Literary Form* (Baton Rouge: Louisiana State University Press, 1967), 293.

77   For a sustained critique of homophobia in the black church, see Michael Eric Dyson, "The Black Church and Sex," in *Race Rules: Navigating the Color Line* (Reading, Mass.: Addison-Wesley, 1996), 77–108.

78   See Darieck Scott, "Jungle Fever? Black Gay Identity Politics, White Dick, and the Utopian Bedroom," *GLQ: A Journal of Lesbian and Gay Studies 1.3* 3 (1994): 299–32.

79   "Gaydar," a pun on "radar," is a term some gays and lesbians use to signal their ability to determine whether or not someone is gay.

80   Zora Neale Hurston, *Their Eyes Were Watching God* (New York: Harper and Row, 1990), 1.

Chapter 7

Roderick A. Ferguson

INTRODUCTION: QUEER OF COLOR CRITIQUE, HISTORICAL MATERIALISM, AND CANONICAL SOCIOLOGY

Roderick A. Ferguson is Professor of American Studies at the University of Minnesota. He is the author of *Aberrations in Black: Toward a Queer of Color Critique* (2004), from which the following excerpt is taken. A sociologist who specializes in American Studies, Ferguson's scholarship examines queer African American culture, contemporary and classical social theory, and ethnic and racial social history.

In this excerpt from his introduction, Ferguson promotes a queer of color analysis that considers how gender and sexual norms are racialized within the context of capitalism. In doing so, Ferguson calls attention to the paradoxical nature of capital—capital's reinforcement of heteropatriarchal universals and its disruption of such universals due to the necessity for surplus labor within a capitalist system. Ferguson discusses the black drag-queen prostitute as a figure that aptly demonstrates not only the racialization of gender and sexual norms, but also the disorganizing effects of capital and the limitations of Marxist analysis in accounting for intersections of race, gender, and sexuality in relation to capital. Despite Ferguson's critique of Marxism, he argues for a revised use of historical materialism—one that acknowledges the formative role that race, gender, and sexuality play in political and economic relations.

IN MARLON RIGGS'S *Tongues Untied*, a black drag-queen prostitute sashays along a waterfront. She has decked herself in a faux leather bomber and a white tiger-striped dress that stops just below her knees. Her face is heavy with foundation as she ponders into the distance. She holds a cigarette between fingers studded with cheap press-on nails, dragging on it with lips painted red. A poem by Essex Hemphill and a ballad by Nina Simone drum in the background. It is difficult to discern whether she is melancholic about her life or simply satisfied. This uncertainty, this hint of pleasure and alrightness, flies in the face of those who say that her life is nothing more than a tangle of pathologies and misfortunes. In the pleasure of her existence lies a critique of commonplace interpretations of her life. Doubtless, she knows that her living is not easy. But that's a long way from reducing the components of her identity to the conditions of her labor. Conceding to the meanness of life, probably for her, is a far cry from assuming that her gender and sexual difference are the reason for her poverty and that who she is attests to the absence of agency.

This scene captures the defining elements of this book. In the film, the drag-queen prostitute is a fixture of urban capitalism. Figures like her, ones that allegedly represent the socially disorganizing effects of capital, play a powerful part in past and contemporary interpretations of political economy. In those narratives, she stands for a larger black culture as it has engaged various economic and social formations. That engagement has borne a range of alienations, each estrangement securing another: her racial difference is inseparable from her sexual incongruity, her gender eccentricity, and her class marginality. Moreover, the country of her birth will call out to "the American people" and never mean her or others like her. She is multiply determined, regulated, and excluded by differences of race, class, sexuality, and gender. As drag-queen prostitute, she embodies the intersections of formations thought to be discrete and transparent, a confusion of that which distinguishes the heterosexual (i.e., "prostitute") from the homosexual (i.e., "drag queen"). She is disciplined by those within and outside African American communities, reviled by leftist-radicals, conservatives, heterosexuals, and mainstream queers alike, erased by those who wish to present or make African American culture the embodiment of all that she is not—respectability, domesticity, heterosexuality, normativity, nationality, universality, and progress. But her estrangements are not hers to own. They are, in fact, the general estrangements of African American culture. In its distance from the ideals upheld by epistemology, nationalisms, and capital, that culture activates forms of critique.

The scene, thus, represents the social heterogeneity that characterizes African American culture. To make sense of that culture as the site of gender and sexual formations that have historically deviated from national ideals, we must situate that culture within the genealogy of liberal capitalist economic and social formations. That genealogy can, in turn, help us perceive how the racialized gender and sexual diversity pertaining to African American cultural formations is part of the secular trends of capitalist modes of production. These are trends that manifest themselves globally, linking terrains separated by time and space.

Queer of color and the critique of liberal capitalism

The preceding paragraphs suggest that African American culture indexes a social heterogeneity that oversteps the boundaries of gender propriety and sexual normativity. That social heterogeneity also indexes formations that are seemingly outside the spatial and temporal bounds of African American culture. These arguments oblige us to ask what mode of analysis would be appropriate for interpreting the drag-queen prostitute as an image that allegorizes and symbolizes that social heterogeneity, a heterogeneity that associates African American culture with gender and sexual variation and critically locates that culture within the genealogy of the West. To assemble such a mode of interpretation, we may begin with the nascent and emergent formation known as queer of color analysis.[1]

In "Home, Houses, Nonidentity: 'Paris Is Burning,'" Chandan Reddy discusses the expulsion of queers of color from literal homes and from the privileges bestowed by the nation as "home." Reddy's essay begins with the silences that both marxism and liberal pluralism share, silences about the intersections of gender, sexual, and racial exclusions. Reddy states,

> Unaccounted for within both Marxist and liberal pluralist discussions of the home and the nation, queers of color as people of color . . . take up the critical task of both remembering and rejecting the model of the "home" offered in the United States in two ways: first, by attending to the ways in which it was defined over and against people of color, and second, by expanding the locations and moments of that critique of the home to interrogate processes of group formation and self-formation from the experience of being expelled from their own dwellings and families for not conforming to the dictation of and demand for uniform gendered and sexual types.[2]

By identifying the nation as the domain determined by racial difference and gender and sexual conformity, Reddy suggests that the decisive intervention of queer of color analysis is that racist practice articulates itself generally as gender and sexual regulation, and that gender and sexual differences variegate racial formations. This articulation, moreover, accounts for the social formations that compose liberal capitalism.

In doing so, queer of color critique approaches culture as one site that compels identifications with and antagonisms to the normative ideals promoted by state and capital. For Reddy, national culture constitutes itself against subjects of color. Alternatively, culture produces houses peopled by queers of color, subjects who have been expelled from home. These subjects in turn "collectively remember home as a site of contradictory demands and conditions."[3] As it fosters both identifications and antagonisms, culture becomes a site of material struggle. As the site of identification, culture becomes the terrain in which formations seemingly antagonistic to liberalism, like marxism and revolutionary nationalism, converge with liberal ideology, precisely through their identification with gender and sexual norms and ideals. Queer of color analysis must examine how culture as a site of identification produces such odd bedfellows and how it—as the location of antagonisms—fosters unimagined alliances.

As an epistemological intervention, queer of color analysis denotes an interest in materiality, but refuses ideologies of transparency and reflection, ideologies that have helped to constitute marxism, revolutionary nationalism, and liberal pluralism. Marxism and revolutionary nationalism, respectively, have often figured nation and property as the transparent outcome of class and racial exclusions. Relatedly, liberal pluralism has traditionally constructed the home as the obvious site of accommodation and confirmation. Queer of color analysis, on the other hand, eschews the transparency of all these formulations and opts instead for an understanding of nation and capital as the outcome of manifold intersections that contradict the idea of the liberal nation-state and capital as sites of resolution, perfection, progress, and confirmation. Indeed, liberal capitalist ideology works to suppress the diverse components of state and capitalist formations. To the extent that marxism and revolutionary nationalism disavow race, gender, and sexuality's mutually formative role in political and economic relations is the extent to which liberal ideology captivates revolutionary nationalism and marxism. To restate, queer of color analysis presumes that liberal ideology occludes the intersecting saliency of race, gender, sexuality, and class in forming social practices. Approaching ideologies of transparency as formations that have worked to conceal those intersections means that queer of color analysis has to debunk the idea that race, class, gender, and sexuality are discrete formations, apparently insulated from one another. As queer of color critique challenges ideologies of discreteness, it attempts to disturb the idea that racial and national formations are obviously disconnected. As an intervention into queer of color analysis, this text attempts to locate African American racial formations alongside other racial formations and within epistemological procedures believed to be unrelated or tangential to African American culture.

To disidentify with historical materialism

By relating queer of color subjects and practices to marxism and liberal pluralism, Reddy suggests that queer of color analysis must critically engage the genealogy of materialist critique. In his book, *Disidentifications: Queers of Color and the Performance of Politics*, José Esteban Muñoz argues, "Disidentification is the hermeneutical performance of decoding mass, high, or any other cultural field from the perspective of a minority subject who is disempowered in such a representational hierarchy."[4] As Muñoz suggests, queer of color critique decodes cultural fields not from a position outside those fields, but from within them, as those fields account for the queer of color subject's historicity. If the intersections of race, gender, sexuality, and class constitute social formations within liberal capitalism, then queer of color analysis obtains its genealogy within a variety of locations. We may say that women of color feminism names a crucial component of that genealogy as women of color theorists have historically theorized intersections as the basis of social formations. Queer of color analysis extends women of color feminism by investigating how intersecting racial, gender, and sexual practices antagonize and/or conspire with the normative investments of nation-states and capital.

As queer of color analysis claims an interest in social formations, it locates itself within the mode of critique known as historical materialism.[5] Since historical materialism has traditionally privileged class over other social relations, queer of color critique cannot take it up without revision, must not employ it without disidentification. If to disidentify means to "[recycle] and [rethink] encoded meaning" and "to use the code [of the majority] as raw material for representing a disempowered politics of positionality that has been rendered unthinkable by the dominant culture,"[6] then disidentification resembles Louis Althusser's rereading of historical materialism. Queer of color analysis disidentifies with historical materialism to *rethink* its categories and how they might conceal the materiality of race, gender, and sexuality. In this instance, to disidentify in no way means to discard.

Addressing the silences within Marx's writings that enable rather than disturb bourgeois ideology, silences produced by Marx's failure to theorize received abstractions like "division of labor, money, value, etc.," Althusser writes in *Reading Capital*,

> This silence is only "heard" at one precise point, just where it goes unperceived: when Marx speaks of the initial abstractions on which the work of transformation is performed. What are these initial abstractions? By what right does Marx accept in these initial abstractions the categories from which Smith and Ricardo started, thus suggesting that he thinks in continuity with their object, and that therefore there is no break in object between them and him? These two questions are really only one single question, precisely the question Marx does not answer, simply because he does not pose it. Here is the site of his silence, and this site, being empty, threatens to be occupied by the "natural" discourse of ideology, in particular, of empiricism. . . . An ideology may gather naturally in the hollow left by this silence, the ideology of a relation of real correspondence between the real and its intuition and representation, and the presence of an "abstraction" which operates on this real in order to disengage from it these "abstract general relations," i.e., an empiricist ideology of abstraction.[7]

As empiricism grants authority to representation, empiricism functions hegemonically, making representations seem natural and objective. To assume that categories conform to reality is to think with, instead of against, hegemony. As he uncritically appropriated the conceptions of political economy formulated by bourgeois economists, Marx abetted liberal ideology. He identified with that ideology instead of disidentifying with it. Disidentifying with historical materialism means determining the silences and ideologies that reside within critical terrains, silences and ideologies that equate representations with reality. Queer of color analysis, therefore, extends Althusser's observations by accounting for the ways in which Marx's critique of capitalist property relations is haunted by silences that make racial, gender, and sexual ideologies and discourses commensurate with reality and suitable for universal ideals.

An ideology has gathered in the silences pertaining to the intersections of race, gender, sexuality, and class. We may locate that silence within one "tendency" of marxism. Writing about that tendency as part of marxism's critique of Western civilization, Raymond Williams states, "'Civilization' had produced not only wealth, order, and refinement, but as part of the same process poverty, disorder, degradation. It was attacked for its 'artificiality'—its glaring contrasts with a 'natural' or 'human' order."[8] As it kept silent about sexuality and gender, historical materialism, along with liberal ideology, took normative heterosexuality as the emblem of order, nature, and universality, making that which deviated from heteropatriarchal ideals the sign of disorder. In doing so, marxism thought in continuity with bourgeois definitions of "Civilization." Moreover, the distinction between civilization as progress versus civilization as disorder obtained meaning along the axes of race, gender, sexuality, and class. Hence, the distinction between normative heterosexuality (as the evidence of progress and development) and non-normative gender and sexual practices and identities (as the woeful signs of social lag and dysfunction) has emerged historically from the field of racialized discourse. Put plainly, racialization has helped to articulate heteropatriarchy as universal.

Marx universalized heteropatriarchy as he theorized property ownership. In *The German Ideology*, he bases the origins of property ownership within the tribe, stating,

> The first form of ownership is tribal . . . ownership. . . . The division of labor
> is at this stage still very elementary and is confined to a further extension of the
> *natural* division of labor existing in the family. The social structure is, therefore,
> limited to an extension of the family; patriarchal family chieftains, below them
> the members of the tribe, finally slaves.[9]

For Marx, tribal ownership presumed a *natural* division of labor symbolized by the heterosexual and patriarchal family. This definition of the "tribe" as a signifier of natural divisions cohered with the use of that category in the nineteenth century. "Tribe" described a "loose *family* or collection headed not by a 'king' but by a 'chief' and denoted a *common essence associated with the premodern*."[10] "Tribe" was a racialized category emerging out of the history of colonial expansion from the seventeenth to the nineteenth centuries. Tribes marked racial difference, securing and transmitting that difference from one person to the next through heteropatriarchal exchange and reproduction. As a racial category, "tribe" illustrates the ways in which racial discourses recruited gender and sexual difference to establish racial identity and essence.

In addition, Marx characterized communal essence and identity as a founding prerequisite for property relations. As he states,

> The spontaneously evolved tribal community, or, if you will, the herd—the
> common ties of blood, language, custom, etc.—is the first precondition of the
> appropriation of the objective conditions of life, and of the activity which gives
> material expression to, or objectifies it (activity as herdsmen, hunters, agricul-
> turalists, etc.).[11]

The property relations presumed within tribal communities suggested a racialized essence garnered through heterosexual and patriarchal familial arrangements. Another way of wording this would be to say that Marx imagined social relations and agency—or as he says, "appropriation" and "activity"—through heteropatriarchy and racial difference simultaneously. Explicating this assumption about social relations and agency, Marx argues in *The German Ideology*, man, who "daily [remakes his] life . . . enters into historical development" by "[making] other men" and "[propagating] their kind."[12] Even earlier, in the *Economic and Philosophic Manuscripts*, Marx stated, "This direct, natural, and necessary relation of person to person is *the relation of man to woman*. In this natural species relationship, man's relation to nature is immediately his relation to man, just as his relation to man is his relation to nature— his own *natural* destination."[13] For Marx, heteropatriarchy was the racialized essence of Man and the standard of sociality and agency.

If a racially secured and dependent heteropatriarchy underlies Marx's origin narrative of social relations and historical agency, then capitalist property relations represent the ultimate obstacle to heteropatriarchal practice and being. In disrupting heteropatriarchy, capital disrupted man's fundamental essence. Locating this disruption within the emergence of the commodity form, Marx argues that

> [p]roduction does not simply produce man as a *commodity*, the *human commodity*, man in the role of *commodity*; it produces him in keeping with this role as a *mentally* and physically *dehumanized* being.—Immorality, deformity, and dulling of the workers and the capitalists.—Its product is the *self-conscious* and *self-acting* commodity . . . the human commodity. Great advance of Ricardo, Mill, etc., on Smith and Say, to declare the existence of the human being—the greater or lesser human productivity of the commodity—to be *indifferent* and even *harmful*.[14]

The commodity disrupts the moral parameters of subjectivity and agency. As Marx states, the commodification produces man as a "mentally and physically dehumanized being," deforming agency and distorting subjectivity.[15]

For Marx, the symbol of that dehumanization could be found in none other than the prostitute. He writes,

> Prostitution is only a *specific* expression of the *general* prostitution of the laborer, and since it is a relationship in which falls not the prostitute alone, but also the one who prostitutes—and the latter's abomination is still greater—the capitalist, etc., also comes under this head. . . . In the approach to woman as the spoil and handmaid of communal lust is expressed the infinite degradation in which man exists for himself.[16]

The prostitute proves capital's defilement of man. She symbolizes man's dehumanization or more specifically, man's feminization under capitalist relations of production. While man's essence in heteropatriarchy suggests undeterred connections with other humans, with one's self, and with nature, the prostitute represents the ways that capital disrupts those connections. Capital now violently mediates man's relationship to himself, to others, and to nature. As a figure of self-interest, the prostitute represents man's descent into vulgar egoism. Suggesting this egoism spawned by capitalist alienation, Marx argues, "[Alienated labor] estranges man's own body from him, as it does external nature and his spiritual essence, his human being."[17] We can see that violent mediation very clearly as the worker who—like all prostitutes—must sell his own labor to survive. Castrated from the means of production, the worker has only that labor that resides in his body to sell. As the prostitute is regarded as the property of "communal lust," the worker is "branded . . . as the property of capital."[18] As Marx imagines capitalist expansion through the disruption of heteropatriarchy, capital implies the mobility of vice, the spread of immorality, and the eruption of social transgressions.

It was precisely this sort of eruption that bourgeois ideologues in nineteenth-century Britain feared the most. During this period, middle-class observers conflated the anarchic possibilities of economic production with a presumably burgeoning sexual deviancy among working-class communities, in general, and working-class women, in particular.[19] The prostitute symbolized poor and working-class communities' potential threat to gender stability and sexual normativity. As mills throughout London employed young British girls, enabling them to buy clothes and other items that were previously inaccessible, middle-class citizens often saw working-class girls' tastes in commodities as signs of awakening sexual appetites. Desires for ribbon, lace, and silks, those citizens reasoned, could entice young girls into a life of prostitution.[20] As Thomas Laqueur notes, "[W]orking-class women were thought to bear the dangers of uncontrolled desire that seemed to flow freely from one domain to another, from legitimate consumption to illegitimate sex."[21] Giving credence to the idea that industrialization was engendering prostitution, the French socialist and feminist Flora Tristan alleged that there were in "'London from 80,000–100,000 women—the flower of the population—living off prostitution'; on the streets and in 'temples raised by English materialism to their gods . . . male guests come to exchange their gold for debauchery.'"[22] Reports of out-of-wedlock births, prenuptial pregnancy, early marriage, masturbation, sexually active youth, and so forth arose during this period and were for the British middle class evidence of a peaking sexual chaos. In doing so, they conflated the reality of changing gender and sexual relations with the representation of the prostitute and the working class as pathologically sexual. As middle-class witnesses to industrialization understood their own families to be sufficiently anchored against the moral disruptions of capital, they regarded the working class as "rootless and uncontrolled—a sort of social correlative to unrestrained id."[23] Corroborating presumptions about industrial capital's encouragement of libertinism, Frederick Engels argued, "[N]ext to the enjoyment of intoxicating liquors, one of the principal faults of the English working-men is sexual license."[24] Marx's use of the prostitute as the apocalyptic symbol of capital's emergence points to his affinity with bourgeois discourses of the day. Both bourgeois ideologues and their radical opponents took the prostitute as the sign for the gendered and sexual chaos that commodification was bound to unleash.

More to the point, pundits understood this gender and sexual chaos to be an explicitly racial phenomenon. Indeed, in nineteenth-century Britain, the prostitute was a racial metaphor for the gender and sexual confusions unleashed by capital, disruptions that destabilized heteropatriarchal conformity and authority.[25] In fact, nineteenth-century iconography used the image of Sarah Bartmann, popularly known as the Hottentot Venus, who was exhibited in freak shows throughout London, to link the figure of the prostitute to the alleged sexual savagery of black women and to install nonwhite sexuality as the axis upon which various notions of womanhood turned.[26] As industrial capital developed and provided working-class white women with limited income and mobility, the prostitute became the racialized figure that could enunciate anxieties about such changes. Conflating the prostitute with the British working class inspired racial mythologies about the supposedly abnormal reproductive capacities and outcomes of that class. One tale suggested that the bodies of British working-class women could produce races heretofore unforeseen. One magistrate warned that if "empty casks were placed along the streets of Whitechapel," it would help spawn species of tub men who would wreak havoc on communities in Britain, creating the conditions by which "savages [would live] in the midst of civilization."[27]

The universalization of heteropatriarchy produces the prostitute as the other of hetero-patriarchal ideals, an other that is simultaneously the effect of racial, gender, sexual, and class discourses, an other that names the social upheavals of capital as racialized disruptions. Unmarried and sexually mobile, the prostitute was eccentric to the gendered and sexual ideals of normative (i.e., patriarchal) heterosexuality. That eccentricity denoted the patholo-gies, disorders, and degradations of an emerging civilization. Rather than embodying hetero-patriarchal ideals, the prostitute was a figure of nonheteronormativity, excluded from the presumed security of heteropatriarchal boundaries.

As such, she and others like her were the targets of both liberal *and* revolutionary regula-tions. Those regulations derived their motives from the fact that both bourgeois and revolu-tionary practices were conceived through heteropatriarchy. We may imagine Marx asking, "How could she—the prostitute—be entrusted with the revolutionary transformation of society?" Likewise, we could imagine the bourgeoisie declaring, "Never could whores ration-ally administer a liberal society." Historical materialism and bourgeois ideology shared the tendency to read modern civilization as the racialized scene of heteronormative disruption. Marx fell into that ideology as he conflated the dominant representation of the prostitute with the social upheavals wrought by capital. Put differently, he equated the hegemonic discourse about the prostitute, a discourse that cast her as the symbol of immorality, vice, and corrup-tion, with the reality of a burgeoning capitalist economy. Taking the prostitute to be the obvious and transparent sign of capital, at what point could Marx approach the prostitute and her alleged pathologies as discursive questions, rather than as the real and objective outcomes of capitalist social relations? At what point might he then consider the prostitute and others like her to be potential sites from which to critique capital?

Naturalizing heteropatriarchy by posing capital as the social threat to heteropatriarchal relations meant that both liberal reform and proletarian revolution sought to recover hetero-patriarchal integrity from the ravages of industrialization. Basing the fundamental conditions of history upon heterosexual reproduction and designating capital as the disruption of heterosexual normativity did more than designate the subject of modern society as hetero-normative. It made the heteronormative subject the goal of liberal and radical practices. Under such a definition of history, political economy became an arena where heteronorma-tive legitimation was the prize. Universalizing heteropatriarchy and constructing a racialized other that required heteropatriarchal regulation was not the peculiar distinction of, or affinity between, Marx and his bourgeois contemporaries. On the contrary, the racialized investment in heteropatriarchy bequeathed itself to liberal and revolutionary projects, to bourgeois and revolutionary nationalisms alike. Queer of color analysis must disidentify with historical materialism so as not to extend this legacy.

The multiplications of surplus: U.S. racial formations, nonheteronormativity, and the overdetermination of political economy

Queer of color analysis can build on the idea that capital produces emergent social formations that exceed the racialized boundaries of gender and sexual ideals, can help explain the emer-gence of subjects like the drag-queen prostitute. At the same time, queer of color critique can and must challenge the idea that those social formations represent the pathologies of modern society. In other words, queer of color work can retain historical materialism's interest in social formations without obliging the silences of historical materialism.

Capital is a formation constituted by discourses of race, gender, and sexuality, discourses that implicate nonheteronormative formations like the prostitute. In addition, capitalist political economies have been scenes for the universalization and, hence, the normalization of sexuality. But those economies have also been the arenas for the disruption of normativity. If we are to be sensitive to the role that those normalizations and disruptions have played within liberal capitalism, we can only take up historical materialism by integrating the critique of normative regimes with the analysis of political economy. In doing so, we must clarify the ways in which our knowledge of liberal capitalism implies this contradiction—that is, the normalization of heteropatriarchy on the one hand, and the emergence of eroticized and gendered racial formations that dispute heteropatriarchy's universality on the other. Understanding the drag-queen prostitute means that we must locate her within a national culture that disavows the configuration of her own racial, gender, class, and sexual particularity and a mode of production that fosters her own formation.

While Marx, like his liberal antagonists, was seduced by the universalization of heteropatriarchy, he can also help us locate procedures of universalization within state formations. As he writes in "On the Jewish Question,"

> [The state] is conscious of being a political state and it manifests its universality only in opposition to these elements [private property, education, occupation, and so forth]. Hegel, therefore, defines the relation of the political state quite correctly when he says: "In order for the state to come in to existence as the self-knowing ethical actuality of spirit, it is essential that it should be distinct from the forms of authority and of faith. But this distinction emerges only in so far as divisions occur within the ecclesiastical sphere itself. It is only in this way that the state, above the particular churches, has attained to the universality of thought—its formal principle—and is bringing this universality into existence."[28]

For Marx, the state establishes its universality in opposition to the particularities of education, property, religion, and occupation. For our own purposes, we may add that this universality exists in opposition to racial, gender, class, and sexual particularities as well. As heteropatriarchy was universalized, it helped to constitute the state and the citizen's universality. Lisa Lowe's arguments about the abstract citizen's relationship to particularity and difference prove instructive here. She writes,

> [The] abstraction of the citizen is always in distinction to the particularity of man's material condition. In this context, for Marx, "political emancipation" of the citizen is the process of relegating to the domain of the private all "nonpolitical" particulars of religion, social rank, education, occupation, and so on in exchange for representation on the political terrain of the state where "man is the imaginary member of an imaginary sovereignty, divested of his real, individual life, and infused with an unreal universality."[29]

The universality of the citizen exists in opposition to the intersecting particularities that account for material existence, particularities of race, gender, class, and sexuality. As a category of universality, normative heteropatriarchy or heteronormativity exists in opposition to the particularities that constitute nonheteronormative racial formations. In this formulation, the citizen is a racialized emblem of heteronormativity whose universality exists at the expense of particularities of race, gender, and sexuality.

Ironically, capital helps produce formations that contradict the universality of citizenship. As the state justifies property through this presumed universality, through claims about access, equivalence, rights, and humanity, capital contradicts that universality by enabling social formations marked by intersecting particularities of race, gender, class, and sexuality. Those formations are the evidence of multiplications. By this I mean the multiplication of racialized discourses of gender and sexuality and the multiplication of labor under capital. Addressing the multiplication of discourses and their relationship to modernity, Foucault argues, "The nineteenth century and our own have been rather the age of multiplication: a dispersion of sexualities, a strengthening of their disparate forms, a multiple implantation of 'perversions.' Our epoch has initiated sexual heterogeneities."[30] For Marx, the multiplication of class divisions and economic exploitation characterizes modernity. As he states, "Growth of capital implies growth of its constituent, in other words, the part invested in labour-power."[31] Despite conventional wisdom, we may think of these two types of multiplication in tandem. For instance, in "On the Jewish Question," Marx states, "Man, in his most *intimate* reality, in civil society, is a profane being. Here, where he appears both to himself and to others as a real individual he is an *illusory* phenomenon."[32] Man, the subject of civil society, is not an unmediated figure. As an illusory phenomenon, Man is constituted within discourse. Like the British prostitute and the race of tub men, Man testifies to capital as a simultaneously discursive and material site. The growth of capital implies the proliferation of discourses.

The gendered and eroticized history of U.S. racialization compels us to address both these versions of multiplication. Indeed, my use of nonheteronormativity attempts to name the intersection between the racialized multiplication of gender and sexual perversions and the dispersion of capitalist property relations. Anxieties about this multiplication characterized American industrialization. The migrations of Asians, Europeans, Mexicans, and African Americans generated anxieties about how emerging racial formations were violating gender and sexual norms. As racialized ethnic minorities became the producers of capitalist surplus value, the American political economy was transformed into an apparatus that implanted and multiplied intersecting racial, gender, and sexual perversions. Nonwhite populations were racialized such that gender and sexual transgressions were not incidental to the production of nonwhite labor, but constitutive of it. For instance, industrial expansion in the southwest from 1910 to 1930, as George Sanchez notes, "created an escalating demand for low-wage labor" and inspired more than one million Mexicans to immigrate to the United States.[33] The entrance of Mexican immigrant labor into the U.S. workforce occasioned the rise of Americanization programs designed to inculcate American ideals into the Mexican household. Those programs were premised on the racialized construction of the Mexican immigrant as primitive in terms of sexuality, and premodern in terms of conjugal rites and domestic habits.[34] In the nineteenth century as well, San Francisco's Chinatown was the site of polymorphous sexual formations that were marked as deviant because they were nonreproductive and nonconjugal. Formed in relation to exclusion laws that prohibited the immigration of Asian women to the United States and out of U.S. capital's designation of Asian immigrants as surplus and redundant labor, Chinatown became known for its bachelor societies, opium dens, and prostitutes. Each one of these formations rearticulated normative familial arrangements and thereby violated a racialized ideal of heteropatriarchal nuclearity.[35] Likewise, as African American urban communities of the North were created out of the demands of northern capital in the early twentieth century, they gave birth to vice districts that in turn transformed gender and sexual ideals and practices in northern cities. As Kevin Mumford notes, spurred by a wartime economy and "in protest of outrageous repression" in the South, the Great Migration—through the production of speakeasies, black and tans, intermarriage, and fallen women—caused a change in "gender roles, standards of sexuality," and conjugal ideals.[36]

As capital solicited Mexican, Asian, Asian American, and African American labor, it provided the material conditions that would ultimately disrupt the gender and sexual ideals upon which citizenship depended. The racialization of Mexican, Asian, Asian American, and African American labor as contrary to gender and sexual normativity positioned such labor outside the image of the American citizen. The state's regulation of nonwhite gender and sexual practices through Americanization programs, vice commissions, residential segregation, and immigration exclusion attempted to press nonwhites into gender and sexual conformity despite the gender and sexual diversity of those racialized groups. That diversity was, in large part, the outcome of capital's demand for labor. As a technology of race, U.S. citizenship has historically ascribed heteronormativity (universality) to certain subjects and non-heteronormativity (particularity) to others. The state worked to regulate the gender and sexual non-normativity of these racialized groups in a variety of ways. In doing so, it produced discourses that pathologized nonheteronormative U.S. racial formations. In the case of Mexican immigrants, Americanization programs attempted to reconstitute the presumably preindustrial Mexican home, believed to be indifferent to domestic arrangements and responsibilities. Doing so meant that the Mexican mother had to be transformed into a proper custodian who would be fit for domestic labor in white homes, as well as her own. As George Sanchez notes, "By encouraging Mexican immigrant women to wash, sew, cook, budget, and mother happily and efficiently, Americans would be assured that Mexican women would be ready to enter the labor market, while simultaneously presiding over a home that nurtured American values of economy."[37] In the case of Asian Americans, immigration exclusion laws worked to ensure that the gender and sexual improprieties of Asian Americans would not transgress U.S. boundaries as residential segregation worked to guarantee that such impropriety among Asian and Asian American residents would not contaminate white middle-class neighborhoods. In like fashion, vice commissions in New York and Chicago, along with anti-miscegenation laws, attempted to insulate middle-class whites from the real and presumed gender and sexual non-normative practices of African Americans and Asian Americans.

Despite his naturalization of gender, sexuality, and race, Marx is useful for thinking about how capital fundamentally disrupts social hierarchies. Those disruptions account for the polymorphous perversions that arise out of the production of labor. Marx defines surplus labor as that labor that capitalist accumulation "constantly produces, and produces indeed in direct relation with its own energy and extent." Surplus populations are populations that are "relatively redundant working populations . . . that is, superfluous to capital's average requirements for its own valorization."[38] Surplus populations exist as future laborers for capital, "always ready for exploitation by capital in the interests of capital's own changing valorization requirements."[39] Both superfluous and indispensable, surplus populations fulfill *and* exceed the demands of capital.

In the United States, racial groups who have a history of being excluded from the rights and privileges of citizenship (African Americans, Asian Americans, Native Americans, and Latinos, particularly) have made up the surplus populations upon which U.S. capital has depended. The production of such populations has accounted for much of the racial heterogeneity within the United States. As mentioned before, the heterogeneity represented by U.S. surplus populations was achieved to a large degree because of capital's need to accumulate labor.

As capital produced surplus populations, it provided the contexts out of which nonheteronormative racial formations emerged.[40] As U.S. capital had to constantly look outside local and national boundaries for labor, it often violated ideals of racial homogeneity held by local communities and the United States at large. As it violated those ideals, capital also inspired worries that such violations would lead to the disruption of gender and sexual proprieties. If racialization has been the "site of a contradiction between the promise of political emancipation and the conditions of economic exploitation,"[41] then much of that contradiction has pivoted on the racialization of working populations as deviant in terms of gender and sexuality. As formations that transgress capitalist political economies, surplus populations become the locations for possible critiques of state and capital.

Marx addresses many of the ways in which capital fosters social heterogeneity and therefore nonequivalent formations. For instance, he states,

> As soon as capitalist production takes possession of agriculture, and in proportion to the extent to which it does so, the demand for a rural working population falls absolutely, while the accumulation of the capital employed in agriculture advances, without this repulsion being compensated for by a greater attraction of workers, as is the case in non-agricultural industries. Part of the agricultural population is therefore constantly on the point of passing over into an urban or manufacturing proletariat, and on the lookout for opportunities to complete this transformation. . . . There is thus a constant flow from this source of the relative surplus population.[42]

Moreover, as capital produced certain working populations as redundant, it inspired rural populations to migrate in search of employment, a move that ensured greater and greater heterogeneity in urban areas. The constant flow of surplus populations from the rural to the urban captures the diverse histories of nonwhite migrations within and to the United States. For instance, this movement from the rural to the urban denotes the history of African American migration.

As well as exceeding local and regional boundaries, surplus populations disrupt social hierarchies of race, gender, age, and sexuality. As it produces surplus, capital compels the transgression of previously established hierarchies and provides the context for the emergence of new social arrangements, identities, and practices. As Marx states,

> We have further seen that the capitalist buys with the same capital a greater mass of labour-power, as he progressively replaces skilled workers by less skilled, mature labour-power by immature, male by female, that of adults by that of young persons or children.

(788)

To adapt this insight to the circumstances of U.S. working populations we might add "immigrant" and "nonwhite" to that of "less skilled," "female," and "child." Hence, the creation of surplus is the violation of the boundaries of age, home, race, and nation.

Surplus populations point to a fundamental feature of capital: It does not rely on normative prescriptions to assemble labor, even while it may use those prescriptions to establish the value of that labor. Capital is based on a logic of reproduction that fundamentally overrides and often violates heteropatriarchy's logic. Subsequently, capital often goes against the state's universalization and normalization of heteropatriarchy. Discussing the ways in which capital bypasses heterosexual means of reproduction, Marx argues,

> The expansion by fits and starts of the scale of production is the precondition for its equally sudden contraction; the latter again evokes the former, but the former is impossible without disposable human material, without an increase in the number of workers, which must occur *independently of the absolute growth of the population*.

(785–86)

Continuing with this argument, he states

> Capitalist production can by no means content itself with the quantity of dispos-
> able labour-power which the natural increase of population yields. It requires
> for its unrestricted activity an industrial reserve army which is *independent of these*
> *natural limits*.

> (788, italics mine)

Capital is based on a fundamentally amoral logic. Capital, without pressures from the state or citizenry, will assemble labor without regard for normative prescriptions of race and gender. Capital, on the other hand, will oblige normative prescriptions, especially in those moments in which it wants to placate the interests of the state.

While capital can only reproduce itself by ultimately transgressing the boundaries of neighborhood, home, and region, the state positions itself as the protector of those boundaries. As the modern nation-state has historically been organized around an illusory universality particularized in terms of race, gender, sexuality, and class, state formations have worked to protect and guarantee this universality. But in its production of surplus populations unevenly marked by a racialized nonconformity with gender and sexual norms, capital constantly disrupts that universality. As the state and heteronormativity work to guarantee and protect that universality, they do so against the productive needs and social conditions set by capital, conditions that produce nonheteronormative racial formations. If heteronormativity is racialized, as I have been arguing, then it is not only gender and sexual integrity that are at stake for heteronormative formations, like the state, but racial integrity and purity as well. As capital disrupts social hierarchies in the production of surplus labor, it disrupts gender ideals and sexual norms that are indices of racial difference. Disrupting those ideals often leads to new racialized gender and sexual formations. To restate, capital requires the transgression of space and the creation of possibilities for intersection and convergence. Capital, therefore, calls for subjects who must transgress the material and ideological boundaries of community, family, and nation. Such transgressions are brought into relief through the capitalist production of labor. As surplus labor becomes the impetus for anxieties about the sanctity of "community," "family," and "nation," it reveals the ways in which these categories are normalized in terms of race, gender, sexuality, and class. Indeed, the production of labor, ultimately, throws the normative boundaries of race, gender, class, and sexuality into confusion.

Nonheteronormative racial formations represent the historic accumulation of contradictions[43] around race, gender, sexuality, and class. The variety of such racial formations (Asian, Asian American, Mexican, Chicano, Native American, African American, and so forth) articulates different racialized, gendered, and eroticized contradictions to the citizen-ideal of the state and the liberatory promise of capital. In doing so, they identify the ways in which race, gender, and sexuality intersect within capitalist political economies and shape the conditions of capital's existence. To address these formations as an accumulation means that we must ask the question of what possibilities they offer for agency. We must see the gendered and eroticized elements of racial formations as offering ruptural—i.e., critical—possibilities. Approaching them as sites of critique means that we must challenge the construction of these formations as monstrous and threatening to others who have no possibility of critical agency and instead engage non-heteronormative racial formations as the site of ruptures, critiques, and alternatives. Racial formations, as they are constituted nonnormatively by gender and sexual differences, over-determine[44] national identity, contradicting its manifold promises of citizenship and prop-erty. This overdetermination could compel intersecting antiracist, feminist, class, and queer struggles to emerge. [. . .]

Notes

1   Queer of color analysis, as I define it in this text, interrogates social formations as the intersections of race, gender, sexuality, and class, with particular interest in how those formations correspond with and diverge from nationalist ideals and practices. Queer of color analysis is a heterogeneous enterprise made up of women of color feminism, materialist analysis, poststructuralist theory, and queer critique.

2   Chandan Reddy, "Home, Houses, Nonidentity: 'Paris Is Burning,'" in *Burning Down the House: Recycling Domesticity*, ed. Rosemary Marangoly George (Boulder: Westview Press, 1997), 356–57.

3   Ibid., 357.

4   José Esteban Muñoz, *Disidentifications: Queers of Color and the Performance of Politics* (Minneapolis: University of Minnesota Press, 1999), 25.

5   Louis Althusser argues, "Historical materialism is the science of social formations." See *For Marx*, trans. Ben Brewster (London and New York: Verso, 1993), 251.

6   Muñoz, *Disidentifications*, 5.

7   Louis Althusser and Étienne Balibar, *Reading Capital*, trans. Ben Brewster (London: Verso, 1979), 88.

8   Raymond Williams, *Marxism and Literature* (Oxford: Oxford University Press, 1977), 18.

9   Karl Marx and Frederick Engels, *The German Ideology*, trans. Dirk J. Struik (New York: International Publishers, 1974), 43–44. Emphasis mine.

10   David Theo Goldberg, *Racist Culture: Philosophy and the Politics of Meaning* (London: Blackwell, 1993), 63.

11   Karl Marx, *Pre-Capitalist Economic Formations*, trans. Jack Cohen (New York: International Publishers, 1964).

12   Marx and Engels, *The German Ideology*, 49.

13   Karl Marx, *Economic and Philosophic Manuscripts of 1844*, ed. Dirk J. Struik, trans. Martin Milligan (New York: International Publishers, 1964), 134.

14   Ibid., 121.

15   The modern conception of subjectivity and agency (liberal and revolutionary) is thoroughly normalized. David Theo Goldberg, for example, makes the following argument: "Moral notions tend to be basic to each sociodiscursive order, for they are key in defining the interactive ways social subjects see others and conceive (of) themselves. Social relations are constitutive of personal and social identity, and a central part of the order of such relations is the perceived need, the requirement for subjects to give an account of their actions. These accounts may assume the bare form of explanation, but they usually tend more imperatively to legitimate or to justify acts (to ourselves and others). Morality is the scene of this legitimation and justification" (*Racist Culture*, 14).

      Indeed the modern conception of agency has historically and consequentially understood formations that fall out of the normative boundaries of morality as incapable of agency and therefore worthy of exclusion and regulation. One of the principal tasks of antiracist queer critique must be to account for those formations expelled from normative calculations of agency and subjectivity. Accounting for those formations means that we must ask what modes of engagement and awareness they enact, modes that normative conceptions of agency and subjectivity can never acknowledge or apprehend.

16   Marx, *Economic and Philosophic Manuscripts of 1844*, 133.

17   Ibid., 114.

18   Karl Marx, *Capital*, vol. 1, *A Critique of Political Economy*, trans. Ben Fowkes (London: Penguin Classics, 1990), 482.

19   Thomas Laqueur, "Sexual Desire and the Market Economy during the Industrial Revolution," in *Discourses of Sexuality: From Aristotle to AIDS*, ed. Domna Stanton (Ann Arbor: University of Michigan Press, 1992), 185–215.

20   Ibid., 208.

21   Ibid.

22   Ibid., 189, quoting Flora Tristan, *London Journal*, trans. Denis Palmer and Giselle Pincetl (1840; reprint, London: George Prior, 1980), 79.

23   Ibid., 208.

24   Ibid., 190, quoting Frederick Engels, *The Condition of the Working Class in England: Karl Marx and Frederick Engels on Britain* (Moscow: Foreign Languages Publishing House, 1962), 61.

25   Anne McClintock, "Screwing the System: Sexwork, Race, and the Law," *Boundary 2* 19, no. 2 (1992): 80–82.

26   Evelyn Brooks Hammonds, "Toward a Genealogy of Black Female Sexuality: The Problematic of Silence," in *Feminist Genealogies, Colonial Legacies, Democratic Futures*, eds. M. Jacqui Alexander and Chandra Talpade Mohanty (New York and London: Routledge, 1997), 172.

27   Laqueur, "Sexual Desire and the Market Economy," 210–11.

28   Karl Marx, "On the Jewish Question," in *The Marx-Engels Reader*, ed. Robert C. Tucker (New York: W.W. Norton and Company, 1978), 33.

29   Lisa Lowe, *Immigrant Acts: On Asian American Cultural Politics* (Durham: Duke University Press, 1996), 25.

30   Michel Foucault, *The History of Sexuality*, vol. 1, *An Introduction*, trans. Robert Hurley (New York: Vintage Books, 1990), 37.

31   Marx, *Capital*, 763.

32   Marx, "On the Jewish Question," 34.

33   George Sanchez, "Go after the Women," in *Unequal Sisters: A Multicultural Reader in U.S. Women's History*, eds. Vicki L. Ruiz and Ellen Carol Du Bois (New York: Routledge, 1994), 285.

34   Ibid., 291–92. Gloria Anzaldúa writes that the borderland is the place for the "squint-eyed, the perverse, the queer, the troublesome, the mongrel, the mulatto, the half-breed, the half dead; in short, those who cross over, pass over, or go through the confines of the 'normal'" (*Borderlands: The New Mestiza-La Frontera* [San Francisco: Aunt Lute Books, 1999], 25).

35   See Nayan Shah, "Perversity, Contamination, and the Dangers of Queer Domesticity," in *Contagious Divides: Epidemics and Race in San Francisco's Chinatown* (Berkeley and Los Angeles: University of California Press, 2001).

36   Kevin Mumford, *Interzones: Black/White Sex Districts in Chicago and New York in the Early Twentieth Century* (New York: Columbia University Press, 1997), xviii.

37   Sanchez, "Go after the Women," 289.

38   Marx, *Capital*, 782.

39   Ibid., 784.

40   By arguing that capital produces gender and sexual heterogeneities as part of its racialized contradiction, I wish neither to privilege a discourse of repression, nor to assume a corollary formulation—that capital is the site of equivalences or uniformities. Indeed, this material and discursive production of surplus is the racialized production of nonheteronormative—and therefore racially differentiated and nonequivalent—sexualities.

41   Lowe, *Immigrant Acts*, 23.

42   Marx, *Capital*, 795–96.

43   Althusser defines contradiction as "the articulation of a practice . . . into the complex whole of the social formation" (*For Marx*, 250). Althusser goes on to state that the accumulation of contradictions may produce the "weakest link" in a system: "If this contradiction is to become 'active' in the strongest sense, to become a ruptural principle, there must be an accumulation of 'circumstances' and 'currents' so that whatever their origin and sense . . . they 'fuse into a ruptural unity'" (*For Marx*, 99).

44   For the theory of overdetermination, see ibid.

Chapter 8

Rosemary Hennessy

THE MATERIAL OF SEX

Rosemary Hennessy is Professor of English and Director of the Center for the Study of Women, Gender, and Sexuality at Rice University. She has authored several books including *NAFTA From Below: Maquiladora Workers, Campesinos, and Indigenous Communities Speak Back* (2006), *Materialist Feminism and the Politics of Discourse* (1993), and *Profit and Pleasure: Sexual Identities in Late Capitalism* (2002), from which this excerpt is taken. Her scholarship encompasses feminist cultural theory, sexuality studies, and U.S.-Mexican studies.

In *Profit and Pleasure*, Hennessy examines how gender and sexual identities are shaped by forces of capitalism. In this excerpt, Hennessy critiques the post-Marxist inclination within queer theory that separates sexuality from capitalism and class. Working against what she considers the "cultural materialism" of leading queer theorists, including Judith Butler and Eve Kosofsky Sedgwick, Hennessy advocates a historical materialist approach to queer theory that emphasizes the tangled histories of capitalism and queer identity formations. In doing so, Hennessy emphasizes the relevance of critiquing heterosexual marriage and family within radical queer politics. A historical analysis of marriage and family highlights the role of capitalism in the formation of family, labor, and consumption—historical formations that also shape queer identities. According to Hennessy, adding capitalism to the discourse of sexual identity "queers" the links between sexual identity and class formation.

The coming of the queer

QUEER THEORY PRESENTED itself in the late eighties as an emphatically post-marxist critique of sexual identity politics. One of the defining features of queer theory is its effort to reorient a cultural and social movement based on identity politics and founded on the categories "gay" and "lesbian" in order to produce "another discursive horizon, another way of thinking the sexual" (de Lauretis 1991, iv). By the early nineties in academic theory, invoking the signifier "queer" paralleled the shift away from the terms "lesbian" and "gay" among some activists (Queer Nation, which gave the signifier "queer" national publicity, was founded in 1990). Claiming a queer identity is an effort to speak from and to the differences that have been suppressed both by heteronorms and by the homo—hetero binary; the transsexual, bisexual, and any other ways of "experiencing" and expressing sensuality and affect that do not conform to the prevailing organization of sexuality. It is an effort to unpack the monolithic identities "lesbian" and "gay," including the intricate ways lesbian and gay sexualities are inflected by heterosexual norms, race, gender, and ethnic differences. Embracing the category used to shame and cast out sexual deviants, queer theory and politics defiantly refuse the terms of the dominant discourse, offering instead an "in your face" rejection of proper sexual identities that is both anti-assimilationist and anti-separatist. Touting queerness is a gesture of rebellion against compulsory heterosexuality's pressure to be either hetero or invisible, either confidently normal or apologetically, shamefully, quietly queer. These knowledges carry an important critical force to the extent that they denaturalize how we think about sexuality and identity. Much of this denaturalizing draws from an array of postmodern theories that see sexuality and identity not as a fact of nature or a libidinal drive but rather as an unstable symbolic construction, a cultural effect. Queer theory distances itself from lesbian and gay identity politics because it sees any identity as internally divided and therefore not an apt or effective rallying point for change. "Queer" is a mark of the instability of identity. It makes visible the ways that heterosexuality functions as a normative power regime and highlights the arbitrariness of the neat distinctions it enforces (between masculine and feminine, straight and gay, for example) in how sexuality and gender—and for some queer theorists race, too—come to be known. In all of these respects queer theory is a significant departure from lesbian and gay studies.

Queer theory is an ensemble of knowledges, many of them contesting knowledges. It is, in other words, a site of struggle, not a monolithic discourse. And yet, underneath the debates, there are some important ways in which the distinguishing features of queer theory share assumptions that are not new. A significant one is the fact that in most of this work capitalism remains completely invisible. Despite their diversity, knowledges that come under the signature "queer theory" invariably and at times insistently separate the primary object of their analysis—sexuality—from capitalism as a class-based system of production. The most widely circulating version of queer theory now is what I will call "avant-garde queer theory." Emerging out of a decade of cultural work on several fronts, affected by new forms of political activism honed in the AIDS-dominated eighties, and tailored by a postmodern academic chic, avant-garde queer theory has challenged and redefined lesbian and gay studies. Some avant-garde queer theory that began to circulate in the early nineties makes no claims to a materialist analysis but remains primarily bound to a more textual approach to identity as signification. (I am thinking here of essays and books by Lee Edelman [1994], Diana Fuss [1991], Wayne Koestenbaum [1993], and Peggy Phelan [1993], for instance.) However, this variant of postmodern theories of identity is now losing credibility and is being displaced as another, more materialist avant-garde strand has become queer theory's dominant discourse.

Michael Warner's "Introduction" to the collection *Fear of a Queer Planet* is an exemplary instance. Unlike versions of queer theory that have been more preoccupied with identity as an effect of language and textuality, Warner's perspective acknowledges the social and political dimensions of sexuality. He even addresses the market mediation of lesbian and gay culture in a "structural environment" where the institutions of queer culture "have been dominated by those with capital" (xvii). We do not learn any more about how Warner understands the power dynamics of domination by capital, the distinction between those with capital and those without, or how this difference shapes queer culture and community, however, because Warner never mentions them again. While Warner hints that capitalism necessarily entails the difference between those who control and those who do not control capital and that this structure plays a determinative role in shaping queer culture, this hint is no substitute for analysis of sexuality's historical relation to capitalism as a class-based system.

In fact, Warner goes on to disavow the need for any such analysis when he asserts that "class is conspicuously useless" for queer theory (xxiv). Warner's dismissive separation of class analysis from sexuality echoes the well-established convention of segregating the history of sexuality from the history of capitalism. This history is most often rendered opaque by appeals to the obviousness of their irrelevance to one another. Much of queer theory now continues this tradition; the very possibility of linking the changing organizations of sexuality to capitalism remains all but unspeakable. Because this strand of queer theory claims to be materialist, the difference between its cultural materialism and marxism's historical materialism needs further clarification.

Both cultural and historical materialist approaches to sexuality call into question cultural categories (gay, straight, butch, femme), oppositions (man vs. woman; hetero vs. homo), or equations (gender = sex) upon which conventional notions of sexual identity rely. Both break from traditional notions of sexuality as a personal or civil rights issue. And both refuse a politics in which identity is understood to be represented in a self-evident way through one's body or collectivity is reduced to group affiliation defined according to the standard of authentic embodiment. Cultural materialist queer theory at times acknowledges the work of materialist feminists. (Monique Wittig, for example, has been claimed by several prominent avant-garde queer theorists.) But the theories of the social and the modes of critical practice offered in cultural materialist queer theory are quite at odds with historical materialism even as it has been embraced and reworked by feminists.

This queer theory of the more cultural materialist sort can be loosely characterized as post-poststructuralist in that it extends poststructuralism's emphatically textual critique of humanism and empiricism to more overtly social concerns, usually framed in terms of cultural politics. (Among those developing this strand of queer theory are Judith Butler, David Halperin, Cindy Patton, Gayle Rubin, and Eve Sedgwick.) Drawing heavily on Michel Foucault's arguments that subjectivity is first of all historical and social, that identities are discursively constructed, and that these constructions are enacted through disciplinary technologies and regimes of power, this strand of queer theory, like Foucault's genealogies, is a version of materialism. But what is meant by materialism here? The answer to this question can take us on a long detour into the history of cultural materialism that is in fact an important supplement to the emergence of queer theory and its post-marxist underpinnings. [. . .] Here [. . .] I want to turn to Judith Butler's work for the exemplary "queer" answer to this question it offers.

Not only has Butler acquired enormous stature in defining queer critiques of heterosexuality, but the explicit endorsement of materialism in her book *Bodies That Matter* situates her arguments squarely within the discourses of post-marxism and characterizes it as a paradigmatic example of Foucauldian avant-garde queer theory. The following reading of Butler is meant to explore some of the informing assumptions of this approach and to question the limits of a post-marxist queer politics. Judith Butler is cited more persistently and pervasively than any other queer theorist. References to her work appear in dissertations, conference papers and journals, and new books and collections, as well as in more popular cosmopolitan venues like the *Voice Literary Supplement*.[1] This attention indicates that her ideas have struck a chord in a certain sector of the public imagination of new ways of knowing sexual identity.

One of the most notable and trenchant features of Butler's analysis is her extension of feminism's theory of gender as culturally constructed to the more radical argument that the internal coherence of the identities "man" or "woman" presumes institutional heterosexuality. Much of the oppositional force of her critique lies in its insistent claim that heteronormativity is absolutely central to the bourgeois ideology of expressive and coherent selfhood. This imaginary representation, she argues, "conceals the gender discontinuities that run rampant within heterosexual, bisexual, gay, and lesbian contexts where gender does not necessarily follow from sex, and desire or sexuality generally does not seem to follow from gender" (1990, 135–36). From this perspective, heterosexuality, which is generally assumed to be an expression of the core of oneself, is exposed as a precarious fabrication always potentially at risk.

In *Gender Trouble* Butler draws on various poststructuralist theories of language to present sexual identification as the effect of *discourses* (acts, gestures, practices) that assemble a provisional coherence on the surface of the body (1990, 136). Her aim is to denaturalize heterosexuality and gender by showing them to be performative features of identity. "Being" lesbian or gay—or straight, for that matter—is for Butler not a mark of one's essential identity but rather the effect of repeated performances of cultural signs and conventions, imitations that are always supplementary, always giving the lie to any original sexual identity. This performativity is not a matter of role playing or mere theatricality, which assumes an "I" that is already in place before the role or act is performed. Rather, identity is radically performative. It is through the repeated performance of certain significations of sex and gender that an "I" continually comes to "be."

In *Bodies That Matter* (1993) Butler extends these arguments about the performativity of identity by casting them in a much more emphatically Foucauldian materialist frame. From the opening pages of *Bodies* she asserts that she began this project trying to consider the materiality of the body, the constraints by which bodies are materialized as sexed, and how to link the materiality of the body to the performativity of gender (xi, 1). It quickly becomes clear, however, that materiality for Butler is simply a matter of norms. The materiality of the body, she argues, is inseparable from regulatory conventions that function in a performative fashion to constitute sex and to materialize the body's sex and sexual difference in the service of a heterosexual imperative (1993, 2). Norms achieve this materialization of sex through their forcible reiteration. It is through the repetition or reiteration of already established norms that one "performs" a sexual identity. In this sense sexual identity is what Butler calls a "citational" practice rather than an ontological or natural essence. Sex is not a raw material on which gender identities are constructed, a drive, physiological configuration, or bodily sensation, but rather a set of cultural conventions by which one becomes visible at all (1993, 2). Norms regulate in part by exclusion, and [. . .] Butler argues that the exclusionary normative matrix by which sex is constructed requires the simultaneous production of a domain of abject categories. Any identification with these abjects is continually disavowed by the norms or laws of the dominant culture. It is that for Butler which constitutes the different citation of the law that this threatening abject puts forward as the critical space of a queer performative politics.

Several concepts are linked in Butler's critique of normative heterosexuality—discourse, materiality, performance—and all are loosely connected to history, power, and the social. Much as it is for Foucault, discourse in *Bodies That Matter* is a complex chain of social practices. These social practices are the vehicles for norms and the vectors of power. Performativity in this sense is the modality of power as discourse. For Butler, the historical force of discourse and of norms is their power over time to enact what they name (1993, 187).

Butler's emphasis on norms injects into poststructuralism's textualized understandings of identity as signification a social and historical analysis more attuned to the workings of power in language. But understanding the materiality of social life as so exclusively normative also limits social relations to the domains of culture and the law. Normative discourses are social practices that regulate action, behavior, rituals, and institutions. And in this sense, they encompass much more than language, speech acts, or signs. But a normative starting point also excludes in advance other important dimensions of social life from critical consideration.

Butler has recently had to address some of the challenges to her way of understanding sexuality. In an essay tellingly entitled "Merely Cultural," which was first given as a talk in

1996 at the Rethinking Marxism Conference in Amherst, Massachusetts, she answers the "explicitly Marxist objection that the cultural focus of leftist politics has abandoned the materialist project of Marxism, failing to address questions of economic equity and redistribution, and failing as well to situate culture in terms of a *systematic* understanding of social and economic modes of production" (265). In response to the charges from what she calls an "orthodox" marxism, Butler (1997a) defends poststructuralism's focus on culture for the interests of a queer politics. She does so by way of a rather high-handed misreading of marxism as aiming for a "racially cleansed notion of class" and deploying a rhetoric of unity that domesticates and subordinates movements that formed in opposition to oppressive efforts to erase their priorities. The problem here is that Butler ignores many of the historical materialist efforts to formulate the complex ways class relations never operate "on their own" or simply "subordinate" certain kinds of social difference. At one point she refers to the need to remember the reasons why new social movements, presumably feminism, gay, and black civil rights movements, "became articulated against a hegemonic Left," as well as against a complicitous "liberal center and a truly threatening right wing" (268). There is a problem here with Butler's presentation of the enemy of new social movements. It obscures some of the ways power was exerted not just through certain political "wings" and "centers" but through the bourgeois ruling bloc who were able to use the repressive power of the state to suppress groups like the Black Panthers and feminists who were forging collectivities based on much more systemic and revolutionary rather than identitarian ways of thinking. It is not clear who exactly Butler includes in the new social movements she refers to, but that she uses the term "semi-autonomous" is interesting. It suggests that identity-based groups can maintain a link to *something*, though the something is unnamed. Is it to class relations? To the ruling bloc? Butler does not say, and the essay goes on to endorse an emphatic cultural politics, but her mention of semi-autonomous political relations is suggestive and important, and I will come back to this point later. What Butler refuses to acknowledge or perhaps even to see is that insisting on the vital role of the extraction of surplus labor in capitalism does not preclude developing analyses of how this process involves highly differentiated and inter-imbricated cultural processes.

It is true that the historical materialist position I am endorsing stresses that capitalism is fundamentally based on social relations of class, relations that are always mediated by other social differences. In other words, yes, class does have a certain priority in capitalism. But it is important to remember that class in this sense is a social relationship, not a reified cultural category. To see this historical materialist analysis as "subordinating" or "domesticating" identitarian interests to class is already to be thinking about class out of the very logic Butler herself disparages, a logic in which differences are "abstracted," made falsely coherent and territorial in relation to one another.

When Butler turns to the topic of sexual difference, she protests against charges that she sees social life as "merely cultural." She counters that, of course, sexuality is central to the functioning of political economy (270–71), then reviews some of the arguments of Marx, Engels, and socialist feminists that systemically tie "the regulation of sexuality" to the mode of production (271). For Butler, these examples serve to show that social reproduction cannot be understood without expanding the economic sphere to include the social reproduction of persons (271). But for her showing that sexuality is central to political economy finally means overwriting political economy with sexuality. The analysis has not advanced any further than the arguments of cultural feminists almost twenty years ago. The examples that she gives tell of lesbians and gays being denied rights—to freedom of assembly and speech, to family, as members of the military, as legitimate committed partners and parents. She is right to foreground that there are rules regulating relations of property and economic entitlement, and she is right to stress that this process is not about specific identities being excluded from cultural recognition but refers rather to a "specific mode of sexual production and exchange that works to maintain the stability of gender, the heterosexuality of desire, and the naturalization of the family" (273). In the end, Butler does not explain how sexuality mediates relations of labor or has anything at all to do with exploitation. Instead she emphatically situates her analysis of economic exchange within culture, using Lévi-Strauss's concept of exchange as the lever to do so. Lévi-Strauss does indeed confound the distinction between the cultural and the economic in his analyses, but the melding of kinship relations and divisions of labor in the societies he describes has not been the prevailing form of production under capitalism. Butler's turn to anthropology allows her to substitute kinship relations—which are cultural relations—for relations of production. This is a familiar ideological shift in the history of feminist encounters with marxism. [. . .] Consequently, in the end, social production remains what it has been all along for Butler—if not "merely," then finally, cultural.

The emphasis on culture and the law in Butler's normative understanding of materiality is quite distinct from what materiality means in historical materialism, and precisely because historical materialism does not "discount the cultural," as Butler charges, the differences between the two are important to consider. Historical materialism understands social life to be historically and materially produced through relations of labor through which people make what is needed to survive. But this process does not happen without the ways of making sense, normative practices (culture–ideology), and the laws (state organization) that are part of the material production of social life. That Butler, like Foucault, entirely drops social relations of labor out of her analysis marks her claims on the material as post-marxist. Indeed, this affiliation with post-marxism is evident in her laudatory appropriation of the work of Ernesto Laclau and Chantal Mouffe. It is helpful to examine this debt to Laclau and Mouffe in sorting out what is at issue in the kind of materialism Butler's queer theory puts forth.

Butler's performative queerity and Laclau and Mouffe's radical democracy share much in common. For Laclau and Mouffe, the material is a performative discourse. In their book *Hegemony and Socialist Strategy* (1985), they develop a version of materialist performativity against the traditions of economic determinism and party vanguardism within marxism. Based on their reading of divisions within marxism, Laclau and Mouffe lay claim to a concept of hegemony more linked to mass (democratic) than class (marxist) politics, a concept whose genealogy they trace through Rosa Luxembourg and Antonio Gramsci. But while their aim is to correct a construction of the class subject in marxism that they claim historically closed out any consideration of the contingent interests of the masses—women, anticolonial and antiracist, sexuality, youth, or ecology movements—their arguments against a reductive economic determinism end up excluding entirely any consideration of capitalism's relationships of exploitation, accumulation, or domination in social life.[2] This exclusion is played out in a social theory that, like Butler's normative materialism, is premised on the notion that social organization is primarily symbolic. We see this in their understanding of class as an articulation of symbolic (subject) positions rather than as an effect of the organization of labor that inflects and is in turn affected by ideology and state. Above all, we see the erasure of capitalism's fundamental relationships of exploitation—the surplus labor capitalism relies on in order to function. The relationship between social differences (of sexuality, race, and gender) and capital's need for surplus labor, as well as the relationship of democratic rights to capitalism's fundamental relations of production, remains unexplained in its overriding attention to the cultural or symbolic dimensions of material life.

This distinctive post-Marxian equation of social life with the symbolic is most evident in the way Laclau and Mouffe unhinge the concept of hegemony from social production, one of the basic premises of historical materialism. Laclau and Mouffe claim that it is necessary to break from historical materialism's starting point—social production—because it conveys that "society" is a totality. Instead, they consider the openness of the social to be its constitutive ground, an openness in which "we are dealing with contingent relations whose nature we have yet to determine" (1985, 96). However, this argument against founding concepts like social production does not acknowledge that the concept of production in historical materialism is not totalizing in the Hegelian sense they imply; rather, it is a way of thinking that recognizes the historical openness of social relations. Moreover, their renunciation of foundational concepts belies that their own contingent social logic is also anchored in a founding concept, namely signification.

Laclau and Mouffe understand the historical materialist notion of production to be totalizing because they equate social production with economic production, which then becomes the Hegelian whole to which all aspects of social production are subsumed. This misreading ignores all of the efforts of contemporary marxists to address cultural practices as part of social production. Indeed, these efforts to theorize cultural production have been central to debates over the uses and limits of the base-superstructure metaphor in Marxism [. . .]. For Laclau and Mouffe, in any social formation there is always a surplus of *meaning* that threatens to interrupt any necessary fixing of the nodal points or discursive axes for identity (e.g., what it means to be a woman, a man, black, or gay). Understanding what constitutes the materiality of this surplus of meanings and the (in)secure fixing of identities refers us to Laclau and Mouffe's founding conception, signification. What establishes the excessive, unstable symbolic dimension of every social identity is for them polysemy: "[S]ociety never manages to be identical to itself, as every nodal point is constituted within an intertextuality that overflows it" (1985, 113).

Drawing on the ideas of Laclau and Mouffe, Butler, too, argues that the constitutive antagonism written into meanings—the nonclosure of definitions and identities—is assured by a contingency or provisionality that underwrites every discursive formation (Butler 1993, 193). This mobilizing incompleteness is guaranteed, she contends, by the instability in "any and all signifying practices" (Butler 1993, 193). Each of these post-marxists insists that the articulation of identities is not simply a linguistic process but pierces the entire density of a discursive formation. But founding their conceptions of materiality only in symbolic processes means that social struggle, or what they call antagonism, is anchored only in the sign—an effect of *differance*. *Differance* is the term Jacques Derrida invented for the continual subversion of any positive meaning (or identity) by the excessive proliferation of signifiers (sound-images in language) that refuse to be attached to a single signified (referent or concept). Laclau and Mouffe, like Butler, contend that the neat oppositions (like heterosexual vs. homosexual or man vs. woman) underlying positive identities are, by virtue of their discursive construction, always open to deconstruction. The materiality of identities, as well as the inevitability of their deconstruction, is presented as a given feature of signification, an effect of the provisional fixing of the sign.

How are we to understand the materiality of this fixing? *Why* are meanings secured in certain ways and not others? *Why* do certain "nodal points" in a culture's logic (heterosexual, for instance) constitute the naturalized axes for identity in some social formations? These questions mark the limits of post-marxism: the unspeakable causal logic elicited by the question "Why?" However, as Althusser's conception of overdetermination suggests, causality need not be reductive, totalizing, or expressive, even as it directs us to consider that the reproduction of the means to meet human needs is never entirely subsumed by cultural or symbolic forms.

Capitalism as a mode of producing the means for survival is tellingly absent in post-marxist cultural materialist analysis. Indeed, it must be if social life is to be seen as constitutively symbolic. This symbolic openness, defined exclusively in relation to political (state) and ideological (normative) processes, is the basis for Butler's enthusiastic endorsement of

Laclau and Mouffe's radical democracy. Butler sets radical democracy against "a causal theory of historical events or social relations" (1993, 192) and insists that the basic ingredient in how we understand the social is its indeterminacy, always leaving open the possible production of new subjects (1993, 193). One problem with this argument for openness is that it potentially endorses *any*—even exploitative—social relations. Giving priority to political reform and to democratic ideals that recognize no relation between state formations, constructions of meaning, *and divisions of labor and wealth* has, of course, a long history in liberal reform movements where questions about "rights for what?" get suppressed under the impetus for equal rights *within* capitalism. If the aim for social movement is to secure democratic rights and privileges *within* capitalism, what responsibility does a radical queer politics have to confront the limits of this endeavor?

I want to approach an answer to this question by testing out Butler's critique of heterosexuality against the "performative" practice of marriage.[3] Although Butler doesn't treat marriage in much detail as the premier institution by which hegemonic heterosexual identity is policed, it is worthy of some consideration as such. Marriage is, of course, regulated by the state and so performed in and through the reiteration of laws. For Butler, it is these laws that secure the normative dimension of heterosexuality through a continual reworking of already operative conventions that are "grounded in no other legitimating authority than the echo-chain of their own re-invocation" (1993, 107). When applied to marriage, Butler's formulation of the performativity of the law suggests that marriage functions as a performative ritual just because it has always done so, and that its reach as a social practice is simply normative.

But is this all that the matrimonial relation to heteronormativity is about? Marriage secures heteronormativity not only through the naturalizing discourses of heterogender but also through the overdetermined relations between gender and class. Of course, marriage never absolutely succeeds in securing heterosexual norms. Many legally married men and women engage in same-sex practices or fantasies. However, according to Butler's performative argument, the myriad everyday rehearsals of the heterosexual imperative in the rituals and customs for honoring married life (ranging from the use of the titles "husband" and "wife" and the required identification of one's "spouse" on a host of bureaucratic forms to expectations about coupling and public celebrations of weddings and anniversaries) belie in their reiteration the possibility that in fact marriage secures desire and affection within the heteronormative conjugal bond. Indeed, the very need to reiterate these rituals, like the monitoring of heterosexual coupling by the state and the church, betrays the insecurity of these social bonds that are in everyday practice continually thrown into crisis, fractured, loosened, or subverted.

Under capitalism the patriarchal heteronorms that the institution of marriage helps secure do not function apart from the relations of production, but the relationship between them and class is not a necessary or neatly causal one. Marriage has historically helped provide a system for ensuring women's unpaid household labor, but there is not a constant, direct, and predictable relationship between marriage, women's labor in and outside the home, and capitalism. Despite the recruitment of more women into the workforce, the division of labor in the home is not being dramatically affected. In the past two decades as vast numbers of middle-class married women have entered the wage-labor force, some of the labor wives once provided has been supplied by consumer markets, paid domestics, and child care providers. Although women's paid employment outside the home has dramatically increased, there has been no appreciable increase in men's participation in household labor. The cleaning, nurturing, and planning necessary for subsistence are still invariably the labor of women, and marriage still remains a prime institution for ensuring this patriarchal hetero-gendered arrangement.[4]

Census figures reveal that the number of unmarried couples in the United States is growing steadily. The state typically takes an ambivalent stance on fluctuations in marriage, at times fostering it, at other times fostering disincentives to marry.[5] The U.S. federal government passed a "Defense of Marriage Act" in 1996, and is currently considering a program for rewarding states that show a decrease in the numbers of unwed women on their welfare rolls. Yet many of the state's practices in defense of marriage can be shown to be inconsistent once you look more closely at exactly which marriages it defends. The state uses marital status to sanction many direct and indirect financial supports to middle-class couples. Among them are lower rates for health benefits and insurance for "partners" and their children, sick leave and parental leave care, reduced rate memberships, property tax exemptions, pension rights, and domestic violence protections (Ingraham 1999, 176). On the other hand, many tax and welfare regulations have made it more economical for the poor not to marry. For those earning minimum wages or living below poverty level, the risk is that even a working husband's earnings may mean that a family exceeds the level to qualify for social welfare programs. The 1997 census data suggest that more and more couples are living together without getting married in order to avoid losing these benefits. As Chrys Ingraham has pointed out in her groundbreaking work on the wedding industrial complex, "marriage primarily benefits groups that are not disproportionately represented among the poor and that are able to maintain goods and property" (Ingraham 1999, 32).

Historically, marriage has protected property by serving as a dense transfer point for land and inheritance, but it has also served property interests by sanctioning the privatization of the production of labor power. In order for a worker to exchange his labor power for wages, he needs to have the capacity for his labor power to be continually nurtured and reproduced. The labor of renewing labor power, that is, the labor of providing directly for subsistence needs, has taken place primarily in the home and has been naturalized as the responsibility of women. It involves preparing food and clean clothing; birthing babies and caring for the young, the sick, and the elderly; educating children; and offering comfort and affection to those who today or tomorrow will go back into the alienating grind of wage work. As the state-sanctioned institution for the normative family, marriage has fostered and protected the ideological construction of this gendered division of labor. In the feudal household structure of private patriarchy, heterogender norms help legitimatize and secure the father/husband's full authority over the wife, his appropriation of her labor, property, and person.[6] To be a wife under private patriarchy is to spend blocks of time in the household preparing food, cleaning, caring, counseling, repairing—performing labor that is appropriated directly for others' use. It is just recently, and only in urban industrialized economies, that for most women there have been any alternatives to marriage as a route to subsistence, since the patriarchal household was the only place where women's economic security was protected, and the social as well as economic position of wife was often preferable to that of unmarried sister, daughter, or aunt. Across the globe, the economic security marriage continues to offer women is often an incentive to marry or for staying married. While 11 percent of households in the United States lived in poverty in 1990, 42 percent of displaced homemakers who headed households and 44 percent of single mothers were impoverished.[7] Single mothers and "displaced homemakers" are four times more likely to live in poverty than the population as a whole, and as wage workers unmarried women are overrepresented in service jobs that offer low pay, few benefits, and part-time employment with little or no job security.

As Butler would have it, women's domestic labor would be seen as a series of continual citations of judicial laws, norms, and discourses, among them naturalized heterosexuality, gender asymmetry, marital duty, motherhood, and romantic love. Under capitalism, however, these domestic activities support more than a history of law and discourses. They provide the labor power for wage work, take care of needs that are not met on the job, and nurture a systemic gendered division of labor outside the household whereby women's labor is exploited and women as a group earn considerably lower wages than men. Capitalism does not structurally require patriarchal gender asymmetry, but historically it has made use of the institution of marriage and the heterosexual norms it regulates to reproduce gendered divisions of labor both in and outside the family. The heteronormative marriage arrangements of private patriarchy secured the bourgeois wife as a domestic worker whose labor, while not directly appropriated by the capitalist in exchange for a wage, was nonetheless essential for reproducing the physical well-being, health, and know-how of the workforce, and it did so through naturalized and racialized ideals of bourgeois womanhood. Throughout the nineteenth century, the heteronorms of private patriarchy also helped secure property relations through marriage and a racialized gender hierarchy required by the economic arrangements of slavery in global capitalism.

The racialized engendering of marriage had very different consequences for white and black women. White women of the elite class were viewed as the means to consolidate property through marriages of alliance, and by birthing and rearing the inheritors of that property. In the U.S. plantation economy in the nineteenth century, female heirs could inherit—sons received land, but daughters slaves (Carby 24). Clearly the slave woman was in a very different relation to the patriarch/plantation owner, as she gave birth directly to capital itself in the form of slaves (Carby 25). As Hazel Carby explains, "The sexual ideology of the period confirmed the differing material circumstances of these two groups of women and resolved the contradiction between the two reproductive positions by balancing opposing definitions of womanhood and motherhood, each dependent on the other for its existence" (25). In the U.S. Deep South where slaves were predominantly agricultural workers, "the slave woman was first a full time worker for her owner, and only incidentally a wife, mother, and homemaker" (Stampp, quoted in Davis 5). Desexed, required to be breeders, and seen as "masculine" as men in their work, black women were positioned outside white normative feminine gender codes in order to facilitate the ruthless exploitation of their labor. They enjoyed few of the benefits of the ideologies of womanhood and motherhood that organized bourgeois heteronorms (Davis 5). The (hetero)sexuality of black men was also not engendered according to the white bourgeois norm. Men and women worked alongside one another, but unlike working-class white men, outside of work black men were ideologically denied the patriarchal positions of family "providers" or family "heads." Of course, as chattel, slaves were forbidden to marry. The norms that regulated family life among slave communities also differed from those governing whites, as did the cultural value of domestic life. While the organization of heterosexual norms through the institution of marriage generally has served the interests of capital, then, it has done so differently for different groups in various social formations, depending on how they are positioned in relations of production that are ideologically organized and justified through racial and gender differences.[8]

Historically the accumulation of profit has relied on the cheap though socially necessary labor of reproducing labor power through women's unpaid or very low paid work in the home. However, in the past few decades, changes in the international sexual division of labor, in marriage law, and in the ideologies of gender suggest that there is no *necessary* relation between a domestic economy organized in terms of the heterosexual marital contract and capital's drive to accumulate wealth for the few. At the same time we acknowledge that patriarchal domestic economies are historically varied and changing, it is important to emphasize that even as more middle-class women enter the paid labor force and private patriarchy's prohibitions around sex outside marriage loosen, heterosexual marriage and the gendered division of labor remain the prevailing, pervasively naturalized social arrangements whose coherence is still assured and legitimized in law and common sense by reference to an abject homosexual other.

Sodomy remains a crime in just under half of the states in the U.S. *Bowers v. Hardwick* brought the state into private sexual spaces in order to reconfirm them as legitimately only heterosexual. Every year thousands of gay teenagers are cast out of their families and are three times more at risk of committing suicide than their straight-identified friends, and lesbian mothers still lose their children in custody battles. Still, there are signs that a transition is under way from the private patriarchy of domestic spaces where heterogender is compulsorily reiterated through the husband's appropriation of the wife's labor and person to a more public patriarchy that may rely less on marriage and heterosexuality. In several cities, local ordinances have been passed that enable hetero- and homosexual couples to register as unmarried domestic partners and to receive some of the rights of married couples.[9] Several corporations have extended insurance benefits to the partners of lesbians and gay men. Without a doubt these are important and necessary achievements of political emancipation that challenge the heterogendered definition of family and household. But it is not enough for a left sexual politics just to focus its agenda on the attainment of these sorts of civil rights within capitalism.

One of the reasons I think it is not brings me back to why a discussion of heterosexual marriage and the family is relevant to a radical queer sexual politics. Avant-garde queer critiques of the arbitrariness of heterosexuality tend to keep invisible how the gendered division of labor has historically secured sexual identities to the family and consumer culture. Domestic partnerships and gay marriages that redefine sexuality only in terms of rights for gays (or straight marriage resisters) leave unquestioned or even indirectly promote capitalism's historical stake in the relations among family, labor, and consumption. The history of gay, lesbian, and queer identities is entangled in changes to the economies of patriarchal households that have accompanied the growth of capitalist consumption and an expanding middle class. Post-marxism does not allow us to address this history, nor does it confront the ways the lives of many lesbians and gays have historically been supported by or involved in the labor of domestics, factory, field, and service workers.

I endorse Judith Butler's argument that repudiating heterosexuals contradicts the anti-essentialism of queer politics (1993, 111–19). It attributes a false unity to heterosexuality (and to homosexual, butch, or femme identities as well) and misses the opportunity to work the weakness in heterosexual identity and to refute its logic of mutual exclusion. Repudiating all heterosexuals is a trap because it suggests, as Butler insightfully demonstrates, that on some level identification with that which is being repudiated (heterosexuals or femmes, for instance) has already taken place and been disavowed. But the politics of repudiation is also a trap because it can keep our understanding of the "economy" of sexual identity and of the grounds for resistance to its hegemonic patriarchal formation restricted to cultural politics.

At issue here is [a] question [. . .] about the limits of radical democracy, limits that are implicit in how we understand the material basis on which hegemonic identities and resistance to them are formulated. If the discourses that construct identities are overdetermined by capitalism's contradictory class processes, the constitutive inability of any identity to secure its referent or to capture what it names—whether that identity be woman, homosexual, heterosexual, or queer—is not the result of an instability inherent to signification, but of the social contradictions on which capitalism is premised and which are condensed in the struggles over naming.[10] Understanding the ground for queer excess so exclusively in terms of the slippages or ambivalences of signification limits the possibility of radical queer intervention to the performative renaming or resignification of norms. Claiming that the materiality of sexual identity is founded on the overdetermined relationship of racialized and gendered discourses of sexuality to class processes does not reduce the history of sexuality to class but rather extends queer politics to queer-y the links between sexual identity and exploitation. From this vantage point, a radical sexual politics is more than a refusal or a resignification of the law. It is also a ruthless interruption of the often less visible relations of labor that have made use of dominant as well as counter-hegemonic sexual identities.

It's my pleasure: consuming desires

As postmodernism is fast becoming the cultural common sense of postindustrial capitalism, it brings in its wake porous, gender-flexible, and playful subjects, subjects more adequate to the complexities of multinational commodity exchange where the expressive self and transcendent morality of liberal humanism have become embarrassingly inadequate (Zavarzadeh 1991, 8). The service sectors of postindustrial economies increasingly require a high-tech systems management consciousness that knows that identity, like knowledge, is performative. This consciousness appears in many zones of postmodern culture from the classroom and boardroom to the fashion runway. Undeniably, performative play with cultural codes is a postmodern fashion statement. Challenges to naturalized notions of identity and difference emanating from Madison Avenue and Wall Street share a certain ideological affiliation with avant-garde queer theory. In fact, I would go so far as to suggest that both indicate the ways in which under late capitalism liberal ambivalence on homosexuality is in the process of being transcoded from the moral and determinate terms of tolerance and disgust to the more postmodern, indeterminate forms of play and pleasure that are helping to consolidate a hegemonic postmodern culture. Postmodern incorporations of a queer "gender fuck" into commodity culture replace the binary logic of liberal moralism's vacillation with the logic of the supplement. Here identities are fluid, open to resignification and re-contextualization. The fixed polarities of liberal morality dissolve into engenderings of pleasure-full erotic indeterminacy. "It is precisely the pleasure produced by the instability of these categories which sustains the various erotic practices that make me a candidate for the category [lesbian] to begin with," announces Judith Butler (1991, 14). For many avant-garde queer theorists, these new cultural and sexual arrangements "occasioned by the movements and transmutations of pleasure in the social field" are not just the occasion for new forms of identity; they also serve as the ground for political organization (Fuss 1991, 5).

Since the late nineteenth century the growth of consumer culture has depended on the formation and continual retooling of a desiring subject, a subject who honors pleasures and may even see them as forces that drive one's existence or as pressing needs. Alexandra Kollontai recognized this effect of capitalism at the turn of the century when she treated the family under capitalism as a legal arrangement concerned only with consumption (Holt 225). The increasing separation of sexuality from class analysis is one component of the cultural production of this desiring subject in the late nineteenth century, as it has helped guarantee that desire take on a life of its own. The important point here is not to dismiss desire and pleasure as bourgeois inventions irrelevant to materialist analysis. Quite the contrary; if we are to understand the historical and material components of sexual identities, we also need to know the social forces out of which the desiring subject and the subject of pleasure are formed.

As it has come to be understood in Western culture, desire has had an uneasy relationship to sexual identity, serving as a labile medium for affective and sensory needs. It is a structure for consciousness that binds sexual subject to sexual object and also perversely disrupts any neatly prescribed links between them. Most theoretical attention to the desiring subject has been developed from a psychologizing/psychoanalytic frame that has been largely responsible for an individualized understanding of desire as a psychic process whose materiality is rooted in the drives and conveyed through the symbolic order. Another strand of queer theory emerges out of postmodern versions of this theoretical frame and foregrounds the disruptive face of desire for interrupting any coherent, generative agency. The effect on sexual identity is that any prescribed relation between sexual subject and sexual object is undone. One sticking point in this formulation of queer identity is how to understand the materiality of this desire.

Gilles Deleuze and Felix Guattari's *Anti-Oedipus: Capitalism and Schizophrenia* (1983) has been embraced by many queer theorists as a monumental explanation of the materiality of desire under capitalism. Even more dramatically than Marcuse and Reich, however, Deleuze and Guattari locate desire outside of history. The libidinal energy that for Marcuse and Reich constituted a life force that is ultimately shaped by history (albeit a too mythic history) becomes for Deleuze and Guattari the very matter of life—manifest in pervasive, natural, human desiring machines. The premise of their argument in *Anti-Oedipus* is that desire in the form of energy that flows between organ-machines—or what they call "desiring production"—is the starting point of social life. No longer understood in terms of lack, desire or libido is the primary connective "labor" of desiring production. Indeed, desiring production *is* social production. Opposed to psychoanalytic theory and practice for the ways it tames or "territorializes" desire by anchoring it in the Oedipus complex, Deleuze and Guattari dis-organize subjectivity, unchain it from socially restrictive forces, and recode it around concepts of plurality, multiplicity, decenteredness. In their schema, desire becomes the basis of social production. Instead of being the product of history, desire is historically invariant matter. The material of desire is the primordial matter of energy flows or of things connected by energy flows—"menstrual flow, amniotic fluid spilling out of the sac; flowing hair; a flow of spittle, a flow of sperm, shit or urine" (5).

Such a premise glorifies desire and makes it impossible to treat the ways its content and the forms the desiring subject has taken change from one historical formation to another and in different phases of capitalism. The desiring subject put forward in *Anti-Oedipus* has been embraced by quite a few queer theorists precisely because this is a subject that has no fixed identity.[11] [. . .] For Deleuze and Guattari, the distinctions between hetero- and homosexual identities are disjunctions forced upon subjects by the Oedipus complex: "Oedipus informs us: if you don't follow the lines of differentiation daddy-mommy-me, you will fall into the black night of the undifferentiated" (78). The Oedipus complex is the representative of a symbolic order that represses desiring production in that it requires exclusive disjunctions (between masculine and feminine terms of identification and desire). Deleuze and Guattari acknowledge that capitalism liberates the flows of desire from the clutches of an oedipalizing culture, but it does so under social conditions that continually reterritorialize the desires it unleashes in order to accrue surplus value. As they see it, desiring production is revolutionary and capable of demolishing social form. But unfortunately and predictably, the alternative it aims for is not social justice but the "body without organs"—the undifferentiated subject of self-enjoyment.

Clearly in Deleuze and Guattari's post-marxist theories we see an intensified emphasis on desire as the motor of history and an elevation of the desiring subject as history's agent. Despite their references to capitalism, however, here the separation of sexuality from historical and material production has become complete. Desire and the desiring subject have assumed the center stage of history, and the structures of exploitation on which capitalist production depends have completely disappeared. Indeed, production has become consumption.

To the extent that they make desire the bedrock of history, Deleuze and Guattari's desiring production shares an affiliation with Foucault's now infamous stance on bodies and pleasures. Foucault argues that power and pleasure in a (post)modern disciplinary regime are entangled in a perpetual relay system. Discourses have traced around bodies and sexes "perpetual spirals of power and pleasure" (Foucault 1978, 45). In the form of an array of discursive mechanisms in the nineteenth-century industrialized West, power "took charge of sexuality, set about contacting bodies, caressing them with its eyes, intensifying areas, electrifying surfaces, dramatizing troubled moments. It wrapped the sexual body in its embrace" (1978, 44). But he also contends that the rallying point for resistance to this web of power– pleasure relations is "bodies and pleasures" (1978, 157). In this much quoted assertion,

Foucault puts forward bodies and pleasures as the ground for resistance to power and in a manner that tends to set them outside their discursive construction and beyond history, much like Deleuze and Guattari's desire.

The turn to pleasure and desire as categories of experience outside culture–ideology and prior to all social production has been one of the most significant features of culture study in the late eighties (Turner 1990, 218), and Foucault's influence in this trend has been considerable. The effort to reclaim the core of identity in the form of an ahistorical pleasure (as *jouissance*, ritual, *chora*, or ambivalent consumer satisfaction) has been a crucial aspect of the formation of a new postmodern subject and needs to be understood in terms of the political and economic arrangements of an emerging neoliberal world order (post-cold war, postcolonial) and its effects on the historical pertinences that shape subjectivities. Recognizing that pleasure does not precede or exceed the social but is itself constituted through the often contradictory economic, political, and ideological production of social life means that its hegemonic articulation is always precarious. Like work, pleasure cannot be or mean as a basis for political affirmation outside its historical organization. But, in fact, this is often how pleasure is understood in the cultural politics of the postmodern left.

For example, in the anthology *Formations of Pleasure*, British cultural critic Colin Mercer argues that the contradictory *play* of ideology can no longer "be reduced to questions of meaning and truth. You can ask whether people 'believe' what they hear on the News or on *Nationwide*, but it's by no means clear what people would 'believe' in light entertainment or comedy. Once enjoyment and pleasure are reintroduced—those jokes in the game—we have to change the rules and go beyond the message" (85). Picking up on his comment, Tania Modleski argues that ideology is effective because it bestows pleasure on its subjects rather than simply conveying messages, "and so it cannot be combated only at the level of meaning" (Modleski 1991, 57). For this reason, she continues, "a theory and practice of the performative are crucial to a politically engaged criticism" (Modleski 1991, 57). Although her comment implies a separation between pleasures and meaning-making that I think never quite occurs, she recognizes that pleasure is an important sensuous-affective dimension of human life that ideology taps into.

Neither the motor of production, nor a prediscursive matter or energy, the human capacity for sensation and affect is the basis for pleasure and it is always historically organized. It is powerfully solicited in the organization of sexual identities as well as in many other areas of culture and deployed in broad-ranging ideologies (of romance, sexuality, religion, patriotism, etc.) and practices (consumption, shaming, entertainment, education, social movement, etc.) that permeate the fabric of individual lives and collectivities. In other words, sensations (including "pleasurable" sensations) never speak for themselves but are always made sense of by the ways of knowing that circulate within a particular social organization or community; pleasures are never entirely outside the "structures of meaning-making." When they are recruited by ideology, sensations and pleasures can be powerful ways to naturalize the historical social relations identities rely on. In part for this reason, they are also especially important areas of social life for a politically engaged criticism. However, to conceptualize the interface between sensation-affect and meaning-making as performative in the terms set forth by cultural materialists risks forfeiting the crucial connection between local and global social structures that the concept of ideology entails. In other words, associated as it is with the cultural materialist notion of discursive play and of culture as the shifting basis for social life, performativity cannot make visible the varied, complex, and uneven historical relationship between pleasure and profit.

Having embraced the potential of sexual pleasure, avant-garde queer theory does indeed "change the rules" by founding its politics on a notion of performance that often not only implies a division between the conceptual and the performative but disparages interrogation and critical analysis. Diana Fuss's assertion that the essays in the anthology *Inside/Out* "mark an important shift away from an interrogative mode and towards a performative mode" in queer theory signals just this sort of displacement of critical concepts (1991, 7).

A materialist approach to sexual identity that reclaims the attention to social totalities that constitutes the radical tradition of the Gay Left—that is, marxism's critique of capitalism and feminism's critique of patriarchy—can resist the pressure to separate sexuality off from capitalism and class relations off from sexuality and desire. It may even read this fragmentation as an ideological symptom. Such an approach to sexuality does not shrink from celebrating the human capacity for sensual pleasure even as it dares to think through—and change—the material relations among identities, norms, state power, and divisions of labor. Of course, by insisting that the more fluid boundaries of postmodern culture have not made patriarchy or capitalism any less viable, the radical sexual politics I am referring to is out of line with the post-marxist mainstream. You might even consider it excessively queer. That excessiveness may well be precisely its challenge and its strength.

Notes

1   See, for example, Michael Warner's report on queer theory in the *Voice Literary Supplement* (1992), which highlights the attention Butler's work was getting in the early nineties as well as the controversy it initially provoked. Routledge is now preparing the tenth anniversary issue of *Gender Trouble* and anticipates record sales.

2   For more detailed critical readings of Laclau and Mouffe see Geras (1987); Hennessy (1993); Larsen (1990).

3   Eve Sedgwick's essay on queer performativity (1993) is another notable example of an argument for queer identity that sets the securing of queer identities through the performative "Shame on you!" against the performative "I do" of marriage. Because she sees both practices merely as individuating speech acts, however, Sedgwick never addresses the material relationships between institutionalized heterogender and the much more diffuse material discourses of shame, between discursive identity performances and other social relations.

4   Several studies support this assertion. One indicates that in recent history women who enter the paid labor force increased their total work time by 14 to 25 hours; another reveals that an overriding majority of working mothers continue to prepare dinner and clean up afterwards alone. For more detailed citations see Fraad, Resnick, and Wolff (1994, 49–50).

5   Associated Press. "More Americans Living out of Wedlock." *Albany Times Union*, 27 July 1998. A1.

6   The concept of the feudal patriarchal domestic economy is developed in Fraad, Resnick, and Wolff. The distinction between private and public patriarchy has been theorized by Ann Ferguson (1989) and also by Walby (1990).

7   According to the *New York Times* (20 February 1994), a study by Women Work.

8   See Spillers (1987) on some of the implications of this history for representations of family and incest in African-American culture.

9   Some of these include visitation rights at hospitals and jails, unpaid leaves for a new child, or rights to the same status as married couples in qualifying for apartments or insurance benefits.

10   Butler alludes to this sort of economy when she addresses the ways the constitutive instability of "woman" is the effect of a dense intersection of paternal social relations (1993, 218). But her normative materiality omits the gendered division of labor from these social relations.

11   Guy Hocquenghem's *Homosexual Desire* extends Deleuze and Guattari's critique of the oedipal family to develop a more specific theory of homosexual oppression as part of a wider system of exploitation; in line with their thinking, he proposes "fusions of desire" as the basis for social revolution.

Works cited

Butler, Judith. 1997. "Merely Cultural." *Social Text* 52/53: 15:3 and 4 (Winter): 265–77.
—. 1993. *Bodies That Matter: On the Discursive Limits of "Sex."* New York: Routledge.

—. 1991. "Imitation and Gender Insubordination." *Inside/Out: Lesbian Theories, Gay Theories*. Ed. Diana Fuss. New York: Routledge. 13–31.

—. 1990. *Gender Trouble: Feminism and the Subversion of Identity*. New York: Routledge.

Carby, Hazel V. 1987. *Reconstructing Womanhood. The Emergence of the Afro-American Woman Novelist*. New York: Oxford.

Davis, Angela Y. 1983. *Women, Race, and Class*. New York: Vintage.

de Lauretis, Teresa. 1991. "Queer Theory: Lesbian and Gay Sexualities: An Introduction." *differences* 3.2: iii–xviii.

Deleuze, Gilles, and Felix Guattari. 1983. *Anti-Oedipus: Capitalism and Schizophrenia*. Minneapolis: University of Minnesota Press.

Edelman, Lee. 1994. *Homographesis: Essays in Gay Literary and Cultural Theory*. New York: Routledge.

Ferguson, Ann. 1989. *Blood at the Root: Motherhood, Sexuality and Male Dominance*. London: Pandora Press.

Foucault, Michel. 1978. *The History of Sexuality*, Vol. 1. Trans. Robert Hurley, New York: Vintage.

Fraad, Harriet, Stephen Resnick, and Richard Wolff. 1994. *Bringing It All Back Home: Class, Gender and Power in the Modern Household*. London: Pluto.

Fuss, Diana, ed. 1991. *Inside/Out Lesbian Theories, Gay Theories*. New York: Routledge.

Geras, Norman. 1987. "Post-Marxism?" *New Left Review* 163: 40–82.

Hennessy, Rosemary. 1993. *Materialist Feminism and the Politics of Discourse*. New York: Routledge.

Hocquenghem, Guy. 1993. *Homosexual Desire*. Durham, N.C.: Duke University Press.

Holt, Alix, ed. 1977. *Selected Writings of Alexandra Kollontai*. New York: Norton.

Ingraham, Chrys. 1999. *White Weddings: Romancing Heterosexuality in Popular Culture*. New York: Routledge.

Koestenbaum, Wayne. 1993. *The Queen's Throat. Opera, Homosexuality, and the Mystery of Desire*. New York: Vintage.

Laclau, Ernesto, and Chantal Mouffe. 1985. *Hegemony and Socialist Strategy: Towards a Radical Democratic Politics*. London: Verso.

Larsen, Neil. 1990. *Modernism and Hegemony: A Materialist Critique of Aesthetic Agencies*. Minnesota: University of Minnesota Press.

Mercer, Colin. 1983. "A Poverty of Desire: Pleasure and Popular Politics." *Formations of Pleasure*. Eds. Tony Bennett, Colin Mercer, and Janet Wollacott. London: Routledge and Kegan Paul.

Modleski, Tanya. 1991. *Feminism without Women: Culture and Criticism in a Post-Feminist Age*. New York: Routledge.

Phelan, Peggy. 1993. *Unmarked: The Politics of Performance*. New York: Routledge.

Sedgwick, Eve Kosotsky. 1993. "Queer Performativity." *GLQ: A Journal of Lesbian and Gay Studies* 1.1: 1–16.

Spillers, Hortense. 1987. "Mama's Baby, Papa's Maybe: An American Grammar Book." *Diacritics* 17:2. 454–81.

Turner, Graeme. 1990. *British Cultural Studies: An Introduction*. New York: Routledge.

Walby, Sylvia. 1990. *Theorizing Patriarchy*. London: Blackwell.

Warner, Michael, ed. 1993. *Fear of a Queer Planet: Queer Politics and Social Theory*. Minneapolis: University of Minnesota Press.

—. 1992. "From Queer to Eternity." *Voice Literary Supplement* (June): 18–19.

Zavarzadeh, Mas'ud. 1991. *Seeing Films Politically*. Albany: State University of New York Press.

Chapter 9

Tim Dean

LACAN MEETS QUEER THEORY

Tim Dean is Professor of English and Director of Humanities Institute at the State University of New York, Buffalo. He is the author of *Unlimited Intimacy: Reflections on the Subculture of Barebacking* (2009) and *Beyond Sexuality* (2000), among other works. In *Beyond Sexuality*, from which the following is excerpted, Dean argues that queer theory and psychoanalysis are not only compatible theoretical frameworks for understanding sexuality, but that psychoanalysis is itself a queer theory.

In "Lacan Meets Queer Theory," Dean argues for the intersection and applicability of Lacanian psychoanalysis and queer theories of sexuality. According to Dean, Lacan's notion of sexuality defines desire not by gender choice, but by the object *a* (*l'object petit a*), which remains separate from gender. The object *a*, as Deans argues later in this chapter, is a term that designates an excess (not lack) that keeps self-identity unattainable, thus perpetuating and prefiguring desire. In doing so, the phallus is displaced from its primacy, which allows the object *a* to be thought as multiple impulses and myriad possibilities, none of which are directly related to gender identification. Desire, then, emerges separately from the binary of homo- or heterosexuality. Through this formulation, Dean works against the notion that psychoanalysis serves as a modern technology that regulates sexuality.

THIS CHAPTER ENVISIONS a dialogue between Lacan and queer theory, a sort of roundtable in which various contemporary theorists of sexuality would directly engage Lacan—and he them. But, of course, Lacan died well before queer theory emerged as such; and, as Thomas Yingling observed, queer theorists prepared to grapple with Freud nonetheless have remained relatively shy of tackling the corpus of speculative work bequeathed by Lacan.[1] Furthermore, I discovered to my disappointment at an International Conference on Sexuation (in New York City, April 1997, where I first presented a preliminary version of this chapter) that for their part Lacanian analysts proved far less willing to engage queer theory than I, perhaps naively, had anticipated. Yet spurred on by my conviction that psychoanalysis *is* a queer theory, I've persisted with this imaginary encounter, a dialogue between—to invoke Yeats—self and antiself.

In *Encore*, his seminar devoted most directly to the topic of sexuality, Lacan speaks often of homosexuality, but with the crucial qualification that as far as love is concerned, gender is irrelevant: *"quand on aime, il ne s'agit pas de sexe"* (*SXX* 27). What should we make of this idea that the gender of object-choice remains ultimately inconsequential in love? Is Lacan merely voicing liberal tolerance, anticipating by a matter of months his transatlantic counterparts' elimination of homosexuality from the *Diagnostic and Statistical Manual of Mental Disorders*, in 1973?[2] Or, more interestingly, could we view Lacan as foreshadowing by a couple of decades the radical move in queer theory to think sexuality outside the terms of gender?[3] Although I consider liberal tolerance far less passé than do most queer theorists, I want to make the case for Lacan as more radical than liberal on the question of homosexuality. I'll make this case by explaining how Lacan's account of sexuality reveals desire as determined not by the gender of object-choice, but by the object *a* (*l'objet petit a*), which remains largely independent of gender. By detaching desire from gender, Lacan helps to free desire from normative hetero-sexuality—that is, from the pervasive assumption that *all* desire, even same-sex attraction, is effectively heterosexual by virtue of its flowing between masculine and feminine subject-positions, regardless of the participants' actual anatomy in any given sexual encounter.

I intend to show how Lacan makes good on certain radical moments in Freud, such as the latter's counterheterosexist observation that "the sexual instinct is in the first instance independent of its object; nor is its origin likely to be due to its object's attractions" (*SE* 7: 148). Through his concept of object *a*, Lacan alters what Freud means when he speaks of sexual objects, and I intend to use Lacan *with* queer theory to mount a critique of the Freudian notion of sexual object-choice as such. It is not so much a question of my isolating those moments in psychoanalytic texts that lend support to a progressive sexual politics, nor even of illuminating the fault lines of these texts in order to reinvigorate them, as psychoanalytic readers from Laplanche to Bersani, Davidson, and de Lauretis have done so brilliantly.[4] Instead, I am concerned to demonstrate how Lacan pursues the logic of Freudian insights about sex to a new destination—and how we may push this logic yet further for contem-porary sexual politics. Thus I shall argue that this radical Freudian tradition discredits the otherwise amazingly durable nineteenth-century notion that homosexual desire expresses "a feminine soul trapped in a masculine body," or vice versa. In so doing, it also discredits the idea that psychoanalysis is a modern technology designed to regulate and normalize sexuality, as some queer theorists, following Foucault, continue to claim.[5] On the contrary, Lacanian psychoanalysis provides a uniquely valuable source of resistance to just such normalization. In what follows, I'll elaborate on Lacan's antinormative potential and try to account for queer theory's failure to exploit that potential.

Nature/nurture—neither

> To encounter desire is first of all to forget the difference in the sexes.
>
> (Guy Hocquenghem, *Homosexual Desire*)

Much of the impasse between Lacan and queer theory stems from problems of translation, difficulties that are as much cultural and ideological as linguistic. To begin with there is the problem of Freud's American reception, which, in seeking to make Viennese speculation about sex palatable in the United States, drastically normalized revolutionary psychoanalytic ideas about sexuality. This is by now a fairly well-known story, told in broad historical terms by Russell Jacoby and elaborated with respect to male homosexuality most notably by Kenneth Lewes and Henry Abelove.[6] In his pioneering study of the American domestication of psycho-analysis, historian Abelove argues that Freud's position on homosexuality was far more progressive than those held by his transatlantic followers, both sympathetic and hostile, later in the century: "Freud was perfectly consistent on the subject of homosexuality," Abelove claims; "[w]hat he told the American mother in his letter of 1935, that it was neither advantage, crime, illness, nor disgrace, he had long believed and acted on."[7] However, once Freudianism migrated to the United States, American analysts promoted a fantasy of eradicating homosexuality altogether, willfully disregarding Freud's conclusion, in his *Three Essays on the Theory of Sexuality*, that "all human beings are capable of making a homosexual object-choice and have in fact made one in their unconscious" (*SE* 7: 145). Considering this emphasis on the unconscious, we can begin to grasp how the efforts of institutionalized psychoanalysis to "cure" homosexuality remain coeval with American psychoanalytic attempts to cure the *unconscious* out of existence. Seen from this vantage point, Lacan's critique of American ego psychology is readily appropriable for queer theory's critique of institutionalized homophobia.

Freud's view that, at least in the unconscious, *we're all a little queer* conforms to what Eve Kosofsky Sedgwick calls the "universalizing" conception of homosexuality—as distinguished from the "minoritizing" conception, which views same-sex object-choice as characterizing a specific group of people, a sexual minority whose identity is thence defined in contradistinction to that of the majority.[8] "Psychoanalytic research is most decidedly opposed to any attempt at separating off homosexuals from the rest of mankind as a group of a special character," insists Freud, explicitly countering the minoritizing conception of sexual inversion propagated in his own time by figures such as Karl Heinrich Ulrichs, Richard von Krafft-Ebing, and Magnus Hirschfeld (*SE* 7: 145). Although the idea of a sexual minority enables a form of political campaigning that culminates in civil rights activism, Abelove's account makes clear how a minoritizing view also serves the American mental health establishment's homophobic purposes by confining homosexuality to a single demographic. And so while I'm persuaded more by the universalizing than by the minoritizing conception of homosexuality, in the end Freud's contention that we've all made a homosexual object-choice (whether we know it or not) doesn't go far enough, because his notion of object-choice remains trapped within the terms of gender. The very possibility of describing object-choice as homosexual or heterosexual takes for granted that the object chosen is gendered and that—no matter how partial or fragmented the object may be—it's somehow identifiable as masculine or feminine. In contrast, Lacan's concept of object *a* radically revises the Freudian notion of object-choice by leaving gender behind, in a move whose far-reaching implications I wish to delineate.

We may approach the ungendered or degendered conception of object-choice by considering a less appreciated dimension of Freud's American reception, one involving the distinction between a psychoanalytic, largely European understanding of sexual difference and a sociological, largely North American understanding of gender. This distinction is raised by Lacan's comment, quoted above, that "*quand on aime, il ne s'agit pas de sexe.*"[9] Although the French word *sexe* roughly conforms to what we mean by gender, this translation elides the specifically psychoanalytic dimension of sex; and so one is forced to confront the conceptual limits of the terms—*sex, gender, sexuality*—available for this discussion.

Conventionally we distinguish sex from gender according to the coordinates of certain well-rehearsed debates—essentialism versus constructionism, or the longer-standing controversy known as nature versus nurture. The force of gender as a concept lies in how it denaturalizes sexual difference, making sex a question of social and historical construction rather than of biological essence. And sexuality, or sexual orientation, tends to be discussed within the framework of these same debates.[10] Indeed, the term *sexuality* is regularly understood to involve questions not only of desire but also of identity, so that the issue of one's sexuality tends to be taken as referring not only to the putative gender of one's object-choice but also to one's *own* gender identity, one's masculinity or femininity. However, we can begin to appreciate the danger of keeping sexuality so closely tied to gender by considering how the diagnosis of "gender identity disorder," in *DSM*, readily takes over the pathologizing role formerly assigned to "homosexuality."[11]

To free a theory of sexuality from the ideological constraints imposed by gender categories also permits us to divorce sexuality from the straitjacket of identity. Another way of putting this would be to say that psychoanalysis enables us to think sexuality apart from the ego. And, as I've suggested, this way of thinking becomes possible only through some concept equivalent to that of the unconscious: it remains a basic psychoanalytic postulate that while there is always sex, there can be no sexuality without the unconscious. Thus for Lacan sexuality is explicable in terms of neither nature *nor* nurture, since the unconscious cannot be considered biological—it isn't part of my body and yet it isn't exactly culturally constructed either. Instead, the unconscious may be grasped as an index of how both biology and culture *fail* to determine subjectivity and sexual desire. Thinking of the unconscious as neither biological nor cultural allows us to distinguish (among other things) a properly psychoanalytic from a merely psychological notion of the unconscious.

In making such distinctions, I consider it important to specify how Lacan's account of sexuality remains unassimilable to the nature/nurture debate, especially since arguments between essentialists and social constructionists have become increasingly polarized in recent years. Yet I want to emphasize that psychoanalysis does not offer some compromise between these polarities; rather, Lacan furnishes the conceptual means for developing a genuine alternative to them. At the essentialist pole of this debate neuroanatomists and geneticists, such as Simon LeVay and Dean Hamer, search for the biological *cause* of homosexuality in hypothalamic structure or chromosomes.[12] At the social constructionist pole philosophers, such as Judith Butler, meticulously deconstruct the sex–gender distinction in order to argue that the ostensibly pregiven, immutable category in this conceptual couple—that is, biological sex—is just as much a result of historically contingent processes of materialization as is gender.[13] As I argued in the previous chapter, the deconstructionist position takes constructionism one step further by arguing that bodies aren't simply the raw material that social processes use to construct gender and sexuality, but rather that corporeal matter itself must be *materialized* through social processes of embodiment. And for this reason the deconstructionist account of sexuality sometimes advertises itself as a critique of and alternative to—rather than simply a refinement of—social constructionism.

But from my point of view the various sides in this debate miss the point of a psychoanalytic critique of sex, gender, and sexuality, since the purpose of such a critique is not (like deconstruction) to devise ever subtler ways of revealing that what seemed natural is in fact cultural or a positive effect of the symbolic order. Thus although Butler uses Lacan to support her argument, in the end psychoanalysis authorizes the constructionist (or deconstructionist) account of sexuality no more than it authorizes the essentialist one. Hence Freud's insistence that "[t]he nature of inversion is explained neither by the hypothesis that it is innate nor by the alternative hypothesis that it is acquired" (*SE* 7: 140). And so while it's possible to identify passages in Freud that appear to support either side of the nature/nurture debate, I prefer to draw out a psychoanalytic logic that remains fundamentally irreducible to this debate's terms, even in their most recent, most advanced form. By describing sexuality in terms of unconscious desire, I wish to separate sexual orientation from questions of identity and of gender roles, practices, and performances, since it is by conceiving sexuality outside the terms of gender *and* identity that we can most thoroughly deheterosexualize desire.

The queer critique of normativity

> Because the logic of the sexual order is so deeply embedded by now in an indescribably wide range of social institutions, and is embedded in the most standard accounts of the

> world, queer struggles aim not just at toleration or equal status but at challenging those
> institutions and accounts.
>
> (Michael Warner, introduction to *Fear of a Queer Planet:*
> *Queer Politics and Social Theory*)

Having reached this point, we should now acknowledge that the problems entailed in confining sexuality to the terms of identity also ignited queer theory, which emerged as an intellectual and political movement only during the 1990s, in the wake of feminism, gay liberation, and the AIDS epidemic.[14] Although queer theory's newness and heterodoxical configurations make hazardous any attempt at definition, we may nevertheless characterize these new epistemological and ideological configurations in order to distinguish their most salient features.[15] Queer theory views with postmodern skepticism the minoritizing conception of sexuality that undergirds gay liberation and women's liberation (and hence academically institutionalized gay studies and women's studies too). Building on the civil rights movements of the 1960s, feminism and gay liberation based their claims for political participation and radical equality, whether assimilationist or separatist, on the foundation of *identity*—female, gay, lesbian, and, more recently, bisexual, transsexual, transgendered identities. By contrast, queer theory and politics begin from a critique of identity and of identity politics, inspired primarily by Foucault's analysis of the disciplinary purposes that sexual identities so easily serve. As Butler encapsulates this Foucaultian critique: "[I]dentity categories tend to be instruments of regulatory regimes, whether as the normalizing categories of oppressive structures or as the rallying points for a liberatory contestation of that very oppression."[16] Or as Foucault himself put it, ventriloquizing Deleuze and Guattari, "Do not demand of politics that it restore the 'rights' of the individual, as philosophy has defined them. The individual is the product of power."[17] We can see immediately how this blunt admonition flies in the face of Enlightenment postulates of individual liberty and autonomous agency, upon which U.S. society and politics are based. Before discussing the political consequences of this reconceptualization, I'd like to consider further its methodological implications.

Queer theory's Foucaultian suspicion of identity *tout court* leads in two competing directions. On one hand, it has inspired a cautious return to psychoanalytic epistemologies among some queer theorists, given how Freud's theory of the unconscious introduces a constitutive subjective division that undermines the possibility of any seamless identity, sexual or otherwise. Even critics with a more thoroughgoing mistrust of psychoanalysis as a heterosexist and homophobic institution have been led, practically despite themselves, to invent conceptual categories tantamount to that of the unconscious.[18]

Yet, on the other hand, queer theory's critique of identity as a regulatory norm has also led diametrically away from psychoanalytic epistemologies, encouraged in large part by Foucault's displacement of attention from identities to practices. Thus although historicism shares with psychoanalysis the view that identities are essentially illusory, historicism resorts to the empiricist solution of investigating discrete social and cultural practices, whereas psychoanalysis focuses on what, though not exactly illusory, nevertheless resists empirical verification, namely, fantasy. Foucault makes this distinction explicit in a 1982 interview:

> I don't try to write an archaeology of sexual fantasies, I try to make an archaeology of discourse about sexuality, which is really the relationship between what we do, what we are obliged to do, what we are allowed to do, what we are forbidden to do in the field of sexuality, and what we are allowed, forbidden, or obliged to say about our sexual behavior. That's the point. It's not a problem of fantasy; it's a problem of verbalization.[19]

[. . . I]t is easy to see how the concrete reality of sexual practices appears to carry greater political weight than the comparative ephemerality of sexual fantasies, which often seem luxurious and trivial in the face of material oppression. [. . . S]uch a hierarchy of political seriousness may itself betoken heterosexist logic: fantasy remains so phenomenologically and conceptually inextricable from perversion that the characteristic relegation of fantasy to zones of secondariness, irrationality, passivity, and immaturity should give us pause. Furthermore, the strong vein of utopianism in queer theory suggests the importance of fantasy to its simultaneously political and sexual agendas—"almost everything that can be called queer theory has been radically anticipatory, trying to bring a world into being," note two of queer theory's most prominent spokespersons.[20]

But before we can specify what's so queer about fantasy, we must grasp more precisely what queerness implies. Far more than a handy moniker covering the rainbow coalition of nonnormative sexualities (lesbian, gay, bisexual, transsexual, and so on), "queer" extends the politics of sexuality beyond sex and sexual minorities' civil rights by insisting that "queer" is opposed not simply to "straight," but more broadly to "normal." Defining itself against the normal, queerness exceeds sexuality, sexual practices, sexual identities; indeed, this is how people whose sexual partners are primarily, even exclusively, of the opposite sex get to count as queer. Queer theory depends on identificatory alliances rather than on identities as such; and queer politics thus involves creating alliances between sexual minorities and other social groups whose marginalization or disenfranchisement isn't necessarily a direct consequence of nonnormative sexuality. Hence the centrality accorded ostensibly nonsexual categories—such as race, ethnicity, and nationality—in queer theory, which isn't so much about being inclusive (under the aegis of an ever expanding liberal tolerance) as it is about connecting one dimension of social exclusion with others. And in light of this commitment to discerning alliances, I have often wondered why queer theorists have not forged more of an alliance with Lacanian psychoanalysts, given the thoroughgoing antinormative bias in Lacan's work. Yet though Lacan reads to me like a queer theorist *avant la lettre*, the institutional history of psychoanalysis, particularly in the United States, has forestalled any such alliance. [. . .]

If *queer* represents more than merely a broader or hipper term for gayness and more than a new form of avant-gardism, then queer theory's principal challenge must be to confront the consequences of defining oneself and one's politics against norms as such.[21] The implications of such a stance are radical indeed, particularly in a society whose ideology of individualism guarantees maximum liberty to pursue one's own version of happiness—on condition only that he or she conform. In view of this ideological double bind, Michael Warner correctly identifies queer theory's paradoxically antisocial utopianism:

> Organizing a movement around queerness also allows [queer theory] to draw on dissatisfaction with the regime of the normal in general. Following Hannah Arendt, we might even say that queer politics opposes society itself . . . The social realm, in short, is a cultural form, interwoven with the political form of the administrative state and with the normalizing methodologies of modern social knowledge. Can we not hear in the resonances of queer protest an objection to the normalization of behavior in this broad sense, and thus to the cultural phenomenon of societalization? If queers, incessantly told to alter their "behavior," can be understood as protesting not just the normal behavior of the social but the *idea* of normal behavior, they will bring skepticism to the methodologies founded on that idea.[22]

The capaciousness and force of queerness stem not simply from its opposing sexual norms—or what, almost two decades ago, Adrienne Rich diagnosed as "compulsory heterosexuality"[23]—but from its resistance to the very idea of the normal as such. Thus by contrast with most gay journalism about sexual politics, queer theory, in its avowed opposition to "society itself," assumes that those who've been socially excluded don't *want* to "fit in" or conform as social beings.[24] It is sometimes hard to decide whether this assumption betrays an elitist disregard for the self-perceptions and desires of nonheterosexuals outside the university (particularly working-class queers), or whether it signals a greater ideological awareness enabled by academic freedom and, indeed, promotes a laudatory shouldering of the political responsibilities that accompany institutional privilege.

Queer theory assumes not only that queers' early sense of alienation effectively renders social conformity impossible, but also that queer opposition to social norms represents far more than an expression of aggressivity or "acting out" under the guise of political activism. Furthermore, queer theory stakes its utopian claims on the conviction that opposing "society itself" doesn't necessarily incur the loneliness of psychosis, foreclosed from all social ties, but that, on the contrary, queer political resistance provides access to alternate forms of community and other social ties—perhaps even other *forms* of social tie, different ways of knotting the subject to society and community.[25] Indeed, more than a decade before queer theory came along, Foucault was already speculating about the radically different kinds of social tie that homosexuals might establish. Distinguishing between homophobic intolerance of gay sex and horror at the possibility of gay sociality, he explained, in a well-publicized interview, that "[i]t is the prospect that gays will create as yet unforeseen kinds of relationships that many people cannot tolerate."[26]

Lacan's critique of normativity

> Strengthening the categories of affective normativity produces disturbing results.
> (Jacques Lacan, *The Seminar of Jacques Lacan,*
> *Book VII: The Ethics of Psychoanalysis*[27])

Rather than directly adjudicating either queer theory's claims or the philosophical presuppositions on which they're based, I want to explore them further by considering how Lacan's account of sexuality harmonizes with queer theory's. In view of its revisionary interventions in social theory, queer politics could be regarded as quintessentially American, as the latest chapter in a long history of native self-invention, utopianism, and experimental communitarianism that characterizes U.S. social politics. Yet on the other hand, queer theory's antinormative, anti-identitarian, and antiliberal commitments make it appear every bit as "un-American" as some of its detractors charge. From this perspective, it is significant that Lacan also directs his critique of norms—including what he pointedly calls "the delusional 'normality' of the genital relation" (*E* 245)—against the American ideology of individualism, particularly as it finds expression in the normalizing ethos of "adaptation to reality" that ego psychology promulgates as the goal of psychoanalytic therapy.

Lacan views the conception of therapy in terms of adaptation as a problem not simply because the reality to which one should adapt turns out to be "heteronormative" (in Warner's terms), but more fundamentally because *reality itself* is *imaginary*. Since we are accustomed to thinking of reality and the imaginary as antithetical, Lacan's paradoxical alignment of the two warrants careful examination. (And even before grasping the full significance of this equation, we can begin to appreciate that what Lacan means by "the real" must be very far from "reality," if reality is imaginary.) It is when one conceives reality in terms of adaptation that it is given over to the imaginary, in that "reality" thus comes to represent a set of norms or ideal forms to which we're supposed to aspire and on the basis of which our egos must be modeled and remodeled. Hence Lacan's objection to the normalizing function of psychology: "Psychology transmits ideals"—to which he adds, "[i]deals are society's slaves" ("Position" 262).

Lacan maintains that so long as psychoanalysts focus exclusively on the ego or individual, they will remain trapped within an essentially prescriptive discourse of norms and normativity. Since the ego comes into being through projective idealization—by means of misrecognitions of images of the other—the ego is nothing but a precipitate of idealized models. Whatever their content, these models are susceptible to idealization insofar as their form appears totalized, bounded, and complete; these imaginary models provide the subject points of coherence with which to identify within a seamless picture of the world. By means of these imaginary identifications the subject finds a place in reality—and so experiences a measure of jubilation, irrespective of how culturally prized or disprized that place may be.[28] Thus "reality" constitutes the sum of these models and norms, the imaginary ideals to which we're supposed to conform not merely in our behavior but in our very existence and perceptions. From this we might say that insofar as reality is imaginary, it is also utopic, a pure projection. Queer theory's counter-utopianism makes more sense in this light. And Lacan himself points out that the American ideology of adaptation mystifies reproductive heterosexuality as the norm: "Goodness only knows how obscure such a pretension as the achievement of genital objecthood (*l'objectalité genitale*) remains, along with what is so imprudently linked to it, namely, adjustment to reality" (*SVII* 293).

However, Lacan's response to normativity is not to produce alternative imaginaries, but to elaborate an alternative of a different order—that of the real, a conceptual category intended to designate everything that *resists* adaptation. As he remarks with characteristic irreverence when alluding to normative accounts of psychosexual development, "what has this absurd hymn to the harmony of the genital got to do with the real?" (*E* 245).[29] Insofar as the real represents that concept through which Lacan challenges heteronormativity, queer theorist Judith Butler is somewhat mistaken in her claim that the Lacanian real *secures* heteronormativity.[30] Of course, it could be objected that Lacan's aligning reality with the imaginary over and against the real simply perpetuates a long metaphysical tradition that associates the world of experience and perceptions (so-called reality) with vain appearances, in contradistinction to an ultimate world of essences beyond appearances. Yet as Lacan conceives it, the real isn't simply *opposed* to reality or the imaginary domain of appearances, since both the imaginary and the real operate only in relation to Lacan's third order, the symbolic (the relation among these three orders—imaginary, symbolic, and real—should be characterized in terms neither of binary opposition nor of dialectic). Furthermore, rather than following the metaphysical tradition, Lacan does not align the order of the real with the world of immutable essences in contrast to an imaginary world of appearances and ephemerality; instead, he situates negativity and mutability on the side of the real rather than on that of appearances. [. . .A]lthough the real has no positive content, it has more to do with sex and death than does the imaginary or the symbolic.

This understanding of the real accounts for my objection to critically analyzing sex and sexuality in terms of the imaginary and symbolic—that is, in terms of the images and discourses that construct sex, sexuality, and desirability in our culture. Hugely powerful though these images and discourses are, sexuality pertains more to the real than to the imaginary or the symbolic.[31] Put another way, sexuality is comprehended better according to the specific modes of these cultural images' and discourses' failure. I'm suggesting that we should think about sexuality in terms of the limits, rather than the power, of these images and discourses—not simply their limits in representing some objective truth of sexuality but, more precisely, their limits in determining human sexuality. Nevertheless, I'm aware that in the face of the constant media barrage of sexualized imagery, this claim may appear particularly counterintuitive. Since the specificity of a Lacanian perspective on sexuality rests on this claim, permit me to elaborate further.

Much of the difficulty—but also the usefulness—of Lacan's concept of the real lies in its de-essentializing, despecifying abstractness. In this regard, the real resonates with the notion of *queer* underlying queer theory. And as a consequence, the Lacanian real, like queerness, is always relational, oppositional in the subversive sense, rather than substantive (there can be no queer without a norm, and vice versa). From this observation we may take another step and note how the Lacanian real functions similarly to the Freudian unconscious in its constantly undermining social and sexual identities. To grasp what Lacan means by this slippery category, whose quotidian connotations remain so hard to dispel, it helps to bear in mind that the real denotes that concept through which, especially in his later work, Lacan implicitly develops certain aspects of Freud's theory of the unconscious. In so doing, Lacan helps to distinguish a psychoanalytic from a more psychological notion of the unconscious as denoting interiority, depth, or the repository of drives and complexes. If we think of the real in light of the *psychoanalytic* unconscious, we will see more clearly how the real is connected with—indeed, remains inseparable from—sexuality.

The paradox of human sexuality, according to Freud, consists in its diphasic emergence: its initial efflorescence in childhood, prior to maturation of the sexual organs, is succeeded by a period of latency before sexuality reemerges alongside, yet forever out of synch with, organic changes in the body. Freud's claims on behalf of infantile sexuality entail recognizing that sex comes before one is ready for it—either physically or psychically. In the case of children it seems relatively clear what being physically unprepared for sex means; psychically it means that the human infant encounters sexual impulses—its own as well as other people's— as alien, unmasterable, unassimilable to its fledgling ego, and hence ultimately traumatic. As a consequence of this capacity to disorganize the ego or coherent self, sexuality becomes part of the unconscious; and it is owing to this subjectively traumatic origin that Lacan aligns sex with the order of the real. The real—like trauma—is what resists assimilation to any imaginary or symbolic universe. Another way of putting this would be to say that the premature emergence of sexuality in humans—its original noncoincidence with biology—splits sexuality off from reality and reassigns it to the domain of fantasy. In so doing, human sexuality is constituted as irremediably perverse.[32] [. . .]

Notes

Abbreviations

DSM: *Diagnostic and Statistical Manual of Mental Disorders*

E: *Écrits: A Selection.* Trans. Alan Sheridan. New York: Norton, 1977.
"Position": *"Position of the Unconscious."* In *Reading Seminar XI: Lacan's Four Fundamental Concepts of Psychoanalysis.* Ed. Richard Felstein, Bruce Fink, and Maire Jaanus, 259-82. Albany: SUNY Press, 1995.

SE: *Standard Edition of the Complete Psychological Works of Sigmund Freud.* 24 vols. Ed. and trans. James Strachey. London: Hogarth, 1953-74.

SVII: *The Seminar of Jacques Lacan. Book 2: The Ego in Freud's Theory and in the Technique of Psychoanalysis, 1954-1955.* Ed. Jacques-Alain Miller, trans. Sylvana Tomaselli. Cambridge: Cambridge University Press, 1988.

SXX: *Le séminaire, livre XX: Encore, 1972-1973.* Paris: Seuil, 1975.

1   Thomas E. Yingling, "Homosexuality and the Uncanny: What's Fishy in Lacan," in *The Gay '90s: Disciplinary and Interdisciplinary Formations in Queer Studies*, eds. Thomas Foster, Carol Siegel, and Ellen E. Berry (New York: New York University Press, 1997), 191.

2   For a detailed account of the American Psychiatric Association's decision to remove homosexuality from its official list of mental disorders, see Ronald Bayer, *Homosexuality and American Psychiatry: The*

Politics of Diagnosis, 2nd ed. (Princeton: Princeton University Press, 1987). For an account of the institutional battles over homosexuality since 1973, see Richard A. Isay, *Becoming Gay: The Journey to Self-Acceptance* (New York: Pantheon, 1996), esp. chap. 7, which suggests that removing homosexuality from *DSM* has not eliminated institutional biases or many psychiatrists' homophobia. Homophobia does not require homosexuality or homosexuals in order to flourish, it just needs signs of queerness.

3   This move to think sexuality outside the terms of gender may be traced to Gayle Rubin's pioneering work, particularly her "Thinking Sex: Notes for a Radical Theory of the Politics of Sexuality," in *Pleasure and Danger: Exploring Female Sexuality*, ed. Carole S. Vance (London: Routledge and Kegan Paul, 1984), 267–319, which argues that feminist theory remains insufficient for conceptualizing sexuality. For an illuminating meditation on Rubin's work, see her interview with Judith Butler: Rubin, "Sexual Traffic," *differences* 6, nos. 2–3 (1994): 62–99. The move to think sexuality outside the terms of gender remains controversial; for example, Biddy Martin, "Sexualities without Genders and Other Queer Utopias," *Diacritics* 24, nos. 2–3 (1994): 104–21, discusses "the potential obfuscation of misogyny by antinormative stances" (119); and Elizabeth Weed, "The More Things Change," *differences* 6, nos. 2–3 (1994): 249–73, whose argument is closer to my own, suggests how queer theory's displacing attention from sexual difference also involves neglecting psychoanalytic ways of thinking.

4   See the following classic readings of Freud's *Three Essays*: Jean Laplanche, *Life and Death in Psychoanalysis*, trans. Jeffrey Mehlman (Baltimore: Johns Hopkins University Press, 1976), chaps. 1, 2; Leo Bersani, *The Freudian Body: Psychoanalysis and Art* (New York: Columbia University Press, 1986), chap. 2; Arnold I. Davidson, "How to Do the History of Psychoanalysis: A Reading of Freud's *Three Essays on the Theory of Sexuality*," in *The Trial(s) of Psychoanalysis*, ed. Françoise Meltzer (Chicago: University of Chicago Press, 1988), 39–64; and Teresa de Lauretis, *The Practice of Love: Lesbian Sexuality and Perverse Desire* (Bloomington: Indiana University Press, 1994), chap. 1.

5   Although Foucault maintained an especially vexed relation to psychoanalysis, this misguided notion derives less from his work than from its Anglo-American reception; as with Freud, Foucault's transatlantic dissemination deformed his thought in a way that has consequences for the reception of other Continental thinkers, including Lacan. Perhaps the best account of the complexities of Foucault's relation to psychoanalysis is Jacques Derrida's "'To Do Justice to Freud': The History of Madness in the Age of Psychoanalysis," trans. Pascale-Anne Brault and Michael Naas, *Critical Inquiry* 20 (1994): 227–66. Although in this text Derrida focuses primarily on Foucault's *Madness and Civilization* and only secondarily on *The History of Sexuality*, much of his analysis can be extended to Foucault's treatment of Freud on the topic of homosexuality. Noting the resonance of Foucault's complete silence concerning Lacan (255 n. 19), Derrida argues that "Foucault's project belongs too much to 'the age of psychoanalysis' in its possibility for [Foucault], when claiming to thematize psychoanalysis, to do anything other than let psychoanalysis continue to speak obliquely of itself" (263). The tensions that Derrida identifies in *Madness and Civilization* should encourage us—by which I mean Lacanians *and* Foucaultians—to read Foucault more carefully, to do justice to Foucault in the way that he insisted on the imperative to "do justice to Freud" (*Madness and Civilization: A History of Insanity in the Age of Reason* [New York: Random House, 1965], 198). The kind of careful reading I have in mind is exemplified by John Murchek, "Foucault and Psychoanalysis: 'Quite Near' " (unpublished manuscript), which pursues a fascinating reading of the first volume of *The History of Sexuality* to argue convincingly that Foucault's concept of power can be understood as a version of Freud's concept of libido; that the scenic account of that power can be read in terms of the psychoanalytic theory of fantasy; and that Foucault's spirals of pleasure and power redescribe the concept of transference.

6   Russell Jacoby, *Social Amnesia: A Critique of Conformist Psychology from Adler to Laing* (Boston: Beacon, 1975), and Jacoby, *The Repression of Psychoanalysis: Otto Fenichel and the Political Freudians* (Chicago: University of Chicago Press, 1986); Kenneth Lewes, *The Psychoanalytic Theory of Male Homosexuality* (New York: Simon and Schuster, 1988); Henry Abelove, "Freud, Male Homosexuality, and the Americans," in *The Lesbian and Gay Studies Reader*, eds. Henry Abelove, Michèle Aina Barale, and David M. Halperin (New York: Routledge, 1993), 381–93. On the most recent chapter of U.S. anti-Freudianism, see Paul Robinson, *Freud and His Critics* (Berkeley and Los Angeles: University of California Press, 1993).

7   Abelove, "Freud, Male Homosexuality, and the Americans," 384.

8   Eve Kosofsky Sedgwick, *Epistemology of the Closet* (Berkeley and Los Angeles: University of California Press, 1990), 40–41.

9   In an English translation of *Encore* published after I wrote this chapter, Bruce Fink renders the passage in question thus: "Last year I played on a slip of the pen I made in a letter addressed to a woman—*tu ne sauras jamais combien je t'ai aimé* ('you will never know how much I loved you')—*é* instead of *ée*. Since then, someone mentioned to me that that could mean that I am a homosexual. But what I articulated quite precisely last year is that when one loves, it has nothing to do with sex." In this

instance, translating *sexe* as *sex* is potentially misleading and so Fink adds this note: "The past participle, *aimé*, is supposed to agree in gender with the sex of the person designated in the phrase by the direct object, *te* (here *t'*); if the person is male, the participle remains *aimé*, if female, an *e* should be added to the end: *aimée*." See Jacques Lacan, *On Feminine Sexuality, The Limits of Love and Knowledge: The Seminar of Jacques Lacan*, Book 20: *Encore, 1972–1973*, ed. Jacques-Alain Miller, trans. Bruce Fink (New York: Norton, 1998), 25.

10   See, for example, the classic contributions collected in Edward Stein, ed., *Forms of Desire: Sexual Orientation and the Social Constructionist Controversy* (New York: Routledge, 1992); and, more recently, Paul R. Abramson and Steven D. Pinkerton, eds., *Sexual Nature, Sexual Culture* (Chicago: University of Chicago Press, 1995). The canonical account of "the construction of homosexuality" is given by David Greenberg in his book of that title (Chicago: University of Chicago Press, 1988), and of heterosexuality in Jonathan Ned Katz, *The Invention of Heterosexuality* (New York: Dutton, 1995).

11   A group of therapists within the American Psychological Association is campaigning to have the category of gender identity disorder removed from the next edition of *DSM*, based on the conviction that this diagnosis, which is used particularly for children, represents a screen for mental health workers' homophobia. See *In the Family: The Magazine for Gays, Lesbians, Bisexuals, and Their Relations*, October 1997, 3.

12   Simon LeVay, *The Sexual Brain* (Cambridge: MIT Press, 1993); Dean Hamer and Peter Copeland, *The Science of Desire: The Search for the Gay Gene and the Biology of Behavior* (New York: Simon and Schuster, 1994). With respect to the search for the gay gene, Guy Hocquenghem's comment almost one quarter-century earlier still holds good: "The chromosome theory [of homosexuality] appears to be less a biological 'discovery' than an ideological regression" (Guy Hocquenghem, *Homosexual Desire* [1972], trans. Daniella Dangoor [Durham: Duke University Press, 1993], 76). More recently, in *Queer Science: The Use and Abuse of Research into Homosexuality* (Cambridge: MIT Press, 1996), LeVay has examined the history and consequences of scientific explanations of sexual orientation, including psychoanalytic ones. As with the overwhelming majority of lesbian and gay people, LeVay favors the conclusion that homosexuality is innate rather than acquired, essential rather than constructed. This conviction about sexual orientation's innateness can be deemed progressive insofar as it discourages a commitment to reorientation therapy, and, furthermore, it discredits the assumption, so common among conservatives, that homosexuals suffer from a febrile will or poor moral fiber. In other words, the essentialist view of sexual orientation ostensibly makes homosexuality easier to accept—for both queers and straights. On the other hand, scientific evidence of sexual orientation's organic innateness also can support a virulently homophobic politics, insofar as genetic engineering and eugenics permit the fantasy of a world in which there would be no homosexuals whatsoever. From this we can see that what attracts both progressives and reactionaries—whether they're experts or laypersons—to scientific evidence concerning the biological innateness of sexual desire is its reassurance that sexuality confers *identity*. This kind of scientific evidence also calms any sense of subjective division, any nagging personal sense that I too could have unconscious conflict about sexual orientation.

13   Judith Butler, *Bodies That Matter: On the Discursive Limits of "Sex"* (New York: Routledge, 1993).

14   On the emergence of queer theory and some ramifications of the term itself, see Teresa de Lauretis, "Queer Theory: Lesbian and Gay Sexualities—An Introduction," *differences* 3, no. 2 (1991): iii–xviii. Because the word *queer* is intended to be gender neutral, I hesitate to offer the customary caveat that I'm focusing here primarily on *either* gay men's *or* lesbians' sexuality. Yet in thus hesitating to specify nonnormative sexualities along gender lines, I want also to emphasize that queer women's and queer men's concerns aren't identical, symmetrical, or analogous—and therefore psychoanalysis should take greater care not to treat them as if they were.

15   On queer theory's resistance to definition, see Lauren Berlant and Michael Warner, "What Does Queer Theory Teach Us about *X*?" *PMLA* 110 (1995): 343–49.

16   Judith Butler, "Imitation and Gender Insubordination," *Inside/Out: Lesbian Theories, Gay Theories*, ed. Diana Fuss (New York: Routledge, 1991), 13–14.

17   Michel Foucault, preface to Gilles Deleuze and Félix Guattari, *Anti-Oedipus: Capitalism and Schizophrenia* (1972), trans. Robert Hurley, Mark Seem, and Helen R. Lane (Minneapolis: University of Minnesota Press, 1983), xiv.

18   I discuss the limits of these queer reinventions of psychoanalysis in "On the Eve of a Queer Future," *Raritan* 15 (1995): 116–34.

19   Michel Foucault, "An Interview with Stephen Riggins," *The Essential Works of Michel Foucault, 1954–1984*, Vol. 1, *Ethics: Subjectivity and Truth*, ed. Paul Rabinow, trans. Robert Hurley et al. (New York: New Press, 1997), 125–26.

20   Berlant and Warner, "What Does Queer Theory Teach Us?" 344.

21   This represents an enormous project, one that bears on the longstanding dispute between Foucault and Jürgen Habermas concerning the function of social norms and normativity. In her stringent critique of Butler's intervention in the feminist version of this debate, Amanda Anderson elaborates a helpful distinction between evaluative norms and normalizing norms. Evaluative norms, associated with the Habermasian position, provide necessary criteria for evaluating the rightness or wrongness of an action or practice. By contrast, normalizing norms, associated with the Foucaultian position, involve mechanisms of social reproduction and identity formation internal to hegemonic social structures (Anderson, "Debatable Performances: Restaging Contentious Feminisms," *Social Text* 54, vol. 16, no. 1 [1998]: 9). This distinction tends to get lost in queer theory's antinormativity, but might prove useful for assessing the role of psychoanalysis as a normalizing discourse or practice, since the reduction of all normativity to normalization—that is, viewing all evaluative criteria as fundamentally insidious—obscures and therefore naturalizes the operation of evaluative norms within queer theory and queer practices themselves.

22   Michael Warner, introduction to *Fear of a Queer Planet: Queer Politics and Social Theory*, ed. Warner (Minneapolis: University of Minnesota Press, 1993), xxvii.

23   Adrienne Rich, "Compulsory Heterosexuality and Lesbian Existence," in *Desire: The Politics of Sexuality*, eds. Ann Snitow, Christine Stansell, and Sharon Thompson (London: Virago, 1984), 212–41.

24   For recent arguments on behalf of the desirability of lesbian and gay assimilation into the social mainstream, see Bruce Bawer, *A Place at the Table: The Gay Individual in American Society* (New York: Poseidon, 1993); and Andrew Sullivan, *Virtually Normal: An Argument about Homosexuality* (New York: Knopf, 1995).

25   For a powerful account of community formation based not on identity but instead on nonbelonging, see Giorgio Agamben, *The Coming Community*, trans. Michael Hardt (Minneapolis: University of Minnesota Press, 1993).

26   Michel Foucault, "Sexual Choice, Sexual Act," in *The Essential Works of Michel Foucault*, 153. In what I take to be the most important work of queer theory to date, Leo Bersani provides a useful gloss on Foucault's comment: "The intolerance of gayness, far from being the displaced expression of the anxieties that nourish misogyny, would be nothing more—by which of course Foucault meant nothing less—than a political anxiety about the subversive, revolutionary social rearrangements that gays may be trying out. Indeed, in this scenario there may be no fantasies—in the psychoanalytic sense—on either side, and if there are, they are insignificant in understanding the threat of gayness." (*Homos* [Cambridge: Harvard University Press, 1995], 78.)

27   Immediately before this, when speaking explicitly of psychoanalytic ethics, Lacan denounces as particularly normalizing those brands of psychoanalysis that aspire to scientific status: "a form of analysis that boasts of its highly scientific distinctiveness gives rise to normative notions that I characterize by evoking the curse Saint Matthew utters on those who make the bundles heavier when they are to be carried by others" (*SVII* 133).

28   See Kaja Silverman, *The Threshold of the Visible World* (New York: Routledge, 1996), for an original psychoanalytic argument on behalf of new political uses of the aesthetic that would enable different modes of idealization—specifically, less violent or exclusionary ways of seeing.

29   In his critique of psychoanalytic ethics, Lacan develops this position, sounding very much like a queer theorist:

> [Y]ou know that I have often taken aim at the approximate and vague character, so tainted with an optimistic moralism, which marks the original articulations taking the form of the genitalization of desire. That is the ideal of genital love—a love that is supposed to be itself alone the model of a satisfying object relation: doctor–love, I would say if I wanted to emphasize in a comical way the tone of this ideology; love as hygiene, I would say, to suggest what analytical ambition seems to be limited to here. (*SVII* 8)

30   Judith Butler, "Arguing with the Real," in *Bodies That Matter*, 187–222.

31   The most compelling demonstration of this distinction—that sex is of the order of the real rather than of the imaginary or symbolic—may be found in Joan Copjec, "Sex and the Euthanasia of Reason," in *Read My Desire: Lacan against the Historicists* (Cambridge: MIT Press, 1994), 201–36, which uses Kant's antinomies of reason to make this argument about sex and the real.

32   In thus characterizing the diphasic emergence of sexuality, I am summarizing Freud's *Three Essays on the Theory of Sexuality* and drawing on Laplanche's reading of Freud, in *Life and Death in Psychoanalysis*, and his subsequent development of ideas concerning generalized seduction and the enigmatic signifier, in *New Foundations for Psychoanalysis*, trans. David Macey (Oxford: Basil Blackwell, 1989). Whereas Lacan describes the traumatically premature emergence of sexuality in terms of the unsym-

bolizable real, Laplanche describes the same phenomenon in terms of the enigmatic signifier—an account he presents especially cogently in "The Theory of Seduction and the Problem of the Other," trans. Luke Thurston, *International Journal of Psychoanalysis* 78, no. 4 (1997): 653–66. Although space prevents me from providing even a brief consideration of the relation between Laplanchean and Lacanian theory here, I would like to note the continuing importance of Laplanche's work for Anglophone theorists of nonnormative sexuality, such as Leo Bersani, Jonathan Dollimore, John Fletcher, Teresa de Lauretis, and Mandy Merck. A thorough account of Laplanche's debt to Lacan might provide the key for understanding why these theorists find Laplanche so much more useful than they find Lacan.

PART 2

Sex

Chapter 10

Lauren Berlant and Michael Warner

SEX IN PUBLIC

Lauren Berlant is George M. Pullman Professor in the Department of English at the University of Chicago and Michael Warner is Seymour H. Knox Professor of English Literature and American Studies at Yale University. The author of *Cruel Optimism* (2011), Berlant's scholarship focuses on race, sexuality, and citizenship in the United States. The author of *Publics and Counterpublics* (2002), Warner's scholarship examines notions of the public sphere, social theory, and print culture. The following essay was jointly authored and first appeared in *Critical Inquiry* (1998).

In "Sex in Public," Berlant and Warner argue that dominant heteronormative social structures conflate "sex" and the "intimate," legitimating a sense of normalcy through the maintenance of protocols that privatize sexual cultures. Heteronormativity is publically mediated in popular, political, and legal discourses and upholds the continuation of hegemonic national heterosexuality. Drawing on Jürgen Habermas's notion of the public sphere, Berlant and Warner advocate a "queer world-making project" through the creation of queer counterpublics. The creation of counterpublics disrupts the heteronormative privatization of intimacy, thereby creating counter-intimacies that are not necessarily associated with socially entitled structures such as domesticity, property laws, kinship, or nation. Queer counterpublics can manifest in literal spaces such as sex shops or clubs and through processes of elaboration such as gossip and print culture. Queer counterpublics include myriad peoples, affiliations, and spaces that together disrupt heterosexual hegemony.

There is nothing more public than privacy

A **PAPER TITLED "SEX IN PUBLIC"** teases with the obscurity of its object and the twisted aim of its narrative. In this paper we will be talking not about the sex people already have clarity about, nor identities and acts, nor a wildness in need of derepression; but rather about sex as it is mediated by publics.[1] Some of these publics have an obvious relation to sex: pornographic cinema, phone sex, "adult" markets for print, lap dancing. Others are organized around sex, but not necessarily sex *acts* in the usual sense: queer zones and other worlds estranged from heterosexual culture, but also more tacit scenes of sexuality like official national culture, which depends on a notion of privacy to cloak its sexualization of national membership.

The aim of this paper is to describe what we want to promote as the radical aspirations of queer culture building: not just a safe zone for queer sex but the changed possibilities of identity, intelligibility, publics, culture, and sex that appear when the heterosexual couple is no longer the referent or the privileged example of sexual culture. Queer social practices like sex and theory try to unsettle the garbled but powerful norms supporting that privilege— including the project of normalization that has made heterosexuality hegemonic—as well as those material practices that, though not explicitly sexual, are implicated in the hierarchies of property and propriety that we will describe as heteronormative.[2] We open with two scenes of sex in public.

Scene 1

In 1993 *Time* magazine published a special issue about immigration called "The New Face of America."[3] The cover girl of this issue was morphed via computer from head shots repre-senting a range of U.S. immigrant groups: an amalgam of "Middle Eastern," "Italian," "African," "Vietnamese," "Anglo-Saxon," "Chinese," and "Hispanic" faces. The new face of America is supposed to represent what the modal citizen will look like when, in the year 2004, it is projected, there is no longer a white statistical majority in the United States. Naked, smiling, and just off-white, *Time*'s divine Frankenstein aims to organize hegemonic optimism about citizenship and the national future. *Time*'s theory is that by the twenty-first century interracial reproductive sex will have taken place in the United States on such a mass scale that racial difference itself will be finally replaced by a kind of family feeling based on blood relations. In the twenty-first century, *Time* imagines, hundreds of millions of hybrid faces will erase American racism altogether; the nation will become a happy racial mono-culture made up of "one (mixed) blood."[4]

The publication of this special issue caused a brief flurry of interest but had no important effects; its very banality calls us to understand the technologies that produce its ordinariness. The fantasy banalized by the image is one that reverberates in the law and in the most intimate crevices of everyday life. Its explicit aim is to help its public process the threat to "normal" or "core" national culture that is currently phrased as "the problem of immigration."[5] But this crisis image of immigrants is also a *racial mirage* generated by a white-dominated society, supplying a specific phobia to organize its public so that a more substantial discussion of exploitation in the United States can be avoided and then remaindered to the part of collec-tive memory sanctified not by nostalgia but by mass aversion. Let's call this the amnesia archive. The motto above the door is Memory Is the Amnesia You Like.

But more than exploitation and racism are forgotten in this whirl of projection and suppression. Central to the transfiguration of the immigrant into a nostalgic image to shore up core national culture and allay white fears of minoritization is something that cannot speak its name, though its signature is everywhere: national heterosexuality. National heterosexu-ality is the mechanism by which a core national culture can be imagined as a sanitized space of sentimental feeling and immaculate behavior, a space of pure citizenship. A familial model of society displaces the recognition of structural racism and other systemic inequalities. This is not entirely new: the family form has functioned as a mediator and metaphor of national existence in the United States since the eighteenth century.[6] We are arguing that its contem-porary deployment increasingly supports the governmentality of the welfare state by sepa-rating the aspirations of national belonging from the critical culture of the public sphere and from political citizenship.[7] Immigration crises have also previously produced feminine icons that function as prostheses for the state—most famously, the Statue of Liberty, which symbolized seamless immigrant assimilation to the metaculture of the United States. In *Time*'s face it is not symbolic femininity but practical heterosexuality that guarantees the monocultural nation.

The nostalgic family values covenant of contemporary American politics stipulates a privatization of citizenship and sex in a number of ways. In law and political ideology, for example, the fetus and the child have been spectacularly elevated to the place of sanctified nationality. The state now sponsors stings and legislation to purify the internet on behalf of children. New welfare and tax "reforms" passed under the cooperation between the Contract with America and Clintonian familialism seek to increase the legal and economic privileges of married couples and parents. Vouchers and privatization rezone education as the domain of parents rather than citizens. Meanwhile, senators such as Ted Kennedy and Jesse Helms support amendments that refuse federal funds to organizations that "promote, disseminate, or produce materials that are obscene or that depict or describe, in a patently offensive way, sexual or excretory activities or organs, including but not limited to obscene depictions of sadomasochism, homo-eroticism, the sexual exploitation of children, or individuals engaged in sexual intercourse."[8] These developments, though distinct, are linked in the way they organize a hegemonic national public around sex. But because this sex public officially claims to act only in order to protect the zone of heterosexual privacy, the institutions of economic privilege and social reproduction informing its practices and organizing its ideal world are protected by the spectacular demonization of any represented sex.

Scene 2

In October 1995, the New York City Council passed a new zoning law by a forty-one to nine vote. The Zoning Text Amendment covers adult book and video stores, eating and drinking establishments, theaters, and other businesses. It allows these businesses only in certain areas zoned as nonresidential, most of which turn out to be on the waterfront. Within the new reserved districts, adult businesses are disallowed within five hundred feet of another adult establishment or within five hundred feet of a house of worship, school, or day-care center. They are limited to one per lot and in size to ten thousand square feet. Signs are limited in size, placement, and illumination. All other adult businesses are required to close within a year. Of the estimated 177 adult businesses in the city, all but 28 may have to close under this law. Enforcement of the bill is entrusted to building inspectors.

A court challenge against the bill was brought by a coalition that also fought it in the political process, formed by anticensorship groups such as the New York Civil Liberties Union (NYCLU), Feminists for Free Expression, People for the American Way, and the National Coalition Against Censorship as well as gay and lesbian organizations such as the Lambda Legal Defense Fund, the Empire State Pride Agenda, and the AIDS Prevention Action League. (An appeal was still pending as of July 1997.) These latter groups joined the anticensorship groups for a simple reason: the impact of rezoning on businesses catering to queers, especially to gay men, will be devastating. All five of the adult businesses on Christopher Street will be shut down, along with the principal venues where men meet men for sex. None of these businesses have been targets of local complaints. Gay men have come to take for granted the availability of explicit sexual materials, theaters, and clubs. That is how they have learned to find each other; to map a commonly accessible world; to construct the architecture of queer space in a homophobic environment; and, for the last fifteen years, to cultivate a collective ethos of safer sex. All of that is about to change. Now, gay men who want sexual materials or who want to meet other men for sex will have two choices: they can cathect the privatized virtual public of phone sex and the internet; or they can travel to small, inaccessible, little-trafficked, badly lit areas, remote from public transportation and from any residences, mostly on the waterfront, where heterosexual porn users will also be relocated and where the risk of violence will consequently be higher.[9] In either case, the result will be a sense of isolation and diminished expectations for queer life, as well as an attenuated capacity for political community. The nascent lesbian sexual culture, including the Clit Club and the only video rental club catering to lesbians, will also disappear. The impact of the sexual purification of New York will fall unequally on those who already have fewest publicly accessible resources.

Normativity and sexual culture

Heterosexuality is not a thing. We speak of heterosexual culture rather than heterosexuality because that culture never has more than a provisional unity.[10] It is neither a single Symbolic nor a single ideology nor a unified set of shared beliefs.[11] The conflicts between these strands are seldom more than dimly perceived in practice, where the givenness of male–female sexual relations is part of the ordinary rightness of the world, its fragility masked in shows of solemn rectitude. Such conflicts have also gone unrecognized in theory, partly because of the metacultural work of the very category of heterosexuality, which consolidates as *a sexuality* widely differing practices, norms, and institutions; and partly because the sciences of social knowledge are themselves so deeply anchored in the process of normalization to which Foucault attributes so much of modern sexuality.[12] Thus when we say that the contemporary United States is saturated by the project of constructing national heterosexuality, we do not mean that national heterosexuality is anything like a simple monoculture. Hegemonies are nothing if not elastic alliances, involving dispersed and contradictory strategies for self-maintenance and reproduction.

Heterosexual culture achieves much of its metacultural intelligibility through the ideologies and institutions of intimacy. We want to argue here that although the intimate relations of private personhood appear to be the realm of sexuality itself, allowing "sex in public" to appear like matter out of place, intimacy is itself publicly mediated, in several senses. First, its conventional spaces presuppose a structural differentiation of "personal life" from work, politics, and the public sphere.[13] Second, the normativity of heterosexual culture links intimacy only to the institutions of personal life, making them the privileged institutions of social reproduction, the accumulation and transfer of capital, and self-development. Third, by making sex seem irrelevant or merely personal, heteronormative conventions of intimacy block the building of nonnormative or explicit public sexual cultures. Finally, those conventions conjure a mirage: a home base of prepolitical humanity from which citizens are thought to come into political discourse and to which they are expected to return in the (always imaginary) future after political conflict. Intimate life is the endlessly cited *elsewhere* of political public discourse, a promised haven that distracts citizens from the unequal conditions of their political and economic lives, consoles them for the damaged humanity of mass society, and shames them for any divergence between their lives and the intimate sphere that is alleged to be simple personhood.

Ideologies and institutions of intimacy are increasingly offered as a vision of the good life for the destabilized and struggling citizenry of the United States, the only (fantasy) zone in which a future might be thought and willed, the only (imaginary) place where good citizens might be produced away from the confusing and unsettling distractions and contradictions of capitalism and politics. Indeed, one of the unforeseen paradoxes of national-capitalist privatization has been that citizens have been led through heterosexual culture to identify both themselves *and their politics* with privacy. In the official public, this involves making sex private; reintensifying blood as a psychic base for identification; replacing state mandates for social justice with a privatized ethics of responsibility, charity, atonement, and "values"; and enforcing boundaries between moral persons and economic ones.[14]

A complex cluster of sexual practices gets confused, in heterosexual culture, with the love plot of intimacy and familialism that signifies belonging to society in a deep and normal way. Community is imagined through scenes of intimacy, coupling, and kinship; a historical relation to futurity is restricted to generational narrative and reproduction.[15] A whole field of social relations becomes intelligible as heterosexuality, and this privatized sexual culture bestows on its sexual practices a tacit sense of rightness and normalcy. This sense of rightness—embedded in things and not just in sex—is what we call heteronormativity. Heteronormativity is more than ideology, or prejudice, or phobia against gays and lesbians; it is produced in almost every aspect of the forms and arrangements of social life: nationality, the state, and the law; commerce; medicine; and education; as well as in the conventions and affects of narrativity, romance, and other protected spaces of culture. It is hard to see these fields as heteronormative because the sexual culture straight people inhabit is so diffuse, a mix of languages they are just developing with premodern notions of sexuality so ancient that their material conditions feel hardwired into personhood.

But intimacy has not always had the meaning it has for contemporary heteronormative culture. Along with Foucault and other historians, the classicist David Halperin, for example, has shown that in ancient Athens sex was a transitive act rather than a fundamental dimension of personhood or an expression of intimacy. The verb for having sex appears on a late antique list of things that are not done in regard to or through others: "namely, speaking, singing, dancing, fist-fighting, competing, hanging oneself, dying, being crucified, diving, finding a treasure, having sex, vomiting, moving one's bowels, sleeping, laughing, crying, talking to the gods, and the like."[16] Halperin points out that the inclusion of fucking on this list shows that sex is not here "knit up in a web of mutuality."[17] In contrast, modern heterosexuality is supposed to refer to relations of intimacy and identification with other persons, and sex acts are supposed to be the most intimate communication of them all.[18] The sex act shielded by the zone of privacy is the affectional nimbus that heterosexual culture protects and from which it abstracts its model of ethics, but this utopia of social belonging is also supported and extended by acts less commonly recognized as part of sexual culture: paying taxes, being disgusted, philandering, bequeathing, celebrating a holiday, investing for the future, teaching, disposing of a corpse, carrying wallet photos, buying economy size, being nepotistic, running for president, divorcing, or owning anything "His" and "Hers."

The elaboration of this list is a project for further study. Meanwhile, to make it and to laugh at it is not immediately to label any practice as oppressive, uncool, or definitive. We are describing a constellation of practices that everywhere disperses heterosexual privilege as a tacit but central organizing index of social membership. Exposing it inevitably produces what we have elsewhere called a "wrenching sense of recontextualization," as its subjects, even its gay and lesbian subjects, begin to piece together how it is that social and economic discourses, institutions, and practices that don't feel especially sexual or familial collaborate to produce as a social norm and ideal an extremely narrow context for living.[19] Heterosexual culture cannot recognize, validate, sustain, incorporate, or remember much of what people know and experience about the cruelty of normal culture even to the people who identify with it.

But that cruelty does not go unregistered. Intimacy, for example, has a whole public environment of therapeutic genres dedicated to witnessing the constant failure of heterosexual ideologies and institutions. Every day, in many countries now, people testify to their failure to sustain or be sustained by institutions of privacy on talk shows, in scandal journalism, even in the ordinary course of mainstream journalism addressed to middlebrow culture. We can learn a lot from these stories of love plots that have gone astray: about the ways quotidian violence is linked to complex pressures from money, racism, histories of sexual violence, cross-generational tensions. We can learn a lot from listening to the increasing demands on love to deliver the good life it promises. And we can learn from the extremely punitive responses that tend to emerge when people seem not to suffer enough for their transgressions and failures.

Maybe we would learn too much. Recently, the proliferation of evidence for hetero-sexuality's failings has produced a backlash against talk show therapy. It has even brought William Bennett to the podium; but rather than confessing his transgressions or making a complaint about someone else's, we find him calling for boycotts and for the suppression of heterosexual therapy culture altogether. Recognition of heterosexuality's daily failures agitates him as much as queerness. "We've forgotten that civilization depends on keeping some of this stuff under wraps," he said. "This is a tropism toward the toilet."[20]

But does civilization need to cover its ass? Or does heterosexual culture actually secure itself through banalizing intimacy? Does belief that normal life is actually possible *require* amnesia and the ludicrous stereotyping of a bottom-feeding culture apparently inadequate to intimacy? On these shows no one ever blames the ideology and institutions of heterosexu-ality. Every day, even the talk show hosts are newly astonished to find that people who are committed to hetero intimacy are nevertheless unhappy. After all is said and done, the pros-pects and promises of heterosexual culture still represent the optimism for optimism, a hope to which people apparently have already pledged their consent—at least in public.

Recently, Biddy Martin has written that some queer social theorists have produced a reductive and pseudoradical antinormativity by actively repudiating the institutions of heterosexuality that have come to oversaturate the social imaginary. She shows that the kinds of arguments that crop up in the writings of people like Andrew Sullivan are not just right-wing fantasies. "In some queer work," she writes, "the very fact of attachment has been cast as only punitive and constraining because already socially constructed. . . . Radical anti-normativity throws out a lot of babies with a lot of bathwater. . . . An enormous fear of ordinariness or normalcy results in superficial accounts of the complex imbrication of sexuality with other aspects of social and psychic life, and in far too little attention to the dilemmas of the average people that we also are."[21]

We think our friend Biddy might be referring to us, although in this segment she cites no one in particular. We would like to clarify the argument. To be against heteronormativity is not to be against norms. To be against the processes of normalization is not to be afraid of ordinariness. Nor is it to advocate the "existence without limit" she sees as produced by bad Foucauldians ("EH," p. 123). Nor is it to decide that sentimental identifications with family and children are waste or garbage, or make people into waste or garbage. Nor is it to say that any sex called "lovemaking" isn't lovemaking; whatever the ideological or historical burdens of sexuality have been, they have not excluded, and indeed may have entailed, the ability of sex to count as intimacy and care. What we have been arguing here is that the space of sexual culture has become obnoxiously cramped from doing the work of maintaining a normal metaculture. When Biddy Martin calls us to recognize ourselves as "average people," to relax from an artificially stimulated "fear of normalcy," the image of average personhood appears to be simply descriptive ("EH," p. 123). But its averageness is also normative, in exactly the sense that Foucault meant by "normalization": not the imposition of an alien will, but a distri-bution around a statistically imagined norm. This deceptive appeal of the average remains heteronormative, measuring deviance from the mass, it can also be consoling, an expression of a utopian desire for unconflicted personhood. But this desire cannot be satisfied in the current conditions of privacy. People feel that the price they must pay for social membership and a relation to the future is identification with the heterosexual life narrative; that they are individually responsible for the rages, instabilities, ambivalences, and failures they experience in their intimate lives, while the fractures of the contemporary United States shame and sabotage them everywhere. Heterosexuality involves so many practices that are not sex that a world in which this hegemonic cluster would not be dominant is, at this point, unimaginable. We are trying to bring that world into being.

Queer counterpublics

By queer culture we mean a world-making project, where "world," like "public," differs from community or group because it necessarily includes more people than can be identified, more spaces than can be mapped beyond a few reference points, modes of feeling that can be learned rather than experienced as a birthright. The queer world is a space of entrances, exits, unsystematized lines of acquaintance, projected horizons, typifying examples, alternate routes, blockages, incommensurate geographies.[22] World making, as much in the mode of dirty talk as of print-mediated representation, is dispersed through incommensurate registers, by definition *unrealizable* as community or identity. Every cultural form, be it a novel or an after-hours club or an academic lecture, indexes a virtual social world, in ways that range from a repertoire of styles and speech genres to referential metaculture. A novel like Andrew Holleran's *Dancer from the Dance* relies much more heavily on referential metaculture than does an after-hours club that survives on word of mouth and may be a major scene because it is only barely coherent *as* a scene. Yet for all their differences, both allow for the concretization of a queer counterpublic. We are trying to promote this world-making project, and a first step in doing so is to recognize that queer culture constitutes itself in many ways other than through the official publics of opinion culture and the state, or through the privatized forms normally associated with sexuality. Queer and other insurgents have long striven, often dangerously or scandalously, to cultivate what good folks used to call criminal intimacies. We have developed relations and narratives that are only recognized as intimate in queer culture: girlfriends, gal pals, fuckbuddies, tricks. Queer culture has learned not only how to sexualize these and other relations, but also to use them as a context for witnessing intense and personal affect while elaborating a public world of belonging and transformation. Making a queer world has required the development of kinds of intimacy that bear no necessary relation to domestic space, to kinship, to the couple form, to property, or to the nation. These intimacies *do* bear a necessary relation to a counterpublic—an indefinitely accessible world conscious of its subordinate relation. They are typical both of the inventiveness of queer world making and of the queer world's fragility.

Nonstandard intimacies would seem less criminal and less fleeting if, as used to be the case, normal intimacies included everything from consorts to courtiers, friends, amours, associates, and coconspirators.[23] Along with the sex it legitimates, intimacy has been privatized; the discourse contexts that narrate true personhood have been segregated from those that represent citizens, workers, or professionals.

This transformation in the cultural forms of intimacy is related both to the history of the modern public sphere and to the modern discourse of sexuality as a fundamental human capacity. In *The Structural Transformation of the Public Sphere*, Habermas shows that the institutions and forms of domestic intimacy made private people private, members of the public sphere of private society rather than the market or the state. Intimacy grounded abstract, disembodied citizens in a sense of universal humanity. In *The History of Sexuality*, Foucault describes the personalization of sex from the other direction: the confessional and expert discourses of civil society continually posit an inner personal essence, equating this true personhood with sex and surrounding that sex with dramas of secrecy and disclosure. There is an instructive convergence here in two thinkers who otherwise seem to be describing different planets.[24] Habermas overlooks the administrative and normalizing dimensions of privatized sex in sciences of social knowledge because he is interested in the norm of a critical relation between state and civil society. Foucault overlooks the critical culture that might enable transformation of sex and other private relations; he wants to show that modern epistemologies of sexual personhood, far from bringing sexual publics into being, are techniques of isolation; they identify persons as normal or perverse, for the purpose of medicalizing or otherwise administering them as individuals. Yet both Habermas and Foucault point to the way a hegemonic public has founded itself by a privatization of sex and the sexualization of private personhood. Both identify the conditions in which sexuality seems like a property of subjectivity rather than a publicly or counterpublicly accessible culture.

Like most ideologies, that of normal intimacy may never have been an accurate description of how people actually live. It was from the beginning mediated not only by a structural separation of economic and domestic space but also by opinion culture, correspondence, novels, and romances; Rousseau's *Confessions* is typical both of the ideology and of its reliance on mediation by print and by new, hybrid forms of life narrative. Habermas notes that "subjectivity, as the innermost core of the private, was always oriented to an audience,"[25] adding that the structure of this intimacy includes a fundamentally contradictory relation to the economy:

> To the autonomy of property owners in the market corresponded a self-presentation of human beings in the family. The latter's intimacy, apparently set free from the constraint of society, was the seal on the truth of a private autonomy exercised in competition. Thus it was a private autonomy denying its economic origins . . . that provided the bourgeois family with its consciousness of itself.[26]

This structural relation is no less normative for being imperfect in practice. Its force is to prevent the recognition, memory, elaboration, or institutionalization of all the nonstandard intimacies that people have in everyday life. Affective life slops over onto work and political life; people have key self-constitutive relations with strangers and acquaintances; and they have eroticism, if not sex, outside of the couple form. These border intimacies give people tremendous pleasure. But when that pleasure is called sexuality, the spillage of eroticism into everyday social life seems transgressive in a way that provokes normal aversion, a hygienic recoil even as contemporary consumer and media cultures increasingly trope toiletward, splattering the matter of intimate life at the highest levels of national culture.

In gay male culture, the principal scenes of criminal intimacy have been tearooms, streets, sex clubs, and parks—a tropism toward the public toilet.[27] Promiscuity is so heavily stigmatized as nonintimate that it is often called anonymous, whether names are used or not. One of the most commonly forgotten lessons of AIDS is that this promiscuous intimacy turned out to be a lifesaving public resource. Unbidden by experts, gay people invented safer sex; and, as Douglas Crimp wrote in 1987

> we were able to invent safe sex because we have always known that sex is not, in an epidemic or not, limited to penetrative sex. Our promiscuity taught us many things, not only about the pleasures of sex, but about the great multiplicity of those pleasures. It is that psychic preparation, that experimentation, that conscious work on our own sexualities that has allowed many of us to change our sexual behaviors—something that brutal "behavioral therapies" tried unsuccessfully for over a century to force us to do—very quickly and very

dramatically. . . . All those who contend that gay male promiscuity is merely sexual *compulsion* resulting from fear of intimacy are now faced with very strong evidence against their prejudices. . . . Gay male promiscuity should be seen instead as a positive model of how sexual pleasures might be pursued by and granted to everyone if those pleasures were not confined within the narrow limits of institutionalized sexuality.[28]

AIDS is a special case, and this model of sexual culture has been typically male. But sexual practice is only one kind of counterintimacy. More important is the critical practical knowledge that allows such relations to count as intimate, to be not empty release or transgression but a common language of self-cultivation, shared knowledge, and the exchange of inwardness.

Queer culture has found it necessary to develop this knowledge in mobile sites of drag, youth culture, music, dance, parades, flaunting, and cruising—sites whose mobility makes them possible but also renders them hard to recognize as world making because they are so fragile and ephemeral. They are paradigmatically trivialized as "lifestyle." But to understand them only as self-expression or as a demand for recognition would be to misrecognize the fundamentally unequal material conditions whereby the institutions of social reproduction are coupled to the forms of hetero culture.[29] Contexts of queer world making depend on parasitic and fugitive elaboration through gossip, dance clubs, softball leagues, and the phone-sex ads that increasingly are the commercial support for print-mediated left culture in general.[30] Queer is difficult to entextualize *as* culture.

This is particularly true of intimate culture. Heteronormative forms of intimacy are supported, as we have argued, not only by overt referential discourse such as love plots and sentimentality but materially, in marriage and family law, in the architecture of the domestic, in the zoning of work and politics. Queer culture, by contrast, has almost no institutional matrix for its counterintimacies. In the absence of marriage and the rituals that organize life around matrimony, improvisation is always necessary for the speech act of pledging, or the narrative practice of dating, or for such apparently noneconomic economies as joint checking. The heteronormativity in such practices may seem weak and indirect. After all, same-sex couples have sometimes been able to invent versions of such practices. But they have done so only by betrothing themselves to the couple form and its language of personal significance, leaving untransformed the material and ideological conditions that divide intimacy from history, politics, and publics. The queer project we imagine is not just to destigmatize those average intimacies, not just to give access to the sentimentality of the couple for persons of the same sex, and definitely not to certify as properly private the personal lives of gays and lesbians.[31] Rather, it is to support forms of affective, erotic, and personal living that are public in the sense of accessible, available to memory, and sustained through collective activity.

Because the heteronormative culture of intimacy leaves queer culture especially dependent on ephemeral elaborations in urban space and print culture, queer publics are also peculiarly vulnerable to initiatives such as Mayor Rudolph Giuliani's new zoning law. The law aims to restrict any counterpublic sexual culture by regulating its economic conditions; its effects will reach far beyond the adult businesses it explicitly controls. The gay bars on Christopher Street draw customers from people who come there because of its sex trade. The street is cruisier because of the sex shops. The boutiques that sell freedom rings and "Don't Panic" T-shirts do more business for the same reasons. Not all of the thousands who migrate or make pilgrimages to Christopher Street use the porn shops, but all benefit from the fact that some do. After a certain point, a quantitative change is a qualitative change. A critical mass develops. The street becomes queer. It develops a dense, publicly accessible sexual culture. It therefore becomes a base for nonporn businesses, like the Oscar Wilde

Bookshop. And it becomes a political base from which to pressure politicians with a gay voting bloc.

No group is more dependent on this kind of pattern in urban space than queers. If we could not concentrate a publicly accessible culture somewhere, we would always be outnumbered and overwhelmed. And because what brings us together is sexual culture, there are very few places in the world that have assembled much of a queer population without a base in sex commerce, and even those that do exist, such as the lesbian culture in Northampton, Massachusetts, are stronger because of their ties to places like the West Village, Dupont Circle, West Hollywood, and the Castro. Respectable gays like to think that they owe nothing to the sexual subculture they think of as sleazy. But their success, their way of living, their political rights, and their very identities would never have been possible but for the existence of the public sexual culture they now despise. Extinguish it, and almost all *out* gay or queer culture will wither on the vine. No one knows this connection better than the right. Conservatives would not so flagrantly contradict their stated belief in a market free from government interference if they did not see this kind of hyperregulation as an important victory.

The point here is not that queer politics needs more free-market ideology, but that heteronormative forms, so central to the accumulation and reproduction of capital, also depend on heavy interventions in the regulation of capital. One of the most disturbing fantasies in the zoning scheme, for example, is the idea that an urban locale is a community of shared interest based on residence and property. The ideology of the neighborhood is politically unchallengeable in the current debate, which is dominated by a fantasy that sexual subjects only reside, that the space relevant to sexual politics is the neighborhood. But a district like Christopher Street is not just a neighborhood affair. The local character of the neighborhood depends on the daily presence of thousands of nonresidents. Those who actually live in the West Village should not forget their debt to these mostly queer pilgrims. And we should not make the mistake of confusing the class of citizens with the class of property owners. Many of those who hang out on Christopher Street—typically young, queer, and African American—couldn't possibly afford to live there. Urban space is always a host space. The right to the city extends to those who use the city.[32] It is not limited to property owners. It is not because of a fluke in the politics of zoning that urban space is so deeply misrecognized; normal sexuality requires such misrecognitions, including their economic and legal enforcement, in order to sustain its illusion of humanity.

Tweaking and thwacking

Queer social theory is committed to sexuality as an inescapable category of analysis, agitation, and refunctioning. Like class relations, which in this moment are mainly visible in the polarized embodiments of identity forms, heteronormativity is a fundamental motor of social organization in the United States, a founding condition of unequal and exploitative relations throughout even straight society. Any social theory that miscomprehends this participates in their reproduction.

The project of thinking about sex in public does not only engage sex when it is disavowed or suppressed. Even if sex practice is not the object domain of queer studies, sex is everywhere present. But where is the tweaking, thwacking, thumping, sliming, and rubbing you might have expected—or dreaded—in a paper on sex? We close with two scenes that might have happened on the same day in our wanderings around the city. One afternoon, we were riding with a young straight couple we know, in their station wagon. Gingerly, after much circumlocution, they brought the conversation around to vibrators. These are people whose reproductivity governs their lives, their aspirations, and their relations to money and entailment, mediating their relations to everyone and everything else. But the woman in this couple had recently read an article in a women's magazine about sex toys and other forms of nonreproductive eroticism. She and her husband did some mail-order shopping and have become increasingly involved in what from most points of view would count as queer sex practices; their bodies have become disorganized and exciting to them. They said to us: you're the only people we can talk to about this; to all of our straight friends this would make us perverts. In order not to feel like perverts, they had to make *us* into a kind of sex public.

Later, the question of aversion and perversion came up again. This time we were in a bar that on most nights is a garden-variety leather bar, but that, on Wednesday nights, hosts a sex performance event called "Pork." Shows typically include spanking, flagellation, shaving, branding, laceration, bondage, humiliation, wrestling—you know, the usual: amateur, everyday practitioners strutting for everyone else's gratification, not unlike an academic conference. This night, word was circulating that the performance was to be erotic vomiting. This sounded like an appetite spoiler, and the thought of leaving early occurred to us but was overcome by a simple curiosity: what would the foreplay be like? Let's stay until it gets messy. Then we can leave.

A boy, twentyish, very skateboard, comes on the low stage at one end of the bar, wearing lycra shorts and a dog collar. He sits loosely in a restraining chair. His partner comes out and tilts the bottom's head up to the ceiling, stretching out his throat. Behind them is an array of foods. The top begins pouring milk down the boy's throat, then food, then more milk. It spills over, down his chest and onto the floor. A dynamic is established between them in which they carefully keep at the threshold of gagging. The bottom struggles to keep taking in more than he really can. The top is careful to give him just enough to stretch his capacities. From time to time a baby bottle is offered as a respite, but soon the rhythm intensifies. The boy's stomach is beginning to rise and pulse, almost convulsively.

It is at this point that we realize we cannot leave, cannot even look away. No one can. The crowd is transfixed by the scene of intimacy and display, control and abandon, ferocity and abjection. People are moaning softly with admiration, then whistling, stomping, screaming encouragements. They have pressed forward in a compact and intimate group. Finally, as the top inserts two, then three fingers in the bottom's throat, insistently offering his own stomach for the repeated climaxes, we realize that we have never seen such a display of trust and violation. We are breathless. But, good academics that we are, we also have some questions to ask. Word has gone around that the boy is straight. We want to know: What does that mean in this context? How did you discover that this is what you want to do? How did you find a male top to do it with? How did you come to do it in a leather bar? Where else do you do this? How do you feel about your new partners, this audience?

We did not get to ask these questions, but we have others that we can pose now, about these scenes where sex appears more sublime than narration itself, neither redemptive nor transgressive, moral nor immoral, hetero nor homo, nor sutured to any axis of social legitimation. We have been arguing that sex opens a wedge to the transformation of those social norms that require only its static intelligibility or its deadness as a source of meaning.[33] In these cases, though, paths through publicity led to the production of nonheteronormative bodily contexts. They intended nonheteronormative worlds because they refused to pretend that privacy was their ground; because they were forms of sociability that unlinked money and family from the scene of the good life; because they made sex the consequence of public mediations and collective self-activity in a way that made for unpredicted pleasures; because, in turn, they attempted to make a context of support for their practices; because their pleasures were not purchased by a redemptive pastoralism of sex, nor by mandatory amnesia about failure, shame, and aversion.[34]

We are used to thinking about sexuality as a form of intimacy and subjectivity, and we have just demonstrated how limited that representation is. But the heteronormativity of U.S. culture is not something that can be easily rezoned or disavowed by individual acts of will, by a subversiveness imagined only as personal rather than as the basis of public-formation, nor even by the lyric moments that interrupt the hostile cultural narrative that we have been staging here. Remembering the utopian wish behind normal intimate life, we also want to remember that we aren't married to it.

Notes

1   On public sex in the standard sense, see Pat Califia, *Public Sex: The Culture of Radical Sex* (Pittsburgh, 1994). On acts and identities, see Janet E. Halley, "The Status/Conduct Distinction in the 1993 Revisions to Military Antigay Policy: A Legal Archaeology," *GLQ* 3 (1996): 159–252. The classic political argument for sexual derepression as a condition of freedom is put forth in Herbert Marcuse, *Eros and Civilization: A Philosophical Inquiry into Freud* (Boston, 1966). In contemporary prosex thought inspired by volume 1 of Michel Foucault's *The History of Sexuality*, the denunciation of "erotic injustice and sexual oppression" is situated less in the freedom of individuals than in analyses of the normative and coercive relations between specific "populations" and the institutions created to manage them (Gayle Rubin, "Thinking Sex: Notes for a Radical Theory of the Politics of Sexuality," in *Pleasure and Danger: Exploring Female Sexuality*, ed. Carole S. Vance [Boston, 1984], p. 275). See also Michel Foucault, *The History of Sexuality: An Introduction*, vol. 1 of *The History of Sexuality*, trans. Robert Hurley (New York, 1978).

2   By heteronormativity we mean the institutions, structures of understanding, and practical orientations that make heterosexuality seem not only coherent—that is, organized as a sexuality—but also privileged. Its coherence is always provisional, and its privilege can take several (sometimes contradictory) forms: unmarked, as the basic idiom of the personal and the social; or marked as a natural state; or projected as an ideal or moral accomplishment. It consists less of norms that could be summarized as a body of doctrine than of a sense of rightness produced in contradictory manifestations—often unconscious, immanent to practice or to institutions. Contexts that have little visible relation to sex practice, such as life narrative and generational identity, can be heteronormative in this sense, while in other contexts forms of sex between men and women might *not* be heteronormative. Heteronormativity is thus a concept distinct from heterosexuality. One of the most conspicuous differences is that it has no parallel, unlike heterosexuality, which organizes homosexuality as its opposite. Because homosexuality can never have the invisible, tacit, society-founding rightness that heterosexuality has, it would not be possible to speak of "homonormativity" in the same sense. See Michael Warner, "Fear of a Queer Planet," *Social Text*, no. 29 (1991): 3–17.

3   See *Time*, special issue, "The New Face of America," Fall 1993. This analysis reworks materials in Lauren Berlant, *The Queen of America Goes to Washington City: Essays on Sex and Citizenship* (Durham, N.C., 1997), pp. 200–208.

4   For a treatment of the centrality of "blood" to U.S. nationalist discourse, see Bonnie Honig, *No Place Like Home: Democracy and the Politics of Foreignness* (forthcoming).

5   See, for example, William J. Bennett, *The De-Valuing of America: The Fight for Our Culture and Our Children* (New York, 1992); Peter Brimelow, *Alien Nation: Common Sense about America's Immigration Disaster* (New York, 1995); and William A. Henry III, *In Defense of Elitism* (New York, 1994).

6   On the family form in national rhetoric, see Jay Fliegelman, *Prodigals and Pilgrims: The American Revolution against Patriarchal Authority, 1750–1800* (Cambridge, 1982), and Shirley Samuels, *Romances of the Republic: Women, the Family, and Violence in the Literature of the Early American Nation* (New York, 1996). On fantasies of genetic assimilation, see Robert S. Tilton, *Pocahontas: The Evolution of an American Narrative* (Cambridge, 1994), pp. 9–33, and Elise Lemire, "Making Miscegenation" (Ph.D. diss., Rutgers University, 1996).

7   The concept of welfare state governmentality has a growing literature. For a concise statement, see Jürgen Habermas, "The New Obscurity: The Crisis of the Welfare State and the Exhaustion of Utopian Energies," *The New Conservatism: Cultural Criticism and the Historians' Debate*, trans. Shierry Weber Nicholsen (Cambridge, Mass., 1989), pp. 48–70. Michael Warner has discussed the relation between this analysis and queer culture in his "Something Queer about the Nation-State," in *After Political Correctness: The Humanities and Society in the 1990s*, eds. Christopher Newfield and Ronald Strickland (Boulder, Colo., 1995), pp. 361–71.

8   *Congressional Record*, 101st Cong., 1st, sess., 1989, 135, pt. 134:12967.

9   Political geography in this way produces systematic effects of violence. Queers are forced to find each other in untrafficked areas because of the combined pressures of propriety, stigma, the closet, and state regulation such as laws against public lewdness. The same areas are known to gay-bashers and other criminals. And they are disregarded by police. The effect is to make both violence and police neglect seem like natural hazards, voluntarily courted by queers. As the 1997 documentary film *Licensed to Kill* illustrates, antigay violence has been difficult to combat by legal means: victims are reluctant to come forward in any public and prosecutorial framework, while bashers can appeal to the geographic circumstances to implicate the victims themselves. The legal system has helped to produce the violence it is called upon to remedy.

10   See Eve Kosofsky Sedgwick, *Epistemology of the Closet* (Berkeley, 1992).

11   Gay and lesbian theory, especially in the humanities, frequently emphasizes psychoanalytic or psychoanalytic-style models of subject-formation, the differences among which are significant and yet all of which tend to elide the difference between the categories male/female and the process and project of heteronormativity. Three prepositional paradigms are relevant here: those that propose that human identity itself is fundamentally organized by gender identifications that are hardwired into infants; those that equate the clarities of gender identity with the domination of a relatively coherent and vertically stable "straight" ideology; and those that focus on a phallocentric Symbolic order that produces gendered subjects who live out the destiny of their positioning in it. The psychoanalytic and philosophical insights and limits of these models (which, we feel, underdescribe the practices, institutions, and incongruities of heteronormativity) require further engagement. For the time being, these works stand in as the most challenging relevant archive: Judith Butler, *Bodies that Matter: On the Discursive Limits of "Sex"* (New York, 1993); Luce Irigaray, *Speculum of the Other Woman*, trans. Gillian C. Gill (Ithaca, N.Y., 1985) and *This Sex Which Is Not One*, trans. Catherine Porter and Carolyn Burke (Ithaca, N.Y., 1985); Teresa de Lauretis, *The Practice of Love: Lesbian Sexuality and Perverse Desire* (Bloomington, Ind., 1994); Kaja Silverman, *Male Subjectivity at the Margins* (New York, 1992); and Monique Wittig, *The Straight Mind and Other Essays* (Boston, 1992). Psychoanalytic work on sexuality does not always latch acts and inclinations to natural or constructed "identity": see, for example, Leo Bersani, *Homos* (Cambridge, Mass., 1995) and "Is the Rectum a Grave?" in *AIDS: Cultural Analysis/Cultural Activism,* ed. Douglas Crimp (Cambridge, Mass., 1988).

12   The notion of metaculture we borrow from Greg Urban. See Greg Urban, *A Discourse-Centered Approach to Culture: Native South American Myths and Rituals* (Austin, Tex., 1991) and *Noumenal Community: Myth and Reality in an Amerindian Brazilian Society* (Austin, Tex., 1996). On normalization, see Foucault, *Discipline and Punish: The Birth of the Prison*, trans. Alan Sheridan (New York, 1979), pp. 184–85 and *The History of Sexuality*, p. 144. Foucault derives his argument here from the revised version of Georges Canguilhem, *The Normal and the Pathological*, trans. Carolyn R. Fawcett and Robert S. Cohen (New York, 1991).

13   Here we are influenced by Eli Zaretsky, *Capitalism, the Family, and Personal Life* (New York, 1986), and Stephanie Coontz, *The Social Origins of Private Life: A History of American Families, 1600–1900* (London, 1988), though heteronormativity is a problem not often made visible in Coontz's work.

14   On privatization and intimacy politics, see Berlant, *The Queen of America Goes to Washington City*, pp. 1–24 and "Feminism and the Institutions of Intimacy," in *The Politics of Research*, eds. E. Ann Kaplan and George Levine (New Brunswick, N.J., 1997), pp. 143–61; Honig, *No Place Like Home*; and Rosalind Pollack Petchesky, "The Body as Property: A Feminist Re-vision," in *Conceiving the New World Order: The Global Politics of Reproduction*, eds. Faye D. Ginsburg and Rayna Rapp (Berkeley, 1995), pp. 387–406. On privatization and national-capitalism, see David Harvey, *The Condition of Postmodernity: An Enquiry into the Origins of Cultural Change* (Oxford, 1989), and Mike Davis, *City of Quartz: Excavating the Future in Los Angeles* (New York, 1992).

15   This language for community is a problem for gay historiography. In otherwise fine and important studies such as Esther Newton's *Cherry Grove, Fire Island: Sixty Years in America's First Gay and Lesbian Town* (Boston, 1993), or Elizabeth Lapovsky Kennedy and Madeline D. Davis's *Boots of Leather, Slippers of Gold: The History of a Lesbian Community* (New York, 1993), or even George Chauncey's *Gay New York: Gender, Urban Culture, and the Makings of the Gay Male World, 1890–1940* (New York, 1994), community is imagined as whole-person, face-to-face relations—local, experiential, proximate, and saturating. But queer worlds seldom manifest themselves in such forms. Cherry Grove—a seasonal resort depending heavily on weekend visits by New Yorkers—may be typical less of a "gay and lesbian town" than of the way queer sites are specialized spaces in which transits can project alternative worlds. John D'Emilio's *Sexual Politics, Sexual Communities: The Making of a Homosexual Minority in the United States, 1940–1970* is an especially interesting example of the imaginative power of the idealization of local community for queers: the book charts the separate tracks of political organizing

and local scenes such as bar life, showing that when the "movement" and the "subculture" began to converge in San Francisco, the result was a new formation with a new utopian appeal: "A 'community,'" D'Emilio writes, "was in fact forming around a shared sexual orientation" (John D'Emilio, *Sexual Politics, Sexual Communities: The Making of a Homosexual Minority in the United States, 1940–1970* [Chicago, 1983], p. 195). D'Emilio (wisely) keeps scare quotes around "community" in the very sentence declaring it to exist in fact.

16   Artemidorus, *Oneirocritica* 1.2, quoted in David M. Halperin, "Sex before Sexuality: Pederasty, Politics, and Power in Classical Athens," in *Hidden from History: Reclaiming the Gay and Lesbian Past*, eds. Martin Bauml Duberman, Martha Vicinus, and George Chauncey (New York, 1989), p. 49.

17   Halperin, "Sex before Sexuality," p. 49.

18   Studies of intimacy that do not assume this "web of mutuality," either as the self-evident nature of intimacy or as a human value, are rare. Roland Barthes's *A Lover's Discourse: Fragments*, trans. Richard Howard (New York, 1978), and Niklas Luhmann's *Love as Passion*, trans. Jeremy Gaines and Doris L. Jones (Cambridge, Mass., 1986) both try, in very different ways, to describe analytically the production of intimacy. More typical is Anthony Giddens's attempt to theorize intimacy as "pure relationship" in *The Transformation of Intimacy: Sexuality, Love, and Eroticism in Modern Societies* (Cambridge, 1992). There, ironically, it is "the gays who are the pioneers" in separating the "pure relationship" of love from extraneous institutions and contexts such as marriage and reproduction.

19   Berlant and Warner, "What Does Queer Theory Teach Us about X?" *PMLA* 110 (May 1995): 345.

20   William Bennett, quoted in Maureen Dowd, "Talk Is Cheap," *New York Times*, 26 Oct. 1995, p. A25.

21   Biddy Martin, "Extraordinary Homosexuals and the Fear of Being Ordinary," *differences* 6 (Summer–Fall 1994): 123; hereafter abbreviated "EH."

22   In some traditions of social theory, the process of world making as we describe it here is seen as common to all social actors. See, for example, Alfred Schutz's emphasis on the practices of typification and projects of action involved in ordinary knowledge of the social in *The Phenomenology of the Social World*, trans. George Walsh and Frederick Lehnert (Evanston, Ill., 1967). Yet in most contexts the social world is understood, not as constructed by reference to types or projects, but as instantiated whole in a form capable of reproducing itself. The family, the state, a neighborhood, the human species, or institutions such as school and church—such images of social being share an appearance of plenitude seldom approached in contexts of queer world making. However much the latter might resemble the process of world construction in ordinary contexts, queer worlds do not have the power to represent a taken-for-granted social existence.

23   See, for example, Alan Bray, "Homosexuality and the Signs of Male Friendship in Elizabethan England," *History Workshop* 29 (Spring 1990): 1–19; Laurie J. Shannon, "Emilia's Argument: Friendship and 'Human Title' in *The Two Noble Kinsmen*," *ELH* 64 (Fall 1997); and *Passions of the Renaissance*, trans. Arthur Goldhammer, ed. Roger Chartier, vol. 3 of *A History of Private Life*, ed. Philippe Ariès and Georges Duby (Cambridge, Mass., 1989).

24   On the relation between Foucault and Habermas, we take inspiration from Tom McCarthy, *Ideals and Illusions* (Cambridge, Mass., 1991), pp. 43–75.

25   Habermas, *The Structural Transformation of the Public Sphere: An Inquiry into a Category of Bourgeois Society*, trans. Thomas Burger and Frederick Lawrence (Cambridge, Mass., 1991), p. 49.

26   Ibid., p. 46.

27   On the centrality of semipublic spaces like tearooms, bathrooms, and bathhouses to gay male life, see Chauncey, *Gay New York*, and Lee Edelman, "Tearooms and Sympathy, or, Epistemology of the Water Closet," in *Nationalisms and Sexualities*, eds. Andrew Parker et al. (New York, 1992), pp. 263–84. The spaces of both gay and lesbian semipublic sexual practices are investigated in *Mapping Desire: Geographies of Sexualities*, eds. David Bell and Gill Valentine (New York, 1995).

28   Douglas Crimp, "How to Have Promiscuity in an Epidemic," *October*, no. 43 (Winter 1987): 253.

29   The notion of a demand for recognition has been recently advanced by a number of thinkers as a way of understanding multicultural politics. See, for example, Axel Honneth, *The Struggle for Recognition: The Moral Grammar of Social Conflicts*, trans. Joel Anderson (Cambridge, 1995), or *Multiculturalism: Examining the Politics of Recognition*, ed. Amy Gutmann (Princeton, N.J., 1994). We are suggesting that although queer politics does contest the terrain of recognition, it cannot be conceived as a politics of recognition *as opposed to* an issue of distributive justice; this is the distinction proposed in Nancy Fraser's "From Redistribution to Recognition? Dilemmas of Justice in a 'Postsocialist' Age," *New Left Review*, no. 212 (July–Aug. 1995): 68–93; rept. in her *Justice Interruptus: Critical Reflections on the "Postsocialist" Condition* (New York, 1997).

30   See Sedgwick, *Epistemology of the Closet*, and Yvonne Zipter, *Diamonds Are a Dyke's Best Friend: Reflections, Reminiscences, and Reports from the Field on the Lesbian National Pastime* (Ithaca, N.Y., 1988).

31   Such a politics is increasingly recommended within the gay movement. See, for example, Andrew
      Sullivan, *Same-Sex Marriage, Pro and Con* (New York, 1997); Michelangelo Signorile, *Life Outside: The
      Signorile Report on Gay Men, Sex, Drugs, Muscles, and the Passages of Life* (New York, 1997); Gabriel
      Rotello, *Sexual Ecology: AIDS and the Destiny of Gay Men* (New York, 1997); William N. Eskridge, Jr.,
      The Case for Same-Sex Marriage: From Sexual Liberty to Civilized Commitment (New York, 1996); *Same-Sex
      Marriage: The Moral and Legal Debate*, ed. Robert M. Baird and Stuart E. Rosenbaum (Amherst, N.Y.,
      1996); and Mark Strasser, *Legally Wed: Same-Sex Marriage and the Constitution* (Ithaca, N.Y., 1997).

32   The phrase "the right to the city" is Henri Lefebvre's, from his *Le Droit à la ville* (Paris, 1968); trans.
      Eleonore Kofman and Elizabeth Lebas, under the title "The Right to the City," *Writings on Cities*
      (Oxford, 1996), pp. 147–59. See also Manuel Castells, *The City and the Grassroots* (Berkeley, 1983).

33   On deadness as an affect and aspiration of normative social membership, see Berlant, "Live Sex Acts
      (Parental Advisory: Explicit Material)," *The Queen of America Goes to Washington City*, pp. 59–60,
      79–81.

34   The classic argument against the redemptive sex pastoralism of normative sexual ideology is made in
      Bersani, "Is the Rectum a Grave?"; on redemptive visions more generally, see his *The Culture of
      Redemption* (Cambridge, Mass., 1990).

Chapter 11

Gregory Tomso

VIRAL SEX AND THE POLITICS OF LIFE

Gregory Tomso is Associate Professor and Associate Director of University Honors at the University of West Florida. Tomso has published essays on American literature, queer and feminist theory, and the cultural study of illness and disease. The following essay was originally published in *South Atlantic Quarterly* in 2008.

In "Viral Sex and the Politics of Life," Tomso explores the political economy of viral sex in public discourse within the context of the HIV/AIDS crisis in the U.S. Tomso defines viral sex as "risky sex between men" wherein "safe sex" practices (condom use, for example) are ignored. Using a Foucauldian framework, Tomso argues that viral sex is an act of biopolitical resistance to state power. The HIV epidemic is a powerful context for the disruption of state power because contemporary liberal discourse shapes HIV as an epidemic that pertains primarily to "risky" subjects whose sexual practices must be "managed" by the state. Through viral sex, life itself becomes politically viable in its refusal to support the state's notion of "well-being," along with discourses of natural rights and sovereign power. Tomso maintains that viral sex as resistance will work to maintain and strengthen gay communities in the face of overwhelming biopolitical surveillance.

> Faced with plague, one can no longer simply go on with business as usual. One is forced to call one's habits, values, and pleasures into question, precisely because the world in which they had a place is in the process of slipping away, disrupted in a way that always feels like an imposition, and seems unjustified, senseless.
>
> (Linda Singer, *Erotic Welfare*)

MEN WHO INTENTIONALLY engage in unsafe sex with other men—barebackers, bug chasers, gift givers, tweakers, virus breeders, those living on the "down low"—are commonly regarded today as murderers and suicides.[1] In the scientific and popular media, "barebackers" and "virus breeders" have been singled out as the targets of moral furor or, among the more liberally minded, as targets of state surveillance and scientific management. In the popular press, outright moral condemnation is not uncommon, nor is the sentimental fearmongering of journalistic exposés.[2] Viral sex, intentionally unsafe sex, produces for all these constituencies the question, "What makes them do it?"[3] Finding an answer to this question is the impetus behind an ever-growing number of public health studies that have, for better and for worse, begun to catalog the reasons why some men choose not to use prophylactics.[4] In short: blame, fear, and the impetus to produce knowledge about the motivations of particular sexual subjects are all part of the first wave of responses to what seems to be a mind-boggling set of sexual behaviors that fly in the face of scientific orthodoxy and the instinct for self-preservation.

As an alternative to these approaches, this essay isolates viral sex in the field of power relations that makes it seem so dangerous in the first place, before particular individuals and their personal lives are submitted to scrutiny by the moralist or researcher. Viral sex, as a Foucauldian condition, constitutes a historical phenomenon, the product of a disciplinary discourse that brings to light three initial observations that are obscured by psychologism and morality. First, since the availability of protease inhibitors in 1996, viral sex has emerged as an object of disavowal, scorn, investigation, and surveillance. Whatever else it may be, viral sex is distinctly the result of changes to technological innovations in the management of HIV. Its origin is therefore historical and material as much as it may be biological or psychological. Second, viral sex is rendered intelligible to a large degree through discourses predicated on identity as opposed to choices or acts. These identities are the latest disciplinary products of a regime knowledge that goes at least as far back as the appearance in the nineteenth century of "the homosexual" himself. Third, approaches that seek to understand the meanings of viral sex in terms of an individual's psychology or personal "experience" internalize, in the figure of the individual risk taker or of his aggregated "risk group," what are quite often relations of power external to the subject and his or her psychology. As a result, power dynamics that contribute to the formation of the subject remain obscure in the current analysis of viral sex.

This essay focuses on the third aspect, the problem of power, or what might be called the political economy of viral sex. Viral sex is analyzed not as a crisis to be solved by morality or social science but as the latest development in the phenomenology of homosexuality as it continues to evolve in the era of what Michel Foucault calls "biopower" and within the domain of liberal political rationality. Thus, the term *viral sex* refers, in this analysis, primarily to the discourses describing risky sex between men. In reading these discourses collectively, and often at face value, I temporarily set aside important epidemiological questions concerning the frequency of, and distinctions among, the risky sexual behaviors they describe.

Viral sex, as a discursive field, provides a philosophical and historical opportunity for thinking about sexual politics in ways not organized around the traditional liberal subject. Instead, it challenges coercive modes of sexual subjugation through a unique form of bio-political resistance to state power. Thinking biopolitically provides a way to organize political resistance around a critique of subjugation as opposed to the state-centered notions of citizenship, rights, and sovereignty. As Andrew Barry and others have noted, a move "beyond the state" leads to "a politics of life, of ethics, which emphasizes the crucial political value of the mobilization and shaping of individual capacities and conduct."[5] Viral sex calls into question the political meanings of life that emerge within the liberal discourse of natural rights and state-centered notions of sovereign power. By doing so, it reopens, in a way not subject to liberalism's constraints, the question of sexual freedom.

As gay men near the end of the third decade of the HIV/AIDS epidemic, what, if anything, is left of the liberal notion of sexual freedom? This is a question that queer theory has inherited, in one important way at least, from Foucault, for whom the answer could not have taken into account the longevity and reach of the epidemic to date. At a time when many gay men no longer feel at liberty to pursue their sexual freedom, at least not in the same way

Foucault did in the late 1970s and early 1980s, it is soberingly clear that liberalism does not guarantee sexual freedom. Rather, as Foucault himself suggests, freedom is a horizon in which we continuously renegotiate the terms of our own subjugation.[6] In its pursuit of sexual freedom, viral sex suggests new forms of political action distinct from the liberal politics of the "new gay center" in the United States—those of the Human Rights Campaign, for example, which ardently pursues the liberal political "good" of same-sex marriage.

Since the rise of protease inhibitors in the mid-1990s, life with HIV has become, for many people in Western countries, immanently more livable, as the possibility of an extended future with HIV unfolds. The new culture of viral sex is one of the most vital and precious products of this technological achievement. While the possibility of a life, or a future, with HIV was practically unthinkable in the first decade of the epidemic, that state of affairs has changed for many of those with the means to afford the new drugs, for those who cannot sustain the panic mentality of the 1980s and early 1990s, and for those who have come of age after the epidemic's initial years of collective mourning and trauma. While viral sex does not lead to an upbeat, liberal politics organized around the "pursuit of happiness" in the Jeffersonian sense, it does invite a serious reconsideration of what a politics of life might look like. Viral sex points in the illiberal direction of a politics of illness and epidemic, a politics of enduring loss that nevertheless still makes room for the pursuit of pleasure. Its most important political "goods" are the literal and symbolic life of the body and the dominant discourses through which such life becomes politically viable.

The political economy of viral sex

The political value of viral sex emerges through its conflicted relationship with liberalism and neoliberalism. Particularly in terms of liberal identity politics in the United States, one of the most radical aspects of the culture of viral sex is the unprecedented proliferation of male sexual identities that it has spawned. Defined by the risk of viral transmission and the pleasures of same-sex eroticism, the new identities of risk endemic to the culture of viral sex are commensurate neither with "homosexuality" nor "gayness," nor even, at least not fully, with the academically mandated, antinormative politics of "queerness." Instead of providing the ground for a relatively stable, politically resonant claim to oppositional sexual identity, the new identities of risk serve in many instances to eschew political recognition. As one barebacking Web site puts it, "Our guys f—k and suck without any barriers, lectures or bullshit."[7] Rather than serving as an embarrassment to mainstream gays (as queens and leather men often do), those who practice viral sex often pursue pleasures that fall outside the purview of gay identity as such. Is viral sex the political vanguard of a postgay world?

Historically coincident with the rise of gay centrism and social assimilationism, viral sex functions as a foil to those gays who see themselves as "virtually normal," challenging the rational, ethical, and identitarian norms of liberal gay politics.[8] To make this claim is not to celebrate barebackers and other risk takers as heroes or as stylish "dissenters," but both to limit and to resist the ethical, moral, social-scientific, and psychological habits of thought that reduce viral sex to a crisis of (gay) sexual subjectivity. Can viral sex not be more productively read as a historical shift in dominant modes of sexual representation and constructions of healthy individualism? Those who engage in risky sex refuse not only to be "virtually normal" but also to be safe and even, at times, to be well. The most radical gesture made by discourses about bug chasing, gift giving, and other forms of risk taking may be, then, not their rejection of gay identity, but their symbolic and sometimes literal refusal of rational, state-supported notions of human well-being. In this regard, viral sex poses ethical challenges to progressives and conservatives alike, regardless of their attitude toward "homosexuality." It is precisely at this point of estrangement from mainstream political values that a stringent critique of the politics of the subject, in both its liberal and neoliberal incarnations, becomes crucial.

Neither liberalism nor neoliberalism can respond to viral sex as anything but a major ethical or moral crisis. Viral sex leads, on the one hand, to a crisis in liberal ethics to the extent that liberals must decide between regard for the sexual freedom of the individual or the sacrifice of such freedom for the good of the many. In this view, the mandates of public health, as dictated by the state, compete with individual and collective claims to sexual freedom. "Super confidential" (as opposed to anonymous) HIV testing and mandatory partner reporting for HIV-positive persons are classic liberal examples of the state's encroachment on individual rights to privacy and personal liberty, and one could say the same about the recent emergence of viral sex as a public health crisis. Public health, in this sense, can be understood as a form of state-sponsored violence against the rights of the individual. Neoliberalism, on the other hand, is far less concerned with the ideal of sexual freedom than classic liberalism. Neoliberalism brings notions of economic efficiency, rationality, and risk aversion to the conduct of affairs not traditionally associated with the economy, such as the management of life and health.[9] According to neoliberal rationality, one should confidently stand behind a state- and corporate-sponsored version of "expert" truths on health and safety while developing "compassion" (if not outright moral condemnation) for those whose needs, desires, and behaviors place them outside the norm. The aim is to ensure the sexual health of individuals who, entitled by the state and within the confines of what the state deems morally acceptable, have access to private assets that allow them to protect their own health. "Compassion" for those who fall outside the boundaries of entitlement (such as certain immigrants) and conventional morality (promiscuous "gay" men) allows for an essentially sentimental response—indeed, one that is cherished within the ethos of Protestant piety—that maintains the social, legal, and political invisibility of the marginal. Those who can become increasingly healthy and feel virtuous for doing so and those who lack the necessary economic, cultural, and social capital experience a widening gap between themselves and the entitled while being blamed for their personal shortcomings.

Nowhere is the cultural influence of neoliberalism more apparent than in the field of public health, focused as it is today on health promotion, risk management, and "lifestyle" change. As a form of governmentality, public health alters self-conduct and self-perception, as when people voluntarily change their behaviors—sexual, dietary, and otherwise—in the pursuit of health and become "health consumers" and "health promoters" in the course of their professions or everyday lives. In its specifically neoliberal incarnation, public health suggests efficient ways to preserve and manage the life of a population by making individuals morally responsible for their own health. Perhaps the most striking example of this rationality in the United States to date appears in recent efforts to reform Medicaid. In the state of West Virginia, for instance, patients must sign a pledge "to do my best to stay healthy," as part of new, federally backed efforts to promote "personal responsibility" in health care.[10] Those who refuse to sign the pledge or to attend mandatory antiobesity or antismoking classes can be denied medical benefits available to other, more "responsible" citizens. Thus, to be unhealthy in a neoliberal, biopolitical regime is not only to be sick or suffering but also to be inefficient, selfish, irresponsible, and irrational—and to be an economic burden on the state.

As the HIV/AIDS epidemic has unfolded in the West, safe-sex education campaigns have augmented neoliberalism's links to the biopolitics of AIDS by creating the idea of a rational actor who, taken as the generic subject of public health, is thought to possess a personal responsibility to protect his or her life and health.[11] As a result, protecting oneself and others from HIV infection today is widely regarded as a moral and legal duty in which rational behavior ensures the well-being of individual and society alike. This focus on the rational subject helps to explain how the political aspects of viral sex have become so difficult to pin down, namely because traditional safe-sex discourses remove viral sex from its cultural context, reducing its fundamentally political and historical tensions to intrinsic qualities of the individual. In effect, neoliberalism makes adhering to the biopolitical norm of health seem like a profoundly personal, ethical choice, to the extent that individual subjects internalize the demand to protect and foster life in accordance with state reason. In other words, neoliberalism helps to naturalize biopolitical aims.

By contrast, in terms of political economy, viral sex is a claim to sexual freedom, a problem in the history of liberalism as it is "haunted" by the contemporary biopolitics of HIV and AIDS.[12] The hegemony of biopolitical governance, facilitated by the proliferation of safer sex campaigns and, more generally, by the rise of the "new" public health with its emphasis on risk management,[13] has clouded the issue of liberal freedom, particularly sexual freedom, in ways that Foucault could not have foreseen, given how early his death came in the epidemic. Yet for many gay men, especially those who have been hit disproportionately hard by the AIDS epidemic and who are now faced with a complicated array of choices regarding their sexual lives, questions of sexual freedom are especially difficult. At stake in any act of sex between two men is a complex series of questions about the economy of health and pleasure, about the interrelation of care of the self and care of others, and about the very meaning and value of life itself. While the same might be said of sex between any two people, gay or straight, male or female, these issues are now weighing heavily on gay men in particular because they face the challenge of rebuilding gay culture, and especially gay sexual culture, after the initial (and ongoing, in some parts of the world) devastation of AIDS.[14] As the thirty-year-old epidemic continues and gay men experiment with alternatives to the safe-sex mantras of "abstinence first" or "use a condom every time," the problem of how to conduct oneself in the face of sexual freedom looms large. One of the most urgent questions facing gay men today is about how to practice sexual freedom in the extended shadow of the epidemic, especially now that strict adherence to the orthodoxy of safe sex is no longer the only imaginable option for the ethical conduct of homosexual life.

If there is a nascent sexual politics to be gleaned from viral sex, it is not, liberally speaking, a politics of the subject, nor is it a politics directed at a single political good, such as the right to marry. Instead, viral sex may constitute, as Foucault would say, a "practice of freedom" in response to configurations of power specific to early-twenty-first-century life in the United States.[15] One way viral sex does this is through its connection to HIV itself. The new identities of risk herald a relocation of the symbolic site of sexual identity within the body, a shift from a conceptual model of biological immanence (where sexuality is contained, privately and inviolately, within the body) to one of exchange and supplementarity (where sexual identity is predicated on bodily states or behaviors that result from shared experiences of transmission and outlaw forms of fluid exchange). The language of feeding, seeding, and breeding commonly used today in Internet chat rooms and personal ads exemplifies this difference. As the personal ad for one would-be virus breeder in San Francisco puts it: "Really get into nasty top men breeding my ass . . . walkin [sic] and use my holes, drop a load and go, Little or no talking. Just dump a load and go. Have one load [of semen] in me now. Seeking a few more tonight. Front door opens in an hour." Another ad reads, "Looking for a RAW top to take out this aggression on my hole! seed me deep and then leave."[16] The emphasis in these examples on exchanging and collecting semen draws on a different set of representational norms from those involved in experiencing, as Foucault would say, the "truth" of one's homosexuality. The eroticism of male–male sexual contact is predicated not on finding another person who shares one's hidden identity but in experiencing the transfer of a charged "load" from one man to another. The ability of semen to "breed" and "seed" does not result, in this case, from its potential to fertilize an egg inside a woman's body, but instead results from its ability to transmit and replicate HIV inside another man. Especially in the first example, the more "loads" the receptive partner collects—hoards, even—the more thrilling the contact with other men becomes.

In addition to the language of breeding and seeding, the discourses of viral sex have given rise to a complicated system of signs in which the signifiers "bug" and "gift" metonymically substitute for the virus itself, highlighting its ties to a metaphorical economy of excess and exchange. "Bug chasing" and "gift giving" are, at their core, economic metaphors, semiotic indicators of excessive forms of exchange or circulation that run counter to the hyperrational economics of risk society. While bugs and gifts may, at first glance, appear to have little in common, they are both closely related in terms of gift economy.[17] Gifts, like bugs and viruses, circulate in society and in the environment in ways that are not easily subject to regulatory laws or to attempts to curtail or monitor their movements. Bugs are especially powerful metaphors in this regard. Bugs are ubiquitous, stalwart, teeming with life; they find ways of reproducing in vast numbers even in the face of extraordinary deprivation; they resist our real and figural attempts to exterminate them; and despite the ravages of nature and technology, they endure. Bugs disrupt our best-laid plans, block our chosen paths, devalue our property and our investments, and imperil our health. They are intelligible almost exclusively in terms of collectivity, refusing the logic of separateness and rendering individualism absurd. Like gifts, bugs confound the terms of both classic and neoliberal economics and challenge the atomism that they foster. Both gifts and bugs make powerful symbols of outlaw forms of exchange, reproduction, and affiliation. Does it come as any surprise that certain Western men, during this interminable middle phase of the AIDS pandemic, would invent the symbolic practices of gift giving and bug chasing not as a psychologically aberrant means of seeking individual death but as a historically contingent, symbolic means of ensuring collective survival?

The emerging signs of excess in the political economy of viral sex are developments consistent with what cultural theorist Linda Singer has called the production of "erotic surplus" in the time of epidemics.[18] Singer's work analyzes the political economy, especially the sexual economy, of the AIDS epidemic. In *Erotic Welfare*, she shows how "sexuality . . . can be thought of as a political economy, a systemic grid of differences which produce, circulate, and order value" (34). Specifically, Singer argues that epidemics produce both an increase in technologies of population management—"a mobilized effort of control" (27)—and a "proliferative surplus" (121) of new forms of pleasures and new demands on the body. Counting "safe sex" as a primary example of that surplus, Singer distrusts such developments to the extent that they solidify neoliberal safeguards that liken bodily management to portfolio management. Analyzing the surplus sexual economies of pornography, prostitution, and addiction, Singer traces the ways in which these economies, shaped in the era of AIDS by what she calls "epidemic logic," have produced new subjects and pleasures incited by the market imperatives of profit making and workforce management that complement efforts at social–sexual control in times of epidemic disease (39). Yet, as Judith Butler notes, "Hegemonic power tends to produce an *excess of value* that it cannot fully control."[19] Barebacking, bug chasing, and gift giving appear to be part of this unanticipated excess, the erotic surplus of the AIDS pandemic.

The symbolic excesses of viral sex function as a kind of political communication—one not necessarily legible at the level of the individual subject—whose semiotic and economic intelligibility is made ripe through the metonymy of "bugs" and "gifts." As such, viral sex represents an intensification and extension, in specifically economic terms, of the politically resistant, identity- and subjectivity-altering effects and of certain forms of male–male sex celebrated by queer theory. David Halperin explains that sadomasochism, for example, was important to Foucault because it "represents a re-mapping of the body's erotic sites . . . a breakup of the erotic monopoly traditionally held by the genitals," adding that sadomasochism "make[s] possible the creation of a masculine sexual identity that need no longer be centered in the penis."[20] It is precisely through such challenges to identity that seemingly private sexual acts become, in effect, political ones.

There are, however, some important differences in the ways sadomasochism and viral sex disrupt the formation of male sexual subjects. Whereas queer theory has traditionally recognized the temporary dissolution of the sexual subject (the experience of jouissance) achieved through sadomasochism, viral sex is not so much a shattering force as it is an additive one. Viral sex could include all or none of the sexual practices traditionally associated with gay jouissance, since what defines viral sex is whether it carries the risk of infection with HIV. This difference highlights the status of HIV as a gift, the sign of a certain excess, or a token of exchange, that alters the traditional economy of male sexual subjectivity in which masculinity must be maintained, conserved, and guarded. In the context of viral sex, the self-shattering of jouissance becomes less important than the process of subjective *supplementation* in which the transmission of the virus (in gift giving, bug chasing, and viral "breeding") or the "raw" exchange of semen permitted by condomless sex (in barebacking) do not so much destroy the masculine subject as alter it by adding something foreign (and potentially fatal) to it.

Research conducted by social scientist Damien Ridge bears out this claim. The following is a description of barebacking offered by "Nic," a participant in a qualitative study of the meanings of male–male sex: "And it's like . . . it's almost like this man is injecting some of his masculinity into me . . . giving me some of that. And so I find it [receptive anal sex] a very augmenting experience as opposed to a diminishing experience. . . . In a sense, it's sort of like me taking something from him."[21] From the perspective of political economy, Nic's response is striking because it highlights the economic terms in which he experiences the thrill of another man's masculinity. Echoing the outlaw economies of bugs and gifts described earlier, Nic suggests here an economy in which masculinity might be "taken" according to the terms of a symbolic order in which semen metonymically stands in for "something" much more valuable, if intangible, perhaps an idealized or authentic masculinity. The thrill of bare-backing results from adding to or "augmenting" one's own limited stores of a precious and desired commodity. Here, the transfer and acquisition of sperm function as a type of commodity fetishism in which sperm magically accesses the fantasmatic ideal of masculinity, creating meanings and pleasures far in excess of sperm's clinical existence as a potentially dangerous bodily excretion. While tightly bound to economic logic and to the structure of the commodity fetish, viral sex resists the intensification of neoliberal subjugation by fully embracing its terms. The economic metaphors of excess—theft, breeding, gift, and augmen-tation—that distinguish viral sex demonstrate the centrality of economic rationality to the erotics of viral and seminal exchange that are crucial to the seemingly individual experience of masculinity.

Despite their differences, the practices of sadomasochism and viral sex serve as good examples of what Foucault calls "becoming homosexual."[22] Becoming homosexual—or, more specifically, "coming out" as gay—is not, in Foucault's view, about adopting a fixed identity, aesthetic style, or psychology, but is about forging new "relational possibilities"[23] or new "affective and relational virtualities."[24] He therefore emphasizes the deliberate choices men might make in the practice of sadomasochism to forge new relations with others that can lead to a new way of life ("mode de vie") ("Triumph," 158). The same could also be said about viral sex, but not without taking stock of the changes in homosexual life due to HIV and AIDS and of the intensification of neoliberal and biopolitical controls in the conduct of everyday life.

As compelling as Foucault's thinking about becoming homosexual remains today, it nevertheless emerges from a particular moment in the history of homosexuality that, just before the dawn of AIDS, is arguably more optimistic than today's. To remain useful, his ideas need to be read in the context of his own historical analysis of liberalism and subject to the very same scrutiny that Foucault himself brings to other forms of discourse. Specifically, the conflict between individual liberty, achieved through the minimization of government, and "reason of state," expressed through biopolitics, became the point of departure for Foucault's later work on the ethics of self-care, which includes his thinking about the conduct of homosexual life. At the heart of Foucauldian ethics is the practice of freedom. "Freedom," he once said, "is the ontological condition of ethics. But ethics is the considered form that freedom takes when it is informed by reflection."[25] Yet in his interviews on homosexuality, Foucault does not often pause to elaborate philosophically or historically on the nature of this freedom. Is sexual freedom, for example, a specifically liberal freedom for Foucault? The answer to this question seems to be yes, at least to the extent that Foucault makes clear in his interviews that homosexual becoming begins with individual freedom achieved in the liberal sense.

Foucault's problem with liberation politics, and what has been called for almost two decades "identity politics," begins when those politics become an end unto themselves. He repeatedly points out that the recognition of sexual identity and of the basic rights of sexual choice should be the beginning, not the end, of homosexual life. In particular, Foucault notes that the danger of liberalism is not that it offers the possibility of freedom, but that it too frequently links the idea of freedom to a discourse of "natural" rights that are thought to be immanent to the liberal subject. As an alternative to the struggle to liberate this mythical force, Foucault suggests that the discourse of liberal rights be altered to encompass "a new relational right that permits all possible types of relations to exist and not be prevented, blocked, or annulled by impoverished relational institutions" ("Triumph," 158). This view helps to explain why Foucault did not necessarily advocate for liberal rights such as gay marriage, since he viewed marriage as an "impoverished" form of social relation.[26] Once a certain measure of liberal freedom has been achieved, Foucault argues that fighting for liberal equality in areas such as the right to marry constitutes only "slight" progress ("Triumph," 158). Thus, it seems fair to say that liberal rights and liberal freedom were not in and of themselves contradictory to Foucault's understanding of homosexual ethics; rather, their achievement constitutes an essential and ongoing part of those ethics, but only insofar as liberalism refrains from positing a natural essence internal to the liberal subject and from imitating the form of existing social institutions.

Viral sex as biopolitical resistance

The enduring political "good" of viral sex is that it points to the possibility of specifically biopolitical forms of resistance to coercive regimes of power. Furthermore, it suggests that the goals of biopolitical resistance will be to challenge the meanings of health or of illness whenever those concepts place unwelcome restrictions on the practice of sexual freedom. Biopolitical resistance moves toward the horizons of life, inhabiting those places where life takes on political meaning, and contests, at their thinnest points, the discourses and practices through which life becomes subjected to political power. This is quite different from seeking "a place at the table" in the liberal body politic.[27] Thinking about resistance biopolitically makes sense today, when liberal appeals to the state seem to be, at best, an endgame. The aim of biopolitical resistance is not liberation from power but a *better form of rule* in which the body and its pleasure can be fruitfully reimagined, experimented with, and rendered unfamiliar.[28]

Surrounding viral sex today is not what Foucault once called the "empty space" of sexual freedom but a bitter political struggle over the meaning of life itself ("Triumph," 160). If biopolitical "reason of state" aims to preserve and foster life for the sake of strengthening the state and sustaining its economic well-being, viral sex presents an immediate challenge to those aims. It resists neoliberal, biopolitical governmentality by calling into question the meanings of health and survival, mobilizing those concepts in direct opposition to the state-supported aims of public health. Eric Rofes has argued that the decision to engage in unsafe sex exposes "fundamental distinctions in the ways gay men conceptualize life in the epidemic," adding that it is "difficult for many to imagine a moral system which prioritizes pleasure or whatever meaning one derives from unprotected anal sex over long-term survival."[29] For this reason, viral sex is likely to remain an intractable problem in contemporary political life, very much like abortion in the United States. Unlike abortion, however, viral sex poses equal challenges to all ideological constituencies, regardless of one's attitude toward "homosexuality" and regardless of whether one espouses a traditional liberal or neoliberal view of government. For those on both the political Right and Left, men who put themselves at risk tend to elicit one of two essentially sentimental responses: either condemnation or compassion. For conservatives, such men appear to be beyond "our" reach and deserve their fate; for progressives, gay men desperately need "our" help. In both instances, those who engage in viral sex become sentimentally bound, by compassion, hate, or fear, to a position of high visibility on the margins of mainstream political life.[30]

Historically speaking, it comes as no surprise that viral sex has emerged as a "problem" at this particular point in time. The early twenty-first century is a time in Western history when the very concept of life itself has been significantly opened to political struggle, in areas such as abortion rights, assisted suicide and vegetative life support, genetic screening and therapy, and stem cell research—to name just a few examples from the United States—the concept of life is a political battleground. While it would be impossible to do justice here to the distinctive but often overlapping histories of these examples, what they suggest is that the early twenty-first century is a time in which a new "vital politics," or a politics of life itself, has begun to emerge.[31] Distinct from but emerging out of the life politics of the eighteenth and nineteenth centuries that focused on birth and death rates, sanitation, and hygiene, this new politics of life, according to Nikolas Rose, "is concerned with our growing capacities to control, manage, engineer, reshape, and modulate the very vital capacities of human beings as living creatures."[32] Especially important to this new politics is the concept of risk. The management of life today focuses on "those individuals, groups or localities where risk is seen to be high. The binary distinctions of normal and pathological, which were central to earlier biopolitical analyses, are now organized within these strategies for the government of risk."[33] The biopolitical problem of viral sex is, quite clearly, a case in point, offering up for biopolitical management a whole new class of risky individuals (barebackers, bug chasers, gift givers, virus breeders, tweakers) as well as the larger and more familiar "risk group" of gay men in general.

The technological and epistemological changes that have, in recent decades, contributed to this new politicization of life have, in the United States, been accompanied by the intensification of an ideological claim on life that links the sustenance of life to the health and strength of the nation. Evidence of this fact can be found in what President George W. Bush calls the "culture of life," something he routinely cites as one of America's most cherished political and moral goods.[34] This particular ideology represents the union of neoconservative social values and biopolitical governmental imperatives whose recent manifestations include the South Dakota legislative challenges to abortion, the acrimonious legal battle over sustaining the life of Terri Schiavo in Florida, and the decision to force-feed prisoners on hunger strike at the U.S. prison camp at Guantánamo Bay, Cuba. Each of these highly politicized events highlights a now familiar, conservative valuation of life frequently defended in the terms of its sanctity, divinity, and preciousness, even in the midst of war. As Dr. William Winkenwerder Jr., U.S. assistant secretary of defense for health affairs, said in defense of the force-feedings at Guantánamo (which many onlookers described as torture), "The objective in any circumstance is to protect and sustain a person's life."[35] As a chief proponent of the culture of life,

Bush has used the phrase literally hundreds of times as part of his official presidential rhetoric. He has, for example, spoken of the nation's "commitment to building a culture of life where all individuals are welcomed in life and protected in law," adding elsewhere that this will be "a welcoming culture, never excluding, never dividing, never despairing and always affirming the goodness of life in all its seasons."[36] The gestures to universality here—"never excluding," "always affirming," "life in all its seasons"—are limited, however, because of their narrow grounding in a conservative vision of liberal inclusiveness that opposes abortion, promotes heterosexual "family values," cuts social services to the poor and needy, and requires abstinence advocacy as a precondition for AIDS relief. Bush's language highlights the way in which neoconservative valuations of life have been naturalized both as moral "goodness" and as properly belonging to the domain of government whose work, it seems, is to ensure that life is "protected in law." Through rhetorical linkages like this one, the biopolitical imperative to preserve and foster life becomes a silent warrant for the neoconservative defense of life.

One might say that, as a political gesture, the power of viral sex lies in its ability to deconstruct the opposition between life and nonlife as it operates within the culture of life. By putting life at risk, viral sex opens the space of *différance* between political life—life as it is explicitly defined through discourses of neoliberalism and biopower, as it is in the culture of life—and bare life. Life deliberately exposed to risk *differs* from healthy life as defined by neoliberal rationalism, as it *defers* from precious, inviolable, and divinely sanctioned life mandated by the culture of life. Thus, life-at-risk, especially when that risk is deliberate, more closely resembles bare life: life that cannot be counted as life in the political sense, yet life that also cannot be adequately mourned, since many see it as life that has been squandered, a death synonymous with suicide or murder.[37] In opposition to this way of thinking, viral sex demonstrates how the meaning of life is violently conflicted and open to revision.

Perhaps the best starting point for biopolitical resistance will be new experiences of mourning.[38] This includes acceptance of the fact that seeking an end to viral sex entails the death of the new pleasures and human relations occasioned by the exchange of HIV. The pursuit of health produces, as a kind of by-product, a certain melancholia. The fact that biomedicine and rational health promotion cannot bring about an end to AIDS is one of the many failures of modern biopolitics, one that produces an unfulfillable longing alongside its most heroic efforts. As the starting point of biopolitical resistance, mourning's most important aim would be to acknowledge biopower's broken promises.

If health, productivity, and longevity mark the success of biopolitical rule, then chronic illness represents the limits of that rule through its detrimental claims on health, work, and life span. Although Foucault argues that death is the ultimate limit to power in the age of biopower, I would add that chronic illness and especially the deliberate choice to become chronically ill are highly effective forms of resistance against such power.[39] One might call out the limit of biopower by choosing to end one's existence, thereby refusing the modes of subjugation associated with the bureaucratic administration of life, but death will always remain a fixed signifier in this particular economy of life. Death is not, in this sense, strategic, but rather is absolute: it marks the limit of power without necessarily intervening in its continued operation. By contrast, chronic illness and HIV infection, in particular, remain a threatening and therefore potentially powerful mode of embodiment. The long, slow engagement with illness that frequently characterizes HIV infection mobilizes, even as it threatens to exhaust, the vast individual and collective resources stockpiled in the name of the biopolitical management of life. While biopolitics aims at optimization of the workforce, ensuring the availability and productivity of labor, chronic illness and death are not, to put it bluntly, good for the bottom line.[40]

Not since the late nineteenth century has chronic illness possessed such strong connections to both cultural and economic capital. Entire industries have sprung up around the management of chronic illness on a global scale, while the cultural integration of chronic illness into the practices of everyday life has been so pervasive that chronicity is now regarded as a "lifestyle" as much as it is a medical condition. These cultural developments coincide with a rising tide of economic complaints—legitimized by the expertise of the social sciences and fiscal watchdogs—that point to the fact that chronic illness is one of the most expensive of all social problems, leading to exorbitant costs for governments, private citizens, hospitals, and insurers. Chronic illness functions, therefore, as a kind of engine within the domain of political economy, affording the movement of capital—measured today in the billions of dollars— while helping to incite new identities and a wide range of cultural productions. The aim of biopolitical resistance is to intervene within this political economy, not to "contain costs" or to "promote health" (the only solutions that ever seem to gain much recognition) but to more fully comprehend HIV as a part of life that must, for the foreseeable future, be endured. In this way, viral sex functions as a "non-instrumental affirmation" of life, that is, of life affirmed not in hopes of an impending cure, or in terms of a "compassionate" reintegration into bourgeois society, or even in those of reincorporation into the optimized workings of capitalist productivity.[41] To the extent that viral sex works against the standards of life's normalization, it poses an alternative to the paucity of options for those whose lives might very well be managed out of existence in societies acutely focused on the containment of risk. The metaphors of bugs and gifts that mark the intransigence of HIV are harbingers of a future in which HIV has not been vanquished by biomedicine and public health. Instead, they function as an imposition, one that insists on making HIV more ubiquitous. They are a sign of the fragility of time, acting counter to the future seen through the biopolitical and neoliberal optimization of life. Coming to terms with the enormity of HIV and AIDS means imagining a time when large numbers of bodies may not be fully optimized for work, for rational living, or for liberal "happiness."

Notes

1   *Barebacking*: intentional unprotected anal sex between two men. *Bug chasing*: intentional unprotected anal sex performed in order to become infected with HIV. *Gift giving*: intentional unprotected anal sex performed in order to infect another person with HIV. *Virus breeding*: the deliberate sexual exchange of HIV between men. *Tweaking*: using crystal methamphetamine, which many see as contributing to unsafe sex among gay men. For more on these practices, see Tim Dean, *Unlimited Intimacy: Reflections on the Subculture of Barebacking* (Chicago: University of Chicago Press, 2009); Perry N. Halkitis et al., *Barebacking: Psychosocial and Public Health Approaches* (Binghamton, NY: Haworth, 2006); David M. Halperin, *What Do Gay Men Want? An Essay on Sex, Risk, and Subjectivity* (Ann Arbor: University of Michigan Press, 2007); Dave Holmes, Patrick O'Byrne, and Denise Gastaldo, "Raw Sex as Limit Experience: A Foucauldian Analysis of Unsafe Anal Sex between Men," *Social Theory and Health* 4.4 (2006): 319–33; David A. Moskowitz and Michael E. Roloff, "The Existence of a Bug Chasing Subculture," *Culture, Health, and Sexuality* 9.4 (2007): 347–57; Frank Sanello, *Tweakers: How Crystal Meth Is Ravaging Gay America* (Los Angeles: Alyson Books, 2005); Michael Shernoff, *Without Condoms: Unprotected Sex, Gay Men, and Barebacking* (New York: Routledge, 2005); and Gregory Tomso, "Barebacking, Bug Chasing, and the Risks of Care," *Literature and Medicine* 23 (Spring 2004): 88–111.

2   See Larry Kramer, *The Tragedy of Today's Gays* (New York: Tarcher, 2005); Dan Savage, "Bug Chasers," Savage Love, *The Stranger* (Seattle), January 30, 2003, www.thestranger.com/seattie/ SavageLove?oid=13241; Gregory A. Freeman, "In Search of Death," *Rolling Stone*, February 6, 2003, 44–48; and *The Gift*, written and directed by Louise Hogarth (Los Angeles: Dream Out Loud Productions, 2000).

3   I am not the first to use the phrase "viral sex." Most notably, it is the title of a book by Jaap Gaudsmit, *Viral Sex: The Nature of AIDS* (New York: Oxford University Press, 1992). I take up the phrase in a different context here.

4   See, for example, Barry D. Adam et al., "AIDS Optimism, Condom Fatigue, or Self-Esteem? Explaining Unsafe Sex among Gay and Bisexual Men," *Journal of Sex Research* 42.3 (2005): 238–48;

Mark Davis, "HIV Prevention Rationalities and Serostatus in the Risk Narratives of Gay Men," *Sexualities* 5.3 (2002): 282–99; Perry N. Halkitis and J. T. Parsons, "Intentional Unsafe Sex (Barebacking) among HIV-Positive Gay Men Who Seek Sexual Partners on the Internet," *AIDS Care* 15.3 (2003): 367–78; Susan Kippax and Kane Race, "Sustaining Safe Practice; Twenty Years On," *Social Science and Medicine* 57 (2003): 1–12; Kane Race, "Revaluation of Risk among Gay Men," *AIDS Education and Prevention* 15 (2003): 4369–81; Damien Thomas Ridge, " 'It Was an Incredible Thrill': The Social Meanings and Dynamics of Younger Gay Men's Experiences of Barebacking in Melbourne," *Sexualities* 7.3 (2004): 259–79; and Nicolas Sheon and G. Michael Crosby, "Ambivalent Tales of HIV Disclosure in San Francisco," *Social Science and Medicine* 58 (2004): 2105–18.

5   Andrew Barry, Thomas Osborne, and Nikolas Rose, *Foucault and Political Reason: Liberalism, Neo-Liberalism, and Rationalities of Government* (London: University College London Press, 1996), 1.

6   Michel Foucault, "The Ethics of the Concern for Self as a Practice of Freedom," in *Ethics: Subjectivity and Truth*, ed. Paul Rabinow (New York: New Press, 1997), 281–301.

7   Bareback.com, www.bareback.com (accessed August 3, 2007).

8   The phrase is the title of a book by Andrew Sullivan, *Virtually Normal* (New York: Vintage, 1996).

9   As Wendy Brown defines it, *neoliberalism* is a political rationality that "while foregrounding the market, is not only or even primarily focused on the economy." Rather, "it involves *extending and disseminating market values to all institutions and social action*, even as the market remains a distinctive player." Brown, "Neoliberalism and the End of Liberal Democracy," in *Edgework: Critical Essays on Knowledge and Politics* (Princeton, NJ: Princeton University Press, 2005), 39–40. Neoliberalism, then, is more than a set of economic priorities; it, too, might best be understood in terms of Foucauldian governmentality, as a rationality "that produces subjects, forms of citizenship and behavior, and a new organization of the social" (37). For more on neoliberalism, see Michel Foucault, "The Birth of Biopolitics," in *Ethics*, 73–80, esp. 74. (This reference is to Foucault's summary of his lectures at the Collège de France in 1979. The full English translation is now available: Michel Foucault, *The Birth of Biopolitics: Lectures at the College de France, 1978-79*, tr. Graham Burchell (Hampshire: Palgrave, 2008). For the full version of the lectures in French, see Foucault, *Naissance de la Biopolitique: Cours au Collège de France (1978–1979)* (Paris: Gallimard and Seuil, 2004). For a useful and readily accessible English overview of these lectures, see Thomas Lemke, "'The Birth of Bio-politics': Michel Foucault's Lectures at the Collège de France on Neo-liberal Governmentality," *Economy and Society* 30.2 (2001): 190–207. For more on neoliberalism, see Lisa Duggan, *The Twilight of Equality? Neoliberalism, Cultural Politics, and the Attack on Identity* (Boston: Beacon, 2003); and David Harvey, *A Brief History of Neoliberalism* (New York: Oxford University Press, 2005).

10   Erick Eckholm, "Medicaid Plan Prods Patients toward Health," *New York Times*, December 1, 2006.

11   For a further elaboration of this point, see Adam et al., "AIDS Optimism, Condom Fatigue, or Self-Esteem?"; and Davis, "HIV Prevention Rationalities." See also Deborah Lupton, ed., *Risk and Sociocultural Theory* (Cambridge: Cambridge University Press, 2005), especially the essay by Mitchell Dean, "Risk, Calculable and Incalculable," 131–59; and Alan Petersen and Robin Bunton, eds., *Foucault, Health and Medicine* (New York: Routledge, 1997).

12   In his 1979 "The Birth of Biopolitics" lectures at the Collège de France, Foucault explores a fundamental tension between "reason of state" and liberalism. One, he says, has always "haunted" the other (79). While liberalism presupposes that government always "governs too much," the rationale of "reason of state" advocates strengthening the state through forms of governmentality that require both growth and more intensive regulation in regard to issues of population (74). Foucault, "The Birth of Biopolitics."

13   For a detailed analysis of the "new" (versus traditional) public health, see Alan Petersen and Deborah Lupton, *The New Public Health: Health and Self in the Age of Risk* (Thousand Oaks, CA: Sage Publications, 1997). See also Alan Petersen, "Risk, Governance, and the New Public Health," in Petersen and Bunton, *Foucault, Health and Medicine*, 189–206.

14   On the rebuilding of gay sexual culture, see Eric Rofes, *Dry Bones Breathe: Gay Men Creating Post-AIDS Identities and Cultures* (New York: Haworth, 1998).

15   The phrase is also the title of a book by Simon Watney, *Practices of Freedom: Selected Writings on HIV/AIDS* (Durham, NC: Duke University Press, 2004). See also Foucault, "The Ethics of the Concern for Self," 284.

16   "BB Bottom seeking tops to breed my ass. Anonymous scene cool," personal ad, Men Seeking Men, Craigslist San Francisco Bay Area, http://sfbay.craigslist.org/cgi-bin/personals.cgi?category=m4m, posting ID 385782984 30 July 2007, 9:31 p.m. PDT (accessed August 1, 2007); and "Looking for a Raw top this AM (concord/pleasant hill/martinez)," personal ad, Men Seeking Men, Craigslist San Francisco Bay Area, http://sfbay.craigslist.org/cgi-bin/personals.cgi?category=m4m, posting ID 381435613 25 July 2007, 7:41 a.m. PDT (accessed August 1, 2007).

17   For the standard explanation of gift economies, see Marcel Mauss, *The Gift: The Form and Reason for Exchange in Archaic Societies* (New York: W.W. Norton, 2000). For an application of Mauss's thinking to online cultures of viral sex, see Michael Graydon, "Don't Bother to Wrap It: Online Giftgiver and Bugchaser Newsgroups, the Social Impact of Gift Exchanges, and the 'Carnivalesque,' " *Culture, Health, and Sexuality* 9.3 (2007): 277–92.

18   Linda Singer, *Erotic Welfare: Sexual Theory and Politics in the Age of Epidemic* (New York: Routledge, 1992). Hereafter cited parenthetically by page number. This is also an example of what Paula Treichler describes as the "epidemic of signification" characteristic of AIDS. Treichler, *How to Have Theory in an Epidemic* (Durham, NC: Duke University Press, 1999).

19   Judith Butler, introduction to Singer, *Erotic Welfare*, 7.

20   David M. Halperin, *Saint Foucault* (Durham, NC: Duke University Press, 1995), 88, 90.

21   Ridge, " 'It Was an Incredible Thrill,' " 266.

22   Michel Foucault, "Friendship as a Way of Life," trans. John Johnston, in *Ethics*, 135–40, 136.

23   Michel Foucault, "Social Triumph of the Sexual Will," in *Ethics*, 157–62, 160. Hereafter cited parenthetically by page number as "Triumph."

24   Foucault, "Friendship," 138.

25   Foucault, "The Ethics of the Concern for Self," 284.

26   Michel Foucault, "Sexual Choice, Sexual Act," in *Ethics*, 141–56, 143.

27   The phrase is a title of a book by Bruce Bawer, *A Place at the Table: The Gay Individual in American Society* (New York: Simon and Schuster, 1994).

28   I am extending here Barry et al.'s claim that freedom, in the Foucauldian sense, is a "formula of rule." See Barry, Osborne, and Rose, *Foucault and Political Reason*, 8.

29   Eric Rofes, *Reviving the Tribe: Regenerating Gay Men's Sexuality and Culture in the Ongoing Epidemic* (New York: Haworth, 1996), 164, 196.

30   These basic responses are an updated version of the logic that, according to Cindy Patton, underwrote first-wave safe-sex education campaigns that identified members of "risk groups" (gays, intravenous drug users, etc.) as opposed to an undifferentiated "everybody else." Patton, *Fatal Advice: How Safe-Sex Education Went Wrong* (Durham, NC: Duke University Press, 1996). One problem with this way of thinking is that it perpetuates a specific form of epistemological violence that, in its need to identify those at risk, discursively produces sexual subjects who, by definition, are categorically different from the undifferentiated subjects who occupy the political center.

31   This argument has been made by Nikolas Rose, from whom I take the term *vital politics*. See Rose, *The Politics of Life Itself: Biomedicine, Power, and Subjectivity in the Twenty-First Century* (Princeton, NJ: Princeton University Press, 2007).

32   Ibid., 3.

33   Ibid., 70.

34   George W. Bush, "National Sanctity of Human Life Day, 2006: A Proclamation by the President of the United States of America," January 20, 2006, www.whitehouse.gov/news/releases/2006/01/20060120–25.html; and George W. Bush, "Remarks by the President at Dedication of the Pope John Paul II Cultural Center," March 22, 2001, www.whitehouse.gov/news/releases/2001/03/20010322–14.html. I am indebted to Troy Urquhart, a participant in a spring 2006 seminar on poststructuralism and sexuality that I taught at the University of West Florida, for these sources and for alerting me to Bush's use of the phrase "culture of life."

35   Tim Golden, "Tough U.S. Steps in Hunger Strike at Camp in Cuba," *New York Times*, February 9, 2006.

36   Bush, "National Sanctity of Human Life Day, 2006"; and Bush, "Remarks by the President at Dedication of the Pope John Paul II Cultural Center."

37   For more on the notion of bare life, see Giorgio Agamben, *Homo Sacer: Sovereign Power and Bare Life*, trans. Daniel Heller-Roazen (Stanford, CA: Stanford University Press, 1998).

38   See Douglas Crimp, "Melancholia and Moralism: An Introduction," in *Melancholia and Moralism: Essays on AIDS and Queer Politics* (Cambridge, MA: MIT Press, 2004), 1–26.

39   Michel Foucault, *The History of Sexuality*, vol. 1, *An Introduction*, trans. Robert Hurley (New York: Vintage, 1990). Foucault writes that in "a society in which political power had assigned itself the task of administering life" (139), death accordingly becomes "power's limit, the moment that escapes [power]" (138). But making this argument comes dangerously close to affirming a belief that Foucault spent much of his late career unraveling, namely, the idea that "sex is worth dying for" (156). To buy into that idea is to participate, Foucault argues, in a naive politics of sexual liberation based on what he calls the "repressive hypothesis," or the idea that sex is something that requires liberation from repression in order to be made free. Thus, embracing death as a queer strategy of

resistance to power remains an unsatisfying political option, however much it might expose the limits of biopower.

40   It is for such reasons that Foucault could argue that the rise of biopolitics is closely linked with the advent of capitalism: "Bio-power was without question an indispensable element in the development of capitalism; the latter would not have been possible without the controlled insertion of bodies into the machinery of production and the adjustment of the phenomena of population to economic processes." Foucault, *History of Sexuality*, vol. 1, 140–41.

41   The phrase comes from Butler, introduction to Singer, *Erotic Welfare*, 3.

Chapter 12

Elizabeth Grosz

EXPERIMENTAL DESIRE: RETHINKING QUEER SUBJECTIVITY

Elizabeth Grosz is Professor of Women's and Gender Studies at Rutgers University. She has published widely on issues relating to sexuality, gender, corporeality, space, time, evolution, and materiality. Grosz has authored many books including *Space, Time and Perversion: Essays on the Politics of Bodies* (1995), in which the following essay appears.

In "Experimental Desire," Grosz considers the universality of oppression and identity within the context of queer subjectivity. Grosz begins with the assertion that positions of subordination are not singular or unidirectional. Instead, she seeks to disentangle the complexity inherent in relations of power and oppression. Borrowing from Deleuze and Guattari's work on affectivity, Grosz argues for the distinction between what the body is and what the body can do. According to Grosz, this distinction structures homophobic oppression: homophobic oppression targets not what one is, but what one does (as opposed to other types of oppressions, such as racial oppression). Eschewing psychoanalytic theories of sexuality that she considers rely on heterosexist libidinal economies, Grosz deploys Nietzschean active/reactive and affirming/negating forces to elucidate the threat posed by non-heterosexual practices (such as lesbianism) to heterosexist power structures. In Grosz's formulation, queer subjectivity is an active, rather than reactive, subject position.

> To me, queer transcends any gender, any sexual persuasion and philosophy. Queerness is a state of being. It is also a lifestyle. It's something that's eternally the alternative. To both the gay and lesbian mainstream. What's queer now may not be queer in five years' time. If transgender queer was accepted by both communities, then there would be no queer. It's a reflection of the times you live in.
>
> (Jasper Laybutt, "male lesbian," female-to-male transsexual who edits the Australian edition of *Wicked Women* in *Capital Q*, October 9, 1992: 9)

I WANT TO LOOK at a set of rather old-fashioned concepts and issues that I believe remain useful and can be revitalized if they are reconsidered in terms of the politics and theory of lesbian and gay sexualities: *oppression*, and *identity*. I do not want to replay the usual anti-humanist critiques of identity which seek to displace, decenter, or even destroy the notion of subjective/sexual "identity," but to work, using their presumptions and insights, on the terrain taken up by notions of oppression, sex, and sexual identity, to rewrite them, to reclaim them in different terms, and, in the process, to clarify some issues that I believe are crucial to the area now known as "queer theory."[1] It is not simply the political history and former power of these terms that I wish to resuscitate: I am not really interested in nostalgic replayings, but in refusing to give up terms, ideas, strategies that still work, whose potentialities have still not been explored, and which are not quite ready to be junked just yet.

Systematic structures of power

For notions like oppression, discrimination, or social positioning to have any meaning, they must be articulated and explained outside any particular form (whether racist, imperialist, sexual, class, or religious). In other words, there must a common strand shared by all the different forms of oppression, something (or many things) that enables them to be described by the same term, even if there is a strong recognition that oppressions may take on massive historical and cultural variations. This core or even "essence," and the range and variability of the term, need to be addressed if one is to come to a clearer understanding of the relations and interactions between different forms of social domination. In short, it requires a very careful and precise understanding if it is not only to be appropriately used to cover a wide variety of different types of oppression; but also, perhaps more politically relevantly, if it is to be able to articulate the interlockings and transformations effected by the convergences, points of reinforcement and/or tension between different forms of oppression. My goal, though, in attempting to render more precise these interlocking systems of oppression is not to set up a kind of hierarchy of oppressed subjects, an index of degrees of oppression,[2] nor to provide a typology which is inclusive of all types of oppression (this seems to be the current trend in much contemporary theorizing about oppressions[3]), but to understand the inflections any particular category must undergo when it is coupled with or related to other categories.

If there is a broad core of meaning to the term, oppression, it must be minimally understood as:

1. The production of systematically differentiated positions for social subjects, which function as modes of specification, constitution, and valuation, within a general structure which distributes to those positions and thus the subjects occupying them, various benefits, power, authority, and value. This implies that whatever skills, capacities, and attributes members of the subordinated groups have, their ability to take up the privileged positions remains extremely limited, if not impossible.

2. These differential positions distribute benefits to those in privileged positions only at the expense of other, subordinated positions. This privilege is possible only because its cost is borne by subordination. This explains why structures of power and authority remain tenaciously difficult to transform: it is not in the interests of the dominant groups, who have benefits without actually paying for them, to readily give up those benefits without struggle. Certainly the impetus and motive for change cannot come from this group, which stands to lose much of its privilege in any realignment of relative positions.

3. Not only are specific groups positioned in differential locations within the social structure (positions that may be interlocked or interdependent, but which serve only the interests of the dominant group), these positions are directly or indirectly linked to values, attributes, benefits, mobility, that are not specifically inscribed in but are preconditioned by these positions. Being born male, white, middle class, Christian, etc. gives one access to wealth, decision-making, and naming capacities that, while not entirely out of the reach of other groups, is made extremely difficult for them, except perhaps at the cost of renouncing or overcoming their definitional linkage to a subordinated group.

4. Relations of domination and subordination are characterized not simply in terms of tangible material benefits, although these could be easily documented, but also in terms of the ease and ability of dominant groups to produce meanings, representations—which present their interests—perspectives, values, and frameworks in positive, self-evident terms, and define their others (non-reciprocally) in terms of these interests. This ease is denied to members of subordinate groups. Here, I do not want to suggest that the capacity to change meaning, to develop new meanings and frameworks, is impossible for dominated groups, but it is nonetheless made considerably more difficult and is a matter of bitter struggle and contestation; and

5. The relations of domination and subordination constituting oppression are more complicated than the occupation of fixed, stable positions of power and powerlessness or centrality and marginality. While they clearly accrue privileges and benefits at the expense of subordinated positions, positions of domination also have their long-term complications, insofar as those who occupy these positions lose access to certain skills of self-determination, skills acquired through struggle, resistance, and the necessary ingenuity of those in subordinated positions. The position of subordination, while it requires the loss or absence of many of the rights and privileges of the dominant position, also produces certain skills and modes of resourcefulness, the capacity precisely for self-sustenance and creativity that are lost for the dominator. They become complaisant and self-satisfied, while the subordinated must sharpen their wits and continuously develop themselves or succumb to their oppressed positions. It is only through the engagement, the encounter between the dominators and the dominated, through the resistances posed by the dominated to the dominators that social change follows a certain direction (even if that direction and the rates of progress to any pre-given goal cannot be guaranteed by members of either or both groups).

The notion of oppression is clearly linked to power, to the relations, forms, and goals that power may take. But since Foucault's genealogies of power, notions of power and oppression have undergone relatively major transformations. The relations between power, domination, and subordination are no longer quite so clear-cut and unambiguous in their status. The subordinated are implicated in power relations even if they are not directly complicit in them: They are implicated in the sense that, as a mobile set of force relations, power requires the structural positions of subordination, not as the outside or limit of its effectivity, but as its internal condition, the "hinge" on which it pivots. Foucault's work, in spite of the by-now well-documented problems in feminist terms,[4] has at least one (but no doubt also many more) insight to offer feminist and lesbian theorists: He has rendered the notion of oppression considerably more sophisticated, he has alerted us to the idea that the attribution of social value is not simply a matter of being rendered passive and compliant, being made into victims, who, occupying certain social positions, cannot be stripped of all capacities and all modes of resistance. The positions of subordination cannot be placed within a singular schema, framework, representation, or universally enforced operation; rather, resistance engenders its own kinds of strategies and counter-strategies, it exerts its own kind of forces (which are not simply the opposite or inverse of domination), its own practices, and knowledges, which, depending on their socio-cultural placement and the contingencies of the power game that we have no choice but to continue playing, may be propelled into positions of power and domination. Foucault, in short, and by no means on his own, has provided a sense of hope, a signal of the possibility, indeed necessity, of a certain agency and efficacy for those classified as oppressed. Admittedly, Foucault's work has the effect of problematizing megalithic understandings of capitalism, patriarchy, racism, and imperialism as systematic, coherent global programs, which makes it more difficult to assert hard and fast allegiances and interlockings between these great systems. He has rendered their interconnections more expedient, less programmed and cohesive, and thus more amenable to realignment and transformation, even if they are now murkier, less clear-cut, less easy to read than any simple assertion of good (politically correct) or bad.

Given this more diffused and less structurally precise understanding of relations of power and domination, notions of oppression and social valuation can be wrenched from humanist history and made to do the work of specifying, rendering visible, the issue of difference, which seems to me to be the fundamental terrain of contestation of our political era. Difference, alterity, otherness are difficult concepts to incorporate into the humanist and phenomenological paradigm of oppression, which seeks to recognize all subjects (or, more commonly, *most* subjects) on the model of a bare or general humanity. Such a conception of humanity has no choice but to cast those different enough from the definition of humanity into the arena of the pre, proto- or non-human. Otherness can enter, at best, as a secondary modification of this basic human nature, a minor detail, but not a fundamental dimension or defining characteristic which alters all the other general capacities attributed to "human" existence. Feminism, along with anti-humanism, is probably the most direct line of assault on that humanism, which took as its standard of the human, the presumptions, perspectives, frameworks, and interests of men.

Sex and sexuality

Are the characteristics I have outlined adequate to outline "sexual oppression," the disqualification, devaluation, and misrepresentation of subjects and practices on the basis of either (or both) their sex and/or their sexuality? Do they encompass the specific modalities of oppression experienced by women in general, by lesbians and gay men, by various perverts, transsexuals, transvestites, drag queens, butches, cross-dressers, and all the other variations of sexual transgression? This is the anti-humanist question: do the apparently universal characteristics common to all modes of oppression include all types of oppression? If they do, then in what ways do they help to explain misogyny and homophobia in their specificity? If they only serve to characterize oppression but not to specify its homophobic dimension, then what needs to be added to them or modified in them to make them appropriate? These questions give rise to a series of further anxieties: is there such a thing as homophobia, and a common oppression for *both* lesbians and gays? Do lesbians experience the same forms of homophobia as gay men? Can we presume that it takes on universal forms? Does the fact that they are women and men (however one chooses to define these terms) alter the forms of homophobia each experiences? Moreover, does the very category of sex/sexuality differ sexually, that is, according to the sex of the subject under question?

Here I want to use these terms, "sex" and "sexuality" in the light of but in variance from Foucault's understanding. For Foucault, and this is one of his major innovations, sex can no longer be understood as the ground, the real, the (biological/natural) foundation of later superstructural ramifications: it is not a base onto which the superstructure of "gender" and of "sexuality" can be securely added. There is no biological substratum onto which to hang a

discursive and cultural overlay. For him, the very notion of sex as origin, as given, as fundamental, to subjectivity, identity and/or cultural harmony, is itself the product or effect of a
socio-discursive regime of sexuality. A well-known quote makes this clear:

> We must not make the mistake of thinking that sex is an autonomous agency
> which secondarily produces manifold effects over the entire length of its surface
> of contact with power. On the contrary, sex is the most speculative, most ideal,
> and most internal element in a deployment of sexuality organized by power in
> its grip on bodies and their materiality, their forces, energies, sensations and
> pleasures.
>
> (Foucault, 1980: 155)

In *Gender Trouble: Feminism and the Subversion of Identity* (1990) and *Bodies That Matter* (1993),
Judith Butler largely affirms Foucault's understanding of sex as an artificial, conventional, or
cultural alignment of disparate elements linked together, not through nature, reason, or
biology, but historical expedience, alignments produced by and required for the deployment
of discourses, knowledges, and forms of power. However, Butler adds a third term to the
Foucauldian pair sex/sexuality, the notion of gender, a concept I see as more antithetical to
Foucault's account than she admits, insofar as gender must be understood as a kind of overlay
on a preestablished foundation of sex, a cultural variation of a more or less fixed and universal
substratum, an overlay that, moreover, can be identified too readily with the notion of
performance, insofar as the body that performs, however much Butler insists it is produced
by the performance itself, must nevertheless abide between performances, existing over and
above the sum total of its performances. For Butler, performance is the mediating term
between sex and gender: gender is the performance of sex. This notion of gender now seems
largely irrelevant or redundant, a term unnecessary for describing the vast social arrangements, contexts, and variations in the ways in which we live, give meaning to, and enact sex.
While not wishing to deny this range of variations in the cross-cultural and historical scope of
sex, nor the performative and self-productive notion of "identity" Butler develops, I am
reluctant to see gender regarded even as the expression of sex, as Butler suggests, insofar as
sex is itself always already expression, which in itself does not require (or forbid) a second
order expression:

> The notion that there might be a "truth" of sex, as Foucault ironically terms it, is
> produced precisely through the regulatory practices that generate coherent
> identities through the matrix of coherent gender norms. The heterosexualiza-
> tion of desire requires and institutes the production of discrete and asymmetrical
> oppositions between "feminine" and "masculine," where these are understood as
> expressive attributes of "male" and "female." The cultural matrix through which
> gender identity has become intelligible requires that certain kinds of "identities"
> cannot "exist"—that is, those in which gender does not "follow" from either sex
> or gender.
>
> (Butler, 1990: 17)

In my understanding, the term "sex" refers, not to sexual impulses, desires, wishes, hopes,
bodies, pleasures, behaviors, and practices: this I reserve for the term "sexuality." "Sex"
refers to the domain of sexual difference, to the question of the *morphologies of bodies*.[5] I do
not want to suggest that sex is in any sense more primordial than or exists independent of
"sexuality." With Foucault, I agree that sex is a product, an end effect, of regimes of sexuality
(which is another way of saying that the inscription, functioning, and practices of a body

constitute what that body is). With Butler, and against Foucault, I want to argue that both sex and sexuality are marked, lived, and function according to whether it is a male or female body that is being discussed. Sex is no longer the label of both sexes in their difference, as in Foucault's writings, a generic term indicating sexed, as opposed to inanimate, existence; it is now the label and terrain of the production and enactment of sexual difference. Gender, it seems, is a redundant category: all its effects, the field that it designates, are covered by the integration of and sometimes the discord between sexuality and sex.

Butler enjoins us to "Consider gender, for instance, as a *corporeal style*, 'act' as it were, which is both intentional and performative, where 'performative' suggests a dramatic and contingent construction of meaning" (1990: 139). She needs the category of gender to mark the discontinuity, the alarming and threatening disjunction of gender from sex, the possibility of masculine behavior in a female subject and feminine behavior in a male subject, the point of tension and uneasiness separating heterocentric demands from the subversive transgressions of the queer subject, the subject in drag, the subject performatively repeating but also subverting heterosexual norms and imperatives, the site of radical disconnection. But all the force and effect of her powerful arguments could, I believe, be strengthened, not through the play generated by a term somehow beyond the dimension of sex, in the order of gender, but within the very instabilities of the category of sex itself, of bodies themselves. Isn't it even more threatening to show, not that gender can be at variance with sex (which implies the possibility or even social desirability or necessity of the Stollerian solution of realigning the one, usually sex, to conform to the other, gender, forcing their readjustment through psychical or surgical means), but that there is an instability at the very heart of sex and bodies, the fact that the body is what it is capable of doing, and what any body is capable of doing is well beyond the tolerance of any given culture?

Affective bodies

Rather than invoke Foucault's *History of Sexuality* to provide an account of the production of sex through the regimes of sexuality, I am more interested at this moment in exploring the relevance of the work of Deleuze, and Deleuze and Guattari, on affectivity, in their understanding the difference between what a body is and what a body can do, between an ontology and a pragmatics, even though Deleuze and Guattari are less vocal and explicit about questions of sexuality, sex, and sexual identity than Foucault. Deleuze's work unsettles the presumptions of what it is to be a stable subject and thus also problematizes any assumption that sex is in some way the center, the secret, or truth of the subject. This unsettling may or may not have positive effects for feminist and queer theory. This will depend on what it enables us to do, to change. If a body is what a body does, then lesbian and gay sexualities, and above all, lifestyles, produce lesbian and gay bodies, bodies not just distinguished by sex, race, and class characteristics, but also by sexual desires and practices.

The second chapter of Deleuze's reading of Nietzsche (Deleuze, 1983) stresses Nietzsche's privileging of affect, force, energy, and impulse over depth, psychology, interiority, or intention. Nietzsche not only corporealizes knowledge, he also reconceptualizes the ways in which these are now judged; philosophy, theory, knowledge are now understood in terms of movement, action, production. Philosophy is best undertaken dancing, with joyous bodily affirmation, with revelry and delight. Knowledge is the unrecognized effect of bodies that, through habits, errors of grammar and cultural imperative, have been somehow misconstrued as conceptual or purely mental. Knowledge is the consequence of bodies, and in turn enables bodies to act or prevents bodies from acting, expanding themselves, overcoming themselves, becoming.

To be very brief: where Nietzsche distinguishes between noble and base impulses, between the moralities of the aristocrat and the slave, Deleuze reads Nietzsche in terms of the distinction between active and reactive forces. In systematizing Nietzsche's openly chaotic and unsystematized writings, Deleuze links the will to power to the functioning of differential forces (in individual and social bodies). These differential forces can be described as either (or variously both) active or reactive depending on their quality. Their qualities, in turn, are a function and effect of the differing quantities of excitation carried by impulses. Not only active forces exhibit the will to power, as if reactive forces have somehow succumbed to them or given them up; rather, both active and reactive are equally effects or products of the will to power. Where active and reactive are terms that express force, corresponding to them, at the level of the will to power (the level of interpretation rather than affect) are affirming and negating: "Affirming and denying, appreciating and depreciating, express the will to power just as acting and reacting express force" (1983: 54). Affirmation clearly functions in some alignment with action, just as negation is reactive, but these alignments are much more tenuous. They do not define entities but processes: "Affirmation is not action but the power of becoming active, *becoming active* personified. Negation is not simply reaction but a *becoming reactive*" (1983: 54).

Reactive forces do not steal the activity from active forces; rather, they convert active forces into the forces of reaction, they separate a force from its effects, through the creation of myth, symbolism, fantasy, and falsification. Reactive forces can be regarded as seductive, enticing: they ensnare active force for their own purposes and procedures, for their own falsifications and rationalizations.

In short, active force is that which stretches itself, takes itself as far as it can go (a limit that cannot be known in advance), moves in its directions without regard for anything other than its own free expansion, mindless of others. It is guileless, open, perhaps even naive in its openness to what befalls it. Reactive forces, on the contrary, are cunning, clandestine, restricting, intervening, secondary, mindless, diligent, and obedient. They function ingenuously, living in modes of sensibility and sentiment (nostalgia, self-justification, and hatred of the other are its primary features). Where active forces affirm, produce, and stretch, reactive forces judge, pontificate, produce ideologies and modes of explanation, devise ingenious theories, compromise. They can be identified with the production of religion, morality, and law, with the systems constrained to endless reproduction of the same, without affirming the infinite nature of chance, change, and transformation. Although it is common to describe affirmative judgments and active force as aristocratic or noble, and negative forces as servile and base—that is, to see affirmation as the domain of the powerful, those *in* power, and negation and *ressentiment* as attributes of the oppressed and the powerless—this is to oversimplify Nietzsche's more sophisticated understanding of these as microforces, alignments, and interactions *within* individuals as much as *between* them. It can just as readily be claimed, as I will, that homophobia, heterosexism, racism, and so on are reactive forces, which function in part to *prevent* alternatives, to negate them and ruminate on how to destroy them; and that gay and lesbian sexualities and lifestyles can be seen as innovative, inventive, productive, and thus active insofar as they aim at their own pleasures, their own distributions, their own free expansion. Heterosexism and homophobia are to be countered insofar as they prevent this and react to it.

Although neither Nietzsche nor Deleuze directly discuss the question of sexual orientations and lifestyles, it is plausible to suggest that those forces, activities, and impulses governed by the regime of compulsory heterosexuality (in all of us—for none of us can remain free of this imperative even as we may choose to defy or transform it) *could* be understood on the model of slavish or reactive forces, forces that separate a body from what it can do, that reduce a body to what it is rather than what it can become; while gay and lesbian sexual practices and lifestyles, insofar as they risk a certain stability, a certain social security and ease, insofar as they refuse these imperatives, can and should be seen as a triumph of active and productive forces. We are prevented, however, from too ready a generalization, too black and white a characterization of straights as the emotionally crippled slaves, and gays, lesbians and other queers as the transgressive sexual radicals if we simply assume there are singular impulses directed solely to conformity or subversion. In each of us there are elements and impulses that strive for conformity and elements which seek instability and change: this is as true for heterosexuals as it is for queers of whatever type, although it may well be less enacted, there may be less external impetus for expansion and change for those who reap its benefits (heterosexual men, primarily). Indeed, one of the avowed reasons why many claim to have adopted the term "queer" was to set themselves outside both the heterosexual as well as the gay communities, which, many claim, function as coercively, and as judgmentally as each other (this sentiment is expressed in the opening quotation of this essay). It is a question of degree or more or less, rather than of type, a matter of varying investments that all of us have, one way or another, in certain types of complicity with stability and social imperative.[6]

This is not, however, to say that all of us, from the 2.2 child suburban family to the queerest of queers, are the same;[7] of course not. Simply that it is a matter of degree, of location, and of will. The heterosexual can, I believe, remain a heterosexual but still undertake subversive or transgressive sexual relations outside the copulative, penetrative, active/passive, stereotyped norm (but does so only rarely); and lesbians and gays can of course produce sexual relations that duplicate as closely as they can the structures, habits, and patterns of the straightest and most suburban heterosexuals (but succeed only rarely). So simply *being straight* or *being queer*, in itself, provides no guarantee of one's position as sexually radical: it depends on how one lives one's queerness, or renders one's straightness, one's heterosexuality as queer.

Regimes of sexuality

If we return to Foucault and his distinction between sex and sexuality, his claim that the discursive regimes of sexuality produce as their historical effect the phenomenon called sex, we see that, although he is at great pains to deny it elsewhere, Foucault does in fact distinguish between the functioning of power (the deployment of sexuality) and a somehow prepower real, a real he describes in terms of a set of timeless "bodies and pleasures." There is a notorious passage in *The History of Sexuality*, one which Butler has also taken as a significant site of tension in and between his works, where he discusses the game called "curdled milk" (which today we would have to regard as a case of child sexual abuse), between the simpleminded farm hand and a young girl:

> At the border of a field, he had obtained a few caresses from a little girl, *just as he had done before* and seen done by the village urchins round him. . . . What is the significant thing about this story? The pettiness of it all; the fact that this *everyday occurrence* in the life of village sexuality, these *inconsequential bucolic pleasures*, could become, from a certain time, the object not only of a collective intolerance but of a judicial action, a medical intervention, a careful clinical examination, and an entire theoretical elaboration.
>
> (Foucault, 1980: 31, emphasis added)[8]

Foucault seems to imply here that there are certain activities, "inconsequential pleasures," the interchange of bodies and pleasures, which are somehow below the threshold of power's reach: these pleasures are relatively innocent, disinvested, and pedestrian. They are everyday occurrences, which only after a certain period become the object of power's ever-intensifying scrutiny. But before this time they exist somehow outside of power's scope. He makes a similar claim, though perhaps with less sinister effects, in one of his more inciteful and direct statements.

> It is the agency of sex that we must break away from, if we aim—through a tactical reversal of the various mechanisms of sexuality—to counter the grips of power with the claims of bodies, pleasures, and knowledges, in their multiplicity and their possibilities of resistance. The rallying point of the counter-attack against the deployment of sexuality ought not to be sex-desire, but bodies and pleasures.
>
> (1980: 157)

To remain within the domain of sexuality (as he implies much of sexual liberationist politics does), is to not only remain complicit in the functioning of power—for there is a constitutive complicity between power and resistance, he insists—but also to extend power's operations. He implies that there is a lever there, as it were, readily at hand, in the multiplicity of possibilities for bodies and pleasures, as if these were no longer somehow bound up with the functioning of the regime of sexuality, as if they were somehow outside. This means that even if sexual liberationists submit themselves uncritically to the domination of the repressive hypothesis and tie liberation to an affirmation of sex, nonetheless gay and lesbian (though he certainly does not mention the latter) bodies, pleasures, practices, and lifestyles may provide precisely the kind of rallying point that he seeks.

This cannot simply be asserted without some explanation of the status and political position of bodies and pleasures. Bodies and pleasures cannot be understood as fixed or biologically given constants, somehow outside of or beyond the constraints of power—no matter how much Foucault himself may have yearned for a disinvested ground, a pure datum, onto which the operations of power can be directed, no matter how much he believed, in spite of himself, in harmless, timeless pleasures and bodies as yet unmarked by power. What Foucault means, on the most generous reading, is that bodies and pleasures are themselves produced and regulated as distinct phenomena, through, if not forms of power as such, at least various interlocking "economies," libidinal, political, economic, significatory, which may congeal and solidify into a sexuality in "our" modern sense of the word, but which also lend themselves to other economies and modes of production and regulation. A different economy of bodies and pleasures may find the organization of sexuality, the implantation of our sex as the secret of our being, curious and intriguing instead of self-evident.[9] The reorganization of this libidinal structure—which Foucault nowhere discusses—is precisely what I believe that psychoanalysis has not been able to adequately address;[10] this may be why Deleuze's distinction between active and reactive forces, and between affirmative and negative judgments or interpretations, may prove useful in rethinking the issue of a different libidinal organization, a mode of living and utilizing bodies and pleasures beyond the regimes of sexuality that establish heterocentrism (and its mode of ideological validation, homophobia) as regulative norms of subjectivity, as well as beyond the regimes of signification and discursivity, the alignments of power/knowledge that Foucault sees as the necessary conditions for the codification, reorganization, and production of bodies into and as a series of sexualities.

Pleasures

Neither Foucault nor Deleuze devote any time to the question of sexual difference, although both appropriate some of the energy generated by this question for their own reconceptualizations of power and desire. Devising a theory of queer pleasures and their relations to the straight (complicity, support, transgression, or subversion) cannot in fact rely on their works even if they have helped mark out the present limits of theorizing sexual politics.

Because we are now dealing with sexual specificities, differences between the sexes, and those differences that constitute each sex, I can no longer afford to generalize about "queerness": this term covers a vast range of sexual practices, partners, aims, and objects (heterosexual as well as homosexual). The term "queer" as it is currently used is basically a reactive category that sees itself in opposition to a straight norm: it is only this norm that defines the others that it cannot tolerate. These others—deviant sexual practices of whatever kind—may find that they share very little in common with each other (indeed they may be the site of profound tension and contradiction). I find it less useful to talk about queerness, or even gayness when theorizing sexed bodies and their sexual relations than specifying at least broadly the kinds of bodies and desires in question.

I must, then, concentrate on lesbian desire and sexual relations between women, the area which still remains the great domain of the untheorized and the inarticulate—something I believe may function to lesbians' advantage rather than to their detriment. It is clear, especially in the era of the AIDS crisis, that there is an ever more detailed analysis, observation, and theorization, not only with the work of sexologists of the 1950s and 1960s on heterosexual couples, but now with the ever-increasing medical and legal investment in gay and bisexual men's sexual practices. Lesbianism still remains untheorized and largely unspecified. It is significant too that while gay men's sexual practices have been under the scrutiny of the law for over a century, in Australia at least, there have never been laws specifically prohibiting lesbianism. Legally, it remained unrecognized until recent equal opportunity and anti-discrimination legislation. I don't want to suggest that lesbians are either more or less oppressed than gay men, that it is better or worse to be recognized or not recognized in the eyes of the law (arguments could be made both ways): my point here is simply that there is no representation of lesbians as lesbians in certain key discourses deeply invested in power relations. This is in the process of change, and of course varies from one state and country to another, but as a generalization, there is a distinct underinvestment in theorizing and extracting knowledge about lesbian sexual practices. This is partly illustrated not only by the status of lesbianism in the eyes of the law, but also in the discourses of medicine, especially those now developing around the AIDS crisis, where the rate of transmission of the virus in lesbian practices is relatively low and the modes of transmission remain unknown.

This same underrepresentation, or failure of representation, occurs in discourses of the erotic, particularly visual pornography, where clearly lesbianism (or a certain male fantasy of lesbianism) is construed and representable only under sanitized, safe, male-oriented terms. There is a manifest inadequacy of erotic language to represent women's sexual organs, sexual pleasures, and sexual practices in terms other than those provided either for male sexuality or by men in their heterosexual (mis)understanding of the sexualities of their female partners. All the terms for orgasm, for corporeal encounters, for sexual exchanges of whatever kind are not only derived and modified from heterosexual models, but, more alarmingly, from the perspective of the men, and not the women involved in these relations. The very terms for sex, for pleasure, for desire—"fucking," "screwing," "coming," "orgasm," etc.— are most appropriate for and are derived from men's experiences of sexuality (both their own and that of women).

But perhaps the solution to this problem is not simply the addition of a set of new words to the vocabulary, new labels to describe "things" that, while they exist as such, are not signified or referred to, are not explicitly named: for such an understanding presumes female sexuality, and especially lesbian sexuality, is readily enumerable and can be described and referred to as distinct entities, objects, and organs. To wish to create a new set of terms implies that one knows in advance what one wants to designate by these terms, that the sexual pleasures, desires, organs, and activities of women together are a known or knowable quantity and that, like the new discoveries of science, now that they have been "discovered," need appropriate names.

This does not seem possible, or entirely desirable: to "know" female sexuality, to "know" what lesbian desire is, is to reduce it to models of subjectivity, sexuality, and corporeality, to notions of self-identity, ontology, and epistemology that are still logically dependent on the ways these terms are defined and have been understood in a male-dominated culture. I don't want to suggest that new terms can't be coined and new labels cannot be created—the regimes of knowledge/power are certainly capable of providing such resources. Perhaps a more interesting question is, given the enormous investment of knowledges in the codification and control of sexuality, why has lesbianism been so decidedly ignored where heterosexuality and male homosexuality are increasingly thoroughly investigated, particularly in medical discourses? Has lesbianism been underestimated, or has it been too threatening (or perhaps too trivial) to be taken seriously? Is this a lapse in the regime of sexuality, a sign of its imperfections and its capacity to create sites of resistance? Or is it a mode of further delegitimizing lesbianism, a ruse of power itself? This is not an idle question, for whether one reads it as a shortfall of power, or as one of its strategies, will dictate whether one seeks to retain the inarticulateness, the indeterminacy of lesbianism, and of female sexuality—my present inclination—or whether one seeks to articulate lesbianism as loudly and as thoroughly as possible, which Marilyn Frye seems to advocate.

Frye seems to believe that the silence on the details of lesbian sexual relations is an effect of the obliteration or subsumption of women under heterosexist sexual norms. In her largely phenomenological reflections on lesbian "sex," Frye seems to yearn for a language and a mode of representation for lesbian sexual practices. She implies that without an adequate language, without appropriate terms, women's experiences themselves are less rich, less rewarding, less determinate than they could be.

> I once perused a large and extensively illustrated book on sexual activity by and for homosexual men. It was astounding for me for one thing in particular, namely, that its pages constituted a huge lexicon of *words*: words for acts and activities, their sub-acts, preludes and denouements, their stylistic variation, their sequences. Gay male sex, I realized then, is *articulate*. It is articulate to a degree that, in my world, lesbian "sex" does not remotely approach. Lesbian "sex" as I have known it, most of the time I have known it, is utterly inarticulate. Most of my lifetime, most of my experience in the realms commonly designated as "sexual" has been pre-linguistic, non-cognitive. I have, in effect, no linguistic community, no language, and therefore in one important sense, no knowledge. . . . The meaning one's life and experience might generate cannot come fully into operation if they are not woven into language: they are fleeting, or they hover, vague, not fully coalesced, not connected, and hence, not *useful* for explaining or grounding interpretations, desires, complaints, theories.
>
> (Frye, 1990: 311)

While I have sympathy for this claim, and recognize that certain delegitimated social and sexual practices may require modes of representation to affirm and render these practices viable and valuable, it is not clear to me that articulateness and representation are in themselves a virtue: the most intense moments of pleasure, the force of their materiality, while certainly broadly evocable in discourse, cannot be reduced to adequate terms, terms which capture their force and intensity. A distinction must be drawn between discourse and experience even with the understanding that language or systems of representation are the prior condition for the intelligibility of experience. Moreover, it is ironic that the very features Frye attributes to the failure of representation for lesbian desire: that these relations and experiences are rendered "fleeting," that they "hover," are "vague," not "coalesced," "connected," or "useful," accord precisely with the more positive characterization accorded to these concepts and to female sexuality itself in the writings of Luce Irigaray,[11] for whom female sexuality is itself non-self-identical, non-enumerable, not made of distinct and separate parts, not one (but indeterminately more than one).

Here we must be careful not to erect a new ontology based on what woman *is*, in and of herself. Irigaray and other theorists of female sexuality have not provided an account of female sexuality in its essence or in its fixed form, but rather have worked on the paradoxes and consequences generated for female sexuality by a culture, a value system, forms of knowledge and systems of representation that can only ever take female sexuality as object, as external, and as alien to the only set of perspectives presenting themselves as true— men's.[12] Female sexuality, lesbian desire, is that which eludes and escapes, that which functions as an excess, a remainder uncontained by and unrepresentable within the terms provided by a sexuality that takes itself as straightforwardly being what it is.

Part of the reason that there is such an explosion of sexual terminology, details, distinctions, nuances, phases, modalities, styles, organs, practices in gay male literature, and especially in pornography and in personal columns in newspapers is that male sexuality, straight and gay, continues to see itself in terms of readily enumerable locations defined around a central core or organizing principle. When sexuality takes on its status as phallic, entities, organs, pleasures, and fantasies associated with it become definitive, distinguishable from their environment or context, separable, nameable, and capable of being reflected on, fantasized, and experienced in isolation from one another. Distinct organs, separable bodily regions, with distinct states, definitive and readily measurable goals, are possible only because of the capacity to have a reflective and analytic relation to one's own body and experiences, to distance oneself as a knowing subject from oneself as the object known. Any experience, any organs, any desire is capable of categorization and organization, but only at the expense of its continuity with the rest of the body and experience, and only at the cost of separating oneself from immersion in its complexity and intensity. To submit one's pleasures and desires to enumeration and definitive articulation is to submit processes and becomings, to entities, locations, and boundaries, to become welded to an organizing nucleus of fantasy and desire whose goal is not simply pleasure and expansion, but control, and the tying of the new to models of what is already known, the production of endless repetition, endless variations of the same.

I think that this is borne out most clearly in the fascination sexology has shown with various (long-term) debates surrounding female sexuality (debates that, in a certain sense, logically precede discussions of lesbianism, insofar as lesbianism in its broadest sense must be understood as female sexual desire directed to other women): a clitoral versus vaginal location for female orgasm, the existence or non-existence of the legendary "G-spot," the homology or lack of it of female stages of sexual arousal and orgasm with the male and so on. I continue to find it astounding that these debates exist at all, that there is such confusion not only among male researchers, but also among the female objects of investigation, that there continues to be such mystery and controversy surrounding the most apparently elementary features of female sexuality. Male sexuality by comparison, *seems* to be completely straightforward, completely uncontentious, knowable, measurable, understandable. This manifest asymmetry cannot be readily explained without the assumption that one already knows what female sexuality is; nonetheless it must clearly be a consequence, in part, of the imposition of models of knowing, of identity, distinctness, and measurability that are in some sense alien to or incapable of adequately explaining female sexuality. Instead of assuming an inherent mystery, an undecipherable enigma, female sexuality must be assumed to be knowable, even if it must wait for other forms of knowledge, different modes of discourse, to provide a framework and the broad parameters of its understanding. There is no object of reference, no concept or term so inherently opaque that it cannot be known. After all, it is language that makes such concepts possible. It cannot be that they are somehow inherently resistant to representation. The question is not, then, simply, *how* to know woman (what theories, concepts, and language are necessary for illuminating this term); but rather, the *cost* and *effects* of such knowledge, what the various processes of knowing *do* to the objects they thereby produce.

One thing remains clear though: whenever the same models are used to discuss female and male sexuality, when sexuality is conceived in generic or human terms, it will remain inadequate for assessing the particularities, the differences that mark female sexuality as other than male sexuality. Lesbianism remains the site of the most threatening challenge to this phallocentrism, which subsumes the female under the generic produced by the male insofar as it evidences the existence of a female sexuality and sexual pleasure outside of male pleasure and control.

Pleasure and subversion

I asked a series of questions at the beginning of this essay that have thus far remained unanswered: Is oppression still a politically and theoretically useful term in the light of postmodern and anti-humanist assaults on the category of identity? Can heterosexism or homophobia be understood as a regional variant of a generic oppression, an oppression also characteristic of racial, ethnic, religious, and ability discrimination? Does homophobia have any distinctive features? Does the term "homophobia" cover different kinds of oppression experienced by gay men and lesbians? Utilizing the work of Foucault, Deleuze, Butler, de Lauretis, and others, at least the broad outlines of some possible answers may be sketched.

The general characteristics of oppression I outlined in the first section of this paper, if they are valid at all, are also appropriate for describing the oppression of lesbians and gay men. But these broad criteria do not seem particularly appropriate for distinguishing the oppression faced under homophobia from other oppressions. What then is it that *distinguishes* the oppression of lesbians and gays from other oppressed groups, bearing in mind that of course many lesbians and gays also suffer from these other modalities in such ways that it may not be possible to always and readily distinguish the features of their homosexual oppression from their oppression as people of color, or from their class, religious, or ethnic oppression. Given an acknowledgement that both homosexuality and homophobia are always invested in other forms of oppression—whether in complicity with them, or as their objects—it also has its own, however precarious, "identity."[13]

I would argue that the oppression of lesbians and gay men has a form quite different from that taken by other oppressions (such a claim can no doubt be made of each particular modality of oppression, for each must have its own distinguishing features). Forms of oppression, to my knowledge, are generally based primarily on what a person *is* quite independent of what they do. Or rather, what they do is inflected and read through who they are. Peoples of color, women, Jews, are discriminated against at least in part because of the fact that whatever they do, it is as people of color, as women, or as Jews, that they do it. Prejudice and oppression dictate that the qualities and achievements of members of most oppressed groups are read, interpreted, to mean something different from that of the privileged group, even if the behavior seems ostensibly identical with that of white, Christian men. Their racial, religious, sexual, and cultural characteristics, characteristics which are in some sense undeniable (although their meanings and significances are the objects of considerable contestation), are used against them, an excuse or rationalization for their being treated inequitably, and for their own phenomenological realities being discounted or unvalued. Sartre argues that such oppression is a fundamental gesture of bad faith, the very opposite, in his understanding, of a scientific attitude (Sartre, 1961). The oppressor refuses to allow anything to count as evidence against his prejudices.

In the case of homosexuals, I believe that it is less a matter of who they *are* than what they do that is considered offensive.[14] This explains the quite common "liberal" attitude of many straights who claim something like: "I don't care what they do, I just wish they would do it only in the privacy of their own homes!" or "What you do in your bedroom is your own business," which more or less means that as long as you don't do queer things, as long as your sexuality is not somehow enacted in public, they don't mind who you are—that is, they can assume you are the same as they. It is this split between what one is and what one does that produces the very possibility of a notion like "the closet," a distinction between private and public that refuses integration. Moreover, it also accounts for the very possibility of coming out—after all, a quite ridiculous concept in most other forms of oppression. This is what enables homosexuals to "pass" as straight with an ease that is extraordinarily rare for other oppressed groups. Homophobia is an oppression based on the *activities* of members of a group, and not on any definitive group attributes.

This is precisely why the forces of cultural reaction are so intent, in the case of homophobia more than in other forms of oppression, on separating a body from what it can (sexually) do. Such an assumption on the one hand affirms that lesbian and gay sexual practices and lifestyles are active and affirmative, that they progress and develop according to their own economies and not simply in reaction to the constraints provided by heterosexism; yet on the other hand, it shows that the forces of reaction have themselves made this choice both immensely difficult and yet also enticingly attractive. The constraints of heterosexism are not simply being reacted to but are obstacles whose overcoming may be self-expanding and positive. Homophobia is an attempt to separate being from doing, existence from action. And if what constitutes homosexuality is not simply a being who *is* homosexual, who has a homosexual personality, a "natural inclination" towards homosexual love objects (the "persona of the homosexual," Foucault claims, is an invention of the nineteenth century), but is a matter of practice, of what one does, how one does it, with whom and with what risks and benefits attached, then it is clear that forces of reaction function by trying to solidify or congeal a personage, a being through and through laden with deviancy. This reduces homosexuality to a legible category in the same way as women (of whatever color) and peoples of color (of either sex) are presumed to be, and in a certain way minimizes the threat that the idea of a labile, indeterminable sexuality, a sexuality based on the contingency of undertaking certain activities and subscribing to certain ideas, has on the very self-constitution of the heterosexual norm.

Lesbianism, for example, attests to the fundamental plasticity of women's (and also presumably men's) desire, its inherent openness not only to changes in its sexual object (male to female or vice-versa), but also its malleability in the forms and types of practices and pleasures available to it. In other words, to the more or less infinite possibilities of becoming. It attests to the rigidity, the fearfulness, the boring, indeed endless repetition, of form in stable male/female Western sex roles, the roles to which stable relationships become accustomed, and to the possibilities of change inherent in them, possibilities that need to be ignored or blotted out in order for them to continue these roles. The threat homosexuality poses to heterosexuality is its own contingency, and openendedness, its own tenuous hold over the multiplicity of sexual impulses and possibilities characterizing all human sexuality. Its own un-naturalness, its compromise and reactive status. Queer pleasures show that one does not have to settle for the predictable, the formulaic, the respected, although these too are not without their cost.

This is both the power and the danger posed by lesbian and gay sexual relations: that what one does, how one does it, with whom, and with what effects are ontologically open questions, that sexuality in and for all of us is fundamentally provisional, tenuous, mobile, igniting in unpredictable contexts with often unsettling effects: its power, attraction, and danger, the fundamental fluidity and transformability of sexuality and its enactment in sexed bodies. In separating what a body is from what a body can do, an essence of sorts is produced, a consolidated nucleus of habits and expectations take over from experiments and innovations. Bodies are sedimented into fixed and repetitive relations, and it is only beyond modes of repetition that any subversion is considered possible.

I am interested instead in the ways in which homosexual relations and lifestyles, expelled from and often ignored by the norms of heterosexuality, nonetheless, seep into, infiltrate the very self-conceptions of what it is to be heterosexual, or at least straight. The rigid alignments of sexual stimuli and responses, the apparently natural coupling of male and female lovers, are unstuck by the existence of lesbians and gays; further, the very existence of a mode of lesbianism not dependent on the phallus or even on a mediated relation with a male sexual subject demonstrates that sexuality as such does not require the phallus, as function or as organ. But more than this flow-on effect—which does effect a certain loosening or contagion of the sphere of sexual "normality," rather than endlessly theorize, explain, analyze, reflect on, reconstruct, reassess, provide new words and concepts for sexuality—we need to experiment with it, to enjoy its various modalities, to seek its moments of heightened intensity, its moments of self-loss where reflection no longer has a place. This is not, I hope and believe, either an anti-intellectualism or a naive return to a 1960s style polysexualism, which sought pleasure with no responsibility, and which moreover, lived out only men's fantasies of sexual freedom while subsuming women's under their imperatives. Rather, it is a refusal to link sexual pleasure with the struggle for freedom, the refusal to validate sexuality in terms of a greater cause or a higher purpose (whether political, spiritual, or reproductive), the desire to enjoy, to experience, to make pleasure for its own sake, for where it takes us, for how it changes and makes us, to see it as one but not the only trajectory or direction in the lives of sexed bodies.

Notes

1   The history of the label "queer theory" has its problems, though it has some appeal. What I think works well in this formulation is an ambiguity about what the term "queer" refers to: that not only are the objects of speculation—lesbian, gay, and other forms of sexuality intolerable to the heterocentric mainstream—"queer," but perhaps more interestingly, the ways in which they are treated are "queer," the knowledges that deal with them are also queer.

But there is also a cost in using this term, a certain loss of specificity, and the capacity for cooption and depoliticization. In her introduction to the "Queer Theory" issue of *differences* (1991), Teresa de Lauretis provides a useful account of the genesis and function of the label "queer," its own self-understanding as distinctively defiant, transgressive, postmodern:

Today we have, on the one hand, the term "lesbian" and "gay" to designate distinct kinds of life-styles, sexualities, sexual practices, communities, issues, publications, and discourses; on the other hand, the phrase "gay and lesbian," or more and more frequently, "lesbian and gay" (ladies first), has become standard currency. . . . In a sense, the term "Queer Theory" was arrived at in the effort to avoid all of these fine distinctions in our discursive protocols, not to adhere to any one of the given terms, not to assume their ideological liabilities, but instead to both transgress and transcend them—or at the very least problematize them. (v)

De Lauretis is of course perfectly correct in her claim that the phrase "Lesbian and Gay" by now has a pre-designated and readily assumed constituency, and a correlative set of identities. And with it, a series of easy presumptions and ready-made political answers. The label "queer" does problematize many of these presumptions; but its risks are greater than simply remaining tied to a set of stale and conventional assumptions. "Lesbian and Gay" has the advantage of straightforwardly articulating its constituency, while "queer" is capable of accommodating, and will no doubt provide a political rationale and coverage in the near future for many of the most blatant and extreme forms of hetero-sexual and patriarchal power games. They too are, in a certain sense, queer, persecuted, ostracized. Heterosexual sadists, pederasts, fetishists, pornographers, pimps, voyeurs suffer from social sanc-tions: in a certain sense they too can be regarded as oppressed. But to claim an oppression of the order of lesbian and gay, women's, or racial oppression is to ignore the very real complicity and phallic rewards of what might be called "deviant sexualities" within patriarchal and heterocentric power relations. It is of the same order as the claim that men too can be the victims of "female chau-vinism": such a claim rests on the denial of a relentless and systematic distribution of values and benefits.

Moreover, underlying the incipient distinction between the labels "lesbian and gay" and "queer" is a series of often unspoken ontological and political assumptions. For example, the question of sexual difference is at the very heart of lesbian and gay theory and politics (the marking of "homosexual" necessarily designates a specific type of love object, male or female); while the proliferation of "queer" sexualities is bound to include bisexuality, heterosexual transvestism, transsexualism, and sado-masochistic heterosexuality. The proliferation of sexualities beyond the notion of two (the assertion of two has been difficult enough!) seems to underlie the rapidly expanding domain and constituency of queerness (*n* sexes). While I do not want to prevent this proliferation, nor to judge the transgressiveness or conservatism of these multiple sexualities, this field of queerness, it seems to me, can only ignore the specificities of sexed bodies at its own peril. Even if we are all composed of a myriad of sexual possibilities, and fluid and changeable forms of sexuality and sexual orientation, nevertheless, these still conform to the configurations of the two sexes. A male sado-masochist does not function in the same way or with the same effect as a female sado-masochist. It *does* make a difference which kind of sexed body enacts the various modes of performance of sexual roles and positions.

2   How one could ever in fact compare different articulations of oppressive structures in order to find out who is more oppressed than whom is entirely unclear to me, particularly in view of the fact that, with the exception of a relatively small minority of white middle class, hetero, Anglo, young men, all of us can in some sense or other understand ourselves as oppressed.

3   In a whole series of current lesbian feminist texts, there seems to be the curious imperative to provide an account of lesbianism, or feminism, from which no category of women is excluded, in which all women are able to find some self-representation. This is a consequence of a drive to all-inclusiveness, which has had the effect, on the one hand, of creating discourses that naively and self-contradictorily claim to speak only for me, not representing anyone, and thus not coercing anyone into accepting a self-representation which is mine alone (see, for example Trebilcot, 1990). This kind of position not only refuses to accept the responsibility for the fact that no discourse or cultural production simply reflects the intentions of its author, insofar as they are read, responded to, and are of interest to others independent of intentions. They are read, and can be effective, only if they are more than mere self-expression. If what I write is true only for myself, it is not true at all ("true for me" is self-contradictory). On the other hand, the opposite extreme is found in many feminist texts that either become embedded in and crippled by their own hyphenization and hybridization as lesbian-feminist-anti-racist-anti-classist-anti-agêst . . . , their aspiration towards all-inclusiveness, or reduced to the kinds of generalizations that, while including everyone, have very little to say about anyone's specifi-cities and differences. A choice has to be made either to refuse to efface specificity (in which case clearly not everyone can be included); or to refuse to efface generality or universality (in which case, no particular form of oppression can be adequately accounted for in its concrete articulations). For a particularly acute analysis of the difficulties of these two extremes, and the political necessity of acknowledging that all subjects are in fact placed in a position (whether they recognize it or not) of speaking on behalf of others, even if their words cannot express or include valid universal claims, see Alcoff, 1992.

4   Most notably, Foucault's inability to acknowledge that the institutions whose genealogies he so well documents—prisons, the insane asylum, the discourses on sexuality and self-production, and so

on—are distinctively male dominated sites, and the privileged subjects whose histories of subordination and insurrection he documents are those of men. See Diamond and Quinby, eds., 1988.

5   On the question of morphologies, and the redundancy of the category of gender, see Grosz, 1994.

6   Deleuze's reading of Nietzsche makes it clear that the forces of the body are only ever a matter of more or less, a question of differential quantities, and through the differential relation between two quantities, the production of qualities. Nietzsche says:

> The attempt should be made to see whether a scientific order of values could be constructed simply on a numerical and quantitative scale of forces. All other "values" are prejudices, naiveties and misunderstandings. They are everywhere reducible to this numerical and quantitative scale. (Nietzsche, 1968: 710)

7   In her intriguing and brilliant paper, "Lesbian 'Sex'," (1990), Marilyn Frye quotes some of the statistics of the sex researchers Philip Blumstein and Pepper Schwartz from their text *American Couples* (William and Morrow Co, New York, 1983) on rates of frequency of sexual activity amongst married, de facto heterosexual, gay, and lesbian couples. Their statistics suggest that 47% of lesbians in a long-term relationship had sex once a month or less while only 15% of married couples had sex once a month or less. Frye's profound insight in her commentary on these statistics is that it is not clear what "having sex" actually means, especially when it emerges that the 85% of married couples who "had sex" more than once a month on the average take less than 8 minutes for such activities. I will return to this crucial paper later in my discussion.

8   Butler argues that Foucault seems to want to say *both* that the regimes of sexuality are what produce sex; and at the same time, that there are bodies and pleasures that are somehow outside the law and the discursive apparatus, there as "raw materials" for the functioning of power. She claims that there is

> . . . an unresolved tension within the *History of Sexuality* itself (he refers to "bucolic" and "innocent" pleasures of intergenerational sexual exchange that exist prior to the imposition of various regulative strategies). On the one hand, Foucault wants to argue that there is no "sex" in itself which is not produced by complex interactions of discourse and power, and yet there does not seem to be a "multiplicity of pleasures" *in itself* which is not the effect of any specific discourse/power exchange. (Butler, 1990: 97)

9   Hence the final paragraph to Foucault's text in which he counterposes the reorganization or realignments of bodies and pleasures to the regime of sexuality:

> we need to consider the possibility that one day, perhaps, in a different economy of bodies and pleasures, people will no longer quite understand how the ruses of sexuality, and the power that sustains its organization, were able to subject us to that austere monarchy of sex, so that we became dedicated to the endless task of forcing its secret, of exacting the truest of confessions from a shadow. (159)

10   It seems stuck within a model that can do nothing but endlessly vary itself around a central core that itself remains inviolable: the domination of the phallus, the structure of power accorded to the position of the father at the expense of the mother's body, the impossibility of a viable position for women as autonomous and self-defining subjects.

11   Most notably in her earlier work (1985a; 1985b). But also in her more recent writings:

> she does not set herself up as *one*, as a (single) female unit. She is not closed up or around one single truth or essence. The essence of a truth remains foreign to her. She neither has nor is being. . . . The/a woman can subsist by already being double in her self: both the one and the other. Not: one plus an other, more than one. More than. She is "foreign" to the unit. And to the countable, to quantification. There to the more than, as it relates to something already quantifiable, even were it a case of disrupting the operations. If it were necessary to count her/them in units—which is impossible—each unit would already be more than doubly (her). But that would have to be understood in another way. The (female) one being the other, without ever being either one or the other. Ceaselessly in the exchange between the one and the other. With the result that she is always already othered but with no possible identification of her, or of the other. (Irigaray, 1991: 86)

12   This is precisely Naomi Schor's and Margaret Whitford's arguments in their separate introductions to their anthology on Irigaray. See Burke, Schor, and Whitford, 1994.

13   Incidentally, there need be no commitment to the presumption of an homogeneity of the objects or victims of homophobia—lesbians and gays may be as varied in these characteristics as any individuals,

indeed, are likely to be members of more or less every constituency, every social category or group; but simply that whatever "identity" is bestowed on lesbians and gay men is the product of relentless forms of oppression, for they produce the homogeneity necessary to single out and define the objects of revulsion and inequity.

14   Indeed, there is a common reaction when someone comes out or is "outed" that they may not be believed—a reaction that is pretty well unimaginable in the case of other oppressions. If someone confessed to being Jewish or Islamic, there could be no disbelief!

Bibliography

Alcoff, Linda. 1992. "On Speaking for Others." In *Cultural Critique* 20: 5–32.

Burke, Carolyn, Naomi Schor and Margaret Whitford, eds. 1994. *Engaging with Irigaray*. New York: Columbia University Press.

Butler, Judith. 1990. *Gender Trouble. Feminism and the Subversion of Identity*. New York: Routledge.

—. 1993. *Bodies That Matter. On the Discursive Limits of "Sex."* New York: Routledge.

de Lauretis, Teresa. ed. 1991. "Queer Theory" issue of *differences* 3, 2.

Deleuze, Gilles. 1983. *Nietzsche and Philosophy*. Trans. Hugh Tomlinson. New York: Columbia University Press.

Diamond, Irene and Lee Quinby, eds. 1988. *Feminism and Foucault. Reflections on Resistance*. New York: Methuen.

Foucault, Michel. 1980. *The History of Sexuality, Volume 1: An Introduction*. Trans. Robert Hurley. New York: Vintage/Random House.

Frye, Marilyn. 1990. "Lesbian 'Sex'." In *Lesbian Philosophies and Cultures*. Ed. Jeffner Allen. Albany: SUNY Press, 305–15.

Grosz, Elizabeth. 1994. *Volatile Bodies. Toward a Corporeal Feminism*. Bloomington: Indiana University Press; and Sydney: Allen and Unwin.

Irigaray, Luce. 1985a. *Speculum of the Other Woman*. Trans. Gillian C. Gill. Ithaca: Cornell University Press.

—. 1985b. *This Sex Which Is Not One*. Trans. Catherine Porter. Ithaca: Cornell University Press.

—. 1991. *Marine Lover of Friedrich Nietzsche*. Trans. Gillian C. Gill. New York: Columbia University Press.

Nietzsche, Friedrich. 1968. *The Will to Power*. Trans. Walter Kaufmann and R.J. Hollingdale. New York: Vintage Books.

Sartre, Jean-Paul. 1961. *Anti-Semite and Jew*. New York: Schocken Books.

Trebilcot, Joyce. 1990, "Dyke Methods." In *Lesbian Philosophies and Cultures*. Ed. Jeffner Allen. Albany: SUNY Press, 15–29.

Chapter 13

Robert Reid-Pharr

DINGE

Robert Reid-Pharr is Distinguished Professor of English at the CUNY Graduate Center. He has published on a variety of topics, including antebellum African American literature and culture and black queer masculinity. Reid-Pharr is the author of *Conjugal Union: The Body, The House, and the Black American* (1999), *Once You Go Black: Desire, Choice and Black Masculinity in Post-War America* (2007), and *Black Gay Man: Essays* (2001), in which the following piece appears.

Sampling autobiography, literary analysis, and queer critique, Reid-Pharr's "Dinge" considers queer theory's inattentiveness to "fucking," or how we actually inhabit our sexually responsive bodies and what we think about as we interact sexually. Specifically, he notes white scholars' inattention to cross-racial desire. According to Reid-Pharr, cross-racial sex offers opportunities for analyzing power, resistance, and domination. Through a reading of cross-racial sexual encounters in James Baldwin's *Another Country*, Reid-Pharr demonstrates that cross-racial sex does not represent the transparency of desire or moments when racial boundaries are transgressed. Instead, whiteness is rendered temporarily visible, and vulnerable, through intimate contact with blackness, thus demonstrating the transformative possibilities of blackness. Yet, he argues, the results of such inquiries are not always liberating and often reify oppressive power structures.

> There is indeed a close interrelation between the predominant Western conception of manhood and that of racial (and species) domination. The notion, originally from myth and fable, is that the summit of masculinity—the "white hero"—achieves his manhood, first and foremost, by winning victory over the "dark beast" (or over the barbarian beasts of other—in some sense, "darker"—races, nations and social castes.)
> (Paul Hoch, *White Hero, Black Beast: Racism, Sexism and the Mask of Masculinity*)

IF **THERE IS** one thing that marks us as queer, a category that is somehow different, if not altogether distinct, from the heterosexual, then it is undoubtedly our relationships to the body, particularly the expansive ways in which we utilize and combine vaginas, penises, breasts, buttocks, hands, arms, feet, stomachs, mouths and tongues in our expressions of not only intimacy, love, and lust but also and importantly shame, contempt, despair, and hate. Because it is impossible to forget that we hold a tangential relationship to what Michael Warner calls heteronormativity, we often are forced to become relatively self-aware about what we are doing when we fuck, suck, go down, go in, get on, go under. Even and especially when I encounter the nameless trick, even and especially when that tricking happens in the blank, barely penetrable atmosphere of the dark room, I am aware of the immense contradictions at play, the pleasure and the danger located at the end of his cock, pleasure and danger that are intimately linked and that work together to produce the electricity of the encounter. Essex Hemphill writes, "Now we think as we fuck. This nut might kill. This kiss could turn to stone."[1]

It is surprising, then, that so little within queer theory has been addressed to the question of how we inhabit our various bodies, especially how we fuck or, rather, what we think when we fuck. In the face of wildly impressive work on gay and lesbian history and historiography, gender roles and politics, queer literature and culture, we have been willing to let stand the most tired and hackneyed notions of what our sex actually means. If you believe the propaganda, it would seem that every time a fag or dyke fingers a vagina or asshole is a demonstration of queer love and community. The exceptions to this rule come almost invariably from what we might think of as the queer margins. Sadomasochistic practice and the debates surrounding it, particularly among lesbians, reminded us that dominance, submission, and violence, real or imagined, are often integral parts of queer sexual practice. The H.I.V./A.I.D.S. community helped focus our thinking about issues of risk, disease, and decay. Further, and more importantly for my purposes here, nearly two decades of writing and film making by people of color, and in particular the work of black gay men, has spoken to the experience of sex with whites, painting it at once as liberatory and repressive.

It is telling that cultural practitioners as distinct as Marlon Riggs, Isaac Julien, and Lyle Harris all found it necessary to identify themselves as snow queens, or some version thereof, in recent years. Indeed, the articulation of a persistent, if diffuse and diverse, black hunger for vanilla has been such a regular aspect of the various discussions of black subjectivities as to seem rather mundane. In 1853, William Wells Brown published the first Black American novel, *Clotel*, in which his near-white female protagonist is first seduced, then abandoned by a handsome young planter. Wallace Thurman continued the theme more than seventy years later as he explored the tension generated by thinly veiled interracial and homosexual desire in his *Infants of the Spring*, tension that is relieved for the white protagonist within the vaginas of several readily available black women and for the black in an ascetic devotion to his art.[2] In the fifties and sixties, Eldridge Cleaver, Piri Thomas, and Malcolm X all confessed their dalliances on the other side of the line, their moments in the sun. Indeed, black queers as diverse as James Baldwin, Audre Lorde, Samuel Delany, and Essex Hemphill have all paid considerable attention to the questions engendered when one "sleeps with the enemy."

What is striking, given the tradition that I have just outlined, is the fact that so few white artists, critics, intellectuals of all stripes, male or female, lesbian or gay, have found it necessary to cover themselves in the mantle of dinge queen, rice queen, or what have you. The desire for black, brown, and yellow flesh remains largely unspoken within either academia, or even within popular publishing. Not since the mid-eighties and the release by Gay Sunshine Press of *Black Men/White Men* have I seen a sustained articulation of cross-racial desire by any white person, though the evidence from the personal ads, the 900 lines, and the porn magazines suggests that dark meat is in exceptionally high demand as we enter the new millennium.[3]

I am not attempting to further police queer sexuality, to suggest that cross-racial desire and fantasy is necessarily a bad or shameful thing. On the contrary, I am enough a product of the "liberal" seventies to imagine that when black dick meets white dick we all are one step closer to the beloved community. Still, the question remains, What do we think when we fuck? Why is it that we often find such sustained discussions of cross-racial desire among people of color, while whites remain largely silent? My attempt to answer this question turns largely on the work that is just beginning to emerge from a variety of scholars in which whiteness is named as a reality, or more accurately, as an ideological structure that stands not so much in contradistinction to blackness, or Latinoness, or Asianness, but in intimate relation to them. David Roediger opens his study of white ethnicity and class consciousness, *The Wages of Whiteness*, with a discussion of the highly overdetermined manner in which stereotypes of black bodies and desires affect white sexuality. Increasing numbers of critics, among them Alexander Saxton, Richard Dyer, Toni Morrison, and Eric Lott, are attempting to open up our understandings of white subjectivity to demonstrate how blackness is indeed the always already lurking in the netherworld of white consciousness.[4] Significantly, each of these scholars has suggested that this reality, the blackness of whiteness, is denied precisely because whiteness itself has been rendered transparent. Whiteness seems incapable of recognizing itself until it is put under extreme pressure, until it is confronted with the hypervisibility of blackness. My contribution to these discussions is to argue that sexuality, no, let me say fucking, is one of the primary nodes at which this process of blackness into whiteness takes place. I contend, in fact, that the tendency to insist upon the innocence of our sex, the transparency of desire at the moment of penetration, is itself part of the complex ideological process by which whiteness is rendered invisible, unremarkable except in the presence of a spectacularized blackness.

> At the Connection in Berlin, I am accosted by a drunk, white American expatriate. He badgers me and my companions: a six-foot-four, 225 pound dark-skinned psychologist and a small, light brown broker, complaining that he cannot attract the attention of the blond Aryan types that he desires because they are overly interested in us. I counter that just beyond our group there is a door that leads to a maze-like backroom in which dozens of men are literally begging to be taken by dark-haired, moderately developed, white thirty-five-year-olds. He persists, pointing to the Gentian fascination with the exotic and the relative ease this affords blacks, particularly Black Americans, in the sexual economy. I remind him that I am from the suburbs and then tell a story about waiting for a bus in Alexanderplatz and people reaching out to touch my skin and hair, at first gingerly, discreetly, and then with passion, eventually forcing me to break away to the other side of the street. I tell him that a few days earlier an East German scared me when he overtook me on the sidewalk, barred my path, insisted on knowing who I was, then begged me to meet him again while friends gruffly pushed him aside and pulled me away. In his stupor, a stupor imported all the way from America, my friend cannot hear me. Mercifully, he leaves, surfacing hours later with a cache of backroom war stories and a huge smudge on his forehead made from the iridescent ink stamped onto the backs of our hands as we entered the club. Even then, I was struck by the irony that this mark of his transgression, this sign of his desirability, of fully inhabiting a clearly raced and gendered body, was visible only under the black light.

What strikes me now in listening to myself relate this episode is not simply how omnipresent racism is within the lives of blacks and other people of color. That is old news. Nor am I attempting to deny the heightened ability of Black American gay men to participate in a sort of cross-racial sexual tourism outside U.S. boundaries. I am not even particularly surprised at how threatened some whites, many whites, most whites are at the spectacle of the visible black, the beautiful black, the black who is desired. What is really stunning, however, is the honesty and clarity with which this man expressed what I take to be a rather profound alienation from his own corporeality, his so-called whiteness, alienation that is focused and transmitted precisely through racist discourse. Upon consideration, what seems to have been taking place, within a sexually tense leather bar in a Germany that always is understood as wildly racist and anti-Semitic, was a breakdown of the very ideological structures by which we construct our various identities: racial, national, sexual, what have you. We were both out of bounds, existing as anomalies in language and culture, freaks to be either exoticized or pitied. My interlocutor seems to have been thrashing about in a fit of anxiety engendered by his will to recapture normality in the face of the intense sense of vertigo that we shared. Strangely enough, I, with all my familiar bestial, intensely sexual blackness, was the only sign by which he seemed capable of reestablishing boundaries, of maintaining a self in the midst of constant erosion. Paul Hoch writes,

> To abandon control over the bestial super-masculinity he has projected outward onto the black male would threaten the racist's control over his own repressed sexuality (which forms the basis for that projection), and overall the bestial niggers and rapists locked within his psyche who threaten to erupt in a mad orgy of sexual violence. The black man must therefore be "kept down," not to protect the white goddesses, but because on the subconscious level his liberation would signify the eruption of the sexuality confined in the racist's own unconscious, hence a catastrophic loss of his conscious self, a "castration."[5]

I stress again the observation that I made earlier in this essay that the process by which the white male might abandon control over what Hoch calls "bestial super-masculinity" is one and the same with the process by which he might lose access to his whiteness. Moreover, the technology that mitigates against this procedure ever occurring is the very technology that renders whiteness transparent. When the black is seen, the white is not. Yet the workings of desire, the will to be recognized, taken, possessed, involves at least a temporary lapse in this invisibility. The black is necessary, then, as a sort of prosthetic, much like the fabricated outer skin manufactured by Orwell's own invisible man. Our presence gives the white form. But always there is the danger that the most sacrosanct boundaries might be crossed, that the man inside might cease to exist as an entity unto himself and become instead a breach, a break, a horrid violation of both self and other. "Now we think as we fuck. This nut might kill us. This kiss could turn to stone."

Interestingly enough, it is James Baldwin who has worked most assiduously to tell us what it is that white men, particularly white queer men, think when they fuck. Vivaldo, Eric, Yves, Giovanni, and David all struggle to speak their desire in the course of Baldwin's narratives. More important, the process by which they come to voice, *if* they come to voice, is always one and the same with the process by which they come to refuse the inevitability of an inarticulate whiteness. Indeed, I suggest that the difficulty that so many critics have when approaching Baldwin is precisely that they seem incapable of maintaining or even acknowledging his intense investment in understanding the manner in which white masculinity is codified in relation to "blackness," understood here as that almost otherworldly existence that is not white. Instead, the rather underdeveloped critical literature surrounding Baldwin tends to turn upon proving or disproving his allegiance to an ill-defined black aesthetic. One must remember always that Baldwin is *the* black author, the paragon of the Black American intellect, the nation's prophet of racial tolerance, one whose queer sexuality presumably stands in such anomalous relation to his racial presence, intellectual and otherwise, that it works only as the exception proving the rule.[6]

Part of the violence that is visited continuously upon Baldwin's work, the body of Baldwin, is a sort of collapsing of ontological and epistemological considerations. The black author thinks black. Baldwin seems, though, to always slip the yoke of his various identities, some self-imposed, others not. He refused, throughout his career, to accept the neat categories into which we deposit our multiple selves, preferring instead to insist upon the funkiness of our existences, or, more to the point, he forces us to consider the shocking manner in which what we think when we fuck is not so much dictated by race, gender, and class but instead acts itself as an articulation of the structures of dominance—and resistance—that create race, gender, and class. Baldwin writes:

> The American ideal, then, of sexuality appears to be rooted in the American ideal of masculinity. This ideal has created cowboys and Indians, good guys and bad guys, punks and studs, tough guys and softies, butch and faggot, black and white. It is an ideal so paralytically infantile that it is virtually forbidden—as an unpatriotic act—that the American boy evolves into the complexity of manhood.[7]

The ideals that Baldwin points to are ones that are constructed through the erection and maintenance of a set of false, if potent, binarisms: good/bad, punk/stud, butch/fag, what have you. For Baldwin, though, the primary binarism, the model from which and through which he filters the presumably natural divisions in the human condition, is none other than the one that both holds together and separates the black and the white.

It is with these ideas in mind that I suggest that we begin to reread Baldwin's *Another Country*, particularly his depiction of the "optically white" Vivaldo. Baldwin so insists throughout the work on forcing consideration of the black/white binarism—white handkerchief in black hands, black tie on white shirt, white dick against black dick against black vagina against white vagina—that the distinctions clearly begin to crumble by the end of the narrative.

> He stared into his cup, noting that black coffee was not black, but deep brown. Not many things in the world were really black, not even the night, not even the mines. And the light was not white, either, even the palest light held within itself some hint of its origins, in fire.[8]

That Italian Vivaldo, who comes from a Brooklyn neighborhood much like the Harlem onto which he has projected so many fantasies, is not "white" is far from being the tragedy of this work. On the contrary, the tragedy, the horror that both the white and the black subject must confront in Baldwin's universe, is the racial fantasy that denies access to the body, that denies access to the beloved, and instead seals each partner into a bizarre competition in which mutual invisibility is the inevitable outcome. Indeed, the "lovemaking" in *Another Country* is as much an act of rage and hate as of adoration and devotion.

> The battle was awful because the girl wished to be awakened but was terrified of the unknown. Every movement that seemed to bring her closer to him, to bring them closer together, had its violent recoil, driving them farther apart. Both clung to a fantasy rather than to each other, tried to suck pleasure from the crannies of the mind, rather than surrender the secrets of the body.
>
> (Baldwin, *Another Country*, 131)

Baldwin has clearly identified the catalytic tension in the labored give and take between the two partners, Vivaldo and Ida, the younger sister of Vivaldo's dead (black) friend, Rufus. Each wants to break, to move beyond identity, not to know, but to surrender to the secrets of the body. Yet their laboring, their performance of intimacy, works only to reconstruct difference. The two are most sealed in their blackness and their whiteness, "in full narcissistic cry," as Fanon would have it, at precisely the moment of their "joining."

And what of Rufus, the ghost who haunts even Vivaldo's most intimate interactions?

It is Rufus whom he tries to save. It is Rufus whom he constantly insists that he loves. It is Rufus whose lost life he carries about as a regretful and irrepressible memory. As Vivaldo fucks Ida, as Vivaldo hires a series of black prostitutes, as Vivaldo seduces/is seduced by Eric, a (white) gay man who is himself a "nigger lover," who himself has loved Rufus, he is haunted not only by remorse and regret at the tragedy suggested by his friend's life and death but by a certain half-acknowledged fear that he neither knew nor particularly loved this man around whom so much in his emotional and social economies was constructed. When confronted with Ida's angry and breathless claim to having loved her brother, Vivaldo responds: "'So did I' . . . too quickly, irrelevantly; and for the first time it occurred to him that, possibly, he was a liar; had never loved Rufus at all, but had only feared and envied him" (Baldwin, *Another Country*, 413).

Vivaldo's fear of Rufus is one and the same with his fear of knowledge. He is afraid to know not only that he never loved Rufus but that the barrier to that love was the very ideology of seamlessness, the insistence that he does not see difference, the "color-blindness," that dictates his relationships with not only Rufus and Ida but Eric, Cass, and her husband, Richard, as well. Rufus embodies not simply difference but, perhaps more important, the knowledge and acknowledgment of the processes through which difference is constructed. Rufus recognizes in his fucking, moreover, an incredible opportunity in which to express this knowledge.

> He wanted her to remember him the longest day she lived. And, shortly, nothing could have stopped him, not the white God himself nor a lynch mob arriving on wings. Under his breath he cursed the milk-white bitch and groaned and rode his weapon between her thighs. She began to cry. I told you, he moaned, I'd give you something to cry about, and at once, he felt himself strangling, about to explode or die. A moan and a curse tore through him while he beat her with all the strength he had and felt the venom shoot out of him, enough for a hundred black-white babies.
>
> (Baldwin, *Another Country*, 22)

Rufus abuses himself, abuses his white lovers, Leona and Eric, then throws his body off the George Washington Bridge. And yet he does not die. He lives always and especially with Vivaldo, who climbs in and out of bed with his lost friend, searching in the bodies of multiple surrogates for some part of himself that he imagines Rufus took with him into the waters of the Hudson.

Again I stress my contention that the difference that haunts Vivaldo is not some free-floating, omnipresent signifier, some pre-given reality. On the contrary, the difference that besets them all is a difference that is constructed—and reconstructed—precisely at those moments of intimate contact. It is almost as if the camp fiction of whiteness, the fiction of the white dick, is put on display at precisely the moment when it presumably is thrown aside. As Vivaldo struggles into the body of Ida, he does not simply find Rufus, or Eric, or any of the faces from his world of sexual experience. Instead, he finds some carnivalesque image of himself, a grotesquely white boy laughing at his feeble efforts to become a man. "It is an ideal so paralytically infantile that it is virtually forbidden—as an unpatriotic act—that the American boy evolves into the complexity of manhood."

It is important here that I guard against the assumption that what I am describing is *simply* a species of racial fetishism. Indeed, the question that I have asked—What do we think when we fuck?—has not been limited to those whites who fuck blacks but instead applies to the entirety of (white, Western, male) sexual desire. If Vivaldo cannot get the Negro off his mind as he fucks black women, the same is true of Eric as he fucks white men and women, of Richard as he fucks Cass, and of Ellis, Richard's business mentor, as he fucks everyone. One of my primary goals is to suggest that, even and especially in those most sacred moments of sexual normativity (white dominant male on white submissive female), the specter of the black beast is omnipresent. As the good white wife, Cass, goes home to tell her dutiful and faithful husband of her affair with the gay, race traitor, Eric, she pauses for a moment in the cab, exchanging glances with the young Puerto Rican driver, taking a moment to allow desire to wash over her before she faces the truth and the violence that she knows are inevitable.

> *Even now, even as we fuck, I smack your buttocks hard. No, not the slight licks that work only to remind us of the fullness of flesh. When I strike out I do mean to hurt, if only to catch your attention for a moment, to startle you with cruelty, to see you writhe on the bed, begging, "Please be gentle." And even so you forget me, disremember laughter and witty conversation about puppets and acting, lose the image of my face as dick passes into rectum. In the morning, no longer drunk, you cannot speak. I leave, your card in hand, scuttle to the subway, a little embarrassed, tired, still hungry.*

What I have been concerned with, in these brief comments, is the question of silence. Why, I have asked, do we see so little work by white gays and lesbians that directly addresses the question of cross-racial desire? I have suggested that we might at least begin an answer by paying attention to the way in which speaking to these issues, admitting to the reality of beauty that is other than white, throws into disarray the idea of whiteness as universal. The point seems easy enough to understand. What is more difficult to accept is the idea that the sexual act, at least as it is performed between queers—and yes, I am nominating Vivaldo as queer—is not necessarily a good, expansive, and liberatory thing, a place in which individuals exist for a moment outside themselves such that new possibilities are at once imagined and actualized. This notion is itself predicated upon the articulation of a set of false boundaries, oddly constructed binarisms in which the black always comes up short. I am fully suspicious, in fact, of the notion of transcendence, of seamless, nonparticu-laristic connection with the rest of existence precisely because it looks so much like the imagined transparence that I have argued defines whiteness. We do not escape race and racism when we fuck. On the contrary, this fantasy of escape is precisely that which marks the sexual act as deeply implicated in the ideological processes by which difference is constructed and maintained. In Berlin there is a white man who cannot get his nut for fear that my black hand might have caressed the flesh of the blond and blue *ubermensch* he so desires. In Baldwin's *Another Country*, Vivaldo cannot connect, cannot come because he is so busy fooling himself that he exists outside his body, in a terrain in which love and desire conquer all.

The task that awaits all of us, then, is to speak desire plainly, to pay attention to what we think when we fuck. It is the particular task of white men to give up the comforts of naivete, of banal gestures to racial inclusion. The work before us is precisely to put our own bodies on the line. We must refuse to allow the production of a queer theory so reified that it does nothing to challenge the way we interact, the way we think, and the way we fuck.

We must insist on a queer theory that takes the queer body and what we do with it as a primary focus, lest we allow for the articulation of a queer subjectivity that never recognizes the differences we create and carry in our bodies, including not only race but gender, health, and age, to name only the most obvious categories. We must not only think as we fuck but also pay close attention to all the implications, good and bad, of those sometimes startling thoughts.

Notes

1   Essex Hemphill, "Now We Think," in Essex Hemphill, *Ceremonies: Prose and Poetry* (New York: Plume, 1992) 155.

2   William Wells Brown, *Clotel, or The President's Daughter* (1853; reprint, New York: University Books, 1969); Wallace Thurman, *Infants of the Spring* (1932; reprint, Boston: Northeastern University Press, 1992).

3   Michael J. Smith, ed., *Black Men / White Men* (San Francisco: Gay Sunshine Press, 1983).

4   David R. Roediger, *The Wages of Whiteness: Race and the Making of the American Working Class* (New York: Verso, 1991); Alexander Saxton, *The Rise and Fall of the White Republic: Class Politics and Mass Culture in Nineteenth-Century America* (New York: Verso, 1990); Richard Dyer, "White," *Screen* 29:4 (1988): 44–64; Toni Morrison, *Playing in the Dark: Whiteness and the Literary Imagination* (Cambridge, Mass.: Harvard University Press, 1992); Eric Lott, *Love and Theft: Blackface Minstrelsy and the American Working Class* (New York: Oxford University Press, 1993).

5   I completed this essay some time before the publication of the rather remarkable collection of new essays on James Baldwin, *James Baldwin Now*, edited by Dwight McBride. It was both stunning and encouraging to find this contribution to Baldwin scholarship and in particular the piece written by Marlon Ross, "White Fantasies of Desire: Baldwin and the Racial Identities of Sexuality," which treats in a much more developed manner some of the themes that I deal with here. On one level I am glad to have come to Ross's essay as late as I did, as I am not certain that, had I known of it before, I would have felt the same need to complete either this piece or the one that follows, "Tearing the Goat's Flesh," both of which are in part attempts to offer readings of Baldwin's corpus that do not distinguish a gay Baldwin from a black Baldwin. See: Dwight McBride, *James Baldwin Now* (New York: New York University Press, 1999).

6   James Baldwin, "Here Be Dragons," in James Baldwin, *The Price of the Ticket: Collected Non-Fiction, 1948–1985* (New York: St. Martin's, 1985) 678.

7   James Baldwin, *Another Country* (New York: Vintage, 1960) 430.

PART 3

Temporalities

Chapter 14

Tavia Nyong'o

DO YOU WANT QUEER THEORY (OR DO YOU WANT THE TRUTH)? INTERSECTIONS OF PUNK AND QUEER IN THE 1970s

Tavia Nyong'o is Associate Professor of Performance Studies in the Tisch School of the Arts at New York University. He is the author *The Amalgamation Waltz: Race, Performance, and the Ruses of Memory* (2009). The following essay originally appeared in *Radical History Review* in 2008.

In this essay Nyong'o examines the intersection between transatlantic punk and queer subcultures in the 1970s. Through a reading of punk subculture, Nyong'o challenges proponents of antirelational queer theory, such as Lee Edelman in his construction of the *sinthomosexual*, a queer subject who embraces the death drive while rejecting political futurity. Nyong'o considers the affinities and discontinuities between punk and queer affect, particularly their shared interest in social rebellion. He notes that punk subcultures resist binaries that make progressive politics and compulsory heteronormativity mutually exclusive. Punk cultural formations borrowed many symbols of queer subcultures, such as the discourse of "rough trade," but did not necessarily reject mainstream scenarios such as family, as is evidenced by Nyong'o's analysis of commentary by punk poet Patti Smith. Using examples such as a Sex Pistols' photo shoot and Guy Hocquenghem's gay liberationist writings, Nyong'o considers intersections between punk and queer subcultures to advocate for a progressive politics and sense of community that are not heteronormative.

IN A MAY 11, 1978, interview on NBC television's late-night talk show *Tomorrow*, the punk poet Patti Smith assured her interviewer, Tom Snyder, that the kids were alright. Smith—whose first single, "Hey Joe/Piss Factory," had been financed by her friend and former lover, Robert Mapplethorpe—told Snyder:

> I want the future to be like, I mean, I just want it to be like an open space
> for children. I mean, for me the future is children, and I feel like, you
> know, when I was younger first I wanted to be a missionary, then I wanted to
> be a schoolteacher, it's like, you know. I couldn't, I couldn't, uh, get through
> all the dogma, and I couldn't really integrate all of the rules and regulations
> of those professions into like my lifestyle and into the, into the generation that
> I was part of. And the really great thing about, umm, doing the work that
> I'm doing now, I have like all the ideals that I ever had to like communicate,
> you know, to, to, to children, or to people in general, to everybody, and to
> communicate with my creator. I, I can do everything all the perverse ends of
> it, and also, you know, all the innocence. It's all inherent in the form that
> I'm doing.[1]

In 1978, Snyder was one of the few cultural arbiters offering a platform to the insolent
and snotty punk rockers who had sprung themselves on a surprised public in the preceding
years. One invited punk set fire to a car live in Snyder's studio, but that stunt was hardly
as jolting as Smith's unexpected paean to family values. The punk diva's statement seems
to confirm the ideological hold of what the queer theorist Lee Edelman calls "reproductive
futurity" even among radical misfits and rebels.[2] Scholars such as Edelman and Lauren
Berlant have called attention to the role that reproductive futurity plays in the infantilization
of politics, turning citizenship, as Berlant puts it, into something "made of and for children."[3]
Because both the nation and its future belong to the child, who is never grown, we are led to
believe that we must sacrifice our adult needs and desires on the altar of perpetual infancy.
Edelman, in his widely discussed book *No Future: Queer Theory and the Death Drive*, identified
this ideology of reproductive futurity as specifically antiqueer and called on queers to "accede"
to our status as a flagrant threat to the future as "an open space for children," a future
that excludes those who are deliberately nonreproductive. Identifying the "homosexual"
with the "death drive"—that is, with the principle that is antagonistic to the very idea of
society, politics, or the future—Edelman's book serves ultimately as a polemic against
increasingly popular forms of lesbian and gay normativity such as marriage, parenting, and
military service.

Edelman's polemic extends and expands on an older strand of gay male critique that
is sometimes referred to as "antisocial" or "antirelational," a project with roots in the gay
liberationist writings of Guy Hocquenghem in the 1970s.[4] The antirelational thesis locates
the power of sexuality in its negativity rather than in any alternative community it may
give rise to. As Hocquenghem argued in *Homosexual Desire*, which was first published in
France in 1972, "the gay movement is thus not seeking recognition as a new political
power on par with others; its own existence contradicts the system of political thought,
because it relates to a different problematic."[5] In a similar vein, Leo Bersani noted in 1987
that "to want sex with another man is not exactly a credential for political radicalism," and
instead valorized homosexuality as an example of "the inestimable value of sex as—at least
in certain of its ineradicable aspects—anticommunal, antiegalitarian, antinurturing, anti-
loving."[6] Tactically embracing the seemingly homophobic charge that "homosexual desire"
subverts the reproduction of the social order, Hocquenghem and Bersani propose what
one of Edelman's critics has labeled a "queer post-politics."[7] Rejecting proposals to articulate
alternative models of queer sociality, community, and utopia, these theorists of antirelationality aim to liberate queers from the normalizing effects of all such progressive and inclu-
sionary ambitions and to instead proclaim a queer radicalism located outside politics as
conventionally conceived, perhaps even outside of politics. As Edelman has put it: "Not that
we are, or ever could be, outside the Symbolic ourselves but we can, nonetheless, make the

choice to accede to our cultural production as figures—*within* the dominant logic of narrative, *within* Symbolic reality—for the dismantling of such a logic and thus for the death drive it harbors within."[8]

In the light of this approach, Patti Smith's comment to Snyder may seem so conventional as to preclude or, at the very least, warn against any retrospective affiliation between punk and queer feelings. Such a precluded affiliation would have less to do with obvious differences in gender, sexual orientation, or parental status than with Smith's choice to figure her rebellion into the dominant logic of symbolic reality. Despite her professed inability to fit into "the dogma" and "the rules" of society, Smith represents her outsiderness as even more faithful to the fantasy of reproductive futurity than a conventional career, such as that of a missionary or schoolteacher, would have been. Retaining "all the ideals that I ever had," Smith finds in punk rock and countercultural poetry precisely the connection that permits her to speak *to*—and perhaps even *through* and *for*—children.

Although Smith's utopian views on reproductive futurity are hardly unusual in themselves, they are startling coming from her. Like Mapplethorpe, Smith was a gifted *provocateuse* and malcontent whose lyrics and stage presence rejected both mainstream and countercultural stereotypes of femininity. On her single "Hey Joe" (1974), Smith fantasized about "Patty Hearst . . . standing there in front of the Symbionese Liberation Army flag with your legs spread . . . wondering will you get it every night from a black revolutionary man and his women." On the single's flip side, "Piss Factory," she sang about wiling away the time on a factory line and thinking that she "would rather smell the way boys smell . . . that odor rising roses and ammonia, and way their dicks droop like lilacs. . . . But no I got, I got pink clammy lady in my nostril." Such deviant and aggressive thoughts did not add up, in Smith's own view, to a thoroughgoing antisocial negativity. On Snyder's couch, Smith's rage, perversion and wild-child persona would paradoxically form the most pure and innocent grounds for preserving the future as "an open space for children." Rather than challenge reproductive futurity, then, punk rebellion could seem to confirm and sustain it.

Smith is an appropriate figure with which to open an exploration of the affinities and discontinuities between punk and queer feelings. I argue that Smith produces both punk and queer affect *through* her perverse narration of reproductive futurity, not despite it. Indeed, the spirit Smith embodies is ultimately one that is inhospitable to the heteronormativity queer theorists censure. In embracing naive futurity, Smith remakes the subject position of "antisocial rebel" and its associated death drive; and, rather than accept the guilt with which the pervert and the rebel are saddled by the social order, she asserts her radical innocence. The innocence Smith extols cannot be fully subsumed into the reproductive futurity that Edelman and others lament, for what is most remarkable about Smith's comment is her suggestion that childlike innocence can be "inherent in the form" of adult perversity. She suggests that, once one abandons the hope of following all the rules and regulations of straight society, the future becomes an open *space* rather than the disciplinary, delayed *temporality* of generational, Oedipal succession. In this heterotopic space of punk feelings, child and adult, pervert and innocent encounter and communicate back and forth continuously. The future is not a disciplinary ideal for Smith so much as it is that most queer of spatial tropes, an ambience.

Studies of queer temporality have reached a new threshold with recent books and essays by Edelman, Judith Halberstam, and Elizabeth Freeman, among others, as well as the appearance of special issues on the topic in journals such as *GLQ* and the present issue of *Radical History Review*.[9] In this essay, I seek to contribute to this conversation through a discussion of one historical intersection or switch point between queer and other subjects: the punk moment of the mid- to late 1970s. At stake in such a crossing of the subject of queer studies is a form of political work that I will associate, following Edelman, with the Lacanian trope of the *sinthome*.[10] Looking back to the cultural politics of the 1970s from which both antirelational theory and punk rock originate, I employ a reading of punk to qualify some of the claims made on exclusive behalf of queer antirelationality. I argue that the figure through which the dismantling of the social is narrated—in a word, the *sinthome*—is more historically multiform and thus both more dangerous and more useful than Edelman's limning of "sinthomosexuality" might suggest.

The critique of reproductive futurity connects compulsory heterosexuality and parenthood with a future-oriented, progressive politics. If one rejects the former, antirelational theory suggests, one must reject the other. This argument has raised a host of objections from within queer studies. Does politics as such require a utopian future orientation that is necessarily disciplined by the tyrannical obligation to reproduce the social? Halberstam, in one published forum on the question, has complained that antirelational theorists "cast material political concerns as crude and pedestrian," leaving little room, in their rush to critique dominant modes of conceptualizing politics, for subaltern and resistant modes of political engagement. She calls for a more expansive archive that includes a robust range of punk, feminist, antiracist, and postcolonial negativities that also subvert the fantasy of reproductive futurity and its sanctified innocent child.[11] Giving up on the future, politics, or both, critics argue, might actually serve a symbolic order if it subsumes the subject that much more securely in the social totality.

This debate about the prospects of a political negativity has gravitated toward a discussion by Edelman, Halberstam, and José Esteban Muñoz, among others, over a series of felt echoes between queer theory and punk rock. But what does punk have to do with either the future or with politics? To answer this question, I want to pursue Halberstam's suggestion that the antirelational call to "accede to our cultural production as figures . . . for the death drive" borrows significant aspects of its affective appeal from punk subcultural formations. On the surface, this suggestion might appear implausible. In one presentation of this essay, a respondent politely inquired into my pursuit of "archival specters" such as the Smith interview, asking whether or not there was a risk of both anachronism and a loss of focus in the pursuit of such an eclectic history of the present. I hope to answer such doubts by hewing to a fairly specific switch point between punk and queer: the queer content of the punk moment of the mid- to late 1970s and its postpunk aftermath. My principal contention, following Halberstam's lead, will be that the antisociality of punk subculture, while not identical to the antisociality of deviant sexuality, nonetheless emerged within a context in which queer and punk affect were continuously and productively confused and conflated by both outsiders and participants. It is the fundamental and productive misprision between punk and queer, even their potential chiasmus, that constitutes grounds for moving queer polities beyond the "binary stalemate" of having to choose between resisting the hegemonic fantasy of the homosexual or acceding to it.[12]

No future . . . for you!

A plausible starting point for exploring the relationship between punk and queer is the shared vocabulary of "rough trade," the phrase denoting the easily recognized casual and sometimes commoditized sexual exchanges found in both subcultures. In Rob Young's excellent new history of the germinal punk music store and record label Rough Trade, he reprints a cartoon that economically summarizes that relation. In it, a cherubic, London-born Geoff Travis hitching through North America pauses to think: "Toronto was pretty cool . . . that band 'Rough Trade' must know the phrase means gay hustlers. That's even trashier than 'Velvet Underground.'"[13] This particular origin story for the label and store's name begs the question: does its founder Travis know that the same etymology of the phrase *rough trade* is also true of the word *punk?* As James Chance bluntly informs viewers of Don Letts's recent documentary *Punk: Attitude* (2003), "originally punk meant, you know, a guy in prison who got fucked up the ass. And that's still what it means to people in prison."[14] At one level, then, queer is to punk as john is to hustler, with both words referencing an established if underground economy of sexual favors and exchanges between men. That Chance could announce his definition as a ribald revelation suggests, however, that the subterranean linkages between punk and queer are as frequently disavowed as they are recognized. This suggests that alongside the "frozen dialectic" between black and white culture that Dick Hebdige famously noticed in British punk, there is also a less frequently noticed but equally furtive set of transactions between queer and punk that is hidden, like Poe's purloined letter, in plain sight.[15]

Punk may be literally impossible to imagine without gender and sexual dissidence. But the secret history, as Chance's comment suggests, also records a history of antagonisms between punk attitude and a male homosexual desire variously cast as predatory and pitiable. In a recent interview, for example, the journalist and author Jon Savage responded to the query about whether or not punk was "a sexy time" by arguing, "No. I thought punk was quite puritan, really. I didn't have a very good time during punk. I spent a lot of time feeling I was worthless . . . it still wasn't great to be gay in the late Seventies."[16] The phrasing of the question, and the whiff of pathos in Savage's response, suggests both a queer eagerness to identify with punk, as well as the hostility with which this desire was frequently met. We might consider as another example of this "53rd and 3rd" (1976) by the New York punk rockers the Ramones, in which Dee Dee Ramone recounts his hustling days at that notorious intersection on the east side of Manhattan and asks his audience, "Don't it make you feel sick?"[17] That line, ironically, is rhymed with "You're the one they never pick," suggesting Ramone's doubled abjection of failing even at being rough trade. But by contrast, Cynthia Fuchs, Mary Kearney, and Halberstam have argued that the affinities between lesbian, feminist, trans, and gay people and the punk subculture was immediate, definitive, and far more enduring.[18]

In a 2006 exchange with Edelman, Halberstam observed that his provocative title, *No Future*, was also the original title for the 1977 Sex Pistols' single, the one known more commonly today as "God Save the Queen." In the chorus to that song, the band front man, Johnny Rotten, snarled that there was "no future in England's dreaming," a line from which Savage drew the title for his celebrated history of British punk.[19] In Halberstam's opinion, Edelman's queer polemic does not stand up well in light of its unacknowledged punk predecessor. "While the Sex Pistols used the refrain 'no future' to reject a formulaic union of nation, monarchy, and fantasy," she argues, "Edelman tends to cast material political concerns as crude and pedestrian, as already a part of the conjuring of futurity that his project must foreclose."[20] Edelman, like Oscar Wilde with his rent boys, stands accused of using punks and then snubbing them as "crude and pedestrian," like the waiter whom Wilde famously, at his trial, denied kissing, dismissing him as "peculiarly plain" and "unfortunately, extremely ugly."[21]

Halberstam's comparison between the political stakes of "No Future" 1977 versus *No Future* 2004 bears some discussion. While rock stars may seem unlikely objects on which to pin our hopes for the expression of material political concerns, historians like Savage and Greil Marcus have situated "God Save the Queen" in a context of political, economic, and cultural crisis, one in which both conventional politics and the countercultural ethos of the sixties appeared exhausted and a time during which the anarchic antipolitics of punk therefore signaled something new.[22] Marcus in particular persuasively susses out the resonances, real and feigned, between anarchism proper and the anarchist poses and iconography of punk shock tactics. The offensive gestures of bands such as the Sex Pistols, the Clash, and Siouxsie and the Banshees, documented in films like Don Letts's *The Punk Rock Movie* (1978) and Julien Temple's *The Filth and the Fury* (2000), sometimes communicated a rejection of political action as traditionally conceived on the Left. But their very popularity inspired attempts, by both the Right and the Left, to appropriate punk attitude for political purposes. Paul Gilroy has given perhaps the definitive account of the contradictions involved in such attempts to incorporate punk, reggae, dancehall, dub, and other genres associated with alterity into a new cultural front in the late 1970s.[23] The absence of formal political incorporation, Gilroy notes, does not immediately negate the possibility of a political reception or deployment.

Furthermore, cultural critiques of the political meanings ascribed to punk often elide the class context of British punk, a component of the subculture that is often missed in the United States where the *sub* in *subculture* seems to stand more often for "suburban" than "subaltern" and where punk is typically read as a mode of middle-class youth alienation. The submerged context of class struggle for British punk, however, comes to the fore in *The Filth and the Fury*'s astonishing footage of Rotten, Sid Vicious, and their bandmates smiling and serving cake to the children of striking firemen in Huddersfield, England, in 1977. Amid the moral panic, physical assaults, and public bans that had followed their incendiary early perform-ances and record releases, the Sex Pistols played a Christmas benefit for the strikers and families. In the film, the Pistols are seen smearing themselves and the children with cake, and then performing, almost unbelievably, "Bodies"—an intensely graphic song about an illegal abortion—as the children and their parents bop around deliriously. Such a truly shocking conflation of the sentimental and the obscene, the perverse and the innocent, produced a moment of saturnalia that served as an outright rejection of the manufactured consensual fantasy of the queen's jubilee year. That moment was political in spite of, or even because of, the absence of a formalized politics among the callow, gangly lads that the pop Svengali Malcolm McLaren had cannily spun into cultural terrorists. Like Patti Smith, the Pistols in Huddersfield did not outright reject the mainstream scenarios of family, child rearing, and working-class politics. Rather, they insinuated themselves into the very space that their rebellious stance ostensibly foreclosed to them. In both cases, Smith's and that of the Pistols, there is a countersymbolic charge to such a performative enactment that cannot simply be subsumed as antisocial behavior.

For Edelman, however, such a countersymbolic charge goes mostly unappreciated. Edelman has objected that the Pistol's "God Save the Queen" "does not really dissent from reproductive futurism," and he has argued that punk rebellion is merely caught up in the Oedipal dynamic of the young claiming the future from their corrupt and complicit elders: "No future . . . for you!" Instead of with the *sinthome*, Edelman associates punk anarchy with the derisive category of kitsch, ever the mandarins' term for that which the masses take seriously but which they consider intellectually or politically puerile. "Taken as political statement," Edelman argues, "God Save the Queen" is "little more than Oedipal kitsch. For violence, shock, assassination, and rage aren't negative or radical in themselves." While Edelman concedes that "punk negativity" may succeed "on the level of style," he takes such success to reinforce rather than undermine his position on the grounds that stylistic revolt is best achieved through the "chiasmic inversions" of his erudite polemic. Edelman warrants that the punks—and Halberstam in her critique—have confused "the abiding negativity that accounts for political negativism with the simpler act of negating particular political posi-tions." We cannot preserve its negativity by making "the swing of the hammer an end in itself," as Edelman puts it, but only if we "face up to political antagonism with the negativity of critical thought."[24] Johnny Rotten, meet Theodor Adorno.

Punk as a mode of revolt indeed begins in fairly blunt affects such as stroppiness and rage. But to reduce its message to the negation of particular political positions (such as repudiating the queen's jubilee) means that Edelman accounts for the Pistols' song only at the level of the lyrics and neglects a consideration of punk in the context of performance. This is a shame, as punk performers are highly cognizant of precisely the challenge of abiding negativism that Edelman raises. In the case of the Pistols, this challenge emerges at least in part from the original negation of musical skill and technical virtuosity that had occasioned punk's three-chord breakthroughs in the mid-1970s. Letts's documentary *Punk: Attitude* reflects retrospectively on the problematic prospect of a virtuoso punk rebellion. If punk rock dissented in part by rejecting musical virtuosity for pure attitude and ecstatic amateurism, how precisely could it sustain that stance? The more committed to punk one was, the quicker one acquired precisely the expressive fluency the genre ostensibly disdains. Either that, or one transforms into a cynical parody of adolescent fumbling such as that exhibited by former Bromley Contingent member Billy Idol, the bottle blond who transformed Vicious's wild snarl into the knowing smirk of eighties megastardom. Punk, like adolescence, quickly becomes its own archival specter, and for many purists, the moment was over almost as soon as the first punk singles were released. Simon Reynolds explores the extremely fruitful terrain of "postpunk" music (some of which preceded punk proper, or developed adjacent to it) that rose to prominence almost as soon as the style of punk had congealed into a recognizable, repeatable form.[25] The challenge of an abiding negativism, whether or not one agrees with the various solutions proposed, is a core feature of punk performance. Punk and postpunk styles are anything but the static, generational revolt caricatured by Edelman's analysis. The punk spirit cannot be decoded from a single lyric, song, or band, no matter how iconic the text or performer seems to be.

Part of this spirit, of course, is the traceable charge of erotic frisson detectable in much of the seemingly hostile overlap between punks and queers, which are often mirrored in the social and economic dynamics that crystallize the relationship between john and hustler. Those dynamics derive from a history of attitudes toward male homosexuality; but it strikes me that 1970s punk represents the moment at which those specifically male homosexual associations lose their exclusivity and punk becomes a role and an affect accessible to people within a range of gendered embodiments who deploy punk for a variety of erotic, aesthetic, and political purposes. The asymmetric, hostile, and desirous relations preserved in punk from the dynamics of rough trade do not always produce an open, inclusive punk community. But the forms of exclusivity punk has historically produced tend to fail abjectly at the reproduction of hegemonic and identitarian logics, even when they seek to engage in it.

For this reason it may prove useful to acknowledge and meditate further on the historical switch points between punk and queer. Let me offer two that would bear a more extensive analysis than I have space for here: a 1975 photo session of the Sex Pistols done by Peter Christopherson, a member of the legendary performance art and music group Throbbing Gristle, and Derek Jarman's 1977 film *Jubilee*. Christopherson, whose early work, by his own description, was "of white trash kids, a bit like Larry Clark's work," was contracted in the summer of 1975 by McLaren to photograph the Sex Pistols. This was at a time when McLaren and his partner, Vivienne Westwood, ran a shop called SEX on Kings Road in London that featured men's and women's street fashions inspired by S-M, gay porn, and various fetishes, like bondage trousers, that were both intentionally shocking and knowingly Warholian. But wearing the iconography or style of the homosexual—such as the gay cowboy T-shirts the Pistols would sometimes sport in concert—was apparently not the same thing as subjecting oneself to the stigma of being perceived as homosexual, or being willingly identified as "gay for pay." When Christopherson posed the Pistols to resemble rent boys in a YMCA toilet, McLaren was apparently shocked and threatened by the explicitly homoerotic images, and he turned down the pictures.[26] The photos nevertheless reside as one archival switch point between the queer and punk seventies.

Similarly, Jarman's *Jubilee* is considered by some the first punk movie, and to make it he recruited a number of nonprofessional actors from the punk scene, including Jordan (Pamela Rooke), Adam Ant, and (in a cameo) Siouxsie Sioux. According to Chuck Warner, the punk Steve Treatment guided Jarman through the punk scene, vouching for the gay outsider when necessary.[27] The film, originally intended as an impressionistic documentary of punk London, evolved into a powerful depiction of urban dystopia as seen from the fantastic vantage point of a time-traveling Queen Elizabeth I. A historically and theatrically erudite iteration of the Pistols' "God Save the Queen," *Jubilee* literalized the disjunction between present-day reality and an anachronistic monarchy by juxtaposing Elizabeth with the anarchic punks. The film proved prophetic in a number of ways, but it was not universally well received at first, with Westwood delivering her review on (where else?) a T-shirt: "The most boring and therefore disgusting film . . . a gay boy jerk off through the titillation of his masochistic tremblings. You pointed your nose in the right direction then you wanked."[28] Westwood's rhetorical condensation of Jarman's camera—first onto his nose, then onto his penis—made particularly explicit the structures of cruising and slumming that made the production of the film possible. And yet to freeze the queen/queer at the other end of a voyeuristic lens would prematurely foreclose the transmissions of desire and affect that were clearly at play in both directions, and to which *Jubilee* stands as an important testament. As Peter Hitchcock notes, while "slumming is an ideologeme of class discourse . . . the slummer also fantasizes what the culture must otherwise hide, the ways in which the porous conditions of class augur the concrete possibilities of change."[29] Rough no doubt, but trade no less.

The three-chord *sinthome*

Chiasmus is a good term with which to capture the relationship between antirelational theory and punk. As a rhetorical figure, chiasmus highlights our entrapment within language, from which neither the future nor the past affords any exit. It is this entrapment within language that belligerent punks want to bust out of. Chiasmus is also the rhetorical instantiation of "sexual inversion," perverting the end of linguistic meaning in the same manner as homosexuality perverts the end of sexuality. The inverted elements of chiasmus are apparent in such formulations as Edelman's Wildean description of homosexuality as that which "leads to no good and has no other end than an end to the good as such." Edelman names the socially and sexually inverted subject of queer theory the "sinthomosexual." This word is a condensation of the word *sinthome*, an archaic way of writing the word *symptom* that Lacan began to use in the course of a seminar on James Joyce (primarily because it seems to offer so many opportunities to make his beloved puns), and the word *homosexual*. Edelman's call for us to "accede" to or "embrace" our social role as "sinthomosexuals" contains more than an echo, I would warrant, of Wilde's famous comment, as recorded by Neil Bartlett, about how delicious the accusations made against him at trial would be if he himself were the one who was making them.[30] In other words, in making sense of affinities and disjunctions between the punk and the queer, it may be useful to unlock this condensation of the *sinthome* and the homosexual and, in so doing, restore greater historical specificity and political pertinence to the discourse of political negativity they both augur.

Without seeking to recuperate the death drive for some dialectically positive and progressive project, I take issue with Edelman's conflation of the homosexual with the *sinthome*, that is, with antisocial, countersymbolic *jouissance* as such. As has repeatedly been suggested, the "queer" in queer theory is most supple when it does not take as its sole referent the homosexual desire of classical psychoanalysis. "Queer" bears at least the potential to name a series of historical intersections at which the body and its potential deviations from the social have been assimilated to the figure of the *sinthome*, and several of those intersections seem to connect with the social imaginary of mid- and late 1970s punk, as we have already seen. But if this is the case, then antirelationality is in part a new articulation of deviancy theory and bears an unspoken debt to the literature emerging from radical sociology and cultural studies. This observation is not in itself a criticism, but it does suggest an expanded purview and deeper historical genealogy than that provided by the presentist and ultimately identitarian basis on which Edelman erects sinthomosexuality.

Antirelational theorists argue that the pursuit of *jouissance* is a quest for self-shattering, not for ego stabilization, and that all attempts to domesticate homosexual desire, rendering it socially productive, are therefore quixotic. Calling this approach to homosexual desire "antirelational" is somewhat misleading, insofar as it is in fact a theory of relationality, albeit not the preferred fantasy of social relations most of us possess. It depends rather on the Lacanian assertion that "there's no such thing as a sexual relationship," by which is meant that we do not relate to each other, but to a third term—the other—and to the other's desire.[31] There is, in other words, a relationship, but just not the one we believe there to be. I make this point to clarify that the virtues and faults of antirelationality lie in nothing so simple as the metaphysical question of whether society, the future, or relationality "exists" but, rather, in what the theory enables us to grasp of a reality that can never truly be grasped. In Lacan's presentation, symptom (*sinthome*) and symbol interlock with each other and provide the joint tether between the real and the imaginary. Not dialectical opposites, they are instead two loops in a complex topology of the psyche and the social. Strictly speaking, the *sinthome* is neither within nor without the symbolic order, neither negating nor sustaining it. If we associate the symbolic with closure and ideology, it might be helpful to associate the *sinthome* with flows of affect such as those Edelman identifies with an embrace of the death drive, and which I wish to extend to certain forms of punk performativity.

Edelman's condensation of *sinthome* and homosexuality, I should note, departs from conventional interpretations of Lacan, who did not originally deploy the term to explain homosexual desire. Rather, as Christine Wertheim writes in an economical summary:

> In Lacan's original knotty model, the psyche is (re)presented as a space bounded by the three interlocked rings of the Real, Symbolic, and Imaginary. However . . . Lacan felt compelled to add a fourth ring to the configuration, turning it from a link into a lock. Called the *sinthome* . . . this fourth element—the symptom—is what keeps a psyche locked up. From this perspective, the aim of Lacanian analysis is to unlock the link by breaking the *sinthome*'s hold. . . . Analysis then, as a practice, rather than a theory, is for Lacan simply the operation of this unlocking—the separation of the *sinthome* from the body of the psychic link.[32]

The *sinthome*, however, holds chiasmic properties that are elided by this therapeutic reading insofar as the separation of the *sinthome* from the psyche can also be thought of as the production of the *sinthome* by the psyche. Unlocking can be a matter not merely of "getting rid" of the *sinthome*, but more ambiguously, of "making" the *sinthome*, as is evident in Lacan's observation that *Ulysses* was Joyce's *sinthome*. Insofar as Lacan and Edelman alike associate the *sinthome* with writing, it is subject to the indefinite deferral of meaning to which deconstruction calls our attention. But if the *sinthome* can include countersymbolic writing or inscription such as that ostensibly represented by Joyce's prose, it is also worth asking whether it can be thought of in relation to expressive forms of creativity, such as music and performance, that are not primarily linguistic in structure. And furthermore, if the *sinthome* is a problem, it may also be perversely, a solution. Hence Edelman's ambiguous instructions to "accede" and "embrace," which sound like a kind of resignation, of letting homophobia have its way, but which alternately can be figured as instructions for queer world making. Edelman's term *reproductive futurity* is helpful to the degree that it highlights a central grievance of the homophobic imaginary: that it is society that is obliged to undergo the labor of reproducing itself so that the homosexual may emerge from within it, while the homosexual is a freeloader under no obligation to reproduce society in turn. Edelman's call for queers to accede to this position is persuasive insofar as it girds us to resist the double blackmail of gay marriage and parenting as homonormative sacrifices to the altar of family values. Only by embracing the antagonism we create by our presence can we bring into view the actual labor of queerness in the processes of world making. Queerness is our *Ulysses*, our *sinthome*.

But queerness was also punk's *sinthome* insofar as punk's most powerful affects were employed in unknotting the body from its psychic link to the social. Here Lacan is especially helpful in moving our analysis beyond semiotic readings of punk subcultures by scholars like Hebdige. The emphasis on reading the symbols of punk, we can now see, elides the complex relationship between symbol and symptom. Here I evoke and diverge from the Chicago School sociologist Ned Polsky's admonition that "the researcher should forget about imputing beliefs, feelings, or motives (conscious or otherwise) to deviants on the basis of the origins of words in their argot."[33] From Polsky's perspective, Chance's connecting of the word *punk* with situational homosexuality would be as illegitimate as reading a junkie's slang for heroin ("shit" and "garbage") as signaling unconscious guilt or internalized inferiority. Even Geoff Travis's conscious borrowing of a phrase like *rough trade* for his record label cannot be read, in such a paradigm, as linking punk and queer, because his motivation was primarily to find a name even trashier than the Velvet Underground. But just because the word does not function symbolically does not prevent it from serving as a *sinthome*, and thinking of queer as punk's *sinthome* gets us further down the road of understanding the frozen dialectic between them.

In conducting my research for this project, I have had to explain repeatedly that I am not seeking to prove or disprove that 1970s punk was gay. Although such information would indeed delight me, my principal interest has been in the transmission of affect, specifically a bad or rebellious attitude, through the paraphernalia and symbols of various queer subcultures. Approaching the circulation of homosexuality or queerness as a symptom of culture has proved enormously helpful for making sense of a late 1970s group like the Homosexuals, who were mostly taking the piss out of the predictability of punk, already visible by 1978.[34] In taking punk's flirtation with overt gay symbols to a switch point with the symptom within punk itself, they ended up serving "as figures—within [punk] for the dismantling of [punk] and thus for the death drive it harbors within."

While my reading so far has accepted much of Edelman's argument, I part ways at his ahistorical presentation of the sinthomosexual. There is a fair amount of nostalgia in Edelman's chiasmic description of homosexuality as that which "leads to no good and has no other end than an end to the good as such." In the era of popular and openly gay musical acts like the Scissor Sisters, television programs like *Queer Eye for the Straight Guy*, and even networks like Logo TV, it stretches credulity to maintain that "the homosexual" as a figure always stands in the cultural imagination for pure and uncompromising complicity with the death drive. To the contrary, it seems that Halberstam is persuasive in arguing that queer theory's bad attitude is a secret sharer of the immature, kitschy, and revolting behavior of punks and other uppity antisocial types.

Historicism gets a bad rap especially from psychoanalytic and deconstructionist critics. Some of this rap is deserved, and it may even be, as with Edelman, necessary to critique the fiction of a "motionless 'movement' of historical procession obedient to origins, intentions, and ends whose authority rules over all."[35] The *sinthome* may indeed obey the logic of repetition (the death drive) that undoes such a fantasy of progressive, developmental time, as Edelman argues; but that atemporal kernel of *jouissance* does not obviate historical time as such. Without historical perspective, we are insufficiently defended from the nostalgic impulse to exaggerate the radical negativity of a given symbol such as queer or homosexual desire. The problem of enduring political negativity is only whisked away by an overreliance on a by now hypostatized moment in queer theory.

A more productive response can be found in a recent album by the Soft Pink Truth, the name of which I have paraphrased for the title of this essay. This self-described "comparative analysis of ideological positions in English punk rock and American hardcore songwriting" provided the sonic ambience that enabled me to complete this essay. The title pays homage to a track from the Minutemen's opus, *Double Nickels on the Dime* (1984), a declaration of hard-core purism that serves as an ironic counterpoint to the Soft Pink Truth's musical hybridizations, which consist of ten cover versions produced out of what is described, in the CD cover art, as a "circular rationale vortex": "Reversing time . . . stopping time . . . street credibility . . . distraction from political misery . . . escapist nostalgia . . . dissertation avoidance . . . suspended dialectics . . . regressive fantasy . . . sweating to the oldies."[36] Such self-parody and free association is suggestive rather than definitive in making a connection between historicist and rhetorical approaches. The Soft Pink Truth's cover versions canvas the range of sometimes ugly feelings that survive in the punk archive, from Nervous Gender's jittery "sex worker rant" ("Confession") to the Angry Samoans' "quasi-parodic hate speech" ("Homo-Sexual"). Like Patti Smith, the Soft Pink Truth performs not so much an ideology as an ambience, one in which the question of political negativity is raised but never definitively answered. The album instead constructs what Josh Kun has called an "audiotopia," a space within sound that both mirrors and negates the world that produced it.[37]

I persist in locating such efforts to produce a usable past between punk and queer, both as a political negativity and an emotive, affective unity. In this, it seems, the songs are more faithful to Hocquenghem's Freudo-Marxian synthesis of the early 1970s than are the antirelational theorists. In chapter 6 of *Homosexual Desire*, "The Homosexual Struggle," Hocquenghem leaves open the space for the delinking of the homosexual and the *sinthome* in a revolutionary praxis founded on a transgressive "subject group," a term he adopts in contrast to the ordinary condition of being a "subjected group": "In the subject group, the opposition between the collective and the individual is transcended; the subject group is stronger than death because the institutions appear to it to be mortal. The homosexual subject group— circular and horizontal, annular and with no signifier—knows that civilization alone is mortal."[38]

"Homosexual desire," he adds in what amounts to a preemptive riposte to Edelman's identification of queer theory with the death drive some three decades later, "is neither on the side of death nor on the side of life; it is the killer of civilized egos."[39] Rather than opposing politics, relationality, and the future in toto, Hocquenghem merely rejected their expression prior to revolutionary transformation.

It is important to remember the original historical context of Hocquenghem's homo-sexual antirelationality because when it is invoked—especially in the early twenty-first century when the possibility of socialist revolution appears to be off the table, to put it mildly—it gives queer theory's rejection of reformist and utopian politics an entirely different meaning. We seem to succumb very easily to a disorienting left melancholy that attempts to substitute a radical critical negativity for the absence of a robust radical politics. In saying this I am not advocating Hocquenghem's particular vision of emancipation. But we may well begin to think about the relations between punk and queer outside of Hocquenghem's own limited horizons of the gay Western male. Chiasmus does such important work in both the Sex Pistols' and Edelman's iterations of "no future" because it apparently stabilizes the infinite play of inversions into a neat paradox to which, as Edelman repeatedly argues, we might ultimately accede. The verbs *accede* and *embrace* constitute critical pivots in Edelman's polemic insofar as they appear to ground his radicalism in something we can do while ensuring that this thing we can do retains its grammatical radicalism only *within* chiasmus. *Accession* and *embrace* serve as potentially positive terms for Edelman only as long as they remain fully reversible. But accession is itself a chiasmic inversion insofar as it can lead *either* to participation in the fantasy of reproductive futurity or the embrace of its stigmatized core of negativity, variously labeled the *sinthome*, the death drive, *jouissance*, and homosexuality itself. By rethinking the grouping or networking expressed across the social figurations of punk and queer in a nonidentitarian way, we may be able to uncouple the *sinthome*-homosexual metonymy, which compels us to see social negativity in an unnecessarily limited frame. Expanding the networks and linkages that produce collective subjects in the present is neither a return to a 1970s-style revolution à la Patty Hearst nor a dewy-eyed faith in perpetual progress. It is a politics of a quite different sort than that which Edelman both rightly disparages and wrongly associates with politics as such.

Notes

The author would like to thank Henry Abelove, Heather Lukes, David Watson, Sheila Ghose, Kevin Murphy, and two anonymous reviewers for comments that strengthened this essay.

1   *The Tomorrow Show with Tom Snyder: Punk and New Wace* (Shout! Factory, 2006), DVD.
2   Lee Edelman, *No Future: Queer Theory and the Death Drive* (Durham, NC: Duke University Press, 2004).
3   Lauren Berlant, *The Queen of America Goes to Washington City: Essays on Sex and Citizenship* (Durham, NC: Duke University Press, 1997), 262.
4   Guy Hocquenghem, *Homosexual Desire* (Durham, NC: Duke University Press, 1993); Leo Bersani, *Homos* (Cambridge, MA: Harvard University Press, 1995).
5   Hocquenghem, *Homosexual Desire*, 137. The English translation of this work contains a useful preface by Jeffrey Weeks that places Hocquenghem within the political and cultural context of his day. For more of an assessment of his relation to queer theory, see the introduction to Tim Dean and Christopher Lane, eds., *Homosexuality and Psychoanalysis* (Chicago: University of Chicago Press, 2001), 3–42.
6   Leo Bersani, "Is the Rectum a Grave?" *October* 43 (1987): 205–15.
7   John Brenkman, "Queer Post-politics," *Narrative* 10 (2002): 174–80.
8   Edelman, *No Future*. 22; emphasis original.
9   Elizabeth Freeman, ed., "Queer Temporalities," special issue, *GLQ* 12 (2007).
10 The *sinthome* was the topic of Lacan's Seminar 23, given in 1975–76. Jacques Lacan, *Livre XXIII: Le sinthome; 1975–1976*, ed. Jacques-Alain Miller, Le Séminaire de Jacques Lacan (Paris: Seuil, 2005). In deference to readers unfamiliar with psychoanalysis, I present the concept here with the aid of (undoubtedly simplified) English-language exegesis.
11 Robert Caserio et al., "Forum: Conference Debates: The Antisocial Thesis in Queer Theory," *Proceedings of the Modern Language Studies Association* 121 (2006): 824. In a comparable vein, in the *GLQ* forum on queer temporality, Annamarie Jagose recommends that we "acknowledge the intellectual traditions in which time has also been influentially thought and experienced as cyclical, interrupted, multilayered, reversible, stalled—and not always in contexts easily recuperated as queer." Carolyn Dinshaw et al., "Theorizing Queer Temporalities: A Roundtable Discussion," *GLQ* 13 (2007): 186–87.
12 José Estaban Muñoz has written about the intersections between punk and queer subcultural spaces in the photographs of Kevin McCarty. See José Esteban Muñoz, "Impossible Spaces: Kevin McCarty's *The Chameleon Club*," *GLQ* 11 (2005): 427–36.
13 Rob Young, *Rough Trade: Labels Unlimited* (London: Black Dog, 2006), 11.
14 For more on *punk* as a keyword, see Tavia Nyong'o, "Punk'd Theory," *Social Text* 23 (2005): 19–34.
15 "For, at the heart of the punk subculture, forever arrested, lies this frozen dialectic between black and white cultures—a dialectic which beyond a certain point (i.e. ethnicity) is incapable of renewal, trapped, as it is, within its own history, imprisoned within its own irreducible antinomies." Dick Hebdige, *Subculture: The Meaning of Style* (London: Routledge, 1979), 70.

16   Alex Needham, "Jon Savage," *Butt*, Winter 2006, 62.

17   The Ramones, "53rd and 3rd," on *The Ramones* (1976), Audio CD, Sire.

18   Judith Halberstam, *In a Queer Time and Place: Transgender Bodies, Subcultural Lives* (New York: New York University Press, 2005); Mary Celeste Kearney, "The Missing Links: Riot Grrrl—Feminism—Lesbian Culture," in *Sexing the Groove: Popular Music and Gender*, ed. Sheila Whiteley (New York: Routledge, 1997) 207–29; Cynthia Fuchs, "If I Had a Dick: Queers, Punks, and Alternative Acts," in *Mapping the Beat: Popular Music and Contemporary Theory*, eds. Thomas Swiss, John Sloop, and Andrew Herman (Malden, MA: Blackwell, 1998) 101–18.

19   Jon Savage, *England's Dreaming: Anarchy, Sex Pistols, Punk Rock, and Beyond* (New York: St. Martin's, 2002).

20   Caserio et al., "Forum," 824.

21   Michael S. Foldy, *The Trials of Oscar Wilde: Deviance, Morality, and Late-Victorian Society* (New Haven, CT: Yale University Press, 1997), 17.

22   Greil Marcus, *Lipstick Traces: A Secret History of the Twentieth Century* (Cambridge, MA: Harvard University Press, 1989).

23   Paul Gilroy, *"There Ain't No Black in the Union Jack": The Cultural Politics of Race and Nation* (London: Hutchinson, 1987).

24   Caserio et al., "Forum," 822.

25   Simon Reynolds, *Rip It Up and Start Again: Postpunk, 1978–1984* (New York: Penguin, 2006).

26   Simon Ford, *Wreckers of Civilisation: The Story of Coum Transmissions and Throbbing Gristle* (London: Black Dog, 2000), 4–10, 5–13. Some of the photos are reproduced in Savage, *England's Dreaming*.

27   Chuck Warner, personal conversation with author, August 13, 2005.

28   Quoted by Tony Peake in "Derek Jarman's *Jubilee* (1977)," an essay accompanying the Criterion Collection release of *Jubilee*, www.criterion.com (accessed May 10, 2007).

29   Peter Hitchcock, "Slumming," in *Passing: Identity and Interpretation in Sexuality, Race, and Religion*, eds. María C. Sánchez and Linda Schlossberg (New York: New York University Press, 2001), 184–85.

30   Neil Bartlett, *Who Was That Man? A Present for Mr. Oscar Wilde* (London: Serpent's Tail, 1988).

31   Bruce Fink, *The Lacanian Subject: Between Language and Jouissance* (Princeton, NJ: Princeton University Press, 1995), 104–25.

32   Christine Wertheim, "To Be or a Knot to Be," *Cabinet* 22 (2006): 35.

33   Ned Polsky, "Research Method, Morality, and Criminology," 1967, in *The Subcultures Reader*, ed. Ken Gelder (New York: Routledge, 2005), 64.

34   The Homosexuals, *Astral Glamour* (Messthetics, 2004), audio CD.

35   Dinshaw et al., "Theorizing Queer Temporalities," 180.

36   The Soft Pink Truth, *Do You Want New Wave or Do You Want the Soft Pink Truth?* (Tigerbeat6, 2004), audio CD.

37   Josh Kun, *Audiotopia: Music, Race, and America* (Berkeley: University of California Press, 2005).

38   Hocquenghem, *Homosexual Desire*, 147.

39   Ibid., 15.

Chapter 15

Elizabeth Freeman

TURN THE BEAT AROUND: SADOMASOCHISM, TEMPORALITY, HISTORY

Elizabeth Freeman is Professor of English at the University of California, Davis. The author of *The Wedding Complex: Forms of Belonging in Modern American Culture* (2002) and *Time Binds: Queer Temporalities, Queer Histories* (2010), Freeman's work explores the intersections of gender, sexuality, and temporality. The following essay originally appeared in *differences: A Journal of Feminist Cultural Studies* in 2008.

In "Turn the Beat Around," Freeman considers the sexually marginalized and under-theorized practice of sadomasochism within temporal terms. She argues for an understanding of sado-masochism as the deployment of bodily sensations wherein the subject's "normative timing" is denaturalized and deconstructed. Through an analysis of Isaac Julien's 1992 film *The Attendant*, Freeman argues that sadomasochistic practices function as "an erotic time machine" that reveals the interweaving and often silenced histories of sexuality, race, nationalism, and imperialism. She suggests that sadomasochism functions within "slow time," a configuration of the temporal that is pre-capitalist and therefore non-normative. Through this process, the queer body transforms into a historiographic tool whereby historical trauma is addressed and acknow-ledged through erotic pleasure. Specifically, sadomasochism elucidates in an affective way the temporal dynamics of power, sexuality, and the possibility of alternative historiographies.

SEXUAL MINORITIES HAVE in many ways been produced by, or at least emerged in tandem with, a sense of "modern" temporality. By this I mean to describe more than just the way that gay men, lesbians, and other "perverts" have served as figures of either civilization's decline or a sublimely futuristic release from nature. Instead, I mean that far from merely functioning as *analogies* for temporal catastrophe, dissident sexual communities and the erotic practices defining them are *historically* tied to the emergence of a kind of time—slow time.

To historicize the correlation between a particular way of being sexual in the world and a particular experience of time, it is helpful to remember that modern temporality engendered a new set of bodily sensations. Critics at least as far back as Walter Benjamin have recognized that modern time, whose emergence he locates in the latter half of the nineteenth century, is a kind of double-time, in which the quick pace of industry shocks a sensory system trained by the slow pace of older production processes.[1] Arguably, of course, this slow temporality is a retroactive formation, an experience of time felt as a lack in the present but imagined as preceding the staccato pace of modernity—particularly as new generations of "moderns" have less and less access to older production processes. But if we follow Benjamin's important insight into how modernity *feels*, we can see another site where slow time seems to offer some kind of respite from the emerging rhythms of mechanized life: the time of emotions themselves.

Thus, in counterpoint to the time of factory life in the antebellum United States, another set of sensations and corporeal forms were imagined, or even felt, as impediments to or bulwarks against the relentless movement of progress. As Dana Luciano argues, in the wake of industrialization in the United States, mourning was newly reconceptualized as an experience outside of ordinary time, as eternal, recurrent, even sacred.[2] But so, I would argue, were any number of other affective modes. Mid-nineteenth-century writers figured maternal love, domestic bliss, romantic attachments, and even bachelorhood as havens from a heartless world and, more importantly, as sensations that moved according to their own beat.[3] This trope is different from the second-wave feminist argument that domestic *labor* was actually a precapitalist production process. (In fact, household manuals from Catharine Beecher and Harriet Beecher Stowe's 1869 *The American Woman's Home* onward show that housework, too, was reorganized according to the principles of time management and productivity, even if women remained outside of the wage system.) In contrast, the emerging *discourse* of domesticity, which included but went beyond labor relations, validated and, in Foucaultian terms, "implanted" a set of feelings—love, security, harmony, peace, romance, sexual satisfaction, motherly instincts—in part by figuring them as timeless, as primal, as a human condition located in and emanating from the psyche's interior.

In this sense, the nineteenth century's celebrated sentimental heart, experienced by its owner as the bearer of archaic or recalcitrant sensations, was the laboring body's double, the flip side of the coin of industrialization. Mourning and romance, empathy and affection, even "family time," were not segmented into clock time, and in this sense, they countered "work time," even if they were also a dialectical product of it. As Eli Zaretsky writes, "The family, attuned to the natural rhythms of eating, sleeping, and child care, can never be wholly synchronized with the mechanized tempo of industrial capitalism" (33). Familial tempos are, if not quite "natural," less amenable to the speeding up and micromanagement that would later characterize the Taylorist system. It is not too much of a leap, I hope, to suggest that Freud's concept of the unconscious later emerged as an even more unruly temporal zone. Appearing in the late nineteenth and early twentieth centuries, as the market put an ever greater premium on novelty, the Freudian unconscious refused to make an experience obsolete or to relegate it to the past. Within the Freudian paradigm of *Nachträglichkeit*, memory recorded the signs of an event when the subject could not consciously process its meaning and preserved these signs for future uses. Freud also reconfigured sexology's perverts, formerly understood as evolutionary throwbacks, as slaves to this unconscious. Psychologizing what had once been biological paradigms, Freud identified "perverse" sexual practices as a kind of stuck or frozen normal behavior: orality, anality, fetishism, and so on are, in the Freudian itinerary, places to visit on the way to reproductive, genital heterosexuality, but not places to stay for long. Henry Abelove and Paul Morrison have also described the way that, as erotic life began to assume the contours of mechanized productivity, specific sexual practices came to be seen as "foreplay," acceptable en route to intercourse but not as a substitute for it.[4] If the denizens of domestic sentimentality resisted the production-time of industrial labor, then, we might say that perverts—melancholically attached to obsolete erotic objects or fetishes they ought to have outgrown, or repeating unproductive bodily behaviors over and over—refused the commodity-time of speedy manufacture and planned obsolescence.

What I want to emphasize here is that sexual deviants, now seen as creatures whose very minds had gone temporally awry, were unimaginable before the modern regime of "progress," a discourse even more totalizing than the "civilizing process" championed by evolutionism. With these changes as background, I want to focus on sadomasochism, an extremely marginalized sexual practice that I understand in predominantly temporal terms, as a deployment of bodily sensations through which the subject's normative timing is disaggregated and denaturalized. As I will argue later in this essay through an analysis of Isaac Julien's 1992 short film *The Attendant*, sadomasochistic sex performs the dialectic of a quick-paced modernity and a slower "premodern," the latter indexed by any number of historical periods. Seen as a kind of erotic time machine, sadomasochism offers sexual metacommentary on the dual emergence of modernity and its others, on the entangled histories of race, nationhood, and imperialism as well as sexuality. Moreover, S/M does this work in simultaneously corporeal and symbolic ways, turning the queer body into a historiographic instrument: more than a cumulative effect of traumatic and/or insidious power relations, the body in sadomasochistic ritual becomes a means of addressing history in an idiom of pleasure.[5]

The beat goes on: timing sadomasochism

Sadomasochism is a sexually "minor" practice, an erotic dialectic between two or more people, that ostensibly focuses on the ritualized exchange of power.[6] But as originally figured by the Marquis de Sade in his fictional writings, S/M also shuttles (or plays at shuttling) between the modern time of the French Revolution and the non- (or pre-) modern time of the ancien régime: Simone de Beauvoir writes that members of the disempowered French aristocracy of which Sade had been a member revived their status of "lone and sovereign feudal despot" symbolically, in the bedroom (16). Indeed, not only did Sade resurrect a "premodern" social system in his orgiastic scenes, but he also wrote his major works in an era that saw the most revolutionary and secular experiment with the Western sociotemporal order—the installation of the French Republican Calendar from 1793 to 1806. Though this new calendar was made law in 1793, it began retroactively on September 22, 1792, replacing the Christian dating framework that began with the birth of Christ. It interrupted the rhythm of the Christian Sabbath by instituting ten-day weeks, while also standardizing the length of months to thirty days and recalibrating days, hours, minutes, and seconds on the decimal system.

Sade, then, lived through, wrote within, and reinvented sex at a moment when time itself was starkly revealed as not eternal or "timeless," but contingent and rationalized.[7] Even as his sexual reinventions depend upon the trappings of the ancien régime, in many ways they also depend upon the Republican conception of time as arbitrary and heterogeneous, and thus malleable, even retroactively. In fact, it is fair to say that Sade used sexual practice itself to measure, mediate, and mimic the historical possibility of competing temporal schemas. Beauvoir, for instance, remarks that within a sadomasochistic scene, a certain depersonalization is mandatory, such that mirrors become central to Sade's sex scenes: the Sadean sadist, she writes, must not "coincide" exactly with her own movements, nor should the masochist merge with his own emotions, or "freedom and consciousness would be lost in the rapture of the flesh" (43). In other words, various techniques of visual distantiation, which in contemporary S/M culture might also include the blindfold, the strobe light, or hallucinogenic drugs, produce a temporal noncoincidence between action and result that, in turn, make possible the awareness of "self," albeit as object. Here, S/M introduces an interval, a liberating gap between effect and a cause one might or might not apprehend as a self.

In sadomasochism, the historical asynchrony achieved by sexually allegorizing a lost form of imperial power meets the temporal asynchrony achieved through such tools as the mirror. In this juncture lies a potential for sex *itself* to become a kind of historiography, perhaps even an "ahistoriography" (Rohy). I recognize that this position seems diametrically opposite from the one taken by Sade's most rigorous admirers, who tend to see him as relentlessly opposed to all things purportedly durational: familial generations, inherited property, even literature.[8] But in my view, in its very insistence upon reanimating historically specific social roles, in the historical elements of its theatrical language, and in using the body as an instrument to rearrange time, Sadean sex becomes a kind of *écriture historique*. It becomes a form of writing history with the body in which the linearity of history may be called into question, but the past does not thereby cease to exist. In this respect, Sade was tacitly ahead of current queer theory, which has shied away from exploring any convergence between this stigmatized form of sexual practice and the seemingly weightier matters of time and history.

Backbeat: theorizing sadomasochism

Queer theory has recently made a striking temporal and historiographical turn.[9] But sadomasochism's absence from this corpus, though S/M was once a staple of queer theorizing "beyond identity," deserves some attention. One reason for this absence may be that S/M was so central to a relatively ahistorical, deconstructive, and psychoanalytic queer theory that was itself responding critically to historically determinist or monolithic analyses. For example, some defenders of sadomasochism refuted Andrea Dworkin and Catharine MacKinnon's description of male sexuality as primally and inevitably rapacious, a description that cast male sexuality as historically unchanging. Furthermore, many radical lesbian feminists and critical race theorists had condemned the sadomasochistic use of icons from the Spanish Inquisition, slavery, and the Holocaust as a perpetuation of genocidal culture.[10] In response, white gay male theorists suggested that the real force of S/M lay in its capacity to undermine psychic structures rather than to shore up historically asymmetrical power relations. Leo Bersani, for instance, has famously argued for the refusal of sex to figure or guarantee an ideal sociality. Instead, he deduces from Freud, Blanchot, Bataille, and to a certain degree from Dworkin and MacKinnon themselves that all sexuality is fundamentally masochistic, insofar as desire and erotic contact threaten the very structure of the ego (*Freudian* 38).[11] Like Lee Edelman, whose recent work on futurity draws from him, Bersani severs the links between erotics and psychic wholeness, sex and revolution, fucking and utopia.

Even when Bersani's early work does invoke the relationship between sexual practice and history, it is only to point out that in Freud the libido's violent disruptions are not the product of a timeless human nature, but rather echo earlier sexual events in the subject's life, so that the unconscious actually contains a "history of the self's structure" (*A Future* 58).[12] Yet, because Freud explains the formation of selfhood temporally, but not quite historically, the undigested past that threatens the coherent self is not a moment experienced collectively; it is merely one point on an individual, if universalized, timeline of developmental events.

Preserving this impetus to think of sex as a politically significant refusal of sociality, in his later work Bersani remarks that sadomasochism detaches the master–slave relation from historically specific "economic and racial superstructures," thereby revealing the sheer eroticism of that relation (*Homos* 89). He hints only in the negative that S/M could potentially reconstitute historical analysis, calling it a bad-faith "theatricalized imitation of history" that proceeds as if collective events could be shorn of the fantasies that animate sadomasochism (90). He does not seem to consider S/M a catalyst for any genuinely historicist inquiry or a mode of connecting otherwise separate historical moments, any more than he considers sex itself a blueprint for community: for Bersani, sex is fundamentally antirelational, both spatially and temporally. Thus it has been easy for critics who would condemn queer theory in the name of a more properly historicist analysis to fasten upon sadomasochism as a socio-sexual and critical fad whose passing ought to be viewed with relief.[13] In this light, the queer theoretical turn toward metacommentary on history and historiography, and away from the psychically negating power of a particular sex act, looks on the face of it like critical and, perhaps more importantly, political progress.

In fact, there is something of a schism in S/M theory itself, and even within individual theorists, between a will to condemn sadomasochism's historical trappings, as second-wave feminists and critical race theorists have tended to do, and a will to ignore or trivialize them, as white gay male theorists who use it as a paradigm for the antirelational thesis have done. But are we truly locked into a choice between viewing sadomasochism as either an equivalent to the historical forces that oppress or the agent of their complete dematerialization and privatization into psychic drives? I would suggest that we need to continue to theorize S/M, to historicize its theorizations, and, most urgently, to *theorize its historicisms*. Even Bersani eventually points out that S/M refuses the very detachment from economic and racial superstructures that he claims for it earlier, insofar as it "profoundly—and in spite of itself—argues for the continuity between [historically specific] political structures of oppression and the body's erotic economy" (*Homos* 90). In this remark, which posits a continuity between history and eroticism rather than a simple causal relationship, bodily response is somehow linked to history. Following this logic, I would like to posit that S/M may bring out the historicity of bodily response itself. By the "historicity" of eroticism, I mean not only the conditioning of sexual response over time, as second-wave feminists and critical race theorists would have it, but the uses of physical sensation to break apart the present into fragments of time that may not be one's "own" or to feel one's present world as both conditioned and contingent. How might we link up sadomasochism's temporary destruction of the subject, then, to the uses of *time*—irreducible to history yet indispensable for any formalization or apprehension of it? The last decade of queer theory has suggested that queer spatial practices open the identity-bound subject up to other coalitional possibilities, other kinds of selves, even to diagonal cuts across the social field. My question, then, is this: do queer uses of time, including but not limited to the queer-of-color uses of time I shall discuss in relation to *The Attendant*, open the subject up to other tenses, to diagonal cuts across the historical field?

Queer theory written by white lesbians offers one way into the question: for these critics, sadomasochism is a mode of (re)constituting a posthumanist self that, in contrast to the ego central to Bersani's analysis, may never have been coherent enough to shatter in the first place. Thus scholars and artists such as Kathy Acker, Lynda Hart, and Ann Cvetkovich have described sadomasochism as a phantasmatic return to a sexual trauma for the purpose of organizing it into an experience.[14] Revisiting S/M's "backwardness" in terms of Freudian *Nachträglichkeit*, Hart has provided the most sophisticated articulation of sadomasochism as a form of psychic healing from sexual trauma. To describe the effect of a sadomasochistic reworking of rape or incest, she invokes Lacan's "future anterior," the grammatical tense expressing something that is not yet present but "will have been so" in the future: "[W]hat takes place [now . . .] is not the past definite of what was, because it is no more, nor is it the present perfect of what has been in what I am, but rather the future anterior of what I will have been or what I am in the process of becoming" (Clément 123; qtd. in Hart 161). In other words, in a sadomasochistic "scene," at least one player gets to articulate a future in terms of the changes that take place as she (re)encounters a sexually violent past. The scene remakes her identity neither as the unchangeable victim of trauma nor as a hero who transcends her past, but as a *process* that can be recognized only retrospectively from the stance of an imagined future in which she is freed from torment but still capable of change. For Hart, who follows Cathy Caruth's theories of trauma, the sadist is *witness to* as well as *executor of* violence, which is also key to this temporal Möbius strip, for this witness secures a different "will have been" for the survivor by embodying that retrospective stance: as with Beauvoir's description of Sade, the witness turns a certain visual distantiation into the kind of temporal dislocation that can secure an open future. In this sense, Hart's analysis seizes upon Sade's depersonalizing techniques as means not only of producing temporal dissonance in the present, but of recasting the future in terms other than those dictated by the past. Here and in other lesbian–queer formulations, sadomasochistic release may have a function somewhat akin to what Luciano attributes to nineteenth-century sentimental culture: just as the mourner slows time down and experiences this slowing as a return to an eternal human condition, the masochist's sensations seem to alter the flow of time so that there is an "after" to violence appearing as its "before," a consensual might-have-been triumphing over a personal history of being victimized.

However problematically redemptive the white lesbian-feminist theoretical move might be in Bersani's or Edelman's view, it is important for my purposes because it restores a temporal axis to what, in the white gay male argument, tends to be S/M's largely structural role as a force of negation. This strand of lesbian queer theory acknowledges, albeit often implicitly, that sadomasochism is a, perhaps *the*, set of sexual practices that most self-consciously manipulates time. But these theorists have predominantly focused on S/M's relationship to the family romance, specifically to incest—and thus not to the signifiers freighted with the more legibly public history that frequently mark sadomasochistic sex. It was earlier, so-called second-wave and third world feminists who in their very condemnations actually confronted the way that sadomasochistic fantasies and/or practices index national and imperial pasts. In their view, using the trappings of violent and even genocidal historical moments was tantamount to repeating them.

Of course, the argument that sadomasochism's "historical" costumes, props, and reenactments aggrandize personal pain by connecting it to collective suffering is not obsolete, nor is an understanding that S/M performs the statement "the personal is political" and thus visually sutures individual trauma to a historically specific structure of systematic oppression. But whatever the uses of Holocaust, slave, or Inquisitor paraphernalia do—whether one approves or disapproves of them—they certainly enact a kind of "time traveling." S/M roles move their players back and forth between some kind of horrific *then* in the past and some kind of redemptive *now* in the present, allegedly in the service of pleasure and a freer future. Sadomasochistic eroticism, then, whatever its moral valences, depends on two linked temporal phenomena. One is a feeling of return to an archaic and more chaotic psychic place, often allegorized as a historical moment that is definitively over: for instance, the powerlessness of a masochist's infancy can be depersonalized and displaced somewhat if it is costumed as an antebellum enslavement he did not go through literally. But conversely, sadomasochism can also aim for a certain visceral fusion, a point of somatic contact between a single erotic body in the present tense and an experience coded as both public and past: for instance, a modern-day Jew might participate in a reenactment of some horror from the Holocaust, experiencing anti-Semitism in more scripted and overt ways than she does in her everyday life, testing her limits, feeling a corporeal, painful, and/or even pleasurable link to her ancestors. Here, the aim is not displacement, but a certain condensation of public and private, collective and individual subjectivities.

In this latter respect, S/M might be a way of feeling historical that exposes the limits of bourgeois-sentimental emotional reactions to historical events.[15] Yet it also refuses to eschew feelings altogether as a mode of knowledge. In other words, S/M, as affect corporealized, rings some changes on what it might mean to theorize historical consciousness—a slippery concept, but one that I take to mean both a latitudinal understanding of individual experience as part of a contingent set of institutional structures (as in Fredric Jameson's "cognitive mapping") and a longitudinal way of connecting that experience to those in a collective past or future, albeit in a relationship other than simple cause and effect. Sadomasochist players may implicitly insist on the body's role, and even the role of sexual pleasure, in such consciousness, for sadomasochism reanimates the erotic dimension of affect that is both solicited and repressed in sentiments like nostalgia, patriotism, or pride in one's heritage. Despite the centrality of sadomasochism to what Eve Sedgwick has called a "paranoid criticism" that often seems to insist on a separation between pleasure and analytic rigor, eroticism and historical memory, S/M relentlessly physicalizes the encounter with history and thereby contributes to a "reparative" criticism that takes up the materials of a traumatic past and remixes them in the interests of new possibilities for being and knowing. Or at least Isaac Julien seems to think so.

A text is being beaten: *The Attendant* and the Marquis de Sade

Isaac Julien's film *The Attendant* was originally made for the BBC series *Time-Code*, which invited filmmakers to produce short, dialogue-free films using the then-new digital technology of Digital D1 (Julien 120). It also appeared within the first wave of what eventually became the New Queer Cinema. This term, apparently coined by film critic B. Ruby Rich, encompassed films that eschewed gay identity as a point of departure or return and instead represented same-sex relations in terms of acts, situations, aesthetics, and unpredictable historical or social collisions.[16] To describe the New Queer Cinema somewhat overschematically, it generally avoided individual coming-out narratives, realistic depictions of urban gay social milieux, and other "expressive" narrative or filmic conventions that would stabilize or contain homoeroticism, correlate particular bodies to particular desires, or reduce erotic practice to sexual identity. It also occasionally, though certainly not always, revealed and troubled the role of whiteness and Western nationalisms in dominant constructions of homosexuality.[17] And crucially, the New Queer Cinema engaged in what Rich called "a reworking of history with social constructionism very much in mind [. . .] a new historiography," about which less has since been written than one might expect (54, 56).[18]

In keeping with what might be called the New Queer Cinema's anti-identitarian (anti) formalism, *The Attendant* features a situational sexual encounter occurring in the off-hours of a museum, a soundtrack shorn of dialogue or voiceover, a fragmented storyline, and characters who travel outside of diegetic time. This film also posits, extremely controversially during the last throes of the "sex wars" of the 1980s and early 1990s, that a black British man might willingly incorporate the iconography of the transatlantic slave trade into his sexual fantasies and activities. When *The Attendant* was first shown, many reviewers saw colonialist history as some kind of catalyst for contemporary sadomasochism, or the latter as a repetition of the former, and read the film as a rebuke to the New Queer Cinema itself. As one reviewer declared, "Insofar as a passion for historical revisionism can be judged a true test of New

Queer cinema, Julien lets us know that he's only queer by half. Some histories are simply a lot harder to revise than others" (Burston 65).

Yet the film's most remarkable quality for a millennial queer audience, over ten years later, may be that it explores sadomasochism as a means not of revising the past but of meeting up with it in the first place. That is, *The Attendant* exploits rather than apologizes for the "historical" excesses of sadomasochistic practices, the subject about which sadomasochism's most radical theoreticians and defenders have remained so silent. Julien seems to recognize that sadomasochism is an unusual sexual practice not only because its rise and elaboration can be traced to a particular historical figure (the Marquis de Sade) and moment in time (the French Revolution) but also because it is a hyperbolically historical, even metahistorical way of having sex. For *The Attendant* bravely solicits the possibilities I have described. It suggests that affect and eroticism themselves may be queer insofar as they refuse to acquiesce in ordinary ways to industrial, commodity, or "modern" time. It intimates that sadomasochism overtly engages with the dialectic between an era's dominant temporal modality and other historical moments and their temporal fields. And it gestures toward the possibility of encountering specific historical moments viscerally, thereby refusing these moments the closure of pastness.

In this eight-minute short, a museum guard, a middle-aged man of African descent played by Thomas Baptiste and referred to in the credits only as the Attendant, has a sexual encounter with a white man played by John Wilson, called the Visitor. Their attraction to one another takes place in relation to F.A. Biard's 1833 abolitionist painting "Slaves on the West Coast of Africa," which is displayed in the museum. This painting, the film's first image, shows a slave market. There, a white, presumably European man straddles a prone, presumably African man, as other black and white men look on or continue their business. In the periphery of this scene, more white men whip, bind, inspect, and brand other black men. During an ordinary day on the job, the Attendant meets the seductive gaze of the Visitor, and the Biard painting suddenly and literally comes alive. It metamorphoses into a tableau vivant of an interracial sexual orgy, with participants posed exactly as they were on the canvas, only now wearing modern S/M gear. After the museum finally closes, the Attendant and the Visitor consummate their lust by whipping one another in a room off the main gallery—or the Attendant may simply imagine this happening; the film leaves this ambiguous.

On the face of it, *The Attendant* is clearly a filmic response to specific critics and intends to trouble several different early 1990s audiences. In the moment of its release, it questioned contemporary antiracist feminist accounts of interracial sadomasochism as a simple repetition and extension of violence against people of color, asking black and white men to examine the traumatic histories encoded in their interracial desires without demanding that they simply give these desires up. In this respect, it also interrogated Kobena Mercer's critique of Robert Mapplethorpe's photographs of black and white men, some in sadomasochistic poses, which Mercer described as fetishistic and racist.[19] And the film critiqued Marlon Riggs's 1989 *Tongues Untied*, which vilified sadomasochism as a white thing and proclaimed that black men loving black men was *the* revolutionary act. *The Attendant* answers Riggs, ironically, with a film containing no dialogue, in which tongues (and bodies) may be tied but speak volumes anyway. Yet Julien's film has much to say about sadomasochism beyond reclaiming the right of black men to fantasize about it and to practice it across the color line, important as that project was and continues to be. Fittingly enough for a film without dialogue, it does not make its claims for sadomasochism on the level of content; it eschews both Riggs's verbal polemic and his straightforward presentation of sexually proper activities. As José Esteban Muñoz has shown in his discussion of *Looking for Langston* (1988), Julien's consummate formalism is part of his counterhistoriographic work: "[T]he concept of time and space that is generated [in *Looking for Langston*] occupies overlapping temporal and geographic coordinates that we can understand as a queer black cultural imaginary [. . .]. Its filaments are historically specific and the overall project is more nearly *trans*historical" (*Disidentifications* 60).

Seen in this light, *The Attendant* brings out a certain formal dialectic within sadomasochism, one that hyperbolically clarifies the *temporal* aspects of power and domination and yet also offers new modes of temporal apprehension and historical consciousness. How does it do this? Hart has written that S/M's "(form)ality depends on a stillness, a waiting that is acted out through both the suspense of deferred gratifications [and] the reenactment of suspense within the sexual scene itself" (103). In other words, sadomasochistic sex pivots on the oxymoron of acting out a passive position: inaction becomes a form of action as the receiver, often forced to lie still, anticipates physical contact or receives it in an unguarded moment. At the same time, following the logic of Hart's analysis, S/M spatializes the temporal rupture of a surprise into something more pictorial, something that is not so much a reenactment but a momentarily arrested presentation, as if for the first time, of a trauma that the player may have lived through but has not yet fully experienced. In the larger argument of which Hart's remark is a part, S/M demands a witness, someone else for whom trauma becomes a spectacle observed at one remove, and is then "handed back" as a legible event to the one who survived it so that she may conjoin it with the moving stream of her life's events. Hart's complicated "stillness" could as easily be a description of *The Attendant*, for Julien exploits film's doubled form, a moving narrative composed of still pictures (or, in the computer-enhanced part of the piece, pixels).

As much as *The Attendant* is concerned with sexual politics, then, it also explores the relationship between film and the static "high arts" of painting, line drawing, and sculpture, which appeared historically prior to the moving, popular art of film, yet continue to inform it even as filmic techniques revivify the still arts. Julien's film is a striking meditation on the passive and active modes not only of sex, but also of perception: it explores the dialectic between contemplation and intervention as they inflect sadomasochistic scenes and then open these scenes into history. For the art forms Julien explores require different and often competing modes of apprehension. In the Kantian tradition, still art solicits a single temporal mode, the slow time of contemplation that lifts the viewer out of her historical moment and into some eternal, disinterested realm of understanding. While film can engage this perceptual practice to a certain extent, it also mobilizes other ways of receiving its sensory input. Crucially, it both solicits a certain bodily mimicry in its audiences and formally reiterates historically specific gestures and bodily experiences. For instance, the material of the projected film negative, segments strung into duration, mirrors the factory assembly line and even, it has been argued, the stopwatch time of Taylorist projects aimed at improving human efficiency.[20] To give another example of how cinematic modes register and reiterate the bodily impact of macrosocial change, the genre of the melodrama certainly engages a slow time of absorption in detail, but not precisely that of disinterested contemplation, for this absorption is tied to the repetitive routines of domestic labor.[21] In another example given by Jameson, the action film invites its viewers to enter a hyperstimulating rapid-fire time that is thoroughly imbricated with the quick time of commodity circulation, its instantaneities promising the spectator a perverse kind of self-sufficiency—a body that, though it can be blown to bits, will still survive the ravages of history ("The End of Temporality"). Julien's innovation is to link the dynamics among film as a temporal medium, the temporalities of the cinema's various narrative genres, and the time of still art to sadomasochistic practice itself.

From the beginning, *The Attendant* plays with the dialectic between spectatorship and participation, perception and action, fixity and motion, timelessness and timing. The film's very title figures this contradiction: to be "attendant" is to wait for, to expect, but also to go, follow, accompany, serve, to be in constant motion on behalf of another. The opening shot of *The Attendant* extends this dynamic. In color, it reveals the Biard painting from afar, glowing in the center of an otherwise black frame. As the picture appears to draw closer, a faint shaft of light to the left reveals that it is actually a zoom shot of a slide projected onto a wall. Julien seems to have filmed the projected slide of a painting not only self-reflexively to indicate the layers of mediation that attend any act of perception but also to bridge the gap between painting and film, thereby prefiguring the scenes where the people in the Biard piece begin to move. The next frame shows a title card reading *The Attendant*, with a shadow flickering across the letters, again juxtaposing stillness and motion. This is followed by still shots of black-and-white photos of a museum from the outside, taken from below and emphasizing the motionlessness of marble steps, white columns, and Greek statuary. Inside, motion is restored as people mill about a room containing paintings and marble busts, each patron walking in a straight line for a while, turning at a right angle, and continuing on. These walkers seem to be imitating both the frames around the pictures and the curatorial practice of producing a linear historical sequence punctuated by moments of spectatorial contemplation. As these scenes clarify, *The Attendant* is certainly a film about film itself, about the rupture of the still image, about arresting a temporal flow and then recatalyzing it—but it eventually reveals the inherent eroticism of this very dynamic.

In that *The Attendant*'s formal properties highlight a dynamic between stasis and motion, stopping and going, the film is not so much sadomasochistic (that is, it does not traffic in the real time of historically specific S/M cultures) as eminently Sadean, a point to which I shall return below. In fact, without ever referencing Sade, *The Attendant* joins a history of critical treatments of this allegedly foundational figure, to whom sexual theorists keep going back to read and develop philosophy in the bedroom, perhaps precisely because this writer's own disruptions of time make him a site and a cite of eternal return.[22] The most pertinent to the film are those of Simone de Beauvoir and Marcel Hénaff. Following up on her own insights about the importance of mirrors in the Sadean scene, Beauvoir argues that Sadean sadomasochism depends upon "tableaux rather than adventures" (45). In her view, Sade's novels and the vignettes within them aim to imitate the image, to create a place outside of narrative wherein the object awakens to the senses without any surrounding explanatory or causal apparatus, which inaugurates an "enchanted domain" outside of time (51). Yet this does not account for Sade's insistence that eroticism consists precisely in *mobilizing* the tableau, as Beauvoir herself seems to recognize when she discusses Sade's use of mirrors to multiply his scenes and achieve a certain temporal asynchronicity. Indeed, Hénaff suggests that the tableau was useful to Sade precisely because of its "double emphasis on motion and motionlessness" (106).

In *The Attendant*, one way that the cross-genre dialectic between still and moving art that I am describing gains erotic force and becomes a form of historiography is by citing the Sadean tableau vivant. This genre of performance art is key to the joinder of Julien and Sade, of sex and a historicized sense of time. In its early-nineteenth-century inception as a parlor game, the tableau vivant involved players frozen into what were called "attitudes," poses that imitated actual paintings or illustrations of either fiction or history and, presumably, conjured forth the original characters' mental states. It thereby brought the high art of painting into scandalous contact with the low art of acting, the cognitive work of apprehending historical events or interpreting fiction into proximity with more visceral, even sexual reactions to the often female bodies on stage. In other words, as film critic James Tweedie writes in his discussion of another New Queer Cinematic film, the tableau vivant is "a medium of historical return that never sloughs off the mediating presence of actual bodies" (380). *The Attendant*, then, makes a historical return to a medium of historical return. The encounter between the Attendant and the Visitor takes place as a set of three tableaux, identifiable as scenes rather than stills only by the slight movements therein: first, we see the Visitor with his whip poised over the prone Attendant, whose mouth and eyes move; then, we see the two lovers in reversed positions with the Attendant on top; and finally, we see the Attendant and the Visitor frozen, standing side by side. This scene of scenes, in turn, takes place in a room with two Tom of Finland drawings on the wall, flanking the tableau with still art as if to emphasize the two-dimensionality of the lovers' encounter. We also see another tableau of sorts in a more opaque aspect of the film: as he checks museum visitors' bags, the Attendant imagines or recalls himself singing an operatic aria from a theater box to an audience consisting of black and white men dressed in disco and S/M gear who are frozen in static poses on a stage below him. I will make more of this last scene a little later, but for now, let me register it as simply one of many moments of the film's play with flow and freeze.

Julien's recapitulations of the Biard paintings as sadomasochistic orgies most obviously evoke Hénaff's description of the tableau: playing on the dual meaning of "table," Hénaff claims that tableaux initially lay out bodies as if on a slab, enabling the viewer to classify part-objects and thereby create a spatialized, cognitive chart of erotic elements (105). After the opening shot, the next time we see the Biard painting of the slave ship, it has come to life. We see the gilded edge of a frame, which has become a kind of moving proscenium, gradually sliding toward the left of the filmic frame to reveal a prone black man wearing a harness that quarters his chest and emphasizes his pectoral muscles. As in Hénaff's description of the tableau as both butcher block and taxonomic chart, the black man at the center of the tableau is laid out for the simultaneous gazes of the cinematic spectator, the Attendant, and a multi-racial group of men who gather around the body. A white man in shining black leather or rubber squats behind the black man, to the right of his head, and cradles his chin. Another kneels, touching the black man's belly with one hand and gesturing with the other. This dynamic recalls and reworks the typical auction scene portrayed in "Slaves on the West Coast of Africa," where white men routinely called spectatorial attention to various parts of slave bodies as signs of their capacity for hard work. But not only does this scene link sadomaso-chism to the history of race slavery, it hints that the aesthetic form of the tableau vivant itself is perversely tied to the intertwined histories of race and sexuality. Perhaps slave auctions were the first tableaux vivants? The film doesn't tell us.[23]

Implicitly contesting Beauvoir's remarks on Sade's alienation-effects, Hénaff suggests that the tableau paradoxically establishes and eliminates distance, presumably because it seems to invite the spectator into the scene. He writes that for Sade, this spatial collapse "is identified with an aggression that forces the engraving to move, features to come to life [. . .]. Engraving becomes scene; the pictorial evolves toward the theatrical, and motionless tableau toward *tableau vivant*" (105). This is exactly what happens to *The Attendant*'s reworked slave auction. As the Attendant enters the gallery and passes by the framed tableau, the characters inside blink and follow him with their eyes, but it is not clear that he sees this. He walks by a second picture, a close-up tableau mimicking a smaller section of the Biard painting. Here, a white man wields a whip over a black man facing away from him, with other black and white men in the background. This group, too, watches him go by. When the men in these two S/M scenes begin to move, it is only their eyes that do so; they leave ambiguous the question of whose desire and aggression mobilize them. Is it the Attendant's? The film viewer's? Or someone else's?

At this point in the film, the live characters remain framed, literally trapped in the still scene of the tableau as though stuck in the historical past, hemmed in by its representation, immobilized by the fixity of a relatively static art. But as Hart reminds us, "[T]he s/m scene is [inevitably] broken up, interrupted" (104). The sadist, especially, must dissolve tableau back into scene in order to recombine elements and introduce surprise, revivifying the encounter. Yet, Hénaff, following Hegel's famous discussion of the master/slave dialectic, contends that the tableau's duality as static and moving picture figures a certain threat to the sadomasochistic master: that in fulfilling his desire to animate the scene, he will thereby cause its end and his own death as a master. How, then, to escape this end? Hart argues that S/M involves "the unexpected element, the *switching* [. . .] which takes the participants by surprise" (141, emphasis hers). *The Attendant* moves beyond simply bringing the dead to life and thereby killing the master by making this switching literal: shortly after the tableaux appear, the crack of a whip announces that the Attendant and the Visitor have begun to play. The two men then appear frozen in the sequence of tableaux vivants I have described, with each playing "top" once before they stand side by side. These men not only wield switches, they *are* switches. Yet, what we miss seeing is, precisely, the "action," the reanimation of sex that would kill off the master entirely. Perversely, the master, too, must play dead to keep the possibility of mastery alive.

By lingering on the frozen image of a man wielding a whip without making contact (though the soundtrack emits "lashing" noises), Julien also correlates two things: (1) the power of still art to "arrest" the development of critical consciousness by demanding contemplation; and (2) the power of the sadomasochist to withhold sensations. Classical theories of aesthetic contemplation suggest that while a spectator's recognition of content and historically specific technique might bring the past to the present momentarily, the object of looking at art is to lift the subject and the artwork out of time and hence beyond the realm of social change, beyond the agency of the spectator. In both contemplation and sadomasochism, a certain lack is temporalized. Kantian art-appreciators feel their contingent, mortal souls transported into eternal, even sacred time; sadomasochists feel their constitutively split subjectivities as delay, suspense, anticipation. But in sadomasochism, delay also spatializes time. Hénaff declares, somewhat obscurely, that "[t]ime is thought to block desire, and waiting is thought to extinguish temptation. The law of time becomes the law in absolute form" (122). Waiting, then, regulates libidinal energy—but it also creates "absolute form," the Law, the ultimate ahistorical structure. The rhythm of Sadian sex, Hénaff continues, consists of accelerating time until it looks like space, linking up strings of sexual pleasures so frenetically as to compact them: "[I]n short, acceleration is to time as saturation is to space" (131). Sade's boring dissertations, unlike his short vignettes that move characters sequentially along a minimal plotline, are in some ways the culmination of this sexual program, for they "say everything, and all at once" (139). So as it turns out, whether by delay or by acceleration, time in the Sadean universe cannot remain itself; it always congeals into space or oscillates with it.

Julien, unlike this particular version of Sade, is unafraid to slow down, and thus in *The Attendant* time does remain itself, interdependent with but not reduced to space. And sex, like film, becomes a time-based art.[24] Sex becomes a time-based art when players withhold bodily pleasure or surprise the body into response; Julien's exploration of sadomasochism dramatizes this aspect of eroticism. In fact, *The Attendant* suggests that a large part of sadomasochism's power lies less in pain itself than in the pause, which the film figures most insistently as the frozen moment of suspense between the crack of a moving whip and its contact with a body that will flinch. And indeed, as Hénaff has perhaps most thoroughly explored and as Julien's film clearly recognizes, genuinely Sadean sadomasochism plays with and literalizes power *as* time. A dynamic between restraint and release shapes sadomasochistic sexual actions, which are syncopated by reward and sometimes punishments; bottoms are rewarded for physical endurance and for waiting; tops for anticipating the bottom's needs and for maintaining suspense. In fact, one of the most powerful aspects of sadomasochism is the way it makes the pause itself corporeal. Here we might recall Gilles Deleuze's description of the masochistic aesthetic. While Deleuze, like Hénaff, describes Sadian sexuality as dependent upon an acceleration and multiplication that aims to annihilate the object, Deleuze also claims that the erotic writings of Leopold von Sacher-Masoch celebrate a suspension of time that preserves the object of desire indefinitely: "The masochist is morose [. . .] by which we mean that he experiences waiting in its pure form" (*Masochism* 63). Finally, S/M exemplifies, celebrates, and turns into a mode of power Freud's description of the perversions as a form of dallying along the way to heterosexuality, as activities that "linger over the intermediate relations to the sexual object which should normally be traversed rapidly on the path towards the final sexual aim" (247). Hurry up and wait then, says the sadist to the masochist, for whom lingering is a virtue.

Here is where history, as opposed to a more abstract or metaphysical temporality, enters the scene. I suggested at this essay's outset that sadomasochism lays bare the dynamic between a historically specific modernity and its precursor, precondition, or repressed double, that its temporal dialectic engages with historicity. In fact, Hénaff, too, locates Sadean acceleration in history, noting that it conforms to an industrial capitalism in which exchange value is increased by shortening the time necessary for production (134). In *The Attendant*, the Biard painting registers the precondition for this shortening of the time of production—the exploitation of labor, which under slavery did not occur in a capitalist mode of production, but nonetheless fed the mechanized textile industry and was instrumental to its profits. Thus we might also read Julien's stoppages as a critical response to the repressed history of industrialization or as a formalistic way of reclaiming bodies that in another era would have been stolen for the making of so-called modern time. He encodes this latter possibility on the soundtrack as an insistent heartbeat, a sonic figure for a body not yet or no longer alienated from artisanal practices or from a biorhythmic pace. Finally, the film has another register, this time visual, for an alternative historiography beyond the "official" histories promulgated within the classical space of a British museum that preserves the work of a heroic abolitionist painter but nothing of the slaves whose freedom he supposedly cherished. Enter the angel of history.

The English beat: attending to history

In *The Attendant*, moments before the Biard painting comes alive and just as the Attendant and the Visitor begin to cruise each other, miniature Cupid-like angels with large wings appear above the two men's heads, frozen in the act of brandishing bows and arrows. These angels turn in small circles like statuettes on a music box or a cuckoo clock.[25] The film, then, marks its transitions from spaces that secure racial purity to those fostering interracial sexual contact, from still art to theater, from present to past, and eventually from the quotidian to the supernatural, with pixellated figures that invoke Walter Benjamin's famous Angel of History, who flies with her back to the future as the human-made catastrophes of the past pile up at her feet (257). One of Julien's angels campily carries a pitchfork, perhaps to shovel up Benjamin's pile of historical debris, perhaps to remind us that history is also the devil's doing.

Yet though these angels turn, they seem to be frozen on an invisible, moving base. This emphasis on stillness might be an example of mere fetishism, or reification, or any number of other modes of obfuscating the social. But in fact, it was Benjamin himself who recognized that the *pause* provides an antidote both to the traditional historicist models of progress that Sade also repudiated and to the "revolutionary" ideology of a complete break from the past that Sade celebrated. Benjamin wrote, "A historical materialist cannot do without the notion of a present which is not a transition, but in which time stands still and has come to a stop" (262). In this formulation, the pause does not signal an interval between one thing and another; it is itself a thing, analytically and experientially available, that reveals the ligaments binding the past and the present. In Benjamin, making time stand still takes the form of recognizing and diagnosing a dialectical image: the pause creates a "configuration [. . .] *pregnant* with tensions" between a heretofore misrecognized or lost element of the past and something occurring right now and, crucially, in a temporal relationship other than causality (262, emphasis mine).

The little angels are not the film's dialectical images. But their arrows literally point us toward one and toward another way of accessing and understanding the convergence of sex and historicist thinking in sadomasochism. The translator of the "Theses on the Philosophy of History" for *Illuminations*, in which the essay first appeared in English, substituted the term *pregnant* for the German *gesättigten* (saturated), which is particularly revealing for *The Attendant*, for the film presents us with a configuration not so much pregnant as "erect" with tensions. Just before the museum closes, before he and the Visitor consummate their lust, the Attendant looks at his pocket watch. The watch casing appears as a gold circlet in an otherwise black-and-white filmic frame. Later, the film cuts to a male body, filmed in color from mid-torso down, wearing crystal beads draped across his belly and gold lamé shorts with a distinct bulge in them. The little frozen angels spin on each thigh of the body whose bulge is on such dramatic display (and who is neither the Attendant nor the Visitor and correlates with nothing inside the museum thus far). They point their arrows down toward this "target." Here, color correspondence between the Attendant's gold watch and the gold-clad bulge has taken the place of narrative continuity: time and sex form what Deleuze has called a crystal-image, glinting up from we do not know what historical moment, even within the film's terms, to meet the Attendant's present (Deleuze 1989: 69).

The bulge corresponds to nothing we have seen before—neither to the slave ship in the painting, nor to the reanimated slave/S/M scene, nor to the flogging scenes between the Visitor and the Attendant. It is, in some ways, a tongue-in-cheek response to Robert Mapplethorpe's famous photograph "Man in the Polyester Suit," which shows a black man shot from the torso down, his flaccid penis emerging from the fly of his trousers. But the bulge also recalls and makes sense of an earlier set of images that had, up to this point in the film, remained entirely incongruous. At the beginning, just before the Attendant checks the Visitor's black leather bag and they exchange their first glance, we hear an extradiegetic chorus singing "Remember me, remember me." A close-up of the Attendant's impassive face and steady gaze fades to a shot of him in a black tuxedo and corsage, standing in an opera box, singing and gesturing outward. He seems to be addressing his performance toward the stage below him, where another, younger black man stands with his arms out, surrounded by black and white men frozen in various poses against a shiny curtain: these are all the same men who will later appear in the sadomasochistic reenactment of the Biard painting. Bare-chested, they are dressed in metallic loincloths. The chorus the Attendant sings to them is the aria "When I Am Laid in Earth," popularly known as "Dido's Lament," from Henry Purcell's opera *Dido and Aeneas*: "Remember me, remember me, but ah, forget my fate."

For several minutes as the seduction scene progresses, this operatic moment hovers entirely outside the film's plot. As it turns out, the gold shorts and the bejeweled torso in the close-up belong to the young black man at the center of the assembled group on the opera stage. The opera scene is one possible referent for the "remember me": perhaps the Attendant is asking the audience to remember his performance but to forget that he ends up curating the art of other people rather than making his own. Perhaps the younger man in the loincloth represents a queer past that the Attendant has temporarily given up. Perhaps the chorus solicits the Anglo segment of Julien's audience to remember the role of their ancestors in the transatlantic slave trade. Or perhaps it is a warning to S/M players about the political implications of mimicking slave relations. Yet later, the "remember me" chorus reappears when the Biard painting comes alive: the chorus seems to be waking up the Attendant, the S/M players in the frame, and Biard's original painted figures, and the heartbeat contributes to this effect. Perhaps, then, what we have is a more complicated injunction. These intertwined sounds seem to implore these men of the past and the present, asking them to move across time and take up their obligations to one another. In keeping with Sade's antagonism toward inheritance, they ask the dead slaves to release any hold on their descendants that would deny later generations the capacity to recalibrate pain into pleasure. In keeping with Benjamin's pursuit of new collective memory-forms, the sounds ask the living players never to confuse pleasure with historical amnesia.

As a figure for and a catalyst of this kind of reciprocal movement across time, the gilt-veiled black phallus functions as the film's critical caesura, a pause that links sex not only to abstract and generic "time" but also to a specifically national history. For it directs our attention toward the Attendant's lament and thereby toward Purcell's opera *Dido and Aeneas* or, as Julien puts it, "another scene on the coast of Africa" (120). Both the libretto and the performance history of this opera tell a story of sex and empire, but not the straightforward story of African slave capture that we might expect from the Biard painting. In fact, seventeenth-century librettist Nahum Tate intended *Dido and Aeneas* to be a gloriously British opera, and he reworked Virgil's *Aeneid* according to Geoffrey of Monmouth's massive *History of the Kings of Britain* (see Price). In the original epic, Aeneas takes advantage of the African Queen Dido's generosity in sharing all the resources of her great city of Carthage. But he eventually abandons her, plunders Carthage with his men, and sails away, intending to use her riches to found Rome. Monmouth wrote that Aeneas was the grandfather of Brutus, whom he named as the founder of Britain—and this "fact" inspired Tate to imbue Virgil's epic with details from English national history.[26]

The opera, then, tells a tale of interracial love, the exploitation of Africa, and European nation making: Joseph Roach has called it an "allegory of Atlantic destiny" (40). He reads Dido's lament as Purcell's paean to European political memory, to conquerors who conveniently remember only their "deep love for the people whose cultures they have left in flames" (46). Moreover, the opera's performance history sits at the disavowed intersection of European and African history: it premiered in 1698, a watershed year in the development of liberal democracy, when a Parliamentary Act confirmed England's first Bill of Rights. Yet this was also the same year that James II, fleeing England, ceded to the original investors the largest share of the Royal Africa Company that captured slaves on the Guinea Coast to trade with the West Indies. This act, in turn, precipitated the defeat of the Royal Africa Company's monopoly over the slave trade, which opened it up to other English companies, allowing the Dutch and French to aggressively pursue trade in the region in a competition that ultimately drove up the price of slaves (42; see Calder 347–48). In sum, the opera *Dido and Aeneas* is an Anglicized tale of European empire-building whose initial performance coincided with signal events in both English liberal democracy and its disavowed prop, the transatlantic slave trade. Thus the lament, even while it appears in the form of an aria that, like all arias, suspends narrative and historical time, can be read as a rebuke to free-market capitalism and its impact on slavery and as an elegy for African cultures.

The Attendant's appropriation of the lament, though, changes the emphasis of the opera somewhat. In beseeching us to "Remember me/but ah, forget my fate," Dido/the Attendant does seem to be asking her audience not to regard her or her city as simply dead, simply "left in flames." In fact, in the original *Aeneid*, Dido promises to return from the dead and makes good on this promise when Aeneas enters the underworld. Julien, unlike Tate, seems to honor her request and her triumph. The reanimations of slave scenes bring the static, supposedly "dead" historical object of slavery and the dead bodies of the enslaved back to life.

In turn, *The Attendant*'s revivifications take place beyond the merely visual, or even sonic, register. They rely on a technique that Alison Landsberg has referred to as "prosthetic memory," or portable, often mass-produced experiences disseminated by films and museums to consumers who never lived through the events represented. Prosthetic memories are neither the scars of originary trauma nor the proprietary result of long, slow cultural inculcation like that of family heritage or ethnic birthright; they belong to nobody and everybody at once and are detachable from the context that produced them.[27] They come from the body's engagement in mimetic activities, participatory affective and sensory relationships that ring changes on, variously, emotions, identity, and affiliation. (Think, for instance, of the Holocaust Museum in Washington, DC, which issues a facsimile identity card and biography to each museum-goer, who proceeds through the exhibit unsure of how the reenacted scenes will affect his or her historical counterpart until reading the last page of the booklet. His or her sensations lose their anchor to any preconceived outcome.) These changes, however momentary, bind and unbind historical subjectivity: collective experiences are implanted and disseminated such that they overflow their containment in and as individual traumas, as events over and done with. Prosthetic memories counter the work of the historical monument, for they travel with and in protean sensations. It is notable, then, that Julien chooses to stage his meditation on colonial oppression and sadomasochistic fantasy in what Landsberg calls the "experiential site" of a museum flanked by statuary (and even an operatic stage populated by frozen actors), suggesting complex relays between sadomasochism and cultural memory, the publics constituted around sex and those hailed by the heritage industries.

However, Landsberg assumes that these spaces try to duplicate the exact sensory and emotional experiences of the original sufferer, with as little modification as possible, and certainly without either humor or eroticism as part of the equation: in her analysis, prosthetic memory is essentially curative. But whatever is going on in a sadomasochistic scene where players appropriate the signs of, say, the Spanish Inquisition, it is not exactly the incorporation of these events into the participants' set of experiential data. It is doubtful that S/M players routinely emerge from their scenes with a sense of having been through a historical process, or feeling empathy for the sufferers they have imitated. Instead, and complicating Landsberg's analysis, even a sadomasochism that eschews historical role-playing openly deals *in* prosthetics—stand-ins, effigies, imitation body parts, extensions of the so-called natural body. Thus, rather than *being* a site for the inculcation of prosthetic memory, S/M may literalize the prosthetic aspect of all memory. In other words, while S/M cannot return its players to a prior historical moment any more than a museum can, it can remind us of what the museum itself represses: memory is not organic or natural at all, but depends on various prompts and even props. In turn, S/M shows us, memory can prop up projects unrelated to the history it supposedly preserves.

To return to Freud for a minute: if one definition of perversion is temporal, a kind of loitering at the way stations toward male orgasm, another definition is spatial and invokes the prosthesis: "[The perversions] extend, in an anatomical sense, beyond the regions of the body that are designed for sexual union" (16). In other words, perverts transport genital sensations outside their proper zones and use other parts of the body (fingers, anuses, fists, nipples) as substitutes for genital satisfaction. Many sadomasochistic players elongate the erotic zones in this way by using parts such as arms, fingers, and hands, and even the entire body itself in ritualized practices of stretching and suspending. These are, again, corporealizations of the experiences of delay or duration. Other sadomasochists extend sex beyond the physiological body itself with props such as dildos, piercing needles, and whips. These spatial extensions of the body, in turn, have a temporal logic of their own. For a butch lesbian top, for example, the dildo can serve as a prop for the prosthetic memory of a masculinity she feels as a birthright but has not lived biologically. The dildo or even the hand itself can restore an "amputated" masculinity, which is often felt as a discontinuous past that has been temporarily interrupted by the butch top's female body but is now resumed in the moment of sexual contact.[28] In other words, the dildo extends the butch or daddy top into her "own" masculine past, the imagined time of another life. Just as S/M exceeds the spatial boundaries of a player's "own" body, it can exceed the temporal boundaries of her "own" lifetime.

There are no dildos visible in Julien's film, which I think arguably does not do justice to female sexuality or lesbian S/M dynamics.[29] What we see instead are whips, predominantly in the hands of white men. This image of the whip travels: appearing first in the original Biard painting, it reappears in the tableau vivant of the sadomasochistic orgy in the hand of the Visitor and is finally wielded by the Attendant. But through a flashback, we learn that when the Attendant originally searched the arriving Visitor's personal items, presumably for cameras or dangerous items, he either saw or fantasized about the shaft of the whip protruding slightly from the black leather case that the Visitor carried, and stroked its length (here, perhaps, is the film's only dildo). This brief scene seems to pun on the historical "baggage" borne by the whip, which, in the hands of the Visitor and the white men in the tableaux, catalyzes a historical flashback, a racial "memory" of the power of actual or de facto ownership that white men once wielded over black men. In the hands of the Attendant, however, the whip invokes and invites the sexual pleasure that white men, however much they disavowed it, may have taken in disciplining black men: the Attendant's whip recalls and reverses the pointing finger of the white man in the earlier tableau of the sadomasochistic orgy. Held by the Attendant, the whip also indexes the erotic energy that enslaved black men managed to preserve and transmit to their successors despite their sufferings.

The whip, like the dildo I have described, works in *The Attendant* as a power line connecting historical as well as personal pasts to the present. As a trope, it not only links sadomasochism's power/sex dynamic to slavery but also suggests that historical memories, whether those forged from connecting personal experiences to larger patterns or those disseminated through mass imagery, can be burned into the body through pleasure as well as pain. This is why Julien reanimates the dead in *sex* scenes rather than in the scenes of revenge or fearmongering in which a classically Derridean "hauntology" usually traffics.[30] Julien's commitment to an eroticized hauntology is, I think, his major contribution to a queer-of-color critique that would hold sensuality and historical accountability in productive tension.[31]

Yet even as Julien figures a mode of corporeal historical cognition in the phallic terms of the whip, it is Benjamin and not he who equates the historical materialist with masculine sexual dominance: "The historical materialist," Benjamin writes in "Theses on the Philosophy of History," "leaves it to others to be drained by the whore called 'Once upon a time' in historicism's bordello. He remains in control of his powers, man enough to blast open the continuum of history" (262). Here Benjamin aligns fiction, fairy tale, and myth with a threatening female sexuality also troped in the commercial terms of a whorehouse: it is as if a (presumably nonmaterialist) "historicism" pimps out a feminized mysticism strong enough to emasculate the scholar, while the genuine materialist practices a spermatic economy that will maximize his own sexualized cognitive power. Julien, on the other hand, suggests that history may enter through the bottom after all—and on the wings of fairies. Indeed, the way his angels do not turn their backs consistently to anything, but turn around and around, suggests a certain opening up of the body to other times, past and future, that Benjamin's work seems sometimes to refuse. In the crotch shot, the historiographic navel of the film's dream, the miniature angels moving in circles on the man's thighs have their bows taut, arrows pointed directly at his bulge, suggesting that he, too, is as likely to be penetrated as to penetrate. Eventually, this dialectical image, juxtaposing real and heavenly bodies, begins to undulate; the man whose torso is in the frame brings his hands around to carefully pull away the crystal beads that cover his stomach, and he moves his hips up and down, up and down, as if to receive penetration from above.

With these images of bodily porosity, Julien also brings forth the possibility of the tactile historicism I have elsewhere called "erotohistoriography."[32] In fact, in his short analytic piece on *The Attendant*, titled "Confessions of a Snow Queen," Julien comments,

> Although the current images of "whips" and "chains" in the representational practices of s/m have been borrowed from [the] colonial iconography [of slavery], the refashioning of these accoutremounts (i.e., rubberization, polished surfaces, latex, polished metal) has transformed them into sexualized, stylized fetish clothing for the queer body.
>
> (122)

In other words, he notes that S/M's restylings occur on the level of the visual *and* the tactile. Here, then, the whip is important not just as an elongation of the body, or merely as a prosthesis, even as sadist's mnemonic device, but as itself the switchily "passive" recipient of a black queer touch that makes it shine with new meanings. In *The Attendant*, the "shine" of the gold lamé bulge resonates with the shine of the rubber and leather worn by the participants in the framed sadomasochistic orgies, the silver boots worn by the angels, the curtain of the opera stage, the gold casing of the watch, the picture frames. This proliferation of visual and tactile "rhymes" cannot be coordinated into anything like a linear historical narrative (backward into slavery, forward into utopia). Instead, they represent a kind of short-circuiting, a jolt seen or felt, a profane illumination or kinetic leap into history otherwise. If S/M in its sensory elements encodes and transmits the bodily knowledge of personal and collective trauma, then, it can also release this knowledge for new bodily experiences in the present tense. In Julien's analysis, the register of touch can literally open up slavery's historical baggage and distribute its contents differently.

   The Attendant also signals the vital role of tactility in a queer-of-color historiography, with the motif of the hand. In one scene, we see a manicured, dark-skinned hand caressing a marble bust on its stony lips, cheek, and chin (we are later to learn that this hand belongs to the Attendant's coworker, an African American woman known as the Conservator and played by Cleo Sylvestre). The next shot shows a hand in a black leather glove, presumably the Attendant's, caressing the hilt of a black whip that is held in a bare white hand; no faces appear in the frame to locate these hands. These images of bare and gloved, black and white hands appear elsewhere in the film: at one point we see a torso (the Attendant's?) wearing a suit, hands smoothing those same black leather gloves; another shot shows the Conservator in long black opera gloves slowly applauding from a balcony; yet another shows the black leather gloves now on the white Visitor, who raises his gloved hands up to dab his eyes. Notably, the hand also plays a central role in Landsberg's analysis of prosthetic memory, for she launches this concept with a reading of the film *The Thieving Hand* (1908), a silent film in which a man's prosthetic arm steals incessantly until he is sent to jail and his false arm leaps off of his body and reattaches itself to the thief to whom it originally belonged. For Landsberg, this film captures the late-nineteenth-century belief in "organic" memory, or the theory that experiences were carried, like our modern genes, along hereditary lines.[33] Seen in light of *The Attendant*, though, *The Thieving Hand* suggests the kind of blind groping, the movement by instinct and "feel," that white queer and queer-of-color historians have had to use as methods for finding and making meaningful the mostly uncatalogued materials of their collective pasts.

   Julien's images of hands, their robing and disrobing, their insistence on touch, invoke just this kind of memorial practice: they figure a memory that is insistently corporeal, but not organic or hereditary. These images also remind us that S/M is at base a practice of skinplay. Its colloquial designation "leathersex" suggests a certain doubling and distantiation of the skin, for even as leather hides the skin, it also is skin. It makes the idea of skin visible, engenders a certain fascination with the epidermal "once removed": thus S/M is always, as Mercer reminds us, a racialized practice ("Skin Head" 174–75). For Mercer, both leathersex and pornography problematically figure the sheen of black skin as an eroticized and incommensurate difference. For Julien, I would argue, this racia*lized*, reduplicative aspect of visual media's history and the iconography of S/M is not always *racist*. First, Julien transfers the "epidermal schema" from people to props: gloved hands, the hilt of a whip wrapped in black leather, the crotch covered by gold lamé. More importantly, he exploits the skinliness of S/M, its ability to capture the way queers polish and rub and elasticize the signs of dominant histories and cultures, to figure interracial eroticism as a tactile practice and not just a visual one. Black skin, here, is rescued from its entrapment in the visual, put back into motion and lambency, given porous qualities that overtake racist fetishizations of color and even shine. This view of S/M as skinplay, in turn, suggests some things about film as a medium and eventually about the temporal in both Julien's film and S/M in general.

In her book *The Skin of the Film*, Laura Marks has persuasively argued for a tactile notion of the medium of film as "impressionable and conductive, like skin" (xi). A material trace of an object—a record of the impression of light upon something—film is also capable of leaving traces upon its viewers. In this view, which literalizes the notion of spectatorial absorption, film takes an impression of the objects it represents and then disseminates this impression into the bodies of viewers.[34] The idea of film as a conduit for the trace is also a distinctly erotic one, as it foregrounds a kind of haptic exchange irreducible to the "purely" visual yet, paradoxically, never fully present as touch. The film stock, the screen, are like membranes between the object and the viewer, at once suggesting and withholding contact (Marks 242). The screen, to put it simply and to stretch Marks's claims a bit, is like the skin of the S/M top. Julien's work resonates with this analysis momentarily, when he shows the Conservator eavesdropping on the encounter between the Visitor and the Attendant, her ear pressed against a wall and her hand touching it. The wall, too, is a porous membrane, for the Conservator seems enchanted, at once part of the scene and apart from it (remember that she, too, may have had fantasies about interracial contact as she caressed the marble bust). Julien calls this "aural voyeurism" (120), but I think its aural sense is ultimately troped as tactile: it is as if, with her white-gloved hand touching the wall that separates her from the sex scene, the Conservator "overfeels" as much as overhears the scene. Likewise, the crotch shot at the center of the film breaks up the merely temporal pause, the still shot, into motion, light, the invitation to touch, and yet withholds full contact with the penis underneath its gold sheath. This tease is what Benjamin's one-way "blasting" into history would disallow. The crotch shot is not only a dialectical image but a dialectical membrane between the viewer and the body that shamelessly beckons us toward the bordellos of myth and history, "Once upon a time" and specific historical moments like the disco era, the painting's 1833, and the opera's 1698.

What does it mean that *The Attendant* ends with a black man apparently suffused with homoerotic and sadomasochistic desire inhabiting the role of a diasporic queen as written by a celebrant of British imperialism? Here is where the temporal aspect of sadomasochism contributes to a different kind of historiography, one that may not be fully containable within the rubric of hauntology. Roach offers a "genealogy of performance" (25) for *Dido and Aeneas*, one centered on the very "Dido's Lament" sung by the Attendant, that obliquely illuminates the role of sexuality in the cultural memory of a conquered people. He notes that the bass line of the lament is a chaconne, which the *OED* defines as a now obsolete, stately dance in one-quarter time that in European usage served as the finale to a ballet or opera. But Roach argues that the European theater's grand finale apparently had its origins as a dance with sexual meanings in Spain and, prior to that, in Peru, the West Indies, or Africa, depending upon the historian one reads (47). Even as Dido prepares for suicide, then, her body carries and transmits the historical memory of pleasures that exceed the parameters of her own lifetime, her individual love affair, her geopolitical location, and her death. This memory, both a "might have been" and a "what could be again," is preserved in the form of a transatlantic beat, however domesticated it has become. In other words, her song performs an even more animate "remember me" than its lyrics, one that appears at the level of meter and bass line. Her lament raises its own dead, even as her words frame the story of England's rise on the backs of dead and dying African slaves.

In putting whips into the hands of the characters who eventually sing and hear this lament, Julien has transposed that bodily memory back into a beat we can see as well as feel, or perhaps that we are enjoined to feel while we see it. The other sonic "beat" that punctuates the film's work on time and history is the aforementioned pounding heartbeat; both the chaconne and the heartbeat are slow, steady, thudding. Perhaps the heartbeat and the dance are, respectively, overly organic or sentimental figures for the feeling body whose recalcitrant rhythms might disrupt the march of national allegory. But the heartbeat, especially, suggests the visceral effect of past history on present bodies and perhaps even vice versa. For the Attendant's lament, floating down to the disco-themed stage, also answers its own call: it beams the stately chaconne back toward the bodies capable of reenlivening it, not in its original form, but in living transformation. These bodies also fulfill in a contemporary idiom Dido's promise to return from the dead, insofar as they register an era before AIDS when disco had the power to connect moving bodies, and they bring that era momentarily back to life. The actors on stage, then, suggest a literal "disco-theque," a library of records unavailable as written text or even visual document, but accessible in and as rhythm. The operatic lament that eddies around them calls to mind Wai Chee Dimock's description of how meaning literally re-sounds over time: "An effect of historical change, noise is a necessary feature of a reader's meaning-making process. And even as it impinges on texts, even as it reverberates through them, it thickens their tonality, multiplies their hearable echoes, makes them significant in unexpected ways" (1063). Only with sadomasochism, "noise" is more than sonic; within the practice of sadomasochism, it becomes kinetic. Whippings, for instance, thicken the body's sensations, multiply its felt responses, and make bodily experience significant in unexpected ways. And one of these ways, I have argued, is in bringing the body to a kind of somatized historical knowledge, one that does not demand or produce correct information about or an original experience of past events, or even engender legibly cognitive understandings of one's place in a historically specific structure, but enacts the oscillation between forms of time and illuminates their historical consequences.

It may seem here that I teeter toward a racist conception of black bodies as the receptors or repositories of some essential beat. Honestly, I think Julien himself may encourage that tilt, challenging his audience's desire not to be racist, its wish to abstract race politics from those of desire or desire from racialization. By playing with the sonic and visceral qualities of "beats" in a film without dialogue, he also refuses us the easy comforts of an authentic "voice." But most important, Julien's association of diasporic African experience and sadomasochistic practices—the latter of which I have argued here are grounded in rhythm—expose rhythm as a form of cultural inculcation and of historical transmission rather than a racial birthright. In fact, here rhythm becomes a nontranscendent, material, nonprocreative means of intergenerational continuity despite the transience of the body and the nonsuccessive emergence of these generations. *The Attendant* figures time as a modality of power rather than a neutral substance, and the body as a perhaps inadvertent conduit for effaced histories of pleasure rather than a figure for some ahistorical essence or a mere mannequin upon which icons of oppression are scandalously hung for fun.

Sadomasochism is, in Julien's final analysis, a complicated form of what Toni Morrison calls "skin memory" (67). Julien offers a particularly synaesthetic mode of historiography, in that he uses the genre of a "silent" film (or more precisely a film without dialogue) to exploit the phenomenological aspects of the temporal politics he explores, to turn what would otherwise be visual representation or sonic resonance into a form of revivification. Invoking the chaconne, the disco beat, the crack of the whip, and the heartbeat, *The Attendant* insists upon the way that sound feels. The film takes black and queer tactile restylings of the visual into yet another sensory realm, demonstrating that S/M's sonic touches and tactile sounds can aggregate temporalities *within* the body rather than simply upon its surfaces, in other words, S/M is not merely drag; it reorganizes the senses and, when it uses icons and equipment from traumatic pasts, reorganizes the relationships among emotion, sensation, and historical understanding, its clash of temporalities ignites historical possibilities other than the ones frozen into the "fate" of official histories.

What I hope to have shown through this analysis of *The Attendant* is how Julien brings out and seizes upon the temporal aspect of sadomasochism, both to undermine the British empire's monumentalizing history of itself *and* to suggest a queer-of-color historiography grounded in bodily memories of a nonoriginary pleasure—one perhaps never experienced "as such"—as well as pain. His methodology and insights might be crucial for a revitalized queer studies in which we recognize the power of temporal as well as spatial demarcations, see temporal difference in relation to subjugated or simply illegible attachments, and view time as itself material for critical and cultural practices that counter the insistent rhythm of (re)production.

These critical and cultural practices include sex itself. The *ars erotica*, as Michel Foucault has called them, are ways of intimating, of understanding and constructing knowledge with the body as instrument. At least in sadomasochism, their object is not only the embodied self but also the structures in which that self is embedded and the contingencies that make a given self possible. As S/M makes particularly clear, these structures and contingencies, the shorthand for which is "history," include prescribed and possible chronometrics of bodily sensation, syntaxes of encounter, and tenses of sociability. As a critical technique or mode of analysis enacted with the body erotic, then, sadomasochism offers up temporal means for reconfiguring the possible: the "slow time" that is at once modernity's double and its undoing, the sensation that discombobulates normative temporal conditionings, the deviant pause that adds a codicil of pleasure to a legacy of suffering. These are not, to be sure, reparations for past damages (as if perfect redress were possible) or the means of transcending all limitations. They are, however, ways of knowing history to which queers might make fierce claim.

Notes

My deepest gratitude goes to the anonymous readers at *differences*, Steven Blevins, Peter Coviello, Heather Love, Heather Lukes, Milly McGarry, Bethany Schneider, Kara Thompson, and audiences at the Dartmouth Institute for American Studies, the University of Pennsylvania Speaker Series on Sexuality, the American Studies Association, and the Penn State Department of English, especially Scott Herring and Robert Caserio, for their help with this essay.

1   This theory of time suffuses Benjamin's work but is especially explicit in "The Work of Art in the Age of Mechanical Reproduction," "The Storyteller," and "On Some Motifs in Baudelaire," all in Benjamin, *Illuminations*.

2   I thank Luciano for permission to view her book in manuscript form.

3   See, for instance, ch. 8, "The Quaker Settlement," in *Uncle Tom's Cabin* and many passages in Donald Mitchell (a.k.a. "Ik Marvel")'s *Reveries of a Bachelor*. Thoreau provides another striking example,

commenting in his 1851 journal that "I am differently timed [. . .]. My spirits [sic] unfolding observes not the pace of nature" (113). Thanks to Peter Coviello for the reference.

4   See Abelove, "Some Speculations." On the narrativization of sex, see Morrison, "End Pleasure."

5   I am indebted to Anne Cheng for providing a succinct account of this essay's aims, some of which has inflected this paragraph, in her initially anonymous reader's report for *differences*.

6   For descriptions of "power exchange" as the basis of sadomasochism, see Califia; Samois; and Thompson.

7   Thus the French Revolution belies Michael O'Malley's claim that this new understanding of time occurred with the inception of railroads and standard times—though he may be right that "modern" secular time was not popularly understood this way in the eighteenth century or in the United States. See his *Keeping Watch*.

8   The positions of Bataille, Blanchot, and Bersani, who see Sade as an antagonist to the idea of durability, especially in the form of the social contract, are elegantly summed up by Frances Ferguson in "Sade and the Pornographic Legacy."

9   Important works following this trajectory include Judith Butler, *The Psychic Life of Power*; Ann Cvetkovich, *An Archive of Feelings*; Carolyn Dinshaw, *Getting Medieval*; Lee Edelman, *No Future*; David Eng and David Kazanjian, *Loss*; Roderick A. Ferguson, *Aberrations in Black*; Carla Freccero, *Queer/Early/Modern*; Elizabeth Grosz, *The Nick of Time*; Judith Halberstam, *In a Queer Time and Place*; Sharon Patricia Holland, *Raising the Dead*; Annamarie Jagose, *Inconsequence*; Heather Love, *Feeling Backward*; Molly McGarry, *Ghosts of Futures Past*; José Esteban Muñoz, *Cruising Utopia*; Christopher Nealon, *Foundlings*; and Kath Weston, *Gender in Real Time*. See also the essays in Elizabeth Freeman, ed., *Queer Temporalities*.

10   See Dworkin; MacKinnon. For arguments that sadomasochism repeats the historical violence it cites, see Miriam; Reti; and Star.

11   In "Is the Rectum a Grave?" Bersani later revises this to describe anal sex as the consummate practice of self-shattering.

12   "The peculiarity of Freudian analysis is to propose a history of the self's structure which includes, as one of its stages, a solidifying of character structures. [It] partially demystifies the notion of such structures by explaining them historically rather than just deducing them from the concept of an ahistorical human nature" (Bersani, *A Future* 58).

13   Critiques of queer theory along these lines include Donald Morton, "Changing the Terms"; Martha Nussbaum, "The Professor of Parody"; and Lee Siegel, "The Gay Science."

14   See Acker's *Blood and Guts in High School*; Cvetkovich's *An Archive of Feelings*; and Hart's *Between the Body and the Flesh*.

15   I thank Dana Luciano for this insight, in conversation. The concept of "feeling historical" is elaborated in Christopher Nealon, *Foundlings*.

16   For a useful description of the formal attributes and temporal politics of the New Queer Cinema, see David Pendleton, "Out of the Ghetto."

17   On the racial politics of the New Queer Cinema, see José Esteban Muñoz, "Dead White."

18   This lacuna is being filled as we speak, though, in cinema studies, particularly in essays on the work of Todd Haynes: see DeAngelis; Gorfinkel; Landy; O'Neill; and Luciano, "Coming Around Again," which cites these pieces.

19   See "Skin Head Sex Thing" and the essay Mercer reconsiders in the latter, "Imaging the Black Man's Sex."

20   See O'Malley, *Keeping Watch*, ch. 5 ("Therbligs and Hieroglyphs"), 200–255.

21   On melodrama and spectatorial absorption, see Doane.

22   I thank H.N. Lukes for this point, in conversation.

23   To the best of my knowledge, the impact of race slavery upon the performance genre of the tableau vivant is a history that remains to be written.

24   Film, video, and television are the paradigmatic time-based arts, as they reproduce motion and cannot he experienced *in toto*, as a painting might, without the forward movement of time. Sadomasochism, with its strong visual elements, metacommentary on power, elaborate system of signs, and theatricality, is the most "artful" of sex practices, the one most available for a claim that sex itself mediates the social world. For an exploration of sex as art, see Foucault.

25   For this description of the angels, see Orgeron 36.

26   Specifically, the ascension of William and Mary to the throne. See Roach 42.

27   In this sense, the concept of prosthetic memory confronts the most conservative implications not only of the antisadomasochistic notion that reenactments of trauma cannot transform the victim but also of Pierre Bourdieu's concept of *habitus*, the lived "memory" of culture as it appears in bodily dispositions forged in repetitive activities over time, or even Judith Butler's "performativity," which

does not fully account for how a liberatory rather than random or reactionary difference might appear in the nonidentical repetitions that constitute identity. Like performativity, prosthetic memories are less than voluntary and more than merely compelled, but as vicarious modes of being they float more freely than either habitus or performativity would allow.

28   Hart cites Stephen Best's description of how prostheses lengthen not only space but time (Best 202; Hart 96). An extraordinary fictional example of experiencing female masculinity as a return to a prior state of being male can be found in Radclyffe Hall's short story "Miss Ogilvy Finds Herself," written in 1926 and published in 1934.

29   For an extended critique of *The Attendant*'s gender and class politics, see hooks.

30   See *Specters of Marx*: "Hauntology" is Jacques Derrida's temporal play on the term "ontology." It describes the unsettling of presence (and the present) by foreclosed, unrealized, or violently repressed past possibilities that "return" as the sign of things to come. Thus hauntings defy both presence and sequence, both the empirical and the purely spiritual.

31   Roderick Ferguson offers a useful definition of queer-of-color critique as a mode of analysis that (1) exposes liberal capitalism's reliance on a tacitly white heterosexual matrix; (2) interrogates the way Marxist analysis naturalizes heterosexuality in order to produce its utopian formulations of property relations untainted by capitalism; and (3) remembers the primacy of racist evolutionary thinking to both liberal and Marxist discourses of progress. In other words, queer-of-color critique is a mode of historical materialism *otherwise*, one that I think Julien anticipates in this and other films. See Ferguson, in this volume, 119–33.

32   See Elizabeth Freeman, "Time Binds, or, Erotohistoriography."

33   See Otis.

34   This is, of course, an indexical view of film, insofar as the concept of index suggests the material presence of the original in the thing itself.

Works cited

Abelove, Henry. "Some Speculations on the History of Sexual Intercourse during the Long Eighteenth Century in England." *Nationalisms and Sexualities*. Eds. Andrew Parker, Mary Russo, Doris Sommer, and Patricia Yeager. New York: Routledge, 1992. 335–42.

Acker, Kathy. *Blood and Guts in High School*. New York: Grove, 1984.

Beauvoir, Simone de. "Must We Burn Sade?" Trans. Anette Michelson. *The Marquis de Sade*. Ed. Paul Dinnage. New York: Grove, 1953. 9–82.

Beecher, Catharine, and Harriet Beecher Stowe. *The American Woman's Home*. [1869]. Ed. Nicole Tonkovich. New Brunswick: Rutgers UP, 2002.

Benjamin, Walter. *Illuminations: Essays and Reflections*. Ed. Hannah Arendt. Trans. Harry Zohn. New York: Schocken, 1969.

Bersani, Leo. *The Freudian Body: Psychoanalysis and Art*. New York: Columbia UP, 1986.

—. *A Future for Astyanax*. Boston: Little, Brown, 1969.

—. *Homos*. Cambridge: Harvard UP, 1995.

—. "Is the Rectum a Grave?" *AIDS: Cultural Analysis, Cultural Activism*. Ed. Douglas Crimp. Cambridge: MIT P, 1988. 197–222.

Best, Stephen. "The Race for Invention: Blackness, Technology, and Turn-of-the-Century Modernity." Diss, U of Pennsylvania, 1997.

Burston, Paul. Rev. of *The Attendant*. *Sight and Sound* 3 (Apr. 1993): 64–65.

Butler, Judith. *The Psychic Life of Power: Theories in Subjection*. Palo Alto: Stanford UP, 1997.

Calder, Angus. *Revolutionary Empire: The Rise of the English-Speaking Empires from the Fifteenth Century to the 1780s*. New York: Dutton, 1987.

Califia, Pat. *Public Sex: The Culture of Radical Sex*. 2nd ed. Pittsburgh: Cleis, 1994.

"Chaconne." *The Oxford English Dictionary*. 2nd ed. 1989. http://www.oed.com (accessed 23 Aug. 2006).

Clément, Catherine. *The Lives and Legends of Jacques Lacan*. Trans. Arthur Goldhammer. New York: Columbia UP, 1983.

Cvetkovich, Ann. *An Archive of Feelings: Trauma, Sexuality, and Lesbian Public Cultures*. Series Q. Durham: Duke UP, 2003.

DeAngelis, Michael. "The Characteristics of New Queer Filmmaking: Case Study—Todd Haynes." *New Queer Cinema: A Critical Reader*. Ed. Michele Aaron. New Jersey: Rutgers UP, 2004. 41–52.

Deleuze, Gilles. *Cinema 2: The Time-Image*. Trans. Hugh Tomlinson and Robert Galeta. Minneapolis: U Minnesota P, 1989.

—. *Masochism: An Interpretation of Coldness and Cruelty*. Trans. Jean McNeil. Together with the entire text of *Venus in Furs* by Leopold von Sacher-Masoch. Trans. Aude Willm. New York: George Braziller, 1971.

Derrida, Jacques. *Specters of Marx: The State of the Debt, the Work of Mourning, and the New International*. Trans. Peggy Kamuf. New York: Routledge, 1994.

Dimock, Wai Chee. "A Theory of Resonance." *PMLA* 112.5 (Oct. 1997): 1060–71.

Dinshaw, Carolyn. *Getting Medieval: Sexualities and Communities, Pre- and Postmodern*. Series Q. Durham: Duke UP, 1999.

Doane, Mary Ann. *The Desire to Desire: The Woman's Film of the 1940s*. Bloomington: Indiana UP, 1987.

Dworkin, Andrea. *Intercourse*. New York: Free Press, 1987.

Edelman, Lee. *No Future: Queer Theory and the Death Drive*. Series Q. Durham: Duke UP, 2004.

Eng, David, and David Kazanjian, eds. *Loss: The Politics of Mourning*. Berkeley: U of California P, 2003.

Ferguson, Frances. "Sade and the Pornographic Legacy." *Representations* 36 (1991): 1–21.

Ferguson, Roderick A. *Aberrations in Black: Toward a Queer of Color Critique*. Critical American Studies Series. Minneapolis: U of Minnesota P, 2004.

Foucault, Michel. *The History of Sexuality, Vol. 3: The Care of the Self*. Trans. Robert Hurley. New York: Vintage, 1988.

Freccero, Carla. *Queer/Early/Modern*. Durham: Duke UP, 2005.

Freeman, Elizabeth. "Time Binds, or, Erotohistoriography." *What's Queer about Queer Studies Now?* Eds. David L. Eng, Judith Halberstam, and José Esteban Muñoz. Spec. issue of *Social Text* 84–85 (Oct. 2005): 57–68.

—, ed. *Queer Temporalities*. Spec, issue of *GLQ: A Journal of Lesbian and Gay Studies* 13.2/3 (2007).

Freud, Sigmund. *Three Essays on the Theory of Sexuality*. Trans. and ed. James Strachey. New York: Basic, 1975.

Gorfinkel, Elena. "The Future of Anachronism: Todd Haynes and the Magnificent Andersons." *Cinephilia: Movies, Love, and Memory*. Eds. Marijke de Valck and Malte Hagener. Amsterdam: Amsterdam UP, 2005. 153–67.

Grosz, Elizabeth. *The Nick of Time: Politics, Evolution, and the Untimely*. Durham: Duke UP, 2004.

Halberstam, Judith. *In a Queer Time and Place: Transgender Bodies, Subcultural Lives*. New York: New York UP, 2005.

Hall, Radclyffe. "Miss Ogilvy Finds Herself." [1928]. *The Norton Anthology of Literature by Women*. Eds. Sandra Gilbert and Susan Gubar. 2nd ed. New York: Norton, 1996. 1394–407.

Hart, Lynda. *Between the Body and the Flesh: Performing Sadomasochism*. New York: Columbia UP, 1998.

Hénaff, Marcel. *Sade: The Invention of the Libertine Body*. Trans. Xavier Callahan. Minneapolis: U Minnesota P, 1999.

Holland, Sharon Patricia. *Raising the Dead: Readings of Death and (Black) Subjectivity*. New Americanists. Durham: Duke UP, 2000.

hooks, bell. "Thinking through Class: Paying Attention to *The Attendant*." *Reel to Real: Race, Sex, and Class at the Movies*. New York: Routledge, 1996. 91–97.

Jagose, Annamarie. *Inconsequence: Lesbian Representation and the Logic of Sexual Sequence*. Ithaca: Cornell UP, 2002.

Jameson, Fredric. "Cognitive Mapping." *Marxism and the Interpretation of Culture*. Eds. Cary Nelson and Lawrence Grossberg. Urbana: U of Illinois P, 1988. 347–57.

—. "The End of Temporality." *Critical Inquiry* 29.4 (Summer 2003): 695–718.

Julien, Isaac, dir. *The Attendant*. 1992. British Film Institute, 1993.

—. "Confessions of a Snow Queen: Notes on the Making of *The Attendant*." *Critical Quarterly* 36.1 (1994): 120–26.

Landsberg, Alison. *Prosthetic Memory: The Transformation of American Remembrance in the Age of Mass Culture*. New York: Columbia UP, 2004.

Landy, Marcia. "'The Dream of the Gesture': The Body of/in Todd Haynes's Films." *Boundary 2* 30.3 (2003): 125–40.

Love, Heather. *Feeling Backward: Loss and the Politics of Queer History*. Cambridge: Harvard UP, 2007.

Luciano, Dana. *Arranging Grief: Sacred Time and the Body in Nineteenth-Century America*. New York: New York UP, 2007.

—. "Coming Around Again: The Queer Momentum of *Far from Heaven*." *GLQ: A Journal of Lesbian and Gay Studies* 13.2–3 (2007): 249–72.

MacKinnon, Catharine A. *Feminism Unmodified: Discourses on Life and Law*. Cambridge: Harvard UP, 1987.

Marks, Laura. *The Skin of the Film: Intercultural Cinema, Embodiment, and the Senses*. Durham: Duke UP, 2000.

McGarry, Molly. *Ghosts of Futures Past*. Berkeley: U of California P, 2007.

Mercer, Kobena. "Imaging the Black Man's Sex." *Photography/Politics: Two*. Eds. Pat Holland, Simon Watney, and Jo Spence. London: Comedia, 1986. 61–69.

—. "Skin Head Sex Thing: Racial Difference and the Homoerotic Imaginary." *How Do I Look? Queer Film and Video*. Ed. Bad Object Choices. Seattle: Bay, 1992. 169–210.

Miriam, Kathy. "From Rage to All the Rage: Lesbian-Feminism, Sadomasochism, and the Politics of Memory." *Unleashing Feminism: Critiquing Lesbian Sadomasochism in the Gay Nineties*. Ed. Irene Reti. Santa Cruz: HerBooks, 1993. 7–70.

Mitchell, Donald ("Ik Marvel"). *Reveries of a Bachelor*. New York: Scribner's, 1850.

Morrison, Paul. "End Pleasure." *GLQ: A Journal of Lesbian and Gay Studies* 1.1 (1993): 53–78.

Morrison, Toni. *Love*. New York: Knopf, 2003.

Morton, Donald. "Changing the Terms: (Virtual) Desire and (Actual) Reality." *The Material Queer: A LesBiGay Cultural Studies Reader*. Ed. Donald Morton. Boulder: Westview, 1996 1–33.

Muñoz, José Esteban. *Cruising Utopia: The Then and There of Queer Futurity*. New York: New York UP, 2009.

—. "Dead White: Notes on the Whiteness of the New Queer Cinema." *GLQ: A Journal of Lesbian and Gay Studies* 4.1 (1998): 127–38.

—. *Disidentifications: Queers of Color and the Performance of Politics*. Minneapolis: U of Minnesota P, 1999.

Nealon, Christopher. *Foundlings: Lesbian and Gay Historical Emotion before Stonewall*. Durham: Duke UP, 2001.

Nussbaum, Martha. "The Professor of Parody: The Hip Defeatism of Judith Butler." *New Republic* 220.8 (22 Feb. 1999): 37–45.

O'Malley, Michael. *Keeping Watch: A History of American Time*. Washington: Smithsonian Institution, 1996.

O'Neill, Edward. "Traumatic Postmodern Histories: *Velvet Goldmine's* Phantasmatic Testimonies." *Camera Obscura* 19.3 (2004): 156–85.

Orgeron, Devin. "Re-membering History in Isaac Julien's *The Attendant*." *Film Quarterly* 53.4 (2000): 32–40.

Otis, Laura. *Organic Memory: History and the Body in the Late Nineteenth and Early Twentieth Centuries.* Nebraska: U of Nebraska P, 1994.

Pendleton, David. "Out of the Ghetto: Queerness, Homosexual Desire, and the Time-Image." *Strategies* 14.1 (2001): 47–62.

Price, Curtis. "Dido and Aeneas in Context." *Dido and Aeneas: An Opera.* Ed. Curtis Price. New York: Norton, 1986. 3–41.

Reti, Irene. "Remember the Fire: Lesbian Sadomasochism in a Post Nazi Holocaust World." *Unleashing Feminism: Critiquing Lesbian Sadomasochism in the Gay Nineties.* Ed. Irene Reti. Santa Cruz: HerBooks, 1993. 79–97.

Rich, B. Ruby. "New Queer Cinema." *New Queer Cinema: A Critical Reader.* Ed. Michele Aaron. Edinburgh: Edinburgh UP, 2004.15–22.

Roach, Joseph. *Cities of the Dead: Circum-Atlantic Performance.* New York: Columbia UP, 1996.

Rohy, Valerie. "Ahistorical." *GLQ: A Journal of Lesbian and Gay Studies* 12.1 (2006): 61–83.

Samois, ed. *Coming to Power: Writings and Graphics on Lesbian S/M.* Boston: Alyson, 1987.

Sedgwick, Eve Kosofsky. "Paranoid Reading and Reparative Reading; or, You're So Paranoid, You Probably Think This Introduction Is about You." *Novel Gazing: Queer Readings of Fiction.* Ed. Eve Kosofsky Sedgwick. Durham: Duke UP, 1997. 1–37.

Siegel, Lee. "The Gay Science: Queer Theory, Literature, and the Sexualization of Everything." *New Republic* 9 (Nov. 1998): 30–42.

Star, Susan Leigh. "Swastikas: The Street and the University." *Against Sadomasochism: A Radical Feminist Analysis.* Eds. Robin Ruth Linden, Darlene R. Pagano, Diana E. H. Russell, and Susan Leigh Star. San Francisco: Frog in the Well, 1982. 131–35.

The Thieving Hand. Dir. unknown. Vitagraph, 1908.

Thompson, Mark, ed. *Leatherfolk: Radical Sex, People, Politics, and Practice.* Boston: Alyson, 1991.

Thoreau, Henry David. *A Year in Thoreau's Journal: 1851.* Ed. Daniel H. Peck. New York: Penguin, 1993.

Tweedie, James. "The Suspended Spectacle of History: The Tableau Vivant in Derek Jarman's *Caravaggio*." *Screen* 44.4 (2003): 379–403.

Weston, Kath. *Gender in Real Time: Power and Transience in a Visual Age.* New York: Routledge, 2002.

Zaretsky, Eli. *Capitalism, the Family, and Personal Life.* Rev. ed. New York: HarperPerennial, 1986.

Chapter 16

David M. Halperin

HOW TO DO THE HISTORY OF MALE HOMOSEXUALITY

David M. Halperin is W.H. Auden Distinguished University Professor of the History and Theory of Sexuality at the University of Michigan. He is a scholar in the fields of comparative literature, critical theory, queer theory, gender studies, and visual and material culture and is a founding editor of *GLQ: A Journal of Lesbian and Gay Studies*, in which the following essay originally appeared. Additionally, Halperin has authored several books including *What Do Gay Men Want? An Essay on Sex, Risk, and Subjectivity* (2007) and a book-length elaboration on this essay, *How to Do the History of Homosexuality* (2002).

In the following essay, Halperin grapples with the difficulties of historiographical work on male homosexuality. Following Foucault, he performs a genealogical analysis of homosexuality in which he creates a flexible paradigm that accounts for the various discourses used to describe male sexual experience throughout Western history. He identifies and traces five different discursive traditions that have been used to describe non-normative sexuality. He begins with four "pre-homosexual" discursive categories: effeminacy, pederasty/sodomy, friendship/love, passivity/inversion, which all place emphasis on gender subversion. He then traces the transformation from "pre-homosexual" categories to the modern category of "homosexuality," which depends less on gender and more on individualization, normalization, and sexuality.

THE HISTORY OF SEXUALITY is now such a respectable academic discipline, or at least such an established one, that its practitioners no longer feel much pressure to defend the enterprise—to rescue it from suspicions of being a palpable absurdity. Once upon a time, the very phrase "the history of sexuality" sounded like a contradiction in terms: how, after all, could sexuality have a history? Nowadays, by contrast, we are so accustomed to the notion that sexuality does indeed have a history that we do not often ask ourselves what kind of history sexuality has. If such questions do come up, they get dealt with cursorily, in the course of the methodological throat clearing that historians ritually perform in the opening paragraphs of scholarly articles. Recently, this exercise has tended to include a more or less obligatory reference to the trouble once caused to historians, long long ago in a country far far away, by theorists who had argued that sexuality was socially constructed— an intriguing idea in its time and place, or so we are reassuringly told, but one that was taken to outlandish extremes and that no one much credits any longer.[1] With the disruptive potential of these metahistorical questions safely relegated to the past, the historian of sexuality can get down, or get back, to the business at hand.

But this new consensus, and the sense of theoretical closure that accompanies it, is premature. I believe that it is more useful than ever to ask how sexuality can have a history. The point of such a question, to be sure, is no longer to register the questioner's skepticism and incredulity (as if to say, "How on earth could such a thing be possible?") but to inquire more closely into the modalities of historical being that sexuality possesses: to ask how exactly—in what terms, by virtue of what temporality, in which of its dimensions or aspects—sexuality does have a history.

That question, of course, has already been answered in a number of ways, each of them manifesting a different strategy for articulating the relation between continuity and discontinuity, identity and difference, in the history of sexuality. The constructionist-essentialist debate of the late 1980s should be seen as a particularly vigorous effort to force a solution to this question, but even after constructionists claimed to have won the debate, and essentialists claimed to have exposed the bad scholarship produced by it, and everyone else claimed to be sick and tired of it, the basic question about the historicity of sexuality has remained. In fact, current work in the history of sexuality still appears to be poised in its emphasis between the two poles of identity and difference, which in my view represent merely reformulated versions of the old essentialist and constructionist positions. Nonetheless, it may be prudent to recast the question in less polemical or old-fashioned terms by acknowledging that any adequate attempt to describe the historicity of sexuality will have to fix on some strategy for accommodating the aspects of sexual life that seem to persist through time as well as the dramatic differences between historically documented forms of sexual experience. Current analytic models that attempt to do this by mapping shifts in the categories or classifications of an otherwise unchanging "sexuality," or by insisting on a historical distinction between premodern sexual acts and modern sexual identities, simply cannot capture the complexity of the issues at stake in the new histories of sexual subjectivity that are available to us.[2]

The tensions between interpretative emphases on continuity and discontinuity, identity and difference, appear with almost painful intensity in the historiography of homosexuality. They reflect not only the high political stakes in any contemporary project that involves producing representations of homosexuality but also the irreducible definitional uncertainty about what homosexuality itself really is.[3] Perhaps the clearest and most explicit articulation of the consequences of this uncertainty for historians is found in the introduction to *Hidden from History*, the pathbreaking anthology of lesbian and gay history:

> Same-sex genital sexuality, love and friendship, gender non-conformity, and a certain aesthetic or political perspective are all considered to have some (often ambiguous and always contested) relationship to that complex of attributes we today designate as homosexuality. . . . much historical research has been an effort to locate the antecedents of those characteristics a given historian believes are constitutive of contemporary gay identity, be they sodomitical acts, cross-dressing, or intimate friendships.[4]

If contemporary gay or lesbian identity seems to hover in suspense between these different and discontinuous discourses of sodomy, gender inversion, and same-sex love, the same can be said even more emphatically about homosexual identity as we attempt to trace it back in time. The essence of the constructionist approach to the history of homosexuality, after all, was to argue that homosexuality is a modern construction, not because no same-sex sexual acts or erotic labels existed before 1869, when the term "homosexuality" first appeared in print, but because no single category of discourse or experience existed in the premodern and non-Western worlds that comprehended exactly the same range of same-sex sexual behaviors, desires, psychologies, and socialities, as well as the various forms of gender deviance, that now fall within the capacious definitional boundaries of homosexuality. Some earlier identity categories attached to same-sex sexual practices occupied some of the discursive territory now claimed by homosexuality; others cut across the frontier between homosexuality and heterosexuality. A number of these identity categories persisted in various forms for thousands of years before the modern term or concept of homosexuality was invented. It is quite possible that the current definitional uncertainty about what homosexuality is, or the uncertainty about what features are constitutive of lesbian or gay male identity, is the result of this long historical process of accumulation, accretion, and overlay. The history of discourses pertaining to forms of *male* intimacy may be especially revealing, because such discourses have been extensively and complexly elaborated over time, and they condense a number of the crosscutting systems of thought at whose intersection we now find ourselves.

In what follows I offer what I believe is a new strategy for approaching the history of sexuality in general and the history of male homosexuality in particular. My strategy is designed to rehabilitate a modified constructionist approach to the history of sexuality by readily acknowledging the existence of transhistorical continuities but refraining them within a genealogical analysis of (homo)sexuality itself. I begin where we must all begin (like it or not), namely, with the modern concept of homosexuality, which, explicitly or implicitly, defines the horizons of our immediate understanding and inevitably shapes our inquiries into same-sex sexual desire and behavior in the past. If we cannot simply escape from the conceptual tyranny of homosexuality by some feat of scholarly rigor—by an insistent methodological suspension of modern categories, by an austerely historicist determination to identify and bracket our own ideological presuppositions so as to describe earlier phenomena in all their irreducible cultural specificity and time-bound purity—we can at least watch our modern definitions of homosexuality dissolve as we attempt to trace them backward in time. A genealogical analysis of homosexuality, in other words, begins with our contemporary notion of homosexuality, incoherent though it may be, not only because such a notion frames our inquiry into same-sex sexual expression in the past but also because it contains within itself genetic traces, as it were, of its own historical evolution. In fact, the very incoherence at the core of the modern notion of homosexuality furnishes the most eloquent indication of the historical accumulation of discontinuous notions sheltered within its specious unity. The genealogist attempts to disaggregate those notions by tracing their separate histories as well as the process of their interrelations, their crossings, and, eventually, their unstable convergence in the present day.

That is what I will make a preliminary attempt to do here. I want to describe, very tentatively, some important prehomosexual discourses, practices, categories, patterns, or models (I am really not sure what to call them) and to sketch their similarities with and differences from what goes by the name of homosexuality nowadays. To do this, I need to be as systematic as I can; that is, I need to distinguish those earlier, prehomosexual traditions of homosexual discourse both from one another and from the modern discourses of homosexuality even as I note overlaps or commonalities among them. This means that I must describe these various categories in all their positivity and build as much specificity as I can into each of them while also accounting for their interrelations. My aim is to capture the play of identities and differences *within* the synchronic multiplicity of different but simultaneous traditions of discourse that have existed through the ages as well as the play of identities and differences *across* the diachronic transition effected during the last three or four centuries by the emergence of the discourses of (homo)sexuality.

Let me not exaggerate my originality. Previous historians and sociologists have identified four principal models according to which same-sex sexual behaviors are culturally constructed around the world (age-differentiated, role-specific, gender-crossing, and homo-sexual), and these four models reveal some obvious correspondences with the categories employed in the genealogy of male homosexuality outlined here.[5] My own approach is distin-guished, I believe, by being explicitly genealogical rather than sociological (or even, in a strict sense, historical) and by making visible a series of discursive figures immanent in the social and cultural traditions of Europe in particular. (I focus here on the history of European discourses, because I am attempting to construct the genealogy of a European notion—that is, homosexuality—but I include non-European material in my survey whenever it seems pertinent.) My most immediate precursors, it turns out, are the editors of *Hidden from History* quoted above: the three models of homosexuality that they enumerate—"same-sex genital sexuality" or "sodomitical acts," "love and friendship" or "intimate friendships," and "gender non-conformity" or "cross-dressing"—closely anticipate the divisions I make here.

I will argue, in any case, that there is no such thing as a history of male homosexuality. At least, there is no such thing as a singular or unitary history of male homosexuality. Instead, there are histories to be written of at least four different but simultaneous categories or traditions of discourse pertaining to aspects of what we now define as homosexuality. Each of these traditions has its own consistency, autonomy, density, particularity, and continuity over time. Each has subsisted more or less independently of the others, although they have routinely interacted with one another, and they have helped constitute one another through their various exclusions. Their separate histories as well as the history of their interrelations have been obscured *but not superseded* by the recent emergence of the discourses of (homo)-sexuality. In fact, what *homosexuality* signifies today is an effect of this cumulative process of historical overlay and accretion. One result of that historical process is what Eve Kosofsky Sedgwick memorably calls "the unrationalized coexistence of different models" of sex and gender in the present day.[6] I believe I am now in a position to offer, as a hypothesis, a historical explanation for the phenomenon that Sedgwick has so brilliantly described. I suggest that if our "understanding of homosexual definition . . . is organized around a radical and irreducible incoherence" (85), owing to "the unrationalized coexistence of different models" of sex and gender, it is because we have retained at least four prehomosexual models of male sexual and gender deviance, all of which derive from a premodern system that privileges gender over sexuality, alongside of (and despite their flagrant conflict with) a more recent homosexual model derived from a modern system that privileges sexuality over gender. If that causal explanation is correct, then a genealogy of contemporary homosexual discourse—which is to say, a *historical* critique of the category of homosexuality, such as I propose to undertake here—can significantly support and expand Sedgwick's influential *discursive* critique of the category of homosexuality in *Epistemology of the Closet* and give it the historical grounding that Sedgwick's critique has, until now, signally lacked.[7]

The four prehomosexual categories of male sex and gender deviance that I have identi-fied so far can be described, very provisionally, as categories of (1) effeminacy, (2) pederasty or "active" sodomy, (3) friendship or male love, and (4) passivity or inversion. A fifth category, the category of homosexuality, is—despite occasional prefigurations in earlier discourses—a modern addition. Each requires a separate analysis. I will concentrate on the history of discourses, because my project is to explore the genealogy of the modern discourses of homosexuality, but, as will become evident, I do not mean to exclude the history of practices, whose relation to the history of discourses remains to be fully considered.

Let me emphasize at the outset that the names I have chosen for the first four of these categories are heuristic, tentative, and ad hoc. My designations are not proper historical descriptors—how could they be, since the first four categories cut across historical periods, geographies, and cultures? Nor will my definitions of the first four categories explicate the historical meanings of those terms. For example, *sodomy*, "that utterly confused category,"[8] was applied historically to masturbation, oral sex, anal sex, and same-sex sexual relations, among other things, but my second category refers to something much more specific—not because I am unaware of the plurality of historical meanings of *sodomy* but because I use the term *active sodomy* specifically to denominate a certain model or structure of male homosexual relations for which there is no single proper name. That is unfortunate, but for the moment I see no alternative. With that as a final warning, let me now begin.

Effeminacy has often functioned as a marker of so-called sexual inversion in men, of transgenderism or sexual role reversal, and thus of homosexual desire. Nonetheless, it is useful to distinguish it from male passivity, inversion, and homosexuality. In particular, effeminacy should be clearly distinguished from homosexual object choice or same-sex sexual preference in men—and not just for the well-known reasons that it is possible for men to be effeminate without being homosexual and to be homosexual without being effeminate. Rather, effeminacy deserves to be treated independently because it was for a long time defined as a symptom of an excess of what we would call *heterosexual* as well as homosexual desire. It is therefore a category unto itself.

Effeminacy has not always implied homosexuality. In various European cultural traditions men could be designated as "soft" or "unmasculine" (*malthakos* in Greek, *mollis* in Latin and its Romance derivatives) either because they were inverts or pathics—because they were *womanly*, or transgendered, and liked being fucked by other men—or because, on the contrary, they were *womanizers*, because they deviated from masculine gender norms insofar as they preferred the soft option of love to the hard option of war. In the culture of the military elites of Europe, at least from the ancient world through the Renaissance, normative masculinity often entailed austerity, resistance to appetite, and mastery of the impulse to pleasure. (The once fashionable American ideal of the Big Man on Campus, the football jock who gets to indulge limitlessly his love of hot showers, cold beer, fast cars, and faster women, would appear in this context not as an emblem of masculinity but of its degraded opposite, as a monster of effeminacy.) A man displayed his true mettle in war, or so it was thought, and more generally in struggles with other men for honor—in politics, business, and other competitive enterprises. Those men who refused to rise to the challenge, who abandoned the competitive society of men for the amorous society of women, who pursued a life of pleasure, who made love instead of war—they incarnated the classical stereotype of effeminacy. This stereotype seems to live on in the American South, where "a redneck queer" is defined as "a boy from Alabama who laks girls better'n football."[9] It is also alive and well in Anglo-Celtic Australia, where a real bloke is a guy who avoids the company of women and prefers to spend all his time with his mates (that's how you can tell he's straight).

This stereotype, which sorts out rather oddly with modern notions of hetero- and homosexuality, goes far back in time. For the ancient Greeks and Romans, a man who indulged his taste for sexual pleasure with women did not necessarily enhance his virility but often undermined it. To please women, such a man was likely to make an effort to appear smooth instead of rough, graceful instead of powerful, and might even compound that effeminate style by using makeup and perfumes, elaborate grooming, and prominent jewelry. In a late antique dialogue ascribed to Lucian, which features a debate between two men as to whether women or boys are better vehicles of male erotic pleasure, it is the advocate of boys who is portrayed as hypervirile, whereas the defender of women, a good-looking young man, is described as exhibiting "a skilful use of cosmetics, so as to be attractive to women."[10]

Similarly, the stereotype of an adulterer in the ancient Greek literary tradition can be judged from the following description in a romance by the Greek prose writer Chariton: "His hair was gleaming and heavily scented; his eyes were made up; he had a soft cloak and fine shoes; heavy rings gleamed on his fingers."[11] Effeminacy has traditionally functioned as a marker of heterosexual excess in men.

It seems that men liked other men to be rough and tough. They may have liked their women and boys to be soft and smooth, but they did not respect these qualities in a mature man. Women, by contrast, seem to have found the soft style of masculinity more appealing. This created a certain tension between gender norms and erotic life for men. The paradigmatic instance, which illustrates the traditional clash between hard and soft styles of masculinity, can be found in the figure of Hercules. Hercules is a hero who oscillates between extremes of hyper-masculinity and effeminacy: he is preternaturally strong, yet he finds himself enslaved by a woman (Queen Omphale); he surpasses all men at feats of strength, yet he is driven mad by love, either for a woman (Iole) or for a boy (Hylas).[12] Hercules sets the stage for such modern figures as Shakespeare's Mark Antony, who claims Hercules as his literal ancestor in *Antony and Cleopatra* and who incurs similar charges of effeminacy when he takes time out from ruling the Roman Empire to live a life of passion and indulgence with Cleopatra. The roles of ruler and lover are made to contrast from the very opening of the play, when Antony is described as "the triple pillar of the world transform'd / Into a strumpet's fool" (1.1.12–13). Antony is not unique in Shakespeare. Othello also voices anxieties about the incapacitating effects of conjugal love on a military leader. But this tension is best represented by Shakespeare's Romeo, who, berating himself for a lack of martial ardor and invoking the traditional opposition between the cold, wet melancholia of love and the hot, dry nature of masculine virtue, exclaims:

> O sweet Juliet,
>   Thy beauty hath made me effeminate,
>   And in my temper softened valour's steel!
>   (3.1.113–15)[13]

The survival and interplay of these different notions of effeminacy may help explain the persistent sexual ambiguity that attaches, even today, to predominantly male institutions, such as fraternities, the armed forces, the church, the corporate boardroom, Congress: is the sort of manhood fostered and expressed there to be considered the truest and most essential form of masculinity, or an exceptional and bizarre perversion of it?

In short, effeminacy needs to be distinguished from homosexuality. This brings me to the second prehomosexual category: pederasty or "active" sodomy. These terms refer to the male sexual penetration of a subordinate male—subordinate in terms of age, social class, gender style, and/or sexual role. The discourses of pederasty or "active" sodomy are shaped by a crucial distinction between the male desire to penetrate and the male desire to be penetrated, and thus between pederasty or sodomy, on the one hand, and male passivity or inversion, on the other. The contrast between these two is reflected in my differentiation here between the second and the fourth of the five categories.

The nineteenth-century sexologists who systematically elaborated the distinction between pederasty ("Greek love") and passivity ("contrary sexual feeling" or "inversion of the sexual instinct") based it on an even more fundamental distinction between perversity and perversion, according to which an inverted, transgendered, or passive sexual orientation always indicated perversion in a man, whereas the sexual penetration of a subordinate male might qualify merely as perversity. These Victorian medical writers, who were still largely untouched by the distinction between homo- and heterosexuality (which had yet to assert its ascendancy over earlier modes of sexual classification), were chiefly interested in determining whether deviant sexual acts proceeded from an individual's morally depraved character (perversity)—whether, that is, they were merely the result of vice, which might be restrained by laws and punished as a crime—or whether they originated in a pathological condition (perversion), a mental disease, a perverted "sexuality," which could only be medically treated. The distinction is expounded by Krafft-Ebing as follows:

> *Perversion* of the sexual instinct . . . is not to be confounded with *perversity* in the sexual act; since the latter may be induced by conditions other than psychopathological. The concrete perverse act, monstrous as it may be, is clinically not decisive. In order to differentiate between disease (perversion) and vice (perversity), one must investigate the whole personality of the individual and the original motive leading to the perverse act. Therein will be found the key to the diagnosis.[14]

The male sexual penetration of a subordinate male certainly represented a perverse act, but it might not in every case signify a perversion of the sexual instinct, a mental illness affecting "the whole personality": it might indicate a morally vicious character rather than a pathological condition.

Implicit in this doctrine was the premise that there was not necessarily anything sexually or psychologically abnormal in itself about the male sexual penetration of a subordinate male. If the man who played an "active" sexual role in sexual intercourse with other males was conventionally masculine in both his appearance and his manner of feeling and acting, if he did not seek to be penetrated by other men, and/or if he also had sexual relations with women, he might not be sick but immoral, not perverted but merely perverse. His penetration of a subordinate male, reprehensible and abominable though it might be, could be reckoned a manifestation of his excessive but otherwise normal male sexual appetite. Like the somewhat earlier, aristocratic figure of the libertine or rake or roué,[15] such a man perversely refused to limit his sexual options to pleasures supposedly prescribed by nature and instead sought out more unusual, unlawful, sophisticated, or elaborate sexual experiences to gratify his jaded sexual tastes. In the case of such men, pederasty or sodomy was a sign of an immoral character but not of a personality disorder, "moral insanity," or psychological abnormality.[16]

The sexologists' distinction between the perverse and the perverted, between the immoral and the pathological, the merely vicious and the diseased, may strike us as quaintly Victorian, but prominent psychologists, sociologists, and jurists today draw similar distinctions between "pseudohomosexuality" and "homosexuality" or between "situational," "opportunistic" homosexuality and what they call, for lack of a better term, "real" homosexuality.[17] The acts of homosexual penetration performed in prison by men who lead heterosexual lives out of prison, for example, are often regarded not as symptoms of a particular psychosexual orientation, as expressions of erotic desire, or even as "homosexuality," but as mere behavioral adaptations by men to a society without women. Such behavior, it is often believed nowadays, simply vouches for the male capacity to enjoy various forms of perverse gratification[18] and, further, to eroticize hierarchy, to be sexually aroused by the opportunity to play a dominant role in structured relations of unequal power.

The distinction between pederasty and sexual inversion that I have derived from nineteenth-century psychiatry and that persists today did not originate in the Victorian period. Rather, it reflects an age-old practice of classifying sexual relations in terms of penetration versus being penetrated, superordinate versus subordinate status, masculinity versus femininity, activity versus passivity—in terms of *hierarchy and gender*, that is, rather than in terms of *sex and sexuality*. Possible evidence for an age-structured, role-specific, hierarchical pattern of sexual relations among males can be found in the Mediterranean basin as early as the Bronze Age civilizations of Minoan Crete in the late second millennium BC[19] and as late as the Renaissance cities of Italy in the fourteenth and fifteenth centuries AD. The best-known and most thoroughly documented historical instances of this pattern are probably ancient Greek and Roman pederasty and early modern European sodomy, but the pattern itself seems to have preexisted them, and it also has outlived them.

The evidence from judicial records in fifteenth-century Florence is sufficiently detailed to afford us a glimpse of the extent and distribution of sodomitical activity in one (admittedly notorious) premodern European community. Between 1432 and 1502 as many as seventeen thousand individuals in Florence, most of them males, were formally incriminated at least once for sodomy, out of a total population of forty thousand men, women, and children: two out of every three men who reached the age of forty in this period were formally incriminated for sodomy. Among those who were indicted, approximately 90 percent of the "passive" partners (including, according to Florentine notions, the insertive partners in oral copulation as well as the receptive partners in anal intercourse) were eighteen or younger, and 93 percent of the "active" partners were nineteen or older—the vast majority of them under the ages of thirty to thirty-five, the time of life at which men customarily married.[20]

This is sex as hierarchy, not mutuality, sex as something done to someone by someone else, not a common search for shared pleasure or a purely personal, private experience in which larger social identities based on age or social status are submerged or lost. Here sex implies difference, not identity, and it turns on a systematic division of labor. It is the younger partner who is considered sexually attractive, while it is the older one who experiences erotic desire for the younger. Although love, emotional intimacy, and tenderness are not necessarily absent from the relationship, the distribution of erotic passion and sexual pleasure is assumed to be more or less lopsided, with the older, "active" partner being the *subject* of desire and the recipient of the greater share of pleasure from a younger partner who figures as a sexual *object*, feels no comparable desire, and derives no comparable pleasure from the contact (unless he is an invert or pathic and therefore belongs to my fourth category). The junior partner's reward must therefore be measured out in other currencies than pleasure, such as praise, assistance, gifts, or money. As an erotic experience, pederasty or sodomy refers to the "active" partner only.[21]

This traditional, hierarchical model of male sexual relations represents sexual preference without sexual orientation. Numbers of texts going back to classical antiquity testify to a conscious erotic preference on the part of men, even to the point of exclusivity, for sexual intercourse with members of one sex rather than the other;[22] indeed, a venerable subgenre of erotic literature consists of formal debates between two men about whether women or boys are superior vehicles of male sexual gratification. Such playful debates are widely distributed in the luxury literatures of traditional male societies: examples can be found in Greek prose works from late antiquity, in medieval European and Arabic poetry and prose, in late imperial Chinese writings, and in the literary productions of the "floating world"—the sophisticated literature of town life in seventeenth-century Japan.[23]

But the explicit and conscious erotic preferences voiced in such contexts should not be equated with declarations of sexual orientation, for at least three reasons. First, they are presented as the outcome of conscious choice, a choice that expresses the male subject's values and preferred way of life, rather than as symptoms of an involuntary psychosexual condition. The men who voice such preferences often see themselves as at least nominally capable of responding to the erotic appeal of both good-looking women and good-looking boys. This is sexual object choice as an expression of ethics or aesthetics, as an exercise in erotic connoisseurship, not as a reflex of sexuality. It is more like vegetarianism than homosexuality. Second, same-sex sexual object choice in and of itself does not necessarily function in this context as a marker of difference. It does not individuate men from one another in terms of their "sexuality." Finally, same-sex sexual object choice in this case does not mark itself visibly on a man's physical appearance or inscribe itself in his personal mannerisms or deportment. Nor does it impugn his masculinity.[24]

Nonetheless, pederasty or sodomy did provide a means for men to express and discuss their sexual tastes, to explore their erotic subjectivities, and to compare their sexual preferences. It is in the context of erotic reflection by socially empowered, superordinate, conventionally masculine males that men have been able to articulate conscious erotic preferences, sometimes to the point of exclusivity, for sexual relations with boys or women, as well as for sexual relations with certain kinds of boys or women. The highly elaborate, ritualistic, conspicuously public practice of courtship and lovemaking provided socially empowered males with a traditional, socially sanctioned discursive space for articulating such preferences and for presenting themselves as conscious *subjects* of desire.

This point is an important one for historians, and it has long been obscured. John Boswell, who influentially defined as "gay sexuality" all same-sex "eroticism associated with a conscious preference," thought that if he could find evidence in premodern Europe of conscious erotic preference by one male for another, he would have documented the existence of gay sexuality in that period as well.[25] Of course, evidence of conscious erotic preferences does exist in abundance, but it tends to be found in the context of discourses linked to the senior partners in hierarchical relations of pederasty or sodomy. It therefore points not to the existence of gay sexuality per se but to one particular discourse and set of practices constituting one aspect of gay sexuality as we currently define it. Declarations of conscious erotic preferences are rarely, if ever, to be found in the contexts of the three other traditional discourses of male same-sex eroticism and gender deviance discussed here. And so conscious same-sex erotic preference ought not be equated with the whole of gay sexuality or male homosexuality. It represents merely one historical tradition among several.[26]

Far removed from the hierarchical world of the sexual penetration of subordinate males by superordinate males is the world of male friendship and love, which can claim an equally ancient discursive tradition. To be sure, hierarchy is not always absent from social relations between male friends: from the heroic comradeships of Gilgamesh and Enkidu in the Babylonian *Epic of Gilgamesh*, David and Jonathan in the biblical Books of Samuel, and Achilles and Patroclus in the *Iliad* to the latest American biracial cop thriller, male friendships often reveal striking patterns of asymmetry.[27] Precisely to the extent, however, that such friendships *are* structured by social divisions or by inequalities of power, to the extent that they approximate patron–client relationships in which the two "friends" are assigned radically different duties, postures, and roles, to just that extent are such friendships opened up to the possibility of being interpreted, then as now, in pederastic or sodomitical terms.[28] Within the horizons of the male world, as we have seen, hierarchy itself is *hot*: it is indissociably bound up with at least the potential for erotic signification. Hence disparities of power between male intimates take on an immediate and inescapable aura of eroticism. No wonder, then, that three and four centuries after the composition of the *Iliad*, some Greeks of the classical period interpreted Achilles and Patroclus as a pederastic couple (although they could not always agree who was the man and who was the boy), while more recently scholars have disputed whether David and Jonathan were lovers. Such disputes, which often have a long history, tend to conflate notions of friendship with notions of erotic hierarchy or sodomy and with notions of homosexuality. It may be useful therefore to distinguish friendship both from erotic hierarchy and from homoerotic desire.

It should be noted that in addition to the tradition of the heroic warrior with his subordinate male pal or sidekick (who inevitably dies), in addition to the patron–client model of male friendship, there is another tradition that emphasizes equality, mutuality, and reciprocity in love between men. Such an egalitarian relation can obtain only between two men who occupy the same social rank, usually an elite one, and who can claim the same status in terms of age, masculinity, and social empowerment. In the eighth and ninth books of his *Nicomachean Ethics*, Aristotle championed precisely such a reciprocal model of friendship between male equals, and he wrote, most influentially, that the best sort of friend is "another self," an *allos autos* or alter ego (9.4 [1166a31]). The sentiment is echoed repeatedly through the centuries: a true friend is part of oneself, indistinguishable from oneself. True friends have a single mind, a single heart in two bodies. As Montaigne writes in his essay "On Friendship," "Our souls mingle and blend with each other so completely that they efface the seam that joined them, and cannot find it again."[29] The friendship of virtuous men is characterized by a disinterested love that leads to a merging of individual identities and hence to an unwillingness to live without the other, a readiness to die with or for the other. We find the theme of the inseparability of male friends in both life and death repeated time and again from representations of Achilles and Patroclus, Orestes and Pylades, Theseus and Pirithous in the ancient world to *Lethal Weapon*'s Mel Gibson and Danny Glover in the modern world.

The language used to convey such passionate male unions often appears to modern sensibilities suspiciously overheated, if not downright erotic. Thus Montaigne can write:

> If you press me to tell why I loved him, I feel that this cannot be expressed, except by answering: Because it was he, because it was I. . . . it is I know not what . . . which, having seized my whole will, led it to plunge and lose itself in his; which, having seized his whole will, led it to plunge and lose itself in mine, with equal hunger, equal rivalry. I say lose, in truth, for neither of us reserved anything for himself, nor was anything either his or mine. . . . Our souls pulled together in such unison, they regarded each other with such ardent affection, and with a like affection revealed themselves to each other to the very depths of our hearts, that not only did I know his soul as well as mine, but I should certainly have trusted myself to him more readily than to myself.[30]

Similarly, in a 1677 drama on a Roman theme by Dryden, *All for Love*, Antony can say about his noble friend Dolabella:

> I was his soul, he lived not but in me.
> We were so closed within each other's breasts,
> The rivets were not found that joined us first.
> That does not reach us yet: we were so mixed
> As meeting streams, both to ourselves were lost;
> We were one mass; we could not give or take
> But from the same, for he was I, I he.
>
> (3.90–96)[31]

It is difficult for us moderns, with our heavily psychologistic model of the human personality, of conscious and unconscious desire, and our heightened sensitivity to anything that might seem to contravene the strict protocols of heterosexual masculinity, to avoid reading into such passionate expressions of male love a suggestion of "homoeroticism" at the very least, if not of "latent homosexuality"—formulations that often act as a cover for our own perplexity about how to interpret the evidence before us. But quite apart from the difficulty of entering into the emotional lives of premodern subjects, we need to reckon with the discursive contexts in which such passionate declarations were produced. The thematic insistence on mutuality and the merging of individual identities, although it may invoke in the minds of modern readers the formulas of heterosexual romantic love (e.g., Cathy's "I am Heathcliff"), in fact situates avowals of reciprocal love between male friends in an honorable, even glamorous tradition of heroic comradeship: precisely by banishing any hint of subordination on the part of one friend to the other, and thus any suggestion of hierarchy, the emphasis on the fusion of two souls into one actually distances such a love from erotic passion. Montaigne never betrays the slightest doubt, in writing about his love for Etienne de La Boétie, that the sentiments he expresses are entirely normative, even admirable and boastworthy (although of course unique in their specifics). Far from offering us clues to his psychopathology, inadvertently revealing to us traces of his suppressed or unconscious desires or expressing his erotic peculiarities (something he freely does elsewhere in his *Essays*), Montaigne seems to have understood that the account of friendship he offers would be immune to disreputable interpretation, in part because his love is so elaborately presented as egalitarian, nonhierarchical, and reciprocal. For by that means he detaches it from the erotic realms of difference and hierarchy, setting it explicitly *against* the sexual love of men and women as well as the male sexual enjoyment of boys.

Sexual love, at least as it is viewed within the cultural horizons of the male world, is all about penetration and therefore all about position, superiority and inferiority, rank and status, gender and difference. Friendship, by contrast, is all about sameness: sameness of rank and status, sameness of sentiment, sameness of identity. It is this very emphasis on identity, similarity, and mutuality that distances the friendship tradition, in its original social and discursive context, from the world of sexual love. So why include it here, in a genealogy of male homosexuality? Because the friendship tradition provided socially empowered men with an established discursive venue in which to express, without social reproach, sentiments of passionate and mutual love for one another, and such passionate, mutual love between persons of the same sex is an important component of what we now call homosexuality.

Both pederasty/sodomy and friendship/love are consonant with masculine gender norms, with conventional masculinity as it has been defined in a number of European cultures. If anything, pederasty and friendship are both traditionally masculinizing, insofar as they express the male subject's virility and imply a thoroughgoing rejection of everything that is feminine. Both can therefore be seen as consolidating male gender identity (although not, of course, in every instance). As such, they belong to a different conceptual, moral, and social universe from what the Greeks called *kinaidia*, the Romans *mollitia*, and the nineteenth-century sexologists "contrary sexual feeling" or "sexual inversion." All these terms refer to the male "inversion" or reversal of masculine gender identity, a wholesale surrender of masculinity in favor of femininity, a transgendered condition expressed in everything from personal comportment and style to physical appearance, manner of feeling, sexual attraction to "normal" men, and preference for a receptive or "passive" role in sexual intercourse with such men.

The mere fact of being sexually penetrated by a man is much less significant for the sexual classification of passives or inverts than the question of the penetrated male's pleasure. In the premodern systems of pederasty and sodomy, boys do not derive much pleasure from the sexual act: they are the more or less willing objects of adult male desire, but they are not conventionally assigned a share of desire equal to that of their senior male partners, nor are they expected to enjoy being penetrated by them. Although they are "passive" in terms of their behavior, then, they are not passive in their overall erotic temperament or attitude: they are not aroused by the prospect or the act of submission. They have to be motivated to submit to their male lovers by a variety of largely nonsexual inducements, such as gifts or threats. So their "passivity" does not extend to their desire, which remains unengaged and can therefore claim to be uncontaminated by any impulse to subordination, any hint of "femininity." *Kinaidoi* (*cinaedi* in Latin) and inverts, by contrast, actively desire to submit their bodies "passively" to sexual penetration by men, and in this sense they are seen as having a woman's desire, subjectivity, and gender identity. The category of male passive or invert applies specifically to subordinate males whose willingness to submit themselves to sexual penetration by men proceeds not from some nonsexual motive but from their own erotic desires and/or from their assumption of a feminine gender identity.

Although the pleasure he takes in being sexually penetrated may be the most flagrant, the most extreme expression of the overall gender reversal that characterizes the male invert, inversion is not necessarily, or even principally, defined by the enjoyment of particular sexual acts. Nor does it have to do strictly with homosexual desire, because inverts may have insertive phallic sex with women without ceasing to be considered inverts. Rather, inversion has to do with deviant gender identity, sensibility, and personal style, one aspect of which is the "womanly" liking for a passive role in sexual intercourse with other men. Therefore notions of inversion do not tend to make a strict separation between specifically sexual manifestations of inversion and other, equally telling deviations from the norms of masculinity, such as the adoption of feminine dress. The emphasis falls on a violation of the protocols of manhood, a characterological failure of grand proportions that cannot be redeemed (as sodomy can) by the enjoyment of sexual relations with women. Inversion is not about sexuality but about gender.[32]

What, then, is the difference between effeminates and passives? What distinguishes those men (belonging to my first category) who affect a "soft" style of masculinity and prefer making love to making war from those men (belonging to this fourth category) who have effeminate mannerisms and wish to submit their bodies, in "womanly" fashion, to the phallic pleasures of other men? The distinction is a subtle one, and it is easily blurred. After all, some stigma of gender deviance, of effeminacy, applies to both types of men. And polarized definitions of the masculine and the feminine, along with the hyperbolic nature of sexual stereotyping, enable the slightest suggestion of gender deviance to be quickly inflated and transformed into an accusation of complete and total gender treason. From *liking* women to wanting to be *like* women is, according to the phobic logic of this masculinist ideology, only a small step—which is why both effeminates and passives ("pathics") can be characterized as "soft" or unmasculine. The common application of the vocabulary of gender deviance to both effeminates and passives complicates for the modern interpreter the problem of distinguishing them.

One way to describe the difference between effeminates and passives is to contrast a universalizing notion of gender deviance with a minoritizing one. "Softness" either may represent the specter of potential gender failure that haunts all normative masculinity, an ever-present threat to the masculinity of every man, or it may represent the disfiguring peculiarity of a small class of deviant individuals.[33] Effeminates are men who succumb to a tendency that all normal men have and that all normal men have to guard against or suppress in themselves, whereas passives are men who are so unequal to the struggle that they can be seen to suffer from a specific constitutional defect, namely, a lack of the masculine capacity to withstand the appeal of pleasure (especially pleasure deemed exceptionally disgraceful or degrading) as well as a tendency to adopt a specifically feminine attitude of surrender in relations with other men.

It is these features that define the invert, even more than his desire or his sexual object choice, because the latter are not unique to him. The desire for a male partner, for example, is something the invert has in common both with the pederast and with the heroic friend, figures vastly removed from him in social and moral status. Inversion also differs from pederasty and friendship in that the love of boys and the love of friends are not necessarily discreditable sentiments, and they may well be confessed or even championed by the subjects themselves, whereas inversion is a shameful condition, never proclaimed about oneself, almost always ascribed to some other by an accuser whose intent is to demean and to vilify.

Moreover, traditional representations of "active" pederasts or sodomites do not necessarily portray them as visibly different in their appearance from normal men. You can't always tell a pederast or sodomite by looking at him. An invert, by contrast, usually stands out, because his reversal of his gender identity affects his personal demeanor and shapes his attitude, gestures, and manner of conducting himself. Unlike the active penetration of boys, which might differentiate the lover of boys from the lover of women in terms of erotic preference but may not mark him as a visibly different sort of person, passivity or inversion stamps itself all over a man's social presentation and identifies him as a spectacularly deviant social type. It is in the context of inversion that we most often find produced and elaborated representations of a peculiar character type or stereotype, a phobic caricature embodying the supposedly visible and flagrant features of male sexual and gender deviance. Although this type is attached to homosexual sex, it is not attached to homosexual sex absolutely, for it is connected much less regularly, if at all, with pederasty or "active" sodomy; rather, it seems to be associated with passive or receptive homosexual sex, seen as merely one aspect of a more generalized gender reversal, an underlying betrayal of masculinity.[34] There is a remarkably consistent emphasis throughout the history of European sexual representation on the deviant morphology of the invert, his visibly different mode of appearance and dress, his feminine style of self-presentation. Inversion manifests itself outwardly.

It doesn't take one to know one. Everybody seems to know what an invert looks like and how he behaves, even if no normal man could possibly impersonate one. As a character in an ancient Greek comedy says, "*I* have absolutely no idea how to use a twittering voice or walk about in an effeminate style, with my head tilted sidewise like all those pathics that I see here in the city smeared with depilatories."[35] Similarly, the Roman orator Quintilian speaks of "the plucked body, the broken walk, the female attire" as "signs of one who is *mollis* [soft] and not a real man."[36] Ancient physiognomists, experts in the learned technique of deciphering a person's character from his or her appearance, provide a more detailed description of the type:

> You may recognize him by his provocatively melting glance and by the rapid movement of his intensely staring eyes. His brow is furrowed while his eyebrows and cheeks are in constant motion. His head is tilted to the side, his loins do not hold still, and his slack limbs never stay in one position. He minces along with little jumping steps; his knees knock together. He carries his hands with palms turned upward. He has a shifting gaze, and his voice is thin, weepy, shrill, and drawling.[37]

All attempts at concealment are useless: "For it is by the twitching of their lips and the rotation of their eyes, by the haphazard and inconsistent shifting of their feet, by the movement of their hips and the fickle motion of their hands, and by the tremor of their voice as it begins with difficulty to speak, that effeminates are most easily revealed."[38]

But the ability to unmask an invert is hardly limited to specialist gender detectives. The Roman leader Scipio Aemilianus, consul in 147 BC and censor in 142, had no difficulty branding an opponent with all the telltale signs: "For the kind of man who adorns himself daily in front of a mirror, wearing perfume; whose eyebrows are shaved off; who walks around with plucked beard and thighs; who when he was a young man reclined at banquets next to his lover, wearing a long-sleeved tunic; who is as fond of men as he is of wine: can anyone doubt that he has done what *cinaedi* are in the habit of doing?"[39] The unmentionable deed of the *cinaedi*, of course, is passive bodily penetration.

The particular markers of inversion may be culture-bound and therefore susceptible to change over time, but the legibility of inversion is one of its perennial features. The medieval and early modern "catamite" (a word sometimes presumed, on the basis of dubious etymological reasoning, to signify the passive partner of a sodomite) is another highly "overt" type, and he seems little more than a *cinaedus* got up in medieval dress. Here, for example, is a retrospective account of the goings-on at the court of the English king William Rufus, at the turn of the twelfth century, by a monastic chronicler named Orderic Vitalis:

> At that time effeminates set the fashion in many parts of the world: foul catamites, doomed to eternal fire, unrestrainedly pursued their revels and shamelessly gave themselves up to the filth of sodomy. They rejected the traditions of honest men, ridiculed the counsel of priests, and persisted in their barbarous way of life and style of dress. They parted their hair from the crown of the head to the forehead, grew long and luxurious locks like women, and loved to deck themselves in long, over-tight shirts and tunics.[40]

From here it is a small step to the Renaissance court of the French king Henri III, where in July 1576 one observer, commenting indignantly on the "effeminate, lewd make-up and adornments" of the king's *mignons*—minions, or darlings (a synonym for "catamite")—remarked that "these fine *mignons* wear their hair long, curled and recurled by means of artifice, with little velvet bonnets on top of it, like the whores of the brothels."[41]

A century and a half later Londoners painted a vivid portrait of the "mollies," the effeminate men who gathered privately in certain taverns called "molly houses." Samuel Stevens, a religious crusader for the reformation of morals, furnished a description in November 1725:

> I found between 40 and 50 men making love to one another, as they called it. Sometimes they would sit in one another's laps, kissing in a lewd manner and using their hands indecently. Then they would get up, dance and make curtsies, and mimic the voices of women. . . . Then they would hug, and play, and toy, and go out by couples into another room on the same floor to be married, as they called it.

Another firsthand account of a molly house includes a description of a costume ball held there:

> The men [were] calling one another "my dear" and hugging, kissing, and tickling each other as if they were a mixture of wanton males and females, and assuming effeminate voices and airs. . . . Some were completely rigged in gowns, petticoats, headcloths, fine laced shoes, furbelowed scarves, and masks; some had riding hoods; some were dressed like milkmaids, others like shepherdesses with green hats, waistcoats, and petticoats; and others had their faces patched and painted and wore very extensive hoop petticoats, which had been very lately introduced.[42]

A literary echo of this stereotype can be found in the figure of Captain Whiffle, in Tobias Smollett's novel *Roderick Random* (1748). But it is a character in John Cleland's *Memoirs of a Woman of Pleasure* (also 1748) who makes this traditional point in terms that look forward to the pathologizing discourses of the modern era. There is, she says, "a plague-spot visibly imprinted on all that are tainted" with this passion.[43]

For it was precisely this visibly disfigured victim of erotic malignancy who provided neurologists and psychiatrists in the latter part of the nineteenth century with the clinical basis for the first systematic scientific conceptualization and definition of pathological (or perverted) sexual orientation. In August 1869, the same year that witnessed the first printed appearance of the word "homosexuality," Karl Friedrich Otto Westphal, a German expert on "the diseases of the nerves" or "nervous system," published an article on "contrary sexual feeling" or "sensibility" [conträre Sexualempfindung], which he presented as a symptom of a neuropathic or psychopathic condition.[44] Specialists continued to argue over the proper scientific designation for this condition, and already by 1878 an Italian specialist by the name of Arrigo Tamassia could speak of "inversion of the sexual instinct," a designation that ultimately proved more popular than Westphal's formula.[45] But we should not be deceived by all this fervor of terminological innovation: despite the newfangled names, the condition that the doctors were busy constructing as a perverted orientation was essentially the same one that had been ascribed from time immemorial to the stigmatized figure of the *kinaidos* or *cinaedus*, the *mollis*, the "catamite," "pathic," "minion," or "molly."[46] It was this venerable category of "folk" belief that was reconstructed by means of the conceptual apparatus of modern sexology into a new scientific classification of sexual and gender deviance, a psycho-sexual orientation.

But sexual inversion, if it was indeed an orientation, still did not equate to homosexuality. "Contrary sexual feeling," for example, was intended to signify a sexual feeling contrary to the sex of the person who experienced it, that is, a feeling of belonging to a different sex from one's own *as well as* a feeling of erotic attraction at odds with the sex to which one belonged (because its object was a member of the same sex as oneself and because it expressed a masculine or feminine attitude proper to members of a sex different from one's own). Westphal, like many of his contemporaries, did not distinguish systematically between sexual deviance and gender deviance. Attraction to members of one's own sex indicated an identification with the opposite sex, and an identification with the opposite sex sometimes expressed itself as a feeling of sexual attraction to members of one's own sex. In this Westphal was reproducing the assumptions of his own culture, but he had also been influenced by the arguments of Karl Heinrich Ulrichs, the first political activist for homosexual emancipation, who in a series of writings composed from about 1862 on described his own condition as that of an *anima muliebris virili corpore inclusa*, a "woman's soul confined by a male body."[47]

Similarly, the concept of sexual inversion treated same-sex sexual desire and object choice as merely one of a number of pathological symptoms exhibited by those who reversed, or "inverted," the sex roles thought appropriate to their own sex: such symptoms, indicating masculine identification in women and feminine identification in men, comprised many different elements of personal style, ranging from the ideologically loaded (women who took an interest in politics and campaigned for the right to vote) to the trivial and bizarre (men who liked cats),[48] but the thread that linked them was sex-role reversal or gender deviance. Sexual preference for a member of one's own sex was not clearly distinguished from other sorts of nonconformity to one's gender identity, as defined by prevailing cultural norms of manliness and womanliness. One implication of this model, which differentiates it strikingly from notions of homosexuality, is that the conventionally masculine and feminine same-sex partners of inverts are not necessarily abnormal or problematic or deviant themselves: the straight-identified male hustler or the fem who allows herself to be pleasured by a butch is merely acting out a proper sexual scenario with an improper partner and may well be sexually normal in his or her own right.[49]

If pederasty or sodomy was traditionally understood as a sexual preference without a sexual orientation, inversion was defined as a psychological orientation without a sexuality. In a footnote at the end of his article Westphal emphasized "the fact that 'contrary sexual feeling' *does not always coincidentally concern the sexual drive as such* but simply the feeling of being alienated, with one's entire inner being, from one's own sex—a less developed stage, as it were, of the pathological phenomenon."[50] For Westphal and his colleagues, "contrary sexual feeling" or sexual inversion was an essentially psychological condition of gender dysphoria that affected the inner life of the individual, an *orientation* not necessarily expressed in the performance or enjoyment of particular (homo)sexual acts. One of Westphal's star examples of "contrary sexual feeling" was in fact an individual who strictly avoided—or at least claimed to avoid—all sexual contact with members of his own sex and was diagnosed as suffering from "contrary sexual feeling" on the basis of his gender style alone, not on the basis of homosexual desire. This was one "Aug. Ha.," who had been arrested at a train station in Berlin in the winter of 1868 while wearing women's clothes. He had worked as a servant for several households, often wearing female attire and even owning fake breasts at some point; he had also stolen women's clothing and toiletries from his employers and had been imprisoned for using false identities. Westphal noted the "almost effeminate conduct of the patient, who speaks with a lisping voice in an effeminate tone" and whose ears bore traces of piercing. Anatomically, Aug. Ha. was hardly exotic: examination revealed strong pubic hair up to the navel; the skin of the penis was strongly pigmented and wrinkled; the testicles were only of "moderate size"; and the anus showed "nothing special." More to the point, Ha. claimed that he "never let himself be used by men and never busied himself with them in a sexual way, even though many offers in this direction reached him." He had simply had a "drive" to dress up as a woman since he was eight years old. He had always had good relations with women and had gone out dancing with them while wearing women's clothes himself. He continued to occupy himself with needlework, embroidering cloths and manufacturing small women's hats, while under observation in the hospital.[51]

Sexual inversion, then, does not represent the same notion as homosexuality, because same-sex sexual object choice, or homosexual desire, is not essential to it: one can be inverted without being homosexual, and one can have homosexual sex, if one is a pederast or sodomite, without qualifying as sexually inverted. Hence, as Kinsey (who was versed in these concepts) insisted, "Inversion and homosexuality are two distinct and not always correlated types of behavior."[52] Instead, the notions of "contrary sexual feeling" and sexual inversion seem to glance back at the long tradition of stigmatized male passivity, effeminacy, and gender deviance, which focuses less on homosexual sex or homosexual desire per se than on an accompanying lack of normative masculinity in one or both of the partners.[53]

Now, at last, we come to homosexuality, a category whose peculiar and distinctive features and ramifications will, I hope, stand out more clearly in contrast to the four discursive traditions already discussed. The word "homosexuality" appeared in print for the first time in German in 1869, in two anonymous pamphlets published in Leipzig by an Austrian translator of Hungarian literature who took the name of Karl Maria Kertbeny. Although Kertbeny claimed publicly to be "sexually normal" himself, his term "homosexuality" can be considered an originally progay coinage, insofar as Kertbeny used it in the course of an unsuccessful political campaign to prevent homosexual sex from being criminalized by the newly formed Federation of North German States.

Unlike "contrary sexual feeling," "sexual inversion," and "Uranian love," "homosexuality" was not coined to interpret the phenomenon it described or to attach a particular psychological or medical theory to it, and Kertbeny himself was vehemently opposed to third-sex or inversion models of homosexual desire. "Homosexuality" simply referred to a sexual drive directed toward persons of the same sex as the sex of the person who was driven by it. Indeed, it was the term's very minimalism, from a theoretical perspective, that made it so easily adaptable by later writers and theorists with a variety of ideological purposes. As a result, the term now condenses a number of different notions about same-sex sexual attraction as well as a number of different conceptual models for defining what homosexuality is.

Specifically, "homosexuality" absorbs and combines at least three distinct and previously uncorrelated concepts: (1) a psychiatric notion of perverted or pathological *orientation*, derived from Westphal and his nineteenth-century colleagues, which is an essentially psychological concept that applies to the inner life of the individual and does not necessarily presume same-sex sexual behavior; (2) a psychoanalytic notion of same-sex *sexual object choice* or desire, derived from Freud and his coworkers, which is a category of erotic intentionality and does not necessarily imply a permanent sexual orientation, let alone a deviant or pathological one (since, according to Freud, most normal individuals make an unconscious homosexual object choice at some point in their fantasy lives); and (3) a sociological notion of sexually *deviant behavior*, derived from nineteenth- and twentieth-century forensic inquiries into "social problems," which focuses on nonstandard sexual practice and does not necessarily refer to erotic psychology or sexual orientation (since same-sex sexual behavior, as Kinsey showed, is not the exclusive property of those with a homosexual sexual orientation, nor is it necessarily pathological, since it is widely represented in the population). So neither a notion of orientation, a notion of object choice, nor a notion of behavior alone is sufficient to generate the modern definition of "homosexuality"; rather, the notion seems to depend on the unstable conjunction of all three. "Homosexuality" is at once a psychological condition, an erotic desire, and a sexual practice (and those are three quite different things).

Furthermore, the very notion of homosexuality implies that same-sex sexual feeling and expression, in all their many forms, constitute a single thing, called "homosexuality," which can be thought of as a single integrated phenomenon, distinct and separate from "heterosexuality." "Homosexuality" refers to *all* same-sex sexual desire and behavior, whether hierarchical or mutual, gender-polarized or ungendered, latent or actual, mental or physical.

The originality of "homosexuality" as a category and a concept appears more vividly in this light. Earlier discourses, whether of sodomy or inversion, referred to only one of the partners: the "active" partner in the case of sodomy, the effeminate male or masculine female in the case of inversion. The other partner, the one who was not motivated by sexual desire or who was not gender-deviant, did not qualify for inclusion in the category. "Homosexuality," by contrast, applies to *both* partners, whether active or passive, whether gendered normatively or deviantly. The hallmark of "homosexuality," in fact, is the refusal to distinguish between same-sex sexual partners or to rank them by treating one of them as more (or less) homosexual than the other.

Kinsey can be taken as representative of this modern outlook. Dismissing as "propaganda" the tendency of some men to define their own sexual identity according to a role-specific, prehomosexual model—to consider themselves straight because they only had fellatio performed on them by other men and never performed it themselves—Kinsey wrote that all "physical contacts with other males" that result in orgasm are "by any strict definition . . . homosexual."[54] According to Kinsey, in other words, it doesn't matter who sucks whom.

In this way homosexuality, both as a concept and as a social practice, significantly re-arranges and reinterprets earlier patterns of erotic organization, and as such it has an additional number of important practical consequences. First, under the aegis of homosexuality, the significance of gender and of gender roles for categorizing sexual acts and sexual actors fades.[55] So one effect of the concept of homosexuality is to detach sexual object choice from any necessary connection with gender identity, making it possible to ascribe homosexuality to women and to men whose gender styles and outward appearance or manner are perfectly normative.

To be sure, this conceptual transformation has not been either total or absolute. Many people nowadays, both gay and nongay, continue to draw a direct connection between gender deviance and homosexuality. Despite the dominance of the categories of homosexuality and heterosexuality, "active" women and "passive" men, as well as effeminate men and masculine women, are still considered somehow *more homosexual* than other, less flamboyantly deviant persons who make homosexual object choices. Here we can discern the force with which earlier, prehomosexual sexual categories continue to exert their authority within the newer conceptual universe of homo- and heterosexuality. In some quarters it still matters a lot who sucks whom. Nonetheless, one effect of the modern homo-/heterosexual model has been to downplay the taxonomic significance of gender identities and sexual roles. Even the most asymmetrical behaviors can get trumped for the purposes of sexual classification by the sameness or difference of the sexes of the persons involved. Witness the anxiety expressed in the following anonymous letter to the sex advice columnist of an alternative newspaper:

> I'm a 200 percent straight guy, married with children. About six months ago, I went to a masseur who finished things with a terrific blow job. If you wonder why I didn't stop him, the truth is, I couldn't, because he was massaging my asshole with his thumb while blowing me. It was so good that I've been going back to this guy just about every week, not for the massage but for the blow job. Now I'm starting to worry that this might label me as gay. I have no interest in blowing this guy, but I wonder if the guy who gets the blow job is as guilty as the one who does it.[56]

The letter writer's worry is a direct effect of the emergent discourses of sexuality and of the recent changes in sexual classification that they have introduced. No such anxieties assail those as yet untouched by the discourses of sexuality.[57]

The homo-/heterosexual model has other consequences. Homosexuality translates same-sex sexual relations into the register of sameness and mutuality. Homosexual relations no longer necessarily imply an asymmetry of social identities or sexual positions, nor are they inevitably articulated in terms of hierarchies of power, age, gender, or sexual role (which, again, is not to deny that such hierarchies may continue to function meaningfully in a lesbian or gay male context).[58] Homosexual relations are not necessarily lopsided in their distribution of erotic pleasure or desire. Rather, like that of heterosexual romantic love, the notion of homosexuality implies that it is possible for sexual partners to bond with one another not on the basis of their difference but on the basis of their sameness, their identity of desire and orientation and "sexuality." Homosexual relations cease to be compulsorily structured by a polarization of identities and roles (active/passive, insertive/receptive, masculine/feminine, or man/boy). Exclusive, lifelong, companionate, romantic, and mutual homosexual love becomes possible for both partners. Homosexual relations are not organized merely according to the requirements or prescriptions of large-scale social institutions, such as kinship systems, age classes, or initiation rituals; rather, they function as principles of social organization in their own right and give rise to freestanding social institutions.[59]

Homosexuality is now set over against heterosexuality. Homosexual object choice, in and of itself, is seen as marking a difference from heterosexual object choice. Homo- and heterosexuality have become more or less mutually exclusive forms of human subjectivity, different kinds of human sexuality, and any feeling or expression of heterosexual desire is thought to rule out any feeling or expression of homosexual desire on the part of the same individual. Sexual object choice attaches to a notion of sexual orientation, such that sexual behavior is seen to express an underlying and permanent psychosexual feature of the human subject. Hence people are routinely assigned to one or the other of two sexual species on the basis of their sexual object choice and orientation.

In short, homosexuality is more than same-sex sexual object choice, more even than conscious erotic same-sex preference. Homosexuality is the specification of same-sex sexual object choice in and of itself as an overriding principle of sexual and social difference. Homosexuality is part of a new system of *sexuality*, which functions as a means of personal individuation: it assigns to each individual a sexual orientation and a sexual identity. As such, homosexuality introduces a novel element into social organization, into the social articulation of human difference, into the social production of desire, and ultimately into the social construction of the self.

It may be easier to grasp some of the overlapping and distinguishing features of our five discursive traditions in the history of (homo)sexual classification by consulting Table 1. As this schematic comparison indicates, each of the five traditions is irreducible to the others. I am not interested in defending the rightness or wrongness of the individual answers I have given to my own set of questions (I acknowledge that my answers are debatable); rather, I wish to show by the way my affirmatives and negatives are scattered across the chart that the patterns I have sketched do not reduce to a single coherent scheme.

One way to make sense of Table 16.1 is to note the radical difference between the final category ("homosexuality") and the four others. All of the first four traditional, postclassical, or premodern categories ("effeminacy," "pederasty/sodomy," "friendship/love," "passivity/inversion") depend crucially on notions of gender. This is obvious in the case of effeminacy and passivity/inversion, but it is also true of pederasty/sodomy and friendship/love, since they are defined by the male subject's embodiment and performance of traditionally masculine and masculinizing norms, just as effeminacy and passivity/inversion are defined by the male subject's violation of them. In premodern systems of sex and gender, the notion of "sexuality" is dispensable, because the regulation of conduct and social status is accomplished by the gender system alone. Of course, social status and class also contribute to the production of the first four categories. For example, effeminacy applies especially to those men who

Table 1 The five categories

	Effeminacy	*Sodomy*	*Friendship*	*Inversion*	*Homosexuality*
Is it an orientation?	No	Not really	No	Yes (?)	Yes
Does it involve gender deviance?	Yes	No (?)	No	Yes	Maybe
Does it involve same-sex genital contact?	Not necessarily	Mostly	No	Sometimes	Mostly
Is it a sexual preference?	No	Sometimes	No	No	Yes
Does it represent a character type?	Yes	No (?)	No	Yes	Maybe
Does it involve homoerotic desire?	Sometimes	Yes, at least for one partner	Maybe	Sometimes	Yes
Does it classify women and men together?	No	No	No	Yes	Yes
Is it constant across a sex or gender transition?	No	No	No	No	Maybe

are high enough in rank and status to be susceptible of suffering a loss or reduction in rank by comporting themselves at variance with the behavior expected of the elite. Friendship/love demands an equality of rank between the partners, whereas pederasty/sodomy depends on a socially significant difference between the partners in age, status, and sexual role. Passivity/inversion defines itself in relation to the gender hierarchy. With the arrival of homosexuality, the systems of difference that were internal to the structure of the previous four categories find themselves externalized and reconstituted at the border between homosexuality and heterosexuality, categories that now represent in and of themselves new strategies of social differentiation and regulation. The homo/hetero categories function not to maintain an already existing hierarchy of gender and status but to manage, by differentiating and disciplining, unranked masses of notionally identical "individuals." One name for this technique of governing individuals en masse is *normalization*.[60]

Perhaps the final irony in all this is that the very word *sex*, which itself may derive from the Latin *secare*, "to cut or divide," and which originally signified the sharpness and cleanness of the division between the natural categories of male and female, has had the fine edge of its meaning so blunted by the historical shifts and rearrangements in our conceptual maps of sexual life that it now represents what is most resistant to clear classification, discrimination, and division.

Notes

The title of my essay pays tribute to the work of Arnold I. Davidson, which has consistently, enduringly, and powerfully shaped my own: see, especially, his essays "How to Do the History of Psychoanalysis: A Reading of Freud's *Three Essays on the Theory of Sexuality*," *Critical Inquiry* 13 (1986–87): 252–77; "Sex and the Emergence of Sexuality," *Critical Inquiry* 14 (1987–88): 16–48; and "Closing Up the Corpses: Diseases of Sexuality and the Emergence of the Psychiatric Style of Reasoning," in *Meaning and Method: Essays in Honor of Hilary Putnam*, ed. George Boolos (Cambridge: Cambridge University Press, 1990), 295–325. In my recent work on the history of sexuality, particularly in this essay and in "Forgetting Foucault: Acts, Identities, and the History of Sexuality," *Representations* 63 (1998): 93–120, I have returned to a set of issues that Davidson's work first opened up for me and that I have pondered for well over a decade now. This essay represents the first installment of what I hope will be a larger project.

Many people have discussed with me the ideas touched on in this essay; I cannot list all their names here, as I would like to do. But I must thank Patricia Crawford and Hilary Fraser, who invited me to participate in their Australian Academy of the Social Sciences Workshop "Gender, Sexualities, and Historical Change," University of Western Australia, 31 July–1 August 1998. Discussions among members of that workshop provided the immediate stimulus for this essay. I owe a particular debt in this regard to Judith M. Bennett.

This essay was written for delivery at the conference "Sex and Conflict: Gay and Lesbian Studies in the Humanities and Social Sciences," Lund University, 9–10 October 1998. I wish to thank Eva Österberg and Johanna Esseveld for giving me that opportunity to present my work and Martha Vicinus and Lillian Faderman, my fellow participants, for encouraging me to persevere with it.

Finally, I would like to thank George E. Haggerty, whose work and conversation originally prompted me to broach some of these ideas. See now his *Men in Love: Masculinity and Sexuality in the Eighteenth Century* (New York: Columbia University Press, 1999), which offers a refreshingly different solution from the one proposed here to a similar question about how to do the history of male homosexuality.

Some of the material and the argumentation presented here also appear in my entry "Sex, Sexuality, Sexual Classification," in *Critical Terms for Gender Studies*, eds. Catharine Stimpson and Gilbert Herdt (Chicago: University of Chicago Press, 1998).

1   See, e.g., Jacqueline Murray, "Twice Marginal and Twice Invisible: Lesbians in the Middle Ages," in *Handbook of Medieval Sexuality*, eds. Vern L. Bullough and James A. Brundage (London: Garland, 1996), 191–222; or the otherwise excellent article by Anna Clark, "Anne Lister's Construction of Lesbian Identity," *Journal of the History of Sexuality* 7 (1996): 23–50.

2   Or so I argue in "Historicizing the Subject of Desire: Sexual Preferences and Erotic Identities in the Pseudo-Lucianic *Erôtes*," in *Foucault and the Writing of History*, ed. Jan Goldstein (Oxford: Blackwell, 1994), 19–34, 255–61; and in "Forgetting Foucault." For a quite different but powerful

and persuasive argument for the importance of emphasizing continuities in women's history see Judith M. Bennett, "Confronting Continuity," *Journal of Women's History* 9, no. 3 (1997): 73–94.

3   The demonstration of the existence of such an irreducible definitional uncertainty is the central, invaluable accomplishment of Eve Kosofsky Sedgwick, *Epistemology of the Closet* (Berkeley: University of California Press, 1990). As will become evident, I have taken on board her critique (45–48) of my earlier work, *One Hundred Years of Homosexuality and Other Essays on Greek Love* (New York: Routledge, 1990), applying her lesson about the irresolvable contradictions in what we are too quick to call "homosexuality as we understand it today." At the same time, however, I will continue to insist on documenting the existence of what she terms, sarcastically, "a Great Paradigm Shift" in the history of homosexuality, namely, the emergence of the discourses of homosexuality themselves in the modern period. Far from seeing a conflict between a historical inquiry into the construction of homosexuality and a discursive analysis of the contradictions in the modern notion of homosexuality, I see such a historical inquiry as helping account for the ineradicable incoherence of the modern notion. Sedgwick's own work, in fact, has enabled me to bring the historical and discursive critiques of homosexuality into closer and more systematic alignment.

4   Martin Bauml Duberman, Martha Vicinus, and George Chauncey Jr., eds., *Hidden from History: Reclaiming the Gay and Lesbian Past* (New York: New American Library, 1989), 8.

5   See Randolph Trumbach, "London's Sodomites: Homosexual Behavior and Western Culture in the Eighteenth Century," *Journal of Social History* 11 (1977): 1–33; Barry D. Adam, "Age, Structure, and Sexuality: Reflections on the Anthropological Evidence on Homosexual Relations," in *Anthropology and Homosexual Behavior*, ed. Evelyn Blackwood (New York: Haworth, 1986), 19–33; Adam, "Structural Foundations of the Gay World," in *Queer Theory / Sociology*, ed. Steven Seidman (Oxford: Blackwell, 1996), 111–26; and David F. Greenberg, *The Construction of Homosexuality* (Chicago: University of Chicago Press, 1988), 25. Greenberg speaks of "transgenderal," "transgenerational," and "egalitarian" types (the last two terms are, in my view, misleading).

6   Sedgwick, *Epistemology of the Closet*, 47.

7   There is a striking irony—no less striking for its having gone, so far as I know, totally unnoticed— in the section of *Epistemology of the Closet* in which Sedgwick justly criticizes social-constructionist historians of homosexuality because, to call attention to the differences between premodern and modern forms of homosexual expression, they typically draw a sharp contrast between earlier sexual categories and a falsely coherent, homogeneous, and unitary notion of "homosexuality as we understand it today," thereby treating the contemporary concept of homosexuality as "a coherent definitional field rather than a space of overlapping, contradictory, and conflictual definitional forces" (45). Sedgwick argues that it is wrong to suppose that earlier sexual categories are simply superseded or wholly replaced by later ones. Rather, she suggests, earlier sexual categories continue to reappear within later ones, producing an ineradicable instability in those later categories. Moreover, she produces an analysis of homosexual discourse in terms of what she regards as a well-nigh perennial tension among and between four definitional axes: minoritizing / universalizing modes of homosexual definition and gender-transitive versus gender-intransitive or gender-separatist modes of homosexual definition. By that means Sedgwick aims "to denarrativize" the narratives written by social-constructionist historians (including, explicitly, myself) by "focusing on a performative space of contradiction" (48). Although I have embraced Sedgwick's critique, as will be evident from this essay, I find it noteworthy that Sedgwick herself seems to ignore her own lesson in the very act of preaching it. For she announces that her intention is to end the essentialist-constructionist debate, "to promote [its] obsolescence" (40). In this she has been largely successful. As Ross Chambers observes in a superb commentary on this very passage in Sedgwick, "Without quite putting an end to the essentialist-constructivist debate, Sedgwick's move has effectively backgrounded it, and allowed an ongoing conversation to bracket it out by, as it were, changing the subject" ("Strategic Constructivism? Sedgwick's Ethics of Inversion," in *Regarding Sedgwick: Essays in Queer Culture and Critical Theory*, eds. Stephen Barber and David L. Clark [New York: Routledge, 2002]). In other words, Sedgwick delib- erately sets aside historical questions about the emergence of modern sexual categories and describes these questions as effectively superseded by her own approach; in a gesture exactly congruent with the one she criticizes, she structures her project in such a way that "the superseded model then drops out of the frame of analysis" (47). But just as the discourses of sodomy or inversion do not disappear with the emergence of the discourses of homosexuality, as Sedgwick rightly argues, so the historical problem of describing the differences between prehomosexual and homosexual formations will not simply disappear with a heightened awareness of the crisis of homo- and heterosexual definition in the present. It is now my turn to insist, against Sedgwick, on her very own axiom: despite her dazzling and important demonstration of the futility of playing the truth game called the essentialist-construc- tionist debate, the terms of that debate have not been superseded for historians by Sedgwick's

"focusing on [homo-heterosexual definition] as a performative space of contradiction." Rather than attempt to reassert the terms of the essentialist-constructionist debate in opposition to Sedgwick, however, I try here to reanimate the constructionist historical project in a more self-aware and theoretical spirit, so as to bring the Foucauldian historical and narratival critique of homosexual essentialism into greater harmony with the denarrativizing and performative critique advocated by Sedgwick.

8   Michel Foucault, *The History of Sexuality*, trans. Robert Hurley, 3 vols. (New York: Pantheon, 1978–86), 1:101.

9   Rosemary Daniell, *Sleeping with Soldiers: In Search of the Macho Man* (New York: Holt, Rinehart, and Winston, 1984), 71.

10   Pseudo-Lucian, *Erôtes* 9, trans. M. D. Macleod, in *Lucian VIII* (Cambridge, Mass.: Harvard University Press, 1967). See, generally, Halperin, "Historicizing the Subject of Desire."

11   Chariton, *Chaereas and Callirhoe* 1.4, trans. B. P. Reardon, in *Collected Ancient Greek Novels*, ed. B.P. Reardon (Berkeley: University of California Press, 1989), 27. Similarly, Artemidorus observes that men who dream that they wear facial makeup, jewelry, or unguents will suffer disgrace (i.e., will be exposed) as adulterers: see 81.15–17, 106.16–107.2, and 269.11–13 Pack, cited with discussion by Suzanne MacAlister, "Gender as Sign and Symbolism in Artemidoros' *Oneirokritika*: Social Aspirations and Anxieties," *Helios* 19 (1992): 140–60, esp. 149–50. Cf. the representations of Agathon in Old Comedy: commentary by Froma I. Zeitlin, "Travesties of Gender and Genre in Aristophanes' *Thesmophorizusae*," in *Playing the Other: Gender and Society in Classical Greek Literature* (Chicago: University of Chicago Press, 1996), 375–416; Frances Muecke, "A Portrait of the Artist as a Young Woman," *Classical Quarterly* 32 (1982): 41–55.

12   See Nicole Loraux, "Herakles: The Super-Male and the Feminine," trans. Robert Lamberton, in *Before Sexuality: The Construction of Erotic Experience in the Ancient Greek World*, eds. David M. Halperin, John J. Winkler, and Froma I. Zeitlin (Princeton: Princeton University Press, 1990), 21–52.

13   See Stephen Orgel, *Impersonations: The Performance of Gender in Shakespeare's England* (Cambridge: Cambridge University Press, 1996), 25–26. I wish to thank Vernon Rosario for suggesting the humoral gloss on this passage. See also Joseph Cady, "The 'Masculine Love' of the 'Princes of Sodom' 'Practising the Art of Ganymede' at Henri III's Court: The Homosexuality of Henri III and His *Mignons* in Pierre de L'Estoile's *Mémoires-Journaux*," in *Desire and Discipline: Sex and Sexuality in the Premodern West*, eds. Jacqueline Murray and Konrad Eisenbichler (Toronto: University of Toronto Press, 1996), 123–54, esp. 132–33: "However, in the Renaissance the word 'effeminate,' when applied to a man, did not automatically connote homosexuality, but instead had a diversity of meaning it lacks today. For instance, the term sometimes designated a kind of hyper or helpless male heterosexuality, a usage that, of course, no longer exists. Donne's remark that he is called 'effeminat' because he 'love[s] womens joyes,' in his epigram 'The Jughler' (1587?–1596?), belongs to this Renaissance tradition." For further details Cady refers to his earlier essay "Renaissance Awareness and Language for Heterosexuality: 'Love' and 'Feminine Love,'" in *Renaissance Discourses of Desire*, ed. Claude J. Summers and Ted-Larry Pebworth (Columbia: University of Missouri Press, 1993), 143–58.

14   Quoted by Davidson, "Closing Up the Corpses," 315.

15   See Randolph Trumbach, "The Birth of the Queen: Sodomy and the Emergence of Gender Equality in Modern Culture, 1660–1750," in Duberman, Vicinus, and Chauncey, *Hidden from History*, 129–40, 509–11.

16   I follow here the arguments of Davidson, "Closing Up the Corpses"; and George Chauncey Jr., "From Sexual Inversion to Homosexuality: Medicine and the Changing Conceptualization of Female Deviance," in *Passion and Power: Sexuality in History*, eds. Kathy Peiss and Christina Simmons, with Robert A. Padgug (Philadelphia: Temple University Press, 1989), 87–117.

17   See, for some recent examples, Thorkil Vanggaard, *Phallos: A Symbol and Its History in the Male World*, trans. from the Danish by the author (New York: International Universities Press, 1972), 17 and passim; Lionel Ovesey, *Homosexuality and Pseudohomosexuality* (New York: Science House, 1969); and Richard A. Posner, *Sex and Reason* (Cambridge, Mass.: Harvard University Press, 1992), esp. 105–7, 152, 296.

18   E.g., Gary W. Dowsett, *Practicing Desire: Homosexual Sex in the Era of AIDS* (Stanford: Stanford University Press, 1996).

19   See Robert B. Koehl, "The Chieftain Cup and a Minoan Rite of Passage," *Journal of Hellenic Studies* 106 (1986): 99–110; and Koehl, "Ephorus and Ritualized Homosexuality in Bronze Age Crete," in *Queer Representations: Reading Lives, Reading Cultures*, ed. Martin Duberman (New York: New York University Press, 1997), 7–13.

20   Michael Rocke, *Forbidden Friendships: Homosexuality and Male Culture in Renaissance Florence* (New York: Oxford University Press, 1996), 4, 96–97.

21   Thus, for example, the fourteenth- and fifteenth-century Florentine definitions of "sodomy" and "sodomite" refer to the "active" or insertive partner in anal intercourse only (ibid., 14, 110).

22   See Halperin, *One Hundred Years of Homosexuality*, 163 n. 53, for an admittedly incomplete list.

23   See Halperin, "Historicizing the Subject of Desire," esp. 24–25, 257–58 nn. 30–32; also Everett K. Rowson, "The Categorization of Gender and Sexual Irregularity in Medieval Arabic Vice Lists," in *Body Guards: The Cultural Politics of Gender Ambiguity*, eds. Julia Epstein and Kristina Straub (New York: Routledge, 1991), 50–79; and J.W. Wright and Everett K. Rowson, eds., *Homoeroticism in Classical Arabic Literature* (New York: Columbia University Press, 1997).

24   See Cynthia B. Herrup, *A House in Gross Disorder: Sex, Law, and the Second Earl of Castlehaven* (New York: Oxford University Press, 1999), 33: "The prosecutions for sodomy about which we have information before the late seventeenth century rarely condemned defendants for effeminate behavior; conversely, reproaches for effeminacy rarely included sexual examples."

25   John Boswell, *Christianity, Social Tolerance, and Homosexuality: Gay People in Western Europe from the Beginning of the Christian Era to the Fourteenth Century* (Chicago: University of Chicago Press, 1980), 44.

26   For an attempt to document several instances of same-sex sexual object choice, and even of conscious erotic preferences for persons of the same sex as oneself, that nonetheless do not satisfy the criteria for homosexuality, see Halperin, "Historicizing the Subject of Desire."

27   See Halperin, "Heroes and Their Pals," in *One Hundred Years of Homosexuality*, 75–87, 176–79.

28   See Alan Bray, "Homosexuality and the Signs of Male Friendship in Elizabethan England," in *Queering the Renaissance*, ed. Jonathan Goldberg (Durham: Duke University Press, 1994), 40–61. I interpret Bray to provide evidence for this claim, although he does not quite make it himself. See also Herrup, *A House in Gross Disorder*, 33: "Whether or not actually pederastic, the sodomitical relationships described in the legal records invariably paired authority and dependency—men and boys, masters and servants, teachers and pupils, patrons and clients."

29   *The Complete Essays of Montaigne*, trans. Donald M. Frame (Stanford: Stanford University Press, 1958), 139.

30   Ibid., 139–40.

31   I owe this citation to Haggerty, *Men in Love*, 25, who interprets it eloquently but almost exactly contrary to the way I do. For a contrasting approach to this topic see C. Stephen Jaeger, *Ennobling Love: In Search of a Lost Sensibility* (Philadelphia: University of Pennsylvania Press, 1999).

32   I overstate for the sake of emphasis. For a more nuanced and complex account of the interrelations of sexuality and gender in transgenderism see Don Kulick, *Travesti: Sex, Gender, and Culture among Brazilian Transgendered Prostitutes* (Chicago: University of Chicago Press, 1998).

33   See Sedgwick, *Epistemology of the Closet*, esp. 1, 9, 85–86, whence I derive the distinction between "universalizing" and "minoritizing" constructions of sexual identity.

34   For a more detailed contrast between the invert and the sodomite as discursive types see Halperin, "Forgetting Foucault."

35   Cited and translated by Maud W. Gleason, *Making Men: Sophists and Self-Presentation in Ancient Rome* (Princeton: Princeton University Press, 1995), 68.

36   Quintilian, *Institutes* 5.9.14, cited and translated by Amy Richlin, "Not before Homosexuality: The Materiality of the *Cinaedus* and the Roman Law against Love between Men," *Journal of the History of Sexuality* 3 (1992–93): 542.

37   This is a composite passage by ancient physiognomic writers, assembled by Gleason, *Making Men*, 63.

38   Another composite passage, ibid., 78.

39   Aulus Gellius, 6.12.5, cited and translated by Craig A. Williams, *Roman Homosexuality: Ideologies of Masculinity in Classical Antiquity* (New York: Oxford University Press, 1999), 23. A measure of the distance between inversion or passivity and male love can be gauged from the fact that Scipio was quite willing to identify himself publicly as bound to his friend Laelius by a "bond of love," according to the Roman historian Valerius Maximus (8.8.1). (I wish to thank Tom Hillard of Macquarie University for this observation and citation.) There would not necessarily have been any inconsistency or hypocrisy in Scipio's attitude.

40   *Historia ecclesiastica* 8.10, cited and translated by Glenn W. Olsen, "St. Anselm and Homosexuality," in *Proceedings of the Fifth International Saint Anselm Conference: St. Anselm and St. Augustine, Episcopi ad Saecula*, ed. Joseph C. Schnaubelt et al. (White Plains, N.Y.: Kraus, 1988), 110. Note that nothing in this passage establishes that the "effeminates" excoriated in it are being condemned specifically for sexual passivity (although the use of the word *catamite* clearly points in that direction). It would be easy enough for an incautious (or essentialist) historian to construe Orderic's reference to "the filth of sodomy" as implying the opposite, namely, that the "effeminates" are also being accused of playing an "active" role in homosexual intercourse. There is plainly no way to settle the question definitively,

but I hope that the historical typology I am constructing here will help resolve such ambiguities and will aid in the decipherment of historical texts. In Orderic's case, the text's insistence on the visible deviance of the catamites, its ascription to them of an effeminate morphology, situates it in a discursive tradition considerably more specific than that of merely "gay male representation." Instead, Orderic's account would seem to belong to a particular European tradition of discourse, a particular discursive mode of representing male inverts or passives. The more we know about the discursive rules and regularities that control the production of statements about historical sexual actors, the easier it may be to figure out what is going on in a particular passage even in the absence of explicit linguistic indications. In this way, attentiveness to the discursive context of Orderic's text makes it possible, I believe, to extract from his ambiguous and indeterminate language a better idea of the transgression for which the "effeminates" are being condemned than we could ever do on the basis of his words alone.

41   Cited and translated (with slight alterations here) by Cady, "'Masculine Love' of the 'Princes of Sodom,'" 133. Cady, of course, draws a different conclusion about the existence of homosexuality in the Renaissance from this and other comments by Pierre de L'Estoile.

42   The two passages are cited and quoted by Alan Bray, *Homosexuality in Renaissance England* (London: Gay Men's, 1982), 81, 87.

43   Quoted and discussed by Lisa L. Moore, *Dangerous Intimacies: Toward a Sapphic History of the British Novel* (Durham: Duke University Press, 1997), 72–74.

44   C. Westphal, "Die conträre Sexualempfindung, Symptom eines neuropathischen (psychopathischen) Zustandes," *Archiv für Psychiatrie und Nervenkrankheiten* 2 (1870): 73–108.

45   Arrigo Tamassia, "Sull' inversione dell' istinto sessuale," *Rivista sperimentale di freniatria e di medicina legale* 4 (1878): 97–117.

46   Of course, the molly himself is a complex figure, already verging on the homosexual, as Trumbach and others have shown. I do not mean to skip over the vexed interpretative issues, merely to make the point that the figure of the molly—however forward-looking he may be in other respects— retains many of the features traditionally ascribed to male inverts or passives.

47   The basic study is Hubert Kennedy, *Ulrichs: The Life and Works of Karl Heinrich Ulrichs, Pioneer of the Modern Gay Movement* (Boston: Alyson, 1988).

48   See Chauncey, "From Sexual Inversion to Homosexuality."

49   My account derives from Chauncey, ibid.

50   Westphal, "Die conträre Sexualempfindung," 107 n; my emphasis.

51   Westphal, "Die conträre Sexualempfindung," 82–84, cited, translated, and discussed by Robert Grimm, "The Dawn of Contrary Sexual Sensitivity," unpublished manuscript.

52   Alfred C. Kinsey, Wardell B. Pomeroy, and Clyde E. Martin, *Sexual Behavior in the Human Male* (Philadelphia: Saunders, 1948), 615. For a detailed elaboration of the distinction between homosexuality and inversion see C.A. Tripp, *The Homosexual Matrix* (New York: McGraw-Hill, 1975), 22–35.

53   In this one respect, at least, Kinsey proves a more reliable historian than Foucault. In *The History of Sexuality* Foucault dated the birth of homosexuality (as a discursive category) to Westphal's article: "We must not forget that the psychological, psychiatric, medical category of homosexuality was constituted from the moment it was characterized—Westphal's famous article of 1870 on 'contrary sexual sensations' can stand as its date of birth—less by a type of sexual relations than by a certain quality of sexual sensibility, a certain way of inverting the masculine and the feminine in oneself. Homosexuality appeared as one of the forms of sexuality when it was transposed from the practice of sodomy onto a kind of interior androgyny, a hermaphrodism of the soul. The sodomite had been a temporary aberration; the homosexual was now a species" (1:43). I believe Foucault was right to see in Westphal the emergence of a modern psychiatric notion of erotic *orientation*, which brought with it a specification of deviant individuals and a shift from a juridical discourse of prohibited acts to a normalizing discourse of perverted psychology. But I also believe Foucault was wrong to identify Westphal's category of "contrary sexual feeling" with *homosexuality*. In *Epistemology of the Closet* Sedgwick ingeniously argued that my "reading of 'homosexuality' as 'we currently understand it' . . . is virtually the opposite of Foucault's," insofar as Foucault has a "gender transitive" understanding of homosexuality, whereas I have a "gender intransitive" one (46). That may well explain why Foucault did not take what I regard as the historically necessary step of systematically differentiating "sexual inversion" from "homosexuality." Still, the ultimate issue here may not be a difference of opinion about what homosexuality is so much as an uncertainty about whether it is possible to draw a meaningful distinction in the history of modern European discourses between an "orientation" and a "sexuality."

54   Kinsey, Pomeroy, and Martin, *Sexual Behavior*, 616, 623.

55   The aptly chosen word *fades* here derives from Adam, who writes that in homosexuality "sex-role definitions fade from interpersonal bonding" ("Structural Foundations," 111). This paragraph and much of what follows have been inspired by Adam.

56   Quoted by Dan Savage, *Savage Love: Straight Answers from America's Most Popular Sex Columnist* (New York: Plume, 1998), 189–90.

57   See, in addition to Kinsey, Pomeroy, and Martin, *Sexual Behavior*, the following: George Chauncey Jr., "Christian Brotherhood or Sexual Perversion? Homosexual Identities and the Construction of Sexual Boundaries in the World War One Era," in Duberman, Vicinus, and Chauncey, *Hidden from History*, 294–317, 541–46; and Michael Bartos, John McLeod, and Phil Nott, *Meanings of Sex between Men: A Study Conducted by the Australian Federation of AIDS Organisations for the Commonwealth Department of Human Services and Health, 1993* (Canberra: Australian Government Publishing Service, 1994).

58   See Barry D. Adam, "Age Preferences among Gay and Bisexual Men," *GLQ* 6 (2000): 413–33.

59   See, once again, Adam, "Structural Foundations."

60   See Michel Foucault, *Discipline and Punish: The Birth of the Prison*, trans. Alan Sheridan (New York: Vintage, 1979), 182–84:

> "In short, under a régime of disciplinary power, the art of punishing . . . brings five quite distinct operations into play: it refers individual acts, performances, and conducts to a group ensemble that is at once a field of comparison, a space of differentiation, and a source of the rule to be followed. It differentiates individuals in relation to one another and in terms of that group rule, whether the rule be made to function as a minimal threshold, as an average to be looked to, or as an optimum to be approximated. It measures in quantitative terms and hierarchizes in terms of value the abilities, the level of attainment, and the 'nature' of individuals. It imposes, through this 'valorizing' measurement, the constraint of a conformity to be achieved. Lastly, it traces the limit that will define difference in relation to all other differences, the external frontier of the abnormal. . . . [To recapitulate, it] compares, differentiates, hierarchizes, homogenizes, excludes. In a word, it normalizes. . . . Like surveillance and together with it, normalization becomes one of the great instruments of power at the end of the classical age. The marks that once indicated status, privilege, and group membership come to be replaced, or at least to be supplemented, by a whole range of degrees of normality: these are signs of membership in a homogeneous social body, but they also play a part themselves in classification, in hierarchization, and in the distribution of ranks. In one sense, the power of normalization enforces homogeneity; but it individualizes by making it possible to measure deviations, to set levels, to define specialties, and to render differences useful by calibrating them one to another. The power of the norm functions easily within a system of formal equality, since within a homogeneity that is the rule, the norm introduces, as a useful imperative and as the result of measurement, all the gradations of individual differences."

Translation extensively modified.

Chapter 17

Lee Edelman

THE FUTURE IS KID STUFF: QUEER THEORY, DISIDENTIFICATION, AND THE DEATH DRIVE

Lee Edelman is the Fletcher Professor of English Literature and Chair of the English Department at Tufts University. A key figure in the dissemination of queer theory, Edelman's publications include *Homographesis: Essays in Gay Literary and Cultural Theory* (1993) and *No Future: Queer Theory and the Death Drive* (2004). His work examines the intersections of sexuality, rhetorical theory, cultural politics, and film.

In "The Future is Kid Stuff," originally published in *Narrative*, Edelman explores the ways in which notions of political futurity are shaped by the image of the child. Using a Lacanian framework, Edelman suggests that the image of the child in political discourse functions to uphold reproductive futurism, which demands the endless deferment of *jouissance* and an ethics that privileges heteronormativity. This discursive framework defines queer identities as embodiments of the death drive. Edelman interrogates the politics that promote the child as a figure of universal value and explores how this trope (and the symbolic order that produces it) can be potentially disputed through a strategic deployment of queer sexualities and queer oppositional politics. Specifically, Edelman argues that queer subjects should embrace political negativity through the role of the *sinthomosexual*, a figure that actively disrupts social order through a rejection of reproductive futurity and progressive politics.

A LLOW ME, BY way of introduction, to call your attention to a recent, minor, and short-lived political controversy, one that citizens of the United States have been rightly unwilling to fret about amid all the other incidents by which the press would have us be scandalized. According to an article in the *New York Times*, a series of public service announcements featuring President and Mrs. Clinton and sponsored by the Ad Council, a nonprofit organization, have "raise[d] questions about where politics stops and public service begins"

(Bennet A18). These "questions," for those who have chosen to raise them, center on a fear that these commercial spots, however briefly and unexpectedly caught in the glare of the media spotlight, might burnish the President's image, and thus increase his political clout, insofar as they show him in a role construed as inherently non-political. By depicting the President, in the words of the *Times*, as "a concerned, hard-working parent," one who attends to the well-being of children unable to protect themselves, these public service announcements on behalf of the "Coalition for America's Children" could have the effect of heightening his moral stature with the American electorate, or so fears Alex Castellanos, a Republican media consultant. "This is the father picture," he fulminates in the pages of the *Times*, "this is the daddy bear, this is the head of the political household. There's nothing that helps him more" (Bennet A18).

But what helps him most in this public appeal for parental involvement with children is the social consensus that such an appeal is *distinct* from the realm of politics; indeed, though these public service announcements conclude with a rhetorical flourish evocative of an ongoing political campaign ("We're fighting for the children. Whose side are you on?"), that rhetoric is intended precisely to assert that this issue *has* only one side. And while such apparently self-evident one-sidedness—the affirmation of so uncontested, because so uncontroversial, a cultural value as that condensed in the figure of the child whose innocence cries out for defense—is precisely what ought to distinguish the public service spots from the more volatile discourse of political persuasion, I want to suggest that this is also what makes them so oppressively, and so dangerously, political: political not in the partisan terms implied by the media consultant, but political in a far more insidious way; political insofar as the universalized fantasy subtending the image of the child coercively shapes the structures within which the "political" itself can be thought. For politics, however radical the means by which some of its practitioners seek to effect a more desirable social order, is conservative insofar as it necessarily works to *affirm* a social order, defining various strategies aimed at actualizing social reality and transmitting it into the future it aims to bequeath to its inner child. What, in that case, would it signify *not* to be "fighting for the children"? How, then, to take the *other* "side" when to take a side at all necessarily constrains one to take the side of, by virtue of taking a side within, a political framework that compulsively returns to the child as the privileged ensign of the future it intends?

In what follows I want to interrogate the politics that informs the pervasive trope of the child as figure for the universal value attributed to political futurity and to pose against it the impossible project of a queer oppositionality that would oppose itself to the structural determinants of politics as such, which is also to say, that would oppose itself to the logic of opposition. This paradoxical formulation suggests the energy of resistance—the characteristically perverse resistance informing the work of queer theory—to the substantialization of identities, especially as defined through opposition, as well as to the political fantasy of shaping history into a narrative in which meaning succeeds in revealing itself, *as itself*, through time. By attempting to resist that coercive faith in political futurity, while refusing as well any hope for the sort of dialectical access to meaning that such resistance, as quintessential political gesture, holds out, I mean to insist that politics is always a politics of the signifier, and that queer theory's interventions in the reproduction of dominant cultural logics must never lose sight of its figural relation to the vicissitudes of signification. Queer theory, as a particular story of where storytelling fails, one that takes the value and burden of that failure upon itself, occupies, I want to suggest, the impossible "other" side where narrative realization and derealization overlap. The rest of this paper aspires to explain the meaning and implications of that assertion, but to do so it must begin by tracing some connections between politics and the politics of the sign.

Like the network of signifying relations Lacan described as the symbolic, politics may function as the register within which we experience social reality, but only insofar as it compels us to experience that reality in the form of a fantasy: the fantasy, precisely, of form as such, of an order, an organization, assuring the stability of our identities as subjects and the consistency of the cultural structures through which those identities are reflected back to us in recognizable form. Though the material conditions of human experience may indeed be at stake in the various conflicts by means of which differing political perspectives vie for the power to name, and by naming to shape, our collective reality, the ceaseless contestation between and among their competing social visions expresses a common will to install as reality itself one libidinally subtended fantasy or another and thus to avoid traumatically confronting the emptiness at the core of the symbolic "reality" produced by the order of the signifier. To put this otherwise: politics designates the ground on which imaginary relations, relations that hark back to a notion of the self misrecognized as enjoying an originary fullness—an undifferentiated presence that is posited retroactively and therefore lost, one might say, from the start—compete for symbolic fulfillment within the dispensation of the signifier. For the mediation of the signifier alone allows us to *articulate* these imaginary relations, though always at the price of introducing the distance that precludes their realization: the distance inherent in the chain of ceaseless deferrals and mediations to which the very structure of the linguistic system must give birth. The signifier, as alienating and meaningless token of our symbolic construction as subjects, as token, that is, of our subjectification through subjection to the prospect of meaning; the signifier, by means of which we always inhabit the order of the Other, the order of a social and linguistic reality articulated from somewhere else; the signifier, which calls us into meaning by seeming to call us to ourselves, only ever confers upon us a sort of *promissory* identity, one with which we never succeed in fully coinciding because we, as subjects of the signifier, can only be signifiers ourselves: can only ever aspire to catch up to—to close the gap that divides and by dividing calls forth—ourselves as subjects. Politics names those processes, then, through which the social subject attempts to secure the conditions of its consolidation by identifying with what is outside it in order to bring it into the presence, deferred perpetually, of itself.

Thus, if politics in the symbolic is always a politics *of* the symbolic, operating in the name, and in the direction, of a future reality, the vision it hopes to realize is rooted in an imaginary past. This not only means that politics conforms to the temporality of desire, to what we might call the inevitable historicity of desire—the successive displacements forward of figures of meaning as nodes of attachment, points of intense metaphoric investment, produced in the hope, however vain, of filling the gap within the subject that the signifier installs—but also that politics is a name for the temporalization of desire, for its translation into a narrative, for its teleological representation. Politics, that is, by externalizing and configuring in the fictive form of a narrative, allegorizes or elaborates sequentially those overdeterminations of libidinal positions and inconsistencies of psychic defenses occasioned by the intractable force of the drives unassimilable to the symbolic's logic of interpretation and meaning-production, drives that carry the destabilizing force of what insists outside or beyond, because foreclosed by, signification. These drives hold the place of what meaning misses in much the same way that the signifier, in its stupidity, its intrinsic meaninglessness, preserves at the heart of the signifying order the irreducible void that order as such undertakes to conceal. Politics, in short, gives us history as the staging of a dream of self-realization through the continuous negotiation and reconstruction of reality itself; but it does so without acknowledging that the future to which it appeals marks the impossible place of an imaginary past exempt from the deferrals intrinsic to the symbolic's signifying regime.

Small wonder then that the post-Kantian era of the universal subject should produce as the figure of politics, because also as the figure of futurity collapsing undecidably into the past, the image of the child as we know it. Historically constructed, as numerous scholars, including Phillipe Ariès, Lawrence Stone, and James Kincaid, have made clear, to serve as the figural repository for sentimentalized cultural identifications, the child has come to embody for us the telos of the social order and been enshrined as the figure for whom that order must be held in perpetual trust. The image itself, however, in its coercive universalization, works to discipline political discourse by consigning it always to accede in advance to the reality of a collective futurity whose figurative status we are never permitted to acknowledge or address. From Delacroix's iconic image of Liberty urging us into a brave new world of revolutionary hope, her bare breast making each spectator the unweaned child to whom it belongs, to the equally universalized waif in the logo that performs in miniature the "politics" of the mega-musical *Les Miz*, we are no more able to conceive of a politics without a fantasy of the future than we are able to conceive of a future without the figure of the child.

And so, for example, when P.D. James, in her novel, *The Children of Men*, attempts to imagine the social effects of a future in which the human race has suffered a seemingly absolute loss of the capacity to reproduce, her narrator not only, predictably enough, attributes this reversal of biological fortune to the putative crisis of sexual values in late twentieth-century democracies—"Pornography and sexual violence on film, on television, in books, in life had increased and became more explicit but less and less in the West we made love and bred children" (James 10), he declares—but also gives voice to the ideological truism that governs our investment in the child as emblem of fantasmatic futurity: "without the hope of posterity, for our race if not for ourselves, without the assurance that we being dead yet live," her narrator notes, "all pleasures of the mind and senses sometimes seem to me no more than pathetic and crumbling defences shored up against our ruins" (13). While the plangent allusion to "The Waste Land" here may recall another of its well-known lines, one for which, apparently, we have Vivienne Eliot to thank, "What you get married for if you don't want children?," it also brings out the function of the child as prop of the secular theology upon which our common reality rests—the secular theology that shapes at once the meaning of our collective narratives and our collective narratives of meaning. Charged, after all, with the task of assuring "that we being dead yet live," the child, as if by nature, indeed as the living promise of a natural transcendence of the limits of nature itself, exudes the very pathos from which the narrator of *The Children of Men* recoils when mirrored back in the non-reproductive "pleasures of the mind and senses." For the "pathetic" quality he projectively locates in all such forms of enjoyment exposes the fetishistic figurations of the child that the narrator offers against them as legible in terms identical to those whereby pleasures pursued in the absence of "hope of posterity" are scorned: legible, that is, as nothing more than so many "pathetic and crumbling defences shored up against our ruins." Indeed, how better to characterize the narrative project of the text itself, which ends as any reader not born yesterday expects, with renewal of the barren world through the miracle of birth.

And if the author of *The Children of Men*, like the parents of mankind's children, succumbs without struggle to the mystifications of the all-pervasive, self-congratulatory, and strategically misrecognized narcissism endlessly animating pronatalism, why should we be the least bit surprised when her narrator insists, with what fully deserves to be characterized as a "straight face," that "sex totally divorced from procreation has become almost meaninglessly acrobatic" (167)? Which is, of course, to say no more than that sexual practice will be made to allegorize the vicissitudes of meaning so long as the heterosexually specific alibi of reproductive necessity covers up the drive *beyond* meaning that drives the symbolic's machinery of sexual meaningfulness and erotic relationality. The child whose pure possibility suffices to spirit away the naked truth of heterosexual sex, seeming to impregnate heterosexuality itself with the future of signification by bestowing upon it the cultural burden of signifying the future, figures an identification with an always about-to-be-realized identity—an identity intent on disavowing the threat to the symbolic order of meaning that inheres in a structure of desire that drives us to seek fulfillment in a meaning unable, *as* meaning, to fulfill us: unable, that is, to close the gap in identity that "meaning" means.

The consequences of such a compulsory identification both of and with the child as the culturally pervasive emblem of the motivating end, albeit endlessly postponed, of every political vision *as a vision of futurity*, must weigh upon the consideration of a queer oppositional politics. For the only queerness that queer sexualities could ever hope to claim would spring from their determined opposition to this underlying structure of the political—their opposition, that is, to the fantasmatic ambition of achieving symbolic closure through the marriage of identity to futurity in order to reproduce the social subject. Conservatives, of course, understand this in ways most liberals never can, since conservatism profoundly imagines the radical rupturing of the social fabric, while liberalism conservatively clings to a faith in its limitless elasticity. The discourse of the right thus tends toward a greater awareness of, and an insistence on, the figural logics implicit in the social relations we inhabit and enact, while the discourse of the left tends to understand better the capacity of the symbolic to accommodate change by displacing those figural logics onto history as the unfolding of narrative sequence.

Consider, for example, a local moment from the ongoing campaign around abortion. Not long ago, on a much-traveled corner in Cambridge, Massachusetts, opponents of the legal right to abortion posted an enormous image of a full-term fetus on a rented billboard accompanied by a simple and unqualified assertion: "It's not a choice; it's a child." Many critics, Barbara Johnson among them, have detailed with powerful insight how such anti-abortion polemics simultaneously rely on and generate tropes that animate, by personifying, the fetus, determining in advance the answer to the juridical question of its personhood by the terms with which the fetus, and thus the question, is addressed. Rather than attempting a deconstruction of this rhetorical instance, however (rather, that is, than note, for example, the collocation of the objectifying pronoun, "it," and the quintessentially humanizing epithet, "child," in order to see how this fragment of discourse maintains the undecidability it seems intended to resolve, casting doubt, therefore, on the truth of its statement by the form of its enunciation), I want to focus instead, for a moment, on the ideological truth its enunciation, unintentionally perhaps, makes clear.

For as strange as it may seem for a gay man to say this, when I first encountered that billboard in Cambridge I read it as addressed to me. The sign, after all, might as well have pronounced, and with the same absolute and invisible authority that testifies to the successfully accomplished work of ideological naturalization, the divine injunction: "Be fruitful and multiply." Like an anamorphotic distortion that only comes into focus when approached from an angle, the slogan acquired, through the obliquity of my subjective relation to it, a logic that served to articulate together the common stake in opposition to abortion and to the practice of queer sexualities—a common stake well understood (if only as the literalization of a figural identity) by radical groups like the one behind the January 1997 bombings of a lesbian bar and an abortion clinic in Atlanta. For the billboard, in this exemplary of the truths that right-wing discourse makes evident, understood what left-wing discourse prefers to keep concealed: that the true compulsion, the imperative that affords us as subjects no meaningful choice, is the compulsion to embrace our own futurity in the privileged form of the child and thereby to imagine the present as pregnant with the child of our identifications, as pregnant, that is, with a meaning to fill up the hole in the signifying order opened up by the distance, the internal division, produced through our subjection to the symbolic's logic of "meaning" itself.

Thus the left no more than the right will speak in *favor* of abortion; it, as the billboard cannily notes, aligns itself only with choice. And who, indeed, would speak *for* abortion, who would speak against reproduction, against futurity, and hence against life? Who would destroy the child and with it the sustaining fantasy of somehow bridging the signifying gap (a fantasy that serves to protect us against the violence of the drives insofar as it distracts us from seeing how thoroughly it compels us to enact them)? The right once again knows the answer, knows that the true oppositional politics implicit in the practice of queer sexualities lies not in the liberal discourse, the patient negotiation, of tolerances and rights, important as these undoubtedly are to all of us still denied them, but rather in the capacity of queer sexualities to figure the radical dissolution of the contract, in every sense social and symbolic, on which the future as guarantee against the return of the real, and so against the insistence of the death drive, depends. It is in this sense that we should listen to, and even perhaps be instructed by, the readings of queer sexualities produced by the forces of reaction. However much we might wish, for example, to reverse the system of values informing the following quotation from Donald Wildmon, founder and head of the deeply reactionary American Family Association, we would surely do well to consider it less as hyperbolic rant and more as a reminder of the disorientation that queer oppositionality entails: "Acceptance or indifference to the homosexual movement will result in society's destruction by allowing civil order to be redefined and by plummeting ourselves, our children and grandchildren into an age of godlessness. Indeed, the very foundation of Western Civilization is at stake" (Wildmon). Before the standard discourse of liberal pluralism spills from our lips, before we supply once more the assurance that ours is another kind of love but a love like his nonetheless, before we piously invoke the litany of our glorious contributions to civilizations of East and West alike, dare we take a moment and concede that Mr. Wildmon might be right, that the queerness of queer theory should tend precisely toward such a redefinition of civil order itself through a rupturing of our foundational faith in the reproduction of futurity?

It is true, of course, that the ranks of lesbian, gay, bisexual, and transgendered parents swell larger now than the belly sufficient to house that anti-abortion billboard's poster child for children. And nothing intrinsic to the constitution of persons who identify as lesbian, gay, bisexual, transgendered, transsexual, or queer predisposes them to resist the appeal of the future, to refuse the temptation to reproduce, or to place themselves outside or against the acculturating logic of the symbolic; neither, indeed, is there any ground we could stand on outside of that logic. But politics, construed as oppositional or not, never rests on essential identities; it centers, instead, on the figurality that is always essential *to* identity, and thus on the figural relations in which social identities are always inscribed. And so, when I argue, as I intend to do here, that the burden of queerness is to be located less in the assertion or reification of an oppositional political identity than in opposition to politics as the fantasy of realizing, in an always indefinite future, imaginary identities foreclosed by the fact of our constitutive subjection to the signifier, I am not suggesting a platform or position from which queer subjects or queer sexualities might finally and truly become themselves, as if they could somehow manage thereby to realize their essential queerness. I am suggesting instead that the efficacy of queerness, its strategic value, resides in its capacity to expose as figural the symbolic reality that invests us as subjects insofar as it simultaneously constrains us in turn to invest ourselves in *it*, to cling to its fictions as reality, since we are only able to live within, and thus may be willing to die to maintain, the figures of meaning that pass as the very material of literal truth.

The child, in the historical epoch of our current epistemological regime, is the figure for that compulsory investment in the misrecognition of figure; it takes its place on the social stage like every adorable Annie gathering her limitless funds of pluck to "stick out her chin/ and grin/ and say/ 'Tomorrow,/ tomorrow,/ I love you tomorrow,/ you're only a day away.'" And lo and behold, as viewed through the distorting prism of the tears she calls forth, the figure of this child seems to shimmer with the iridescent promise of Noah's rainbow, serving, like the rainbow, as the pledge of a covenant to shield us against the threat of apocalypse now—or apocalypse later. Recall, for example, the end of *Philadelphia*, Jonathan Demme's cinematic atonement for what some construed as the homophobia of *The Silence of the Lambs*. After saintly Tom Hanks, last seen on his deathbed in an oxygen mask that slyly alludes to, if only by virtue of troping upon, Hannibal Lecter's more memorable muzzle, has shuffled off this mortal coil to stand, as we are led to suppose, before a higher law, we find ourselves in, if not at, his wake surveying a room in his family home crowded with children and pregnant women whose reassuringly bulging bellies, lingered upon by the camera, displace the bulging basket (unseen) of the HIV-positive gay man (unseen) from whom, as the filmic text suggests, in a cinema given over, unlike the one in which we sit taking in *Philadelphia*, to explicit depictions of gay male sex, our Tom himself was infected by the virus that finally cost him his life. And when, in the film's final sequence, we look at the videotaped representation of our dead hero as a boy, can the tears that this shot would solicit fail to burn with an indignation directed not only against the homophobic world that sought to crush the man this boy was destined to become, but also against the homosexual world within which boys like this grow up to have crushes on other men? For the cult of the child permits no shrines to the queerness of boys or girls, since queerness, for the culture at large, as for *Philadelphia* in particular, is understood as bringing children and childhood to an end. The occasion of a gay man's death thus provides a perfect opportunity to unleash once more the disciplinary force of the figure of the child performing the mandatory cultural labor of social reproduction, a force we encounter continuously as the lives, the speech, and the freedoms of adults, especially queer adults, continue to suffer restriction out of deference to imaginary children whose futures, as if they were permitted to have them except insofar as they consist in transmitting them to children of their own, could only be endangered by the social disease as which queer sexualities register. Nor should we forget the extent to which AIDS, for which to this day the most effective name to be associated with the appropriation of funds in the U.S. Congress is that of a child, Ryan White, reinforces a much older linkage, as old as the gay-inflection given to the Biblical narrative of Sodom, between practices of gay sexuality and disappropriation from the promise of futurity, a linkage on which Anita Bryant could draw in waging her anti-gay campaign under the rubric of "Save Our Children."

While lesbians and gay men by the thousands work for the right to marry, to serve in the military, to adopt and raise children of their own, the right simply opens its closet and asks us to kneel at the shrine of the child: the child who might be subjected to physical or intellectual molestation; the child who might witness lewd or inappropriately intimate behavior; the child who might discover information about queer sexualities on the internet; the child who might choose a provocative book from the shelves of the public library; the child, in short, who might find an enjoyment that would nullify the figural value invested by the force of adult desire in the child as unmarked by the adult's adulterating implication in desire itself; the child, that is, compelled to image, for the satisfaction of adults, an imaginary fullness thought to want, and thus to want for, nothing. As Lauren Berlant puts it cogently in the introduction to *The Queen of America Goes to Washington City*, "a nation made for adult citizens has been replaced by one imagined for fetuses and children" (1). On every side, the present enjoyment of our liberties as citizens is eclipsed by the lengthening shadow of the child whose phantasmatic freedom to develop unmarked by encounters with an "otherness" of which its parents either do not or *should* not approve, unimpaired by any collision with the reality of alien desires, terroristically holds us all in check and determines that political discourse conform to the logic of a narrative in which history unfolds the future for a figural child who must never grow up. That child, immured in an innocence seen as continuously under siege, embodies a fantasy unable to withstand the queerness of queer sexualities precisely insofar as it promises the perpetuation of the same, the return, by way of the future, to an imaginary past. It denotes, in this, the *homo* sexuality intrinsic to the proper functioning of the heterosexual order: the erotically charged investment in the sameness of identity that is guaranteed oppositionally and realized in the narrative of reproductive futurity. And so, the radical right insists, the battle to preserve what Michael Warner describes as "heteronormativity" amounts to a life and death struggle over the future of the child whose ruin feminists, queers, and pro-choice activists intend. Indeed, according to the bomb-making guide produced by the so-called Army of God, the group that claimed, correctly or not, responsibility for attacks on an abortion clinic and a lesbian bar in Atlanta, their purpose was to "disrupt and ultimately destroy Satan's power to kill our children, God's children" (Sack A13).

While we continue to refute the lies that pervade these insidious right-wing diatribes, do we also have the courage to acknowledge, and embrace, their correlative truths? Are we willing, as queers, to be sufficiently oppositional to the structural logic of opposition— oppositional, that is, to the logic by which political engagement serves always as the medium for reproducing our social reality—to accept that the figural burden of queerness, the burden that queerness is phobically produced in order to represent, is that of the agency of disfiguration that punctures the fictions of the symbolic, shattering its persistent fantasy of recapturing a lost imaginary unity, by obtruding upon it the void of what remains necessarily unsymbolizable, the gap or wound of the real that insists as a death drive within the symbolic? Not that we are—or, indeed, could be—committed to living outside the figures that constitute the symbolic; but perhaps we can begin to explore the possibilities of acceding to our construction as figures bodying forth, within the logic of narrative, the dissolution of that very logic.

The death drive, after all, refers to an energy of mechanistic compulsion whose structural armature exceeds the specific object, the specific content, toward which we might feel that it impels us. That object, that content, is never "it," and could never, possessed, truly satisfy; for the drive itself insists, and whatever the thing to which we mistakenly interpret its insistence to pertain, it is always only a grammatical placeholder deceiving us into reading the drive's compulsive insistence as transitive. But the structural mandate of the drive within the order of the symbolic produces that content, that thing, as mere displacement: as allegorization, within the governing logic of narrative transitivity, of its own differential force. That is why Lacan can declare that "if everything that is immanent or implicit in the chain of natural events may be considered as subject to the so-called death drive, it is only because there is a signifying chain" (1992, 212). And we can locate this reading of the death drive in terms of the figural economy inherent in the "chain of natural events" central to narrative if we conceptualize the play and place of the death drive in relation to a theory of irony, that queerest of rhetorical devices, especially as construed by Paul de Man. Proposing that "any theory of irony is the undoing, the necessary undoing, of any theory of narrative," de Man asserts a tension between irony as a particular trope and narrative as the representational mode he construes as the allegory of tropes, as the attempt to account for trope systematically by reading it as the site of a meaning that reflects a dialectical consciousness confronting its status as subject to the signifier (176–77). The corrosive force of irony carries a charge for de Man quite similar to that of the death drive for Lacan. "Words have a way of saying things which are not at all what you want them to say," de Man observes; "There is a machine there, a text machine, an implacable determination and a total arbitrariness . . . which inhabits words on the level of the play of the signifier, which undoes any narrative consistency of lines, and which undoes the reflexive and dialectical model, both of which are, as you know, the basis of any narration" (181). This mindless violence of the textual machine, implacable and arbitrary, threatens, like a guillotine, to sever the integrity of narrative genealogy, recasting its narrative "chain of . . . events" as merely a "signifying chain" that inscribes in the realm of signification, along with unwanted meanings, the meaninglessness of the machinery that puts signification into play.

What is this but the death drive, which Barbara Johnson in a different context evokes as "a kind of unthought remainder . . . a formal overdetermination that is, in Freud's case, going to produce repetition or, in deconstruction's case, may inhere in linguistic structures that don't correspond to anything else" (98)? Irony may be one of the names for the force of that unthought remainder; queerness is surely another. Queer theory, then, should be viewed as a site at which a culturally repudiated irony, phobically displaced by the dominant culture onto the figure of the queer, is uncannily returned by those who propose to embrace such a figural identity with the *figuralization* of identity itself. Where the critical interventions of identitarian minorities, not excluding those seeking to substantialize the identities of lesbians, bisexuals, and gay men, may properly take shape as oppositional, reassuringly confronting the dominant order with the symmetrical image of its own achieved identity as social authority, queer theory's opposition, instead, is to the logic of oppositionality; its proper task the perpetual disappropriation of propriety.

It is not, therefore, a matter of either being or becoming, but rather of *embodying*, within the historical moment that imposes upon us such a figural association, the unsymbolizable remainder of the real produced by the order of meaning as the token of what that order is necessarily barred from being able to signify. One name given to this unnameable remainder by Lacan is "jouissance," occasionally translated as "enjoyment": the sense of a violent passage beyond the circumscriptions inherent in meaning that can have the effect, insofar as it gets attached, fetishistically, to a privileged object, of defining and congealing our experiential identities around fantasies of fulfillment through that object, but that also can function, insofar as it escapes such fetishistic reification, to rupture, or at least to seem to rupture, the consistency of a symbolic reality organized around the signifier as substantial identity, as name. Hence there is another name that can designate the unnameability to which the experience of jouissance can appear to give us access: "behind what is named, there is the unnameable," writes Lacan. "It is in fact because it is unnameable, with all the resonances you can give to this name, that it's akin to the quintessential unnameable, that is to say to death" (1991, 211). The death drive, then, manifests itself, though in radically different guises, in both versions of jouissance. To the extent that jouissance, as fantasmatic escape from the alienation intrinsic to meaning, and thus to the symbolic, lodges itself in an object on which our identities then come to depend, it produces those identities as mortifications, reenactments of the very constraints of meaning they were intended to help us escape. But to the extent that jouissance as a tear in the fabric of symbolic reality as we know it unravels the solidity of every object, including the object as which the subject necessarily takes itself, it evokes the death drive that always insists on the void both in and of the subject beyond its fantasy of self-realization in the domain of the pleasure principle.

Bound up with the first of these death drives we find the figure of the child, enacting the law of perpetual repetition as it fixes our identity through identification with the futurity of the social order; bound up with the second, the figure of the queer localizes that order's traumatic encounter with its own inescapable failure, its encounter, that is, with the illusory status of its faith in the future as suture, as balm for the wound as which the subject of the signifier experiences its alienation in meaning. In the preface to *Homographesis*, I wrote that "gay," understood "as a figure for the textuality, the rhetoricity, of the sexual . . . designates the gap or incoherence that every discourse of 'sexuality' or 'sexual identity' would master" (xv); I am now extending that claim by suggesting that queer sexualities, within the framework of the social text we inhabit, figure the gap in which the symbolic confronts what its discourse can never know. It is certainly the case that this production of the queer as the figural signifier of what the signifying system constitutively fails to name reassures by seeming to span the abyss opened up by the signifier itself, reassures by giving a name to the unnameable—a name such as "faggot," or "dyke," or "queer"—and construing in the form of an object what threatens the consistency of objects as such. But it is also the case that the righteous protestations against this figural positioning by those called upon historically to personify it, while enabling the gradual extension of rights and benefits to those denied them, *similarly* reassures by suggesting the seamless coherence of the symbolic, suggesting that its logic of narrative supersedes the corrosive force of our irony. For every expression of opposition to the figural status to which we are called affirms the triumph of history as story, as the narrative allegorization of the irony that is trope.

It may seem, from within this structure, that the symbolic can only win; but that, of course, is to ignore the fact that it also can only lose. For the division on which the subject rests, opening it to incursions of anxiety in which the reality conjured by the signifier quakes, can never be conjured away. The order of social reality demands some figural repository for what the structural logic of its articulation is destined to foreclose, for the fracture that persistently haunts it as the death within itself. By refusing to identify with this death drive, by refuting the tropology that aligns us with this disidentification from the logic of futurity, those of us occupying the place of the queer can only, at best, displace that figural burden onto someone else; only by making the ethical choice of acceding to that position, only by assuming the truth of our queer capacity to figure the undoing of the symbolic and the subject of the symbolic can we undertake the impossible project of imagining an oppositional political position exempt from the repetitive necessity of reproducing the politics of the signifier—the politics aimed at eliminating the gap opened up by the signifier itself—which can only return us, by way of the child, to the politics of reproduction.

In Boston last year, Cardinal Bernard Law, mistaking, or perhaps understanding too well, the authority of identity bestowed by the signifier that constitutes his own name, declared his opposition to domestic benefits assuring the availability of health care to same-sex partners of municipal workers by offering us the following piece of rancid piety in the sky: "Society has a special interest in the protection, care and upbringing of children. Because marriage remains the principal, and the best, framework for the nurture, education and socialization of children, the state has a special interest in marriage" (Slattery 68). If Cardinal Law, by adducing this bitter concentrate of a governing futurism so fully invested in the figure of the child that it manages to justify refusing health care to the adults that those children become, if Cardinal Law can thus give voice to the mortifying mantra of a communal jouissance committed to the fetishization of the child at the expense of whatever it renders queer, then we must respond not only by insisting on our right to enjoy on an equal footing the various prerogatives of the social order, not only by avowing our capacity to confirm the integrity of the social order by demonstrating the selfless and enduring love we bestow on the partners we'd gladly fly to Hawaii in order to marry or on the children we'd as eagerly fly to China or Guatemala in order to adopt, but also by saying explicitly what Law and the law of the symbolic he represents here, more clearly even than we do perhaps, in every public avowal of queer sexuality or identity: fuck the social order and the figural children paraded before us as its terroristic emblem; fuck Annie; fuck the waif from *Les Miz*; fuck the poor innocent kid on the 'Net; fuck Laws both with capital "l"s and with small; fuck the whole network of symbolic relations and the future that serves as its prop.

Choosing to stand, as many of us do, outside the cycles of reproduction, choosing to stand, as we also do, by the side of those living and dying each day with the complications of AIDS, we know the deception of the societal lie that endlessly looks toward a future whose promise is always a day away. We can tell ourselves that with patience, with work, with generous contributions to lobbying groups, or generous participation in activist groups, or generous doses of political savvy and electoral sophistication, the future will hold a place for us—a place at the political table that won't have to come, as it were, at the cost of our place in the bed, or the bar, or the baths. But there are no *queers* in that future as there can be no future for queers. The future itself is kid stuff, reborn each day to postpone the encounter with the gap, the void, the emptiness, that gapes like a grave from within the lifeless mechanism of the signifier that animates the subject by spinning the gossamer web of the social reality within which that subject lives. If the fate of the queer is to figure the fate that cuts the thread of futurity, if the jouissance, the excess enjoyment, by which we are defined would destroy the other, fetishistic, identity-confirming jouissance through which the social order congeals around the rituals of its own reproduction, then the only oppositional status to which our queerness can properly lead us depends on our taking seriously the place of the death drive as which we figure and insisting, against the cult of the child and the political culture it supports, that we are not, to quote Guy Hocquenghem, "the signifier of what might become a new form of 'social organization'" (138), that we do not intend a new politics, a better society, a brighter future, since all of these fantasies reproduce the past, through displacement, in the form of the future by construing futurity itself as merely a form of reproduction. Instead we choose not to choose the child, as image of the imaginary past or as identificatory link to the symbolic future; we would bury the subject in the tomb that waits in the hollow of the signifier and pronounce at last the words we are condemned from the outset for having said anyway: that *we* are the advocates of abortion; that the child as figure of futurity must die; that we have seen the future and it's every bit as lethal as the past; and thus what is queerest about us, queerest within us, and queerest despite us, is our willingness to insist intransitively: to insist that the future stops here.

Note

This paper was delivered at the Narrative conference at the University of Florida in April 1997. I wish to thank the other plenary speakers, Nancy Armstrong and Rey Chow, for their valuable comments and enjoyable company. I would also like to thank D.A. Miller, Diana Fuss, and Joseph Litvak for their generous readings of the text.

Works cited

Bennet, James. "Clinton, in Ad, Lifts Image of Parent." *New York Times*. 4 March 1997: New England Edition, A18.

Berlant, Lauren. *The Queen of America Goes to Washington City*. Durham: Duke Univ. Press, 1997.

de Man, Paul. *Aesthetic Ideology*. Edited by Andrzej Warminski. Minneapolis: Univ. of Minnesota Press, 1996.

Edelman, Lee. *Homographesis: Essays in Gay Literary and Cultural Theory*. New York: Routledge, 1994.

Hocquenghem, Guy. *Homosexual Desire*. Translated by Daniella Dangoor. Durham: Duke Univ. Press, 1993.

James, P.D. *The Children of Men*. New York: Warner Books, 1994.

Johnson, Barbara. *The Wake of Deconstruction*. Cambridge: Basil Blackwell, 1994.

Lacan, Jacques. *The Seminar of Jacques Lacan; Book II: The Ego in Freud's Theory and in the Technique of Psychoanalysis, 1954–1955*. Translated by Sylvana Tomaselli. New York: W.W. Norton: 1991.

—. *The Seminar of Jacques Lacan; Book VII: The Ethics of Psychoanalysis, 1959–1960*. Edited by Jacques-Alain Miller. Translated by Dennis Potter. New York: W.W. Norton, 1992.

Sack, Kevin. "Officials Look For Any Links in Bombings in Atlanta." *New York Times*. 2 February 1997: New England Edition, A13.

Slattery, Ryan. "Cardinal Law Urges Menino to Veto Bill Giving Benefits to City Workers' Partners." *Boston Sunday Globe*. 17 March 1996, 68.

Wildmon, Donald. "Hope '97 Tour to Counter Pro-Homosexual Philosophy in American Culture." Lkd. *American Family Association Action Alert*. <http://www.cfnweb.com/head-line.htm> (25 February 1997).

PART 4

Kinship

Chapter 18

David L. Eng

TRANSNATIONAL ADOPTION
AND QUEER DIASPORAS

David Eng is Professor of English, Comparative Literature, and Asian American Studies at the University of Pennsylvania. He is the author of *Racial Castration: Managing Masculinity in Asian America* (2001) and *The Feeling of Kinship: Queer Liberalism and the Racialization of Intimacy* (2010), and a co-editor of *Q&A: Queer in Asian America* (1998), *Loss: The Politics of Mourning* (2002), and a special issue of *Social Text*, "What's Queer about Queer Studies Now?" (2005).

In this essay, Eng undertakes a queer critique of the political, material, psychic, and affective contradictions and repressions that cohere in the practice of transnational adoption. Focusing on Deann Borshay Liem's film *First Person Plural* (2000), Eng demonstrates how the families and queer kinships enabled by new forms of consumer capitalism function as intimate sites through which imperial and national discourses are managed in order to buttress the ideological force of the white heterosexual nuclear family. Borshay Liem is unable to sustain the idea of having two mothers and Eng explores the sexual and racial implications of this psychic symptom. In Eng's reimagining of queer kinship, it is the necessity of creating the psychic and political space for two—or more—mothers that holds out the possibility for a new kind of ethical multicultural and queer politics.

DEANN BORSHAY LIEM'S 2000 documentary on transnational adoption, *First Person Plural*, recounts the filmmaker's 1966 adoption from a Korean orphanage by Alveen and Donald Borshay, a white American couple in Fremont, California, as well as Borshay Liem's eventual discovery some twenty years later of her birth mother in Kunsan, Korea.[1] With the hopes of alleviating the clinical depression from which she has suffered since college, Borshay Liem decides that she must see her two families together, in one room, in the same physical space. And so she orchestrates what can be described only as an excruciating "reunion" between her American parents and her Korean family, a journey of recuperation and return to origins compelled as much by fantasy as by fact. Midway through *First Person Plural*, however, Borshay Liem halts her narrative of reunion to offer this painful disclosure. Looking straight into the camera lens, she bluntly admits: "There wasn't room in my mind for two mothers."

I begin with this statement of a *psychic* predicament—the dearth of space in Borshay Liem's psyche for two mothers—because I am struck by the complicated ways by which female subjectivity and maternal blame become the site for working out a host of material and psychic contradictions associated with the practice of transnational adoption. This practice, in which infants are entangled in transnational flows of human capital, is a post-World War II phenomenon closely associated with American liberalism, postwar prosperity, and Cold War politics. In the late twentieth century, transnational adoption has proliferated alongside global consumer markets, becoming a popular and viable option not only for heterosexual but also—and increasingly—for homosexual couples and singles seeking to (re)-consolidate and (re)occupy conventional structures of family and kinship.

Through this contemporary emergence of new family and kinship relations, we come to recognize transnational adoption as one of the most privileged forms of diaspora and immigration in the late twentieth century. In turn, we are confronted with an interlocking set of gender, racial, national, political, economic, and cultural questions. Is the transnational adoptee an immigrant? Is she, as in those cases such as Borshay Liem's, an Asian American? Even more, is her adoptive family Asian American? How is the "otherness" of the transnational adoptee absorbed into the intimate space of the familial? And how are international and group histories of gender, race, poverty, and nation managed or erased within the "privatized" sphere of the domestic?

Attempts to answer these questions often result in significant confusion, and this difficulty suggests that transnational adoption must be analyzed not only in terms of "private" family and kinship dynamics but also in relation to larger "public" imperialist histories of race, gender, capitalism, and nation. Amy Kaplan, in the context of new Americanist studies of nineteenth-century practices of U.S. imperialism, argues that "imperialism as a political or economic process abroad is inseparable from the social relations and cultural discourses of race, gender, ethnicity, and class at home."[2] The vexing issues invoked by transnational adoption suggest that this practice might be usefully considered in relation to Kaplan's formulation. What would it mean to think about transnational adoption as a paradigmatic late-twentieth-century phenomenon situated at the intersection of imperialist processes "over there" and social relations "over here"? How might transnational adoption help us understand contemporary contradictions between processes of globalization and discourses of nationalism? For instance, how might late capitalist modes of flexible production and accumulation (in which the practice of transnational adoption must be situated) relate to the scaling back of civil rights and liberties in the U.S. nation-state, including access to the public sphere and participation in civil society, as well as claims to privacy, parenthood, and family?

It is crucial to investigate the material implications and effects of transnational adoption. However, it is equally important, as Borshay Liem's maternal predicament insists, to explore the psychic dimensions of the practice. And while we have a growing body of scholarship analyzing the political economy of transnational adoption, we lack a sustained analysis of its psychic range and limits. This essay explores both the political and the psychic economies of transnational adoption. It brings historical, anthropological, and legal scholarship on transnational adoption together with psychoanalysis—a rather unorthodox but, I would contend, necessary theoretical combination.

The essay begins with a description of the evolving politics of family and kinship relations in the late twentieth century. It examines, through an analysis of a recent John Hancock commercial depicting American lesbians adopting a Chinese baby, the historical conditions and contradictions of transnational adoption that make new social formations of family and kinship thinkable. In the second part of this essay, I elaborate upon the psychic structures that support these new social formations—that make them inhabitable and reproducible or, perhaps more accurately in Borshay Liem's recounting, unlivable and barren. Offering a theory of racial melancholia as well as a reading of Freud's essays on femininity and the negative Oedipus complex, I explore questions of origin and the psychic genealogy of Borshay Liem's maternal dilemma.

I recognize that Borshay Liem's documentary represents a singular set of experiences that may at first seem remote from the heterogeneous experiences of different transnational adoptees and their families. Nevertheless, I hope that my particular analyses of *First Person Plural* will not only resonate with the social and psychological issues of many of these various groups but also provide some new critical approaches to reframe and to broaden current discourses exploring this phenomenon.[3] Ever since the National Association of Black Social Workers (NABSW) issued a position paper in 1972 advocating the adoption of black children only by black families, there has been a contentious and long-standing debate concerning the politics of race in black/white transracial adoption and foster care. In comparison, little critical attention has been paid to the politics of race (not to mention the psychic issues) regarding transnational adoption of Asian children by white families. While transnational adoption practices implicate some of our most deeply held beliefs about family and identity and some of our most deeply held values about community and nation, there remains a dearth of available vocabularies to investigate this critical juncture of private and public.

The adoption of a child, domestically or from abroad, is a material and an affective enterprise of great magnitude. In unpacking its implications and effects, I do not want to be construed as either an advocate or an adversary of transnational adoption. Instead, the relentless moralizing that characterizes much of our contemporary debate on the erosion of "family values"—of traditional white, middle-class parenthood and the nuclear family—must give way to a sustained discussion of the ethics of multiculturalism in relation to the current emergence of what I call the "new global family." It is in this spirit that I offer a sustained analysis of transnational adoption's material contours and affective crossings. For without such examination, we will have few theoretical ways to understand and few therapeutic resources to alleviate the psychic pain associated with Borshay Liem's striking—indeed, heartbreaking—confession. How might the transnational adoptee come to have psychic space for two mothers? And what, in turn, would such an expansion of the psyche mean for the sociopolitical domain of contemporary family and kinship relations and the politics of diaspora?

Queer diasporas

This essay is part of a book-length project, "Queer Diasporas/Psychic Diasporas," exploring structures of family and kinship in the late twentieth century. "Queer Diasporas/Psychic Diasporas" investigates what might be gained politically by reconceptualizing diaspora not in conventional terms of ethnic dispersion, filiation, and biological traceability, but rather in terms of queerness, affiliation, and social contingency. By doing so, "queer diaspora" emerges as a concept providing new methods of contesting traditional family and kinship structures— of reorganizing national and transnational communities based not on origin, filiation, and genetics but on destination, affiliation, and the assumption of a common set of social practices or political commitments.[4]

"Queer Diasporas/Psychic Diasporas" focuses upon this theoretical question: Why do we have numerous poststructuralist accounts of language but few poststructuralist accounts of kinship? In the 1970s, feminist anthropologists such as Gayle Rubin turned to structuralist accounts of kinship, most notably those of Claude Lévi-Strauss, to compare the exchange of women to the exchange of words.[5] Judith Butler observes that, when the study of kinship was combined with the study of structural linguistics, the exchange of women was likened to the trafficking of a sign, the linguistic currency facilitating a symbolic and communicative bond among men. "To recast particular structures of kinship as 'symbolic,'" Butler warns, "is precisely to posit them as preconditions of linguistic intelligibility and to suggest that these 'positions' bear an intractability that does not apply to contingent social norms."[6] In this manner, these structuralist accounts burdened us with traditional kinship relations under-written by the Oedipal—a structuralist legacy establishing "certain forms of kinship as the only intelligible and livable ones."[7]

We have moved beyond structuralist accounts of language, but have we moved beyond structuralist accounts of kinship? Collectively, feminists have done much to challenge the idea of kinship as the exchange of women *tout court*. But insofar as there continues to be a privileged relationship between the exchange of women and the exchange of words, it would be difficult to imagine a poststructuralist accounting of kinship not predicated on the subordination of women and normative forms of Oedipalization. What would such a poststructuralist project look like?

"Queer Diasporas/Psychic Diasporas" explores these questions through an investigation of Asian transnational as well as gay and lesbian/queer social movements. The late twentieth century has witnessed the emergence of a spectrum of new social formations and identities. While idealized notions of family and kinship have been under duress throughout history, at this contemporary moment two of the most notable challenges to traditional orderings of family and kinship have come in the form of Asian transnational movements as well as queer reorganization of familial norms.

For instance, a distinct theoretical vocabulary has arisen in the fields of Asian and Asian American studies to describe transnational shifts, on the side of both capital and labor, in conventional orderings of family and kinship. The late twentieth century has witnessed not only the increasing proliferation of cheap and flexible Asian immigrant labor across the globe (in the form of free trade zones and global sweatshops) but also the concomitant expansion of Asian immigration into spheres of transnational and global capitalism. "Mail-order brides" and "domestic servants" are two of the more significant terms in a global age associated with the exploitation of Third World women in an ever increasing international gendered division of labor supporting First World middle-class family households. In contrast, "satellite people," "parachute kids," "reverse settlers," and "flexible citizenship" are some of the more prevalent concepts connected to the rise of a distinct Asian transnational capitalist and mana-gerial class.[8] How do we situate another emerging term—*transnational adoptee*—in relation to these social constellations of exploitation and privilege? On which side—capital or labor—does the transnational adoptee fall?

At the same historical moment, U.S.-based gay and lesbian activist movements have culminated in demands for legal rights to same-sex marriage, adoption, custody, and inherit-ance, for antidiscrimination employment legislation, and for service in the military. Paradoxically, prior historical efforts to defy state oppression have, to a striking extent, given way to the desire for state legitimacy and inclusion, for the backing of mainstream gay and lesbian political and policy aims. It is in this climate of heightened assimilation and state sanc-tion, as well as through the rhetorics of equal opportunity and multicultural inclusion, that contemporary permutations of family and kinship must be rethought.

We can approach this dynamic from another angle. In his well-known essay "Capitalism and Gay Identity," John D'Emilio argues that gay identity first emerged at the turn of the last century through the ascent of wage labor in industrializing cities and the independent sexual lifestyle this wage labor afforded.[9] The creation of urban zones of gay and lesbian life was facilitated by the movement of individuals away from agrarian-based familial units and actualized through the severing of family and kinship bonds—a severing later mirrored, even embraced, in the politics of gay liberation and "coming out."

To come out of the closet today still places family and kinship bonds at risk. At the same time, however, gays and lesbians are reinhabiting structures of family and kinship not only in growing numbers but also in increasingly public and visible ways (such as being included in the recently renamed "Weddings/Celebrations" announcements section of the Sunday *New York Times*).[10] The continuing AIDS crisis, the lesbian baby boom of the 1980s, the emergence of same-sex partnership recognition on the corporate and municipal levels, and present-day legal claims to gay marriage, adoption, and custody have remade the politics of kinship into "Families We Choose," to invoke anthropologist Kath Weston's important study of queer kinship in 1980s San Francisco.

If gays and lesbians today are no longer eccentric to structures of family and kinship, we need to consider whether this reformulation of traditional social formations can be justifiably described as "poststructuralist" or whether it must be thought about in terms of a constrained (material and psychic) assimilation to dominant social customs and norms. What are the contemporary political, economic, and cultural conditions that allow for this queer reinhabitation of family and kinship? Significantly, in moving from the politics of the closet to the "privileges" of family, and from prewar industrialization to postwar globalization, gays and lesbians are also said to have moved from wage labor to particular modes of consumer capitalism. While it is clear that gays and lesbians have always come from varied class backgrounds, the historical development and public visibility of queer family and kinship demand a concerted analysis of the ways in which contemporary forms of capitalism, flexible accumulation, and exploitation might be the very conditions of possibility for this emergence.

Indeed, both this analysis and the status of the transnational adoptee as complicating the borders between exploitation and privilege can be elaborated remarkably in the present context of the transnational adoption of Chinese baby girls by Western couples and singles. A John Hancock commercial that aired nationally during the 2000 Olympics and World Series illustrates this crossing of queerness and diaspora—of contemporary sexual and racial formation—in the global system and domestic sphere of the nation-state. First broadcast during the U.S. women's gymnastics championships, the commercial depicts a white American lesbian couple at a major U.S. metropolitan airport with their newly arrived Chinese baby girl.[11] Interspersed between shots of busy white immigration officers, a close-up of the U.S. flag, and throngs of anonymous Asian faces restlessly waiting to gain entry into the country, we spy the couple with their nameless infant waiting patiently in line. The commercial then moves to a close-up of the trio.

"This is your new home," coos the dark-haired lesbian as she rocks the sleeping infant. "Don't tell her that; she's going to want to go back," jokes the other, a gangly blonde. "Hi, baby," the blonde whispers, as her partner asks, "Do you have her papers?" "Yeah, they're in the diaper bag," she responds. As the scene cuts away to a black screen, on which appears the list "Mutual Funds, Annuities, Life Insurance, Long Term Care Insurance," the dark-haired lesbian is heard in a voice-over stating wondrously, "Can you believe this? We're a family." The commercial cuts to her placing a tender kiss on the baby girl's head, as a second black screen appears with the words, "Insurance for the unexpected / Investments for the opportunities." A third black screen with the John Hancock logo comes into view as we hear a final off-screen exchange between the couple: "You're going to make a great mom." "So are you."

Given the long U.S. history of Chinese immigration exclusion and bars to naturalization and citizenship, and given the recent public outcry and legal repudiation of gay and lesbian parenting, we must pause to wonder exactly what John Hancock, one of the world's largest financial services companies, is seeking to insure. How does this depiction of transnational adoption and circuits of (human) exchange not only resignify past and present histories of exploited Asian immigrant labor but also situate the adoption of Chinese baby girls by an emerging consumer niche group—white lesbians with capital—as one of the late twentieth century's most privileged forms of immigration?

The commercial implies that, in crossing an invisible national boundary, a needy "object" left to wither in the dark corners of a Chinese orphanage is miraculously transformed into a treasured U.S. "subject" worthy of investment—economic protection (capital accumulation), political rights (citizenship), and social recognition (family). In this regard, we should note that, in the face of immediate right-wing outrage at the commercial, a John Hancock spokesman, waxing liberal-poetic about the company's advertisement, announced, "However a child comes into a family, that child is entitled to financial protection, and John Hancock can help."[12] How is the rhetoric of "financial protection" functioning here as moral justification for the ever greater accumulation and conflation of (economic) property and (legal) rights, including at this juncture child and family as property and rights for lesbians and gays?[13] How is this respectable lesbian couple with money being positioned as the idealized inhabitants of an increasingly acceptable gay version of the nuclear family? How, in other words, is "financial protection" inextricably bound together with political citizenship and social belonging as the prerequisite for queer kinship?

Anthropologist Ann Anagnost suggests that, for white middle-class subjects in the era of late capitalism, the position of parent has become increasingly a measure of value, self-worth, and "completion."[14] Indeed, I would suggest that the possession of a child, whether biological or adopted, has today become the sign of guarantee not only for family but also for full and robust citizenship—for being a fully realized political, economic, and social subject in American life. ("Can you believe this? We're a family.") The desire for parenthood as economic entitlement and legal right (transnational adoption requiring immigration visas, along with the termination and transfer of parental rights for naturalization and citizenship) not only by heterosexuals but also, and increasingly, by homosexuals seems to stem in large part from an unexamined belief in the traditional ideals of the nuclear family as the primary contemporary measure of social respectability and value. This enjoyment of rights is, of course, ghosted by those queers and diasporic subjects—unacknowledged lovers, illegal immigrants, indentured laborers, infants left behind—consigned to outcast status and confined to the edges of globalization; they have attenuated, and often no, legal claims to "family," "home," or "nation."

Legally, U.S. citizenship is granted on the basis of either birthplace (jus soli) or descent (jus sanguinis), deriving from parent to child. What does it mean that, in our present age, full and robust citizenship is *socially* effected from child to parent and, in many cases, through the position of the adoptee, its visible possession and spectacular display? In this regard, what does it mean consciously to ask that the transnational adoptee operate as a guarantee for her parents' access to full social recognition and rights to participation in the public sphere and civil society? Indeed, given the history of Asian immigration exclusion, how is it possible that this Chinese baby could effect such a transformation? The John Hancock commercial illustrates how capitalism colonizes idealized notions of family and familial sentiment to sell its products and services to newly emergent transnational families. But we must wonder, along with Anagnost, how the figure of the child can function "so relentlessly in U.S. political rhetoric as emblematizing the current state of emergency, even as public support for the needs of children is rapidly eroding?"[15] In this context, we need to ask again, is this version of queer family "poststructuralist"? On which side—capital or labor—does the transnational adoptee fall?

The baby's tenuous transformation from object to subject and her need for citizenship papers ("Do you have her papers?" "Yeah, they're in the diaper bag") insist that we consider the transnational adoptee an immigrant, thus realigning her with the anonymous Asian crowd from which she is individuated (an individuation, we might note, that emerges from the dross of the diaper bag). At the same time, this transformation demands us to entertain the possibility that the transnational adoptee is a form of embodied value, a special type of property uneasily straddling both subjecthood and objecthood. Her movement across invisible national boundaries, east to west and south to north, thus places her on the threshold of a tenuous subjectivity continually threatening to undo itself, to unmask the history of its commodification. If the adoptee's miraculous political, economic, and social transformation obscures the commodification of infant girls as a gendered form of embodied value bought and sold, what cultural alibis about Chinese otherness and gender abuse must be produced so as to efface the history of this transaction in the global marketplace? How do generalized narratives of salvation—from poverty, disease, and the barbarism of the Third World—often attached to narratives of transnational adoption displace global and local histories of colonialism, military intervention, capitalist exploitation, racism, and gender discrimination? In this particular crossing of queerness and diaspora, what kind of global and local histories must be managed and erased?

The movement of the transnational adoptee from "over there" to "over here," and from "orphanage" to "family," not only individuates her ever so tenuously but also contracts imperialist histories and their domestic embodiments into the privatized space of the family. Through this process, the political is contracted into "private" life, and this contraction makes more collective forms of political activism seem untenable and extreme. This sphere is what Lauren Berlant, analyzing the conservative regulation and privatization of family, heterosexuality, and good citizenship during the Reagan/Thatcher era, has labeled the "intimate public sphere."[16] Significantly, as Borshay Liem's example indicates, global and domestic histories contracted into the intimate public sphere of the reconstituted white heterosexual nuclear family are often psychically displaced. They reemerge in symptomatic form within the dynamics of what I will call the "imperial psychic sphere."

Before turning to a more detailed investigation of the imperial psychic sphere in *First Person Plural*, I consider what kind of histories and historical contradictions might be returned to the practice of transnational adoption in order to analyze more fully its global and domestic genealogies. I offer the following brief historical sketch, as it is crucial to link transnational adoption not just to humanitarian or religious narratives of love, altruism, salvation, and redemption but also to specific pre- and post-World War II histories of imperialism, immigration, racialized exploitation, and gendered commodification.

The history of transnational adoption is a recent one. Initiated in the aftermath of World War II as a humanitarian response by a prospering North America, transnational adoption to the United States first began with the emigration of European orphans from Germany and Poland.[17] However, it was only after the Korean War (1950–53), and under the shadow of Cold War politics, that the largest wave of transnational adoptions was to take place. Since then, South Korea, with the help of Western religious and social service agencies, has expedited the adoption of over 200,000 South Korean children (150,000 of whom are now residing in the United States and 50,000 of whom are currently living in Western Europe, Canada, and Australia). Until 1991, South Korean children constituted the largest number of transnational adoptees to enter the United States on an annual basis. Transnational adoptions from South Korea have been followed by adoptions from other Asian countries (such as Vietnam, Cambodia, and China) in which the United States has had a notable military presence and/or strong political and economic interests. In 2000, China (5,053), Russia (4,269), and South Korea (1,794) ranked first, second, and third in U.S. transnational adoptions.[18]

Scholarship in postcolonial and transnational feminism links the historical emergence of war brides and mail-order brides to foundations of military prostitution and the commodification of Third World female bodies for First World male consumption and pleasure.[19] From this perspective, we might say that the historical phenomena of war brides and mail-order brides make explicit what is often only implicit or absent in traditional analyses of transnational adoption (the majority of adoptees being baby girls). Parents adopting infants in China are expected to make a cash contribution of U.S.$3,000–$4,000 to the orphanage in which the child resides. These costs are now partially underwritten by many private corporations and by the U.S. government. In 1997, adoptive U.S. parents of foreign-born children began to qualify for a one-time tax credit of U.S.$5,000–$86,000.[20]

While feminist critics in general have been reluctant to associate the purchase of a wife with the "heroic" act of saving a (female) child, transnational adoptions occur predominantly in areas where not only women but also nations themselves cannot care for their own children. Numerous national as well as international declarations on the rights of children demand that poverty alone should not justify the loss of parental authority.[21] Legal scholar Twila Perry asks us: "Could it be argued that, rather than transferring the children of the poor to economically better-off people in other countries, there should be a transfer of wealth from rich countries to poor ones to enable the mothers of poor children to continue to take care of their children themselves?"[22] Dissociating transnational adoption from the historical and economic legacy of war brides and mail-order brides thus obscures an understanding of this practice as one of the more recent forms of gendered commodification—an enduring symptom of an increasing international gendered division of labor under the shadows of globalization.

From the perspective of Asian American studies and history, we might consider how transnational adoption from Asia fits not only within a gendered postwar pattern of privileged immigration (war brides, mail-order brides, transnational adoptees) but also within nineteenth-century histories of anti-Asian immigration and bars to naturalization and citizenship. The period from 1882 to 1943 is often cited as the "official" years of Asian exclusion. However, legal scholar Leti Volpp has suggested that the Page Law of 1875, largely banning Chinese female immigration to the United States, might be a more appropriate historical date to mark the *gendered* form in which racialized exclusion of Asian immigrants from the U.S. nation-state took place.[23] In this regard, the privileged migration of Chinese baby girls in our contemporary moment marks not only a striking gendered reversal of this history of racialized exclusion but also an emergent form of Asian American subjectivity of considerable consequence to Asian American politics, history, and community. Indeed, this reversal suggests not only that the transnational adoptee must be considered a "proper" subject of Asian American studies but also that the field has evolved to a point where a "subjectless" critique—a critique that does not rely upon an assumed and naturalized set of Asian American bodies—is indispensable.

What, we might ask, accounts for this gendered reversal of the Page Law? Further, how might we rethink time-honored paradigms relating to racial formation, gender subordination, and labor exploitation in Asian American studies in regard to the practice of transnational adoption? The historical period from the late nineteenth century to World War II—the era of the "Asian Alien" and "Yellow Peril"—is one during which a rapidly industrializing U.S. nation-state produced cheap and flexible labor through Asian exclusion laws and the creation of the "illegal (Asian) immigrant" outside the rights and privileges of citizenship.[24] If the transnational adoptee is, in fact, an Asian American immigrant, what kind of labor is she performing for the family, and for the nation?

Here, we need to broaden yet again our historical perspective to consider the intersection of transnational and domestic histories of race and racial formation. Due to declining birth rates in the post-World War II West, greater access to abortion and reliable methods of contraception, and an easing of the stigma against women bearing children outside of marriage, fewer white children are now available for domestic adoption.[25] As a result, white parents reluctant or unwilling to adopt black children in the United States (and/or fearful of domestic child custody battles with birth parents) have turned increasingly to transnational adoption as an alternative.[26] In this way, the Asian transnational adoptee serves to triangulate the domestic landscape of black–white race relations. Indeed, she might be described as performing a type of crucial ideological labor: the shoring up of an idealized notion of kinship, the making good of the white heterosexual nuclear family.

Hence, transnational adoption need not be understood as historically disparate from the prewar period of Asian exclusion, with its bars to naturalization and citizenship. In the postwar period of the Asian American *citizen* the practice of transnational adoption expands wage labor into arenas of consumer capitalism meant to effect a different type of labor power. We might describe this form not as "productive labor," in the traditional Marxian sense, but as "consumptive labor." Miranda Joseph argues that "consumptive labor is productive, but it is organized very differently from productive labor: it is not organized, procured, or exploited as wage labor."[27] Instead, as Joseph observes, in the shift to globalization and modes of flexible production and accumulation, consumptive labor serves to produce and to organize social community as a supplement to capital.

In the context of transnational adoption, consumptive labor produces and shores up the social and psychic boundaries of the white heterosexual nuclear family, guaranteeing its integrity and the sanctity of its ideals. Under the shadows of this imperative, then, we need to consider how transnational parenting might underwrite powerful regimes of racial, sexual, and economic containment. In constructing a cultural "identity" for their adoptee, for instance, how do parents utilize discourses of multiculturalism to absorb difference into the intimate space of the familial? How are discourses of multiculturalism being invoked to manage, to aestheticize, to reinscribe, and finally to deracinate culture of all meaningful difference?

In the context of this analysis, the practice of transnational adoption suggests that Asian baby girls *are* more easily folded into the imagined community of the white, heterosexual, middle-class nuclear family than black children. All the more, then, we need to consider the multiple ways in which economic agency, political power, and social recognition are becoming increasingly privatized as a function of capital, while civil society continues to shrink and priorities are shifted from social services to capital maximization. Moreover, we need to explore how the racial management of gender and the gendered management of race assimilate the Asian adoptee into the intimate public sphere of the white nuclear family—into traditional, recognizable, and idealized family and kinship structures. How does the model minority myth help to facilitate this fit? How does the stereotype of the hard-working, agreeable, and passive Asian girl, ever eager to please, work to smooth over political problems, economic disparities, and cultural differences?[28]

These questions demand a deconstructive rereading of the Asian American model minority myth, whose genealogy is said to date from the Cold War necessity to produce "good" (anti-Communist) Asian subjects, as well as to the reformation of the 1965 Immigration and Nationality Act and its subsequent initiation of a professional "brain drain" from Asia. How do war brides, mail-order brides, and transnational adoptees collectively challenge, broaden, and reorient traditional accountings of the transformation of "Asian alien" into "Asian American citizen"?

Relating this gendered history of Asian immigration, as well as white/black/yellow race relations, to the model minority discourse suggests that global histories of gendered commodification do in fact effect and affect domestic genealogies of race, racialization, and citizenship. Indeed, the practice of transnational adoption marks a contemporary crossing of global processes of flexible specialization and the production of new racialized communities—new global families—that must be considered against a politics of weak multiculturalism. This is a politics focused not on issues of social justice, material redistribution, and substantive equality, but on economic entitlement and the privileges of family for an emergent class of multicultural elites. In this current state of emergency, to paraphrase Walter Benjamin, what are the psychic costs and burdens that underwrite transnational adoption's political, economic, and social contradictions? What is the psychic scaffolding that makes transnational adoption an inhabitable and livable, or an uninhabitable and barren, condition of existence? Let us return to the psychic dilemma—to the imperial psychic sphere—of "two mothers."

Psychic diasporas

For the transnational adoptee, where does history begin?

In the opening minutes of *First Person Plural*, we are given several conflicting answers to this question. The filmmaker presents a complex montage sequence that combines family photographs, her adoptive father's home movies, including scenes of Borshay Liem's arrival at the San Francisco airport on 3 March 1966, and her own interview footage of her American parents and siblings some thirty years later as they watch these home movies and recall their memories and feelings of that fateful day. The sequence begins with Denise, Borshay Liem's sister, explaining the excitement of "getting" a sister, "someone to play with," as she puts it. "I remember getting my hair done to go pick you up at the airport, and I was really jazzed about that," Denise tells us. But despite her "excitement" about picking up Cha Jung Hee, her new little sister from Korea, Denise's investment in (feminine) self-display belies a narcissistic logic that as a whole underwrites the entirety of the Borshay family's initial encounter with the eight-year-old adoptee. "I think mother went up to the wrong person," Denise admits. "Yeah. I think we didn't know until we checked your name tag or something who told us who you were. It didn't matter. I mean, one of them was ours."

Here, the language of ownership, as well as the assumed interchangeability of the variously "tagged" adoptees, constitutes a clear violation of the exclusive bond thought to exist between mother and child. This violation opens immediately upon the terrain of commodification—one of exchangeability and substitutability. Significantly, Borshay Liem's "acquisition" is accompanied by the simultaneous erasure of Cha Jung Hee's Korean identity through the dismissal of her prior history and family. "You know, to us an orphanage meant that you had no family," Alveen Borshay explains. "This way you were going to have a family." Suggesting that Borshay Liem's history begins only with her entry into their particular family unit, Denise concludes: "From the moment you came here, you were my sister and we were your family and that was it. And even though we look different—different nationality or whatever—we were your family."

Echoing Alveen's and Denise's sentiments, Donald Borshay's account is notably similar. And although the father recalls a momentary wrinkle in Borshay Liem's initial arrival, this problem is quickly smoothed out through its concerted willing away: "I remember very clearly your first meal," Donald recalls. "Mother prepared something that was very nice. And we were sitting at the table and you just kind of dropped your head and the tears started to come down. No words were spoken. Mother could see what was happening, and she simply took you away from the table and you were excused and from then on it was perfect."

"*From then on it was perfect.*" I have spent some time detailing the various recollections of the "from then on" moment of Borshay Liem's arrival in the United States. I do so because these comments collectively illustrate the ways in which the transnational adoptee is commodified as an object to be enjoyed, while at the same time the particular histories of her past are denied, repressed, and effaced. In Denise's, Alveen's, and Donald's recollections, history "proper" begins only at the moment of Borshay Liem's arrival "over here," the privatized language of family working to overwrite histories of Korea as well as the particularities of Cha Jung Hee's Korean past. Alveen admits quite forthrightly that her initial desire to adopt stemmed from watching Gary Moore commercials on NBC television advertising Foster Parents Plan through the plight of Korean War orphans. However, this history cannot be easily reconciled with Borshay Liem's past. Public histories of war, imperialism, domestic conflict, and poverty in Korea cannot be easily connected to the private sphere of the prosperous American family.

Moreover, while there is no such thing as a motherless child, the opening sequence of *First Person Plural* highlights the management of Borshay Liem's past history through the valence of the "proper" name. Sent to the United States at eight, Borshay Liem has a series of identities and proper names that are erased through her transnational exchange. "My Name is Kang Ok Jin," Borshay Liem begins in the opening lines of *First Person Plural*. As her face flashes onto the screen and fades into an eerie solarized silhouette, she continues: "I was born on 14 June 1957. I feel like I've been several different people in one life. My name is Cha Jung Hee. I was born on 5 November 1956. I've had three names, three different sets of histories. My name is Deann Borshay. I was born 3 March 1966, the moment I stepped off the airplane in San Francisco. I've spoken different languages and I've had different families." First "Kang Ok Jin" and then deliberately substituted for another child, "Cha Jung Hee," by the Korean adoption agency, "Deann Borshay" is finally "born" on 3 March 1966, not by her Korean birth mother but by her arrival on the San Francisco jetway. Ultimately, through the animating desires and projections of her American family, she enters what they consider to be her "proper" history.

It is important to note that the repression of Borshay Liem's past is carried out not only as a collective family project but also, and more importantly, through the *strict management of the adoptee's affect*. That is, the contraction of Korean history into the privatized boundaries of the white American family is finessed through the repression and erasure of Borshay Liem's emotions. The silent tears that mark Borshay Liem's arrival as well as the negation of her past cannot have linguistic expression and thus have no symbolic life. These tears must necessarily be refused, as Donald Borshay does indeed refuse and then "excuse" them, such that Borshay Liem has little psychic recourse to work through her considerable losses. (Attitudes toward open adoption have shifted considerably from thirty years ago. However, given the ways in which difference is often appropriated and reinscribed by a politics of weak multiculturalism, the current acknowledgement of the adoptee's past may not have shifted this management of affect in any significant manner.)

How might we begin to analyze Borshay Liem's affective losses? Several years ago, in response to a series of Asian American student suicides at a university where I had been teaching, I cowrote with Shinhee Han, a clinical psychotherapist, an essay entitled "A Dialogue on Racial Melancholia."[29] In this article, we analyze Freud's theories of mourning and melancholia as presenting a compelling framework to conceptualize registers of loss and depression attendant to the conflicts and struggles associated with immigration, assimilation, and racialization for Asian Americans. In contrast to "normal" mourning, where libido is eventually withdrawn from a lost object to be invested elsewhere, melancholia as described by Freud is a "pathological" mourning without end. As Freud's privileged theory of unresolved grief, melancholia delineates a psychic condition whereby certain losses can never be avowed and, hence, can never be properly mourned. In our argument, racial melancholia describes both social and psychic structures of loss emerging from Asian immigrant experiences that can be worked through only with the greatest of considerable pain and difficulty.

Here it is important to emphasize that the experience of immigration is based on a structure of loss. In "Mourning and Melancholia," Freud describes the lost object as embodying a person, place, or ideal. When one leaves a country of origin, voluntarily or involuntarily (as in the case of transnational adoptees), a host of losses both concrete and abstract must be mourned. To the extent lost ideals of Asianness (including homeland, family, language, property, identity, custom, status) are irrecoverable, immigration, assimilation, and racialization are placed within a melancholic framework—a state of suspension between "over there" and "over here." In Freud's theory of mourning, one works through and finds closure to these losses by investing in new objects and ideals—in the American dream, for example.

To the extent, however, that Asian Americans are perpetually consigned to foreigner status and considered eccentric to the nation (as the recent Wen Ho Lee case illustrates), and to the extent that ideals of whiteness remain unattainable and thus lost for Asian Americans, it might be said that they are denied the capacity to invest in new people, places, and ideals. This inability to invest in new objects is a crucial part of Freud's definition of melancholia. Racial melancholia thus describes a psychic process by which vexed identification and affiliations with lost objects, places, and ideals of both Asianness *and* whiteness remain estranged and unresolved.

In *First Person Plural*, we witness the numerous ways in which Borshay Liem's past is repressed, the continuous ways in which her racial difference and past history are managed and denied, so that she cannot mourn what she has lost in Korea. Furthermore, the documentary portrays Borshay Liem's frustrating and impossible identifications with ideals of whiteness that remain perpetually elusive. Speaking about her vain attempts to mimic the "American ways" of her siblings, Duncan and Denise, Borshay Liem presents us with numerous home movies documenting her torturous adolescent development: Deann sitting amid her white dolls; Deann dressed up like a Korean doll; Deann the prom queen; Deann with her towering white high school boyfriend; Deann as a perky college cheerleader.

Throughout the documentary, we witness in everyday acts, gestures, and offhand comments by her entire family the active production of Borshay Liem's Korean difference, accompanied by a simultaneous reinscription—an effacing and a whitewashing—of this difference. In the very opening minutes of Borshay Liem's documentary, her brother Duncan, in what can be described only as a smug tone of self-congratulation, tells her: "You didn't come from my mommy's womb. You don't have the family eyes, but you've got the family smile. Color and look doesn't make any difference. It's who you are. You're my sister." Duncan's statement underwrites a philosophy of weak multiculturalism, what Homi Bhabha describes as the irreducible failure of mimicry: "*Almost the same, but not quite . . . Almost the same but not white.*"[30]

In an especially disturbing episode recounted by her mother, a young Borshay Liem is shown in a home movie combing the very blond hair of a doll. In a voice-over commentary that could easily be described as an Asian version of *The Bluest Eye*, Alveen tells Borshay Liem, "You said, 'Mother, my ears always stick out. I hate that.' I said, 'Honey, that can be fixed if you want,' and you wanted." At this point, Donald Borshay chimes in, "So we went to the plastic surgeon in San Jose . . . and when they went to take the bandages off, then you began to cry." Again, the family is faced with tears, an overflow of affect that is met with bafflement, without real understanding.

Freud maintains in "Mourning and Melancholia" that melancholia emerges from a "pathological" disposition and can be distinguished from regular mourning by its inability to end.[31] In "A Dialogue on Racial Melancholia," Han and I contest Freud's distinction between mourning and melancholia. If experiences of immigration, assimilation, and racialization in the United States are fundamentally determined through both the forced relinquishing of lost but unspeakable Asian ideals and foreclosed investments in whiteness, then we might justifiably describe racial melancholia as a "normal" everyday group experience for Asian Americans. This insight places Asian American subjectivity and racial melancholia on the terrain of conflict, not damage. In this respect, racial melancholia might be better described as a depathologized "structure of feeling," to cite Raymond Williams's term for those unidentified affects marking emergent group formations and identities.[32] Operating less as an individual than a group dynamic, racial melancholia for Asian Americans, we conclude, involves not just mourning or melancholia but a continual negotiation between mourning *and* melancholia.

Significantly, this negotiation is often and even exclusively configured within Asian American cultural politics as an *intergenerational* and *intersubjective* negotiation. That is, problems and contradictions arising from Asian American immigration are often interpreted in terms of master narratives of intergenerational conflict between parents and children, between the older and younger generation. The tendency to reduce all social issues, including those resulting from institutional racism and economic exploitation, to first-generation versus second-generation struggles threatens to displace them within the privatized space of the family. At the same time, it denies what are necessarily public problems and absolves the state and mainstream community from proper address or redress.

While I flag this palpable danger, what I would like to emphasize in this analysis of transnational adoption is the elimination of this intergenerational and intersubjective process, the loss of the communal nature of racial melancholia. As a collective unit, the family cannot recognize Borshay Liem's racial melancholia. Borshay Liem's losses remain unaffirmed and unacknowledged by those closest to her, by her own family, by those most affectively immediate to her. This is the striking difference between the ways in which racial melancholia is negotiated within Asian American immigrant families and the ways loss is negotiated by the Asian transnational adoptee. Earlier, I asked whether the transnational adoptee, as well as her adoptive family, was Asian American. To the extent that Borshay Liem's adoptive family recognizes her as a racialized subject, while not recognizing themselves as such, we witness an emotional gap of significant consequence in the intimate space of the family. That is, this failure of recognition serves to redouble racial melancholia's consequences, effectively severing Borshay Liem from the family unit, affectively segregating her, and ultimately forcing her to negotiate her losses in isolation. What should necessarily be an intergenerational and intersubjective negotiation of loss is thus reduced to intrasubjective isolation and silence.

"There was an unspoken contract between us, which we had all agreed upon—that I was an orphan with no family ties to Korea," Borshay Liem explains, using the "public" language of contracts and exchange to pierce the "private" bubble of the nuclear family.

> I belonged only to my American parents. It meant I didn't have a Korean history or Korean identity. . . . I think being adopted into my family in some ways brought a lot of happiness for both me and for my parents, my American family. But there was also something that was—there was also a lot of sadness that we couldn't deal with as a family. And a lot of that sadness had to do with loss.

"I was never able to mourn what I had lost [in Korea] with my American parents," Borshay Liem adds, explaining the years of clinical depression that she suffered after leaving Fremont and her family to attend college at Berkeley.

What is especially disturbing here is not just the fact that the family cannot recognize Borshay Liem's racial melancholia, cannot easily conceive of her adoption as involving loss, cannot easily imagine her arrival in the United States as anything but a gain. Equally distressing is the fact that Borshay Liem's continual melancholy is a sadness that is read by many involved as ingratitude, serving to exacerbate Borshay Liem's enduring feelings of disloyalty and shame. What, after all, could be less "grateful" on the part of an adoptee than depression?

Hence, what is justifiably felt to be a happy event from the point of view of the parents and siblings comes to overdetermine the adoptee's affect. Deann's melancholia is countered by an overpowering joy on the part of the other family members, such that their collective will comes to overwrite her emotional states and experiences. In the end, Borshay Liem tells us, "I forgot everything. I forgot how to speak Korean. I forgot any memory of ever having had a family. And I even forgot my real name. . . . The only memories I have of my child-hood are the images my father filmed while growing up. I relegated my real memories into the category of dreams."[33]

For Borshay Liem, racial melancholia involves the effacing and overwriting of her child-hood memories and affective commitments. In this regard, transnational adoption's psychic predicament radically reduces any sense of the adoptee's agency. Indeed, though I earlier described the practice of transnational adoption as one of the most privileged forms of contemporary immigration, it is one largely devoid of emotional agency for the adoptee. In her attempts to mourn the unspeakable losses initiated by her (involuntary) exchange, the transnational adoptee might also be said to experience an affective curtailment that prevents her from transforming melancholy ever gradually into mourning. Here, I am delineating a profound form of racial melancholia, one that reduces memories to dreams, and agency to fantasy.

Importantly, it is only the mother who ultimately recognizes Borshay Liem's affective discrepancy. Reviewing the family movie of Borshay Liem's arrival, Alveen finally notices some thirty years later Borshay Liem's stricken facial expression. In a voice-over, she admits to her daughter, "When you arrived—little stoic face and bundled up in all those clothes. We couldn't talk to you. You couldn't talk to us. I realize now that you were terrified. Because we were so happy, we just didn't think about that." As we witness in *First Person Plural*, the emotional clash between the Borshay family's affective joy and the young adoptee's obvious terror eventually becomes a "return of the repressed," a repetition compulsion that is psychically displaced and negotiated between mother and daughter.

Here, let us remember that adoption is often bound up with questions of faltering maternity—of failed reproduction and proper mothering. To the extent that adoption (rather than having no children) is often viewed as the last alternative to biological reproduc-tion the maternal bond with the adoptee is already overdetermined. In the case of transna-tional adoption, these issues become especially problematic because of the child's tenuous place within the biologized ideal of the nuclear family. Because the racialized link between the white mother and the Asian daughter elicits comment, because it becomes something that must be continually and repeatedly explained, the maternal bond appears as something not only unnatural but also in need of continual support.[34] "Some people would ask and others would kind of look," Alveen tells Borshay Liem, "and you knew they were wondering, but we didn't care." Given the challenge to negotiate radical alterity and racism within the inti-mate public sphere of the white family, Alveen's reaction is unfortunately less rather than more ideal, less rather than more caring, a wasted opportunity. In the final analysis, the mother is not just responsible for removing Borshay Liem from the dinner table—literally burdened with handling her daughter's disjunctive affect. Indeed, the mother is ultimately blamed for the daughter's psychic condition. "Emotionally," Borshay Liem concludes, "there wasn't room in my mind for two mothers." Let us try to explore this mother/daughter predicament more carefully.

In psychoanalysis, of course, origin and history begin with the mother. It is important to recall that, in Freud's traditional narrative of the little girl's separation from the maternal, there is not only an account of two mothers, the phallic and the lacking, but also a genealogy of unrelenting recrimination and blame. Summarizing his views on the "riddle" of female subjectivity, Freud writes in "Femininity":

> A woman's identification with her mother allows us to distinguish two strata: the pre-Oedipus one which rests on her affectionate attachment to her mother and takes her as a model, and the latter one from the Oedipus complex which seeks to get rid of her mother and take her place with her father. We are no doubt justified in saying that much of both of them is left over for the future and that neither of them is adequately surmounted in the course of development. But the phase of the affectionate pre-Oedipus attachment is the decisive one for a woman's future: during it preparations are made for the acquisition of the characteristics with which she will later fulfill her role in the sexual function and perform her invaluable social tasks. It is in this identification too that she acquires her attractiveness to a man, whose Oedipus attachment to his mother it kindles into passion. How often it happens, however, that it is only his son who obtains what he himself aspired to! One gets the impression that a man's love and a woman's are a phase apart psychologically.[35]

Commentators typically gloss Freud's famous lament—"that a man's love and a woman's are a phase apart psychologically"—as the notion that "women direct toward their children the love which their husbands desire for themselves."[36] What accounts for this cleaving and generational displacement of affect? What psychic mechanism forces the little girl to shift her desire for and pleasurable identifications with the pre-Oedipal mother to invest, ever so reluctantly, in the unforgiving figure and the name of the father?

According to Freud, the castration crisis and the subsequent penis envy it activates in the little girl work to alienate her from an affectionate attachment to the pre-Oedipal mother, or what Freud elsewhere labels the "negative Oedipus complex." In surrendering the negative-Oedipal mother to identify with the symbolic mother of lack, the little girl is not just exiled from activity into passivity, but also forced into an impossible psychic trajectory of contempt. "The suppression of women's aggressiveness which is prescribed for them constitutionally and imposed on them socially," Freud observes, "favors the development of powerful masochistic impulses, which succeed . . . in binding erotically the destructive trends which have been diverted inward."[37] Here, Freud delineates the emergence of the normative female subject as not just profoundly masochistic but melancholic. She is a subject not only estranged from the loved phallic mother and the pleasurable passion she represents but also narcissistically wounded and, finally, alienated from her own self, the psychic life of her original erotic investments.

The legacy of the little girl's severed history with the negative-Oedipal mother is one in which the affective bonds to the phallic nonlacking mother are melancholically transformed from intense love to magnified hate, such that it becomes, Freud observes, "very striking and [may] last all through life."[38] In covering up the passionate bonds of attachment between the little girl and her loved mother, the castration crisis inaugurates and makes way for the symbolic mother of lack, the positive-Oedipal mother, whom the little girl blames for her "mutilated" condition. This is an endless cycle of vilification. For every daughter who comes to blame her mother for her subordinated position is also liable to censure should she become a mother and thus be forced to relive this psychic rejection from the receiving end. This process of maternal melancholy explains how it is that the little girl comes to have no psychic room in her mind for two mothers. That is, it explains how the little girl comes to have no psychic room for the nonlacking negative-Oedipal mother but only psychic space for the castrated positive-Oedipal mother and the diminished world she comes to signify.

How might this paradigm of the negative and positive Oedipus complex play out specifically in terms of Borshay Liem's psychic predicament? How are the negative and positive Oedipus complex negotiated between the bodies of two mothers—Korean and white? What should be immediately clear in Borshay Liem's psychic predicament is that the negative and positive Oedipus complexes necessarily map not only a sexual but also a racial divide. This racial divide creates distinctions between Asianness and whiteness that must also be traced back to a kind of castration crisis where whiteness emerges as a symbolic and governing trope. For the Asian transnational adoptee, whose racialization might be said to be produced and denied by her family at once, issues of blame and recrimination are remarkably complicated.

Melanie Klein's notion of reinstatement of the mother to a world of loved internal objects is critical to understanding Borshay Liem's psychic dilemma. Klein tells us that psychic stability and health depend upon a subject's ability to align and to test continually the "real" mother against her phantasmatic images—both good and bad. In "The Psychogenesis of Manic-Depressive States," Klein writes,

> In some patients who had turned away from their mother in dislike or hate, or used other mechanisms to get away from her, I have found that there existed in their minds nevertheless a beautiful picture of the mother, but one which was felt to be a *picture* of her only, not her real self. The real object was felt to be unattractive—really an injured, incurable, and therefore dreaded person. The beautiful picture had been dissociated from the real object but had never been given up, and played a great part in the specific ways of their sublimations.[39]

What must be shorn away from the mother in order for reinstatement to occur, in order for Borshay Liem to create a beautiful picture of the mother? In "A Dialogue on Racial Melancholia," Han and I found that, in the case of biological Asian American immigrant children, race and sexuality must often cleave—that racial difference must often be dissociated from the figure of the "real" mother—for reinstatement to occur. But, for the transnational adoptee, who is the "real" mother? And what might her beautiful picture look like?

In the case of Borshay Liem, the negotiation of the good and the bad mother must be brokered across two maternal bodies, Korean and white. "I had a particular difficulty talking to my American mother about my Korean mother. . . . I didn't know how to talk about my mother with my mother because she was my mother," Borshay Liem states confusedly. For her, the question of who is the "real" mother oscillates wildly, so that recrimination and blame abound to the point that any creation of a beautiful picture is inevitably constrained. Borshay Liem admits that, even though "it was as if I had been born to them somehow," she cannot, as an adult, accept Alveen and Donald Borshay as her parents (even though, as we must remember, it is Alveen who largely lives through and negotiates Borshay Liem's recriminations and blame). Ultimately, Deann feels as if she must choose one family over the other, one mother over the other. Hoping to alleviate these feelings of "disloyalty," Borshay Liem confesses, "I felt if I could actually see them come together in real life that somehow both families could then live within myself. So I asked my parents to go to Korea with me."

However, Borshay Liem's attempt to merge her two mothers through her long-anticipated "reunion" with both women illustrates the difficulty of her psychic dilemma of the maternal and the racial. Her attempts to achieve psychic integration are met on the part of her two families with confusion and resistance, as well as a dearth of understanding about the absolute need to move beyond the singularity of the "real" mother. In fact, much of Borshay Liem's reunion in Korea is spent trying to determine who the "real" mother really is. As such, the initial trauma of Borshay Liem's transnational adoption is not just reenacted but redoubled through her initial rejection of the (white) mother and, in turn, her own repeated rejection by *both* mothers.

"You look like your mother," Alveen tells Borshay Liem upon their arrival at the birth mother's residence in Kunsan, Korea. However, Alveen's "gracious" relinquishing of Borshay Liem to her biological mother is met with equally "gracious" ambivalence and resistance. "She [the birth mother] says it's natural because she's her daughter," the translator first relates. "Yes," Alveen responds. But then the translator adds, turning to Borshay Liem: "She [the birth mother] says that although she is your mother, she only gave birth to you so you should really love and do everything you can for your adoptive parents . . . She wants you to be happy with your parents, your adopted parents." At this imperative, we see Borshay Liem wince. Having rejected her white mother, Borshay Liem, in turn, is rejected.

According to her Korean brother, who speaks on behalf of the Kang family (the father having died), Borshay Liem was sent away for a "better life." "It's not that important anymore. We are not very proud of what happened. She really needs to consider the cultural differences between us. Only then will she understand us," he rationalizes. "We have been apart for thirty years. It would be easier to close the gap between us if we spoke the same language. However, our cultural differences are difficult to overcome." Configuring her adoption as both an alienation from her "native" Korean culture and a gain, a "better life" for Borshay Liem in the United States, the Korean brother's attitude is remarkably similar to that of Donald Borshay insofar as neither man is capable of recognizing Borshay Liem's emotional injuries or needs. They cannot acknowledge her inability to negotiate the affective losses of her transnational exchange. (Tellingly, Borshay Liem does not state that "there wasn't room in my mind for two fathers.")

In *First Person Plural* affective responsibility is highly gendered, a psychic dynamic of which the mothers are not only aware but also for which they are both finally held accountable. "She [Borshay Liem] is filled with heartache," the Korean birth mother recognizes, "so I am very sad." Though she is "unable to express" this sadness in adequate ways, having "no words to describe the agonizing years" after she relinquished Borshay Liem for adoption, the Korean birth mother, like Alveen Borshay, must tend to the affective dissonance of the event, assuming blame for the situation. The Korean birth mother thanks the white mother for raising Borshay Liem, and in this way her sorrow and gratitude become, in the words of Alveen Borshay, "our joy." As such, Borshay Liem's "reunion" and fantasy of return disturb the notion of completion and closure, revealing in the process the asymmetry separating women in Third World nations who relinquish their children and those in First World nations who receive them. This racialized asymmetry between First and Third World comes to underpin the gendered dilemma of maternal melancholy delineated by Freud. That is, the endless cycle of maternal vilification is compounded by racial disparities that ultimately force a rethinking of the category of the "real" as well as Klein's notion of the good and the bad mother.[40]

Psychically pushed and pulled away by both her Korean mother and her American mother, Borshay Liem is unable to create space in her mind for two mothers. While there is a proliferation of multiple sites of the "real" in this reunion, there is nevertheless absolute psychic fidelity on the part of everyone involved that the position of the "real" mother can be only singular and not multiple. Indeed, the predicament of Borshay Liem's maternal melancholy, compounded by the dissonance of the "real" (Korean or white) mother, ultimately renders the question of the "real" impossible. That is, Borshay Liem ultimately does not have space in her mind for *any* "real" mother at all. In Klein's vocabulary, while she cannot have room in her mind for two good mothers, she does indeed have room in her mind for two bad mothers. One—the Korean mother—is blamed for abandoning her to her fate; the other—the white mother—is blamed for being unable to mirror her emotional (racial) predicaments. Hence, Borshay Liem cannot create a beautiful picture from either, rendering the question of reinstatement extraordinarily tenuous. Rejected by both mothers she, too, must reject them. (Here let me gesture to Gail Dolgin and Vincente Franco's 2002 *Daughter from Danang*, another recent documentary exploring transnational adoption in the wake of the Vietnam War. The film is an elaborate disquisition on adoptee Heidi Bub's successive rejection of two "bad" mothers—first her adoptive mother and then her birth mother.)

The singularity of the "real" mother, as well as the question of blame, continues to haunt Borshay Liem through the very end of *First Person Plural*. Confessing that, with her parents in the room, she felt more like a "temporary visitor" with her Korean family, Borshay Liem admits that "the only way I can actually be closer to my Korean mother is to admit that she's not my mother anymore. The only way to be close to her is to acknowledge that she hasn't been my mother for over thirty years, and that my other mother has been my mother for—in a way my real mother." Borshay Liem's speech expresses the will to move forward psychically, but it is riddled with ambivalence and continues to be marked by the notion of singularity, origin, and return—the need to choose between the two mothers. Responding to Alveen Borshay's statement that "after all, that's your real mother [the Korean mother]," Borshay Liem attempts to broker a truce, stating cautiously, "I think you're my real mother." "Well, I feel that way," Alveen Borshay responds, "I really do." Again, we witness a certain asymmetry between mother and daughter, between language and emotion. While Alveen can affectively *feel* like Borshay Liem's mother, Borshay Liem can still only *think* this possibility.

The question of the singularity of the "real" mother is not only the kernel of the psychic dilemma of two mothers but also the key to imagining a poststructuralist theory of family and kinship predicated not on origin but on destination. However, this moving beyond fidelity to the singular, this moving forward from the fixity of the "real," is complicated by two powerful and compelling fantasies of return that simultaneously underwrite the psychic dynamics of transnational adoption: the return to the birth mother and the return to the motherland. In transnational adoption's crossing of sexuality and diaspora, we are presented with both the desire to return to the "real" mother and the desire to return to the place of origins. These intersecting discourses of return underwrite a personal narrative of self-realization, completion, and closure that, as *First Person Plural* illustrates, is not only an impossible task to accomplish but also creates fragmentation and further displacement rather than wholeness. In returning to Korea for her "reunion," Borshay Liem is forced to acknowledge the fact that confronting the past is always double-edged, challenging any sense of recoupable stability. On the social level, these discourses of return resist notions of authenticity and belonging that support conservative notions of diaspora. Configuring diaspora in terms of heterosexuality, filiation, and ethnic purity, discourses of return as "completion" and "recuperation" deny issues of queerness, affiliation, and social contingency that define contemporary formations of new global families and flexible kinship underwriting queer diasporas.

Following this family "reunion" Borshay Liem admits that she has given up "that childhood fantasy of returning to my family," of "somehow be[ing] sent back to Korea." Although Borshay Liem recognizes that she must "develop another relationship, a different relationship with my Korean family," the conclusion of *First Person Plural* does not seem to endorse such a moving forward. Indeed, the documentary ends with Borshay Liem's marriage ceremony and the birth of a son, Nick. The sentimental "resolution" to Borshay Liem's social and psychic predicament is an entitled Oedipal structure legislating only one privileged place for mother, father, and child. Hence, Borshay Liem's "cure" to her dilemma of two mothers does not move beyond either notions of the singular or the traditional structures of family and kinship. Rather, this marriage allows her to create and to inhabit a conventional nuclear family structure of her own, to make good on what she believes she never had. While Borshay Liem's marriage to her Asian husband, Paul Liem, significantly complicates questions of return to cultural origins, the final image Borshay Liem leaves us with in *First Person Plural* comes in the form of a family photo of this naturalized Oedipal trio. Ironically, this Oedipal trio subscribes to the very psychic and material structure at the heart of Borshay Liem's maternal and diasporic predicament.

Here, let me conclude by way of my own return to the negative Oedipus complex. In "Girl Love," Kaja Silverman reminds us of Freud's insistence that it is only by accessing a woman at the level of her negative Oedipus complex that a man can love her. "It is in this identification," Silverman quotes Freud, "that she acquires her attractiveness to man, whose Oedipus attachment to his mother it kindles into passion." Silverman then observes that "so long as the negative Oedipus complex remains hidden from the female subject herself, she will not be able to respond to the desire it arouses in the male subject."[41] Hence, the melancholy to which the female subjectivity typically leads is based not just upon the impossibility of any reciprocal relationship between the sexes; it is equally based upon the loss of the loved mother, the forfeiting of a realm of extraordinary affective intensity, and the closing down of the possibility of any redemptive form of female love. The castration crisis inaugurates this form of pathological sexuality in the little girl who, like her lacking mother, finally becomes a subject who cannot love and a subject no one else could love.

What would it mean for the little girl to have access to the passionate psychic intensity of her negative Oedipus complex? What would it mean for the little girl, like the little boy, to have equal and reciprocal access to the affective realm of the loved mother, to refuse to devalue the negative-Oedipal mother, to repudiate the logic of maternal blame and recrimination? It would mean, of course, that she would have room in her psyche for two good mothers. Silverman proposes that the symbolic recovery of the affect associated with the negative-Oedipal mother is indeed possible, not just for men but for women, too, in a signifying process she labels "girl love."

In both *The Interpretation of Dreams* and *The Unconscious*, Freud maintains that every signifying act in a given subject's life refers back in some ultimate sense to a primally repressed term, which, as we witness in *First Person Plural*, is still primarily the mother. But, while she is configured as our ground of desire, the mother in fact provides the first signifier for a more primordial loss: the loss of what Jacques Lacan variously calls "presence," "being," or the "here and now." Silverman writes,

> Unlike the other signifiers of the *hic et nunc*, though, she has nothing to refer back to. What she stands in for psychically cannot provide this function, since it is precisely what escapes signification. Although serving as the support for libidinal symbolization, the mother is consequently devoid of semantic value. It is not she who gives all of the other signifiers of desire their meaning; it is, rather, *they* who determine what *she* can mean. To go "backward," libidinally speaking, is also not finally to touch "ground"; it is, instead, to apprehend the groundlessness of all signification.[42]

"Girl love" represents a signifying process whereby one recuperates the loved and lost negative-Oedipal mother not by moving backward toward the recuperation of origins but by moving forward, "to symbolize lack in a way that is utterly our own."[43] It is a signifying process that is quickening of disparaged creatures and things, that endows devalued others, the bad Korean and the bad white mother, with new and alternate meaning. "There is nothing primordial about this relationship," Silverman writes. "It does not represent a continuation of the female's early love for the mother, but rather its symbolic recovery from a later moment in time, and there is no limit on when that can occur."[44] Like Silverman, what I am proposing here is not the recuperation of a lost origin in the recaptured figure of the negative-Oedipal mother, but the deployment of the affective intensity associated with this loved figure for a forgotten though crucial new form of symbolization.

Were it not for the castration crisis, Silverman concludes, we would all, men and women alike, have permanent access to the affective intensity of the negative Oedipus complex. "Girl love" thus recuperates a lost form of symbolization represented by the negative Oedipus complex, where libidinal "openness" rather than fixity reigns, and where words rather than binding affect come under the influence of their unconscious desire. By symbolizing lack in highly personalized and alternate forms we can create psychic space for two *good* mothers. While our words would still induce the "fading" of being, they would also induce a kind of "second coming." They would not only open psychic space for but also lend symbolic sustenance to two good mothers—two *good enough* mothers—not just the mother of lack but the mother of love, not just the Korean mother or the white mother but, indeed, both. The maternal resignification facilitated by "girl love" thus provides a crucial corrective to conservative (hetero)sexual and diasporic politics. We return to mother and motherland not by going back but by moving forward. We do not bring the present into the past. Rather, we bring the past into the present. In fact, we keep the past alive in the present by signifying and quickening through our desire those creatures and things that conventional culture would disavow or bury.

In the introduction to this essay, I stated that while we have numerous poststructuralist accounts of language, we have few poststructuralist accounts of kinship. Why is this so? I have spent some time analyzing the material and psychic contradictions of transnational adoption in *First Person Plural*, for I think the practice manifests the broader paradoxes of globalization and contemporary crossings of sexuality, racial formation, economic exploitation, and nation on both an international and a domestic level. As an instance of globalization and its discontents, transnational adoption also opens upon the difficult affective terrain of poststructuralist notions of family and kinship. While the age of late capitalism has given rise to numerous material reconfigurations of family, I fear that these new forms of kinship and social identity do not have any concomitant psychic support.[45] To the extent that the transnational adoptee functions as guarantee to conventional ideals of the white nuclear family, and to the extent that she cannot in turn create space in her mind for two good mothers, the possibility of a poststructuralist kinship is dubious at best. To the extent, however, that transnational adoption allows us to denaturalize powerful myths of return animating (hetero)sexual and diasporic politics in a global age, we are left with several possible alternatives.

As a contemporary phenomenon, transnational adoption installs racial alterity and otherness squarely into the privatized space of the white American nuclear family, even as our national borders continue to be sealed in unprecedented ways. The contemporary formation of interracial First and Third World families represents a tremendous opportunity to question the conservative impulses of (hetero)sexuality and diaspora. In the context of *First Person Plural*, the disjunctive experiences of the transnational adoptee open upon a painful though potentially productive social and psychic terrain exceeding the privatized boundaries of the family unit. There is no smooth translatability, that is, between the ideological demands of the white nuclear family structure and the adoptee's disjunctive affect, her psychic protest. By creating new global families and racial formations at once, the presence of the Asian child in the space of the white family necessarily erodes the boundaries between the public and private spheres, between public and private histories. If, as Berlant contends, the political sphere has been largely contracted into private life, then the practice of transnational adoption provides one crucial site to reengage with questions of the political.

Under the shadows of globalization, this erosion of boundaries separating public from private calls for a broader response to racism, gender subordination, and economic exploitation that goes beyond, in Anagnost's words, "merely asserting one's entitlement to be a [transnational] parent."[46] Parents of transnational adoptees should not be held any more accountable than the rest of us to the political, economic, and social vicissitudes of globalization. Nevertheless, the practice of transnational adoption presents an exemplary—perhaps radical—opportunity for white, middle-class subjects to confront and to negotiate difference ethically within the social configurations of the new global family.

Restoring collective history to the process of a transnational adoptee's social and psychic development is crucial to the survival of the global family. It is also crucial to an ethical multiculturalism that rejects the model of the white heterobiological nuclear family as the standard against which all social orderings must be measured. Positing such an ethical multiculturalism may not just lead to powerful alliances for a progressive politics but could conceivably cut across historically constituted divisions of gender, race, and class to create important international and domestic political coalitions. In the process, it may also help us to create new material and psychic structures, a poststructuralist account and accounting of family and kinship, and of identity, community, and nation. Reimagining family and kinship, as well as recasting diaspora, in these terms offers a host of political opportunities, economic responsibilities, and cultural commitments.

Here, let me return to queer diasporas—to the John Hancock commercial and two dykes and a baby. We exist in a time when transnational adoption of Chinese baby girls by white lesbians can be aired on prime-time television during the Olympics. In this representation lies a nascent possibility, the possibility that this child might grow up to exist in a world where the psychic structure of two—indeed, three, four, five, or perhaps no—mothers of various races could be accommodated. Let us try to imagine—indeed, to live—these other possibilities, these other possible structures.

Notes

I would like to thank the following friends and colleagues for their insightful feedback and support: Shinhee Han, Fred Moten, Mae Ngai, Teemu Ruskola, Mari Ruti, Josie Saldaña, Kaja Silverman, and Leti Volpp. I have been fortunate to present this essay to various university audiences and seminars at Harvard University, Dartmouth College, the University of Illinois at Urbana-Champaign, and the University of California at San Diego. I would like to thank Brian Axel, Donald Pease, Robyn Wiegman, Martin Manalansan, Catherine Prendergast, Kent Ono, Lisa Lowe, Judith Halberstam, and Gayatri Gopinath for being ideal hosts as well as rigorous interlocutors. I would also like to thank the *Social Text* collective, especially Brent Edwards and Cindi Katz, for their helpful comments.

1   Deann Borshay, dir., *First Person Plural* (San Francisco: National Asian American Telecommunications Association, 2000).

2   Amy Kaplan, introduction to *Cultures of United States Imperialisms*, eds. Amy Kaplan and Donald E. Pease (Durham, N.C.: Duke University Press, 1993), 16.

3   See *Social Text*, no. 74 (2003), a special issue on transnational parenting curated from the disciplinary angle of anthropology. My essay, in part, is a response to what I see as a necessary critical reframing of current approaches to analyzing transnational adoption ethnographies and memoirs, as well as the broadening of the political, economic, and cultural issues they raise.

4   For an elaboration of the concept of "queer diaspora," see JeeYeun Lee, "Toward a Queer Korean American Diaspora," in *Q&A: Queer in Asian America*, eds. David L. Eng and Alice Y. Hom (Philadelphia: Temple University Press, 1998); David L. Eng, "Out Here and Over There: Queerness and Diaspora in Asian American Studies," in *Racial Castration: Managing Masculinity in Asian America* (Durham, N.C.: Duke University Press, 2001); Cindy Patton and Benigno Sanchez-Eppler, eds., *Queer Diasporas* (Durham, N.C.: Duke University Press, 2000); and Arnaldo Cruz-Malavé and Martin F. Manalansan IV, eds., *Queer Globalizations: Citizenship and the Afterlife of Colonialism* (New York: New York University Press, 2002).

5   See Gayle Rubin, "The Traffic in Women: Notes on the 'Political Economy' of Sex," in *Toward an Anthropology of Women*, ed. Rayna R. Reiter (New York: Monthly Review, 1975); and Claude Lévi-Strauss, *The Elementary Structures of Kinship*, trans. James Harle Bell and John Richard von Sturmer (Boston: Beacon, 1969).

6   Judith Butler, *Antigone's Claim: Kinship between Life and Death* (New York: Columbia University Press, 2000), 29–30.

7   Butler, *Antigone's Claim*, 70.

8   See, e.g., Rhacel Salazar Parreñas, *Servants of Globalization: Women, Migration, Domestic Work* (Stanford, Calif.: Stanford University Press, 2001), and Aihwa Ong, *Flexible Citizenship: The Cultural Logics of Transnationality* (Durham, N.C.: Duke University Press, 1999).

9   John D'Emilio, "Capitalism and Gay Identity," in *The Lesbian and Gay Studies Reader*, eds. Henry Abelove, Michèle Aina Barale, and David M. Halperin (New York: Routledge, 1993).

10   See "Times Will Begin Reporting Gay Couples' Ceremonies," *New York Times*, 18 August 2002.

11   John Hancock Financial Services (Agency: Hill Holiday, Region: North America), 2000. To view this commercial, go to www2.commercialcloset.org/cgi-bin/iowa/portrayals.html?record = 216.

12   See "Hancock Ad Raises Alarm in Adoption Communities," *Wall Street Journal*, 14 September 2000. After protests from right-wing conservatives, the commercial was reedited without the final exchange about being great mothers. In addition, fearing reprisals from Chinese authorities that lesbians were snatching up Chinese infants, John Hancock added an audio track stating that a flight from Phnom Penh, Cambodia, had just arrived.

13   We need to dissociate the relationship between economic entitlement and political rights. That is, the current practice of transnational adoption suggests that family is available to those gays and lesbians with access to capital. However, the legal treatment of this group by courts has by and large excluded them from the sphere of noneconomic rights (adoption, marriage, inheritance, service in the military, consensual sex). As a legal matter, adoption is a privilege. Hence, the contemporary reconsolidation of family by gays and lesbians has become an economic privilege and entitlement for few rather than a political right for all.

14   Ann Anagnost, "Scenes of Misrecognition: Maternal Citizenship in the Age of Transnational Adoption," *positions* 8.2 (Fall 2000): 389–421.

15   Ibid., 395.

16   Lauren Berlant, *The Queen of America Goes to Washington City: Essays on Sex and Citizenship* (Durham, N.C.: Duke University Press, 1997), 4–24.

17   The practice of transnational adoption does have a longer history than its post-World War II and current globalized incarnations. See, for instance, Linda Gordon, *The Great Arizona Orphan Abduction* (Cambridge: Harvard University Press, 1999). Gordon's book chronicles the adoption of Irish orphans by Mexican mineworker families in Arizona at the turn of the last century, as well as their subsequent kidnapping by white vigilantes who were determined to "save" them from the darker races.

18   These figures are based on INS Statistics for IR3 and IR4 Immigrant Visas Issued to Orphans. See the Holt International Web site at www.holtintl.org/insstats.shtml.

19   See, for instance, Cynthia H. Enloe, *Bananas, Beaches, and Bases: Making Feminist Sense of International Politics* (Berkeley: University of California Press, 2000).

20   Robert S. Gordon, "The New Chinese Export: Orphaned Children, an Overview of Adopting Children from China," *Transnational Law* 10 (spring 1997): 121–51. In the 1990s, Americans spent over U.S.$300 million to adopt 18,751 children from China. In 1999, adoption costs from China per child were approximately $20,000–27,000.

       From another angle, the economic profits from transnational adoption are central for understanding the political development and economic transformations marking the advent of Asian modernity. How, for instance, does transnational adoption relate to Korea's official narratives of its postwar economic miracle as one of Asia's "four tigers," its prolonged struggles for democratic rule, and its more recent and visible debates on the plight of "comfort women"?

21   For instance, see the 1989 United Nations Convention on the Rights of the Child (www.unicef.org/crc/crc.htm), the 1993 Hague Convention on the Protection of Children and the Cooperation in Respect of Intercountry Adoption (travel.state.gov/hagueinfo2002.html), and Brazil's 1990 Children's Code (Estatuto de Criança e do Adolescente, lei n 8.069 de 13 de julho de 1990, Diário Oficial de Uniã de 16.07.1990).

22   Twila L. Perry, "Transracial and International Adoptions: Mothers, Hierarchy, Race, and Feminist Legal Theory," *Yale Journal of Law and Feminism* 10 (1998): 101–64.

23   Leti Volpp, "Dependent Citizens and Marital Expatriates," unpublished manuscript.

24   See Lisa Lowe, *Immigrant Acts: On Asian American Cultural Politics* (Durham, N.C.: Duke University

Press, 1996), and Mae Ngai, *Impossible Subjects: Illegal Aliens and the Making of Modern America* (Princeton, N.J.: Princeton University Press, 2004).

25   Of course, the question of availability is not absolute but a discursive phenomenon. For a controversial analysis of the supply-and-demand aspect of baby adoption, see Elisabeth M. Landes and Richard A. Posner, "The Economics of the Baby Shortage," *Journal of Legal Studies* 7.2 (June 1978): 323–48. For a critique of Landes and Posner, see Patricia Williams, "Spare Parts, Family Values, Old Children, Cheap," *New England Law Review* 28 (Summer 1994): 913–27, and Laura Briggs and Ana Ortiz, "The Culture of Poverty, Crack Babies, and Welfare Cheats: The Making of the 'Healthy White Baby Crisis,'" *Social Text* 21.3 (Fall 2003): 39–57. Briggs and Ortiz write eloquently on how the 1980s emergent discourse on "crack babies," damaged beyond repair, also fuels the desire to adopt "safe" babies from abroad.

26   For an excellent discussion of the politics of interracial white parents/black child adoption, see R. Richard Banks, "The Color of Desire: Fulfilling Adoptive Parents' Racial Preferences through Discriminatory State Action," *Yale Law Journal* 107 (January 1998): 875–964.

27   Miranda Joseph, *Against the Romance of Community* (Minneapolis: University of Minnesota Press, 2002), 43.

28   In *First Person Plural*, Donald Borshay tells Deann: "You were so determined to learn. I guess to please us, whatever, I'm not sure. You actually made yourself ill and you became jaundiced. You got kind of yellow-looking. And the only thing we could think of was that you really tried too hard and were trying too hard."

29   See David L. Eng and Shinhee Han, "A Dialogue on Racial Melancholia," *Psychoanalytic Dialogues: A Journal of Relational Perspectives* 10.4 (2000): 667–700.

30   Homi Bhabha, "Of Mimicry and Man: The Ambivalence of Colonial Discourse," *October* 28 (Spring 1984): 126, 130; Bhabha's emphasis.

31   See Sigmund Freud, "Mourning and Melancholia," in *The Standard Edition of the Complete Psychological Works of Sigmund Freud*, vol. 14, ed. James Strachey (London: Hogarth, 1957), 243–58. Later, in *The Ego and the Id* (1923), Freud comes to revise this distinction between mourning and melancholia, noting that the ego is, in fact, comprised of its abandoned and lost objects.

32   See Raymond Williams, *Marxism and Literature* (New York: Oxford University Press, 1977), 128–35.

33   In another part of *First Person Plural*, Borshay Liem adds, "When I had learned enough English to talk to my parents, I decided that I should tell them who I really was. I remember going up to my mother and telling her 'I'm not who you think I am, I'm not Cha Jung Hee. And I think I have a mother and brother and sisters in Korea still.' And she turned to me and said, 'Oh, honey, you've just been dreaming. You don't have a mother. And you never had brothers and sisters. Look at these adoption documents. It says that you're Cha Jung Hee and your mother died giving birth to you.' And she said, 'You know what, this is just a natural part of you getting used to living in a new country. Don't worry about it. They're just bad dreams. They're going to go away soon.'"

34   Here, I draw on this argument from Anagnost, "Scenes of Misrecognition," 395.

35   Sigmund Freud, "Femininity," in *New Introductory Lectures on Psychoanalysis*, ed. James Strachey (New York: W.W. Norton, 1965), 118.

36   Kaja Silverman, "Girl Love," in *James Coleman* (Munich: Lebhachhaus München, 2002), 159. I am indebted to Kaja Silverman for a series of conversations on the negative Oedipus complex and "girl love" that have influenced my arguments on *First Person Plural*.

37   Freud, "Femininity," 102.

38   Ibid.

39   Melanie Klein, *The Selected Melanie Klein*, ed. Juliet Mitchell (New York: Free Press, 1986), 125; Klein's emphasis.

40   It also complicates the notion of the "gift" that often attaches itself to (transnational) adoption—a notion that the infant is a "gift" from the birth mother to the adoptive mother, a gift that can never be repaid. See Barbara Yngvesson, "Placing the 'Gift Child' in Transnational Adoption," *Law and Society Review* 36.2 (2002): 227–56.

41   Silverman, "Girl Love," 159.

42   Ibid., 156–57, Silverman's emphasis.

43   Ibid., 166.

44   Ibid., 161.

45   See Ken Corbett, "Nontraditional Family Romance," *Psychoanalytic Quarterly*, no. 70 (2001): 599–624.

46   Anagnost, "Scenes of Misrecognition," 395.

Chapter 19

Richard T. Rodríguez

MAKING QUEER *FAMILIA*

Richard T. Rodríguez is Associate Professor of English and Latina/Latino Studies in the Department of English at University of Illinois of Urbana-Champaign. His book, *Next of Kin: The Family in Chicano/a Cultural Politics* (2009), explores the central role of *la familia* in Chicano/a politics since the emergence of the Mexican American civil rights movement in the late 1960s.

In this essay Rodríguez considers the difficulties and tensions of the notion of the "chosen family" that is central to Chicano/a queer politics. Rodríguez argues that for Chicano/a queers, indeed for all queers of colour, disengaging from one's given biological family is a near impossible task given the comfort and security family offers in a dominant, and often hostile, white culture. Analyzing various cultural productions, political groups and social spaces, he traces how Chicano/a queers have taken up and reworked Cherríe Moraga's notion of "chosen family," one animated by a dialectic—rather than a choice—between biological families and sociopolitical groupings. For Rodríguez, the gay Latino bar emerges as a generative but conflicted "diasporic space." Enabling the formation of new queer Chicano/a counterpublics, the bar can potentially transform traditional familial relationships even as it also repeats other structures of gendered inequality.

> These spaces of *familia* have all made this moment of conclusion possible; they have taught me almost everything I now know about queer, about desire, about bodies on the margins, and dance floors creating momentary centers.
> (Juana María Rodríguez, *Queer Latinidad: Identity Practices, Discursive Spaces*, 2003)

IN HER FOUNDATIONAL essay, "The Traffic in Women: Notes on the 'Political Economy' of Sex," anthropologist Gayle Rubin (1975, 169) maintains that kinship is not "a list of biological relatives" but rather "a system of categories and statuses that often contradict actual genetic relationships." While I argue that *la familia* has been deployed as a means of maintaining normative kinship arrangements, I also want to demonstrate how reconfigured kinship arrangements need not be established in mutual exclusivity from biological relations. Kath Weston has identified this as enacting "chosen families." For Weston (1992, 137), "chosen families do not directly oppose genealogical modes of reckoning kinship. Instead, they undercut procreation's status as a master term imagined to provide the template for all possible kinship relations." Indeed, chosen families lie at the heart of Chicano/a queer politics so much so that it has become virtually impossible to articulate notions of community without signaling their import. And while [I aim] to show how "queer familia" as a chosen family might contest the heteropatriarchal stronghold on communitarian thought in Chicano/a cultural politics, [I] must also end with a cautionary note given how "queer" reconfigurations are always provisional.

The work of Cherríe Moraga is an important guidepost for charting the conceptual terrain of queer familia. As a way of making more tangible her dream for "Queer Aztlán," Moraga adopts la familia to foreground its potential for collective empowerment and social change. Her comprehension of empowerment, however, does not focus exclusively on the blood family entrenched within the domestic sphere, nor does it substitute such a family with a sociosymbolic kinship network mobilized within the public sphere. Instead, as Moraga's reworking of la familia breaks from the heteropatriarchal expectations that characterize the typical desires to utilize "private" matters for "public" values, she additionally scrambles kinship with the family to formulate a radical dialectic. Moraga, I believe, succeeds in disengaging their usual hard-and-fast categorization that also separates the private from the public by situating la familia within a genealogy conjoining individuals relatively immediate and socially extended.

Coterminous with her critique of Chicano nationalism, Moraga (1993, 157) points out that "the preservation of the Chicano familia became the Movimiento's mandate and within this constricted 'familia' structure Chicano políticos ensured that the patriarchal father figure remained in charge both in their private and political lives." Yet Moraga's insistence on utilizing the idea of la familia shows how belonging to *la raza* need not be contained by a male nationalist desire. Thus her troping of the family frequently shifts between her biologically given family and her sociopolitical family of choice, privileging neither relation over the other in the final analysis but rather animating the notion of a "chosen family." Importantly, Moraga's deployment of the family always reveals a radical departure from conventional nationalist appeals found in early movement texts.

For Chicana/o queers—as Moraga has shown—disinheriting one's biologically given family is a near impossible task considering how blood ties often prove invaluable. As Sunil Gupta has remarked in the case of Black and Asian gay men in Britain,

> the family was the source of both material and communal well-being. In a hostile white environment, for the first generation the community was their only hope of comfort and security. To turn your backs on it was to cut yourself off from both this security in real terms and from a sense of identity that was/is separate from the whites.
>
> (1989, 176)

In response to the exclusionary practices of white queer communities, the work of Moraga echoes Gupta in its desire to maintain family connections. Moreover, Moraga (1993, 147) acknowledges finding a "sense of place among la Chicanada," which, "not always a safe place . . . is unequivocally the original familial place from which [she is] compelled to write, which [she] reach[es] toward in [her] audiences, and which serves as [her] source of inspiration, voice, and lucha." In turn, Moraga's "Queer Aztlán" amplifies this family relationship and recasts it within the public sphere as a strategy for contesting the inequalities faced by queer members of la raza. Despite the questions it provokes and, indeed, its limitations and exclusions, Moraga's new nationalism does part ways with conventional demands for national consciousness since it is premised on a democratic egalitarianism for Chicanos and Chicanas in spite of—or most likely because of—class, gender, and sexual differences.

While Moraga insists that "la Chicana Indígena must stand at the center" of her new nationalism, "Queer Aztlán" nonetheless encompasses heterosexuals (who are no doubt rehabilitated) as well as gay men. Indeed, her nation-based kinship network is fundamentally concerned with the role of Chicano gay men in enacting a liberatory politics. Although critical of gay men and their inherent male privilege ("Being gay does not preclude gay men from harboring the same sexism evident in heterosexual men" [1993, 161]), Moraga nevertheless closely aligns them with lesbians given their shared marginalization from blood families and the Chicano community at large. "When 'El Plan Espiritual de Aztlán' was conceived a generation ago," she writes, "lesbians and gay men were not envisioned as members of the 'house'; we were not recognized as the sisters planting the seeds, the brothers gathering the crops. We were not counted as members of the 'bronze continent'" (159). Here Moraga signals a bond between the queer outcast "siblings"; yet she simultaneously puts pressure on Chicano gay men "to recognize and acknowledge that their freedom is intricately connected to the freedom of women." By doing so, "gay men can do their part to unravel how both men and women have been formed and deformed" by racism, misogyny, and homophobia (162).

Various cultural productions reveal that Chicano/a queers have taken up and extended Moraga's attempt to recast and conjoin our understanding of kinship and the family (albeit at times confirming her point about the gay male potential to wield power over women). To provide illustration, I want to engage with Augie Robles's and Valentín Aguirre's 1994 documentary video, ¡Viva 16! Yet let me briefly digress to discuss John D'Emilio's influential essay "Capitalism and Gay Identity" (1983), which importantly illustrates how the conjugal relationship of capitalism and family tends to suppress gay and lesbian identities yet simultaneously enables their emergence via new modes of kinship.

D'Emilio suggests that gay and lesbian communities exist on terrain beyond the boundaries of the heterosexual family, on terrain where social and sexual collectivity and collaboration become possible. Noting the declining centrality of the family's economic stronghold given men's and women's participation in the capitalist free-labor system, D'Emilio traces the emergence of literary societies, private social clubs, drag balls, and bars as social spaces where gay men and lesbians ultimately came together in the early twentieth century. A parallel socioeconomic phenomenon, of course, holds true in the late twentieth and early twenty-first century for Chicano/a and Latino/a queers, particularly those migrating to, and residing and working within, urban spaces in the United States. Indeed, for as much as D'Emilio's historical account is insightful, especially when translated for a context in which queer communities of color and their specific experiences take center stage, it is important nonetheless to signal his essay's blind spots. Scott Bravmann (1990, 70), for instance, observes how the "newly gay identity and social action" tracked in D'Emilio's essay ultimately "reflect the same differentiation based on gender, race, and class that pervades capitalist societies." In other words, in D'Emilio's conceptual frame, "when it first emerged, gay life was the domain of middle-class urban white men." While Bravmann is also right to note that "the formation of a modern gay identity must have depended on the subjugation of people of color" (71), it is imperative to grasp how gay identity formation depended upon a split from the families to which these gay men once belonged. Alan Sinfield's discussion on the rise of "metropolitan gay identities" in his book Gay and After resonates with D'Emilio's project, yet parts ways with it when he correctly argues that the "metropolitan disaffiliation from family does not suit members of racial minorities" (1998, 7). Thus when considering the convergence of metropolitan identities of racial-ethnic gay men and lesbians, one must always consider the sustained relevance of family and kinship in their discrepant articulations.

This is evident in *¡Viva 16!* (1994), Augie Robles's and Valentín Aguirre's video documentary "focusing on the queens, drag performers, and home-boys of San Francisco's gay Latino strip," the Mission District.[1] Along with spotlighting two neighboring gay bars—Esta Noche and La India Bonita—that lie on 16th Street (hence the video's title), the documentary maps the emergence of a San Francisco queer Latino community coterminous with—and not necessarily exclusive from—the Chicano movement.[2] *¡Viva 16!* opens with shots that frame a distinct cultural terrain as well as the iconography particular to the Mission District and other urban Latino hubs (for example, fruit stands, run-down buildings, and Virgen de Guadalupe and Aztec calendar T-shirts). Aguirre and Robles admit that the "primary focus" of the video "is Chicanos" (Brandley 1994); yet the video also brings into focus the overlapping histories and experiences of those composing a diasporic, transnational Latino cultural citizenship.

In the introduction to their edited collection, *Latino Cultural Citizenship: Claiming Identity, Space, and Rights,* William V. Flores and Rina Benmayor (1997, 1) define Latino cultural citizenship as "a range of social practices which, taken together, claim and establish a distinct social space for Latinos in this country. Latino social space is evolving and developing new forms, many of them contributing to an emergent Latino consciousness and social and political development." Extrapolating from the work of Arjun Appadurai, Puerto Rican theorist Juan Flores (1997, 221) argues that though it is important to view "lo Latino ('Latinoness') from the optic of the particular national groups, the social and cultural perspective of each group also evokes some relation to a Latino 'ethnoscape' of transnational dimensions." Although viewed from a Chicano optic, the video ultimately—and necessarily—examines a distinctly Latino ethnoscape given the transnational dimensions of the Mission and the Latino gay scene in general, and the gay bar scene in particular, in San Francisco.[3] Indeed, Andres Camacho Contreras, one of the video's interviewees, points out that Esta Noche and La India Bonita are spaces occupied not only by "Mexicanos" but by Latinos whose roots stem from various regions of the United States (including, of course, Aztlán) and Central and South America (as well as "Americanos" and Filipinos).

To make further sense of these spaces, Avtar Brah's *Cartographies of Diaspora: Contesting Identities* offers an important conceptual frame in which to situate the dynamics captured in *¡Viva 16!* In her book, Brah (1996, 16) employs the "immanent" concepts of diaspora, border, and politics of location, which, taken together, "mark conceptual connections for historicised analyses of contemporary trans/national movements of people, information, cultures, commodities and capital." From this site "a new concept" is initiated: "diaspora space." Diaspora space is, as she argues, "a point of confluence of economic, political, cultural, and psychic processes." Moreover,

> it is where multiple subject positions are juxtaposed, contested, proclaimed or disavowed; where the permitted and the prohibited perpetually interrogate; and where the accepted and the transgressive imperceptibly mingle even while these syncretic forms may be disclaimed in the name of purity and tradition. Here, tradition is itself continually invented even as it may be hailed as originating from the mists of time.
>
> (Brah 1996, 208)

"Distinct from the concept of diaspora," diaspora space "is 'inhabited' not only by diasporic subjects but equally by those who are constructed and represented as 'indigenous'" (16). Diaspora space, then, is an effective concept that situates the intersecting local Chicano and transnational Latino community formations evident in *¡Viva 16!*, the Mission, and, most importantly, specific geopolitical moments.[4] Likewise, given the way familial traditions are "continually invented" within diaspora space, we can also register its "new" manifestation in rooted, yet spliced, genealogies.

As with most documentaries, *¡Viva 16!* employs talking heads, voice-over narration, shots of still photographs, and an assemblage of archival footage. Significantly, the video begins with family photographs and a personal memoir of activist and health administrator Diane Felix. She begins with a personal anecdote about the evolution of her lesbianism. We then hear from Chris Sandoval and Ricky Rubio, who elaborate on the emergent Chicano/a gay and lesbian community in San Francisco in the early 1970s. When Rubio discusses GALA, The Gay Latino Alliance, the language of kinship central to queer Latino community formation is instantly detected. Rubio declares: "I really didn't want to become a part of GALA, it became a part of me." GALA members also understood "the family" as "their source of strength"—"At the core of GALA's philosophy is not to alienate ourselves from our families and community but to help them come to understand our gayness in a Latino context."[5] In *¡Viva 16!*, Felix, Sandoval, and Rubio collectively detail how GALA was a departure point for the eventual creation of the bar Esta Noche, which endeavored to establish a queer Chicano/Latino counterpublic.[6]

For Michael Warner (2005, 121–22) one of the distinguishing features of counterpublics is that they attempt "to supply different ways of imagining stranger sociability and its reflexivity . . . oriented to stranger-circulation in a way that is not just strategic but also constitutive of membership and its affects." Premised on "imagining stranger sociability," the video reveals how Esta Noche's owners sell their house so as to create a space where, as Felix conveys, "the bar became home and strangers became family." In a related vein, we might invoke Manuel Guzmán [. . .] who reads the New York bar La Escuelita as "the house of gay Latino men in the city of New York," a "house" where generative schemes such as "the principles on which the production of thought, perception, and action are based" (1997, 215). *¡Viva 16!* offers a view of queer Latino kinship networks that counter dislocation within the inhabited space of the house-*cum*-bar, hinging on the strategy to forego domestic private property for communal public space.[7] Indeed, throughout the video, the subjects of *¡Viva 16!* elaborate on the pleasures and politics of Latino/a queer bodies in a communal public. To invoke Juana María Rodríguez, whose words opened [this essay] (words that were fittingly inspired within bars like Esta Noche), such spaces supply a sense of *familia* because of the ways in which they foster a sense of Latino/a queer belonging. Moreover, the video's overarching narrative recalls Cherríe Moraga's attempt to recast the rhetoric of Chicano/a cultural nationalism in "Queer Aztlán": situating the Chicano homeland of Aztlán in a sexually democratic—that is, an antiheterosexist and antihomophobic—frame. At the start of the video, *¡Viva 16!* fittingly identifies itself as a twenty-first-century Aztlán production. However, the ethnoscape of a transnational queer Latino/a counterpublic begs a rethinking of Chicano cultural nationalist objectives given the more expansive, transnational alliances invariably forged.

Akin to Moraga's scrambling of kinship networks chosen and given, the queer Latino bar is not off-limits to biological family members. In writing about La Escuelita, Manuel Guzmán argues that for men in the bar, "the articulation and the negotiation of sexual desire must perforce blend in the matrix of social interactions found there." Yet,

> while sitting or dancing, men must negotiate their sexual desires in the presence of homosexual women, heterosexuals, and their relatives. Mothers and their mothers, *nuestras abuelas*, are members familiar to the audience. According to Raúl [La Escuelita's co-owner], "we, Hispanics, do not have any shame or *complejos* with regards to our children. We love them as they are. They [Hispanic families] have heard so much about La Escuelita that they come to see where it

is their children go to. I know that is the case because I receive them at the door where they always ask for a table."

(Guzmán 1997, 215)

Although Raúl claims that *all* "Hispanic families" do not harbor shame or complexes about their gay children (a sweeping claim to be sure), his observations are nonetheless useful to ascertain how Latino/a queer spaces might not always be exclusively queer. Indeed, listed on a flier for GALA's first anniversary dance, along with the traditional features one would expect to find at gay dances such as live music and food, is child-care. As is the case with La Escuelita, the families present at La India Bonita and Esta Noche must ultimately meet the challenges to heteronormativity posed by a queer public culture. Focusing on "the mother of a Chicano drag queen," Ramón García's poem "Miss Primavera Contest," published in *The Americas Review* in 1994—the same year of *¡Viva 16!*'s release—takes place at La India Bonita. In it, García highlights how a Fellini-like surrealism mixes with the familiar sights and sounds of a queer Latino bar (where "machismo and being maricón are blurred/as the tough cholo dances with the drag queen"); and yet this space does not require detachment from "traditional" family relationships. Within the queer space of La India Bonita, for example, an alternative identification between mother and son emerges. García writes, "Miss Primavera's mother/must have been a little like/Miss Primavera herself, her son/and deep inside this must please her/for her hijo to turn out/so much like her/when she was in the Spring of her life—a little bit loca" (and "*loca*" is, fittingly, a term used by Latino/a queers to refer to someone *as* queer). The mother's identification with her son also offers a refreshing reversal of traditional parent–child sexual difference models, namely the Oedipus complex and the passage it requires in obtaining normative familial and sexual status.[8]

Judith Butler (1993, 124) argues that the rearticulation of kinship by the transgender African Americans and Latinos who comprise the New York subcultural drag ball scene in the film *Paris Is Burning* "might be understood as repetitions of hegemonic forms of power which fail to repeat loyally and, in that failure, open possibilities for resignifying the terms of violation against their violating aims."[9] In other words, it is possible to acknowledge "the force of repetition" as "the very condition of an affirmative response to violation" (124).[10] Importantly, Butler also emphasizes that there are moments in which these strategic repetitions cannot be called subversive. Such a moment in *¡Viva 16!* is when the men are unwilling to understand the necessity of a women's component in GALA. In a moment of finely honed crosscutting, Felix and Rubio elaborate on the tensions between men and women within the group around the creation of a women's component. Rubio insists the group had to be a group undivided, "all for one," as it were, "fighting for one goal." Felix, though, insists that women also required a separate space given the male-dominant composition of the group. Felix relates the situation to that of a family feud, chalking it up to an instance of unconditional love, a moment in which women must negotiate the presence of brothers whose gender socialization affects their relationships with women. Certainly, this moment of a gay-inflected paternalism symbolically keeps the divisive bar in between gay and lesbian communities firmly intact. Furthermore, the space of the bar (like diaspora space, cultural nationalism, or la familia) is never inherently devoid of inequality. Consider, then, how the number of women in this space, as captured in the documentary, is minimal at best in contrast to the number of men. Reflective of GALA's gender politics, women in the bar scenes showcased in *¡Viva 16!* are relegated to secondary status. As Horacio Roque Ramírez's research on GALA has shown, the marginalization of women in GALA extended into the space of Esta Noche (which "undermined GALA's social and political fundraising efforts") since the bar was inevitably regarded as a business and not a political organization, thus destabilizing the potential of democratic kinship in light of proprietorship. Thus women's protest and demand for equal treatment would be further ignored and dismissed (Roque Ramírez 2003, 256). Clearly evident is the provisional status of queer (read here as gay male) constitutions of community, including the fact that nonheteronormative attempts at collectivity are never inherently liberatory or automatically given. Indeed, the gendered hierarchies particular to the domestic sphere can indeed extend into the public domain of a bar that for some might be home sweet home whereas others may desire to burn it down.

[My work] has sought to unveil the complexities in maintaining la familia as an organizing principle for Chicano/a cultural politics. It is not hard to see why its retention proves difficult given its placement at the heart of heteropatriarchal value systems. Yet the significance of kinship becomes evident when taking into account the myriad forces of subordination faced by Chicano/a and Latino/a communities. In particular, the queer folk within these communities will undoubtedly continue to critically assess and negotiate their relationships with the families to whom they are born as well as to those with whom they are joined by necessity. In his book, *Against Nature: Essays on History, Sexuality, and Identity*, Jeffrey Weeks (1991, 135) argues that it is within the "subterranean social order" that genuine alternative families are created. It is my hope that the Chicano/a and Latino/a subterranean social order reflected in the texts and cultural practices with which [my work] has grappled precisely illustrates how community is made, and remade, ideally over and against normative familia romances whose hopeful passing will call forth its next of kin.

Notes

1   This description of the film is Aguirre's and Robles's from a synopsis submitted to Frameline for inclusion in the annual San Francisco International Lesbian and Gay Film Festival. *¡Viva 16!* screened at the festival in 1994.

2   Significant to note is that while Esta Noche still exists at the time of this writing, La India Bonita does not as a result of the drastic gentrification in the area since the tape's release. In *Queer Latinidad: Identity Practices, Discursive Spaces* (2003), Juana María Rodríguez discusses how the Mission District "has become a more desirable and chic neighborhood as the quality of life for its Latina/o residents worsens." Furthermore, according to Rodríguez, "La India Bonita . . . is now a yuppie bar called Skylark" (175).

3   Importantly, the term "Queer Raza" has been used to crystallize a transnational Latino alliance. See the essay by Bustamante and Rodríguez (1995) in the exhibition catalog *Queer Raza*.

4   That *¡Viva 16!* retains its Chicano specificity is important given how, in many discussions of Latino gay male cultural production (including that which is U.S. Latino), Chicano identity is often subsumed under a banner that may tout itself as "all encompassing," yet this banner may also gloss over differences within that category, thus eliminating differences of race and class among Latinos and treating privileged Latin Americans and working-class Mexicans and Chicanos as one and the same. It must also be noted that diaspora and nationalism are never mutually exclusive categories. For more on this point, see James Clifford's "Diasporas" (1997).

5   This is taken from a letter GALA wrote in protest of a gay white man who criticized the organization's politics and Latino culture in general. See GALA, "GALA: In the Community," *Coming Up!* February 1982, 4, cited in Horacio Roque Ramírez, "'That's *My* Place!': Negotiating Racial, Sexual, and Gender Politics in San Francisco's Gay Latino Alliance, 1975–83," 250–51. Roque Ramírez's essay also perceptively reveals the complexity and pervasiveness of kinship dynamics in and around the organization.

6   See Rodrigo Reyes's "Latino Gays: Coming Out and Coming Home" (1981) for a first-person account of GALA's formation in the late 1970s and early 1980s. Horacio N. Roque Ramírez (2003) provides an excellent account of GALA in the context of Latino/a queer history and further elaborates on the gendered tensions between gay men and lesbians raised in *¡Viva 16!*

7   Spaces that foster racial or ethnic specificity are pivotal within a larger queer cultural economy. Two young men in *¡Viva 16!* confess that, unlike in the predominantly white Castro District, they felt a sense of belonging at Esta Noche. The work of Marlon Riggs and Luis Alfaro, for example, has shown that predominantly white gay bars have been known to adopt exclusionary practices toward people

of color by asking for three pieces of identification for entrance or simply turning them away at the door. In a similar vein, the largely white San Francisco gay bar The Stud held an event in 1999 called "Wet Back Night." Needless to say, protests were staged by members of the local queer Latino community. Furthermore, the San Francisco Human Rights Commission received formal complaints of discrimination regarding the event.

8   Mark Doty (1993, 18–20) similarly pays homage to a drag performer (identified as "la fabulosa Lola") at Esta Noche in his poem named after the bar in *My Alexandria*. Fittingly, Doty contrasts "Esta Noche, a Latin drag bar in the Mission" with "neighborhood storefront windows" displaying items such as "wedding dresses, First Communion's frothing lace," thus highlighting how Lola's extravagant presence in the neighborhood jostles with signifiers of Catholicism and heteronormativity.

9   In an argumentative vein similar to Butler's, Manuel Guzmán (1997, 18–20) extends Pierre Bourdieu's formulation of the dialectical body/space "mythico-ritual oppositions" to account for the Latino gay patrons of La Escuelita who "find their bodies engaged not with homologous, mythico-ritual oppositions, but their inversion."

10 In *Homos*, Leo Bersani (1995, 49) takes issue with Judith Butler, arguing that the families formed by the "drag queens" in the film "remain tributes to the heterosexual ideal of the family itself." Bersani is correct to the extent that the queens in the film aspire to "get out of the drag family and become a success in the real (straight) fashion and entertainment world" (49), yet his contention is also largely anchored by his belief that attempts to "'resignify' the family for communities that defy the usual assumptions about what constitutes a family…have assimilative rather than subversive consequences" (5). Although Bersani's version of gay community may reject family tropes, it is, however, almost exclusively—and unapologetically—homogeneous (read white and middle-class). We must therefore question *his* community's ideological trappings in relation to queer people of color.

Bibliography

Bersani, Leo. 1995. *Homos*. Cambridge, Mass.: Harvard University Press.

Brah, Avtar. 1996. *Cartographies of Diaspora: Contesting Identities*. London: Routledge.

Brandley, Kent. 1994. "Gay and Latin on the Sixteenth Street Corridor." *Bay Area Reporter* 24 (August 25): 13.

Bravmann, Scott. 1990. "Telling (Hi)stories." *Out/Look* 8 (Spring): 68–74.

Bustamante, Nao, and Eugene Rodríguez. 1995. "El Corazón Me Dio Un Salto." *Queer Raza: El Corazón Me Dio Un Salto*. Exhibition catalog. San Francisco: Galería de la Raza.

Butler, Judith. 1993. *Bodies That Matter: On the Discursive Limits of "Sex"*. New York: Routledge.

Clifford, James. 1997. "Diasporas." *Routes: Travel and Translation in the Late Twentieth Century*, 244–77. Cambridge, Mass.: Harvard University Press.

D'Emilio, John. 1983. "Capitalism and Gay Identity." In *Powers of Desire: The Politics of Sexuality*, Ann Snitow, Christine Stansell, and Sharon Thompson, eds., 100–113. New York: Monthly Review Press.

Doty, Mark. 1993. *My Alexandria*. Urbana: University of Illinois Press.

Flores, Juan. 1997. "Latino Studies: New Contexts, New Concepts." *Harvard Educational Review* 67 (Summer): 208–21.

Flores, William V., and Rina Benmayor, eds. 1997. *Latino Cultural Citizenship: Claiming Identity, Space, and Rights*. Boston: Beacon.

García, Ramón. 1994. "Miss Primavera Contest." *Americas Review* 22 (3–4): 71–72.

Gupta, Sunil. 1989. "Black, Brown and White." In *Coming On Strong: Gay Politics and Culture*, Simon Shepherd and Mick Wallis, eds., 163–79. London: Unwin Hyman.

Guzmán, Manuel. 1997. "'Pa La Escuelita con Mucho Cuida'o y por la Orillita': A Journey through the Contested Terrains of the Nation and Sexual Orientation." In *Puerto Rican Jam: Essays on Culture and Politics*, Frances Negrón-Muntaner and Ramón Grosfoguel eds., 209–28. Minneapolis: University of Minnesota Press.

Moraga, Cherríe. 1993. "Queer Aztlán: The Re-formation of Chicano Tribe." In *The Last Generation*, 145–74. Boston: South End Press.

Reyes, Rodrigo. 1981. "Latino Gays: Coming Out and Coming Home." *Nuestro* 5 (3): 42–45, 64.

Rodríguez, Juana María. 2003. *Queer Latinidad: Identity Practices, Discursive Spaces*. New York: New York University Press.

Roque Ramírez, Horacio N. 2003. "'That's *My* Place!': Negotiating Racial, Sexual, and Gender Politics in San Francisco's Gay Latino Alliance, 1975–83." *Journal of the History of Sexuality* 12 (April): 224–58.

Rubin, Gayle. 1975. "The Traffic in Women: Notes on the 'Political Economy' of Sex." In *Toward an Anthropology of Women*, Rayna R. Reiter, ed., 157–210. New York: Monthly Review Press.

Sinfield, Alan. 1998. *Gay and After*. London: Serpent's Tail.

¡Viva 16! (directed by Augie Robles and Valentín Aguirre, 1994).

Warner, Michael. 2005. *Publics and Counterpublics*. New York: Zone Books.

Weeks, Jeffrey. 1991. *Against Nature: Essays on History, Sexuality, and Identity*. London: Rivers Oram Press.

Weston, Kath. 1992. "The Politics of Gay Families." In *Rethinking the Family: Some Feminist Questions*, Barrie Thorn and Marilyn Yalom, eds., 119–39. Boston: Northeastern University Press.

Chapter 20

Mark Rifkin

ROMANCING KINSHIP: A QUEER READING OF INDIAN EDUCATION AND ZITKALA-ŠA'S *AMERICAN INDIAN STORIES*

Mark Rifkin is Assistant Professor in the Department of English at the University of North Carolina, Greensboro. The author of *Manifesting America: The Imperial Construction of U.S. National Space* (2009), he is currently working on a project entitled "When Did Indians Become Straight? Kinship, the History of Sexuality, and Native Sovereignty."

In "Romancing Kinship" Rifkin undertakes a queer critique of Native American education policy, as well as the strategies of detribalization associated with it, arguing that the policy can be understood as enforcing compulsory heterosexuality by means of a romance narrative, in which Native Americans are asked to exchange traditional forms of erotic relations and kinship ties in return for the alleged benefits of individuality, bourgeois respectability and the nuclear heterosexual family that cohere in marriage. Rifkin argues that two late nineteenth-century stories written by Zitkala-Ša resist this compulsory heterosexuality by redeploying the romance plot to make Sioux forms of kinship, affection, and social ties intelligible to white readers, subordinating romance to broader social ties and community-making, while also problematically eliding practices of "polygamy," flexible gender identity and homoeroticism. Rifkin's essay foregrounds heteronormativity's racializing and imperial project, and its dependence on the material force of the homo–hetero binary.

> By kinship all Dakota people were held together in a great relationship that was theoretically all-inclusive and co-extensive with the Dakota domain. . . . Before going further, I can safely say that the ultimate aim of Dakota life, stripped of accessories, was quite simple: One must obey kinship rules; one must be a good relative.
>
> (Ella Deloria, *Speaking of Indians*)

CAN DAKOTA KINSHIP be included under the rubric of heterosexuality? In *The Invention of Heterosexuality* Jonathan Ned Katz argues, "The intimidating notion that heterosexuality refers to everything differently sexed and gendered and eroticized is, it turns out, one of the conceptual dodges that keeps heterosexuality from becoming the focus of sustained, critical analysis."[1] Following this logic, what are heterosexuality's contours and boundaries, and where in relation to them do indigenous forms, especially traditional forms, of sex, gender, and eroticism lie?[2] Pushing the matter further, can the coordinated assault on native kinship in U.S. policy in the late nineteenth century be understood as an organized effort to make heterosexuality compulsory as a key part of breaking up indigenous landhold-ings and "detribalizing" native peoples, and what would such a formulation mean for rethinking the scope and direction of queer studies?[3]

In her provocative and ground-clearing essay "Punks, Bulldaggers, and Welfare Queens," Cathy J. Cohen observes, "Queer politics has often been built around a simple dichotomy between those deemed queer and those deemed heterosexual"; some queer activists and critics have used this dichotomy to "map the power and entitlement of normative hetero-sexuality onto the bodies of all heterosexuals," thereby failing to recognize that "'nonnorma-tive' procreation patterns and family structures of people who are labeled heterosexual have also been used to regulate and exclude *them*." Cohen further argues that "many of the roots of heteronormativity are in white supremacist ideologies which sought (and continue) to use the state and its regulation of sexuality, in particular through the institution of heterosexual marriage, to designate which individuals were truly 'fit' for full rights and privileges of citizenship."[4] Pointing to a larger problematic in the history of sexuality, this trenchant critique suggests that the ideological structure and regulatory force of heteronormativity cannot be grasped through versions of the homo/hetero binary.[5] In this vein, the effort to "civilize" American Indians and the attendant repudiation of indigenous traditions can be understood as significantly contributing to the institutionalization of the "heterosexual imaginary," in Chrys Ingraham's evocative phrase, helping build a network of interlocking state-sanctioned policies and ideologies that positioned monogamous hetero couplehood and the privatized single-family household as official national ideals by the late nineteenth century.[6] Such an analysis of the history of federal Indian policy enables discussion of the ways that questions of kinship, residency, and land tenure lie at the unspoken center of the heteronorm, which itself then can be understood as always already bound up in racializing and imperial projects.[7]

This kind of queer critique, tracing the unacknowledged genealogies and lineaments of heteronormativity, also builds on recent work in American Indian studies that seeks to reconstruct traditional forms of gender diversity. In *Changing Ones* Will Roscoe argues that the study of indigenous sex/gender configurations, particularly their development and normalization of nonprocreative statuses and identities, "helps break the cycle of projection in which Western observers constantly replicate heterosexual binarism wherever they turn their gaze."[8] While rejecting the use of Euro-American sexological vocabularies in under-standing native sex/gender systems, though, this scholarship only minimally develops a crucial corollary: that traditional romantic or erotic relationships between men and women in native societies are not heterosexual. Put another way, the heterosexual imaginary is just as inappropriate and obfuscatory in considerations of native marriage, family, and procrea-tion as it is in treatments of more "queer" topics, such as transvestism and homosexuality. More than making visible the lives of "queer" persons in native communities (historically and in the present), engaging with the forms of critique found in queer studies opens the possibility within American Indian studies of a more expansive and integrated analysis of the U.S. assault on indigenous social formations.[9] Such an approach helps foreground the processes through which a particular configuration of "home" and "family" is naturalized and administratively implemented, while also emphasizing the discursive and institutional connections between what might otherwise appear as distinct forms of imperial abjection (e.g., attacks on "berdaches," polygamy, and kinship-based governance).

The "heterosexual binarism" Roscoe cites, then, functions not just as a conceptual block to comparative intellectual work but as a material force; it imposes an alien configuration on native cultures and provides ideological cohesion for a disparate collection of detribalizing initiatives in federal Indian policy. The discourse of Indian education in particular presents the emotional connection and the division of labor between husband and wife as the paradigmatic model for social order and interaction, and the construction of a bourgeois home predicated on legally recognized matrimony is continually cited as the goal of boarding school training in ways that link the acquisition of a proper understanding of family life to the splintering of tribal territory into single-family households. Thus education policy can be said to be structured as a romance plot in which the abandonment of indigenous kinship networks, patterns of residence, and forms of communal identification appears as a self-evidently desirable exchange of "degraded" traditional sociality for the marital bliss and private homeownership portrayed as constitutive of civilized life.

The writings of Zitkala-Ŝa (Gertrude Simmons Bonnin), a self-identified Dakota born on the Yankton reservation in 1876, provide an excellent starting place for an examination of how native writers opposed this institutionalized representation of tradition as degenerate.[10] A former pupil at Josiah White's Manual Institute and an instructor at the Carlisle Institute, the first and most famous of the off-reservation boarding schools, Zitkala-Ŝa was an adamant and well-known native critic of Indian education, publishing essays and stories that focused on the horrors of the boarding school system, the pitfalls of assimilation, and the role of indigenous family formations in sustaining tribal communities.[11] *American Indian Stories* (1921) reprints many of these turn-of-the-century pieces. Of these, "The Trial Path" and "A Warrior's Daughter" are the only ones that involve love stories.[12] In these stories, romance does not mark an isolating passion between individuals; rather, it highlights the ways that couples remain intimately entwined in the web of social relations and responsibilities organized through kinship networks. In these writings Zitkala-Ŝa, I contend, offers a counternarrative to administrative efforts to impose a detribalizing teleology justified as the achievement of real and stable love, home, and family, instead connecting romance to the maintenance of indigenous collective identity and forms of self-determination.[13]

While I pursue a self-consciously queer analysis in this essay, I do not argue that *American Indian Stories* should be interpreted as a queer text. The difference for me lies in the distinction between mobilizing critical tools and questions that have emerged most clearly in queer studies and asserting de facto forms of continuity between nonnative sexual minorities and native peoples. (I am also wary about the potential for annexing native texts to critical and political agendas shaped primarily by and for nonnatives.) Elaborating how federal policy functions as a romance plot indicates the ways that the representation of heterosexual desire in U.S. discourses is imbricated in a set of assumptions and associations hostile to native traditions and extended kinship formations, and elucidating Zitkala-Ŝa's rejection of this vision of privatized couplehood illustrates how alternative figurations of home and family in native writing contest the political economy of imperial domesticity. Through these readings, then, my essay demonstrates (1) how a sustained engagement with American Indian histories and forms of self-representation as part of the history of sexuality in the United States can aid in rethinking what constitutes heteronormativity and (2) how queer critique of federal Indian policy as compulsory heterosexuality can contribute to an understanding of its organizing ideological and institutional structure as well as strategies of native opposition to it. I will close, however, with an investigation of the ways that *American Indian Stories* also disavows Sioux social identities and practices that might be taken by white readers as *sexually* nonnormative. In this reading I explore how the text's effort to rehabilitate tradition illustrates the layered quality of the heterosexual imaginary and the ways that the bribe of normality can lead native peoples to disavow the elements of their communities deemed most perverse by the white power structure.[14]

Killing the Indian, saving the heterosexual homesteader

> They must stand or fall as men and women, not as Indians.
> (Commissioner of Indian Affairs Thomas J. Morgan,
> "Supplemental Report on Indian Education")

In *Ethnocriticism* Arnold Krupat argues that law "seeks to *make* history by *imposing* a story."[15] Specifically, addressing the Indian Removal Act (1830) and Cherokee responses to it, he asserts that legal discourse should be understood not merely as a set of juridical propositions or directives but as a mode of emplotment, narrating the relationship between persons, groups, and institutions in ways that enforce particular kinds of social interactions and outcomes while casting the effects of such coercive management as natural and inevitable. In this vein, one can understand the vision of social order articulated in federal Indian policy as a romance plot—a narration organized around the ineluctable movement toward marriage as the culmination of the education or civilization process.[16] More than justifying particular legislative enactments, heteronormative emplotment works to deny the possibility of registering indigenous residential and kinship formations as *political*, positioning the adoption of legally recognized, monogamous, companionate marriage and heterogendered bourgeois domesticity as the self-evident basis of American political identity.

Indian education policy, and the boarding school system in particular, was one of the main avenues for generating and institutionalizing this imperial narrative. By the early 1890s Indian education had transformed from a primarily missionary-led affair on treaty-guaranteed land to a federally sponsored bureaucratic infrastructure with over one thousand employees and almost ten thousand students enrolled in boarding schools located on and off reservation.[17] As part of a reoriented formulation of "the Indian problem," education would play a key role by breaking native children's connection to "backward" traditions and teaching them how to be individuals, while justifying the clearing of millions of acres of "surplus" land for settlement and development. The drive toward the creation of a formal Indian education program began in the late 1870s with the founding of a number of Indian reform associations in the east, the enrollment of native students at the Hampton Institute in Virginia, and the creation of the Carlisle Institute by Colonel Richard Henry Pratt.[18] Pratt's education program was based on two major organizational principles: mandating that classroom activity and manual training, strictly differentiated by gender, would each take up half of the school day; and creating what came to be known as the "outing" system, described by Pratt as "by far the most important feature of our work," in which students would be placed with white families over school breaks to help them "receive an adequate idea of civilized home-life" that they could not get from boarding school alone.[19]

Scholars have tended to focus on the language of "individualism" and its centrality to education discourse and the broader assault on indigenous governance and land tenure, contrasting such an atomized notion of selfhood with traditional communal conceptions of identity among native peoples. However, this line of critique often overlooks or minimizes the extent to which monogamous marriage, the nuclear family, and privatized homemaking are necessary conditions for the ideological and material (re)production of this generic individual. In his well-researched and compelling analysis of the social vision imagined and implemented at Carlisle under Pratt, Joel Pfister argues, "Those who sought to 'individualize' Indians . . . developed strategies of subjectivity and emotion production that aimed to prescribe how an 'individual' should properly pursue happiness, meaningfulness, and work."[20] While recognizing that the normalization of "sentimental American life" organized around lifelong hetero coupling was an important aspect of the education process, Pfister treats notions of "home" and "family" as components of a "stage" "for the performance of productive individuality," rather than interpreting the individual subject as an (after)effect of a primary restructuring of kinship and household formations (59–63). Presenting "individualization" as the goal of federal Indian policy seems to me to perform an intellectual inversion, accepting the terms of individualism by subordinating discussion of the contours and significance of the material conditions that enable and sustain such subjectivity. "Productive individuality" presupposes the installation of a political economy in which land tenure, subsistence, and residency have been reorganized in ways that break down extended social networks and break up shared territory and in which affective ties have been rerouted from larger communal formations to the nuclear family. In other words, individualism is inseparable from the broader process of privatization, which is naturalized through the representation of monogamous marriage and the single-family dwelling as the self-evident basis for true intimacy and human reproduction. I contend, then, that we need to examine the ways that reference to the generic individual in the discourse of Indian policy condenses a larger heteronormative matrix, which is the horizon for the imperial restructuring of native social relations. As David Wallace Adams notes, "In the eyes of reformers no sphere of Indian life was more reprehensible than the relations between the sexes."[21]

The writings of Thomas J. Morgan provide an excellent index of the de facto consensus among officials and reformers as well as the policy goals of Indian education in the late nineteenth century. Commissioner of Indian affairs from 1887 to 1892, Morgan was a major force in the expansion and standardization of the boarding school system; his activities included campaigning to make such schooling compulsory and drafting the first official curriculum for federally funded Indian schools in 1890.[22] As the leading figure in federal Indian policy at a time when the scope of the government's civilization program increased exponentially, he was well positioned to exert immense influence on the shape it took. Morgan's ideas about Indian education, shared by most reformers and officials connected to the boarding school system, are presented perhaps most succinctly and forcefully in his "Supplemental Report on Indian Education," included in his annual report to Congress in 1889.[23] Persistently invoking home and family as key figures for what Indians lack and what must be inculcated through education, the text uses this supposed absence to justify the broader imperial program of detribalization.

According to Morgan, tribal identity must be eradicated utterly. He offers some sense of how to achieve this goal in his description of the education program's primary aims:

> That which is fundamental in all this is the recognition of the complete manhood of the Indians, their individuality. . . . They should be free to make for themselves homes wherever they will. The reservation system is an anachronism which has no place in our modern civilization. The Indian youth should be instructed in their rights, privileges, and duties as American citizens; . . . should be imbued with a genuine patriotism, and made to feel that the United States, and not some paltry reservation, is their home.
>
> (95–96)

Sketching a correlation between the literal building of houses and a patriotic investment in national identity, the passage indicates that Indian conceptions of home perpetuate affective bonds to reservations. To gain "individuality," Indians must shift the horizon of their thinking and, more importantly, their feeling, connecting "home" not to specific tribal territories but to the great expanse of the entire United States. Broadening the Indian's perspective in this way trades a vision of "home" based on sustained connections within native communities for an abstract and metonymic relation between privatized households and the nation. Moreover, Morgan asserts, "owing to the peculiar surroundings of the mass of Indian children, they are homeless and are ignorant of those simplest arts that make home possible" (99). Thus he reduces native kinship and residency to "peculiar" deviations.

The larger project of reordering native affect, of "arous[ing] the feeling that they are Americans" (102), is to be accomplished through the fostering of a sense of self-reliance inextricably tied to the performance of heterogender, itself represented as alien to native peoples.[24] "No pains should be spared to teach them that their future must depend chiefly upon their own exertions, character, and endeavors. They will be entitled to what they earn. . . . They must stand or fall as men and women, not as Indians" (102). Most notably, Morgan sets "Indians" apart from "men and women," tying contradistinguished gender identity to forms of production and social organization that native societies apparently lack. The (re)gendering of native students is further linked to the creation of appropriate states of feeling, with romance as the paradigm: "Co-education of the sexes is the surest and perhaps only way in which Indian women can be lifted out of that position of servility and degradation which most of them now occupy, on to a plane where their husbands and the men generally will treat them with the same gallantry and respect which is accorded to their more favored white sisters" (96).

Morgan's vision of "the sexes" channels affect toward companionate marriage, casting the division of labor among native peoples as virtual slavery and presenting native relationships as though they lacked affection. The central relationship between "men and women" is that of husband and wife; all other interactions between the sexes are to be modeled on this one, which is understood as emblematic rather than contextualized as one in the vast network of relationships that constitute a given community. Morgan encapsulates the connection between right feeling, marriage, and property in his discussion of the goals of Indian grammar schools: "It is during this period particularly that it will be possible to inculcate in the minds of pupils of both sexes that mutual respect that lies at the base[of a happy home life, and of social purity" (101). Teaching Indians to be "men and women" means developing in them a sense of "respect" that reaches its apogee in marriage, which itself regulates gender expression, promotes seclusion through a clearly demarcated and privatized home, and ties the latter to self-provision disconnected from one's tribe. Such training presents itself as imparting the self-evident truths of intimate life in the nation while making monogamous bourgeois marriage the framework through which to imagine relations to place.[25]

Additionally, the school must regulate social interaction between the sexes. They are to be kept entirely apart (classes and meals excepted), but "at stated times, under suitable supervision, they may enjoy each other's society": "Such occasions should be used to teach them to show each other due respect and consideration . . . and to acquire habits of politeness, refinement, and self-possession."[26] In essence, the schools are to orchestrate and manage the process of courting, forbidding virtually all communication between boys and girls unless it is superintended by teachers and matrons,[27] and there is little to no concern about relations among boys and among girls. Hetero association is positioned as the primal scene of socialization, and cross-sex connections with nonkin are implicitly cast as the center of one's social world.

Beyond working to make Indian children's perception of normal social relations conform to a vision of "gallantry" hostile to their own tradition, school policy reinforces the federal program of allotment. The General Allotment Act of 1887, otherwise known as the Dawes

Act, sought to divide native territory into privately owned plots, which would cease to be under tribal control of any kind.[28] One of the chief mechanisms for eliminating tribal control was the institutional erasure of native forms of kinship and the collective geographies established and maintained through webs of attachment and obligation. Allotments were parceled out to each "head of a family," thereby soldering occupancy to a particular vision of what constitutes a family unit, and the act mandated that "the law of descent and partition in force in the State or Territory where such lands are situated shall apply thereto." Thus it created a barrier to native efforts to merge land claims through extended chains of familial belonging or to maintain ties of lineage and tribal identification through the transfer of land along alternate lines of descent or affiliation.

Indian education directly participates in this attack on native kinship and on associated forms of collective mapping and self-representation by extending the terminologies employed in allotment.[29] In addition to interrupting the transmission of traditional knowledge and social logics to native children, the education program adopts the system of naming used to remake Indians as Americans. Morgan observes, "When Indians become citizens of the United States, under the allotment act, the inheritance of property will be governed by the laws of the respective States, and it will cause needless confusion and, doubtless, considerable ultimate loss to the Indians if no attempt is made to have the different members of a family known by the same family name on the records and by general reputation" (clx). The act of naming functions as a way of reconstellating "family" while speaking as if it merely acknowledged the fact of relatedness: members of the same family should be known by the same name. The implicit structure of this normative model of kinship—which, despite its supposed self-evidence, needs to be imposed institutionally by way of Morgan's order—is made clear directly: "If agents and school superintendents will systematically endeavor, so far as practicable, to have children and wives known by the names of the fathers and husbands, very great improvement in this respect will be brought about within a few years" (clx). This imagined family unit, then, is to be defined by the connection between husband and wife and their offspring. Beyond disavowing the matrilineal bonds that regulate belonging and social position in many tribes, this insistence on the name of the father/husband makes marriage and biological parenthood the core of personal and social identity in ways that both atomize tribes into aggregations of hetero pairings and proscribe more collective forms of subjectivity articulated within familial idioms. Noting the broader significance of naming as part of the project of dismantling native polities, Morgan argues, "The matter is important . . . because it will tend strongly toward the breaking up of the Indian tribal system which is perpetuated and ever kept in mind by the Indian's own system of names" (clxi).[30] Indian education policy, then, plays a crucial part in this process of hetero naming, literally extending the bureaucratic mandates of allotment while training students to see these institutionalized terminologies as expressive of normal, natural, and healthful forms of sentiment and civilized social order.

Romance (counter)plots

The potential of American Indians to circulate radical counternarratives of home and family was greatly curtailed by the institutionalization of the romance plot in federal Indian policy, which in depicting traditional social life as "degraded" denied its legitimacy as a subject position from which to critique capitalist hetero homemaking and the program of detribalization. Native writers publishing during the heyday of the Indian education program did offer positive descriptions of traditional practices and community dynamics. Such loving accounts, however, were presented as scenes of bygone days, set either prior to the narrator's own entry into white-run schooling or before substantial contact with whites. These textual moments can appear coded as nostalgia for childhood, childish naïveté, ethnography, or quasi fairy tales separated by an unbridgeable gap from the writer's and reader's own life. Thus, in response to the official depiction of traditional kinship as a savage anachronism, native writers cast their own favorable representation of such networks as an evocation of the past.[31]

One can see this dynamic at work in Zitkala-Ša's writing. The pieces of hers that have received the most critical attention are three autobiographical sketches of her life before her decision to attend boarding school, her time as a student, and her stint as a teacher at Carlisle.[32] These three pieces and six others were collected and reprinted in 1921 as *American Indian Stories*. As Susan Bernardin notes, there is an "omission of romance and marriage plots" in the three autobiographical selections.[33] This absence of "romance," however, does not characterize the collection as a whole. In fact, two pieces, "The Trial Path" and "A Warrior's Daughter," are structured around love plots. What also marks these two as different from the rest is that they are set before the advent of the reservation system. In a March 1901 letter to her then fiancé, Carlos Montezuma, Zitkala-Ša justifies her choice of setting: "Already I've heard that at Carlisle my story ['The Soft-Hearted Sioux'] is pronounced 'trash' and I—'worse than Pagan.' . . . Last week *Harper's* [sic] accepted another story of mine—'The Trial Path'—that is purely Ancient history and won't bear hard on anyone's pet co[nc]erns."[34] In response to the harsh criticism incurred by "The Soft-Hearted Sioux's" endorsement of Dakota spirituality and its condemnation of overzealous and missionizing Christian converts, Zitkala-Ša declares her intent to sidestep the "pet concerns" of the proponents of Indian education and reform by reaching back to "Ancient history."[35] Rather than denoting a disengagement from U.S.–Indian politics or the tale's actual location in the remote past, however, this phrase suggests a particular strategy for circumventing white "concerns."[36] In other words, "Ancient history" is less a straightforward description of when the story takes place than an ironic comment on the kinds of temporal disjunction necessary in order to depict elements of traditional Dakota life while avoiding censure by white officials, reformers, and publishers.

That the stories set in the distant past (or rather, before the routine appearance of whites among the Yankton) are also the only ones that contain romance plots, then, is no coincidence. This alignment suggests the ways that narrative projections into the past allow a bracketing of the civilizing imperatives of white readers and their assumptions about the nature of home and family so as to tell a different story about the possibilities of and for Dakota life. Moreover, focusing on the writings of hers that neither feature white characters nor reference U.S. policy directly requires a greater awareness of and attention to tradition as an enduring force in Dakota life.[37] While appearing less explicitly or recognizably *political* than the other pieces in the collection, "The Trial Path" and "A Warrior's Daughter" implicitly challenge the pathologization of native kinship networks in U.S. legal and political discourse. They emphasize the disparity between U.S. ideologies of sexuality and domesticity, on the one hand, and traditional Dakota social organization, on the other, foregrounding the latter's sustaining sense of community and thereby seeking to render it publicly intelligible as something other than the degraded absence of civilized normality.

While "The Trial Path" tells the story of a man who kills his best friend to eliminate a rival for the woman he loves, the text repeatedly displaces discussion of the romance that inspires this crime of passion in favor of making the tale of the murder and its aftermath the occasion for an explanation of the workings of kinship. The story opens with a late-night conversation between a woman and her twenty-year-old granddaughter, and in response to the younger woman's description of one of the stars as "my dear old grandfather" (127), the older woman recalls the tragic events of her youth:

> Listen! I am young again. It is the day of your grandfather's death. The elder one, I mean, for there were two of them. They were like twins, though they were not brothers. They were friends inseparable! All things, good and bad, they shared together, save one, which made them mad. In that heated frenzy the younger man slew his most intimate friend. He killed his elder brother, for long had their affection made them kin.
>
> (128)

Although the killing ostensibly is motivated by jealousy, the emphasis here is not on the romantic fervor that leads to violence but on the nature and strength of the bond severed in the name of love—or rather, on the idea that one profound love gains expression only through the destruction of another. The deep "affection" between the men and the ways that mutual feeling made them "kin" is given more weight in the grandmother's account than her love for either of them. In fact, readers are given no background on the romantic relationship that inspires the murderous act at the center of the story. Moreover, the grandmother's claim that her granddaughter has two grandfathers reaffirms the persistence of the men's bond even in death. In some sense, the text introduces the love story only to subordinate it to an elaboration of the creation of kinship bonds, particularly the process of adopting people into familial networks in ways that make them virtually indistinguishable socially from blood relations. Rather than highlight the construction of a new family unit through companionate marriage, then, the romance plot is detoured into a commentary on the capaciousness of Dakota family to absorb new members along lines dissociated from procreation and heterogendered pairing.[38]

As the grandmother's initial description implies, her narrative focuses not on the emotional exchange between her and the man who killed to get her but on the potentially destructive impact of this rash act on the community and the social mechanisms of adoption through which it is resolved. The means of communal resolution is the trial path of the title. The murdered man's father, who is given control of the life of the murderer, decides that the killer must ride a horse from the home of the murdered man's family to the outer ring of the camp circle. If he falls, he must die, but if he completes the ride, his life will be spared. Although the horse races and bucks and the rider almost loses his grip, he meets the challenge. At this point, the murdered man's father rises, goes to the murderer, and "cries, with compassionate voice, 'My son!'" (133), thereby incorporating the killer into his family in place of his dead child. While the story is set in motion by an expression of individual passion as part of what may seem hetero romance, then, its dramatic arc is constituted by the struggle over how and whether this individual can be reintegrated into Dakota life. The title reinforces the sense that the love plot functions as a background against which to stage the resiliency of Yankton tradition, structured by a kinship system flexible enough to respond to change and durable enough to maintain social cohesion.

Rather than merely surprise white readers with a generic bait and switch by presenting them with the beginnings of a love story only to steer them into another sort of tale entirely, Zitkala-Ša circulates and capitalizes on the markers of hetero romantic feeling to help make potentially alien forms of sociality affectively intelligible; she uses sentiment in this way as a teaching tool. After readers are told of the murder, they are given some insight into the grandmother's emotional state. When a messenger arrives with the news of the murder, she notes, "How fast, how loud my heart beats," adding that "I longed to ask what doom awaited the young murderer, but dared not open my lips, lest I burst forth into screams instead" and that "my temples throbbed like a pair of hearts!" (129–30). Later during the trial, she thinks, "Do not fall! Choose life and me!" while holding her "thick blanket" over her lips (132). These moments that give readers access to her consciousness suggest an interior life whose terms conform to a certain set of romantic conventions: the repeated figure of "hearts"; an all-consuming desire that leaves her speechless; the depiction of her feelings as inhabiting a private realm separate from, and in conflict with, public life; and the portrayal of coupling as the ultimate horizon of personal fulfillment. These gestures draw readers into the story by implicitly affirming marriage as the goal of the emotional trajectory that the text seems to chart. Yet the story pivots away from the question of whether the killer will survive to be paired with his lover and toward the question of whether he will be accepted by the family of his victim. The lover's fear and passion slide into the emotional response of the women in the murdered man's family to the prospect of accepting the murderer as one of them. The mother addresses him as "My son!" but "on the second word her voice shook, and she turned away in sobs" (133). The dead man's sister, having been instructed by her father to embrace her brother's killer, "cries, with twitching lips, 'My brother!'"—upon which, we are told simply, "the trial ends" (134). The trial, then, is not merely the successful riding of the horse but the resolution of a social crisis produced by passion through the processes of kin making, and the lover/grandmother's romantic feelings for the murderer are eclipsed by the drama of familial re-formation. The mother's and the sister's expression of pain and act of forgiveness suggest as powerful an emotional investment as that of the lover/storyteller's and illustrate a negotiation between personal emotion and collective well-being in which kinship is the mediator. In other words, rather than affectively saturating the love plot as the greatest expression of sentiment, the story juxtaposes romantic feeling with that of kinship distinct from companionate coupling, privileging nonmatrimonial kin making as a site of reconciliation and somewhat noble self-sacrifice for the sake of communal harmony.

The story, however, does not end here. After noting in passing "the fifteen winters of our wedded life," the grandmother moves to a discussion of how Ohiyesa, the horse that her lover rode, "was a constant member of our family" (134). Describing her narration of the horse's burial with her husband as "sacred knowledge," she observes that her granddaughter has fallen asleep, although she had been awake for the end of the tale of the trial itself.[39] The grandmother bemoans her granddaughter's lapse in attention—"I did wish the girl would plant in her head this sacred tale" (135)—implying that the extension of kinship to the horse, and the attendant sense of kinship as the central social form and force of Dakota life, is the primary "knowledge" that she sought to convey.[40] In this sense, the girl serves as a figure for the reader who is interested only or primarily in the romance plot, the tale of her grand-parents' love. By chastising her for missing the point, the grandmother further frames the story as an intergenerational lesson in ways that implicitly critique the paradigms at work in federal Indian education. Invoking and then displacing romance while staging the act of story-telling as a pedagogical effort within the family to instill the value of kinship, the text serves as a challenge and a corrective to U.S. policy in its effort to interpellate native youth into heteronormative affect.

In addition to contesting the heterosexual imaginary of the boarding school system, Zitkala-Ŝa's stories respond to changing conditions on the Yankton reservation. Looking at the annual reports of J.F. Kinney, the agent to the Yankton, one can see how the official weave between education, allotment, and bourgeois marriage and homemaking in federal Indian discourse was brought to the reservation.[41] Moreover, an attention to these reports acknowledges Zitkala-Ŝa's presence on the Yankton reservation during most of her child-hood.[42] One of the agent's primary aims was to supplant the chiefs, a project to which the dispersion of the Yankton on privately owned plots was crucial. "One of the prime objects of the Government in the management of Indians, and to make them self-supporting, is to break up the old tribal relations and effectually destroy tribal authority over them," and the "divi-sion of land separates the people from the chiefs."[43] More important, tribal members needed to be separated from each other: "Successful farming requires isolation, and their habits and disposition lead them into gangs. They want to be together."[44] Of course, this dissolution of social ties is cast as liberating: "Farming, a home, the accumulation of property, a higher social and political status, a feeling of manhood, a consciousness that they have the capacity to do and act for themselves, freed from tribal dictation, will wean them from these old customs."[45] The reason behind this repudiation of cooperative farming, though, is that "gangs" are the backbone of native identity. More than allegiance to the chiefs themselves, the framework of traditional life and governance is sustained through webs of intimate affiliation that provide an alternative to the abstract individualism of U.S. citizenship. As the agent notes, "The fraternal feelings existing between the Yanktons was [sic] much stronger than the obligations imposed by official duty; nor is this strange when it is understood that by marriage and blood the Yanktons are nearly all connected."[46] Given the linkage of traditional affective bonds to extensive networks created "by marriage and blood," the reordering of Yankton land tenure must be accompanied by a reconfiguration of kinship. The attempt to replace native geopolitics with a political economy based on isolated (bourgeois) households and centralized governance, then, is conducted through a coordinated attack on the material conditions that sustain kinship, including restricting travel to visit relatives both on and off the reservation.[47]

If the severing of kinship bonds is structurally necessary to the imperial transformation of Yankton political identification and land tenure, the depiction of plural marriage and native gatherings as depraved and unnatural legitimizes such intervention. Dances are characterized as "weekly orgies." "Here in feathers and paint, with the jingling of bells and beating of drums, the men dance, recounting their deeds of valor in speech and song. At last, carried away by frenzied excitement, they at times give away their property, and occasionally their wives." Such events are "entirely at variance with progressive industry and civilization."[48] These "carnivals of vice" also were charged with "corrupting" women and "the young."[49] Thus the agent's reports represent Yankton sociality itself as promoting rampant immorality, defining tradition not just as a lack of "civilization" but as its active antithesis. More broadly, beyond inciting "depraved lusts," dances were seen as a structural impediment to the implementation of the privatizing imaginary ("the blessings of home and family") discussed above; the agent sought to interest "the Indians in farming to such an extent as should wean them from the dance."[50] Dances, like communal labor, promoted and helped concretize a feeling of collectivity that militated against the material reorganization of production, homemaking, and land tenure and that undercut attempts to euphemize this process as the acquisition of a sense of individual identity.

Often dances are listed with other practices that contribute to "the utter unsanctity of the marital relations," most notably polygamy. "While Indians are . . . born and reared to abhor manual labor, in morals, they come into the world with the polygamous taint attached to them," which would suggest that plural marriage is less a sociosexual system than a form of congenital stigma.[51] Polygamy stands in here for original sin, connecting moral bankruptcy to heredity, and monogamy implicitly is cast as salvational, cleansing native children of their (racial) "taint." The practice of having multiple wives is offered as a hyperbolic example of the overarching insecurity of "the family relations between husband and wife."[52] The campaign against polygamy, then, is the most visible part of the project of reconstructing Yankton "family relations" in ways that sever them from traditional practices and formations in order to subject them to the ostensibly sacralizing and stabilizing force of U.S. (marriage) law. Such transformation privileges the companionate couple over the more diffuse webs of "fraternal feeling" that organize residence and labor; it also participates in discursively soldering the remapping of Yankton economies and land tenure to the promotion of marital and moral purity, thereby reaffirming a capitalist vision in which the isolated nuclear family staves off the chaos of a surrender to degeneracy.[53] The reports, however, also reveal that the Yankton did not simply adopt "civilized" ways. They largely continued their traditions—including collective labor, dances, visiting, and polygamy—except when directly punished by the agent, implicitly illustrating the persistence of the kinship networks at stake in all of these practices despite the government's insistence on the nuclear logic of detribalization.

In response to such imperial efforts to reorganize Dakota social life, Zitkala-Ŝa further emphasizes the importance of extended family relations to virtually all aspects of Dakota life in "The Warrior's Daughter," in which kinship connections make possible the romance at the center of the story. The text opens up the hetero pairing at its heart by illustrating how its consummation relies on a broader affective and affiliative network, suggesting that the social bonds constitutive of Dakota tradition are crucial to the maintenance of home and family rather than, in Morgan's terms, acting as "peculiar" impediments to them. The text begins by introducing the reader to "a warrior father" sitting with his wife and his eight-year-old daughter in the camp circle. The young girl, Tusee, "is taking her first dancing lesson" in preparation for participation in a ceremony that will take place that evening. We also are told that the father "was the chieftain's bravest warrior" but that his status in the community largely comes from his being "one of the most generous gift givers to the toothless old people" (137–38). In situating the father's bravery and this vision of familial comfort within a framework of social responsibility and interdependence, the text suggests that it will complicate the image of the Dakota household with which the story opens.

Into this domestic scene the text inserts another figure, "an elderly man" who rides up to the tepee and speaks "with a stranger's accent" (138–39). His history is as follows: "From an enemy's camp he was taken captive long years ago by Tusee's father. But the unusual qualities of the slave had won the Sioux warrior's heart, and for the last three winters the man had had his freedom. He was made [a] real man again. His hair was allowed to grow. However, he himself had chosen to stay in the warrior's family" (139). Not only does "family" appear as a flexible concept here, defined in ways that are not routed exclusively through marriage and procreation, but it serves as a mechanism through which the Dakota negotiate relations with outsiders. In addition to allowing for intraband realignments of feeling and responsibility, as in "The Trial Path," articulations of kinship provide a means for crossing the gulf marked by war, thereby positioning kinship as a mode of political identification.[54] Emphasizing the primacy of familial relations to Dakota identity, the discussion of the unnamed character's incorporation into the warrior's family indicates the unity between Dakota band or tribal belonging and the matrix of kinship: one is either kin or captive. Being Dakota, being incorporated as a full member of the band (indexed here by the right to be a "real man" and to grow out one's hair), is dependent on one's acceptance as part of a Dakota family. Kinship appears here as the immanent nexus of native sociality, encompassing yet exceeding romantic pairings.[55]

More than illustrating the elasticity of kinship and its role in defining Dakota identity, the former slave's inclusion in the warrior's family as Tusee's "uncle" is the linchpin of the romance plot. After introducing the reader to Tusee and her family, the text abruptly skips an indeterminate number of years and resumes after Tusee has acquired her own tepee. However, she "is not alone in her dwelling. Near the entranceway a young brave is half reclining on a mat" (141–42). Described as "her lover," he explains that he has had a confrontation with her father, who has told the young man that he must get "an enemy's scalp-lock, plucked fresh with your own hand" before he can make her his "wife" (143). Early the next morning the warriors set out to attack their enemies, traveling "southward" to their territory (144). This elliptical directional reference to the identity of their foe recalls the description of Tusee's uncle as having "features . . . of the Southern type" (139), implying that the warriors (including Tusee's father and her lover) are going off to do battle with the former people of this slave cum kinsman. A number of women, including Tusee, go along on the campaign, waiting hidden in a nearby ravine while the men attack. Two Dakota are killed, and one, Tusee's lover, is captured. As the others pack up and begin the journey homeward, she resolves to stay and save him.[56] Blending into the crowd at the enemies' victory celebration, she discerns the man responsible for capturing her lover. After flirting with him during the evening, she lures him "out into the night" by "speak[ing] to him in his own tongue" (149), and once they are far enough away from the camp ground, she leaps toward him, "like a panther for its prey," revealing her identity to him ("I am a Dakota woman!") just before stabbing him to death (150–51). Then, disguised as an old woman, she sneaks back while everyone is asleep, cuts her lover free, and carries him toward home.

The relationship between Tusee and the young-would-be warrior is the backbone of the story, driving the dramatic action, and their reunion takes place at the story's close, implying a somewhat conventional happily-ever-after coupledom, albeit one in which she has saved him rather than the reverse. Yet if the romance is the point, the story's opening seems incongruous, given its focus on Tusee's childhood and her relationship with her uncle, the former captive. Additionally, the love plot references elements of the opening scene: the implication that the enemy is the uncle's former tribe and that Tusee can speak to the warrior she kills "in his own tongue" because she has learned it from her uncle (having spoken to him "in the man's own tongue" [141]; note the parallel phrasing).[57] Moreover, the initial scene with the former slave is alluded to later when the uncle is described as having been a "captive" (139), the same term used to designate Tusee's lover, and when the uncle proves his affection for Tusee by his willingness to go out to capture one of her father's ponies so that she can have the necessary gift to bring to participate in her "first dance" (140)—a dance being the context in which she later uses his language and rescues her lover.[58]

What do these repetitions and resonances mean? The text does not make these connections explicit by offering commentary on them. Instead, it allows them to appear as echoes of the story's preface, suggesting how the romance plot is built out of the relationships and dynamics described at the outset. The subtlety of these traces may itself point toward the obviousness of kinship as the foundation of Dakota social life; its presence is everywhere and is unremarked on because it is so self-evident. If in "The Trial Path" the reader implicitly is compared to the young woman who falls asleep at the end of the love story, thereby missing the "sacred" lesson about kinship, in "The Warrior's Daughter" the reader is called on to remember the framework of kinship that precedes and makes possible the romance. Otherwise, the tale's climax—the luring of the enemy warrior in his own language—would be inexplicable. The story at the text's heart, then, is assembled from elements of what can be described as the kinship plot with which it opens. Rather than initiating a process of breaking away from her family and tribe to create an independent household, as in the romance plot of federal policy, Tusee's reunion with her lover reaffirms her identity as Dakota and underscores the fact that expansive notions of family suffuse all Dakota relationships, providing a shared conceptual and political basis for individual and collective action.

In light of the efforts in education and reservation policy to inculcate proper forms of affect by associating interpersonal intimacy and self-sufficiency with bourgeois marriage and homemaking, the link in Zitkala-Ša's stories between evoking romantic feeling and illustrating its embeddedness in the webs of Dakota kinship works to open room in U.S. public discourse for valuing otherwise abjected native subjectivities. By combining love stories with temporal displacement, these tales cannibalize and reconstellate the central elements of official narratives (marriage, home, and family) in ways that affirm tradition and disjoint the heteronormative logics organizing policy, but they do so without explicitly condemning government initiatives. Adopting a less immediately political framework allows for a tacit denunciation of detribalization and affirmation of the political economy of Dakota kinship without appearing to engage in what could be dismissed as a perverse repudiation of civilized homemaking. In other words, Zitkala-Ša's writing can be seen as trying to make traditional native social formations and modes of self-representation intelligible to white readers by avoiding an outright rejection of compulsory heterosexuality. Though seeking to depathologize native family formations by offering an alternative to their representation in federal discourse as the absence of civilization, this oblique mode of (non)confrontation risks emphasizing the potential normality of the Yankton. That danger and its implications for contemporary queer reading are the topics of the next section.

Multiple wives and *winktes*; or, the naughty bits of tradition

While the tales I have examined resist the official forms of romantic emplotment that lend coherence to and help validate the federal assault on native sovereignty, these stories also have couples at their center. Actually, they have couples at the periphery as well, leaving readers with the impression that male–female pairing is the lone form of romantic association among the Dakota. Zitkala-Ša's use of romance to highlight traditional kinship networks can be seen as part of an effort to shift the perceptions of her predominantly white readership and to open some room for representing oppositional native subjectivities. Yet one must also ask how in the process she strategically simplifies Yankton gender and sexuality, making tradition more palatable to a white audience while effacing elements that might be more objectionable to them. In the title of one piece she proudly proclaims herself a "pagan," offering a principled argument against conversion to Christianity,[59] but in the texts collected in *American Indian Stories* she makes no reference to the other P word with which natives were connected: polygamy. The coordinated legal and military attacks on the Mormons in the latter half of the nineteenth century, including several U.S. Supreme Court decisions that speak of monogamous marriage as central to civilized social order, would have given anyone pause in discussing familial and residential arrangements in which someone has multiple sexual partners.[60] Yet the possession of several spouses by Yankton men was neither unusual nor condemned within the tribe, and the absence of any mention of such relationships in Zitkala-Ša's stories, especially those set before sustained contact with whites, such as "The Trial Path" and "A Warrior's Daughter," suggests an effort on her part to make Yankton practices fit certain white and/or Christian notions of respectability.[61] While registering native challenges to the imperially imposed heteronorm, queer critique should also track where such accounts engage in a process of straightening or editing indigenous histories and cultures in response to U.S. pressures or attendant internalized moral strictures.

The issue, though, is less a failure to mention everything than an apparently systemic elision—a consistent effort not to discuss particular beliefs, practices, and/or identities. What is the boundary of acceptability? How does Zitkala-Ša represent tradition in ways that push against readers' assumptions even as she refuses to cross a certain line, creating a dialectic of anti-imperial critique and self-censorship? In *American Indian Stories* she stops short of addressing forms of gender expressivity and desire that point toward the regularity of homoeroticism, critiquing the imposition of privatizing notions of kinship and residence organized around marriage while concomitantly producing a zone of perversity. To gain readers' sympathy, Zitkala-Ša sometimes rigidifies Dakota masculinity in ways that play to dominant assumptions about sex and gender, erasing forms of male identity and practice that involve same-sex eroticism—specifically, those surrounding the *winkte*. The term *winkte* denotes someone classified as male who occupies a non-masculine gender status associated with, among other things, a vision in which the person is called to this status, the adoption of alternate clothing, and the performance of specialized roles in religious ritual and child care.

Winktes traditionally were recognized and respected members of Sioux communities.[62] While the category is based on gender expression rather than sexual object choice, *winktes* most often engaged in romantic relationships with non-*winkte* men, whose own social identities were not affected by this sexual activity.[63] In offering a portrait of Dakota masculinity that effaces the existence of *winktes*, Zitkala-Ša not only circumscribes the representation of Dakota gender permutations to conform to white expectations but edits out the nonstigmatized participation of non-*winkte* men in forms of same-sex eroticism with *winktes*, thereby ignoring the ways that such sexual activity and romance (including marriage) were acceptable parts of normal Dakota masculinity.

This process of accommodation/elision is most evident in "The Soft-Hearted Sioux." The story, which follows a Dakota man from the time that he is a sixteen-year-old boy living with his parents and grandmother to his return to the reservation as a missionary after nine years spent in Indian schools, notes the community's hostility toward him (including the moving of the camp circle away from him and his family) and his inability to provide food for his sick father and elderly mother. The drama of the text rests on the unnamed title character's failure to fulfill what are presented as the gender ideals of Dakota manhood. The story begins with the young man and his family clustered around the fire in their tepee, and the first bit of dialogue is his grandmother's inquiry "When are you going to bring here a handsome young woman?" (110). Over her grandson's protestations ("Not yet!"), she continues in this vein, and his parents join in, his father noting that "learn[ing] to provide much buffalo meat" is a necessary precursor to "bring[ing] home a wife" (111). Impending adulthood is connected to finding a female partner and becoming an adequate provider, the latter serving as a signal of maturation toward matrimony. The main character, who is also the first-person narrator, observes, "My heart was too much stirred by their words, and [I was] sorely troubled with a fear lest I should disappoint them" (111). His expression of fear is tied to his concern about his ability to fulfill a social role expected of him, although he does not say whether his trepidation is about his relationship to women, his prowess as a hunter, or both.

Here the narrative breaks off, skipping "nine winters' snows" in which the narrator "hunt[s] for the soft heart of Christ" (112). Returning to preach Christianity to his people, he exhibits signs of anxiety, including "nervous fingers" and sweating before speaking (113, 116), and is continually described as "soft-hearted." While explicitly marking his lack of hunting skills, the multiple references to his softness by members of the reservation community and his family suggest a broader failure to live up to the terms of Dakota manhood, casting his Christianization as an unacceptable feminization and as evidence that he is a "traitor to his people" (117). The failure properly to perform masculinity is represented as the sign of his abandonment of Dakota ways, reciprocally implying that the role of husband/provider lies at the core of native male identity.

More than bemoaning how Indian education disrupts the transmission of tradition and condemning the misguided effort to eradicate native beliefs and customs, "The Soft-Hearted Sioux" fuses this twofold critique to a representation of the resulting deracination as an unnatural gender inversion. Opposition to federal Indian policy here works through a form of gender baiting that appeals not only to white stereotypes of native masculinity but to dominant notions of dimorphic gender identity and its inherent fulfillment in the hetero coupling of marriage.[64] The main character's later fears about killing allude to his earlier concerns about both hunting and courting (118), so the story encourages readers to see his distancing of himself from his tribe as a sort of perversion. The text, then, creates an equivalency among his inability to connect with his people, to support himself and his family (his father starves because he, the son, cannot find food in time), and to "bring home a wife." This chain of association, however, depends on the assumption that to become and remain an accepted member of traditional Dakota society, a boy must follow a hetero-gendered path toward monogamous marriage. Such an assumption simply makes no sense in light of the role of *winkte* as an acknowledged and valued social option for boys. In addition, the emotional force and logic of the story require a merging of Dakota manhood with hetero romance so as to pathologize, implicitly but powerfully, the "soft-hearted" convert, even though normative masculinity did not preclude having sex with or indeed marrying people of the same sex.

While not claiming that the central character of "The Soft-Hearted Sioux" is a *winkte*, I am suggesting that the story's efforts to generate white feeling against U.S. policy relies on the erasure of *winktes* from Dakota communities and a consequent straightening of Dakota sex/gender, especially for men, so as to cast the civilization program, rather than tradition, as perverse. While rejecting the image of the isolated household and the notion of the married couple as an independent family unit, *American Indian Stories* does not displace hetero romance as a lens through which to represent Dakota tradition, in some cases fetishizing it so as to heighten reader sympathy for resistance to white intrusion. In the effort to oppose the pathol-ogization of native kinship, residency, and collective identity, Zitkala-Ša offers a truncated representation of Dakota gender identities that screens out forms of eroticism and romantic attachment that might trouble white readers.

Rather than suggest that *American Indian Stories* constructs something like a queer subjectivity, I have argued that Zitkala-Ša uses romance to preserve and transmit embattled tradition in response to a sustained imperial assault. Yet in rejecting the privatizing imaginary and nuclear political economy of normality, she also effaces what could be taken by whites as the most perverse or queer elements of Dakota culture. This complex dialectic between championing and censoring tradition reflects the layered quality of compulsory heterosexu-ality and suggests the need for multipronged forms of queer analysis that are not focused exclusively on sexual identity/diversity but that do not overlook its suppression, either. Focusing on the ideological structure of federal Indian policy—its organization as a romance plot—and the attendant political implications of native representations of kinship, then, works to provide greater leverage in defining and dislocating the force of heteronormativity while also marking how straight privilege functions as a bribe within imperial efforts to persuade native peoples to disidentify from tradition.

Notes

1   Jonathan Ned Katz, *The Invention of Heterosexuality* (New York: Dutton, 1995), 13.
2   By *traditional* I mean the ways that native peoples maintain their political and cultural distinctiveness against various modes of imperial intervention, integrating new beliefs and practices while envisioning a continuity between the past and the present. See Simon Ortiz, "Towards a National Indian Literature: Cultural Authenticity in Nationalism," *MELUS* 8, no. 2 (1981): 7–12; Taiaiake Alfred, *Peace, Power, Righteousness: An Indigenous Manifesto* (Don Mills, ON: Oxford University Press, 1999); M. Annette Jaimes, "American Indian Studies: Toward an Indigenous Model," *American Indian Culture and Research Journal* 11, no. 3 (1987): 1–16; and Beth Brant, *Writing as Witness: Essay and Talk* (Toronto: Women's, 1994).
3   The concept of compulsory heterosexuality is borrowed from Adrienne Rich's essay "Compulsory Heterosexuality and Lesbian Existence," in *Adrienne Rich's Poetry and Prose: Poems, Prose, Reviews, and Criticism*, ed. Barbara Charlesworth Gelpi and Albert Gelpi (New York: Norton, 1993), 203–24.
4   Cathy J. Cohen, "Punks, Bulldaggers, and Welfare Queens: The Radical Potential of Queer Politics?" in this volume, 77, 82, 86. For a fuller theoretical elaboration of this position with respect to African Americans in the twentieth century see Roderick A. Ferguson, *Aberrations in Black: Toward a Queer of Color Critique* (Minneapolis: University of Minnesota Press, 2004). For useful accounts of the intersection of nineteenth-century sexological discourses and racial ideologies and imageries see Siobhan B. Somerville, *Queering the Color Line: Race and the Invention of Homosexuality in American Culture* (Durham:

Duke University Press, 2000); Will Roscoe, *Changing Ones: Third and Fourth Genders in Native North America* (New York: St. Martin's, 1998); Mason Stokes, *The Color of Sex: Whiteness, Heterosexuality, and the Fictions of White Supremacy* (Durham: Duke University Press, 2001); and Lisa Duggan, *Sapphic Slashers: Sex, Violence, and American Modernity* (Durham: Duke University Press, 2000). For discussion of how Mormons ceased to be considered white due to their polygamous unions see Nancy Bentley, "Marriage as Treason: Polygamy, Nation, and the Novel," in *The Futures of American Studies*, eds. Donald E. Pease and Robyn Wiegman (Durham: Duke University Press, 2002), 341–70.

5   Michael Warner's introduction to the collection *Fear of a Queer Planet: Queer Politics and Social Theory*, ed. Michael Warner (Minneapolis: University of Minnesota Press, 1993), vii–xxxi, is usually cited as the first publication in which the term *heteronormativity* appeared.

6   See Chrys Ingraham, "The Heterosexual Imaginary: Feminist Sociology and Theories of Gender," *Sociological Theory* 12 (1994): 203–19. For the imposition of the family ideal in early federal Indian policy see Reginald Horsman, *Expansion and American Indian Policy, 1783–1812* (East Lansing: Michigan State University Press, 1967); and Theda Perdue, *Cherokee Women: Gender and Culture Change, 1700–1835* (Lincoln: University of Nebraska Press, 1998). For the impact of negative representations of native peoples' practices on institutionalized U.S. sexual norms, especially in terms of promiscuity and polygamy, see Nancy F. Cott, *Public Vows: A History of Marriage and the Nation* (Cambridge, MA: Harvard University Press, 2000); Joan Smyth Iversen, "A Debate on the American Home: The Antipolygamy Controversy, 1880–90," in *American Sexual Politics: Sex, Gender, and Race since the Civil War*, eds. John C. Fout and Maura Shaw Tantillo (Chicago: University of Chicago Press, 1993), 123–40; and David Wallace Adams, *Education for Extinction: American Indians and the Boarding School Experience, 1875–1928* (Lawrence: University Press of Kansas, 1995). For discussion of the ways that American Indians served as prominent examples or models for sexological discourse in the late nineteenth century see Roscoe, *Changing Ones*, 167–200. On transformations in residency and kinship in the nineteenth-century United States via marriage law and ideology see Cott, *Public Vows*, 24–131; John D'Emilio and Estelle B. Freedman, *Intimate Matters: A History of Sexuality in America*, 2nd ed. (Chicago: University of Chicago Press, 1997); Michael Grossberg, *Governing the Hearth: Law and the Family in Nineteenth-Century America* (Chapel Hill: University of North Carolina Press, 1985); Jeanne Boydston, *Home and Work: Housework, Wages, and the Ideology of Labor in the Early Republic* (New York: Oxford University Press, 1990); Elizabeth Freeman, *The Wedding Complex: Forms of Belonging in Modern American Culture* (Durham: Duke University Press, 2002); Paul A. Gilje, ed., *Wages of Independence: Capitalism in the Early American Republic* (Madison, WI: Madison House, 1997); and Amy Dru Stanley, *From Bondage to Contract: Wage Labor, Marriage, and the Market in the Age of Slave Emancipation* (New York: Cambridge University Press, 1998).

7   A growing number of scholars are taking up the question or concept of kinship as a vehicle of queer critique. See Judith Butler, *Undoing Gender* (New York: Routledge, 2004); Kath Weston, *Families We Choose: Lesbians, Gays, Kinship* (New York: Columbia University Press, 1991); Scott Tucker, *The Queer Question: Essays on Desire and Democracy* (Boston: South End, 1997); Michael Warner, *The Trouble with Normal: Sex, Politics, and the Ethics of Queer Life* (New York: Free, 1999); Shane Phelan, *Sexual Strangers: Gays, Lesbians, and Dilemmas of Citizenship* (Philadelphia: Temple University Press, 2001); Lisa Duggan and Nan D. Hunter, *Sex Wars: Sexual Dissent and Political Culture* (New York: Routledge, 1995); and Freeman, *Wedding Complex*. This excellent body of work, though, tends to ask questions about how queers fit into kinship systems rather than seeing the question of kinship as undergirding the heteronorm separate from the queer/straight binary per se.

8   Roscoe, *Changing Ones*, 210. For other scholarly work on gender diversity in American Indian cultures see Sabine Lang, *Men as Women, Women as Men: Changing Gender in Native American Cultures*, trans. John L. Vantine (Austin: University of Texas Press, 1998); Walter L. Williams, *The Spirit and the Flesh: Sexual Diversity in American Indian Culture* (Boston: Beacon, 1986); Sue-Ellen Jacobs, Wesley Thomas, and Sabine Lang, eds., *Two-Spirit People: Native American Gender Identity, Sexuality, and Spirituality* (Urbana: University of Illinois Press, 1997); Evelyn Blackwood, "Sexuality and Gender in Certain Native American Tribes: The Case of Cross-Gender Females," *Signs* 10 (1984): 27–42; and Beatrice Medicine, "'Warrior Women': Sex Role Alternatives for Plains Indian Women," in *The Hidden Half: Studies of Plains Indian Women*, eds. Patricia Albers and Beatrice Medicine (Lanham, MD: University Press of America, 1983), 267–80.

9   To achieve such visibility is an important project on its own, given both the existence of heterosexism in native communities and the general tendency of the outside world to see native peoples as presumptively straight. See Brant, *Writing as Witness*; Qwo-Li Driskill, "Stolen from Our Bodies: First Nations Two-Spirits/Queers and the Journey to a Sovereign Erotic," *SAIL*, ser. 2, 16, no. 2 (2004): 50–64; Craig S. Womack, *Red on Red: Native American Literary Separatism* (Minneapolis: University of Minnesota Press, 1999), 271–303; Will Roscoe, ed., *Living the Spirit: A Gay American Indian Anthology*

(New York: St. Martin's, 1988); and Jacobs, Thomas, and Lang, *Two-Spirit People*. In particular, I would like to thank Craig Womack for drawing my attention to this point.

10   For background on Bonnin see Dexter Fisher, foreword to *American Indian Stories*, by Zitkala-Ŝa (Lincoln: University of Nebraska Press, 1985), v–xx; Cathy N. Davidson and Ada Norris, introduction to *American Indian Stories, Legends, and Other Writings*, by Zitkala-Ŝa (New York: Penguin, 2003), v–xlvi; Ruth Spack, "Dis/engagement: Zitkala-Ŝa's Letters to Carlos Montezuma, 1901–2," *MELUS* 26, no. 1 (2001): 173–204; Susan Bernardin, "The Lessons of a Sentimental Education: Zitkala-Ŝa's Autobiographical Narratives," *Western American Literature* 32 (1997): 213–38; and Ruth J. Heflin, *I Remain Alive: The Sioux Literary Renaissance* (Syracuse, NY: Syracuse University Press, 2000). In the present essay I refer to her by her chosen pseudonym. Several critics have misidentified her as Lakota, possibly because her pen name is from that language. See Jeanne Smith, " 'A Second Tongue': The Trickster's Voice in the Works of Zitkala-Ŝa," in *Tricksterism in Turn-of-the-Century American Literature: A Multicultural Perspective*, eds. Elizabeth Ammons and Annette White-Parks (Hanover, NH: University Press of New England, 1994), 46–60; and Ruth Spack, "Re-visioning Sioux Women: Zitkala-Ŝa's Revolutionary *American Indian Stories*," *Legacy* 14 (1997): 25–42. Yankton is the Gallicized version of the name of one of the seven tribes of the Sioux, although *Sioux* itself is a misnomer—a French derivation of an Ojibwa insult for the tribes whose long-standing (ethnic?) alliance the term denotes. The Yankton are often included in the term *Dakota*, which also has been used to refer to all seven tribes, most notably by Ella Deloria. The terms *Dakota, Nakota*, and *Lakota* (the latter usually refers to the westernmost Sioux tribe, the Teton) often have been used to designate different groupings of the seven tribes, but these terms more properly refer to dialects of the language they all speak. For a good overview of nomenclatures and their philologies see Raymond J. DeMallie, "Sioux until 1850" and "Yankton and Yanktonai," in *Plains*, vol. 13.2 of *Handbook of North American Indians*, ed. Raymond J. DeMallie (Washington, DC: Smithsonian Institution, 2001), 718–60, 777–93. I use *Sioux* when referring to this collection of tribes or to characteristics that apply to most of these groups, since it currently is the most common term among natives and nonnatives.

11   Scholars have disagreed about how to interpret Zitkala-Ŝa's political commitments, especially after she joined the Society of American Indians. For conflicting interpretations see Deborah Welch, "Gertrude Simmons Bonnin (Zitkala-Ŝa)," in *The New Warriors: Native American Leaders since 1900*, ed. R. David Edmunds (Lincoln: University of Nebraska Press, 2001), 35–53; and Robert Allen Warrior, *Tribal Secrets: Recovering American Indian Intellectual Traditions* (Minneapolis: University of Minnesota Press, 1995). Warrior tends to emphasize Zitkala-Ŝa's resistance to the Peyote movement and to overlook her intermittent residence on the Yankton reservation, her defense of the traditional government, and her resistance to the supplanting of that government under the Indian Reorganization Act.

12   Zitkala-Ŝa, *American Indian Stories*. Pages will be cited parenthetically.

13   As Patricia C. Albers asserts, kinship serves as the "primary idiom through which the Sioux and other Native Americans ordered their social relations of production, trade, war, ceremony, and recreation" ("Sioux Kinship in a Colonial Setting," *Dialectical Anthropology* 6 [1982]: 254). For broader discussion and theorization of the politics of kinship, especially as it is articulated with gender, see Eleanor Burke Leacock, *Myths of Male Dominance: Collected Articles on Women Cross-Culturally* (New York: Monthly Review Press, 1981); and Jane Fishburne Collier and Sylvia Junko Yanagisako, eds., *Gender and Kinship: Essays toward a Unified Analysis* (Stanford: Stanford University Press, 1987). For discussion of the difference between kinship-based and capitalist economies see Eric Cheyfitz, *The Poetics of Imperialism: Translation and Colonization from "The Tempest" to "Tarzan,"* enl. ed. (Philadelphia: University of Pennsylvania Press, 1997); and Eric R. Wolf, *Europe and the People without History* (Berkeley: University of California Press, 1997), 73–100. My argument here with respect to heteronormativity follows Laura Wexler's similar move with respect to the "culture of sentiment" ("Tender Violence: Literary Eavesdropping, Domestic Fiction, and Educational Reform," in *The Culture of Sentiment: Race, Gender, and Sentimentality in Nineteenth-Century America*, ed. Shirley Samuels [New York: Oxford University Press, 1992], 9–38).

14   For an exploration of this process of marginalization in relation to AIDS in African American communities see Cathy J. Cohen, *The Boundaries of Blackness: AIDS and the Breakdown of Black Politics* (Chicago: University of Chicago Press, 1999).

15   Arnold Krupat, *Ethnocriticism: Ethnography, History, Literature* (Berkeley: University of California Press, 1992), 132. While the law "requires particular acts" and is shaped by the narratives it proposes, however, Krupat finds that it still "remains open to interpretation" (130).

16   Bentley offers a similar formulation in her discussion of the ways that late-nineteenth-century opposition to Mormon polygamy "helped to give American nationalism the structure of a domestic novel" ("Marriage as Treason," 343).

17   Adams, *Education for Extinction*, 61, 58.

18 Soon after introducing Indians to a formerly all-black school, Pratt received permission from Congress to open a school exclusively dedicated to Indian education in Carlisle, Pennsylvania. This school became the model for the twenty-four off-reservation Indian boarding schools that opened across the country during the next twenty-five years. On Pratt and the history of Indian education more broadly see Adams, *Education for Extinction*; Frederick E. Hoxie, *A Final Promise: The Campaign to Assimilate the Indians, 1880–1920* (Cambridge: Cambridge University Press, 1995); Joel Pfister, *Individuality Incorporated: Indians and the Multicultural Modern* (Durham: Duke University Press, 2004): Richard Henry Pratt, *Battlefield and Classroom: Four Decades with the American Indian, 1867–1904*, ed. Robert M. Utley (New Haven: Yale University Press, 1964); Frederick J. Stefon, "Richard Henry Pratt and His Indians," *Journal of Ethnic Studies* 15, no. 2 (1987): 87–112; Robert A. Trennert, "Educating Indian Girls at Nonreservation Boarding Schools, 1878–1920," in *Unequal Sisters: A Multicultural Reader in U.S. Women's History*, eds. Vicki L. Ruiz and Ellen Carol DuBois (New York: Routledge, 1990), 224–37; Trennert, "From Carlisle to Phoenix: The Rise and Fall of the Indian Outing System, 1878–1930," *Pacific Historical Review* 52 (1983): 267–91; Alice Littlefield, "Learning to Labor: Native American Education in the United States, 1880–1930," in *The Political Economy of North American Indians*, ed. John H. Moore (Norman: University of Oklahoma Press, 1993), 43–59; and K. Tsianina Lomawaima, "Domesticity in the Federal Indian Schools: The Power of Authority over Mind and Body," *American Ethnologist* 20 (1993): 227–40. The Annual Report of the Commissioner of Indian Affairs (ARCIA) (Washington, DC: Office of Indian Affairs, 1869–1940) is another rich source, containing the commissioners' comments on education as well as reports by superintendents of Indian education and from the various boarding schools.

19 ARCIA, 1884, 186; ARCIA, 1888, xix. While the idea of acculturating native children through white bourgeois homemaking dominated the outing program in the east, the system out west often degenerated into a means of providing cheap Indian labor to the communities surrounding the boarding schools. See Trennert, "From Carlisle to Phoenix"; Littlefield, "Learning to Labor"; Adams, *Education for Extinction*, 162–63; and Hoxie, *Final Promise*, 189–210.

20 Pfister, *Individuality Incorporated*, 12.

21 Adams, *Education for Extinction*, 173. The experiment at Hampton and Carlisle was championed by eastern reform organizations, and in 1883 they founded the Lake Mohonk Conference, an annual meeting at which the self-designated "Friends of the Indian" could gather to discuss the proper shape and direction of the civilization program—especially education. The most powerful figures in federal Indian policy, such as the various commissioners of Indian affairs and Senator Henry Dawes, were regular attendees.

22 On Morgan's background and influence see Adams, *Education for Extinction*, 61–64.

23 ARCIA, 1889, 93–114. Hereafter pages are cited parenthetically.

24 The term *heterogender* was coined by Ingraham to address the inseparability of contemporary Euro-American understandings of gender from a conceptual and institutional investment in heterosexuality ("Heterosexual Imaginary," 204).

25 For expressions of fear by those within the Indian education system of the threat of students giving in to "licentiousness" (especially polygamy) when they return home see ARCIA, 1884, 200; ARCIA, 1885, 220; and ARCIA, 1889, 335. In fact, legal marriage, as opposed to "marr[ying] in the Indian way," was a major criterion used by both Carlisle and Hampton to assess the success of former students. See Adams, *Education for Extinction*, 287–88.

26 Thomas J. Morgan, "Rules for Indian Schools," ARCIA, 1890, cli. Hereafter pages are cited parenthetically.

27 On how girls in the boarding schools resisted such superintendence see Lomawaima, "Domesticity in the Federal Indian Schools." On students' forms of opposition more broadly see Adams, *Education for Extinction*, 209–38; and Pfister, *Individuality Incorporated*, 66–78.

28 On allotment see Hoxie, *Final Promise*, 41–81, 147–87. The allotment program caused native land-holding to decline from more than 138 million acres in the early 1880s to about 52 million acres in 1934 (Adams, *Education for Extinction*, 344). For an edited text of the Dawes Act see Francis Paul Prucha, ed., *Documents of United States Indian Policy*, 3rd ed. (Lincoln: University of Nebraska Press, 2000), 170–73.

29 Students at boarding schools annually were required to commemorate the passage of the Dawes Act—referred to as Indian Citizenship Day or Franchise Day. For Morgan's original order on this point see ARCIA, 1890, clxvii–clxviii; for discussion of how the "holiday" was celebrated see Adams, *Education for Extinction*, 196–201.

30 For more on the process and importance of renaming in education and allotment see Adams, *Education for Extinction*, 108–11. For an alternate reading of official renaming as compatible with certain native traditions see Pfister, *Individuality Incorporated*, 107–8.

31   Recent scholarship in queer studies has begun to explore what are formulated as queer philosophies of and relations to time and history. See Freeman, *Wedding Complex*; Elizabeth Freeman, "Packing History, Count(er)ing Generations," *New Literary History* 31 (2000): 727–44; Judith Halberstam, *In a Queer Time and Place: Transgender Bodies, Subcultural Lives* (New York: New York University Press, 2005); and Lee Edelman, *No Future: Queer Theory and the Death Drive* (Durham: Duke University Press, 2004). While demonstrating how self-consciously "queer" projects of individual and collective self-fashioning challenge dominant conceptions of reproduction, maturation, and generational differentiation, some of this work repeats the larger (and I think ultimately unhelpful) trend within queer studies of presenting "family" as an inherently normative and normalizing formulation against which to define queerness—in this case, queer temporality. Instead, I suggest that exploring the different logics of kinship and household organization present in different practices of family formation, and examining the ways that certain family formations institutionally are privileged as natural, yields a better sense of the political economy of the heteronorm while opening up potential lines of alliance organized not around resistance to reproductivity and blood relation per se but around the ideological soldering of child care, intimacy, and nurturance to a particular social framework (hetero marriage, the nuclear family, the bourgeois household). Rather than suggesting that because heteronormativity is justified as natural by reference to reproduction, we need to distance ourselves from reproductivity (or, in Edelman's terms, "reproductive futurism"), queer critique can challenge the equation of the creation of children with institutionalized marriage and privatized homemaking while also turning away from a developmentalist relation to the future (subtended as much by the civilizing mission as by heterosexism) and toward an engagement not only with the past (the nuclear family as marginal in human history) but with understandings of kinship whose orientation is grounded in the past (shared ancestors as the basis for expansive kin networks and flexible notions of relatedness based on shared experience). Moreover, the kind of temporality I am exploring here is not a self-consciously "queer" renunciation of reproductivity or of generational breaks but the work of tradition—the survival of native peoples and their cultures through the recirculation of stories, rituals, objects, languages, etc. that keep the past alive in the present and thereby sustain a sense of collective identity.

32   On Zitkala-Ša's autobiographical writing see Bernardin, "Lessons of a Sentimental Education"; Charles Hannon, "Zitkala-Sa and the Commercial Magazine Apparatus," in *"The Only Efficient Instrument": American Women Writers and the Periodical, 1837–1916*, eds. Aleta Feinsod Cane and Susan Alves (Iowa City: University of Iowa Press, 2001), 179–229; Patricia Okker, "Native American Literatures and the Canon: The Case of Zitkala-Ša," in *American Realism and the Canon*, eds. Tom Quirk and Gary Scharnhorst (Newark: University of Delaware Press, 1994), 87–101; Roumiana Velikova, "Troping in Zitkala-Ša's Autobiographical Writings, 1900–921," *Arizona Quarterly* 56 (2000): 49–64; Jessica Enoch, "Resisting the Script of Indian Education: Zitkala-Ša and the Carlisle Indian School," *College English* 65 (2002): 117–41; and Wexler, "Tender Violence."

33   Bernardin, "Lessons of a Sentimental Education," 229.

34   Quoted ibid., 215–16.

35   When referring to her people, Zitkala-Ša uses the term *Dakota*, and it is unclear whether she means all seven Sioux tribes, the groups to the east (excluding the Teton), or the Yankton specifically. My sense is that she is speaking from or about Yankton experience but that her comments are meant to apply broadly across tribal divisions. I therefore move back and forth between *Yankton* and *Dakota*, most often employing the latter term, given that it is the one she uses.

36   In fact, the stories probably are set less than a century prior to their publication. Bernardin takes Zitkala-Ša's statement at face value, claiming that "The Trial Path" is "set in the precontact past" ("Lessons of a Sentimental Education," 216). However, the story prominently features horses as a routine part of Dakota life, and horses themselves were introduced to the continent by Europeans and were not integrated into Dakota culture until the late eighteenth century. Moreover, the use of beads in "A Warrior's Daughter" suggests that it takes place no earlier than the nineteenth century. See DeMallie, "Sioux until 1850"; Ella Deloria, *Speaking of Indians* (1944) (Lincoln: University of Nebraska Press, 1998); Herbert T. Hoover, in collaboration with Leonard R. Bruguier, *The Yankton Sioux* (New York: Chelsea House, 1988); and Patricia C. Albers, "Symbiosis, Merger, and War: Contrasting Forms of Intertribal Relationship among Historic Plains Indians," in Moore, *Political Economy of North American Indians*, 94–132.

37   These stories also differ greatly from Zitkala-Ša's later writings, especially those in *American Indian Magazine*, which tend to speak to current affairs much more directly, often advocating for particular positions on political issues. See Davidson and Norris, introduction to *American Indian Stories*. I would argue, though, that we should neither see her earlier work, especially the versions of traditional tales, as somehow apolitical in light of her later participation in national organizations and

public commentary on current events, nor read her later work and activism as the true expression of her politics in ways that make the earlier acts of storytelling simply a cover for an agenda that later becomes explicit. A more productive move is to consider the different kinds of cultural work performed by different genres and the sorts of commentary and critique enabled by them.

38   On the prominence of inter- and intragenerational kin making as a mainstay of Sioux social life see Raymond J. DeMallie, "Kinship and Biology in Sioux Culture," in *North American Indian Anthropology: Essays on Society and Culture*, eds. Raymond J. DeMallie and Alfonso Ortiz (Norman: University of Oklahoma Press, 1994), 125–46; James R. Walker, *Lakota Society*, ed. Raymond J. DeMallie (Lincoln: University of Nebraska Press, 1982); and Deloria, *Speaking of Indians*. As these sources note, adoptees could be distinguished terminologically from blood relations but usually were not.

39   As Deloria notes, the Dakota words for "to address a relative" and "to pray" are the same (*Speaking of Indians*, 28–29).

40   See Heflin, *I Remain Alive*, 128–29.

41   At one time the Yankton possessed thirteen to fourteen million acres in what is now the Dakotas. In 1858, however, a headman named Struck by the Ree (who two years earlier had been appointed principal chief of the Yankton by General William S. Harney) led a party that negotiated a treaty selling more than eleven million acres to the United States, also creating the Yankton reservation. Three of the seven bands that composed the Yankton publicly condemned the treaty that authorized the transaction, because it was signed without their knowledge while they were out on their annual buffalo hunt. The terms of the treaty defined Yankton territory until the beginning of the allotment program in the 1880s. The Yankton were the only Sioux tribe that never went to war against the United States; thus "they have never experienced that chastisement which has served to make the Santees and other branches of the great Sioux family submissive and easily governed" (ARCIA, 1887, 65). On Yankton history see Renée Sansom-Flood, *Lessons from Chouteau Creek: Yankton Memories of Dakota Territorial Intrigue* (Sioux Falls, SD: Center for Western Studies, 1986); Hoover, *Yankton Sioux*; DeMallie, "Sioux until 1850"; DeMallie, "Yankton and Yanktonai"; and Guy Gibbon, *The Sioux: The Dakota and Lakota Nations* (Malden, MA: Blackwell, 2003).

42   Zitkala-Ŝa left for White's Manual Institute in 1884; returned to the reservation in 1887 and remained there until 1891; and then went back to the school for another three years before attending Earlham College for two years. See Fisher, foreword to *American Indian Stories*. On White's see John W. Parker and Ruth Ann Parker, *Josiah White's Institute: The Interpretation and Implementation of His Vision* (Dublin, IN: Prinit, 1983).

43   ARCIA, 1887, 58. By 1885 Kinney had handpicked a ruling council, described as "the board of advisors," but the people on the reservation continued to look to and support traditional leaders (ARCIA, 1885, 59–60).

44   ARCIA, 1887, 56.

45   ARCIA, 1888, 65.

46   ARCIA, 1886, 100.

47   On the home–house connection see ARCIA, 1887, 58; and ARCIA, 1884, 58. On visiting see ARCIA 1885, 58, 62; ARCIA, 1886, 94; and ARCIA, 1888, 64.

48   ARCIA, 1884, 60. The giving away of wives probably refers to the sexual sharing of one's wife with close friends as a gesture of intimacy. However, if the woman objected, divorce was a simple process, since she owned the tepee and virtually all the household goods; she simply left her husband's possessions outside the tepee or, if they were living with his kin, moved back to her parents' band. See Raymond J. DeMallie, "Male and Female in Traditional Lakota Culture," in Albers and Medicine, *Hidden Half*, 237–65; and Walker, *Lakota Society*, 40–44, 56.

49   ARCIA, 1886, 99; ARCIA, 1885, 60.

50   ARCIA, 1887, 60; ARCIA, 1888, 65. In fact, as prominent events in Yankton life, dances may well have functioned as spaces for coordinating opposition to U.S. policy initiatives, and this suggests an alternative motive for the official condemnation of them. See ARCIA, 1887, 59. The accusations leveled at dances usually appear in the context of the agent's admitted failure to control them.

51   ARCIA, 1887, 53. While the proper term for a man's marriage to more than one woman is *polygyny*, I use the term *polygamy* because it is more familiar and was used at the time.

52   ARCIA, 1888, 65. Many, if not most, of the cases brought before the Indian court set up by the agent had to do with illegal cohabitation and divorce. See ARCIA, 1886, 98; ARCIA, 1889, 174; and ARCIA, 1890, 72–74.

53   Moreover, the agent repeatedly emphasizes that education is the vehicle through which the Yankton will be elevated from their savage state. See ARCIA, 1887, 61. His reports include discussions of Yankton efforts to resist the removal of their children, to which Kinney responded by withholding annuities, including rations.

54   See Deloria, *Speaking of Indians*; DeMallie, "Kinship and Biology"; DeMallie, "Sioux until 1850"; Hoover, *Yankton Sioux*; and Walker, *Lakota Society*. Yankton and other Sioux tribes tended to be divided into kinship units called *tiôspaye*, comprising a shifting number of blood and other relatives. A variable number of *tiôspaye*, themselves linked by more distant kinship ties, would combine to form a camp circle with its own council, whose rule for the most part was by persuasion rather than coercion. In this way, belonging to the camp circle as a geopolitical entity was defined by kinship.

55   This reading challenges Spack's contention that "The Warrior's Daughter" relies on "cultural and romantic language" instead of "political discourse" ("Re-visioning Sioux Women," 36).

56   While Tusee's choice to stay behind to rescue her lover is depicted as exceptional, the presence of women among the war party seems to be taken as fairly conventional: "Astride their ponies laden with food and deerskins, brave elderly women follow after their warriors"; "the war party of Indian men and their faithful women vanish beyond the southern skyline" (144). On Sioux women's participation in war see Medicine, "'Warrior Women'"; Blackwood, "Sexuality and Gender"; and Lang, *Men as Women*, 268, 275, 277–78, 304.

57   For brief readings that tend to focus on the story's gender dynamics, often in ways that underestimate the potential flexibility of gender identity among the Sioux, see Spack, "Re-visioning Sioux Women"; Spack, "Dis/engagement"; Okker, "Native American Literatures"; and Smith, "'Second Tongue.'"

58   The reference to dances also recalls the attack on them led by the federal agent to the Yankton.

59   For discussion of "Why I Am a Pagan" and the revisions made to it under the title "The Great Spirit" in *American Indian Stories*, see Velikova, "Troping."

60   See Bentley, "Marriage as Treason"; Cott, *Public Vows*, 105–31; and Iversen, "Debate on the American Home." There is evidence that Zitkala-Ša was in fact a Mormon. See P. Jane Hafen, "Zitkala Sa: Sentimentality and Sovereignty," *Wicazo Sa Review* 12, no. 2 (1997): 41.

61   See DeMallie, "Male and Female"; and Walker, *Lakota Society*, 53, 55.

62   On the traditional cultural role of the *winkte* see Williams, *Spirit and the Flesh*, esp. 31–86; Medicine, "'Warrior Women'"; and Lang, *Men as Women*, esp. 57–255. For discussion of *winkte* identity today, of its uneasy relationship to gay or queer identification, and of its uneven acknowledgment on reservations see the articles by Michael Red Earth and Doyle V. Robertson in Jacobs, Thomas, and Lang, *Two-Spirit People*, 210–16, 228–35; and Lang, *Men as Women*, 311–22.

63   In fact, *winktes* often were married to non-*winkte* men and had similar relationships to them as their wives had. See Williams, *Spirit and the Flesh*, 100–101, 112, 118–19; and Lang, *Men as Women*, 198–203. "Homosexuality" as a concept, then, does not apply to this arrangement, since the relevant distinction was based not on object choice but on gender identity: two men could have a relationship with each other, but not two non-*winkte* men. For further theorization of this distinction see Lang, *Men as Women*, 3–55, 323–30; and Roscoe, *Changing Ones*, 3–21, 119–36.

64   On white visions or fetishizations of native masculinity in the late nineteenth and early twentieth centuries see Gail Bederman, *Manliness and Civilization: A Cultural History of Gender and Race in the United States, 1880–1917* (Chicago: University of Chicago Press, 1995); and Philip J. Deloria, *Playing Indian* (New Haven: Yale University Press, 1998). For a compelling discussion of how people who went through the Indian education system sought to "Indianize themselves," tactically deploying white images of native peoples to their own ends, see Pfister, *Individuality Incorporated*, 97–132.

Chapter 21

Elizabeth A. Povinelli

NOTES ON GRIDLOCK: GENEALOGY, INTIMACY, SEXUALITY

Elizabeth A. Povinelli is a Professor in the Department of Anthropology and the Institute for Research on Women and Gender at Columbia University, New York. A former editor of the interdisciplinary cultural studies journal *Public Culture*, Povinelli has written a number of books, including *The Empire of Love: Toward a Theory of Intimacy, Genealogy and Carnality* (2006) and *Economies of Abandonment: Social Belonging and Endurance in Late Liberalism* (2011).

In "Notes on Gridlock," Povinelli argues that the histories of genealogy and intimacy are not clearly distinct, successive or oppositional fields of power, but rather work as dynamic, over-lapping and dispersed "grids" that constitute certain people and sexual practices as legitimate, human, and social. Povinelli's essay is framed by her everyday encounter with two, seemingly incommensurate, family archives: the diagrammatic family tree of an Australian Aboriginal "local descent group" and the autobiography of a lesbian mother's fight to adopt her partner's son. Povinelli articulates the ways in which each is differently bound to and apprehended by genealogical discourse, and its colonial and postcolonial extensions. Using the radical anti-relational ethic of a third (anti-family) archive—Jean Genet's novel *Querelle*—Povinelli demonstrates how the interlocking machinery of intimacy and genealogy founds the modern legitimation of sex acts and other forms of corporeal sociality.

> We're tired of trees. We should stop believing in trees, roots, and radicals. They've made us suffer too much. . . . Thought is not arborescent, and the brain is not a rooted or ramified matter.
>
> (Gilles Deleuze and Felix Guattari, *A Thousand Plateaus: Capitalism and Schizophrenia*)

WHY DOES THE RECOGNITION of peoples' worth, of their human and civil rights, always seem to be hanging on the more or less fragile branches of a family tree? Why must we be held by these limbs? The two archives prompting this meditation are not new to me or to anyone else. Moreover, the social worlds and visions of these two archives are, geographically speaking, worlds apart. Stacks of land claim documents sit to the left of me. Some of these documents concern an Australian indigenous claim I am currently working on. Others compose the archives of claims already heard that I hope to use as a precedent for what I am trying to argue in the current case. All of them demand a diagram of a "local descent group." That is what I am doing right now, drawing a genealogical diagram, a family tree, using now-standard icons for sex and sexual relationship: a diamond represents a man; a circle, a woman; an upside-down staple, sibling relations; a right-side-up staple, marriage; and a small perpendicular line between these two staples, heterosexual reproduction.

The book I am currently reading, *Family Values: Two Moms and Their Son*, lies to the right of me. *Family Values* is a first-person account of the radicalization of a lesbian mother as she fights to adopt her partner's son. The author, Phyllis Burke (1993: 6), figures lesbian mother-hood in terms of a morbid chiasma: "Eight thousand gay men were prematurely dead in San Francisco by the time Jesse [Burke's son] was two, and yet behind what was almost a shadowy membrane there was a lesbian baby boom. Lesbians were giving birth, adopting children, and building families with gay men" (see also Lewin 1993). As I read across these texts I remember a T-shirt that the Society for Lesbian and Gay Anthropologists (SOLGA) printed a few years ago. It schematically represents gay families with the same kinship iconography I am using in these land claims. When I finish *Family Values*, I plan to reread *Querelle*, Jean Genet's (1974: 4) tale about a "sailor's mortal flesh," about the sea, murder, and criminality, and about love against nature. The values in *Querelle* are hardly about the families gay men build. Whenever I read Genet I think of Alexandre Kojeve's (1969: 6) carnal description of human desire: "Man 'feeds' on Desires as an animal feeds on real things. And the human I, realized by the active satisfaction of its human Desires, is as much a function of its 'food' as the body of an animal is of its food."

Clear differences separate the two family archives in which I am immersed. The family diagrams I am drafting for the land claim do not indicate the love, desire, affect, or intimacy that exist between indigenous persons reproductively related. Nor do they document nonsexual corporeal relations. There is no standard icon for "intimacy," "desire," or "love." What makes these indigenous families felicitous in law is the principle of descent that regiments them (e.g., patrilineality, matrilineality). In contrast, Burke argues that true families and just nations are made by love—not by laws of adoption and descent or social, sexual, and gender status. Can Genet's vision of a world of sailors take root in this queer kinship?

What follows are notes on how we might examine the presuppositions and global circulations of what I call genealogical and intimacy grids, some suggestions about their connectivities and irreducibilities, and a few comments on the social worlds made possible and interrupted by their functionings. Why are these the grids that appear across such diverse social and geographical spaces in the public struggle for recognition? How are they distributed across different populations in such a way that I can make sense of the two archives staring at me today? How, in their seeming oppositionality, have they more effectively colonized social imaginaries and territorialized regional social worlds? This essay looks at how these grids have made possible not only the thinking of sex acts as legitimate social acts, but also the restricting and recirculating of the imagination of a counterethics of national and everyday life. The end of this exercise is not the essay itself. The larger goal is to understand: the presuppositions of global forms of felicitous sexual activity, the history of these presuppositions' emergence, and the distribution of them across specific social groups.

Genealogical grids

From the perspective of their roots, genealogical trees have been moving with Europeans for a very long time. The size and characteristics of these European trees, and how they may be legitimately planted, have changed dramatically as marriage reforms progressed from the fifteenth century onward, and as new market and civil forms displaced blood and rank as the defining grid of power and sociality (Goody 1983; Plakans 1984; Macfarlane 1986). The causal history of this transformation is well rehearsed, albeit in competing versions (Foucault 1980; Habermas 1989; Taylor 2002). Humanity as a concept was slowly freed from the grip of familial kinship, descent, and rank; and as a concept and practice it came to define emergent modern social orders. Membership in an abstract human order, rather than in a family (aristocratic) grid, increasingly defined civil, social, and political rights and obligations. As opposed to the social solidarity premised on a genealogical grid, the European diaspora seemed increasingly bent on stranger-sociability.

Of particular importance to this essay, for reasons indicated below, is the function that a specific characterization of nature played in disembedding the individuated human from his or her social role, function, and status. The infamous state of nature: Charles Taylor (2002) points to the role Hugo Grotius and John Locke played in producing a disembedded individual by projecting the individual against a natural world stripped of all social encumbrances. The meaning and use of this conceptual move continued to echo in the eighteenth century. Adam Smith (1976: 140–41), for instance, thought that people should not observe each other from the point of view of "something separate and detached" but as "Man . . . citizens of the world," made equal by being projected against "the vast commonwealth of nature."

I am not so interested here in whether this abstract individual emerged from new forms of market circulation ("the traffic in commodities and news"[1]) that broke down previous forms of social organization or from the migration of theoretical imaginings into broader social imaginings. Instead, I am interested in the alleyways of this progress narrative, in a set of genealogical intensions and extensions inside and outside Europe that accompanied the emergence of the individualized human and its polity. For instance, inside Europe the genealogical grid did not simply disappear as a means of governmentality; rather it was imaginatively reduced, regrounded, and dispersed. For one thing, it is clear that citizenship continues to have a strong genealogical component in many nation-states (birth in the national body gives persons citizenship rights that then descend genealogically). Moreover, though the political relevance of family trees was narrowed and relocated, their social relevance was in fact democratized and dispersed into the life-world of ordinary people and the seams of homogenous national space-time (Anderson 1991).

We could argue that, in being democratized, the genealogical grid has become more vital and real to the political order, whether it is attacked or defended. Certainly, the genealogical grid ceased to function as a broadcast model in which concentric circles of genealogical ranks and associations radiated from the apical crown. Polity no longer unfolded out of the (fictive) ranked affiliations of the people from the point of view of the sovereign family. But now everyone could have a little heritage of his or her own—diagrammed as a personal tree—a stake in some plot that tracked generationally. And, remember, though a petite cosmology, the genealogical grid now organizes democratic state dispensations like inheritance, marriage, child welfare, and capital gains. And not only does it organize the distribution of material goods within each of these agencies, the genealogical grid also provides a mode of translation among them. Genealogy allows governments and social agencies to coordinate people across social practices (e.g., the regulatory fields of inheritance and welfare). Moreover, though the linkage between family and cosmology is of a very different order from that experienced by Duncan in Shakespeare's *Macbeth*, many Christian fundamentalists believe the connection to be as tight.

In its reduced and dispersed form, however, the genealogical grid that operates as the presupposition of national life is not the same grid that operated prior to the seventeenth century. Here Jacques Le Goff's (1989) discussion of the king's body and Jürgen Habermas's (1989) discussion of intimacy—"saturated and free interiority"—are crucial (see also Landes 1988 and Berlant 1997). The aristocratic genealogy was rich in distinctions of rank, role, and kinship that both ordered persons and allowed them multiple avenues for contestation, elaboration, and negotiation. The genealogical grid inherited by market society was only unevenly deracinated from social status and rearticulated to *humanity*, a term intended to suggest equivalence. Questions about the internal dynamic of hierarchy within the new bourgeois family arose almost immediately, as did questions about the grounds for building these new families. What forms of subordination should extend out of the reduced differences among men and women, parents and children? What could— and should—be the presuppositional grounds for forming these petite genealogies if not the social or religious status of the contracting members? Who should be included and excluded from the ranks of blood and money, property and inheritance, love and affection, and sex?

The emergence of democratic genealogies in the eighteenth and nineteenth centuries and debates about what could serve as their legitimate foundations do not provide the history of the genealogical grid, nor even the interior history of Western elaborations of their own genealogical imagination. Dynamic transpositions between old regimes of genealogy and new regimes of citizenship occurred in colonial and European worlds. Both of these worlds ramified into European conceptualizations of their own genealogical systems. Here we return to the complex and uneven deployment of the state of nature in Western social theory. Though the state of nature was originally the empty backdrop against which seventeenth-century legal theorists abstracted persons from all social relations of superiority and inferiority, eventually the state of nature was recollapsed into a genealogical grid through the mediating function of savage society. When applied to so-called savage societies, the state of nature was no longer empty. The savage slot, as Michel-Rolph Trouillot (1991) has called it, was identified as coterminous with nature. In other words, subjects of empire provided the site in which a family, a sexual form, and a governmentality based on them were naturalized. The social organization projected into this new state of nature was soon said to be dependent on the relations of superiority and inferiority projected out of "the elementary family" (Radcliffe-Brown 1965). Two histories need to be told in relation to these developments: one to examine the theoretical elaboration of human society as a divide between descriptive (real) and classificatory kinship societies and subsequent rewritings of the state of the state of nature, the other to examine the dissemination of the genealogical grid with empire, and the resulting territorializations and reterritorializations of metropole and colony. Let me sketch the contours of these two histories.

> Mr. G.F. Bridgman's native servant, before mentioned, who had travelled far and wide throughout Australia, told him that he was furnished with temporary wives by the various tribes with whom he sojourned in his travels; that his right to those women was recognized as a matter of course; and that he could always ascertain whether they belonged to the division into which he could legally marry, "though the places were 1000 miles apart, and the languages quite different." Many pages might be filled with similar testimony.
>
> (Fison and Howitt 1991: 53–54)

In Lorimer Fison and A.W. Howitt's slightly overheated reports, an infinitely extendable collectivity of possible female sexual partners exists for male indigenous Australians not because indigenous groups lacked orderly social relations ("marriage classes") but because the entire world was enclosed within them. So Fison and Howitt famously described the endless horizon of kinship and marriage in savage epistemology.

Kant's question of governance (How should we be governed once detached from the tutelage of social rank?) developed an imperial form: How are societies functionally held together and reproduced without the formal structures of government? In 1871, Lewis Henry Morgan, a lawyer from New York, published an account of how colonial societies ordered and reproduced themselves. Morgan began with the already deracinated ego: "Around every person there is a circle or group of kindred of which such person is the centre, the Ego, from which the degree of the relationship is reckoned, and to whom the relationship itself returns" (10). There were "but two radically distinct forms of consanguinity." On the one hand were descriptive systems, such as "the Aryan, Semitic, and Uralian families." This system recognized only the "primary terms of relationship . . . which are those for husband and wife, father and mother, brother and sister, and son and daughter, to which must be added, in such languages as possess them, grandfather, grandmother, and grandson and granddaughter. . . . Each relationship is thus made independent and distinct from every other." On the other hand were the classificatory systems of consanguinity, such as the Turanian, American Indian, and Malayan families. These rejected "descriptive phrase in every instance, and reducing consanguinei to great classes by a series of apparently arbitrary generalizations, [applied] the same terms to all the members of the same class. It thus confounds relationships, which, under the descriptive system, are distinct, and enlarges the signification both of the primary and secondary terms beyond their seemingly appropriate sense" (12). In her 1989 Lewis H. Morgan lectures, Marilyn Strathern noted that Morgan's vision was critical to the collapse of the state of nature into the state of colonial societies: "Morgan conceived the contrast as between those closer to and more distant from nature. . . . Indeed the draft opening chapter of *Systems of Consanguinity* referred to family relationship existing in nature independently of human creation" (1992: 16; see also Fortes 1969 and Kuper 1988).

The comparative study of kinship was revitalized and made the foundation of the emergent science of anthropology, when, in 1910, the British psychologist W.H.R. Rivers announced a major methodological breakthrough in the study of "savage" societies. Shortly after returning from a collaborative study of the Torres Strait Islanders off northeast Australia, Rivers announced new procedures for collecting and analyzing data that allowed the scientific study of man to move beyond conjectural history. Rivers recommended the genealogical method to the emergent anthropological community on the basis of its simplicity and the minimal impact local systems of meaning would make on the collection of social data. Rendered into its reduced modern and democratic form, the genealogical grid's utility to social science was clear. A couple of assumptions about human beings (sex difference and heterosexual reproduction), assumptions that could be claimed to be the universal preconditions of human life, provided just enough structure for the maximal comparison among societies.[2] The comparative reach, the territorial possibilities of this new demographic method, stretched as far as the British Empire.

What was initially a research method soon became a full-fledged social theory, as Rivers's student, A.R. Radcliffe-Brown, transformed a tool for generating social data into a theory of the generative structure of social systems. Harking back to Morgan, Radcliffe-Brown posited that genealogy (kinship and affinity) provided the structural principle out of which a social system unfolded, operated, and was reproduced.

> The existence of the elementary family creates three special kinds of social relationship, that between parent and child, that between children of the same parents (siblings), and that between the husband and wife as parents of the same child or children. A person is born or adopted into a family in which he or she is son or daughter and brother or sister. When a man marries and has children he now belongs to a second elementary family, in which he is husband and father. This interlocking of elementary families creates a network of what I call, for lack of any better term, genealogical relations, spreading out indefinitely. . . . in any given society a certain number of these relationships are recognised for social purposes, i.e. they have attached to them certain rights and duties, or certain distinctive modes of behavior.
>
> (Radcliffe-Brown 1965: 51–52)

All the great and small societies of Africa, Australia, and the Americas provided clear demonstrations of the social elaborations of the "elementary family," a structure presupposing the same two principles: sex difference and heterosexual reproduction. These two principles provided the minimal dual pairs out of which all other social differences, such as rank, status, and duty, were built. Both principles had to be in play for a family to exist as such. Thus a childless couple fell off the genealogical grid for Radcliffe-Brown—just as they sometimes do in contemporary land claim practices in Australia, where consanguineous ancestors who did not reproduce are often left off the genealogies, for clarity's sake.

In *The Elementary Structures of Kinship* (1969), dedicated to Lewis H. Morgan, Claude Lévi-Strauss goes one step further, seemingly decapitating the sovereign subject from the logic of kinship. Kinship systems were not projections out of the elementary family or the sovereign ego, but out of a deeper structural semantics of restricted exchange. Indeed, Lévi-Strauss transformed the possibility of associating the human being and natural being ("the state of nature") by arguing that the human existed not prior to but alongside kinship. Humanity and kinship, culture and nature, emerged as such in the transformation, or transition, marked by the advent of the first rule of exchange, first announced in a negative form: the prohibition of incest. This rule of rules is, of course, dependent on another: a "deep polygamous tendency, which exists in all men," which "always makes the number of available women seem insufficient" (38). Homosexuality, polyandry, and wife swapping were immediately transformed into solutions to the seeming scarcity of women. More social forms and relations fell off the grid or were recast as mere by-products of its logic, as the atom of kinship and the very nature of culture emerged as the dialectic of binary exchanges that constituted I and thou; man and woman; parent and child; and wife-givers and -takers.

Of course, this short overview simplifies the more complicated history of genealogy theory in the social sciences. The French schools argued with the British over generality and comparison (see, for instance, Leach 1966: 2). And in the United States, a generation of scholars argued heatedly whether kinship was a cultural category or whether it reflected a human universal—each proposition controversial in some way or another (Schneider 1968; Scheffler 2001; Strathern 1992; Collier and Yanagisako 1987). With every new argument, the interior complexity of the genealogical grid intensified. Indeed, building careers was one of the means by which the genealogical imaginary was elaborated and spread. New discursive contours, possibilities, and lines of flight emerged. And, insofar as scholars struggled to characterize the essential properties that determined the applicability of the genealogical grid, they cast the grid itself into the background.

Alongside this analysis of the theoretical intensions and extensions within the Western academy, we need an analysis of how the genealogical grid was inlaid into and diversified by the life-worlds of colonial subjects. Here we can return to the first of the two cases prompting my reflections in this essay. All the land claim documents I am shuffling through contain a description of the genealogical principles by which Australian indigenous persons are recruited into the "local descent group" said to own the land. The Australian Parliament and courts demand that indigenous people present some principle of descent as the grounds for a successful land claim. They do not demand any specific principle of descent. They simply demand descent, typically understood as "a relationship defined by connection to an ancestor (or ancestors) through a culturally recognized sequence of parent–child links" (Keesing 1975: 148; see also Sutton 1998). It is also generally understood that the relationships defined by these parent–child links provide the presuppositional grounds for a number of other social relations, such as property, affect, and ritual. Culture is conceived as an incrustation on the parent–child link. What, if any, presuppositions ground the self-evident social fact of the parent–child link is not typically discussed (that is, rarely does anyone query the universal application of the parent–child connection).

Putting aside this problem for now, we find an impressive variety of principles of descent that indigenous people and anthropologists have presented to the courts as local principles of social recruitment. Indeed, it is a lesson in the power of generative grammar, itself an analogical extension of the family tree. Based on nothing more than two assumptions—sex difference and heterosexual reproduction—anthropologists have introduced a range of descent models beyond the patrilineal clan, originally the only model of descent recognized as traditional by land commissioners and many anthropologists. Over the course of twenty-six years of land claim hearings, the tree has grown many branches: cognatic, ambilineal, patrilineal with one-step matrifiliation, matrilineal with one-step patrifiliation. Diversity in the content of the genealogical grammar is supported and sanctified by one influential strand of legal interpretation. In paragraph 89 of his 1982 report on the Finniss River Land Claim, Toohey J. stated that the land commissioner should base an understanding of recruitment into a local descent group "on a principle of descent deemed relevant by the claimants," not on anthropological theory or debate. The words local, descent, and group should be considered ordinary English words rather than anthropological terms. Of course, they have to be considered; that is, making the meaning of "local descent group" local did not relieve locals from the demand that they give these terms meaning. Recognition has an implicit command structure. The third land commissioner, Michael Maurice, sanctified descent, arguing in paragraph 92 of the 1985 Timber Creek Land Claim report that "it is [the] religious bond with the world . . . that the Parliament has endeavored to recognize by its definition of traditional Aboriginal owner with its three elements: family ties to land; religious ties; and economic rights, i.e., to forage."

Recognizing the local meanings of the local descent group, of family, and of family ties and the principles upon which they are constructed is one of the key means by which the genealogical grid is inlaid locally. Recognition connects the genealogical grid to simple human desires, such as the desire to live and be recognized as being worthy, to have personal and social value, and to reclaim lands once owned. The fulfillment of these large and small desires depends on the ability of indigenous people to produce a "descent group" recognizable as such by lawyers, land commissioners, and anthropologists. And insofar as they do, the law of recognition demonstrates the delicate processes by which local identities are constituted and mediated and the extraordinary delicacy with which local protocols for building and sustaining communities are displaced (see also Povinelli 2002).

But land claims were not the first forum in which the genealogical imaginary was localized. Before the *Aboriginal Land Rights (Northern Territory) Act 1976* was passed, other social practices like welfare and child care addressed colonial subjects through the genealogical imaginary and demanded a response in kind. And, not only were genealogical relations the presuppositional grounds for address, they were also the bureaucratic means by which administrators could coordinate colonial subjects. To be sure, the very nature of political administrative and scholarly practice, its open rather than closed structure, provided colonial subjects room to maneuver. For instance, administrative debates over social policy provided an opening through which subject populations could present countervisions of their social worlds. And, in the case of scholarly regimes, the conversation between ethnographer and subject often teetered between real and fictive dialogical partners. Nevertheless, the discursive protocols of asking, testing, and arguing about the difference between Western forms of genealogy and local practices of corporeality wove genealogical and nongenealogical modes of social organization firmly into the fabric of the possible (see also the exchange between Blowes and Secretary in Povinelli 1999: 43).

Something else happened when Morgan projected European-based genealogical grids onto the empire. Insofar as colonial political and scholarly communities took advantage of differences the colony afforded to advance their own projects, a back draft was felt in the metropole. As Marilyn Strathern (1992) has noted, European forms of kinship and affinity could no longer be taken as singular or natural. They were simply a type of genealogical system, a type that was dissociated from the universal by queer forms of kinship. True, most kinship theorists distinguish between descriptive ("real") and classificatory kinship—from the nineteenth century onward. But the European heterosexual family became more explicitly theorized and politically elaborated as the core institution of the nation-state even while the genealogical surface of that family was being diversified. Eric Fassin's recent discussion of debates in France and the United States over the adoption of children by homosexual couples exemplifies this point, as does Kath Weston's ethnography, *Families We Choose* (Fassin 2001; Weston 1991). As Fassin relates, the French have grounded their arguments in Lévi-Straussian and Lacanian models of the linkage between the family, nature, and culture. But discussions about new reproductive technologies and kinship would do equally well (Franklin and Ragoné 1998; Ginsburg and Rapp 1995). In these new technologies, kinship and affinal relations proliferate, but this proliferation seems only to elaborate and more thoroughly disperse the genealogical grid. Indeed, we can hardly call kinship and affiliation a theory anymore, so thoroughly has it reterritorialized modern social life.

Intimacy grids

Though saturated with intimations of the intimate sanctity that Aboriginal families share with their country, neither Maurice's commentaries nor those of any other land commissioner have concluded that the indigenous family is the result of anything more than an (un)conscious calculus of social inclusion and exclusion undertaken by indigenous people factoring their local principles of heterorelationality (kinship, affinity, and descent). Love does not make an indigenous family qua traditional family according to the Australian Parliament and the courts, nor do local notions of corporeality, proximity, affect, place, context, or spirituality. The Aboriginal family recognized by the Australian Parliament and courts as the basis of indigenous property is a typological projection of classic British structural-functional accounts of "kinship societies." The organization of social life is based on ever more elaborate extensions out of the elementary family (a man, his wife, and their children). The richness of indigenous social imaginations and practices arising out of local notions of the proximities and potencies of various bodies are not relevant to the state imaginaries informing material redistribution schemes. Indeed, practices and relations that fall off the genealogical grid receive very little attention in court hearings because they, like the nonreproductive ancestor, are thematized as irrelevant to the task at hand.

Although members of Australian courts and Parliament do not grant nongenealogical-based corporeal potencies a formative function in the making of indigenous social worlds, they nevertheless assume that social life depends on the exchange of intimate forms of recognition. The formative function of intimacy in state-based property negotiations reappears when we shift our focus away from what the courts recognize as the basis of an indigenous social order and toward what they presume is the basis of a just national order. At this level we see the rhetoric of recognition moving across juridical and public genres, filling the public sphere with calls for mutuality in cultural love, tolerance, intimacy, and under-standing. We hear that the Australian nation is threatened by the interruption of mutual displays of cultural worth. The intimate recognition I am talking about here is not between an I and a Thou but between their abstracted plural counterparts: We-the-People distended from ourselves in being alienated from the best version of ourselves by You-the-Other.[3]

The constitutive character of intimate love in the formation of true families and just nations is, of course, a central debate within U.S. gay politics. The Australian case seems turned on its head: in mainstream America, it is said that love makes families elemental(ly). *Family Values*, for instance, hinges together family and nation through an argument about the value of intimate recognition. The dust jacket thematizes the story of *Family Values* as the threat posed to the nation by the denial of the fundamental role human love plays in family-formation (parent and child).

> Painfully aware of the fact that the law did not acknowledge her ties to the child she loved and helped raise like any other "natural" parent, Burke began adoption proceedings to win recognition as Jesse's second legal mother. The court's resistance to her request was a powerful blow to her ability to quietly endure the treatment lesbians and gays receive in mainstream society. Inspired by her love for and pride in her family, Burke, who had formerly been unnerved by the militant stance of gay activist groups like Queer Nation, now found their riotous tactics and "in your face" attitude a source of strength.

The limbs holding Burke and her family are the unexpected extensions of an army of love(rs). The polemic is fairly clear. State, public, and personal worth of a family should be based on the intimate recognition that occurs between two people, on the choice to love and the love that circulates through this choice. No matter that one of the major distinguishing features of modern intimacy is an expectation of a blurring of choice and compulsion in the context of love, of a dynamic among self-risk and self-elaboration, personal transcendence, and the fall back onto the self. Indeed, *love* thematizes and indicates the affective site where choice and compulsion are blurred. Still, *Family Values* and countless other public pronounce-ments in the United States make a similar argument. Love makes a family. And laws that stifle the natural connection between love and family by restricting reproductive technologies (with adoption as a legal reproductive technology) are therefore perverse and antidemocratic.

Of course, *Family Values* could easily be described as part of a conservative bent in American gaylesbian politics. Moreover, though it refers to gays and lesbians, the book does not capture the rich jargons, dialects, and speech genres characterizing contemporary gay and lesbian social life (much less the modern novel and some modern [auto]biographies). Genet offers a welcome alternative. The self-professed pied piper of criminality, Genet's goal never was "to gain entrance into your houses, your factories, your laws and holy sacraments, but to violate them"—and to help children violate them. Genet is well known in France for his support of the Algerian revolution, the PLO, and the Black Panther movement and, more generally, his anticolonial, antimilitary, and antiracist politics (Sartre 1964; White 1994; Le Sueur 2001). Still, for Genet, the act of love was not for self-recognition or for a pure relay of recognition with an other but for self-evacuation and self-murder through the murder of an other. A void created through the self-executing exercises of sexuality—this was the pure vision of Genet's sexuality. No surprise that it is difficult to produce a community out of Genet's work, or even a boatload of sailors. They just do not add up. Indeed, Genet's vision sometimes seems completely washed out of contemporary U.S. political discussions by the flood of discourse about whether it takes Adam and Eve to make a family or whether it just takes a little love.

Intimacy is not absent in *Querelle*. Reproduced throughout it are the private journal entries that Lieutenant Seblon of the *Vengeur* keeps on Georges Querelle, the protagonist of the book. These journal entries ache with the desire for intimacy. "I shall not know peace until he makes love to me, but only when he enters me and then lets me stretch out on my side across his thighs, holding me the way the dead Jesus is held in a pietà" (1974: 275). And yet Genet insists that Seblon is not "in the book." This claim is odd because we are reading selections from Seblon's journal, which Genet refers to as a book within the book, as a "book of prayers" and "meditations" on Querelle. There between the spines that signal the space of the book we find the soft pornographic interior of Lieutenant Seblon's languid stroll over Querelle's "muscles, his rounded parts, his teeth, his guessed-at genitals" (11). But Genet is careful to distinguish Seblon's mood from that of the other characters. "While the other characters are incapable of lyricism which we are using in order to recreate them more vividly within you, Lieutenant Seblon himself is solely responsible for what flows from his pen" (23). Seblon's lyricism, what could be wrong with that? Why does Genet write Seblon into *Querelle* only to deny him?

As we know, Habermas pivoted the rise of modern forms of the public sphere on the development and circulation of new forms of textually mediated intimate address, exemplified, in many ways, by the lyric genre. Intimacy came to mark a particular movement and elaboration of the deracinated ego in relation to a deracinated other. "From the beginning, the psychological interest increased in the dual relation to both one's self and the other: self-observation entered a union partly curious, partly sympathetic with the emotional stirrings of the other I. The diary became the letter addressed to the sender, and the first-person narrative became a conversation with one's self, addressed to another person. These were the experiments with the subjectivity discovered in the close relationships of the conjugal family" (Habermas 1989: 49). These experiments with subjectivity arose in the period when the grounds for building genealogy were detached from social status, rank, and religion. They provided a means, not of doing away with genealogy, but of hinging it onto emergent humanist narratives of the citizen/subject (the *I*) and his or her relationship to We-the-People. As a result, one of the questions that arose was: What could, and should, be the presuppositional foundations for forming petite genealogies once marriage on the basis of social, economic, or religious contracts was delegitimated? And one of the answers was: intimate recognition. *Intimate love* was the phrase used to refer to and entail the feelings associated with a person's worth based solely on his or her capacities and qualities as a human being. Eventually, *love* absorbed the semantics of *intimacy* and stood as if on its own, opposed to interested attachment, to use, to usury. To assert a bond of love was to assert simultaneously a rejection of social utility. And, simultaneously, nationalism absorbed the structures of this recognition: We-the-People emerged as a transposition and lifting-up (*Aufhebung*) of the dialectic of the intimate I and thou.

These experiments in subjectivity make specific narrative demands on the personal and national subject. We know some aspects of the form that modern intimacy demands. Intimacy, and personal sexual intimacy in particular, has come to be characterized by a form of pronominalized interiority. As numerous people have noted, the intimate interiority is characterized by a second-order critical reflexivity, by the *I* that emerges in the asking of the question, What do I feel toward you? In other words, the I who asks, What do I feel toward you? How do I desire you? contours the intimate interior. Along with being a form of orientation and attachment, intimacy is the dialectic of this self-elaboration. Who am I in relation to you?—this question and its cognates lift up a reflexive ego in the act of asking and stitch it into the world of others. The question is a performative in the strict sense. In the act of asking, Who am I? the I is constituted. This I and its labor with an other provide the micropragmatic architecture out of which We-the-People and other mass subjects unfold.[4] Indeed, the I of the modern self has become so closely associated with this particular narrative form that challenges to intimacy seriously threaten the modes of attachment the subject has to herself and others, and thus challenge the basis of social coherence. Where would the I be without this intimate form of reflexivity? Where would we be? At sea—cast adrift, without nationality and without recognition?

"Where" is one way of asking the question; "when" is another. In other words, crucial aspects of the intimate subject emerge when we examine the changing temporalities of asking, Who am I in relation to you and what do I feel? And when we ask, What are the changing stakes of my answer in relation to my social bonds? Understanding the temporality of the intimate subject moves us away from intimacy and toward what we might describe as the temporality of modern sexual contract and consent. Taylor notes that Grotius and Locke disagreed about the temporality of consent in the governance of man. According to Taylor, Grotius understood political authority to be legitimate insofar as it was consented to by individuals. This original contract created binding obligations by virtue of the preexisting principle that promises ought to be kept. It is Locke who changed the temporal rhythm of consent, setting government according to its clock and justifying revolution when that timing is thrown off. "Consent is not just an original agreement to set up government, but a continuing right to agree to taxation" (Taylor 2002: 93). Consent must now be continually re-theatricalized in the form of the franchise. We see an interesting parallel in Catholic and Protestant approaches to the marriage contract. Does the original marriage contract create binding obligations between the two persons, or must they continually reaffirm their commitment? How does an approach to marriage that necessitates a continual consent as opposed to a "done deal" change the orientation of the I in relation to itself and the other? Isn't the demand for a continual inspection of the intimate contract one of the technologies producing, rather than resulting from, the intimate interiority? And how does the I of intimate love change (or not) in the light cast from the new temporalities figured within derivative contracts? Are some people called upon to re-contract to their commitments in a different way? Do some people conceptualize their intimacies as premised on a series of conditions, distributions of accountabilities, increasing or decreasing portfolios?

No matter how we answer these questions, it does seem clear that the intimacy grid is unevenly distributed across global populations. We must therefore follow the migration of intimacy with the European diaspora. Some scholars have already begun to track this history of sexual diaspora. The recent diasporic and transnational turn in queer studies has contested the history of sexuality as written in the West. This diasporic and transnational turn aspires to displace the history of sexuality by engaging its colonial and postcolonial scenes of circulation and inscription. But queer national and diasporic studies of sexuality share many common orientations. Both forms of queer studies turn away from the catalog of sex acts and identities toward a view of counternormative sex publics as a condition and site, where new political, social, and economic worlds are imagined and where the practices of world-building are elaborated. Insofar as they share this orientation, these scholars follow their subjects into rich worlds of sexual imaginings and new corporeal economies. The object, however, is not simply to enumerate the variety of gaylesbian worlds, but to understand the conditions of their intelligibility as human worlds within a larger liberal diaspora in which such intelligibility is increasingly demanded. To do this it is helpful to return to Genet's stance toward intimate recognition before we enter the postcolony.

It is clear that Genet was experimenting with subjectivity or, more precisely, desubjectification, in a way that was quite different from that of eighteenth- and nineteenth-century Europe and of many in the contemporary gaylesbian movement. His was an experiment in an unnatural love that emptied the body, devisaged the face. Genet's love betrayed its usury, and made intimacy, as a relay of recognition, impossible. Stirrings resonate throughout *Querelle*, but as waves that anesthetize the curious self or as positions that annul the possibilities that these emotional stirrings will move into human relationality. Thus when Querelle approaches his friend Vic to kill him after Vic has helped him smuggle opium off the ship: "No longer was any part of Querelle present within his body. It was empty. Facing Vic, there was no one. . . . He was free to leave his body, that audacious scaffolding for his balls. Their weight and beauty he knew. With one hand, calmly, he opened the folding knife he had in the pocket of his peacoat" (Genet 1974: 59). And, when Querelle symbolically executes himself for his murderous crime by allowing Norbert (the owner of the bar where Querelle will sell his drugs) to fuck him, the position of their act enables the momentary desire for a facial relation but bars its consummation. "In a vague way [Querelle] felt grateful toward Norbert for protecting him, in thus covering him. A sense of some degree of affection for his executioner occurred to him. He turned his head slightly, hoping, after all, and despite his anxiety, that Norbert might kiss him on the mouth; but he couldn't even manage to see his face" (75). These de-facializations enrich the social in a way that is different from the Hegelian fight for recognition. It is a richness of bogs, pungent with odors, stench, and despair.

Of course, Genet's experiment with desubjectification was made possible by the success of the earlier bourgeois experiment with intimate recognition. Habermas is surely right that "the jeopardy into which the idea of the community of love was thereby put, up to our day, occupied the literature (and not only the literature) as the conflict between marriage for love and marriage for reason, that is, for economic or social considerations" (Habermas 1989: 47). This conflict remains. For instance, I am surprised reading Burke's autobiography. It is less syrupy than I expected, and shot through with the cynical subjectivity of love (see also Williamson 1991). And yet, in the European diaspora that Genet addressed, this conflict between intimate love and instrumental marriage was unequally fought, for intimate love soon became the tender of the democratic marriage contract, the true grounds for the union between persons, and a necessary basis for a community of people. Love of persons and love of country are the twin contracts of modernity that sailors circumnavigate, or so Genet might say. Thus, Seblon's stylization of love, his lyrical, virile lassitude, is indeed the backdrop Genet wishes to bypass if not surpass, in the desubjectifying rituals of sailors. Gone is the sublimation of I and Thou into We-the-Couple or We-the-People. Kojeve's carnal construction of desire no longer seems an appropriate partner for Genet. No one is home in this unnatural sex. And no one is homesick. Two men having sex. What comes of sailors (de)facing thusly? In other words, if Genet was experimenting with desubjectification, what is the outcome of this experiment? To what would the social refer if the relay of recognition between you and me were cut, if *entre nous* were blocked by the practices of sex?

These are questions that numerous readers of Genet and his legacy have asked. Leo Bersani has argued quite definitely that Genet forecloses the possibility of a humanist answer to these questions. He argues that Genet refuses "cultural relationality" in order to imagine "a form of revolt that has no relation whatsoever to the laws, categories, and values it would contest and, ideally, destroy" (Bersani 1995: 152). This nonrelational ethics allows Genet to be radically alone, and absolutely distinguishes him from "the tame demand for recognition on the part of our own gay community" (161).

Genet and Bersani are not the only persons experimenting with or beyond intimacy. Candace Vogler has characterized certain modern styles of sex as seeking depersonalized intimacy; Michael Warner, stranger intimacy; Lauren Berlant, critical Utopian intimacy (Vogler 1998; Warner 2002; Berlant 1998). When we supplement these forms of intimacy emerging in the United States with emergent styles and stylizations outside its hegemony, we see the edge of contemporary theoretical and social experimentation. And we see a vague glimmer of the dispersion of intimacy surrounding us.

The dispersion of the intimacy grid is especially apparent when we examine historical linkages among intimacy, sexuality, and recognition in the shadow of the postcolony. Remembering the lesson from Genet that to be human is to engage in practices of intimate recognition, let us return to the postcolony. There some people are foreclosed from entering the human realm in order that a nation can be made more human(e). It is in this light that we return to our earlier discussion of state forms of recognition of indigenous social organization, this time focusing on the dehumanizing gesture embedded within it. Remember, in legal precedents pertaining to traditional forms of tenure, indigenous persons are recognized as organizing their sexualities or socialities not on the basis of intimate recognition but rather on the basis of social status—kinship, religion, economic utility. Ashis Nandy (1983) has discussed with great insight the shattering of the intimate self in this colonial relation. Indeed, Western recognition of the worth of other cultures within the nation and among nations was meant, in one of its ideal forms, to repair these distensions. What irony then that state recognition of traditional forms of indigenous social organization works by acknowledging the humanity of indigenous social organization (the local descent group) even as it evacuates the prima facie indices of that humanity: intimacy (Habermas 1989: 47). The double bind in which persons are placed multiplies. It might not be the intent of legislators within the liberal Australian state, but in the context of indigenous Australia—where life chances are closely tied to state aid—indigenous persons must in fact dehumanize themselves into pure genealogy to gain the recognition of courts. And so tightly has the narrative *I* of intimacy become associated with the human and humanity that to be without it is to risk being dehumanized and subject to all the harms of the dehumanizing practices of modernity. What wonder that we now know that all people have feelings. We might conclude by noting that the gay families Burke promotes do not escape these binds. They just approach them from another angle. To be sure, intimate love makes a family human, but love must still culminate in a family, a domestic or communal plot, a social group that adheres. It is Genet who pulls apart the intimate and genealogical plot, by creating narrative spaces in which intimacy and the subjective *I* separate and in which love refuses to build into the grammar of genealogy. Thus, in the end,

> As soon as the thought crossed her mind, she felt deeply ashamed. Then, numbly, Madame Lysiane saw her own words written out in front of her, in her own inimitable grammar. "They is singing." Looking at Querelle, Madame Lysiane no longer felt what fencing masters call the hunger of the rapier. She was alone.

> (Genet 1974: 276)

Coda

The genealogical imaginary did not die when the sovereign's head tumbled. Nor was it replaced by intimacy as a new form of association and attachment. Something more—and less—interesting is happening. Both genealogy and intimacy have emerged as semiautonomous foundations for legitimating sex acts and other forms of corporeal sociality, even as both have been dispersed in and by colonial and postcolonial worlds. Sociality seems unthinkable not only without one or the other of these two grids, but without them working as twin pairs, intertwined, twisting, struggling against each other in the empty horizon of the Universal.

Notes

1   Habermas 1989: 15.
2   Rivers (1910: 1) writes:

> The first point to be attended to is that, owing to the great difference between the systems of relationship of savage and civilised peoples, it is desirable to use as few terms denoting kinship as possible, and complete pedigrees can be obtained when the terms are limited to the following: father, mother, child, husband and wife.

3   Note, however, that even this mode of address is fictional. In the public sphere of newspapers, talk shows, and government reportage, the Other is typically not addressed. Rather, the mode of address is oriented to the assumed and entailed We-the-People who beseech one another to incorporate or expel the nonperson plural They-the-Other. (The significance of the We–Them form is suggested by Benveniste 1971.)
4   If, according to Alexandre Kojeve (1969: 4), it is in, by, and as desire that man is formed and revealed to himself and others as a (human) I—the I that is essentially different from, and radically opposed to, the non-(human) I—then the intimate interior I is built on top of that, as the I that reflects, discerns, and differentiates its desires.

References

Anderson, Benedict. 1991. *Imagined communities: Reflections on the origin and spread of nationalism.* Rev. ed. London: Verso.

Benveniste, Emile. 1971. *Problems in general linguistics*, translated by Mary Elizabeth Meek. Coral Gables, Fla.: University of Miami Press.

Berlant, Lauren. 1997. *The queen of America goes to Washington City: Essays on sex and citizenship.* Durham, N.C.: Duke University Press.

—. 1998. Intimacy. *Critical Inquiry* 24: 281–88.

Bersani, Leo. 1995. *Homos.* Cambridge: Harvard University Press.

Burke, Phyllis. 1993. *Family values: Two moms and their son.* New York: Random House.

Collier, Jane Fishburne, and Sylvia Junko Yanagisako, eds. 1987. *Gender and kinship: Essays toward a unified analysis.* Stanford, Calif.: Stanford University Press.

Fassin, Eric. 2001. Same sex, different politics: "Gay marriage" debates in France and the United States. *Public Culture* 13: 215–23.

Fison, Lorimer, and A.W. Howitt. 1991. *Kamilaroi and Kurnai: Group-marriage and relationship, and marriage by elopement drawn chiefly from the usage of the Australian Aborigines; also, the Kurnai tribe, their customs in peace and war.* Canberra: Aboriginal Studies Press.

Fortes, Meyer. 1969. *Kinship and the social order: The legacy of Lewis Henry Morgan.* Chicago: Aldine.

Foucault, Michel. 1980. *The history of sexuality, Volume 1: An introduction*, translated by Robert Hurley. New York: Vintage.

Franklin, Sarah, and Helena Ragoné, eds. 1998. *Reproducing reproduction: Kinship, power, and technological innovation.* Philadelphia: University of Pennsylvania Press.

Genet, Jean. 1974. *Querelle*, translated by Anselm Hollo. New York: Grove.

Ginsburg, Faye D., and Rayna Rapp, eds. 1995. *Conceiving the new world order: The global politics of reproduction.* Berkeley: University of California Press.

Goody, Jack. 1983. *Development of the family and marriage in Europe*. Cambridge: Cambridge University Press.

Habermas, Jürgen. 1989. *The structural transformation of the public sphere: An inquiry into a category of bourgeois society*, translated by Thomas Burger with Frederick Lawrence. Cambridge: MIT Press.

Keesing, Roger M. 1975. *Kin groups and social structure*. New York: Harcourt Brace Jovanovich College Publishers.

Kojeve, Alexandre. 1969. *Introduction to the reading of Hegel*, edited by Allan Bloom, translated by James H. Nichols. Ithaca, N.Y.: Cornell University Press.

Kuper, Adam. 1988. *The invention of primitive society, transformations of an illusion*. London: Routledge.

Landes, Joan B. 1988. *Women and the public sphere in the age of the French Revolution*. Ithaca, N.Y.: Cornell University Press.

Leach, Edmund. 1966. *Rethinking anthropology*. London School of Economics Monograph of Social Anthropology, no. 22. New York: Athlone.

Le Goff, Jacques. 1989. Head or heart? The political use of body metaphors in the Middle Ages. In *Fragments for a history of the human body*, edited by Michael Feher. New York: Zone.

Le Sueur, James D. 2001. *Uncivil War: Intellectuals and identity politics during the decolonization of Algeria*. Philadelphia: University of Pennsylvania Press.

Lévi-Strauss, Claude. 1969. *The elementary structures of kinship*, translated by James Harle Bell. Boston: Beacon.

Lewin, Ellen. 1993. *Lesbian mothers: Accounts of gender in American culture*. Ithaca, N.Y.: Cornell University Press.

Macfarlane, Alan. 1986. *Marriage and love in England: Modes of reproduction, 1300–1840*. New York: Blackwell.

Morgan, Lewis Henry. 1871. *Systems of consanguinity and affinity of the human family*. Washington, D.C.: Smithsonian Institution Press.

Nandy, Ashis. 1983. *The intimate enemy: Loss and recovery of self under colonialism*. Oxford: Oxford University Press.

Plakans, Andrejs. 1984. *Kinship in the past: An anthropology of European family life, 1500–1900*. New York: Blackwell.

Povinelli, Elizabeth A. 1999. Settler modernity and the quest for indigenous traditions. *Public Culture* 11: 19–47.

—. 2001. Sexuality at risk: Psychoanalysis metapragmatically. In *Homosexuality and psychoanalysis*, edited by Tim Dean and Christopher Lane. Chicago: University of Chicago Press.

—. 2002. The poetics of ghosts: Social reproduction in the archive of the nation. In *The cunning of recognition: Indigenous alterities and the making of Australian multiculturalism*. Durham, N.C.: Duke University Press.

Radcliffe-Brown, A. R. 1965. The study of kinship systems. In *Structure and function in primitive society: Essays and addresses*. New York: Free Press.

Rivers, W. H. R. 1910. The genealogical method of anthropological inquiry. *Sociological Review* 3: 1–12.

Sartre, Jean-Paul. 1964. *Saint Genet: Actor and martyr*. New York: New American Library.

Scheffler, Harold W. 2001. *Filiation and affiliation*. Boulder, Colo.: Westview.

Schneider, David Murray. 1968. *American kinship: A cultural account*. Englewood Cliffs, N.J.: Prentice-Hall.

Smith, Adam. 1976. *The theory of moral sentiments*. Indianapolis, Ind.: Liberty Classics.

Strathern, Marilyn. 1992. *After nature: English kinship in the late twentieth century*. Cambridge: Cambridge University Press.

Sutton, Peter. 1998. *Native title and the descent of rights*. Perth, Australia: National Native Title Tribunal.

Taylor, Charles. 2002. Modern social imaginaries. *Public Culture* 14: 91–124.

Trouillot, Michel-Rolph. 1991. Anthropology and the savage slot: The poetics and politics of otherness. In *Recapturing anthropology: Working in the present*, edited by Richard Fox. Santa Fe, N.M.: School of American Research.

Vogler, Candace. 1998. Sex and talk. *Critical Inquiry* 24: 328–65.

Warner, Michael. 2002. Publics and counterpublics. *Public Culture* 14: 49–90.

Weston, Kath. 1991. *Families we choose: Lesbians, gays, kinship*. New York: Columbia University Press.

White, Edmund. 1994. *Genet: A biography*. New York: Random House.

Williamson, Donald S. 1991. *The intimacy paradox: Personal authority in the family system*. New York: Guilford.

PART 5

Affect

Chapter 22

Ann Cvetkovich

AIDS ACTIVISM AND PUBLIC FEELINGS: DOCUMENTING ACT UP'S LESBIANS

Ann Cvetkovich is the Garwood Centennial Professor of English and Professor of Women's and Gender Studies at the University of Texas at Austin. Formerly co-editor of *GLQ: A Journal of Lesbian and Gay Studies*, in her research Cvetkovich explores the historical, public, and political dimensions of queer feelings.

In this excerpt from *An Archive of Feelings: Trauma, Sexuality, and Lesbian Public Cultures* (2003), Cvetkovich uses oral history to create a counterpublic archive of the affective politics of AIDS activism, and specifically of ACT UP New York's lesbian activists. Excluded from more public and national AIDS memorializations yet also dismissed as not radical enough because of its predominantly white, gay middle-class membership, ACT UP/NY emerges as a complex and diverse enterprise in sexual politics and queer community-making when viewed from the "minority" position of its lesbian and women members. For Cvetkovich, oral history becomes a radical methodology able to document not only the emotional intensities of friendship, anger, and ambivalence testified to by AIDS activists, but also more difficult feelings often articulated in the gaps and silences caught on tape. While celebrating ACT UP/NY's accomplishments, Cvetkovich suggests that her counterhistory of these difficult queer political feelings provides a resource for present and future queer activism.

THE AIDS CRISIS, like other traumatic encounters with death, has challenged strategies for remembering the dead, forcing the invention of new forms of mourning and commemoration. The same is true, I would argue, for AIDS activism. What is the current meaning of the slogan "the AIDS crisis is not over" in the context of treatment with protease inhibitors and an ever widening gap, of transnational proportions, between medical possibility and political and economic reality that has significantly shifted the early associations of

AIDS with gay men? Like activism itself, the slogan's meaning is constantly shifting. In March 1997, ACT UP/NY marked its tenth anniversary with a return to the site of its inaugural Wall Street protest; while the event suggested an ongoing AIDS activism, it was also an occasion for looking back on a time that seemed now located in the past. What kind of memorial would be appropriate for a movement that while not exactly dead, since ACT UP/NY and other chapters, for example, continue to meet, is dramatically changed? When is it important to move on and when is it useful, if painful, to return to the past? I ask these questions about ACT UP in particular because in the process whereby AIDS activism was the catalyst for what has now become mainstream gay politics and consumer visibility, something got lost along the way, and I'm mourning that loss along with the loss of so many lives.

Another of my interests in approaching the wide range of traumas produced by AIDS through the more specific topic of activism is to explore the assumption that trauma is best addressed by public and collective formations, rather than private or therapeutic ones. Such formulations pit affective and political solutions to social problems against one another. There is often good reason to do so; my own work on sensationalism has suggested as much in examining the affective powers of melodramatic, sentimental, and sensational representations as a displaced response to social problems.[1] Lauren Berlant continues this line of argument when she proposes that within sentimental culture, "the authenticity of overwhelming pain that can be textually performed and shared is disseminated as a prophylactic against the reproduction of a shocking and numbing mass violence."[2] My goal here, though, is to challenge such paradigms by scrutinizing activism for its affective and even therapeutic dimensions, and to question the divisions between public and private, affective and political, on which such distinctions rest.[3] ACT UP is a suggestive example for this project insofar as the group was forged out of the emotional crucible of anger and grief created by homophobic neglect and an escalating number of deaths. Only with a fuller sense of the affective life of politics can one avoid too easy assertions of a "political" solution to the affective consequences of trauma in which politics becomes a phantasmatic structure that effects its own forms of displacement.

I feel a particular urgency about remembering and documenting ACT UP because as someone who grew up in the shadow of the 1960s—old enough to have vivid memories of the new social movements but too young to have participated in them directly—AIDS activism represented a significant instance of post-1960s' movement activism. It built on the models of direct action established by the civil rights, antiwar, women's, and gay and lesbian movements, thus proving they were still viable, but it was not simply repeating the past since it also created new forms of cultural and media activism, and incorporated a distinctive flair for the visual and performative. As a member of Austin's ACT UP group from 1989, when it started, until 1991, when it became less active, I have been trying to figure out what to make of an experience that has had a changing though persistent and indelible impact on my life. I also can't forget ACT UP because it is entwined with the experience of death; I was drawn to it because of my relationship with two friends, one of whom was the first person I knew closely who was HIV+ and the other of whom, his lover, helped found ACT UP/Austin shortly after he tested positive. When first one and then the other got sick, I spent less time doing activism and more time taking care of them; after their deaths, I didn't really return to ACT UP. Remembering ACT UP has become a way of keeping their memories alive.

Throughout this period and even well after it, I was fascinated with ACT UP/NY, which operated on a far grander scale than Austin's group. I attended meetings whenever I was in New York, and during the summer of 1990, participated in the activities of what was then the Women's Caucus. I was enormously affected by the energy, passion, and productivity of the Monday night meetings at the Lesbian and Gay Community Center. (As it turns out I was not alone; the excitement and intensity of ACT UP meetings, as much as the demonstrations, are a frequent topic in the interviews cited below.) In New York, AIDS activism was also a particularly vital site of cultural activism, which appealed to my intellectual interests; the videos produced by ACT UP's DIVA-TV collective and the Testing the Limits collective, the *Living with AIDS* series produced by Gay Men's Health Crisis (GMHC), as well as its *Safer Sex* shorts, Video Data Bank's collection *Video against AIDS*, and an array of graphics, documented in Douglas Crimp and Adam Rolston's *AIDS Demo Graphics*, extended the reach of ACT UP and fostered a public culture organized around AIDS activism.[4] I was also intrigued by the strong presence of women and lesbians in ACT UP, some of whom were working specifically on women and AIDS issues. Cultural documents such as the book *Women, AIDS, and Activism*, a publication that grew out of the *Women and AIDS Handbook* first developed for teach-ins, and Maria Maggenti and Jean Carlomusto's video *Doctors, Liars, and Women*, about ACT UP's 1988 demonstration against *Cosmopolitan* magazine, drew attention to work that might otherwise have remained invisible except to those directly involved in ACT UP/NY.[5]

It has seemed all the more urgent to provide a history of ACT UP's lesbians when, with the passage of time, ACT UP is in danger of being remembered as a group of privileged gay white men without a strong political sensibility, and sometimes critiqued on those grounds.[6] Once again lesbians, many of whom came to ACT UP with considerable political experience, seem to be some of the first to disappear from ACT UP's history. Also troubling is the dismissal of ACT UP as too radical, internally divided, or even a failure. Carlomusto worries about "reductive" representations that "flatten the complexities": "After a while we've seen so much footage of demonstrations and people yelling at buildings, and doing 'die-ins,' that it's almost used the way images of bra burning were used to reduce feminism to a one-note kind of deal."[7] Watching ACT UP's history become prone to disappearance and misrepresentation has made me wonder about how other activisms have been (mis)represented. And I have also pondered how best to document AIDS activism both in its time and for the future since its preservation makes the claim that it mattered, that it made a difference.[8]

Over time, I also kept noticing the ongoing productivity of ACT UP/NY's lesbians, especially in the context of New York's urban cultural scene; they were making films, videos, and visual art, writing novels and creating magazines, tending to the Lesbian Herstory Archives, and forming new activist groups such as the Lesbian Avengers. Sometimes the work addressed AIDS and activism explicitly, as in the case of Sarah Schulman's novels *People in Trouble* and *Rat Bohemia* or Anne D'Adesky's publication of the magazine *HIV Plus*, but even when the connections were more diffuse, as in the case of Ellen Spiro's move from safe sex videos to trailer park life or Zoe Leonard's photographs of the trees on the streets of the Lower East Side, I could see the legacy of AIDS activism and death.[9] But even this rich archive of cultural materials couldn't answer all my questions. I wanted to know how people looked back on their experience with ACT UP, whether they missed it, and whether it continued to inspire and sustain them.

Uncertain of my own answers to these questions, I decided to consult with others, and thus embarked on an experiment in ethnography and oral history by interviewing AIDS activists and, more specifically, lesbians involved with ACT UP/NY [. . .]. I focused on ACT UP's most visible and well-documented chapter because I wanted to get a sense of the more ephemeral network of friendships and publics that accompanied its vast archive of graphics, documentaries, and papers, and to explore how those affective networks support the political, cultural, and sexual publics that are also fostered by New York's urban environment.[10] Here's a compressed list of questions and concerns I brought to the task of interviewing ACT UP's lesbians: How was it that AIDS and ACT UP fostered distinctive coalitions between lesbians and gay men—coalitions that brought new understandings to the word *queer*? If the erotic and affective bonds that underlie political affiliations were heightened by ACT UP's reputation as a cruising ground as well as its proximity to death, what was the role of lesbians as friends, lovers, allies, and caretakers? From the vantage point of lesbian participation, what does the tension within ACT UP between whether to focus on AIDS and treatment issues exclusively or to tackle other related political issues look like? Examining the trauma of AIDS as it affects not just gay men but lesbians as caretakers and activists is a way of casting a wide net for trauma's everyday effects. One outcome of AIDS activism for lesbians is that they have a legacy; they have the privilege of moving on because they have remained alive. What does this experience of survival reveal about the particular mix of death and burnout that some people cite as reasons for ACT UP's waning? And for those lesbians involved with ACT UP's cultural projects, including graphic arts and media, what has been its impact on their subsequent work as artists?

I aim not to provide a representative picture of ACT UP but to intervene against the construction of such a thing, to capture something of the many specificities of its history and legacy. Although my use of oral history is inspired by my particular emotional needs, my most ambitious aspiration has been to use it to create a collective public sphere out of the individual stories of people who once worked collectively and are now more dispersed. Bringing the stories together serves as a reminder that the experiences they document are historically significant and shared.

AIDS and trauma cultures

[. . .I]t is something of a relief, however odd or inappropriate that feeling might be, to turn to the subject of AIDS because its status as trauma seems relatively uncontested. Even sexual abuse can be more complicated to legitimate as social trauma, fraught as it is with distinctions between private and public pain, and between emotional damage and the hard fact of death. Of course, AIDS is no different, especially as a specifically sexual trauma. Public recognition of traumatic experience has often been achieved only through cultural struggle, and one way to view AIDS activism, particularly in the 1980s, is as the demand for such recognition. That battle has involved combating, among other forms of oppression, homophobia, which has ignored the experiences of those disproportionately affected by AIDS by casting them as outside the general public.

AIDS has thus achieved the status of what I call national trauma, standing alongside the Holocaust, the Vietnam War, World War I, and other nation- and world-defining events as having a profound impact on history and politics. Surely, national attention to AIDS constitutes a considerable victory given the early association of AIDS with gay men and hence its central place in the politics of homophobia. Moreover, AIDS has produced renewed forms of a radical politics of sexuality through its links to "vices" and "perversions" such as drug use and sex work. Through issues such as immigration, the prison system, and the national and global economics of health care, it has also required an analysis and a political strategy that connects sexuality to race, class, and nation. But it seems that only some versions of AIDS make it into the national public sphere or archive, which includes cultural artifacts such as red ribbons, *Rent*, and *Philadelphia*. Even the NAMES Project AIDS Memorial Quilt and *Angels in America*, which are complex cases worthy of the considerable critical and public scrutiny they have received, are on a different order from ACT UP and its cultural archive of *AIDS Demo Graphics*, DIVA-TV videos, and Gran Fury public art projects. And even that specialized archive does not always clearly reveal a lesbian presence.

In what form, then, does AIDS achieve its status as national trauma? While connected to the insidious and everyday forms of trauma generated by sexism, racism, and other forms of oppression, the spectacular body count of AIDS commands attention, and indeed comparisons with the body counts in wars are often used to underscore its devastating impact. More so even than the sexual trauma of incest, which occupies the ambiguous terrain of what Berlant has called the "intimate public sphere," it seems to have made its way into the canon of national public culture.[11] Within the university and cultural studies approaches to trauma, the inclusion of AIDS in, for example, Cathy Caruth's important collection *Trauma: Explorations in Memory* or Marita Sturken's *Tangled Memories* can be taken as signs of the success of this effort.[12] Rooted strongly, yet not exclusively in Holocaust studies, Caruth's collection includes an interview with AIDS activists Gregg Bordowitz and Douglas Crimp about the current state of the health crisis, thereby facilitating the production of trauma studies as an interdisciplinary field that crosses many national and cultural sites.[13] Sturken focuses on the Vietnam War and AIDS as defining moments that generate "cultural memory," a process of politicized history making in which the nation uses representation in order to work through trauma. Precisely because it is so consonant with my own project, Sturken's book also provides an important point of contrast with it. Among the valuable contributions of *Tangled Memories* is its argument for the centrality of both memory and culture in the national public sphere, and the strategic and legitimating effects of equating the AIDS crisis with the Vietnam War cannot be underestimated. In chapters that explore representations of AIDS, the AIDS Memorial Quilt (as comparable to the Vietnam War memorial), and discourses of immunology, Sturken includes consideration of ACT UP and the cultural theory that surrounds it. But while Sturken's inclusive approach accomplishes a great deal—indeed, it offers the legitimating attention sought by AIDS activism—it also mutes the critical and oppositional force of the more marginal(ized) forms of activism that are my emphasis. ACT UP's memory is not the nation's memory, and my more selective focus aims to illuminate a counterpublic memory that has a critical relation to the more prominent national representations of AIDS that threaten to overshadow it.

One of the most significant contributions of this more specifically gay and activist AIDS culture to understandings of trauma has been its insights about mourning. Still occupying a canonical position in my AIDS/trauma archive is Crimp's essay "Mourning and Militancy."[14] I first heard it presented as a keynote address at the 1989 Gay and Lesbian Studies conference at Yale University, where it marked an occasion when activists and academics were in close communication and something only later named queer theory was taking off. Returning to it now, I am reminded of Carlomusto's remarks in Bordowitz's 1993 video, *Fast Trip, Long Drop*, about how the activist documentaries of an earlier period have taken on new meanings, as the footage that once offered proud testimony of a robust and angry resistance becomes a memorial because it depicts those who are now dead.

Crimp's essay can conjure feelings of mourning as well as nostalgia for a lost community and past moment of activism, but it also remains powerful and relevant for trauma studies. Grounded in activism, it offers an achingly concrete as well as novel validation of the famous Freud essay it invokes and provides a fresh approach to cultural theory's longstanding preoccupation with the tensions between psychic and political accounts of social problems. Crimp maintains that militancy cannot ease every psychic burden and that the persistence of mourning, if not also melancholy, must be reckoned with in the context of activism. Turning around a familiar opposition between private therapy and public activism (exemplified by the slogan "Don't mourn, organize!"), he reads militancy as an emotional response and a possible mode of containment of an irremediable psychic distress. His essay is part of a range of texts and practices, including Simon Watney's observations about the politics of funerals in which gay men remain closeted and David Wojnarowicz's vision of throwing dead bodies onto the steps of the White House, that have scrambled the relations between mourning and militancy, between affect and activism.[15] Adding new resonance to the term *intimate public sphere*, these practices counter the invisibility of and indifference to feelings of loss by making them extravagantly public as well as building collective cultural practices that can acknowledge and showcase them.

Crimp also notes that trauma takes many forms, that AIDS means not just the specter of death but also the loss of particular forms of sexual contact and culture, and that one might mourn the loss of unsafe sex as much as the death of one's friends or prospect of one's own death. His argument echoes Laura Brown's essay on the implications of gendered experience for definitions of trauma, in which she introduces the term *insidious* trauma to encompass the ways in which punctual events, such as rape and sexual abuse, are linked to more pervasive and everyday experiences of sexism.[16] She argues that definitions of trauma as "outside the range of human experience" cannot do justice to the traumatic effects of a sexism that does its work precisely by being constructed as normal.[17] Brown's argument can be bolstered and extended by queer theory's critique of "normativity" along with the myriad ways in which it is embedded in practices of sexuality and intimacy. Crimp's attention to the insidious traumas that pervade sexual practices and funerals in a time of AIDS is startlingly material. In making a claim for not being able to use Crisco or not being able to fuck without a condom as one of the losses of AIDS, he introduces the everyday life of sexual practices into the discourse of trauma in a particularly graphic way. Moreover, the claim that safe sex constitutes a loss challenges the dismissal of certain practices as decadent or perverse as well as the tendency to think that only certain forms or magnitudes of loss count as real. Trauma makes itself felt in everyday practices and nowhere more insidiously or insistently than in converting what was once pleasure into the specter of loss or in preventing the acknowledgment of such losses. It may be a necessity rather than a luxury to consider trauma's impact on sexual life or how its effects are mediated through forms of oppression such as homophobia. This insight seems all the more relevant in the context of the shifting cultures of safe and unsafe sex; recent controversies about barebacking don't make sense without some sympathetic understanding of the attractions of unsafe sex and the significance of its loss.

Crimp emphasizes the ways in which putatively normal practices of mourning are foreclosed for gay men—because they are faced with the prospect of their own deaths, because gay identities are erased at funerals organized by families, because they have been at too many funerals—and thus suggests not only that psychic processes are profoundly affected by social circumstances but also that Freud's production of the normal in relation to mourning might be challenged from the vantage point of queer theory. Although he is suspicious of the category of melancholy because Freud constructs it as an instance of "pathological mourning," and Crimp wants to resist pathologizing accounts of homosexuality, another strategy for a queer reading of Freud might be to return to melancholy and its supposed abnormalities. David Eng and David Kazanjian propose just such a revisionist reading of Freud:

> Were one to understand melancholia better, Freud implies, one would no longer insist on its pathological nature. . . . We suggest that a better understanding of melancholic attachments to loss might depathologize those attachments, making visible not only their social bases but also their productive, unpredictable, political aspects. . . . In this regard, we find in Freud's conception of melancholia's persistent struggle with its lost objects not simply a "grasping" and "holding" on to a fixed notion of the past but rather continuous engagement with loss and its remains.[18]

Like Eng and Kazanjian, I refuse the sharp distinction between mourning and melancholy that leads Dominick LaCapra, for example, to differentiate between "working through," the successful resolution of trauma, and "acting out," the repetition of trauma that does not lead to transformation.[19] Not only does the distinction often seem tautological—good responses to trauma are cases of working through; bad ones are instances of acting out—but the verbal link between acting out and ACT UP indicates that activism's modes of acting out, especially its performative and expressive functions, are a crucial resource for responding to trauma.

Using a richer and more sympathetic sense of melancholy to revisit Crimp's distinction between mourning and militancy not only bolsters his argument but also explains its continued relevance. Crimp ultimately argues that mourning and militancy are intertwined rather than opposed; by looking at activism as a response to psychic needs, one that emerges from a desire to project the internal externally, he is in a position to see it as open-ended and ambiguous. Such insight is crucial to understanding the emotions produced by the persistence of AIDS and social injustice amid the waning of AIDS activism.[20] While this current state of affairs can generate debilitating forms of melancholy, Eng and Kazanjian's approach suggests that this need not be the case. Returning to ACT UP's history in order to find what remains does not have to be a nostalgic holding on to the past but can instead be a productive resource for the present and future. In the aftermath of activism, emotional life can be more subtle and ambivalent because there is no longer the clear enemy or fixed target for activism that creates righteous indignation and anger. Just as Crimp highlights the insidious effects of AIDS on sexual practices, so too would the documentation of activism require attention to a range of everyday emotions that might otherwise fly under the radar screen of trauma studies. To remain attentive to these emotions is to ward off the sense of political failure that can add one more dull blow to the loss from death. Furthermore, the continued relevance of an essay such as "Mourning and Militancy" is another reminder that the archive of activism remains alive.

An experiment in queer ethnography

My project can't really be appreciated without some sense of how unusual, and hence experimental, my choice of interviews as a research method has been. At the risk of reinventing the wheels of oral history, ethnography, and even social science research, I have approached an unfamiliar methodology from the vantage point of a cultural critic accustomed to working with an already existing archive rather than creating one. In fact, I came to oral history with a certain amount of resistance given that my theoretical background had taught me to be suspicious of what Joan Scott calls "the evidence of experience."[21] If our identities as intellectuals are revealed by the texts we love, then you should know that one of my all-time-favorite essays is Gayatri Spivak's "Can the Subaltern Speak?"—a critique of the presumptions that the disempowered can speak the conditions of their exploitation (or be known to intellectuals through their personal testimony).[22] But one of the great, and often misunderstood, lessons of deconstruction is that far from undermining the grounds for inquiry, it is at its most interesting when applied to concrete decisions such as those demanded by the practice of oral history. Doing oral history, like doing activism, presents an endless array of practical challenges, including not just who to interview and what to ask but, as I learned the hard way, where to do the interview and when to turn the tape recorder off. I quickly discovered that the material logistics of interviewing were not going to produce "evidence" that was in any way "transparent."

Despite my methodological hesitations, I was also intrigued by the radical potential of oral history to document lost histories and histories of loss. Both gay and lesbian as well as activist history have ephemeral, unorthodox, and frequently suppressed archives, and in both cases, oral history can be a crucial tool for the preservation of history through memory. It can help create the public culture that turns what seems like idiosyncratic feeling into historical experience. I have been inspired by the model of ethnographic works such as *Cherry Grove* and *Boots of Leather, Slippers of Gold*, in which queer scholars such as Esther Newton, Madeline Davis, and Liz Kennedy come to oral history as members of the communities they document and unabashedly acknowledge their personal investment in their material.[23] Another compelling influence has been documentary film, and in particular queer autoethnographies, including work by Carlomusto, Bordowitz, Marlon Riggs, and Ellen Spiro, in which the documentary maker's story enters the frame, and in which the process of collecting and archiving is charged with affect.[24] Thus, mixed in with my skepticism about oral history were curiosity and fascination. I was driven by the compulsion to document that is so frequently, I think, engendered by the ephemerality of queer communities and counterpublics; alongside the fierce conviction of how meaningful and palpable these alternative life worlds can be lies the fear that they will remain invisible or be lost. Oral history can capture something of the lived experience of participating in a counterpublic, offering, if nothing else, testimony to the fact that it existed. Often as ephemeral as the very cultures it seeks to document (since both tapes and transcripts are records of a live event that is past), oral history is loaded with emotional urgency and need.[25]

In this respect, queer community histories share something with testimony, the genre that brings together trauma studies and oral history. Testimony has been viewed by some as an impossible genre, an attempt to represent the unrepresentable.[26] Trauma poses limits and challenges for oral history, forcing consideration of how the interview process itself may be traumatically invasive or marked by forms of self-censorship and the work of the unconscious. Gay and lesbian oral histories, as forms of insider ethnography, have much to contribute to this project, including a sense of the complexity of gathering information about sexual intimacy that can be applied to the study of trauma's emotional intimacies. I have wanted to see for myself how the process of testimony works by interviewing a group of people who, while they may not be trauma survivors themselves, have lived, as activists and lesbians, in close proximity to a national trauma. My goal has been to use interviews to create political history as affective history, a history that captures activism's felt and even traumatic dimensions. In forging a collective knowledge built on memory, I hope to produce not only a version of history but also an archive of the emotions, which is one of trauma's most important, but most difficult to preserve, legacies.

Freighted with methodological, theoretical, and psychic baggage, the interview process was always both humbling and revelatory. The burden of intimacy, of encouraging people to talk about their emotional experience even when I didn't know them especially well, was an ongoing challenge. The labor of sympathetic listening in order to facilitate someone else's articulation of her experience was often exhausting, and I felt myself overwhelmed by all the voices in my head. Even with the help of the protocols for gathering life histories, where the emphasis is on open-ended questions that enable interviewees to tell their stories as they see fit, I worried about being too invasive and not representing people's stories adequately, especially since I also had my own agendas and wanted the interviews to address my concerns. The actual labor and practice of interviewing has informed this project as much as the content of the interviews themselves has, giving me a healthy respect for the difficulty of gathering archives of testimony as well as a passionate conviction that they are valuable precisely because so ephemeral.

What follows is an account of my research, based on interviews with twenty-four women, almost all of them lesbians.[27] Most of them were members of ACT UP/NY during its initial and most active years, from 1987 to 1992, but some of them were involved even after that. Extremely significant for my thinking has been a cluster of interviews with women who were not members of ACT UP but were involved with AIDS activism; in addition to having valuable comments about ACT UP, their stories about AIDS activism in the years prior to ACT UP's formation are a reminder not to make the mistake of equating ACT UP with AIDS activism. This is not a reconstruction of ACT UP's history, complete with chronologies and important events. Instead, it is an exploration of the ongoing uses of that history in the lives of those who participated in it. My focus is on the affective life of ACT UP, including experiences of both love and loss, and especially on relationships and political controversies that are marked by ambivalence and conflict, and thus resistant to documentation.

The affective public culture of ACT UP

> There was a time in my life when I didn't know anybody who wasn't queer. I didn't know anybody who wasn't involved in ACT UP. I didn't have time for you if you didn't talk about or want to hear about what was going on with AIDS. . . . We all seemed to be living and breathing the AIDS crisis.
>
> (Alexis Danzig)[28]

> I have so much fondness and respect for the people I worked with in ACT UP. I feel like there's something really special when I run into them. I don't know. It's not like going to school together. It's something else. You took a stand with this person. It's knowing that in some very, very important way you shared at least some basic values with this person. You may not have had a friendship, you may have had other, outside interests. You may like different movies, you may dress in different clothes, but at some point you shared some very important values with this person, and we built something incredible together.
>
> (Zoe Leonard)

> I decided at some point early on that ACT UP was a collection of really idiosyncratic weirdos, myself included—that it is a group of fringe types who don't fit in in a lot of other places. That's one reason they're at ACT UP. It is an activist group that came into existence and survived because it attracted a particular kind of person who didn't need social approval, who had never gotten the social approval, and therefore, was willing to step out and do civil disobedience, confront authority. I think that there are a finite number of people in the world who will act like that, and that it may be no more than 10 percent of any given population, and maybe even, a lot less than that. . . . It is a great gift to find those other people, and you develop an enormous respect and love for every one of them.
>
> (Ann Northrop)

> People were so angry because there really had not been a place to vent your rage about what was going on. It's so hard to remember what it was like then, with people just getting sick and dying. There were no drugs available, and there was a lot of blame—blaming gay men for having the disease, for promiscuity, for anal sex. [ACT UP] gave people a place to be with other people who were as angry as they were. In most people's lives—at work and with friends—it's not really possible to have that level of venting. People look at you like you're crazy. So [ACT UP] was a really cathartic place.
>
> (Amy Bauer)

It really did take on an urgency that made you want to do anything. I began to live in this world where you got to know people, and you got to love them, and you laughed with them and found out how beautiful they were, and they were going to die. In some cases you watched them fucking die. That just seemed immensely unfair. In sort of a naive way, it's like, "You've got to be kidding." I suddenly have this place where who I am is validated, where I can be who I am, as a lesbian, as kind of a crazy, mad person, as a very emotional person, and there are people like me there. They like me and they love me, and they're there for me. We have fun together, this is a blast, and you're telling me they're going to be fucking dead in a few months, or a year, or two years? No way. That just made you enraged. That made you want to do anything, and it made you want to break the glass in the limo as it was coming up to the demonstration. It was crazy making.

(Heidi Dorow)

I think ACT UP did provide a psychic healing, or comfort, or community that was useful during a time of crisis for a lot of people, but not all the people. It's like the high school thing. You run into people and you say, "Oh, what have you been doing since high school?" . . . One thing that's become clear to me is that there were people who did find what they needed or made what they needed, either within the leadership of ACT UP or in an affinity group. For women and people of color, there were so few of us that we found it among each other. . . . And now, talking to a lot of people who weren't part of any of those things—a lot of white guys—again, I realize women and people of color really had a different relation to ACT UP. But to talk to some of these guys—it was difficult for them too. It really did feel like high school for them too. Few of their needs were being satisfied, they felt left out, they were desperate, they didn't know where else to go, and they just felt shitty about themselves all the time because there were so many cliques, including a popular clique.

(Catherine Gund)

I felt like around women's issues you really had to watch your step. I came into ACT UP with that attitude, and that definitely permeated my interaction with people, and maybe I also wondered a little bit, as I became more involved in the organization, "Who are these women who were initially in ACT UP?" They really wanted to work with men, and that was very strange to me. I couldn't really understand it, as drawn as I was to the power of the organization, the ability to get things done, its far-reaching political agenda—these were things I respected.

I wasn't so sure I wanted to work with men. So that was the rub. Yet I did develop many close friendships with men, of course. Knee-jerk reactions aside, reality takes over and you have friendships. But I think the women in ACT UP, who were there from the start, must have trusted men politically in a way that I didn't. That would be my guess. Not that they weren't feminists. I'm not saying that at all, or that they didn't have radical politics or understand the oppression and power between men and women. Maybe they just had more trust or something.

(Tracy Morgan)

Every time I would come down there with my two dark-skinned little boys, and my red and orange hair from Miss Clairol, from the South Bronx, never once did I feel like I didn't belong there. Never. On the contrary. I was always made to feel so welcome. We bickered about how to put things together, or this issue was more important than that one, but I never felt that sense of "she doesn't belong here."

(Marina Alvarez)

Some things that happened at these actions were lousy. Because going to prison is horrible. Socializing was great because there was a good chance you would know someone in your prison cell if you had to sit there all day. It was scary being in there. There is always that uneasy feeling when the door slams. I'm really locked in. It's not pleasant. The social networks helped sustain me, give me the extra oomph of wanting to do these things.

(Jean Carlomusto)

I think doing activism, particularly on the level that we do it, gives you a personal trust in people. We used to joke in ACT UP that we would judge people by, if you were thrown into a cell for forty-eight hours, who would you want to be with? Both who would be fun to be with, but also who would you trust not to get you killed in that time?

(Amy Bauer)

So the passion with which, the emotion with which people came into this movement and this organization, which was personal—"Either I'm going to die, or someone I love is going to die"—really forces you to cut through the bullshit when it comes to friendship and relationships. You are in it. There's stuff you're dealing with that most friendships don't deal with in a lifetime. And they were all compressed. It was all compressed into this tight, extraordinary little four-year period. Every single week, every Monday night. There was a big joke: "Does the virus take a vacation?" We used to joke, "You can't take a vacation. The virus doesn't take a vacation." That was another thing. There was a great sense of humor and irony. I learned what irony was in that group, from gay men.

(Maria Maggenti)

Of the whole group of people whom I was really friends with, there is definitely a feeling of incredible shared history. At the same time, there are also friendships that for me are over for natural causes. We came together at a certain moment and our lives have changed significantly, and we're no longer in each other's spheres. But the intensity was really intense. It sounds sort of lame to say that. . . . But it was simply the way we all seemed to be living at the time. It felt very normal.

(Alexis Danzig)

For a lot of people, ACT UP was like a zombie from outer space that ate away at the rest of their life. . . . It got in the way of their job. It got in the way of their relationships or their other friendships, and since ACT UP couldn't meet their needs, eventually they got really mad at it and they burned out.

(Amy Bauer)

Collaborative work is so important—but it's like relationships. They're so important, but you have to be so careful about who you get involved with because it can be a complete disaster. It's a relationship. It's made me think more seriously about who I choose to collaborate with.

(Jean Carlomusto)

Years later it was hard to see some of the people with whom I had shared so much—jail time, tears, and sex. It was too emotional. It was extraordinary. . . . The whole thing was so intense. . . . My life now is intense but I've learned how to live it. I can get in it, understand it, enjoy it, accept it, and make something of it—and be relaxed. And I don't feel relaxed around some people from that time because it was just so crazy. Our friends started dying in our early twenties and there we were in no way prepared for that.

(Catherine Gund)

We also went to one motel on that same trip, I'll never forget, where we were refused. In fact, we were refused at a number of motels because they saw that there were obviously gay men with us. And somebody asked, "Does anybody in this group have AIDS?" and we said, "Yeah, just about everybody does." And they said, "We're sorry. We don't have any rooms." We moved on and on and on until we found a place. Some gay men in one town loaned us their house. We all took a day off and went to the beach. We had a great time. I have pictures from it. It was hilarious. We went swimming. It was amazing.

That to me was the glue that kept that group together. From the outside, it looked like everyone was always yelling, "Fuck you, government, and fuck you—," but in fact, the kind of behind-the-scenes of it was a lot of parties, a lot of drinking, a lot of eating, a lot of love affairs, and extraordinary friendships. That's what kept me in it for so long. It couldn't just have been "doing the right thing," although that was obviously a motivating factor, and a significant factor. That was also the glue. But it was also a lot of fun.

(Maria Maggenti)

I've started by quoting at length from the interviews in order to give as much prominence as possible to the words of the activists themselves. The interviews have a life of their own, and both here and elsewhere I include long blocks of quotations without commentary in order to convey a sense of the larger archive. I think of these sections as themselves an archive installed within the body of my text. Although the editorial process of excision and juxtaposition inserts my own agenda into this archive, the resulting montage creates many layers of meaning, and I especially like the way the quotations speak to one another not only in their agreements but their disagreements.[29] They have a cumulative force beyond their individual meanings.

The above montage is meant to convey the passion and excitement inspired by ACT UP, and the highs and lows of its vibrant social life. Explaining her attraction, Amy Bauer says: "It was a very queer place. It was really queer, you know, to the core, and that was very appealing. I sort of instantaneously liked a lot of the people in it, or felt at home in it." Ann Northrop describes not only her initial enthusiasm but also her ongoing commitment: "I just fell in love, my first night in the room. . . . It was stunning to me to be able to walk into a room where I agreed with everyone there. That's what has kept me there for eleven years now [fifteen years in 2002], because it's the one place I can count on going and having an honest conversation with people whose values I share." The women talk about going dancing in clubs with ACT UP men after meetings, developing beloved friendships and even romances, and building rituals and traditions such as the annual queer Jewish seder hosted by Alexis Danzig and Gregg Bordowitz; they discuss a wide array of affective networks that underpin activism. Their remarks express the sense that the bonds formed through activism, through sharing a jail cell or values, are particular and special. Jean Carlomusto offers a reminder of how friendship compensates for the unpleasant aspects of activism. Moreover, in ACT UP, the specter of death added to the stakes of friendship; as Heidi Dorow observes, it was impossible to believe that the precious community she had just found was going to be taken away from her. Thus, ACT UP's camaraderie was central to its activism, and it fostered strong bonds between gay men and lesbians that gave substance to newly emerging notions of queer identities and politics. Maxine Wolfe says, "It created a community more than simply a political group."

If friendships and affective networks were a crucial source of ACT UP's power, they were a volatile source, although no more so than the desires and investments that underpin any relationship. References (such as Catherine Gund's) to high school figure prominently in representations of ACT UP as a social milieu in which some people were "in" and others were "out." Says Cynthia Schneider, "I always had such mixed feelings about it, and I think I did at the time. The whole ACT UP scene was such a 'star culture.' It was so much like, 'Who's been out there and who's performing for the whole group?' . . . There were certain people who were so much trying to get attention." The powerful sense of belonging that some people found is therefore matched by the ambivalence of others. Tracy Morgan, for example, was reluctant to work with men and couldn't understand the enthusiasm of the other women she encountered in the group. Involved with a man when she came to ACT UP, she remarked that, "it felt like if you were going to be a woman in this place, you should be a lesbian." There were identifications and disidentifications, including the shared sense of disidentification indicated by Northrop's portrait of the "idiosyncratic weirdos" who made common cause in ACT UP. The lines of inclusion and exclusion are not predictable; for example, Marina Alvarez's comments about her sense of belonging provide a cautionary note against generalizing about ACT UP's racial politics. Moreover, it would appear that if friendship was ACT UP's strength, it was also a liability. As Maggenti and others attest, their activism became so absorbing that they had no other life beyond it, and they could only be friends with those who shared their activist lives. For some people, such as Bauer and Northrop, who remained active members of ACT UP well past its prime, the key to long-term involvement was not to make ACT UP the center of their social life. Offered in hindsight, the comments in this archive convey a vivid sense of both the preciousness of activist relationships and their transitoriness; not only were they interrupted by death but they were specific to the context of activism, and in many cases their intensity could not be sustained. Yet this ephemerality does not make them any less real or important, and descriptions of relationships lost are matched by those of lasting friendships forged in ACT UP.

Although ACT UP's formation of a queer community is distinctive, a focus on its lesbian members also reveals strong ties to histories of feminist organizing. The lesbians in ACT UP had a crucial and visible role, disproportionate to their numbers, because so many of them came to ACT UP with previous political experience and contributed organizing skills. Ranging in age from their early twenties to forties when they got involved in AIDS activism, they had experience with the civil rights and antiwar movements, feminism and the women's reproductive health movement of the 1970s and 1980s—including the Feminist Women's Health Centers, Women's Pentagon Action, and Seneca Peace Camp—the gay rights movement, and the sex wars. Even younger women who were just out of college (a common trajectory for arriving in ACT UP and a sign of its class profile) had experience with lesbian and gay organizations, divestment protests, and other kinds of campus activism. Some women first got involved with ACT UP because their specific skills led to invitations; Bauer came to the first Wall Street protest in March 1987 because she knew how to organize a demonstration, and Carlomusto was there because she could operate a video camera. In some cases, ACT UP provided an important respite from fractures within political communities, especially feminist ones. Kim Christensen, for instance, had been ostracized by the lesbian community in Northampton, Massachusetts, in part because of her self-identification as bisexual. Wolfe and Sarah Schulman had been driven out of the Committee for Abortion Rights and Against Sterilization Abuse (CARASA) for homophobic reasons. And Amber Hollibaugh, one of the people outside ACT UP whom I interviewed, turned to AIDS activism in flight from the vehemence and bitterness of the feminist sex wars of the early 1980s.

Almost unanimously, these experienced women note how dramatically ACT UP differed from other kinds of activism. After many years of working within left organizations, Wolfe was impressed with how ACT UP "cut an incredibly broad stripe across the lesbian and gay community in New York," and represented an unprecedented case of "organizing the unorganized." She says, "I felt like I was organizing in there as well as outside of there, that it was an opportunity to open the minds of people who had their minds opened, and that anyone could stand up and say anything, and if you had a good idea, people would do it." Coming from years of experience with Feminist Women's Health Centers and radical left groups, Marion Banzhaf had been determined not to join another group in which one person was the leader:

> ACT UP, even very early on, was very exciting because this was a different kind of group. It was not a top-down group, it was a bottom-up group, even though there were hierarchies within ACT UP about who was cool and who got to cruise who and who got to do what. It was still a very democratic group. . . . So ACT UP was thrilling. Because, also, it was about people actually fighting for their lives, so it was very immediate.

Speaking about AIDS activism more generally, Hollibaugh emphasizes how dramatically it challenged movement politics and changed the relation between insiders and outsiders:

> None of our movements had done the kind of work you ended up having to do in order to guarantee the most fundamental rights for someone who was getting sick. So it was really an extraordinary thing for me. It changed the way I understood activism. There's no way that you have the privilege of just being an outsider when you're fighting an epidemic. You can always be right when you're in an outsider position. Your placard can always sound clever. Your chants can always sound correct. But when you've got to make sure that somebody gets bathed in a hospital, you've got to try to figure out how to maintain that radical position and how to get inside that hospital at the same time, so that when you're not there, that person is still getting cleaned in a way that respects their dignity.

Although Hollibaugh did not find ACT UP a compelling arena for her own AIDS activism (in the 1980s, she worked in the AIDS Discrimination Unit of the New York City Commission on Human Rights), her sentiments echo those of many of ACT UP's members who have long histories of political experience—that AIDS activism was an arena of tremendous possibility for them, and that rather than finding it wanting compared with other political causes or organizations, they are grateful for its lessons.

If political experience and cultural capital made ACT UP a "powerful and volatile" organization (in Christensen's words), another element in the mix was the urgency of illness and death. Like many of the men, a large number of women mention coming to ACT UP out of the immediacy of emotional need. Their anecdotes tell a collective story about the importance of friendships between lesbians and gay men, and between artists, both of which occur within public cultures that frequently overlap in New York. David Wojnarowicz had been telling Zoe Leonard how exciting ACT UP was, and she came with him to a meeting on the same day that he told her he was HIV+. Schneider went with Todd Haynes, who was one of her best friends from Brown University and with whom she had collaborated on the short film *Superstar*. Gund came with Ray Navarro, who along with Ellen Spiro and others who joined ACT UP, was her fellow student in the Whitney Program. Not to be underestimated, then, is the concrete power of a specific individual relationship to serve as an entrée into ACT UP. The result, according to Leonard, was an extremely diverse mix:

> I think there were some conscious efforts later to try to expand our vision and expand who felt comfortable in that room. That's something I'm sure you've heard from a lot of people. A big problem with ACT UP was its racial and economic limitations. But I do think it gained from a certain kind of mix, where someone like me came into that room because I knew people who were dying. I had friends who were dying. I didn't come into that room because I was involved in a certain college, and I didn't come into that room because I was queer. I met people in that room who were older than me, younger than me, who had different backgrounds from me, because we had this one, other thing in common: that someone we knew or loved was either dead or dying of AIDS.

I would suggest that coming to ACT UP for either political or personal reasons, to the extent they are separable, were both equally essential to the power of the organization. In the face of hostile questions, sometimes from other feminists, about why lesbians would be interested in AIDS activism, they entered a culture in which, as some assert, the distinction between being HIV+ and HIV− was often far more salient than differences in gender. Within the many stories lesbians tell about why they came to ACT UP are insights about disidentifications with feminism, the origins of queer social formations in friendships between gay men and lesbians that assumed public visibility in the AIDS crisis, and the way a diversity of motives and resources strengthened the group.

My focus on ACT UP's lesbians both confirms and disrupts the presumption that ACT UP is predominantly white, middle class, and privileged. Although all but one of the women I interviewed is white, almost half of them are also Jewish, which inflects the ways in which they live their ethnic and political identities. College education, the mark of both class and cultural capital, figures prominently in the stories that many of them tell about their activist histories, but a great number of them, including those with college degrees, also mention coming from poor or working-class backgrounds. Also significant as a mark of cultural privilege is ACT UP's location in New York. Dorow and Polly Thistlethwaite both mention coming from small towns and being drawn to as well as overwhelmed by New York City; Dorow talks about feeling like a "hick" in ACT UP. The number of artists I interviewed is also notable since this category can mean high cultural capital but low economic status, and is thus complicated to gauge in terms of class. Ultimately, it seems reductive to describe ACT UP as white and middle class or to do so dismissively rather than as an entry point into a more detailed account of what white, middle-class politics looks like, especially when crossed with other categories such as being Jewish, an artist, or queer, or living in New York.

At the same time, the demographics of ACT UP's lesbians are relatively homogeneous when compared with the profile of Marina Alvarez, who was the only Puerto Rican and person of color, as well as the only HIV+ person I interviewed. Her story is distinctive within the interviews; she is a recovering drug addict who learned of her HIV status while in prison and later found her way to an AIDS peer-education program in the South Bronx after having been through a twelve-step program. Through her work with the peer-education program, she met members of ACT UP's Latino Caucus and began to attend ACT UP meetings in addition to becoming an outspoken person with AIDS (PWA) at conferences and government meetings, especially those pertaining to women with HIV. Alvarez has collaborated with Spiro on the video *(In)Visible Women* about women with AIDS; she has been involved with Gund's *Positive: Life With HIV* television series and has acted as a consultant to pharmaceutical. companies. As her comments in the opening section suggest, she felt very much a part of ACT UP and responded passionately to its organizational power and style of direct action. But her remarks also redefine the meaning of activism, when she talks, for example, about her response to other HIV+ women in prison:

> Right in the prison, something happened for me, and I know today, when I think back, that my activism started right there. First of all, as a person, I say I speak three languages. I speak Spanish, English, and compassion. From the way that my life is and my personality, I've always been a very, very compassionate person. So when women who had AIDS in 1985, in this particular institution, were ostracized—which is literally what happened to them—their food was placed in front of their cell. They were not touched. They were "skived." Nobody wanted to be around them. People would talk about them, make comments about them. Immediately. Immediately, in my heart, I felt the compassion for them.

Alvarez proceeded to help these other women, demonstrating the activism that arises from the needs of daily life. She also strongly identifies as a mother and credits her children with giving her the motivation to get off drugs and survive. Notable, too, is the way her activism is an extension of providing the emotional support and care for people that she learned from her twelve-step support groups. As she puts it in an interview with Ginetta Candelario, "Among Latina/os, the family itself often becomes part of the care of HIV-positive family members. This is a form of activism because there is a group of people involved in care, not just the patient and a doctor. Also, there's an implicit challenge to community denial of the existence of AIDS through caregiving activities."[30]

When I made the trip to the South Bronx, where I had never been before, I not only acutely felt my own whiteness but was reminded of the extent to which most of my other interviews were a form of insider ethnography where I felt comfortable with my narrators because of a range of shared experiences that often went without saying. The difference is also apparent in geographic terms; I only did one other interview outside of Manhattan (Wolfe is happily ensconced in Brooklyn just down the street from the Lesbian Herstory Archives), and within Manhattan, Chelsea was as far north as I got. While I had thought that some of the pitfalls of ethnographic research could be avoided by sticking close to home and interviewing people like me, it was absolutely invaluable to take the risk of making a mistake and hearing from someone whose experience is utterly unlike mine. Interviewing Alvarez was also a reminder that there were other women of color with HIV who were prominent activists, women like Iris de la Cruz or Katrina Haslip, whom I couldn't interview because they have died. Moreover, Alvarez debunked any presumption that ACT UP was exclusionary by enthusiastically claiming a sense of kinship. In fact, at least as powerful as feelings of exclusion based on differences of identity such as gender or race were cases of what

Freud would call a "narcissism of small differences," feelings of not being liked, of being out and not in.

In some cases, the sense of ACT UP as an exclusive social arena was enough to keep people out of the group. Alisa Lebow, for example, mentions ACT UP's social style as one reason that it was not for her, although she also extends her observations to comment on ACT UP's political limitations:

> What I was not able to swallow in the few ACT UP meetings I went to were the group dynamics and the cliquishness. It felt too much like a "scene" for me. There were a lot of cute boys and girls who thought they were being really hip, mostly upper middle class and white, and it was as much a party as it was politics. And while I don't object to partying and politicking, at the same time it just was not for me. . . . The kind of activism that was needed then and is needed now has never really been done, and that is being able to mobilize the poor and working-class communities of color in the city and around the country. I think I always felt that with ACT UP. They were never going to touch those communities in any significant way.

Hollibaugh, with whom Lebow worked at the New York City Commission on Human Rights doing AIDS education and media work, expressed similar reservations about ACT UP's failure to address issues of class and race fully.[31] Hollibaugh's and Lebow's comments are also a reminder that some people were not more involved with ACT UP because they were already intensively involved with other kinds of AIDS activism (Lebow, for example, also worked at GMHC with Gregg Bordowitz and Jean Carlomusto) and thus didn't need ACT UP as a point of entry into the fight against AIDS.

Another example is the case of Jane Rosett, who was immersed in her work in the People with AIDS Coalition (PWAC) of which she was a founding member more than four years before ACT UP began. (Rosett was the only founder of PWAC who did not have AIDS, and the only woman.) Also a cofounder of the Community Research Initiative and People With AIDS Health Group, Rosett was already deeply involved, as both a treatment activist and a photographer, in issues pertaining to the underground AIDS treatment community. Because of her awareness of the political ramifications of her status as a non-PWA working within the PWA movement, Rosett chose to play a more invisible role.

> Because of my unique access to less public—often underground—activities, I believed that the greatest contribution I had to offer was to continue my less visible activist work within the people with AIDS movement. I had already been entrenched for over four years within the PWA movement—as distinct from the broader AIDS movement—when ACT UP came along. And my early PWA movement work was a natural extension of my ongoing disability rights work.
>
> So, while I was involved with the town meeting at which ACT UP was born and attended the first several actions, very soon after it became obvious that ACT UP was quite well saturated, specifically with documentarians. Too often people mark the beginning of AIDS activism with the founding of ACT UP. But by then, generations of PWAs had died fighting for their lives.
>
> Until ACT UP rendered AIDS activism "chic" within the dyke world, lesbians working in the early AIDies were often dismissed as confused fag hags and, far from experiencing any sense of "community," we were quite isolated from other lesbian activists, who had specifically chosen not to do AIDS work.

(Jane Rosett)[32]

Rosett's remarks, like those of other non-ACT UPers, offer valuable testimony to the vital forms of AIDS activism that preceded ACT UP's formation and that also need to be part of the historical record.

Viewed from the "minority" position of its lesbian and women members, ACT UP emerges as more complex and diverse than it might otherwise appear to be, and as a group whose members are well aware of its possible limitations. For example, the reasons for tensions between men and women in ACT UP were perceptively analyzed by Christensen, who maintains that ACT UP was an interesting coalition not just across gender but also class lines, in which women with political experience collaborated with men who had access to cultural and economic resources.

> I think what made ACT UP both powerful and eventually what made it fall apart was that it was the coming together of men of predominantly one class background and women of predominantly lower-class backgrounds—not low-class backgrounds, not like where some of us were coming from. But a lot of the men in ACT UP were coming from what I would call at least PMC [professional managerial class] and sometimes higher. . . . They had access to people, to resources, to media outlets. . . . But it's also then combined—and this is what I think made it both powerful and volatile—combined with a lot of people, predominantly women and some men of color, who were not from that class background but who had the political skills that these white guys needed. They knew how to put out a press release, but they didn't know how to organize a demonstration. Peter organize a demonstration? Please. He couldn't have done it to save his damn life, literally. I think what made it work so well was that those of us from the political backgrounds brought those skills. But we could not call the *New York Times* the way that Larry Kramer could. But Larry could make the phone call, and we could be kicking his ass to tell him what to say. I think that's what made it actually work for as long as it did. . . . A lot of things that in retrospect were very much about class looked like they were just about gender and got fought out in terms of gender. . . . I think the intersection of class and gender in that organization was complicated, very complicated, and often kind of subterranean.

While offering a critical appraisal of the men's privilege, Christensen also appreciates their cultural access in constituting ACT UP as what she calls an "uneasy coalition." She is not alone in articulating a critique of ACT UP's class and gender politics from within—a critique, however, that can see the group's tensions and precariousness as part of its power. Not only does gender become more complicated when linked to class but class is also a nuanced category. Christensen draws distinctions within middle-class identities to articulate the differences between the men and women since even if they were of "predominantly lower-class backgrounds" than the men, many women had middle-class jobs as well as the cultural capital that comes with being college graduates, artists, and writers. Like the distinctions between being "in" and "out," these nuanced differences suggest the complexity of affinities within political groups—affinities that are as refined as personal tastes and sensibilities. These "queer" affections produced unusual forms of fierce love and bonding, but also points of conflict and distress.

[. . .]

Activist shame

My decision to write about conflicts within ACT UP has been a difficult one, pervaded by the fear of "airing dirty laundry" and creating a picture of ACT UP that detracts from its many accomplishments. I take inspiration, however, from Amber Hollibaugh, who recognizes the powerful dynamics of shame within political movements, and I'd like to close [. . .] by considering not only her comments in my interviews but her recent work on the concept of "dangerous desires."[33] [. . .] I was eager to interview Hollibaugh not only to get a sense of her work with two projects outside ACT UP—the AIDS Discrimination Unit of the New York City Commission on Human Rights in the 1980s and the Lesbian AIDS Project at GMHC in the 1990s—but also because I was curious about the connection between her earlier history with the sex wars and her subsequent move to AIDS activism. Hollibaugh is no stranger to the feeling of being "uncomfortable" in political organizations that is described by some of the other AIDS activists. She cites many experiences—as a lesbian within leftist and antiwar politics, as a high femme in gay and lesbian movements of the 1970s, as a working-class sex radical in feminist movements of the early 1980s—of being an outsider within her own movement. She describes how the sex wars brought her to AIDS activism, as "the one place I could figure out where my activism, my sexual politics, and my understanding of class and gender and race would be valued contributions rather than making me 'other,' and to be isolated and stayed away from."

Hollibaugh speaks passionately about the terrible consequences of movements that ostracize and shame people, and when I asked her about whether sexual desires and identities are particularly prone to such dynamics, she responded by making links between sexual desire and activism:

> Around sexuality, I think people believe very quickly that they're deviant, and that they're not part of a collective experience that they can use to buffer some of the impact of criticism. So when you say to somebody, "There's something wrong with you. There's something deviant or perverse about your desires," it's the loneliest, most dangerous, and most vulnerable place, and the place I think people are least able to resist and come to terms with themselves and still be open about their own issues. . . . I think the loneliness of that early sex radical politics was exactly—I think we were brave there in a way that was different than other kinds of slights and humiliations that come in political movements, which I think aren't good. But around sexuality I think people are more vulnerable, more isolatable, and more prone to believe that they are in the wrong. Being a sexual minority in your own movement is a very uncomfortable position. I've been out now as a high femme for twenty years almost, and this is not a point of pleasure for me. It's given me great pleasure, but it's an extraordinarily difficult place to defend. . . . It's very hard to hold out for the right to be profoundly sexual; to hold out for your own desires; to figure out what they mean and claim them, when they even seem a little dicey to you. It's not gay pride.

Closely connected to sexuality are feelings of belonging and vulnerability that are fundamental to political organizing. Hollibaugh's remarks name humiliation and shame as problems for political movements, which can purport to embrace freedom while making people fearful of articulating their most deeply held desires and feelings. They help explain why my interviews might contain only fleeting hints of personal experiences of both love and death, and especially those experiences where one has felt most isolated or alone. Included in this category are political conflicts that can also leave people feeling isolated by the convictions that are most dear to them.

As Hollibaugh contends, "Our refusal to take on sex is one of the fundamental reasons we have not created a larger movement. Because we refuse to incorporate the dynamic of danger and vulnerability and sexuality into our organizing, and that is what sex represents in most people's eyes. It's the thing that they either never have or that they lose everything in order to have." In both her interview with me and *Dangerous Desires*, Hollibaugh dramatizes this point by telling the story of how she attempted suicide after a Gay Pride march in San Francisco in 1978 that was a show of force against Anita Bryant's antigay campaigns in Florida.

> I was proud to be part of it that year, angry and defiant about all the homophobia surrounding us. I was also full of inarticulate grief. The fundamental importance of gay liberation was unequivocally clear to me. But my desires, the way I felt and expressed my own queer femme sexuality, now positioned me outside the rights I was marching to defend. My internal erotic identity made me an alien to the politics of my own movement—a movement I had helped start, a movement whose growth and survival I was committed to.[34]

Hollibaugh's willingness to make her own story public underscores the persistence of vulnerability and isolation even for an experienced activist dedicated to sexual liberation. "When individual desire rides that fiercely through a person's intrinsic, intimate set of principles, there can be no resolution of the crisis without an extraordinary self-confrontation, a coming to terms. Because of that, this story is important to tell and remember."[35] Her testimony and use of it offer legitimation of what might seem like painfully personal stories as a crucial part of the archive of activism.

Hollibaugh's comments suggest that one of the contributions of sexual politics can be models of organizing that are more attentive to the dynamics of shame and isolation that complicate activism. My use of oral history to investigate the affective complexity of activism complements Hollibaugh's call for new forms of political organizing that can do justice to sexuality, and by implication, emotion. Even when the interviews point to places where things cannot be said or articulated, they are a way into an understanding of activism that can accommodate the full range of its affects, including not just its camaraderie and righteous indignation but also its ambivalences and disagreements. While an oral history of ACT UP constitutes a record of its accomplishments, it is a tool for exploring political difficulties and challenges as well. As such, oral history is itself a complex tool, sometimes revealing these issues only through gaps and silences within the interviews and conflicts between them. But this material, too, is part of the archive of activism, particularly an archive that focuses on feelings.

Notes

1   See Cvetkovich, *Mixed Feelings*.
2   Berlant, "Poor Eliza," 657.
3   For another investigation of how ACT UP combines emotion and politics, see Deborah Gould, "Sex, Death, and the Politics of Anger: Emotion and Reason in ACT UP's Fight Against AIDS" (Ph.D. diss., University of Chicago, 2000). I thank Gould for sharing her work with me.
4   For a discussion of cultural activism, see Douglas Crimp, ed. *AIDS: Cultural Analysis/Cultural Activism* (Cambridge: MIT Press, 1997). The DIVA-TV (Damned Interfering Video Activists) collective made *Target City Hall* (1989), *Pride* (1989), and *Like a Prayer* (1991). The compilation *Video against AIDS*

(Video Data Bank, 1989), available from Video Data Bank at 112 South Michigan Avenue, Chicago, Ill. 60603, includes many important videos from this period, including *Testing the Limits: NYC* (Part One) (1987) and segments of Gay Men's Health Crisis's *Living with AIDS* series, which was coproduced by Gregg Bordowitz and Jean Carlomusto. For a graphics archive and an account of major ACT UP demonstrations between 1987 and 1990, see Douglas Crimp and Adam Rolston, *AIDS Demo Graphics* (Seattle: Bay Press, 1990). (Indicative, though, of the danger of losing access to ACT UP's history is the fact that this book is out of print.) A key guide to AIDS activist video is Alexandra Juhasz, *AIDS TV: Identity, Community, and Alternative Video* (Durham, N.C.: Duke University Press, 1995), which includes an annotated videography by Catherine Saalfield. Many of these videos are included in the Royal S. Marks Collection in the New York Public Library, which was assembled with support from the Estate Project for Artists with AIDS.

5   See ACT UP/NY Women and AIDS Book Group, *Women, AIDS, and Activism* (Boston: South End Press, 1990); and *Doctors, Liars, and Women*, dir. Jean Carlomusto and Maria Maggenti, on *Video against AIDS* (Video Data Bank, 1989). For a discussion of these works and other AIDS activist videos, see Ann Cvetkovich, "AIDS and Video Activism," in *Art, Activism, and Oppositionality: Essays from Afterimage*, ed. Grant Kester (Durham, N.C.: Duke University Press, 1998), 182–98. On women and AIDS activism, as well as *Doctors, Liars, and Women*, see Paula A. Treichler, "Beyond *Cosmo*: AIDS, Identity, and Inscriptions of Gender," *How to Have Theory in an Epidemic: Cultural Chronicles of AIDS* (Durham, N.C.: Duke University Press, 1999), 235–77.

6   See, for example, Peter F. Cohen, *Love and Anger: Essays on AIDS, Activism, and Politics* (New York: Harrington Park Press, 1998).

7   Jean Carlomusto, interview with the author, 31 January 2000. [. . .]

8   I have been helped in this enterprise by an ongoing body of scholarship on AIDS and AIDS activism. Sources that have been especially important for my work include John Nguyet Erni, *Unstable Frontiers: Technomedicine and the Cultural Politics of "Curing" AIDS* (Minneapolis: University of Minnesota Press, 1994); Cindy Patton, *Fatal Advice: How Safe-Sex Education Went Wrong* (Durham, N.C.: Duke University Press, 1994); Steven Epstein, *Impure Science: AIDS, Activism, and the Politics of Knowledge* (Berkeley: University of California Press, 1996); David Román, *Acts of Intervention: Performance, Gay Culture, and AIDS* (Bloomington: Indiana University Press, 1998); Treichler, *How to Have Theory in an Epidemic*; and Cathy J. Cohen, *The Boundaries of Blackness: AIDS and the Breakdown of Black Politics* (Chicago: University of Chicago Press, 1999).

9   See Sarah Schulman, *People in Trouble* (New York: Dutton, 1990), and *Rat Bohemia* (New York: Dutton, 1995); *DiAna's Hair Ego: AIDS Info Up Front*, dir. Ellen Spiro (Women Make Movies, 1989); *(In)Visible Women*, dir. Marina Alvarez and Ellen Spiro (Women Make Movies, 1991); *Greetings from out Here*, dir. Ellen Spiro (Video Data Bank, 1993); *Roam Sweet Home*, dir. Ellen Spiro (1996); and Zoe Leonard, *Strange Fruit* (New York: Paula Cooper Gallery, 1995), and *Secession: Zoe Leonard* (Vienna: Wiener Secession, 1997). Other examples include Catherine (Saalfield) Gund's video work, including the *Positive: Life with HIV* (1995) television series and *Hallelujah! The Ron Athey Story* (1998); and Jean Carlomusto's videos *To Catch a Glimpse* (1997) and *Shatzi Is Dying* (2000). [. . .]

10   ACT UP/NY's files are now cataloged and available in the manuscript collections of the New York Public Library.

11   See Berlant, *The Queen of America Goes to Washington City*.

12   See Caruth, *Trauma*; and Sturken, *Tangled Memories*.

13   Cathy Caruth and Thomas Keenan, "The AIDS Crisis Is-Not Over: A Conversation with Gregg Bordowitz, Douglas Crimp, and Laura Pinsky," in *Trauma: Explorations in Memory*, ed. Cathy Caruth (Baltimore, Md.: Johns Hopkins University Press, 1995), 256–71.

14   Douglas Crimp, "Mourning and Militancy," *October* 51 (Winter 1989), 3–18.

15   See Watney, *Policing Desire*, 7–8; and Wojnarowicz, *Close to the Knives*, 121–22.

16   See L. Brown, "Not outside the Range," 100–112.

17   This was some of the language used to describe the symptoms of PTSD in the 1980 DSM-III, but it was subsequently removed from the 1994 DSM-IV in part because of this problem. For an overview of the history of the diagnosis, see Young, *The Harmony of Illusions*.

18   See Eng and Kazanjian, introduction to *Loss*, 1–25.

19   See Dominick LaCapra, *Representing the Holocaust*, esp. 14–15, and "Conclusion: Acting-Out and Working-Through," 205–23.

20   For Douglas Crimp's own reflections on the current state of militancy, mourning, and the AIDS crisis, see "Melancholy and Moralism," in *Loss*, eds. David Eng and David Kazanjian (Berkeley: University of California Press, 2002), 188–202.

21   See Joan Scott, "The Evidence of Experience," in *The Lesbian and Gay Studies Reader*, eds. Henry Abelove, Michèle Aina Barale, and David M. Halperin (New York: Routledge, 1993), 397–415.

22 Gayatri Chakravorty Spivak, "Can the Subaltern Speak?" in *Marxism and the Interpretation of Culture*, eds. Lawrence Grossberg and Cary Nelson (Urbana and Chicago: University of Illinois Press, 1988), 271–313.

23 See Esther Newton, *Cherry Grove, Fire Island: Sixty Years in America's First Gay and Lesbian Town* (Boston: Beacon Press, 1993); and Davis and Kennedy, *Boots of Leather, Slippers of Gold*. My work has also been informed by experimental ethnography and the influence of cultural theory on anthropology, including the following works: James Clifford and George E. Marcus, *Writing Culture: The Poetic and Politics of Ethnography* (Berkeley: University of California Press, 1986); James Clifford, *The Predicament of Culture: Twentieth-Century Ethnography, Literature, and Art* (Cambridge: Harvard University Press, 1988); Kamala Visweswaran, *Fictions of Feminist Ethnography* (Minneapolis: University of Minnesota Press, 1994); Ruth Behar and Deborah Gordon, eds., *Women Writing Culture* (Berkeley: University of California Press, 1995); Ruth Behar, *The Vulnerable Observer: Anthropology That Breaks Your Heart* (Boston: Beacon Press, 1996); and Stewart, *A Space on the Side of the Road*. Especially important has been work on the role of sexuality and gay and lesbian identities in anthropological field-work such as William L. Leap and Ellen Lewin, eds., *Out in the Field: Reflections of Lesbian and Gay Anthropologists* (Urbana: University of Illinois Press, 1996); Don Kulick and Margaret Wilson, eds., *Taboo: Sex, Identity, and Erotic Subjectivity in Anthropological Fieldwork* (New York: Routledge, 1995); and Newton, *Margaret Mead Made Me Gay*. Much of my knowledge of oral history was provided firsthand by Ron Grele and Mary Marshall Clark, the director and associate director of Columbia University's Oral History Research Office, during my time as a Rockefeller Fellow there in 1999–2000. Important textual resources include Paul Thompson, *The Voice of the Past: Oral History*, 3rd ed. (New York: Oxford University Press, 2000); Ron Grele, *Envelopes of Sound: The Art of Oral History*, 2nd ed. (Chicago: Precedent Publishing, 1985); Alessandro Portelli, *The Death of Luigi Trastulli: Form and Meaning in Oral History* (Albany: State University of New York Press, 1991); Sherna Gluck and Daphne Patai, eds., *Women's Words: The Feminist Practice of Oral History* (New York: Routledge, 1991); and Robert Perks and Alistair Thompson, eds., *Oral History Reader* (New York: Routledge, 1998). Finally, my experiment in ethnography would be unimaginable without the advice and inspiration of my aunt, Celia Haig-Brown, author of *Resistance and Renewal: Surviving the Indian Residential School* (Vancouver: Tillacum Library, 1988), and *Taking Control: Power and Contradiction in First Nations Adult Education* (Vancouver: University of British Columbia Press, 1995).

24 See, for example, Jean Carlomusto, *To Catch a Glimpse* (1997) and *Shatzi Is Dying* (2000); Gregg Bordowitz, *Fast Trip, Long Drop* (1993); Marlon Riggs, *Tongues Untied* (1989) and *Black Is, Black Ain't* (1995); Ellen Spiro, *Greetings From Out Here* (1993).

25 My sense of the ephemerality of oral history is informed by work in performance studies that focuses on the difficulty of archiving live events; the oral history interview can usefully be understood on the model of performance. See, for example, Peggy Phelan, *Unmarked* (New York: Routledge, 1993). On the combined ephemerality of queer cultures and performance, see Muñoz, "Ephemera as Evidence."

26 See Felman and Laub, *Testimony*; and Langer, *Holocaust Testimonies*.

27 Naming identity presents a bit of a challenge here since many of the women I talked to had relationships with men before, during, and after their ACT UP involvement: some might identify as bisexual, others as lesbians who have relationships with men, still others as having changed sexual identity over time. There's also some slippage between lesbians and women in my research; the interviews focus primarily on lesbians not simply because I restricted my inquiry to lesbians but also because so many of the women central to ACT UP were lesbians.

28 The names of those interviewed will be cited parenthetically in the text.

29 One inspiration for my use of montage is Alessandro Portelli, *Ordine e Gia Stato Esequito Roma le Fosse Ardeatine la Memoria* (Rome: Donzelli, 1999), which includes many long blocks of quotations from interviews. I had access to the manuscript of the English translation.

30 Marina Alvarez and Ginetta Candelario, "(Re)visiones: A Dialogue through the Eyes of AIDS, Activism, and Empowerment," in *Talking Visions: Multicultural Feminism in a Transnational Age*, ed. Ella Shohat (Cambridge: MIT Press, 1998), 250. This interview offers important redefinitions of what constitutes activism. Alvarez's comments come in response to the following remarks by Candelario: "Traditionally, when we think of activism we envision protest marches, sit-ins, and more formal lobbying activities. If we limit ourselves to that definition, we fail to recognize the kind of quiet, often familial activism that takes place in Latina/o communities. Resistance to oppression and oppressive conditions occurs in many forms" (250).

31 For more on the Commission on Human Rights's AIDS Discrimination Unit, which was established in 1983, see Amber Hollibaugh, Mitchell Karp, and Katy Taylor, "The Second Epidemic," in *AIDS: Cultural Analysis/Cultural Activism*, ed. Douglas Crimp, 127–42.

32   Jane Rosett, phone conversation and e-mail with the author, 8 July 2002.
33   See Hollibaugh's essays and interviews, recently collected as *My Dangerous Desires*.
34   Ibid., 256.
35   Ibid., 258.

Bibliography

ACT UP/NY Women and AIDS Book Group. *Women, AIDS, and Activism*. Boston: South End Press, 1990.

Alvarez, Marina, and Ginetta Candelario. "(Re)visiones: A Dialogue through the Eyes of AIDS, Activism, and Empowerment." In *Talking Visions: Multicultural Feminism in a Transnational Age*, edited by Ella Shohat. Cambridge: MIT Press, 1998.

Behar, Ruth. *The Vulnerable Observer: Anthropology That Breaks Your Heart*. Boston: Beacon Press, 1996.

Behar, Ruth, and Deborah Gordan, eds. *Women Writing Culture*. Berkeley: University of California Press, 1995.

Berlant, Lauren. *The Queen of America Goes to Washington City*. Durham, N.C.: Duke University Press, 1997.

—. "Poor Eliza." *American Literature* 70, no. 3 (September 1998): 635–38.

Brown, Laura S. "Not outside the Range: One Feminist Perspective on Psychic Trauma." In *Trauma: Explorations in Memory*, edited by Cathy Caruth. Baltimore, Md.: Johns Hopkins University Press, 1995.

Caruth, Cathy, ed. *Trauma: Explorations in Memory*. Baltimore, Md.: Johns Hopkins University Press, 1995.

Clifford, James. *The Predicament of Culture: Twentieth-Century Ethnography, Literature, and Art*. Cambridge: Harvard University Press, 1988.

Clifford, James, and George E. Marcus. *Writing Culture: The Poetics and Politics of Ethnography*. Berkeley: University of California Press, 1986.

Cohen, Cathy J. *The Boundaries of Blackness: AIDS and the Breakdown of Black Politics*. Chicago: University of Chicago Press, 1999.

Cohen, Peter F. *Love and Anger: Essays on AIDS, Activism, and Politics*. New York: Harrington Park Press, 1998.

Crimp, Douglas. "Mourning and Militancy." *October* 51 (Winter 1989): 3–18.

—. "Melancholy and Moralism." In *Loss*, edited by David Eng and David Kazanjian. Berkeley: University of California Press, 2002.

—, ed. *AIDS: Cultural Analysis, Cultural Activism*. Cambridge: MIT Press, 1987.

Crimp, Douglas, and Adam Rolston. *AIDS Demo Graphics*. Seattle: Bay Press, 1990.

Cvetkovich, Ann. *Mixed Feelings: Feminism, Mass Culture, and Victorian Sensationalism*. New Brunswick, N.J.: Rutgers University Press, 1992.

—. "AIDS and Video Activism." In *Art, Activism, and Oppositionality: Essays from Afterimage*, edited by Grant Kester. Durham, N.C.: Duke University Press, 1998.

Davis, Madeline D., and Elizabeth Lapovsky Kennedy. *Boots of Leather, Slippers of Gold: The History of a Lesbian Community*. New York: Routledge, 1993.

Eng, David L., and David Kazanjian, eds. *Loss*. Berkeley: University of California Press, 2002.

Epstein, Steven. *Impure Science: AIDS, Activism, and the Politics of Knowledge*. Berkeley: University of California Press, 1996.

Erni, John Nguyet. *Unstable Frontiers: Technomedicine and the Cultural Politics of "Curing" AIDS*. Minneapolis: University of Minnesota Press, 1994.

Felman, Shoshana, and Dori Laub. *Testimony: Crises of Witnessing in Literature, Psychoanalysis, and History*. New York: Routledge, 1992.

Gluck, Sherna, and Daphne Patai, eds. *Women's Words: The Feminist Practice of Oral History*. New York: Routledge, 1991.

Grele, Ron. *Envelopes of Sound: The Art of Oral History*. 2nd ed. Chicago: Precedent Publishing, 1985.

Haig-Brown, Celia. *Resistance and Renewal: Surviving the Indian Residential School*. Vancouver: Tillacum Library, 1988.

——. *Taking Control: Power and Contradiction in First Nations Adult Education*. Vancouver: University of British Columbia Press, 1995.

Hollibaugh, Amber. *My Dangerous Desires: A Queer Girl Dreaming Her Way Home*. Durham, N.C.: Duke University Press, 2000.

Juhasz, Alexandra. *AIDS TV: Identity, Community, and Alternative Video*. Durham, N.C.: Duke University Press, 1995.

Kulick, Don, and Margaret Wilson, eds. *Taboo: Sex, Identity, and Erotic Subjectivity in Anthropological Fieldwork*. New York: Routledge, 1995.

LaCapra, Dominick. *Representing the Holocaust: History, Theory, Trauma*. Ithaca, N.Y.: Cornell University Press, 1994.

Langer, Lawrence. *Holocaust Testimonies: The Ruins of Memory*. New Haven, Conn.: Yale University Press, 1991.

Leap, William L., and Ellen Lewin, eds. *Out in the Field: Reflections of Lesbian and Gay Anthropologists*. Urbana: University of Illinois Press, 1996.

Muñoz, José Esteban. "Ephemera as Evidence: Introductory Notes to Queer Acts." *Women and Performance* 16 (1996): 5–16.

Newton, Esther, *Cherry Grove, Fire Island: Sixty Years in America's First Gay and Lesbian Town*. Boston: Beacon Press, 1993.

——. *Margaret Mead Made Me Gay: Personal Essays, Public Ideas*. Durham, N.C.: Duke University Press, 2000.

Patton, Cindy. *Fatal Advice: How Safe-Sex Education Went Wrong*. Durham, N.C. Duke University Press, 1994.

Perks, Robert, and Alistair Thompson, eds. *Oral History Reader*. New York: Routledge, 1998.

Phelan, Peggy. *Unmarked*. New York: Routledge, 1993.

Portelli, Alessandro. *The Death of Luigi Trastulli: Form and Meaning in Oral History*. Albany: State University of New York Press, 1991.

Román, David. *Acts of Intervention: Performance, Gay Culture, and AIDS*. Bloomington: Indiana University Press, 1998.

Schulman, Sarah. *People in Trouble*. New York: Dutton, 1996.

——. *Rat Bohemia*. New York: Dutton, 1995.

Scott, Joan. "The Evidence of Experience." In *The Lesbian and Gay Studies Reader*, edited by Henry Abelove, Michèle Aina Barale, and David M. Halperin. New York: Routledge, 1993.

Spivak, Gayatri Chakravorty. "Can the Subaltern Speak?" in *Marxism and the Interpretation of Culture*, edited by Cary Nelson and Lawrence Grossberg. Urbana: University of Illinois Press, 1987.

Stewart, Kathleen. *A Space on the Side of the Road: Cultural Poetics in an "Other" America*. Princeton, N.J.: Princeton University Press, 1996.

Sturken, Marita. *Tangled Memories: The Vietnam War, the AIDS Epidemic, and the Politics of Remembering*. Berkeley: University of California Press, 1997.

Thompson, Paul. *The Voice of the Past: Oral History*. 3rd ed. New York: Oxford University Press, 2000.

Treichler, Paula A. *How to Have Theory in an Epidemic: Cultural Chronicles of AIDS*. Durham, N.C.: Duke University Press, 1999.

Visweswaran, Kamala. *Fictions of Feminist Ethnography*. Minneapolis: University of Minnesota Press, 1994.

Watney, Simon. *Policing Desire: Pornography, AIDS, and the Media*. Minneapolis: University of Minnesota Press, 1987.

Wojnarowicz, David. *Close to the Knives: A Memoir of Disintegration*. New York: Vintage Books, 1991.

Young, Allan. *The Harmony of Illusions. Inventing Post-Traumatic Stress Disorder*. Princeton, N.J.: Princeton University Press, 1995.

Chapter 23

Helen Hok-Sze Leung

ARCHIVING QUEER FEELINGS IN HONG KONG

Associate Professor of Gender, Sexuality, and Women's Studies at Simon Fraser University, Helen Hok-Sze Leung writes on cinema, sexuality, and queer cultural politics, with a particular emphasis on Hong Kong. She is the author of two books, *Undercurrents: Queer Culture and Postcolonial Hong Kong* (2009) and *Farewell My Concubine: A Queer Film Classic* (2010).

In this essay Leung considers how three marginal, if not already forgotten, Hong Kong texts— Samshasha's *History of Homosexuality in China* (1997), Chou Wah-Shan's *The Postcolonial Tongzhi* (1998), and Anson Mak's *Bisexual Desire* (2000)—archive local queer feelings of discomfort, unease, and failure. These texts also constitute, Leung argues, local queer theoretical projects. Hong Kong culture is particularly productive in this sense because, unlike Taiwan for example, it recognizes no coherent critical field that can be understood as 'queer theory.' Mindful of the impacts of academic institutionalization, and in particular the often unexamined category of theory in queer theory, Leung aims to revitalize the original radical provocation of the gap between "queer" and "theory." For Leung this strategy is integral to transforming what counts as knowledge and, in localizing theory, bringing us closer to what is local about the "global queer."

What counts as theory?

ASKING THIS QUESTION at the beginning of her book *Theory in its Feminist Travels*, Katie King examines "theory" as a historically and politically contingent sign deployed and defended for various investments and interests. King's study makes clear that what counts as "theory" is never governed by an objective or universalist standard. Contextualized within the politics of publication, King examines the specific strategies through which particular forms of theory become "marked" as such, how they travel globally, and how local and unmarked "theory" may be made invisible—but may also in turn challenge or alter—generic theoretical forms (King 1994: 2). With a frankness not found too often in academic publications, King also exposes the ways in which the works of feminists of color had been appropriated through improper citations and produced *as* theory *only* when those ideas were attributed to prominent white academic "stars" (King 1994: 146–47). For King, "theory" should ultimately only be thought with this qualification in mind:

> Thus, this term "theory" has to be bracketed in feminist thinking now, used ironically and proudly, shamedfacedly and shrewdly, gloriously and preposterously, if it is really to convey anything like what feminists are doing in the academy and elsewhere.
>
> (King 1994: 147)

King's insights and caution about what counts as "theory" in feminist contexts are just as relevant to a consideration of theory in its queer travels. The institutionalization of queer theory has made proper objects out of bodies, pleasures, identities, emotions, and practices that were hitherto considered deviant, unruly, rude, dangerous. At the same time, these are constituted as objects of theory only in so far as they are articulated in recognizable theoretical forms, within specific intellectual trajectories, and by theorists working in bona fide academic positions. It has often seemed to me that queer theory is defined more by the institutional parameters of "theory" than by the critical reach of "queer" which can deform those very parameters. For instance, in the conclusion to her lucid and concise account of the discursive formation of queer theory, Annamarie Jagose advocates the continual potential of queer as a term of self-critique, an "identity under construction, a site of permanent becoming" and a means of "interrogating both the preconditions of identity and its effects"(Jagose 1997: 131–32). Yet, there is surprisingly no consideration of the possibility that the category theory—in other words, the form and not just the content of queer theory—may also benefit from similar processes of self-critique. In "The normalization of queer theory," David Halperin recalls queer theory's "scandalous" origin, which he attributes to a moment at a conference in 1990 when Teresa de Lauretis paired the "scurrilous term ['queer'] with the academic holy word 'theory'" (Halperin 2003: 339–40). Halperin argues that this initially radical provocation gradually undergoes a process of domestication as queer theory becomes institutionally acceptable:

> The first step is for the "theory" in queer theory to prevail over the "queer," for "queer" to become a harmless qualifier of "theory" . . . It can [then] be folded back into the standard practice of literary and cultural studies, without impeding academic business as usual. The next step was to despecify the lesbian, gay, bisexual, transgender, or transgressive content of queerness, thereby abstracting queer and turning it into a generic badge of subversiveness, a more trendy version of "liberal".
>
> (Halperin 2003: 341)

The ease with which "queer theory" is now consumed within the academy belies its radical inception which, as Halperin reminds us, was motivated "first and foremost by an impulse to *transform* what could count as knowledge" (Halperin 2003: 343, my emphasis). It is all the more crucial that this impulse to transform—marked in queer theory's original formulation by the (then) offensive incompatibility of the two irreverently juxtaposed terms—should not be forgotten as we turn to a consideration of "local theories." Lest such an endeavor becomes nothing more than a continual institutionalization of queer theory, the qualifier "local" must not be taken to simply denote local variants of a globally intelligible body of knowledge.

Rather, the anxiety-laden exploration of what exactly constitutes the "local queer"—a process John Erni argues is always structured by lines of discontinuities, divided loyalties and ambiguous subject-positions (Erni 2003: 384)—behooves us *also* to rethink the relation between "queer" and "theory." In fact, one way for "local theories" to bring "global queer" to a productive crisis is to reinvigorate the *distance* between "queer" and "theory" such that their very juxtaposition may provoke unease, embarrassment or even offense – as it once did when de Lauretis first uttered those terms together in a conference room, almost two decades ago.

Hong Kong provides a challenging but potentially rewarding context for such an undertaking. Unlike the critical scene in Taiwan, there is no comparably coherent formation of a field that can be readily named "queer theory" in Hong Kong. First of all, academic studies on issues related to sexual and gender minorities have remained scattered on the margins of a handful of disciplines—notably Social Work, Sociology, Cultural Studies and Gender Studies—with no "critical mass" to form a viable field on its own. These scattered scholarly efforts also tend to be disseminated primarily in English: colonial legacy and the corporate university's drive towards internationalization ensure that academic publications in English "count" much more significantly towards tenure and promotion. As a result, critical writings on queer issues in English, even when penned by Hong Kong-based scholars (such as Sik-Ying Ho, Travis Kong, John Erni and Mirana Szeto) tend to be published in international journals and, by necessity, reflect the critical priorities of English-language debates. Chinese-language writings that are disseminated locally are often authored by activists and creative writers whose concerns with queer issues are not primarily academic. Even the Chinese-language works by academic writers (such as, for instance, Yau Ching who in addition to being a film-maker also holds a university faculty position) often appear in non-academic venues (newspaper columns, magazine articles, and non-academic publications) and are adapted to the stylistic demands of those media. While these writings form a rich repository of queer thought, they do not fit academic publishers' lists, conform to the demands of peer review, or establish positions within current academic debates. With a categorically different kind of political and emotional investment than that of generic theory, they reflect concerns that are entangled with local developments of a specific place and time, address an audience not limited to the academic community, and are written with a degree of stylistic freedom, critical ambiguity, and emotional frankness far greater than what is usually allowed in academic theoretical writings. By bringing these writings into a consideration of "local theories," I am not arguing for their inclusion as theory in order to elevate their status within the academy. Nor am I suggesting that all forms of thought should be approached as theory *tout court*. Rather, I am led by a queer impulse to pervert the boundaries of queer theory—now respectably distant from its scandalous origin—by attending to precisely what appears to be outside its proper domain. What queer effects may result from this critical impropriety? What dimensions of (local) queer life may be uncovered when (global) theory is made to bend out of its habitual shape? Most of all, how may our understanding of "what counts as theory"—what constitutes theoretical efforts—be transformed by queering the generic boundaries of a recently institutionalized field of knowledge? In my exploration of these questions, I deliberately turn away from the argumentative and towards the archival and affective aspects of local queer writings. I argue that they constitute significant interventions into current theoretical debates, albeit in unusual guises. After all, collecting things and experiencing emotions are not usually seen as means of advancing theoretical positions. My point though is that they *can be*, particularly when recognizing that they do calls upon us to read, use, and do theory a bit more strangely.

In *An Archive of Feelings*, Ann Cvetkovich examines what she calls an "unusual archive," the materials of which point to ephemeral phenomena and are themselves ephemeral. Indeed, ephemerality is a defining feature of Cvetkovich's twin objects of study: trauma and queer culture. While the former is rendered unspeakable and unrepresentable in mainstream and therapy culture, the latter risks being forgotten due to institutional marginalization and neglect. By undertaking a study that recovers and makes visible cultural traces that have hitherto remained obscured in public spheres, Cvetkovich's critical work examines as well as *produces* an archive of queer trauma (Cvetkovich 2003: 7–8). In her analysis and documentation of queer subculture, Judith Halberstam further suggests that an archive serves as a "theory of cultural relevance, a construction of collective memory, and a complex record of queer activity" (Halberstam 2005: 169–70). For Halberstam, queer archival efforts are also *theoretical efforts*: they reconceptualize the boundaries of what is deemed culturally relevant (and thus worthy of being archived). Halberstam demonstrates that archival activities take place not only in academic writings but also in cultural productions that invoke genealogical influences and community memories in both their content and in the continuation and mutual influences between forms (Halberstam 2005: 170–71). Thus, for both Cvetkovich and Halberstam, queer archives are constituted dialogically: through the subject as well as object of their critical writing. Likewise, my efforts in this article to analyze scattered fragments of Hong Kong's local queer thought attempt to archive works that stay only fleetingly in print and have by and large remained outside established academic circuits of exchange (e.g. published citations, conference mentions, and classroom uses). At the same time, the very works that I discuss are *themselves* archival efforts at documenting queer lives and queer cultures. The dialogic interplay between these textual efforts—their impulse to archive queer phenomena as well as my impulse to "collect" these writings in this essay and by extension in an emergent archive of "local theories"—bespeaks a form of theoretical intervention: a way to re-examine what is worthy of research and what counts as knowledge.

Cvetkovich also describes the materials she analyzes as an archive of *feelings* in order to highlight the function of cultural texts as a repository of feelings and emotions. Cvetkovich suggests that this affective dimension is encoded not only in the content of the texts, but also in the practices that surround their production and reception (Cvetkovich 2003: 7). Her study shows that experiences and articulation of trauma are often constitutive of a rich and fulfilling queer culture. As her analysis focuses on ways in which traumatic emotions are culturally *productive*, it avoids value judgments over whether an emotion—be it anger, shame, hatred—is positive or negative. In *The Cultural Politics of Emotions*, Sara Ahmed makes an important intervention into the frequently debated opposition between queer assimilation (i.e. efforts to be included into normative structures such as marriage) and queer resistance (i.e. efforts to maintain a stance against *all* norms). For Ahmed, while assimilation upholds the normative distinction between legitimate and illegitimate lives, the queer ideal of perpetually maintaining a "transgressive" life against norms is a possibility available only to some and one that, even for those few, may exact too great a physical, psychical, and economic toll. Instead of understanding assimilation and resistance as conservative or radical choices in queer lives, Ahmed draws our attention instead to the possibly productive and generative condition of queer subjects—willing or otherwise—inhabiting norms. Ahmed understands "queer feelings" as *discomfort*: queer lives are uncomfortable as they must inhabit structures whose contours they misfit and live by narratives whose scripts they fail to reproduce. The pressure such queer discomfort brings to bear on the norms it fails to reproduce becomes, for Ahmed, a sign of how queer lives may affect and "work on" the social structures they neither embrace nor reject (Ahmed 2004: 146–55). Guided by both Cvetkovich's and Ahmed's ideas, I choose to focus on the emotions generated in the texts I examine while opting out of the critical authority that adjudicates between good and bad arguments. In fact, I want to show that both good and bad—or for that matter, strong or weak, daring or timid— arguments can generate intriguingly queer feelings that are manifest as discomfort, unease, and anxiety.

I now turn to three texts to explore successive "moments" of queer thought in Hong Kong. Not only are these writings representative of particular local contexts, they also bear an uneasy or tenuous relation to academic publishing: Samshasha's *History of Homosexuality in China* (1997) has been allegedly plagiarized and is no longer in print; Chou Wah-Shan's self-published *The Postcolonial Tongzhi* (1998) has garnered severe criticism as an academic work; while Anson Mak's *Bisexual Desire* (2000), which straddles the generic boundaries of creative and critical writings, has remained largely unknown (and is rarely referenced) in academic studies. At the same time, these unwitting or—as I will argue in Mak's case—self-conscious moments of "failure," along with the discomfort and anxiety they signal, constitute the most theoretically productive dimensions of these writings. As part of a necessarily incomplete and open-ended archive of queer feelings in Hong Kong, these works warrant quite a bit more of our critical attention.

Queer history and its discontent

In a new preface written for the 1997 edition of *History of Homosexuality in China*, the late writer and activist Samshasha expresses a series of anxieties around the reception and social influence of his 1984 work. Bringing together an extensive collection of textual and anthropological evidence drawn from official court records, apocryphal accounts, religious documents, legal codes, medical manuals, literature, paintings, the plastic arts, ritual artifacts, accounts by foreign missionaries and spanning thousands of years of recorded history from the Zhou Dynasty (1122–1500 BC) to the present day, the book purports to archive "abandoned" fragments of history to prove that there has always been a tradition of "same-sex love" in China. Samshasha's expressed anxieties in the revised edition illustrate both the possibilities and the peril inspired by this massive historiographic project, one that was undertaken independent of academic institutions and disseminated through an alternative press.

In the preface, Samshasha first sketches the social change that has taken place between the two editions of the book: in the 1980s, social attitudes towards homosexuality had "improved," yet the discussion around AIDS had revived the claim that "like AIDS, homosexuality was imported from the West"; by the late 1990s, even though homosexuality was no longer viewed as a foreign import while social movements for gay rights were flourishing in both Hong Kong and Taiwan, there were new concerns with "Mainland Chinese attitude towards homosexuals in Hong Kong after July 1, 1997" (Samshasha 1997: 1). Samshasha then presents the most significant change in the new edition: a reformulation of his theory in the original book that "homophobia [was] imported from the West." Samshasha claims that his theory is now "defunct" and should be reframed as the "Westernization of homophobia" in China. Towards the end of the preface, Samshasha refers to the suspected plagiarism of his book by an American academic (Samshasha 1997: 2) as well as his reluctance to include erotic images from the Ming and Qing dynasties lest the theme of homosexuality becomes exclusively associated with sex (Samshasha 1997: 3). The content of the historical evidence gathered in the book has remained essentially the same between the two editions. However, the author's rather awkward re-positioning of this material as well as his anxieties over how this material has been (and may in future be) received or appropriated illustrate how shifts in local/global discursive relations affect the significance of a queer archive.

At the time of the book's first edition, homosexual acts between men under all circumstances were still illegal in Hong Kong. A series of scandals involving prominent British civil servants (most notably the MacLennan Incident in 1980, in which a police officer under investigation on charges of alleged homosexuality "committed suicide" under very suspicious circumstances) prompted the colonial government to introduce legal reforms to bring about decriminalization. The actual bill which legalized consensual homosexual acts in private was enacted only in 1991, after nearly a decade of fierce debates and hostile opposition. One of the most commonly heard objections to decriminalization was the charge that homosexuality is essentially a product of the West. The colonial government's attempt to legalize this alien behavior, according to this view, posed a threat to traditional Chinese values. It was in indignant response to this kind of thinking that Samshasha rushed to finish the research that he started some years ago while studying in the U.S. Writing as an "angry Chinese" (Samshasha 1997: 4), Samshasha argues that it is not so much homosexuality but homophobia which is an import from the West. His argument is built on two fronts: from the material he has assembled to prove that same-sex love has flourished for thousands of years alongside the Confucian order, and from the fact that the law against consensual homosexual behavior that the government was trying to repeal in the 1980s was inherited from British laws and deviates significantly from the pre-modern Chinese legal tradition. Samshasha is aware of the "illicit sex" (*jian*) laws during the Ming and Qing dynasties and the juridical construction of sodomy as a "pollution" of chastity (Samshasha 1997: 10, 20–21). However, not unlike the interpretation of Kang Zhengguo (Kang 1996: 109–62) and Matthew Sommer (Sommer 2000: 114–65), Samshasha understands Chinese laws to be regulatory mechanisms that protect the gendered hierarchies of the Confucian household rather than a proscription of homosexuality per se. (In fact, Samshasha will suggest that this regulatory impulse paradoxically also functions to *sanction* certain gendered forms of what we would now call homosexuality—an argument he makes explicit in the revised edition and which I will return to in the next section.) Samshasha's polemic was a powerful rebuttal at a time when the majority of oppositional arguments, including those made from religious or moral perspectives, invoked "Chinese tradition" to appeal to anti-colonial sentiments and patriotic cultural pride (Ho 1997: 80–82). Anti-coloniality and homophobia were constructed as each other's alibi and Samshasha's sweeping historiographic efforts aimed at undoing that relation. Yet, by the time the revised edition came out on the eve of Hong Kong's sovereignty transfer from British to Chinese hands in 1997, the discursive relationship between homophobia, coloniality and nationalism had shifted considerably. Anti-colonial sentiments had been displaced by fears over the uncertainty of impending Chinese rule and by the pressure (or temptation) to become "suddenly patriotic" (*huran aiguo*) as many opportunistic ex-colonials had done, to great personal benefits. Meanwhile, the social movement for sexual minorities—now dubbed the *tongzhi* movement—had been flourishing with a decidedly nativist cast. The imperative to "find our own path" dominated the agenda of the first Chinese Tongzhi Conference in Hong Kong (Loo 1999: 392–424) and continued to exert influence on subsequent rhetoric. Parallel to these local developments was the concurrent and continuing globalization of an increasingly universalist conception of homosexuality. Although not explicitly stated in his book, Samshasha was clearly also concerned with the latter development: in an interview with Mark McLelland for the journal *Intersections*, he laments that modern gay movements all over the world seem to be primarily influenced by Western notions of sexuality and are ignorant of indigenous expressions of alternative forms of sexuality (Samshasha 2000: para. 41).

The anxiety-ridden preface of the 1997 edition of *History of Homosexuality in China* was produced by the convergence of all these discursive currents: a very recent history of homophobia appropriated as a form of anti-colonial discourse, the advent of Chinese nationalism replacing colonial ideology as the new hegemony, and the rise of a global homosexual identity that threatens to subsume all sexual variance in its monolithic image. While the original intention of the project was to prove the existence of a Chinese tradition of homosexuality, Samshasha's awareness of the discursive shifts in Hong Kong society and the potential for nativist tendencies in *tongzhi* discourse to be appropriated into a newly hegemonic Chinese nationalism prompts him to reframe his understanding of homophobia in Hong Kong as a Western*ized* rather than Western phenomenon. This modification allows Samshasha to theorize that, prior to Westernization, homophobia in Chinese culture functioned "implicitly" through a "fuzzy transgender-transsexual pansexualism" (Samshasha 1997: 12) that sanctioned same-sex love but only in so far as it involved a transgender feminization of the male partner and the coexistence of heterosexual familial relationships. This new formulation theorizes a unique—but not unproblematic—system of sexual regulation in pre-modern China. It reflects Samshaha's attempt to launch an argument for the uniqueness of Chinese homosexuality while at the same time refrains from celebrating it as a solely positive tradition. While this attempt helps Samshasha resolve one source of tension, it also immediately breeds others. The explanation reduces transgender embodiments and bisexual desire as merely regulatory mechanisms that facilitate same-sex love under a regime of "implicit homophobia." This blind spot is further reinforced by the retention of the book's original title, which categorizes its diverse historical material under the sign homosexuality (or "same-sex love" [*tongxingai*] in Chinese) even though Samshasha has pointed out elsewhere that "there isn't even an exact term for *homosexual* in Chinese history and we certainly don't have any precedent for the concept *gay*" (Samshasha 2000: para. 39). Yet, what is most productive about the book's shifting tension and anxiety is what they reveal about the book's (and more generally queer historiography's) negotiation with crisscrossing discursive currents. From his angry assertion of cultural uniqueness to the cautionary repositioning of that uniqueness, Samshasha exposes the need to signify an archive in relation to the discursive alignment of power at any given time. The naming and organization of historical material is never complete and the anxiety-ridden "tic" to *continually* rename and reframe that material may ultimately be the only productive strategy for doing queer history.

Aside from the anxious repositioning of the book's central argument, the 1997 preface also betrays the author's anger over an alleged case of plagiarism. Samshasha explains that he did not pursue legal action only because of limited financial resources. He also thanks two American scholars for their published discussion of the case which "brought a correct understanding to the international academic circle" (Samshasha 1997: 2–3). The alleged work of plagiarism refers to Bret Hinsch's *Passions of the Cut Sleeve* (1992) which assembles similar archival material and advances a similar argument about the Western "origin" of homophobia in China (Samshasha 2000: para. 61–64). Samshasha's self-construction as an injured party in this case prompts us to ask questions regarding the politics of publication and its impact on the circulation and adaptation of knowledge. In her review of Hinsch's book in 1991, Charlotte Furth approaches the plagiarism charge from two angles. First, she attributes it to Chinese gays and lesbians' resistance against "powerful outsiders" appropriating a local cause. Second, she faults Hinsch not for plagiarism but for relying on secondary material without tracing their primary sources: the parallels between Hinsch's and Samshasha's works in Furth's view result from their reliance on the same secondary source (Furth 1991: 912). What I find missing in Furth's discussion, regardless of whether Hinsch's work can actually be considered an act of plagiarism, is the unequal power dynamic between scholarly studies with institutional support and independent research conducted outside of the academy. Not only do English-language works already enjoy a global reach of dissemination while Chinese-language works tend to get ghettoized (because rarely translated) within local regions, a work by an author with a Ph.D. and published by a prestigious university press automatically accrues more scholarly credential and longevity than an amateur historian's work published by a little-known independent press with few print runs. (Hinsch's book is still in print and widely cited in the field while Samshasha's is no longer easily available.) Moreover, the boundary between citation, translation, and outright plagiarism is more easily disrespected when one party is outside of the established academic circuit of exchange. It would likely have been unthinkable for Hinsch to use the material in the same way had Samshasha's work been that of an established sinologist published in English. Samshasha's anger and desolate dependence on other scholars' efforts to adjudicate over the case in the international scene reveal the hierarchical politics of publication and the immense difficulty for local queer works, especially those conducted outside of established academic circles, to enter into the international scene of scholarly debates as equal and respected partners in dialogue (as opposed to being appropriated or consumed as raw material). This unequal politics of publi-cation also spawns other unexpected (and seemingly unrelated) effects. In the book, Samshasha mentions his extensive collection of erotic images from the Ming and Qing period, which he has deliberately excluded from both editions of the book (Samshasha 1997: 3). He explains that the images are left out because he does not wish the theme of homosexuality always to be associated with sex. This reflects an uncharacteristically prudish concern that reproduces the normative distinction between good/chaste (hetero)sexuality and bad/promiscuous (homo)sexuality. Yet, as my discussion of Sara Ahmed's work previously has shown, those in relative positions of privilege can more often afford to practice the queer ideal of transgression. This seemingly prudish gesture likely reflects a prudent impulse to protect his historiographic work from being pushed further beyond the realm of respectable scholarship. More than anything else in the book, this easily overlooked act of self-censorship signifies the most heightened form of queer discomfort. It also serves as a somewhat grim reminder that theoretical agency is always contingent on one's relative position within the hierarchical politics of publication.

Heterosexual melancholia

If Samshasha had been concerned that an overly celebratory cultural essentialism would result from the influence of his historical work, then the Chinese-language writings of sociologist Chou Wah-Shan signal a period of queer thought in Hong Kong that rides precisely on the wave of such an influence. Aside from a handful of articles in English, Chou's main publica-tions during 1993–97 were in Chinese. This voluminous body of work (over ten books) represents a problematic but visibly productive period in queer theorizing in Hong Kong. Furthermore, while Chou held a faculty position in the University of Hong Kong during this time, his works in Chinese were self-published by a now defunct small press, Tongzhi Studies Group (Tongzhi yanjiu she), that appeared to be devoted to the publication of Chou's own work. The status of Chou's Chinese-language works is thus ambiguous: while Chou occupied an established academic position, his Chinese-language publications were not disseminated through accredited academic channels and not held up to standardized processes of scrutiny. While this "freedom" has certainly resulted in major problems in Chou's work as scholarship, it also gives queer issues an unprecedentedly popular visibility in Hong Kong. As I will argue later, it also allows Chou an affective outlet that sheds light on some intriguing issues.

In her study of radicalism in contemporary Chinese societies, Mirana Szeto offers a meticulous critique of Chou's works, in particular his conceptualization of "Chinese *tongzhi*" as a theoretical category. Szeto exposes the complicity between Chou's self-positioned racial-ized and colonialized victimhood and a problematic reassertion of hegemonic ideologies, amongst which are: a neo-Confucian "familism"; frequent instances of cultural essentialism despite repeated denials; an essentialist consolidation of *tongzhi* as a monolithic identity, often at the expense of women; an anti-colonial hysteria that may be a pathological after-effect of the colonial condition (Szeto 2004: 378–441). Szeto's work provides a critical look at what has often appeared in mainstream culture at the time to be the only possible queer discourse in Hong Kong. Szeto's critique is unrelentingly harsh: not only does she disagree with Chou on almost every single issue, she also questions his work on *ethical* grounds while characterizing his argumentative flaws in pathological terms. Ironically Szeto's critique (perhaps unintentionally) accords a form of academic respect towards Chou's works: through citations and serious critical engagement, Szeto's discussion actually serves to archive Chou's work as a form of serious scholarship, albeit one with which she is in fierce contention. What interests me most, however, is Szeto's intense aversion to Chou's persistent rhetoric of self-positioned victimhood, which betrays *her* unease towards a fundamental question: what is at stake in a self-identified straight man's decade-long affective investment in queer lives? Moreover, Szeto's unease is evidently, if unwittingly, *shared* by Chou himself who displays throughout his work these paradoxical emotions: an intense shame over his heterosexuality on the one hand and an equally intense fear of homosexuality (not in theory but evidently in practice) on the other. How may we best approach this affective investment in (and simultaneous disavowal of) queerness? How may Chou's work serve as an archive of queer feelings?

In *Postcolonial Tongzhi*, Chou advocates several "resistant" strategies of self-identification for heterosexuals (especially men) who work in the *tongzhi* movement. First, he suggests that they should not immediately disclose their heterosexuality and should "actively explore intimate relations with members of the same sex" (Chou 1998: 45). Second, they should also "tease" those who are homophobic with deliberately ambivalent replies such as: "You guessed it about me, aren't you also?" "How do you know you aren't as well?" or "Which parts of me make me look bi or gay?" (Chou 1998: 45). While Chou advocates these strategies for others, his *own* experience in practicing these strategies often results in expressions of anger, bitterness, and tortuous self-examination. Several examples of such expressions are found in the autobiographical introductions that precede Chou's ethnographic accounts in *Hong Kong Tongzhi Stories* (1996) and *Postcolonial Tongzhi* (1998). In these texts, Chou recurrently betrays his intense discomfort with being a straight man involved in queer research. This discomfort provokes an initial questioning of his heterosexuality which is in turn followed by a vehement disavowal of his possible homosexuality and a tortuous re-embracing of straightness.

In the preface to *Hong Kong Tongzhi Stories*, Chou gives an account of what he feels is an instance of homophobia towards him from a colleague. Prefaced by a reference to a T-shirt slogan "You don't know I'm straight," he describes how a colleague, on seeing a visibly gay man in Chou's office, raised her voice to announce with unmistaken innuendo: "Someone is waiting for you in your office." Chou interprets her expression to mean she has "caught him out" (Chou 1996: 2). Chou notes that he had to suppress his intense disappointment at his colleague's apparently homophobic intimation that Chou was gay by association. Yet, isn't the situation entirely Chou's own making and a re-enactment of what he advocates as a strategy of resistance? By remaining ambivalently silent about his heterosexuality while conducting queer research, he is virtually inviting his colleague to make the normative assumption that he is "not straight" and "therefore gay." Such a moment would appear to be precisely the opportunity of critical engagement that Chou supposedly wants. Yet the situation only signals for Chou a sense of disappointment. Examples of his *other* strategy—not to immediately disclose one's heterosexuality while living and working amongst queer folks—backfire in even more dramatic ways. In the first section of *Postcolonial Tongzhi*, Chou describes in detail the behavior of a white man who thought Chou was gay:

> He stared at my calf, thigh, waist, chest, neck, face, eyes and skillfully pushed
> my hands away to hug me tightly for five seconds, then let go . . . While we

were in the car, he lightly and very slowly ran his fingers on my hair and neck and said, "Sweetheart, we're almost there."

(Chou 1998: 10)

Chou then recounts the man's reaction when Chou disclosed to him that he was in fact not gay: the man became enraged and said that everyone who knew Chou had told him Chou was gay. He also accused Chou of concocting his theory of Chinese *tongzhi* only as a justification for remaining closeted (Chou 1998: 10). Subsequently in the same section, Chou describes his own association with queer research as a "tattoo" that follows him everywhere. Queerness, he claims, "runs in [his] veins" so much so that he "would make great efforts to force [himself] to try, even to push [himself] to develop a relationship with another man" but to no avail. He then wonders if "subconscious homophobia prevents [him] from being sexually attracted to men or whether genetic factors have rendered [him] a hopeless heterosexual" (Chou 1998: 34). Eventually, Chou claims he realizes it is not "a sin" to be heterosexual and thus begins to publicly hold his female partner's hands without feeling guilty about his heterosexual privilege (Chou 1998: 35). While Chou interprets the white man's angry response as a racist reaction (which could of course be accurate), the above statements also show that Chou would intentionally use another man's attraction as a "test case" for his possible homosexuality, a possibility he would then disavow while conceding that, for ideological or genetic reasons, he disidentifies completely with same-sex attraction in practice. What Chou does not seem to realize, or at least is reluctant to admit in print, is that in these instances he is using his queer scholarship *as a sexual tease*. His subsequent declaration of straight identification would thus be taken as a wounding rejection from those who are unlucky enough to have taken the bait. At the same time, Chou's entire career of researching queer lives seems to signal a long struggle to come to terms with his own shame at "(not) being gay." (I use this neither-nor identity formulation as a parody of Chou's preferred identities throughout the first section of *Postcolonial Tongzhi* as "(not) British . . . (not) Chinese . . . (not) Christian . . . (not) a queer scholar and (not) straight" [Chou 1998: 7–45].) The affective narrative assembled from the previously cited passages runs like this: Chou is paralyzed with guilt and shame about being heterosexual, then implicates himself in situations in which he knows he would frequently be mistaken for gay (obsessively researching queer lives, "forcing" himself to "test" his attraction to men, playfully refusing to affirm he is straight), then disavows the gay identity others attribute to him, and *then* reclaims a form of heterosexuality without the prior sense of guilt and shame. Yet, clearly this strategy does not resolve his discomfort once and for all. Rather, it has to be performatively reiterated, over and over again to purge his shame and reaffirm his "(not) gay" identification.

This repeated narrative may be understood through Judith Butler's formulation of drag and melancholy, albeit in modified terms. In the seminal essay "Critically Queer," Butler cautions against theorizing cross-gender drag through a Freudian notion of melancholia, as a form of ungrieved loss for a rejected object which also becomes manifest in a heightened identification with that very object (Butler 1993: 234). To do so, Butler suggests, would run the risk of consolidating the assumption that a man performing femininity has some attachment to and prior rejection of the figure of femininity (Butler 1993: 235). In other words, to apply the Freudian understanding of melancholia *only* to cross-gender drag would reinforce the conventionally homophobic interpretation of male homosexuality as ungrieved loss for femininity and lesbianism as ungrieved loss for masculinity while heterosexuality remains "natural." In her famous reversal, Butler stands this formulation of melancholia on its head by applying the paradigm to *same-gender* performance. As Butler understands *all* acts of gender to be a form of drag, she characterizes a straight masculine man's heightened identification with masculinity (itself a form of drag) and concurrent rejection of masculinity as an object of love as a form of "heterosexual melancholy" (Butler 1993: 235). According to this formulation, the straight masculine man incorporates masculinity into his embodiment out of an ungrieved loss for (and which is manifest as a rejection of) the same masculinity as an object of love. If we further modify this formulation to approach queerness itself (however gendered) as a sexual performance and interpret Chou's queer scholarship as a form of critical drag, then Chou's melancholia is manifest in his incorporation of (and heightened identification with) queerness in *theory* via a simultaneous *exclusion* of queerness as a possible object of love in *practice*. Chou intensely identifies with queerness in theory, an identification he reiterates and performs over and over. Yet, in practice, he repeatedly disavows and rejects queerness only to reconsolidate what is ultimately a melancholic reassertion of being "(not) gay."

What would constitute a far more productive project, both for Chou and for those critical of him, is an exploration of the originary trauma of heterosexuality, of which Chou's melancholia may well be an important and instructive part. What conditions produce Chou's sense of guilt, shame, and frustration about being heterosexual? What *other than* melancholia may resolve his persistent identification with queerness in theory but inexorable disavowal in practice? What lives other than Chou's are similarly affected? These are the stories that could emerge from our engagement with—rather than wholesale disavowal of—the complex queer feelings in Chou's works.

Creative failure and queer discomfort

After Chou's departure from the University of Hong Kong in the late 1990s, he had by and large stopped researching and writing on queer lives. The publication in 2000 of *Bisexual Desire* signals a new era of queer writing in Hong Kong without Chou's hitherto dominant presence. *Bisexual Desire* is an eclectic, semi-collaborative work by Anson Mak, an activist and multimedia artist as well as one-time collaborator and later sharp critic of Chou Wah-Shan. In Mirana Szeto's critique of Chou Wah-Shan, she contrasts Mak's non-identitarian formation of "bi/*bai*" to Chou's essentialist formation of *tongzhi*. Szeto characterizes bi/*bai* as a "bicultural and strange 'creole'" term that appropriates the negative meanings of "failure" and "defeat" in the service of transgressive activities such as "ruining, messing up and the active attempt to make boundaries fail and dysfunction" (Szeto 2004: 412). I am particularly interested in exploring Mak's creative use of "failure" as a queer trope in relation to Ahmed's formulation of "queer feelings." In contrast to the unspoken anxiety that pervades the works of the previous two authors, Mak consciously *deploys* her feelings of anxiety as a form of creative expression. Mak's insistence on not cohering an identity while at the same time invoking such non-coherence as a form of failure produces unease. Yet, as Ahmed has demonstrated, we do not necessarily have to take an active stance against identity *or* be uncritically invested in identity to feel the queer discomfort of "failing" (willingly or otherwise) to inhabit normative zones of comfort. For me, then, the most productive of Mak's formulation of "bi/*bai*" involves a profound engagement with these feelings of failure/discomfort even as the book itself searches for ways to alleviate such feelings.

The second chapter of Mak's book is titled with this phrase: "it began simply with a search for comforting/appropriate [*shu(he)shi*] language . . . " (Mak 2000: 6). In the chapter, Mak describes how bi/*bai* exposes various conditions of discomfort. The first is a linguistic discomfort:

> Speaking of "bi" or *bai*, one doesn't even know if one's speaking in English or Chinese. Hong Kong people often use words which can be spoken aloud but have no corresponding written characters. Even if these are Chinese words, they

only exist in Cantonese. I don't even know whether to be happy about such hyper localism or anxious about its exclusivity. Speaking of "bi" or *bai* is difficult not only because there is a lack of discussion on sexuality and desire in Hong Kong culture and hence a lack of adequate vocabulary, but also because there is no acknowledgment that bisexual desire even exists.

(Mak 2000: 6)

Many of the most nuanced theorists of Hong Kong culture such as Leung Ping-Kwan, Li Siu-Leung, Ackbar Abbas and Rey Chow have written on the linguistic and cultural difficulty of representing Hong Kong. Their scholarship aims at capturing the hybrid, mediated, and layered expressions that writers, songwriters, and filmmakers must deploy to represent a rapidly changing city, the specificity of which seems to defy easy representation. Mak understands a similar difficulty in representing what she provisionally calls bi/*bai*, a form of desire that is uncomfortable to speak about because it is not even recognized as existent, a predicament quite close to what Abbas theorizes as "disappearance": a form of "reverse hallucination"; a failure to see what is actually there (Abbas 1997: 6). Mak goes on to describe the difficulty (*nan*) of articulating this desire even in *tongzhi* circles:

This kind of difficulty involves the difficulty of speaking, the difficulty of not having words even if one speaks, and the difficulty of facilitating any development culturally. There is nothing to be done [*wunai*] and it is painful.

(Mak 2000: 7)

Mak explains that her decision to speak of "bisexual desire" rather than a "bisexual identity" is to "allow our lives to be better" (Mak 2000: 9). Ironically, what Mak documents throughout her book is the utter discomfort and difficulties her choice causes. Yet, it may precisely be through these difficult experiences that life could become "better" – or at least filled with more possibilities. A narrative of queer feelings is woven through Mak's documentation of queer social activism in Hong Kong which she narrates as a series of autobiographical reflections. In particular, in the concluding section, Mak vividly evokes the dynamics of the contemporary activist scene through the utter discomfort and immense difficulties she experiences while trying to sustain activist communities, create new space for thought, and juggle school, work and physical well-being:

The fiftieth anniversary of the U.N. Declaration of Human Rights . . . I was asked by the Hong Kong Christian Women's Association to write a report on sexual orientation. . . . I thought of what to write, the fact that I had to write in English. . . . I did not use the word *queer* . . . or *tongzhi* . . . homosexuals are homosexuals, bisexuals are bisexuals! Why mix all these together under *queer* or *tongzhi* when we are all so different . . .

1998 *Tongzhi* Conference . . . Before the conference I was so sick I had to go to the ER . . . and then rushed to Lantau Island for the meeting. It was so hard physically. I didn't say much . . . I felt so uncomfortable, like an outsider . . . Why did I put myself in these uncomfortable surroundings . . .

I feel that Queer Sisters should be rebuilt but it's hard to push through the proposal, hard to assemble more people, hard to properly represent everyone's views. As for bisexual theorizing, there're not a lot of opportunities to involve more people. I fear that I have failed. I feel guilty and terribly uneasy. Still, I have to work on my thesis. If I don't complete it I can't graduate . . . I don't know what to do.

I fell sick. This time for real. I could not get up. I thought I would die. Sick. Still sick.

Everything has to quiet down. Everything has to be still.

(Mak 2000: 30)

Mak's long illness then becomes a queer trope: the "normal" working life becomes utterly uninhabitable for a sick person. The discomfort Mak endures while being sick seems to signify the heart of her activist project. Her illness has led her to let go of her anxiety about the theoretical and political importance of all of this work:

A book is just a book. It's the reader's heart that is most important. Hope can first aim for the heart, then culture, then politics.

It's all to make life a bit better. A mouthful of rice, a good night's sleep, a blue sky, a star, a whiff of wind, a cat, a love for both sexes. It's all just to fill life with love.

(Mak 2000: 33)

Ironically, Mak reaches a state of comfort (which denotes open possibilities and hope) only through her experiences of discomfort, both physically (being ill), emotionally (feeling uneasy, disheartened, guilty) and critically (inhabiting theoretical spaces that are demanding). This paradoxical state echoes what Sara Ahmed theorizes as the trajectory of queer feeling, "along with an excitement in the face of uncertainty of where the discomfort may take us" (Ahmed 2004: 155). For Mak, such "excitement" does not cause agitation but rather instills cat-like grace:

Between critical self-awareness and a soul at peace, I just want to be a cat, a cat with a sense of justice, that lives lovingly and tenderly. At ease, careful, at peace. Like a cat, that's enough.

(Mak 2000: 20)

This enigmatic and beautifully simple wish radiates ease and resilience at the heart of a book that predominantly documents discomfort and difficulty. The eccentricity of its humor (mis) fits (in)appropriately into the more cautious formality of my own academic prose. This uneasy distance between how I write and what I write about takes me back to the beginning of this essay, where I speak of the necessity to revitalize what was once an uncertain *gap* between "queer" and "theory." Inhabiting rather than avoiding this gap—in the face of all the queer feelings this endeavor may entail—will bring us far closer to what is local about the global queer, in Hong Kong and elsewhere.

References

Abbas, Ackbar (1997) *Hong Kong: Culture and the Politics of Disappearance*, Minneapolis: University of Minnesota Press.

Ahmed, Sara (2004) *The Cultural Politics of Emotions*, New York and London: Routledge.

Butler, Judith (1993) *Bodies That Matter: On the Discursive Limits of "Sex"*, New York: Routledge.

Chou, Wah-Shan (1996) *Hong Kong Tongzhi Stories* (*Xianggnag tongzhi gushi*), Hong Kong: Tongzhi yanjiu she.

— (1998) *Postcolonial Tongzhi* (*Hou zhimin tongzhi*) Hong Kong: Tongzhi yanjiu she.

Cvetkovich, Ann (2003) *An Archive of Feelings: Trauma, Sexuality, and Lesbian Public Culture*, Durham: Duke University Press.

Erni, John (2003) "Run queer Asia run," *Journal of Homosexuality* 45(2/3/4): 381–84.

Furth, Charlotte (1991) "Review of *Passions of the Cut Sleeve* by Bret Hinsch," *The Journal of Asian Studies* 50(4): 911–12.

Halberstam, Judith (2005) *In a Queer Time and Place: Transgender Bodies, Subcultural Lives*, New York and London: New York University Press.

Halperin, David M. (2003) "The normalization of queer theory," *Journal of Homosexuality* 45(2/3/4): 339–43.

Hinsch, Bret (1992) *Passions of the Cut Sleeve: The Male Homosexual Tradition in China*, Berkeley and Los Angeles, California: University of California Press.

Ho, Petula Sik-Ying (1997) "Policing identity: decriminalization of homosexuality and the emergence of gay identity in Hong Kong," Dissertation, Essex University.

Jagose, Annamarie (1997) *Queer Theory: An Introduction*, New York: New York University Press.

Kang Zhengguo (1996) *Aspects of Sexuality and Literature in Ancient China*, Taipei: Rye Field Publishing.

King, Katie (1994) *Theory in its Feminist Travels: Conversations in U.S. Women's Movements*, Bloomington: Indiana University Press.

Loo, John (ed) (1999) *New Reader on Chinese Tongzhi* (*Huaren tongzhi xin dupin*), Hong Kong: Worldson.

Mak, Anson (2000) *Bisexual Desire* (*Shuangxing qingyu*), Hong Kong: Hong Kong Christian Women Association.

Samshasha (1997) *History of Homosexuality in China* (*Zhongguo tongxinglian shilu*), Hong Kong Rosa Winkel Press (Revised Edition).

— (2000) Interview with Mark McLelland, *Intersections* 4, http://intersections.anu.edu.au/issue4/interview_mclelland.html.

Sommer, Matthew H. (2000) *Sex, Law and Society in Late Imperial China*, Stanford: Stanford University Press.

Szeto, Mirana May (2004) "The radical itch: rethinking radicalism in contemporary Chinese societies," Dissertation, University of California, Los Angeles.

Chapter 24

José Esteban Muñoz

FEELING BROWN, FEELING DOWN: LATINA AFFECT, THE PERFORMATIVITY OF RACE, AND THE DEPRESSIVE POSITION

José Esteban Muñoz is Professor and Chair of the Department of Performance Studies at Tisch School of the Arts, New York University. The author of *Disidentifications: Queers of Color and the Performance of Politics* (1999) and *Cruising Utopia: The Then and There of Queer Futurity* (2009), Muñoz works at the intersections of queer theory, performance studies, Latina/o studies, and critical race theory.

Drawing an analogy with the homely crocheted coverings that form part of Nao Bustamante's video performance art piece *Neapolitan* (2003), Muñoz stitches critical race theories, Kleinian object-relations theory, and queer critique into a provisional exploration of the feelings encapsulated in his rhyming title. The essay demonstrates how Bustamante's work performs "feeling brown, feeling down" as a depressive position, rather than a stage to be moved through. Muñoz argues that this position offers minoritarian subjects a better ethical mode of being and becoming than the paranoid one that has become routinized in some queer critique. Queerness never occupies central ground in Muñoz's analysis but emerges at specific moments as a corrective to the other theories he engages, and as part of the particularities of history and loss registered by brown feelings.

DEPRESSION HAS BECOME one of the dominant affective positions addressed within the cultural field of contemporary global capitalism. However, such a blanket statement requires fine-tuning. While art and media that depict the affective contours of depression have certainly become more prevalent, it is nonetheless important to be attentive to the ways in which the current historical moment is able to mimetically render various depictions of the problem of depression that plagues the contemporary citizen subject with a crypto-universalist script. Certainly depression is gendered. Female depression and male depression resonate quite differently. While female depression is more squarely framed as a problem, the depression that plagues men is often described as a full-on condition, registering beyond the sphere of the individual, linked to a sort of angst and longing that are often described as endemic to postmodernism. However, that statement also requires some amending insofar as such a distinction reproduces a default white subject. The topic of depression has not often been discussed in relation to the question of racial formations in critical theory. This essay dwells on a particular depiction of depression that most certainly speaks to the general moment but resists the pull of crypto-universalism. The art project at the center of this essay considers how depression itself is formed and organized around various historical and material contingencies that include race, gender, and sex.

The work of Nao Bustamante does not conform to our associations of art practices that emerged at the moment of identity politics, nor does it represent an avoidance of the various antagonisms within the social that define our recognition and belonging as racialized, gendered, and sexed subjects. Bustamante's work tells us a story about the problems of belonging in alterity. I contend that her oeuvre meditates on our particularities, both shared and divergent, particularities that are central to the choreography of self and other that organizes our reality.[1] This, as I will contend, is negotiated through a particular affective circuit. The version of depression I consider in this essay is marked by a depression that is not one. I am provisionally naming this affective site a feeling of brownness that transmits and is structured through a depressive stance, a kind of feeling down, thus my rhyming title, "Feeling Brown, Feeling Down."

Bustamante's video installation *Neapolitan* (2003) includes an eleven-minute-long loop tape.[2] The tape shows the artist breaking out into seemingly spontaneous sobbing as she watches the end of a movie. As she cries, the viewer witnesses the somatic signs of depressive sadness: her eyes well up, her nose runs. The video is shown on a monitor that sits on an old-fashioned table, which sits on a sculpture block. The monitor is covered by a multicolored cozy that was crocheted by the artist. On top of the cozy sits a crocheted basket filled with crocheted flowers. Above the basket rests an artificial crow; the artificial bird wears a matching crocheted hat. A power plug, connected to the wall, is also snugly covered in a crocheted caddy. The movie being watched by the artist is Tomás Gutiérrez Alea's *Fresa y chocolate*, a film set in the 1970s in Cuba and focused on a difficult and fragile friendship between a proper revolutionary subject and a gay bohemian. As the artist watches the film, it is lightly projected on her face, giving the sense that the glow of the screen she is watching is bouncing off her face. After the film is over, the artist rewinds it again and again, continuing to cry.

In this essay I will suggest that this installation can be read as an illustration of the depressive position and its connection to minoritarian aesthetic and political practice. Toward this end I will draw from certain aspects of Kleinian object-relations theory. Thus, I will address a very particular mode of depression, not depression in its more general or clinical sense. Describing the depressive position in relation to what I am calling "brown feeling" chronicles a certain ethics of the self that is utilized and deployed by people of color and other minoritarian subjects who don't feel quite right within the protocols of normative affect and comportment. While the work of Melanie Klein (1986) and her circle is not tailored to attend to the vicissitudes of racialization and ethnic particularity, I nonetheless find some of her formulations suggestive and helpful when trying to discuss what I'm calling "brown feelings."

The larger project of this essay engages different psychological and phenomenological discourses in an effort to theorize affective particularity and belonging. Jonathan Flatley (2004) has recently described his own interest in affective particularity in relation to the social as affective mapping. Affective mapping is Flatley's amplification and amendment of Fredric Jameson's (1981) theory of cognitive mapping. To some degree such a description would hold sway with this analysis. My endeavor, more descriptively, is intended to enable a project that imagines a position or narrative of being and becoming that can resist the pull of identitarian models of relationality. Affect is not meant to be a simple placeholder for identity in my work. Indeed, it is supposed to be something altogether different; it is, instead, supposed to be descriptive of the receptors we use to hear each other and the frequencies on which certain subalterns speak and are heard or, more importantly, felt. This leaves us to amend Gayatri Chakravorty Spivak's famous question, "Can the subaltern speak?" (1988, 1999) to ask How does the subaltern feel? How might subalterns feel each other? Toward this end, modified theories of object relations can potentially translate into productive ways in which to consider relationality within a larger social sphere.

Certain acts of translation must happen if we are to use Klein to consider feeling brown or any other modality of minoritarian being or becoming. This entails addressing what I have mentioned as the crypto-universal aspect of various aesthetic and hermeneutical projects. A touchstone for this aspect of my work is the writing of Hortense Spillers. In her powerful meditation on psychoanalysis and race, "All the Things You Could Be by Now if Sigmund Freud's Wife Was Your Mother," the literary theorist deuniversalizes psychoanalytic tools in generative ways:

> Is it not, then, the task of a psychoanalytical protocol to effect a translation from the muteness of desire/wish—that which shames and baffles the subject, even if its origins are dim, not especially known—into an articulated syntactic particularity? This seems to me a passable psychoanalytic goal, but perhaps there is more to it than simply a nice thing to happen? At the very least I am suggesting that an aspect of the emancipatory project hinges on what would appear to be a simple self-attention, except that reaching the articulation requires a process, that of making one's subjectness the object of a disciplined and potentially displaceable attentiveness.
>
> (2003, 400)

Her understatement here is poignant—it would indeed be much more than "simply a nice thing" for groups and circuits of belonging to leave the realm of muteness and attain a valuable "articulated syntactic particularity" that is tuned to group identification. Thus for Spillers, the psychoanalytical protocol is laden with an emancipatory potentiality in that it helps one combat a certain muteness that social logics like homophobia, racism, and sexism would project onto the minoritarian subject. This move to identify the radical impulse in developmental theories aims to recast the theories outside the parameters of positivism and enact their political performativity for circuits of belonging that do not conform to a crypto-universalism associated with the universal white subject. Spillers's argument confirms that a hermeneutical approach that is indeed attentive to psychoanalytic questions may provide descriptions of our own recognition via the route of racial performativity. Racial performativity is the final key concept that this essay foregrounds. The meaning I am assigning to the term *racial performativity* is intended to get at an aspect of race that is "a doing."[3] More precisely, I mean to describe a political doing, the effects that the recognition of racial belonging, coherence, and divergence present in the world. This turn to the performativity of race has to do with the fact that during this moment where the discourse of race is prone to the corrosive forces of corporate multiculturalism and other manifestations of globalization, it seems especially important to consider racial formations through a lens that is not hamstrung by positivism, insofar as the discourse of positivism is at best reductive and unresponsive to the particularities of racial formations. The epistemological core of what race is has become less and less accessible during these tumultuous times. It is therefore expedient to consider what race does. Furthermore, to look at race as a performative enterprise, one that can best be accessed by its effects, may lead us out of political and conceptual impasses that have dogged racial discourse. A critical project attuned to knowing the performativity of race is indeed better suited to decipher what work race does in the world.

What I am describing as "feeling brown, feeling down" is a modality of recognizing the racial performativity generated by an affective particularity that is coded to specific historical subjects who can provisionally be recognized by the term *Latina*. Feeling brown in my analysis is descriptive of the ways in which minoritarian affect is always, no matter what its register, partially illegible in relation to the normative affect performed by normative citizen subjects. The notion of brownness has been rendered differently by essayist Richard Rodriguez, who is also interested in describing brownness in relation to a certain antinormativity. In his most recent (2003) book, the Mexican American memoirist revisits the scene of his racialized upbringing in California and his feelings of nonbelonging to a majoritarian sphere. His narrative uses race (and to a much lesser degree queerness) as a springboard to discuss the particularity of being brown. Yet he leaps so far away from a racially situated notion of this affective phenomenon that brownness becomes the justification for Rodriguez's identification with Richard Nixon over John F. Kennedy during their famous televised debate of 1960. My approach to brownness does not correspond with Rodriguez's work on this ideological level. More nearly, thinking through brownness is akin to what Spillers describes as the "making of one's subjectness the object of a disciplined and potentially displaceable attentiveness" (2003, 400). Brown feelings are not individualized affective particularity; they more nearly express this "displaceable attentiveness," which is to say a larger collective mapping of self and other. Aesthetic practices enable these mapping protocols. In my current research project, I am interested in all sorts of antinormative feelings that correspond to minoritarian becoming. In some cases aesthetic practices and performances offer a particular theoretical lens to understand the ways in which different circuits of belonging connect, which is to say that recognition flickers between minoritarian subjects. Brownness is not white, and it is not black either, yet it does not simply sit midway between them. Brownness, like all forms of racialized attentiveness in North America, is enabled by practices of self-knowing formatted by the nation's imaginary through the powerful spikes in the North American consciousness identified with the public life of blackness. At the same time, brownness is a mode of attentiveness to the self for others that is cognizant of the way in which it is not and can never be whiteness. Whiteness in my analysis is also very specific: I read it as a cultural logic that prescribes and regulates national feelings and comportment. White is thus an affective gauge that helps us understand some modes of emotional countenance and comportment as good or bad. It should go without saying that some modes of whiteness—for example, working-class whiteness—are stigmatized within the majoritarian public sphere. Modes of white womanhood or white ethnicities do not correspond with the affective ruler that measures and naturalizes white feelings as the norm.

Depression is not brown, but there are modalities of depression that seem quite brown. Psychoanalytic critic Antonio Viego (2003) has looked at how American ego psychology attempts to perform a certain kind of therapeutic work on Latino/a subjects. The telos of that project is to achieve a gradually realized whole and well-adjusted minority self. The majority of ego-psychological work explored by Viego attempts to translate notions of traditional Latino maladies—*los nervios* and *attaques*—into ethnically named translations of disorders analyzed as depression and anxiety disorder in English and North American institutional formats. Viego's critique dismantles this wish for an ego that is not shattered in Latino psychology. For Viego, such a desire would be an escape from the social. Thus, any social theory that posits happiness as its goal is a flawed theory. Viego's use of psychoanalytic protocols functions as a displaceable attentiveness that imagines a mode of brown politics not invested in the narrative of a whole and well-adjusted subject.

My notion of feeling down is meant to be a translation of the idea of a depressive position. Thus, down is a way to link position with feeling. The use of the concept of positions, rather than the more developmental discourses on stages, is one of Klein's (1986) amendments to Freud. Scholars interested in Klein or object-relations psychology view positions, as opposed to stages, as less turgid trajectories of emotional development. In this instance Klein's contribution resonates alongside one of Antonio Gramsci's most substantial contributions to social theory, namely, his thinking about the war of positions as a mode of resistance that is different from the classical Marxian revolt described as a war of maneuvers ([1992] 1996). Positions in both theorists' lexicons are provisional and flexible demarcations, practices of being.

The depressive position for Klein is not a stage that must be moved beyond. There are ways in which such occupations of the depressive position lead to reparation, where love helps one surpass paranoid and schizoid feelings. In infancy the child splits the maternal other into two objects. One is a good breast that represents a continuous flow of fulfillment—a sense of being one with the mother. Yet the fact that such a flow is not continuous leads to feelings of resentment and hate toward what becomes the bad breast. For Klein these destructive feelings vector into a sort of cannibalistic or sadistic urge. The infant later feels considerable guilt about possessing such destructive feelings. At some point the split object becomes, once again, whole, and the child is able to once again introject it. The object, like the subject, is never whole, but the fiction or feeling of wholeness is crucial for survival within the social. In her 1946 paper "Notes on Some Schizoid Mechanisms" Klein explains that "the drive to make reparation, which comes to the fore at this stage, can be regarded as a consequence of a greater insight into psychic reality and of growing synthesis, for it shows a more realistic response to feelings of grief, guilt and fear of loss resulting from the loved object. Since the drive to repair or protect the injured object paves the way for more satisfactory object relations and sublimations, it in turn increases synthesis between inner and external situations" ([1946] 1986, 189).

The depressive position is, in Kleinian theory, associated with a kind of interjection, which is a stark opposite to the practice of projecting menace or threat as exterior to the self. The depressive position is not a linear or task-oriented sense of developmental closure. It is instead a position that we live in, and it describes the ways in which we attempt to enter psychic reality, where we can see objects as whole, both interior and exterior, not simply as something that hums outside our existence. To extend, or in Spillers's phraseology, "displace," this attentiveness of the self to others is to begin to understand one of the deep functions of brown feelings, to see the other in alterity as existing in a relational field to the self. In this sense I am proposing an ethics of brownness, one that attempts to incorporate understandings of the psychic in the service of understanding the social. The whole object that is interjected in the depressive position is not real, or more nearly, not firmly bound. One always feels its drive toward fragmentation, but taking up the depressive position is one way in which, as subjects, we resist a disrepair within the social that would lead to a breakdown in one's ability to see and know the other. That would certainly be a mode of clinical depression.

In queer studies Eve Kosofsky Sedgwick (2003) has recently turned to the divide between paranoia and reparation. Sedgwick has argued that paranoia has become a standardized posture taken in queer critique and that it thus has become routine rather than critical thinking. The paranoid move is always about a certain hermeneutic unveiling of an external threat. Such a move becomes routine, or numb repetition, and renders the paranoid subject unable to participate in what Spillers would call the intramural protocol of a displaceable self-attentiveness. Spillers (2003) wishes to turn away from a critique of "the man" and turn to a theory of the way in which relational skills are organized around "the one." The one, for Spillers, is interior to the life world of the black community, the lives we have among one another within racial formations. This is not to say that there are not multiple threats presented by an outsider, by the man, but Spillers wants us to understand the ways in which our own sense of relationality and practices of belonging within communities of color are threatened from within. Spillers in this instance is once again insisting on repealing a certain paranoid sense of being in the world where menace is exterior to our world of intraracial or ethnic experience and instead wants to linger or dwell in the realm of this enabling fantasy of a whole object.

Sedgwick invites her readers and the field of queer critique to consider reparation. In this same intervention Sedgwick wishes to consider how certain strong theories of the social, theories that can be codified as prescriptive and totalizing, might not be as advantageous at this particular moment as weak theories that do not position themselves in the same masterful, totalizing fashion. I would align a Gramscian war of positions with this weak theory. I understand the theory-making impulse that propels my description of feeling brown as resisting the strong-theory model. The stitching I am doing between critical race theories, queer critique, and psychological object-relations theory is a provisional and heuristic approach that wishes to stave off the totalizing aspect of all those modes of critique.

I want to suggest that the ethics of "the one" that Spillers rehearses is a mode of intramural depressive positionality that gives us the ability to know and experience the other who shares a particular affective or emotional valence with us. The reparation staged in Spillers's theoretical work is informed by a desire to return to another place that she describes as "old-fashioned." *Old-fashioned* is associated with the nonsecular belonging that in turn is associated with the history of the black church (2003). Spillers explicitly desires a secular space where such relationality is possible, but *old-fashioned* is not only deployed in its conventional usage, it is also written in a psychic sense—the desire for a moment before communities of color lapsed into functional impasse. This functional impasse is certainly relational to a well-founded sense of paranoia and also to the ways in which such continuous challenges within the social spur a disconnect from psychic reality where our relational potentiality is diminished. This turn to the old-fashioned in Spillers, this desire for "the one," is a desire that is relational to a depressive position that does not succumb to a paranoid-schizoid position. The depressive position in Klein is the ethical position. Taking that point into account, I would argue that feeling brown, feeling down is an ethical position within the social for the minoritarian subject.

My stitching together of theories, my attempt at weaving together a provisional whole that is indeed not a whole but rather an enabling sense of wholeness that allows a certain level of social recognition, is a reparative performance. However, one should be cognizant of the three different modes of reparation that Klein distinguishes. It is useful to break these types down. One is a kind of manic reparation that carries a sense of triumph, since it essentially flips over the child–parent relationship at the parent's expense. Another notion of the reparative is a mode of obsessive reparation that can be characterized as compulsive repetition, a sort of placating magical thinking. Finally, there is the type of reparation that I wish to promote for the fields of inquiry discussed in this essay. This modality is what I see at work in Bustamante's installation. This would be a form of reparation that is grounded in love for the object. Klein argues that "one moment after we have seen the most sadistic impulses, we meet with performances showing the greatest capacity for love and the wish to make all possible sacrifices to be loved" ([1935] 1986, 124). Utilizing Klein as a theorist of

relationality is advantageous because she is true to the facts of violence, division, and hierarchy that punctuate the social, yet she is, at another moment, a deeply idealistic thinker who
understands the need to not simply cleanse negativity but instead to promote the desire that
the subject has in the wake of the negative to reconstruct a relational field. Love for Klein is
thus not just a romantic abstraction; it is indeed a kind of striving for belonging that does not
ignore the various obstacles that the subject must overcome to achieve the most provisional
belonging.

Neapolitan, Bustamante's installation, is stitched together by a homey crocheted binding
that seems elastic and permeable, its texture reminiscent of a nostalgia for a mode of domesticity associated with hobbyism, with craft and domestic forms of belonging. The texture of
the installation is meant to connote a sense of home and belonging that is perhaps squarely in
the past, yet it nonetheless wishes to recirculate that sense of belonging in relation to our
presentness and our futurity. While not a cynical assemblage, the object is not without a
sense of humor. The sad crow of depression, a species that is quite apart from the bluebird of
happiness, wears a snug little bonnet that links him to the odd object over which he sits
watch. It is a construct as elaborate and provisional as the selves we perform within the social.
The fact that a monitor is enshrouded by a homemade covering indexes the ways in which
televisual reality is linked to real life and fantasy. The homey fabric enfolding the television
set indicates that home is where the heart is, and at the center of this home we will find a
television set.

The video on the loop and the performance of sobbing, rewinding, and sobbing again is
a performance of repetition. Repetition is the piece's most obvious depressive quality. It
describes the ways in which subjects occupy and dwell within the depressive position. The
piece's play of light, the illumination bathing the artist's face, and the illumination that the
object itself offers comment on a complicated choreography of interjection and projection.
The sound track that washes over the artist and, in turn, the viewer is the familiar swelling
associated with melodrama, the weepy, the woman's film, and this track, in relation to this
installation, is the sound of brown feelings.

The film being screened in the video, the source of the sadness and somatic excess, is a
Cuban film about homosexuality and revolution. Its tragedy has to do with the way in which
queerness can finally not be held by the nation-state. This is the rip, the moment of breakdown in a revolutionary imaginary. In a similar fashion, this is a rip or break in the object-
relation theories that I have been considering. In the bulk of this work, in Klein, D.W.
Winnicott, and others who came after Freud, homosexuality is a primitive condition that
needs to be contained, managed, or surpassed. Queerness is the site of emotional breakdown
and the activation of the melodrama in the installation. I would thus position Bustamante's
art object as a corrective in relation to the homophobic developmental plot. Queerness, the
installation shows, never fully disappears; instead, it haunts the present. More nearly, it is
something whose mourning is a condition of possibility for other modes of sexuality that are
less problematic.

All of this mourning comes out of a specific time and place, which is to say that it is
historically situated. To illustrate this point, I turn to a moment in London, during a
question-and-answer session following an artist's talk in which Bustamante discussed
Neapolitan. When the artist fielded the question "How is your work different from that of
Bas Jan Ader, another artist who represented his tears?" I wanted to answer the question for
the artist, but, fulfilling my role as critic and onlooker, I could not. I nonetheless take this
opportunity to do so in hope of explaining not only the difference between two art projects,
spread apart by thirty years, but also to remark on the value of displaceable attentiveness in
relation to aesthetics and psychoanalysis. Ader mysteriously disappeared at sea in 1975 as
part of his performance project. Depression, sadness, and loss saturate his work. The

three-minute black-and-white film *I Am Too Sad to Tell You* (1971) is reminiscent of Bustamante's crying tape. It portrays the artist driven to tears and crying for a prolonged time. The motivation behind his emotion is left even more ambiguous than the themes that constitute Bustamante's installation. Ader's performance rehearses something that is very much like the ethics of Klein's depressive position. Ader's work is beautiful and moving. It seduces us with the lure of the universal. These tears are not wrapped up in the kind of affective particularity that I associate with brownness and queerness in my reading of *Neapolitan*. I reference *I Am Too Sad to Tell You* in an effort to illustrate the ways in which some tears access a universal sadness or loss that offers us a generalized story of the world of affect, stopping short of linking affect to historical loss. What motivates these tears? Loss and history become untethered in Ader's film. While *Neapolitan* certainly speaks across particularities within the social, it addresses a historical particularity, one that I describe as a feeling, feeling down.

Jennifer Doyle (2005) skillfully compares Ader's work with that of feminist artist Marina Abramovic's video performance *The Onion* (1995) and Hayley Newman's *Crying Glasses (An Aid to Melancholia)* (1995). In Abramovic's piece the lauded performance artist lists complaints about her life, ones that are not very interesting, banalities like time spent in waiting rooms and the annoyances that accompany travel. Newman's performance is one of her artificial performances, fake performances that are documented as if they were real in a series she calls Connotations Performance. However, the distinction between the two women artists' works and Ader's, as described by Doyle, is instructive when thinking through the historicizing of affect and tears:

> As the title reminds us (telling us that the artist won't tell us), we do not know why Ader is crying. As a male artist with a particular mythology (he disappeared while attempting to sail across the Atlantic in execution of a performance), Bas Jan Ader is closer to the eighteenth-century ideal of the gentlemanly "man of feeling" than he is to the female melodrama cited by Abramovic. The portrait is an extension of his interest in the subject of his own vulnerability (as in a series of short films that document the artist falling over—riding a bicycle into a canal, falling from a tree, standing and swaying from side to side until he falls down). His film, when compared with Newman's photograph or Abramovic's perform-ance, comes off as more purely seductive—and as somehow more private—in part because nothing in the film indicates that we must read it as "produced" for the camera.

> (2005, 48–49)

The man of feeling is a universal subject. The spectator cannot know what his tears are about because they are deeply private, as Doyle indicates, as is the very nature of the tear. However, they are also universal tears in the ways in which Newman's are false tears (the tears of feminine deception) or Abramovic's are onion-peeling kitchen tears (the tears that mark women's work). Doyle, citing Jameson (1981), reminds readers that "history is what hurts" (Doyle 2005, 50). We are then left to contemplate which histories are marked by particular tears and which histories are elided. In the remainder of this essay, I will discuss an attempt to get at the performativity of brownness that marks Bustamante's tears.

In a review for *Artweek*, Lindsay Westbrook discusses the installation in terms that help make visible what outside contingencies get projected onto Bustamante's piece by its audi-ence: "Nao Bustamante's *Neapolitan* is also brand new and deals with several themes that recur in her work; emotionality, vulnerability and stereotypes of gender and Mexican-American culture; we watch her watching a scene from the Cuban film *Strawberries and*

Chocolate. She is making herself cry, periodically rewinding the tape and wiping her eyes on a Mexican flag hanky. The work is profoundly self-conscious, of course, and, for that reason, cynical. But it is also genuinely sad, expressing sorrow and mourning, perhaps, for the current world situation" (2003, 14).

The dynamics of projection in this thumbnail sketch are worth looking at for a couple of reasons. The hanky that the reviewer identifies as the Mexican flag is no such thing. It is merely a colored dish towel. The fact that Bustamante's Mexicanness was projected onto her installation does in fact make a case for the various ways in which brown paranoia is not something that can be wished away, no matter how much we would like to fully escape the regime of paranoia. Indeed, the brown depressive position I'm describing is called into being in relation to the various projections screened on the embodied self from the outside. The formulation, in which self-consciousness equals cynicism, is odd. Yet the lines with which Westbrook closes her analysis do bear remembering. Indeed this mode of sadness has a great deal to do with the "world situation." That is, the video represents and performs a political depression, which is neither a clinical depression nor a literal breakdown. This political recognition contains a reparative impulse that I want to describe as enabling and liberatory, in the same way that an attentiveness to those things mute within us, brought into language and given a syntax, can potentially lead to an insistence on change and political transformation.

In discussing the depressive position, Julia Kristeva (2004) reminds Klein's readers that reparation is far from idyllic, since the purportedly whole object is tainted with despair. The object's state of disintegration is never fully resolved. It is instead worked through. Certainly *Neapolitan* is nothing like an ideal aesthetic object, but it does represent a creative impulse, where grief is temporally conjoined to ideas. In this essay I've attempted to suggest the various ways in which the depressive position is a site of potentiality and not simply a break-down of the self or the social fabric. Reparation is part of the depressive position; it signals a certain kind of hope. The depressive position is a tolerance of the loss and guilt that underlies the subject's sense of self—which is to say that it does not avoid or wish away loss and guilt. It is a position in which the subject negotiates reality, resisting the instinct to fall into the delusional realm of the paranoid schizoid. I have also attempted to call attention to the ways in which minoritarian chains of recognition can benefit from avoiding paranoid positions that keep them from engaging the necessary project of being attentive to the self in an effort to know the other, but indeed my central goal has been one of enacting and performing a sort of reparative analysis that describes and bolsters the project of feeling brown. The depressive position, as described in the work of Klein and adjusted through Spillers's questions, offers a useful insight into one dimension of what I am calling feeling brown. Feeling brown is a mode of racial performativity, a doing within the social that surpasses limitations of epistemological renderings of race.

Notes

1   This word usage is calibrated to address a minoritarian subject. For more on this particular narrative of subjectivity, see Muñoz 1999.

2   See http://www.naobustamante.com/art_neapolitan.html.

3   This idea of performativity as "a doing" is indebted to a line of thought in the postdisciplinary field of performance studies that engages the work of the philosopher of everyday speech, J.L. Austin, and his book *How to Do Things with Words* (1962). See Parker and Sedgwick 1995 for a useful introduction to some of Austin's postdisciplinary relevance.

References

Austin, J.L. 1962. *How to Do Things with Words*. Oxford: Clarendon.

Crying Glasses (An Aid to Melancholia). 1995. Performance art by Hayley Newman. From the series Connotations Performance. Screened at the Ikon Gallery, Birmingham, U.K.

Doyle, Jennifer. 2005. "Critical Tears: Melodrama and Museums." In *Getting Emotional*, ed. Nicholas Baume, 42–53. Boston: Institute of Contemporary Art.

Flatley, Jonathan. 2004. "Reading into Henry James." *Criticism* 46 (1): 103–23.

Gramsci, Antonio. (1992) 1996. *The Prison Notebooks*. Trans. Joseph A. Buttigieg and Antonio Callari. Ed. Joseph A. Buttigieg. New York: Columbia University Press.

I Am Too Sad to Tell You. 1971. Directed by Bas Jan Ader. 16 mm black-and-white film, silent; 3 minutes 21 seconds. Independently produced.

Jameson, Fredric. 1981. *The Political Unconscious: Narrative as a Socially Symbolic Act*. Ithaca, NY: Cornell University Press.

Klein, Melanie. (1935) 1986. "The Psychogenesis of Manic-Depressive States." In Klein 1986, 115–45.

—. (1946) 1986. "Notes on Schizoid Mechanisms." In Klein 1986, 175–200.

—. 1986. *The Selected Melanie Klein*. Ed. Juliet Mitchell. New York: Free Press.

Kristeva, Julia. 2004. *Melanie Klein*. Trans. Ross Guberman. New York: Columbia University Press.

Muñoz, José Esteban. 1999. *Disidentifications: Queers of Color and the Performance of Politics*. Minneapolis: University of Minnesota Press.

Neopolitan. 2003. Performance art by Nao Bustamante. Independently produced.

The Onion. 1995. Marina Abramovic. Video still. Independently produced.

Parker, Andrew, and Eve Kosofsky Sedgwick. 1995. "Introduction: Performativity and Performance." In their *Performativity and Performance*, 1–18. New York: Routledge.

Rodriguez, Richard. 2003. *Brown: The Last Discovery of America*. New York: Penguin.

Sedgwick, Eve Kosofsky. 2003. *Touching Feeling: Affect, Pedagogy, Performativity*. Durham, NC: Duke University Press.

Spillers, Hortense. 2003. "All the things you could be by now if Sigmund Freud's wife was your mother": Psychoanalysis and Race. In her *Black, White, and in Color: Essays on American Literature and Culture*, 376–428. Chicago: University of Chicago Press.

Spivak, Gayatri Chakravorty. 1988. "Can the Subaltern Speak?" In *Marxism and the Interpretation of Culture*, eds. Cary Nelson and Lawrence Grossberg, 271–313. Chicago: University of Chicago Press.

—. 1999. *A Critique of Postcolonial Reason*. Cambridge, MA: Harvard University Press.

Viego, Antonio. 2003. "The Unconscious of Latino/a Studies." *Latino Studies* 1 (3): 333–36.

Westbrook, Lindsay. 2003. "Review." *Artweek* 34 (10): 14.

Chapter 25

Sara Ahmed

QUEER FEELINGS

Sara Ahmed is Professor of Race and Cultural Studies in the Department of Media and Communications at Goldsmiths University of London. Keyed to the body and its experience of the world, her research intersects with phenomenology, critical race studies, feminism, and queer theory.

In this essay, originally a chapter from her book *The Cultural Politics of Emotion* (2004), Ahmed explores the political potential of queer feeling in heteronormative culture. Through a phenomenological and performative account of the formation of bodies and identities, social and public spaces, and the enforcement of norms, Ahmed traces how queer feelings are produced. Arguing that living with norms produces queer affects of shame and melancholia, Ahmed considers how queers inhabit norms differently in relation to the idealization of the family, processes of grieving, and the distributions of pleasures. While agreeing that queer theory is anti-normative, Ahmed argues that queer does not have to mean a choice between assimilation or transgression; neither can it be free from norms or transcend the global circuits of capital. Her claim is that it is rather in the moment of queer's proximity to (hetero) normativity—the uncomfortable fit of queer bodies to heteronormative spaces—that queer can be at its most transformative.

> As the immigrant makes visible the processes of production, she also exemplifies the idea that the family is in need of protection because it is losing its viability, increasingly posed in the horrors of the imaginary as needing ever more fierce strategies of security to ensure its ideal of reproducing itself. It is this connection that is hidden – a relation between the production of life (both discursive and reproductive) and global production.
>
> (Goodman 2001: 194)

THE REPRODUCTION OF LIFE itself, where life is conflated with a social ideal ("life as we know it") is often represented as threatened by the existence of others: immigrants, queers, other others. These others become sources of fascination that allow the ideal to be posited as ideal through their embodiment of the failure of the ideal to be translated into being or action. We might note that "reproduction" itself comes under question.

The reproduction of life—in the form of the future generation—becomes bound up with the reproduction of culture, through the stabilisation of specific arrangements for living ("the family"). The family is idealisable through the narrative of threat and insecurity; the family is presented as vulnerable, and as needing to be defended against others who violate the conditions of its reproduction. As Goodman shows us, the moral defence of the family as a way of life becomes a matter of "global politics". [. . .] What needs closer examination is how heterosexuality becomes a script that binds the familial with the global: the coupling of man and woman becomes a kind of "birthing", a giving birth not only to new life, but to ways of living that are already recognisable as forms of civilisation. It is this narrative of coupling as a condition for the reproduction of life, culture and value that explains the slide in racist narratives between the fear of strangers and immigrants (xenophobia), the fear of queers (homophobia) and the fear of miscegenation (as well as other illegitimate couplings).

These narratives or scripts do not, of course, simply exist "out there" to legislate the political actions of states. They also shape bodies and lives, including those that follow and depart from such narratives in the ways in which they love and live, in the decisions that they make and take within the intimate spheres of home and work. It is important to consider how compulsory heterosexuality—defined as the accumulative effect of the repetition of the narrative of heterosexuality as an ideal coupling—shapes what it is possible for bodies to do,[1] even if it does not contain what it is possible to be. Bodies take the shape of norms that are repeated over time and with force. The work of repetition involves the concealment of labour under the sign of nature. I want to argue that norms surface *as* the surfaces of bodies; norms are a matter of impressions, of how bodies are "impressed upon" by the world, as a world made up of others. In other words, such impressions are effects of labour; how bodies work and are worked upon shapes the surfaces of bodies. Regulative norms function in a way as "repetitive strain injuries" (RSIs). Through repeating some gestures and not others, or through being orientated in some directions and not others, bodies become contorted; they get twisted into shapes that enable some action only insofar as they restrict capacity for other kinds of action.

I would suggest that heteronormativity also affects the surfaces of bodies, which surface through impressions made by others. Compulsory heterosexuality shapes bodies by the assumption that a body "must" orient itself towards some objects and not others, objects that are secured as ideal through the fantasy of difference. Hence compulsory heterosexuality shapes which bodies one "can" legitimately approach as would-be lovers and which one cannot. In shaping one's approach to others, compulsory heterosexuality also shapes one's own body, *as a congealed history of past approaches*. Sexual orientation is not then simply about the direction one takes towards an object of desire, as if this direction does not affect other things that we do. Sexual orientation involves bodies that leak into worlds; it involves a way of orientating the body towards and away from others, which affects how one can enter different kinds of social spaces (which presumes certain bodies, certain directions, certain ways of loving and living), even if it does not lead bodies to the same places. To make a simple but important point: orientations affect what it is that bodies can do.[2] Hence, the failure to orient oneself "towards" the ideal sexual object affects how we live in the world, an affect that is readable as the failure to reproduce, and as a threat to the social ordering of life itself.

Of course, one does not have to do what one is compelled to do: for something to be compulsory shows that it is not necessary. But to refuse to be compelled by the narratives of ideal heterosexuality in one's orientation to others is still to be affected by those narratives; they work to script one's orientation as a form of disobedience. The affects of "not following" the scripts can be multiple. We can consider, for example, the psychic as well as social costs of loving a body that is supposed to be unloveable for the subject I am, or loving a body that I was "supposed to" repudiate, which may include shame and melancholia (Butler 1997a;

Braidotti 2002: 53). The negative affects of "not quite" living in the norms show us how loving loves that are not "normative" involves being subject to such norms precisely in the costs and damage that are incurred when not following them. Do queer moments happen when this failure to reproduce norms as forms of life is embraced or affirmed as a political and ethical alternative? Such affirmation would not be about the conversion of shame into pride, but the enjoyment of the negativity of shame, an enjoyment of that which has been designated shameful by normative culture (see Barber and Clark 2002: 22–29).

I could ask the question: How does it feel to inhabit a body that fails to reproduce an ideal? But this is not my question. Instead, I wish to explore "queer feelings" without translating such an exploration into a matter of "feeling queer". Such a translation would assume "queerness" involves a particular emotional life, or that there are feelings that bodies "have" given their failure to inhabit or follow a heterosexual ideal. Of course, one can feel queer. There are feelings involved in the self-perception of "queerness", a self-perception that is bodily, as well as bound up with "taking on" a name. But these feelings are mediated and they are attached to the category "queer" in ways that are complex and contingent, precisely because the category is produced in relation to histories that render it a sign of failed being or "non-being".[3] In examining the affective potential of queer, I will firstly consider the relationship between norms and affects in debates on queer families. I will then discuss the role of grief in queer politics with specific reference to queer responses to September 11. And finally, I will reflect on the role of pleasure in queer lifestyles or countercultures, and will ask how the enjoyment of social and sexual relations that are designated as "non-(re)productive" can function as forms of political disturbance in an affective economy organised around the principle that pleasure is only ethical as an incentive or reward for good conduct.

(Dis)comfort and norms

It is important to consider how heterosexuality functions powerfully not only as a series of norms and ideals, but also through emotions that shape bodies as well as worlds: (hetero) norms are investments, which are "taken on" and "taken in" by subjects. To practise heterosexuality by following its scripts in one's choice of some love objects—and refusal of others—is also to become invested in the reproduction of heterosexuality. Of course, one does not "do" heterosexuality simply through whom one does and does not have sex with. Heterosexuality as a script for an ideal life makes much stronger claims. It is assumed that all arrangements will follow from the arrangement of the couple: man/woman. It is no accident that compulsory heterosexuality works powerfully in the most casual modes of conversation. One asks: "Do you have a boyfriend?" (to a girl), or one asks: "Do you have a girlfriend?" (to a boy). Queer subjects feel the tiredness of making corrections and departures; the pressure of this insistence, this presumption, this demand that asks either for a "passing over" (a moment of passing, which is not always available) or for direct or indirect forms of self-revelation ("but actually, he's a she" or "she's a he", or just saying "she" instead of "he" or "he" instead of "she" at the "obvious" moment). No matter how "out" you may be, how (un)comfortably queer you may feel, those moments of interpellation get repeated over time, and can be experienced as a bodily injury; moments which position queer subjects as failed in their failure to live up to the "hey you too" of heterosexual self-narration. The everydayness of compulsory heterosexuality is also its affectiveness, wrapped up as it is with moments of ceremony (birth, marriage, death), which bind families together, and with the ongoing investment in the sentimentality of friendship and romance. Of course, such sentimentality is deeply embedded with public as well as private culture; stories of heterosexual romance proliferate as a matter of human interest. As Lauren Berlant and Michael Warner argue:

"National heterosexuality is the mechanism by which a core national culture can be imagined as a sanitised space of sentimental feeling" (Berlant and Warner 2000: 313).

We can consider the sanitised space as a comfort zone. Normativity is comfortable for those who can inhabit it. The word "comfort" suggests well-being and satisfaction, but it also suggests an ease and easiness. To follow the rules of heterosexuality is to be at ease in a world that reflects back the couple form one inhabits as an ideal. Of course, one can be made to feel uneasy by one's inhabitance of an ideal. One can be made uncomfortable by one's own comforts. To see heterosexuality as an ideal that one might or might not follow—or to be uncomfortable by the privileges one is given by inhabiting a heterosexual world—is a less comforting form of comfort. But comfort it remains and comfort is very hard to notice when one experiences it. Having uncomfortably inhabited the comforts of heterosexuality for many years, I know this too well. Now, living a queer life, I can reflect on many comforts that I did not even begin to notice despite my "felt" discomforts. We don't tend to notice what is comfortable, even when we think we do.

Thinking about comfort is hence always a useful starting place for thinking. So let's think about how it feels to be comfortable. Say you are sinking into a comfortable chair. Note I already have transferred the affect to an object ("it is comfortable"). But comfort is about the fit between body and object: my comfortable chair may be awkward for you, with your differently shaped body. Comfort is about an encounter between more than one body, which is the promise of a "sinking" feeling. It is, after all, pain or discomfort that return one's atten-tion to the surfaces of the body *as body*. To be comfortable is to be so at ease with one's environment that it is hard to distinguish where one's body ends and the world begins. One fits, and by fitting, the surfaces of bodies disappear from view. The disappearance of the surface is instructive: in feelings of comfort, bodies extend into spaces, and spaces extend into bodies. The sinking feeling involves a seamless space, or a space where you can't see the "stitches" between bodies.

Heteronormativity functions as a form of public comfort by allowing bodies to extend into spaces that have already taken their shape. Those spaces are lived as comfortable as they allow bodies to fit in; the surfaces of social space are already impressed upon by the shape of such bodies (like a chair that acquires its shape by the repetition of some bodies inhabiting it: we can almost see the shape of bodies as "impressions" on the surface). The impressions acquired by surfaces function as traces of bodies. We can even see this process in social spaces. As Gill Valentine has argued, the "heterosexualisation" of public spaces such as streets is naturalised by the repetition of different forms of heterosexual conduct (images on billboards, music played, displays of heterosexual intimacy and so on), a process which goes unnoticed by heterosexual subjects (Valentine 1996: 149). The surfaces of social as well as bodily space "record" the repetition of acts, and the passing by of some bodies and not others.

Heteronormativity also becomes a form of comforting: one feels better by the warmth of being faced by a world one has already taken in. One does not notice this *as a world* when one has been shaped by that world, and even acquired its shape. Norms may not only have a way of disappearing from view, but may also be that which we do not consciously feel. Queer subjects, when faced by the "comforts" of heterosexuality may feel uncomfortable (the body does not "sink into" a space that has already taken its shape). Discomfort is a feeling of disorientation: one's body feels out of place, awkward, unsettled. I know that feeling too well, the sense of out-of-place-ness and estrangement involves an acute awareness of the surface of one's body, which appears *as* surface, when one cannot inhabit the social skin, which is shaped by some bodies, and not others. Furthermore, queer subjects may also be "asked" not to make heterosexuals feel uncomfortable by avoiding the display of signs of queer intimacy, which is itself an uncomfortable feeling, a restriction on what one can do with one's body, and another's body, in social space.[4] The availability of comfort for some bodies may depend on the labour of others, and the burden of concealment. Comfort may operate as a form of "feeling fetishism": some bodies can "have" comfort, only as an effect of the work of others, where the work itself is concealed from view.[5]

It is hence for very good reasons that queer theory has been defined not only as anti-heteronormative, but as anti-normative. As Tim Dean and Christopher Lane argue, queer theory "advocates a politics based on resistance to all norms" (Dean and Lane 2001: 7). Importantly, heteronormativity refers to more than simply the presumption that it is normal to be heterosexual. The "norm" is regulative, and is supported by an "ideal" that associates sexual conduct with other forms of conduct. We can consider, for example, how the restriction of the love object is not simply about the desirability of *any* heterosexual coupling. The couple should be "a good match" (a judgement that often exercises conventional class and racial assumptions about the importance of "matching" the backgrounds of partners) and they should exclude others from the realm of sexual intimacy (an idealisation of monogamy, that often equates intimacy with property rights or rights to the intimate other as property). Furthermore, a heterosexual coupling may only approximate an ideal through being sanctioned by marriage, by participating in the ritual of reproduction and good parenting, by being good neighbours as well as lovers and parents, and by being even better citizens. In this way, normative culture involves the differentiation between legitimate and illegitimate ways of living whereby the preservation of what is legitimate ("life as we know it") is assumed to be necessary for the well-being of the next generation. Heteronormativity involves the reproduction or transmission of culture through how one lives one's life in relation to others.

For queer theorists, it is hence important that queer lives do not follow the scripts of heteronormative culture: they do not become, in Judith Halberstam's provocative and compelling term, "homonormative" lives (Halberstam 2003: 331). Such lives would not desire access to comfort; they would maintain their discomfort with all aspects of normative culture in how they live. Ideally, they would not have families, get married, settle down into unthinking coupledom, give birth to and raise children, join neighbourhood watch, or pray for the nation in times of war. Each of these acts would "support" the ideals that script such lives as queer, failed and unliveable in the first place. The aspiration to ideals of conduct that is central to the reproduction of heteronormativity has been called, quite understandably, a form of assimilation.

Take, for instance, the work of Andrew Sullivan. In his *Virtually Normal* he argues that most gay people want to be normal; and that being gay does not mean being not normal, even if one is not quite as normal as a straight person (to paraphrase Homi Bhabha, "almost normal, but not quite"). So he suggests that one can aspire to *have* a heterosexual life without *being* heterosexual: the only difference would be the choice of one's love object. As he puts it:

> It's perfectly possible to combine a celebration of the traditional family with the celebration of a stable homosexual relationship. The one, after all, is modelled on the other. If constructed carefully as a conservative social ideology, the notion of stable gay relationships might even serve to buttress the ethic of heterosexual marriage, by showing how even those excluded from it can wish to model themselves on its shape and structure.
>
> (Sullivan 1996: 112)

Here, gay relationships are valued and celebrated insofar as they are "modelled" on the traditional model of the heterosexual family. Indeed, Sullivan explicitly defines his project as a way of supporting and extending the ideal of the family by showing how those who are "not it" seek to "become it". Gay relationships, by miming the forms of heterosexual coupling, hence pledge their allegiance to the very forms they cannot inhabit. This mimicry is, as Douglas Crimp (2002) has argued, a way of sustaining the psychic conditions of melancholia insofar as Sullivan identifies with that which he cannot be, and indeed with what has already rejected him. As Crimp remarks, Sullivan is "incapable of recognising the intractability of homophobia because his melancholia consists precisely in his identification with the homophobe's repudiation of him" (Crimp 2002: 6). Assimilation involves a desire to approximate an ideal that one has already failed; an identification with one's designation as a failed subject. The choice of assimilation—queer skin, straight masks—is clearly about supporting the violence of heteronormative distinctions between legitimate and illegitimate lives.[6]

As Judith Butler has argued, one of the biggest problems in campaigns for gay marriage is precisely the way that they may strengthen the hierarchy between legitimate and illegitimate lives. Rather than the hierarchy resting on a distinction between gay and straight, it becomes displaced onto a new distinction between more and less legitimate queer relationships (Butler 2002: 18). As she asks, does gay marriage "only become an 'option' by extending itself as a norm (and thus foreclosing options), one which also extends property relations and renders the social forms for sexuality more conservative?" (Butler 2002: 21). In other words, if some of the rights of heterosexuality are extended to queers, what happens to queers who don't take up those rights; whose life choices and sexual desires cannot be translated into the form of marriage, even when emptied of its predication on heterosexual coupling? Do these (non-married) queers become the illegitimate others against which the ideal of marriage is supported?

Of course, the question of gay marriage remains a political dilemma. For not to support the extension of the right of marriage to gay relationships could give support to the status quo, which maintains the distinction between legitimate and illegitimate lives on the grounds of sexual orientation. As Judith Butler (2002) argues, the social and psychic costs of not having one's relationship recognised by others (whether or not the recognition is determined by law) are enormous especially in situations of loss and bereavement (see the following section). I want to enter this debate by considering how the political choice of being queer or straight (or an assimilated queer) can be contested. Butler herself contests the choice through adopting a position of ambivalence. Whilst I recognise the value of such ambivalence, I want to suggest that more reflection on queer attachments might allow us to avoid positing assimilation or transgression as choices.

To begin with, we can return to my description of what we might call a queer life. I suggested that "ideally" such lives will maintain a discomfort with the scripts of heteronormative existence. The reliance on this word is telling. For already in describing what may be queer, I am also defining grounds of an ideality, in which to have an ideal queer life, or even to be legitimately queer, people must act in some ways rather than others. We need to ask: How does defining a queer ideal rely on the existence of others who fail the ideal? Who can and cannot embody the queer ideal? Such an ideal is not equally accessible to all, even all those who identify with the sign "queer" or other "signs" of non-normative sexuality. Gayatri Gopinath (2003), for example, reflects on how public and visible forms of "queerness" may not be available to lesbians from South Asia, where it may be in the private spaces of home that bodies can explore homo-erotic pleasures. Her argument shows how queer bodies have different access to public forms of culture, which affect how they can inhabit those publics. Indeed, whilst being queer may feel uncomfortable within heterosexual space, it does not then follow that queers always feel comfortable in queer spaces. I have felt discomfort in some queer spaces, again, as a feeling of being out of place. This is not to say that I have been *made* to feel uncomfortable; the discomfort is itself a sign that queer spaces may extend some bodies more than others (for example, some queer spaces might extend the mobility of white, middle-class bodies). At times, I feel uncomfortable about inhabiting the word "queer", worrying that I am not queer enough, or have not been queer for long enough, or am just not the right kind of queer. We can feel uncomfortable in the categories we inhabit, even categories that are shaped by their refusal of public comfort.

Furthermore, the positing of an ideal of being free from scripts that define what counts as a legitimate life seems to presume a negative model of freedom; defined here as *freedom from norms*. Such a negative model of freedom idealises movement and detachment, constructing a mobile form of subjectivity that could escape from the norms that constrain what it is that bodies can do. Others have criticised queer theory for its idealisation of movement (Epps 2001: 412; Fortier 2003). As Epps puts it: "Queer theory tends to place great stock in movement, especially when it is movement against, beyond, or away from rules and regulations, norms and conventions, borders and limits . . . it makes fluidity a fetish" (Epps 2001: 413). The idealisation of movement, or transformation of movement into a fetish, depends upon the exclusion of others who are already positioned as *not free in the same way*. Bodies that can move with more ease may also more easily shape and be shaped by the sign "queer". It is for this reason that Biddy Martin suggests that we need to "stop defining queerness as mobile and fluid in relation to what then gets construed as stagnant and ensnaring" (Martin 1996: 46). Indeed, the idealisation of movement depends upon a prior model of what counts as a queer life, which may exclude others, those who have attachments that are not readable as queer, or indeed those who may lack the (cultural as well as economic) capital to support the "risk" of maintaining antinormativity as a permanent orientation.

Queer lives do not suspend the attachments that are crucial to the reproduction of heteronormativity, and this does not diminish "queerness", but intensifies the work that it can do. Queer lives remain shaped by that which they fail to reproduce. To turn this around, queer lives shape what gets reproduced: in the very failure to reproduce the norms through how they inhabit them, queer lives produce different effects. For example, the care work of lesbian parents may involve "having" to live in close proximity to heterosexual cultures (in the negotiation with schools, other mothers, local communities), whilst not being able to inhabit the heterosexual ideal. The gap between the script and the body, including the bodily form of "the family", may involve discomfort and hence may "rework" the script. The reworking is not inevitable, as it is dependent or contingent on other social factors (especially class) and it does not necessarily involve conscious political acts.

We can return to my point about comfort: comfort is the effect of bodies being able to "sink" into spaces that have already taken their shape. Discomfort is not simply a choice or decision—"I feel uncomfortable about this or that"—but an effect of bodies inhabiting spaces that do not take or "extend" their shape. So the closer that queer subjects get to the spaces defined by heteronormativity the more *potential* there is for a reworking of the heteronormative,[7] partly as the proximity "shows" how the spaces extend some bodies rather than others. Such extensions are usually concealed by what they produce: public comfort. What happens when bodies fail to "sink into" spaces, a failure that we can describe as a "queering" of space?[8] When does this potential for "queering" get translated into a transformation of the scripts of compulsory heterosexuality?

It is important, when considering how this potential is translated into transformation, that we do not create a political imperative; for example, by arguing that all lesbian parents should actively work to interrupt the scripts of compulsory heterosexuality. As Jacqui Gabb shows, some lesbian parents may perceive their families to be "just like other families" (Gabb 2002: 6; see also Lewin 1993). Now, is this a sign of their assimilation and their political failure? Of course, such data could be read in this way. But it also shows the lack of any direct translation between political struggle and the contours of everyday life given the ways in which queer subjects occupy very different places within the social order. Maintaining an active positive of "transgression" not only takes time, but may not be psychically, socially or materially possible for some individuals and groups given their ongoing and unfinished commitments and histories. Some working-class lesbian parents, for example, might not be able to afford being placed outside the kinship networks within local neighbourhoods: being recognised as "like any other family" might not simply be strategic, but necessary for survival. Other working-class lesbian parents might not wish to be "like other families": what might feel necessary for some, could be impossible for others. Assimilation and transgression are not choices that are available to individuals, but are effects of how subjects can and cannot inhabit social norms and ideals.[9] Even when queer families may wish to be recognised as "families like other families", their difference from the ideal script produces disturbances— moments of "non-sinking"—that will require active forms of negotiation in different times and places.

To define a family as queer is already to interrupt one ideal image of the family, based on the heterosexual union, procreation and the biological tie. Rather than thinking of queer families as an extension of an ideal (and hence as a form of assimilation that supports the ideal), we can begin to reflect on the exposure of the failure of the ideal as part of the work that queer families are doing. As Weeks, Heaphy and Donovan suggest, we can consider families as social practices, and "more as an adjective or, possibly, a verb" (Weeks, Heaphy and Donovan 2001: 37). Families are *a doing word and a word for doing*. Indeed, thinking of families as what people do in their intimate lives allows us to avoid positing queer families as an alternative ideal, for example, in the assumption that queer families are necessarily more egalitarian (Carrington 1999: 13). Queer lives involve issues of power, responsibility, work and inequalities and, importantly, do not and cannot transcend the social relations of global capitalism (Carrington 1999: 218). Reflecting on the work that is done in queer families, as well as what queer families do, allows us to disrupt the idealisation of the family form.

This argument seems to suggest that queer families may be just like other families in their shared failure to inhabit an ideal. But of course such an argument would neutralise the differences between queer and non-queer families, as well as the differences between queer families. Families may not "be" the ideal, which is itself an impossible fantasy, but they have a different relation of proximity to that ideal. For some families the ideal takes the shape of their form (as being heterosexual, white, middle-class, and so on). The "failure" to inhabit an ideal may or may not be visible to others, and this visibility has effects on the contours of everyday existence. Learning to live with the effects and affects of heterosexism and homo-phobia may be crucial to what makes queer families different from non-queer families. Such forms of discrimination can have negative effects, involving pain, anxiety, fear, depression and shame, all of which can restrict bodily and social mobility. However, the effects of this failure to embody an ideal are not simply negative. As Kath Weston has argued, queer families often narrate the excitement of creating intimacies that are not based on biological ties, or on established gender relations: "Far from viewing families we choose as imitations or derivatives of family ties created elsewhere in their society, many lesbians and gay men alluded to the difficulty and excitement of constructing kinship in the *absence* of what they called 'models' " (Weston 1991: 116, see also Weston 1995: 93). The absence of models that are appropriate does not mean an absence of models. In fact, it is in "not fitting" the model of the nuclear family that queer families can work to transform what it is that families can do. The "non-fitting" or discomfort opens up possibilities, an opening up which can be difficult and exciting.

There remains a risk that "queer families" could be posited as an ideal within the queer community. If queer families were idealised within the queer community, then fleeting queer encounters, or more casual forms of friendship and alliance, could become seen as failures, or less significant forms of attachment. Queer politics needs to stay open to different ways of doing queer in order to maintain the possibility that differences are not converted into failure. Queer subjects do use different names for what they find significant in their lives and they find significance in different places, including those that are deemed illegitimate in heteronormative cultures. The word "families" may allow some queers to differentiate between their more and less significant bonds, where significance is not assumed to follow a form that is already given in advance. For others, the word "families" may be too saturated with affects to be usable in this way. Eve Kosofsky Sedgwick's vision of the family, for instance, is "elastic enough to do justice to the depth and sometimes durability of nonmarital and/or nonprocreative bonds, same-sex bonds, nondyadic bonds, bonds not defined by genitality, 'step'-bonds, adult sibling bonds, nonbiological bonds across generations, etc" (Sedgwick 1994: 71). But hope cannot be placed simply in the elasticity of the word "family": that elasticity should not become a fetish, and held in place as an object in which we must all be invested. The hope of "the family" for queer subjects may exist only insofar as it is not the only object of hope (see Chapter 8 [of *The Cultural Politics of Emotion*], for an analysis of hope). If we do not legislate what forms queer bonds take—and presume the ontological difference between legitimate and illegitimate bonds—then it is possible for queer bonds to be named as bonds without the demand that other queers "return" those bonds in the form of shared investment.

It is, after all, the bonds between queers that "stop" queer bodies from feeling comfortable in spaces that extend the form of the heterosexual couple. We can posit the effects of "not fitting" as a form of queer discomfort, but a discomfort which is generative, rather than simply constraining or negative. To feel uncomfortable is precisely to be affected by that which persists in the shaping of bodies and lives. Discomfort is hence not about assimilation or resistance, *but about inhabiting norms differently*. The inhabitance is generative or productive insofar as it does not end with the failure of norms to be secured, but with possibilities of living that do not "follow" those norms through. Queer is not, then, about transcendence or freedom from the (hetero)normative. Queer feelings are "affected" by the repetition of the scripts that they fail to reproduce, and this "affect" is also a sign of what queer can do, of how it can work *by working on* the (hetero)normative. The failure to be non-normative is then not the failure of queer to be queer, but a sign of attachments that are the condition of possibility for queer. Queer feelings may embrace a sense of discomfort, a lack of ease with the available scripts for living and loving, along with an excitement in the face of the uncertainty of where the discomfort may take us.

Queer grief

The debate about whether queer relationships should be recognised by law acquires a crucial significance at times of loss. Queer histories tell us of inescapable injustices, for example, when gay or lesbian mourners are not recognised as mourners in hospitals, by families, in law courts. In this section, I want to clarify how the recognition of queer lives might work in a way that avoids assimilation by examining the role of grief within queer politics. There has already been a strong case made for how grief supports, or even forms, the heterosexuality of the normative subject. For example, Judith Butler argues that the heterosexual subject must "give up" the potential of queer love, but this loss cannot be grieved, and is foreclosed or barred permanently from the subject (Butler 1997a: 135). As such, homosexuality becomes an "ungrievable loss", which returns to haunt the heterosexual subject through its melancholic identification with that which has been permanently cast out. For Butler, this ungrievable loss gets displaced: heterosexual culture, having given up its capacity to grieve its own lost queerness, cannot grieve the loss of queer lives; it cannot admit that queer lives are lives that could be lost.

Simply put, queer lives have to be recognised as lives in order to be grieved. In a way, it is not that queer lives exist as "ungrievable loss", but that queer losses cannot "be admitted" as forms of loss in the first place, as queer lives are not recognised as lives "to be lost". One has to recognise oneself as having something before one can recognise oneself as losing something. Of course, loss does not simply imply having something that has been taken away. The meanings of loss slide from "ceasing to have", to suffering, and being deprived. Loss implies the acknowledgement of the desirability of what was once had: one may have to love in order to lose. As such, the failure to recognise queer loss *as* loss is also a failure to recognise queer relationships as significant bonds, or that queer lives are lives worth living, or that queers are more than failed heterosexuals, heterosexuals who have failed "to be". Given that queer becomes read as a form of "non-life"—with the death implied by being seen as non-reproductive—then queers are perhaps even already dead and cannot die. As Jeff Nunokawa suggests, heteronormative culture implies queer death, "from the start" (Nunokawa 1991: 319). Queer loss may not count *because it precedes a relation of having*.

Queer activism has consequently been bound up with the politics of grief, with the question of what losses are counted as grievable. This politicisation of grief was crucial to the activism around AIDS and the transformation of mourning into militancy (see Crimp 2002). As Ann Cvetkovich puts it: "The AIDS crisis, like other traumatic encounters with death, has challenged our strategies for remembering the dead, forcing the invention of new forms of mourning and commemoration" (Cvetkovich 2003: 427). The activism around AIDS produced works of collective mourning, which sought to make present the loss of queer lives within public culture: for example, with the Names Project Quilt, in which each quilt signifies a loss that is joined to others, in a potentially limitless display of collective loss. But what are the political effects of contesting the failure to recognise queer loss by displaying that loss?

In order to address this question, I want to examine public forms of grief displayed in response to September 11 2001. As Marita Sturken has argued, the rush to memorialise in response to the event not only sought to replace an absence with a presence, but also served to represent the absence through some losses and not others. On the one hand, individual losses of loved others were grieved, and surfaced as threads in the fabric of collective grief. The individual portraits of grief in the *New York Times*, and the memorials to individual losses posted around the city, work as a form of testimony; a way of making individual loss present to others. Each life is painted in order to transform a number into a being, one who has been lost to someone; so the person who is lost *is not only missing, but also missed*. But at the same time, some losses more than others came to embody the collective loss. Sturken suggests that a "hierarchy of the dead" was constructed: "The media coverage of September 11 establishes a hierarchy of the dead, with, for instance, the privileging of the stories of public servants, such as firefighters over office workers, of policemen over security guards, and the stories of those with economic capital over those without, of traders over janitors" (Sturken 2002: 383–84). Whilst some losses are privileged over others, some don't appear as losses at all. Some losses get taken in (as "ours"), thereby excluding other losses from counting as losses in the first place.[10]

Queer losses were among the losses excluded from the public cultures of grief. As David L. Eng has argued, the public scripts of grief after September 11 were full of signs of heteronormativity: "The rhetoric of the loss of 'fathers and mothers', 'sons and daughters', and 'brothers and sisters' attempts to trace the smooth alignment between the nation-state and the nuclear family, the symbolics of blood relations and nationalist domesticity" (Eng 2002: 90). It is because of this erasure that some queer groups have intervened, by naming queer losses. The president of the National Lesbian and Gay Journalists Association,[11] for example, names queer loss both by naming individual queers who were lost in September 11, and by describing that event as a loss for the queer community. What is interesting about this response is how it addresses two communities: the nation and the queer community, using inclusive pronouns to describe both. The first community is that of all Americans: "This unimaginable loss has struck at the very core of our sense of safety and order." Here, September 11 is viewed as striking "us" in the same place. But even in this use of inclusive language, the difference of GLBT Americans is affirmed: "Even on a good day, many GLBT Americans felt unsafe or at least vulnerable in ways large and small. Now, that feeling has grown even more acute and has blanketed the nation." The feelings of vulnerability that are specific to queer communities are first named, and then get extended into a feeling that blankets the nation, covering over the differences. The extension relies on an analogy between queer feelings (unsafety, vulnerability) and the feelings of citizens living with the threat of terrorism. The narrative implies that the nation is almost made queer by terrorism: heterosexuals "join" queers in feeling vulnerable and fearful of attack. Of course, in "becoming" queer, the nation remains differentiated from those who "are"already queer.

This tension between the "we" of the nation and the "we" of the queer community is also expressed through the evocation of "hate": "Like others, our community knows all too well the devastating effects of hate." This is a complicated utterance. On the one hand, this statement draws attention to experiences of being hated that trouble the national imaginary, which assumes a distinction between tolerant multicultural subjects who "love" and fundamentalists and racists who "hate" By showing how queers are a community "that is hated" by the imagined nation, the statement breaches the ideal image the nation has of itself ("America can hate others ([queers]), as well as be hated by others" But at the same time, this narrative repeats the dominant one: the tragedy of the event is the consequence of "their hate" for "us" ("Why do they hate us?"). The construction of the queer community as a hated community, which splits the nation, slides into a construction of the nation as "being" hated by others. The nation is reinstalled as a coherent subject within the utterance: together, we are hated, and in being hated, we are together.

Within this queer response, mourning responds to the loss of "every life" which includes "members of our own community". Individual names are given, and the losses are named as queer losses: "They include an American Airlines co-pilot on the flight that crashed into the Pentagon; a nurse from New Hampshire; a couple travelling with their 3-year-old son." Furthermore, the losses are evoked through the language of heroism and courage: "Father Mychal Judge, the New York Fire Department chaplain, who died whilst administering last rites to a fallen fire fighter, and Mark Bingham, a San Francisco public relations executive, who helped thwart the hijackers". Certainly, the call for a recognition of queer courage and queer loss works to "mark" the others already named as losses. That is, the very necessity of identifying some losses *as* queer losses reveals how most losses were narrated as heterosexual losses in the first place. The apparently unmarked individual losses privileged in the media are here marked by naming these other losses *as* queer losses. The risk of the "marking" is that queer loss is then named as loss *alongside* those other losses; the use of humanist language of individual courage and bravery makes these losses *like the others*. Hence, queer loss becomes incorporated into the loss of the nation, in which the "we" is always a "we too". The utterance, "we too", implies both a recognition of a past exclusion (the "too" shows how the "we" must be supplemented), and a claim for inclusion (we are like you in having lost). Although such grief challenges the established "hierarchy between the dead" (Sturken 2002: 384), it also works as a form of covering; the expression of grief "blankets" the nation. Queer lives are grieved *as* queer lives only to support the grief of the nation, which perpetuates the concealment of other losses (such as, for example, the losses in Afghanistan, Iraq, Palestine).

So whilst the NLGJA response to September 11 challenges the way in which the nation is secured by making visible some losses more than others, it allows the naming of queer losses to support the narrative it implicitly critiques. But our response cannot be to suspend the demand for the recognition of queer grief. We have already registered the psychic and social costs of unrecognised loss. The challenge for queer politics becomes finding a different way of grieving, and responding to the grief of others. In order to think differently about the ethics and politics of queer grief, I want to reconsider the complexity of grief as a psycho-social process of coming to terms with loss.

Freud's distinction between mourning and melancholia might help us here. For Freud, mourning is a healthy response to loss, as it is about "letting go" of the lost object, which may include a loved person or an abstraction which has taken the place of one (Freud 1934: 153). Melancholia is pathological: the ego refuses to let go of the object, and preserves the object "inside itself" (Freud 1934: 153). In the former "the world becomes poor and empty", whilst in the latter, "it is the ego itself" (Freud 1934: 155). Melancholia involves assimilation: the object persists, but only insofar as it is taken within the subject, as a kind of ghostly death. The central assumption behind Freud's distinction is that it is good or healthy to "let go" of the lost object (to "let go" of that which is already "gone"). Letting go of the lost object may seem an ethical as well as "healthy" response to the alterity of the other.

But the idea that "letting go" is "better" has been challenged. For example, the collection *Continuing Bonds*, "reexamines the idea that the purpose of grief is to sever the bonds with the deceased in order to free the survivor to make new attachments" (Silverman and Klass 1996: 3). Silverman and Klass suggest that the purpose of grief is not to let go, but lies in "negotiating and renegotiating the meaning of the loss over time" (Silverman and Klass 1996: 19). In other words, melancholia should not be seen as pathological; the desire to maintain attachments with the lost other is enabling, rather than blocking new forms of attachment. Indeed, some have argued that the refusal to let go is an ethical response to loss. Eng and Kazanjian, for example, accept Freud's distinction between mourning and melancholia, but argue that melancholia is preferable as a way of responding to loss. Mourning enables gradual withdrawal from the object and hence denies the other through forgetting its trace. In contrast, melancholia is "an enduring devotion on the part of the ego to the lost object", and as such is a way of keeping the other, and with it the past, alive in the present (Eng and Kazanjian 2003: 3). In this model, keeping the past alive, even as that which has been lost, is ethical: the object is not severed from history, or encrypted, but can acquire new meanings and possibilities in the present. To let go might even be to kill again (see Eng and Han 2003: 365).

Eng and Han's work points to an ethical duty to keep the dead other alive. The question of how to respond to loss requires us to rethink what it means to live with death. In Freud's critique of melancholia, the emphasis is on a lost external object, that which is other to me, being preserved by becoming internal to the ego. As Judith Butler puts it, the object is not abandoned, but transferred from the external to the internal (Butler 1997a: 134). However, the passage in grief is not simply about what is "outside" being "taken in". For the object to be lost, *it must already have existed within the subject*. It would be too narrow to see this "insideness" only in terms of a history of past assimilation ("taking in" as "the making of likeness"), although assimilation remains crucial to love as well as grief, as I have already suggested. We can also think of this "insideness" as an effect of the "withness" of intimacy, which involves the process of being affected by others. As feminist critics in particular have argued, we are "with others" before we are defined as "apart from" others (Benjamin 1988). Each of us, in being shaped by others, carries with us "impressions" of those others. Such impressions are certainly memories of this or that other, to which we return in the sticky metonymy of our thoughts and dreams, and through prompting either by conversations with others or through the visual form of photographs. Such "withness" also shapes our bodies, our gestures, our turns of phrase: we pick up bits and pieces of each other as the effect of nearness or proximity (see Diprose 2002). Of course, to some extent this proximity involves the making of likeness. But the hybrid work of identity-making is never about pure resemblance of one to another. It involves a dynamic process of perpetual resurfacing: the parts of me that involve "impressions" of you can never be reduced to the "you-ness" of "you", but they are "more" than just me. The creation of the subject hence depends upon the impressions of others, and these "impressions" cannot be conflated with the character of "others". The others exist within me and apart from me at the same time. Taking you in will not necessarily be "becoming like you" or "making you like me", as other others have also impressed upon me, shaping my surfaces in this way and that.

So to lose another is not to lose one's impressions, not all of which are even conscious. To preserve an attachment is not to make an external other internal, *but to keep one's impressions alive*, as aspects of one's self that are both oneself and more than oneself, as a sign of one's debt to others. One can let go of another as an outsider, but maintain one's attachments, by keeping alive one's impressions of the lost other. This does not mean that the "impressions" stand in for the other, as a false and deadly substitute. And nor do such "impressions" have to stay the same. Although the other may not be alive to create new impressions, the impressions move as I move: the new slant provided by a conversation, when I hear something I did not know; the flickering of an image through the passage of time, as an image that is both your image, and my image of you. To grieve for others is to keep their impressions alive in the midst of their death.

The ethical and political question for queer subjects might, then, not be *whether* to grieve but *how* to grieve. In some queer responses to September 11, the public display of grief installs queer loss as an object, alongside other losses, and in this way constructs the nation as the true subject of grief. But queer subjects can also share their impressions of those they have lost without transforming those impressions into objects that can be appropriated or taken in by the nation. For some, this was precisely the work of the Names Project Quilt, despite the reservations theorists such as Crimp have expressed about the way it sanitised loss for the mainstream audience (Crimp 2002: 196). As Ken Plummer has argued, the Project might matter not because of how it addresses the nation, as an imagined subject who might yet take this grief on as its own, but because of the process of working through loss with others. He suggests that "stories help organise the flow of interaction, binding together or disrupting the relation of self to other and community" (Plummer 1995: 174). Perhaps queer forms of grief sustain the impressions of those who have been lost by sharing impressions with others. Sharing impressions may only be possible if the loss is not transformed into "Our loss", or converted into an object: when the loss becomes "ours", it is taken away from others. Not to name "my" or "your" loss as "our loss" does not mean the privatisation of loss, but the generation of a public in which sharing is not based on the presumption of shared ownership. A queer politics of grief needs to allow others, those whose losses are not recognised by the nation, to have the space and time to grieve, rather than grieving for those others, or even asking "the nation" to grieve for them. In such a politics, recognition does still matter, not of the other's grief, but of the other as a griever, as the subject rather than the object of grief, a subject that is not alone in its grief, since grief is both about and directed to others.[12]

It is because of the refusal to recognise queer loss (let alone queer grief), that it is important to find ways of sharing queer grief with others. As Nancy A. Naples shows us in her intimate and moving ethnography of her father's death, feeling pushed out by her family during her father's funeral made support from her queer family of carers even more important (Naples 2001: 31). To support others as grievers—not by grieving for them but allowing them the space and time to grieve—becomes even more important when those others are excluded from the everyday networks of legitimation and support. The ongoing work of grief helps to keep alive the memories of those who have gone, provide care for those who are grieving, and allow the impressions of others to touch the surface of queer communities. This queer community resists becoming one, and aligned with the patriotic "we" of the nation, only when loss is recognised as that which cannot simply be converted into an object, and yet is with and for others. Here, your loss would not be translated into "our loss", but would prompt me to turn towards you, and allow you to impress upon me, again.

Queer pleasures

Of course, queer feelings are not simply about the space of negativity, even when that negativity gets translated into the work of care for others. Queer politics are also about enjoyment, where the "non" offers hope and possibility for other ways of inhabiting bodies. How do the pleasures of queer intimacies challenge the designation of queer as abject, as that which is "cast out from the domain of the liveable" (Butler 1993: 9), or even as the "death" made inevitable by the failure to reproduce life itself? This is a risky question. Whilst queers have been constructed as abject beings, they are also sources of desire and fascination. Michael Bronski explores the tension between "heterosexual fear of homosexuality and gay culture (and the pleasure they represent) and the equally strong envy of and desire to enjoy that freedom and pleasure" (Bronski 1998: 2). Žižek also examines the ambivalence of the investment in "the other" as the one "who enjoys", and whose enjoyment exceeds the economies of investment and return (Žižek 1991: 2). The racist or homophobe tries to steal this enjoyment, which he assumes was taken from him, through the aggression of his hatred (see also Chapters 2 and 6 [of *The Cultural Politics of Emotion*]). To speak of queer pleasure as potentially a site for political transformation risks confirming constructions of queerness that sustain the place of the (hetero)normative subject.

Equally though, others can be envied for their lack of enjoyment, for the authenticity of their suffering, their vulnerability, and their pain. I have examined, for example, how the investment in the figure of the suffering other gives the Western subject the pleasures of being charitable (see Chapter 1 [of *The Cultural Politics of Emotion*]). Within the Leninist theory of the vanguard party, or the work of the Subaltern Studies group, there also seems to be an investment in the pain and struggle of the proletariat or peasant. Here the investment allows the project of speaking for the other, whose silence is read as an injury (Spivak 1988). In other words, the other becomes an investment by providing the normative subject with a vision of what is lacking, whether that lack is a form of suffering or deprivation (poverty, pain), or excess (pleasure, enjoyment). The other is attributed with affect (as being *in* pain, or *having* pleasure) as a means of subject constitution. I will not suggest that what makes queers "queer" is their pleasure (from which straight subjects are barred), but will examine how the bodily and social practices of queer pleasure might challenge the economies that distribute pleasure as a form of property—as a feeling we have—in the first place.

In mainstream culture, it is certainly not the case that pleasure is excluded or taboo (there are official events and places where the public is required to display pleasure—where pleasure is a matter of being "a good sport"). Indeed within global capitalism the imperative is to have more pleasure (through the consumption of products designed to tantalise the senses). And yet alongside this imperative to enjoy, there is a warning: pleasures can distract you, and turn you away from obligations, duties and responsibilities. Hedonism does not get a good press, certainly. Pleasure becomes an imperative only as an incentive and reward for good conduct, or as an "appropriate outlet" for bodies that are busy being productive ("work hard play hard"). This imperative is not only about having pleasure as a reward, but also about having the right kind of pleasure, in which rightness is determined as an orientation towards an object. Pleasure is "good" only if it is orientated towards some objects, not others. The "orientation" of the pleasure economy is bound up with heterosexuality: women and men "should" experience a surplus of pleasure, but only when exploring each other's bodies under the phallic sign of difference (pleasure as the enjoyment of sexual difference). Whilst sexual pleasure within the West may now be separated from the task or duty of reproduction, it remains tied in some way *to the fantasy of being reproductive*: one can enjoy sex with a body that it is imagined one *could be* reproductive with. Queer pleasures might be legitimate here, as long as "the queer" is only a passing moment in the story of heterosexual coupling ("queer as an enjoyable distraction"). The promise of this pleasure resides in its convertibility to reproduction and the accumulation of value.

We might assume that queer pleasures, because they are "orientated" towards an illegitimate object, will not return an investment. But this is not always or only the case. As Rosemary Hennessy has argued, "queer" can be commodified, which means that queer pleasures can be profitable within global capitalism: the pink pound, after all, does accumulate value (Hennessy 1995: 143). Hennessy argues that money and not liberation is crucial to recent gay visibility. As she puts it: "The freeing up of sensory-affective capacities from family alliances was simultaneously rebinding desire into new commodified forms" (Hennessy 2000: 104). The opening up of non-familial desires allows new forms of commodification; the "non" of the "non-normative" is not outside existing circuits of exchange, but may even intensify the movement of commodities, which converts into capital (see Chapter 2 [of *The Cultural Politics of Emotion*]). Global capitalism involves the relentless search for new markets, and queer consumers provide such a market. The production of surplus value relies, as Marx argued, on the exploitation of the labour of others. The commodification of queer involves histories of exploitation: the leisure industries that support queer leisure styles, as with other industries, depend upon class and racial hierarchies. So it is important not to identify queer as outside the global economy, which transforms "pleasures" into "profit" by exploiting the labour of others.

Such an argument challenges the way in which sexual pleasure is idealised—as almost revolutionary in and of itself—within some versions of queer theory. For example, Douglas Crimp offers a vision of gay male promiscuity as "a positive model of how sexual pleasures might be pursued" (Crimp 2002: 65), while Michael Warner defines sexual autonomy as "access to pleasures" (Warner 1999: 7). Michael Bronski sees the "pleasure principle" as the reason for the fear of homosexuality and also for its power: "Homosexuality offers a vision of sexual pleasure completely divorced from the burden of reproduction: sex for its own sake, a distillation of the pleasure principle" (Bronski 1998: 8). This idealisation of pleasure supports a version of sexual freedom that is not equally available to all: such an idealisation may even extend rather than challenge the "freedoms" of masculinity. A negative model of freedom is offered in such work, according to which queers are free to have pleasure as they are assumed to be free *from* the scripts of (hetero)normative existence: "Because gay social life is not as ritualised and institutionalised as straight life, each relation is an adventure in nearly uncharted territory" (Warner 1999: 115; see also Bell and Binnie 2000: 133). Ironically, such a reading turns queer pleasure into a discovery narrative that is not far off genres that narrated the pleasures of colonialism: as a journey into uncharted territory. Who is the explorer here? And who provides the territory?

And yet, despite the way in which queer pleasures can circulate as commodities within global capitalism, I want to suggest that they can also work to challenge social norms, as forms of investment. To make this argument, we need to reconsider how bodies are shaped by pleasure and take the shape of pleasures. I have elsewhere addressed the phenomenology of pain arguing that pain reshapes the surfaces of the body through the way in which the body turns in on itself. Pleasure also brings attention to surfaces, which surface as impressions through encounters with others. But the intensification of the surface has a very different effect in experiences of pleasure: the enjoyment of the other's touch opens my body up, opens me up. As Drew Leder has argued, pleasure is experienced in and from the world, not merely in relation to one's own body. Pleasure is expansive: "We fill our bodies with what they lack, open up to the stream of the world, reach out to others" (Leder 1990: 75).

Pleasures open bodies to worlds through an opening up of the body to others. As such, pleasures can allow bodies to take up more space. It is interesting to consider, for example, how the display of enjoyment and pleasure by football fans can take over a city, excluding others who do not "share" their joy, or return that joy through the performance of pleasure. Indeed, the publicness of pleasure can function as a form of aggression; as a declaration of "We are here." Beverley Skeggs (1999) shows how the display of pleasure by heterosexuals in queer space can also work as a form of colonisation; a "taking over" of queer space, which leaves queer subjects, especially lesbians, feeling unsettled, displaced and exposed. These examples demonstrate an important capacity to enter into, or inhabit with ease, social space, but also functions as a form of entitlement and belonging. Spaces are claimed through enjoyment, an enjoyment that is returned by being witnessed by others. Recalling my argument in the first section [. . .], the display of queer pleasure may generate discomfort in spaces that remain premised on the "pleasures" of heterosexuality. For queers, to display pleasure through what we do with our bodies is to make the comforts of heterosexuality less comfortable.

Further, pleasure involves an opening towards others; pleasure orientates bodies towards other bodies in a way that impresses on the surface, and creates surface tensions. But pleasure is not simply about any body opening up to any body. The contact is itself dependent on differences that already impress upon the surfaces of bodies. Pleasures are about the contact between bodies that are already shaped by past histories of contact. Some forms of contact don't have the same effects as others. Queer pleasures put bodies into contact that have been kept apart by the scripts of compulsory heterosexuality. I am not sure that this makes the genitals "weapons of pleasure against their own oppression" (Berlant and Freeman 1997: 158). However queer pleasures in the enjoyment of forbidden or barred contact engender the possibility of different kinds of impressions. When bodies touch and give pleasure to bodies that have been barred from contact, then those bodies are reshaped. The hope of queer is that the reshaping of bodies through the enjoyment of what or who has been barred can "impress" differently upon the surfaces of social space, creating the possibility of social forms that are not constrained by the form of the heterosexual couple.

Queer pleasures are not just about the coming together of bodies in sexual intimacy. Queer bodies "gather" in spaces, through the pleasure of opening up to other bodies. These queer gatherings involve forms of activism; ways of claiming back the street, as well as the spaces of clubs, bars, parks and homes. The hope of queer politics is that bringing us closer to others, from whom we have been barred, might also bring us to different ways of living with others. Such possibilities are not about being free from norms, or being outside the circuits of exchange within global capitalism. *It is the non-transcendence of queer that allows queer to do its work.* A queer hope is not, then, sentimental. It is affective precisely in the face of the persistence of forms of life that endure in the negative attachment of "the not". Queer maintains its hope for "non-repetition" only insofar as it announces the persistence of the norms and values that make queer feelings queer in the first place.

Notes

1   I borrow this phrase, of course, from Adrienne Rich. I am indebted to her work, which demonstrates the structural and institutional nature of heterosexuality.

2   A queer phenomenology might offer an approach to "sexual orientation" by rethinking the place of the object in sexual desire, attending to how bodily directions "towards" some objects and not others affects how bodies inhabit spaces, and how spaces inhabit bodies.

3   To reflect on queer feelings is also to reflect on "queer" as a sticky sign. As Butler points put, the word "queer" is performative: through repetition, it has acquired new meanings (Butler 1997b). Queer, once a term of abuse (where to be queer was to be not us, not straight, not normal, not human) has become a name for an alternative political orientation. Importantly, as a sticky sign, "queer" acquires new meanings not by being cut off from its previous contexts of utterance, but by preserving them. In queer politics, the force of insult is retained; "the not" is not negated ("we are positive"), but embraced, and is taken on as a name. The possibility of generating new meanings, or new orientations to "old" meanings, depends on collective activism, on the process of gathering together to clear spaces or ground for action. In other words, it takes more than one body to open up semantic as well as political possibilities. Furthermore, we should remember that queer still remains a term of abuse, and that not all those whose orientations we might regard as queer, can or would identify with this name, or even be able to "hear" the name without hearing the history of its use as an injurious term: "Now, the word *queer* emerges. But other than referring to it in quotations, I will never use the term *queer* to identify myself or any other homosexual. It's a word that my generation—and my companion, who's twenty-five years younger than I am, feels the same way—will never hear without evoked connotations—of violence, gay-bashings, arrest, murder" (Rechy 2000: 319). What we hear when we hear words such as "queer" depends on complex psycho-biographical as well as institutional histories.

4   Of course, heterosexual subjects may experience discomfort when faced by queers, and queer forms of coupling, in the event of the failure to conceal signs of queerness. A queer politics might embrace this discomfort: it might seek to make people feel uncomfortable through making queer bodies more visible. Not all queers will be comfortable with the imperative to make others uncomfortable. Especially given that "families of origin" are crucial spaces for queer experiences of discomfort, it may be in the name of love, or care, that signs of queerness are concealed. Thanks to Nicole Vittelone who helped me to clarify this argument. [. . .]

5   Global capitalism relies on the "feeling fetish" of comfort: for consumers to be comfortable, others must work hard, including cleaners as well as other manual workers. This division of labour and leisure (as well as between mental and manual labour) functions as an instrument of power between and within nation states. But the "work" relation is concealed by the transformation of comfort into property and entitlement. We can especially see this in the tourism industry: the signs of work are removed from the commodity itself, such as the tourist package, as a way of increasing its value. See McClintock (1995) for an analysis of commodification and fetishism and Hochschild (1983: 7) for an analysis of the emotional labour that is required for the well-being of consumers.

6   I am, of course, paraphrasing Frantz Fanon's *Black Skin, White Masks*. The analogy has its limits: assimilation into whiteness and assimilation into straightness cannot be assumed to be equivalent, partly given the different relation of race and sexuality to signs of visibility. See Lorde 1984.

7   Thanks to Jackie Stacey whose astute comments during a conversation helped me to formulate this argument.

8   Of course, some queer bodies can pass, which means passing into straight space. Passing as a technology entails the work of concealment: to pass might produce an effect of comfort (we can't see the difference), but not for the subject who passes, who may be feeling a sense of discomfort, or not being at ease, given the constant threat of "being seen" or caught out. See Ahmed (1999).

9   The debate about queer families has also been defined in terms of the opposition between assimilation and resistance (Goss 1997; Sandell 1994; Phelan 1997: 1; Weston 1991: 2; Weston 1998).

10   Of course, a question remains as to whether "others" would want collective grief to be extended to them. What would it mean for the ungrieved to be grieved? The other might not want my grief precisely because such a grief might "take in" what was not, in the first place, "allowed near". Would Iraqis, Afghanistanis want the force of Western grief to transform them into losses? Would this not risk another violent form of appropriation, one which claims their losses as "ours", a claim that conceals rather than reveals our responsibility for loss? Expressions of nostalgia and regret by colonisers for that which has been lost as an effect of colonisation are of course mainstream (see hooks 1992). Recognising the other *as* grieving, as having experienced losses (for which we might have responsibility) might be more ethically and politically viable than grieving for the other, *or claiming their grief as our own*. [. . .]

11   The National Lesbian and Gay Journalists Association "is an organization of journalists, online media professionals, and students that works from within the journalism industry to foster fair and accurate coverage of lesbian, gay, bisexual and transgender issues. NLGJA opposes workplace bias against all minorities and provides professional development for its members." Their web site is available on: http://www.nlgja.org/. Accessed 22 December 2003.

12   The political and legal battle for the recognition of queer partners in claims for compensation post September 11 is crucial. However, so far no such recognition has been offered. Recognising queer

losses, and queers as the subjects of grief would mean recognising the significance of queer attachments. Bill Berkowitz interprets the 9/11 Victim Compensation Fund, which leaves the determination of eligibility for compensation to states, as follows: "In essence, in a rather complicated and
convoluted decision, families of gays and lesbians will not be given federal compensation unless they
have wills, or the states they live in have laws recognizing domestic partnerships, which of course
most states do not." "Victims of 9/11 and Discrimination", http://www.workingforchange.com/
article.cfm?ItemId=13001 Accessed 6 January 2004.

References

Ahmed, S. (1999), "Passing Through Hybridity", *Theory, Culture and Society* 16 (2): 87–106.

Barber, S.M. and Clark, D.L. (2002), "Queer Moments: The Performative Temporalities of Eve
Kosofsky Sedgwick" in S. M. Barber and D.L. Clark (eds.), *Regarding Sedgwick: Essays on
Queer Culture and Critical Theory*, New York: Routledge.

Bell, D. and Binnie, J. (2000), *The Sexual Citizen: Queer Politics and Beyond*, Cambridge: Polity.

Benjamin, J. (1988), *The Bonds of Love: Psychoanalysis, Feminism, and the Problem of Domination*, New
York: Pantheon Books.

Berlant, L. and Freeman, E. (1997), "Queer Nationality" in L. Berlant, *The Queen of America Goes
to Washington City: Essays on Sex and Citizenship*, Durham, NC: Duke University Press.

— and Warner, M. (2000), "Sex in Public" in L. Berlant (ed.), *Intimacy*, Chicago: University of
Chicago Press.

Braidotti, R. (2002), *Metamorphoses: Towards a Materialist Theory of Becoming*, Cambridge: Polity
Press.

Bronski, M. (1998), *The Pleasure Principle: Sex, Backlash, and the Struggle for Gay Freedom*, New York:
St. Martin's Press.

Butler, J. (1993), *Bodies that Matter: On the Discursive Limits of "Sex"*, New York: Routledge.

—. (1997a), *The Psychic Life of Power: Theories in Subjection*, Stanford: Stanford University Press.

—. (1997b), "Critically Queer" in S. Phelan (ed.), *Playing with Fire: Queer Politics, Queer Theories*,
London: Routledge.

—. (2002), "Is Kinship Always Already Heterosexual?" *differences: A Journal of Feminist Cultural
Studies* 13 (1): 14–44.

Carrington, C. (1999), *No Place Like Home: Relationships and Family Life Among Lesbians and Gay Men*,
Chicago: University of Chicago Press.

Crimp, D. (2002), *Melancholia and Moralism: Essays on AIDS and Queer Politics*, Cambridge, MA:
The MIT Press.

Cvetkovich, A. (2003), "Legacies of Trauma, Legacies of Activism: ACT UP's Lesbians" in D.L.
Eng and D. Kazanjian (eds.), *Loss: The Politics of Mourning*, Berkeley: University of California
Press.

Dean, T. and Lane, C. (2001), "Homosexuality and Psychoanalysis: An Introduction" in T. Dean
and C. Lane (eds.), *Homosexuality and Psychoanalysis*, Chicago: University of Chicago Press.

Diprose, R. (2002), *Corporeal Generosity: On Giving with Nietzsche, Merleau-Ponty, and Levinas*, New
York: SUNY.

Eng, D.L. (2002), "The Value of Silence", *Theatre Journal* 54 (1): 85–94.

— and Han, S. (2003), "A Dialogue on Racial Melancholia" in D.L. Eng and D. Kazanjian (eds.),
Loss: The Politics of Mourning, Berkeley: University of California Press.

— and Kazanjian, D. (2003), "Introduction: Mourning Remains" in D.L. Eng and D. Kazanjian
(eds.), *Loss: The Politics of Mourning*, Berkeley: University of California Press.

Epps, B. (2001), "The Fetish of Fluidity" in T. Dean and C. Lane (eds.), *Homosexuality and
Psychoanalysis*, Chicago: University of Chicago Press.

Fanon, F. (1986), *Black Skin, White Masks*, trans. C.L. Markmann, London: Pluto Press.

Fortier, A.-M. (2003), "Making Home: Queer Migrations and Motions of Attachment" in S. Ahmed, C. Castañeda, A.-M. Fortier and M. Sheller (eds.), *Uprootings/Regroundings: Questions of Home and Migration*, Oxford: Berg.

Freud, S. (1934), "Mourning and Melancholia", *Collected Papers*, vol. 4, ed. E. Jones, trans. J. Riviere, London: The Hogarth Press.

Gabb, J. (2002), "Telling Tales: Troubling Sexuality within Analyses of the 'Lesbian Community' and 'Lesbian Families' ", paper presented at "Re-Imagining Communities" conference, Lancaster University, May 2002.

Goodman, R.T. (2001), *Infertilities: Exploring Fictions of Barren Bodies*, Minneapolis: University of Minnesota Press.

Gopinath, G. (2003), "Nostalgia, Desire, Diaspora: South Asian Sexualities in Motion" in S. Ahmed, C. Castañeda, A.-M. Fortier and M. Sheller (eds.), *Uprootings / Regroundings: Questions of Home and Migration*, Oxford: Berg.

Goss, R.E. (1997), "Queering Procreative Privilege: Coming Out as Families" in R.E. Goss and A.A.S. Strongheart (eds.), *Our Families, Our Values: Snapshots of Queer Kinship*, New York: The Harrington Park Press.

Halberstam, J. (2003), "What's That Smell? Queer Temporalities and Subcultural Lives", *International Journal of Cultural Studies* 6 (3): 313–33.

Hennessy, R. (1995), "Queer Visibility in Commodity Culture" in L. Nicholson and S. Seidman (eds.), *Social Postmodernism: Beyond Identity Politics*, Cambridge: Cambridge University Press.

—. (2000), *Profit and Pleasure: Sexual Identities in Late Capitalism*, New York: Routledge.

Hochschild, A.R. (1983), *The Managed Heart: Commercialisation of Human Feeling*, Berkeley: University of California Press.

hooks, b. (1992), *Black Looks: Race and Representation*, Boston: South End Press.

Leder, D. (1990), *The Absent Body*, Chicago: University of Chicago Press.

Lewin, E. (1993), *Lesbian Mothers: Accounts of Gender in American Culture*, Ithaca: Cornell University Press.

Lorde, A. (1984), *Sister Outsider: Essays and Speeches*, Trumansburg, NY: The Crossing Press.

McClintock, A. (1995), *Imperial Leather: Race, Gender and Sexuality in the Colonial Contest*, New York: Routledge.

Martin, B. (1996), *Femininity Played Straight: The Significance of Being Lesbian*, New York: Routledge.

Naples, N.A. (2001), "A Member of the Funeral: An Introspective Ethnography" in M. Bernstein and R. Reimann (eds.), *Queer Families, Queer Politics: Challenging Culture and the State*, New York: Columbia University Press.

Nunokawa, J. (1991), "'All the Sad Young Men': AIDS and the Work of Mourning" in D. Fuss (ed.), *Inside/Out: Lesbian Theories, Gay Theories*, New York: Routledge.

Phelan, S. (1997), "Introduction" in S. Phelan (ed.), *Playing with Fire: Queer Politics, Queer Theories*, London: Routledge.

Plummer, K. (1995), *Telling Sexual Stories: Power, Change and Social Worlds*, London: Routledge.

Rechy, J. (2000), Comments in "The Final Frontier: A Roundtable Discussion", moderator T. Modleski, in J.A. Boone, M. Dupuis, M. Meeker, K. Quimby, C. Sarver, D. Silverman and R. Weatherston (eds.), *Queer Frontiers: Millennial Geographic, Genders, and Generations*, Madison: The University of Wisconsin Press.

Sandell, J. (1994), "The Cultural Necessity of Queer Families", *Bad Subjects* 12: http://eserver.org/bs/12/sandell.html.

Sedgwick, E. K. (1994), *Tendencies*, London: Routledge.

Silverman, P.R. and Klass, D. (1996), "Introduction: What's the Problem?" in D. Klass, P.R. Silverman and S.L. Nickman (eds.), *Continuing Bonds: New Understandings of Grief*, Philadelphia: Taylor and Francis.

Skeggs, B. (1999), "Matter out of Place: Visibility and Sexualities in Leisure Spaces", *Leisure Studies* 18: 213–32.

Spivak, G. C. (1988), "Can the Subaltern Speak?" in C. Nelson and L. Grossberg (eds.), *Marxism and the Interpretation of Culture*, Urbana: University of Illinois Press.

Sturken, M. (2002), "Memorialising Absence" in C. Calhoun, P. Price and A. Timmer (eds.), *Understanding September 11*, New York: The New Press.

Sullivan, A. (1996), *Virtually Normal: An Argument about Homosexuality*, New York: Vintage Books.

Valentine, G. (1996), "(Re)Negotiating the 'Heterosexual Street': Lesbian Productions of Space" in N. Duncan (ed.), *Bodyspace: Destabilising Geographies of Gender and Sexuality*, London: Routledge.

Warner, M. (1999), *The Trouble with Normal: Sex, Politics, and the Ethics of Queer Life*, Cambridge, MA: Harvard University Press.

Weeks, J., Heaphy, B. and Donovan, C. (2001), *Same Sex Intimacies: Families of Choice and Other Life Experiments*, London: Routledge.

Weston, K. (1991), *Families We Choose: Lesbians, Gays, Kinship*, New York: Columbia University Press.

—. (1995), "Forever is a Long Time: Romancing the Real in Gay Kinship Ideologies" in S. Yanagisako and C. Delaney (eds.), *Naturalizing Power: Essays in Feminist Cultural Analysis*, New York: Routledge.

—. (1998), *Long Slow Burn: Sexuality and Social Science*, London: Routledge.

Žižek, S. (1991), *For They Know Not What They Do: Enjoyment as a Political Factor*, London: Verso.

PART 6

Bodies

Chapter 26

Iain Morland

WHAT CAN QUEER THEORY DO FOR INTERSEX?

Iain Morland is Lecturer at the Cardiff University School of English, Communication, and Philosophy. A co-founder of the London Critical Sexology seminar series, Morland has published extensively on the history and ethics of the medical management of intersex.

With its interrogatory title, Morland's essay announces its aim to test queer theory's adequacy to intersex bodies. Morland argues that queer theory's valorization of pleasure risks characterizing postsurgical intersex bodies as irrevocably impoverished. Conversely, its discourse on shame allows an ethical recognition of the persistent effects of genital surgery on intersex bodies. The critical impact of queer theory's reliance on sensorial modes of critique, a critique premised on the interrelatedness of pleasure and shame, emerges in Morland's consideration of the queer discourse on touch. While queer touch offers a way to criticize the surgical emphasis on appearance and function, for Morland queer touching remains bounded by its unexamined reliance on the simultaneity of touch and tactility, obscuring the fact that touch requires a sensate body. Instead, Morland finds that queer theory's critical value lies in its theorization of desire independent of tactility. Morland figures this desire not as touching but as reaching, exceeding surgical attempts to discipline the intersex body.

The time of the touch

TO QUEERS AND nonqueers alike the visceral immediacy of the sexual touch might appear to be self-evident; contact between a lover's body and one's own is typically coincident with the mutual sensation of such contact. Even an unwelcome sexual advance is recognizable by its tactile impression—for instance, the brush of a hand from which one immediately recoils. In short, touching and feeling happen live.

My starting point in this essay is that when the nerves in one's genitalia have been damaged by surgery, the time of the touch changes. For example, one sees a lover's hand touching one's genitalia, but one does not feel it. Hence the apparently real time of sexual experience—in which, as Sarah E. Chinn claims in an essay about queer touching, "our bodies feel and are felt outside solely visual perception"—turns into the contemplative voyeurism of pornography.[1] Touching happens, but it is seen rather than sensed, and in Chinn's opinion vision "is virtually useless when it comes to figuring out and describing the experience of sexual pleasure" (182). I know from direct personal experience that this is profoundly disorienting; when genitalia are insensate, the time of the touch stretches infinitely away from the moment of physical contact. Perhaps one can recall how it felt to be touched prior to genital surgery, or imagine how it might feel if sensation were to return in the future to one's genitalia—either way, touching and feeling are riven, too late or too early to coincide.

Consider in this regard a 1996 letter to the influential *Journal of Urology*, in which the founder of the Intersex Society of North America (ISNA), Cheryl Chase, described some of the postsurgical problems reported by society members. Several had experienced either diminished or extinguished genital sensation following surgery for intersex. One member whose clitoris was reduced in childhood found orgasm "so difficult to reach and so rarely attained" that she regarded her "sexual function as being destroyed."[2] Disturbingly, another felt "intense genital pain" following sexual stimulation (1140). More recently, a study by a London-based medical team evaluated clitoral sensation in six intersex women whose clitorises had been surgically reduced. The study was innovative because it used not merely a sexual satisfaction questionnaire but also electronic devices to measure clitoral sensitivity to temperature and vibration. These provided gradually increasing stimuli until participants pressed a button to register sensation. It was the first time that such "objective sensory testing" had been performed on individuals with a history of genital surgery.[3] Postsurgical clitoral sensation in the six women was found to be "profoundly abnormal" (138). All had atypical results for the sensation of cold, and five participants had abnormal results for the sensation of warmth and vibration. In response to the questionnaire four women said they had problems achieving orgasm. Worryingly, this was not the legacy of outdated surgical techniques: the authors of the study cautioned that "there is currently no justification for the optimism that modern surgical techniques are better for preserving clitoral sensation than previous operations" (138). The caution was an implicit rejoinder to the criticism by earlier clinicians that the individuals discussed in Chase's letter had not benefited from "changes in the surgical approach" since the mid-1970s.[4] Even if scholars in the theoretical humanities might query the London team's claim to objectivity, it's still pragmatically useful in making their study authoritative to other doctors, as well as in substantiating Chase's letter.

What kinds of critiques of genital surgery does queer theory enable or substantiate? In this essay I investigate what queer theory can do for intersex bodies that have been desensitized by genital surgery. Of course, surgery for intersex does not wholly desensitize entire bodies, but in what follows I refer often to desensitized postsurgical *bodies* rather than merely genitalia for three reasons. The first reason isn't specific to intersex: any experience of surgery extends beyond the scalpel's cut. Even anesthesia can cause postoperative nausea and vomiting.[5] The second and third reasons are more specific. Nerve damage can alter the perception and tactility of areas other than those where cutting has been performed.[6] Finally, surgery for intersex does not operate solely on exterior genitalia: it can also change, reposition, or remove internal structures, for instance by creating a vagina from a segment of colon.[7] In short, the whole body undergoes surgery, and the experience of surgery is lived by the body as a whole, even if the body is cut in only a small area—hence one ISNA member's claim that clitoral surgery had destroyed "sexual function" in general. My aim, then, is not to use queer theory to undo the diverse bodily effects of genital surgery. Rather, I evaluate whether a critique of surgery's effects is possible from a queer theoretical perspective on the body.

To this end I make four key claims, beginning with my reservations about queer discourses of pleasure and shame. My first claim is that the desensitized postsurgical body cannot be accounted for by a queer discourse in which sexual pleasure is a form of hedonistic activism. Consequently, I seek to follow Robert Jensen's recommendation that our task as sexual dissidents "is not necessarily imagining new ways of touching but always being attentive to the ethics and politics of the touch."[8] In other words, a queer reaction to the problems of intersex surgery cannot be simply the advocacy of more and better sex, because that's precisely what intersex surgery can make at best pointless and at worst impossible. Instead we must proceed with careful awareness of how previous touches on intersexed bodies, such as the desensitizing touch of the surgeon, change those bodies and thereby constrain the possibilities for queer critique. My second claim is that a queer discourse of shame enables a critical engagement with the surgical creation of atypically sensate bodies. As Sara Ahmed has commented, an ethics of touch is not just about touching others but about sensitivity to the way others have already been touched and affected—in this instance how bodies obdurately remember the shameful touch of surgery, no matter how desperately we may wish to brush its effects away.[9] Nevertheless I do not wish to suggest that queer critics need simply to choose between theorizing intersex in terms of either pleasure or shame. There is really no such opposition. My third key claim, then, is that queerness is characterized by the sensory interrelation of pleasure and shame, for as David M. Halperin puts it, "the genius of gay sex—and not only *gay* sex—lies precisely in its ability to transmute otherwise unpleasant experiences of social degradation into experiences of pleasure."[10] If there exists "a queer ethic of dignity in shame," in Michael Warner's words, my interest lies not in revealing shame to be a kind of pleasure or vice versa.[11] I am interested instead in the fact that shame and pleasure are both queer *sensations*; I argue that queer theory's assumption of a sensorial basis to cultural critique flounders when confronted with the desensitized intersex body. In the light of this, my fourth and final claim is that if queer theory is figured as a kind of reaching—but not necessarily touching—then it can be of greater use in accounting for the problematic effects of intersex surgery. Thus the reach is queerer than the touch, for it is a recognition that, as Lee Edelman has written, "queer theory can only remain a desire, and like desire it depends for its energy, for its continuing power to grip us, on the impossibility of knowing its boundaries, of knowing its coherence as a state."[12] In my opinion, desire is what queer theory and the postsurgical intersex body have in common. But for this reason I think Edelman's idea of "gripping" isn't quite right; I would say that desire *reaches* through queer and intersex bodies alike. I argue in closing that desire's reach confounds the surgical project of touching atypical bodies in order to make them sexually normal.

Queer pleasures

Queer theory would appear to facilitate a critique of diminished sexual pleasure following intersex surgery. This is because queer theory, together with related strands of third-wave feminism, is the academic discourse that has had the most to say about the cultural significance and experience of human sexual pleasure: it is a "vision of social production that engages the libidinal," in Edelman's words (344). Unlike the emphasis within second-wave feminism on gender, and specifically in "antisex" feminism on sexual pleasure as a ruse of gender oppression, queer theory has taken the sexual and its pleasures as central objects of study. In her groundbreaking 1979 essay "A Secret Side of Lesbian Sexuality," Pat Califia drew a contrast between the "pleasure" of sadomasochism and "real slavery or exploitation."[13] The contrast would become a central issue for both third-wave feminism and queer theory. Significantly, Califia described as "ephemeral" sadomasochism's pleasures, unlike "economic control or forced reproduction" (166). The opposition here was not only between pleasure and displeasure but also between the felt immediacy of sexual activities and the protracted historicity of institutionalized heterosexuality. In this way sadomasochism is "time-consuming and absorbing," in Califia's words (166), paradoxically because its pleasures are transitory—a series of present moments that viscerally envelop the sexual subject, rather than a history of sexuality of which the regulated sexual subject is the effect. By equating sadomasochism with a unique time of pleasure, Califia was able to articulate a feminism that was distinctively neither heterosexual nor antisex. During the 1980s and 1990s such counter-cultural possibilities of sexual pleasure would be analyzed and celebrated by third-wave feminism and in turn queer theory. Of course other queer theories would also emerge—such as those centered upon shame, loss, drag, and temporality, on which I'll draw later in this article—but I want to discuss pleasure first because the diminution of pleasure seems to be the defining problem with genital desensitization. If queer theory can tell us why pleasure is valuable, then it follows that a queer discourse of pleasure can pinpoint why the diminution of pleasure makes genital desensitization wrong.

The central theme of Califia's account—sexual pleasure as converse to sexuality's institutional formations—has shaped the interface between queer theory and intersex. An important axiom of queer theory has been that sex acts can be pleasurable even if—or perhaps because—they occur outside mainstream norms. This is demonstrated by Califia's contrast between subcultural sadomasochism and institutionalized heterosexuality. Just as a queer discourse of pleasure prioritizes transient sexual activities over stable gender identities, so too has intersex activism emphasized healthy sexual functioning as an alternative to reforming gender categories.[14] Thus intersex activism and much queer theory have in common the project of "opening up a new space for the subject of desire," as one commentator on queer theory has described.[15] In this regard both discourses address a subject for whom sexuality functions without adherence to mainstream norms. Now this does not mean that individuals with intersex anatomies necessarily have queer desires; rather, several intersex activists and scholars have called intersex bodies queer in their deviation from norms of embodiment.[16] Queer theory and intersex activism converge on the belief that such deviation is not an obstacle to sexual pleasure, contrary to what medicine has traditionally assumed. A queer discourse of pleasure, then, is useful in critiquing the normalizing use of genital surgery—for instance, when clinicians have evaluated vaginal surgery in terms of whether "adequate intercourse . . . defined as successful vaginal penetration" is possible postoperatively, or when they have reported in childhood surgical outcome studies on whether patients have subsequently entered into heterosexual marriages.[17] As Morgan Holmes complains, "When parents sign consent forms, allowing doctors to remove the erotogenic tissue of their children, they are willingly following a heterosexist requirement that humans live as either male or female."[18] The sacrifice of sensation ("erotogenic tissue") to the norm ("heterosexist requirement") is opposed by Holmes. Nevertheless, to enjoy sexual pleasure outside mainstream norms is not the same as to enjoy sexual pleasure in the absence of all constraints; I return to this caveat shortly.

Another queer axiom presciently thematized in Califia's essay is less a simple rejection of heterosexuality than a deployment of pleasure to resist sexuality's institutionalized forms, of which mainstream heterosexuality is one formation among others. For example, Douglas Crimp has eschewed the perceived institutionalism of gay marriage in favor of the "life-affirming and pleasure-filled world" of homosexual subculture.[19] More than a critique of gender identity, queer theory has enabled an understanding and experience of sex acts as signifiers of pleasure, not signifiers of sexual identity. Sex acts can therefore be resignified within a queer discourse of pleasure, much as the word *queer* has itself undergone countercultural reclamation and revision.[20] Such resignification encompasses acts commonly considered heterosexual, for as Califia has argued, "a belief in sex differences and a dependence on them for sexual pleasure is the most common perversion."[21] In this view heterosexual sex is not motivated by heterosexual identity; it is merely one perversion among many, pursued for pleasure while overlaid by privilege. When heterosexual sex is cast as a pleasure like any other, the institutionalized privileges of heterosexuality are highlighted as unwarranted. The surgical sacrifice of genital sensation to heterosexuality is therefore not only a curtailment of individual pleasure, but also a fundamental misrecognition of the individual as the institution. For the former, heterosexual sex is a source of pleasure; in the latter, heterosexual identity is a source of privilege. Consequently, to create a heterosexual individual through desensitizing genital surgery is a contradiction in terms.

The work of Michel Foucault has been instrumental in the politics of resignification. Despite some leftist resistance to the first volume of Foucault's *History of Sexuality* for its incongruous coupling of a sweeping account of sex and power with an obtusely brisk discussion of how such power can be resisted, Halperin argues that "lesbian and gay militants" have been perhaps the most receptive audience for Foucault's thought.[22] This includes such activists as the AIDS Coalition to Unleash Power, because as Halperin notes, "the public response to AIDS" in the United States in the 1980s perfectly illustrated "the mutual imbrication of power and knowledge" concerning sex that Foucault analyzed—for example, the "endless relays between expert discourse and institutional authority . . . and local struggles for survival and resistance" (27). Consequently, Halperin envisages AIDS activism as accelerating "a multiplication of the sites of political contestation beyond such traditional arenas as the electoral process" to "ultimately the public and the private administration of the body and its pleasures." This strategy, which includes critical interventions into medical practice, is Foucauldian to the extent that volume 1 of *The History of Sexuality* "had already treated the body as a site of political struggle" (28). There Foucault asserted that sexuality is "organized by power in its grip on bodies and their materiality, their forces, energies, sensations, and pleasures," and famously recommended that "the grips of power" should be resisted by "bodies and pleasures."[23] Foucault argued, in other words, for bodily pleasure as a way to resist power.

Within queer theory there have emerged two distinct views on the relation between bodies and pleasures. According to one view, pleasure is obtained exclusively or most effectively through use of the genitalia. Hence for Queer Nation, in the words of Lauren Berlant, genitalia were "not just organs of erotic thanksgiving, but weapons of pleasure against their own oppression."[24] What makes such genital terrorism queer is the combination of genitalia in a given sex act; queer sex for that reason can shock heterosexual culture. This is what Tim Dean has called queer theory's "insistence on the specificity of genital contact as the basis for all political work."[25] According to the other view of the relation between bodies and pleasures, queer pleasure is characterized by a focus not on genitalia but on the body as a whole. For example, according to Mark Blasius, homosexual relations become queer when they use "every part of the body as a sexual instrument in order to achieve the greatest intensification of pleasure possible."[26] The result is what Halperin called "a multiplication of the sites of political contestation" on the level of the body. In this distinctly Foucauldian view, queer sex can effect cultural change through its stylized attention to reciprocal "erotic pleasure," quite aside from the genital morphologies of its participants.[27] The latter view is notable also for the continuity that it signals between queer theory and third-wave feminism, in which heterosexual relations are often acceptable so long as they are similarly "nongenitally organized."[28] For writers like Califia, sadomasochism is paradigmatic of such relations.

In both views, the valorization of pleasure in queer subcultures can be a source of pride. But the capacity of the postsurgical body to participate in such subcultures is unclear. Chase, anorgasmic after genital surgery for intersex, has criticized "sex radicals and activists" who claim that she is having "vaginal" or "full-body" orgasms despite her insistence to the contrary. Understandably, Chase finds highly patronizing their assumption that she will "learn how to orgasm."[29] A queer theory focused on pleasure alone, whether exclusively genital or diffusely "full-body," risks characterizing postsurgical intersex bodies as irrevocably impoverished.[30] Correspondingly, a queer critique of intersex treatment, advanced on the grounds that presurgical intersex bodies are queer in their physical sexual dissidence, may cast postsurgical intersex bodies as *less* queer—or not queer at all. To clarify this assertion, I don't mean that after surgery intersex bodies are less queer because surgery successfully eliminates a queer presurgical anatomy. Rather, I am making a point about physiological functioning: the post-surgical body, irrespective of the degree to which it still looks sexually ambiguous, may be less amenable to queer analysis and political participation because of its diminished capacity for sexual pleasure.

Queer shame

Readers might object that my discussion in the previous section presumed sex between bodies that *haven't* had intersex surgery to be straightforwardly pleasurable, and further that the presence of pleasure is inversely proportional to pleasure's absence. But as I discuss now, not all queer discourse has conceived of sex in this way, so different queer theories of the postsurgical intersex body are possible.

One's conception of sexual pleasure determines one's conception of desensitizing genital surgery as injurious. Although the discourses of pleasure discussed above enable a queer critique of surgery on the grounds that the loss of sexual pleasure is bad, such criticism depends on the conception of sexual pleasure as something that can be lost. Likewise, within those queer discourses the diminution of sexual pleasure is objectionable in part because it raises the possibility of sexual pleasure's extinction. Now if sex is purely pleasurable, and pleasure is the opposite of no pleasure, then it is indeed possible to lose the capacity for, and hence the experience of, sexual pleasure. However, if sex is something more or other than pleasurable, then pleasure's presence and absence are not necessarily opposed, and accordingly the idea of lost sexual pleasure is far less straightforward. While some queer theory, in line with much gay pride discourse, has measured the effects of homophobia by the extent to which homophobia limits subcultural sexual pleasures, other queer theorizations of sex have been more ambivalent. Specifically, they have queried the Foucauldian conception of sex as a matter of bodies and pleasures, for as Sally Munt argues, however "strategically essential" pride in sexual dissidence may be, "the presence of shame has been repressed in the discourse of homosexual rights in an unhelpful way, and in order to gain greater agency, we must learn to revisit its ambivalent effects."[31] In light of Munt's claim I want to evaluate what queer attention to shame, rather than to pleasure, might do for intersex.

Within queer theory the most well-known account of sex—and not merely queer sex—as an experience more ambivalent than pleasurable was given by Leo Bersani in his 1987 essay "Is the Rectum a Grave?" The essay's provocative title reflects the fact that Bersani was writing in reaction to the AIDS crisis. Although, as I've shown, Halperin has presented a Foucauldian turn to bodies and pleasures as resistant to those structures of power and knowledge that conflated homosexuality with social collapse and death, Bersani's incendiary response to the same epidemic was to query whether homosexuality is, after all, in some way antithetical to the social as it has been defined in mainstream Western culture. The big secret about sex, Bersani advances, is that "most people don't like it"—which is to say neither that people don't think about sex a lot, nor that people don't want to have a lot of sex.[32] Instead, Bersani's point is that sex is not as pleasurable as it might seem to us while we're daydreaming about it. When we actually have sex, Bersani claims, we are no longer self-contained subjects enjoying an easily quantifiable experience of pleasure that we have contemplated beforehand. Quite the reverse: for Bersani, sex is an experience of radical dissolution that he calls "self-shattering" (222). Sexuality is therefore "socially dysfunctional," in Bersani's words, not because it can sometimes be the genital terrorism of Queer Nation but because it always undoes "the supposed relationality or community of the couple (which depends on self-hood)," as a commentator on Bersani's essay puts it.[33] Regardless of the number of partici-pants, sex is a profoundly solipsistic experience. So in Bersani's account the passive "suicidal ecstasy" of the gay bottom exemplifies a general theory of sex as nonrelational.[34] This has subsequently become known as the "antisocial thesis" in queer theory.[35]

The antisocial account of sex puts in question the apparently self-evident badness of desensitizing genital surgery. If sex isn't pleasurable anyway, then the diminution or loss of sexual pleasure is at least a misnomer and perhaps also a contradiction. It is a misnomer if something other than pleasure—a shattering—is lost to postsurgical sex; it is a contradiction if a loss of pleasure—again, a shattering—characterizes sex in general. An obvious way to resolve this conundrum would be to say simply that shattering is just another name for pleasure, which is what Bersani argues elsewhere about the apparent pain of masochism: we might then say that self-shattering describes only the transformation of "stimuli generally associated with the production of pain into stimuli that set off intense processes identified as pleasurable," as Bersani comments on masochism.[36] But rather than try to sanitize shattering by defending it as a "pleasurable debasement," the antisocial thesis in queer theory has devel-oped into a complex discourse about negativity, futurity, and—most significantly for my argument—shame.[37] In short, the antisocial character of sex—debasing, disintegrating, demeaning—makes sex shameful. Queer subcultures, it has been argued, have a distinctive relationship to such shame; if sex for both queers and nonqueers is a kind of shattering, then what distinguishes queer subcultures isn't the performance of certain sex acts (genital terrorism, whole-body sadomasochism, or anything else) but a particular attitude toward the antisocial experience of sex. In queer subcultures, according to Warner, "one doesn't pretend to be *above* the indignity of sex," since "we're all in it together."[38] In this way, an "acknowledgement of all that is most abject and least reputable in oneself"—namely, the solipsistic evacuation described by Bersani—perversely enables "the special kind of soci-ability that holds queer culture together" (35). That is, queer subcultures are characterized by the recognition that sex is antisocial.

Nonetheless, if sex is really as shamefully antisocial as Bersani describes, one has to wonder why people have sex at all. I'm not raising this issue in order to retreat from Bersani's claim to a version of queer sex that is cuddly hand-holding; his claim is important and deserves interrogation. Even though Bersani aims to "desexualize the erotic" by casting it as antisocial, his account remains resolutely sexualized in its valorization of gay anal penetration as the exemplary "intensification or . . . mode of revelation of an always-already shattering self," as Kathryn Bond Stockton writes in her book about shame.[39] As a consequence, there is a circu-larity in Bersani's argument. He explains, through reference to sex, why "most people don't like sex," as if most people don't like it because they've had it, but didn't like the way in which it shattered them. This doesn't account for those people who haven't had sex, can't have it, or don't want to have it in the first place. Yet I think those people may be no less queer. A critique of queer theory by Heather Love is useful on this point. Love has argued that "queer desire is often figured as . . . excessive, dissonant desire. But it would also make sense to understand queerness as an absence of or aversion to sex."[40] Both types of queerness presented by Love are possible on the basis of the antisocial thesis, but much queer theory has alighted on the first (queerness as an excessive embrace of shameful shattering) while failing to investigate the second (queerness as a rejection of, or withdrawal from, sex). The absence of sex, as Love admits, is "not very sexy," and for that reason has received little critical attention (175n22). But if queer theory is to do anything for intersex, it needs to theorize the ways in which postsurgical bodies may be asexual, and even downright unsexy to some people—including sometimes those who dwell in such bodies. The shattering experience of sex might be shameful—the antisocial thesis teaches us that much—but not having sex, or having sex without shattering, can be shameful, too.

In queer discourse the body of the stone butch is sometimes presented as the somatic personalization of the absence of or aversion to sex described by Love. Traditionally, a stone butch makes love to her femme partner but refuses to be touched in return.[41] In a ground-breaking essay on the subject, Judith Halberstam has criticized any simplistic conception of stone butch "impenetrability" as a "closed" sexuality (63, 68). In an argument that may seem equivalent to Chase's rejection of claims that she will learn how to orgasm, Halberstam contests the representation of stoneness as "a wall that has been built up and could come down with the right femme" (68).

Despite the stone butch body's closure to genital penetration, Halberstam suggests that it is "open to rubbing or friction," and in this regard "butch untouchability multiplies the possibilities of touch," as one commentator on Halberstam notes.[42] To be stone, then, is "a courageous and imaginative way of dealing with the contradictory demands and impulses of being a butch in a woman's body," according to Halberstam (69). But for this very reason there are two critical differences between stone butch and intersex. The former is a "sexual identity" (71), whereas the latter is an anatomy. I agree with Ellen K. Feder, [. . .] that there are not "intersex individuals" in the same way that there are "homosexual individuals."[43] Further, because the queerness of the stone butch lies not in sexual "closure" but in the performance and reception of certain kinds of touching, the stone butch body is still a tactile body. It is therefore vital to examine whether there is a similar place for the postsurgical intersex body in the relation between queerness, tactility, and touch.

Queer touching

The idea that queer theory is a kind of touch has been formatively elaborated by Carolyn Dinshaw in an essay titled "Chaucer's Queer Touches/A Queer Touches Chaucer."[44] For Dinshaw, queerness can touch on bodies and cultural structures alike, and its force on both is transformative. In this section I consider the critical context of Dinshaw's argument, as well as its implications for the difficult relation between queer theory and intersex bodies of diminished tactility. To be clear: I am not referring here to a postsurgical diminution of sexuality or sex drive, even if impaired tactility may sometimes correlate with such diminution.

Writing on touch is often an occasion to comment on the human condition. For instance, in a major book on the subject, the anthropologist Ashley Montagu has advised gravely that "inadequate tactile experience will result in . . . inability to relate to others in many fundamental human ways."[45] In this fashion touching has frequently been presented as both figure and ground for interpersonal relations: it at once exemplifies relations and makes them possible. This is because the touch, in Margrit Shildrick's words, is "an undecidable moment of exchange" during which one's "sense of wholeness and self-sufficiency dissolve."[46] Here is shattering not as asocial but conversely as the basis for sociality. Accordingly, several feminists and queer theorists have celebrated the "conjoining power of touch" as ethically and sexually superior to what Shildrick calls an "anaesthetic" ethic grounded in "separation and division" that some critics have associated with vision.[47] Conjoining is suggested by the syntax of Dinshaw's title "Chaucer's Queer Touches/A Queer Touches Chaucer": it indicates that queer criticism will emerge where author and critic touch. Undecidable exchange is stressed by Dinshaw's substitution of an ambivalent slash for the conventional academic colon that would hierarchize title and subtitle.

The nonhierarchical configuration of text and critic indicates how touching connotes equality between individuals; similarly, Warner has used a spatial metaphor to claim that there is equality in shame, since in queer subcultures the indignity of sex is "spread around the room, leaving no one out, and in fact binding them together."[48] Shame here touches individuals and connects them, without separation and division, weblike. And just as there is no "sub" in Dinshaw's title, so too has Califia argued that queer sexual practices focused on touching are mutually respectful and nonhierarchical. During gay sex, writes Califia, "there's good sex, which includes lots of touching, and there's bad sex, which is nonsensual": touching is more than mere foreplay.[49] Consequently, in both the queer views on the relationship between bodies and pleasures that I discussed above, touching is crucial. While Blasius's model of sex that engages the entire body does demote the genitalia as the primary location of sexual activity, it simultaneously promotes touching just as much as the genital-centered behavior that it is intended to supersede.

Queer attention to touch is certainly an effective counterpoint to the medical project of making genitalia look normal at the cost of desensitization.[50] For example, in an anthology of writings on queer body image, Chase has eschewed the cultural use of "infant genitals . . . for discriminating male from female infants" on the grounds that "*my* genitals are for *my* pleasure."[51] In this respect queer theory lets us argue that desensitization is not an acceptable side effect of normalizing surgery, because genitalia are for touching, not for looking at. But implicit in this type of critique, whereby a medical concern for appearance is distinguished from a queer concern with touching, is a highly significant conflation of touch and tactility.[52] Touch and tactility are not the same: the former is an action, whereas the latter is a sense. Hence a body can touch without tactility, for instance, if one's hands are numb from exposure to cold weather. Likewise, a tactile body is not necessarily a body that is touched, as the figure of the stone butch exemplifies. Then again some bodies are indeed tactile, touching, and touched, all at once. My point is that touching and tactility are different, so they do not always coincide, although I recognize that for many bodies they do. Crucially, then, the conflation of touch and tactility is what enables a queer critique of surgery. This is because surgical desensitization impairs touching only if touching is assumed to entail tactility. After all, desensitized genitals can still touch and be touched; it is their tactility that surgery damages.

More than arguing for a queer critique of the impairment of tactility, I want to consider whether queerness itself is a kind of tactility or sensitivity to impressions. Elizabeth Freeman has recently called queer history "a structure of *tactile* feeling," and I am interested in whether postsurgical bodies can find a place within such a queer sensorial structure.[53] The shattering experience described by Bersani demonstrates that queer pleasure and shame are not necessarily opposed, for pleasure and shame are both "sensations of minority," to borrow a delightful phrase from Berlant.[54] As sensations, pleasure and shame have in common a position of exteriority to the social. In making this claim, my interest lies not in determining whether such sensations are inexorably antisocial but merely in suggesting that if pleasure and shame are embodied sensations, then by definition they are situated outside the social. They are in the body. For instance, critics have described shame as "an embodied emotion" that "makes our bodies horribly sensitive."[55] Meanwhile, Foucault has criticized the failure of "modern Western societies" to recognize "the reality of the body and the intensity of its pleasures."[56] All the same, the relation of exteriority that I'm describing is more complex than an opposition between body and society. I argue that queer sensations are exterior to the social as it has been defined in mainstream Western culture, because such sensations are cultivated through embodied participation in queer communities.[57]

Consider in this connection an account by Berlant and Warner of watching a performance of "erotic vomiting" at a leather bar. Describing the audience's transfixion, Berlant and Warner comment that "people are moaning softly with admiration, then whistling, stomping, screaming encouragements."[58] In other words, both the bodies of the performers and those of the audience are affected by the scene. For Berlant and Warner, this is the production, via sex in public, of "nonheteronormative bodily contexts" (208). The result is a queer community as the audience presses forward into "a compact and intimate group" of bodies before the performers (207). In light of this attention to the embodied sensations of minority, we can understand the Foucauldian emphasis on pleasure and the antisocial emphasis on shame (for surely both are in circulation during the erotic vomiting performance) as ways to privilege minority sensations. To be precise, such sensations not only signal but actually constitute a resistant relation to mainstream society. In other words, they have countercultural force.

Cultural change for Dinshaw is correspondingly accomplished not through touching alone but through the queer *sensation* of the touch. Berlant and Warner remark that heteronormativity can be unmarked, naturalized, and/or idealized (209n3), and it's Dinshaw's queer contestation of the second of these attributes—naturalization—that interests me most. She states that the "disillusioning force" of a queer character like Chaucer's Pardoner "shakes with his touch the heterocultural edifice": these sensory metaphors of shaking and force describe not only touching but moreover the tactile impression of being touched.[59] Similarly, Dinshaw asserts that twentieth-century readers of the Pardoner "can feel the shock" of the character's discourse and thereby "appropriate that power for queer use" (79). I suggest that queerness in Dinshaw's argument names the simultaneity of touching and tactility. Because of this simultaneity, queerness for Dinshaw can "provoke perceptual shifts and subsequent corporeal response in those touched" (76). It is through queer sensations, then, that cultural change is accomplished. As Dinshaw explains: "Queerness articulates not a determinate thing but a relation to existent structures of power. Despite its positioning on the other side of the law, it is arresting: it makes people stop and look at what they have been taking as natural" (77). It is as if bringing into relation "existent structures of power" and "the other side of the law" would enable some intermingling between these positions—as if making queerness and heteroculture touch could reveal the natural to be a construction after all. Now if one can relate to Shildrick's description of touching as an undecidable exchange in which self-sufficiency dissolves, then it's easy to imagine that when queerness and heteroculture touch, cultural change will happen. But with genitalia of diminished tactility, the catalytic (or shattering) potential of touching is far less clear. Dinshaw claims later that the queer touch renders strange "what has passed until now without comment" (79). I agree that queerness can have that disorienting effect, but what remains absolutely *not* strange in Dinshaw's queer analysis is the simultaneity of touching and tactility.

In summary, queerness as a critical kind of touching requires a tactile surface—whether of an individual subject or a cultural structure—for the registration of its contact. Evidently the conflation of touch and tactility may stigmatize as less than fully human (unable "to relate to others," as Montagu speculates) those individuals whose genitalia are without sensation. But that's not my main quarrel with this discourse. Rather, I would query the assumption that the body produced by normalizing genital surgery "passes without comment" and so is susceptible to queer denaturalization in the manner described by Dinshaw. If we think of surgery itself as touching, its effects are more ambivalent, so a different kind of critique will be necessary.

Queering surgery

My critique of surgery in this section is intended to show why most queer accounts of touch are, in my view, insufficient for theorizing intersex. This is because not only recognizably queer touches defamiliarize. Indeed, touching may be defamiliarizing quite aside from its simultaneity with any particular sensation, as the surgical creation of insensate genitalia demonstrates. Put differently, the surgeon's desensitizing touch makes bodies strange.

To understand how genital surgery is a kind of touching, it's necessary first to analyze an implicit distinction in accounts such as Dinshaw's of the queer touch. The queer touch as discussed above is implicitly organized around a difference between cultural and natural, and therein lies a contradiction. On the one hand, the queer touch is cultural, in its opposition to naturalized cultural structures: it transmits a denaturalizing constructivist force. But, on the other hand, the fact that the simultaneity of touching and tactility passes without comment in queer discourse is naturalizing: in this regard the queer touch seems beyond construction. This contradiction doesn't mean that we should give up trying to theorize queer touching, but it does suggest that we should shift the terms in which the touch is theorized away from the distinction between cultural and natural. This enables a more interesting critique of genital surgery, because such a critique will not depend on a judgment about whether surgery naturalizes or denaturalizes intersex genitalia.

With this purpose in mind I find extremely useful the "minoritizing" and "universalizing" terminology that Eve Kosofsky Sedgwick proposes in *Epistemology of the Closet*. The aim of her terminology is to address the question, "in whose lives is homo/heterosexual definition an issue of continuing centrality and difficulty?"[60] Or put another way: to whom is homosexuality important—homosexuals (in a minoritizing view) or everyone (in a universalizing view)? Whether one argues that the importance of homosexuality is natural or cultural is secondary. For example, everyone may be naturally homosexual, but most people may be socialized into heterosexuality; or only some people may be naturally homosexual, and the rest may be naturally heterosexual; or homosexuality may be an entirely cultural phenomenon; and so on. The value of Sedgwick's terminology is that it permits analysis of how and why the distinction between natural and cultural is used, rather than using that distinction as an explanatory framework. Sedgwick therefore offers these unusual terms as a wholesale alternative to "essentialist versus constructivist understandings of homosexuality" (40): whereas those understandings can lead to contradictions similar to the one I've identified in the queer touch, universalizing and minoritizing views of homosexuality can coexist without contradiction. Hence we can now see that Dinshaw universalizes the queer touch as "no one's property," shifting between characters and readers while simultaneously minoritizing it to twentieth-century critical readers who alone "can feel the shock" of a character such as the Pardoner.[61] The coexistence of universalization and minoritization in Dinshaw's account generates the denaturalizing power of the touch and also its naturalization: it is uniquely queer, yet it queers things for everybody. So the question I wish to ask is, to whom is touching important—queers or everyone?

Genital surgery for intersex is an example of how bodies touch. It is an embodied encounter between patients and surgeons.[62] The operating room, a space of stylized hygiene, makes possible extraordinarily intimate touches in which normally unseen and inaccessible bodily interiors are touched by other bodies and their technological prostheses.[63] Technology such as the scalpel extends the temporal reach of the surgeon's touch. The scalpel lends the surgeon's touch a force of which durability is an effect: by having the power to cut the body, the surgeon's touch persists in ways that would be impossible otherwise, changing for life the patient's genitalia.[64] In Ahmed's words, "the wound functions as a trace of where the surface of another entity . . . has impressed upon the body."[65] The corollary of this is the immobility of the patient's anesthetized body, which in its meaty docility is receptive to the impression of the touch. Giving willingly to the surgeon and medical team the ability to see oneself without being seen, during the time of anesthesia, is a corporeal gift that subverts the assumption by some critics that "the ability to see without being seen" is a "masculinist and imperialist" fascination.[66] Later, as the pain of wounds fades, the formation of scars constitutes a visual record of the cutting that anesthesia has hidden from the patient's memory.

In my opinion the touch of genital surgery on the body is strikingly similar to Esther Newton's account of how drag performers incongruously mix "sex-role referents" such as a tuxedo and earrings.[67] The performers in Newton's study called this "working with (feminine) pieces" (101), a phrase that I think describes what surgeons do when operating on intersex anatomies, although the "pieces" are not sartorial items but body parts, and not only feminine ones are manipulated. The surgeon's touch has the force to detach, move, reshape, and even injure such pieces. The resultant "drag" of surgery may take the form of contrasts between conventionally masculine and feminine genital parts, such as a phallus and labia, or it may take the form of juxtapositions between scarred tissue and undamaged flesh. Now it could be argued that genital surgery is a drag act that performatively produces gender by "dragging on" in the life of the postsurgical subject. In some instances this may be true. However, this is not my main point because I don't think we can assume that genital surgery necessarily has anything to do with gender. It may simply be stigmatizing, and that is all; gender may be formed by other means.[68]

Therefore this is drag not as disguise or impersonation but as a fragmentary working with pieces whereby the postsurgical body neither remains intersex nor becomes convincingly nonintersex. It is readable incongruously as both at once. The lived experience of this is that one's sexual anatomy seems both glaringly unusual and yet brutally normalized—one reason why postsurgical individuals may be fearful of sexual relations.[69] Surgery can leave one unsure as to whether an explanation for one's genital appearance and function needs to be offered to sexual partners—and if so, whether such an explanation should presume that partners have already noticed the effects of intersex, of surgery, or of both. The deficiency of the distinction between cultural and natural as a critical framework for understanding genital surgery also becomes apparent here: the postsurgical body is neither successfully constructed by surgery into a clearly male or female form, nor is it still naturally intersex. At the same time, depending on who is looking, the body's intersex condition may seem an unnatural residue that has not been adequately naturalized by surgery.[70] So the effect of the surgeon's touch is highly ambivalent in its production of persistently incongruous bodily "pieces"—masculine and feminine, intersexed and nonintersexed, presurgical and postsurgical.

For these reasons, one might even conclude that genital surgery makes bodies *more* intersex than they started out, as Holmes brilliantly puts it.[71] Certainly genital surgery can render strange anatomies that would otherwise have passed without comment. For instance, when I was about eleven, in the school locker-room (that fabled location on which some surgeons base judgments about the fate of intersexed people who don't receive surgery) I was teased *not* because of intersex characteristics that remained after surgery but specifically because of scars *caused* by surgery.[72] The copresence on my body's surface of presurgical and postsurgical times—the pieces of intersex alongside the pieces of surgery—made my intersex condition less notable but my body more strange. This was a nonheteronormative bodily context, in Berlant and Warner's phrase, if ever there was one. So although surgery is evidently an instrument of what Dinshaw calls heteroculture, I'd argue that it's nonetheless a queer practice according to her own definition. Surgery is an example of what Freeman has named "temporal drag"—the registration of "the co-presence of several historically specific events" on bodily surfaces.[73]

The diminution of genital tactility is one way in which a historically specific event persists on the body's surface. As Ahmed explains in her book on the cultural politics of emotions, "It is through the recognition or interpretation of sensations, which are responses to the impressions of objects and others, that bodily surfaces take shape."[74] I think Ahmed is right, but she tells only half the story: I argue further that the body's very capacity for sensation is shaped by the impressions of objects and others on its surfaces. One such object is the surgeon's scalpel. It is not simply that we feel touches but that certain touches, depending on their force and durability, determine what we are able to feel. In this way I concur with Gayle Salamon that "as a perceived and perceiving entity, the body depends on a substratum of history."[75] Surgery's effects show how tactility, far from being simultaneous with touching, always has a constitutive history. A history of surgery forecloses the kinds of touches that a body can feel and drags the genitalia permanently back into the time of anesthetized insensitivity when surgery took place. Genital surgery thereby limits the extent to which the queer touch can be universalized to people with intersex bodies. Whether one regards surgery's aims and outcomes as naturalizing or denaturalizing, in matters of touch surgery is minoritizing, and I think this is reason enough to object to it.

The time of the reach

In this final section I consider what constraints desensitizing surgery places on the future for intersex bodies and show how queer theory might engage with desires that curiously persist after surgery. Halberstam has suggested that queer subcultures allow their participants "to believe that their futures can be imagined according to logics that lie outside of those paradigmatic markers of life experience—namely, birth, marriage, reproduction, and death."[76] There is an affinity here between queerness and intersex because both phenomena can disrupt the heterocultural scripts for birth, marriage, and reproduction. However, to accomplish this, queer subcultures tend to emphasize "flexibility" in desires, practices, and identifications, as Halberstam has noted elsewhere.[77] This leads to an opposition between flexibility and inflexibility, which in Halberstam's words "ascribes mobility over time to some notion of liberation and casts stubborn identification as a way of being stuck in time, unevolved, not versatile" (190). My concern as I draw to a close is not with identification (either as queer or as intersex) but with the flexible/inflexible binary itself. The queer touch is emblematic of flexibility because in Dinshaw's formulation it "moves around, is transferable," and can even work "across time."[78] I discuss whether the postsurgical body may be more flexible than a queer account might suggest, but I also argue that its flexibility shouldn't be the only measure of its future—or indeed the measure of only its future.

Even though the postsurgical body of diminished tactility is unquestionably material, it is still constructed, and in a queer reading this may imply a capacity for future change. As I've demonstrated, to say that the intersex body is constructed is to describe its materiality as contingent on the enduring touch of genital surgery. It's not to imply that the body is unreal but to tell the history of its realness—and thereby to insist that its realness is worth explaining. Contrary to most commentaries in the humanities on intersex, I offer this account not as a rejoinder to medicine but as a caution to queer theory. Queer theory as much as medicine has overlooked the construction of the tactile body (which includes the nurturing of tactility for some bodies as well as the destruction of tactility for others), despite the queer constructivist agenda and its attention to other aspects of the body's cultural formation. Moreover, there is no necessary relation between the revelation of the postsurgical body's construction and its deconstruction or reconstruction as something else. It may resist such constructive flexibility. So whereas queer theory often assumes that change follows from the revelation of construction, revealing the constructed character of the postsurgical intersex body makes possible no change: the insensate genitalia remain.[79]

In much queer theory, the idea of cultural change is sexualized as the hope for a future in which sex will take place, whether inside or outside the social. For example, Amber Hollibaugh has declared that "there is no human hope without the promise of ecstasy."[80] In this respect, I think Donald Morton was correct to state in his notorious 1995 *PMLA* essay on queer theory that "when queer theorists envision a future, they portray an ever-expanding region of sensuous pleasure, ignoring the historical constraints need places on pleasure."[81] Although I disagree with much of Morton's essay—in particular its simplification of the problems with queer politics to a flimsy opposition between "ludic" postmodernism and materialism (372)—I think he was right to critique the assumption that a queer future must be a "sensuous" one. But whereas Morton characterized the historical constraints on queer sensations as matters of material need, in the case of intersex a sensuous future is apparently closed down by the body's history of surgery. In other words, the problem with genital surgery for a queer account of intersex is surgery's foreclosure of the flexibility privileged in queer subcultures and exemplified by touching.

Nevertheless, to align what Salamon calls the body's "sedimented history" with material need versus ludic sensuality would be to give the postsurgical body an unwarranted inevitability.[82] My objection to this is not, for the reasons I explained in the previous section, that it would naturalize the body. Rather, I am concerned that a critique of queer sensations from the point of view of Morton's "historical materialism" would turn that critique into a reiteration of surgery's enduring effects.[83] Put another way, history would come to mean inflexibility. In Morton's attack on queer theory, history (as if this were a singular "systematic development," in his phrase [369]) becomes an explanation for pleasure's limits, and thereby imposes a limit of its own on critical analysis: history becomes the boundary beyond which critique cannot pass. Although Morton doesn't say so, this is because critique itself is a historical formation. So while history may explain why a sensuous future could be problematic, history's force as an explanation cannot be theorized in Morton's critical framework. Similarly, to represent the desensitized intersex body as the historical cause of a future without sex is to fail to imagine that anything other than tactility might organize sex. Therefore instead of critiquing queer theory in Morton's style by hammering it over the head with historical materialism, we might usefully unravel the opposition between historical inflexibility and queer flexibility.

Desire unravels this opposition, I believe. Consider that a diminution or loss of genital sensation may have nothing to do with desire, which might function independently of tactility. David Reimer, whose alleged sex reassignment from male to female after a circumcision accident was often cited as proof of surgery's capacity to change gender identity in children with unusual genitalia, has described the persistence of desire following the removal of his penis.[84] "If you lose your arm," he explained to his biographer, "and you're dying of thirst, that stump is still going to move toward that glass of water to try to get it. It's instinct. It's in you."[85] In this comment Reimer differentiates between desire and history, but for Reimer, unlike Morton, these are not mutually exclusive. Morton regards desire in queer and postmodern theory as "an autonomous entity outside history," opposed to historically determined need.[86] Desire in Reimer's account, though, is neither wholly inside nor wholly outside history, for it is the experience of the past's failure to determine fully the present.

Therefore although history persists in the present by leaving the postsurgical individual with a "stump" (whether literally or metaphorically), the stump may be invested with desire in ways that could not be anticipated by a historical materialist explanation of how the stump came to be. Put another way, desire arises from the difference between past and present, but it cannot be reduced to an effect of the past on the present. Desire in my analysis is therefore separate from the question of how we might imagine and reach a queer future.[87] It is a matter of how we reach and inhabit the present.

So desire is also distinct from the issue of how we might pursue and archive a queer history as Dinshaw envisages it.[88] At first glance, Reimer's account is akin to Dinshaw's theory of the queer touch: a text such as the *Canterbury Tales* may activate and engage readerly desires that cannot be explained by history of the text. These desires arise when text and critic come into contact across time, as Dinshaw states. Yet there is a key difference between Dinshaw and Reimer: the former describes touching; the latter, reaching. Although the reach doesn't "move around" quite like the touch, it is nevertheless a dynamic "moving toward," to use Reimer's phrase. Desire in this way cannot be reduced to an embodied affect, for its situation is neither in the postsurgical body nor in the presurgical body. Instead, desire names a relation between these bodies for the individual who inhabits the narrative of their succession. Reimer's narrative of reaching interestingly demonstrates both the flexibility of desire and also desire's stubbornness—its persistence after genital modification signals its adaptability just as much as its intractability. This account of desire thereby confounds the canonical, queer binary between flexibility and immobility.

Edelman has argued that queer theory should "remind us that we are inhabited always by states of desire that exceed our capacity to name them."[89] If Edelman is correct, then I think a queer understanding of the postsurgical body need *not* attend to the genitalia on which surgery operates, and which surgery attempts to name as female or male for heterosexist ends. Other types of critique, such as those from feminist science studies, can make those complaints.[90] A queer understanding ought to attend instead to the desires that exceed such naming. Otherwise, queer theory may echo the medical attempt to normalize bodies as markers of dichotomously sexed heterosexual desire by attempting to locate in bodies the nonheteronormative sensations of minority. What queer theory can do for intersex, then, is critique genital surgery without presuming to know in advance what comes after surgery, after desensitization, or even after queer theory—shame or pleasure; naturalization or denaturalization; familiarization or defamiliarization.[91] Queerness is useful instead for its interrogation of the meaning of the "after," which is the flexibility and inflexibility of history in the present.

Notes

I thank Neil Badmington, Jake Buckley, Sarah Creighton, Rebecca Munford, and Margrit Shildrick for helpful information and discussions, and the *GLQ* anonymous reviewers for perceptive feedback.

1   Sarah E. Chinn, "Feeling Her Way: Audre Lorde and the Power of Touch," *GLQ* 9 (2003): 192.

2   Cheryl Chase, letter to the editor, *Journal of Urology* 156 (1996): 1139; see also Morgan Holmes, "Rethinking the Meaning and Management of Intersexuality," *Sexualities* 5 (2002): 163.

3   N.S. Crouch et al., "Genital Sensation after Feminizing Genitoplasty for Congenital Adrenal Hyperplasia: A Pilot Study," *British Journal of Urology International* 93 (2004): 137.

4   J.P. Gearhart, A. Burnett, and J.H. Owen, letter to the editor, *Journal of Urology* 156 (1996): 1140.

5   Alain Borgeat, Georgios Ekatodramis, and Carlo A. Schenker, "Postoperative Nausea and Vomiting in Regional Anesthesia: A Review," *Anesthesiology* 98 (2003): 530–47.

6   Gillian Einstein, "From Body to Brain: Considering the Neurobiological Effects of Female Genital Cutting," *Perspectives in Biology and Medicine* 51 (2008): 84–97.

7   Rakesh Kapoor et al., "Sigmoid Vaginoplasty: Long-Term Results," *Journal of Urology* 67 (2006):
        1212–15.

8   Robert Jensen, "Getting It Up for Politics: Gay Male Sexuality and Radical Lesbian Feminism," in
        Opposite Sex: Gay Men on Lesbians, Lesbians on Gay Men, eds. Sara Miles and Eric Rofes (New York: New
        York University Press, 1998), 165.

9   Sara Ahmed, *Strange Encounters: Embodied Others in Post-Coloniality* (New York: Routledge, 2000),
        155.

10   David M. Halperin, *What Do Gay Men Want? An Essay on Sex, Risk, and Subjectivity* (Ann Arbor:
        University of Michigan Press, 2007), 86.

11   Michael Warner, *The Trouble with Normal: Sex, Politics, and the Ethics of Queer Life* (Cambridge, MA:
        Harvard University Press, 1999), 37.

12   Lee Edelman, "Queer Theory: Unstating Desire," *GLQ* 2 (1995): 345.

13   Pat Califia, "A Secret Side of Lesbian Sexuality," in *Public Sex: The Culture of Radical Sex*, 2nd ed. (San
        Francisco: Cleis, 2000), 166.

14   Intersex Society of North America, "Why Doesn't ISNA Want to Eradicate Gender?" (2006), www.
        isna.org/faq/not_eradicating_gender. My claim here is not that queer theory has had nothing to say
        about gender but that it has critiqued gender for the perceived limitations that it places on sex and
        sexuality. Accordingly, and unlike much second-wave feminism, queer theory has generally argued
        that gender identities should be "fucked" (blended, dissolved, crossed, and so on) instead of more
        equitably defined. See, for example, Stephen Whittle, "Gender Fucking or Fucking Gender?" in *Queer
        Theory*, eds. Iain Morland and Annabelle Willox (Basingstoke: Palgrave, 2005), 115–29.

15   Donald Morton, "Birth of the Cyberqueer," *PMLA* 110 (1995): 370. Although I think Morton is right
        on this point, I have reservations about much of his essay, which I discuss below.

16   See, for example, Betsy Driver, preface to special issue, *Cardozo Journal of Law and Gender* 12 (2005):
        3; Peter Hegarty in conversation with Cheryl Chase, "Intersex Activism, Feminism, and Psychology:
        Opening a Dialogue on Theory, Research, and Clinical Practice," *Feminism & Psychology* 10 (2000):
        127; M. Morgan Holmes, "Queer Cut Bodies," in *Queer Frontiers: Millennial Geographies, Genders, and
        Generations*, ed. Joseph A. Boone et al. (Madison: University of Wisconsin Press, 2000), 98; Emi
        Koyama, *Intersex Critiques: Notes on Intersex, Disability, and Biomedical Ethics* (Portland: Confluere,
        2003), 3, 7, 15.

17   John P. Gearhart, quoted in M. M. Bailez et al., "Vaginal Reconstruction after Initial Construction of
        the External Genitalia in Girls with Salt-Wasting Adrenal Hyperplasia," *Journal of Urology* 148 (1992):
        684; W. Hardy Hendren and Anthony Atala, "Repair of High Vagina in Girls with Severely
        Masculinized Anatomy from the Adrenogenital Syndrome," *Journal of Pediatric Surgery* 30 (1995): 91.

18   M. Morgan Holmes, "Queer Cut Bodies: Intersexuality and Homophobia in Medical Practice"
        (1995), tinyurl.com/6aw334. Note that this version differs from Holmes's chapter of the same name
        in *Queer Frontiers*.

19   Douglas Crimp, "Melancholia and Moralism," in *Loss: The Politics of Mourning*, eds. David L. Eng and
        David Kazanjian (Berkeley: University of California Press, 2002), 199.

20   The most influential articulation of "resignification" as a third-wave feminist/queer practice is in
        Judith Butler's *Gender Trouble: Feminism and the Subversion of Identity*, 2nd ed. (New York: Routledge,
        1999), 42.

21   Pat Califia, "Genderbending: Playing with Roles and Reversals," in *Public Sex: The Culture of Radical
        Sex*, 2nd ed. (San Francisco: Cleis, 2000), 185.

22   David M. Halperin, *Saint Foucault: Towards a Gay Hagiography* (New York: Oxford University Press,
        1995), 26. I find Halperin's account informative, but it also has limitations, which are demonstrated
        by Halperin's suggestion that "Foucault's focus on sexuality, and his refusal to subordinate the
        analysis of its instrumentality to the politics of gender, race, or class, made his work particularly
        useful for addressing the irreducibly *sexual* politics of the AIDS crisis" (27). While this focus on the
        sexual may seem paradigmatically queer (and as Halperin clarifies in a note, it enables an analysis of
        homophobia [195n26]), it for the same reason fails to consider how the other kinds of politics
        mentioned by Halperin not only affect sexuality but constitute the sexual *as* irreducible for particular
        subjects. In fact in his later book *What Do Gay Men Want?* Halperin acknowledges that "the focus on
        gay subjectivity [in public discourse on HIV/AIDS prevention] is sharpest in the case of white,
        socially privileged gay men, whose agency and autonomy are not likely to have been compromised by
        political oppression or external constraint and whose behavior therefore cannot be explained by
        other social factors" (23). But even this later formulation is somewhat unsatisfactory; I would suggest
        that uncompromised agency and autonomy are indeed explicable by "other social factors" such as
        race, class, and gender (see, for example, Damien W. Riggs, *Priscilla, (White) Queen of the Desert: Queer
        Rights/Race Privilege* [New York: Peter Lang, 2006]). Judith Halberstam offers a provocative analysis

of such ongoing tensions in queer identity politics in "Shame and Gay White Masculinity," *Social Text* 23, nos. 3–4 (2005): 219–33.

23   Michel Foucault, *The Will to Knowledge*, vol. 1 of *The History of Sexuality*, trans. Robert Hurley (Harmondsworth, UK: Penguin, 1998), 155, 157.

24   Lauren Berlant, *The Queen of America Goes to Washington City: Essays on Sex and Citizenship* (Durham, NC: Duke University Press, 1997), 158.

25   Tim Dean, *Beyond Sexuality* (Chicago: University of Chicago Press, 2000), 172.

26   Mark Blasius, *Gay and Lesbian Politics: Sexuality and the Emergence of a New Ethic* (Philadelphia: Temple University Press, 1994), 110. See also pages 125 and 221 on the "queerness" of Blasius's "new ethic."

27   Blasius, *Gay and Lesbian Politics*, 125; see also Michael Bronski, *The Pleasure Principle: Sex, Backlash, and the Struggle for Gay Freedom* (New York: St. Martin's, 1998), 157. On the Foucauldian basis of this claim, see Michel Foucault, "Sex, Power, and the Politics of Identity," interview by B. Gallagher and A. Wilson, in *Ethics: Subjectivity and Truth*, vol. 1 of *The Essential Works of Foucault, 1954–1984*, ed. Paul Rabinow, trans. Robert Hurley et al. (New York: New Press, 1997), 163–73, esp. 164–65.

28   Amber Hollibaugh, in Deirdre English, Amber Hollibaugh, and Gayle Rubin, "Talking Sex: A Conversation on Sexuality and Feminism," *Feminist Review* 11 (June 1982): 44.

29   Cheryl Chase, "Affronting Reason," in *Looking Queer*, ed. Dawn Atkins (New York: Harrington Park, 1998), 207.

30   Beyond the context of intersex, Jensen has made a comparable criticism of gay male culture ("Getting It Up for Politics," 166).

31   Sally R. Munt, "Shame/Pride Dichotomies in *Queer as Folk*," *Textual Practice* 14 (2000): 533, 536.

32   Leo Bersani, "Is the Rectum a Grave?" in *AIDS: Cultural Analysis/Cultural Activism*, ed. Douglas Crimp (Cambridge, MA: MIT Press, 1988), 197–98.

33   Bersani, "Is the Rectum a Grave?" 222; Kathryn Bond Stockton, *Beautiful Bottom, Beautiful Shame: Where "Black" Meets "Queer"* (Durham, NC: Duke University Press, 2006), 15.

34   Bersani, "Is the Rectum a Grave?" 212; see also Stockton, *Beautiful Bottom*, 15.

35   Robert L. Caserio, "The Antisocial Thesis in Queer Theory," *PMLA* 121 (2006): 819–21.

36   Leo Bersani, *Homos* (Cambridge, MA: Harvard University Press, 1995), 93; see also 94.

37   Stockton, *Beautiful Bottom*, 15. The antisocial relationship between negativity and futurity has been most polemically explored by Lee Edelman in *No Future: Queer Theory and the Death Drive* (Durham, NC: Duke University Press, 2004).

38   Warner, *Trouble with Normal*, 35, 36.

39   Bersani, *Homos*, 80; Stockton, *Beautiful Bottom*, 15.

40   Heather Love, *Feeling Backward: Loss and the Politics of Queer History* (Cambridge, MA: Harvard University Press, 2007), 40. However, Love does ultimately seem to recuperate as "bound up with pleasure" the emotions associated with an aversion to sex (161).

41   Judith Halberstam, "Lesbian Masculinity, or Even Stone Butches Get the Blues," *Women and Performance* 8, no. 2 (1996): 64.

42   Halberstam, "Lesbian Masculinity," 68; Ann Cvetkovich, *An Archive of Feelings: Trauma, Sexuality, and Lesbian Public Cultures* (Durham, NC: Duke University Press, 2003), 67.

43   Ellen K. Feder, "Imperatives of Normality: From 'Intersex' to 'Disorders of Sex Development,' " *GLQ* 15.2 (2009): 225–47. Some people do identify as "intersex" or "intersexual," of course, and I used both terms throughout "Is Intersexuality Real?" (*Textual Practice* 15 [2001]: 527–47). But I still don't think either term is comparable to *homosexual* because a sexual identity is just one of many things to which the terms could refer—anatomies (pre- and postsurgical), desires, gender identifications and roles, and so on. In particular to say that "intersex" names a sexual identity specific to a certain anatomy is to insinuate that all sexual identities are based in anatomy.

44   Carolyn Dinshaw, "Chaucer's Queer Touches/A Queer Touches Chaucer," *Exemplaria* 7 (1995): 75–92.

45   Ashley Montagu, *Touching: The Human Significance of the Skin* (New York: Columbia University Press, 1971), 292.

46   Margrit Shildrick, "Unreformed Bodies: Normative Anxiety and the Denial of Pleasure," *Women's Studies* 34 (2005): 329.

47   Chinn, "Feeling Her Way," 195; Margrit Shildrick, *Embodying the Monster: Encounters with the Vulnerable Self* (London: Sage, 2002), 119; Iris Marion Young, "The Scaling of Bodies and the Politics of Identity," in *Space, Gender, Knowledge: Feminist Readings*, eds. Linda McDowell and Joanne P. Sharp (London: Arnold, 1997), 221.

48   Warner, *Trouble with Normal*, 36.

49   Pat Califia, "Gay Men, Lesbians, and Sex: Doing It Together," in *Public Sex: The Culture of Radical Sex*, 2nd ed. (San Francisco: Cleis, 2000), 194.

50   For a further analysis of the extent to which surgery creates "normal-looking" genitalia, see Iain Morland, "The Injustice of Intersex: Feminist Science Studies and the Writing of a Wrong," in *Toward a Critique of Guilt: Perspectives from Law and the Humanities*, ed. Matthew Anderson (New York: Elsevier, 2005), 60–62.

51   Chase, "Affronting Reason," 210.

52   In this discussion I use the term *tactility* rather than *feeling* to avoid additional conflation with affect. Other critics have argued for the interrelation of tactility and affect. Eve Sedgwick in a book called *Touching Feeling* has suggested that the verbs in her book's title carry a double meaning, "tactile plus emotional." To be sure, the words may bear double meanings, but it doesn't follow that the tactile and affective realms are necessarily interconnected. Nonetheless, Sedgwick continues that "a particular intimacy seems to subsist between textures and emotions." Even though she advances this claim as "intuition" rather than a fact, it's unsatisfactorily circular because it attempts to explain touching (as tactile, textural) in terms of touching (as the affective intuition of a proximate "intimacy"). See Eve Kosofsky Sedgwick, *Touching Feeling: Affect, Pedagogy, Performativity* (Durham, NC: Duke University Press, 2003), 17. For a further argument about the significance of affect to queer theory and sexualities, see Ann Cvetkovich, "Public Feelings," *South Atlantic Quarterly* 106 (2007): 459–68.

53   Elizabeth Freeman, "Time Binds, or, Erotohistoriography," *Social Text* 23, nos. 3–4 (2005): 66; emphasis in original.

54   Lauren Berlant, "'68 or The Revolution of Little Queers," in *Feminism Beside Itself*, eds. Diane Elam and Robyn Wiegman (New York: Routledge, 1995), 301.

55   Noreen Giffney, preface (with Michael O'Rourke) to Sally R. Munt, *Queer Attachments: The Cultural Politics of Shame* (Aldershot, UK: Ashgate, 2008), ix; Elspeth Probyn, *Blush: Faces of Shame* (Minneapolis: University of Minnesota Press, 2005), 127.

56   Michel Foucault, introduction to *Herculine Barbin: Being the Recently Discovered Memoirs of a Nineteenth-Century French Hermaphrodite*, trans. Richard McDougall (New York: Pantheon, 1980), vii.

57   Of course, sensations of pleasure and shame can equally be firmly mainstream—for example, the visceral titillation, for some, of watching a heteronormative movie.

58   Lauren Berlant and Michael Warner, "Sex in Public," in *Publics and Counterpublics*, by Michael Warner (New York: Zone, 2002), 207.

59   Dinshaw, "Chaucer's Queer Touches," 92, 89.

60   Eve Kosofsky Sedgwick, *Epistemology of the Closet* (Berkeley: University of California Press, 1990), 40.

61   Dinshaw, "Chaucer's Queer Touches," 79.

62   Rosalyn Diprose, *Corporeal Generosity: On Giving with Nietzsche, Merleau-Ponty, and Levinas* (New York: State University of New York Press, 2002), 107–21.

63   For a seminal account of the stylized aspects of the operating room, see Pearl Katz, "Ritual in the Operating Room," *Ethnology* 20 (1981): 335–50.

64   Another way to theorize this durability is as a kind of writing. See Iain Morland, "The Glans Opens Like a Book': Writing and Reading the Intersexed Body," *Continuum* 19 (2005): 335–48.

65   Sara Ahmed, *The Cultural Politics of Emotion* (Edinburgh: Edinburgh University Press, 2004), 27.

66   Chinn, "Feeling Her Way," 195.

67   Esther Newton, *Mother Camp: Female Impersonators in America* (Chicago: University of Chicago Press, 1979), 101.

68   Alice Domurat Dreger, *Hermaphrodites and the Medical Invention of Sex* (Cambridge, MA: Harvard University Press, 1998), 200.

69   See, for example, Mary E. Boyle, Susan Smith, and Lih-Mei Liao, "Adult Genital Surgery for Intersex: A Solution to What Problem?" *Journal of Health Psychology* 10 (2005): 573–84; and Lih-Mei Liao, "Learning to Assist Women Born with Atypical Genitalia: Journey through Ignorance, Taboo, and Dilemma," *Journal of Reproductive and Infant Psychology* 21 (2003): 233.

70   For another account of how intersex is "constructed," see Morland, "Is Intersexuality Real?" 533.

71   Holmes, "Rethinking the Meaning," 174; on the failure of surgery to "normalize," see also Holmes, "Queer Cut Bodies" (*Queer Frontiers* version), 104.

72   On the rhetoric of the "locker-room" in medical discourse about intersex, see Iain Morland, "Plastic Man: Intersex, Humanism, and the Reimer Case," *Subject Matters* 3–4 (2007): 82–83.

73   Elizabeth Freeman, "Packing History, Count(er)ing Generations," *New Literary History* 31 (2000): 728, 729; see also Freeman's ingenious analysis of Frankenstein's monster's body as the literalization of the queer touch ("Time Binds," 60). I'd prefer not to argue that postsurgical bodies are Frankensteinian. In future work I'll discuss in more detail the bodily coexistence of different time periods after surgery, including the relation between body parts with and without tactility.

74   Ahmed, *Cultural Politics*, 25.

75 Gayle Salamon, "Boys of the Lex: Transgenderism and Rhetorics of Materiality," *GLQ* 12 (2006): 583.

76 Judith Halberstam, *In a Queer Time and Place: Transgender Bodies, Subcultural Lives* (New York: New York University Press, 2005), 2.

77 Judith Halberstam, "Theorizing Queer Temporalities: A Roundtable Discussion," Carolyn Dinshaw et al., *GLQ* 13 (2007): 190.

78 Dinshaw, "Chaucer's Queer Touches," 79; Carolyn Dinshaw, *Getting Medieval: Sexualities and Communities, Pre- and Postmodern* (Durham, NC: Duke University Press, 1999), 21.

79 As Love argues, "Critics [in queer studies] have ignored what they could not transform" (*Feeling Backward*, 147).

80 Amber Hollibaugh, "My Dangerous Desires: Falling in Love with Stone Butches, Passing Women, and Girls (Who Are Guys) Who Catch My Eye," in *Queer Cultures*, eds. Deborah Carlin and Jennifer DiGrazia (Upper Saddle River, NJ: Pearson Prentice Hall, 2004), 383.

81 Morton, "Birth of the Cyberqueer," 375.

82 Salamon, "Boys of the Lex," 583.

83 Morton, "Birth of the Cyberqueer," 369.

84 For a full account of the Reimer case in relation to intersex treatment, see Morland, "Plastic Man."

85 John Colapinto, *As Nature Made Him: The Boy Who Was Raised as a Girl* (London: Quartet, 2000), 148.

86 Morton, "Birth of the Cyberqueer," 371.

87 Kate Thomas has described the movement to a queer future as a sensation of reaching—a "muscular, epistemic stretch" ("Post Sex: On Being Too Slow, Too Stupid, Too Soon," *South Atlantic Quarterly* 106 [2007]: 623–24).

88 Desire in my account is also slightly different to the psychoanalytic argument about historical practice and the past made by Valerie Traub in *The Renaissance of Lesbianism in Early Modern England* (Cambridge: Cambridge University Press, 2002), 353–54.

89 Edelman, "Queer Theory," 345.

90 See Morland, "Injustice of Intersex."

91 A recent special issue of *South Atlantic Quarterly*, titled "After Queer Theory," engages with some of these questions of queerness, although intersex is mentioned only once, and in passing, in the issue (Carla Freccero, "Queer Times," *South Atlantic Quarterly* 106 [2007]: 491).

Chapter 27

Judith Halberstam

TRANSGENDER BUTCH: BUTCH/FTM BORDER WARS AND THE MASCULINE CONTINUUM

Judith Halberstam is Professor of English, American Studies, and Ethnicity and Gender Studies at the University of Southern California. Her most recent books are *In a Queer Time and Place: Transgender Bodies, Subcultural Lives* (2005) and *The Queer Art of Failure* (2011).

In this chapter from *Female Masculinity* (1998), Halberstam considers how the public emergence of FTM (female-to-male) transsexualities complicates other identifications and experiences of female masculinity, such as the tomboy, butch lesbian, and stone butch. Problematizing the notion of gender and the crossing of sexual borders, Halberstam reveals how conservative transsexual discourses depend not only on essentialized understandings of sex and gender, but also on whiteness and class privilege. In attending to those moments in transsexual discourse that threaten to reconsolidate dominant forms of masculinity via the desire for an authentic transsexual body, Halberstam demonstrates the complex and at times contradictory dynamics of cross-identification, sexual preference, and gendered embodiment. Meditating on what possible future gender-queer identities transsexual discourse may both enable and foreclose, Halberstam finds in the relatively new category of transgender a progressive rubric that promises dialogue and cohabitation in gender-queer worlds.

In addition to the definitional and legal wars, there are less obvious forms of sexual political conflict which I call the territorial or border wars. The processes by which erotic minorities form communities and the forces that seek to inhibit them lead to struggles over the nature and boundaries of sexual zones.

(Gayle Rubin, "Thinking Sex," Pleasure and Danger: Exploring Female Sexuality [1984])

The wrong body

IN 1995 THE BBC broadcast a series called *The Wrong Body*. One episode in the series dealt with a young person called Fredd, a biological female, who claimed to have been born into the wrong body. Nine-year-old Fredd claimed that "she" was really a male and demanded that his family, friends, teachers, and other social contacts deal with him as a boy. The program followed Fredd's quest for gender reassignment over a period of three years until at age twelve, Fredd trembled on the verge of female puberty. Fredd expressed incredible anxiety about the possibility that his efforts to be resocialized as a male were to be thwarted by the persistence of the flesh, and he sought hormone-blocking drugs to stave off the onset of puberty and testosterone shots to produce desired male secondary characteristics in and on his body. The BBC program dealt with Fredd's condition as a medical problem that presented certain ethical conundrums when it came to prescribing treatment. Should Fredd be forced to be a woman before he could decide to become a man? Could a twelve year old know enough about embodiment, gender, and sexuality to demand a sex change? What were the implications of Fredd's case for other seemingly commonplace cases of tomboyism?

Over the three-year period covered by the documentary, Fredd spent a considerable amount of time attending a child psychiatrist. We watched as Fredd carefully reeducated his doctor about the trials and tribulations of gender dysphoria and led his doctor through the protocols of gender reassignment, making sure that the doctor used the correct gender pronouns and refusing to allow the doctor to regender him as female. The doctor suggested at various moments that Fredd may be experiencing a severe stage of tomboy identification and that he may change his mind about his gender identity once his sexuality developed within a female adolescent growing spurt. Fredd firmly distinguished for the doctor between sexuality and gender and insisted that his sexual preference would make no difference to his sense of a core male gender identity. The doctor sometimes referred to Fredd by his female name and was calmly corrected as Fredd maintained a consistent and focused sense of himself as male and as a boy. Fredd's case made for a riveting documentary, and although the BBC interviewers did not push in these directions, questions about childhood cross-identification, about the effects of visible transsexualities, and about early childhood gender selection all crowded in on the body of this young person. What gender is Fredd as he waits for his medical authorization to begin hormones? What kind of refusal of gender and what kind of confirmation of conventional gender does Fredd's battle with the medical authorities represent? Finally, what do articulations of the notion of a wrong body and the persistent belief in the possibility of a "right" body register in relation to the emergence of other genders, transgenders?

[Here], I take up some of the questions raised by contemporary discussions of transsexuality about the relations between identity, embodiment, and gender. In an extended consideration of the differences and continuities between transsexual, transgender, and lesbian masculinities, I approach the thorny questions of identity raised by the public emergence of the female-to-male transsexual (FTM) in the last decade or so. If some female-born people now articulate clear desires to become men, what is the effect of their transitions on both male masculinity and on the category of butch? What will be the effect of a visible transsexual population on young people who cross-identify? Will more tomboys announce their transsexual aspirations if the stigma is removed from the category?

In the last part of this century, the invention of transsexuality as a medical category has partly drained gender variance out of the category of homosexuality and located gender variance very specifically within the category of transsexuality. Whereas in [other] chapters [in *Female Masculinity*] I have attempted to trace and historically locate some of the intersections between medical definitions of transsexuality and homosexual inversion, I want to analyze here the surprising continuities and unpredictable discontinuities between gender variance that retains the birth body (for example, butchness) and gender variance that necessitates sex reassignment. Medical descriptions of transsexuality throughout the last forty years have been preoccupied with a discourse of "the wrong body" that describes transsexual embodiment in terms of an error of nature whereby gender identity and biological sex are not only discontinuous but catastrophically at odds. The technological availabilities of surgeries to reassign gender have made the option of gender transition available to those who understand themselves to be tragically and severely at odds with their bodies, and particularly for male-to-female transsexuals (MTFs), these surgical transitions have been embraced by increasing numbers of gender-variant people. The recent visibility of female-to-male transsexuals has immensely complicated the discussions around transsexuality because gender transition from female to male allows biological women to access male privilege within their reassigned genders. Although few commentators would be so foolish as to ascribe FTM transition solely to the aspiration for mobility within a gender hierarchy, the fact is that gender reassignment for FTMs does have social and political consequences.

If we study the fault lines between masculine women and transsexual men, we discover, I point out, that as transsexual men become associated with real and desperate desires for reembodiment, so butch women become associated with a playful desire for masculinity and a casual form of gender deviance. Although homosexuality was removed from the DSM III manual in 1973, transsexuality remains firmly in the control of medical and psychological technologies.[1] However, all too often, such a fact is used to argue that more cultural anxiety focuses on the transsexual than on the homosexual. I believe that the confusing overlaps between some forms of transsexuality and some gender-deviant forms of lesbianism have created not only definitional confusion for so-called medical experts but also a strange struggle between FTMs and lesbian butches who accuse each other of gender normativity. I am attempting here to unravel some of the most complicated of these arguments.

I use the term "transgender butch" to describe a form of gender transitivity that could be crucial to many butches' sense of embodiment, sexual subjectivity, and even gender legitimacy. As the visibility of a transsexual community grows at the end of the twentieth century and as FTMs become increasingly visible within that community, questions about the viability of queer butch identities become unavoidable. Some lesbians seem to see FTMs as traitors to a "woman's" movement who cross over and become the enemy. Some FTMs see lesbian feminism as a discourse that has demonized FTMs and their masculinity. Some butches consider FTMs to be butches who believe in anatomy, and some FTMs consider butches to be FTMs who are too afraid to make the "transition" from female to male. The border wars between transgender butches and FTMs presume that masculinity is a limited resource, available to only a few in ever decreasing quantities. Or else we see masculinity as a set of protocols that should be agreed on in advance. Masculinity, of course, is what we make it; it has important relations to maleness, increasingly interesting relations to transsexual maleness, and a historical debt to lesbian butchness. At least one of the issues I want to take up here is what model of masculinity is at stake in debates between butches and FTMs and what, if anything, separates butch masculinity from transsexual masculinities. I will examine some of the identifications that we have argued about (the stone butch in particular) and attempt to open dialogue between FTM and butch subject positions that allows for cohabitation in the territories of queer gender. I will also look at the language of these arguments and try to call attention to the importance of the metaphors of border, territory, crossing, and transitivity.

Recently, transsexual communities have become visible in many urban areas, and a transsexual activist response to transphobia (as separate from homophobia and not assimilable under the banner "queer") has animated demands for special health care considerations and legal rights. Although one might expect the emergence of transsexual activism to fulfill the promise of a "queer" alliance between sexual minorities by extending the definition of sexual minority beyond gay and lesbian, in fact there is considerable antipathy between gays and lesbians and transsexuals, and the term "queer" has not managed to bridge the divide. Whereas transsexuals seem suspicious of a gay and lesbian hegemony under the queer banner, gays and lesbians fear that some forms of transsexualism represent a homophobic restoration of gender normativity. But there is possibly another group in this standoff who maintain the utility of queer definition without privileging either side of the gay/lesbian versus transsexual divide. This group may be identified as transgender or gender-queer. The gender-queer position, often also called queer theory or postmodernism, has been cast in many different theoretical locations as the blithe opponent of the real, the player who fails to understand the life-and-death struggle around gender definition. While I contest such a characterization of the transgender position, I do want to consider what kind of symbolic burden we force on the transsexual body within postmodernism and how such bodies resist or defy the weight of signifying the technological constructions of otherness.

Transgender butch

Transsexuality has become something of a favored topic for gender studies nowadays because it seems to offer case studies for demonstrations of various gender theories. Because transsexual self-accountings are all too often left out of the theorizations of gender variance, some critical animosity has developed between transsexual and nontranssexual theorists. Jacob Hale has informally published a set of rules for nontranssexuals writing about trans-sexuality (http://www.actlab.utexas.edu/ sandy/hale.rules.html), and these rules suggest that parameters are necessary and important for nonidentity-based writings. As a nontrans-sexual who has written about transsexuality, I would like to comment in this section about the important skirmishes between FTM and butch theorists, my role in those skirmishes, and the kinds of knowledge they produce.

In 1994 I published an essay called "F2M; The Making of Female Masculinity" in a volume called *The Lesbian Postmodern*.[2] The avowed intention of the article was to examine the various representations of transsexual bodies and transgender butch bodies that surfaced around 1990 to 1991, largely within lesbian contexts. The essay was speculative and concen-trated on films, videos, and narratives about gender-ambiguous characters. Much to my surprise, the essay was regarded with much suspicion and hostility by some members of FTM International, a San Francisco-based transsexual men's group; these reactions caused me to look carefully at the kinds of assumptions I was making about transsexuality and about the kinds of continuities or overlaps that I presumed between the categories of FTM and butch. My intention here is not to apologize for that essay or simply to explain again my position; rather, I want to use the constructive criticism I received about that article to reconsider the various relations and nonrelations between FTM and butch subjectivities and bodies. Ultimately, I believe that "F2M" was actually trying to carve out a subject position that we might usefully call transgender butch to signify the transition that the identity requires from female identity to masculine embodiment. At present, the moniker "FTM" names a radical shift in both identity and body base within the context of transsexuality that by comparison makes "butch" look like a stable signifier. But the shifts and accommodations made in most cross-gender identifications, whether aided by surgery or hormones or not, involve a great deal of instability and transitivity. Transgender butch conveys some of this movement.

In "F2M," I attempted to describe the multiple versions of masculinity that seemed to be emerging simultaneously out of both lesbian and transsexual contexts. My project was not a fact-finding ethnography about FTM; nor did it examine the mechanics, trials, tribulations, benefits, and necessities of body alteration. Rather, I asked discursive and possibly naive questions such as: Why, in this age of gender transitivity, when many queers and feminists have agreed that gender is a social construct, is transsexuality a widespread phenomenon? Why has there been so little discussion of the shared experiences of masculine lesbians and FTMs? And, finally, why are we not in what Sandy Stone has called a "posttranssexual era"?[3] My questions presumed that some forms of transsexuality represented gender essentialism, but from this assertion, some people understood me to be saying that butchness was postmodern and subversive whereas transsexualism was dated and deluded. I think, rather, that I was trying to create a theoretical and cultural space for the transgender butch that did not presume transsexuality as its epistemological frame. I was also implicitly examining the possibility of the non-operated-upon transgender person.

My article was received, as I suggested, as a clumsy and ignorant attack on the viability of FTM transsexuality, and there was a small debate about it in the pages of the *FTM Newsletter*. The editor, James Green, took me to task for speaking for FTMs, and in a review essay, a writer called Isabella cast me in the role of the lesbian feminist who wanted transsexuals to disappear within some postmodern proliferation of queer identities.[4] Isabella noted that I focused on film and video in my essay (on representations, in other words, as opposed to "real" accounts), and she accused me of failing to integrate the real lives and words of "the successfully integrated post-op FTM" into my theory.[5] She went on to suggest that I was not interested in the reality of transsexuality because "it is the fluidity, the creation and dissolution of gender 'fictions' that is so fascinating" (14). I took this criticism very seriously, if only because I had been trying to do the very opposite of what she accused me of doing and because my position on transsexuality is not really akin to the kinds of lesbian feminist paranoias articulated by the likes of Janice Raymond.[6] By arguing that "desire has a terrifying precision" ("F2M," 212), I was trying to get away from the tendency within queer popular culture and some queer writing to privilege gender fluidity (being butch *and* femme for example) as the goal of some ongoing gender rebellion, and I was trying to talk about the ways in which desire and gender and sexuality tend to be remarkably rigid.[7] Rather than consent to the terms of this debate, I wanted to question the belief in fluid selves and the belief, moreover, that fluidity and flexibility are always and everywhere desirable. At the same time, I was trying to show that many, if not most, sexual and gender identities involve some degree of movement (not free-flowing but very scripted) between bodies, desires, transgressions, and conformities; we do not necessarily shuttle back and forth between sexual roles and practices at will, but we do tend to adjust, accommodate, change, reverse, slide, and move in general between moods and modes of desire. Finally, Isabella's charge that I had not accounted for the experiences of "the successfully integrated post-op FTM" assumes that this particular mode of transsexuality—integrated and post-op—represents the apex of cross-gender transition and indeed represents its success. The in-between bodies that I had focused on in my essay can only be read in such a context as preoperative versions of the real thing, as bodies that fail to integrate.

Another more recent article critiquing "F2M" also accused the essay of advocating some simple celebratory mode of border crossing. In "No Place like Home: The Transgendered

Narrative of Leslie Feinberg's *Stone Butch Blues*," Jay Prosser sets up "F2M" as a prime example of queer theory's fixation on the transgender body.[8] This article pits queer theory against transgender identity in a polemic: queer theory represents gender within some notion of postmodern fluidity and fragmentation, but transgender theory eschews such theoretical free fall and focuses instead on "subjective experience" (490). Queer theories of gender, in Prosser's account, emphasize the performative, and transgender theories emphasize narrative. Queer theories of gender are constructivist, and transgender theories are essentialist. Ultimately, Prosser proposes that transgender be separated from "genetic queerness" to build a transgender community (508).

The shaky foundation of Prosser's polemic is revealed in his reading of Feinberg's novel, in which it becomes clear that *Stone Butch Blues* represents both essential and constructed genders, both performative gender and genetic embodiment. Accordingly, when the main character, Jess Goldberg, chooses to halt his transition from female to male, we see the necessary insufficiency of binary gender rather than the solidity of transsexual identification. But Prosser uses Goldberg's transition to claim a continuity between this novel and transsexual autobiography. Even though Jess says, "I didn't feel like a man trapped in a woman's body, I just felt trapped," Prosser reads this as a transsexual paradigm "driven by the subject's sense of not being home in his/her body" ("No Place like Home," 490). The point here is that many subjects, not only transsexual subjects, do not feel at home in their bodies, and Prosser even cites from Feinberg a list of such gender outlaws at the end of his essay: "Transvestites, transsexuals, drag queens and drag kings, cross-dressers, bull-daggers, stone butches, androgynes etc."[9] But this was exactly my point in "F2M," and it is also what I recognize by using the term "transgender butch"—there are a variety of gender-deviant bodies under the sign of nonnormative masculinities and femininities, and the task at hand is not to decide which represents the place of most resistance but to begin the work of documenting their distinctive features. The place from which I chose to begin the work of examining the specificity of embodied desires was the butch, indeed the stone butch; I examined FTM subjectivity in that essay only as it compared to butch identifications. The place from which one theorizes "home," as Prosser calls it, completely alters the models of gender and sexuality one produces. As I discuss later, when theorized from the perspective of the FTM, the stone butch becomes pre-FTM, a penultimate stage along the way to the comfort of transsexual transformation; however, when theorized from the perspective of the butch, the stone butch becomes a nonsurgical and nonhormonal version of transgender identification and does away with the necessity of sex reassignment surgery for some people.

My essay also found a supporter in the *FTM Newsletter*. Jordy Jones, an FTM performance artist from San Francisco, responded to some of the criticisms of my article by suggesting that the notion that I had advanced of gender as a fiction did not necessarily erase the real-life experiences of transsexuals; rather, he suggested, it describes the approximate relation between concepts and bodies.[10] Furthermore, Jones objected to the very idea that transsexual experience could be represented in any totalizing or universal way:

> Not everyone who experiences gender dysphoria experiences it in the same way, and not everyone deals with it in the same way. Not all transgendered individuals take hormones, and not everyone who takes hormones is transgendered. I have a (genetically female) friend who identifies as male and passes perfectly. He's never had a shot. I certainly know dykes who are butcher than I could ever be, but who wouldn't consider identifying as anything other than women.

(15)

Jones, eloquently and forcefully, articulates here the limits of a monolithic model of transsexuality. His description of the wild variability of masculinities and identifications across butch and transsexual bodies refuses any notion of a butch–FTM continuum on the one hand, but on the other hand, it acknowledges the ways in which butch and FTM bodies are read against and through each other for better or for worse. Jones's understanding of transgender variability produces an almost fractal model of cross-gender identifications that can never return to the binary models of before and after, or transsexual and nontranssexual, or butch and FTM.

Needless to say, I have learned a great deal from these various interactions and textual conversations, and I want to use them here to resituate "F2M: The Making of Female Masculinity" in terms of a continuing "border war," to use Gayle Rubin's term, between butches and FTMs. [Here], I try again to create an interpretive model of transgender butchness that refuses to invest in the notion of some fundamental antagonism between lesbian and FTM subjectivities. This is not to ignore, however, the history of lesbian feminist opposition to transsexuals, which has been well documented by Sandy Stone. In "A Posttranssexual Manifesto," Stone shows how Janice Raymond and other feminists in the 1970s and 1980s (Mary Daly, for example) saw male-to-female transsexuals as phallocratic agents who were trying to infiltrate women-only space.[11] More recently, some lesbians have voiced their opposition to FTM transsexuals and characterized them as traitors and as women who literally become the enemy.[12] More insidiously, lesbians have tended to erase FTMs by claiming transsexual males as lesbians who lack access to a liberating lesbian discourse. So, for example, Billie Tipton, the jazz musician who lived his life as a man and who married a woman, is often represented within lesbian history as a lesbian woman forced to hide her gender to advance within his profession rather than as a transsexual man living within his chosen gender identity. In "The Politics of Passing," for example, Elaine K. Ginsberg rationalizes Tipton's life: "He lived his professional life as a man, presumably because his chosen profession was not open to women."[13] Many revisionist accounts of transgender lives rationalize them out of existence in this way or through the misuse of female pronouns and do real damage to the project of mapping transgender histories.

So while it is true that transgender and transsexual men have been wrongly folded into lesbian history, it is also true that the distinctions between some transsexual identities and some lesbian identities may at times become quite blurry. Many FTMs do come out as lesbians before they come out as transsexuals (many, it must also be said, do not). And for this reason alone, one cannot always maintain hard and fast and definitive distinctions between lesbians and transsexuals. In the collection *Dagger: On Butch Women*, for example, the editors include a chapter of interviews with FTMs as part of their survey of an urban butch scene.[14] The five FTMs in the interview testify to a period of lesbian identification. Shadow admits that "the dyke community's been really great, keeping me around for the last 12 years" (154); Mike says that he never really identified as female but that he did "identif[y] as a lesbian for a while" because "being a dyke gave me options" (155). Similarly, Billy claims that he feels neither male nor female but that he did "go through the whole lesbian separatist bullshit" (155). Like Shadow, Eric feels that for a while, "the lesbian place was really good for me" (156), and finally Sky suggests that although certain individuals in the dyke community are hostile to him, "I'm forty years old and I've been involved with dykes for nearly half my life. I'm not going to give that up" (158). Obviously, these FTM voices are quite particular and in no way represent a consensus or even a dominant version of the relations between FTM and dyke communities. Also, these versions of FTM history have been carefully chosen to fit into a collection of essays about lesbian masculinities. However, these transgender men do articulate one very important line of affiliation between transsexualities and lesbian identities. Many transgender men, quite possibly, successfully identify as butch in a queer female community before they decide to transition. Once they have transitioned, many transsexual men want to maintain their ties to their queer lesbian communities. Much transsexual discourse now circulating tries to cast the lesbian pasts of FTM as instances of mistaken identities or as an effort to find temporary refuge within some queer gender-variant notion of "butchness."[15]

In this FTM chapter of *Dagger*, just to complicate matters further, the transgender men also tell of finding the limits of lesbian identification. Billy, for one, hints at the kinds of problems some pretransition transgender men experience when they identify as lesbians. Billy recalls: "I've had this problem for ten years now with women being attracted to my boyishness and my masculinity, but once they get involved with me they tell me I'm too male" (156). Billy crosses the line for many of his lovers because he wants a real moustache and a real beard and does not experience his masculinity as temporary or theatrical. Billy's experience testifies to the ways in which masculinity within some lesbian contexts presents a problem when it becomes too "real," or when some imaginary line has been crossed between play and seriousness. This also makes lesbian masculinity sound like a matter of degree. Again, this kind of limited understanding of lesbian masculinity has a history within lesbian feminism. As many historians have pointed out, male identification was an accusation leveled at many butches in the early days of lesbian feminism, and so it is hardly surprising to find a residue of this charge in the kinds of judgments made against FTMs by lesbians in contemporary settings.[16] The real problem with this notion of lesbian and transgender masculinities lies in the way it suggests a masculine continuum that looks something like this:

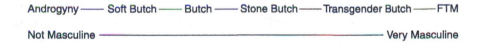

Androgyny —— Soft Butch —— Butch —— Stone Butch —— Transgender Butch ——FTM

Not Masculine ————————————————————————— Very Masculine

Such a model clearly has no interpretive power when we return to Jordy Jones's catalog of transgender variety. For Jones, the intensity of masculinity was not accounted for by transsexual identification. Furthermore, as Jones points out, "not everyone who experiences gender dysphoria deals with it in the same way"; gender dysphoria can be read all the way along the continuum, and it would not be accurate to make gender dysphoria the exclusive property of transsexual bodies or to surmise that the greater the gender dysphoria, the likelier a transsexual identification. At the transgender end of the spectrum, the continuum model miscalculates the relation between bodily alteration and degree of masculinity; at the butch end, the continuum model makes it seem as if butchness is sometimes just an early stage of transsexual aspiration. Stone butchness, for example, is very often seen as a compromise category between lesbian and FTM and is therefore defined by sexual dysfunction rather than sexual practice. As a compromise category, stone butch may be seen as a last-ditch effort to maintain masculinity within female embodiment: the expectation, of course, is that such an effort will fail and the stone butch will become fully functional once she takes steps toward transitioning to be a transsexual man.

In the essay "Stone Butch Now" (as opposed to stone butch in the 1950s), Heather Findlay interviews stone butches about their various modes of gender and sexual identification. For the purposes of the article, stone butch occupies "a gray area" between lesbian and FTM.[17] One of Findlay's informants simply calls him/herself Jay and relates that s/he is considering transitioning.[18] Jay tries to define the difference between being stone and being transsexual: "As a stone butch you have a sense of humor about your discomfort in the world. As an FTM, however, you lose that sense of humor. Situations that were funny suddenly get very tragic" (44). Obviously, in this comment, Jay already seems to be speaking from the perspective of an FTM. To do so, s/he must cast the stone butch as playful in comparison to the seriousness of the FTM transsexual. The stone butch laughs at her gender discomfort whereas the FTM finds his discomfort to be a source of great pain. The stone butch manages her gender dysphoria, according to such a model, but the FTM cannot. Again, these oppositions between FTM and butch come at the expense of a complex butch subjectivity and also work to totalize both categories in relation to a set of experiences. As other stone butches interviewed in the article attest, being stone may mean moving in and out of gender comfort and may mean a very unstable sense of identification with lesbianism or femaleness. To separate the category of FTM from the category of butch, Jay must assign butch to femaleness and FTM to maleness.

My aim here and in my earlier essay has been to focus on certain categories of butchness without presuming that they represent early stages of transsexual identity within some progressive model of sexual transidentity and without losing their specificity as masculine identifications within a female body. Just as there is obviously much tension between the categories "lesbian" and "FTM," there are even tensions between "lesbian" and "butch." As I have been using butch here, it obviously refers to some form of dyke masculinity and refers to a historical equation of female homosexuality with female masculinity. But this history of overlap between sexual and gender variance does not mean that female masculinity has not often been cast as a thorn in the side of contemporary lesbian definition. All too often, as Billy suggests, the lesbian butch has been pressured to forgo her masculinity and attest to positive female embodiment. In *Stone Butch Blues*, for example, [. . .] the he-she, Jess Goldberg, fights with her femme-turned-feminist girlfriend about acceptable forms of female masculinity. "You're a woman," Theresa tells Jess, but Jess responds, "I'm a he-she, that's different."[19] Jess goes on to tell her girlfriend that s/he is not a lesbian in the terms that Theresa has used for lesbian definition. The distinction that butches have made throughout the last twenty years between lesbianism and female masculinity hinges on a mounting perception of distinct differences between gender and sexual identities. "Lesbian," since the rise of lesbian feminism, refers to sexual preference and refers to some version of the "woman-loving woman." Butch, on the other hand, bears a complex relation to femaleness and, in terms of sexual orientation, could refer to a "woman-loving butch" or a "butch-loving butch."

The places where the divisions between butch and FTM become blurry, on the other hand, have less to do with the identity politics of lesbian feminism and more to do with embodiment. As Jordy Jones suggests, many individuals who take hormones may not be transgendered, and many transgendered men may not take hormones. In fact, although in "F2M" I tried to make visible some of the gender fictions that prop up contemporary gender binarism, in the disputes between different groups of queers, we see that the labels "butch" and "transsexual" mark another gender fiction, the fiction of clear distinctions. In "F2M" I used the refrain "There are no transsexuals. We are all transsexuals" to point to the inadequacy of such a category in an age of profound gender trouble. I recognize, of course, the real and particular history of the transsexual and of transsexual surgery, hormone treatment, and transsexual rights discourse. I also recognize that there are huge and important differences between genetic females who specifically identify as transsexual and genetic females who feel comfortable with female masculinity. There are real and physical differences between female-born men who take hormones, have surgery, and live as men and female-born butches who live some version of gender ambiguity. But there are also many situations in which those differences are less clear than one might expect, and there are many butches who pass as men and many transsexuals who present as gender ambiguous and many bodies that cannot be classified by the options transsexual and butch. We are not all transsexual, I admit, but many bodies are gender strange to some degree or another, and it is time to complicate on the one hand the transsexual models that assign gender deviance only to transsexual bodies and gender normativity to all other bodies, and on the other hand the hetero-normative models that see transsexuality as the solution to gender deviance and homosexuality as a pathological perversion.

Female-to-male

While many female-to-male transsexuals (FTMs) live out their masculinity in deliberately ambiguous bodies, many others desire complete transitions from female to male (and these people I will call transsexual males or transsexual men). Some of those transgender people who retain the label "FTM" (rather than becoming "men") have mastectomies and hysterectomies and take testosterone on a regular basis and are quite satisfied with the male secondary characteristics that such treatments produce. These transgender subjects are not attempting to slide seamlessly into manhood, and their retention of the FTM label suggests the emergence of a new gender position marked by this term. However, another strand of male transsexualism has produced a new discourse on masculinity that depends in part on startlingly conservative pronouncements about the differences between themselves and transgender butches. These conservative notions are betrayed in the tendency of some trans-sexual males to make distinct gender assignations to extremely and deliberately gender-ambiguous bodies, and this tendency has a history within transsexual male autobiography; indeed, the denigration of the category "butch" is a standard feature of the genre.

In Mario Martino's autobiography *Emergence* (1977), Martino goes to great lengths to distinguish himself from lesbians and from butches in particular as he negotiates the compli-cations of pretransition identifications. Before his transition, Mario falls in love with a young woman; s/he tells the girlfriend, Becky: "You and I are not lesbians. We relate to each other as man to woman, woman to man."[20] One day, Becky comes home from work and asks: "Mario, what's a butch?" (141). Mario writes, "I could actually feel my skin bristle" (141). Becky tells Mario that the head nurse on the ward where Becky works asked her about her "butch," and in effect she wants to know the difference between Mario and a butch. Mario gives her a simple answer: "A butch is the masculine member of a lesbian team. That would make you the feminine member. But, Becky, honest-to-God, I don't feel that we're lesbians. I still maintain I should have been a male" (141). Becky seems satisfied with the answer, but the question itself plagues Mario long into the night: "The word *butch* magnified itself before my eyes. *Butch* implied female—and I had never thought of myself as such" (142). In *Emergence*, lesbianism haunts the protagonist and threatens to swallow his gender specificity and disallow his transsexuality. Unfortunately, as we see in the passages I have quoted, Martino's efforts to disentangle his maleness from lesbian masculinity tend to turn butchness into a stable female category and tend to overemphasize the differences between butch womanhood and transsexual manhood.

Another transsexual autobiography also magnifies the gulf between butch and trans-sexual male to mark out the boundaries of transsexual masculinity. In *Dear Sir or Madam*, Mark Rees obsessively marks out his difference from lesbians. On attending a lesbian club before transition, sometime in the early 1960s, he feels assured in his sense of difference because, he notes, "the women there didn't want to be men; they were happy in their gender role."[21] He goes on to identify lesbianism in terms of two feminine women whose attraction is based on sameness, not difference. It is hard to imagine what Rees thinks he saw when he entered the lesbian bar. In the 1960s, butch–femme would still have been a cultural dominant in British lesbian bar culture, and it is unlikely that the scene that presented itself to Rees was a kind of "Bargirls" scene of lipstick lesbians. What probably characterized the scene before him was an array of gender-deviant bodies in recognizable butch–femme couplings. Because he needs to assert a crucial difference between himself and lesbians, Rees tries to deny the possibility of cross-identifying butch women.

In his desperation to hold the terms "lesbian" and "transsexual" apart, however, Rees goes one step further than just making lesbianism into a category for women who were "happy in their gender role." He also marks out the difference in terms of sexual aim as well as sexual and gender identity; he focuses, in other words, on the partner of the transsexual male for evidence of the distinctiveness of transsexual maleness. Rees claims to find a medical report confirming that lesbians and transsexuals are totally different. The report suggests that transsexuals "do not see themselves as lesbians before treatment, hate their partners seeing their bodies. It added that the partners of female-to-males are normal heterosexual women, not lesbians, and see their lovers as men, in spite of their lack of a penis. The partners were feminine, many had earlier relations with genetic males and often experienced orgasms with their female-to-male partners for the first time" (*Dear Sir or Madam*, 59). This passage should signal some of the problems attendant on this venture of making transsexual man and transgender butch into totally separate entities. Although one is extremely sympathetic to the sense of being misidentified, the need to stress the lack of identification inevitably leads to a conservative attempt to reorder the sex and gender categories that are in danger of becoming scrambled. Here Rees attempts to locate difference in the desires of the transsexual male's partner and unwittingly makes a distinction between these women as "normal heterosexual women" and lesbians. Lesbianism suddenly becomes a category of pathology next to the properly heterosexual and gender-normative aims of the transsexual man and his feminine partner. Furthermore, this "normal heterosexual woman" finds her perfect mate in the transsexual man and indeed, we are told, often experiences orgasm with him "for the first time."

The jarring need to identify the feminine partner of the transsexual man with normal sexual aims and desires unravels a little later in the book when Rees reports his difficulty in finding a relationship. After several disastrous relationships, he resigns himself to living alone and asexually, and he tries to admit his own responsibility in the string of bad relationships: "My conclusion is that my lack of success must be due to my lack of acceptability as a person" (134). However, he quickly turns this judgment onto his partners: "One flaw has been my appalling lack of judgement." In other words, Rees has not found a good relationship because he has made bad choices, and ultimately the women are to blame. The distinction between lesbian and transsexual is undoubtedly an important one to sketch out, but there is always the danger that the effort to mark the territory of transsexual male subjectivity may fall into homophobic assertions about lesbians and sexist formulations of women in general.

Rees's categorical distinctions between lesbians and partners of transsexual men and both his and Martino's horror of the slippage between homosexual and transsexual also echo in various informal bulletins that circulate on transsexual discussion lists on the Internet. In some bulletins, transsexual men send each other tips on how to pass as a man, and many of these tips focus almost obsessively on the care that must be taken by the transsexual man not to look like a butch lesbian. Some tips tell guys[22] to dress preppy as opposed to the standard jeans and leather jacket look of the butch; in other instances, transsexual men are warned against certain haircuts (punk styles or crew cuts) that are supposedly popular among butches. These tips, obviously, steer the transsexual man away from transgression or alternative masculine styles and toward a conservative masculinity. One wonders whether another list of tips should circulate advising transsexual men of how not to be mistaken for straight, or worse a Republican or a banker. Most of these lists seem to place no particular political or even cultural value on the kinds of masculinity they mandate.[23]

Finally, in relation to the conservative project of making concrete distinctions between butch women and transsexual males, such distinctions all too often serve the cause of hetero-normativity by consigning homosexuality to pathology and by linking transsexuality to a new form of heterosexuality. In a popular article on transsexual men that appeared in the *New Yorker*, for example, reporter Amy Bloom interviews several transsexual men and some sex reassignment surgeons to try to uncover the motivations and mechanics of so-called "high intensity transsexualism."[24] Bloom comments on the history of transsexualism, the process of transition, and the multiple, highly invasive surgeries required for sex reassignment from female to male. She interviews a young white transsexual male who sees his transsexualism as a birth defect that needs correction and several older white transsexual males, one Latino trans-sexual man, and one black transsexual man, who have varying accounts of their gender identi-ties. Bloom spends much time detailing the looks of the men she interviews: a young transsexual man, Lyle, is "a handsome, shaggy graduating senior," and James Green is a chivalrous man with a "Jack Nicholson smile" (40); Loren Cameron is "a not uncommon type of handsome, cocky, possibly gay man" with "a tight, perfect build" (40); Luis is a "slightly built, gentle South American man" (40). So what, you might think, these are some important descriptions of what transsexual men look like. They look, in fact, like other men, and Bloom quickly admits that she finds herself in flirtatious heterosexual dynamics with her charming companions, dynamics that quickly shore up the essential differences between men and women. Bloom, for example, reports that she was sitting in her rental car with James Green and could not find the dimmer switch for the headlights; when James finds it for her, she comments: "He looks at me exactly as my husband has on hundreds of occasions; affectionate, pleased, a little charmed by this blind spot of mine" (40). Later, over dinner with Green, she notices: "He does not say, 'Gee, this is a lot of food,' or anything like that. Like a man he just starts eating" (40).

Bloom's descriptions of her interviewees and her accounts of her interactions with them raise questions about mainstream attitudes toward male transsexuals versus mainstream attitudes toward masculine lesbians. Would Bloom, in a similar article on butch lesbians, comment so approvingly on their masculinity? Would she notice a woman's muscular build, another butch's wink, another's "Jack Nicholson smile"? Would she be aware of their eating habits, their mechanical aptitudes? The answer, of course, is a resounding "no," and indeed I find confirmation for my suspicions further down the page. Bloom reflects on her meetings with these handsome transsexual men as follows:

> I expected to find psychologically disturbed, male-identified women so filled with self-loathing that it had even spilled into their physical selves, leading them to self-mutilating, self-punishing surgery. Maybe I would meet some very butch lesbians, in ties and jackets and chest binders, who could not, would not accept their female bodies. I didn't meet these people. I met men.
>
> (41)

What a relief for Bloom that she was spared interaction with those self-hating masculine women and graced instead by the dignified presence of men! Posttransition, we must remember at all times, many transsexual men become heterosexual men, living so-called normal lives, and for folks like Amy Bloom, this is a cause for some celebration.

In her interaction with a black transsexual man, Bloom asks questions that actually raise some interesting issues, however. Michael, unlike James and Loren, is not part of an urban FTM community; he lives a quiet and somewhat secretive life and shies away from anything that may reveal his transsexuality. Michael finds a degree of acceptance from his family and coworkers and strives for nothing more than this tolerance. He articulates his difference from some other transsexuals:

> I was born black. I don't expect people to like me, to accept me. Some trans-
> sexuals, especially the white MTF's—they're in shock after the transition. Loss
> of privilege, loss of status; they think people should be thrilled to work side by
> side with them. Well, people do not go to work in mainstream America hoping
> for an educational experience. I didn't expect anyone to be happy to see me—I
> just expected, I demanded a little tolerance.
>
> (49)

Michael is the only person in the whole article to mention privilege and the change in social
status experienced by transsexuals who pass. He clearly identifies the differences between
transsexuals in terms of race and class, and he speaks of lowered expectations on account of
a lifetime of experiencing various forms of intolerance. Bloom makes little comment on
Michael's testimony, and she does not make a connection between what he says and what the
other white men say. But Michael's experience is crucial to the politics of transsexualism. In
America there is a huge difference between becoming a black man or a man of color and
becoming a white man, and these differences are bound to create gulfs within transsexual
communities and will undoubtedly resonate in the border wars between butches and
transsexual men. The politics of transsexuality, quite obviously, reproduce other political
struggles in other locations, and while some transsexuals find strength in the notion of identity politics, others find their identities and loyalties divided by their various affiliations. As in
so many other identity-based activist projects, one axis of identification is a luxury most
people cannot afford.

   We are presently in the midst of a "reverse discourse" of transsexuality. In *The History
of Sexuality*, Michel Foucault analyzes the strategic production of sexualities and sexual
identities, and he proposes a model of a "reverse discourse" to explain the web of relations
between power, discourse, sexuality, and resistance. He argues that resistance is always
already embedded in power "as an irreducible opposite" and that therefore resistance cannot
come from an outside; the multiplicity of power means that there is no opposite, no site of
resistance where power has not already been.[25] There is, Foucault suggests, a "reverse
discourse" in which one empowers a category that might have been used to oppress one—
one transforms a debased position into a challenging presence. As a reverse discourse takes
shape around the definitions of transsexual and transgender, it is extremely important to
recognize the queerness of these categories, their instability and their interpretability. While
identity obviously continues to be the best basis for political organizing, we have seen within
various social movements of the last decade that identity politics must give way to some form
of coalition if a political movement is to be successful. The current discourse in some transsexual circles, therefore, of setting up gay and lesbian politics and communities as the enemy
to transgender definition is as pernicious as the gay and lesbian tendencies to ignore the
specificities of transsexual political needs and demands.[26] Furthermore, the simple opposition
of transsexual versus gay and lesbian masks many other lines of affiliation and coalition that
already exist within multiple queer communities: it masks, for example, that the gay/lesbian
versus transsexual/transgender opposition is very much a concern in white queer contexts
but not necessarily in queer communities of color. Many immigrant queer groups have
successfully integrated transgender definition into their conceptions of community.[27]

The right body?

My intent is not to vilify male transsexualism as simply a reconsolidation of dominant
masculinity. But I do want to point carefully to the places where such a reconsolidation

threatens to take place. In academic conversations, transsexualism has been used as both the place of gender transgression and the marker of gender conservatism. Obviously, transsexualism is neither essentially transgressive nor essentially conservative, and perhaps it becomes a site of such contestation because it is not yet clear what the politics of transsexualism will look like. Indeed, the history of FTM transsexuality is still being written, and as FTM communities emerge in urban settings, it becomes clear that their relations to the history of medicine, the history of sexuality, and the history of gender are only now taking shape. One attempt to chart this history in relation to a more general history of transsexualism and medical technology reveals what we might call the essentially contradictory politics of transsexualism. In *Changing Sex*, Bernice Hausman meticulously details the dependence of the category "transsexual" on medical technologies and in turn the dependence of the very concept of gender on the emergence of the transsexual. Several times in the book, Hausman rejects the notion that we can read gender as an ideology without also considering it as a product of technological relations. This argument marks a crucial contribution to the study of gender and technology, but unfortunately Hausman quite simply tends to attribute too much power to the medical configuration of transsexual definition. She claims that the transsexual and the doctor codependently produce transsexual definitions and that therefore transsexual agency can be read "through their doctor's discourses." She develops this notion of an interdependent relationship between transsexuals and medical technology to build to a rather astounding conclusion:

> By demanding technological intervention to "change sex," transsexuals demonstrate that their relationship to technology is a dependent one . . . demanding sex change is therefore part of what constructs the subject as a transsexual: it is the mechanism through which transsexuals come to identify themselves under the sign of transsexualism and construct themselves as subjects. Because of this we can read transsexuals' agency through their doctor's discourses, as the demand for sex change was instantiated as the primary symptom (and sign) of the transsexual.[28]

Sex change itself has become a static signifier in this paragraph, and no distinction is upheld between FTM sex change and MTF sex change. No power is granted to the kinds of ideological commitments that doctors may have that influence their thinking about making vaginas versus making penises, and because sex change rhetoric has been mostly used in relation to MTF bodies, the FTM and his relation to the very uncertain process of sex change, demanding sex change, and completing sex change is completely lost.

Hausman's book, I should stress, is careful and historically rich and will undoubtedly change the way that gender is conceived in relation to transsexual and nontranssexual bodies. But the particular border wars between butches and transsexual men that concern me both here and in my earlier essay have been lost in a study of this kind. Future studies of transsexuality and of lesbianism must attempt to account for historical moments when the difference between gender deviance and sexual deviance is hard to discern.[29] The history of inversion and of people who identified as inverts (Radclyffe Hall, for example) still represents a tangle of cross-identification and sexual preference that is neither easily separated nor comfortably accounted for under the heading of "lesbian." There is not, furthermore, one history to be told here (the history of medical technology) about one subject (the transsexual). There are many histories of bodies that escape and elude medical taxonomies, of bodies that never present themselves to the physician's gaze, of subjects who identify within categories that emerge as a consequence of sexual communities and not in relation to medical or psychosexual research.

Because these categories are so difficult to disentangle, perhaps, a new category has emerged in recent years, "transgender." Transgender describes a gender identity that is at least partially defined by transitivity but that may well stop short of transsexual surgery. Inevitably, the term becomes a catchall, and this somewhat lessens its effect. Toward the end of her book, Hausman attempts to stave off criticisms of her work that may be based on an emergent notion of transgenderism. She acknowledges that transgender discourse seems to counter her claims that transsexuals are produced solely within medical discourse and that this discourse actually suggests "a fundamental antipathy to the regulatory mode of medical surveillance" (*Changing Sex*, 195). Hausman manages to discount such an effect of transgender discourse by arguing that "the desire to celebrate and proliferate individual performances as a way to destabilize 'gender' at large is based on liberal humanist assumptions of self-determination" (197). This is an easy dismissal of a much more complicated and ongoing project. Transgender discourse in no way argues that people should just pick up new genders and eliminate old ones or proliferate at will because gendering is available as a self-determining practice; rather, transgender discourse asks only that we recognize the nonmale and nonfemale genders already in circulation and presently under construction.

Hausman's real stakes in this seemingly historical project slip out at the end of her chapter "Transsexual Autobiographies." Having argued strenuously that transsexual autobiographies collude in the construction of notions of an authentic sex, Hausman attempts to ease off her critical tone and express some empathy for the transsexual condition. She comments earnestly: "Those of us who are not transsexuals may wonder what it is like to feel oneself in the 'wrong body'" (174). The idea that only transsexuals experience the pain of a "wrong body" shows an incredible myopia about the trials and tribulations of many varieties of perverse embodiment.[30] It neatly ascribes gender confusion and dysphoria once again to transsexuals and efficiently constructs a model of "right body" experience that applies, presumably, to people such as Hausman. Part of the motivation of a transgender discourse is to produce what Sedgwick calls in *Epistemology of the Closet* "universalist" models of gender identity in which all gender identities fall under scrutiny rather than simply the unorthodox ones. Hausman resists a universalist model of gender identification and ensures that transsexual and pathology remain annexed while her book maintains the fiction of proper and normal genders.

Border wars

Because the production of gender and sexual deviance takes place in multiple locations (the doctor's office, the operating room, the sex club, the bedroom, the bathroom) and because the discourses to which gender and sexual deviance are bound also emerge in many different contexts (medical tracts, queer magazines, advice columns, films and videos, autobiographies), the categories of transsexual, transgender, and butch are constantly under construction. However, in the border wars between butches and transsexual men, transsexuals are often cast as those who cross borders (of sex, gender, bodily coherence), and butches are left as those who stay in one place, possibly a border space of nonidentity. The terminology of "border war" is both apt and problematic for this reason. On the one hand, the idea of a border war sets up some notion of territories to be defended, ground to be held or lost, permeability to be defended against. On the other hand, a border war suggests that the border is at best slippery and permeable. As I mentioned earlier, in "No Place like Home," Prosser critiques queer theory for fixing on "the transgendered crossing in order to denaturalize gender" (484), and he claims that queer border crossing positions itself against "the homeliness of identity politics" (486). For Prosser, such a move leaves the transsexual man with no place to go and leaves him languishing in the "uninhabitable space—the borderlands in between, where passing as either gender might prove quite a challenge" (488–89). Whereas queers might celebrate the space in between, Prosser suggests, the transsexual rushes onward to find the space beyond, "the promise of home on the other side" (489). "Home," as one might imagine in relation to Prosser's model, is represented as the place in which one finally settles into the comfort of one's true and authentic gender.

Prosser thinks that queer theory (specifically, actually, my earlier essay "F2M") celebrates the in-between space as full of promise and "freedom and mobility for the subject" ("No Place like Home," 499), whereas transsexual theory embraces place, location, and specificity. The queer butch, in other words, represents fluidity to the transsexual man's stability, and stability (staying in a female body) to the transsexual man's fluidity (gender crossing). Prosser makes little or no recognition of the trials and tribulations that confront the butch who for whatever reasons (concerns about surgery or hormones, feminist scruples, desire to remain in a lesbian community, lack of funds, lack of successful phalloplasty models) decides to make a home in the body with which she was born. Even more alarming, he makes little or no recognition of the fact that many FTMs also live and die in those inhospitable territories in between. It is true that many transsexuals do transition to go somewhere, to be somewhere, and to leave geographies of ambiguity behind. However, many post-op MTFs are in-between because they cannot pass as women; many FTMs who pass fully clothed have bodies that are totally ambiguous; some transsexuals cannot afford all the surgeries necessary to full sex reassignment (if there is such a thing), and these people make their home where they are; some transsexual folks do not define their transsexuality in relation to a strong desire for penises or vaginas, and they may experience the desire to be trans or queer more strongly than the desire to be male or female.

If the borderlands are uninhabitable for some transsexuals who imagine that home is just across the border, imagine what a challenge they present to those subjects who do not believe that such a home exists, either metaphorically or literally. Prosser's cartography of gender relies on a belief in the two territories of male and female, divided by a flesh border and crossed by surgery and endocrinology. The queer cartography that he rejects prefers the charting of hybridity. Queer hybridity is far from the ludic and giddy mixing that Prosser imagines and more of a recognition of the dangers of investing in comforting but tendentious notions of home. Some bodies are never at home, some bodies cannot simply cross from A to B, some bodies recognize and live with the inherent instability of identity.

So far, I have noted the ways in which transsexual males and butch lesbians regard each other with some suspicion and the ways in which the two categories blur and separate. I have argued against stable and coherent definitions of sexual identity and tried to suggest the ways in which the lines between the transsexual and the gender-deviant lesbian inevitably crisscross each other and intersect, even producing a new category: transgender. I want to turn now to the rhetoric itself in the debate between transsexuals and butches to try to identify some of the dangers in demanding discrete and coherent sexual and gender identities. Much of the rhetoric surrounding transsexualism plays with the sense of transitivity and sees transsexuality as a passage or journey. Along the way, predictably enough, borders are crossed, and one leaves a foreign country to return, as we saw in Prosser's essay, to the home of one's true body.

If we return for the moment to the BBC series *The Wrong Body*, it offers an interesting example of the power of this kind of rhetoric. In one remarkable confrontation between Fredd and his psychiatrist, the psychiatrist used an extended simile to try to express his understanding of the relation of Fredd's female and male gender identities. He said: "You, Fredd, are like someone who has learned to speak French perfectly and who immigrates to France and lives there as a Frenchman. But just because you speak French and learn to imitate

Frenchness and live among French people, you are still English." Fredd countered with: "No, I don't just speak French having moved there, I AM French." In this exchange, the doctor deploys what has become a common metaphor for transsexualism as a crossing of national borders from one place to another, from one state to another, from one gender to another. Fredd rejects such a rhetorical move and insists that his expression of his boy self is not a transition but rather the expression of a self that he has always inhabited. That Fredd is young and indeed preadolescent allows him to articulate his transsexualism very differently from many adult transsexuals. He is passing into manhood not from one adult body to another but from an almost pregendered body into a fully gendered male body. The rhetoric of passing and crossing and transitioning has only a limited use for him.

Metaphors of travel and border crossings are inevitable within a discourse of transsexuality. But they are also laden with the histories of other identity negotiations, and they carry the burden of national and colonial discursive histories. What does it mean, then, to discuss gender variance and gender transitivity as a journey from one country to another or from a foreign country toward home or from illegal status to naturalized citizenship? How useful or how limiting are metaphors of the border and crossing and belonging to questions of gender identity? How does gender transitivity rely on the stability of other identity markers?

Within discussions of postmodernism, the transsexual body has often come to represent contradictory identity per se in the twentieth century and has been discussed using precisely the rhetoric of colonialism. Whereas Janice Raymond identified the transsexual body in 1979 as part of a patriarchal empire intent on colonizing female bodies and feminist souls,[31] Sandy Stone responded in her "Posttranssexual Manifesto" by allowing the "empire" to "strike back" and calling for a "counterdiscourse" within which the transsexual might speak as transsexual. Whereas Bernice Hausman reads transsexual autobiographies as evidence that to a certain extent "transsexuals are the dupes of gender,"[32] Jay Prosser sees these narratives as "driven by the attempt to realize the fantasy of belonging in the sexed body and the world."[33] Many contemporary discussions of plastic surgery and body manipulation take transsexuality as a privileged signifier of the productive effects of body manipulation, and many theories of postmodern subjectivity understand the fragmentation of the body in terms of a paradigmatic transsexuality. Transsexuality, in other words, seems burdened not only by an excess of meaning but also by the weight of contradictory and competing discourses. If we sort through the contradictions, we find transsexuals represented as "empire" and the subaltern, as gender dupes and gender deviants, and as consolidated identities and fragmented bodies.

Jay Prosser, as we saw, critiques postmodern queer theory in particular for fixing on "the transgendered crossing in order to denaturalize gender" ("No Place like Home," 484), and he claims that queer affirmations of the "trans journey" celebrate "opposition to a narrative centered upon home" (486). Female-to-male transsexual theorist Henry Rubin provides an even more polarized opposition than the queer versus transgender split produced by Prosser. For Rubin, the division that is most meaningful is between transsexuals and transgenders: "Although it is often assumed that 'transgender' is an umbrella term that refers to cross-dressers, drag queens, butch dykes, gender blenders, and transsexuals, among others, there is a tension between transsexual and transgenders."[34] For Rubin, the tension lies between the transsexual's quest for "'home,' a place of belonging to one sex or the other," and the transgender quest for "a world without gender" (7). According to such logic, the transgender person is just playing with gender and trying to deconstruct the naturalness of gender, but the transsexual bravely reaffirms the notion of stable gender and fortifies the reality of biology. The people who fall under the "umbrella" of transgender definition represent for Rubin a nonserious quest for gender instability that comes at the expense of a transsexual quest for "a place of belonging." To hold up what might seem an unlikely division between transgender and transsexual, Rubin models his argument on the various debates about lesbian identity. In the 1970s, it became quite common for women to call themselves "lesbian" as a mark of solidarity rather than a statement of sexual practice, and Rubin suggests that transgenders are like political lesbians. Again, such an argument collapses the historical differences between the lesbian sex debates and contemporary identity skirmishes, and it also renders transgenders as well-meaning, but transsexuals as the real thing.

One other essay that typifies this concern about gender realness and the symbolic uses of transsexualism within postmodernism is "Fin de Siecle, Fin de Sexe: Transsexuality, Postmodernism, and the Death of History," by Rita Felski. Felski notes the ways in which transsexuality is invoked at this fin de siècle to "describe the dissolution of once stable polarities of male and female."[35] But she warns against the elevation of transsexualism to the status of universal signifier because it runs the risk of "homogenizing differences that matter politically: the differences between men and women, the difference between those who occasionally play with the trope of transsexuality and those others for whom it is a matter of life and death" (347). In other words, if queer theorists take up transsexualism as a trope for the breakdown of identity, they unwittingly shore up a postmodern evacuation of political activism by detaching transsexualism from the hard facts of gender and embodiment. Felski's warning is well taken, but to whom is it directed? Who, in other words, occasionally plays with transsexuality rather than taking it seriously? Felski finds such play to be dangerous and necessarily a sign of privilege: "Not all social subjects, after all, have equal freedom to play with and subvert the signs of gender, even as many do not perceive such play as a necessary condition of their freedom" (347). Felski identifies Arthur and Marilouise Kroker and Jean Baudrillard as being those postmodernists playing with transsexuality and therefore, we presume, failing to take seriously the differences between men and women and the differences between gender players, and gender realists.[36] I have no wish to defend Baudrillard's vacuous postmodern visions or the Krokers' notions of porno sex, but I do want to challenge the depiction of a postmodern queer constituency who play happily in some gender borderlands while others diligently and seriously refuse to take part in the celebration. What or who is missing from Felski's earnest picture of the "fin de sexe" at the "fin de siècle"?

The people, presumably, who play with transsexuality and gleefully subvert the signs of gender are nontranssexuals who see "such play as a necessary condition of their freedom." They are indeed the transgenders of Henry Rubin's article and the queers in Jay Prosser's. I wonder if it strikes anyone else as ironic that the very people, gays and lesbians and gender deviants, who have been identified as historically the victims of heteronormativity are here invoked as dilettantes and recreationalists in the game of gender. Suddenly the transsexual has been resituated as the central figure in gender deviance, the one body that suffers, the only body that believes in gender and as an antidote to queer mobility. But the transgender butch in particular has long been a literary tragic hero who is martyred by her sense of being out of place. Whether it is Stephen Gordon in Radclyffe Hall's *The Well of Loneliness* (1928) discovering that "the loneliest place in this world is the no-man's-land of sex,"[37] or the 1950s butch Jess Goldberg in Leslie Feinberg's *Stone Butch Blues* (1993) finding herself out of time and place in contemporary lesbian New York, the narrative of the transgender or inverted butch has been one of loss, loneliness, and disconnection.[38] The butches in these narratives are hardly playful gender hedonists, and indeed they share with many FTMs a serious quest for place and belonging. In the novel *Sacred Country* (1992), Rose Tremain's female-to-male transsexual character, Marty, counters her grandfather's claim that "everything important in life was dual, like being and not being, male and female, and that there was no country in between." Marty thinks to him/herself: "Cord is wrong, there is a country in between, a country that no one sees, and I am in it."[39] The literary narrative of gender transitivity and gender dysphoria, then, has understood the experience of the "wrong body" in terms of a complex rhetoric of unbelonging and nonidentity. In response to this fundamental sense of being out of place, Tremain's transsexual man and Hall's invert and Feinberg's transgender butch conjure up images of imaginary lands, both countries in between and border worlds of the dispossessed.

Transition and mobility have themselves long been the alibi of many a female-to-male cross-dresser: female adventurers and fortune hunters have, over the last three hundred years, donned men's clothing, very often military uniforms, and made their way in the world passing back and forth between places and genders. Some passing women in the eighteenth and nineteenth centuries went to sea and lived as pirates; others joined the army and lived as men among men; still others used their disguises to enter male professions, take female lovers, or travel the world.[40] In other words, cross-dressing, passing, and gender transitivity work in and through other forms of mobility: a woman who accesses mobility through cross-dressing may well destabilize economies of masculinity, but she may simultaneously restabilize certain forms of racism or particular class antagonisms. To give just one example of such a nest of contradictory crossings, we could consider the abundance of turn-of-the-century cross-dressing and cross-identifying aristocratic women in Europe who took up the fascist cause in very active ways that I discussed in chapter 3 [of *Female Masculinity*].

The contradictions of cross-identification and its mobilities are further exemplified in a highly renowned autobiographical transsexual text, Jan Morris's *Conundrum*. Jan Morris was at one time known as James Morris, a travel writer and, in the 1950s, foreign correspondent for the *London Times*. Morris uses her skills as a travel writer to take the metaphor of travel and migration to its logical end in relation to questions of gender transition. She describes every aspect of her transition from male to female as a journey and characterizes not only gender identity in terms of countries but also national identities in terms of gender. "I was a child of imperial times," writes Morris at one point to explain her impression of "Black Africa" as "everything I wanted not to be."[41] While cities like Venice represent the feminine (and therefore a desired female self) to the pre-transsexual James Morris, Black Africa represents a masculinity that scares him because it is "alien" and "vicious." In this transsexual autobiography, the space in between male and female is represented as monstrous. Jan Morris describes herself between genders as "a kind of nonhuman, a sprite or monster" (114), and the space of gender is described as "identity itself."

Morris, world traveler and travel writer, understands national identity in much the same way that she understands gender identity; national identities are stable, legible, and all established through the ruling consciousness of empire. Accordingly, Morris collates different reactions to her gender ambiguity according to country: "Americans," she tells us, "generally assumed me to be female" (111); however, in a manner reminiscent of a whole history of colonial travel narratives, Morris tells us casually: "Among the guileless people, the problem was minimal. They simply asked. After a flight from Darjeeling to Calcutta, for instance, during which I had enjoyed the company of an Indian family, the daughter walked over to me at the baggage counter and asked . . . 'whether you are a boy or a girl'" (111). In her essay on transsexuality, Sandy Stone does mention the "Oriental" quality of Morris's travel narrative, and Marjorie Garber upgrades this assessment to "Orientalist" in her discussion of Morris's description of her sex change in Casablanca. In general, however, there has been little consideration of this transsexual autobiography as a colonial artifact, as, indeed, a record of a journey that does not upend either gender conventionality or the conventions of the travelogue.[42] Ultimately, *Conundrum* is a rather unremarkable modernist narrative about the struggle to maintain identity in the face of a crumbling empire. It is, paradoxically, a narrative of change that struggles to preserve the status quo. I want to stress that Morris's narrative in no way represents "*the* transsexual autobiography." Plenty of other transsexual fictions and autobiographies contradict Morris's travelogue, and many such narratives combine a profound sense of dislocation with a brave attempt to make do with the status of unbelonging. The narrative of the female-to-male transsexual, furthermore, differs in significant ways from, and in no way mirrors, the narrative of the male-to-female. Morris's book serves less as a representative narrative and more as a caution against detaching the metaphors of travel and home and migration from the actual experience of immigration in a world full of borders.

Indeed, we might do well to be wary of such a unidirectional politics of home and of such divisions between sexual minorities. As Fredd's story shows, transsexuality requires often long periods of transition, periods within which one must live between genders. The place where transgender ends and transsexual begins is not as clear as either Morris's text or Rubin's essay assumes, and the spaces between genders, which some queer theory claims, do not represent giddy zones of mobility and freedom but represent lives reconciled to gender queerness and bodies committed to making do with the essential discomforts of embodiment. Although the language of home and location in Prosser's and Henry Rubin's essays sounds unimpeachable, as in the Morris text, there is little or no recognition here of the danger of transposing an already loaded conceptual frame—place, travel, location, home, borders—onto another contested site. In *Conundrum*, the equation of transsexuality with travel, and gender with place, produced a colonialist narrative in which both gender identity and national identity are rendered immutable and essential. Of the male, Morris writes: "It is this feeling of unfluctuating control, I think, that women cannot share, and it springs of course not from the intellect or the personality . . . but specifically from the body" (82). On becoming female, she comments: "My body then was made to push and initiate, it is made now to yield and accept, and the outside change has had its inner consequences" (153). The politics of home for Morris are simply the politics of colonialism, and the risk of essentialism that she takes by changing sex turns out to be no risk at all. The language that Prosser and Rubin use to defend their particular transsexual project from queer appropriations runs the risk not only of essence and even colonialism but, in their case, of using the loaded language of migration and homecoming to ratify new, distinctly unqueer models of manliness.

Analyses of transsexual subjectivity by critics such as Prosser and Rubin, I am arguing, are implicated in the colonial framework that organizes Morris's account of transsexuality, if only because both texts seem unaware of the discussions of borders and migration that have raged in other theoretical locations. In Chicano/a studies and postcolonial studies in particular, the politics of migration have been fiercely debated, and what has emerged is a careful refusal of the dialectic of home and border. If home has represented the comfort of place and the politics of location and the stability of belonging within such a dialectic, the border has stood for the politics of displacement, the hybridity of identity and the economics of undocumented labor. There is little to be gained theoretically or materially from identifying either home or border as the true place of resistance. In the context of a discussion of Asian American theater, Dorinne Kondo notes "home for many people on the margins is what we cannot not want."[43] In this context, home represents the belated construction of a safe haven in the absence of such a place in the present or the past. Home becomes a mythic site, a place to anchor some racial and ethnic identities even as those identities are wrenched out of context or pressured into assimilation. But for the queer subject, or what Gloria Anzaldúa calls the border dweller, home is what the person living in the margins cannot want: "She leaves the familiar and safe home ground to venture into the unknown and possibly dangerous terrain. This is her home / this thin edge / of barbwire."[44] Clearly, home can be a fantasy space, a remembered place of stable origin and a nostalgic dream of community; it can as easily be a space of exclusion whose very comforts depend on the invisible labor of migrant border dwellers. To move back to the debate around transsexualism and queers, the journey home for the transsexual may come at the expense of a recognition that others are permanently dislocated.

When nine-year-old Fredd rejects his doctor's simile of naturalized citizenship for his transsexual condition, Fredd rejects both the history of the rhetorical containment of transsexuality within conventional medical taxonomies and a recent attempt to translate the rhetoric of transsexuality into the language of home and belonging. Fredd does not, however, reject the popular formulation of being a "boy trapped in a girl's body," and he holds on to his fantasy of male adulthood even as his body begins to betray him. We might do well to work on other formulations of gender and body, right body, and right gender to provide children such as Fredd, queer cross-identifying children, with futures and bodies that seem habitable. Obviously, the metaphor of crossing over and indeed migrating to the right body from the wrong body merely leaves the politics of stable gender identities, and therefore stable gender hierarchies, completely intact. The BBC program avoided the more general questions raised by the topic of transsexuality by emphasizing Fredd's individual needs and his urgent desire for maleness. When Fredd was shown in dialogue with other transsexual men, the group as a whole expressed their desire simply to be "normal" boys and men and to live like other male subjects. None of the group expressed homosexual desires, and all expected to live "normal lives" in the future once their sex reassignment surgery was complete.

Transsexuality currently represents an immensely complicated web of identifications and embodiments and gendered phenomena and cannot reduce down to Fredd's narrative of prepubescent angst or Jan Morris's narrative of colonial melancholy. However, as "transgender" becomes a popularly recognized term for cross-identification, the sexual politics of transgenderism and transsexualism must be carefully considered. Because much of the discussion currently circulates around the male-to-female experience of transsexuality, we have yet to consider the gender politics of transitioning from female to male. In this section, I have tried to argue that wholesale adoptions of the rhetoric of home and migration within some transsexual aesthetic practices alongside the rejection of a queer border politics can have the uncanny effect of using postcolonial rhetorics to redeem colonial texts (such as Morris's) or of using formulations of home and essence advanced by feminists of color to ratify the location of white transsexual men. Such rhetoric also assumes that the proper solution to "painful wrong embodiment" (Prosser) is moving to the right body, where "rightness" may as easily depend on whiteness or class privilege as it does on being regendered. Who, we might ask, can afford to dream of a right body? Who believes that such a body exists? Finally, as long as migration and borders and home remain metaphorical figures within such discourse, transsexuals and transgendered people who actually are border dwellers or who really do work as undocumented laborers or who really have migrated from their homelands never to return must always remain just outside discourse, invisible and unrecognized, always inhabiting the wrong body.

Conclusion

As Gayle Rubin remarks in her essay on the varieties of butchness: "Butches vary in how they relate to their female bodies" ("Thinking Sex," 470). She goes on to show that "forms of masculinity are molded by experiences and expectations of class, race, ethnicity, religion, occupation, age, subculture, and individual personality" (470). Rubin also casts the tensions between butches and FTMs as border wars (she calls them "frontier fears") and notes that the border between these two modes of identification is permeable at least in part because "no system of classification can successfully catalogue or explain the infinite vagaries of human diversity" (473). Rubin's conclusion in this essay advocates gender and sexual (and other kinds of) diversity not only as a political strategy but as simply the only proper response to the enormous range of masculinities and genders that we produce.

I also want to argue against monolithic models of gender variance that seem to emerge from the loaded and intense discussions between and among transgender butches and transsexual males at present, and I also want to support some call for diversity. However, at the same time, it is important to stress that not all models of masculinity are equal, and as butches and transsexuals begin to lay claims to the kinds of masculinities they have produced in the past and are generating in the present, it is crucial that we also pay careful attention to the function of homophobia and sexism in particular within the new masculinities. There are transsexuals, and we are not all transsexuals; gender is not fluid, and gender variance is not the same wherever we may find it. Specificity is all. As gender-queer practices and forms continue to emerge, presumably the definitions of "gay," "lesbian," and "transsexual" will not remain static, and we will produce new terms to delineate what they cannot. In the meantime, gender variance, like sexual variance, cannot be relied on to produce a radical and oppositional politics simply by virtue of representing difference. Radical interventions come from careful consideration of racial and class constructions of sexual identities and gender identities and from a consideration of the politics of mobility outlined by that potent prefix "trans." Who, in other words, can afford transition, whether that transition be a move from female to male, a journey across the border and back, a holiday in the sun, a trip to the moon, a passage to a new body, a one-way ticket to white manhood? Who, on the other hand, can afford to stay home, who can afford to make a home, build a new home, move homes, have no home, leave home? Who can afford metaphors? I suggest we think carefully, butches and FTMs alike, about the kinds of men or masculine beings that we become and lay claim to: alternative masculinities, ultimately, will fail to change existing gender hierarchies to the extent to which they fail to be feminist, antiracist, and queer.

Notes

1   For more on this see Phyllis Burke, *Gender Shock: Exploding the Myths of Male and Female* (New York: Doubleday, 1996), 60–66.

2   Judith Halberstam, "F2M: The Making of Female Masculinity," in *The Lesbian Postmodern*, ed. Laura Doan (New York: Columbia University Press, 1994), 210–28.

3   Sandy Stone, "The 'Empire' Strikes Back: A Posttranssexual Manifesto," in *Body Guards: The Cultural Politics of Gender Ambiguity*, eds. Julia Epstein and Kristina Straub (New York: Routledge, 1993), 280–304.

4   See *FTM International Newsletter* 29 (January 1995).

5   Isabella, "Review Essay," *FTM Newsletter* 29 (January 1995): 13–14.

6   Janice Raymond, *The Transsexual Empire: The Making of the She-Male* (Boston: Beacon Press, 1979).

7   The tendency to equate lesbian desire with fluidity is too general to trace in all its specificity, but it surfaces most clearly in the so-called sex debates documented by critics such as Alice Echols and Lisa Duggan and Nan Hunter (see Alice Echols, "The Taming of the Id: Feminist Sexual Politics, 1968–83," in *Pleasure and Danger: Exploring Female Sexuality*, ed. Carole Vance [New York: Routledge, Kegan and Paul, 1984], 50–72; Lisa Duggan and Nan D. Hunter, *Sex Wars: Sexual Dissent and Political Culture* [New York: Routledge, 1995]). The idea that lesbian sex should be autonomous from male sexuality and from butch–femme roles has also been articulated by sex-negative feminists such as Sheila Jeffreys (see chapter 3 [of *Female Masculinity*]). My point here, however, is that the belief in the sexual fluidity of lesbian desire cannot be limited to the puritanical impulses of a few feminists. Rather, in magazines, zines, and all manner of popular lesbian representation, androgyny or the movement back and forth between femininity and masculinity has been held up as a virtue.

8   Jay Prosser, "No Place like Home: The Transgendered Narrative of Leslie Feinberg's *Stone Butch Blues*," *Modern Fiction Studies* 41, nos. 3–4 (1995). I should say here that I find Prosser's work challenging and

provocative, and I believe that his book on transsexual body narratives will be a crucial intervention into transgender discourse. My disagreements with Prosser are particular to this article. See Prosser, *Second Skins: The Body Narratives of Transsexuals* (New York: Columbia University Press, 1998).

9   Leslie Feinberg, *Transgender Liberation: A Movement Whose Time Has Come* (New York: World View Forum, 1992), 5.

10 Jordy Jones, "Another View of F2M," *FTM Newsletter* 29 (January 1995): 14–15.

11 See Stone, "Empire Strikes Back."

12 An example of an article that represented this kind of hostile attitude toward FTMs by lesbians appeared in the *Village Voice* in response to the horrifying murders of transgender man Brandon Teena, his girlfriend Lisa Lewis, and another friend, Philip DeVine (see Donna Minkowitz, "Gender Outlaw," *Village Voice*, 19 April 1994, 24–30). Many people wrote to the *Village Voice* charging Minkowitz with insensitivity to the chosen gender of Teena.

13 See Elaine K. Ginsberg, "Introduction: The Politics of Passing," in *Passing and the Fictions of Identity*, ed. Elaine K. Ginsberg (Durham, N.C.: Duke University Press, 1996), 3. Ginsberg also blurs the lines between racial and gendered passing in this essay and makes the two analogous, thereby losing the very different social and political structures of gender and race.

14 Deva, "FTM/Female-to-Male: An Interview with Mike, Eric, Billy, Sky, and Shadow," in *Dagger: On Butch Women*, eds. Lily Burana, Roxxie, and Linnea Due (Pittsburgh and San Francisco: Cleis Press, 1994), 154–67.

15 For an example of this tendency see Henry Rubin, *Self-Made Men: Identity and Embodiment among Transsexual Men* (Nashville: Vanderbilt University Press, 2003).

16 See chapter 4 [in *Female Masculinity*] for more on this history. See also Elizabeth Lapovsky Kennedy and Madeline Davis, *Boots of Leather, Slippers of Gold: The History of a Lesbian Community* (New York: Routledge, 1993).

17 Heather Findlay, "Stone Butch Now," *Girlfriends Magazine*, March/April, 1995, 45.

18 I have maintained the female gender pronouns used in the article here until I refer to Jay as FTM, and then I use male pronouns.

19 Leslie Feinberg, *Stone Butch Blues: A Novel* (New York: Firebrand, 1993), 147.

20 Mario Martino, with Harriet, *Emergence: A Transsexual Autobiography* (New York: Crown Publishers, 1977), 132.

21 Mark Rees, *Dear Sir or Madam: The Autobiography of a Female-to-Male Transsexual* (London: Cassell, 1996), 59.

22 "Guys" is an insider term used between FTMs and within transsexual circles.

23 Unfortunately, I cannot provide a citation for such a list because the lists are often anonymous and circulate only within a limited list with no intention of becoming public.

24 Amy Bloom, "The Body Lies," *New Yorker* 70, no. 21 (18 July 1994): 38–49.

25 Michel Foucault, *The History of Sexuality, Volume 1: An Introduction*, trans. Robert Hurley (New York: Vintage, 1980), 96.

26 Again, this is difficult to document, if only because transsexual discourse is still in the making. I am thinking of one particular conference I attended on transsexual and transgender issues in which a group of transsexual panelists insistently defined their political strategies in opposition to gay and lesbian political aims, which they considered to be mainstream and transsexual insensitive: "Transformations" Conference, CLAGS, Thursday, 2 May 1996.

27 For example, one critic comments on the effect of immigration on the Filipino third gender category of *bakla* (see Martin Manalansan, "Under the Shadows of Stonewall: Gay Transnational Politics and the Diasporic Dilemma," in *Worlds Aligned: Politics and Culture in the Shadow of Capital*, eds. David Lloyd and Lisa Lowe [Durham, N.C.: Duke University Press, 1997]).

28 Bernice Hausman, *Changing Sex: Transsexualism, Technology, and the Idea of Gender* (Durham, N.C.: Duke University Press, 1995), 110.

29 Hausman, to her credit, does look at this shared history in a section on early-twentieth-century sexology. She studies the language of inversion and claims: "'Transsexual' is not a term that can accurately be used to describe subjects exhibiting cross-sex behaviors prior to the technical capacity for sex reassignment . . . there is no transsexuality without the surgeon" (117).

30 Holly Devor, "Female Gender Dysphoria in Context: Social Problem or Personal Problem?" *Annual Review of Sex Research* 7 (1997): 44–89.

31 Raymond, *Transsexual Empire*.

32 Hausman, *Changing Sex*, 140.

33 Prosser, "No Place like Home," 489.

34 Henry S. Rubin, "Do You Believe in Gender?" *Sojourner* 21, no. 6 (February 1996): 7–8.

35   Rita Felski, "Fin de Siecle, Fin de Sexe: Transsexuality, Postmodernism, and the Death of History," *New Literary History* 27, no. 2 (spring 1996): 337.

36   See Jean Baudrillard's comments on transsexualism in *The Transparency of Evil* (New York: Verso, 1993); see also Arthur Kroker and Marilouise Kroker, *Body Invaders: Panic Sex in America* (New York: St. Martin's Press, 1987), and their *The Last Sex* (New York: St. Martin's Press, 1993).

37   Radclyffe Hall, *The Well of Loneliness* (1928; reprint, New York: Anchor, 1990), 79.

38   Feinberg, *Stone Butch Blues*.

39   Rose Tremain, *Sacred Country* (New York: Washington Square Press, 1992), 179.

40   In an essay on one such passing woman, Loreta Velazquez, Elizabeth Young comments on the complex of meanings that arise from the history of women who engage in the so-called scandal of cross-dressing but do so often for patriotic or nationalist purposes. Velazquez commemorated her cross-dressed adventures in a mammoth first-person narrative called *The Woman in Battle*, in which she recorded her adventures as a man, her marriages as a woman, the battles she fights as a Confederate soldier, romances she carries on with women as a man, childbirth, her experiences as a Confederate spy in the Union army, and other multiply contradictory experiences. Young carefully and assiduously sorts through the details of *The Woman in Battle* and concludes: "Confederate cross-dressing is simultaneously and inseparably a question of gender, sexuality, race, region and nation, and the constitutive presence of metaphor in each of these realms can have both reactionary and radical consequences" (Young, "Confederate Counterfeit: The Case of the Cross-Dressed Civil War Soldier," in *Passing and the Fictions of Identity*, ed. Elaine K. Ginsberg [Durham, N.C.: Duke University Press, 1996], 213).

41   Jan Morris, *Conundrum: An Extraordinary Narrative of Transsexualism* (New York: Henry Holt, 1986), 99.

42   Stone, "Empire Strikes Back"; Marjorie Garber, "The Chic of Araby: Transvestism, Transsexualism, and the Erotics of Cultural Appropriation," in *Body Guards: The Cultural Politics of Gender Ambiguity*, eds. Julia Epstein and Kristina Straub (New York: Routledge, 1994), 223–47.

43   Dorinne Kondo, "The Narrative Production of 'Home,' Community, and Political Identity in Asian American Theater," in *Displacement, Diaspora, and Geographies of Identity*, ed. Smadar Lavie and Ted Swedenburg (Durham, N.C.: Duke University Press, 1996), 97.

44   Gloria Anzaldúa, *Borderlands/La Frontera: The New Mestiza* (San Francisco: Spinsters/Aunt Lute Foundation, 1987), 13.

Chapter 28

Robert McRuer

COMPULSORY ABLE-BODIEDNESS AND QUEER/DISABLED EXISTENCE

Robert McRuer is Professor of English at George Washington University. He is the author of *The Queer Renaissance: Contemporary American Literature and the Reinvention of Lesbian and Gay Identities* (1997), and *Crip Theory: Cultural Signs of Queerness and Disability* (2006).

Taking his critical lead from Adrienne Rich's ground-breaking 1980 essay "Compulsory Heterosexuality and Lesbian Existence," McRuer develops a theory of compulsory able-bodiedness as a system, inextricably bound up with compulsory heterosexuality. Tracing the queer and disabled critique of normalcy, he argues that normalcy drives the compulsion that supports both intertwined systems. As a normalization that rests on the performative repetition of able-bodied identities, able-bodiedness is even more normalized than heterosexuality. In an audacious move, McRuer resignifies Judith Butler's famous theory of "gender trouble" as "ability trouble," drawing attention to the impossibility of the cultural ideal of able-bodiedness. Noting the frequency of cultural representations in which queerness and disability cohere in a single figure, he argues that such formations work to naturalize able-bodiedness and heterosexuality as universally desirable. Interweaving the subversive potential of critically queer positionalities and the political activism of disabled movements, McRuer develops what he calls "severely disabled" critique as a defiant resistance to straight/able norms.

Contextualizing disability

IN HER FAMOUS critique of compulsory heterosexuality Adrienne Rich opens with the suggestion that lesbian existence has often been "simply rendered invisible" (178), but the bulk of her analysis belies that rendering. In fact, throughout "Compulsory Heterosexuality and Lesbian Existence," one of Rich's points seems to be that compulsory heterosexuality depends as much on the ways in which lesbian identities are made visible (or, we might say, comprehensible) as on the ways in which they are made invisible or incomprehensible. She writes:

> Any theory of cultural/political creation that treats lesbian existence as a marginal or less "natural" phenomenon, as mere "sexual preference," or as the mirror image of either heterosexual or male homosexual relations is profoundly weakened thereby, whatever its other contributions. Feminist theory can no longer afford merely to voice a toleration of "lesbianism" as an "alternative lifestyle," or make token allusion to lesbians. A feminist critique of compulsory heterosexual orientation for women is long overdue.
>
> (178)

The critique that Rich calls for proceeds not through a simple recognition or even valuation of "lesbian existence" but rather through an interrogation of how the system of compulsory heterosexuality utilizes that existence. Indeed, I would extract from her suspicion of mere "toleration" confirmation for the idea that one of the ways in which heterosexuality is currently constituted or founded, established as the foundational sexual identity for women, is precisely through the deployment of lesbian existence as always and everywhere supplementary—the margin to heterosexuality's center, the mere reflection of (straight and gay) patriarchal realities. Compulsory heterosexuality's casting of some identities as alternatives ironically buttresses the ideological notion that dominant identities are not really alternatives but rather the natural order of things.[1]

More than twenty years after it was initially published, Rich's critique of compulsory heterosexuality is indispensable, the criticisms of her ahistorical notion of a "lesbian continuum" notwithstanding.[2] Despite its continued relevance, however, the realm of compulsory heterosexuality might seem to be an unlikely place to begin contextualizing disability.[3] I want to challenge that by considering what might be gained by understanding "compulsory heterosexuality" as a key concept in disability studies. Through a reading of compulsory heterosexuality, I want to put forward a theory of what I call compulsory able-bodiedness. The Latin root for *contextualize* denotes the act of weaving together, interweaving, joining together, or composing. This essay thus contextualizes disability in the root sense of the word, because I argue that the system of compulsory able-bodiedness that produces disability is thoroughly interwoven with the system of compulsory heterosexuality that produces queerness; that—in fact—compulsory heterosexuality is contingent on compulsory able-bodiedness and vice versa. And, although I reiterate it in my conclusion, I want to make it clear at the outset that this particular contextualizing of disability is offered as part of a much larger and collective project of unraveling and decomposing both systems.[4]

The idea of imbricated systems is of course not new—Rich's own analysis repeatedly stresses the imbrication of compulsory heterosexuality and patriarchy. I would argue, however, as others have, that feminist and queer theories (and cultural theories generally) are not yet accustomed to figuring ability/disability into the equation, and thus this theory of compulsory able-bodiedness is offered as a preliminary contribution to that much-needed conversation.[5]

Able-bodied heterosexuality

In his introduction to *Keywords: A Vocabulary of Culture and Society*, Raymond Williams describes his project as

> the record of an inquiry into a vocabulary: a shared body of words and meanings in our most general discussions, in English, of the practices and institutions which we group as culture and society. Every word which I have included has at some time, in the course of some argument, virtually forced itself on my attention because the problems of its meaning seemed to me inextricably bound up with the problems it was being used to discuss.
>
> (15)

Although Williams is not particularly concerned in *Keywords* with feminism or gay and lesbian liberation, the processes he describes should be recognizable to feminists and queer theorists, as well as to scholars and activists in other contemporary movements, such as African American studies or critical race theory. As these movements have developed, increasing numbers of words have indeed forced themselves on our attention, so that an inquiry into not just the marginalized identity but also the dominant identity has become necessary. The problem of the meaning of masculinity (or even maleness), of whiteness, of heterosexuality has increasingly been understood as inextricably bound up with the problems the term is being used to discuss.

One need go no further than the *Oxford English Dictionary* to locate problems with the meaning of heterosexuality. In 1971 the *OED Supplement* defined *heterosexual* as "pertaining to or characterized by the normal relations of the sexes; opp. to homosexual." At this point, of course, a few decades of critical work by feminists and queer theorists have made it possible to acknowledge quite readily that heterosexual and homosexual are in fact not equal and opposite identities. Rather, the ongoing subordination of homosexuality (and bisexuality) to heterosexuality allows heterosexuality to be institutionalized as "the normal relations of the sexes," while the institutionalization of heterosexuality as the "normal relations of the sexes" allows homosexuality (and bisexuality) to be subordinated. And, as queer theory continues to demonstrate, it is precisely the introduction of normalcy into the system that introduces compulsion. "Nearly everyone," Michael Warner writes in *The Trouble with Normal: Sex, Politics, and the Ethics of Queer Life*, "wants to be normal. And who can blame them, if the alternative is being abnormal, or deviant, or not being one of the rest of us? Put in those terms, there doesn't seem to be a choice at all. Especially in America where [being] normal probably outranks all other social aspirations" (53). Compulsion is here produced and covered over, with the appearance of choice (sexual preference) mystifying a system in which there actually is no choice.

A critique of normalcy has similarly been central to the disability rights movement and to disability studies, with—for example—Lennard Davis's overview and critique of the historical emergence of normalcy (*Enforcing* 23–49) or Rosemarie Garland-Thomson's introduction of the concept of the "normate" (*Extraordinary Bodies* 8–9). Such scholarly and activist work positions us to locate the problems of able-bodied identity, to see the problem of the meaning of able-bodiedness as bound up with the problems it is being used to discuss. Arguably, able-bodied identity is at this juncture even more naturalized than heterosexual identity. At the very least, many people not sympathetic to queer theory will concede that ways of being heterosexual are culturally produced and culturally variable, even if and even as they understand heterosexual identity itself to be entirely natural. The same cannot be said, on the whole, for able-bodied identity. An extreme example that nonetheless encapsulates currently hegemonic thought on ability and disability is a notorious *Salon* article attacking disability studies that appeared online in the summer of 1999. Nora Vincent writes, "It's hard to deny that something called normalcy exists. The human body is a machine, after all—one that has evolved functional parts: lungs for breathing, legs for walking, eyes for seeing, ears for hearing, a tongue for speaking and most crucially for all the academics concerned, a brain for thinking. This is science, not culture" ("Enabling").[6] In a nutshell, you either have an able body or you don't.

Yet the desire for definitional clarity might unleash more problems than it contains; if it's hard to deny that something called normalcy exists, it's even harder to pinpoint what that something is. The *OED* defines *able-bodied* redundantly and negatively as "having an able body, i.e. one free from physical disability, and capable of the physical exertions required of it; in bodily health; robust." Able-bodiedness, in turn, is defined vaguely as "soundness of bodily health; ability to work; robustness." The parallel structure of the definitions of ability and sexuality is quite striking: first, to be able-bodied is to be "free from physical disability," just as to be heterosexual is to be "the opposite of homosexual." Second, even though the language of "the normal relations" expected of human beings is not present in the definition of able-bodied, the sense of normal relations is, especially with the emphasis on work: being able-bodied means being capable of the normal physical exertions required in a particular system of labor. It is here, in fact, that both able-bodied identity and the *Oxford English Dictionary* betray their origins in the nineteenth century and the rise of industrial capitalism. It is here as well that we can begin to understand the compulsory nature of able-bodiedness: in the emergent industrial capitalist system, free to sell one's labor but not free to do anything else effectively meant free to have an able body but not particularly free to have anything else.

Like compulsory heterosexuality, then, compulsory able-bodiedness functions by covering over, with the appearance of choice, a system in which there actually is no choice. I would not locate this compulsion, moreover, solely in the past, with the rise of industrial capitalism. Just as the origins of heterosexual/homosexual identity are now obscured for most people so that compulsory heterosexuality functions as a disciplinary formation seemingly emanating from everywhere and nowhere, so too are the origins of able-bodied/disabled identity obscured, allowing what Susan Wendell calls "the disciplines of normality" (87) to cohere in a system of compulsory able-bodiedness that similarly emanates from everywhere and nowhere. Able-bodied dilutions and misunderstandings of the minority thesis put forward in the disability rights movement and disability studies have even, in some ways, strengthened the system: the dutiful (or docile) able-bodied subject now recognizes that some groups of people have chosen to adjust to or even take pride in their "condition," but that recognition, and the tolerance that undergirds it, covers over the compulsory nature of the able-bodied subject's own identity.[7]

Michael Bérubé's memoir about his son Jamie, who has Down's syndrome, helps exemplify some of the ideological demands currently sustaining compulsory able-bodiedness. Bérubé writes of how he "sometimes feel[s] cornered by talking about Jamie's intelligence, as if the burden of proof is on me, official spokesman on his behalf." The subtext of these encounters always seems to be the same: "In the end, aren't you disappointed to have a retarded child? [. . .] Do we really have to give this person our full attention?" (180). Bérubé's excavation of this subtext pinpoints an important common experience that links all people with disabilities under a system of compulsory able-bodiedness—the experience of the able-bodied need for an agreed-on common ground. I can imagine that answers might be incredibly varied to similar questions—"In the end, wouldn't you rather be hearing?" and "In the end, wouldn't you rather not be HIV positive?" would seem, after all, to be very different questions, the first (with its thinly veiled desire for deafness not to exist) more obviously genocidal than the second. But they are not really different questions, in that their constant repetition (or their presence as ongoing subtexts) reveals more about the able-bodied culture doing the asking than about the bodies being interrogated. The culture asking such questions assumes in advance that we all agree: able-bodied identities, able-bodied perspectives are preferable and what we all, collectively, are aiming for. A system of compulsory able-bodiedness repeatedly demands that people with disabilities embody for others an affirmative answer to the unspoken question, Yes, but in the end, wouldn't you rather be more like me?

It is with this repetition that we can begin to locate both the ways in which compulsory able-bodiedness and compulsory heterosexuality are interwoven and the ways in which they might be contested. In queer theory, Judith Butler is most famous for identifying the repetition required to maintain heterosexual hegemony:

> The "reality" of heterosexual identities is performatively constituted through an imitation that sets itself up as the origin and the ground of all imitations. In other words, heterosexuality is always in the process of imitating and approximating its own phantasmatic idealization of itself—and failing. Precisely because it is bound to fail, and yet endeavors to succeed, the project of heterosexual identity is propelled into an endless repetition of itself.
>
> ("Imitation" 21)

If anything, the emphasis on identities that are constituted through repetitive performances is even more central to compulsory able-bodiedness—think, after all, of how many institutions in our culture are showcases for able-bodied performance. Moreover, as with heterosexuality, this repetition is bound to fail, as the ideal able-bodied identity can never, once and for all, be achieved. Able-bodied identity and heterosexual identity are linked in their mutual impossibility and in their mutual incomprehensibility—they are incomprehensible in that each is an identity that is simultaneously the ground on which all identities supposedly rest and an impressive achievement that is always deferred and thus never really guaranteed. Hence Butler's queer theories of gender performativity could be easily extended to disability studies, as this slightly paraphrased excerpt from *Gender Trouble* suggests (I substitute, by bracketing, terms having to do literally with embodiment for Butler's terms of gender and sexuality):

> [Able-bodiedness] "offers normative [. . .] positions that are intrinsically impossible to embody, and the persistent failure to identify fully and without incoherence with these positions reveals [able-bodiedness] itself not only as a compulsory law, but as an inevitable comedy. Indeed, I would offer this insight into [able-bodied identity] as both a compulsory system and an intrinsic comedy, a constant parody of itself, as an alternative [disabled] perspective.
>
> (122)

In short, Butler's theory of gender trouble might be resignified in the context of queer/disability studies as what we could call "ability trouble"—meaning not the so-called problem of disability but the inevitable impossibility, even as it is made compulsory, of an able-bodied identity.

Queer/disabled existence

The cultural management of the endemic crisis surrounding the performance of both heterosexual and able-bodied identity effects a panicked consolidation of hegemonic identities. The most successful heterosexual subject is the one whose sexuality is not compromised by disability (metaphorized as queerness); the most successful able-bodied subject is the one whose ability is not compromised by queerness (metaphorized as disability). This consolidation occurs through complex processes of conflation and stereotype: people with disabilities are often understood as somehow queer (as paradoxical stereotypes of the asexual or oversexual person with disabilities would suggest), while queers are often understood as somehow disabled (as an ongoing medicalization of identity, similar to what people with disabilities more generally encounter, would suggest). Once these conflations are available in the popular imagination, queer/disabled figures can be tolerated and, in fact, utilized in order to maintain the fiction that able-bodied heterosexuality is not in crisis. As lesbian exist- ence is deployed, in Rich's analysis, to reflect back heterosexual and patriarchal "realities," queer/disabled existence can be deployed to buttress compulsory able-bodiedness. Since queerness and disability both have the potential to disrupt the performance of able-bodied heterosexuality, both must be safely contained—embodied—in such figures.

In the 1997 film *As Good As It Gets*, for example, although Melvin Udall (Jack Nicholson), who is diagnosed in the film as obsessive-compulsive, is represented visually in many ways that initially position him in what Martin F. Norden calls "the cinema of isolation" (i.e. Melvin is represented in ways that link him to other representations of people with disabilities), the trajectory of the film is toward able-bodied heterosexuality. To effect the consolidation of heterosexual and able-bodied norms, disability and queerness in the film are visibly located elsewhere, in the gay character Simon Bishop (Greg Kinnear). Over the course of the film, Melvin progressively sheds his sense of inhabiting an anomalous body, and disability is firmly located in the nonheterosexual character, who is initially represented as able-bodied but ends up, after he is attacked and beaten by a group of burglars, using a wheelchair and cane for most of the film. More important, the disabled/queer figure, as in many other contemporary cultural representations, facilitates the heterosexual romance: Melvin first learns to accept the differences Simon comes to embody, and Simon then encour- ages Melvin to reconcile with his girlfriend, Carol Connelly (Helen Hunt). Having served their purpose, Simon, disability, and queerness are all hustled offstage together. The film concludes with a fairly traditional romantic reunion between the (able-bodied) male and female leads.[8]

Critically queer, severely disabled

The crisis surrounding heterosexual identity and able-bodied identity does not automatically lead to their undoing. Indeed, as this brief consideration of *As Good As It Gets* should suggest, this crisis and the anxieties that accompany it can be invoked in a wide range of cultural texts precisely to be (temporarily) resolved or alleviated. Neither gender trouble nor ability trouble is sufficient in and of itself to unravel compulsory heterosexuality or compulsory able-bodiedness. Butler acknowledges this problem: "This failure to approximate the norm [. . .] is not the same as the subversion of the norm. There is no promise that subversion will follow from the reiteration of constitutive norms; there is no guarantee that exposing the naturalized status of heterosexuality will lead to its subversion" ("Critically Queer" 22; qtd. in Warner, "Normal and Normaller" 168–69 n87). For Warner, this acknowledgment in Butler locates a potential gap in her theory, "let us say, between virtually queer and critically queer" (Warner 168–69 n87). In contrast to a virtually queer identity, which would be experienced by anyone who failed to perform heterosexuality without contradiction and incoherence (i.e. everyone), a critically queer perspective could presumably mobilize the inevitable failure to approximate the norm, collectively "*working the weakness in the norm*," to use Butler's phrase ("Critically Queer" 26).[9]

A similar gap can be located if we appropriate Butler's theories for disability studies. Everyone is virtually disabled, both in the sense that able-bodied norms are "intrinsically impossible to embody" fully and in the sense that able-bodied status is always temporary, disability being the one identity category that all people will embody if they live long enough. What we might call a critically disabled position, however, would differ from such a virtually disabled position; it would call attention to the ways in which the disability rights movement and disability studies have resisted the demands of compulsory able-bodiedness and have demanded access to a newly imagined and newly configured public sphere where full participation is not contingent on an able body.

We might, in fact, extend the concept and see such a perspective not as critically disabled but rather as severely disabled, with *severe* performing work similar to the critically queer work performed by *fabulous*. Tony Kushner writes:

> *Fabulous* became a popular word in the queer community—well, it was never unpopular, but for a while it became a battle cry of a new queer politics, carnival and camp, aggressively fruity, celebratory and tough like a streetwise drag queen: *"FAAAAABULOUS!"* [. . .] *Fabulous* is one of those words that provide a measure of the degree to which a person or event manifests a particular, usually oppressed, subculture's most distinctive, invigorating features.
>
> (vii)

Severe, though less common than *fabulous*, has a similar queer history: a severe critique is a fierce critique, a defiant critique, one that thoroughly and carefully reads a situation—and I mean reading in the street sense of loudly calling out the inadequacies of a given situation, person, text, or ideology. "Severely disabled," according to such a queer conception, would reverse the able-bodied understanding of severely disabled bodies as the most marginalized, the most excluded from a privileged and always elusive normalcy, and would instead suggest that it is precisely those bodies that are best positioned to refuse "mere toleration" and to call out the inadequacies of compulsory able-bodiedness. Whether it is the "army of one-breasted women" Audre Lorde imagines descending on the Capitol; the Rolling Quads, whose resistance sparked the independent living movement in Berkeley, California; deaf students shutting down Gallaudet University in the Deaf President Now action; or ACT UP storming the National Institutes of Health or the Food and Drug Administration, severely disabled/critically queer bodies have already generated ability trouble that remaps the public sphere and reimagines and reshapes the limited forms of embodiment and desire proffered by the systems that would contain us all.[10]

Compulsory heterosexuality is intertwined with compulsory able-bodiedness; both systems work to (re)produce the able body and heterosexuality. But precisely because they depend on a queer/disabled existence that can never quite be contained, able-bodied heterosexuality's hegemony is always in danger of being disrupted. I draw attention to critically queer, severely disabled possibilities to further an incorporation of the two fields, queer theory and disability studies, in the hope that such a collaboration (which in some cases is already occurring, even when it is not acknowledged or explicitly named as such) will exacerbate, in more productive ways, the crisis of authority that currently besets heterosexual/able-bodied norms. Instead of invoking the crisis in order to resolve it (as in a film like *As Good As It Gets*), I would argue that a queer/disability studies (in productive conversations with disabled/queer movements outside the academy) can continuously invoke, in order to further the crisis, the inadequate resolutions that compulsory heterosexuality and compulsory able-bodiedness offer us. And in contrast to an able-bodied culture that holds out the promise of a substantive (but paradoxically always elusive) ideal, a queer/disabled perspective would resist delimiting the kinds of bodies and abilities that are acceptable or that will bring about change. Ideally, a queer/disability studies—like the term *queer* itself—might function "oppositionally and relationally but not necessarily substantively, not as a positivity but as a positionality, not as a thing, but as a resistance to the norm" (Halperin 66). Of course, in calling for a queer/disability studies without a necessary substance, I hope it is clear that I do not mean to deny the materiality of queer/disabled bodies, as it is precisely those material bodies that have populated the movements and brought about the changes detailed above. Rather, I mean to argue that critical queerness and severe disability are about collectively transforming (in ways that cannot necessarily be predicted in advance) the substantive uses to which queer/disabled existence has been put by a system of compulsory able-bodiedness, about insisting that such a system is never as good as it gets, and about imagining bodies and desires otherwise.

Notes

1   In 1976, the Brussels Tribunal on Crimes against Women identified "compulsory heterosexuality" as one such crime (Katz, "Invention" 26). A year earlier, in her important article "The Traffic in Women: Notes on the 'Political Economy' of Sex," Gayle Rubin examined the ways in which "obligatory heterosexuality" and "compulsory heterosexuality" function in what she theorized as a larger sex/gender system (179, 198; qtd. in Katz, *Invention* 132). Rich's 1980 article, which has been widely cited and reproduced since its initial publication, was one of the most extensive analyses of compulsory heterosexuality in feminism. I agree with Jonathan Ned Katz's insistence that the concept is redundant because "any society split between heterosexual and homosexual is compulsory" (*Invention* 164), but I also acknowledge the historical and critical usefulness of the phrase. It is easier to understand the ways in which a society split between heterosexual and homosexual is compulsory precisely because of feminist deployments of the redundancy of compulsory heterosexuality. I would also suggest that popular queer theorizing outside the academy (from drag performances to activist street theater) has often employed redundancy performatively to make a critical point.

2   In an effort to forge a political connection among all women, Rich uses the terms "lesbian" and "lesbian continuum" to describe a vast array of sexual and affectional connections throughout history, many of which emerge from historical and cultural conditions quite different from those that have made possible the identity of lesbian ("Compulsory Heterosexuality" 192–99). Moreover, by using "lesbian continuum" to affirm the connection between lesbian and heterosexual women, Rich effaces the cultural and sexual specificity of contemporary lesbian existence.

3   The incorporation of queer theory and disability studies that I argue for here is still in its infancy. It is in cultural activism and cultural theory about AIDS (such as John Nguyet Erni's *Unstable Frontiers* or Cindy Patton's *Fatal Advice*) that a collaboration between queer theory and disability studies is already proceeding and has been for some time, even though it is not yet acknowledged or explicitly named as such. Michael Davidson's "Strange Blood: Hemophobia and the Unexplored Boundaries of Queer Nation" is one of the finest analyses to date of the connections between disability studies and queer theory.

4   The collective projects that I refer to are, of course, the projects of gay liberation and queer studies in the academy and the disability rights movement and disability studies in the academy. [. . .]

5   David Mitchell and Sharon Snyder are in line with many scholars working in disability studies when they point out the "ominous silence in the humanities" on the subject of disability (*Body* 1). See, for other examples, Simi Linton's discussion of the "divided curriculum" (71–116) and assertions by Rosemarie Garland-Thomson and by Lennard Davis about the necessity of examining disability alongside other categories of difference such as race, class, gender, and sexuality (Garland-Thomson, *Extraordinary Bodies* 5; Davis, *Enforcing Normalcy* xi).

6   Disability studies is not the only field Vincent has attacked in the mainstream media; see her article "The Future of Queer: Wedded to Orthodoxy," which mocks academic queer theory. Neither being disabled nor being gay or lesbian in and of itself guarantees the critical consciousness generated in the disability rights or queer movements or in queer theory or disability studies: Vincent is a lesbian journalist, but her writing clearly supports both able-bodied and heterosexual norms. Instead of showing a stigmaphilic response to queer/disabled existence, finding "a commonality with those who suffer from stigma, and in this alternative realm [learning] to value the very things the rest of the world despises" (Warner, *Trouble* 43), Vincent reproduces the dominant culture's stigmaphobic response. See Warner's discussion of Erving Goffman's concepts of stigmaphobe and stigmaphile (41–45).

7   Michel Foucault's discussion of "docile bodies" and his theories of disciplinary practices are in the background of much of my analysis here (*Discipline* 135–69).
8   The consolidation of able-bodied and heterosexual identity is probably most common in mainstream films and television movies about AIDS, even—or perhaps especially—when those films are marketed as new and daring. The 1997 Christopher Reeve-directed HBO film *In the Gloaming* is an example. In the film, the disabled/queer character (yet again, in a tradition that reaches back to *An Early Frost* [1985]) is eliminated at the end but not before effecting a healing of the heteronormative family. As Simon Watney writes about *An Early Frost*, "The closing shot [. . .] shows a 'family album' picture. [. . .] A traumatic episode is over. The family closes ranks, with the problem son conveniently dispatched, and life getting back to normal" (114). I am focusing on a non-AIDS-related film about disability and homosexuality, because I think the processes I theorize here have a much wider currency and can be found in many cultural texts that attempt to represent queerness or disability. There is not space here to analyze *As Good As It Gets* fully; for a more comprehensive close reading of how heterosexual/able-bodied consolidation works in the film and other cultural texts, see my article "As Good As It Gets: Queer Theory and Critical Disability." I do not, incidentally, think that these processes are unique to fictional texts: the MLA's annual *Job Information List*, for instance, provides evidence of other locations where heterosexual and able-bodied norms support each other while ostensibly allowing for tolerance of queerness and disability. The recent high visibility of queer studies and disability studies on university press lists, conference proceedings, and even syllabi has not translated into more jobs for disabled/queer scholars.
9   See my discussion of Butler, Gloria Anzaldúa, and critical queerness in *Queer Renaissance* 149–53.
10   On the history of the AIDS Coalition to Unleash Power (ACT UP), see Douglas Crimp and Adam Rolston's *AIDS DemoGraphics*. Lorde recounts her experiences with breast cancer and imagines a movement of one-breasted women in *The Cancer Journals*. Joseph P. Shapiro recounts both the history of the Rolling Quads and the Independent Living Movement and the Deaf President Now action in *No Pity: People with Disabilities Forging a New Civil Rights Movement* (41–58, 74–85). Deaf activists have insisted for some time that deafness should not be understood as a disability and that people living with deafness, instead, should be seen as having a distinct language and culture. As the disability rights movement has matured, however, some deaf activists and scholars in deaf studies have rethought this position and have claimed disability (that is, disability revalued by a disability rights movement and disability studies) in an attempt to affirm a coalition with other people with disabilities. It is precisely such a reclaiming of disability that I want to stress here with my emphasis on severe disability.

Works cited

Bérubé, Michael. *Life As We Know It: A Father, a Family, and an Exceptional Child.* 1996. New York: Vintage, 1998.

Butler, Judith. "Critically Queer." *GLQ: A Journal of Lesbian and Gay Studies* 1.1 (1993): 17–32.

—. *Gender Trouble: Feminism and the Subversion of Identity.* New York: Routledge, 1990.

—. "Imitation and Gender Insubordination." *Inside/Out: Lesbian Theories, Gay Theories.* Ed. Diana Fuss. New York: Routledge, 1991. 13–31.

Crimp, Douglas, and Adam Rolston. *AIDS DemoGraphics.* Seattle: Bay, 1990.

Davidson, Michael. "Strange Blood: Hemophobia and the Unexplored Boundaries of Queer Nation." *Beyond the Binary: Reconstructing Cultural Identity in a Multicultural Context.* Ed. Timothy Powell. New Brunswick: Rutgers UP, 1999. 39–60.

Davis, Lennard J. *Enforcing Normalcy: Disability, Deafness, and the Body.* New York: Verso, 1995.

Erni, John Nguyet. *Unstable Frontiers: Technomedicine and the Cultural Politics of "Curing" AIDS.* Minneapolis: U of Minnesota P, 1994.

Foucault, Michel. *Discipline and Punish: The Birth of the Prison.* Trans. Alan Sheridan. New York: Vintage, 1977.

Garland-Thomson, Rosemarie. *Extraordinary Bodies: Figuring Physical Disability in American Culture and Literature.* New York: Columbia UP, 1997.

Halperin, David M. *Saint Foucault: Towards a Gay Hagiography.* New York: Oxford UP, 1995.

Katz, Jonathan Ned. "The Invention of Heterosexuality." *Socialist Review* 20 (1990): 7–34.

—. *The Invention of Heterosexuality*. New York: Dutton, 1995.

Kushner, Tony. "Foreword: Notes toward a Theater of the Fabulous." *Staging Lives: An Anthology of Contemporary Gay Theater*. Ed. John M. Clum. Boulder: Westview, 1996. vii–ix.

Linton, Simi. *Claiming Disability: Knowledge and Identity*. New York: New York UP, 1998.

Lorde, Audre. *The Cancer Journals*. San Francisco: Aunt Lute, 1980.

McRuer, Robert. *The Queer Renaissance: Contemporary American Literature and the Reinvention of Lesbian and Gay Identities*. New York: New York UP, 1997.

—. "As Good As It Gets: Queer Theory and Critical Disability." *GLQ: A Journal of Lesbian and Gay Studies* 9.1–2 (2003): 79–105.

Mitchell, David T., and Sharon L. Snyder, eds. *The Body and Physical Difference: Discourses of Disability in the Humanities*. The Body, in Theory: Histories of Cultural Materialism. Ann Arbor: U of Michigan P, 1997.

Norden, Martin F. *The Cinema of Isolation: A History of Physical Disability in the Movies*. New Brunswick: Rutgers UP, 1994.

Patton, Cindy. *Fatal Advice: How Safe-Sex Education Went Wrong*, Durham: Duke UP, 1997.

Rich, Adrienne. "Compulsory Heterosexuality and Lesbian Existence." *Powers of Desire: The Politics of Sexuality*. Eds. Ann Snitow, Christine Stansell, and Sharon Thompson. New York: Monthly Rev., 1983. 177–205.

Rubin, Gayle. "The Traffic in Women: Notes on the 'Political Economy' of Sex." *Toward an Anthropology of Women*. Ed. Rayna R. Reiter. New York: Monthly Rev., 1975. 157–210.

Shapiro, Joseph P. *No Pity: People with Disabilities Forging a New Civil Rights Movement*. New York: Times, 1993.

Vincent, Nora. "Enabling Disabled Scholarship." *Salon*. 18 Aug. 1999 <http://www.salon.com/books/it/1999/08/18/disability>.

—. "The Future of Queer: Wedded to Orthodoxy." *Village Voice* 22 Feb. 2000: 16.

Warner, Michael. "Normal and Normaller: Beyond Gay Marriage." *GLQ: A Journal of Lesbian and Gay Studies* 5.2 (1999): 119–71.

—. *The Trouble with Normal: Sex, Politics, and the Ethics of Queer Life*. New York: Free, 1999.

Watney, Simon. *Policing Desire: Pornography, AIDS, and the Media*. 2nd ed. Minneapolis: U of Minnesota P, 1989.

Wendell, Susan. *The Rejected Body: Feminist Philosophical Reflections on Disability*. London: Routledge, 1996.

Williams, Raymond. *Keywords: A Vocabulary of Culture and Society*. Rev. ed. New York: Oxford UP, 1983.

Chapter 29

Elizabeth A. Wilson

HYPOTHALAMIC PREFERENCE: LEVAY'S STUDY OF SEXUAL ORIENTATION

Elizabeth A. Wilson is Professor of Women's Studies at the Emory College of Arts and Sciences, Emory University. She works at the interface of science and the humanities, exploring how biology, and the neurosciences in particular, might open up new ways of thinking about gender and sexuality. She is the author of *Neural Geographies: Feminism and the Microstructure of Cognition* (1998) and *Affect and Artificial Intelligence* (2010).

In this essay, originally a chapter in her book *Psychosomatic: Feminism and the Neurological Body* (2004), Wilson reconsiders a notorious scientific study by Simon LeVay that found hypothalamic nuclei in the brains of homosexual men to be smaller than those of heterosexual men. Scientific and humanities-based responses to the study's data are divided, Wilson argues, between the former's statistical interpretation, which favors the dimorphism of homo- and heterosexual preference, and the latter's emphasis on exceptional data, which supports a distributed understanding of diverse sexualities. Wilson intervenes by arguing that LeVay's data suggest that dimorphism—in contradistinction to binarism—and distribution are not antithetical choices but are instead productively conjoined in a reticulated, chiasmatic relation. Wilson argues that more than establishing a neurobiological basis for sexual preference, LeVay's data suggest that sexuality might be regulated by other biological processes, such as body temperature or appetite, meaning that sexuality is even more perverse, and diverse, than we currently think.

The discovery that a nucleus differs in size between heterosexual and homosexual men illustrates that sexual orientation in humans is amenable to study at the biological level, and this discovery opens the door to studies of neurotransmitters or receptors that might be involved in regulating this aspect of personality.[1] Further interpretation of the results of this study must be considered speculative.

(LeVay 1991)

SIMON LEVAY'S CAVEAT that interpretation of his data should be delimited has been widely disregarded. In the wake of his 1991 report in *Science* there has been little in the way of new data on the neurotransmitters and receptors that may be involved in regulating sexuality, and to date there has been no published replication of LeVay's key findings.[2] There has, however, been much in the way of further interpretation of his report by academic, scientific, political, legal, and media commentators.[3]

For a study that is reliant on simple symmetrical axes of analysis (hetero vs. homo; male-typical vs. female-typical), LeVay's article has incited a curiously variant set of responses: gay activists who welcome the political implications of a biologically conferred homosexuality (Pillard in Stein 1993), feminist scientists who doubt the robustness of LeVay's data (Fausto-Sterling 1992), critics who broach the antihomophobic possibilities of biological research into sexuality while maintaining reservations about the particularities of LeVay's study (Rosario 1997; Stein 1999), scientists who integrate LeVay's results into a contentious body of research on the causes of homosexuality (Swaab, Zhou, Fodor, and Hofman 1997), cultural critics who find LeVay's conceptualization of sexuality and sexual identity too static (Garber 1995; Terry 2000), psychologists who argue that LeVay's work could be read as latent poststructuralist genealogy (Gordo-López and Cleminson 1999), a psychologist who argues that LeVay's work is a conventional reiteration of heterosexist norms (Hegarty 1997), a philosopher who compares LeVay to Monique Wittig (Zita 1998), a legal theorist who warns against the use of biological theories of sexual orientation in pro-gay litigation (Halley 1994), and a neuroscientific colleague who was harshly critical of LeVay's article—arguing that it should not have been published—but who later replicated a key finding of that study (Byne 1995; Byne et al. 2000).

Within the humanities-bound literature there has been extensive commentary on the ways LeVay's original study is limited both methodologically and conceptually. For example, it has been argued that the medical records of postmortem individuals contain insufficient data to reliably allocate those individuals to different categories of sexual identity, that LeVay's use of the categories heterosexual and homosexual is modeled on outdated notions of sexual identity, that the brains of many of the subjects may have been modified by complications from AIDS, that LeVay conflates male homosexuality with femininity, that the sample size is too small for reliable comparisons between groups to be made, that LeVay's hypothesis can be supported only when data from the brains of homosexual women are included in the comparative schema, and that LeVay's assertion that studies of rodent and primate sexuality offer useful behavioral and neurological homologies for humans is not valid.[4]

[I do] not offer more in the way of this kind of commentary. Nor am I concerned with the debates about the nature and nurture of homosexuality that have been reignited by LeVay's report and by genetic studies of homosexuality published about the same time (Bailey and Pillard 1991; Hamer, Hu, Magnuson, Hu, and Pattatucci 1993; LeVay and Hamer 1994). Instead, this chapter offers some speculations about the kind of neurological substance that is revealed in LeVay's study. By paying close attention to the specifics of LeVay's data, I hope to show one way that neurological substrate and sexuality can be allied. I clarify the relation between, on the one hand, the inertly dimorphic forms of sexuality that LeVay's methodology uses and, on the other hand, the exceptional (distributed) neurological and sexual forms in his data. It has been typical in commentaries on the 1991 study that only one of these patterns is respected. Pro-LeVay commentators tend to focus on the dimorphic distribution of his data and thus endorse simplistic notions of homosexuality and heterosexuality. Anti-LeVay commentators attempt to refute the validity of this dimorphic pattern by discussing the ways sexualities breach the confines of hetero/homo definition. [I make] a case that this analytic choice (dimorphic vs. distributed) obscures a more useful reading of the data. I argue that it is the relationship between dimorphic and distributed forms that is most instructive in LeVay's study.

This analysis of the dimorphic (n = 2) and the divergent (n > 2) serves as a template for examining the convergence of brain and sexuality. I leave to one side an analysis of what LeVay's data might be able to tell us about sexuality; by and large, LeVay presumes a conventional theory of gender-bound sexuality.[5] I am more interested in how this study of sexuality and the brain might reorganize our expectations about the character of neurology; specifically, how the reticulation of the hypothalamus by a dimorphic sexuality may provide insight into the nature of neurological substrata.

I recruit "reticulation" as a way of elucidating the relationship between dimorphic articulations (homo/hetero; large/small) on the one hand and the circuitry of neurological structures and the exceptionality of outlying data on the other. "Reticulate, v. 1. To divide or mark in such a way as to resemble [a] network. 2. To divide so as to form a network, or something having that appearance" (OED).[6] Rather than argue that there is an interpretive choice (or a political imperative) to favor dissemination over dimorphism, I suggest that these two kinds of neurological forms are in a reticulated relationship, wherein dimorphic divisions are irreducibly, agonistically, generatively conjoined with networks of divergence.

A difference in hypothalamic structure in heterosexual and homosexual men

First of all, and as a way of introducing some particularity to the discussion of LeVay's data about the hypothalamus and sexual orientation, let's consider the empirical antecedents, method, and outcomes of the 1991 study.

LeVay drew on two sets of empirical evidence to establish his hypothesis about the hypothalamus and sexuality. First, animal studies suggested that the medial zone of the anterior hypothalamus is implicated in what the literature nominates as "male-typical" sexual behavior (i.e., mounting). Second, one study indicated that lesions to this area impaired heterosexual behavior but did not eliminate sexual drive per se. Lesions to the medial preoptic anterior hypothalamus in male rhesus monkeys resulted in decreased frequency of sexual contact with female monkeys (measured as levels of manual contact, mounting, intromission, and ejaculation); however, there was no decrease in the frequency of masturbation (Slimp, Hart, and Goy 1978).[7] These data have been used to argue that this part of the hypothalamus controls heterosexuality, but not sexual drive in general.

Following on from this research, LeVay contended that an area in the human hypothalamus homologous to this area in other animals may be involved in regulating sexual behavior in men and women. Importantly for LeVay, these homologous nuclei in the human hypothalamus had already been reported to be significantly larger in men than in women (Allen, Hines, Shryne, and Gorski 1989). Moreover, this dimorphism in size had been interpreted as evidence that these nuclei may contribute to functional differences not only between men and women, but also between individuals of different sexual orientation: "Morphological analysis of the brains from humans with different sexual orientations and identities . . . may lead to further deductions concerning the possible influences of sex hormones on the structure and function of the human brain" (Allen et al. 1989, 504).[8] LeVay took up Allen et al.'s suggestion, but inverted the primacy accorded to gender in their study. He hypothesized that the reported dimorphism in certain hypothalamic nuclei in humans may be primarily related not to gender differences, but to differences in sexual orientation: "Specifically, I hypothesized that INAH [interstitial nuclei of the anterior hypothalamus] 2 or INAH 3 is large in individuals sexually oriented towards women (heterosexual men and homosexual women) and small in individuals sexually oriented towards men (heterosexual women and homosexual men)" (1991, 1035).

To test this hypothesis, LeVay measured the volume of the four hypothalamic nuclei that Allen et al. had investigated. They had named these "previously undescribed cell groups" (1989, 497) the interstitial nuclei of the anterior hypothalamus: INAH 1, 2, 3, 4. LeVay obtained brain tissue from forty-one subjects: nineteen homosexual men (their homosexuality was noted in their medical records), sixteen (presumed) heterosexual men, and six (presumed) heterosexual women.[9] The brain tissue was chemically fixed, the area containing the hypothalamic nuclei was dissected, and sliced sections were mounted on slides and stained. Measurement of the nuclei was undertaken by projecting magnifications of each section of tissue onto paper so that the nucleus is clearly visible, and then tracing an outline around that structure: "The outline of each nucleus was drawn as the shortest line that included every cell of the type characteristic for that nucleus, regardless of cell density . . . the volume of each nucleus was calculated as the summed area of the serial outlines multiplied by the section thickness" (LeVay 1991, 1035).[10]

LeVay's 1991 report has two micrographs that illustrate the differences in the volume of these nuclei. The micrograph of INAH 3 from a heterosexual man shows a well-defined, densely packed area; the micrograph of INAH 3 from a homosexual man, on the other hand, "is poorly recognizable as a distinct nucleus, but scattered cells similar to those constituting the nucleus in the heterosexual men were found" (1035). Indeed, "in most of the homosexual men (and most of the women) the nucleus was represented by only scattered cells" (1036).

Statistical analysis of the differences in volume among the nuclei of the women, heterosexual men, and homosexual men showed that, on average, INAH 3 was "more than twice as large in heterosexual men . . . as in the homosexual men" and that "there was a similar difference between the heterosexual men and the women" (LeVay 1991, 1035). There were no significant differences in the other nuclei studied (INAH 1, 2, 4). From these data LeVay claims some tentative support for the hypothesis that INAH 3 is dimorphic in relation to sexual orientation rather than in relation to gender; that is, small in those individuals, men or women, sexually oriented to men and large in those individuals, men or women, sexually oriented to women. He is unable to fully support such a conclusion as he requires data from the brains of lesbians to complete the comparative schema. Nonetheless, the established anatomical dimorphism is presumed to entail a functional dimorphism of INAH 3, and so imply that, at least in men, "sexual orientation has a biological substrate" (1034).

Reticulating neurology

In the final paragraphs of the 1991 report, LeVay discussed a number of factors that may contaminate his data: the difficulty in actually defining which cells belonged to a nucleus, the absence of brain tissue from homosexual women, the effects of AIDS and AIDS-related conditions on the volume of the nuclei in some of his subjects, the possibility that individuals who have died from AIDS are an unrepresentative sample of the male homosexual population, and the limitations that postmortem medical records place on representing "the diversity of sexual behavior that undoubtedly exists within the homosexual and heterosexual populations" (1036).

These concerns have been exploited in many critical commentaries, although perhaps they represent no more than the usual limitations that any empirical study of this kind has to

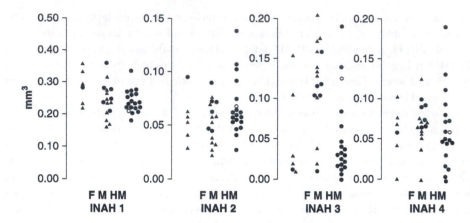

Fig. 29.1 Volumes of the four hypothalamic nuclei studied (INAH 1, 2, 3, and 4) for the three subject groups: females (F), presumed heterosexual males (M), and homosexual males (HM). Individuals who died of complications of AIDS, ●; individuals who died of causes other than AIDS, ▲; and an individual who was a bisexual male and died of AIDS, O. For statistical purposes this bisexual individual was included with the homosexual men.

endure. It is LeVay's final reservation that strikes me as more engaging, as it foregrounds the complexity in his data and the dynamic organization of neurological substrate: "The existence of 'exceptions' in the present sample (that is, presumed heterosexual men with small INAH 3 nuclei, and homosexual men with large ones) hints at the possibility that sexual orientation, although an important variable, may not be the sole determinant of INAH 3 size" (1036).

Leaving aside the question of what determines the size of INAH 3 (as there just are not sufficient data here or in the literature generally to adjudicate on this matter), the existence of "exceptions" in the sample is important. The INAH 3 data show a fair degree of variation. The second largest INAH 3 was in a homosexual man (when the trend was for INAH 3 in homosexual men to be small); the volumes of the three smallest nuclei in the heterosexual men closely matched those of the homosexual men (whereas most of the nuclei from heterosexual men were significantly larger than the nuclei of homosexual men); and two of the six female nuclei were similar in volume to the heterosexual men's (though, as a group, the female nuclei were similar in size to the smaller nuclei of homosexual men; see Figure 29.1). LeVay offers the suggestion that these exceptions may be due to "technical shortcomings or to misassignment of subjects to their subject groups" (1036). However, his prior recognition of "the diversity of sexual behavior that undoubtedly exists within the homosexual and heterosexual populations" preempts any expectation that subjects will fall naturally into two discretely contained categories. And herein lies the interpretive crux of LeVay's study: how to account for a body of data that both clusters in a statistically significant dimorphic pattern and manifests exceptional, outlying measurements that directly contradict this pattern.

The preference for analyzing data in terms of dimorphisms was well established in the neurobiological literature prior to LeVay's study. Sexual dimorphisms—the existence of anatomical and functional differences between male and female brains—had been alleged for over 150 years (Fausto-Sterling 2000). In the years prior to LeVay's study there had been increasing interest in male/female differences in various hypothalamic nuclei (Swaab, Chung, Kruijver, Hofman, and Ishunina 2001; Swaab, Gooren, and Hofman 1992).[11] LeVay conscripts this conceptual framework into his study on sexual orientation, hypothesizing that a hetero/homo dimorphism will also be evident in the hypothalamus. I am interested in engaging this conceptual proclivity for dimorphisms (n = 2) a little further—to see what dimorphic structures might generate in relation to neurology and sexuality. It is true enough that n = 2 has often been the very worst place to start and end interpretation about sexual difference and differences in sexual orientation. But it is not therefore a place to be avoided altogether: a comprehensive understanding of sexual differentiation needn't require the abandonment of this remarkably powerful figuration.[12] My challenge in relation to LeVay's data is not to recite the heteronormative aspects of n = 2, but to explore how the simplicity of a dimorphic pattern contributes to the elaborations, refractions, and de-evolutions of neurological substance.

Standard statistical interpretation guarantees that the dimorphic pattern predominates over the outlying data. Exceptional data require explanation, but they do not disrupt the robustness of the main division in nucleic volume in the sample. By all regular scientific and statistical conventions, LeVay's data manifest a dimorphic division in the size of INAH 3.[13] The conventions of critical, humanities-based commentary, on the other hand, dispute this statistical interpretation. For these commentators, sexuality is constituted according to a more distributed logic; sexualities are not ordered into two symmetrical groupings (hetero/ homo). Outlying data are not evidence of technical slips or methodological aberrations, they are part of the natural diversity of human sexualities. In this vein, Janet Halley (1994) has been particularly articulate:

> LeVay's method excludes from consideration the complex social patterns of identity profession and ascription, the refracting layers of representation in which the image of sexual orientation is managed, groomed, appropriated, negotiated, and captured. He reduced this complexity to a single characteristic: essential sexual orientation lodged neatly within the atomized individual who has died.
>
> This exclusion of the social and representational aspects of sexual orientation identity makes LeVay's handling of his bipolar categories, homosexual and heterosexual, almost startlingly crude . . . Whatever the ultimate resolution of those debates about experimental technique, LeVay's deployment of his categ- ories remains open to cultural criticism for ignoring the complexity of his subject. By making his heterosexual class a universal default, LeVay insists that all persons are indeed located in one of his two classifications. As a matter of theoretical assumption, he eliminates the possibility of a person with a sexuality neither heterosexual nor homosexual . . . LeVay's error was more grave than simply misclassifying some subjects who are "really" heterosexual as homosexual, or vice versa. He has changed the nature of his categories from the merely lexical to the ontological. His method forced these categories to describe and conclude the entire range of human possibility—to constitute us, no matter who we are and what we do or feel.
>
> (536–37)

For Halley, the dimorphic pattern in LeVay's data misrepresents the range of human possibility; human sexualities manifest a complexity that is not reducible to the bipolar categories hetero/homo. Halley's cultural orientation directly refutes the statistically based claim that a reliable dimorphic difference exists in the data. In a manner that is exemplary of the humanities-bound commentaries on the LeVay study, Halley annuls the dimorphic pattern in the data in favor of a more distributed organization. Jennifer Terry (2000) notes that researchers like LeVay rely too much on animal models of gender-typical sexual behavior (mounting and lordosis): "Assuming that gender typicality is the same across species allows researchers to ignore or misunderstand variance among individual animals and across species. This is precisely what happens in much of the research on human sexuality and sexual orientation that relies on the use of rodents" (161). Variance is lost or misrepresented when a dimorphic approach to sexual behavior (mounting and lordosis) is enacted. Timothy Murphy's (1997) commentary on the outlying data in LeVay's study reaffirms this inclination for variation. He emphasizes general differentiation over dimorphic difference: "There is no INAH 3 size at which sexual orientation divides neatly into homosexual and heterosexual categories, with the single bisexual man in the study straddling a dividing point between the two. Sizes of INAH 3 range, for gay men and straight men alike, over almost the entire gamut possible for that nucleus" (28). For Murphy, the statistically authorized dimorphic pattern is a ruse: there is no "two," there is in fact "almost the entire gamut." Nucleic volumes are not seen to "divide" but rather to "range" across a continuum of possible sizes. For Murphy, Halley, Terry, and many other critics of LeVay's work, the logic of the range is offered in order to replace or invalidate the logic of the divide. That is, the pattern of dimorphic division is repudiated as an interpretive possibility in favor of an interpretation of more divergent sexual forms.

The analyses that Halley, Terry, and Murphy construct are on target: clearly, LeVay gives no attention to the originary and constitutive nature of variation in sexual orientation. As Halley notes, dimorphism is a conceptual a priori for this research: it is assumed (male-typical, female-typical) rather than demonstrated. My comments are not intended to contest the general validity of the critiques offered by Halley, Terry, or Murphy. Nonetheless, I would like to suggest that LeVay's data might be more usefully interpreted according to an axis askew to both these critical concerns and the conventional statistical claims. What LeVay's data show is neither two discretely sexualized nuclei nor an aimless pattern of nucleic volumes. Rather, the data demonstrate a reticulating pattern, a coimplication of the disseminated (ranging) with the dimorphic (divided). In this reticulating structure neither of these patterns governs the field of neurological possibilities to the exclusion of the other. Instead, the data invite another, more difficult, interpretive challenge: to envisage how dimorphic patterns might relate to, be implicated in, arrest and cleave, but also be partially generative of, more distributed organizations.

In a set of literatures that is preoccupied with binarized concerns (either in scientific attempts to deploy crudely dyadic forms of sexuality or in critical attempts to definitively disrupt any form that might risk a familiarity with binarization), this reticulation of dimorphism with differentiation is an important point of departure: How does a simple division—large/small—participate in an expansive field of neurological and sexual ontologies? Is a dimorphic analytic axis simply an error, a failure to accommodate difference, or does it offer a particular approach to the notion of (sexual and neurological) difference that, though rudimentary, is nonetheless generative? The argument following on from here presumes that a nontrivial distinction can be made between a dimorphism (the division into two forms, e.g., large/small) and a binary (wherein there is less a cleaving into two forms than an ordering according to one form and its supplement, e.g., man/woman, human/technology, speech/writing). Hetero/homo distinctions are commonly ordered according to binarized concerns, but their alliance in LeVay with a dimorphic difference (large/small) suggests another manner in which the couplet homo/hetero may be instantiated. And rather than simply obliterating binarization, this dimorphic pattern brings the awkward, insistent, constitutively inconstant effects of binarization to the fore.

In this regard, the work of Eve Kosofsky Sedgwick has been particularly illuminating. Her readings of homo/heterosexual definition understand the dual logic of its "potent incoherences" (1990, 2). These readings document how the instability of homo/hetero as either a binarized or dimorphic coupling is precisely the source of—rather than the obstacle to—its generative power.[14] Moreover, Sedgwick's mobilization of queer has been singularly effective for its ability to account for how any queer (disseminated) articulation has a close and vital relation to the cleaving nature of homo/hetero organization. In a preamble on the term queer, Sedgwick notes, "Given the historical and contemporary force of the prohibitions against *every* same-sex sexual expression, for anyone to disavow those meanings, or to displace them from [queer's] definitional center, would be to dematerialize any possibility of queerness itself" (1993, 8). That is, the couplet homo/hetero stands in a reticulating relation to queer; the dimorphic and binarized instantiations of homosexuality and heterosexuality are not an impediment to queer materializations, but rather are peculiarly incoherent, peculiarly potent mechanisms of sexual generativity as such.

I am also guided by Sedgwick's petition for "a political vision of difference that might resist both binary homogenization and infinitizing trivialization" (Sedgwick and Frank 1995, 15). What gives Sedgwick and Frank's analysis particular purchase is their recognition that biology and biologism are an indispensable part of this vision. Recounting the instinctive resistance provoked in humanities-trained commentators by the di- or polymorphic essentialisms of biological explanation, Sedgwick and Frank note, "The resistance occurs because there seems to be some strong adhesion between the specification 'finitely many (n > 2) values' and that conversation-stopping word, innate . . . Somehow it's hard to hold on to the concept of eight or thirteen (and yet not infinite) different kinds of—of anything important—without having a biological model somewhere in the vicinity. The adhesion may well be a historical development, as though some momentum of modernity . . . has so evacuated the conceptual space between two and infinity that it may require the inertial friction of a biologism to even suggest the possibility of reinhabiting that space" (15).

In relation to LeVay's study, the conceptual space I am attempting to reinhabit is one where the possibility of a dimorphic pattern (n = 2) isn't obliterated by an imperative for debinarized organization. That is, I am attempting to take seriously the impact—generative and degenerative—of dimorphic ontologies.

To put this another way, heterogeneity isn't simply the opposite (or negation) of a dimorphic pattern. The relationship between dimorphism and its others is more, well, heterogeneous than simple contrariety. Michael Fortun's (2003) work on genomics provides one method for thinking about the relationship of dimorphic and distributed forms—the chiasmus: "One of its operations in rhetoric is to join and distinguish, combine and reverse two terms. The chiasmus marks a folding into each other that, like any of a number of M.C. Escher prints, never settles down into a *first this, then that* image, statement, or concept. Rhetorically, the chiasmus marks the spot where two distinct concepts can't be distinguished from each other, but feed off each other, send silent coded messages between themselves, and set possibilities in motion: not the smooth and simple interaction between distinct entities (nature and nurture, to cite just one familiar example), but the inescapably volatile and generative operations of an aporia" (23).

Fortun literalizes the chiasmus in the notation χ (chi), and uses it as a central analytic tool in examining how genomics, technoscience, governmentality, economics, and speculation have crossbred during the trading of Icelandic genetic and genealogical information. Referring to his neologism lavaχland, Fortun says: "The χ in lavaχland marks the fissure out of which emerges both flowing lava and solid land. The figure marks the spot of volatility and speculation. It marks the place where lava and land are joined, in sameness while separated, in difference . . . It marks an *and*—lava and land—although it would be better to say that the χ marks the not—not lava, not land" (2001, 23).

Fortun's analysis is organized according to a series of chiasmatic formulations (deconstructionχbiology; geneχome; epistemologyχstock options; maniaχfundamentals; open futureχsafe harbor; promisingχgenomics; presumedχconsent; speculationχ speculation), and for each of these paired formulations, he offers a diagram of "irreducible complexities" (8). What the chiasmus delivers in this context is a means for diagramming complexity (n > 2: "the massive amounts of genetic and other information now routinely pouring out of corporate, university, and government labs," 9) within a bilateral structure (aχb). This linking of complexity to the classical simplicity of a pair provides a powerful model for those of us working under threat of being analytically underwhelmed by formulations of difference where n = 2 and analytically overwhelmed by the explosion of data, theories, and cross-disciplinary affiliations that characterize the contemporary scientific scene.

So too with LeVay. The patterns in his data, and the ontological organizations that they attempt to delineate, don't offer up an interpretive or political choice of either divided structurations or eccentric distributions. The data suggest a more complex structuration of rudimentary divisions and their vicissitudes: dimorphismχdivergence. This reticulating-chiasmatic configuration is not simply a continuum in which dimorphic and disseminating forms benignly cohabit (a bell curve of standard data and their deviations). What is interesting in the data is neither the demonstration of a clear distinction of hetero/homo differences (as LeVay would hope) nor the demonstration of exhaustively debinarized sexualities (as many of LeVay's critics have hoped), but rather the more confounding, less readily identifiable reticulation of conventionalized and exceptional neurological constitutions.

Hypothalamic preference

My foregoing interest in the interpretations of pattern in LeVay's data is an attempt to approach the reticulating nature of neurological material. By containing my reflections to the substrate of neurology (that is, without taking immediate interpretive recourse to cultural, social, psychological, or representational contingencies), I hope to amplify neurology's natural intricacies.

The mammalian brain is a reticulating structure. Its most obvious morphological feature—the division into two cerebral hemispheres—cohabits with a divergent array of synaptic connections, neural pathways, functional and histological differentiations, and biochemical communications. If we consider simply the anatomy of neuronal connections, this complexity is almost beyond comprehension: by one estimation (Edelman 1992), there are around 10 billion neurons in the cortex alone, and each of these neurons has between 1,000 and 10,000 synaptic connections from other neurons. There are, then, about 1 trillion connections in the cortex; a sample of tissue the size of a match head contains around a billion connections. Edelman notes that "if we consider how connections might be variously combined, the number would be hyperastronomical—on the order of ten followed by millions of zeros. (There are about ten followed by eighty zeros' worth of positively charged particles in the whole known universe!)" (17).

Yet, at the same time, the brain is radically underconnected: neurons don't just connect anywhere, or at a great distance—their connections are typically made within locally defined functional and anatomical constraints. So while the anatomy of neuronal connections suggests an almost boundless functional capacity, it is also the case that there are constraints in terms of which neurons can participate in what functions. The visual areas of the brain, for example, have an architectural structure quite different from that of subcortical regions such as the hypothalamus, and in a rudimentary way, the cortex itself is divided into areas of functional specialization: motor cortex, association cortex, visual cortex, and so on. Much of the popular commentary on the brain is an attempt to negotiate one side or other of this reticulating puzzle: the brain is seen as either one of the most complex structures in the universe, or as an organ delimitable to simple, localized constraints.

The hypothalamus also instantiates this reticulating entanglement of symmetrical, localized, and disseminating organizations. The hypothalamus is a subcortical structure in the vertebrate forebrain that contains a number of nucleic foci. The nuclei of the hypothalamus are thought to control a number of different activities, many of which are homeostatic. The hypothalamus

> integrates the autonomic nervous system, with centers for sympathetic and parasympathetic control; receives impulses from the viscera. Ideally situated to act as an integration center for the endocrine and nervous systems, secreting various releasing factors into the pituitary portal system and neurosecretions into the posterior pituitary . . . Contains control centers for feeding and satiety—the latter inhibiting the former after feeding, in higher vertebrates, is a center for aggressive emotions and feelings and for psychosomatic effects. Contains a thirst center responding to extracellular fluid volume; helps regulate sleeping and waking patterns; monitors blood pH and concentration and, in homeotherms, body temperature.
>
> (Thain and Hickman 1996, 319)

At the same time, however, this functional heterogeneity is housed in symmetrical form: the hypothalamus is divided into left and right halves. Each nucleus within the hypothalamus is duplicated on the right and left, although there are no known functional or anatomical differences between the nuclei.[15] And although the hypothalamus is widely connected biochemically to the cortex and to other organs (e.g., the pituitary gland, and through it to the gonads), most of the information that the hypothalamus receives comes from itself (LeVay 1993).

This relationality between simple, symmetrical forms and widely dispersing circuits is precisely what needs to be excavated from LeVay's 1991 data. The injection of a dimorphic sexuality into this field need not have the effect of arresting divergent neurological pathways. Although LeVay's transmogrification of sexual orientation into nucleic volume appears to be a hopelessly reductive gesture, the deployment of neurologically dimorphic forms need not in itself enact reductionism. If the brain does, in places, coalesce into symmetrical and localized organizations, it does so only within a wider circuitry that reticulates this localizing symmetry. Likewise, these circuits are themselves constituted through an intimate adhesion to localized dimorphisms. As I have attempted to argue, dimorphic, symmetrical forms are not necessarily degenerate, reductive, or inflexible, but may be generative constituents of overall neurological structure and function.

LeVay's study opens up at least two avenues for approaching the conjunction of neurology and sexuality. First, it allows the embodiment of sexual preference to be instantiated neurologically. It is parochial to expect that sexualities circulate only in nonbiological realms, that they could be contained to cultural domains, or that they could be arrested at the cell membrane or synaptic gap. If sexuality is sequestered within nonbiological organizations (culture, economics, semiosis), then the communicability of sexuality and the possibilities for perversion have been considerably diminished. Second (and following on from this first point), LeVay's insistence on the intimacy of INAH and sexuality opens sexuality up to a range of hypothalamic possibilities. It canvases the possible links between sexuality and, for example, body temperature, appetite, and circadian rhythms in ways that promise perverse and disseminated sexual forms. Not surprisingly, perhaps, LeVay has ruled out such a divergent biological substrate for sexuality. At the beginning of his 1991 study he notes that there have been a number of unsuccessful attempts to establish a biological basis for sexual orientation, and he footnotes the following example: "The suprachiasmatic nucleus (SCN) of the hypothalamus has been reported to be larger in homosexual than in heterosexual men . . . There is little evidence, however, to suggest that SCN is involved in regulation of sexual behavior aside from its circadian rhythmicity" (1036).

It seems to me, however, that sexuality cannot be partitioned within the hypothalamus in this way: orientation here, circadian rhythms there. The extent to which any hypothalamic function can be aside from sexuality is the very question that LeVay's study most fruitfully put into circulation. More recently, attempts have been made to study this interface between sexuality and broader hypothalamic functions. Rahman and Silber (2000) note that the SCN of the human hypothalamus is "the principal neural substrate of circadian rhythmicity" (127), and it has been found to be significantly larger in homosexual men than in heterosexual men. It follows, they argue, that sleep cycles in heterosexual and homosexual men might be different. Their data suggest that homosexual men have much shorter sleep duration than heterosexual men, the former going to sleep later and waking earlier. For a number of reasons, the data don't seem that strong (they were collected through self-report, for example). The biggest problem of the study, however, is how Rahman and Silber preserve a detached relationship among sexuality, circadian rhythms, and the hypothalamus. They remark on the correlation of sexuality and circadian rhythms and they postulate that this correlation "warrants an interpretation at the neurological level" (132), but they don't imagine the co-contamination of these events: how they might chiasmatically cross each other, constituting each other according to unusual ontologies and rhythms.

Although LeVay's data have facilitated a literature that reduces sexuality to binarized forms (Ellis and Ebertz 1997), it also opens sexuality into a broader material field. Through the LeVay study we could be provoked to think about the neurology/sexuality interface more exhaustively—not as an insular coupling, but as a node in a chiasmatic-reticulating physiological organization. It is clear enough that LeVay's 1991 report seriously simplifies sexuality and does not provide data sufficiently robust to support the conclusions that he draws there and in other contexts. It is also the case, however, that the data, generated through a conceptually awkward attempt to envisage the conjunction of neurology and sexuality, reveal a neurological complexity that LeVay has been able to record but not fully elucidate.

Notes

1   In this context, the term nucleus refers to an aggregation of nerve cells. Such nuclei (or ganglia) are anatomically distinct areas in the brain and spinal cord. Here, LeVay is referring to nuclei in the human hypothalamus. In conjunction with the endocrine system, the hypothalamic nuclei are thought to be involved in homeostatic regulation (e.g., eating, diurnal rhythms, aggression, sexuality, body temperature).

2   Rahman and Wilson (2003) give an overview of psychobiological research on sexual orientation since LeVay's study. There has been no replication of LeVay's findings. There has been some interest in the dimorphism of other hypothalamic nuclei in relation to sexual orientation, and there also seems to be increasing interest in the hypothalamic structures of the brains of transsexuals. Byne et al. (2000) have reported a sexual dimorphism in one of the hypothalamic nuclei LeVay studied, but they did not investigate differences in sexual orientation (see n. 10 below).

3   In violation of his own directive, LeVay has been a prolific contributor to the further interpretation of the original data. In 1992 he resigned from his position at the Salk Institute, where the hypothalamic research was conducted. He lists the 1991 *Science* report as the second to last of his scientific publications. It was, however, the first study he had conducted on sexuality; his usual area of neurological expertise was the visual cortex (http://hometown.aol.com/slevay). From 1992 onward LeVay commented extensively on the nature and implications of his 1991 study. He has appeared on TV news programs (*MacNeil/Lehrer NewsHour*, *Primetime Live*, *Nightline*) and talk shows (*Donahue*,

Oprah), he has written a syndicated column for gay newspapers, he has given legal testimony, he has been a presenter for a Channel 4 documentary (*Born That Way?*), he has given lectures to universities and community organizations about the biology of sexual orientation, and he has written two popular nonfiction books and a novel about the scientific context and cultural implications of neurobiological research on sexuality (*The Sexual Brain*, 1993; *Queer Science*, 1996; *Albrick's Gold*, 1997). *Science* and *Nature* also disregarded LeVay's interdiction; they immediately published further commentary and speculation on his data (Barinaga 1991; Maddox 1991).

4   See Byne (1995), De Cecco and Parker (1995), Fausto-Sterling (1992), Murphy (1997), and Stein (1999) for academic critiques that discuss these methodological and conceptual limitations in LeVay's study. Gallagher (1991) and Gessen and McGowan (1992) in *The Advocate* canvas the variety of political/activist responses to LeVay's study.

5   LeVay's most sustained account of his theoretical commitments, in relation to sexuality, is to be found in *Queer Science* (1996), where he makes his partiality for Hirschfeld's sexology explicit: "a profound admiration for the man, his ideas and his cause" (40). However, it is unclear whether Hirschfeld's research helped structure LeVay's original approach to the study of the hypothalamus and sexual orientation, or whether it has been a post hoc theoretical foundation: "LeVay, who is gay, readily acknowledges that at the root of his inquiry into the origins of sexuality was 'just my own gut feeling that I share with, I think, many gay men. It's not a feeling that has much scientific documentation at the moment' " (Gessen and McGowan 1992, 60).

6   The OED cites "reticulate" in the eighteenth century, but it was used most commonly in the nineteenth century in reference to geographical and geological structure: "1833 *Lyell Princ.* Geol. III. 356 The granite, in this locality, often sends forth so many veins as to reticulate the limestone and schist . . . 1871 Alabaster *Wheel of Law*. 252 The numerous canals and branches of the river which reticulate the flat alluvial plain . . . 1876 Page *Adv. Text-bk. Geol.* iii. 54 Showing a thousand reticulating fissures." In these contexts, reticulate seems to mean the secondary differentiation of a uniform surface by branching geological features. Here, I use reticulate more to emphasize the way in which division, specifically dimorphic division, is a constitutive or originary aspect of a networking structure.

7   See Terry (2000) for an excellent analysis of this study and a general discussion of the limitations and implications of using animal data in studies about human sexuality.

8   There has been considerable confusion in the neurobiological literature on sexual orientation about whether or not a homology between these rodent hypothalamic nuclei and human hypothalamic nuclei exists. In the first instance, the naming of these structures has changed over the years. Gorski, Gordon, Shryne, and Southam (1978) reported sex difference in the medial preoptic nucleus of the rat (MPON); this area was significantly larger in male than female rats. This area became known as the sexually dimorphic nucleus of the preoptic area (SDN-POA). Eleven years later, Allen et al. (1989) reported two sexually dimorphic nuclei in the human hypothalamus. They abandoned the idea of a single sexually dimorphic nucleus in the human brain and focused their attention on a group of nuclei, the interstitial nuclei of the anterior hypothalamus, of which they isolated four: INAH 1, 2, 3, 4. Allen et al. found that INAH 2 and INAH 3 were sexually dimorphic (larger in males than in females). The homology between the structures described in the 1978 and 1989 reports is complicated further by Allen et al.'s acknowledgment that "it is unclear which, if either, of the 2 nuclei we found to be sexually dimorphic in the human brain corresponds to the SDN-POA of the rat" (501). They also advise against using the term INAH 1 interchangeably with SDN-POA: "There is presently no indication that INAH 1 is homologous to the SDN-POA of the rat" (503). Nonetheless, two prominent researchers in the field, Swaab and Hofman (1995), have retained the old nomenclature: "The sexually dimorphic nucleus of the preoptic area (SDN-POA) of the hypothalamus, as first described in the rat by Gorski and colleagues, is still the most conspicuous morphological sex difference in the mammalian brain" (266); they equate the SDN-POA with INAH 1. Byne et al. (2000) canvas the possibility that the SDN-POA in the rat may be homologous to INAH 3 in humans. It is by no means clear that similar structures in the rat and human brains are being compared, nor even that the same structure within the human brain is being described in these different papers.

9   All of the homosexual subjects had died of AIDS; six of the heterosexual men and one of the heterosexual women had died of AIDS. See LeVay (1991, n. 8) for details concerning the causes of death in the other subjects.

10   Volume rather than cell number or cell density was used as the measure of size because of "the difficulty in precisely defining the neurons belonging to INAH 3" (LeVay 1991, 1036). See Allen et al. (1989, 489) for a full description of this measurement technique. Swaab and Hofman (1995) consider that there are difficulties with such a method: "Volume is susceptible to various pre- and post-mortem factors, such as differences in agonal state and fixation time, but also to histological procedures and

methods such as section thickness. Therefore it is essential to include data on total cell numbers of hypothalamic nuclei, since this parameter is not influenced by such factors" (266–67).

11   Leaving aside putative sexual dimorphisms in other hypothalamic nuclei (e.g., the suprachiasmatic nucleus), it is still unclear whether there is a sexual dimorphism in the INAH structures that LeVay studied. Swaab's early work on the dimorphism of the SDN-POA/INAH 1 (Swaab and Fliers 1985) initiated much of the interest in the hypothalamus and sex differences. However, this finding has not been replicated by another research group, even though Swaab et al. (2001) claim the sex difference in this area in the rat "is so evident that it can even be observed with the naked eye" (93). Other researchers have reported a sexual dimorphism in INAH 2 or 3, but not in INAH 1.

Table 29.1

	INAH 1 (SDN-POA)	INAH 2	INAH 3	INAH 4
Swaab and Fliers 1985	Larger in men	Not studied	Not studied	Not studied
Allen et al. 1989	No sex difference	Larger in men	Larger in men	No sex difference
Hofman and Swaab 1989	Larger in men	Not studied	Not studied	Not studied
LeVay 1991	No sex difference	No sex difference	Larger in men	No sex difference
Byne et al. 2000	No sex difference	No sex difference	Larger in men	No sex difference

12   The template n = 2 includes pairs, dimorphisms, divisions, and bilateralities. Think of paired nucleotides and the double helix or lungs and kidneys. Bilaterality is a common organization of human biology: the limbs, the sense organs, the cortical hemispheres are all paired, although they are often asymmetrical. One particularly important mode of bilateral organization of limbs, sense organs, and neurology is the optic chiasma: the crossing of the right optic nerve to the left side of the brain, and the left optic nerve to the right side of the brain.

13   Hegarty (1997) has suggested that LeVay's statistical analysis could have been conducted more rigorously. Hegarty's alternative analysis (which confines itself to the data from subjects who died of AIDS and measures differences across all four INAH volumes) does not register a statistically significant difference in relation to sexual orientation in the volumes of INAH 3. Any body of data can be subject to different batteries of statistical testing, and in some cases differences between groups may be statistically significant under one test, but not under another. LeVay, for example, notes that if the comparison between heterosexual and homosexual subjects is restricted to those who died of AIDS (thus eliminating any confounding influence of AIDS vs. non-AIDS deaths), then the statistical significance of the difference in nucleic volumes drops markedly (from p < 0.001 to p < 0.028). This difference between LeVay's own reanalysis and Hegarty's reanalysis discloses the essentially equivocal nature of all statistical analysis. It is not one of the ambitions of this essay to adjudicate on the appropriate statistical analysis for LeVay's data. However, I take LeVay's original analysis to indicate a division of some kind in the data. What LeVay's statistical test certifies is that the probability that two clusters in the INAH 3 data would emerge by chance (i.e., if subjects were assigned randomly to each category) is less than 1 in 1,000 (p < 0.001). It seems substantially more likely, then, that something may differentiate the hypothalamic structures of these forty-one individuals into a dimorphic pattern. Other commentators seem also to concur about the reliability of LeVay's statistical analysis of this sample; for example, Suppe (1994) comments favorably on LeVay's statistical testing in a paper that is otherwise hostile to LeVay's study. The concerns of these commentators have been either that this is not a representative sample of the general population or that we are unable to infer specific functional differences from this anatomical difference.

14   For a meticulous reading of Sedgwick and Halley on this issue, see Deutscher (1997, chap. 1).

15   LeVay (1991) measured both the left and right INAH in fewer than half of his subjects: "In 15 cases the nuclei in both left and right hypothalami were traced. In 12 cases only the left hypothalamus was studied, and in 14 cases only the right" (1035). In a later text he comments, "As far as we know, the two members of each [nucleic] pair have the same structure, the same connections and the same function, so they are often casually referred to in the singular" (1993, 40).

References

Allen, Laura, Melissa Hines, James Shryne, and Roger Gorski. 1989. Two sexually dimorphic cell groups in the human brain. *Journal of Neuroscience* 9: 497–506.

Bailey, Michael, and Richard Pillard. 1991. A genetic study of male sexual orientation. *Archives of General Psychiatry* 48: 1089–96.

Barinaga, Marsha. 1991. Is homosexuality biological? *Science* 253: 956–57.

Byne, William. 1995. Science and belief: Psychobiological research on sexual orientation. In *Sex, cells, and same-sex desire: The biology of sexual preference*, edited by John De Cecco and David Allen Parker. New York: Haworth.

Byne, William, Mitchell Lasco, Eileen Kemether, Akbar Shinwair, Mark Edgar, Susan Morgello, Liesl Jones, and Stuart Tobet. 2000. The interstitial nuclei of the human anterior hypothalamus: An investigation of sexual variation in volume and cell size, number and density. *Brain Research* 856: 254–58.

De Cecco, John, and David Allen Parker. 1995. The biology of homosexuality: Sexual orientation or sexual preference? In *Sex, cells, and same-sex desire: The biology of sexual preference*, edited by John De Cecco and David Allen Parker. New York: Haworth.

Deutscher, Penelope. 1997. *Yielding gender: Feminism, deconstruction and the history of philosophy*. London: Routledge.

Edelman, Gerald. 1992. *Bright air, brilliant fire*. Harmondsworth, England: Penguin.

Ellis, Lee, and Linda Ebertz, eds. 1997. *Sexual orientation: Toward biological understanding*. Westport, Conn.: Praeger.

Fausto-Sterling, Anne. 1992. *Myths of gender: Biological theories about men and women*. Revised ed. New York: Basic Books.

——— 2000. *Sexing the body: Gender politics and the construction of sexuality*. New York: Basic Books.

Fortun, Michael. 2003. *To speculate—on genomics*. Occasional paper, School for Social Science, Institute for Advanced Study. http://www.ss.ias.edu/home/papers.html.

Gallagher, John. 1991. Hypothalamus study and the coverage of it may attract many barbs. *Advocate* October 8 (no. 587): 14–15.

Garber, Marjorie, 1995. *Vice versa: Bisexuality and the eroticism of everyday life*. New York: Simon and Schuster.

Gessen, Masha, and David McGowan. 1992. Raiders of the gay gene. *Advocate* March 24 (no. 599): 60–62.

Gordo-López, Angel, and Richard Cleminson. 1999. Queer science/queer psychology: A biosocial inoculation project. *Theory and Psychology* 9(2): 282–88.

Gorski, Roger, J.H. Gordon, J.E. Shryne, and A.M. Southam. 1978. Evidence for a morphological sex difference within the medial preoptic area of the rat brain. *Brain Research* 148: 333–46.

Halley, Janet. 1994. Sexual orientation and the politics of biology: A critique of the argument from immutability. *Stanford Law Review* 46: 503–68.

Hamer, Dean, Stella Hu, Victoria Magnuson, Nan Hu, and Angela Pattatucci. 1993. A linkage, between DNA markers on the X chromosome and male sexual orientation. *Science* 261: 321–27.

Hegarty, Peter. 1997. Materializing the hypothalamus: A performative account of the "gay brain." *Feminism and Psychology* 7(3): 355–72.

Hofman, Michel, and Dick Swaab. 1989. The sexually dimorphic nucleus of the preoptic area in the human brain: A comparative morphometric study. *Journal of Anatomy* 164: 55–72.

LeVay, Simon. 1991. A difference in hypothalamic structure between heterosexual and homosexual men. *Science* 253: 1034–37.

——. 1993. *The sexual brain*. Cambridge, Mass: MIT Press.

——. 1996. *Queer science: The use and abuse of research into homosexuality*. Cambridge, Mass.: MIT Press.

——. 1997. *Albrick's gold*. London: Hodder Headline.

LeVay, Simon, and Dean Hamer. 1994. Evidence for a biological influence in male homosexuality. *Scientific American* 270: 44–49.

Maddox, John. 1991. Is homosexuality hard-wired? *Nature* 353(6339): 13.

Murphy, Timothy. 1997. *Gay science: The ethics of sexual orientation research*. New York: Columbia University Press.

Rahman, Qazi, and Ken Silber. 2000. Sexual orientation and the sleep-wake cycle: A preliminary investigation. *Archives of Sexual Behavior* 29(2): 127–34.

Rahman, Qazi, and Glenn Wilson. 2003. Born gay? The psychobiology of human sexual orientation. *Personality and Individual Differences* 34(8) 1337–82.

Rosario, Vernon. 1997. Homosexual bio-histories: Genetic nostalgias and the quest for paternity. In *Science and homosexualities*, edited by Vernon Rosario. New York: Routledge.

Sedgwick, Eve Kosofsky. 1990. *Epistemology of the closet*. Berkeley: University of California Press.

—. 1993. Queer and now. In *Tendencies*. Durham, N.C.: Duke University Press.

Sedgwick, Eve Kosofsky, and Adam Frank. 1995. Shame in the cybernetic fold: Reading Silvan Tomkins. In *Shame and its sisters: A Silvan Tomkins reader*, edited by Eve Kosofsky Sedgwick and Adam Frank. Durham, N.C.: Duke University Press.

Slimp, Jefferson, Benjamin Hart, and Robert Goy. 1978. Heterosexual, autosexual and social behavior of adult male rhesus monkeys with medial preoptic-anterior hypothalamus lesions. *Brain Research* 142: 105–22.

Stein, Edward. 1993. Evidence for queer genes: An interview with Richard Pillard. *GLQ: A Journal of Lesbian and Gay Studies* 1(1): 93–110.

—. 1999. *The mismeasure of desire: The science, theory and ethics of sexual orientation*. Oxford: Oxford University Press.

Suppe, Frederick. 1994. Explaining homosexuality: Philosophical issues, and who cares anyhow? *Journal of Homosexuality* 27(3/4): 223–68.

Swaab, Dick, Wilson Chung, Frank Kruijver, Michel Hofman, and Tatjana Ishunina. 2001. Structural and functional sex differences in the human hypothalamus. *Hormones and Behavior* 40: 93–98.

Swaab, Dick, and E. Fliers. 1985. A sexually dimorphic nucleus in the human brain. *Science* 228: 1112–15.

Swaab, Dick, L. Gooren, and Michel Hofman. 1992. The human hypothalamus in relation to gender and sexual orientation. *Progress in Brain Research* 93: 205–19.

Swaab, Dick, and Michel Hofman. 1995. Sexual differentiation of the human hypothalamus in relation to gender and sexual orientation. *Trends in Neuroscience* 18(6): 264–70.

Swaab, Dick, Jiang-Ning Zhou, Mariann Fodor, and Michel Hofman. 1997. Sexual differentiation of the human hypothalamus: Differences according to sex, sexual orientation, and transsexuality. In *Sexual orientation: Toward biological understanding*, edited by Lee Ellis and Linda Ebertz. Westport, Conn.: Praeger.

Terry, Jennifer. 2000. "Unnatural acts" in nature: The scientific fascination with queer animals. *GLQ: A Journal of Lesbian and Gay Studies* 6(2): 151–93.

Thain, Michael, and Michael Hickman. 1996. *Dictionary of biology*. Harmondsworth, England: Penguin.

Zita, Jacqueline N. 1998. *Body talk: Philosophical reflections on sex and gender*. New York: Columbia University Press.

PART 7

Borders

Chapter 30

Jasbir K. Puar

QUEER TIMES, QUEER ASSEMBLAGES

Jasbir K. Puar is Professor of Women's and Gender Studies at Rutgers, the State University of New Jersey. Well known in queer studies for her book *Terrorist Assemblages: Homonationalism in Queer Times* (2007), she has also edited special journal issues on queer terrorism, and sexuality and space.

Written as part of Puar's critical response to 9/11 and the U.S. "war on terror," this essay argues for the "queerness," and thus the radical political force, of two figures who seem unlikely queer candidates: the terrorist figure of the suicide bomber, and the terrorist-like figure of the turban-wearing Sikh. Puar argues that both figures should be considered not in identitarian terms, as comprehensible at the intersection of certain forms of race, gender, class, sexuality, and religion, but rather, after Gilles Deleuze and Félix Guattari, as "queer assemblages." Puar's methodology seeks to undermine dominant, normative and nationalist claims of the U.S.'s sexual and racial "exceptionalisms," which underpin its self-representations as a uniquely liberal, progressive democracy. Occupying a space of post-identity, Puar's essay produces a radical version of queer theory whereby the queer assemblages of these terrorist and terrorist-like figures enable the articulation and disruption of intertwined discourses of U.S. sexual liberalism and nationalism.

T**HESE ARE QUEER** times indeed. The war on terror is an assemblage hooked into an array of enduring modernist paradigms (civilizing teleologies, orientalisms, xenophobia, militarization, border anxieties) and postmodernist eruptions (suicide bombers, biometric surveillance strategies, emergent corporealities, counterterrorism gone over-board). With its emphases on bodies, desires, pleasures, tactility, rhythms, echoes, textures, deaths, morbidity, torture, pain, sensation, and punishment, our necropolitical present-future deems it imperative to rearticulate what queer theory and studies of sexuality have to say about the metatheories and the "real-politiks" of Empire, often understood, as Joan Scott observes, as "the real business of politics."[1] Queer times require even queerer modalities of thought, analysis, creativity, and expression in order to elaborate on nationalist, patriotic, and terrorist formations and their intertwined forms of racialized perverse sexualities and gender dysphorias. What about the war on terrorism, and its attendant assemblages of racism, nationalism, patriotism, and terrorism, is already profoundly queer? Through an examination of queerness in various terrorist corporealities, I contend that queernesses proliferate even, or especially, as they remain denied or unacknowledged. I take up these types of inquiries not only to argue that discourses of counterterrorism are intrinsically gendered, raced, sexualized, and nationalized but also to demonstrate the production of normative patriot bodies that cohere against and through queer terrorist corporealities. In the speculative, exploratory endeavor that follows, I foreground three manifestations of this imbrication. One, I examine discourses of queerness where problematic conceptualizations of queer corporealities, especially via Muslim sexualities, are reproduced in the service of discourses of U.S. exceptionalisms. Two, I rearticulate a terrorist body, in this case the suicide bomber, as a queer assemblage that resists queerness-as-sexual-identity (or anti-identity)—in other words, intersectional and identitarian paradigms—in favor of spatial, temporal, and corporeal convergences, implosions, and rearrangements. Queerness as an assemblage moves away from excavation work, deprivileges a binary opposition between queer and not-queer subjects, and, instead of retaining queerness exclusively as dissenting, resistant, and alternative (all of which queerness importantly is and does), it underscores contingency and complicity with dominant formations. Finally, I argue that a focus on queerness as assemblage enables attention to ontology in tandem with epistemology, affect in conjunction with representational economies, within which bodies, such as the turbaned Sikh terrorist, interpenetrate, swirl together, and transmit affects to each other. Through affect and ontology, the turbaned Sikh terrorist in particular, I argue, as a queer assemblage, is reshaping the terrain of South Asian queer diasporas.

Queer narratives of U.S. exceptionalism

As a critique, "queer liberalism" notes an unsettling but not entirely unexpected reconciliation of the radical convictions of queerness as a post-structuralist anti- and transidentity critique with the liberal demands of national subject formation. We can map out a couple of different yet overlapping genealogies of queer liberal subjects. The first is the rise of the queer consumer-citizen, hailed with force in the late 1980s and early 1990s, fueled by the fantasy of enormous disposable incomes for unburdened-by-kinship gays and lesbians. The second genealogy, of the queer liberal subject before the law, culminates with the 2003 decriminalizing of sodomy through *Lawrence and Garner v. Texas*. While both consumptive and juridical lineages reflect heavily on the status of the nation, I argue that one very concise way queer liberalism is inhabited is through stagings of U.S. nationalism via a praxis of sexual othering that unwittingly exceptionalizes the identities of U.S. queernesses vis-à-vis Islamophobic constructions of sexuality in the Middle East. This is not a critique of the racisms and other constitutive exclusions of conservative lesbian, gay, bisexual, transgender, queer, and questioning (LGBTQ) discourses. Rather, I am taking issue with queer theorizing that, despite (and perhaps because of) a commitment to an intersectional analytic, fails to interrogate the epistemological will to knowledge that invariably reproduces the disciplinary interests of the U.S. nation-state. Forms of U.S. sexual exceptionalism from purportedly progressive spaces have historically surfaced through feminist constructions of "third world" women; what we have now, however, is the production of a sexual exceptionalism through normative as well as nonnormative (queer) bodies. That is, queerness is proffered as a sexually exceptional form of American national sexuality through a rhetoric of sexual modernization that is simultaneously able to castigate the other as homophobic *and* perverse, and construct the imperialist center as "tolerant" but sexually, racially, and gendered normal.

Queerness colludes with U.S. exceptionalisms embedded in nationalist foreign policy via the articulation and production of whiteness as a queer norm and the tacit acceptance of U.S. imperialist expansion. For example, national LGBTQ organizations such as the National Gay and Lesbian Task Force (NGLTF) and the Human Rights Commission (HRC) have been far more preoccupied with gay marriage and gays in the military than the war on terrorism or even the "homosexual sex" torture scandal at Abu Ghraib.[2] In fact, Mubarak Dahir suggests that some organizations have actually harnessed the oppression of LGBTQ Arabs to justify the war, and calls on gays and lesbians who support the war in Iraq to "stop using the guise of caring about the plight of gay Arabs to rationalize their support."[3] For Queer Left organizing not to center people of color borders dangerously on eliding a critique of the racist, imperialist war, or conversely reenacting forms of colonial and multiculturalist fetishisms, for example, in relation to queer Filipino war resister Stephen Funk, who has become the poster queer for LGBTQ antiwar sloganeering. Are LGBTQ communities addressing the war on terrorism as a "gay issue"?[4] If so, are they articulating a politics of race, empire, and globalization?

The most explicit production of this queer exceptionalism can be found in numerous instances of the responsive commentary to the Abu Ghraib "sexual torture scandal." The Abu Ghraib saga demonstrates that sexuality is at once absolutely crucial to the production of the geopolitics of American exceptionalism, and despite this critical role, or perhaps because of it, it is an undertheorized, underrated, and often avoided aspect of the debate on the war on terror. Very shortly after the first release of the photos in May 2004, the descriptions of the torture cathected within the specter of "homosexual acts," prompting a flurry of interviews with queer theorists, organizational press releases from LGBTQ associations, and articles within the gay press, all of which, incredibly enough, demonstrated no hesitations about speaking knowledgeably of "Muslim sexuality." In the gay press, the Abu Ghraib photos were hailed as "evidence of rampant homophobia in the armed forces,"[5] with scarce mention of the linked processes of racism and sexism. Even more troubling was the reason given for the particular efficacy of the torture: the taboo, outlawed, banned, disavowed status of homosexuality in Iraq and the Middle East, complemented by an aversion to nudity, male-on-male contact, and sexual modesty with the rarely seen opposite sex. It is exactly this unsophisticated notion of Arab/Muslim/Islamic (does it matter which one?) cultural difference that military intelligence capitalized on to create what they believed to be a culturally specific "effective" matrix of torture techniques. What we have here, then, is the paralleling of the Pentagon's strategies, which used among other materials an anthropology study, *The Arab Mind*, and the discourses that emanate from progressive queers. For example, Faisal Alam, founder and director of the international Muslim lesbian, gay, bisexual, transgender, intersex, queer, and questioning (LGBTIQ) organization Al-Fatiha, states that "sexual humiliation is perhaps the worst form of torture for any Muslim." The press release from Al-Fatiha continues: "Islam places a high emphasis on modesty and sexual privacy. Iraq, much like the rest of the Arab world, places great importance on notions of masculinity. Forcing men to masturbate in front of each other and to mock same-sex acts or homosexual sex, is perverse and sadistic, in the eyes of many Muslims." In another interview Alam reiterates the focus on the violation of proper gender norms, maintaining that the torture is an "affront to their masculinity."[6]

I take issue with Al-Fatiha's statements, as they along with many other statements relied on an orientalist notion of "Muslim sexuality" that foregrounded sexual repression and upheld versions of normative masculinity—that is, the feminized *passivo* positioning is naturalized as humiliating, producing a muscular nationalism of sorts. In displays of solidarity, Al-Fatiha's comments were uncritically embraced by various queer sectors: the Center for Lesbian and Gay Studies newsletter used them to authenticate its perspective through that of the native informant, while the gay press endlessly reproduced the appropriate masculinity and sexual conservatism lines. I want to underscore the complex dance of positionality that Muslim and Arab groups such as Al-Fatiha must perform in these times, whereby a defense of "Muslim sexuality" through the lens of culture is easily co-opted into racist agendas.[7] Given their place at the crossroads of queerness and Arabness, Al-Fatiha was, and still is, under the most duress to authenticate orientalist paradigms of Muslim sexuality, thus reproducing narratives of U.S. sexual exceptionalism. Reinforcing a homogenous notion of Muslim sexual repression vis-à-vis homosexuality and the notion of "modesty" works to resituate the United States, in contrast, as a place free of such sexual constraints. For Al-Fatiha to have elaborated on the issues of Islam and sexuality more complexly would have not only missed the orientalist resonance so eagerly awaited by the mass media—that is, there is almost no way to get media attention unless this resonance is met—it would have also considerably endangered a population already navigating the pernicious racist effects of the Patriot Act: surveillance, deportations, detentions, registrations, preemptive migrations, and departures. Thus Al-Fatiha's performance of a particular allegiance with American sexual exceptionalism is the result of a demand, not a suggestion. The proliferation of diverse U.S. subjects, such as the Muslim American, and their epistemological conditions of existence, are mandates of homeland security.

The point to be argued is not how to qualify the status of homosexuality across the broad historical and geographic, not to mention religious, regional, class, national, and political variances, of the Middle East (a term I hesitate to use, given its area studies implications). We must consider instead how the production of "homosexuality as taboo" is situated within the history of encounter with the Western gaze. The Orient, once conceived in Foucault's *ars erotica* and Said's deconstructive work as the place of original release, unfettered sin, and acts with no attendant identities or consequences, now symbolizes the space of repression *and* perversion, and the site of freedom has been relocated to Western identity. For example, the queer theorist Patrick Moore, author of *Beyond Shame: Reclaiming the Abandoned History of Radical Gay Sex*, opines:

> Because "gay" implies an identity and a culture, in addition to describing a sexual act, it is difficult for a gay man in the West to completely understand the level of disgrace endured by the Iraqi prisoners. But in the Arab world, the humiliating techniques now on display are particularly effective because of Islam's troubled relationship with homosexuality. This is not to say that sex between men does not occur in Islamic society—the shame lies in the gay identity rather than the act itself. As long as a man does not accept the supposedly female (passive) role in sex with another man, there is no shame in the behavior. Reports indicate that the prisoners were not only physically abused but also accused of actually being homosexuals, which is a far greater degradation to them.[8]

The act to identity telos spun out by Moore delineates the West as the space of identity (disregarding the confusion of act–identity relations at the heart of U.S. homosexualities), while the Arab world is relegated, apparently because of "Islam's troubled relationship to homosexuality," to the backward realm of acts. The presence of gay- and lesbian-identified Muslims in the "Arab world" is inconceivable. Given the lack of any evidence that being called a homosexual is much more degrading than being tortured, Moore's rationalization reads as an orientalist projection that conveys much more about the constraints and imaginaries of identity in the "West" than anything else. Furthermore, in the uncritical face-value acceptance of the notion of Islamic sexual repression, we see the trenchant replay of what Foucault termed the "repressive hypothesis": the notion that a lack of discussion or openness about sexuality reflects a repressive, censorship-driven apparatus of deflated sexual desire.[9] While in Said's *Orientalism* the illicit sex found in the Orient was sought out in order to liberate the Occident from its own performance of the repressive hypothesis, in the case of Abu Ghraib, conversely, it is the repression of the Arab prisoners that is highlighted in order to efface the rampant hypersexual excesses of the U.S. prison guards.

Given the unbridled homophobia, racism, and misogyny demonstrated by the U.S. guards, it is indeed ironic, yet predictable, that the United States nonetheless emerges exceptionally, as more tolerant of homosexuality (and less tainted by misogyny and fundamentalism) than the repressed, modest, nudity-shy "Middle East." We have a clear view of the performative privileges of Foucault's "speaker's benefit": those who are able to articulate sexual knowledge (especially of oneself, but in this case, also of others) then appear to be freed, through the act of speech, from the space of repression.[10] Through the insistent and frantic manufacturing of "homosexuality" and "Muslim" as mutually exclusive discrete categories, queerness colludes with the delineation of exceptional U.S. sexual norms, produced against the intolerable forms of the sexualities of "terrorist" bodies. Furthermore, queer exceptionalism works to suture U.S. nationalism through the perpetual fissuring of race from sexuality—the race of the (presumptively sexually repressed, perverse, or both) terrorist and the sexuality of the national (presumptively white, gender normative) queer: the two dare not converge.

Terrorist corporealities

José Esteban Muñoz's writing on the "terrorist drag" of the Los Angeles-based performance artist Vaginal Davis harks back to another political era—bizarrely as if it were long ago, although in measured time we are talking about the mid-1990s—when the notion of the terrorist had a trenchant but distant quality to it.[11] Muñoz argues that Davis's drag performance, encompassing "cross-sex, cross-race minstrelsy," is terrorist on two levels. Aesthetically, Davis rejects glamour-girl feminine drag in favor of "ground level guerrilla representational strategies" such as white supremacist militiamen and black welfare queen hookers, what Muñoz calls "the nation's most dangerous citizens." This alludes to the second plane of meaning, the reenactment of the "nation's internal terrors around race, gender, and sexuality." It is imperative in a post-9/11 climate of counterterrorism to note that guerrillas and terrorists have vastly different racial valences, the former bringing to mind the phantasmic landscapes of Central and South America, while the latter, the enduring legacy of orientalist imaginaries. In the context of these geographies it is notable that Davis as the white militiaman astutely brings terrorism home—to Oklahoma City, in fact—and in doing so dislodges, at least momentarily, this orientalist legacy.

Muñoz's description of this terrorist drag points to the historical convergences between queers and terror—homosexuals have been the traitors to the nation, figures of espionage and double agents, associated with Communists during the McCarthy era, and, as with suicide bombers, bring on and desire death (both are figured as always already dying, although for homosexuals it is through the AIDS pandemic). More recent exhortations place gay marriage as "the worst form of terrorism" and gay couples as "domestic terrorists."[12] Clearly, one can already ask, what is terrorist about the queer? But the more salient and urgent question is what is queer about the terrorist? And what is queer about terrorist corporealities? The depictions of masculinity most rapidly disseminated and globalized through the war on terrorism are terrorist masculinities: failed and perverse, these emasculated bodies always have femininity as their reference point of malfunction and are metonymically tied to all sorts of pathologies of the mind and body—homosexuality, incest, pedophilia, madness, and disease. We see, for example, the queer physicality of terrorist monsters haunting the U.S. State Department counterterrorism Web site.[13] With the unfurling, viruslike, explosive mass of the terrorist network, tentacles ever regenerating despite efforts to truncate them, the terrorist is concurrently an unfathomable, unknowable, and hysterical monstrosity, and yet one that only the exceptional capacities of U.S. intelligence and security systems can quell. This unknowable monstrosity is not a casual bystander or parasite; the nation assimilates this effusive discomfort with the unknowability of these bodies, thus effectively producing new normativities and exceptionalisms through the cataloging of unknowables. It is not, then, that we must engage in the practice of excavating the queer terrorist or queering the terrorist; rather, queerness is always already installed in the project of naming the terrorist; the terrorist does not appear as such without the concurrent entrance of perversion, deviance, deformity. The strategy of encouraging subjects of study to appear in all their queernesses, rather than primarily to queer the subjects of study, provides a subject-driven temporality in tandem with a method-driven temporality. Playing on this difference, between the subject being queered versus queerness already existing within the subject (and thus dissipating the subject as such) allows for both the temporality of being and the temporality of always becoming.

As there is no entity, no identity to queer, rather queerness coming forth at us from all directions, screaming its defiance, suggests to me a move from intersectionality to assemblage. The Deleuzian assemblage, as a series of dispersed but mutually implicated networks, draws together enunciation and dissolution, causality and effect. As opposed to an intersectional model of identity, which presumes components—race, class, gender, sexuality, nation, age, religion—are separable analytics and can be thus disassembled, an assemblage is more attuned to interwoven forces that merge and dissipate time, space, and body against linearity, coherency, and permanency. Intersectionality demands the knowing, naming, and thus stabilizing of identity across space and time, generating narratives of progress that deny the fictive and performative of identification: you become an identity, yes, but also timelessness works to consolidate the fiction of a seamless stable identity in every space. As a tool of diversity management, and a mantra of liberal multiculturalism, intersectionality colludes with the disciplinary apparatus of the state—census, demography, racial profiling, surveillance—in that "difference" is encased within a structural container that simply wishes the messiness of identity into a formulaic grid. Displacing queerness as an identity or modality that is visibly, audibly, legibly, or tangibly evident, assemblages allow us to attune to intensities, emotions, energies, affectivities, textures as they inhabit events, spatiality, and corporealities. Intersectionality privileges naming, visuality, epistemology, representation, and meaning, while assemblage underscores feeling, tactility, ontology, affect, and information. Most important, given the heightened death-machine aspect of nationalism in our contemporary political terrain—a heightened sensorial and anatomical domination described by Achille Mbembe as "necropolitics"—assemblages work against narratives of U.S. exceptionalism that secure empire, challenging the fixity of racial and sexual taxonomies that inform practices of state surveillance and control, and befuddling the "us versus them" of the war on terror. For while intersectionality and its underpinnings—an unrelenting epistemological will to truth—presupposes identity and thus disavows futurity, assemblage, in its debt to ontology and its espousal of what cannot be known, seen, or heard, or has yet to be known, seen, or heard, allows for becoming/s beyond being/s.[14]

Queer assemblages appear in Mbembe's devastating and brilliant meditation on the necropolitics of our current infinite war positioning. Mbembe argues for a shift from biopower to necropolitics (the subjugation of life to the power of death), noting that the historical basis of sovereignty that is reliant on a notion of (Western) political rationality begs for a more accurate framing: that of life and death.[15] He asks, "What place is given to life, death, and the human body (especially the wounded or slain body)?" Mbembe attends to the informational productivity of the (Palestinian) suicide bomber. In pondering the queer modalities of this kind of terrorist, one notes a pastiche of oddities: a body machined together through metal and flesh, an assemblage of the organic and the inorganic; a death not of the self or of the other, but both simultaneously; self-annihilation as the ultimate form of resistance and self-preservation. This body forces a reconciliation of opposites through their inevitable collapse—a perverse habitation of contradiction. As a figure in the midst of always already dying even as it is in the midst of becoming, like the homosexual afflicted with HIV, the suicide bomber sutures his or her status as sexually perverse.[16] Mbembe also points to the queer becomings of a suicide bomber—a corporeal experiential of "ballistics." The dynamite strapped onto the body of a suicide bomber is not merely an appendage; the "intimacy" of weapon with body reorients the assumed spatial integrity (coherence and concreteness) and individuality of the body that is the mandate of intersectional identities: instead we have the body-weapon. The ontological affect of the body renders it a newly becoming body, queerly:

> The candidate for martyrdom transforms his or her body into a mask that hides
> the soon-to-be-detonated weapon. Unlike the tank or the missile that is clearly
> visible, the weapon carried in the shape of the body is invisible. Thus concealed,
> it forms part of the body. It is so intimately part of the body that at the time of
> its detonation it annihilates the body of its bearer, who carries with it the bodies
> of others when it does not reduce them to pieces. The body does not simply
> conceal a weapon. The body is transformed into a weapon, not in a metaphorical
> sense but in a truly ballistic sense.[17]

Temporal narratives of progression are upturned as death and becoming fuse into one: as one's body dies, one's body becomes the mask, the weapon, the suicide bomber, not before. Not only does the ballistic body come into being without the aid of visual cues marking its transformation, it also "carries with it the bodies of others." Its own penetrative energy sends shards of metal and torn flesh spinning off into the ether. The body-weapon does not play as metaphor, or in the realm of meaning and epistemology, but rather forces us ontologically anew to ask: what kinds of information does the ballistic body impart? These bodies, being in the midst of becoming, blur the insides and the outsides, infecting transformation through sensation, echoing knowledge via reverberation and vibration. The echo is a queer temporality; in the relay of affective information between and amid beings, the sequence of reflection, repetition, resound, and return (but with a difference, as in mimicry), and brings forth waves of the future breaking into the present. Gayatri Spivak, prescient in drawing our attention to the multivalent textuality of suicide in "Can the Subaltern Speak?" reminds us in her latest ruminations that suicide terrorism, as a relay of affective information, is a modality of expression and communication for the subaltern:

> Suicidal resistance is a message inscribed on the body when no other means will
> get through. It is both execution and mourning, for both self and other. For you
> die with me for the same cause, no matter which side you are on. Because no
> matter who you are, there are no designated killees in suicide bombing. No matter
> what side you are on, because I cannot talk to you, you won't respond to me, with
> the implication that there is no dishonor in such shared and innocent death.[18]

We have the proposal that there are no sides, and that the sides are forever shifting, crumpling, and multiplying, disappearing and reappearing—unable to satisfactorily delineate between here and there. The spatial collapse of sides is due to the queer temporal interruption of the suicide bomber, projectiles spewing every which way. As a queer assemblage—distinct from the "queering" of an entity or identity—race and sexuality are denaturalized through the impermanence, the transience of the suicide bomber; the fleeting identity replayed backward through its dissolution. This dissolution of self into other/s and other/s into self not only effaces the absolute mark of self and other/s in the war on terror, it produces a systemic challenge to the entire order of Manichaean rationality that organizes the rubric of good versus evil. Delivering "a message inscribed on the body when no other means will get through," suicide bombers do not transcend or claim the rational or accept the demarcation of the irrational. Rather, they foreground the flawed temporal, spatial, and ontological presumptions on which such distinctions flourish.

The body of Mbembe's suicide bomber is still, however, a male one and, in that universalized masculinity, ontologically pure regardless of location, history, and context. Whereas, for Mbembe, sexuality—as the dissolution of bodily boundaries—is elaborated through the ballistic event of death, for female suicide bombers, sexuality is always announced in advance: the petite manicured hands, mystical beauty ("beauty mixed with violence"), and features of her face and body are commented on in a manner not requisite for male suicide bombers; the political import of the female suicide bomber's actions are gendered out or into delusions about her purported irrational emotional and mental distress.[19] Female suicide bombers disrupt the prosaic proposition that terrorism is bred directly of patriarchy and that women are intrinsically manifesting peace. This rationale is reinscribed, however, when observers proclaim that women cast out of or shunned by traditional compositions of gender and sexuality (often accused of being lesbians) are most likely predisposed toward violence. These discursive and bodily identity markers reflect the enduring capacities of intersectionality—we cannot leave it completely behind—but also its limitations.

Mbembe and Spivak each articulate, implicitly, how queerness is constitutive of the suicide bomber: delinked from sexual identity to signal instead temporal, spatial, and corporeal schisms, queerness is installed within as a prerequisite for the body to function symbolically, pedagogically, and performatively as it does. The dispersion of the boundaries of bodies forces a completely chaotic challenge to normative conventions of gender, sexuality, and race, disobeying normative conventions of "appropriate" bodily practices and the sanctity of the able body. Here then is a possible rereading of these terrorist bodies, typically understood as culturally, ethnically, and religiously nationalist, fundamentalist, patriarchal, and, often even homophobic, as queer corporealities. The political import of this queer rereading should not be underestimated: in the upheaval of the "with us or against us" rhetoric of the war on terror, queer praxis of assemblage allows for a scrambling of sides that is illegible to state practices of surveillance, control, banishment, and extermination. These nonexceptional, terrorist bodies are nonheteronormative, if we consider nation and citizenship to be implicit in the privilege of heteronormativity, as we should. Following from Cathy Cohen's argument that heteronormativity is as much about (white) racial and (middle-to upper-) class privilege as it is about sexual identities, identifications, and acts,[20] the (American imperialist) nation also figures as an important axis of psychic and material identification, repeatedly casting these bodies into the spotlight of sexual perversity. Through the reclamation of the nation's perverse beings across homo–hetero divides, the tenor of queerness is intrinsically antinationalist. In attending to affective corporeal queernesses, ones that foreground normativizing and resistant bodily practices beyond sex, gender, and sexual object choice, queerness is expanded as a field, a vector, a terrain, one that must consistently, not sporadically, account for nationalism and race within its purview, as well as insistently disentangle the relations between queer representation and queer affectivity. What does this rereading and rearticulation do to Cohen's already expansive notion of queer coalitional politics? What types of affiliative networks could be imagined and spawned if we embrace the already queer mechanics and assemblages—threats to nation, to race, to sanctioned bodily practices—of terrorist bodies?

Affective queerness

These bodies are old, no doubt, but their queernesses are suggested by the intense anxieties they provoke; they trouble the nation's perimeters, from within and also from the outside, and appear to be rife with, as well as generative of, fear and danger. Why, in the name of a secular state, ban the use of head scarves for Muslim women in France, with allusions to the next targets: turbans and beards?[21] What kinds of monstrous bodies are visualized when daily the papers are plastered with turbaned al-Qaeda operatives? Why scream, "Take that turban off, you fucking terrorist"?[22] What is lost, gained, and retained in the act of shaving Saddam Hussein's beard off just hours after his purported capture? (See also the picture "Saddam's Queer Eye Makeover" and "Queer Eye for Saddam," aka "Queer Eye for the Hopeless Guy."[23]) Who is appeased through the motions of shaving the facial and head hair of prisoners before they are taken to Guantánamo Bay? These bodies are not only being commanded to the restoration of the properly visible. (The name of the detention site, Camp X-Ray, suggests in itself a profound yearning for the transparency of these bodies, the capacity to see through them and render them known, taciturn, disembodied.) In the act of removing Hussein's battered, overgrown beard, Hussein's monstrosity is renewed. We do not recognize in him the decrepit, worn, tired man found in a hole, a man whose capture has more symbolic than material utility and entails the erasure of decades of U.S. imperialist violence in the "Middle East." But do not look too closely at his eyes, for his familiarity may be lost. And it is the reterritorialization of the body that must be performed through the ritual of cutting and shaving hair, the prodding medical examinations, the prayer quarters proximate to arrows pointing to Mecca, and other forms of apparently "humane" incarceration tactics that supplement those of torture. The "detained body" is thus a machination of ceremonial scrutiny and sheer domination.

Terrorist look-alike bodies may allude to the illegible and incommensurable affect of queerness—bodies that are in some sense machined together, remarkable beyond identity, visuality, and visibility, to the realms of affect and ontology, the tactile and the sensorial. Brian Massumi concisely pinpoints the effect of affect: "The primacy of the affective is marked by a gap between content and effect: it would appear that the strength or duration of an image's effect is not logically connected to the content in any straightforward way. This is not to say there is no connection and no logic."[24] Beyond what the body looks like, then, this is also about what the queer body feels like, for the embodied and for the spectator. Reworking Michael Taussig's notion of "tactile knowing,"[25] May Joseph eloquently asserts,

> For cultures whose forms of social knowledge have been fragmented and mutated by multiple experiences of conquest and cultural contact . . . tactile practices are difficult to read and contain multiple meanings. Such exchanges are frequently informal events intrinsic to everyday life through which cultural knowledge gets cited, transmitted or re-appropriated. The senses acquire texture.[26]

As that which "immerses the senses beyond the structuring logic of vision and dislodges memory as the fascia of history,"[27] tactile knowledges install normativizing traces of danger, fear, and melancholia into the bodies of racialized terrorist look-alikes. The turban, for example, is not merely an appendage to the body. It is always in the state of becoming, the becoming of a turbaned body, the turban becoming part of the body. The head scarf, similarly (along with the burka and the hijab, often decried as masks), has become a perverse fetish object—a point of fixation—a kind of centripetal force, a strange attractor through which the density of anxiety accrues and accumulates. For the wearer, the rituals and sensations attached to these parts of the body—the smells during the weekly starching of the linens, the stretching of yards of coarse fabric to induce some softening, the wrapping and pinning of the turban into place—these are experiences in the midst of becoming qualitatively different than before.

Through queerly affective and tactile realms, the Sikh *pagri*, or turban, is acquiring the inscriptions of a (terrorist) masculinity, much in the way that veiling has been read as indicative of an other femininity. The turbaned man, no longer merely the mark of a durable and misguided tradition, a resistant antiassimilationist (albeit patriarchal) stance, now inhabits the space and history of monstrosity, that which can never become civilized. The turban is not only imbued with the nationalist, religious, and cultural symbolics of the other. The turban both reveals and hides the terrorist. Despite the taxonomies of turbans, their specific regional and locational genealogies, their placement in time and space, their singularity and their multiplicity, the turban as monolith profoundly troubles and disturbs the nation and its notions of security. Since 9/11, Sikh men wearing turbans, and mistaken for kin of Osama bin Laden, have been disproportionately affected by backlash racist hate crimes targeting Muslims and other South Asians. As a sign of guilt and also the potential redemption of that guilt, the elusive, dubious character of the turbaned man or woman could drive the onlooker crazy. It is not for nothing that in one hate crime incident after another, turbans are clawed at viciously, and hair is pulled, occasionally even cut off. The intimacy of such violence cannot be overstated. The attack functions as a double emasculation: the disrobing is an insult to the (usually) male representative (Sikh or Muslim) of the community, while the removal of hair entails submission by and to normative patriotic masculinities. The turban insinuates the constant sliding between that which can be disciplined and that which must be outlawed. Sometimes death ensues.

In relation to Sikhs, misnamed "Hindoo" during the first migrations of Sikhs to the Northwest and California in the early 1900s and now mistaken as Muslim, the hypothesis of mistaken identity as the main causal factor for post-9/11 hate crimes has been embraced by conservative and progressive factions alike. The Bush administration and progressive Sikh advocacy groups have promoted education as the primary vehicle through which to ameliorate this situation. The notion of mistaken identity relies on multiple premises: that the viewer is open to and willing to discern the visual differences between Sikh turbans and Muslim turbans; that the ideals of multiculturalism as promulgated by liberal education acknowledge that differences within difference matter. The focus on mistaken identity favors the visual experience of the turban over its affective experience, one that hails historical formations of orientalism and elicits fear, loathing, and disgust. Tactile economies reassert ontological rather than epistemological knowing and highlight touch, texture, sensation, smell, feeling, and affect over what is assumed to be legible through the visible. Furthermore, the turban wearer, usually male, bears the typically female burden of safeguarding and transmitting culture and of symbolizing the purity of nation. But this does not automatically or only feminize him; instead, the fusion of hair, oil, cloth, skin, the organic with the nonorganic, renders the turban a queer part of the body. It is this assemblage of visuality, affect, feminized position, and bodily nonorganicity that accounts for its queer figuration in the execution of a hate crime.

This queer assemblage of the turbaned terrorist speaks to the prolific fertilization and crosshatching of terrorist corporealities amid queer South Asian diasporas, bodies that must be reclaimed as queer. South Asian queer diasporas may mimic forms of (U.S.) model minority exceptionalism that posit queerness as an exemplary or libratory site devoid of nationalist impulses, an exceptionalism that narrates queerness as emulating the highest transgressive potential of diaspora. But the tensions—and overlaps—between the now-fetishized desi drag queen and the turbaned or otherwise Sikh or Muslim terrorist temper this exceptionalism. Brian Keith Axel, in his ground-clearing essay "The Diasporic Imaginary," poses two radical modifications to the study of diaspora as it has been conceived in anthropology, cultural studies, and interdisciplinary forums. Referencing his study of Sikh diasporas, he argues that "rather than conceiving of the homeland as something that creates the diaspora, it may be more productive to consider the diaspora as something that creates the homeland."[28] Axel is gesturing beyond the material locational pragmatics of the myth of return, the economic and symbolic importance of the NRI (nonresident Indian), Khalistan and Hindutva nationalist movements funded by diasporic money, or the modalities of homeland that are re-created in the diaspora. The homeland, he proposes, "must be understood as an affective and temporal process rather than a place."[29] But if not the fact of place, what impels a diasporic sensibility or collectivity?

In situating "different bodies or corporeal images and historical formations of sexuality, gender and violence" as deeply and equally constitutive of the diasporic imaginary as the place of the homeland, Axel's formulation can be productively reworked to further queer the habitus of nation and its geographic coordinates. The notion of queer diaspora retools diaspora to account for connectivity beyond or different from sharing a common ancestral homeland.[30] That is, to shift away from origin for a moment allows other forms of diasporic affiliative and cathartic entities, for Axel (and also Mbembe) primarily that of bodies and the traumas that haunt them, to show their affiliative powers. Furthermore, an unsettling of the site of origin, that is, nation as one of the two binding terms of diaspora, de facto punctures the homeland-to-diaspora telos and wrenches ancestral progression out of the automatic purview of diaspora, allowing for queer narratives of kinship, belonging, and home. The sensation of place is thus one of manifold intensities cathected through distance. The diaspora, then, for Axel, is not represented only as a demographic, a geographic place, or primarily through history, memory, or even trauma. It is cohered through sensation, vibrations, echoes, speed, feedback loops, and recursive folds and feelings, coalescing through corporealities, affectivities, and, I would add, multiple and contingent temporalities: not through an identity but an assemblage.

The corporeal images in question for Axel are the tortured bodies, not unlike those of Abu Ghraib, of Sikh male Amritdharies, those caught in civil unrest in Punjab in the mid-1980s to early 1990s and arbitrarily incarcerated by the Indian government. Again we have the appearance of the turbaned Sikh male. Axel details the mechanics of the torture:

> Often the first act is to cast off the detainee's turban. . . . For many victims, the displacement of the turban, along with the use of the hair to tie the victim down, is one of the deepest gestures of dishonor (beizatti). But after surrender and dishonor are enacted on the head, focus shifts to the genitals and anus, which become the objects of taunts and violation.[31]

Collectively, the turban, genitals, and anus take on the force of the phallus: the sexual shaming begins with the nakedness of the head and use of the otherwise pride-engendering hair to subjugate, then continues on to the habitual objects of sex. In particular, torture of the anus seeks to simulate anal sex and, thus, arouse the specter of homosexuality. The turbaned male body, now the tortured deturbaned body, is effectively rendered religiously impotent and unable to repeat its threat to national boundaries:

National-normative sexuality provides the sanctioned heterosexual means for reproducing the nation's community, whereas antinational sexuality interrupts and threatens that community. Torture casts national-normative sexuality as a fundamental modality of citizen production in relation to an antinational sexuality that postulates sex as a "cause" of not only sexual experience but also of subversive behavior and extraterritorial desire ("now you can't be married, you can't produce any more terrorists").[32]

Sexual violence, not place, is the dominant constitutive factor of Axel's diasporic imaginary. This violence is performative in that queerness of the body is confirmed on several fronts: first, there is the queer inversion of reproductive capacity to the male terrorist body, away from the normative focus on women as reproducers of nation and culture; second, the body is symbolically stripped of its reproductive capacities, propelled into the queer realm of an antinational sexuality; temporality is re-planed because the assumption of normative familial kinship forms as engendered by generational continuity is ruptured. But, third, in line with the queer figuration of the turbaned Sikh body, this body already appears as queer, and thus the torture performs, in the citational sense, the very queer assemblage that instantiates it. The assemblage is possible not through the identity markers that encapsulate this body— Sikh, male, turbaned, heterosexual but perverse—but, rather, the temporal and spatial reorderings that the body reiterates as it is tortured. There is the doubling of time and space as the body is simultaneously refashioned for normative (Indian) national aesthetics yet cast from the nation as its reproductive capacity is castrated. Spatially situated both within and outside nation, temporally always becoming both national and its antithesis, the assemblage is momentary, fleeting even, and gives way to normative identity markers even in the midst of its newly becoming state.

It is this shift from national and regional origin to corporeal affectivity—from South Asia as unifying homeland to the assemblage of the monster-terrorist-fag[33]—in South Asia and in the diasporas, as they work together, that dislodges identity-based notions of queerness, thus problematizing queer diasporic exceptionalisms but also motivating their exponential fortification and proliferation in the first place. Queer occupation of the turbaned Sikh male and other terrorist assemblages not only counters sexual exceptionalisms by reclaiming perversion—the nonexceptional—within the gaze of national security. In the comingling of queer monstrosity and queer modernity, it also creatively, powerfully, and unexpectedly scrambles the terrain of the political within organizing and intellectual projects. These terrorist assemblages, a cacophony of informational flows, energetic intensities, bodies, and practices that undermine coherent identity and even queer anti-identity narratives, bypass entirely the Foucauldian "act to identity" continuum that informs much global LGBTIQ organizing, a continuum that privileges the pole of identity as the evolved form of Western modernity. Yet reclaiming the nonexceptional is only partially the point, for assemblages allow for complicities of privilege and the production of new normativities even as they cannot anticipate spaces and moments of resistance. Opening up to the fantastical wonders of futurity is the most powerful of political and critical strategies, whether it be through assemblage or to something as yet unknown, perhaps even forever unknowable.

Notes

Many thanks to Patricia Clough for her inspirational thinking on affect and assemblages, to Julie Rajan for her research assistance, and to Amit Rai, Katherine Sugg, David Eng, and Kelly Coogan for their feedback on earlier drafts. In memory of my brother, Sandeep.

1   Joan Scott, "Gender: A Useful Category of Historical Analysis," in *Gender and the Politics of History* (New York: Columbia University Press, 1988), 28–52.

2   In an article titled "Highlighting the Q in Iraq" ("Letters from Camp Rehoboth," 18 October 2002, www.camprehoboth.com/issue0_18_02/capitalletters.htm), Hastings Wyman argues that "for gay groups such as HRC, NGLTF, and others to take a position on a major issue that affects gay people no differently from the rest of society ultimately divides our community, dilutes our resources, and risks undermining our standing with the public."

3   Mubarak Dahir, "Stop Using Gay 'Liberation' as a War Guise," *Windy City Times*, 23 April 2003. Noting that the "forces that are supposedly emancipating our downtrodden GLBT brethren are themselves hyper-homophobic," Dahir asks, "How can anyone seriously argue that the United States military is an instrument for glbt liberation?" According to Dahir, "gay hawks" have pointed out the oppressiveness toward homosexuality of regimes in Syria and Iraq while conveniently forgetting those in Saudi Arabia and Egypt. Claiming that the lives of gays and lesbians in Iraq will change very little regardless of the ousting of Hussein, Dahir writes: "The final and perhaps most personally infuriating aspect of the hypocrisy around the argument that we are invading foreign countries in the interest of freeing gay people is the way we treat gay Arabs and gay Muslims here in the United States."

4   On gay issue versus not-gay issue organizing, see Michael Bronski, "Gay Goes Mainstream," *Boston Phoenix*, 16–23 January 2003, www.bostonphoenix.com/boston/news_features/other_stories/documents/02653048.htm.

5   Joe Crea, "Gay Sex Used to Humiliate Iraqis," *Washington Blade*, 7 May 2004.

6   Ibid.

7   Andrew Sullivan, "Daily Dish," www.andrewsullivan.com (accessed 4 May 2004).

8   Patrick Moore, "Gay Sexuality," *Newsday*, 7 May 2004.

9   In the face of the centrality of Foucault's *History of Sexuality* to the field of queer studies, it is somewhat baffling that some queer theorists have accepted at face value the discourse of Islamic sexual repression. That is not to imply that Foucault's work should be transparently applied to other cultural and historical contexts, especially as he himself perpetuates a pernicious form of orientalism in his formulation of the *ars erotica*. Rather, Foucault's insights deserve evaluation as a methodological hypothesis about discourse.

10 But are the acts specifically and only referential of gay sex (and here, gay means sex between men)? Certainly this rendition evades a conversation about what exactly constitutes the distinction between gay sex and straight sex, and also presumes some static normativity about gender roles as well. Amnesty International is among the few that did not mention homosexuality, homosexual acts, or same-sex sexuality in its press release condemning the torture. See "USA: Pattern of Brutality and Cruelty—War Crimes at Abu Ghraib," web.amnesty.org/library/index/ENGAMR510772004.

11 José Esteban Muñoz, *Disidentifications: Queers of Color and the Performance of Politics* (Minneapolis: University of Minnesota Press, 1999), 108.

12 "Bauer Compares Vermont Gay Rights Decision to Terrorism," 27 December 1999, www.cnn.com/1999/ALLPOLITICS/storeis/12/27/campaign.wrap[??1009]/Concerned   Women   of America (accessed 2 April 2003; this site is no longer available).

13 See usinfo.state.gov/topical/pol/terror/. For a detailed analysis of this Web site, see Jasbir K. Puar and Amit S. Rai, "The Remaking of a Model Minority: Perverse Projectiles under the Spectre of (Counter)Terrorism" *Social Text*, no. 80 (2004): 75–104.

14 This is not to disavow or minimize the important interventions that intersectional theorizing makes possible and continues to stage, or the feminist critical spaces that gave rise to intersectional analyses.

15 Achille Mbembe, "Necropolitics," *Public Culture* 15 (2003): 11–40.

16 Judith Butler, in "Sexual Inversions," writes: "The male homosexual is figured time and time again as one whose desire is somehow structured by death, either as the desire to die, or as one whose desire is inherently punishable by death" (Butler, "Sexual Inversions," in *Discourses of Sexuality: From Aristotle to AIDS*, ed. Donna Stanon [Ann Arbor: University of Michigan Press, 1992], 83).

17 Mbembe, "Necropolitics," 36.

18 Gayatri Spivak, "Class and Culture in Diaspora" (conference keynote address, "Translating Class, Altering Hospitality," Leeds University, England, June 2002).

19 Sudha Ramachandran, "Women Suicide Bombers Defy Israel," *Asia Times*, 25 October 2003, www.atimes.com/atimes/Middle_East/EJ25Ak02.html; www.guardian.co.uk/israel/Story/0,2763,428563,00.html.

20 Cathy J. Cohen, "Punks, Bulldaggers, and Welfare Queens: The Radical Potential of Queer Politics?" *GLQ* 3 (1997): 437–65.

21 *Times of India*, 23 January 2004.

22   From *Targeting the Turban: Sikh Americans and the Aversion Spiral after September 11* (2002), a documentary about hate crimes against Sikh Americans since 9/11, directed by Valarie Kaur Brar.

23   See politicalhumor.about.com/library/images/blsaddamqueereye.htm.

24   Brian Massurmi, *Parables for the Virtual: Movement, Affect, Sensation* (Durham, NC: Duke University Press, 2002), 24.

25   Michael Taussig, *Mimesis and Alterity* (New York: Routledge, 1993).

26   May Joseph, "Old Routes, Mnemonic Traces," *UTS Review* 6, no. 2 (2000): 46.

27   Ibid.

28   Brian Keith Axel, "The Diasporic Imaginary," *Public Culture* 14 (2002): 426.

29   Ibid.

30   Ibid.

31   Ibid., 420.

32   Cynthia Keppley Mahmood, *Fighting for Faith and Nation: Dialogues With Sikh Militants* (Philadelphia: University of Pennsylvania Press, 1996), 40, quoted in Axel, "The Diasporic Imaginary," 420.

33   See Jasbir K. Puar and Amit Rai, "Monster-Terrorist-Fag: The War on Terrorism and the Production of Docile Patriots," *Social Text*, no. 72 (2002): 117–48.

Chapter 31

Martin F. Manalansan IV

QUEER INTERSECTIONS: SEXUALITY AND GENDER IN MIGRATION STUDIES

Martin F. Manalansan IV is Associate Professor of Anthropology and Asian American Studies at the University of Illinois at Urbana-Champaign. Trained in social anthropology, Manalansan has been writing on the Filipino gay experience in the U.S. since the early 1990s. He is the author of *Global Divas: Filipino Gay Men in the Diaspora* (2003).

"Queer Intersections" offers a challenge to migration studies and its rubrics of gender and sexuality, calling for a transformation in its critical frameworks and research agendas. Manalansan deploys a multifaceted queer perspective, defining sexuality as a normative institution while also foregrounding queer as a marginal social category. He argues that in gender-focused migration research, sexuality is inadequately conceptualized, not only confined to reproductive sex, abstinence, abuse, and rape, but also sustaining normatively gendered understandings of domesticity and affect. In part a critique of the inadequacy of gender in analyzing sexuality, Manalansan's essay also insists that a queer perspective on sexuality can complicate the operation of gender in different contexts. Through a case study on Filipino domestic workers, Manalansan demonstrates how a queer perspective can expand the field of migrant research beyond labor to include desires and pleasures as part of the more contradictory and complex terrain of migrant experience.

Introduction

SEXUALITY HAS TRAVERSED a circuitous historical route as a topic for social research in general and as a unit of analysis in migration studies in particular. While gender has been stereotypically rendered as female in many works, until very recently sexuality has almost always been relegated to and equated with the realms of heterosexual reproduction and family life. Additionally, sexuality has been submerged under or closeted within concepts and rubrics like gender roles, morals, deviance, and pathology.

Recent works on sexuality and migration, particularly those that document queer sexualities, have emphasized not only the viability and importance of sexuality as an object of study, but also pointed to its constitutive role in the formation and definitions of citizenship and nation. In other words, sexuality, specifically as it is understood in queer studies[1] terms not only expands the meaning of migration but also alters our understanding of gender and challenges migration studies' reliance on heteronormative meanings, institutions, and practices (Luibhéid, 2004). This essay investigates how a queer perspective on sexuality can enrich gender and migration research by unraveling underexamined assumptions about kinship, marriage, desires, and social roles.

By "queer" I do not mean merely adding homosexual identities and practices to the mix. Rather, I am positing a political and theoretical perspective that suggests that sexuality is disciplined by social institutions and practices that normalize and naturalize heterosexuality and heterosexual practices including marriage, family, and biological reproduction by marginalizing persons, institutions, or practices that deviate from these norms. Queer scholars argue that all social discourses—including some scholarly works by politically progressive feminists—more often privilege, if not exclusively promote, heteronormative ideas, practices, and institutions. One of the tasks then for queer studies scholars is to expose these privileging and normalizing tendencies in institutions and texts. In this spirit, this paper attempts to delineate the theoretical, methodological, and conceptual slippages and underlying assumptions that permeate recent works in gender and migration studies. The aim is not to diminish their contributions, but rather to highlight alternative frameworks of analysis and to demonstrate the contested boundaries between gender and sexuality.

I also use "queer" both as an anti-normative signifier as well as a social category produced through the "intersectionality" of identities, practices, and institutions. Political theorist Cathy Cohen, echoing feminists of the seventies and eighties, underscores the interconnections between the predicaments of marginalized figures such as the welfare queen and the lesbian bulldyke and advocates for a "broadened understanding of queerness . . . based on an intersectional analysis that recognizes how numerous systems of oppression interact to regulate . . . the lives of most people" (1997:441; see also Harper et al., 1997).

Following this logic, I would argue that sexuality and sexual identities, practices, and desires may be pivotal factors for migration. Hector Carillo (2004:58) suggests that sexuality, broadly conceived, can be the indirect or direct motivation for international relocation and movement. Carillo (2004) calls this concept "sexual migration." He proposes that "sexual migration," far from a normalizing process where migrants move for the purposes of biological and heterosexual reproduction, suggests that transnational movements enable queer practices, identities, and subjectivities.

This paper examines the various ways in which a queer perspective on sexuality can positively influence gender and migration studies. The first section of the essay will briefly trace the historical antecedents of the study of sexuality in gender and migration research. While neither an exhaustive chronological examination nor broad-ranging literature review, the next couple of sections will highlight scholarly themes in the research that articulate with specific historical moments. The study of sexuality in migration emerged in the past ten to fifteen years due to numerous intellectual, political, and historical conditions, specifically the rise of the AIDS pandemic and the emergence of intellectual currents in feminism, race/ethnic studies, and LGBTQ (lesbian, gay, bisexual, transgender, and queer) studies.

The following section of the paper will briefly examine dominant themes in gender and migration research and focus on specific works that have advanced the study of sexuality in the field. [. . .] This essay will not be a comprehensive review of all possible bodies of research. As the other essays in the Spring 2006 special issue of *International Migration Review* suggest, there are many exciting new projects that are advancing the field of sexuality and gender in migration research, but more work needs to be done.

The primary aim of this paper is to illustrate how sexuality is an important factor in the migration process and how migration researchers might reconceptualize prevailing notions in gender and migration studies not only by including queer people but also by utilizing the tools of queer studies as a way to complicate and reexamine assumptions and concepts that unwittingly reify normative notions of gender and sexuality. To emphasize the value of a queer perspective to the study of sexuality in gender and migration research, I present a case study or a "queer reading" of a particular body of literature in gender and migration studies that focuses on Filipina domestic workers. While researchers in this area of gender and migration research have been successful in showcasing the gendered dimensions and experiences of Filipina labor migrants, they have unwittingly ignored the normalizing and naturalizing tendencies in their own concepts and methods. In the final section, I enumerate the various ways this perspective may help expand and complicate gender and migration research.

Thinking sex, thinking gender: from feminism to transnational studies

A pressing question comes to [. . .]: why "think sex" and not think sex in tandem with gender? Can gender subsume sexuality conceptually and theoretically? In other words, why devote a section to sexuality in a collection of works that aims to review the valences of gender in migration studies? Can we think of gender separate from sexuality? In her seminal essay "Thinking Sex," Gayle Rubin (1993) calls for a conceptual and theoretical separation of gender from sexuality. She suggests that sexual oppression and regulation demanded an alternative explanatory framework beyond familiar feminist culprits such as patriarchy and male dominance. Therefore, sexuality demands a separate investigative path while still maintaining a critical dialogue with gender. The development of contemporary research on sexuality and migration reflects the complicated tensions between gender and sexuality (see Valentine, 2004). To better understand these tensions, it is important to look into the historical and cultural contexts in which these categories developed in the late 20th and early 21st centuries.

The overlapping histories of feminism, the AIDS pandemic, and lesbian and gay studies were important sources of a conglomeration of ideas, situations, and practices that shaped and influenced the contemporary study of sexuality. Significant developments in feminist studies in the seventies and eighties were important milestones in the trajectory of queer sexuality research. Feminists during this period departed from a universalized notion of "woman" and acknowledged how particular groups of women, particularly those from the third world, have specific struggles and experiences that are not similar to those of their Western counterparts.

An emergent cohort of feminists in the late seventies and early eighties attempted to dislodge the universalizing tone of early "second wave" feminism by arguing for the intersectionality of sexuality and gender or their contextual definition and operation in conjunction with other identities and practices such as race and class. Adrienne Rich (1986) attempted to dismantle monolithic constructions of gendered and sexualized experiences by positing the notion of the "politics of location." The "politics of location" suggests the specificity and particularity of gendering and sexualizing processes and how they are important in trying to understand and transform women's predicament. Women and their experiences, she argued, are always situated, positioned, and marked by race, class, and ethnicity (Lewis and Mill, 2003:5).

The emergence of feminists of color and the third-world feminist movement was the catalyst for a new path or divergent strand of feminist and sexuality studies as they confronted the vicissitudes and diversity of women's oppression. For example, the African American writer and lesbian feminist Audre Lorde argued that women should recognize the relative privilege of white women that was achieved in part at the cost of black and third-world women's lives. She further suggested that this recognition should also lead to a political process for change (Lewis and Mill, 2003; see also Hull, Scott, and Smith, 1982; Anzaldúa, 1987; Mohanty, 2003). Therefore, these feminist scholars argued against universal and fixed notions of "woman" and "gender," and instead pointed to divergences and cleavages due to social, cultural, and historical conditions.

Shifts in understanding sexuality and gender, particularly in terms of their cultural and social inflections, found their way to another body of literature that emerged out of the AIDS pandemic in the mid-eighties. AIDS as a global phenomenon shaped the development of the research agenda on sexuality as one that is not merely about physical contacts, but about culturally mediated behaviors and identities. Human travel and movement were singled out to be crucial vectors in the spread of the disease. While simplistic and problematic, this notion of the disease's "mobility" did provide the grist for new research that broadened the scope and range of sexual ideologies, practices, and identities. AIDS became a catalyst in the transformation of the research agenda by both public health professionals and academic scholars. The change in research direction was based on the realization that Western models of sexual orientation were untenable in various cultural contexts. While anthropological studies in various non-Western societies had advanced this idea long before the eighties, it was only in the later half of the first decade of the pandemic in the U.S. when it became apparent that AIDS—which was first labeled GRID (gay-related immune deficiency) when it was first thought to be affecting primarily white gay men—started to devastate communities of color and immigrant communities. The radical changes in the epidemiology showed how the disease also affected "heterosexuals" or several groups of men and women who eventually were found to have been involved in same-sex relations but did not identify as either homosexual or gay/lesbian.

Beyond discrepancies in identities and behavior, epidemiologists and social scientists found that the meanings and valences of "straight," "gay," or "lesbian" in communities of color and immigrant communities were radically different from mainstream American society (Herdt, 1997; Parker, 2001; Patton, 2002b). More importantly, specific migrant groups such as Haitians were given special epidemiological labels because they could not be easily classified into existing risk behaviors and identity categories. The radical shift in AIDS epidemiology in the mid to late eighties when communities of color and immigrant communities started showing signs of the pandemic's ravages led epidemiologists and social scientists on a mad rush to try to understand non-Western and non-mainstream identities, values, and practices around sex and gender.

At the same time, migrants, who have been historically held as culprits in various epidemics in history, have also become one of the exemplary figures of the pandemic. The disease and the organizing around various sexual minorities, including gays, lesbians, and sex workers, highlighted the idea that not only did migration bring cultural and racial differences into the mix but that the movement of people around the world and the globalizing of cultural economic and political institutions have brought divergent sexual ideologies and identities into sharp relief (Mishra, Connor, and Magaña, 1996; see also Patton, 1990, 1992, 2002b). These realities established new research avenues for AIDS tracking and prevention, and also shaped the parallel emergence of the academic discipline of gay and lesbian studies and eventually queer studies. Not only were academic and health researchers acknowledging the bias in the usage of such terms as "gay," "lesbian," and/or "homosexual," they were also trying to understand how migration can be an important factor in the creation of a variety of sexual identity categories and practices that do not depend on Western conceptions of selfhood and community. This shift in understanding can be likened to the situation with feminists of color and third-world feminists in the late seventies and early nineties. Therefore, departing from a popular notion of universal categories of sexual orientation, research during the early eighties up till the mid-nineties eventually strongly advocated for the cultural "situatedness" of sexuality (Weston, 1998:168–73).

Queer studies in particular and sexuality research in general were influenced by changes in the pandemic and also by a growing realization about the effects of globalization. While Rubin (1993) hinted at the importance of migration, it was only in the past ten years that the study of sexuality in a transnational and global perspective gained ground (Altman, 1997, 2001; Adam, Duyvendak, and Krouwel, 1999; Bell and Binnie, 2000). Povinelli and Chauncey (1999) in their introduction to an important collection of essays interrogated the question of how sexuality can be unmoored from a static geographic frame to a mobile one by demonstrating how the sexual provides a better understanding of global movements and "flows" by positing the notion of "subjective mediation." In other words, they go against the abstraction of flows and mass group movement and emphasize the ways in which people as agentive subjects negotiate sexual and gender identities in processes that include immigration, tourism, business travel, etc.

Part of the new emerging attitude toward sexuality, mirroring that of gender, is to understand the particular factors, conditions, and ideologies that shape sexual identities and practices, and how these permeate social institutions. Film and other forms of mass media, the Internet, tourism, and migration of people have created a stage on which to scrutinize sexual phenomena as part of globalization and transnationalism. Scholars who examine the transnationalization of sexuality and sexual identities have shown that far from a homogenizing or McDonaldization of sexual mores and practices, globalization and rapid transnational movements have created emergent hybrid forms that interact with Western or Euro-American sexual ideologies. In other words, non-Western sexual ideologies do not follow a unilinear assimilative process into Western modern sexual ideologies but rather are involved in syncretic processes that create alternative sexual politics, cultures, and identities (Manalansan, 1994, 1995, 1997, 2000, 2003; Eng and Hom, 1998; Cruz-Malavé and Manalansan, 2002; Luibhéid, 2002, 2005). Following this idea, feminist theorists Grewal and Kaplan (1994) and queer studies scholars Patton and Sánchez-Eppler (2000:2) have suggested that transnational travel and movement have not diminished the influence of indigenous local practices and institutions but rather created situations where ideologies, identities, and practices highlight the crucial articulation between the local and the global.

In sum, this rather abbreviated genealogy of theories and research on sexuality showcases the shifting meaning of sexuality in research texts from a universalized biological and psychological reflex of static bodies into a constitutive element of cross-cultural, cross-national migrant experiences. These main ideas provide broad hints to the specific themes and processes of existing works that incorporate a sexuality perspective in migration research.

Sex and migration: a glimpse of the landscape

A quick perusal of the empirical literature on sexuality and migration will readily show how particular disciplines such as anthropology, history, and sociology have been at the forefront of research on sexuality and migration. Sociology's specialized subfield of deviance and anthropology's interest in non-Western practices, and history's focus on the development and provenance of identities and communities have been the foundational bases for the development and accumulation of knowledge. Other disciplines have contributed to the corpus of work on sexuality and migration. These disciplines include psychology and social psychology, which deal with migrant sexual attitudes after settlement (Suárez-Orozco and Qin, 2006). Sexual mores and attitudes in addition to family and community restrictions were seen as the barometer of migrants' adjustments to their new homes (Espín, 1997, 1999; Ahmadi, 2003).

Historical research on sexuality and migration is particularly notable. Specifically the reinterpretation of specific events such as Chinese migration to the United States were reinterpreted and portrayed not merely as symptoms of political and economic factors, but rather as a product of intersecting processes of racialization and sexualization (Hing, 1993). Nayan Shah's (2001) study of San Francisco's Chinatown showed how struggles around public hygiene and health in the late nineteenth and early twentieth centuries were suffused with overt Orientalized images of the Chinese during this period that were inflected by sex and gender. Therefore, Chinese women, who were virtually barred from the United States until the middle of the twentieth century, were portrayed as embodiments of illicit sex, loose morals, and disease (Peffer, 1986, 1999). At the same time, Shah (2001) suggests that Chinese men were feminized in such a way that they were easily figured into an American domesticity yet rendered in conflicting images of asexuality and threatening heterosexuality at various times during this period of antimiscegenation (see also Hodes, 1999; Ngai, 2003).

The history of U.S. immigration shows how various laws restricted entry of particular groups by constructing them as sexually deviant and morally corrupt. For example, the Page Law of 1882, which restricted Chinese migration, included barring Chinese women for being alleged prostitutes (Luibhéid, 2005:xiv). The McCarren-Walter Act was an important act of immigration legislation that, among other things, specifically barred homosexuals since homosexuality was considered to be a pathological or psychopathic condition akin to an infectious disease (Luibhéid, 2005:xii).

The landscape of sexuality in gender and migration research is too broad to cover in this essay. [. . .] Here, I would like to highlight three important trends and themes in recent research that provide new vantage points on popular theoretical frameworks, concepts, and methodologies in gender and migration research. While the following discussion points to some of the more exciting research, it also calls for more work to be done.

Queer asylum

Apart from antimiscegenation laws and migrants' struggle for citizenship, research around refugees and asylum cases has become a prominent part of the literature on sexuality. Issues around asylum gained ground during the height of the AIDS pandemic, particularly in relation to undocumented immigrants who have come down with the disease. Legal measures were promulgated to allow these immigrants to have a stay of deportation for humanitarian purposes, while at the same time ironically maintaining strict quarantine rules that prevented visitors and immigrants with HIV/AIDS from crossing U.S. borders (Herdt, 1997).

Political organizing around AIDS and gay rights enabled the establishment of immigration provisions for refugee/asylum cases based on sexual orientation. This legal development was double-edged. The laws required the asylum petitioners to assert and document the horrible conditions that existed in their home countries. Of particular importance are the dossiers developed based on social science expert testimony on the conditions for nonnormative sexualities in Muslim societies and other non-Western nations. This created a dilemma because it appeared to effectively demonize specific societies and in the words of legal scholar Sonia Katyal (2002) led to the process of "exporting identities" from the West to other countries. Sexual orientation and labels such as gay, lesbian, and homosexual were uncritically deployed in legal proceedings, thereby creating an East—West dichotomy that was morally and culturally hierarchical. At the same time, this development allowed for the inclusion of sexuality as a possible basis for acquiring asylum status. This broadened the definition of conditions for the granting of asylum and in turn transformed the idea of what it meant to be a refugee. Practices around LGBT asylum reinforced and encouraged the idea that the home country, typically located in the non-West, is essentially homophobic and inhumane in their treatment of queers. Such practices enabled court proceedings to regard LGBT asylum seekers as essentially victims of homophobic violence and ignorant pre-modern cultural norms in dire need of liberation. It is also possible that both lawyers and petitioners actually believed in the universal nature of gender and sexual identities by couching the whole project in terms of human rights (Human Rights Watch, 1992; Bhabha, 1996, 2002; Welch, 2002).

However, a counter argument by Juana Rodriguez (2003) in her analysis of the case, *In Re Tenorio*, about the asylum application of a Brazilian black man, serves to advance a different understanding of the process of queer asylum. She argues that asylum need not be read in terms of a national portrait of "evil" or "backward" societies but in terms of the complex arrangements of events and statuses—such as the concatenation of race and class in the case of Marcelo Tenorio, the petitioner who grew up poor and racially marginalized in Brazil. Her contention therefore echoes the need to read queer asylum as being not merely about the protection of people from persecution due to their sexual predilections but more broadly in the context of the intersection of marginalized racialized and classed sexualities.

The current conservative and anti immigration political climate, especially after September 11, 2001, may in fact reverse if not halt the progress in the legal domain, particularly for asylum seekers from the Middle East (Randazzo, 2005:51–53). However, there are efforts to offset this unfortunate turn of events both in the form of new writing on the topic (Randazzo, 2005) and through the political work of nonprofit organizations like the Audre Lorde Project in New York City, which combines feminist concerns about migration and asylum (particularly female genital mutilation and domestic abuse) and those of queer sexual orientation. However, more work clearly needs to be done in this area.

Shifting notions of female sexuality in sex tourism, pen pal brides, and second-generation young women

While it is beyond the purview of this essay to map out the full range of the burgeoning literature on the shifting notions of female sexuality [. . .], I would like to briefly focus on specific research on women involved in tourism and sex work, pen pal or Internet romances, and second-generation young women. It is important to highlight some general trends that are relevant to the discussion of sexuality and migration. Female sexuality is not merely the conduit for biological reproduction but is also the site for the contestation of various group and institutional norms. In other words, female migrant sexuality is the arena for the contestation of tradition, assimilation, and the travails of transnational migration.

Recent research literature challenges the earlier myth of women's lack of agency and their image as unwilling and unwitting victims of circumstance by moving toward the detailing of strategies employed by many women who are involved in transnational sex work and "pen pal" marriages, thus actively contesting received ideas and situations. In other words, new works suggests that these women are not innocent victims in these situations but are in some ways complicit with as well as active resisters of powerful structural arrangements and ideas.

Recent literature has focused on affect and most importantly on "love" as important arenas through which female sex workers are in fact creating and then manipulating situations that will enable them to garner material and cultural capital through emotional and monetary relationships with foreign men who may eventually enable the women to live more comfortable lives. Brennan (2004) conducted an ethnographic study of Dominican women who have sexual relationships with Western men and how "love" as an idiom is manipulated to rationalize work, pleasure, suffering, and eventual migration. What is fascinating in this ethnography and other works like it is the decentering of heterosexual reproduction and the troubling of the heterosexual dyad. In other words, love and coupling are enabled not by romance on the ground but through the influences of economic plight, mass media representations of love, and the objectification of desire as located in the West.

Recent works illustrate the various conduits to the sexual commodification of women and queers that lead to their migration across national borders. Women and third-world queers are active participants in sex tourism and in the Internet. By exposure to the ideas, practices, and images of the West through tourism and through exploring the Web, third-world women and queers are involved in new forms of recruitment where the impulse to migrate and the desire for life outside the homeland are seen through the lenses of sexual desire and pleasures. Constable (2003) conducted an ethnographic study of Filipina and Chinese women who were involved in romantic Internet relationships with Western men. She suggests that these women are able to narrate their relationships in terms of romance and fairy tales by manipulating idioms of love, sex, and money. At the same time, the Internet affords these women the ability to get to know and fall in "love" with their partners before actually migrating or meeting them in person.

The Internet is the medium that gives rise to the desire to migrate by creating new and efficient ways of navigating cultural, racial, and class differences as well as physical distance. Third-world and immigrant queers are also utilizing the Internet to negotiate the racial and cultural divides in the sexual communities. At the same time, sex tourism also becomes a site for the reification of racial and economic differences (Alexander, 1994, 1997; Cantú, 2002; Giorgi, 2002). For example, Jasbir Puar (2002) illustrates how non-Western queers are exposed to gay and lesbian cultures through established tours and mass media connected to such industries. These may lead to the visualization of the West as a haven for various queers.

Research suggests that there is still a moral dimension attached to traditional practices from the homeland and a resistance to the seemingly amoral racialized dimensions of gender and sexual practices in the new land of settlement. Yen Le Espiritu (2003) demonstrated this theme in her study of Filipina second-generation girls in California who see themselves as being pitted against white girls in terms of normative moral behavior. Oliva Espín's (1997, 1999) pioneering studies of Latina lesbian migrants suggest that they are caught between their own communities' homophobic and misogynist tendencies and the larger new homeland's racialized, classed, and ethnicized attitudes and practices. As such, their struggle to negotiate their own identities can be seen as not mere passive assimilation to or adoption of lesbian and/or American identities. Second-generation and young immigrant women are held to be the repositories of their communities' traditions and their sexual behavior as "evidence" of the groups' worth and are therefore highly policed (Luibhéid, 2005:xxvi–xxvii).

Again, more work needs to be done on these aspects of migrant female sexuality, particularly those that go beyond normative conceptions of marriage and family. However, Jennifer

Hirsch's (2004) work on Mexican transnational families provides a strong innovative model for future research by demonstrating that reproductive choices and gender relations among Mexican migrants are experiencing dramatic transformation due to mobility. She shows the ways in which female roles, family relationships, and male—female interactions among Mexican migrants have departed from the focus on biological reproduction and economic concerns to one that highlights struggles around marital intimacy and the construction of companionate marriages. Therefore, reproductive choices, including the use of contraception and birthing methods, are set within the shifting cultural, emotional, and economic contexts of Mexican female sexuality, family dynamics, and marriage.

In sum, female sexuality in migration situations functions not as mere symbol of homeland traditions but rather as the site of ideological and material struggles that shape the impetus to migrate and influence the manner of settlement and assimilation. Female migrant sexuality therefore deflects the imputed normative meanings of reproduction and mothering, and poses new ways of thinking about female sexual agency and the redefinition of gender roles in a transnational context. More importantly, this section suggests that new works should also look into how migrant lives and conditions set the stage for dramatically altering normalized ideas of the family primarily as reproductive units, marriage as economic transactions, and sexuality as always and already heterosexual.

Queer settlement and the question of assimilation

In her pioneering work *Entry Denied*, Eithne Luibhéid (2002:xii–xv) notes that the state regulates migration through legal, political, cultural, and economic means that in turn reproduce sexual identities, practices, and categories. Luibhéid suggests that the movements of migrants are not only monitored and controlled by state authorities by specific racial, ethnic, and gender preferences and prohibitions, but also mediated through implicit sexualized ideas in law and immigration proceedings. Therefore, she suggests that the migrant body is the site where the racialized, ethnicized, and gendered disciplinary measures employed by various states and their agents come together and is also the venue for promoting as well as repressing sexualized images, desires, and stereotypes (see Minter, 1993).

The renaissance of research on queer immigrant cultures and sexuality in the past ten years illustrates the complicated ways in which migrants understand, make sense of, and engage with the prevailing practices of the new land of settlement. As I have argued above, several important themes arise out of these encounters. First, studies of Filipino and Latino gay migrant men (Manalansan, 1994, 1997; Cantú, 1999, 2000; Roque Ramirez, 2001) demonstrate how they evaluate their experiences with the gay community in terms of the conflict between tradition and modernity. Second, third-world migrant queers are often conflicted over issues regarding home and family. Far from having a "natural affiliation" with their biological families, these men and women establish complex fictive family networks of friends and lovers to mitigate the violence and rejection of the former (Cantú, 1999; Manalansan, 2000, 2003). At the same time, coming from biological families who still live in the homeland and who depend on their remittances and other kinds of support, these queers need to negotiate conflicting emotions and attitudes to mark the economic transnational binds that connect them to each other (Cantú, 1999, 2001). Third, migrant queers experience discrimination and stigma from both their own communities as well as from mainstream culture. These experiences extend the marginalization of migrant queers even within the "gay and lesbian" communities in the United States (Gopinath, 1996, 2005; Puar, 1998; Reddy and Syed, 2001; Wat, 2002). As migrants of color, these queers are gendered and racialized accordingly by these communities. Unable to be easily located in normalized acceptable identities and categories, these migrants of color are establishing multiple hybrid cultures and creating spaces for community activities and new cultural "traditions" that depart from both their own migrant communities and from mainstream "straight" and "gay and lesbian" cultures.

In sum, this section provides a brief glimpse of the various issues and modes of thinking around sexuality in migration research and suggests the need for more work on sexuality and migration. This subsection on queer settlement points to the innovative ways queer migrants are reconfiguring family and social networks, as well as negotiating stigma and ostracism from mainstream communities. That migrant queers are creating nonnormative family formations and hybrid cultural arrangements is an important fact. Its utility extends beyond the confines of queer migrant lives. The next section will demonstrate how a queer perspective can provide new avenues for research and critical insight for a significant body of migration literature on Filipina domestic workers.

Heteronormativity across borders: the case of Filipina domestic workers

Global labor migration has become increasingly female. This reality has led to particular themes and concepts in the migration literature that address the issue of gender but ironically reify normative notions of both gender and sexuality. A major part of this burgeoning litera-ture has focused on female migrant workers from the Philippines and their dispersal into various parts of the world and has formed over the past eight to ten years. A good number of these works have focused primarily on the travails and experiences of Filipina domestic workers. While most of the research conducted about these women attempts to engender the processes of migration, several themes in the research can be characterized by the following heteronormative tendencies.

The literature has tended to focus on heterosexual married mothers. While this had led to interesting follow-up work on the children of transnational families, it has also led to the neglect of the experiences of gay and straight men and single women. In fact the implication seems to be that the nuclear family is the primary model of the transnational family and that heterosexual marriage or heterosexual partnering are only plausible cornerstones of family life with parenthood gendered in static biological terms and motherhood or maternal love, the province solely of biological (typically married) women with children.

A critical examination of this body of literature from the perspective of queer sexuality studies and theory will illustrate how these themes are played out in the research texts focusing on Filipinas who have been constructed as the "servants of globalization" in the best known study on the topic, by Rhacel Parreñas (2001). I will show that while women from the Philippines have been the most thoroughly studied female migrant laborers in the world, they have also been subject to an implicit gendering and sexualizing even from the most politically progressive and analytically sophisticated feminist researchers.

My purpose here is not to disparage these works but to forge an agenda that might push the research into a more critical and reflective stage. Indeed, the works I will be engaging with are those that have clearly made important contributions to the study of gender and migration. The research by Parreñas (2001) and Nicole Constable (1997) are among the notable works that have provided moving and incisive ethnographic portraits of Filipina domestic workers in Rome, Los Angeles, and Hong Kong. The authors are clearly sensitive to the economic and social realities of these women and are focused on how Filipina migrants are actively engaging transnational issues of labor, family obligations, and "caring." These pioneering works have successfully mapped the unique transnational labor market for nannies and maids in the "first world," to which third-world women go to work as cooks, cleaners, and housekeepers—labor that is always feminized or widely recognized as the province of women.

At the heart of these workers' dilemma is the "chain of care." Not only are Filipina domestic workers expending physical energy for salaries, they are also involved in providing emotional or "caring" work by looking after the children of more affluent first-world families. At the same time, they are displaced and torn away from their biological families and forced to leave their children in the care of poorer women in the homeland. Hence, this "chain" is forged primarily through links constituted by biologically reproducing women of the first and third worlds and the displacement of their labor from their biological families.

Unfortunately, despite the excellent work that has been done in documenting and analyzing these women's transnational dilemma, researchers have conceptualized the maternal and affective labor inherent in the "chain of care" of the global domestic service industry as being embodied in married mothers from the third world. In other words, the work of the home, including caring for children, cooking, cleaning, and other domestic chores, is rendered in heteronormative terms.

For example, Rhacel Parreñas (2001) in her study of Filipina domestics in Rome and Los Angeles unwittingly reifies stereotypical gendered conceptions of domesticity and affect. Her methodology section argues for a preponderance of married women in her sample and case studies, despite the fact that nearly half of the respondents are single women. While she provides several case studies of single women, they are eventually marginalized when the idea of children and transnational mothering gains dominance in the ethnography. Additionally, she conducted a nonrandom survey of domestic workers in Rome with 222 women at least half of whom were single. The sample also included 79 men (Parreñas, 2001:16). While she conducted ten interviews with male domestic workers, single female and lesbian domestic workers, these interviews are eventually sidelined in relation to the dominant stories of Filipina migrant mothers.

Of course, it is not a methodological error to focus on married mothers, but without the necessary contextualization this focus creates naturalized and normalized conceptions of motherhood, domesticity, child care, and reproduction. Parreñas seems to imply that married women with children are the only possible and logical links in this "chain of care." But the presence of single women and men (be they queer or heterosexual) among migrant domestic workers disrupts the neat synchronicity of the "chain of care" in which third-world mothers take up the "reproductive labor" of their first-world counterparts while in turn employing poorer relations or other more destitute women in their countries to take care of the children they left behind.

I am not arguing for merely adding more analyses of single and/or queer migrant domestics, but questioning how the "chain of care" framework unwittingly privileges the experiences of migrant women with children. Note for example that in the concluding section of the chapter on intergenerational and gender relations where she presents a couple of case studies of single women, Parreñas creates a monolithic construction of the migrant laborers when she writes "emotional repression enables parents to delay reunification, the more they aggravate the intergenerational strains of the transnational household formation and the harder it is for them to return to the Philippines, face their children and confront the tensions that migration has caused the family" (Parreñas, 2001:149). This statement starkly illustrates how the biological nuclear family is the pivot around which the dynamics of the so-called chain of care migration operate.

In another work, Barbara Ehrenreich and Arlie Hochschild (2003) argue that the "chain of care" of the international domestic labor industry has created "a crisis of care" or a "care drain." In *Global Woman*, Ehrenreich and Hochschild (2003:1–13) suggest that this crisis is not caused by the departure of women or of domestic workers per se, but by the departure of third-world mothers and wives. The problem is that the authors perceive the gender, reproductive, and marital status of these laborers as the all-encompassing rationale for the inequality of labor conditions left behind in the homeland. In doing so, these researchers again construct the international care industry by privileging a heterosexual (mostly) married third-world mother.

One way to complicate this deceptively simple picture is to commit to changes in the research agenda. First, it is important to examine the work of male domestic workers. Second, new works need to focus on gender fluidity and the role of women as sexual and gendered agentive subjects. If [. . .] gender is relational, then my move to include the work of male domestic workers does *not* in any way disavow the strong gender factor in labor market segmentation nor dismiss issues of sexism and gender inequality. Rather, including the labor of male domestic workers can help nuance and complicate our understanding of the idea and process of "gendering" in the domestic industry. While the easy answer to the question of gender in domestic work could be that not too many men are involved in it, placing the experiences of these men alongside that of women highlights the continuities and discontinuities of domestic work. In other words, my purpose here is not to valorize the male domestic labor but to show how it complicates the idea of carework and prevents us from falling into the normative and universalizing trap of implicitly regarding women as natural nurturers.

In the recent years, it has become apparent that the Filipina or Filipino woman as the global careworker par excellence exists hand in hand with the figure of male migrant careworker, specifically gay Filipino men, who are becoming the new figure of foreign careworkers. An example is the nurses and unskilled domestic workers, who according to recent accounts are tending to the elderly in Israel. A television documentary produced in Tel Aviv entitled "Paper Dolls" chronicles the travails of these men (who are not professional nurses but unskilled domestic careworkers for the elderly) as they contend with the racializing, gendering, and sexualizing processes in Israel.

Therefore, current works on Filipino migrant labor do not take into consideration the present and shifting terrain of gender (broadly construed) in the global care industry. In care industry fields such as nursing, recent trends in the past five years indicate that Filipino male doctors are retraining themselves to become nurses to find employment in the United States and Europe. At the same time, anecdotal accounts suggest that an increasing number of Filipino nurses in the U.S. are gay men. I do not intend to equate the work of nurses with those of domestic workers, but I am interested in the ways in which gender operates when third-world migrant men work in unskilled, paraprofessional, and professional fields that have been traditionally constructed as female. Indeed, in order to get a comprehensive idea of the gendered dimension of domestic work, it is necessary for future work to move away from this oversight of migrant male labor and examine how such relationships are in fact crucial and constitutive elements of gendering processes in the international care industry.

Parreñas (2001:77) and Hochschild (2003:29) depict the Filipino (and other third-world) male as being pathologically prevented by cultural "tradition" from participating in domestic affairs while at the same time rendering the domestic sphere as always and already female. Hochschild (2003:29) suggests a solution to this "problem" by advocating for an educational program that will train these men to become more involved in domestic activities. This supposed pathological condition of men "traditionally" avoiding and being discouraged from domestic affairs is not only ethnographically erroneous, it belies a particular kind of knowledge "imperialism," to use Hochschild's term, since it portrays third-world men as lacking the cultural knowledge to be authentic modern fathers. A related problem is

Hochschild's tendency to implicitly create a context in which third-world male and female migrants are seen as premodern or wallowing in tradition only to move as domestic workers into Western modernity. Therefore, Hochschild's proposed educational program unwittingly portrays third-world cultures as primarily archaic patriarchies that can only be transformed through the infusion of Western gender equalities. This idea reifies gender and sexism in static black-and-white terms. While I strongly believe in the existence of gender inequalities, statements such as Hochschild's provide a rather inflexible gender script that actually inhibits the politicizing of female domestics by rendering their status as "natural" and inevitable.

My point here is not to excuse or deny the existence of sexism in the Philippines, but to contest the universalizing claim that third-world men are not involved in domestic work and, more importantly, to demonstrate the variation in cultural ideologies regarding men and domestic work that can potentially dislodge normative universalizing notions of gender scripts and domesticity. Ethnographic evidence on gender relations in Southeast Asia actually points to more fluid notions of male and female that counter simplistic conceptions of gender roles (see Errington and Atkinson, 1990; Brenner, 1998; Cannell, 1999). Alicia Pingol's (2001) study of husbands in the northern part of the Philippines whose wives are overseas contract workers (a good number of them domestics) showed a significant number of the men taking over the work of "mothering" and suggests a shift or "re-making" of masculinities. Pingol is not describing a liberatory process happening to male roles in the Philippines, but rather, her work implies that there are shifting, oftentimes messy and contradictory relationships between ideal conditions and everyday practices within transnational families and in gender relations in migration.

At the same time, it is useful to note that in most of the literature on Filipina domestic workers, the notions of motherhood and fatherhood are determined solely by the biological features of specific bodies and not as disciplinary results of social and cultural norms. These researchers are unable to seriously consider motherhood without biological reproduction and/or marriage. Feminist researchers of gender and migration might benefit from unsettling their normative conceptions of parenthood, maternal love, and care by not locking them into specific gendered and married bodies. The focus on biological parenthood also means that sexuality in this body of migration research is relegated to either reproductive sex, forced abstinence brought about by migration, and sexual abuse, or rape. There have been very limited discussions of sexuality and pleasure (either heterosexual or homosexual) in the lives of these women.

The gendering of these women is rendered on the basis of rigid or stereotypical notions of being "feminine." Constable (1997:95–99) documented the disciplining of Filipina women's bodies by their Hong Kong employers by obscuring or deemphasizing their femininity including by forbidding nail polish, prescribing daily wear, and having their hair cut short like a boy. The prescribed defeminization of these women is seen solely in terms of employers' discipline and there is no consideration or further investigation as to whether any of these women found either pleasure in it or had some positive reaction. In other words, is it not possible that the disciplining of the feminine aspects of their appearance might also present the opportunity for gender insubordination and gender-crossing behavior, or a source of agency or even pleasure for these women? Another interesting project would be to reexamine these women's weekly gatherings, which are typically seen as merely leisure activities or sometimes as politically oriented meetings and to entertain the possibility that these occasions offer homosocial sites for same-sex affection, intimacy, and romance and how these erotic entanglements can destabilize dominant notions of femininity, female roles, and reproduction.

In a more recent work, Constable (2002) examined how women constantly negotiated the disciplining of their appearances by their employers attempting to achieve a balance between the overtly "sexy" feminine look that could label them as "easy" prey for male sexual advances and an excessively masculine look that could lead them to be mistaken for a "T-bird" or lesbian. This promising path of research could benefit from actually looking at how lesbian and/or gender-insubordinate "female" workers actually perceive these defeminizing disciplinary measures in relation to desire and erotic practices. Feminist researchers of gender and migration might want to consider third-world women and men in the international care industry as viable desiring subjects without imputing compulsory heterosexuality and middle-class domesticity and thus locating them within the very patriarchal confines that these researchers have implicitly vowed to critique.

While more work needs to be done to move away from these heteronormative presuppositions, new work is beginning to appear as a way to counteract these tendencies. Rhacel Parreñas's (2005) recent work *The Children of Global Migration*, on the children in transnational families, provides a useful starting point for future works. She begins the book by narrating her unique fieldwork experiences in the Philippines, where she encountered situations of gender and sexual misrecognition—that is, she was mistaken for a bakla, which is a Tagalog gloss for a homosexual, transvestite, and effeminate "man." Again, toward the end of the book, she points to the idea of the limits and possibilities of gender fluidity as one important vantage point for understanding and engaging with the plight of these children. These observations build on Parreñas's earlier pioneering work and can potentially be the first steps toward new provocative insights.

In sum, a critical queer reading reveals the gaps and fissures in this emergent literature on Filipina migrant workers and shows that even recent research that purports to sensitively bring gender to the center of migration studies fails to consider how specific normalizing and naturalizing ideas around reproduction, parenting, carework, and family formation create discrepant and incomplete understandings of third-world female migrant labor. While new works are starting to emerge in response to this gap, more research needs to be done to create a more expansive and provocative body of literature that engages with the dynamic aspects of migrants' institutions, bodies, and desires.

Sexuality as part of the research equation: added value or complicating factor?

As I have argued above, far from being a conservative force that leaves bodies and cultures intact, migration creates specific dilemmas and contradictory situations that disturb static notions of gender and sexuality. Therefore, it is important to see how a radical repositioning and reexamination of heteronormative premises in gender and migration research can yield expansive and provocative insights. This essay then is not about mere documentation, but aims to strongly push for migration scholars to step back and reflect on their works in the face of these hegemonic premises.

To summarize the mains points of this essay, the following are the main contributions of a queer analysis of gender and migration research. First, the queer perspective suggests going beyond a laboring gendered agent and highlighting a desiring and pleasure-seeking migrant subject. As seen through the queer reading of Filipina migrant laborers above, migrants are not just displaced caretakers and mothering workers but in fact possess sexual desires and erotic practices that must be taken into consideration. These desires are not limited to migrants' search for material and social advancement but also are often pivotal reasons for the decision to migrate.

Secondly, the queer perspective suggests that sexuality is not an all-encompassing reality but one that intersects with and through other social, economic, and cultural practices and identities. At the same time, a queer notion of sexuality enables migration research to go beyond normative and universalized family patterns and biological rationales. I have argued that the crises around migrant laborers do not have to center on nuclear and biological family bonds nor to firmly ground caring and maternal love in biologically reproducing women. The rather provocative questions in the preceding section were meant to disentangle parenting and affect from biologically deterministic notions of male and female.

Finally, a queer perspective of sexuality expands the notions of refugee, asylum, recruit- ment, and assimilation particularly as to what constitutes factors that force people to migrate or flee particular spaces for other places. The growing importance of the Internet, sex tourism, and other global cultural flows showcases the influence on people's imagination about the rest of the world beyond their immediate locality, thus expanding the terms of their longings and desires. A queer perspective complicates conceptions of integration or assimilation particularly when citizenship and alien status are marked by racialized, classed, sexualized, and gendered images of specific migrant groups. For example, figures who are portrayed as simultaneously sexually deviant, gendered, foreign, and dangerous are Middle Eastern or South Asian males of a certain age range who, after September 11, 2001, were seen to be part of a profile that is labeled as "terrorist" and, as such, unable to be incorporated into the idea of nationhood and patriotism (Puar and Rai, 2002).

These aforementioned ideas are already part of the new emerging works in the field, and scholars are beginning to heed the call for critical analysis that includes sexuality as part of migration research, thereby charting new provocative theoretical and conceptual terrains and resulting in relevant empirical research and interventions. Despite all these accomplish- ments, a lot more work remains to be done. Researchers should remain vigilant in guarding against the reification of the heteronormative and be active in opening new and alternative ways of understanding sexuality and gender in migration studies.

Note

1   I use "queer studies" and not "lesbian and gay studies" to emphasize the fact that queer studies go beyond lesbian and gay identities to question and undermine the idea of sexual identities and orientation.

References

Adam, B.D., J.W. Duyvendak, and A. Krouwel (1999) *The Global Emergence of Gay and Lesbian Politics: National Imprints of a Worldwide Movement*. Philadelphia: Temple University Press.

Ahmadi, N. (2003) "Migration Challenges Views on Sexuality." *Ethnic and Racial Studies* 26(4):684–706.

Alexander, M.J. (1997) "Erotic Autonomy as a Politics of Decolonization." In *Feminist Genealogies, Colonial Legacies, Democratic Futures*. Eds. C.T. Mohanty and M.J. Alexander. New York: Routledge.

—— (1994) "Not Just (Any) Body Can Be a Citizen: The Politics of Law, Sexuality and Postcoloniality in Trinidad and Tobago and the Bahamas." *Feminist Review* 48:5–23.

Altman, D. (2001) *Global Sex*. Chicago: University of Chicago Press.

—— (1997) "Global Gaze/Global Gays." *GLQ* 3(4):417–36.

Anzaldúa, G. (1987) *Borderlands/La Frontera. The New Mestiza*. San Francisco: Aunt Lute.

Bell, D., and J. Binnie (2000) *The Sexual Citizen: Queer Politics and Beyond*. London: Polity Press.

Bhabha, J. (2002) "Boundaries in the Field of Human Rights: International Gatekeepers? The Tension Between Asylum Advocacy and Human Rights." *Harvard Human Rights Law Review* 15:155–81.

— (1996) "Embodied Rights: Gender Persecution, State Sovereignty, and Refugees." *Public Culture* 9(1):8.

Brennan, D. (2004) *What's Love Got to Do with It?: Transnational Desires and Sex Tourism in the Dominican Republic*. Durham NC: Duke University Press.

Brenner, S. (1998) *The Domestication of Desire: Women, Wealth, and Modernity in Java*. Princeton NJ: Princeton University Press.

Cannell, F. (1999) *Power and Intimacy in the Christian Philippines*. Cambridge: Cambridge University Press.

Cantú, L. (2002) "De Ambiente: Queer Tourism and the Shifting Boundaries of Mexican Male Sexualities." *GLQ* 8(1–2):139–66.

— (2001) "A Place Called Home: A Queer Political Economy of Mexican Immigrant Men's Family Experiences." In *Queer Families, Queer Politics: Challenging Culture and the State*. New York: Columbia University Press.

— (2000) "Entre Hombres/Between Men. Latino Masculinities and Homosexualities." In *Gay Masculinities*. Ed. P. Nardi. Thousand Oaks CA: Sage.

— (1999) "Border Crossings: Mexican Men and the Sexuality of Migration." Unpublished Ph.D. Dissertation. University of California, Irvine.

Carillo, H. (2004) "Sexual Migration, Cross-Cultural Sexual Encounters, and Sexual Health." *Sexuality Research and Social Policy* 1(3):58–70.

Cohen, C. (1997) "Punks, Bulldaggers, and Welfare Queens: The Radical Potential of Queer Politics?" *GLQ* 3(4):437–85.

Constable, N. (2003) *Romance on a Global Stage: Pen Pals, Virtual Ethnography, and "Mail Order" Brides*. Berkeley: University of California Press.

— (2002) "Sexuality and Discipline among Filipina Domestic Workers in Hong Kong." In *Filipinos in Global Migrations at Home in the World*. Ed. F. Aguilar. Quezon City, the Philippines: Philippine Migration Research/Philippine Social Science Research Council.

— (1997) *Maid to Order in Hong Kong: Stories of Filipina Workers*. Ithaca NY: Cornell University Press.

Cruz-Malavé, A., and M.F. Manalansan IV, eds. (2002) *Queer Globalizations: Citizenship and the Afterlife of Colonialism*. New York: New York University Press.

Ehrenreich, B., and A.R. Hochschild (2003) *Global Woman: Nannies, Maids and Sex Workers in the New Economy*. New York: Metropolitan Books.

Errington, S., and J.M. Atkinson, eds. (1990) *Power and Difference: Gender in Island Southeast Asia*. Stanford CA: Stanford University Press.

Eng, D., and Alice Hom (1998) "Introduction: Q&A: Notes on Queer Asian America." In *Q & A: Queer in Asian America*. Eds. D. Eng and A. Hom. Philadelphia: Temple University Press.

Espín, O. (1999) *Women Crossing Boundaries: A Psychology of Immigration and Transformation*. New York: Routledge.

— (1997) *Latina Realities: Essays on Healing, Migration and Sexuality*. Boulder CO: Westview Press.

Espiritu, Y.L. (2003) *Home Bound: Filipino American Lives Across Cultures, Communities, and Countries*. Berkeley: University of California Press.

Giorgi, G. (2002) "Madrid en Tránsito: Travelers, Visibility, and Gay Identity." *GLQ* 8(1–2): 57–79.

Gopinath, G. (2005) *Impossible Desires: Queer Diasporas and South Asian Public Cultures*. Durham NC: Duke University Press.

— (1996) "Funny Boys and Girls: Notes on a Queer South Asian Planet." In *Asian American Sexualities: Dimensions of Gay and Lesbian Experience*. Ed. R. Leong. New York: Routledge. Pp. 119–27.

Grewal, I., and C. Kaplan, eds. (1994) *Scattered Hegemonies: Postmodernity and Transnational Feminist Practices*. Minneapolis: University of Minnesota Press.

Harper, P.B., A. McClintock, J.E. Muñoz, and T. Rosen (1997) "Queer Transexions of Race, Nation and Gender." *Social Text* (52–53):3.

Herdt, G., ed. (1997) *Sexual Cultures and Migration in the Era of AIDS*. Oxford: Clarendon Press.

Hing, B.O. (1993) *Making and Re-Making Asian America Through Immigration Policy*. Stanford CA: Stanford University Press.

Hirsch, J. (2004) *A Courtship After Marriage: Sexuality and Love in Mexican Transnational Families*. Berkeley: University of California Press.

Hochschild, A. (2003) "Love and Gold." In *Global Woman: Nannies, Maids and Sex Workers in the New Economy*. Eds. B. Ehrenreich and A. Hochschild. New York: Metropolitan Books. Pp. 15–30.

Hodes, M., ed. (1999) *Sex, Race, Love: Crossing Boundaries in North American History*. New York: New York University Press.

Hull, G.T., P.B. Scott, and B. Smith, eds. (1982) *All the Women Are White, All the Blacks Are Men, But Some of Us Are Brave: Black Women's Studies*. New York: Feminist Press.

Human Rights Watch (1992) *Brutality Unchecked: Human Rights Abuses Along the U.S. Border With Mexico*. New York and Washington DC: Human Rights Watch.

Katyal, S. (2002) "Exporting Identity." *Yale Journal of Law and Feminism* 14(1):98–176.

Lewis, R., and S. Mill, eds. (2003) "Introduction." *Feminist Postcolonial Theory: A Reader*. New York: Routledge. Pp. 1–21.

Luibhéid, E. (2005) "Queering Migration and Citizenship." In *Queer Migrations: Sexuality, U.S. Citizenship and Border Crossing*. Eds. E. Luibhéid and L. Cantu. Minneapolis: University of Minnesota Press. Pp. ix–xlvi.

— (2004) "Heternormativity and Immigration Scholarship: A Call for Change." *GLQ* 10(2):227–35.

— (2002) *Entry Denied: Controlling Sexuality at the Border*. Minneapolis: University of Minnesota Press.

Manalansan IV, M.F. (2003) *Global Divas: Filipino Gay Men in Diaspora*. Durham NC: Duke University Press.

— (2000) "Diasporic Deviants/Divas: How Filipino Gay Transmigrants 'Play With the World'." In *Queer Diasporas*. Eds. C. Patton and B. Sánchez-Eppler. Durham NC: Duke University Press. Pp. 183–203.

— (1997) "In the Shadows of Stonewall: Examining Gay Transnational Politics and the Diasporic Dilemma." In *The Politics of Culture in the Shadow of Capital*. Eds. L. Lowe and D. Lloyd. Durham NC: Duke University Press. Pp. 485–505.

— (1995) "Speaking of AIDS: Language and the Filipino Gay Experience in America." In *Discrepant Histories: Translocal Essays on Filipino Cultures*. Ed. V. Rafael. Philadelphia: Temple University Press. Pp. 193–220.

— (1994) "Searching for Community: Filipino Gay Men in New York City." *Amerasia Journal* 20(1):59–73.

Minter, S. (1993) "Sodomy and Public Morality Offenses Under U.S. Immigration Law." *Cornell International Law Journal* 26:771–818.

Mishra, S.I., R.F. Connor, and J.R. Magaña, eds. (1996) *AIDS Crossing Borders: The Spread of HIV Among Migrant Latinos*. Boulder CO: Westview Press.

Mohanty, C.T. (2003) *Feminism without Borders*. Durham NC: Duke University Press.

Ngai, M. (2003) *Impossible Subjects: Illegal Aliens and the Making of Modern America*. Princeton NJ: Princeton University Press.

Parker, R. (2001) "Sexuality, Culture, and Power in HIV/AIDS Research." *Annual Review of Anthropology* 30:163–79.

Parreñas, R.S. (2005) *Children of Global Migration*. Stanford: Stanford University Press.

— (2001) *Servants of Globalization: Women, Migration and Domestic Work*. Stanford: Stanford University Press.

Patton, C. (2002a) "Stealth Bombers of Desire: The Globalization of 'Alterity' in Emerging Democracies." In *Queer Globalizations. Citizenship and the Afterlife of Colonialism*. Eds. A. Cruz-Malavé and M.F. Manalansan IV. New York: New York University Press. Pp. 195–218.

— (2002b) *Globalizing AIDS*. Minneapolis: University of Minnesota Press.

— (1992) "From Nation to Family: Containing 'African AIDS'." In *Nationalisms and Sexualities*. Eds. A. Parker et al. New York: Routledge. Pp. 218–34.

— (1990) *Inventing AIDS*. New York: Routledge.

Patton, C., and B. Sánchez-Eppler, eds. (2000) *Queer Diasporas*. Durham NC: Duke University Press.

Peffer, G. (1999) *If They Don't Bring Their Women Here*. Urbana: University of Illinois Press.

— (1986) "Forbidden Families: Emigration Experiences of Chinese Women Under the Page Law, 1875–82." *Journal of American Ethnic History* 6(1):28–46.

Pingol, A. (2001) *Remaking Masculinities: Identity, Power, and Gender Dynamics in Families with Migrant Wives and Househusbands*. Quezon City, the Philippines: University Center for Women's Studies, University of the Philippines.

Povinelli, E., and G. Chauncey, eds. (1999) "Thinking Sexuality Transnationally: An Introduction." *GLQ* 5(4):439–50.

Puar, J.K. (2002) "Queer Tourism: Geographies of Globalization." *GLQ* 8(1–2):1–6.

—(1998) "Transnational Sexualities: South Asian (Trans)nation(alism)s and Queer Diasporas." In *Q & A: Queer in Asian America*. Eds. D. Eng and A. Hom. Philadelphia: Temple University Press. Pp. 185–209.

Puar, J.K., and A.S. Rai (2002) "Monster, Terrorist, Fag: The War on Terrorism and the Production of Docile Patriots." *Social Text* 20(72):117–48.

Randazzo, T. (2005) "Social and Legal Barriers: Sexual Orientation and Asylum in the United States." In *Queer Migrations: Sexuality, U.S. Citizenship and Border Crossings*. Eds. E. Luibhéid and L. Cantu. Minneapolis: University of Minnesota Press. Pp. 30–60.

Reddy, C., and J. Syed (2001) "I Left My Country for This?" *Rice Combo* 20(April/May). <www.apiwellness.org/v20/ricecombo/mycountry.html>.

Rich, A. (1986) *Blood, Bread, Poetry: Selected Prose. 1979–1985*. New York: Norton.

Rodriguez, J.M. (2003) *Queer Latinidad: Identity, Practices, Discursive Spaces*. New York: New York University Press.

Roque Ramirez, H.N. (2001) "Communities of Desire: Queer Latina/Latino History and Memory, San Francisco Bay Area, 1960s to 1990s." Unpublished Ph.D. Dissertation. University of California, Berkeley.

Rubin, G.S. (1993 [1984]) "Thinking Sex: Notes for a Radical Theory of the Politics of Sexuality." In *The Lesbian and Gay Studies Reader*. Eds. H. Abelove, M. Barale, and D. Halperin. New York: Routledge. Pp. 3–44.

Shah, N. (2001) *Contagious Divides: Epidemics and Race in San Francisco's Chinatown*. Berkeley: University of California Press.

Suárez-Orozco, C. and D.B. Qin (2006) "Gendered Perspectives in Psychology: Immigrant Origin Youth." *International Migration Review* 40(1):165–98.

Valentine, D. (2004) "The Categories Themselves." *GLQ* 10(2):215–20.

Wat, E.C. (2002) *The Making of a Gay Asian Community: An Oral History of Pre-AIDS Los Angeles*. Lanham MD: Rowman and Littlefield.

Welch, M. (2002) *Detained: Immigration Laws and the Expanding I.N.S. Jail Complex*. Philadelphia: Temple University Press.

Weston, K. (1998) *Long Slow Burn: Sexuality and Social Science*. New York: Routledge.

Chapter 32

Anjali Arondekar

BORDER/LINE SEX: QUEER POSTCOLONIALITIES OR HOW RACE MATTERS OUTSIDE THE U.S.

Anjali Arondekar is Associate Professor of Feminist Studies at the University of California, Santa Cruz. Her monograph, *For the Record: On Sexuality and the Colonial Archive in India* (2009), won the 2010 Alan Bray Memorial Book Award for best book in lesbian, gay, or queer studies in literature and cultural studies from the GL/Q Caucus of the Modern Language Association.

In "Border/Line Sex" Arondekar critiques the institutionalization in human rights discourses of analogies between race and sex. In what is partly a critique of the translatability of American-based scholarship to other places, Arondekar argues that the language of analogy cannot achieve true intersectionality given the epistemic violence with which it flattens social and geopolitical differences. It also tends to universalize the resolutely heterogeneous category of queer. In response, Arondekar suggests reorienting the analogy between race and queer as an active transaction between oppositions that question those oppositions. Most promising, Arondekar suggests, is scholarship that takes account of the simultaneity of multiple local and global spatialities, without homogenizing or essentializing "native" or "indigenous" experience. Despite problems with some of this work, Arondekar suggests that in exhaustively evidencing the local, such studies open up new terrain for critical race/queer studies[1].

The compulsion to translate, to think the world in the categories of the Euro imperial modern is real and deeply rooted in institutional practices. One cannot simply opt out of this problem, or [one cannot simply] not suffer by a sheer act of will, the epistemic violence that is necessary to nation and empire making drives. . . . I think of it as Barthes once said with reference to Shaharazad of the Arabian Nights, more as a merchandise, a narrative traded for one more day of life. . . . It is to say to every perpetrator of epistemic violence and in the voice of the woman subject Shaharazad: don't fuck me yet, for I still have another story to tell.

(Patel 1998)[2]

Necessarily, we must dismiss those tendencies that encourage the consoling play of recognitions.

(Foucault 1977)

Preamble: 'Interested but not involved'

IN AN INTERVIEW RECORDED just a few months before the November 2004 presidential elections, Arundhati Roy was asked what she thought of John Kerry as presidential candidate. More precisely, the interviewer, David Barsaimian, was keen to hear if Roy agreed with the writer Tariq Ali who, though critical of Kerry, had declared: "If the American population were to vote Bush out of office, it would have a tremendous impact on world opinion. Our option at the moment is limited. Do we defeat a warmonger government or not?" Pressed into response, Roy exasperatedly comments: "I feel sometimes when I'm asked this question like I imagine that a gay person must feel when they're watching straight sex: I'm sort of interested but not involved." Being gay is comparable here to a location of strategized disavowal, where the imaginary "gay person" bears witness, but not presence. For Roy, the recourse to the metaphoric space of homosexuality translates her refusal of the terms of the political debate into a language of misplaced affect, desire and agency. Given that this is the only reference to sexuality and/or "gayness" in an interview that examines the emergence of a "New Racism" perpetuated by the "New Imperialism" of the United States, Roy's curious choice of analogy certainly bears further scrutiny (Roy 2004: 9). In other words, what are the elisions that must be carried out in order to so metaphorize homosexuality?

Such a singular reference to homosexuality seems particularly jarring in an interview that is otherwise careful to warn against the language of a seductive "New Racism" reliant on structures of similitude and displacement. The "New Racism" no longer needs antiquated formal policies of apartheid or segregation, but instead relies on complex global systems of shared representation and trade that institutionalize inequity much more efficaciously. For example, Roy stresses the political perils of facilely equating the electoral defeat of the Hindu right in India, with the possible defeat of George W. Bush. While both governments share the rise of an "outright fascism" and an embrace of "corporate globalization", they differ critically in their racialization of Muslims. In India, Roy reminds us, the racialization of Muslims is linked to a covert communalism that is at the heart of the political process, while in the United States, "terrorist" Muslims function specifically as the best allegory for Bush-style democratic reform. To succumb to an easy comparison between the two geopolitical sites is to collapse the differentiated racial logics at work, and to give in to a simple "them versus us" narrative of progress.

Throughout the interview, Roy returns repeatedly to the importance of her particular location as a scholar-activist, based in India. Within such careful formulations, Roy's "gay" analogy thus appears even more out of place, and opens up several urgent and unanswered questions through the structure of its utterance: What does it mean to *imagine* oneself gay? Does the invocation of a "gay person" mark a similarity that renders irrelevant the specificities of the local? Is the identity of a "gay person" rhetorically interchangeable with any and all locations? In what way, one could ask, are such invocations of homosexuality also about new forms of racisms and transnationality?[3] Let me turn now to those questions.

Transacting sex

At the 2001 United Nations Conference against Racism, Racial Discrimination, Xenophobia and Related Intolerance in Durban, South Africa, Pravin Rashtrapal, a prominent Gujarat Congress Member of Parliament, and renowned Dalit activist from India made the following comment: "Racism is rape without a condom and casteism is rape with a condom." Needless to say, this remark sparked off much controversy. Dalit activists, both from India and elsewhere, distanced themselves from what they saw as a crass and inappropriate analogy, adding fuel to the already heated discussions around the location of the category of "casteism" within the hierarchies of discrimination and intolerance outlined by the conference organizers. Yet, for many Dalit activists, the difficulty still lay in convincing the attendees at the conference of the brutalities of the "disease of casteism", which they argued produced human rights violations and degradations akin to the horrors of "racial lynching" in the United States. Defending his words, Rashtrapal also argued that the analogy with rape and sexual violation was necessary to drive home the connections between casteism and racism, while still maintaining the differences between the two spheres of human violence. "Race as rape without a condom" was clearly the greater of the two evils, but casteism too contained the same violations, albeit to a lesser degree, where the safety valve of the condom only partially mediated the brutality of rape (Kaur 2001).

Embedded in these struggles for the advocacy and articulation of "casteism" are two critical yet fraught analogies: casteism is both like and not like racism; and casteism and racism are both like and not like rape. Here, the terrains of gender and sexuality disturbingly provide the lexicon through which gradations of human violation can be measured and evaluated, with the threat of sexually transmitted diseases ("without a condom") providing contemporary reminders of a different order of death and destruction.[4] I belabor the particular example of the Dalits at the United Nations Conference to foreground the current critical emphasis on the language of intersectionality and analogy, especially with respect to the discourse of rights and discrimination (for a more detailed discussion of the term "intersectionality", see Crenshaw 1993). Such language uses "racism" and "race" as stable registers of oppression, whereby a range of discriminatory practices gather representational and judicial validity through their linkage and similarity to such registers. Hence, casteism makes sense as a human rights violation *only* when weighed alongside an established understanding of racism.

A second example of such thinking finds articulation in the manifold organizing work done by LGBT and/or queer groups in the United States. In 2001, the International Gay Lesbian Human Rights Commission (IGLHRC) issued a statement to be distributed at the United Nations Conference proposing such intersectional thinking as being foundational to their mission and advocacy of queer rights in the global arena. In the statement entitled "The Intersection of Race and Sexuality: A Background Paper", the authors argue that "the struggle to win legal protection for people who are discriminated against or stigmatized due to their sexual identity or behavior is integrally linked with the struggle to win rights and legal protections for groups who experience racial discrimination".[5] The remainder of the statement then addresses itself to transforming the "linkage" between sexual and racial discrimination to an equation whereby discrimination based on sexual orientation and discrimination based on race become parallel structures of oppression, and thus privy to the same judicial processes and advocacy. In the case of organizations such as IGLHRC, such analytical shifts are particularly hazardous as these American-based "international" groups emphasize the global and transnational reach of their arguments, haphazardly including postcolonial and neo-colonial locations within the same raced landscape.

In this article, I do not advocate an "against race" argument, but instead outline an analytical strategy where the conjoining of the categories of queer and race within discourses of globalization needs to be rethought and rearticulated. I focus, in particular, on the institutionalization of the "linkages" of queer and race studies in current geopolitical formulations, and the utilization of discourses of human rights and discrimination in such a project. Buried, in such "linkages", is the very mathematical paradox of parallelism that forecloses any true intersection, even as it invites lines of common origin and travel. Hence, we are often left with a language of analogy and repetition where race as sex and sex as race become parallel political formations only through a constant reminder of their irreconcilable separation. Instead, I wish to theorize the productive possibility of a Spivakian "transactional reading" that articulates the analogical imperative as a "site of the displacement of function between sign systems". Within such transactional readings, the linking of sex and race becomes a dynamic dilation of difference, even as it speaks the language of similarity and kinship. Such a reading elaborates the very act of analogy as an active transaction between oppositions, even as it puts these oppositions into question, in "the breaking and relinking of the [signifying] chain" (Spivak 1985: 333–37).

What I want to do here, with the help of the murky genealogies of sex and race that my opening examples have already outlined for us, is ask the following questions: Given the rise of queer transnational work, of which I am a hesitant producer, how do we translate the analytical paradigm of "race" outside of its formations in the United States? Do queer transnational projects fall easily under the umbrella of the queer/race project, or do their theoretical formulations require a different rendering of the project? If "race", for instance, as understood in the context of a geography like India is a model of analysis that works only in relation to either colonial or neo-colonial structures of knowledge (i.e., Indians are "raced" in relation to their construction in colonial or neo-colonial epistemes), how do we read "race" through a grid of similarities instead of differences as in the case of postcolonial India? In order to answer these questions and more, I examine some contemporary mobilizations of the race/sex nexus, especially after the events of 9/11.

Fags not flags: thank God for the West

One problematic effect of the "international" project of global queering, or what Joseph Massad has called the emergence of "Gay International", has been the growing public presence of Al-Fatiha, a non-profit organization for gay Muslims based in the United States. Founded in 1997 by Faisal Alam, a Pakistani-American Muslim, Al-Fatiha's mission statement reads as follows:

> Al-Fatiha is an international organization dedicated to Muslims who are gay, lesbian, bisexual, transgendered, those questioning their sexual orientation and/or gender identity, and aims to support LGBTQ Muslims in reconciling their sexual orientation or gender identity with Islam. Al-Fatiha promotes the Islamic notions of social justice, peace, and tolerance through its work, to bring all closer to a world that is free from injustice, prejudice, and discrimination.[6]

Al-Fatiha follows in the footsteps of GLAS (Gay and Lesbian Arabic [sic] Society), founded in 1989, to help gay Muslims be "part of the global gay and lesbian movement" (quoted in

Massad 2002). Both organizations clearly articulate their links to some avatar of global queer solidarity, albeit based on what they outline as their corrective view of Islamic ideology and heritage. The critical impulse, especially behind the mission statement of Al-Fatiha, is that the organization merely seeks to explicate, make "right" what is misread, "wrong" in fundamentalist and Western readings of Islam. Joseph Massad, in his work on the linkages between the Gay International and the Arab World, argues that Al-Fatiha's gestures of ideological reform *vis à vis* Islam merely echo the missionary zeal embedded in the rhetoric of organizations such as ILGHRC and ILGA (International Lesbian and Gay Association). For Massad, just as Muslims within pre-modern Western articulations were attacked for their sexual licentiousness, the modern West now reorders that attack on the grounds of Islam's alleged repression of sexual freedoms. Organizations such as Al-Fatiha thus merely continue the hegemony of the sexual epistemology of identity over practice, so necessary to the establishment of an identity-based global queer movement emanating from the West.

Since its inception in November 1997, Al-Fatiha has also received extensive publicity in major queer-friendly and queer-focused newspapers and magazines in North America and Europe, ranging from *The Advocate*, *Trikone* magazine, *The Gay Times* (UK) and *The New York Times*, to name a select few. The Al-Fatiha website also proudly (and indiscriminately) proclaims its coverage in a range of non-Western media sites in Bangladesh, Turkey and India, underlining through such claims that its membership is growing and spreading globally. The website does not describe the particular discursive locations of this much-touted coverage in Bangladesh and/or India, for instance, disavowing, as it were, any sites of local challenge. In fact, Al-Fatiha has been heavily criticized by the main grassroots lesbian rights group, Stree Sangam, in Mumbai, India, for producing "dangerously communal rhetoric" around essential religious identities (Shah 2001). In a metropolitan space like Mumbai, India, which has still not entirely recovered from the Hindu-right's hysterical denouncements of a lesbian relationship depicted in Deepa Mehta's *Fire*, Al-Fatiha's mission, however tolerantly imagined, still comes up short. By claiming to speak for all Muslims, and in the name of a corrective Islam, Al-Fatiha produces merely another equally flattening order of things, delinking geopolitical landscapes from the racialization and sexualization of bodies. Arab Muslims stand in for South Asian Muslims and so on, producing the symbolic corpus of gay Muslim identity that continuously overlooks its own geographical and historical fractures.

A dangerous effect of such elisions of differences within and between what is articulated as "Muslim", "gay", "queer", "Arab", "South Asian" can be most markedly seen in the responses of public cultures after the events of 9/11. In the weeks following the World Trade Center and Pentagon attacks, media and activist groups recorded the increasing proliferation of hate-crimes against Arab-Americans, Sikhs and various "others" who come under the purview of difference ("mistaken identity") as broadly conceived and stretched within gender and racial terms. In the aftermath of 9/11, the consolation of a racially motivated crime replaces the specter of gay bashing in a proudly liberal urban space such as San Francisco. Hence, in San Francisco, for example, a Latino gay man was reportedly beaten up for appearing Middle Eastern by a gang of Latino youngsters in early October, while the media quietly ignored the presence of his gay white lover who accompanied him and was also similarly brutalized by the same group of individuals. Such misrecognitions of civil rights have been accompanied by a concurrent and visible remasculinization of American culture as strong, turban-less, aggressively heterosexual, and refueled with a newer, more bellicose version of the colonial *mission civilisatrice*. On a visit to New York, two weeks after the attacks, a friend who lives and works in midtown Manhattan, passed on a poster of a caricatured Bin Laden being anally penetrated by the Empire State Building. The scribbled text accompanying the poster read: "So you like them big, bitch?" A few days later, the poster reappeared as a sardonic, anonymous Internet image on my computer screen from my local queer watch group, courtesy of a subject title that read: "The Empire Strikes Back." Here the nexus of race and sex had reappeared in a more vicious version of racialized homophobia where American reprisals render homosexuality into the ultimate form of punishment. Fags not flags were to be the answer to the attacks against the United States. Clearly, such representations of the enemy as the demonized faggot figure are not unusual. During the Gulf War, Saddam Hussein suffered similar treatment at the hands of Internet cartoonists and other resident public commentators (see Puar and Rai 2004).

Interestingly, within such times of representational peril, Al-Fatiha has taken on the role of producing itself as the ideal secular body in response to what it sees as senseless hate-crimes against those perceived as Muslims. Al-Fatiha members have routinely adopted the voice of the new, secularized Islamic body, espousing what they see as a much-needed liberal and Western-friendly reading of Islam and Muslim identity. Faisal Alam, the young founder of the group which now has six chapters in the United States, two in Canada, and one in the United Kingdom, defends his organization's efforts by emphasizing the linkages between his efforts to democratize and domesticate Islam (by accepting homosexuality) and the crackdown in the United States on Islamic militants: "We're trying to make this our home. We like the freedom here. And we don't want to seem like a foreign entity."[7] Alam's efforts have gained much press primarily after a "*fatwa*" was issued by Sheikh Omar Bakri Mohammed, head of the British Islamic group Al-Muharjiroun, after Al-Fatiha publicized an open conference for gay Muslims in 2001. The decree in the much publicized "*fatwa*" rejected the very existence of Al-Fatiha as illegitimate, condemning its members to the death sentence, anticipating as it were the very language that Al-Qaeda, Bin-Laden's network would use to denounce the United States and its allies.

An article in the 18 October 2001 issue of *The Guardian* extends this American logic of incorporation to its British allies. The article boldly titled "An Islamic Revolutionary" is a feature on Adnan Ali, founder of the British branch of Al-Fatiha, and portrays him as the selfless new hero of secular Muslims, and by extension of the secular West. Adnan Ali, in response to a question on the relationship of gay Muslims to the larger (read: white) community, answers: "There's a lot of Islamophobia, to them [gay Muslims], everyone is like the Taliban." Here, the confusions of communalism, bigotry and terrorism collude to produce the gay Muslim as the modern revolutionary, fighting against the absolutism of competing systems of intolerant whiteness and Islamic fundamentalism. And in case the reader becomes too disturbed by this image, the author, Tania Branigan, coyly adds that Ali is "clean-shaven" and gentle as he thoughtfully strokes his hairless chin in response to her questions. In this case, fags, Al-Fatiha's gay Muslim subjects become the new purveyors of Western democracy, the Bin-Ladenesque Islamic revolutionaries domesticated to clean-shaven, secular subjects of the Union Jack (Branigan 2001).

Even as faith-based queer organizations like Al-Fatiha placate American liberal sentiment, there are others who continue to join the fray, in louder and more visible form. The heavily orchestrated publication of Irshad Manji's *The Trouble with Islam: A Muslim's Call for Reform in Her Faith* (Manji 2003) in the United States and Canada is one such striking example. Manji, a self-designated "Muslim refusnik" is a prominent lesbian talk-show host in Canada who claims she wrote the book because "Islam is on very thin ice with me" (Manji 2003: 1). Manji argues for an Islamic reformation, substituting *jihad*, or religious war, with *ijtihad*, independent critical thinking for Muslims. And of course, it is no small coincidence that such reform can only take place in countries such as the United States where Muslims are wildly free from the suffocating totalitarianism of the Islamic world (Manji 2003: 2–24). Under Manji's "Western eyes", to slightly misquote Chandra Talpade-Mohanty here, globalization is the new freedom. As she glibly writes: "Maybe in your steely-eyed revolt against globalization . . . you've concluded that the universality of freedom is a slick euphemism for the uniformity of culture. Get real. Under globalization's "uniformity," nobody forces me on pain of execution to patronize the golden arches. I can choose *not* to read a McDonald's menu" (Manji 2003: 202).

While there is much to be said about the problematic and dangerous success of Manji's book in the United States and Canada, I want to restrict my comments here to the strategic mobilization of her "Muslim queer" identity. Manji's website (www.irshadmanji.com) carefully documents the transnational reach of her book – the book has been published in over ten countries – and contains links to free downloadable Urdu and Arabic translations of the text. We are told that bookstores in Pakistan, for example, are afraid to sell the book, and Manji's American-based website, with its free Arabic and Urdu translations, is designed to make such material hurdles disappear. The website also provides multiple testimonies, letters and links that attest to Manji's impact on Muslim communities, from young straight girls thanking her for her bravery, to angry Mullahs berating her for her vilification of Islam. What is fascinating about the website, and Manji's book in particular, is her management of her lesbianism. In a book that takes on the most sensationalized aspects of islam (*hijab*, *fatwas*, adultery, fanaticism), Manji's own publicized identity as a lesbian remains curiously uninter-rogated, emerging only as an occasional marker of interest. It is as if being a queer Muslim is paradoxically a topic of least and most interest. That is to say, Manji's call for reform in Islam is most successful because she is understood as a lesbian, a context that somehow needs the least explanation. Islam's "troubles" can thus only be articulated through the voice of a lesbian, as Manji herself says, "in appreciation of what the West has done for me. I owe the West my willingness to help reform Islam. In all honesty, my fellow Muslims, you do too" (Manji 2003: 203).

Critical queer/race studies: some interventions

Thus far, I have outlined some symptomatic debates through which the facile (and sometimes not so facile) conflations of race and sex produce gross misrepresentations of historical and geopolitical subjects and issues. What I want to do now is to provide some examples of critical work where the epistemic violence of such analogical gestures is being interrogated and negotiated. One such intellectual space of intervention is the burgeoning arena of critical queer/race studies in the United States. Critical queer/race studies, broadly defined, explores the interrelated, epistemological frameworks of critical race studies and queer studies. Through the study of a range of philosophical, scientific, literary and cinematic texts, to name a select few, it rigorously historicizes and theorizes nineteenth-, twentieth- and twenty-first-century efforts to simultaneously link and separate theories of race and sexuality. Overall, this is an interdisciplinary field, where the interstices between "factual" and "fictional" materials on sexuality and race are constantly exploded and expanded upon. Building on the work of critical race studies scholars like Kimberle Crenshaw, Richard Delgado, Kendall Thomas and Patricia Williams, critical queer/race studies extends interrogations of intersectionality and legal interpretation to questions of sexuality and race, as they emerge both in equal rights discourse, as well as the intellectual space of the academy. Recent collections such as *Q and A: Queer in Asian America* (1998), *Queer Diasporas* (Patton and Sánchez-Eppler 2000), the special issue of *Callaloo* on black queer studies (Vol. 23, No. 1) and *Queer Globalizations: Citizenship and the Afterlife of Colonialism* (2002) elaborate on the relationship of racial difference to the constitution of sexuality, and could, to some extent, be excellent examples of critical queer/race scholarship within the academic arena.

The past decade in queer scholarship has also witnessed a perceptible shift in queer studies to include questions of transnationalism, and its effects on the impact of queer movements globally. Such shifts have been in response to the growing sense that the proliferation of transnational sexual diasporas is challenging the ways in which we understand and disseminate categories of the sexual, the nation, and the subject. Thus, *GLQ: A Journal of Gay and Lesbian Studies* produced a special issue entitled "Thinking Sexuality Transnationally" (Povinelli and Chauncey 1999) with the explicit goal of placing critical studies of sex along-side discourses of globalization and transnationalism, and by extension, urging the literatures of globalization to also incorporate theorizations of mediated cultural forms such as sexuality in their analysis of social phenomena. Much of these efforts to critically "transnationalize" queer studies in the United States have also emerged in response to severe criticism from international scholars about the provinciality of American-based queer criticism.

An example of the kinds of international criticism the new work in queer studies in the United States is attempting to address can be best understood through the terms of the continued debate on the issue of "global queering". This debate attempts to formulate, albeit awkwardly and generally, the uneven relationship between the United States' neo-colonialist, capital presence and the onslaught of a proliferating "queer subjects", produced and encouraged, partially, through the dissemination of vehicles such as "queer theory". The debate was most aggressively rehearsed in the August 1996 issue of the *Australian Humanities Review* where Dennis Altman argued for a renewed skepticism toward the liberating claims of "queer theory", pointing to the pervasiveness of the North American (read: American) model of gayness and its appropriation in the post-industrial, and more interestingly, the industrializing world (Altman 1996a). Altman's piece raised much ire and discussion, and was accompanied by a host of responses from queer scholars such as David Halperin, Christopher Lane and so on. Altman has since then followed this piece with a similar one in an issue of *Social Text* where he takes us on a dizzyingly haphazard tour of the "homosexual world" in countries such as Thailand, the Philippines and Japan, suggesting, rather banally, I would argue, for closer attention to the political economy of sexuality in each of the specific locations. For Altman, there are "indigenous" movements and subcultures that need to be read in their "original" state before the arresting contamination of global queering "Westernizes" them beyond reprieve (Altman 1996b).

In Altman's view, "Westernization" in this new queer version is continuing the process of capitalist exploitation that these "Third World" countries have always experienced at the hands of First World economies. And queer theory, despite its assumed radicalness and political underpinnings, Altman argues, has done little to address these concerns – a fact not helped by the old bugbear of all theory: its arcane language – as he says "one might compliment Eve Sedgwick for her intelligence, but hardly for her style . . . this theory is totally ignored by the vast majority of people whose life it purports to describe" (Altman 1996a). Altman's most recent addition to the debate is his new book, *Global Sex*, which once again continues (in more taxingly detailed form) the theoretical questions he outlined in his earlier pieces (Altman 2001).

I elaborate the terms of Altman's critique because, first, it does signal important lacunae in queer studies which (despite the texts I have cited earlier) is still prominently American-based and ostensibly disinterested in geopolitical formations and in any possible intersectionalities with the kinds of historicist and materialist questions that postcolonial critics such as, for example, the Subaltern Studies group continue to pose. Second, what is equally interesting are the flaws in Altman's attempt to expose and remedy what he sees at fault in current queer work. While championing the cause of the "indigenous" or the "native" (categories whose demarcations have always eluded me), Altman assumes that there is no indigenous greed, or alternative market space, or consumer culture – that it is only Westernization and its American-created queer cultures that create such economic formations. The limits of such observations are evident in the work of transnational studies scholars such as Aihwa Ong who have repeatedly emphasized the need to decenter the hegemony of the American impact model, and to instead articulate the simultaneity of multiple local and global spatialities. Thus, Ong's work in China, specifically Shanghai, foregrounds the upheavals brought on by the entry of Japanese and Korean entrepreneurs into local economies that far outweigh any damage American multinationals are doing (Ong 1999). Ong's focus on a differentiated locale could thus reorient American-based prescriptions about sexuality and geopolitics.

Altman's (1997) construction of the United States crippling "global gaze/gays" phenomenon can be challenged further through an examination of the specific work of queer scholars whose work originates, as it were, in his eulogized and privileged space of authentic nativist production. In this example, so-called "indigenous theorization" suffers from an equally constraining homogenization and/or essentialization. I am referring here to Giti Thadani's *Sakhiyani: Lesbian Desire in Ancient and Modern India* (Thadani 1996). Postcolonial queer critics such as Ruth Vanita have pointed out that American-based theory is often dismissed within Indian intellectual circles as politically suspect and unworthy of serious intellectual labor and recovery, a skepticism that extends beyond just the provenance of queer theory (Vanita 1996). Within such a framework, what does it then mean for Giti Thadani, the Indian founder of an openly lesbian collective, SAKHI, to author a book from a postcolonial geographical location that deploys the same theoretical gestures that Altman and the Indian academy repudiate? Thadani's book recuperates the strategies of historical genealogy, lesbian invisibility and identity and deploys them in her reading of lesbian culture in India. Her project is also remarkably guilt-free of its own complicity in these so-called "Western" critical gestures. In fact, Thadani begins sections of her book with quotations from Edward Said's *Orientalism* and crafts the lesbian movement in India in the same stylized ways as the gay movement in the United States. The significant and useful difference is her exhaustive evidence of, and gesture to, the specificity of her context. Thadani provides specific Indian models to all the so-called "Western critical manners" being adopted, resurrecting an eerie shadow of what Homi Bhabha has called the concept of "colonial mimicry". While Thadani's book is fraught with historical and scholarly inaccuracies, and gross schematizations of the archives she has uncovered, her book still opens up new terrains for investigation – a first major exploration of lesbians in South Asia, especially in the space of queer transnational work where the deemed preoccupation – by necessity, or by choice – is still the histories and anthropologies of gay men.

A second model of critical queer/race studies would be the one we see emblazoned in recent gay rights discourse such as that of IGLHRC, what Janet Halley has recently called the "like race" advocacy language that "joins sexual constituencies to race constituencies". Halley (2000: 46) argues that the "central legal achievement of litigation waged on behalf of the black civil rights movement was a historic succession of equal protection holdings". Attempting to work with such equal rights precedents, gay and lesbian advocates frequently reiterate that sexual orientation is like race, or that gay men and lesbians are like a racial group, or that anti-gay policies are like racist policies, or that homophobia is like racism. While it is obvious that the analogical imperative is in some ways inbuilt into American case law (within the logic of legal precedent) and perhaps all public discourse, Halley cautions against the dangers of such liaisons, not just in terms of a critique of rights discourse (which scholars such as Wendy Brown have done so well) but more in terms of the damage it does to the complexity of the queer model. Thus, "like race" arguments produce a perilous universalizing structure to understand queers, what Halley (2000: 49) categorizes as the "integrationalist model". Such a model clearly works against the very notion of "queer" activism which relies on a fractured, non-cohesive identity formation. An additional problem with the "like race" argument is an assumption that one knows what "race" is in legal terms. And within our current milieu of anti-affirmative action policies, many activists have strategically chosen to organize their claims for equal protection rights within the new form, "not like race". Halley (2000: 68) cites the example of a Native Hawaiian rights claim where the special programs dedicated under federal law to federally maintained Indian tribes and under Hawaiian state law to Native Hawaiian cultural preservation could be erased from the landscape if native groups were understood to be "like race".

Stuart Hall's formulations suggest some additional strategies through which these questions of race, cultural power and political struggle could be imagined *within*, rather than against the grain of "the postcolonial" or, in our case, of "the queer" (Hall 1996). Here my invocation of "queer" alongside "the postcolonial" works more as a rhetorical and political juxtaposition than as violent analogical conflation. In other words, just as India, Brazil, Mexico, on the one hand, and Britain, Canada and the United States are not raced in the same ways, does not mean that they are not raced in any way. To extrapolate from Hall, the very constitution of the idea of queer/race studies as in the general discourse of all theoretical and political projects is always already operating, in Derridean terms, "under erasure" (Hall 1996: 255). To assume, then, for example, that the continued critique of racism, of hetero-sexuality and of Europe in both queer and postcolonial studies contradicts its desire to be "over" precisely those preoccupations misses Hall's point. The project of queer/race studies is no exception, and as practitioners and contributors to such a project, we are particularly aware of the dangers of analogical and telos-driven thinking. Our goal as queer scholars and teachers must then be to make sexuality co-constitutive with writing on labor, race and colonialism, and intervene in discursive formations that would disarticulate queer/race subjects. Thus, even as the repetitions of colonial epistemes rework themselves in the language of analogy, we must think of these echoes more as transactions, as necessary narratives traded for one more day of life.

Notes

1   The first incarnation of this piece was given as a talk at the inaugural conference of the Center for Sexual Cultures at the University of California at Berkeley, 8 March 2002.

2   Quoted here is a transmuted citation. Geeta Patel rewrites Dipesh Chakraborty, "The difference-differal of a colonial modernity: Public debates on domesticity in British India", *Subaltern Studies VIII* (1994): 50–88. Chakraborty, himself, is rewriting Roland Barthes.

3   It is important to note here that Roy's casual reference to being a "gay person" also comes on the heels of a well-publicized High Court decision in Delhi to uphold Section 377 of the Indian Penal Code. Section 377 deems all "unnatural sexual conduct" punishable by law. Roy's "gay person watching straight sex" analogy thus seems even more politically problematic.

4   This discursive gesture is repeated in the formulations of nation and terrorism in the crisis in Afghanistan. One Pakistani diplomat registered some skepticism at the United States' new alignment with Pakistan and noted that "Pakistan was simply the condom that the US is using to penetrate Afghanistan. Once they are done, they will toss us aside, as they have done in the past" ("Quotables", *Frontline*, 25 September 2001).

5   The Intersection of Race and Sexuality: A Background Paper with Amendments and Proposals for the Draft Declaration and Programme of Action for the World Conference against Racism, Racial Discrimination, Xenophobia and Related Intolerance, IGLHRC, 27 August 2001. Available on their website at: www.ighlhrc.org.

6   *Al-Fatiha Home Page*, www.al-fatiha.net/ (accessed 30 October 2001).

7   See www.thegully.com/essays/gaymundo/011027_gay_muslims.html (accessed 27 October 2001).

References

Altman, Dennis (1996a) "On global queering", *Australian Humanities Review* (August). Available online at: www.lib.latrobe.edu.au/AHR.

— (1996b) "The internationalization of gay identities", *Social Text* 48(14/3): 77–94.

— (1997) "Global gaze/global gays", *Gay and Lesbian Quarterly* 3: 417–36.

— (2001) *Global Sex*, Chicago, IL: University of Chicago Press.

Branigan, Tania (2001) "An Islamic revolutionary", *The Guardian*, 18 October.

Campaign for Lesbian Rights (1999) "Introduction", in *Campaign for Lesbian Rights: Lesbian Emergence*, Bombay, pp. 1–4.

Crenshaw, Kimberle (1993) "Demarginaliziing the intersection of race and sex: A black feminist critique of antidiscrimination doctrine, feminist theory and antiracist polities", in D. Kelly Weisburg (ed.) *Feminist Legal Theory: Foundations*, Philadelphia, PA: Temple University Press, pp. 383–98.

Foucault, Michel (1977) "Nietzsche, genealogy, history", in *Language, Countermemory, Practice: Selected Essays and Interviews by Michel Foucault*, ed. and trans. Donald F. Bouchard, Ithaca, NY: Cornell University Press, pp. 139–64.

Hall, Stuart (1996) "When was the 'post-colonial'? Thinking at the limit", in Iain Chambers and Lidia Curti (eds.) *The Post-Colonial Question: Common Skies, Divided Horizons*, London/New York: Routledge, pp. 242–60.

Halley, Janet E. (2000) "'Like race' arguments", in Judith Butler, John Guillory and Kendall Thomas (eds.) *What's Left of Theory? New Work on the Politics of Literary Theory*, New York: Routledge, pp. 40–74.

Kaur, Davinder (2001) "Grumble of distant drums", *Outlook* (17 September): 22–27.

Manji, Irshad (2003) *The Trouble with Islam: A Muslim's Call for Reform in Her Faith*, New York: St. Martin's Press.

Massad, Joseph (2002) "Re-orienting desire: The Gay International and the Arab world", *Public Culture* 14(2): 361–85.

Ong, Aihwa (1999) *Flexible Citizenship: The Cultural Logic of Transnationality*, Durham, NC: Duke University Press.

Patel, Geeta (1998) 'Ghostly Appearances: Time Tales Tallied Up'. Unpublished manuscript.

Patton, Cindy and Sánchez-Eppler, Benigno (2000) *Queer Diasporas*, Durham, NC: Duke University Press.

Povinelli, Elizabeth and Chauncey, George (1999) "Thinking sexuality transnationally", *Gay and Lesbian Quarterly* 5(4): 439–50.

Puar, Jasbir and Rai, Amit (2004) "The remaking of a model minority: Perverse projectiles under the specter of (counter)terrorism", *Social Text* 2(3): 75–104.

Roy, Arundhati (2004) "Seize the time: An interview", *International Socialist Review* 38: 1–13.

Shah, Tejal (2001) Member of Stree Sangam, Mumbai. Personal Interview, 6 November.

Spivak, Gayatri Chakravorty (1985) "Subaltern studies: Deconstructing historiography", in Ranajit Guha (ed.) *Subaltern Studies IV: Writings on South Asian History and Society*, Delhi: Oxford University Press, pp. 330–63.

Thadani, Giti (1996) *Sakhiyani: Lesbian Desire in Ancient and Modern India*, London: Cassell.

Vanita, Ruth (1996) Queer Readings of Suniti Namjoshi. Paper presented at the MLA Panel "All Quiet on the Queer Front: In the Closets of Post-Colonial Theory".

Chapter 33

Lucas Cassidy Crawford

TRANSGENDER WITHOUT ORGANS? MOBILIZING A GEO-AFFECTIVE THEORY OF GENDER MODIFICATION

Lucas Cassidy Crawford is an academic, poet, performance artist, and community activist. A former Trudeau Scholar at the University of Alberta, Crawford's work has appeared in a range of scholarly and non-academic publications, including *Women's Studies Quarterly*, the *Journal of Gender Studies*, and the *Seattle Journal for Social Justice*.

With its reference to Gilles Deleuze and Félix Guattari's "body without organs," "Transgender without Organs?" argues for an alternative model of transsexual subjectivity, one less dependent on urban relocation, financial resources for surgery, or even queer community recognition. While a dominant mode of transgender experience is the feeling of being trapped in the wrong body, Crawford observes that experiences of body modification have also produced metaphors of territoriality. Arguing that this dominant feeling obscures a potentially more radical understanding of trans bodily sensations, and that such metaphors valorize the city and all that it purportedly guarantees, Crawford compels us to understand that bodily affect and its surrounding environment are generative of each other. If transgender subjectivity is no longer a matter of individual psyche or altered body parts, choosing where and how to live, particularly the inhabitation of rural spaces, become modes of body/gender modification, modes that are likely to be more reassuring, even galvanizing, for gender-fuckers everywhere.

1977, HALIFAX, NOVA SCOTIA. My parents will work in their hometown, Halifax, until they save enough money to move to the country: not the neopastoral country of idyllic retirement, leisure, or quaintness, but rather a place of quietude, crops, and the moral high ground that (at least reportedly) makes the country such a good place to raise kids. But just now, my mother works in the emergency room of the Halifax Infirmary, has recently married my father, and remembers having had a crush on Billy Conway in high school. Billy comes by Outpatients almost biweekly, and receives a day of psychiatric treatment when he asks the sympathetic but distant doctor for a sex change. One day, Billy arrives with his severed penis wrapped in a Kleenex, is made to dwell slightly longer in the psych ward before once again being released; he then promptly hangs himself in his boarding room in the city's North End. Soon after, when Billy's former doctor plans to marry an ex-nun (dyke?) he knows, a man who claims to be the doctor's lover arrives in the emergency room after his own suicide attempt. The doctor comes out as gay, but dies a year later of a then unfathomable virus. The infirmary closed in 1998 and was demolished in 2005, after Ron Russell, the minister of transportation and public works, condemned the building as "unsafe and unusable."

When the ruggedly boyish character Moira debuted in season three of Showtime's (in) famous program *The L Word*, many of us working-class, rural, or butch dykes finally undid the collective knot in our boxers. Moira's impromptu move from Skokie to Los Angeles coincided with hir transsexual awakening, however, and s/he transitions to become "Max" in subsequent episodes. Relocating from Illinois to California puts Moira not only literally but also figuratively in different states: of mind, of identity, and of desire. The queer pilgrimage to the city is a far from innovative motif, and even in theories that are attuned to the role of place in queer life, the role of the rural is presumed to be inconsequential. For instance, Jay Prosser (1998) claims that narratives of pre- and post-operative transsexuality belie their authors' nostalgia for bodily homes that never existed, a style of feeling that not only shores up the power we attribute to hominess but also traces on our bodies a one-way journey home. As this model configures gender modification as a safe return rather than a risky exploit or experiment in embodied selfhood, Prosser finds relief in the "transgender ambivalence" (177) he finds in the narratives of non-operative gender-variant writers. Their ambivalence towards place, he argues, reflects and generates their nonteleological orientation to practices of gender modification. For both varieties of trans life, styles of affect are constitutive technologies of embodiment; how one is moved emotionally informs and illustrates the mobility of one's gender and one's home.

Even in the transgender texts Prosser analyzes, however, the reader encounters linear and one-way trips from the country to the city—supplemented, at best, with a short trip or two back to the protagonist's hometown. As an (albeit far more interesting) forerunner to *The L Word*'s Max, Leslie Feinberg's character Jess in *Stone Butch Blues* moves from "the desert" (15) to Buffalo and eventually to New York City, while the protagonist of her other novel, *Drag King Dreams*, lives out her days in this same urban center. The many representations of Brandon Teena's life (especially in *Boys Don't Cry*) work in tandem with such representations of urban queer freedom, attributing Brandon's murder to regressive, purportedly rural, attitudes that are seldom imagined as characteristics of urban communities.

Philosophical and political accounts of queerness all too often corroborate these valorizations of the urban; Kath Weston describes and decries the "Great Gay Migration" to the city (1995, 253), while Douglas Victor Janoff suggests in *Pink Blood: Homophobic Violence in Canada* that "smaller communities . . . would benefit from [the] strategy of reaching out to isolated citizens and connecting them with support and services in larger centres" (2005, 243). The link between the city and the queer seems ineluctable in both instances; in the former, smart queers will eventually come to the city, while in the latter, the city eventually comes to all queers. As a small-town trans person whose life is becoming urban and mobile (in various senses), this link certainly feels experientially true for me, as my cities get bigger and my old dot on the map looks smaller.

Given the filmic and literary examples cited above, an attraction to the urban undoubtedly rings true for many other transgender or transsexual people who crave the emotional and medical resources seemingly unavailable in rural spaces. In this ubiquitous city of queer imaginings, such people might join a movement like Queer Nation; change their gender "citizenship," as Susan Stryker recently described transition at a lecture at the University of Alberta; and read Janice G. Raymond's renowned polemic *The Transsexual Empire* or Sandy

Stone's famous reply, "The Empire Strikes Back: A Posttranssexual Manifesto." Curiously, the experience of gender modification seemingly demands metaphors of sovereign territoriality as well as literal movement from place to place by those who practice it. This coincidence of various kinds of mobility with various kinds of space motivates some preliminary questions: How do geographical or nationist metaphors of transgender community—empire, citizenship, nation, home—both reflect and reify the apparent need for a transgender person's geographical (urban) relocation? Might something more nuanced than access to medical resources, anonymity, and communities based on identity politics or rooted in urban subcultural practices lie behind the geographical relocation of transgender people? If we can imagine that trans people may remain (or wish to remain) in the country by choice and not by accident or unfortunate circumstances, we could see instead that holding our ground says something about our styles of affect: that each bodily transition (from gender to gender or place to place) may be a matter of spatial ethics as much as sexual ones, of orientation to place as much as to the body, of being moved in certain ways as much as moving.

This essay is animated, then, by the question of how our styles of affect and movement may become "trans" in ways that cast doubt upon our current valorization of cities in representations of queer space. How might we trouble our certainty that small towns need to be escaped, that less populous cities can never quite do the trick or ever offer us enough tricks, that migrating to big cities is an unproblematically happy experience untainted by culture shock, or that one's desire to be there is unsullied by contributory conditions such as class or economic need? My motivation for raising such questions is neither to archive nor to justify existent modes of living gender rurally, but rather to point towards new creative potentials. Drawing on Deleuze and Guattari, my aim is to unsettle—their word, significantly, is "deterritorialize" (1987, 156)—the model of the transgender or transsexual subject, if only because this increasingly coherent model of the subject entails practices that demand medical, subcultural, and financial resources often unavailable to (or undesired by) some rural genderfuckers—and probably many urban ones as well.[1] Prying open the terms "transgender" and "transsexual" in a way that might allow more people to belong to them or to desire them is an important project; however, the vignettes and theoretical interventions that constitute this essay also revel in the deterritorializing potential of *not* being recognized, *not* being counted, of being ignored by urban trans theories and cultures, and of finding or crafting ceaseless mobility in seemingly static and conservative locales in ways that may never move trans-urbanites.

How trans moves us

1996, Kingston, Nova Scotia (population twenty-five hundred). Women in this village wear ties daily—they work at the military base. After I am issued my air cadet uniform, I even wear my tie to school sometimes. I excel at being an air cadet, perhaps because the first year of training could be called "How to Be a (Versatile) Butch Bottom" and summarized thus: 1. No long hair. 2. No insubordination within our playful little roles. 3. No makeup. 4. No fancy jewelry. 5. No problem! Air cadet camp is the sleepaway summer program for twelve-year-old proto-butch kids itching for queer kitsch, for boot-campy kids who wax nostalgic for the drag days of summer drill team when August oranges into rural-school September, and for everyone else who wants to black boots and train their bodies for years to earn the privilege of being called Sir or (like me) Ma'am. In ostensibly impersonal militaristic interactions, more than a few queer kids (who always seem to take the top ranks) thrive on feeling very much in the right body and never quite at home with it in the barracks, parade square, or semiformal dances. We, like the other cadets, cry, but with more grit than melancholy, perhaps because we want a witness to our imperceptible gender-fucking. Perhaps we simply miss our small hometowns. But is "homesickness" just a pessimist's way of describing restlessness, a fever for frequent redeployment? Perhaps we cry because we know the secret of it all. But more often than not, queer cadets can't stop laughing.

In what are probably the three most recognizable transgender narratives in contemporary culture—*Boys Don't Cry*, *The Crying Game*, and *Stone Butch Blues*—even the titles signal the affect of sadness: characters move from place to place and gender to gender as readers and viewers are moved to tears by these transitions. The concurrence of these different kinds of "being moved" is not simply coincidental; Prosser notes that the "metaphoric territorializing of gender and literal territorializations of physical space have often gone hand in hand" in transgender narrative (1998, 171), an unsurprising collapse, perhaps, given that the singular site of the body is the affective space where both cycles of reification are produced and played out.

If my affective account of the relationship between transgender subjectivity and spatiality seems counterintuitive, two theorists of queer affect may help clarify the precedents as well as the stakes of such a project. Ann Cvetkovich's *An Archive of Feelings: Trauma, Sexuality, and Lesbian Public Cultures* recoups a number of ostensibly negative feelings. Cvetkovich argues: "Affect, including the affects associated with trauma, serves as the foundation for the formation of public cultures. . . . Rather than a model in which privatized responses displace collective or political ones, my book proposes a collapsing of these distinctions so that affective life can be seen to pervade public life" (2003, 10). Cvetkovich's text deftly illustrates the productive and creative work that can be generated by treating feelings as publicly significant acts. In her earlier text, *Mixed Feelings: Feminism, Mass Culture, and Victorian Sensationalism* (1992), she reminds readers that while the personal may be political, the political is not necessarily subversive. Thus, the affective experience of transgender may always be political, but the narratives we craft from these affects, and the actions we take in response to them, are not always or obviously resistant. The danger in this conflation of affect and action, Cvetkovich warns, is that any phenomenon that generates a specifically physical response is all too often used to affirm the supposed naturalness of that feeling—a tautological maneuver that shores up, among other things, the notion of an inborn gender identity that we "feel" to be "true."

While Prosser's work exemplifies the applicability of affect studies to trans life, it also demonstrates the liability of treating affect as an explanation for actions and identities. As he makes clear in *Second Skins: The Body Narratives of Transsexuality* (1998), the feelings associated with inhabiting the "wrong body" are the ones that have, in the manner Cvetkovich describes, formed the most accessible public narrative of transsexuality. Prosser vindicates the transsexual's desire to change sex by way of analyzing and trusting the ways in which the body feels and responds to certain procedures of gender modification, or, conversely, by the lack of such responses. Responding to the widely held assumption that transsexuals are pathological at worst, or falsely conscious Cartesian dupes at best, Prosser states his contention "that transsexuals continue to deploy the image of wrong embodiment because being trapped in the wrong body is simply what transsexuality feels like" (69). In this account, affect is not an expression of transsexuality but is, rather, the definitive condition of it. Prosser arrives at this formulation of affect via his interest in psychoanalyst Didier Anzieu's *The Skin Ego*, which holds that one's ego is a mental projection of what one feels (as the title suggests) through one's skin. Against those who believe that transsexuals are the worst kind of body/mind dualists, Prosser argues that a self who feels accommodated by the wrong body is already corporeal through and through: "Body image . . . clearly already has a material force for transsexuals" (69), insofar as the ego "is ultimately derived from bodily sensations" (65).

This is a challenging formulation of affect insofar as it implies that feelings are generative rather than reflective, productive rather than derivative, and innovative rather than symptomatic of something less corporeal or more pathological. It is surprising, then, that Prosser thinks that affects "simply" (69) occur or are simply translated into the narratives and conventional procedures of gender modification. Aside from the point that living in the wrong body is certainly not "what transsexuality feels like" (69) *for everyone*, it is worth noting that no bodily sensation carries its own self-evident meaning or orders for action prior to our reformulating these affects into narratives. While the present essay is premised on Prosser's insistence that transsexuality is a matter of affect at least as much as it is a matter of certain procedures of gender transition, Prosser's defense of the wrong-body narrative runs the risk not only of settling on just one definition of the "right" trans affect, but also of figuring affect as an extremely personal phenomenon that has very little to do with others, or with places outside of one's (embodied) home.

The role of Prosser's Freudianism, which trusts that one's psyche will speak through words or through one's signifying body, is obvious in his assumption that a wrong-body narrative is simply a verbal translation of a particular affect. Prosser comes dangerously close to suggesting that wrong-body narratives emanate from our skin without the effects of other people or places, or external ideas about gender. If Freud's taken-for-granted equation of signification and affect allows the latter term to figure unproblematically in our analyses of desire, then it is entirely appropriate to turn to Deleuze and Guattari, whose complex oeuvre aims in part to formulate a specifically anti-Freudian theory of affect, to begin refiguring the relationship between affect and signification. As Freud and Prosser would have it, the formation of the self occurs when one creates a mental projection of the sensations one feels. Affects, for Deleuze and Guattari, operate in precisely the opposite way: they *undo* the subject "like weapons" (1987, 400): they "open a way out" (258) and mount a "counterattack" (400) to even our best attempts to settle on identities and desires. These dangerous bodily occurrences—"arrows," "weapons," and "projectiles" (400), as they are described—are not simply the raw or pre-verbal form of the emotions we know as love, envy, anger, or even the bodily uncanniness that inspires wrong-body narratives. Rather, for Deleuze and Guattari, these narratives of feelings are attempts to harness (and transform) the destructive quality of affect. As they write, "Affect is the active discharge of emotion, the counterattack, whereas feeling is an always displaced, retarded, resisting emotion" (400). As Bonta and Protevi note in *Deleuze and Geophilosophy*, affect is "the capacity to become" (2004, 50), whereas feeling is the reterritorialization of becoming, by means of coding and ultimately controlling it.

Deleuze and Guattari insist vehemently on "an affectability that is no longer that of subjects," but has instead to do with crafting an "assemblage," and with relationships of "symbiosis" (1987, 258). In other words, if affects are generated by proximity, movement, and symbiosis with or between other organisms and environments—a style of relationality that threatens the borders of bodies and identities—why then are they recouped, tamed, and privatized in the name of the subject? This "displaced" and "retarded" (400) harnessing of affect into feelings in fact constitutes "subjectivization," the process through which affect is controlled in order to hold the subject together. For Deleuze and Guattari, affect is the body's capacity to *undermine* our best attempts at deciding on identities and selves. If, in this account, what we call feelings are quite far from bodily sensation, and are actually attempts to maintain the coherence of the subject, then, perhaps Prosser is right to say that "being trapped, in the wrong body is simply what transsexuality *feels* like" (1998, 69, emphasis mine). When Prosser claims that transsexual transition is a "coming home to the self through body" (83), he describes a spatial trajectory that is the opposite of Bonta and Protevi's gloss on deterritorialization: "the process of leaving home, of altering your habits, of learning new tricks" (2004, 78), a series of exploits that sound much more like camp.

Smooth bodies

January 2007, Edmonton, Alberta. In a Jasper Avenue bar connected to a Catholic church, I try to convince a pretty (and) brilliant architect that cities built on grids probably help us become straight, insofar as how we move must affect how we are moved, and that the comfortable feeling of knowing where our bodies are at all times might not in fact be a very queer feeling. His soused-up lecture on what was so radical, in the first instance, about the nonmimetic clean straight lines of modern architecture will earn him footnotes later. For now, leaning back on the men's room toilet for a pause, I see his shoes, hear his gentleman's cough at the urinal. I think about him, and his girlfriend, who has reminded me of the excitement of a reciprocated crush.

I will write about this crooked washroom moment and read it at our first drag king show at our one dank and lovely dyke bar—"the last of its kind in Canada," the owner never fails to mention. There have been other shows in years past but nobody seems to know quite when, who, or what they were. "Smooth space does not have a long-term memory with all that that entails, so only microhistories are possible" (Bonta and Protevi 2004, 145).

"You might be able to fill the [thirty] seats," a friend says before the show, but the owner has to lock the door for the first time ever, when this remote back alley bar is almost triple its legal capacity, filled with enthralling people dressed for the occasion of the first drag king show they've ever seen. At intermission I bump into the architect and his girlfriend. "Yep, this is Edmonton, all right," I think: nobody is avoidable and I almost always love this way in which rural accountability permeates our semi-urban space.

A year later, I avoid the temptation to tell the architect that Sara Ahmed (2006) argues in Queer Phenomenology *that desire and affect are generated by our various habits of turning and directing the body, writing that "the etymology of 'direct' relates to 'being straight' or getting 'straight to the point.' To go directly is to follow a line without a detour, without mediation. Within the concept of direction is a concept of 'straightness.' To follow a line might be a way of becoming straight, by not deviating at any point" (16). But I don't call the architect, or his girlfriend. Instead, I'll smile obliquely at their summer wedding as they walk down the narrow aisle, looking gorgeously aslant.*

Insofar as Deleuze and Guattari consider the affect of a body and its surrounding environment to be mutually constitutive, it is not for rhetorical flourish alone that they continually employ geographical vocabulary and geo-oriented descriptions of the spaces in which affects occur, including their figure of the nomad who "clings to the smooth space left by the receding forest, where the steppe or the desert advances" (1987, 381). It's worth repeating that the word they use to denote the disruptive force of affect is "deterritorialization" (142). In his recent essay, "Space in the Age of Non-place," Ian Buchanan notes that "deterritorialization names the process whereby the very basis of one's identity, the proverbial ground beneath our feet, is eroded, washed away like the bank of a river swollen by floodwater" (2005, 23). In this decidedly pastoral metaphor, Buchanan reminds us that, just as trans life seems to demand literal and figural movement, so does Deleuze and Guattari's deterritorialization of the subject implicate both body and space. In this sense, the literal shapes we impose upon bodies, buildings, or hillsides are constitutive of how we will be able to move and be moved.

If these nonurban motifs are not accidental, how might a kind of gender nomadism—of refusing home, of refusing the straightest and quickest path between two points—demand a reconfiguration of how we think and feel about space? Deleuze and Guattari's distinction between smooth and striated space suggests that, against any simple rural/urban dichotomy (which is itself instituted only through the boundary-tracing authority of the city), nomadic and radical ways of living with/in (or as) space can happen in any locale, including a rather rural city of a million dispersed people such as Edmonton. To think through the usefulness of this model of striated/smooth for trans relationships to space, I cite at length first Bonta and Protevi, then Deleuze and Guattari:

> Striated space is first griddled and delineated, then occupied, by the drawing of rigid lines that compartmentalize reality into segments, all controlled to a

greater or lesser extent through a nested hierarchy of center. . . . Thus striated
space, because it is composed of centers, is productive of remoteness, of the
entire idea that there are places of more and of less importance. Striation imparts
the "truth" that "place" is an immobile point and that immobility (dwelling) is
always better than "aimless" voyaging, wandering, itinerancy, and of course
nomadism. . . . The city . . . is what allows the striation of a larger territory.

(Bonta and Protevi 2004, 154)

Smooth space is precisely the space of the smallest deviation: therefore it has no
homogeneity, except between infinitely proximate points, and the linking of
proximity is effected independently of any determined path. It is a space of
contact, of small tactile or manual actions of contact, rather than a visual
space. . . . Smooth space is a field without conduits or channels. A field, a
heterogeneous smooth space, is wedded to a very particular type of multiplicity:
nonmetric, acentered, rhizomatic multiplicities that occupy space without
"counting" it and can "be explored only by legwork." They do not meet the
visual condition of being observable from a point in space external to them.

(Deleuze and Guattari 1987, 371)

With their coded roads, maps, and high straight buildings from which one might see the
streets without moving, urban centers seem just what Deleuze and Guattari have in mind
when they describe striated space. Perhaps their smooth or nomadic space may not be the
random gay bars or drag shows to which one roves in a strange city, but instead, quite literally "a field" (371), the kind where rural queers might have first kisses or redneck trannies
might roam, work, or play. In valorizing the work of *Queer Nation*, Lauren Berlant and
Elizabeth Freeman suggest that this activist group succeeds in confounding the question of
"where" the nation itself might be located; "it names," they say, "multiple local and national
publics; it does not look for a theoretical coherence to regulate in advance all of its tactics: all
politics in the *Queer Nation* are imagined on the street" (Berlant and Freeman 1997, 151). This
is all too true, insofar as *Queer Nation*'s tactics (such as claiming the public space of a shopping
mall to hand out pro-queer information) are achieved by using certain versions of publicity,
by assuming the possibility of anonymity, and by imagining that "the *street*" somehow belongs
and speaks to all queers. Indeed, to the disapproval of Deleuze and Guattari and their privileging of smoothness, this popular model of queer nationhood—and indeed, the very institution of the Pride Parade—assumes the presence of "street" (Berlant and Freeman 1997, 151)
and its "direct" centrality to bent queer life.

Interpreting Deleuze and Guattari's distinction of smooth and striated space as merely
another way of saying rural and urban would be to oversimplify. To hick trannies for whom
public transit is a mere abstraction, a space "explored only by legwork" (Deleuze and Guattari
1987, 371) is concretely familiar. Likewise, while a field appears meticulously organized to a
farmer, or a series of landmarks may function as striations for local residents, these people
"are not necessarily forces for imparting" the effect of these markings "beyond their own
neighbourhood" (Bonta and Protevi 2004, 154), as urban thinkers or planners might be.
Insofar as the striation of space is not conducive to becoming, this imperative needs to be
actively resisted. That which is striated is, by definition, not remote. Perhaps an overarching
revaluing of the very concept of "remoteness" is required to rethink the value of the rural
realm and the bodies that (choose to) assemble with/in it. If, for Deleuze and Guattari, "the
body or assemblage in question is co-constituted along with the space it occupies" (Bonta and
Protevi 2004, 146), it is clear that where one lives and moves is more than a blank space into
which subjects arrive fully formed; rather, choosing where to live and how to live with/in its

spaces are technologies of the (undoing of the) subject, equally as much as those surgical and hormonal technologies we recognize more easily as body/gender modification.

The suggestion that we ought to roam and fuck with the grids and codes of striated spaces deterritorializes the valorization of city dwelling, ownership, and organized urban life that often accompanies representations or expectations of trans life. Regarding space and movement as constitutive of one's gender presupposes that, contra Prosser, gender identity is neither simply a matter of the psyche or the skin nor a way in which the subject ought to shore up his or her sense of body hominess. But, if our modes of moving and being moved are indeed so closely intertwined, what ethic of body modification does this reconsideration of remoteness and smooth spaces evoke? Significantly, Bonta and Protevi suggest that "we need to emphasize that striated (and smooth) can be features of non-geographic assemblages (desire, music, and cloth, to cite examples from *A Thousand Plateaus*) and so are not restricted to spaces of interest to geographical pursuits at the scale of the human or the landscape" (2004, 155). In other words, given that processes of gender modification may also be smooth or striated, how do we engage in practices of body morphology that strive toward the smooth, that aim to deterritorialize the subject rather than settle it, to become a nomad rather than come "home to the self through body" (Prosser 1998, 83)? Conceiving of practices of body modification—including gender transition—as a move from one point to another by the straightest line possible seems antithetical to that project. To striate one's body (indeed, even to regard it as so discrete as to call it that) into literal organs and imbue certain of these with a surplus of signifying power also puts one at danger for codifying embodiment in a way that creates remoteness—both of parts of one's "own" body, affect itself, and also those bodies that live elsewhere and morph in different ways. If, instead, one prioritized traits over forms, movement over stasis, and smoothness over striation, gender modification would seem to be at its most deterritorializing when we are emphatically unconcerned with moving from one fixed point to another on the path of least distance and detour. In this sense, an ethics of mobility and spatiality is entailed in and illustrated by any ethics or practice of gender modification. If, by productively unsettling the geo-affective subject, we could create new potentialities for the body, it follows that there is something lacking in our focus on reproducing existent bodies, in the very concept of transition, and in the increasingly coherent practices we pursue in transition's ubiquitously urban home.

Hopefully the applicability of such ideas to rural trans life is becoming clear. Many rural gender-fucking people find—in unconventional ways—unconventional allies, lovers, and mentors in their towns and villages, many of which don't even have geographically accessible hospitals, let alone the legion of certified psychiatrists, surgeons, and endocrinologists who preside over the processes of urban gender transition. What kind of phenomenon is "transgender" if it exists without hormones, surgery, or the extensive medical documentation that accompanies these identifiably trans procedures? Deleuze and Guattari offer resistance to those who might assume such things impossible. In one of their more (in)famous plateaus, "How Do you Make Yourself a Body without Organs?" they speak explicitly about the dangers of reducing a body to a series of cooperative organs. Their phrase "body without organs," (abbreviated BwO in specialist literature) offers resistance to the notion of bodily integrity or unity and calls to mind the dynamic character of transgender bodies—even though its dispensing of a definitive bodily organization clashes with the aspirations of those trans people for whom the acquisition or removal of certain organs constitutes the authenticity of trans subjectivity. While Deleuze and Guattari write of bodies and organs in general, their comments are especially resonant with surgical sex/gender modification. Imbuing certain parts of the body with certain meanings, what they call a focus on "part-objects," is "the approach of a demented experimenter who flays, slices, and anatomizes everything in sight, and then proceeds to sew things randomly back together again" (1987, 171). They contrast the part-object approach and its "fragmented body" (171) with the BwO by arguing that the latter neither presupposes an original unity, nor, more enigmatically, can be contained within one organism or controlled by one singular body. On this last point, they suggest that "it is not 'my' body without organs, instead the 'me' (*moi*) is on it, or what remains of me" (161). The BwO is infinitely unfinished, and it presumes that our environments move us as much as we move through them.

There is nothing necessarily deterritorializing about the gender or body of someone who lives out this kind of transgender without organs.[2] That such a configuration of trans-gender is possible, however—where passing, nightlife, community, and transition seem or are impossible—reminds us that policing gender identity on the basis of medical procedures also entails a policing of class, race, and a plethora of other cultural and bodily conditions, and also of location. Deterritorializing the system of subjectivity that would have us privilege certain organs and see the body as an integral whole (an idea that undermines trans life in the first instance) does not necessarily entail turning one's body into an assemblage of parts or series of seeming fragments, though this may well be involved. As Deleuze and Guattari note, functioning as a subject is necessary to effect change: "You have to keep small supplies of significance and subjectification, if only to turn them against their own systems when the circumstances demand it" (1987, 160). Transgender and transsexual subjects clearly do and will continue to exist, and for good reason—but hopefully as a way to deterritorialize gender rather than settle it, to take apart their own habits and territories, to help us experiment rather than solve a problem, and to take us wayward rather than directly from one point to the next.

Imperceptible transgenders

October 2007, Los Angeles, California. Like most rural kids I feel frantic here at first, compelled to take advantage of everything offered by a new strange city—lest I not make the most of this opportunity to travel. A few hours after the hotel concierge accepts my credit card, following a ten-minute conversation about how "strange it is you use Laura as a man's name in Canada!," I visit the Los Angeles Holocaust Museum. I shuffle tentatively about the empty rooms until an older woman approaches me, introduces herself as a child survivor, and implores me to sit with her on a bench to hear her story. As she speaks about hiding with her parents in France, and tells me what a fine young man I am for coming to the museum, I think: How will I tell her my name if she asks? Might she consider the incongruence between my acceptance of her appellation, "young man," and my self-naming as "Laura" to be duplicitous? I ask whether, as a child of nine years old, she had a sense of what was going on around her, as she and her mother hid in a non-Jewish household and snuck food to her father, who lived in a cave nearby. Her response echoes one I have offered to others, when trying to explain the perils and pleasures of my new urban transgender experiences: "Do you have any idea what it's like to never know what people are thinking when they look at you? To be afraid that you'll be found out?" A staff member announcing closing time abbreviates what might have been a considerably difficult and important conversation. Later that day, I stroll to a nearly deserted Sunset Boulevard and pass an establishment called Dr. Tea's. An employee on the sidewalk offers me a sample cup and says, "Sir, I'm convinced you need some tea!" I sense he's not alone in that belief. But I don't quite agree. "Could what the drug user or masochist obtains also be obtained in a different fashion . . . so it would even be possible to use drugs without using drugs, to get soused on pure water?" (Deleuze and Guattari 1987, 166).

I think of the way in which "passing" is a void notion in a small town where everyone knows you, and I wonder if the way in which rural people are largely ignored by urban queer theory lets us experience something more exhilarating than passing: imperceptibility. Deleuze and Guattari write: "What does becoming-imperceptible signify. . . . A first response would be: to be like everyone else. . . . After a real rupture, one succeeds . . . in being just like everyone else. To go unnoticed is by no means easy. . . . it is an affair of becoming" (1987, 279).[3]

If rural social lives occur in homes, backyards, and dark fields "rather than [in] a visual space" (371) like a city street, club, organization, or parade, we might ask ourselves a question that any urban postflâneur hasn't been able to ask for some time: What *is* it like to remain unseen, both by urban-centered theories of queerness and by our culture at large? While this "indiscernibility" (279) may sound like the kind of gender illegibility proffered by some postmodern theories of gender, that sort of unreadability may well be the "too-much-to-be-perceived" (279) of which Deleuze and Guattari write, though visible excess of ambiguous gender undoubtedly has its own value. Instead, the imperceptible lies beneath notice but is still only "like" (280) everybody else. In this account, imperceptibility is something entirely different from being "in the closet," as rural queers are so often read. By seeing imperceptibility as something other than a stopover on the way to a satisfying queer life, this equation of imperceptibility and becoming disrupts the teleology of coming out and transitioning. In so doing, Deleuze and Guattari offer a version of imperceptible trans life (rather than passing) that rural (or otherwise seemingly invisible) trans people might find reassuring or galvanizing: that continually navigating one's imperceptibility, rather than seeking out places where one feels readable or acknowledged as transgender[4] is not necessarily an unmitigated sign of self-loathing or the inability to move to a city; rather, it may be precisely this imperceptibility and lack of recognition that enables rural styles of transgender and the very different affects and lives that could be realized there—ones in which childhood vignettes do not add up to a narrative or to an adult, in which affects don't add up to a fully formed and settled subject, in which body parts and supposed bodily integrity are not cause for premature death, and where bodies that pass or bodies that are imperceptible each assemble in unexpectedly deterritorializing fashion, if only on the way to the next stop, the next desire, the next gender, the next . . .?

Notes

1   While I use "transgender" as an umbrella term, I also understand the slippage between the terms "transgender," "transsexual," "gender-fucking," and even "queer" as an indication of the molecular, affective, unsettled, and non-identity-politics version of gender modification that I try to imagine in these pages. It is also worth noting that while these words may have very specific definitions and conventions in some communities, their meanings, and even their importance, vary from place to place. For instance, in a rural maritime village of a few hundred people—where technologies of transsexuality are unavailable or largely unaffordable (financially or otherwise), is the (urban?) distinction between transsexuality and transgender a difference that bears on the lives of local gender-fuckers in the same way? Are these definitions yet more ways to organize gender—to craft a coherent grid of identities? I follow Prosser (1998), then, in regarding different practices of place, movement, and affect as equally (and, at times, more) constitutive of trans life as are discrete operations, hormone therapies, and passing.

2   The pun here on genitals as "organs" relies on Deleuze and Guattari's "body without organs" (BwO), mentioned above, by which they hope to inspire an orientation to embodiment and assemblage that is not based on being a complete organism or focusing on "parts-objects" (1987, 171). Harnessing organs into an organism (or, in more useful words for this analysis, organizing body parts into a particular kind of coherent subject) would illustrate the kind of striation (centering, bringing home) of the body against which Deleuze and Guattari write, and which promotes the very sense of remoteness that marginalizes others genders and (their) locales. Therefore, while "organs" are not reducible to genitals, there are certainly particular orientations to (and practices of/with) genitals that may be more or less likely to strive towards the BwO. The question posed by the pun is, then, In what ways does the concept of transgender-without-organs demand that we rethink the centrality of sexual "organs" to gender?

3   There is one paragraph in *A Thousand Plateaus* in which Deleuze and Guattari address transsexuality explicitly, to suggest the differences—but also the possible connections—between transition and their phrase "becoming-woman": "What we term a molar entity is, for example, the woman as defined by her form, endowed with organs and functions and assigned as a subject. Becoming-woman is not imitating this entity or even transforming oneself into it. We are not, however, overlooking the importance of imitation, or moments of imitation, among certain homosexual males, much less the prodigious attempt at a real transformation on the part of certain transvestites. All we are saying is that these indissociable aspects of becoming-woman must first be understood as a function of something else: not imitating or assuming the female form, but emitting particles that enter the relation of movement and rest, or the zone of proximity, of a microfemininity, in other words, that produce in us a molecular woman, create the molecular woman."

      Holding together this version of imperceptibility with transgender modes of passing offers a third way of interpreting the Deleuzian sense of "becoming-woman" (279), a phrase so easily either misunderstood as transsexuality or relegated to the realm of metaphor. If transgender passing has the potential to be a kind of Deleuzian imperceptibility, it is clear that their radical process of becoming-woman does, indeed, have everything to do with a literal form of gender transgression.

4   This version of imperceptibility is revisited by Kelly Oliver (2001) in her argument for a postrecognition model of subjectivity in *Witnessing: Beyond Recognition*. In the following, she could remind rural trans people to be wary of political projects that take recognition by urbanites as our main goal. As she writes, "While it seems obvious that oppressed people may engage in struggles for recognition in response to their lack of recognition from the dominant culture, it is less obvious that recognition itself is part of the pathology of oppression and domination" (23).

Works cited

Ahmed, Sara. 2006. *Queer Phenomenology: Orientations, Objects, Others*. Durham: Duke University Press.

Berlant, Lauren, and Elizabeth Freeman. 1997. "Queer Nationality." In *The Queen of America Goes to Washington City: Essays on Sex and Citizenship*. Durham: Duke University Press.

Bonta, Mark, and John Protevi. 2004. *Deleuze and Geophilosophy: A Guide and Glossary*. Edinburgh: Edinburgh University Press.

Buchanan, Ian. 2005. "Space in the Age of Non-place." In *Deleuze and Space*, eds. I. Buchanan and G. Lambert. Edinburgh: Edinburgh University Press.

Cvetkovich, Ann. 1992. *Mixed Feelings: Feminism, Mass Culture, and Victorian Sensationalism*. New Brunswick: Rutgers University Press.

— 2003. *An Archive of Feelings: Trauma, Sexuality, and Lesbian Public Cultures*. Durham: Duke University Press.

Deleuze, Gilles, and Félix Guattari. 1987. *A Thousand Plateaus: Capitalism and Schizophrenia*. Trans. Brian Massumi. London: Athlone Press.

Janoff, Douglas Victor. 2005. *Pink Blood: Homophobic Violence in Canada*. Toronto: University of Toronto Press.

Oliver, Kelly. 2001. *Witnessing: Beyond Recognition*. Minneapolis: University of Minnesota Press.

Prosser, Jay. 1998. *Second Skins: The Body Narratives of Transsexuality*. New York: Columbia University Press.

Stryker, Susan. 2007. "Transgender Feminism: Queering the Woman Question." Lecture delivered at Edmonton, University of Alberta, March 8.

Weston, Kath. 1995. "Get Thee to a Big City: Sexual Imaginary and the Great Gay Migration." *GLQ* 2(3):253–78.

Index